LIVERPOOL STUDIES IN INTERNATIONAL SLAVERY, 8

Tropics of Haiti

Race and the Literary History
of the Haitian Revolution in the Atlantic World,
1789–1865

Marlene L. Daut

Liverpool University Press

For my two Samys and Sébastien

First published 2015 by
Liverpool University Press
4 Cambridge Street
Liverpool
L69 7ZU

Copyright © 2015 Marlene L. Daut

The right of Marlene L. Daut to be identified as the author of this book has been asserted by her in accordance with the Copyright, Designs and Patents Act 1988.

All rights reserved. No part of this book may be reproduced, stored in a retrieval system, or transmitted, in any form or by any means, electronic, mechanical, photocopying, recording, or otherwise, without the prior written permission of the publisher.

British Library Cataloguing-in-Publication data
A British Library CIP record is available

ISBN 978-1-78138-184-7 cased
ISBN 978-1-78138-185-4 limp

Typeset by Carnegie Book Production, Lancaster
Printed and bound by CPI Group (UK) Ltd, Croydon, CR0 4YY

Contents

List of Figures   vii
Acknowledgments   ix

Introduction: The "Mulatto/a" Vengeance of 'Haitian Exceptionalism'   1

Part One: From "Monstrous Hybridity" to Enlightenment Literacy   49
Chapter One: "Monstrous Hybridity" in Colonial and Revolutionary Writing from Saint-Domingue   73
Chapter Two: Baron de Vastey, Colonial Discourse, and the Global "Scientific" Sphere   110
Chapter Three: Victor Hugo and the Rhetorical Possibilities of "Monstrous Hybridity" in Nineteenth-Century Revolutionary Fiction   152

Part Two: Transgressing the Trope of the "Tropical Temptress": Representation and Resistance in Colonial Saint-Domingue   197
Chapter Four: Moreau de Saint-Méry's Daughter and the Anti-Slavery Muse of *La Mulâtre comme il y a beaucoup de blanches* (1803)   220
Chapter Five: 'Born to Command': Leonora Sansay and the Paradoxes of Female Benevolence as Resistance in *Zelica; the Creole*   253
Chapter Six: 'Theresa' to the Rescue! African American Women's Resistance and the Literary History of the Haitian Revolution   288

Part Three: The Trope of the Tragic "Mulatto/a" and the Haitian Revolution   329

Chapter Seven: "Black" Son, "White" Father: The Tragic "Mulatto/a" and the Haitian Revolution in Victor Séjour's 'Le Mulâtre'   345

Chapter Eight: Between the Family and the Nation: Lamartine, Toussaint Louverture, and the "Interracial" Family Romance of the Haitian Revolution   373

Chapter Nine: A 'Quarrel Between Two Brothers': Eméric Bergeaud's Ideal History of the Haitian Revolution   412

Part Four: Requiem for the "Colored Historian"; or the 'Mulatto Legend of History'   459

Chapter Ten: The Color of History: The Transatlantic Abolitionist Movement and the 'Never-to-be-Forgiven Course of the Mulattoes'   474

Chapter Eleven: Victor Schoelcher, 'L'imagination Jaune,' and the Francophone Genealogy of the 'Mulatto Legend of History'   524

Chapter Twelve: 'Let us be Humane after the Victory': Pierre Faubert's 'New Humanism'   568

Coda: Today's 'Haitian Exceptionalism'   605

Bibliography   613
Index   679

List of Figures

'Toussaint Reading the Abbé Raynal's Work,' from John Relly
Beard's *The Life of Toussaint L'Ouverture* (1853).   53

Aménaïde Moreau de Saint-Méry, 'Ritratto del Padre' (1802), oil on
canvas.   240

'La couleur de mon corps nuit-elle à mon honneur et à ma bravoure?'
from Joseph Saint-Rémy's *Mémoires du Général Toussaint-
L'Ouverture, écrits par lui-même* (1853).   389

Guillaume Guillon-Lethière, 'Le Serment des ancêtres' (1822),
oil on canvas.   448

'The Colored Historian,' from William Wells Brown's *The Rising Son;
or, the Antecedents and Advancement of the Colored Race* (1882)   461

Flyleaf inscription from Juste Chanlatte's *La Partie de chasse du roi*
(1820).   585

Acknowledgments

I have carried this book around with me for a little over ten years. Stacks and piles of papers, disks and computer drives, internet files and countless USB sticks went with me to family dinners, birthday parties, holiday celebrations, barbeques, picnics, beaches, mountains, on airplanes, subways, and trains, on vacation, in cars, and to the hospital. This book was with me for the births of my precious nieces, and my own treasured children, and it was by my side after the pain of losing my dear grandmother. It was sustained at every moment by the love and support of parents, siblings, a patient spouse, and kind friends. But I have also carried this book with me in much less literal ways. I felt that it was living inside of me alongside my two children, Samy and Sébastien, who probably at least unconsciously know more about the interiority that this book and I share than perhaps anyone else. I dedicate this book to these sons of mine, and to my wonderful husband, partner, and the father of these children as a brief acknowledgment of the time among us, I hope, not lost, but merely postponed; the tears of joy, frustration, anger, and pain that we have all shared, now turned into relief, pride, and even joy. Finishing this book has been almost as emotional as the long journey of bringing it into existence. I have acquired so many intellectual debts along the way, along with the physical, emotional, and spiritual ones, that I find myself at times overwhelmed with feelings of good fortune.

It seems that I have somehow managed to be in many of the right places at many of the right times. Almost immediately upon arriving at Notre Dame, I had the amazing luck to meet Karen Richman, who taught me to *pale nan lang maman mwen an*, and it was Karen who brought the Haitian Studies Association into my life and therefore brought me also friends and fellow Haitianists to whom I am ever grateful: Chantalle Verna, Marc Prou, Nadège Clitandre, Claudine Michel, Matthew Smith, Gina Athena Ulysse, Valerie Kaussen, Mark Schuller, Kate Ramsey, and Régine Jean-Charles.

In a discipline of English-language literatures that has not always been receptive to multilingual literary studies, at Notre Dame I was also extremely gratified to have the unwavering support of my advisor, Glenn Hendler. His patient reflections and academic backing throughout these years of revision have sustained me at various trying moments in my career. Julia Douthwaite also supported this work throughout the years in a variety of different ways and has been a practical and gracious reader as well as a wonderful role model as a scholar-mother herself. I am forever grateful to Jean Jonassaint for taking me under his wing when he had zero institutional obligation to do so. The ever-judicious and pragmatic Ivy Wilson also helped at different phases of this work and, along with Cyraina Johnson-Roullier, helped to make comparative American studies at Notre Dame feasible.

Chance also brought Deborah Jenson and Jeremy Popkin into my life, both of whom I first began to know at the meeting of the 2008 Haitian Studies Association Conference, and I am grateful for the helpful advice they have subsequently been able to offer. Thanks also to Deborah for inviting me to be so seamlessly involved with Duke University's unmatched experiment in creating a humanities-based Haiti Lab. Through my involvement with the Haiti Lab, funded by the Franklin Humanities Institute, I came to know the ever-generous historian and Lab co-director, Laurent Dubois, as well as scholars Nick Nesbitt, Carey Hector, Jeremy Leglaunec, Doris Garraway, and many, many wonderful then graduate students, including Lesley Curtis and Julia Gaffield. I would be remiss not to mention that it was through the Haiti Lab that I also got to know one of the most humorous, bighearted people I now know, Jean Casimir, who has helped to bring my work to the Haitian people and to bring the Haitian people to me: *honè toujou*. I also came to know Chris Bongie during this time, who is perhaps one of the most generous scholars I have ever met. Even though Chris and I have often engaged in spirited intellectual disagreements about the nature and consequences of the 'mulatto legend of history,' Chris has been a patient reader of my work whose own work taught me so much about the meaning of rigor in the context of literary-historical studies. Despite having all of these brilliant and talented scholars in my life as mentors and friends, any mistakes, oversights, and ineptitudes to be found in this monograph are certainly mine alone.

I would now like to thank various colleagues, mentors, and friends who have collaborated with me in much more amorphous, but no less important, ways on this journey: Suzanne Lovering from El Dorado High School; and Véronique Flambard-Weisbart and Marc Lony from the French Department at Loyola Marymount University. Back in 2005, John Garrigus furnished me with a photocopy of *La Mulâtre comme il y a beaucoup de blanches*, thus facilitating its incorporation into my dissertation and now into this

Acknowledgments

book. Benjamin Hebblewaithe and Jacques Pierre helped me to learn to write in Haitian Kreyol through FIU's Haiti Seminar in the summer of 2005. Richard Pierce, Diane Pinderhughes, and Heidi Ardizonne of the University of Notre Dame brought the Erskine Peters Fellowship into my life, and it was through this fellowship that I made one of my most lasting friendships with fellow Peters scholar Nazera Wright. J. Michael Dash, Anna Brickhouse, and Kirsten Silva-Gruesz graciously agreed to appear at a conference I organized in 2005 at Notre Dame and offered helpful advice in the years that followed. Elizabeth Maddock Dillon, Michael Drexler, Karen Salt, Bob Fanuzzi, Gretchen Woertendyke, and Michelle Burnham have welcomed me into the field of early American studies. Kimberly Manganelli has been a supportive friend ever since we met at ASECS in Richmond, Virginia in 2009. Daniel Desormeaux gave me one of the first opportunities to present my research on Vastey at the Kentucky Foreign Language Conference in 2007, and I have much more recently made the acquaintance of Patrick Bellegarde-Smith and Grégory Pierrot, the latter of whom is fast becoming one of my most frequent intellectual sounding boards.

My years at Notre Dame were sustained by friendships with Gina Rho, Misty Schieberle, Marion Rohrleitner, Thomas (Tommy) Davis, and Reanna Ursin. My experience at the University of Miami was strengthened by friendship and advice from Pat Saunders, Sandra Pouchet Pacquet, Tim Watson, Chrissy Arce, Carlos Fernandez, and John Funchion. At Claremont Graduate University I have enjoyed the support of so many of my colleagues, especially David Luis-Brown, Eve Oishi, Joshua Goode, Linda Perkins, Henry Krips, Lori Anne Ferrell, Janet Farrell Brodie, Tammi Schneider, and Eric Bulson. I must thank the entire Intercollegiate Department of Africana Studies at the Claremont Colleges as well, but most especially our fearless and ever-resourceful chair, Sheila Walker, as well as fellow Haitianist Marie-Denise Shelton, in addition to April Mayes and Sidney Lemelle. I am also grateful to my writing group at the Claremont Colleges, in particular Ellen Rentz, and to Kyla Wanzana Tompkins of Pomona College. It would be negligent not to thank also the various research assistants who have helped with mundane tasks over the years: Shona Ganguly, Berniece Bruinius, and Denise Groce.

This project has received funding at various stages from the Kellogg Institute of Latin American Studies and the Nanovic Institute for European Studies, in addition to the departments of English and Africana studies, all at Notre Dame. This book has also received financial support in both doctoral and post-doctoral phases from the Ford Foundation. The National Endowment for the Humanities also provided me with a summer stipend for research. Various entities at the Claremont Graduate University have provided much-needed research funds as well as a book subvention, including the School of Arts and Humanities and the Program in Transdisciplinary Studies.

A different version of chapter eight appeared in the journal *Nineteenth-Century Literature* and parts of chapter two have appeared in *Comparative Literature*. Thanks to these journals for the opportunity to reprint and revise, and also to Anthony Cond and Alison Welsby of Liverpool University Press for making this long book happen, and to the two anonymous readers for helpful critiques and suggestions.

I am so fortunate to have a gaggle of hilarious siblings to keep me laughing: Rodney Martin Daut II, Tatiana Kelly, Austin Daut, Erika Stewart, and David Kemper. My parents, Rodney M. Daut and Leydy Kemper, along with my stepfather Donald Kemper, have never failed in their encouragement. My in-laws, Samy Zaka, Sr., Chantal Temple, and Roselinde and Dean Otto, have also been wonderfully supportive. Friends, Maxine Reger and Sara Lee, have been a part of my amazing support system since the fourth and fifth grades, respectively. My cousins from the families of Marcelin, Lalanne, Rousseau, Jean-Louis, Louis, Guillaume, and Coulter have always been awesome. But it is to the numerous *allomothers* who patiently cared for my children as if they were their own when I was working long hours or when I was away at conferences to whom I am the most grateful: my mother, my sister, and my mother-in-law, along with Manon, Nina, and Rachel. It may be a *cliché* now to say that 'it takes a village,' but that does not make it any less true for the working parent. I always knew that, for me, having children would bring unimaginable meanings into my life, but what I did not anticipate are the meanings and purpose that these children have brought to my work. I started this work for me, but I finished it for you, dear children, with the hopes that you will help to make of this world the kind in which we all want to live.

Introduction:
The "Mulatto/a" Vengeance of 'Haitian Exceptionalism'[1]

'Haiti is just like everyplace else ... except it's Haiti.'
—Herbert Gold, *Haiti: Best Nightmare on Earth* (1991)

'Haiti, like most of the world's poorest nations, suffers from a complex web of progress-resistant cultural influences. There is the influence of the voodoo religion, which spreads the message that life is capricious and planning futile. There are high levels of social mistrust. Responsibility is often not internalized ... We're all supposed to politely respect each other's cultures. But some cultures are more progress-resistant than others, and a horrible tragedy was just exacerbated by one of them.'
—David Brooks, 'The Underlying Tragedy' (2010)

'Haiti is not that weird. It is the fiction of Haitian exceptionalism that is weird.'
—Michel-Rolph Trouillot, 'The Odd and the Ordinary' (1990)

It is by now rather commonplace in academic circles to refer to the idea that the Haitian Revolution has been 'silenced' for the past two centuries in both scholarship and popular history. The concept of 'silencing' refers to the work of the late Michel-Rolph Trouillot, who, in his landmark *Silencing the Past: Power and the Production of History* (1995), argued that through both a 'formula of banalization' and a 'formula of erasure,' the 'silencing' of the Haitian Revolution has become merely one 'chapter within a narrative of global domination' (96). This form of 'silencing,' he writes—'"It" did not

---

[1] All translations mine unless otherwise indicated.

really happen; it was not that bad, or that important' (96)—is 'a part of the history of the West, and it is likely to persist, even in attenuated form, as long as the history of the West is not retold in ways that bring forward the perspective of the world' (107). While acknowledging that these silences exist has proved to be extraordinarily important to restoring the Haitian Revolution to its proper place among the most world-historical events of the eighteenth-century Atlantic World, in recent years a proliferation of writings have challenged Trouillot's premise of 'silencing' itself. Ada Ferrer, for example, has written:

> if Trouillot has provided a much-needed and powerful condemnation of the relative silence that has surrounded the Haitian Revolution to the present, other authors have shown that at the time, as news of the slaves' actions erupted onto the world stage, everyone seemed to be talking and thinking about events in Saint-Domingue. (22)

As historian David Geggus (1983), and more recently Jeremy Popkin (2007) and Philippe Girard (2012), have pointed out, when it comes to the eighteenth and nineteenth centuries there is almost too much written material on the Haitian Revolution.[2] Popkin writes, '[i]f the story of the Saint-Domingue insurrection fell into the realm of silence ... this is not because no one tried to speak of it at the time. In fact, these events provoked the composition of a large body of literature' (2007, 3).

Indeed, the onset of the Haitian Revolution (or the events that would come to be designated as such) sparked the creation of a corpus of hundreds, perhaps even thousands, of written texts that took the form of eye-witness accounts, letters, memoirs, histories, novels, poetry, plays, and newspaper articles. Even so, if we interpret Trouillot's thesis of 'silencing' as having produced the actual absence of utterance or conversation, rather than as having reinforced certain perceptions of the Revolution at the expense or sublimation of other perceptions, it seems to me that we might be missing the point. As Sibylle Fischer has argued, 'attempts to suppress certain memories of [the] Haitian Revolution,' in both its own day and our own, have 'rarely produced silence' (2004, 38). Trouillot infinitely understood this when he clarified that the form of 'silencing' under discussion in his monograph was that which resulted from, '[o]fficial debates and publications of the times, including the long list of pamphlets published in France from 1790 to 1804, [which] reveal the incapacity of most contemporaries to understand the revolution on its own terms.' He continues, '[t]hey could

---

2 For more philosophical and semantic challenges to the idea of the Haitian Revolution as 'unthinkable,' see also, Geggus, (2009, 3–4), Ghachem (2012, 4–9), and Nesbitt, (2013, 31).

Introduction

read the news only with their ready-made categories, and these categories were incompatible with the idea of a slave revolution' (1995, 73). The object of Trouillot's study was less to chart the history and general features of these 'ready-made categories' than it was to argue that the sublimation of the role of the slaves and former slaves in histories of the Age of Revolution has something to tell us about not only the worldview of the former colonists, but that of nineteenth- and twentieth-century historians: 'the contention that enslaved Africans and their descendants could not envision freedom—let alone formulate strategies for gaining and securing such freedom—was based not so much on empirical evidence as on an ontology, an implicit organization of the world and its inhabitants' (1995, 73).

The aim of *Tropics of Haiti* is precisely to elaborate upon some of the 'ready-made' categories that inform the 'ontology of the world and its inhabitants' that was developed in late eighteenth- to mid-nineteenth-century writing about the Haitian Revolution, whether written by pro-slavery advocates, the French colonists themselves, former Haitian revolutionaries and their descendants, or British, U.S., and French abolitionists. The goal of examining the vast and varied multitude of printed material that circulated about the Haitian Revolution is not to contradict the idea that the Revolution has been 'silenced,' but rather to probe what this immense body of writing might tell us about the way in which the revolution in Saint-Domingue was abundantly discussed as it unfolded and in the half-century after Haitian independence, a period of time which saw not only the creation of the first independent "black" nation in the American hemisphere in 1804, but which saw the formal end of slavery throughout most of the Atlantic World: first, in the colonies of Great Britain (1833), next in those of France (1848), and, finally, in the United States (1865). This necessarily comparative body of writing—what I am calling a *transatlantic print culture of the Haitian Revolution*[3]—reveals that these events were perhaps less 'silenced' in literal terms than they were incessantly narrated in a particularly 'racialized' way that had the ultimate effect of subordinating the position of the Haitian Revolution to the French and American revolutions. If, as Simon P. Newman has written, 'the Haitian

---

3 By 'print culture,' I mean to evoke much less the kind of book history, scribal politics, or history of print that have all been used to define the term and that have incited much heated debate over its meanings (Dane, 2003, 3). Instead, I mean to call forth what Meredith McGill might call a 'culture of reprinting,' where during the Haitian Revolution and the 60 or so years afterward, adapting, modifying, reprinting, translating, and circulating texts that had been written about the Haitian Revolution, often, to use McGill's words, 'outstripped authorial and editorial control' (2). In other words, many of the Haitian revolutionary texts that will be examined here often featured large passages that had been copied or closely paraphrased from prior works, making discussing authorship with respect to this corpus unwieldy and complicated.

Revolution racialized the age of revolution' (72), then it was only because the Age of Enlightenment had 'racialized' Saint-Domingue/Haiti.

The racialization of Saint-Domingue owes its historical genealogy to the kinds of organizational taxonomies that were created by naturalist travel writers, who, after descending upon the French Caribbean islands beginning in the seventeenth century, attempted to categorize by "race" or "type" the different varieties of inhabitant one might find there. Early narratives of the Haitian Revolution were directly linked to the vocabulary of these naturalists and, especially, to that of the colonist M.L.E. Moreau de Saint-Méry, who would claim that there were at least 128 different kinds of "racial mixes" to be found in Saint-Domingue resulting from sex between "negroes," "whites," and their descendants. This naturalist lexicon, which eventually grew to include words like, "mulatto," "quadroon," "octoroon," "griffes," "saccatras," among other variations, would be borrowed not only by early nineteenth-century writers who sought to describe the "racial" make up of colonial Caribbean societies, but also by those who sought to explain the impetus for the Haitian Revolution.

Up until at least the American Civil War, in fact, the literature of the Haitian Revolution demonstrates a dogged obsession with "mulatto" or other "mixed-race" beings, and, more specifically, with understanding the initial revolt and subsequent rebellion as one of children of "color" against their "white" fathers, and not as an antislavery revolution led by predominantly "negro" slaves. As we will see, the majority of colonial European and U.S. American authors who referenced the Haitian Revolution in their writing before 1865 argued that these events were the result of a putative natural desire for vengeance on the part of people of color—what I am calling a "mulatto/a vengeance narrative"—rather than a desire for liberty or equality as connected to the Enlightenment—or what I have called the "Enlightenment literacy narrative." This "mulatto/a" vengeance narrative often more specifically made the Haitian Revolution a result of the desire for revenge on the part of people of "mixed race," whose French colonist fathers had refused to recognize or pass down to them the rights of citizenship, rather than a desire on the part of slaves for the philosophical ideals of liberty and equality as set forth in the *Declaration of the Rights of Man*. If H.L. Malchow has written that ideas about 'miscegenation' or 'racial contamination' in British gothic literature 'establish[ed] a naturalistic explanation for moral depravity and aberration' (172), similarly, what we might call a 'structure of attitude and reference' (Said, 1993, xxiii) about "racial mixing" in early writing on the Haitian Revolution established a pseudoscientific "racial" framework for understanding revolutionary motivations. This was a way of seeing whereby people of "mixed race" were narrated as the parricidal and innately violent agitators who had caused the Haitian Revolution due to the

Introduction

degradations and instabilities occasioned by their putative "racial hybridity." Such a racialized perspective of the Haitian Revolution meant that it was not only most often understood to have been a revolution for "mulatto/a" revenge rather than for "black" freedom, but also caused these events to be narrated as an "interracial" family conflict involving "whites" and their children or other kin of "color."

As the most often repeated story of the Haitian Revolution in the archive of writing examined here, one face of the "mulatto/a" vengeance narrative focuses squarely on the vengeance *of* "mulatto/as," but because it was also a way to express disdain and disgust for racial "miscegenation" in general, the other face narrates vengeance *for* "mulatto/as." People described as being of "mixed race," therefore, occupy a dual role in early narratives about the Haitian Revolution. They are both historical actors described as having encouraged and/or participated in revolutionary violence owing to their deep-seated feelings of aggression and revenge towards their fathers, who were often their own masters, and they stand as metaphors for the anxieties aroused about the Haitian Revolution as a conflict in which there were no clear political, familial, or "racial" dividing lines, and in which political allegiances could never be assumed on the basis of color, class, and kinship alone. According to these portrayals, it was "mulatto" biology—a depraved and degraded mixture of the "whiteness" of their fathers and the "blackness" of their mothers—which caused them to pursue the purportedly parricidal and tragic objectives of the Haitian Revolution.

Because of the tropological, metonymic power of the word "mulatto" (rather than solely the literal, physical body of the "mulatto") to call forth such ideas of vengeance in the context of the Haitian Revolution, this is what I call a "tropics of Haiti." The word "tropics" is especially apt since, as Michelle Stephens observes, it all at once 'connotes both the ideological work of language and tropes in the colonial enterprise, and the geographical space of the Caribbean' (294).[4] In the transatlantic print culture inspired by the events of the Haitian Revolution, we find the same four "racial tropics," and the pseudoscientific vocabulary upon which writers relied, anxiously repeated as symbols of the epistemological uncertainty wrought by the merging of the concept of revolution and the idea of "racial mixing" in colonial Caribbean

---

4 Stephens was influenced here by Peter Hulme, who wrote in his article, 'Hurricane in the Caribeees,' that the word tropics refers to both the physical designation of the 'torrid zone and parts immediately adjacent,' a definition which Hulme quotes from the *Oxford English Dictionary* (qtd. in Hulme, 55), and the ideological work that tropes perform in the tropics, which for Hulme can be explained using Hayden White's idea of 'tropics [as] the process by which all discourse *constitutes* the objects which it pretends only to describe realistically and to analyze objectively' (qtd. in Hulme 55, emphasis in original)

space: the "monstrous hybrid," whose incongruity and degradation (whether owing to "mulatto" vengeance or "black" savagery) supposedly leads him to seek equally the destruction of "whites," "blacks," and other "mulattoes"; the "tropical temptress," a naturally dangerous and seductive woman of color whose innate lasciviousness often makes her an agent of radical revolution in her own right; and the stereotype of the tragic "mulatto/a," whose tormented position as an intermediary between his or her "white" colonist father and the "black" revolutionaries through his or her mother becomes his *raison d'être* for committing parricide, suicide, or infanticide during the Revolution. The incessant repetition of the first three tropes in early narrative descriptions of Saint-Domingue and the Haitian Revolution led precisely to the mid-nineteenth-century development of the fourth and final figure of "mulatto/a" vengeance: the "colored historian," a trope which narrates the putatively inherent desire for "mulattoes" and "negroes" to dominate one another, not only physically, but politically and discursively as well. All of these tropes, while not necessarily dependent upon literal acts of "miscegenation" or on "mulatto" identity itself, rely upon the same language of incongruity, "hybridity," and uncertainty found in eighteenth- and nineteenth-century conversations about "racial mixing" in the "tropics" to narrate the history of the Haitian Revolution as a "racial" Revolution.

Because it was the sometimes vague notion of "hybridity" that was viewed as having led to incongruity, immorality, concupiscence, degradation, aggression, rebellion, and even parricide, such radical monstrosity could be attached to people described as "creole," "negro," and "mulatto" in the literary history of the Haitian Revolution. *Tropics of Haiti* is therefore not a study of "mulatto identity"; nor can it be deemed a "mulatto history." In my view, doing this would only reify these pseudoscientific ideas of "race" as a valid way to classify social groups or people with phenotypical similarities. Nor does *Tropics of Haiti* provide an account of representations of "mulattoes" in the literary history of the Haitian Revolution, which, on the contrary, would be a perfectly valid way to establish "mulatto" identity as a discourse that must be deconstructed rather than as a *commonsense* political, social, or phenotypical marker that must be accepted. Instead, this study is a systematic examination of the ways in which a vocabulary inspired by naturalist travel writing and, later, "scientific" debates about "race," much of which had to do with ideas about "racial mixing" or "hybridity," dominated the way that people understood the Haitian Revolution in the eighteenth and nineteenth centuries.

Such a "racial tropics," although it may have relied upon a vocabulary that carried all the weight of scientific authority in the eighteenth and nineteenth centuries, must still be referred to as a pseudoscience. This is not only because the original creators of the "racial" taxonomies under

Introduction

consideration here made distinctions describing nothing that could be considered scientific today, but because, as we shall soon see, many of the naturalists who initially contributed to such a "science" produced theories of "race" that were riddled with hesitations, contradictions, qualifications, and exceptions.[5] The writing of the novelists, dramatists, poets, historians, and other contributors to the transatlantic print culture of the Haitian Revolution would in turn not only repeatedly assert these naturalist theories as unquestioned *truths*, but would also mirror the same kinds of ambivalence about "race" to be found in the works of those from whom they copied. As Homi Bhabha has written, 'it is the force of ambivalence that gives the colonial stereotype its currency: ensures its repeatability in changing historical and discursive conjunctures ... for the stereotype must always be in *excess* of what can be empirically proved or logically construed' (1994, 95). This ambivalence is precisely what helped to establish as equally authoritative both the fictional and historical accounts of the "racial" motivations of revolutionary actors under discussion here.

The idea that the "racial" taxonomies found in seventeenth-century naturalist travel writing gained their authority, however ambivalent, in mid-eighteenth-century metropolitan European natural history debates by people like Buffon, has been argued by Jean-Luc Benniol and Jean Benoist (1994), Robert Young (1995), Wernor Sollors (1997), Pierre Boulle (2007, 1985), Andrew S. Curran (2011), and others. However, I suggest that these debates about "race," which 'by settling on the possibility or impossibility of hybridity, focused explicitly on the issue of sexuality and the issue of sexual unions between whites and blacks' (Young, 1995, 9), only became widely available for co-optation and dissemination to the reading public when they began to appear with earnest insistence in the transatlantic print culture of the Haitian Revolution. The casual "racial" vernacular developed in the works of early contributors to the literary history of the Haitian Revolution demonstrates how formal debates about "racial mixing" acted in the popular consciousness to produce people of color as at once fascinating objects of study, desirable sexual partners, and dangerously degraded and volatile specimens of the New World to be feared, enslaved, or destroyed.[6] Thus, while many of the early fiction writers and historians

---

5 Although it is beyond the purview of this study to distinguish between the many different kinds of writing that might be called naturalist, my usage of the term focuses specifically on that category of travel writing whose primary aim was first to chart the physical terrain of the Americas, including its geography, along with its wildlife and the flora and fauna, particularly, of the island of Hispaniola and later, more specifically, of colonial Saint-Domingue.

6 My use of the idea of "racial" vernacular has been influenced by Sue Peabody's development of the idea of vernaculars of law. She writes, 'I am interested not only

of the Revolution under study here would not have considered themselves to have been contributing to any kind of "science" of "race" when they used the "racial" taxonomies found in naturalist travel writing and more formal debates about "miscegenation," it is still important to examine what James McClellan might call the 'vaguely scientific' (5) authority produced in such works since the idea of "race" established in the late eighteenth-century print culture of revolutionary Saint-Domingue would wield enormous influence over nineteenth-century understandings of the Haitian Revolution.

The nineteenth-century transatlantic reading public appears not only to have gained their understanding of the Haitian Revolution from reading various kinds of biographical and eyewitness histories, but they also appears to have gained their understanding of the consequences of "miscegenation" from reading works we might categorize today as unquestionably fictional. Léon-François Hoffmann has recently written of the relationship between 'history' and nineteenth-century French fictional representations of the Haitian Revolution:

> most of the writers whom we are discussing not only claim to be just as historical much more so than they do to be fictional, but they do not hesitate to cite their sources. It is therefore likely that the general public became aware of the events of Saint-Domingue and the names, Jean-Louis, Biassou, Toussaint Louverture, Henri Christophe or Dessalines, through works of imagination wherein they are named as characters, or at least that make reference to their existence. (2010, 14)[7]

And, as Pratima Prasad pointed out in one chapter of her book *Colonialism, Race, and the French Romantic Imagination* (2009), "racial" taxonomies ended up in romantic novels in ways that often 'present a more amorphous picture of some of the other underlying epistemologies of race' (48). It is precisely the vague, ill-organized shapes that thinking about "miscegenation" embodied in the historical literature of the Haitian Revolution that allowed the tropics of Haiti, which has always also been a tropics of "race," to be easily swallowed,

---

in what legal ideas and principles held valence for formally trained jurists, such as the lawyers and magistrates, but also what we might call "vernacular law", that is, legal understandings shared by common people without formal training but which influence formal legal culture' (2008, 3).

7 This fact alone has made it difficult to heed Margarita Zamora's call to pay attention to what 'each text "thinks it is"' before applying the genres of 'contemporary culture' (346). A great portion of the texts within the transatlantic print culture of the Haitian Revolution reveal themselves, upon closer examination, to be unsure about what they 'think' they are: novels or memoirs, histories or dramatizations. All of the texts under consideration here, in some way, therefore, blur the lines between history and fiction, biography and memoir, philosophy and science.

Introduction

digested, and regurgitated. The body of writing under study here has something to tell us not only about how ideas about "racial mixing" became explicitly attached to the Haitian Revolution, but how these ideas eventually found their way into the vocabulary of modern "racial" tropologies.

That such a tropological narrative of "mulatto/a" vengeance was the dominant hermeneutic of the nineteenth-century transatlantic print culture of the Haitian Revolution will no doubt come as a surprise to many literary critics and historians since, at least from the time of C.L.R. James, scholars have tended to narrate the Haitian Revolution as the ultimate triumph of "black" slaves over their "white" masters, or of the universalist principles of freedom over the capitalist economics of slavery. The desire to trumpet the slaves' successes can be demonstrated by the provocatively titled works of not only James himself, in *The Black Jacobins: Toussaint L'Ouverture and the San Domingo Revolution* (1938), but also Carolyn Fick, who in 1990 produced *Making Haiti: The Saint-Domingue Revolution from Below*; Laurent Dubois, who published *Avengers of the New World: The Story of the Haitian Revolution* in 2004; Nick Nesbitt, who penned *Universal Emancipation: The Haitian Revolution and the Radical Enlightenment* (2008); and, more recently, Philippe Girard, who gave us *The Slaves Who Defeated Napoleon: Toussaint Louverture and the Haitian War of Independence* (2011). The present study does not seek to contradict the idea that the slaves and former slaves of Saint-Domingue were the veritable authors of Haitian independence, who, in the words of Nesbitt, 'were able actively to construct their right to autonomy because they were able to represent to themselves the discrepancy between a received symbolic object (the *Déclaration [of the Rights of Man]*) and their own situation' (2004, 22). My aim instead is to point out the crushing significance of ideas about "racial mixing" in early narratives of the Haitian Revolution and to show how the various meanings attached to the idea of the "mulatto" became the primary *topos* through which to understand the epistemological problems of the Haitian Revolution. The vast archive of early writing produced about the Haitian Revolution suggests overwhelmingly that duplicitous and parricidal "mulattoes"—even as a simple metaphor for people whose identity or loyalties were suspect or unknown—actually initiated the rebellion.

The competing and itself popular narrative of Enlightenment literacy, or the widespread claim that Louverture read Enlightenment philosophy and was consequently inspired to lead a slave rebellion, surfaced simultaneously with the narrative of "mulatto/a" vengeance and can often be found alongside it. Yet this particular version of the literacy narrative of the Haitian Revolution has been repeated, debated, critiqued, and even refuted from a variety of different corners (Aravamudan, 1999, 302; Trouillot, 1995, 170; D. Scott, 2004, 101–102; Nesbitt, 2005, 28; Fick, 1997, 70; L. Dubois,

2004, 105; A. Hunt, 1988 120; C. Miller, 2008, 36; Fouchard, 1972, 17, 84; Geggus, 2007a, 85; Geggus, 2007b, 304).[8] In contrast, the narrative of "mulatto/a" vengeance has rarely warranted the same kind of deep scrutiny, either by way of interpretation or through positivist examination. With the exception of the woman of "mixed race" in colonial writings from Saint-Domingue (Dayan, 1998; Garraway, 2005; Garrigus, 2006; Jenson, 2011), there has never been a systematic study into the ways in which naturalist travel writing about "race" might have influenced popular understandings of the Haitian Revolution and vice versa.[9] In addition, while the tragic woman of "mixed race" comprises one of the most famous and studied tropes in Atlantic (largely, U.S. American) literary history (Sollors, 1997; Brody, 1998; Manganelli, 2012; Clark, 2013), there has never been a comprehensive exploration of how such a figure operated as a metaphor for anxieties that were not solely about "miscegenation," as such, but were also about epistemological uncertainty during the Haitian Revolution and the parricidal consequences of revolution in general.[10] Along these lines, in *Undoing Empire: Race and Nation in the Mulatto Caribbean* (2003), José Buscaglia-Salgado has observed:

8 In a different version of the literacy narrative, Nick Nesbitt has told of how a plantation owner in Saint-Domingue named Parham wrote in his diary that he had captured an unnamed rebel slave on his plantation upon his return from France. The planter wrote that he punished the slave but that the slave, 'who met death without any fear or complaint,' had 'in one of his pockets pamphlets printed in France, filled with commonplaces about the Rights of Man and the Sacred Revolution' (qtd. in Nesbitt, 2004, 28). In addition, Laurent Dubois suggests that some slaves may indeed have read or known about the *Declaration of the Rights of Man* since, 'in a few cases, slave insurgents explicitly phrased their demands in the language of Republican rights' (2004, 105).

9 Although Malchow does reference Haiti several times in connection with British debates about the putative 'moral depravity' of the 'mulatto' (172), the author does not actually discuss any works of fiction about the Haitian Revolution. Even while drawing a related conclusion, that, 'the ever present danger of black revolt in the Caribbean, well focused by sensational press accounts of the maroon wars of the 1790s in Jamaica and the bloody revolution in Haiti, made the issue of the *half-breed* or mulatto infinitely more problematical for whites in the [British] islands' (185), Malchow uses a nationalist perspective in limiting himself to British literature. *Tropics of Haiti* takes a much more expansive approach to the 'problematical' 'mulatto' in examining British, U.S. American, French, Haitian, and, in at least one case, German, literary productions about the Haitian Revolution.

10 In her 1999 study, Françoise Vergès does treat the idea of *métissage* as a metaphor for the kinds of 'family romance' that characterized the French and Haitian revolutions. However, this premise is only a theoretical starting point for her study, which is actually focused on the French colony of Réunion, especially after it became a department of France in the twentieth century and particularly as it relates to the author's own family history there.

Introduction

> As a whole, the subject of mulatto history and identity has been neglected and poorly studied. When it has been dealt with, scholars have often unknowingly reproduced some of the precepts of the Negro codes. Almost invariably a certain aversion to 'racial mixture' is reflected in attempts to reinforce the lines that separate white and black, free and slave, 'good' and 'evil,' no matter what the ideological position of the author might be. (203)

Wernor Sollors adds that "mulattoes" may have remained relatively 'unstudied' 'because of their apparently referential character and their deceptive familiarity,' such that 'they may appear to be self-evident or to pose no problem' (1999, 28). In the context of Haitian revolutionary studies, the result of the seemingly 'self-evident' meaning of the "mulatto" in the nineteenth century, is that even though more than two decades have passed since McClellan argued that 'science more than "Enlightenment" seems the appropriate criterion by which to analyze French colonialism in the eighteenth century' (292), and examinations of racism have often been features of studies about late nineteenth- and early twentieth-century Haiti (Dash, 1988; Plummer, 1988; and Farmer, 1994), and three newer studies of natural science in the West Indies (Schiebinger, 2004; Iannini, 2012; Allewaert, 2013), along with a monograph on medicine in revolutionary Saint-Domingue (Weaver, 2006), have been recently published, the widespread idea about "mulatto" biology as a catalyst for revolutionary violence and the oft-cited inherent divide between people with *dark* skin and people with *light* skin in contemporary Haiti has rarely been challenged. As such, "race," as a concept that was unmistakably informed by pseudo-scientific or biological understandings of "hybridity," has never been fully examined in the context of the Haitian Revolution, let alone in the context of present-day Haiti.[11]

One reason for this may be that the nineteenth-century interpretation of the Haitian Revolution as a "mulatto/a" revolution for vengeance is, in many respects, incompatible with its reception as a "black" slave revolution today. I contend that this gap between past and present understandings of the Haitian Revolution has something to tell us about the dramatically

---

11 Bruce Dain's well-researched 2003 study is about ideas of "race" in the United States and thus only one chapter is devoted to U.S. responses to the Haitian Revolution. Although Dain asks the question, 'Were pure blacks or free mulattoes the danger?' (82), this chapter is actually about how 'Saint-Domingue' and 'Haiti' became code words in the U.S. for people who wanted to discuss the threat of slave revolts and rebellion on U.S. shores. Furthermore, because Dain's book is largely an intellectual and cultural history of "race" in the U.S., its author does not consider any works of fiction, nor does he make an attempt to create or explicate a systematic literary history of the Haitian Revolution.

different effects on interpretation produced by the modern understanding of "race" as a social category versus understanding "race" as the biological determinant that it was figured to be in the eighteenth- and nineteenth-century Atlantic World. Most contemporary studies of both colonial and revolutionary Saint-Domingue are informed by an understanding of "race" as sociological and therefore understand "race" to have primarily social, legal, and cultural effects.[12] This stands in opposition to the eighteenth- and nineteenth-century belief that "race" was a biologically produced phenomenon, whose most serious consequences were physiological. When understood as biological, "race" produces not only physical and phenotypical inequalities,[13] but ontological ones as well, in the form of various mental, intellectual, spiritual, psychological, and emotional differences; whereas thinking about "race" as a social tool reveals that variations in phenotype could be used to justify and rationalize uneven access to education, medicine, justice, freedom, marriage, and the law. "Race" as *social* could also be used to produce a counter-narrative capable of contesting dominant epistemologies of "race" as something *biological* by conversely organizing people into various cultural and political groups on the basis of shared histories, languages, religions, politics, and other worldviews.

While understanding "race" as social or cultural in this way reveals a lot about how ideas of "race" can be *used* to produce or contest various social and legal consequences, it tells us very little about the third-person imagined and first-person expressed shared interiority of various "racial" groups; which is to say that it often tells us nothing about the way that being a "mulatto" or "negro" was supposed to have made a person *feel*. In other words, divorcing "racial" thinking from its origins in quasi-biological principles does not allow us to fully examine the various kinds of sensibilities that were narrated as having supposedly been aroused both as a result of *being* a "negro" or a "mulatto," and as a result of having one's entire *being*

---

[12] Perhaps the only exception comes from Jeremy Popkin, who briefly acknowledged that 'Revolutionary Saint-Domingue was one of the birthplaces of modern, pseudoscientific racism' (2008, 25). Yet, beyond this recognition, in what is primarily an anthology of what Popkin calls first-person accounts of the Haitian Revolution, little treatment is given to the radical implications of such a statement.

[13] I am drawing on the Rousseauean understanding of the term 'inequality.' In *Discourse on the Origin and Foundations of Inequality among Men* (1755), Rousseau writes, 'I conceive of two kinds of inequality in the human species: one which I call natural or physical, because it is established by nature and consists in the difference of age, health, bodily strength, and qualities of mind or soul. The other may be called moral or political inequality, because it depends on a kind of convention and is established, or at least authorized, by the consent of men. This latter type of inequality consists in the different privileges enjoyed by some at the expense of others' (1992, 16).

Introduction

legally, conceptually, physically, and spiritually determined by ideas that others had about "negroes" and "mulattoes." One of the things that we are seeking to determine, then, is how the biological idea of "race" produced in early modern and eighteenth-century travel writing helped to produce a distinctive interiority for people of color that became attached to ideas about the Haitian Revolution from the 1790s onward. That is to say, if other scholars of colonial and revolutionary Saint-Domingue have focused on the social, legal, and cultural outcomes produced by "racial" thinking, especially in the realms of policy, law, economics, and culture, *Tropics of Haiti* seeks to unfold the consequences for interiority produced by naturalist pseudoscientific understandings of "race." Specifically, this study documents how understandings of "race" as biological were represented as affecting the personal experiences, individual lives, and family histories of various people who were narrated as having been involved in the Haitian Revolution.

The belief that the effects of "race" were most easily seen in the body and in the mind, so to speak, as opposed to chiefly in the law and in the community, remains at the center of the *décalage* between the literary archive that produced the Haitian Revolution as the culmination of repressed "mulatto/a" vengeance and the popular and social histories that have produced the Haitian Revolution as a slave rebellion for liberty. We find "race" being explained as having primarily social consequences rather than innate existential implications in John Garrigus's groundbreaking study, *Before Haiti: Race and Citizenship in French Saint-Domingue* (2006). One of Garrigus's most intriguing findings is that free women of color, some of whom were courtesans or plantation owners, were able to successfully use their status as property owners or as wealthy city dwellers, to bring lawsuits against those who had defrauded them (77–85). This leads Garrigus to conclude that many of these free women of color enjoyed both relative agency and economic independence, which is a far cry from the kinds of depredation that the nineteenth-century Haitian writer Baron de Vastey (a former free person of color from Saint-Domingue) claimed all free people of color had experienced as a result of their "race" rather than their class, when he wrote, 'we will not make any distinction between these so-called free people [and the slaves], because even if they didn't have distinct masters, the *white* public was their master' (1814a, 74). Additionally, Garrigus describes the way in which participating in 'armed service' was still 'another way free people of color' could 'distance … themselves from slavery and reinforce their social status vis-à-vis whites' (85). My reading of the function of "race" in colonial Saint-Domingue is not that as sometime markers of class, determinations of a person's status as "mulatto" or "negro" never produced the kinds of distinctive social and economic consequences that made the revolutionary motivations of free people of color often vastly different from that of the slaves. Rather, I am emphasizing that because these terms were more often understood to be ontological, that is, having to do much more with the nature of a person's *being*, rather than with a person's *being rich*, "race" was not imagined in the literary culture of Saint-Domingue to have produced or to have been capable of producing the kind of distinct separation implied by the terms "white," "negro" and "mulatto," consistently or without great nuance, caveat, and exception.

The naturalist Michel-René Hilliard d'Auberteuil (2:88), followed by the former French colonial planters Peter Francis Venault de Charmilly (35) and Pierre-Victor Malouet (baron de) (4:10), for instance, argued that the creation of a "racially" intermediary population of free "mulattoes" could help to consolidate the powerful position of the numerical minority "white" colonists in Saint-Domingue and to further subject to slavery the numerical majority slaves. This kind of colonialist logic, which will be further discussed in chapter one of this monograph, assumed that out of gratitude for their freedom, "mulattoes" would be beholden to the "white" colonists to whom they were putatively related. Consequently, such planters also presumed that these same "mulattoes" would be naturally opposed to "negroes" (and therefore help to subdue them) in order to distance themselves from the slave status that being related to "Africans" always had the ability to confer. According to many colonial writers, the plan to create this intermediary class was a spectacular failure, precisely because of the purportedly innate biological vices occasioned by being of "mixed race," in the first place. This was precisely the sentiment behind Venault de Charmilly's venomous reply to the Jamaican planter Bryan Edwards about the actions of the free people of color during some of the first revolts in Saint-Domingue: 'If you had really understood the conduct of the Men of Color [*des Hommes de Couleur*] in every circumstance,' the French colonist writes, 'it would be easy for you to see how the essence of their character is a mixture of all the vices; dominated by cowardice ... soiled already with the most atrocious of crimes and there is every reason to be afraid of them [*le fond de leur caractère est un mélange de tous les vices; dominé par la lâcheté ... souillés déjà par les crimes les plus atroces, & tout à craindre*]' (57). Venault de Charmilly's comments demonstrate that the mere fact that a person of color could be a property owner, and even a slave owner, did not mean that this same person was never subject to the kinds of "racial" thinking that undergirded plantation slavery and about which Baron de Vastey would complain. Malouet would seem to have confirmed this conclusion when, after outlining his specious plan for restoring slavery to the erstwhile colony by ensuring that all people of "mixed race," of whatever degree, would be manumitted, he clarified, 'I am not saying that we should consider as equals the two colors' (4:141).

As if to punctuate the very premise that wealth and social status had little

Introduction

ability to eradicate the kind of biological thinking about "race" that would lead to what I call the *genocidal imaginings* of the "mulatto/a" vengeance narrative in chapter one of this volume, in his 1791 *Réponse aux considérations de M. Moreau, dit Saint-Méry*, Julien Raimond, another free person of color from Saint-Domingue, tried to link the consequences of such "racial" thinking, namely, that treacherous free people of color were trying to instigate a slave rebellion, to physical violence against them.[14] He wrote, 'Oh, how many false ideas, false fears, and false suspicions, has this caused to be born! how many innocent victims will have to be sacrificed for these atrocious beliefs [*perfides avis*]' (6). 'The *petits blancs*,' Raimond said, 'have obtained the right to pursue [free people of color], to steal from them, to destroy them even' (1791, 8). Thus, even though Garrigus, too, acknowledges that despite his status as perhaps the wealthiest free person of color in all of Saint-Domingue, the 'colonial elite defined Raimond as a man of color and sought to humiliate him' (2006, 4), I think that Garrigus tends to downplay the cumulative psychological costs of this humiliating racism when he finds, 'Decades before the outbreak of the French and Haitian revolutions, men and women [of color] with very little power used public texts to successfully protect their liberty and demand justice' (2006, 12). As Chris Bongie has insightfully remarked, 'The experience of color prejudice is something that has to be lived to be understood' (1998, 286). Where Garrigus sees only a confounding "racial" paradox that made 'Saint-Domingue's history [...] exceptional' (2006, 11)—he writes, 'What is harder to explain is why, in Saint-Domingue, the idea of racial impurity triumphed over slave-owners' solidarity' (2006, 7)— I see only the final outcome of the logic of colonial "science;" an organizational rationale that was used to ensure not only the continuation of "race"-based slavery in the colony of Saint-Domingue, but to encourage the creation of *genocidal* policies of "race"-based extermination.

The pages of the literary history of the Haitian Revolution that will be unfolded here suggest that the idea of "race" as biological produced a narrative of the Haitian Revolution and later Haitian independence that was dominated by fantasies of parricide, ethnic cleansing, and "interracial" warfare. At the same time, these narratives of "mulatto/a" vengeance also left us a record of the imagined and expressed subjectivities of various people of

---

14 Raimond was a metropolitan-educated free man of color from Aquin, who, according to Hénock Trouillot, was considered to be the 'head of the free people of color' (1962, 88). Raimond was also a spirited enemy of Moreau de Saint-Méry who, in his daring *Réponses aux considérations de M. Moreau, dit Saint-Méry* (1791), wrote that his goal was to 'destroy all the falsehoods of Mr. M—concerning the origins of the people of color, their population, their release from slavery; ... [and] prove the necessity of restoring to them their rights as active citizens' (2).

color who had experienced and often described themselves as having to live with the brute force of conceptions of their "race" deep within their psyche, whether they were slaves or free. That is to say that while Deborah Jenson has detailed in *Beyond the Slave Narrative* (2011) how 'the French colonial and early postcolonial tradition' created by the slaves and former slaves of Saint-Domingue 'offer ... particularly detailed accounts of *unbecoming* the legal property of another human being' (3), this study examines how writers of color, both the formerly enslaved turned masters, like Louverture, and those who were from prominent slave-owning families from Saint-Domingue, like Vastey and Raimond, provided moving accounts of their experiences under the same color prejudices that supported the colonialism and slavery from which they had clearly benefited, and which made them targets of extermination.

In *The Libertine Colony: Creolization in the Early French Caribbean* (2005), Doris Garraway, too, even while charting the legal implications of "racial mixing" as codified in early modern naturalist travel writing, primarily treats the cultural and social rather than biological or psychological dimensions of "racial" attitudes. Her brilliant theoretically oriented study elucidates how naturalist travel writers to the French colonies of America, and colonial administrators, used ideas about hybridity to 'coerce ... radically different ethnic and national groups' into 'social relations of domination based on race' (xii). These forced or coerced relations had the ultimate effect of paradoxically producing a 'common culture,' Garraway says, and she views the "racial" taxonomies that she so expertly connects to both European travel writing and colonial legal documents as having led principally to a creolized 'social system marked by asymmetrical power relations and the threat of violence' (1). One of the aims of her study is to question the ways in which a 'libidinal economy undergirds exploitative power relations among whites, free nonwhites, and slaves in the colonies' (26). Nevertheless, because she focuses solely on 'French narrative sources' that were 'produced almost exclusively from the perspective of those in power' (2005, 21), the corpus under study in Garraway's work understandably tells us little about the effects of "racial" thinking on the subjects of those narratives. Those who created eighteenth- and nineteenth-century "racial" terminologies not only helped to produce a biology of being "negro," "mulatto," or "white," that could legally or socially justify the violence and subjugation of people of color that plantation slavery always entails, but they occasioned an immense interpersonal devastation in the minds of those they sought to subjugate with these beliefs.

If Toni Morrison has written that *Playing in the Dark* (1992) was intended to be a study about 'the impact of racism on those who perpetuate it' rather than upon those who experience it (11), *Tropics of Haiti* is an inquiry into

Introduction

both, which is to ask how it felt 'to be a problem' (Du Bois, 1986, 363) in colonial and later revolutionary Saint-Domingue. I am interested in the effects of what we might call pseuodoscientific 'race-thinking' (Gilroy, 2000, 12) on both the seer and the seen in the context of the Haitian Revolution. In many ways, the "mulatto/a" vengeance narrative was an able distraction from the very substantive complaints occasioned by both the slaves and the free people of color about the color prejudices that had been encoded into the laws of Saint-Domingue. The "mulatto/a" vengeance narrative helped to displace the feelings occasioned by having experienced color prejudice and slavery onto the biology of being "black" or "mulatto/a," making it seem as though the aggressive act of war that constituted the Haitian Revolution was about the innate consequences of "blacknesss" or "mulattoness" rather than about freedom from the twin oppressions of slavery and colonial racism.

Of course, two of the most famous works that tell us about the effect of "racial thinking" on people considered to be "of color" come from W.E.B. Du Bois in *The Souls of Black Folk* (1903) and Frantz Fanon in *Peau Noire, Masques Blancs* (1952), but it is my contention that long before these twentieth-century writers the former slaves and free people of color from Saint-Domingue, and later the Haitian revolutionists themselves, would give us poignant accounts of the entrenched hostility that the experience of color prejudice occasioned in people whose bodies were marked as being "of color." In many ways, after the publication of *The Interesting Narrative of the Life of Olaudah Equiano* in 1789, it was through the writing of people of color from Saint-Domingue, including Toussaint Louverture, Juste Chanlatte, Baron de Vastey, Julien Raimond, Boisrond-Tonnerre, and Jean-Jacques Dessalines, that the nineteenth-century reading public became aware of subaltern subjectivities (see, Daut, 2008 and 2012; and Jenson, 2011). For example, nearly all scholars of the Haitian Revolution acknowledge that in Saint-Domingue 'the signifier *mulatto* became synonymous with the entire population of free people of color, as whites constructed the free class in terms of sex between whites and blacks' (Garraway, 2005, 212). What has been less acknowledged or downplayed, however, is that this word "mulatto" was largely understood not to have been a simple and interchangeable stand-in for free people of color, but was actually viewed as a way to demean them. The Frenchman Jean-Philippe Garran de Coulon wrote exactly this in his *Rapport sur les troubles de Saint-Domingue* (1797–99):

> According to the degree in which this intermediary race could be considered closer to blacks or whites [*cette race intermédiaire tenait aux blancs ou aux noirs*], the pride of the white colonists was centered on taking pleasure in humiliating them with the derogatory names of *mulâtres, grifs, quarterons,*

marabouts, tiercerons, métis, mameloucs, etc.; they did not even consider the fact that it was their own family members and their own blood whom they were insulting in this way. (1:17)

A former free person of color, Guy Joseph Bonnet, who also served as a soldier under General André Rigaud, gestured toward the inherent insult that these "racial" taxonomies carried within them as well when he wrote in his posthumously published memoir, '… this word mulatto … recalls nothing more than the idea of slavery' (1864, 430). The purposefully and inherently insulting nature of the term "mulatto," in particular, because it was also a signifier for the inhuman condition of slavery, probably also explains Raimond's own quarrel with being called *'mulâtre'* when in his *Réponse aux considerations de M. Moreau, dit Saint-Méry* (1791), Raimond noted of his adversary, 'he believes that he is also insulting me by calling me a mulatto [*Il croit m'en accabler aussi en m'appelant mulâtre*] … If I were, I would not blush at all; but I am the legitimate son and grandson of European fathers who were property owners in Saint-Domingue' (16). It was not only Raimond and Bonnet who would take issue, specifically, with the "racial" terminologies used to describe people of color in colonial writing. Much of nineteenth-century Haitian literature was dedicated to pointing out the cruelty of biological beliefs about "race" and the ontological effects for all people "of color" occasioned by the terms "negro" and "mulatto" themselves.

If the notion that people living in the eighteenth and nineteenth centuries understood "race" to be biological and ontological seems obvious, and because of that, much of the writing that will be examined here has often been dismissed as uninteresting because it can be deemed racist, this is also the main reason why the meaning of "race" in revolutionary Saint-Domingue has nearly always been taken for granted. A tendency to take "race" for granted, meaning that we understand that our eighteenth- and nineteenth-century sources viewed "race" as biological, while we ourselves view it as "social," "political," and/or "historical," is problematic because it seems to rest upon a false distinction between biological and sociological understandings of "race," where one is understood to be undesirable and racist, while the other is understood to be ideologically benign and even academic. In order to understand the consequences for Haitian revolutionary historiography of understanding "racial" thinking *against* rather than *with* its disreputable origins in pseudoscience, it is worth pointing out that according to the sociologist Howard Winant, the twentieth-century transformation in thinking that led to "race" being understood as sociological rather than physiological has had the effect of producing "race" as a category that appears to be a relevant and permissive way to distinguish among various groups because it may refer to certain 'social types' rather than different phenotypes.

Introduction

Winant writes, however, that not only is there 'no biological basis for distinguishing human groups along the lines of "race,"' but 'the sociohistorical categories employed to differentiate among these groups reveal themselves, upon serious examination, to be imprecise if not completely arbitrary' (172).

The words "black," "negro," and "mulatto," "homme de couleur" and "sang-mêlé," were not only used as often arbitrary and inconsistent markers of "race" and "class" in eighteenth-century Saint-Domingue, as Garrigus acknowledges (2006, 3), but were terms that had been contrived first to subject all the slaves to all the planters and the free colored planters to the "white" colonists, and later to subjugate all the Haitian people in the larger world order by dividing them into "mulattoes" and "negroes." It must therefore be recognized that the contemporary usage of these colonialist terms in scholarship, even if used solely to produce social, political, and historical distinctions, still relies upon a vocabulary whose genesis lies in racist pseudoscience. That is to say that even when understanding "race" as primarily a social instrument used to justify chattel slavery, an often unselfconscious and divisive vocabulary of "mulattoes," "negroes," and "whites," calls forth the biological tropologies that are indelible parts of these terms. Adopting these seemingly precise "racial" neologisms to impose commonality among people from often wildly different social, economic, and political groups (just as when colonial writers used the term, "mulatto," to refer to all free people of color, even as they acknowledged many "mulattoes" were slaves and many people considered to have been "negroes" were free), allows a number of "racial" essentialisms to creep into contemporary historical works about Haiti, confusing to the point of being virtually irrelevant the distinction between understanding "race" as a biological category versus understanding it as a socially and historically informed phenomenon. Producing "race" as sociological is not only a problem because it might lead us unwittingly to discount the experience of color prejudice by people like Raimond—whom Garrigus has accused of 'exaggerat[ing] the legal disabilities borne by free men of colour' (2007b, 5)—but also because it tends to reproduce the same colonialist framework about which we have seen Trouillot passionately complain.[15]

No study of the implications of differing conceptions of "race" in revolutionary Saint-Domingue and nineteenth-century Haiti should fail to mention the pioneering work of David Nicholls in *From Dessalines to Duvalier: Race, Colour and National Independence in Haiti* (1979). This vastly influential history was probably the first monograph of the twentieth century to attempt to link

---

[15] Moreau de Saint-Méry had actually accused Raimond and the free people of color in general of exaggerating the effects of color prejudice in his *Considérations présentées aux vrais amis du repos et du bonheur de la France* (1791).

sociological conceptions of "race," not solely to the Haitian Revolution, but to Haitian independence, and to acknowledge the writing of nineteenth-century Haitian historians like Joseph Saint-Rémy and Beaubrun Ardouin. However, Nicholls's work is beset by a number of problems with respect to his attempt to produce "mulatto" and "noir" identities as valid binaries for understanding post-independence Haiti. Despite the fact that, as Kwame Anthony Appiah has written, 'there is a fairly widespread consensus in the sciences of biology and anthropology that the word "race," at least as it is used in most unscientific discussions, refers to nothing that science should recognize as real' (1989, 227), Nicholls begins his study by recognizing as 'real' a distinction between 'race' and 'colour.' For Nicholls, the former refers to 'a set of persons who regard themselves and are generally regarded as being connected in some significant way by extrafamilial common descent' (1), whereas the latter should be understood as referring to 'phenotypical or somatic characteristics, specifically to skin colour, type of hair, nose, and lips' (2). Alex Dupuy has provided the most spirited critique of these distinctions by arguing:

> The difference Nicholls makes between race and color, however, does not hold. First, both definitions are based on the premise that people who share a common biological heritage expressed in the idea of 'common blood' belong to the same race. But this assumes that someone who is said to belong to a race, say in the nineteenth or the twenty-first century, is connected to a member of that same race in the fifteenth or seventeenth century through an invariant common line of descent. Going that far back in history, however, would surely mean that everyone who lived in the nineteenth or the twenty-first century would be descended from many people by more than one route, as modern DNA testing is starting to reveal, thereby making it impossible to hold that those who belong to a particular race today shared a common biological or genetic heritage with the presumed members of that same race several centuries removed. (45)

In short, since the colonialist understanding of skin color or phenotype was always connected to both genealogy and biology, we cannot claim to use either genealogy or biology in isolation in our discussions of "race" since to use one *is* to imply the other. Moreover, Nicholls's belief that skin color could reliably reveal and predict Haitian behavior and beliefs is hardly different from the way in which the former French colonists had written about colonial Saint-Domingue.

One of the functions of naturalist "racial" taxonomies was to reassure the colonists, planters, and colonial administrators that they could know something objectively just by looking at a person's skin color; that all the "negroes" were slaves, for example. People wanted to believe that there was

Introduction

an easy way to figure out not only who was a slave and who was free, but, later, who was on what side of the Revolution, who was likely to rebel, and who was likely to remain "loyal." The "mulatto/a" vengeance narrative and the 'taxonomic lunacy' (Fischer, 2004, 232) it borrowed from naturalist writings about "race," represents not only a reflection of this desire to classify and therefore to *know*, but reflects the deep fissures or cracks in the colonialist logic of "racial" determinacy itself. Ann Laura Stoler has written:

> Colonial authority was constructed on two powerful but false premises. The first was the notion that Europeans in the colonies made up an identifiable and discrete biological and social entity—a 'natural' community of common class interests, racial attributes, political affinities, and superior culture. The second was the related notion that the boundaries separating colonizer from colonized were thus self-evident and easily drawn. Neither premise reflected colonial realities. (2010b, 42)

In much the same way, the post-independence Haiti that Nicholls paints, one where people were and are clear about who was "black" and who was "mulatto," simply did not and does not now reflect reality.[16]

The best example of the problems attending Nicholls's adoption of the essentialist premises of colonial pseudoscience surfaces when relying on the popular understanding that both Ardouin and Saint-Rémy had *light* skin, Nicholls points to their position as "mulattoes" in order to cast a shadow of doubt over their authority as objective scholars. Nicholls said that both Haitian historians subscribed to something that he called a 'mulatto legend of history,' or a 'stylized version of the past,' which was 'presented in order to explain and justify the predominant position enjoyed by the mulatto elite, and thereby to consolidate its position' (1979, 89). He argued that the origin of this legend—the idea that it was the '*affranchis*' rather than the slaves who were the true 'pioneers' of Haitian independence and freedom (95)—went back to Pétion's republic and that the scholarship produced under the aegis of this kind of 'history' was characterized by a 'practical' rather than an

---

16 A point that is illustrated with a full sense of irony by the contemporary Haitian proverb *nèg rich, se milàt, milàt pòv, se nèg* or a 'poor mulatto is a black man; a rich black man is a mulatto,' which, according to Laurent Dubois, is merely a 'revision of the nineteenth-century form: "The rich black who can read and write is a mulatto; the poor mulatto who can't read or write is black"' (qtd. in Gates, Jr., 2011, 150). Furthermore, even though Nicholls's claims that he uses the "racial" categories of 'mulatto' and 'black' 'partly because Haitians themselves frequently use them' (1979, 2), the fact that Haitians use these terms does not mean that they are not inherently pseudoscientific and also offensive. While the word *nigger* has been culturally re-appropriated as a form of resistance in some U.S. communities of color, it is certainly indisputable that many, many people (this scholar included) remain deeply offended by the word.

'academic' interest in the topic (91). For Nicholls, the creation of the 'mulatto legend,' whereby Pétion was portrayed as 'virtuous' and 'humane,' along with Rigaud and Ogé and Chavannes, while Dessalines and Christophe were demonized (91), 'stimulated the creation of a black legend' that was 'eventually incorporated into a negritude ideology.' He writes: 'Associated with this *noiriste* ideology, was a whole black legend of the past, according to which the heroes [of the Haitian Revolution] were Toussaint, Dessalines, Christophe ...' (11).

Reading Haitian writing with this colonialist framework allows Nicholls to claim that nearly all nineteenth-century Haitian writers exhibited prejudice when it came to the topic of continental Africa, but that these prejudices took on a distinctly racialized quality depending upon the skin color or "race" of those who expressed them. Nicholls argues that 'mulatto' writers took an 'ambivalent' stance with respect to European colonization of Africa because 'of course, [they] were partly of European origin and valued this link with Europe'; while, on the contrary, 'most of the blacks were creoles and shared to some degree the colonial prejudice against Africa' and they 'often assumed that Africa was a barbarous continent' (42). These "racial," political, and literary taxonomies are issued as support for Nicholls's broader thesis that since independence there have been 'two main parties which were contending for power, distinguished broadly by colour' (10): 'a mulatto, city-based, commercial elite, and a black, rural, and military elite' (8). Independence in Haiti, he concludes, has been continuously threatened by these 'deep divisions' based on 'colour distinctions' that have helped to create, exacerbate, and encourage the country's political divisions (7–8).

Nicholls's entirely *colorized* understanding of Haitian society is hardly surprising when we consider that his highly influential argument is actually a mere repetition of the kinds of colonialist understandings of "race" that we find in the texts of nineteenth-century U.S. American and European writers. The celebrated nineteenth-century French abolitionist Victor Schoelcher, for instance, had something to say about "mulatto" prejudices in Haiti when he accused the Haitian poet and playwright Pierre Faubert of exalting the accomplishments of Haiti's 'yellow men' in his play *Ogé, ou le préjugé de couleur*, in order to maintain caste divisions (1843, 2:228). In his *Life of Toussaint L'Ouverture* (1853), John Relly Beard went even further when he accused the Haitian historian Joseph Saint-Rémy, 'a mulatto,' of 'obviously' 'valu[ing] his caste more than his country or his kind' in his 'biased' writings on Haitian history (vi). Like Nicholls, Beard and Schoelcher also appear to blame nineteenth-century Haitians (and especially those whom they identify as "mulattoes") rather than the legacy of colonialism and slavery, or even the continuing threat of French invasion in the two decades after independence, for the country's "racial" divisions, which were in all reality actively pursued

Introduction

and encouraged by the French, as Baron de Vastey would go on to prove (see chapter two of this volume). Beard, for his part, even argued that color prejudice in nineteenth-century Haiti stemmed from the days of the Haitian Revolution and had retarded' Haiti's progress in the 'arts' and 'paved the way for a renewal of strife and bloodshed' (144).

Unlike these nineteenth-century authors, in any event, Nicholls acknowledges that the earlier noted divisions between "mulattoes" and "blacks" were not without exception. He writes after all that many of Christophe's ministers, including Baron de Vastey, were people of "mixed race," and he points out that 'although there was a general coincidence between colour, status and class—so that light skin tended to go with high status and wealth—divisions based on status or ("caste"), colour and economic class did not wholly reinforce one another' (109). Moreover, influenced by Vastey himself, Nicholls observes that regional divisions have often been much more important than class or color distinctions in both revolutionary and post-independence Haiti (110–11). Yet what Stoler might call these same kinds of 'loud aside in the imperative tense ... wedged between the folds of truth-claims' (2010a, 23) can also be found in eighteenth- and nineteenth-century narrative descriptions of both the "white" Creoles and people of color in the colony and, therefore, do not absolve one of the charge of having been essentialist in the first place.

After describing "white" Creole women as generally indolent, pleasure loving beings, the French colonist Gabriel-François Brueys d'Aigalliers writes, 'You will ask me no doubt if ... all the female inhabitants resemble the portrait that I have just given you. Certainly not; in this, as in everything, there are exceptions, and we have women here who have not contributed a single feature to my portrait' (47). We find the same sort of qualification in the work of Moreau de Saint-Méry, who is most famous for having created in his *Description topographique, physique, civile, politique et historique de la partie française de l'isle Saint-Domingue* (1797) that elaborate 128-part racial taxonomy to which I earlier referred, and in which he characterized by ascending and degrees of "whiteness" and "blackness" the personalities, physical, and mental attributes of the many different kinds of people of color he said one might encounter in Saint-Domingue. Although Moreau de Saint-Méry had explained that successive "racial mixing" had resulted in both corruption and degradation of people of color, he prefaced his study by reminding his readers that to take his descriptions too literally 'would be to have a really false idea of this Colony' (1:6). Later in the text he added, 'In a colony where everyone, having brought his vices and virtues, is guided to the temple of fortune according to his opinions, needs, and circumstances, there will necessarily be noticeable differences, even absolute dissimilarities' (1:23). The absurdity of trying to classify people based upon the rather arbitrary attribute of skin color, not to mention the even more spurious, biological notion of "race," shines through in these 'hesitant asides' (Stoler, 2010a, 23), but the futility of such statements to undo their authors' earlier racialist generalizations is perhaps best punctuated by way of analogy. To say that all light-skinned people behave in one way and all dark-skinned people behave in another, with the caveat that these are simply general observations and should not be taken at face value, is much like saying that in the United States baseball is a "white" sport and basketball is a "black" sport, except that "blacks" and "whites" can be found among the players and viewers of each. Such caveats to statements that are themselves so general, so essentialist, so stereotypical, and therefore so in need of qualification as to be virtually meaningless, have little ability to actually undo the *truth-claims* to which they are opposed.

It is not enough to merely call attention to the implausibility of Nicholls's idea of the sharp 'colour' divisions among nineteenth-century Haitian historians, authors, and politicians, which, as we will see in chapter ten, seems to owe its genealogy to the nineteenth-century publisher James Redpath's idea that 'there are three versions of Haytian history—the white, the black, and the yellow' (1863, 4). This theory must also be analyzed and deconstructed as a part of the "mulatto/a" vengeance narrative itself since it is my claim that Nicholls's idea of the 'mulatto legend' is in large part responsible for present-day understandings of nineteenth-century Haitian writing, especially since *From Dessalines to Duvalier* is considered to be 'essential reading for all serious students of Haitian history' (Dupuy, 43). Even the most rudimentary perusal of a handful of contemporary articles and books that mention nineteenth-century Haitian historical writing will reveal uncritical references (without any sense of irony and even tinged with just a hint of self-righteousness) to *'noiriste'* and 'mulattoist' or *'mulatrist'* ideologies, the "mulatto" and "black" versions or 'legends' of history, and pithy references to the biased scholarship of a 'Haitian elite' or 'light-skinned intellectuals.' In his recent survey of the field, for example, historian Philippe Girard evokes the 'mulatto legend of history' when he writes, 'The historian's country of origin also matters, with parochialism being the norm.' He elaborates on this viewpoint by claiming, 'Haitian historians have tended to focus on their national heroes (black or mixed race, depending on the author's skin color), French historians on colonial debates' ties to the French Revolution and US historians on the Haitian Revolution's repercussions in the USA' (2012, 2). With even more insistence, Léon-François Hoffmann has written that in Haiti, 'The tensions between the older mulatto elite, who tended to perpetuate the ideology of Pétion, and the black middle class, who favored Christophe's, have survived down to the present.' He continues by complaining about the 'weaknesses of Haitian historical writings about

Introduction

the origins of the country: they are either blatantly partisan (especially in the case of the first mulatto historians, Beaubrun Ardouin and Thomas Madiou), or indiscriminately hagiographic' (1994, 368).

Is there a reason why we should preface a gloss of Ardouin's works by clarifying that he was a 'mulatto historian,' if we do not also feel it necessary to first note that Jules Michelet was a "white" one? Knowing someone's skin color or "race" would only be important if we wanted that knowledge to do some kind of tropological work, which is precisely what claims about a person's "mulatto" status do: they discount Haitian historians by making exceptions out of them, which ultimately results in silencing—an issue to which I will return in just a moment. That's the thing about tropes, one needn't go on and on about them, as Nicholls does, to call forth the argument (and power) lying beneath the surface of any argument about "racial" determinacy. Just calling someone a 'mulatto historian' or a *'noiriste'* is usually all it takes to call into question his or her objectivity. This is because tropes are metonymic. If I say that someone is a *'noiriste'* historian, I have essentially called forth the idea that this person is against "mulattoes," or is working against "mulatto history" or "mulatto politics" at the very least, and therefore cannot be trusted to be unbiased. All of this, in my opinion, plays right back into the stereotype that Haitians of yesterday and today are hopelessly prejudiced against one another and that this is one of the biggest, if not the primary, problem of their society. Indeed, references to the 'mulatto legend of history' or what I call, in Part Four of the present work, the trope of the "colored historian," is the primary way in which the narrative of "mulatto/a" vengeance operates in present-day scholarship about Haiti.

Uncritically repeated statements about the uncanny "racial" biases of Haitian historians are reminiscent of Trouillot's theory of 'Haitian exceptionalism,' defined as the idea that 'Haiti is unique, bizarre, unnatural, odd, queer, freakish, or grotesque … that it is unnatural, erratic, and therefore unexplainable … that Haiti is so special that modes of investigation applicable to other societies are not relevant here' (1990, 6). Trouillot found that such 'Haitian exceptionalism … tends to function at the level of subtext in most books published outside of the country in the second half of the [twentieth] century,' since '[w]hile it permeates the entire work, there are very few sentences that actually articulate it' (1990, 6). Trouillot doubled down on this criticism in *Silencing the Past* when he pointed out the distinct relationship between eighteenth- and twentieth-century historical writing about Haiti:

> the history produced outside of Haiti is increasingly sophisticated and rich empirically. Yet its vocabulary and often its entire discursive framework recall frighteningly those of the eighteenth century. Papers and monographs

take the tone of plantation records. Analyses of the Revolution recall the letters of La Barre, the pamphlets of French politicians, the messages of Leclerc to Bonaparte, or, at best, the speeches of Blangilly. I am quite willing to concede that the conscious political motives are not the same. Indeed, again, that is part of my point. Effective silencing does not require a conspiracy, not even a political consensus. Its roots are structural. Beyond a stated—and most often sincere—political generosity, best described in U.S. parlance within a liberal continuum, the narrative structures of Western historiography have not broken with the ontological order of the Renaissance. This exercise of power is much more important than the alleged conservative or liberal adherence of the historians involved. (1995, 106)

Trouillot has not been the only historian to notice that 'silencing the past' often also involves deep layers of echoing the past as well. In an article published in a special issue of the *Journal of Haitian Studies* devoted entirely to examining the life and works of Michel-Rolph Trouillot, Alyssa Goldstein Sepinwall observed that though *Silencing the Past* 'helped to make the Haitian Revolution more widely known, when non-Haitian scholars write about the Revolution, they often still do so in ways that Trouillot would denounce as "banalizing,"' because they write about the events in 'unwittingly trivializing ways' (2013, 76). Although nineteenth-century Haitian writers have happily found their way into several newer studies of Atlantic literary culture, many scholars have still managed to 'unwittingly trivialize' their works, as when Hoffmann calls much of Haitian writing 'hagiographic,' or when Chris Dixon reduces all Haitian historiographical differences to "racial" squabbles. After evoking Nicholls's theory, Dixon writes, 'Perhaps predictably, mulatto versions of the black republic's past emphasized the roles by mulattoes in establishing and maintaining Haitian independence and liberty ... And although mulatto writers shared Haitians' sense of racial pride, an undercurrent of color prejudice toward their more dark-skinned compatriot's was evident among many mulatto historians' (2008, 341).

My aim is not to take anything away from the remarkable works of scholarship that have been produced on the Haitian Revolution and nineteenth-century Haiti, much of which has directly influenced this study, since the wide array of comments about 'mulatto historians' and the biases of Haitian authors are often made in passing in works that otherwise provide new and challenging ways to understand the Haitian Revolution and Haitian independence. I hope merely to signal how "racial" thinking continues to operate in our understandings of Haiti in a way that is so implicit as to appear to be 'common sense' (Omi and Winant, 13). As Appiah has written, 'racialism' or the belief in a sort of 'racial essence' that involves

Introduction

'heritable characteristics' and can therefore account for 'more than the visible morphological characteristics—skin color, hair type, facial features,' was 'at the heart of nineteenth-century attempts to develop a science of racial difference; but it appears to have been believed by others—for example, Hegel, before then, and many in other parts of the non-Western world since—who have had no interest in developing scientific theories' (1990, 5). I suggest that it is precisely because of the implicitly accepted 'common sense' of 'racialism' that essentialist ideas about "race"—the idea that there were groups of people who could be classified generically and with any sort of precision as "negro" or "black," as "mulatto" or of "mixed race"—have passed into Haitian historiography and popular history as unchecked, unchallenged vernacular *truths* rather than as ways of storytelling that have had various ideological and practical implications not only for the many different kinds of Haitians whose story was being told, but for the storytellers themselves.

The nineteenth-century storytellers whose accounts of the Haitian Revolution will be under scrutiny here, whether intended to be fictional or biographical, interpretive or historical, often deliberately or unwittingly used a language of blame that was tinged with the influence of colonialist ideas about race to, in the words of Trouillot, 'mask the contribution of the Western powers to the Haitian situation' (1990, 7). The argument that "mulatto" writers associated with Pétion developed the narrative that free people of color were the first authors of the insurrection in Saint-Domingue, for example, is simply not borne out by the evidence. As we will see, such claims were made as early as the start of the insurrection by nearly all of the French colonists, who, according to Raimond, used this narrative to distract from the real cause of slave rebellions, which was the rampant abuses the slaves had suffered under the colonial yoke. Raimond essentially argued that the slaves did not need the free people of color or the Société des Amis des Noirs to incite them to insurrection since, 'would it not be natural to fear that the blacks, in thinking about their own situation, would have wanted to demand their liberty? [*n'était-il pas naturel de craindre que les noirs, par un retour sur eux-mêmes sur leur cruelle situation, voudraient aussi revendiquer leur liberté*]' (1791b, 12).

The widely influential Gros[17] was one such colonist who, in using the

---

[17] According to Jeremy Popkin, Gros's account had 'more immediate impact than any other first-person narrative of the insurrection' (2007, 105), and it has also had the 'greatest impact on the historiography of the Haitian insurrection' (11) and 'has continued to influence depictions of that event down to the present day' (105). See also the colonist Guillaume François Mahy, Baron de Cormeré's *Histoire de la révolution, de la partie française de St. Domingue* (1794), wherein the author writes that the 'mulatto Ogé,' along with the 'mulatto Chavannes, and a free negro, savage men, who only drew breath for the murder of the white population [*la génération blanche*]' (77), had first been

"mulatto/a" vengeance narrative, attempted to write away or distract from the inevitable agency of the slaves. Gros wrote in his *Historick Recital* in 1792 that of 'all of the People of Colour none were more to blame than the Outlaws of Ogé ... It has been proved that these were the Persons employed by the Government to instruct the Negroes, and prepare them for Rebellion' (92–93).[18] If writers associated with Pétion later made the same argument, it was likely because they had borrowed such claims from a colonial archive that incessantly narrated such "mulatto/a" vengeance as an incontestable *truth*, but it was almost certainly not because they were people who were called and may have even called themselves "mulattoes," any more than Gros read the events the way he did *because* his skin may have been "white." Having said that, I do not wish to make the argument that there were no lingering color prejudices or 'racisms,' to use Appiah's term (1990, 3–4), in nineteenth-century Haiti, let alone in contemporary Haiti.[19] As a person of color living in the United States, who, like all people of color here, suffers endless microaggressions on a daily basis, and had the unfortunate experience of witnessing macroaggression against my colleagues being shouted down as

---

engaged in a 'propaganda' campaign designed to encourage the 'insurrection of the mulattoes' and later, 'in November of 1790, the mulattoes of Grande-Rivière, a parish of the Northern section, about four leagues from Cap, were led into insurrection by he whose name was Ogé, recently arrived from France, with a plan designed to incite both this revolt and that of the slaves in all of the colony' (78).

18 Gros refers here to Vincent Ogé, a wealthy merchant of color from Cap-Français who is most famous for having led a revolt, ostensibly aimed at achieving political rights for free people of color, in October of 1790, along with Jean-Baptiste Chavannes and around 250 free men of color. However, the result of Ogé's revolt was ambiguous (see, Garrigus, 2010, 37), causing him to flee to the Spanish side of the island. Upon his successful extradition back to French Saint-Domingue in December of 1790, Ogé and many of his allies were publicly 'broken on the wheel' by the French government in a square in Cap-Français. See chapters eleven and twelve of this volume for further context.

19 Appiah says that there are at least two main types of 'racism,' the first being 'extrinsic racism' or the belief that one can 'make moral distinctions between members of different races because ... the racial essence entails certain morally relevant qualities' (1990, 5). He continues by saying, 'the basis for the extrinsic racists' discrimination between people is their belief that members of different races differ in respects that *warrant* the differential treatment' (5). 'Intrinsic racists,' by contrast, 'are people who differentiate morally between members of different races because they believe that each race has a different moral status, quite independent of the moral characteristics entailed by its racial essence' (5). Importantly, '[f]or an intrinsic racist, no amount of evidence that a member of another race is capable of great moral, intellectual, or cultural achievements, or has characteristics that, in members of one's own race, would make them admirable or attractive, offers any ground for treating that person as he or she would treat similarly endowed members of his or her own race' (6).

Introduction

niggers! at the 2009 Indiana HSA conference at IU-Bloomington, I would be the last person to tell anyone about the kinds of color prejudice that do or do not exist in their own country. I am simply saying that if we really listen to what Ardouin and Saint-Rémy, and many other Haitian authors both before and after them, were trying to tell us about the role outsiders were playing in encouraging the replication in independent Haiti of the "racial" divisions of the colonial era, it will be hard not to see the color prejudices of nineteenth-century Haiti that were ceaselessly reported to be *true* by outside observers as anything other than performative, in the sense that the supporters of this narrative of "mulatto/a" vengeance—one where "blacks" and "mulattoes" seek out endless aggression against one another—attempted to create the 'reality' they 'discursively constitute[d]' (Butler, 2006, 156).

Moreover, I think it will be plain to see after reading this literary history that mid-nineteenth-century Haitian historians did not create something we can reliably call a 'mulatto legend of history.' The arguments that Ardouin and Saint-Rémy made in the mid-nineteenth century were already at least 40 or 50 years old by the time they got around to discussing the Haitian Revolution. It is therefore a-historical, at the very least, to suggest that in order to dominate their "black" compatriots, these "mulatto" historians were the ones who invented the ideas that Ogé had been the primary instigator of slave rebellion in Saint-Domingue and that Toussaint Louverture betrayed the cause of the slaves. Believing that Ardouin and Saint-Rémy, in particular, wrote the way they did because of their skin color and because they wanted to discursively, if not politically, dominate "blacks," not only evokes the narrative of "mulatto/a" vengeance as the vengeance *of* "mulattoes," but it forecloses our ability to think about or understand their historical contributions to Haitian revolutionary historiography as anything other than propaganda; it also sets up an untenable relationship among their works and the vastly derivative literary history of the Haitian Revolution.

It is at this point that I would like to stress that the narrative of "mulatto/a" vengeance is not strictly a colonial discourse. In other words, it is not a discourse solely from "white" people about "black" people (even though it may have begun that way) or from "colonizers" about the "colonized," nor is it solely a narrative from the rest of the world about Haiti. The narrative of "mulatto/a" vengeance is a vocabulary, a kind of 'implicit racial grammar' (Stoler, 1995, 12), which underwrites nearly all writing about the Haitian Revolution. To ignore the contributions of Haitian authors, and people otherwise identified as "black" or "mulatto," to such a discourse would be to once again contribute to the 'silencing of the past' and to the broader concept of 'Haitian exceptionalism.'

Early Haitian authors, many of whom either participated in or were witnesses to the events of the Revolution, have often been dismissed as irrelevant to Haitian historiography because of their putative biases; both their fictional and biographical works have therefore often been considered minor, when they have been considered at all, using both what Trouillot has called a 'formula of banalization' and a 'formula of erasure'—either they did not *really* write these narratives, a charge that Daniel Desormeaux shows has been often made against Toussaint Louverture (2005, 135), or they are not *really* that important, which up until very recently had historically been the case with mentions of the works of Vastey. However, perhaps even more disconcerting is that when Haitian writers have been considered it is often in the name of making an *exception* out of them, which promotes isolation of their work rather than comparative study of it (Trouillot, 1990, 9).[20] Such isolation was historically anachronistic for Trouillot since,

20 When I first began to study early nineteenth-century Haitian literary history, other than the works of J. Michael Dash (1988), Léon-François Hoffmann (1984), and Colin (Joan) Dayan (1995), there was little comparative consideration of nineteenth-century Haitian authors, and when there was, it was often dismissive. Thankfully, much has changed since that time. The early Americanist Anna Brickhouse (2004), for example, provided a useful comparison between Pierre Faubert's *Ogé; ou le préjugé de couleur* and Stowe's *Uncle Tom's Cabin*. Wigmore Francis (2003) considered Haitian authorship in a comparative Caribbean context in his discussion of the writings of Baron de Vastey in an article about representations of masculinity in the early Caribbean. Chris Bongie has also taken an interest in the writings of Baron de Vastey, publishing both an article (2005) and a book chapter in which he compares the former secretary of Christophe's writings (2008) to Derek Walcott's *Haitian Trilogy*. In addition, Bongie has also recently published and edited the first English-language translation of Vastey's *Le Système colonial dévoilé* (1814), which includes four articles on Vastey by Bongie, Garraway, Nick Nesbitt, and me (2014). Daniel Desormeaux has also recently contributed to the accessibility of early Haitian writing with his edited edition of Toussaint Louverture's memoirs (2011), which follows a very spirited article about the authorship of the memoirs in the context of the French historiographical tradition, first published in a special edition of *Yale French Studies*. In *Claims to Memory* (2006), Catherine A. Reinhardt examined some of the memoirs of free people of color like Julien Raimond, along with plays, letters, and pamphlets, in order to interrogate the ways in which what she calls 'claims to memory' have shaped historical discourses. More recently, in *Beyond the Slave Narrative* (2011) Deborah Jenson has incorporated into her study of early Haitian manuscripts what she calls a 'heteroclite corpus of political texts and correspondence' (1), much of it written in Haitian Creole by 'French colonial slaves, former slaves, and their descendants in the early postcolonial period' (2011, 3). In one chapter of *The Fear of French Negroes* (2012), Sara Johnson briefly takes up the long-neglected topic of early Haitian print culture with her examination of the mid-nineteenth-century Haitian newspaper *L'Union* as part of an Atlantic, 'transcolonial,' and African diasporic network. Finally, Lesley Curtis and Christen Mucher will soon publish the only English translation of the first Haitian novel, *Stella* (1859), written by Eméric Bergeaud, in order to bring this text to an Anglophone

Introduction

as he acknowledged, 'before the twentieth century, Haitian writers rarely if ever promoted singularity. In fact, quite the opposite' (1990, 7). Trouillot added that while 'nineteenth-century studies have been unjustly outflanked by the dual emphasis on the slave revolution of 1791 and twentieth-century politics,' we should pay more attention to early Haitian writers since, 'with their faith in universals and their desire to defend Haiti in a context of open ostracism, [they] may have given us the most potent antidote to the myth of Haitian exceptionalism: specific questions, tuned to Haitian particulars but informed by the international debates of the times' (1990, 11).

The stark reality, in any case, is that people of color living in Saint-Domingue and later nineteenth-century Haitian authors themselves, even with all of their 'ideals' and 'desire to defend Haiti' and people of color, also contributed to an implicitly racialized language of the Revolution and therefore to the dissemination of popular ideas about "race." Sometimes, the contributions of early Haitian authors to the "racial" stereotypes that undergird the narrative of "mulatto/a" vengeance were made in the name of refuting them. This is often the case in the written works of the revolutionary figures André Rigaud, who insisted upon using the term 'citoyens de couleur' over 'mulâtre' (iii–iv), and Julien Raimond, who issued his own variation of a racial taxonomy in his 1791 *Observations sur l'origine et les progrès du préjugé des colons blancs contre les citoyens de couleur* (16–17). Other times, nineteenth-century Haitian authors unwittingly affirmed the idea that "blacks" and "mulattoes" in Haiti were hopelessly divided by "race," even as they attempted to dismantle this argument, as is the case in much of Vastey's post-revolutionary writing about Christophe's nemesis Pétion, wherein Vastey characterizes the latter as behaving in a way that is 'whiter than the French themselves' and as having 'change[d] from one day to the next his color and shape in order to perpetuate this civil war [against Christophe]' (1815c, 15). Saint-Rémy also used a similarly racialized language when he described the famous secretary of Dessalines, Louis-Félix Boisrond-Tonnerre, as 'half wolf ... half jackal' with a 'violent complexion'

---

audience for the first time (forthcoming, 2015). There are also two recently published monographs that seek to access nineteenth-century Haiti largely through twentieth-century writing: John Patrick Walsh's *Free and French in the Caribbean* (2013) and Philip Kaisary's *The Haitian Revolution in the Literary Imagination* (2014). Yet even with these renewed efforts to incorporate early Haitian writing into studies not only of Haiti, but the Americas and the broader Atlantic World, nineteenth-century fiction, poetry, and drama from Haiti is still woefully understudied. Not only is there no comprehensive and multilingual literary study of representations of the Haitian Revolution in the nineteenth century, but few studies that do discuss nineteenth-century representations or evocations of the Haitian Revolution consider any Haitian authors at all.

(1851, ix) and consequently blamed him for all the 'antagonisms' of 'race' and 'class' in mid-nineteenth-century Haiti (1851, xx).

The point of examining nineteenth-century Haitian writing about "race" as a part of the narrative of "mulatto/a" vengeance, in which the implicit "racial" understandings that undergird the author's writing provide the analytical frame rather than the skin color or "race" of the author himself, is precisely to underscore the fact that excluding Haitian authors from the narrative of "mulatto/a" vengeance because it provides an unflattering portrait, or in order to mark them out as singularly prejudiced against one another because of such a discourse (as in the 'mulatto legend'), is actually to distort the literary history of the Haitian Revolution. Such distortions have the effect not only of continuing to produce a very perverse picture of Haiti and Haitians, but cause us to miss crucial factors in understanding just how deeply ideas of "race" permeated understandings of the Haitian Revolution all across the Atlantic World, as well as how ideas about "hybridity" have affected popular discourse on both Haiti and "race" today. People did not and do not use racist language and "racial" stereotypes about Haiti *because* they are "black," "mulatto," or "white" (which would be to buy into *scientist* ideas about "race"), but rather because this pseudoscientific language has been implicitly accepted as *true*, even by many of those who have been the primary targets of its discourse.

By calling attention to the "racial" understandings that lie beneath nearly all writing about Haiti, then, I hope to show that as it unfolded and in the half century after Haitian independence, the Revolution was overwhelmingly read to be the result of some kind of "mulatto/a" vengeance rather than as a slave rebellion for freedom. Because this narrative of "mulatto/a" vengeance was the primary way in which the Haitian Revolution was understood in its day by virtually everyone who wrote about these events, nineteenth-century Haitian authors were not promoting a 'mulatto legend' of history designed to affirm their rule over a "black" majority when they emphasized the blame that had been placed on people of "mixed race," discussed the role that free people of color were understood to have played in the early days of the Revolution, or defended themselves from the stereotypes that had become attached to people called "mulattoes." Some Haitian authors did contribute to the pervasive transatlantic print culture of the Haitian Revolution and the narrative of "mulatto/a" vengeance that it catalyzed, and this contribution is what needs to be analyzed, not their putative, unsubstantiated, and supposedly collective desire to dominate all people with darker or lighter skin than their own.

Even though some nineteenth-century Haitian authors did contribute to the discourse of "'mulatto/a' vengeance," many writers from the early Haitian literary tradition quite conscientiously tried not to engage with

Introduction

this discourse. I submit that these authors have something to teach us all about how to understand the Haitian Revolution as something other than a "racial" insurrection. Taking seriously the criticism of Said's *Orientalism* (to which this study owes a great intellectual debt) that its representational scope was too one-sided, *Tropics of Haiti* acknowledges that, like Berlant's 'diva citizens,' various Haitian authors almost incessantly disrupted the 'voice-over' (Berlant, 223) of colonial discourse, even if their remonstrations could barely be heard above the constant din. One of the related goals of this study is to write early nineteenth-century Haitian authors back into the literary history of the Haitian Revolution as more than simple victims or vengeful aggressors, in the hope not only of uncovering the myriad ways in which a variety of people who lived during the Haitian Revolution or in the world created by its immediate aftermath understood these events as they unfolded and tried to make sense of them, but how we might make better sense of them today.

Many nineteenth-century Haitian authors provided ardent counter-narratives of "mulatto/a" vengeance in which they passionately pleaded for an eradication of the terms "mulatto" and "negro" to refer to any divisions in their society, as when Baron de Vastey implored his compatriots to, 'scorn these insulting epithets [*méprisez ces épithètes injurieuses*] of *negroes* of the North and *mulattoes* of the South that they have given us' (1815b). I believe that we should heed these calls and must seriously consider relinquishing any unexamined usage of the language of "racial" taxonomies in our scholarship. As scholar Florence Gauthier has written, using the word "mulatto" as either a distinct category of identity or as a label for entire movements of historiography, literature, and politics, is to return to a historically violent method of organizing the world: 'The term mulatto had been used by segregationists to denote the category of all people of *mixed-blood*: it is therefore a word that reeks of the language of color prejudice.' She continues by observing, 'It is regrettable, even dangerous, to see it employed today as a common historical category' (2013). Moreover, I dare say that as a "racial," social, or political category, the word "mulatto" is every bit as inflammatory and prejudicial as the word "negro," and we should all not only care about any unexamined usage of the term in our society and in our scholarship, where it often masquerades as either a completely innocent or relatively benign marker, but we should work to eradicate it. Paul Gilroy has persuasively argued in *Against Race*, on similar grounds, that 'raciology' or 'the lore that brings the virtual realties of "race" to dismal and destructive life' has been so successful at 'saturat[ing] the discourses in which it circulates' that 'it cannot be readily re-signified or de-signified, and to imagine that its dangerous meanings can be easily rearticulated into benign democratic forms would be to exaggerate the power of critical and oppositional interests' (2000, 11–12). If

Frantz Fanon's philosophy teacher implored his young student, 'Whenever you hear anyone abuse the Jews, pay attention, because he is talking about you" (1967, 122), in much the same way we must pay attention to anyone who encourages us to divide large swaths of people into "mulattoes" and "negroes" because he is talking about dividing all of us. Such divisions are not just invariably racist, but they are as anti-human as the slavery the words "white," "mulatto," and "negro" supported. I do not know if we can 'liberate humankind from race-thinking' any time soon and without the kinds of unintended consequences that Gilroy describes (2000, 12), but I am encouraged that we can 'liberate' our scholarship from such a destructive and divisive hermeneutic.

But we are getting ahead of ourselves here. We have a whole lot of work to do before we can conclude that over two centuries of writing about the Haitian Revolution inflected with colonialist ideas about "race" have kept the "mulatto/a" vengeance narrative alive. So, let us back up now. To get to the end, we must find our way to the beginning. The "mulatto/a" vengeance narrative of the Haitian Revolution is a palimpsest that has been written, rewritten, copied, recopied, and then written again many times over since the onset of insurrection in Saint-Domingue in August of 1791. If it is true that, as Martin Heidegger has written, 'In essential history, the beginning comes last' (1), it will only be by painstakingly peeling back the many layers of the various different kinds of writing about the Haitian Revolution that the idea of Haiti itself will surface as intimately connected to a narrative of "mulatto/a" vengeance. Ultimately, this literary history of the Haitian Revolution will be hermeneutic in structure. That is to say that it will circulate around what Luanne T. Frank has called the 'meanings to come' (1) that arise out of the complex interplay between the past of the texts we are examining and the present of the future in which we are living. In the words of Anthony Kerby, '[t]he goal of a hermeneutic understanding' is finding out what an 'artefact' 'can mean to us in the present.' He writes, 'Hermeneutical understanding is the result of an authentic dialogue between the past and our present, which occurs when there is a "fusion of horizons" between the two. In the end, this is an act of self-understanding, of understanding our own historical reality and its continuity with the past' (91). Like Tzvetan Todorov in *The Conquest of America*, 'the present is more important to me than the past' (4), precisely because I believe that all of the ways in which the Haitian Revolution has historically been read as a "racial" revolution have everything to tell us about readings of present-day Haiti as the land of continuous political, economic, and "racial" strife. In unearthing this painful narrative, I have every confidence that we will see the harm in continuing to use the vocabulary of "racial" taxonomers to describe, classify, and decode the behavior of human beings. To echo Fanon again, *Humankind, I believe in you!*

Introduction

Tropics of the Haitian Revolution

This study of what I have been calling the "mulatto/a" vengeance narrative of the Haitian Revolution and the four "racial" tropes of it examined here—the "monstrous hybrid," the "tropical temptresses," the tragic "mulatto/a", and the "colored historian"—operates under the premise that those who wrote about the Haitian Revolution in the long nineteenth century gave recourse to these "racial" tropologies in order to make sense of the events to which they were either witness or about which in their aftermath they were deeply fascinated, horrified, or confused. If these "racial" tropes have something to tell us about the experience—expressed or imagined—of living in a "raced" body, then, they also have something to tell us about the experience—expressed or imagined—of having lived through the Haitian Revolution and its aftermath. These racialized tropes do more than simply reflect understandings people had of pseudoscientific theories of "race" and "hybridity" circulating in the Atlantic World. Importantly, they helped to create and sustain a long-standing cultural vocabulary about revolutions. This particular vocabulary, which took the Haitian Revolution as a central point of reference, is one that became infinitely useful to individual nation-states as they constructed national narratives based around policies of inclusion and exclusion and to the slave-holding Atlantic World as it grasped to hold on to its many lucrative plantation economies. Although national distinctions and concerns did matter, they were often subordinated to transnational concerns about the continuation of the slave trade, the capacity of "blacks" for self-rule, and the familial implications of plantation culture. That is to say that the U.S., French, Haitian, German, and British authors whose works are under examination here, though they may have had different overt reasons for writing about the Revolution, still wrote about it with largely the same implicit "racial" tropics.

My particular usage of the concept of "racial" tropes in relationship to the Haitian Revolution has been heavily influenced by Hayden White's ideas concerning the 'tropological theory of discourse.' White has written that tropes 'gives us understanding, or to put it another way, imagination and thought.' He explains:

> For too long the relationship between these two pairs has been conceived as an opposition. The tropological theory of discourse helps us to understand how speech mediates between these supposed oppositions, just as discourse itself mediates between our apprehension of those aspects of experience still 'strange' to us and those aspects of it which we 'understand' because we have found an order of words adequate to its domestication. (21)

In examining what White refers to as 'verbal artifacts,' I have identified four of the most dominant tropes that people in the eighteenth and nineteenth centuries used to understand the events of the Haitian Revolution; tropes that rendered those 'aspects of experience' that might have been 'strange' into 'an order of words' that made them infinitely understandable. This literary history is not so much strictly historical as it is basically interpretive, and it will be far less positive in any of its conclusions than it will be evocative. For, importantly, understanding tropology is not 'a matter of choosing between objectivity and distortion, but rather between different strategies for constituting "reality" in thought' (22). To take just one example, in the first part of *Tropics of Haiti*, by placing the "mulatto/a" vengeance narrative up against what I have referred to as the Enlightenment literacy narrative, I do not suggest that one is more accurate or plausible than the other, but rather that both depend upon 'different strategies' of narration, and therefore different tropics of representation.

The subject of this literary history is simultaneously the reaction and/or response of individuals to the Haitian Revolution as it occurred and what Ronald Paulson has called 'the problem of representing the phenomenon in words and images' afterward (4). These are writers and observers who were sometimes for, sometimes against, and very often ambivalent in their ways of seeing the Revolution. Therefore, 'referentially,' what must be taken into account when using the concept of representation or troping as a frame is not, as Paulson notes, '(except for purposes of difference) what actually happened but what was thought to have happened, as reported in available sources—what served as referent and as analogue ... and the concepts and abstractions to which [the writer] had access and for which he sought equivalents' (5). For our purposes, we are not so much concerned with the *truth* of what 'actually happened' but rather with the ways in which writers found the means to express what they 'thought' had happened, what they wished had happened, or what they hoped to convince others had happened.

For many of those living in the nineteenth-century Atlantic World, it appears to have scarcely mattered, in the end, what the *truth* about the Haitian Revolution might actually have been. The 'system of knowledge' that was in common circulation in the transatlantic print culture of the Haitian Revolution was, as with *orientalism*, not '"truth" but representations' (1978, 21). In Said's words, when we examine the 'authority' that is 'formed, irradiated, [and] disseminated' (20) by these kinds of representations, '[t]he things to look at are style, figures of speech, setting, narrative, devices, historical and social circumstances, *not* the correctness of the representation nor its fidelity to some great original' (21). In this light, taken together, the words 'Haitian' and 'Revolution,' like the words 'French' and 'Revolution,'

Introduction

took on the 'associations' of a 'particular series of events' (Paulson, 4) in the late eighteenth and nineteenth centuries. In the case of Haiti, these events were the thwarted insurrection of the revolutionary Vincent Ogé in October of 1790 and his subsequent execution in February of 1791; the fiery insurrection of the slaves in August of 1791 who burned Cap-Français, now Cap-Haïtien; the French commissioners Léger Félicité Sonthonax and Etienne Polverel's qualified declaration of the abolition of slavery in 1793; the War of the South between General André Rigaud and General Toussaint Louverture beginning in 1799; Louverture's ascension to power in 1794 and his governorship of the colony until 1802, when, under the orders of Napoleon Bonaparte, the Leclerc expedition arrived in Saint-Domingue to reinstate slavery and kidnap Louverture; and finally, Dessalines's renaming of Saint-Domingue as Haiti, his proclamation of independence from France in the fall of 1803, the Haitian revolutionists' creation of an independent state in 1804, and the subsequent driving out of the French colonists from the country in the spring of 1804.

The "racial" tropes that would eventually be used to assign meaning to the above events were not necessarily created by the authors who wrote about them, but rather the writers examined here adapted and changed many of these already existing narratives and metaphors about "race" to make the Revolution more 'bearable' or even 'usable' (Paulson, 6). The tropes and referents used to talk about the Haitian Revolution provided a language for understanding these events that became infused with distinctly "racial" meaning. As we will see throughout this literary history, Ogé's revolt would be characterized as the prime piece of evidence for the fact that the free people of color had sought to raise the slaves of the colony against their masters, while the War of the South between Louverture and Rigaud would be attributed to an innate hatred of "mulattoes" for *pure* "blacks" and vice versa ("monstrous hybridity"); Louverture's kidnapping would often be interpreted as a capitulation owing to his supposedly *pure* "African" nobility (juxtaposed with André Rigaud's "mulatto" vengeance) or as the result of a heartbreaking "interracial" family romance involving Louverture's sons Isaac and Placide, along the order of the tragic "mulatto/a." At the same time, the abolition of slavery would often be attributed to ("white") French benevolence and the revolt of the "negro" slaves would be associated with "mulatto" influence ("monstrous hybridity" and the "colored historian"); the participation of women of color would also be "racially" codified in terms of seduction and reproduction, benevolence, and betrayal ("the tropical temptress"); and finally, Dessalines's ascension to power and, later, the division of the country into two distinct states by Pétion and Christophe would serve at once as the ultimate culmination of "mulatto/a" vengeance as vengeance both *of* and *for* "mulattoes." Ironically, any attempt by Haitian authors to read this history beyond the boundaries of a slave rebellion would come to be labeled as a part of a "colored" or racist "mulatto" history, coterminous with Nicholls's argument about the 'mulatto legend of history.'

Part One of this monograph, 'From Enlightenment Literacy to "Mulatto/a" Vengeance,' examines the relationship between the seemingly counterpoised idea of literate "black" slaves who were inspired to revolt by Enlightenment principles and vengeful "mulatto" children who rebelled out of a desire for parricide, showing how both the Enlightenment literacy narrative and the "mulatto/a" vengeance narrative were beholden to a pseudoscientific vocabulary of "race."

In the first chapter of *Tropics of Haiti*, I take up the figure of the "mulatto" as both a stereotypical object of fears about "racial" mixing and as a destabilizing symbol of Enlightenment justifications for transgression and resistance on the part of slaves. Many depictions of "mulattoes" as monstrous "racial" hybrids were ultimately connected to an author's unease about the rational nature of slave rebellion. The epistemological uncertainty that nearly always accompanied descriptions of the behavior of the Haitian revolutionists—whether considered "mulatto" or "black"—promoted a vocabulary of incongruity and uncertainty with respect to the ultimate meaning of revolutionary violence. Portrayals of the Haitian revolutionaries as "monstrous hybrids," therefore, reflect larger questions circulating in the Atlantic World about the meaning of both revolution and racial "miscegenation": would it cause regeneration or degeneration of the "black race," and to whose side of a revolution would "mulattoes" belong, to the side of their slave-mothers or to the figurative and literal side of their father-masters?

It is precisely due to the different "racial" meanings that have been attached to the events of the Revolution in many European, U.S. American, West Indian, and Haitian sources that these tropes are also related to the notion of stereotyping. As Homi Bhabha has written, the concept of the 'stereotype' implies a '"fixity" in the ideological construction of otherness' (1994, 94) that is characterized by 'ambivalence.' Bhabha writes that stereotyping, 'vacillates between what is always "in place", already known, and something that must be anxiously repeated' (1994, 95). Even so, as a 'complex, ambivalent, contradictory mode of representation' (1994, 100), the colonial stereotype also provides an unwitting, but probably unconscious, opportunity for resistance. In the context of the Haitian Revolution, writings *about* Baron de Vastey and writings *from* Baron de Vastey provide perhaps the best examples of the way in which the real-life words of revolutionary actors forced the reading public to confront a rhetoric of the Haitian Revolution that was at once *supra*-logical and painstakingly violent. In chapter two, for example, we see that Baron de Vastey anticipated the negative potential of the tropology of the "monstrous hybrid" and sought to combat it in his important and

Introduction

widely reviewed political memoir, *Le Système colonial dévoilé* (1814), when he unequivocally defended the violent actions of the revolutionaries, arguing that these acts were solely a reaction to the violence of the colonial system and not the perfidious result of being of "African" or of "mixed race." Even though Vastey's memoir can be considered one of the founding documents of anti-colonial discourse, we will also see that it was Vastey himself whose image as a vengeful "mulatto" revolutionary became one of the most pervasive symbols of "monstrous hybridity" in nineteenth-century Haitian revolutionary historiography.

Chapter three describes how using information found in the captivity narratives of Michel Etienne Descourtilz and the colonist Gros, as well as their storytelling techniques, in *Bug-Jargal* (1826) Victor Hugo reproduces the idea that "mixed-race" revolutionaries were naturally "monstrous hybrids" who had degenerated precisely because of their admixture of "blood." However, Hugo's novel also provides a probably unconscious moment of resistance, when Habibrah, a character identified as being of "mixed race," challenges the authority of Enlightenment humanism using a similar rhetoric to the real-life revolutionary Vastey, by asking his oppressors in the language of transnational abolition, 'Am I not a man?'

In Part Two, 'Transgressing the Trope of the "Tropical Temptress": Representation and Resistance in Revolutionary Saint-Domingue,' I examine the pervasive image of the "tropical temptress"—or the dangerously beautiful woman of color—found in nearly all travel writing dealing with Saint-Domingue. This figure was used in the literature of the Haitian Revolution to explain the idea that devious women of color had had helped to facilitate the loss of the colony through their powers of seduction and reproduction. Heinrich von Kleist, in his 'Betrothal in Santo Domingo' (1811), simultaneously exhibited a fascination and disgust with "interracial" sex by suggesting that it had created "tropical temptresses," who had literally given birth to the Revolution in the form of "mixed-race" revolutionaries. Leonora Sansay (Mary Hassal) was also influenced by natural historians and travel writing in her *Secret History; or the Horrors of Santo Domingo* (1808), when she positioned the "mulatta" as a figure to be simultaneously admired for her economic and sexual power over "white" men and feared for the innate vengeance she might visit upon them in the revolutionary hour. Each of the anonymously published texts under analysis in this section, when examined more closely, actually complicate the stereotypical theory of the "tropical temptress" as a figure of seduction, offering her instead as a figure of rebellion. I argue that this reflects the Janus face of representations of women of color in the literary history of the Haitian Revolution, the about-face of which was her unbridled sexuality, the shadowed-face having been her radical transgression of patriarchal authority. While the woman of color's supposedly innate lasciviousness is by far the most often discussed issue with respect to women in the modern historiography of colonial and revolutionary Saint-Domingue, the chapters in Part Two suggest that reading against this stereotype produces a radically different literary history of the woman of color from Saint-Domingue.

Chapter Four considers, to that end, the anonymously published, *La Mulâtre comme il y a beaucoup de blanches* (1803), in which the character Mimi takes up a passionate defense of women of color through her deconstruction of the "racial" theories about the dangerous, deviant, and singular sexual agency of women of "mixed race" put forth by eighteenth-century travel writers. Mimi radically inserts herself into the civic life of the colony when she argues for non-violent reform of colonial laws and legislative abolition of slavery rather than revolution.

Chapter Five turns to the three-volume novel *Zelica; the Creole* (1820), most often attributed to Leonora Sansay, which ambivalently constructs a narrative in which during the Revolution, women of color become the principle guardians of "white" women, whom they protect from both men of color and male European colonists. In addition, the novel provokes questions about the nature of a gendered revolution that often made no room for benevolence and kindness as a form of rebellion against authority.

Chapter Six is all about 'Theresa; a Haytien Tale' (1828), which was serialized and published anonymously in the first African American newspaper *Freedom's Journal*, and is now considered to be the first African American short story. I argue that this brief text provides an even more redemptive role for women of color. 'Theresa' imagines women as central to the liberation of the colony through their unfailing and unquestioning allegiance to the revolutionary cause. 'Theresa' is therefore not buttressed by pseudoscientific claims of the innate savagery or hyper-sexuality of "black" women, but instead unequivocally celebrates their ability to contribute to slave rebellions, imagining a hitherto denied active role for women of color in the events of the Haitian Revolution.

Part Three, 'The Trope of the Tragic "Mulatto/a" and the Haitian Revolution' argues that though the stereotype of the tragic "mulatto/a" is usually considered a U.S. phenomenon, it can also be traced to eighteenth- and nineteenth-century Francophone literature, where the trope surfaced in conjunction with the image of the Haitian Revolution as a tragic and parricidal "race" war.

In Chapter Seven, the Louisiana-born Victor Séjour's short story, 'Le Mulâtre' (1837), represents my primary example of the ways in which debates over the effects of "racial mixing" were mediated simultaneously through the image of the tragic "mulatto/a" and the Haitian Revolution. Rather than celebrating the desire of the slaves to achieve freedom at any cost,

Introduction

Séjour's narrative laments the psychosocial consequences of such a parricidal revolution, suggesting that slavery and "miscegenation" were ultimately responsible for the corruption, degradation, and eventual destruction of the family.

In Chapter Eight, which considers the French abolitionist Alphonse de Lamartine's verse drama, *Toussaint Louverture* (1850), I show how writing that narrates the life of Louverture as not simply a 'colonial family romance,' but as an "interracial" family romance further demonstrates anxieties about the psychological effects of the plantation system. Attempts to explain Louverture's life using a grammar beholden to the "mulatto/a" vengeance narrative, and especially that of the tragic "mulatto/a," suggests that the epistemological problems created by slavery and revolution engendered an Oedipal tendency in people of color who, in the revolutionary hour, might either symbolically or literally occasion the death of their parents and vice versa when faced with a choice between their family and the nation.

In Chapter Nine, the Haitian author Eméric Bergeaud's historical romance of the Revolution, *Stella* (1859), complicates the archetypal portrait of the tragic "mulatto/a." *Stella* provides a passionate reversal of the notion that differences in skin color encouraged family (read: national) conflicts. *Stella* offers a celebration of Haiti's diversity by arguing that the union between people of different skin color during the War of Independence was the productive process responsible for the liberation of the country. Bergeaud's novel consequently forces us to recognize the complicated and indeed conflicting meanings of the "mulatto," which was the primary symbol of the both the family tragedy and violent rebellion (and, therefore, national uncertainty) in nineteenth-century European and U.S. American depictions of people of color, yet is described as an empty "racial" signifier left over from colonialism in much of post-revolutionary Haitian letters.

Part Four, 'Requiem for the "Colored Historian"; or the "Mulatto Legend of History,"' circles back to the thesis of David Nicholls's *From Dessalines to Duvalier*. This section shows not only the deep uncertainty inherent in Nicholls's own account of the general features of this 'legend' and its corollary in the 'black' or '*noiriste*' legend of history, but exposes its relationship to nineteenth-century 'racisms' with respect to the widespread idea of the "colored historian."

Chapter Ten looks at the way in which Nicholls's vocabulary about the 'mulatto legend' was almost entirely derived from that of nineteenth-century transatlantic abolitionist writing about Haiti, where the idea was first proffered that history itself could have a "color" or a "race." Beginning with John Beard's biography of Louverture and its representative status in the transatlantic print culture of the Haitian Revolution, I examine the influence of this text on the American abolitionists William Wells

Brown and James Redpath. Finally, I undertake what is the first systematic examination of Beard's, and later C.L.R. James's, claims that the Haitian historian Joseph Saint-Rémy was a biased "mulatto" historian whose account of Louverture's life should be entirely dismissed.

In Chapter Eleven, I expose more fully the relationship of Nicholls's thought to nineteenth-century 'racisms' by connecting the genealogy of the 'mulatto legend of history' to the French abolitionist Victor Schoelcher's claims about the 'yellow imagination' of "mulatto" writers in nineteenth-century Haiti. If the vocabulary of Nicholls's argument came from Beard and Redpath, the ideological construct of that argument, particularly the idea that such a history was *legendary*, can be traced directly to Schoelcher's idea about the 'imagination jaune' of Boyer-era Haiti's historians and writers, including Beaubrun Ardouin and Pierre Faubert. I suggest that the 'racisms' expressed in Schoelcher's writings remain precisely that which has prevented us from being able to consider nineteenth-century Haitian historiography and literature outside of colonial epistemologies.

In Chapter Twelve, in part to show what we have missed when our readings of nineteenth-century literary texts are circumscribed by an *a priori* idea about what is contained therein based on the author's skin color or "race," I take a look at Pierre Faubert's *Ogé, ou le préjugé de couleur* (1841/1856). I offer this play as a prime example of how the trope of the "colored historian" has led to an obfuscation of Faubert's much more important contribution to what is now called *critical race theory*, on the one hand, and, on the other, his position as one of the first writers in what I have called a tradition of Black Atlantic Humanism that emanated from nineteenth-century Haitian authors.

While each of these chapters zooms *in* on a particular text to provide a sustained close reading, my focus will also zoom *out* many times to survey the landscape of writing in a particular genre like fiction or a specific subset, such as examining writing about the children of Louverture. Because of its palimpsestic, referential nature, many of the works initially discussed in one place in *Tropics of Haiti*, will be mentioned again, often in several different places, entering this study of the connection between the idea of "race" and the idea of the Haitian Revolution whenever they are most relevant to the analysis.

The years 1789 and 1865 mark the chronological boundaries of this study, as well as two important moments in the literary history of the Atlantic World. 1789, of course, signals the formal beginning of the French Revolution, which, along with the narrative of "mulatto/a" vengeance, and the narrative of Enlightenment literacy, was often represented as one of the primary catalysts for the start of the Haitian Revolution; the year 1865 marks the end of the U.S. Civil War and the final abolition of plantation slavery in

Introduction

the U.S. Because this was an age of slavery, the majority of representations of the Haitian Revolution examined in this literary history were composed mostly in support or in condemnation of ideas of slavery and revolution, with a multitude of ambivalences in-between. Choosing these boundaries that in many ways reflect Euro-American points of historical reference constitutes a compromise on my part, but one that I recognize and am willing to live with. While I could have chosen to begin this study at 1790, reflecting the year of Ogé's rebellion, I ultimately chose not to because of the highly controversial nature of that rebellion (which will be discussed in chapter eleven), but also because in many ways choosing that date closes off a conversation about revolution that was taking place long before Ogé and long before the formal start of the slave insurrection in 1791. Choosing the much more evocative date of 1789 allows me to posit this year less as a historical starting point, since many of the works that will be discussed far predate that year itself, and more as a theoretical starting point for a tropics of Haiti. The year 1804, the birth of Haitian independence, carries with it a similar evocative rather than literal quality, but choosing that year would have been, in my opinion, to overshadow too much of what was written at the end of the eighteenth century by making it seem as if this study had to do with literary history of the Haitian Revolution only *after* it had taken place rather than while it was actually unfolding.

The authors whose works fall within these chronological boundaries and upon whom I have primarily chosen to focus have been chosen precisely because of their ambivalences and contradictions. The texts I consider in-depth in the individual chapters have been selected because, in my opinion, they represent the best examples of the kinds of complex representations of "race" that the revolution in Saint-Domingue called forth. Even though each chapter deals deeply with only a few specific works, because representations of the Haitian Revolution span many textual genres, including poetry, drama, the epistolary romance, the short story, the novel, the memoir, and abolitionist pamphlets and speeches, I have worked in and across these genres in every chapter, weaving them together as much as possible, in order to show the ways in which the era's struggles with issues of "interracial" political and intimate relationships and the changing conception of the family and the nation charged the Haitian Revolution with distinctly "racial" meaning. That is to say, I have not hesitated to examine as *literary* travelogues, personal letters, historical essays, encyclopedias, or legal writing when I have needed them to interrogate the connection between pseudo-scientific theories of "race" and popular understandings of the Haitian Revolution.

This analysis does privilege the written word (whether published or private) since I rarely consider visual, audio, or physical material and cultural artifacts like dress and dance. One of the primary benefits of working with written texts is that, as Christopher Iannini has written, 'it creates a clearer picture of how natural history reached a wider audience—beyond a circle of intimate correspondents' (15), making it possible to imagine, in this case, how the Haitian Revolution entered the living rooms of literate people living in the Atlantic World. One of the downsides, of course, is that focusing on the *literary* tends to obscure other types of response to the Haitian Revolution by the non-literate, whether by slaves or people who were otherwise without access to book knowledge, and especially by subaltern peoples excluded from what Gayatri Spivak referred to, in a famous interview with Leon de Kock, as the 'culture of imperialism' (qtd. in de Kock, 1992, 45).

Therefore, although I believe *Tropics of Haiti* to be the most comprehensive literary history of the Haitian Revolution to date, I recognize that it is by no means exhaustive or all-inclusive; nor does it pretend to provide the definitive word on interpreting representations of the Haitian Revolution of any kind as a type of history. This is not least because for reasons of linguistic obstacle I have not been able to fully examine the various Dutch (and in at least one case, Polish!)[21] representations of the Haitian Revolution that circulated in the Atlantic World; nor is it because, for limitations of time and space, I have not been able to delve into the world of German, Italian[22] and Spanish-language representations of the Revolution or to fully extend my analysis beyond 1865 in order to discover what other tropes almost assuredly surfaced in the post-slavery and later postcolonial Atlantic World; but rather, such a caveat is meant to imply that I view this work as merely the beginning of what I hope will become a tradition of thinking about the early representations of the Haitian Revolution—whether in art, music, dance, or artifact, in addition to the written word—as a largely uncharted comparative field in need of more critical attention. I have no doubt, for example, that before this book is even in the galleys, additional literary representations of the Haitian Revolution will be unearthed in the physical archives of libraries or in the pages of under-examined nineteenth-century newspapers and journals or even in previously unknown private family troves. The reach of the Haitian Revolution was so wide that it may never be possible to uncover everything that has been written and preserved about the events.

21 In 1818, Lithuanian author Sophie de Choiseul-Gouffier (née Tyzenhauzów) published *Le Polonais à Saint-Domingue, ou la Jeune Créole*. The novel was original written in French, but was published in Warsaw. It was almost immediately translated into Polish where it appeared under the title *Polak w St. Domingo, czyli Młoda Mulatka* (1819) and much later it was translated into German as *Der Pole auf St. Domingo oder die junge Creolin* (1858).

22 For example, Gaetano Donizetti et al., *Il Furioso nell Isola di S. Domingo; melodramma in due atti* (1833).

Introduction

A Word on Reflexivity and a Note on Terminology

It is now in vogue to practice self-reflexivity, or self-positioning, with respect to one's work. While I can appreciate the value of asking, as did the anthropologist and performer Gina Ulysse in a plenary session at the Haitian Studies Association given at Indiana University-Bloomington in 2009, 'You're studying us, but who's studying you?' I am also skeptical that such information is always used in the way that Ulysse intended. Such reflexivity can be used at times to proclaim special powers of seeing for one's self as a neutral outsider in contrast to an embattled insider rather than to remove the idea of the unbiased, un-embodied, and objective scholar who benevolently provides (knowledge and supplies) rather than procures (prestige and money in the form of academic compensation) from the community he or she studies. Such information can also, perhaps more perniciously, be used for the purposes of predetermining a person's ideology.

As a first-generation U.S. born Haitian woman through my mother who is also of distant German and Irish descent through my father, I have often been asked by mostly well-meaning U.S. and European scholars as well as foreign aid workers to Haiti about the "class" and/or "race" of my Haitian family. Those who view me as *milàt*, in the way that it suggests both class and skin color in Haitian Creole, have often been skeptical of my ideological leanings. But my skin color cannot tell them about the ideologies and class positions of either me or the majority of my Haitian family members, whose lives can hardly be characterized as "elite": my grandmother was a seamstress who, compelled to escape the social and economic repressions of the Duvalierist regime, left her entire family in Haiti (including my mother and uncle) for eight long years to work in the United States, eventually saving up enough money to bring her children and extended family out of Haiti, one by painstaking one. Furthermore, even though as a U.S.-based academic with a Ph.D., I now exist in a privileged position relative to the people whom I study and to whom I am related, in no way do I share the belief attributed to much of the so-called "Haitian elite" that either French or U.S. imperialism had anything but disastrous consequences for Haiti. Therefore, I probably tend to resent the inference, perhaps more than others, that Haitian writers and scholars, particularly those with *light* skin like me, were and are necessarily more biased or *francophilic* than anyone else.

As a result of my cynicism about the utility of "race" or skin color to tell us anything benign about a person in advance, like Georges Fouron (2006), I have risked annoying my readers by using double quotation marks throughout this work to exhibit my skepticism for the words "race," "mulatto," "black," and "white," and the utterly unfortunate term "miscegenation," even while finding their usage practically unavoidable in a work about "racial" classification systems and popular understandings of "race."[23] For, like Fred Constant, I believe that 'race is a socially constructed category, if not ... a practical device for policy implementation' (x), and not the preconceived, wholly deterministic, biological or sociological entity that it pretends to be. Even so, I have also had to appreciate the fact that, as Appiah has written, 'races are like witches: however *unreal* witches are, belief in witches, like belief in races has had—and in many communities continues to have—profound consequences for human social life' (1989, 277). It is for this reason that I have adopted the generic term "of color" when not referring to the ways in which people whose bodies were marked by beliefs in racial inferiority had been divided into "mulattoes" and "negroes."

Though I believe that referring to people as being "of color" is an entirely imperfect solution to the problem of "race," since if we must be against "race," we must also be against "color," and all other essentially organizational notions of identity, there must still be some way to describe those who were collectively oppressed by the kinds of prejudices that made a person subject to dominant epistemologies of "race"; there must also be some way to discuss the consciously constructed movements of solidarity created by exploited communities to oppose the material effects of these dominant epistemologies. The only thing that perhaps occasions more psychological and physical violence against marginalized people today than 'race-thinking' itself is the belief that we now live in a "post-racial" world or in a "colorblind" society. These are beliefs in which racism, rather than "race," is what appears not to exist, and therefore the former is no longer considered to be a factor that influences opportunity, well-being, safety, justice, and freedom. Such *post-racist* thinking has the perhaps unintended effect of trying to force us to forget the brutalities that we, and our ancestors, as human beings, have suffered at the hands of "racial" thinking. *De-racing* our understanding of the Haitian Revolution, on the contrary, means that we must affirm at every turn that racism has had horribly deleterious effects on exploited populations, and that it is alive and festering today. This recognition also requires of us that

---

23 The creation of the word "miscegenation" in 1863 was part of an elaborate hoax perpetrated by an anonymous U.S. author who wrote a satirical pamphlet in which he claimed to promote "racial mixing." The purpose of the pamphlet, however, was actually to show the dangers of such 'miscegenation,' defined as 'the mixture of two or more races.' The author explained the creation of this word by writing, 'There is as yet no word in the language which expresses exactly the idea' and the word 'express[es] nothing else' (*Miscegenation*, ii). As Malchow has written of this, 'If *half-breed* implied inadequacy, incompleteness, and failure, miscegenation ... suggested through its pseudoscientific resonance that the act of engendering such creatures was itself not merely individually culpable and shameful but a biological confusion, an error that set in train the process of racial degeneration' (184).

Introduction

we deliberately and quite self-consciously untangle our understandings of the individual ideologies, politics, intellect, beauty, capability, and humanity of various revolutionary actors from their appearance or phenotype, or what is commonly called "race."

While this study looks at a variety of different kinds of writing about the Haitian Revolution from authors who have been variously identified as "mulatto," "black," or "white," I have looked to the texts themselves rather than the author's "racial" identity or skin color—self-identified or not—to provide information about his or her reading of the Revolution. As Laurent Dubois has written, 'Understanding the Haitian Revolution ... requires avoiding using racial designations—white, mulatto, black—as categories that can generate explanations rather than as social artifacts that demand them' (2004, 5). Similarly, understanding representations of the Haitian Revolution, whether published as fiction or nonfiction, requires avoiding using "race" as any kind of key that can reveal the motives and ideologies of their authors. If, as Jean Casimir has written, '"A Negro" is the result of a socialization process,' because '"Negroes" as such never disembarked in Saint-Domingue' (xiv), the "mulatto" is the result of the same process of 'socialization.' In other words, one is not a "mulatto" or a "negro" in the womb, which is to say, 'there are no genes for whiteness, mulattoness, blackness, or other classifications, only ideological interpretations of phenotype' (Dupuy, 46). One can only become "mulatto," "negro," and even "white" in the pseudoscientific sense that will be examined here after centuries of historical understandings about "race" become grafted onto identity and are used to explicate physiognomy, behavior, and ideology. It is precisely for this reason that in the era of mid-nineteenth-century abolition we will see Louverture's pure "negro" identity stressed by many anti-slavery writers. In his biography, *The Life of Toussaint L'Ouverture* (1853), Beard sought to use Louverture's image as an 'African' to shirk theories of what Paul Gilmore has called, 'mulatto exceptionalism' (59–60) when he wrote, 'Toussaint was a negro. We wish emphatically to mark the fact that he was wholly without white blood. Whatever he was, and whatever he did, he achieved all in virtue of qualities which in kind are common to the African race' (23). It is because of the same process of 'socialization' that we will see Louverture's *pure* "blackness" challenged in the twentieth-century era of U.S. segregation by authors like Hesketh Prichard, who, in order to prove a theory of "mulatto" superiority, and therefore white supremacy, argued that '[j]udging from his pictures, you cannot but form the opinion that Toussaint was not a pure-blooded negro' (278).[24]

---

24 See also Edward Byron Reuters, *The Mulatto in the United States: including a study of the role of the mixed-blood races throughout the world* (1918), where the author argues that the vast majority of the people listed in W.E.B. Du Bois's theory of the 'talented tenth'

Although I do provide detailed biographical and genealogical information about many of the authors I discuss, which often includes popular understandings of an author's "race," when I believe it enriches our understanding of the national literary histories out of which these texts emerged or when it provides identifying information about the production of a text itself or even clues about the identity of an anonymous author, I have tried to avoid using that person's "racial" biography as a legend that might tell us how to interpret his or her writings. I view the texts under analysis here as mostly closed artifacts, which themselves reveal everything we need to know about their author's interpretation of the Haitian Revolution and its connection to "race." What I have found through my examination of this vast body of writing is that the kinds of fissures exposed by looking to identity to explain contradictions and gaps in a person's writings, are usually already present in the texts themselves and therefore we need not rely upon biographical details largely provided by third parties to reveal the *truth*, since these biographical interpretations were undoubtedly influenced by the biographer or *witness's* own understandings of both "race" and the Haitian Revolution.

In the same vein, I have also tried to avoid reductively labeling the people I study as 'apologists,' 'ideologues,' or 'propagandists,' as a way not to have to deal with or interpret what they actually say, especially since I find that these terms have been mostly used to disavow the utility of early Haitian authorship. Most often, these terms surface as code words that allow a writer to feel justified in dismissing the work in question on either formal or methodological grounds or even on the grounds of simply not liking what the author in question has to say.

To conclude, in Herbert Gold's *Haiti: Best Nightmare on Earth* (1991), a book whose politics I do not at all share, I cannot help but find resonance in the character Cindy's statement that 'Haiti is just like everyplace else … except it's Haiti' (223). To me, combating both Haitian exceptionalism and the 'silencing of the past' requires showing that Haiti is not 'odd' exactly by placing it in a comparative—transatlantic and hemispheric—framework. Such a framework allows for us to see the ways in which Haiti's cultural, national, and linguistic specificity is not *exceptional* in the sense that it is utterly beyond all comprehension, belief, or rationality, but rather that Haiti's particularity is utterly understandable once we also comprehend the comparative historical and cultural conditions that brought it into existence, as well as the internal and external pressures that have shaped its development, which, I dare say, is exactly the same way that we should try to understand 'everyplace else.'

---

were actually of "mixed race." In the course of such an argument, the author identifies Louverture as a 'mulatto' because of the 'reasonable doubt' about his 'ancestry' alluded to by Prichard (64, 189, 197).

PART ONE
From "Monstrous Hybridity" to Enlightenment Literacy

'Le yo vle tiye chen, yo di li fou.'

—Haitian proverb

'... il y a un proverbe parmi les nègres des Antilles, qui dit:
Dieu a fait blanc, Dieu a fait noir, diable a fait mulâtre.'

—Drouin de Bercy, *De Saint-Domingue: de ses guerres, de ses révolutions, de ses ressources et des moyens à prendre pour y rétablir la paix et l'industrie* (1814)

My research into the vast world of eighteenth- and nineteenth-century Haitian revolutionary print culture reveals that literary texts dealing with the Haitian Revolution from 1789 to 1865, whether published as fiction or nonfiction, had a broad influence on not only early understandings of the events, but on later popular historiographies like C.L.R James's widely consulted *The Black Jacobins* (1938). James's highly influential text, which explicitly references the writings of some of the most infamous promoters of taxonomic thinking with respect to "race" in Saint-Domingue, such as Moreau de Saint-Méry, Baron de Wimpffen, Hilliard D'Auberteuil, and Pamphile de Lacroix, also bears the uncanny influence of the British naval officer Marcus Rainsford's *An Historical Account of the Black Empire of Hayti* (1805). Even though James refers to Rainsford's history as a 'panegyric' and a 'propaganda pamphlet,' like Rainsford long before him, James famously promulgated the idea that Toussaint Louverture's ascent to leadership depended in great part on the act of literacy, and specifically, on the act of Louverture's reading and interpretation of the famous 'Black Spartacus' passage contained in works signed by the abbé Guillaume-Thomas Raynal.[1]

---

1 Srinivas Aravamudan has pointed out that the excerpts published in the many

From "Monstrous Hybridity" to Enlightenment Literacy

The most salient and widely utilized example of the 'Black Spartacus' comes from Raynal's celebrated compilation, *Histoire des deux Indes* (1770–1780), wherein he foreshadowed that a 'grand homme' would liberate the slaves and lead them towards revenge. Raynal writes:

> Your slaves do not have a need for your generosity nor for your advice to break the sacrilegious yoke that oppresses them. Nature speaks louder than philosophy and vested interest … the negroes only want a courageous leader to transport them to vengeance and to carnage. Where is he, this great man whom nature owes to her vexed, oppressed, and tormented children? Where is he, this new Spartacus? (6:206–08)

Rainsford's history of the revolution in Saint-Domingue, which may very well be the first 'complete' book-length English-language history of the Haitian Revolution, as the editors of the newly published 2013 version contend (Youngquist and Pierrot, 2013, xvii), and remains one of the most widely referenced works on the Revolution up until this day,[2] helped to spread the idea that Louverture was inspired to rebellion through his Enlightenment education or what I have called the "Enlightenment literacy narrative" of the Haitian Revolution. Rainsford helped to accomplish the dissemination of this narrative throughout the Anglophone world when he wrote of the revolutionary general: he had 'acquired the knowledge of new sources, and the relish for books of a superior order … the author of whom he became the most speedily enamored was the abbé Raynal, on

---

editions of the *Histoire des deux Indes* dealing with what has been called the 'Black Spartacus' passage were actually partially plagiarized from Louis-Sébastien Mercier's *L'An deux mille quatre cent quarante* (1771) (Aravamudan, 1999, 302). For a reading of Mercier's 'Black Spartacus' passage in relation to Saint-Domingue and abolitionism see, Laure Marcellesi (2011); Catherine Salles (1990, 163–73). For comparisons of the different versions of the works attributed to Raynal, as well as questions about and explanations of Diderot, Pechméja, and Malouet's contributions to works attributed to Raynal, see Anatole Feugère (1922); Yves Benot (1963, 37–53); and, more recently, Andrew S. Curran (2011, 167–215).

2 In their recent edited edition of *An Historical Account of the Black Empire of Hayti* (2013), Paul Youngquist and Grégory Pierrot write that Rainsford first detailed his life as a soldier during the British occupation and subsequent evacuation of Saint-Domingue in a widely reviewed publication entitled *A Memoir of Transactions That Took Place in St. Domingo in the Spring of 1799* (1802) (Youngquist and Pierrot, xxx). Later, in 1802, a second and a third edition of the memoir, which were 'thirty pages longer than the first' (Youngquist and Pierrot, xxxi), would be published under the title of *St. Domingo; Or an Historical, Political and Military Sketch of the Black Republic*. Even though the 1805 *An Historical Account of the Black Empire of Hayti* would also be widely reviewed and even translated into two languages, Rainsford's last history of Haiti would never be reprinted after its first run (Youngquist and Pierrot, xxxii).

whose history and speculations in philosophy he was intent for weeks, and never quitted.' Rainsford added more details by saying that Louverture also enjoyed reading a 'French translation of Epictetus' and the following works, among others, composed by 'ancient historians': 'Caesar's Commentaries,' 'Marshall Saxe's Military Reveries,' and Herodotus's 'Histories of the Wars of the Persians against the Greeks' (244). Rainsford concluded by writing, 'General Laveaux called [Louverture] "the negro, the Spartacus foretold by Raynal, whose destiny it *was* to avenge the wrongs committed on his race"' (247).

The idea that Louverture, or any other former slave for that matter, could have been inspired to revolt by reading Raynal or other works of philosophy far predates Rainsford.[3] In his passionate refutation of the idea that the free people of color of Saint-Domingue, in concert with the Société des Amis des Noirs, had sought to incite a general slave rebellion in the colony, Julien Raimond wrote, 'Oh! When the insurrection happens, will we really have to go so far as to point to the existence of this society in order to explain the cause?' Raimond continued by vaguely evoking the 'Black Spartacus' narrative when he said:

> For two centuries the blacks [*les noirs*] have attempted uprisings in multiple areas; and yet there was not even a *société des amis des noirs*; and if anti-slavery writing could bring the slaves to rebel, the work of the abbé Raynal, which was in the hands of all of the inhabitants of the islands, was, it goes without saying, the most proper to bring them to it. (1791b, 12)

It would be nearly a decade later, though, in another early version of the Enlightenment literacy narrative, that the life of Toussaint Louverture would become specifically tied to reading Raynal. On January 9, 1799 (20 *nivôse* an VII), one newspaper source claimed to have personally observed Louverture with his 'eyes on' Enlightenment philosophy. The French republican newspaper, *La Gazette Nationale ou le Moniteur Universel*,[4]

---

3 The number of texts that either refer to Louverture as a 'Spartacus' or evoke the 'black Spartacus' passage of Raynal in some way are far too numerous to list. Nevertheless, some varied mentions (rather than mere repetitions) can be found in works by the following authors: Vastey (1819, 19); Saint-Rémy (1850, 13, 145, 171); de Saillet (83); Gabrielle de P*** (1:45, 3:234); A. Michelet (161); Bergeaud (1859, 44); Carteau (75–76); Lamartine (1850, line 2469); Beard (170); and Brown (1854, 23). There is also a little-known handwritten manuscript by George Didbin Pitt called *Toussaint L'Ouverture, or the Black Spartacus, A Military Drama in Two Acts, Taken from the Historical Account of the Tale of St. Domingo, or Hayti* (1846).

4 The article from the *Gazette Nationale* has been cited in Victor Schoelcher's 1889 *Vie de Toussaint Louverture* (286), as well as in Geggus (2007b, 305); and Girard and Donnadieu (2013).

From "Monstrous Hybridity" to Enlightenment Literacy

published an article, which Philippe Girard and Jean-Louis Donnadieu have recently called 'more mythmaking than journalism' (42). In the article, 'a citizen newly arrived from Saint-Domingue,' provided the following account of Louverture's *awakening*:

> Toussaint, whose intellectual faculties had been ripened because of his habitual proximity to the class of free men, turned his thoughts to the degradations of his brothers. He could not conceive by what destiny slavery could be found so close to liberty [*Il ne pouvait concevoir par quelle fatalité l'esclavage se trouvait si près de la liberté*], and how a difference in skin color had placed such an enormous distance between one man and another. His ideas became further enlarged when he heard several passages from Raynal cited. He went about procuring his work. This book kindled his enthusiasm for general liberty. He often had his eyes on that page where Raynal seems to announce the liberator who would tear off the shackles of a large part of the human race. He returned incessantly to this prediction that struck him so much. (448)

After more than a century of narratives about Haiti in which the Enlightenment literacy narrative appeared as one of the major causes of the Haitian Revolution, C.L.R. James rendered Louverture's revolutionary consciousness into terms that bore the influence of the tropology of the 'Black Spartacus' in a variety of ways. In a passage that was clearly influenced by the writing of Rainsford, James wrote of the slaves of Saint-Domingue:

> Revolutionary literature was circulating among them ... Of the men who were to lead their brothers to freedom none of them as far as we know was yet active ... Toussaint alone read his Raynal. 'A courageous chief only is wanted.' He said afterwards that, from the time the troubles began, he felt he was destined for great things. (82)

James's characterization of Louverture's radical interpretation of Enlightenment texts as a call to violent revolution and leadership of the colony continues when he writes:

> He had read Caesar's Commentaries, which had given him some idea of politics and the military art and the connection between them. Having read and re-read the long volume by the Abbé Raynal on the East and West Indies, he had a thorough grounding in the economics and politics, not only of San Domingo, but of all the great empires of Europe. (91)

In a subsequent passage that explicitly demonstrates the influence of not only Rainsford, but the French historian Louis Dubroca, James wrote that it was the French general and frequent correspondent of Louverture,

From "Monstrous Hybridity" to Enlightenment Literacy

'Toussaint Reading the Abbé Raynal's Work,' from John Relly Beard's
The Life of Toussaint L'Ouverture (1853).
Reprinted from John Relly Beard's *The Life of Toussaint L'Ouverture* (1853)
with permission from the Rare Book Collection, Wilson Library,
The University of North Carolina at Chapel Hill.

Etienne Laveaux, who had first called the revolutionary hero the 'saviour of constituted authority, the Black Spartacus, the Negro predicted by Raynal who would avenge the outrages done to his race' (171).[5]

This last idea, that it was Laveaux who had called Louverture the black Spartacus predicted by Raynal, rather than Louverture himself, provides a lens through which to understand how the Enlightenment literacy narrative did not always depend upon the literal act of reading. In many representations of the Haitian Revolution that circulated in early nineteenth-century metropolitan France, even though Louverture was often portrayed as barely literate, vengeful, and equally hateful of "blacks" as of "mulattoes," his call to arms was often still connected to a much more amorphous narrative of Enlightenment literacy.[6] In *La Vie de Toussaint L'Ouverture* (1802), for example, Dubroca, who was a professional writer for Napoleon Bonaparte (and is, incidentally, cited by Rainsford as a source for the literacy narrative), also evoked the 'Black Spartacus' tropology, but he attributed the connection between Louverture and Raynal solely to Laveaux. Moreover, Dubroca did not even consider the possibility that Louverture, whom he says could only read 'passablement' (3) and spoke French very poorly (1802, 50), may have ever read the *Histoire des deux Indes*. Instead, Dubroca wrote that it was Laveaux, who 'intoxicated with appreciation, proclaimed [Toussaint Louverture] the avenger [*le vengeur*] of constituted authority' (1802, 16). Dubroca then quoted from a letter written by Laveaux in which the latter said of Louverture: 'he was ... the Spartacus predicted by Raynal, whose destiny it would be to avenge the outrages committed against his race' (1802, qtd. in 16).[7]

---

5 As Chris Bongie (2004, 203 n. 31) and Kirsten Silva Gruesz and Susan Gillman (2011, 242) have pointed out, many of the other biographical details of the Haitian Revolution found in *The Black Jacobins* can be sourced to Pamphile de Lacroix's *Mémoires pour Servir à l'Histoire de la Révolution de Saint-Domingue* (1819).

6 For the way in which Louverture was characterized in the nineteenth-century French media, in general, see also Deborah Jenson (2008, 41–62).

7 In 1814, the British writer James Stephen wrote in *The History of Toussaint L'Ouverture* that Dubroca 'was employed by [Napoleon] Buonaparte's government to slander the unfortunate Toussaint L'Ouverture, in a libel called his Life, published at Paris while they were offering rewards for his head in St. Domingo' (318). Two years later, Dubroca repeats the same version of the 'Black Spartacus' narrative in *La Vie de J.J. Dessalines, chef des noirs révoltés de Saint-Domingue* (1804, 42). Yet almost a century later, French historian Georges Le Gorgeu wrote that it was Louverture who 'who believed himself to be the *emancipator of the blacks*, announced by the abbé Raynal' (qtd. at 9, emphasis in original). Le Gorgeu went on to suggest that Laveaux had more specifically evoked the idea of Louverture as '*the Spartacus of the black race*,' when, in what Le Gorgeu calls a 'memorable harangue,' Laveaux wrote, 'The negroes were only wanting a leader, Raynal had shouted in a fit of enthusiasm. Where is he, this great man? He will appear, have

From "Monstrous Hybridity" to Enlightenment Literacy

Cousin d'Avallon, in his *Histoire de Toussaint L'Ouverture, chef des insurgés* (1802), while still characterizing Louverture as a traitor to the French, also has Laveaux calling the former slave turned general the 'Black Spartacus' 'predicted by the abbé Raynal' (36, 138). Cousin d'Avallon offers Louverture as having been at least Enlightenment literate when he writes:

> *Toussaint-L'Ouverture* had become the most declared partisan of Raynal; the work of this philosopher had become, so to speak, his guidebook [*son bréviaire*]. He believed that he there read his destiny, in the chapters that spoke of the eventual independence of the colonies of the New World. He strongly recommended reading it. (37)

Of course, Louverture's supposed knowledge of Raynal is here characterized in wholly negative terms when Cousin d'Avallon tells us, 'We should notice here that all of the theories of our modern philosophers end by instilling trouble and division within nations. Their principles, beautiful in theory, are and will always be followed by the greatest of disasters whenever we try to put them into practice' (138). These two passages from Dubroca and Cousin d'Avallon, in stressing the incongruity and the monstrosity produced by thinking about Louverture as a 'Black Spartacus,' go a long way towards explaining how the "mulatto/a" vengeance narrative and the Enlightenment literacy narrative could appear not as diametrically opposed in the vast majority of early attempts to craft a history of the Haitian Revolution, but wholly complementary. If "mulatto/a" vengeance depended upon the idea that "blacks" and "mulattoes," *because* they were "blacks" and "mulattoes," sought the wholesale destruction not only of one another, but of "whites" as well, it also depended to a certain extent on thinking about how Enlightenment literacy could either prevent the genocidal imaginings of "racial" revolution or exacerbate them.

The French soldier Pamphile de Lacroix, whose writings after those of Moreau de Saint-Méry, did more to inflect understandings of the Haitian Revolution than any other written work until that of C.L.R. James, characterized Louverture in the terms of both Enlightenment literacy and "mulatto/a" vengeance. In his 1819 *Mémoire*, Lacroix described Louverture as having once said that at the time of the start of the insurrection in Saint-Domingue he was a quasi-illiterate 54-year-old whose rise to power was divinely sanctioned: 'A secret voice was saying to me,' said Louverture, according to Lacroix, 'Since the blacks are free, they now need a leader, and it is me who must be that leader predicted by the abbé Raynal' (1:405). Like Dubroca, Lacroix downplayed the idea that Louverture may have been

no doubt about it; he will raise the standard of liberty' (qtd. in Le Gorgeu, 9, emphasis in original).

enlightened through literacy by portraying him instead as wholly insensible and utterly vengeful against 'whites.' Lacroix writes:

> an infinity of other examples prove at the same time the ferocious resentment of TOUSSAINT-LOUVERTURE towards our [white] color and the cold calculation of a ruthless politics, by which he would sacrifice the last white man who had remained with him ... Is it possible to believe that DESSALINES and the other black leaders ... would have dared to strike with such inhumanity, if the atrocious system of TOUSSAINT-LOUVERTURE had not encouraged their homicidal methods? [*si le système désespéré de TOUSSAINT-LOUVERTURE n'eût poussé leurs bras homicides*]. (2:183)

Lacroix's counter to the idea of an enlightened and therefore humane Louverture overtly relies upon a language of "racial" monstrosity in order to destabilize the idea that Louverture had been *civilized* or *humanized* through acts of reading.

If Lacroix's reliance on this racialized vocabulary of revolution is in some ways exactly what we might expect from an author who supported the idea that the French should attempt to re-conquer Saint-Domingue (see chapter one of this volume), Rainsford's adoption of a similar vocabulary of "racial" revolution might strike as much more surprising on precisely that score, especially, given the role that Rainsford would later play in exposing France's duplicity, when he translated Baron de Vastey's *Communication officielle de trois lettres de Catineau Laroche: ex-colon, agent de Pétion; imprimées et publiées par ordre du gouvernement* (1816).[8] Still, despite the fact that Rainsford's sympathies were clearly with Haiti throughout his life—as evidenced by the

---

8 Pierrot and Youngquist also note that in his translation of Vastey's work, *Translation of an Official Communication from the Government of Haiti* (Vastey, 1816c, 3; qtd. in Pierrot and Youngquist, xxxiii), Rainsford claimed to have been appointed 'lieutenant general in the Haytean [sic] army'. Youngquist and Pierrot write, however, that this was 'obviously an honorary appointment, and its duties (if there were any) remain a mystery' (xxxiii). Their speculation about the honorific nature of Rainsford's post-revolutionary military involvement is strengthened by the fact that Rainsford is not listed in the 1814, 1815, 1816, 1817, or 1818 editions of the fascinatingly documented *Almanach Royale d'Hayti*. These almanacs, which bibliophile Ralph T. Esterquest has called the 'Burke's Peerage for Christophe's grandiose kingdom,' are invaluable sources of information about the role foreigners like Rainsford might have had in Christophe's kingdom, since the different versions of the *Almanach* list, as Esterquest acknowledges, 'down to the least of them, every member of the king's household, bureaucracy, and military staff..., along with his title, honors, and rank' (176). For a British reference and review of Rainsford's translation of Vastey's *Communication Officielle*, see the British newspaper *The Military Register*, November 8, 1815, 571. See also Pierrot (2008, 591).

From "Monstrous Hybridity" to Enlightenment Literacy

Comte de Saint-Louis's toast to Rainsford as being one who was 'brave and virtuous,' and had always 'offered' to 'defend the cause of the Haitians,' as reported in the November 19, 1814 issue of the *Gazette Royale d'Hayti—An Historical Account of the Black Empire of Hayti* did just as much to popularize and historicize the narrative of "mulatto/a" vengeance as it would do for the narrative of Enlightenment literacy. As Youngquist and Pierrot have written, 'The stark engravings in *An Historical Account of the Black Empire of Hayti* remain to this day the best known contemporary representations of the Haitian Revolution' (xlii). What may be even less recognized, however, is that Rainsford's history also contributed to widespread beliefs about "race" and "miscegenation" found in natural history and later in the texts of formal "scientific" racists like the Comte de Gobineau. Rainsford's ideas about not only the revolution, but about "race" too, would also find their way into the writings of James's *The Black Jacobins*, arguably the most influential text written on the Haitian Revolution in the twentieth century.

Rainsford adopted the essentialism of taxonomic categories about "race" when he employed a language of "mulatto/a" vengeance to describe any divisions found between the people whom he called 'mulattoes' and 'negroes.' Rainsford explicitly mentioned, in this respect, that he owed his ideas about the 'manners of the inhabitants of the colony' of Saint-Domingue to the descriptions found in the naturalist travel writing of father Jean-Baptiste Le Pers (1805, 88), and the abbés du Tertre, Labat, and Raynal (xii, 225), whose works will be examined in more detail in chapter one. Reference to the pseudoscientific debates about "race" found in these naturalist texts provided Rainsford with the authority to make his own "racial" characterizations of the 'inhabitants' of French Saint-Domingue, whom he described as consisting of 'pure whites; people of colour; ... blacks of free condition; and negroes in a state of slavery.' Rainsford added that the 'whole of the intermediate grades were called generally mulattoes' (87). Rainsford categorized the different inhabitants of the 'Spanish' side of the island by "race" as well when he wrote that these consisted of: 'pure Spaniards ... who looked down with disdain upon every other order of men ... the Creoles or descendants of Europeans settled in America,' whom he described as living in the 'vilest sloth'; 'the third [class] was the offspring of an European with an Indian, or a negro: the former called Mulattoes, the latter Mestizos,' who were a 'robust and hardy race ... lively, well-tempered, and frequently accomplished'; and finally, he said, 'The Negroes [who] compose the fourth rank' were 'rendered so subservient to vanity that they became themselves, more silly, vain, and imperious, than their masters' (73–74). Later in the text, Rainsford also clarified that he 'use[s] the term[s] *negro* and *brigand* (both derogatory of the ruling power of St. Domingo,) not as by any means appropriate to the people they describe at present, but as the means of distinguishing them to the European, who cannot so easily assimilate himself with their present condition' (224).

Rainsford's description of Louverture as 'black' rather than 'negro,' and as learned, benevolent, and humane, stands in stark contrast to his characterization of various 'mulatto' revolutionaries in French Saint-Domingue. In particular, Rainsford characterizes the entire revolt of the Ogé brothers using a vocabulary of "monstrous hybridity" or "racial" incongruity, including words like 'ferocity' and 'terror,' along with 'enlightened' and 'education,' contradictions which would come to be distinctly associated in his mind with 'mulattoes.' Rainsford tells us that Ogé, 'a mulatto; whose mother owned a coffee plantation,' had 'imbibed' in Paris, where he was sent 'for the purposes of education,' both the 'natural feelings of his class' and 'all the prejudices entertained at this period against the white planters in the mother country' (121).[9] As a result of these 'natural' and 'imbibed' feelings of rebellion, owing ostensibly to the corrosive combination of his "natural" biology and his French (Enlightenment) education, according to Rainsford, Ogé 'took upon himself the character of the Protector of the Mulattoes,' and upon returning to Saint-Domingue, he subsequently 'appointed his two brothers, and another mulatto of a ferocious character, named Mark Chavanne [sic], as lieutenants' (122).[10] These 'mulattoes,' Rainsford tells us, 'commenced their unruly operation by the murder of two white men, whom they met accidentally, and by punishing with extreme cruelty those of their complexion not disposed to revolt' (122).[11]

9 In this passage, Rainsford mistakenly refers to Vincent Ogé's older brother Jacques as having organized the rebellion, probably because, as John Garrigus has written, 'in 1793 Saint-Domingue refugees in Philadelphia published a document claiming to be "Ogé's Confession". But this was a statement that the older brother Jacques made to colonial authorities just before his own execution' (2010, 22). Bryan Edwards also published the document in volume 4 of his *The History, Civil and Commercial, of the British Colonies* (205).

10 Rainsford borrows this language, in part, from Edwards, who wrote of Ogé in his sketch of the revolt in Saint-Domingue, which covers the years 1789–94, that in 1790 Ogé 'declares himself the protector of the mulattoes, and announces his intention of taking up arms in their behalf, unless their wrongs should be redressed' (3:46). Edwards goes on to describe Chavannes as 'fierce, intrepid, active, and enterprising; prone to mischief and thirsty for vengeance' (3:47).

11 This information appears also to come from Edwards, who explains that while Ogé was 'mild and humane,' his followers were exceedingly cruel: 'the first white man that fell in their way they murdered on the spot,' Edwards writes, 'a second, of the name of Sicard, met the same fate; and it is related that their cruelty towards such persons of their own complexion as refused to join in the revolt was extreme' (3:47). In 1818, Sir James Barskett, who acknowledged that he derived the "racial" taxonomy of the colony he recites from Edwards (106), would also merely repeat a rendition of Edwards's story about Chavannes and company, noting that '… they committed many murders and

From "Monstrous Hybridity" to Enlightenment Literacy

André Rigaud fared no better in Rainsford's estimation since he is described as being motivated mostly by a 'pathetic' desire to protect his property rather than for the ideals of liberty and equality. Rainsford even went on to describe Rigaud in immediately genocidal terms when he wrote that the future Haitian general was inclined to desire the 'extermination' of the French colonists and that under his command the free people of color 'put to death all the French planters who fell in their way' (194).[12]

These are not the only places in Rainsford's narrative where 'mulattoes' are described as singularly 'ferocious.' In the course of his description of the capture of the commander of a U.S. ship, Rainsford described the prison guards as 'four blacks, and a mulatto officer of great ferocity' (230). We know that 'ferocity' is attached to being uncivilized in Rainsford's mind because he used the same language to admonish the French for their terrifying military tactics, including the usage of 'ferocious animals' (xviii). In contrast to the natural 'ferocity' of the 'mulattoes,' French 'ferocity' is wholly 'unnatural' to their character, arising as a result of the diminishing 'power' of the French military during the final days of the Leclerc-Rochambeau expedition (338). In the following lengthy passage, in which Rainsford refers to the French army's practice of throwing their enemies to 'blood-hounds...to be devoured alive!' (339), he absolved the 'blacks' of any of this 'ferocity.' The passage punctuates the qualitatively racialized character of Rainsford's earlier descriptions of 'mulatto' behavior during the Revolution:

> Thus ended the siege and blockade, which had cost the French army much, by the loss of some of her best generals and finest troops, but in nothing so much as in the exercise of a ferocious spirit unknown among civilized people. Besides the cruelties in cold blood which have been recited, and which were exultingly acknowledged in the dispatches of General Le Clerc, were numerous acts of private barbarity, the recital of which could answer no good purpose, while the blacks, in this instance, are not charged, even by their enemies, with the commission of any of these enormities. ... The remembrance of this affair will long be found on the banks of the Artibonité [*sic*], to the disgrace of the one party, and the praise of the other. (302)

Often facile comparisons like this one help Rainsford to use "monstrous hybridity"—whether on the part of the French, who went against their own

---

exercised severe despotism with unhesitating cruelty. A mulatto man of some property being urged to follow them, excused himself by pointing to his wife and children, which being considered as contumacious, the man and his whole family were massacred' (131).

12 The phrase about murdering 'all the white inhabitants that fell in their way' (without any mention of Rigaud) appears also in Edwards (3:125).

nature, or on the part of "mulattoes" who were merely, it seems, giving in to their own—in addition to Louverture, the latter's literacy, and ultimately his "blackness" as *chiaroscuros* that would end up producing a narrative that was much less about the nobility of "blackness" or the evil of "mulattoness" than it was about the honor of Britishness.

The British abolitionist Harriet Martineau's three-volume *The Hour and the Man* (1841), which was highly praised by her contemporaries, including Thomas Carlyle (even though he was an ardent detractor of Haitian society), Maria Edgeworth, Florence Nightingale, Wendell Phillips, and Lydia Maria Child (Belasco, 160), and was perhaps the most influential novel written on Haiti in the nineteenth century (Langerwerf, 6), provides a distinct example of how the trope of "monstrous hybridity" that we find in Rainsford's work could circulate alongside a narrative of Enlightenment literacy. Martineau also helped to popularize the idea that the Haitian Revolution was catalyzed by an act of reading on the part of Toussaint Louverture.[13] In so doing, like nearly all contributors to the literary history of the Haitian Revolution, Martineau narrated "mulatto/a vengeance." Clearly directly influenced by the writing of Rainsford, Martineau describes Louverture as having read 'Plutarch, Caesar's Commentaries, Epictetus, and Marshall Saxe's Military Reveries' (1:4). She goes on to describe his valorous behavior as the result of the learning that he 'got out of books' (1:50), and later she posits that Louverture 'was surely the black, the Spartacus predicted by Raynal, whose

---

13 Martineau's novel, which, John Herbert Nelson has written, was composed mostly for a U.S. audience (13), exercised broad influence over understandings of the Haitian Revolution in the nineteenth century. Some examples of Martineau's influence can be found in the work of John R. Beard, whose *The Life of Toussaint L'Ouverture* (1853) shows clearly Martineau's influence when he writes, 'Yes, here is the man, and the hour is coming' (74). In his 1863 revision and republication of Beard's biography, the abolitionist James Redpath also added significant material to Beard's original text in a section entitled 'Martineau and Wordsworth' (337). The section is noteworthy because, as in the work of Rainsford and Martineau, it contains a long list of books supposedly read by Louverture. Moreover, according to the editor of Kate Stone's journals *The Hour and the Man* was called an 'early *Uncle Tom's Cabin*.' Stone, a confederate sympathizer who wrote of her impressions of the novel in the journal she kept from 1861 to 1868, and which were published under the title of *Brokenburn* in 1955, however, was not a fan of the novel. She wrote, 'Have just finished *The Hour and the Man* by Miss Martineau, purporting to be a historical novel with Toussaint L'Ouverture, the leader of the insurrection in San Domingo as the hero. He is represented as superhumanly good and great beyond all heroes of ancient or modern times. He and Napoleon were contemporaries and comparisons are constantly drawn between them, all in favor of this darkie saint. Napoleon is completely overshadowed by Toussaint. It is a disgusting book. The Negroes are all represented as angelic beings, while all the whites are the fiends who entered in and took possession of their Eden, Haiti' (313–14).

destiny it should be to avenge the wrongs of his race' (1:191). Precisely in order to labor against the idea that Louverture had been inspired to revolt by vengeance or hatred for 'whites,' Martineau's well-read Toussaint Louverture contradicts Laveaux's reading of his behavior by saying, 'It seems as if I were the one who I myself have spoken of as likely to arise— not, as Laveaux says after Raynal, to avenge, but to repair the wrongs of my color' (1:197). Like Martineau after him, Rainsford had also aimed to redeem Toussaint Louverture of the charge of vengeance against 'whites.' According to Rainsford, unlike the slaves who 'retaliate their wrongs and sufferings on their owners' (245) or who, because 'their female slaves' were often forced into licentious intercourse with white masters, would putatively inevitably try to seek vengeance through rape of 'white' women (138), Louverture is not motivated by such 'sanguinary revenge.' Rainsford explains that it was 'probable that his manly heart revolted from cruelties' when he saw that the 'innocent would suffer with the guilty; and that the effects of the revolution regarded future more than present justice' (245).

Yet, also like its precursor in Rainsford's book, *The Hour and the Man* is filled with an understanding of people of "mixed race" as the initial catalysts for revolutionary violence, being hopelessly and equally prejudiced against "blacks" and "whites." Martineau describes "mulattoes" using a vocabulary of degradation that can be linked to the same kind of naturalist travel writing evoked in Rainsford's account. In Martineau's adaptation, Madame Ogé, a fictionalized version of the real-life Haitian revolutionary figure Vincent Ogé's mother, is filled with a desire for a "white" massacre that would have the effect of 'avenging her sons' (49), and later in the novel, a character refers to 'mulattoes' as 'devils' (188). Allusions to the supposed enmity between "mulattoes" and *pure* "blacks," which forms one of the core stereotypes in the trope of "monstrous hybridity," are also demonstrated by the fictional daughter of color of one of the Raymond brothers, whom we are supposed to understand to be of "mixed race."[14] Afra Raymond fearfully writes to her friend Euphrosyne, 'L'Ouverture is all in all. We shall have every office filled with blacks; and the only chance for our *degraded* color is in the fields or in the removal of this black' (1:167, emphasis added). An unnamed 'mulatto' character acknowledges the perfidy attributed to people of "mixed race" when he states, 'To our being mulattoes we owe our disgrace' (239); and Martineau's Louverture constantly suspects that the 'mulattoes' seek to betray him, as when he tells a group of them, 'I have beloved friends of your

---

14 Martineau refers to the family of the same Julien Raimond, who wrote several revolutionary pamphlets, including a spirited response to Moreau de Saint-Méry in which he directly refuted charges that people of "mixed race" were characterized by degradation, inferiority, and treachery. See Raimond (1791a, 1791b, and 1793a).

color. ... Believe me, however, the complexion of your souls is so disgusting that I have no attention to spare for your faces' (1:109). In contrast, the putatively *pure* "black" beauty of Toussaint Louverture's daughter, Génifrède (an invented character), is exalted precisely because 'in her might be seen, and in her was seen by the Europeans ... what the negro face and form may be when seen in their native climate, unhardened by degradation, undebased by ignorance, unspoiled by oppression' (1:98).

Although James, like Rainsford and Martineau, subscribed to the seemingly flattering Enlightenment literacy narrative of the Revolution, his text also contains an understanding of both "black" and "mulatto" vengeance that is filled with the kinds of prejudices that eighteenth- and nineteenth-century discourses of "race" had encouraged. That is to say that if we are able to recognize that James's contestation of 'Eurocentric representations of colonial history ... does not merely revise but perpetuates nineteenth-century historiography' (Bongie, 1998, 270), what we have been less able to see is that his representations of "race" merely perpetuate beliefs in "mulatto/a" vengeance and the pseudoscience of "race" that nineteenth-century narratives of the Haitian Revolution nearly always entailed. In *The Black Jacobins*, James recited Moreau de Saint-Méry's "racial" classification system when he wrote that 'the offspring of white[s] and black[s]' were 'divided ... into 128 divisions. The true Mulatto was the child of the pure black and the pure white. The child of the white and the Mulatto woman was a quarteron with 96 parts white and 32 parts black. But the quarteron could be produced by the white and the marabou in the proportion of 88 to 40, or by the white and the sacatra' and on and on (39). Even though James called these classifications an 'elaborate tom-foolery,' his rendition of the Revolution is filled with the kinds of pseudoscientific understanding about "race" found in the works of many of the very people who, in their own histories of the Haitian Revolution, had adopted the terminology that James purports to despise.

James not only believed that 'Black slaves and Mulattoes hated each other' (43), but much like Rainsford he also imputed the start of the Revolution to such 'mulattoes' like Rigaud, who, he claimed, 'hated the whites ... for the indignities which he, an educated and widely-traveled soldier, had to suffer' (96). James even wrote that Louverture and Rigaud were at odds because of their different "racial" statuses, and he hyperbolically charged Rigaud with the majority of the blame for the conflict by telling us that the 'mulatto' general was too 'narrow-minded' and had a clear bias that caused him to defect to the side of France and 'ruin himself, his caste, and his country for a generation' (207).[15] James's adoption of the idea that the 'mulatto'—who, he

---

15 Both Rigaud and Louverture, on the contrary, denied that any antagonisms between

had earlier written, 'despise[d] th[e] half of his origin' that was connected to the slaves, even though he found himself 'at home' among them (38)—and *pure* "blacks" had an innate enmity for one another is most obvious, however, when he writes:

> The free blacks, comparatively speaking, were not many, and so despised was the black skin that even a Mulatto slave felt himself superior to the free black man. The mulatto, rather than be slave to a black, would have killed himself. It all reads like a cross between a nightmare and a bad joke. (43)[16]

James observed nevertheless that such 'distinctions' based on skin color were a far cry from being mere memories of eighteenth-century colonialism since they 'continue to exercise their influence in the West Indies today' (43). Though such a statement suggests that James is well aware that the blatantly racist language of eighteenth-century colonialism had produced material consequences for twentieth-century West Indians, he continued to adopt that very language of 'distinctions' when he praised Beard's above mentioned problematic biography of Louverture for its putative objectivity. Without any mention of the author's "race" or skin color, he called Beard's work 'on the whole, accurate' (389), while pointing out that the aforementioned Saint-Rémy's *Vie de Toussaint L'Ouverture* (1850) was written by a 'Mulatto' who 'hated L'Ouverture like poison' (James, 388).

We could hardly say that every statement like James's, identifying people by their "color" or "race" in the context of the Haitian Revolution, was explicitly meant to be racist. However, certainly every statement that identified whole groups of people primarily using terms like "mulatto," "quadroon," "octoroon," "negro," "yellow," "black," or "sang-mêlé," literally, "mixed blood," does actually enter either explicitly or implicitly into the 'elaborate tom-foolery' of "racial" debates and the tropologies they inherently imply by virtue of an adoption of what Werner Sollors has called 'the calculus of color' (1997, 113). According to Sollors, this 'calculus' is characterized by 'thinking in racial fractions,' like one-fourth black or half-white, 'and the invention of new terms to go along with them,' like "mulatto," "quadroon," and "octoroon" (1997, 123). Even though this kind of terminology appears to be scientific, technical, and official, and has been accepted into common parlance about "race," as James's history shows, Sollors cautions

---

them were based upon color prejudice. For more on the 'War of the South,' also called the 'war of knives' and the denials of these two generals, see L. Dubois (2004, 233).

16 Later, James walks back from this pseudoscientific language when he weakly notes, 'Mulatto instability lies not in their blood but in their intermediate position in society' (207).

that such 'classification schemes are primarily *social* instruments—and not the scientific or biological findings that they appear to be,' evidenced by the fact that 'such genealogies are hardly part of a continued scientific interest' (1997, 123). Appiah further explains the pseudoscientific implications not only of the idea of "race" itself, but more specifically of pseudoscientific "racial" taxonomies, when he writes:

> And it is not just the claim that there is a 'racial' essence that can explain a person's moral, intellectual or literary aptitudes that scientists have rejected. They also believe that such classifications as *Negro, Caucasian,* and *Mongoloid,* are of no importance for biological purposes. First, because there are simply too many people who do not fit into such a category; and second, because even when you in succeed in assigning someone to one of these categories—on the basis of skin-pigmentation and hair, say—that implies very little about most of their other biological characteristics. Even those scientists who still have a use for the term 'race' agree that a good deal of what is popularly believed about races is false—often wildly false. (1989, 227)

Yet, in the eighteenth and nineteenth centuries, such classifications were considered scientific and therefore *real*. In fact, in chapter one we will see that by couching such a seemingly *scientific* terminology about human *types* or "races" in works that were largely about systematically classifying plants and animals or studying the geography and topography of Saint-Domingue, eighteenth-century naturalists and travel writers captured either explicitly or implicitly what the French historian Pierre Boulle has called the 'aura of unimpeachable scientific authority' (Boulle, 1988, 224). Two good examples of how naturalist 'authority' could be extended from plants to people can be found in the writing of the Jesuit *curé* Jean-Baptiste Le Pers (1675–1735), 'the first of the missionary naturalists to be permanently stationed in Saint-Domingue' (McClellan, 112), and in the later work of the naturalist Thierry de Menonville. In volume three of the *Histoire de l'Isle espagnole ou de Saint-Domingue*, a publication based on the recorded observations of Le Pers, we find elaborate descriptions not only of the animal and plant life of Saint-Domingue, but of the many different types of 'Nègres' whose forced labor provided the manpower on colonial plantations. These descriptions are noteworthy because of the way in which questions of *worth* with respect to the plantation economy of Saint-Domingue continuously surface as connected to the varying and unequal degrees of humanity that separated, in Le Pers's mind, 'des Nègres' from Senegal and Madagascar, for instance. Le Pers tells us that the former were 'the most spiritual' and therefore the 'easiest to discipline' (3:362), while the latter had never been able to 'be of any worth to their Masters' because they were 'practically untamable' (3: 363).

From "Monstrous Hybridity" to Enlightenment Literacy

In his preface to Menonville's *Traité de la culture du nopal et de l'éducation de la cochenille dans les colonies française de l'Amérique*, which was published by Le Cercle des Philadelphes, the official scientific body of Saint-Domingue, Charles Arthaud, the organization's founder (McClellan, 200), claimed that the cultivation of the 'nopal cactus' could best be mandated by the government to free people of color, who, as intermediaries between the European colonists and the slaves, were 'almost French.' Arthaud wrote, 'He [Menonville] also knew that in the colonies there was a class of men (the people of color), that is multiplying every day, and that since they have not, in the least, the same obligations of the Europeans, could be put to use for this cultivation' [*une classes d'hommes (les gens de couleur), qui se multiplient tous les jours, & qui n'ayant pas, à beaucoup près, l'activité des européens, pouraient être occupés utilement à cette culture*] (Arthaud, 1: civ).[17] James McClellan has argued that naturalists priests like Le Pers wrote 'the first chapter in the scientific study of Saint-Domingue' (114), which set the stage for writers like Menonville, offering that 'a major moral of this tale is that science and organized knowledge did not come to Saint Domingue as something separate from the rest of the colonizing process but, rather, formed an inherent part of French colonialism from the beginning' (7).[18]

In much the same way, in the literary history of the Haitian Revolution, ideas about "race" as variously biological, social, or economic instruments that supported colonialism and imperialism, as the famous Trinidadian historian Eric Williams has argued of slavery in general (7), were discourses that would end up supporting "racial" interpretations of the Haitian Revolution and later of independent Haiti, as to be found in the works of Rainsford, Martineau, and James. The ideas about the natural "racial" enmities, for example, that supposedly existed on the part of a 'mulatto' historian like Saint-Rémy towards a 'black' revolutionary like Louverture, and the 'calculus of color' that descriptions of this conflict evoked in concert with the trope of "monstrous hybridity," did not find their way

---

17 Le Pers's manuscript was published in four volumes from 1730-31 by his Jesuit colleague Pierre Francois Xavier de Charlevoix (1682–1761) with 'government support' (McClellan, 112). In 1787 Arthaud, a medical doctor from Saint-Domingue, who eventually became the 'permanent secretary' of the Cercle des Philadelphes (McClellan, 20), published Thierry de Menonville's *Traité de la culture du nopal et de l'éducation de la cochenille dans les colonies française de l'Amérique*. Menonville's work provides its own brief gloss of the "racial" conditions of the various French American colonies. See, for example, Menonville on the differences between 'Africans' and 'Americans' (182–84). For more on Menonville in general, see also Londa Shiebinger (2007, 33–34).

18 As McClellan reminds us, '... despite an aura of liberalism, the Cercle des Philadelphes was a profoundly racist institution and an unquestioning supporter of the slave society out of which it emerged' (239).

into our modern vocabulary about Haiti as something separate from the colonial "scientific" sphere that had produced the Haitian Revolution as a "racial" revolution. Instead, it was a constitutive and contrived element of the conversation at the outset. To take merely one brief example, in 1814, Drouin de Bercy argued that the French could easily re-conquer their former colony by encouraging the supposedly natural hatred that "mulattoes" had for "negroes" and vice versa. He wrote:

> We understand how easy it would be, by sending into their countryside, their farms, their city, intelligent agents of color who are devoted to France, to ferment jealousy and the natural hatred of the black for the mulatto, his oppressor and exploiter, and to make them [Haitians] desire the return of the domination of the whites ... even under slavery. (61)

Drouin de Bercy's claim that 'blacks' and 'mulattoes' in Haiti 'naturally' 'hate[d]' one another, even to the point of accepting the reinstatement of slavery, was endlessly repeated in the transatlantic print culture of the Haitian Revolution, and in many cases, as with Drouin de Bercy, such enmities were actively sought. Claims like Drouin de Bercy's do more than simply establish one person's belief in the trope of "monstrous hybridity," since the underlying ideology shows precisely how hard proponents of colonial discourses of race were working to promote certain "races" as 'friends' and others as 'enemies.' In his *Friends and Enemies* (2008), Bongie has written, 'the existence of two rival Haitis' in the period following Haitian independence, one ruled by 'the "mulatto" Alexandre Pétion' and the other by 'the "black" Henry Christophe,' 'troublingly replicates the binary between friends (the colonized) and enemies (the colonizers) upon which the world-historical outcome of the Haitian Revolution depended' (2008, 25). Drouin de Bercy, for his part, had labored hard to present the French as 'friends' to the 'negroes' or slaves and thus the 'mulattoes' as the true enemies of both the colonists and the slaves, making the latter two seem to be allies.

Thus, even though Rainsford, Martineau, and James's narratives span more than a century and were written by people whose ideologies were vastly different from Drouin de Bercy's, with respect to slavery—the first was written by a person who freely admitted that he was no abolitionist (Rainsford, 1805, 102), the second by an avowed abolitionist, and the third was the work an ardent critic of colonial slavery—each of these narratives show how, if we look into the interstices and shadows of the most seemingly radical analyses of the Haitian Revolution, as equally as the seemingly most apologetic characterizations of certain revolutionaries, we find that beliefs about "race" wrought by pseudoscientific debates have seeped in and affected an author's portrayal of people of color as either 'friends' or 'enemies' of the

Haitian Revolution and/or post-independence Haiti. This means that even in developing a narrative of Enlightenment literacy that had come to be associated in many ways with a radical justification for the action of slaves overthrowing their masters, authors writing in the tradition of Haitian revolutionary historiography and literature were almost always beholden to a narrative of "mulatto/a" vengeance that not only barely disguised their disdain for the "monstrous hybridity" of so-called "mulattoes," but revealed their own anxieties about revolutionary violence and the epistemological problems that revolutions always entailed.[19]

It is because of the epistemological anxieties occasioned by the Haitian Revolution that Louverture can have so easily been written about as a "mulatto" in both the nineteenth and twentieth centuries. The trope of "monstrous hybridity" does not necessarily depend upon a literal idea of "racial mixing" or solely upon people who might be described as being of "mixed race." It is much more about the kinds of ambivalence, incongruity, anxiety, and fear that accompanied taxonomic thinking about such people in the literary history of the Haitian Revolution. A vocabulary of "monstrous hybridity" and the degradations and violence that it called forth often came to symbolize much more than a simultaneous desire and repulsion for "'racial mixing" or what Robert Young has called a colonial 'desiring machine' (98). In representations of the Haitian Revolution, the word "mulatto" also came to stand in for the fact that it was often difficult to know to whose side of the Revolution any given person, regardless of skin color, belonged at any particular moment during the nearly 15 years of violent conflict in Saint-Domingue. This is to say that, as José Buscaglia-Salgado has written of eighteenth-century Mexico, 'the body of the mulatto' was 'the most prominent site, where the tensions and contradictions, the divergences and overlap between master and slave, colonizer and colonized, white and non-White, Christian and non-Christian, acted upon each other' (183). In the transatlantic print culture of the Haitian Revolution, it often was merely the idea of the "mulatto" that provided a stand-in for revolutionary tensions and even

---

19 In Madison Smartt Bell's critically acclaimed *Master of the Crossroads*, for example, the character Isabelle (with much irony on the part of Bell, no doubt) laments the 'harm' of '[b]lacks reading books—reading the newspapers. Taking on notions of Liberty. Equality,' saying, in particular, 'Your Toussaint ... they now say that he has read Raynal, and Epictetus, and so has come to picture himself a black Spartacus come to lead his people to their liberation. A black Moses, possibly' (255). For various versions of the Enlightenment literacy narrative in twentieth-century fiction, see Leslie Pinkney Hill (1928); Aimé Césaire (1960); Madison Smartt Bell (2004); Madison Smartt Bell (2008). In twentieth-century scholarship, see T. Lothrop Stoddard (1914); Healy (1953); Shelby McCloy (1957); Thomas Ott (1973); Robin Blackburn (2006); and Michael Sonenscher (2009).

From "Monstrous Hybridity" to Enlightenment Literacy

paranoia. If, as Edward Said has written, 'Orientalism is a form of paranoia, knowledge of another kind, say, from ordinary historical knowledge' (Said, 1979, 72), so, too, was the narrative of "mulatto/a" vengeance. As Malchow has observed: 'The ever present danger of black revolt in the Caribbean,' occasioned the following question about 'mulattoes' and other '*half-breeds:*' 'Where did his or her loyalties lie?' Malchow concludes that 'Such doubts paralleled the difficulty of reading the "racial" identity of the half-breed' (185). In much the same way, the trope of the "monstrous hybrid" uses a vocabulary that had originally been assigned to the body of the "mulatto" to demonstrate the epistemological problems occasioned by a revolution whose most famous leaders were sometimes fighting on the side of the French, at others on the side of the Spanish, and still yet, had been on the side of the British; a revolution in which skin color could hardly identify a person as a slave or free, or reveal to which of these national powers he or she belonged.

Though people described as being of "mixed race," "mulattoes," or "*affranchis*" were the most likely to be characterized in representations of the Haitian Revolution as treacherously oscillating between the political and "racial" loyalties that their symbolic position as the link between "whites" and "blacks," the "slaves" and the "free," appeared to confer, many historians have argued that French officials and soldiers from the metropole, former free people of color, slaves, and famous Haitian revolutionists like Louverture, Dessalines, and Christophe, were just as likely to have switched or changed sides as "mulattoes" like Rigaud, Boyer, and Pétion. Girard writes, for example, that 'race played a far smaller role in determining the behavior of revolutionary actors than is generally assumed … the color of one's skin was merely one element of a person's profile, along with one's gender, nationality, family network, political ideas, and—crucially—social class' (2011, 345). Girard continues:

> Many people of color fought on the French side until the very end of the war. Conversely, the rebel army included Polish and French defectors, was backed by the (itself multiracial) British navy, and was supplied by U.S. merchants, all of whom pursued ideological, strategic, and commercial goals that had little to do with race. (2011, 9)

Girard contends that even when it came to the topic of slavery and abolition, the loyalties and ideologies of different revolutionary actors were not clearly drawn lines in the sand. He writes, 'Contrary to popular belief, many members of the expedition (including Leclerc) opposed slavery; Louverture, by contrast, had owned slaves,' adding that 'most people in authority—whether black, mixed race, or white—fell in some intermediate category' (9). Girard's interpretation of the Haitian Revolution, therefore, is that a

From "Monstrous Hybridity" to Enlightenment Literacy

'kaleidoscope' rather than bifurcation provides a more apt metaphor for describing the allegiances of the people who lived through the Haitian Revolution (8), since their 'affiliations' could change 'depending on the issue du jour' (8).

Antoine Métral had characterized the free people of color using this very kaleidoscopic language of indeterminacy and instability, but to quite different effect, when he described the free people of color as 'impitoyables' towards their own friends, writing that they

> slaughtered those with whom the night before, they had shared the same camp and with whom they had fought for the same cause. From this union [of slaves and free people of color] was born even more terrible revenge: friends preferred to sink the blade [*enfoncer de préférence le fer*] in the breasts of their own friends. Valor, tenderness, appreciation, hospitality, everything was desecrated by such bloody cruelty: crime respects not a single virtue. (1818, 92)

When we consider the "mulatto" as the primary metaphor for the Janus face of these revolutionary (dis)loyalties, we can see how it was a language that codified hybridity as incongruity, instability, and vengeance *of* "mulatto/as," as well as vengeance *for* "mulatto/as," which also allowed Lovuerture's contemporary Dubroca to describe the character of the famous Haitian general in the quasi-racialized terms of "monstrous hybridity."

Dubroca had characterized Louverture as possessing 'a terrifying mixture of fanaticism and atrocious inclinations; he moves coldly,' Dubroca wrote:

> from the altar to carnage, from prayer to dark combinations of perfidy ... all of these outward signs of devotion were nothing but a mask he believed necessary to cover up the depraved intentions of his heart, in order to take advantage of, with more success, the blind credulity of the blacks. Moreover, Toussaint L'Ouverture wants neither the liberty of the blacks, nor the domination of the whites; he hates to death the mulattoes, whom he almost entirely extinguished as a race; he despises those of his own [race], whom he makes use of as tools to further his ambitions, and then coldly orders them massacred ... he betrayed his own party, he betrayed the Spanish, England, the mulattoes, the whites, France under the government of the kings, republican France, blood, country, and religion. (1802, 50–52)

By painting Louverture in this way, Dubroca helps to firmly establish the trope of "monstrous hybridity" as any set of ideologically conflicting, "racially" confusing, and epistemologically confounding circumstances that help an author to portray a person as not only baffling and inscrutable, in various ways, but as actually demonic and genocidal.

From "Monstrous Hybridity" to Enlightenment Literacy

Because the transatlantic theory of "race" that informs the literary history of the Haitian Revolution was vastly derivative, Dubroca would appear to have borrowed his unhallowed language about the "monstrous hybridity" of Louverture from the proclamation issued by André Rigaud on 23 *ventôse* or March 14, 1800. In this proclamation, Rigaud characterized Louverture, his political opponent, in the following way:

> All the true friends of France should rise up together *en masse*, so that this triple-faced monster who has betrayed Spain, English, France, and his brothers, who has even betrayed the *émigrés* whom he spared or whom he recalled to Saint-Domingue, so that this atrocious fanatic who feeds on the blood of divinity and on the blood of men, should dare to show himself, and so that the earth will be purged of his abominable presence, and nature will be avenged of the mistake that it committed in giving him a human face. (qtd. in Saint-Rémy, 1850, 269)[20]

Dubroca may also have been influenced in his reading of Louverture as hateful of 'mulattoes' by the 1802 translation of Edwards's writing on Saint-Domingue. Edwards had written of Louverture:

> On the departure of the English, Toussaint made a public declaration, signifying that it was his intention not to leave a Mulatto man alive in the country; and with respect to such of these unhappy people as have since fallen into his hands, I am assured that he has kept his word; not an individual of them has been spared. (3:420)

Louverture, for his part, appears to have been aware as early as 1796 that what he considered to have been misinformation was being spread about him regarding the *hommes de couleur*. In a letter from Louverture to General Laveaux dated 11 May 1796, Louverture wrote:

> The wicked had made [the people of Saint-Louis] believe that I wanted to give the country to the English and to put them back into slavery, and that to this end, I had destroyed, in this department as well as elsewhere, all the *hommes de couleur*; they have been so misinformed that my name is horrifying to them [*on les avait si fort égarés que mon nom était en horreur chez eux*]. (rpt. in Laurent, 387)

---

20 Interestingly enough, even though he wrote explicitly that his history of Louverture was meant to provide a counter to that of Dubroca, who had only provided a 'weak and very imperfect sketch of the life and actions of this leader of the blacks' (ii), Cousin D'Avallon appears to have borrowed his description of Louverture's duplicity directly from Dubroca, who had likely copied from Rigaud (16).

From "Monstrous Hybridity" to Enlightenment Literacy

Thinking about the epistemic uncertainty and *genocidal imaginings* that the life of Louverture evoked in the course of the revolution in Saint-Domingue, per Dubroca, Rigaud, and Edwards, allows Girard to present him in much more cerebral rather than evocative terms of "racial hybridity" as well. Girard writes, 'the inscrutable, towering Louverture was a hard man to befriend; his peculiar position at the juncture of African, Creole, and European influences further isolated him, leaving him as a white man in a black man's skin, feared but not loved, alone and lonely' (2011, 25). It is Buscaglia-Salgado, however, who connects interpretations of Louverture's life more directly to the language of "racial hybridity." Buscaglia-Salgado makes the tragedy of Louverture a potent symbol for a vocabulary of "racial mixing":

> He owed his authority both to his African father and to his European master ... he had to weigh and check the forces of both those loyalties all his life ... He was a conciliator and translator, liberator and enforcer, father, brother, and son. Could anyone but the mulatto, in all his subjective disposition to metaphoricity, wear so many disguises? (206–07)

The 'mulatto' as a pervasive icon of 'social camouflage' and 'agent provocateur of social instability' (Buscaglia-Salgado, 183, 184), which Dubroca, Rigaud, Métral, Girard, and Buscaglia-Salgado's characterizations all suggest across great divides of time, provide perfect examples of the anxiousness of revolutionary discourse about Haiti. The Revolution's actors, witnesses, and bystanders were never quite sure if the ends justified the means, and the work of those who wrote about the revolutionary events in Saint-Domingue often bear out the confused and conflicted goals of the insurrection as well as the prejudices of slavery itself.

These explicit references to the myriad versions of the trope of "monstrous hybridity" that we find in various kinds of writing published about the Haitian Revolution in the Atlantic World are hardly outliers. As the three subsequent chapters in this section will show, using the language of "monstrous hybridity" to provide explanations for the bloody character and epistemological blur of revolutionary loyalties during the Haitian Revolution was one of the most abiding features of both historical and fictional descriptions of these events. It is precisely because the idea of "monstrous hybridity" was so widespread and nearly ubiquitous in eighteenth- and nineteenth-century Atlantic discourse that it could so easily be repeated in the transatlantic print culture of the Haitian Revolution as an uncontested and even inconsequential fact rather than as a myth or stereotype. The troping upon which the entire narrative of "mulatto/a" vengeance depends, like mythology, might be considered a form of what Patrick Brantlinger has called 'depoliticized speech' in the sense that it 'treats its subjects as universally accepted, scientifically established, and therefore no longer open to criticism' (168). In an era in which copyright was practically nonexistent and plagiarism did not constitute nearly the intellectual and even legal crime that it does today, the ideas about "race" that we find in various representations of the Haitian Revolution were reproduced, copied, and repackaged over and over again to the extent that they not only became accepted as *truths*, but have become immune to criticism.

CHAPTER ONE

"Monstrous Hybridity" in Colonial and Revolutionary Writing from Saint-Domingue

'On trouve sur la Côte d'Or, comme sur les autres parties de la Guinée, une sorte d'homme qui s'appellent Mulâtres; race qui vient du Commerce des Européens avec les femmes du pays. Cette espèce bâtard forme un tas de brigands, qui n'ont aucun notion de fidélité & d'honneur; ni pour les Nègres, ni pour entr'eux ... Cette race est composée de tout ce qu'il y a de mauvais dans les Européens et dans les Nègres. Elle en est comme le cloaque.'

—abbé Prévost, *Histoire générale des voyages, ou, Nouvelle collection de toutes les relations de Voyages par Mer et par Terre* (1748, Volume 13)

'Il existe aux îles une caste particulière, mélange impur du blanc et du noir, et connu sous le nom de mulâtres. La nature, épouvantée d'horreur à la vue de ce monstre empreignit sur cet être en caractères ineffaçables, les traits de la férocité, joints à ceux de la perfidie la plus insigne. Jaloux du blanc qu'il ne saurait égaler, le mulâtre s'irrite à la vue du noir qui lui a donné le jour, vil rebut de la nature, il ne voit dans ces deux couleurs que la preuve incontestable de sa dégradation, et le reproche éternel de son existence, le Mulâtre en un mot possède les traits et les vices du blanc et du noir, sans en avoir aucune des vertus. Cette caste, contre nature, monument affreux de l'avilissement des blancs, disparaîtra si le gouvernement approuve les envois que je propose.'

—Drouin de Bercy, *De Saint-Domingue: de ses guerres, de ses révolutions, de ses ressources et des moyens à prendre pour y rétablir la paix et l'industrie* (1814)

The trope of "monstrous hybridity" was not actually born in representations of the Haitian Revolution, as shown by the abbé Antoine François

Prévost's 1748 description of 'mulattoes' on the Gold Coast of Africa as a 'bastard species' of brigands 'composed of everything that is awful in Europeans and Negroes' (13: 304) The seeds for this trope were in fact first sown in late seventeenth- and early eighteenth-century travel writing, where ambivalent and often cruel descriptions of "racial mixing" were espoused by naturalist European travel writers and Catholic missionary priests who traveled to and lived in the French overseas colonies. The Dominican missionary Jean-Baptiste Labat, for example, who 'spent the years 1694–1706 traveling throughout the colonial and pirate worlds of the French Antilles,' mostly living in Martinique (McClellan, 112) until he arrived in Saint-Domingue in 1701 (Garrigus, 2006, 21), recorded his observations of the flora and fauna of the islands of the Americas alongside his own theory of "racial mixing." In his *Nouveau voyage aux isles de l'Amérique* (1722), Labat identified 'the mulatto' as a 'child born of a black mother and a white father' (and, in very rare cases, of a 'black' father and a 'white' mother), and argued:

> this libertinage of whites with *des négresses* is the source of an infinity of crimes. The color of children who are born of this mixture is both white and black and produces a kind of blackish-brown tint [*participe du blanc et du noir, et produit une espèce de bistre*] … The Mulattoes are ordinarily well-made, of a good height, vigorous, strong, adroit, industrious, courageous, and daring beyond imagination, they have a lot of vivacity, but they are addicted to their pleasures, flighty, sly, mean, and capable of the greatest crimes. (2:120)

Labat continues by telling us that by the 'third generation' of intermixture we would only be able to distinguish a person 'born of this mixture' by the haziness of their eyes ('*le blanc des yeux qui paraîtra toujours un peu battu*'), but that such a person's descendants could return to a *pure* 'negro' state within 'three generations' (2:128).

Labat's characterization of 'mulattoes' as wholly incongruous and therefore 'capable of the greatest crimes' would find similar expression in the works of the first of the 'missionary naturalists' to be permanently sent to Saint-Domingue by the French government: the aforementioned Father Jean-Baptiste Le Pers, who 'served as a parish priest in the north of Saint-Domingue, where he supervised the building of ten churches' from 1704 until his death in 1735 (McClellan, 112). Le Pers's four-volume *Histoire de l'Isle espagnole ou de Saint-Domingue* (1730-31) contains the following description of the population of the Spanish side of the island:

> They know nothing of and barely even recognize the name of Spain with which they now have very little dealing [*ils n'ont presque plus de commerce*].

"Monstrous Hybridity" in Colonial and Revolutionary Writing

> Moreover, as they have extremely mixed their blood, first with the islanders, then with the Negroes, they now appear in a variety of colors, depending upon whether they contain more of the European, the African, or the American. The nature of their mind partakes of all three also, and they have above all contracted the majority of their vices. (2:479)

Le Pers's description of the way in which the 'extremely mixed blood' of those living in Spanish Saint-Domingue had created a schism between the inhabitants of the eastern part of the island and their European mother country (whom 'they barely even recognize') speaks volumes about his disdain for non-Europeans. Le Pers paints as barely human both the 'Indians,' whom he constantly refers to as 'barbarians' (1:87) and calls practically 'men of another species' [*hommes d'une autre nature*] (1.2:107), and the 'Negroes,' whom he portrays with the utmost cupidity for having 'sold' their own brethren (1:423). He elsewhere calls 'negroes' the 'opprobrium of mankind' and the 'dregs of nature' [*le rebut de la nature*] (2:497). Le Pers's ideas about the savagery of 'negroes' and 'Indians,' helped to support his ultimate conclusion that 'amalgamation' would result in the contraction of the 'vice[s]' of all three races.

Le Pers's text had a long-lasting influence in creating a picture of the "racial" makeup of the Spanish-controlled part of Hispaniola. For example, in 1802, Malouet echoed Le Pers's "racial" summation of those living on the Spanish side of the island when he attempted to provide prescriptions that could end the violence in the colony in his five-volume *Collection de mémoires sur les colonies, et particulièrement sur Saint-Domingue*, 'The Spaniards are, or are nearly so, of the same species as the negroes. There are very few Europeans among them and a very small number of slaves: their blood has been mixed to the point that you can no longer even distinguish any nuance' (4:347). Barré de Saint-Venant, also writing about the problems of revolutionary Saint-Domingue in 1802, characterized 'Les Espagnols de Saint-Domingue' using a vocabulary of "monstrous hybridity" when he wrote that they were 'a bastardized race, originating with the negroes of Africa, some Europeans and some of the ancient indigenous population of the country, whose infirmity is known. We can find within them all shades from black to brown' (207). Le Pers's writing continued to exercise influence in texts dealing with the Haitian Revolution throughout the nineteenth century, evidenced by Jean-Baptiste Lemonnier-Delafosse's gloss of Spanish Saint-Dominguans in his 1846 *Seconde campagne de Saint-Domingue ... précédée de Souvenirs historiques et succincts de la première campagne* (1846): 'We believe them to possess a profound respect for religion,' he writes, 'that they know how to align with an excessive libertinage: their blood was mixed at first with the islanders, during the period of the discovery, then with the negro, so that their character and their color resemble all at once the three races of Europe, Africa, and America' (290).[1]

Each of these evocations of the degradations attached to people who could be described as neither fully "white" nor completely "black" as well as their authors' demonstrable interests in the long-term effects of "miscegenation" reflect the fact that, as Claude Blanckaert has written, 'the question of human crossbreeding' provoked 'a kind of critical secular interest' during the Enlightenment as naturalists and proto-anthropologists asked the questions: 'Are métis viable or not? Do they inherit the best "qualities" from their parents, or are they a vehicle of degeneration?' (43). Yet while these Le Pers influenced descriptions of people who had 'extremely mixed their blood' suggests that the 'métis' almost exclusively derived the worst qualities from the mishmash of their myriad ancestral 'parents,' on the contrary, Labat's characterization of 'the Mulattoes' as possessing an uncanny mixture of positive and negative qualities provides a double answer to these questions. In representing the simultaneously positive and negative dimensions of people of "mixed race," Labat links his writing not only to what would become one of the most central concerns in pseudoscientific debates about "miscegenation," but to one of the central tropes of the Haitian Revolution—"monstrous hybridity."[2] Whether represented in the discourse of "miscegenation" as degenerative, regenerative, or a combination thereof, the trope of "monstrous hybridity" responds to and attempts to regulate

---

[1] The influence of Le Pers's work appears to have been extremely broad, as his words were also echoed by Raynal who wrote that in the early eighteenth century the eastern part of Saint-Domingue was made up of roughly 18,000 'inhabitants, Spaniards, *métis*, *nègres*, or *mulâtres*' and '[t]heir color and their character resembled more or less the American, the European, or the African, depending upon the level of mixture present in their blood of these three peoples' [*en raison du mélange qui s'était fait du sang de ces trois peuples*] (1780, 6: 317).

[2] Labat's description of the way in which "monstrous hybridity" worked to produce the incongruity of simultaneously negative and positive qualities, continued to exert influence over popular understandings of "race" in the nineteenth century. Writing in 1853, the abbé Alphonse Cordier reprinted Labat's very own assessment about 'mulattoes' when without attribution he wrote in his *Voyage de la France à la Guadeloupe*, 'I will say a few words about the people of color [*la caste de couleur*], resulting from the libertinage of the negroes and the whites, who find themselves altogether despised by the one and the other. *On entend par mulâtre les enfants qui naissent de une mère noire et d'un père blanc, ou bien d'un père noir et d'une mère blanche. Ce dernier est très rare ... La couleur des enfants qui naissent de ce mélange participe du blanc et du noir, et produit une espèce de bistre.*' Like Labat, Cordier concluded that even these people of mixed race had some positive qualities, but that, on the whole, 'mulattoes' were '*méchant et capable des plus grands crimes*' (369). I have left the French portion here because I translate it above (see, Labat sections), and the italics have been added by me to indicate the plagiarized portion.

the incongruity of an assemblage of traits perceived as clashing, dissonant, and incompatible, with the epistemological problems generated by the idea of "racial mixing" or the unknowability involved in identifying phenotypically ambiguous people of color as either "white" or "black." Such a vocabulary of monstrosity, as demonstrated by Drouin de Bercy's rendering of "mulattoes" as irrevocably 'imprinted' by 'nature' with the 'incontestable signs of degradation and eternal reproach,' would soon become one of the abiding features of narrative descriptions of rebellion with respect to the people of color living in the colonies, whether slave or free.

Garraway (2005a), Garrigus (2006a), and, to a lesser extent, Sollors (1997) and Dayan (1995b) have examined the relationship between eighteenth-century travel writing to the French colonies and the legal and social ramifications that the "racial" taxonomies produced therein would later have for the colony of Saint-Domingue. However, the perceived existential threat that these people of "mixed race" appear to have posed for European planters has rarely received the same attention. The trope of "monstrous hybridity" had profound ideological implications not only for the naturalist travel writers whose development of the figure would go on to provide a distinctive vocabulary of "mulatto/a" vengeance, but for the way in which later nineteenth-century authors would narrate the history of the Haitian Revolution as a parricidal conflict with "racial" undertones. The crucial story here is the overwhelming importance of the idea that it was a feeling natural to "mulatto/as" that caused such individuals to behave in unstable, degraded, duplicitous, and inscrutable ways, even against their own kin. The purportedly innately vengeful mind of the "mulatto/a" in early narratives of the Haitian Revolution became the primary lens through which to understand not only the causes, but the fundamental political problems of a revolution that often appeared to pit children of "color" against their "white" parents.

As it stands now, the fact that the *hommes de couleur*, and especially those who could be described as "mixed," were understood to be acting violently and vengefully against their parents, both "black" and "white," has been subordinated in favor of the study of the social, political, and economic circumstances that certainly contributed to the sense of resentment and indignation felt by the all of exploited peoples of Saint-Domingue. This is simply to say that the problem of knowing that became attached to the idea of the "mulatto/a" as a way to express anxieties about the instability of political loyalties during the Haitian Revolution has been passed over in most contemporary studies that seek to understand the social and political causes of rebellion on the part of both the enslaved and the free. The epistemological conundrum that the idea of the "mulatto" came to symbolize in early narratives of the Haitian Revolution is, however, far more important. There is a hidden dynamism in early naturalist narratives about "race" that reinforced the idea of a natural phenotypic enmity between "mulattoes" or people of lighter skin hue and "negroes" or people of darker skin hue. The reiteration of these claims in early nineteenth-century writings about the Haitian Revolution would later be used to explain the political distinctions to be found in the territories of Haitian leaders Alexandre Pétion and Henry Christophe, and to justify French attempts to retake the colony up until at least the mid-nineteenth century. As we will see in this chapter, the existence of two Haitis in the early nineteenth century became one of the most prominently evoked examples of "monstrous hybridity" in all of the Atlantic World.

The disturbingly memorable tales of the innate hatred that "mulattoes" supposedly felt equally towards "whites" and "blacks," and vice versa, and that were often buried in the writing of naturalist travel writers, expressed a marked anxiety about the certainty that "racial" taxonomies presupposed. This uncertainty and anxiety would take center stage in narrative descriptions of the free people of color of Saint-Domingue as parricidal "monstrous hybrids" whose loyalties, like their "races," were subject to interpretation and change. The idea first produced in travel writing, that "mulattoes" and other people of "mixed race" were at once naturally violent, vengeful, and 'capable of the greatest crimes,' but also baffling, untrustworthy, and erratic, has never been explicitly linked to the blame that the first writers of the Revolution attached to its "mulatto" participants, and that later writers would link to the "mulatto" government of Alexandre Pétion. The language of incongruity, confusion, and blame used to describe vengeful people of color who were committing what appeared to eighteenth-century travel writers to be the unconscionable crimes of abortion, infanticide, and homicide, would eventually become much more explicitly linked to slave revolts and rebellion in Saint-Domingue, as well as to the Haitian Revolution itself through the trope of the "monstrous hybrid." By tracing "monstrous hybridity" to various little-regarded episodes in some of the most studied naturalist travel writing from various overseas colonies, and later to writings from colonial and revolutionary Saint-Domingue, and, finally, to writings about independent Haiti, this chapter provides a roadmap for how the narrative of "mulatto/a" vengeance would become the most casual vernacular with which to explain not only the impetus for the Haitian Revolution and the problems of knowing that it unleashed, but the political problems of early nineteenth-century Haiti.

*

If the work of the seventeenth-century missionary Father Jean-Baptiste Du Tertre, who was living in the lesser Antilles when he wrote his *Histoire générale des Antilles habitées par les Français* (1667–71), offers a 'repressed

"Monstrous Hybridity" in Colonial and Revolutionary Writing

narrative of French colonialism in the Caribbean' (Garraway, 2005, 57); we might also say that this text produces a 'repressed narrative' of "mulatto/a" vengeance. One of Du Tertre's accounts, which has received little critical attention, involves the 'story of a *Métif* named Waernard,' the 'bastard' son of a certain General Waernard then living on the island of Dominica in the mid-1600s. According to Du Tertre, the general had decided not only to officially recognize his son, the '*Métif*,' but 'allow him to take his name, and have him raised in the house with his other children' (3:82). Du Tertre considered the younger Waernard, who would eventually become governor of the island of Dominica, to have been appointed to such a high position exactly because his existence lay between the 'civilization' of the European 'races' and the 'savagery' of the "American" 'races.' Du Tertre describes the son as having been born of a 'savage slave woman,' yet he also remarks that 'there did not appear to be anything of the savage within him except for the color of the skin and hair' (3:82). Although the color of his skin and the texture of his hair should have signaled his savagery, according to the naturalist priest, Waernard was able to mask these traits by having 'untangled, looped, and curled' [*déliez, annelez, & bouclez*] his 'very black hair,' 'contrary to the ordinary practices of the other Savages' (3:82). However, without any sense of irony, Du Tertre intimates that the general's son does eventually either regress into savagery or reveal his true 'savage' nature when, after his father's death and Madame Waernard's attempt to enslave him, he runs away to join the 'maroons' and 'other fugitive slaves' (3:83).

Having been captured by Madame Waernard, who 'had him chained, and made him wear a ghastly pair of leg irons and even forced him to work wearing this equipment,' the general's son eventually 'follows the advice of his mother, which was to take refuge among the Savages of Dominica' (3:83). Du Tertre writes that the younger Waernard not only reconciled these 'Savages' to the English with whom they were at war, but managed and led them to such an extent that he became 'admired' by them and was eventually appointed their principal leader. 'He had ascended to such an extent,' remarked Du Tertre, 'that he encouraged them with a marvelous ease to carry out the most difficult tasks and cruelties that conformed to his nature, which had almost nothing human in it' (3:83). Du Tertre continues by saying that he himself believed General Waernard's son to have been the 'author of the massacre that the Savages perpetrated against the French on the island of Marigalande in the year 1653' and claimed that M. du Lion, who was then the governor of the island of Guadeloupe (Lafleur, 47), told him that the younger Waernard was 'the author of many evils and guilty of a great deal of murders' (3:83–84). The leap here is unmistakable for Du Tertre, who notes that cruelty, murder, and rebellion were 'natural' to this son who had 'almost nothing human in him' just like the 'Savages' whom his appearance and behavior would eventually putatively approximate. Du Tertre goes on to describe the failure of Lord Willoughby's attempt to Christianize the younger Waernard, sending him to live in England to become educated and Christianized, having recognized his 'capability.'[3] Du Tertre writes, 'he lived as a Christian with the English, & had dressed like them; but upon his return, he quit his clothes, & lived as an Infidel with the Savages & walked barefoot' (3:84).

Du Tertre was hardly the only 'naturalist priest' (McClellan, 114) who would help to develop the trope of "monstrous hybridity" by connecting it to tales of the ineffaceable savagery of people of color. Dominican missionary J.-B.-M. Nicholson (1734–73) served as the superior cleric in Léogane from 1769 until his death in 1773. According to McClellan, upon royal command from Louis XV, Nicholson's family published his manuscript posthumously in 1776 as the *Essai sur l'Histoire Naturelle de Saint-Domingue* (114). In this text, Nicholson's adoption of the language of "monstrous hybridity" as an expression of incongruity, dissonance, and savagery shines through in his description of 'Negresses' who performed self-abortions in order to revenge themselves against their masters. Nicholson writes:

> We see black women who have given themselves abortions, so that the barbaric master whom they serve does not profit from their descendants [*le maître barbare qu'elles servent ne profitent pas d'une posterité*], whose existence could only be miserable; since it would be just like their own. A sort of compassion was combined together with the pleasure of vengeance at outraging nature in this way. Inhuman hearts! this heinous crime is upon you. You are more barbaric than these homicidal mothers if you hear me without shuddering in horror. (55)

Nicholson describes these slave women using the vocabulary of "monstrous hybridity" when he notes that somehow they are able to abort their unborn children equally out of a 'sort of compassion' for them and out of a sheer sense of pleasure at simultaneously 'outraging nature.' The combined 'vengeance' and 'compassion' of these women who, according to Nicholson's portrayal, may have been aborting pregnancies that were the result of sexual relations with their own masters—supported by the idea that the women wanted to prevent their masters from 'profiting' from *their own* 'descendants'—also allows Nicholson to implicate "race," in addition to slavery, as the impetus for a kind of matricide that seemed to him otherwise inexplicable,

---

[3] Lord Francis Willoughby served twice as governor of the English colonies in the West Indies. For more on Willoughby's life and tenure, see volume two of the anonymously published *Antigua and the Antiguans, A Full Account of the Island and its Inhabitants* (1844, 350–51). For more on Waernard, see Lafleur (1992, 47–56).

confusing, and horrifying. Nicholson's narration provides a rich example of how narratives of "mulatto/a" vengeance often detailed attempts to prevent the very birth of "monstrous hybrids."

If Nicholson's contribution to troping the "monstrous hybrid" rests vaguely on the idea of "negro" women avenging nature by disallowing the potential for their slave-masters to enslave their own children, it was the French soldier Alexandre-Stanislaus, Baron de Wimpffen, stationed in Saint-Domingue until 1790, who more explicitly connected ideas about "monstrous hybridity" to the studied duplicity of "mulatto" psychology. In his *Voyage à Saint-Domingue* (1797), under the pretext of explaining the suicide of one of his acquaintances, de Wimpffen, who frequently cited Labat (1797, 2:28–29), describes 'a married mulatto' who decided to take for a mistress a 'single female mulatto.' De Wimpffen recounts how when the man, 'be it out of disgust or repentance,' ultimately decided to go back to his wife, his mistress, 'the olive-complexioned Medea hid her rage, in order to more effectively ensure her vengeance.' Apparently, the so-called 'female mulatto' 'continued to maintain friendly relations with the couple, in order to lure them to her house, where, at a dinner that she gave for them, she poisoned them both' (2:16). Though it may seem like this passage has more to tell us about individual jealousy than the innate psychology of "mulattoes," in an earlier letter, de Wimpffen explicitly noted that in his study of the colored population of Saint-Domingue he sought to answer ontological questions about the "negro." Firstly, de Wimpffen wanted to know 'about the ideas that, in the mind of the negro, form the foundation of his opinion of right and wrong'; secondly, he was curious about 'the perspective from which we must consider his existence'; and finally, 'about the use I imagine he would make of his liberty' (2:38). The fact that the above episode concerning the vengeance of the 'female mulatto' is one of only a few such descriptions of people described as being of "mixed race" in the two-volume work, suggests that these examples were similarly meant to be considered representative. At the end of the description of the 'female mulatto,' de Wimpffen even vaguely inferred that such scenes were commonplace. He said that this event, along with the aforementioned suicide, were spoken of so casually in Saint-Domingue that they might simply constitute the 'news of the day,' and 'no one even thought to report such an atrocious deed [*personne ne songe à constater un fait aussi atroce*]; there you have it,' de Wimpffen exclaimed, 'the *way of life* [*mœurs*] *of the lucky* inhabitants of Saint-Domingue!' (2:16; italics in the original).

What naturalist accounts of inherent criminality, vice, and duplicity on the part of people of color, and especially "mulattoes" or "métis," take for granted is that "Africans" or "Indians" and all of their descendants of whatever degree had the capacity to return not only to the savage state characterized by their ancestral connection to either Africa or the Americas, but to develop a penchant for the kind of vengeance described by de Wimpffen. Even though the scene recounted above was categorized in the index of de Wimpffen's *Voyage* under the simple heading of 'Vengeance' (2:265), the trope of "monstrous hybridity," and the narrative of "mulatto/a" vengeance upon which it relies, actually depends first upon a narrative of savagery. Both "mulatto/a" vengeance and "monstrous hybridity" refer back to ideas of savagery precisely because they suggest that people of color, regardless of any genealogical connection to "whiteness," would never be able to rid themselves of the 'original stain' of their barbarity, no matter how near to such "whiteness" they might approach (Sollors, 1997, 120–24). Moreover, what Pierre de Vassière had referred to as the "'law of regression'" or "'reversion'," which implied 'blackening' (qtd. in Dayan, 1995, 25), more specifically, was a persistent fear in the eighteenth and nineteenth centuries, especially after the initial uprising of the slaves in Saint-Domingue.

In 1794, the Jamaican slave owner, travel writer, and British colonist Bryan Edwards described the first days of the slave insurrection in Saint-Domingue in the following manner: 'Upwards of one hundred thousand savage people,' he wrote, 'habituated to the barbarities of Africa, avail themselves of the silence and obscurity of the night, and fall on the peaceful and unsuspicious planters, like so many famished tigers thirsting for human blood' (3:67). The French naturalist travel writer and medical doctor Michel Etienne Descourtilz, who also visited Saint-Domingue during the insurrection, also ascribed native vengeance, codified as savage inferiority, to 'negro' slaves, when he wrote in his *Voyage d'un naturaliste et ses observations ...* (1809):

> The negroes have other means [than poison] of avenging themselves, and they use the pitiful instruments with which their rude souls have furnished them [*emploient les tristes instruments qui leur fournit leur âme peu délicate*]; that is why they take advantage of their current numerical supremacy to harass the whites, [and] humiliate them in every circumstance which presents itself through exploitation [*des actions d'éclat*], theft, or injuries that remain unpunished. (453)

The narratives of 'negro' savagery called forth by the writing of both Edwards and Descourtilz recalls the putative barbarity attributed to mere contact between 'Africans' and 'whites,' by eighteenth-century naturalist travel writers. The French explorer François Le Vaillant, who also espoused a theory of "mixed-race" degeneracy (2:171) in his *Voyage de M. Le Vaillant dans l'Intérieur de l'Afrique par Le Cap de Bonne Espérance, dans Les années 1783, 84 & 85* (1790), described the way in which the initial contact with European civilization was detrimental to the 'childish curiosity' (1:307),

"Monstrous Hybridity" in Colonial and Revolutionary Writing

'original innocence,' and 'purity of manners' (1:306) of most African nations. He wrote, 'In every part where the natives live entirely unconnected with the whites, their manners are mild and amiable; on the contrary, an acquaintance with the Europeans alters and corrupts their natural character, which degenerates amazingly; and this remark, which is a melancholy truth, seldom admits of an exception' (1:306–07).[4] The French writer Hilliard d'Auberteuil, who arrived in Saint-Domingue at the age of 14 (Garraway, 2005, 219), believed that "racial mixing" was shameful and degrading also (2:82); and, much like Le Vaillant, he, too, thought that it was contact with Europeans and not nature that had produced what he considered to be the vile condition of the 'Negro.' Like Nicholson, D'Auberteuil complained of slave women who performed abortions, but the latter wrote, 'If the *négresses* often give themselves abortions, it is almost always the fault of their masters' (2:66). Hilliard d'Auberteuil further blamed the colonists of the New World for the level of savagery and libertinage present on the plantations when he wrote:

> One should not be surprised at all that the *negroes*, in becoming our slaves, contract an infinity of vices *that they did not have* in their natural state; they lose, with respect to us, the sentiment of *pity*, it is equally certain that *we do not at all have* this sentiment for them, because we have divorced ourselves from nature. (1:130; italics in the original)[5]

When such ideas of innate savagery as a lack of civilization were joined together with the agency of vengeance as the result of contact with "white" civilization, the resulting language produced the effect of "monstrous hybridity." In his famous 1818 history of the Haitian Revolution, Antoine Métral wrote of the marriage of savagery and civilization, symbolized by the difference between native Africans and creolized Africans, in precisely these terms when he said:

> The child born of a slave was different from one born to a free father; and as these negroes went from a savage nature to a corrupt nature [*et à mésure que ces nègres passaient de la nature sauvage à la nature corrompue*], their virtues changed into vices and their vices into crimes, without us being able to see among them any of the graces of civilization. (1818, 46)

---

4 All quotations from Le Vaillant are taken from Elizabeth Helme's English translation, *Travels from the Cape of Good Hope, into the interior parts of Africa* (1841).

5 Hilliard D'Auberteuil's remarks about pity are almost certainly inflected by Jean-Jacques Rousseau's *Discours sur l'origine et les fondements de l'inégalité parmi les hommes* (1755), wherein the French *philosophe* declared that what marked the distinction between human beings and animals was the sentiment of pity (2002, 31).

From "Monstrous Hybridity" to Enlightenment Literacy

While 'Negroes' and Africans were variously codified as monstrous savages, nobly innocent, or 'childish[ly]' inferior beings in much of the writing of the period, it was almost certainly Jean-Jacques Dessalines who became the primary symbol, in the narrative descriptions of the Haitian Revolution in which he appears, of the "negro" savage's tendency to turn these imbibed 'vices' into 'crimes.' Many of those who lived through the Haitian Revolution described Dessalines as a warrior from Africa, a man who was illiterate, knew no French, and was only thirsty for "white" blood. Armand Levasseur, a French lieutenant in Saint-Domingue during the Leclerc expedition, for example, described Dessalines in the following way: 'He was a former Bossale slave ... from the coast of Africa [who] did not known how to read or write' (25).[6] 'He is angry by nature,' Levasseur writes, 'his face is hideous, and his physiognomy is horrendous' (26). Levasseur evoked more fully the language of "monstrous hybridity" in his subsequent impression of Dessalines as a barely human 'criminal' in a passage that is so telling with respect to the way in which the troping of "racial" monstrosity relies upon a narrative of "black" savagery and was not used solely to describe the vengeance and perfidy of people considered to be of "mixed race" that it is worth quoting at length:

> This man, who has none of those passions that ordinarily drive the individual over whom they reign with force, is nevertheless one of the most criminal. Is humankind not revolted to witness how it is in the murder of one of his own that he finds his Happiness? ... This man (must I give him this title?) is so thirsty for blood [*tellement altéré de sang*] that he can only go a few days without seeing it flow. For him, it is such a compelling need that when there are no more whites to sacrifice, he chooses his victims from among his own race. (26–27)

In many ways, Levasseur's description of Dessalines provides just a mere peek into the proliferate defamation machine that was the transatlantic print culture of the Haitian Revolution and which produced seemingly infinite descriptions of this revolutionary hero as a "monstrous hybrid." After Dessalines's proclamation of April 28, which mandated the expulsion or death of all remaining French colonists on the island, Dessalines would become the Haitian Revolution's most infamous "monstrous hybrid."[7] One

---

6 The term 'Bossale' was used to describe those slaves who had recently arrived from Africa and was often pejorative. See, for example, Gérard Barthélemy's explication of the word (1997, 841).

7 In part to combat such a tendency, the French abolitionist Victor Schoelcher would seem to defend Dessalines when he writes in his *Colonies étrangères et Haïti*: 'The entire history of the life of Dessalines proves that he was not naturally ruthless [*impitoyable*],

"Monstrous Hybridity" in Colonial and Revolutionary Writing

good example of the tendency for nineteenth-century writers to make of Dessalines an incomprehensible demon comes in H. Furcy de Bremoy's *Evrard; ou Saint-Domingue au 19ème siècle*. In this former French planter's novel, Dessalines is called 'the living incarnation of Satan' [*l'image vivante de Satan*] (26), and Furcy de Bremoy continues by noting, 'Every one of his thoughts became a crime; every one of his speeches became a death writ. Coldly meditated by this cannibal; the destruction of men is subject to a mathematical calculation, and this massacre is regularly organized' (26–27). After recounting Dessalines's expulsion of the 'whites' from the island, Furcy de Bremoy said of Dessalines, 'the exterminator of the white race is on the move' [*l'exterminateur de la race blanche est en marche*] (27). The belief that Dessalines had perpetrated a wholesale extermination of 'the white race' was extremely widely held in the nineteenth century. Alfred Hunt notes, in fact, that after the transnational circulation[8] of Dessalines's declaration of Haitian independence,

> Several [U.S. American] journals carried a story in which Dessalines was a man of 'wild and flighty mind' who killed 'whites' on sight. In this fictional and emotional account, Dessalines captured Toussaint's former master after Toussaint had helped him escape. Toussaint pleaded for his former master's life, but Dessalines replied, 'He must perish because he is white. His color is his guilt.' (91)

Comparing him to Louverture, the French soldier Pamphile de Lacroix also described Dessalines as having 'preside[d] over the massacres of Saint-Marc, Verettes, and la Petite-Rivière' during the Haitian Revolution, and as having caused 'innocent' blood to be shed (183).

Deborah Jenson has observed that after Dessalines's famous proclamation of April 28, 1804 was printed in France in the *Journal des débats*—a document in which the Haitian leader famously explained his ejection of the French colonists from the island by either forced deportation or extermination, 'we have returned to these true cannibals war for war, crime for crimes, outrage for outrage. Yes, I saved my country, I have avenged America'—the French journalist Benjamin Constant wrote, 'There is something savage in this negro style that grips those of us who are accustomed to the forms and hypocrisy of the social world with a particular kind of terror' (qtd. in Jenson, 2011, 46–47). These descriptions of the terrorizing behavior of Dessalines,

> despite the barbaric acts of vengeance that dishonored him; for the memory of his servitude threw his ardent soul and his uncultivated mind into a dizzy rage. He wanted to place between Haiti and its former metropole a sea more impassable than the Ocean, a sea of blood' (1843, 2: 142).

8 For the transnational circulation of this document see Jenson (2011, 122–60).

whose frankness—he acknowledges in the Haitian *Acte d'Indépendance* 'that my name has become a horror to all people who want to continue slavery, and that despots and tyrants pronounce it only in cursing the day that I was born' (1804, 7)—supposedly lay outside of U.S. sentimentalism and European understandings of their 'social world,' reflect the "racial" hierarchies in place in colonial pseudoscientific debates about "race." These were debates in which some people were defined as natural slaves (because they were "savages") owing to their alleged ignorance, simplicity, and lack of human emotions, and others were described as natural masters owing to their purported knowledge, sophistication, and sympathy. These descriptions also bear the influence of the "racial" hierarchies based on climate and geography, often referred to as climatology, that proliferated in metropolitan debates about "race."

Eighteenth- and nineteenth-century pseudoscientific discourses of "race" in the Atlantic World centered on the debate between polygenists like the Swedish naturalist Carl von Linné (Linnaeus) and Thomas Jefferson, who believed that 'negroes' were of an entirely different species and consequently had a different origin than 'Caucasians,' and monogenists like the Comte de Buffon and Johann Friedrich Blumenbach, who believed in one common origin (genus/species) and therefore, for Buffon at least, that if some Africans were inferior it was because they had degenerated due to climate changes (Dain, 7–30).[9] At the heart of this debate about the origins of mankind was really a debate about whether or not, and to what effect, "white" Europeans and "black" Africans could reproduce with one another. Such debates, therefore, often centered on fertility, or whether or not "whites" and "blacks" could produce progeny who could themselves reproduce. Robert Young has written that 'by settling on the possibility or impossibility of hybridity,' these debates 'focused explicitly on the issue of sexuality and the issue of sexual unions between whites and blacks' (9). Such a focus can

---

9 Linnaeus had divided humanity into four distinct groups (Americanus, Asiaticus, Africanus, and Europeaeus) in his 1735 *Systema naturae*, which would be refined by subsequent naturalists, such as Johann Friedrich Blumenbach, to establish a more explicitly hierarchical system of classifying human beings. For Blumenbach, there were 'five "racial" types': 'Caucasian, Mongolian, Ethiopian, American, and Malay.' According to Michael Yudell, 'Blumenbach's addition posited the Caucasian as the ideal, or mean race, and on either side of that mean were "racial" extremes; the Mongolian and Ethiopian on one side and the American and Malay on the other. Both divergences from the Caucasian ideal were considered inferior' (16). Nevertheless, it is Buffon's theory of hybrid regeneration as opposed to degeneration to be found in his *Histoire Naturelle*, which was read not only by Europeans, but by 'educated Americans' (Dain, 18), that most influenced the development of the trope of the "monstrous hybrid" and its subsequent appearance in the print culture of the Haitian Revolution.

be seen in the writings of Edward Long, an ardent supporter of colonial slavery, who argued that the 'White man' and the 'Negro' were actually two distinct species and therefore could not together produce progeny capable of producing their own progeny. In other words, a 'mulatto' would not be able to have children with another 'mulatto' (2:336). Contrary to Long, the Martinican colonist Moreau de Saint-Méry, another unabashed advocate of colonial slavery, believed that women of color and 'white' men could and did produce children who could reproduce themselves, but that after the first instance of 'white' and 'black' procreation (resulting in the "mulatto/a"), each successive generation would be less fertile than the preceding one. Thus, the child of a *mulâtresse* who coupled with a 'white man' would not be as fertile as her *pure* 'negro' counterparts, and 'quadroons' who did so would be even less fertile and on and on until eventually complete infertility would result.

Regardless of their ultimate conclusions, these kinds of argument served the ends of colonialism and slavery since if it could be proven that "whites" and "blacks" could not produce children who could reproduce themselves, then the logic of the period maintained that it could be proven that they did not derive from one common origin.[10] If it could be proven that there was no common origin for Africans and Europeans, some would take this as proof that 'negroes' were hopelessly inferior and were therefore somehow obviously more destined to be slaves. This last sentiment is exemplified by the abbé Raynal, who concluded not only that 'The colour of the negroes is falsely supposed to be owing to the climate' (1776, 3: 102), but that they were a 'particular species of men' in whom 'the passions ... of fear and love are carried to excess ... and this is the reason why they are more effeminate, more indolent, more weak, and unhappily more fit for slavery' (1776, 1:101). Influenced by the writing of Thomas Jefferson, whom he cites (Mazères, 63–64), the French colonist Mazères would even argue that 'negroes' were not only better off under formal chattel slavery, but that they were meant to be slaves, since the 'negative color of their skin ... already proclaims the darkness of their intelligence' (61).[11] The idea that the actual physiology supposedly responsible for "racial" identities was also responsible for the feelings of the mind or that "blackness" was not just an outward appearance, but also way of *being*, would provide fodder for keeping the free people of

---

10 Wernor Sollors has shown that the 'mulatto' population was steadily increasing and not decreasing throughout the eighteenth century (1997, 130), which appears to contradict the claim of a writer like Moreau de Saint-Méry, who maintained that 'this class' was susceptible to 'disappearing' (1:95). Sollors also tells us that these kinds of mistaken claims about 'mulatto degeneration' were repeated in mid-nineteenth-century U.S. scientific theories of "race" by people like Josiah Nott (1997, 130).

11 Jefferson wrote, 'This unfortunate difference of color, and perhaps of faculty, is a powerful obstacle to the emancipation of these people' (1781, 141).

color in a subordinate state to "whites." Garran de Coulon tells us to that end that 'the difference of color' [*la nuance des couleurs*], and ostensibly the link to slavery that it called forth, 'did not permit us to consider them as the equals of the whites in the political order' (1:21–22).

The furious practice of trying to determine the proper terminology for and meaning of the "negro" reveals some of the inherent anxieties of an Enlightenment strain of thought that prided itself on the ability to *know*. It is precisely the uncertainty and unknowabilty of "race" that sparked some of the most heated debates in the eighteenth century as metropolitan naturalists sought to create "racial" taxonomies that were in many ways more elaborate than any that had been thus far created by those living in the colonies. The practice of claiming authority to describe those whom they had never even seen was so pervasive that even Buffon, while proclaiming the utmost authority for himself, scoffed at those like a certain M.P., most likely the Dutch philosopher Cornelius de Pauw, who 'affirmatively make claims about a great number of things without citing [their] sources.' Buffon quotes M.P. as having written, 'It would absolutely take four mixed generations to make entirely disappear the color of the negroes' (qtd. in Buffon, 1838, 2:661).[12] Yet what Buffon really took issue with was M.P.'s "interracial" taxonomy since M.P. had not simply provided names for the different generations of "interracial" mixtures (Buffon had been frustrated at his own inability to do so [1838, 2:661]) but had also described the hair and precise skin color of such people. M.P. had written, for example, 'From a Negro and a white woman is born the mulatto who is half white with long hair,' while 'From the mulatto and the white woman comes the swarthy quadroon with long hair' (qtd. in Buffon, 1838, 2:661). Buffon contested the certainty with which M.P. could have so distinctly described people of 'mixed generations' since neither one of them had ever been to the New World. Buffon wrote, 'I do not want to contradict the assertions of M.P.; I would only have liked for him to have told us from where he drew these observations, all the more since I was not able to procure any descriptions that were this precise' (1838, 2:661).

Buffon's ultimate argument was that the precise terminology used to describe different generations of "interracial" mixture had hardly been decided upon because there was a lack of 'a sufficient number of well-made observations' (2:661). To prove his point, Buffon quoted from a 1724 notice published in the *Histoire de l'Académie des Sciences*, which had used quite a different "racial" taxonomy. The notice stated:

---

12 Buffon is actually quoting from the first volume of de Pauw's *Recherches philosophiques sur les américains ou Mémoires intéressants pour servir à l'histoire de l'espèce humaine* (London: 1771), which the author signed 'M. de P***' (217–18).

"Monstrous Hybridity" in Colonial and Revolutionary Writing

> Everyone knows that the children of a white man and a black woman, or of a black man and a white woman, which is the same thing, are yellow in color, and that they have hair that is black, short, and curly; we call them *mulattoes*. The children of a mulatto man and a black woman [*un mulâtre et une noire*], or of a black man and a mulatto woman [*un noir et une mulâtresse*], which we call *griffes*, are of a yellow that is more black and have black hair: to the extent that a nation that had been originally formed of blacks and mulattoes would eventually return to perfect blackness. The children of mulattoes [together], which we call *casques*, are of a yellow that is lighter than that of the *griffes*: and apparently, a nation that had been originally formed by them would return to whiteness. (qtd. in 1838, 2:662)

Such debates about the characteristics and precise terminology to be used in describing people of color continued to be called forth with anxious uncertainty throughout the nineteenth century, as evidenced by abbé Migne's reference to both Buffon and M.P. in his 1853 *Nouvelle Encyclopédie théologique*. Under the entry 'Ethiopique,' and prefacing a reprinting of the whole of M.P.'s "racial" taxonomy, Migne wrote: 'The successive mixing of mulattoes and negroes has given way to complications and varieties that are rather inexplicable, which an author cited by Buffon has already tried to clear up' (42:480).

While armchair naturalists like Buffon and M.P. were constrained by their lack of empirical evidence, travel writers to Saint-Domingue, on the contrary, tried to proclaim the utmost authority for themselves based on the very act of seeing. Baron de Wimpffen, for example, after describing the intellectual, moral, and physical characteristics of the '*mulâtresse*' (which will be further taken up in Part Two of this volume), wrote: 'If this portrait should chance to differ from those you have seen elsewhere, you will please remember, Sir, that I sketch it on the spot, that the model is before my eyes, and that I have neither the talent nor the ambition of amusing you with ideal beauties' (115). The baron also exhibited the anxious ambivalence of desiring to *know* with certainty that often accompanies narrative descriptions of "mulattoes" when he specifically denied that he had ever fallen prey to the seduction and charms of such a '*mulâtresse*:' 'On this subject, however, I wish to refer to such as have entered into connections with them, with sufficient discernment to judge—for my own part, I freely confess that I do not now speak from experience' (113). While the first statement appears to contradict his stated lack of experience, it also paradoxically helps him to claim a distinctly ambivalent authority to represent. Such ambivalent claims of authority—as if to say, even though my eyes don't lie, I can't be certain—would continuously resurface in attempts to codify, quantify, and contain the kind of threat that "racial mixing" appears to have presented for the colonists of Saint-Domingue.

From "Monstrous Hybridity" to Enlightenment Literacy

In his daunting two-volume *Description... de la partie française de l'isle Saint-Domingue* (1797), Moreau de Saint-Méry's own claim to authority, that he was writing with 'certitude' and was the only such person who could undertake this endeavor of describing the colony (1:ix–xii), made him what Mary Louise Pratt might call the 'monarch-of-all-I-survey' (202), and allowed him to turn what were really his personal, rather than "scientific," observations into the kind of 'knowledge' used to support the system of slavery and that would eventually dominate understandings of the Haitian Revolution. Even though Moreau de Saint-Méry prefaced his *Description* by claiming that he merely wanted to offer some 'useful truths' about the 'past splendor of the colony' to his compatriots so that the errors of the past might be avoided (1:iii), he did much more than provide a "racial" taxonomy that could be used to classify and describe all of the different kinds of people present in Saint-Domingue: the 'negro' slaves, the 'white' colonists, and the free people of color. He also provided an elaborate tableau of personality characteristics for such people that has everything to tell us about how "mulatto/a" vengeance became explicitly attached to the Haitian Revolution.

The first 100 pages of the first volume of Moreau de Saint-Méry's *Description* are almost entirely devoted to the topic of skin color or 'class' and its effect on the colony, the majority of these pages being used to elaborate upon a theory of "interracial" mixing. Moreau de Saint-Méry begins by describing the product of a *pure* 'Blanc' with a *pure* 'Négresse' as a 'Mulâtre' (those who have between 49 and 70 parts of "white" ancestry) and the 'Quarteron' as the product of a *pure* 'Blanc' with a 'Mulâtresse,' but after this his system becomes more complex (1:77). Moreau de Saint-Méry writes, 'By the fifth nuance the *Métis* is born, called *Métif* in Saint-Domingue, who principally, if he is the son of a white man, has a very white skin and long hair, but this whiteness is not at all animated' (1:77). He follows by noting that the 'Mameluke' has between 113 and 120 parts "whiteness" (out of 128 parts total); the 'Sacatras' has between 8 and 24 parts of "whiteness"; the 'Griffes' has between 24 and 39 parts of "whiteness"; the 'Marabous' has between 40 and 48 parts of "whiteness," and so on (1:86).

In this intricate "racial" classification system that, like most of the debates of the era, settled on 'the possibility or impossibility of hybridity,' and in doing so betrayed what Robert Young would call a distinct 'fascination' with people having "interracial" sex (181), Moreau de Saint-Méry also provides a regular compendium of detailed personality and psychological characteristics for both "mixed-race" men and women that did more to affect discussions of "race" in the writing of the Haitian Revolution than any other published text. Moreau de Saint-Méry tells us, for example, that 'mulatto' men are 'indolent' and have a 'love of rest' even though they are relatively

"Monstrous Hybridity" in Colonial and Revolutionary Writing

'well-made,' 'strong' (1:90) and make 'excellent soldier[s]' (1:91). Yet Moreau de Saint-Méry will spend only two pages describing the physical and moral characteristics of 'mulatto' men, while devoting eight pages to describing female 'mulattoes' and their 'illegitimate commerce' with white men, which, he writes, 'offends principles and religious morals' (1:91). The same sense of incongruity and "monstrous hybridity" pervades his description of these women as well. After describing the '*mulâtresse*' as a 'Goddess' whose 'entire being' was 'given over to sensual pleasure,' 'seductive raptures' and dangerous 'charms' (1:92), Moreau de Saint-Méry concludes that these desirable women remain 'almost generally condemned, and ... are associated with the female slaves' (1:94).

Such descriptions of women of color as simultaneously desirable and disgusting provides not only another example which bolsters Young's theory of 'colonial desire' as a discourse that 'circulate[s] around an ambivalent axis of desire and aversion: a structure of attraction, where people and cultures intermix and merge ... and a structure of repulsion, where the different elements remain distinct and are set against each other dialogically' (19), but also reveals the way in which Moreau de Saint-Méry had co-opted a version of Buffon's theories of degeneracy and regeneracy to paint a narrative of "mulatto/a" vengeance.[13] Moreau de Saint-Méry's public disdain for the free people of color and the *sang-mêlés* was well known, owing to his *Observations*

---

13 In the mid-eighteenth century, Georges Louis Leclerc, the Comte de Buffon began to publish his *Histoire naturelle, générale et particulière* (1749–88) in which he categorized human beings, among other animals, based on climate. However, unlike his polygenist counterparts, Buffon affirmed his belief that "Negroes" and "Whites" indeed shared a common origin and focused his energy upon elaborating a theory of "racial mixing": 'If the mulatto was a real mule, there would be actually two species, quite distinct; the negro would be to man what the donkey is to the horse; or rather, if Whites were men, Negroes would no longer be; it would be an animal apart like the monkey, and we would be right to think that the White man and the Negro could not at all have had a common origin; but this supposition itself is contradicted by the fact that since all men can procreate and reproduce together, that all men come from the same stock and are of the same family' (4:389). Buffon wrote that even though 'Negroes' in the interior of Africa were more degenerate than those on the coast, both could be improved through sexual contact with the 'White Man' and thereby eventually 'return' to "whiteness." According to Buffon, "whiteness" was preferable because it was the "hue of heaven" [*la teinture du ciel*] (*Histoire*, 14:316). Buffon tells us that if "mulattoes" could continue in this way to reproduce themselves with whites down to the third and fourth generations they could benefit from "whiteness" in proportion to how far they could distance themselves from "blackness." He wrote, to that end, that eventually 'the Mulatto would have only a light trace of brown that would disappear all together within the next generations' and 'it would only take therefore 150 or 200 years to clean the skin of a Negro by this method of mixing with white blood' (*Histoire*, 14:313–14).

d'un habitant des Colonies sur le Mémoire en faveur des gens de couleur par M. Grégoire (1789). Moreau de Saint-Méry had anonymously published this pamphlet as a refutation of the abbé Grégoire's earlier defense of the free people of color.[14] In his *Observations*, Moreau de Saint-Méry acknowledged that 'the exclusion' of the free people of color from certain 'public offices' 'showed the strength of prejudice' [*le préjugé se montre dans toute sa force*] (1789, 18), but he went on to argue that 'It is not possible that beings, who were yesterday enslaved, could be today in the highest ranks of society' (1789, 19). Later in his 1791 *Considérations présentées aux vrais amis du repos et du bonheur de la France* Moreau de Saint-Méry, this time under his own name, wrote that if the slaves ever determined that 'the mulattoes had become or should become our equals, there is no longer any hope that France will be able to conserve its colonies' [*les mulâtres sont devenus ou doivent devenir nos égaux, il n'est plus d'espoir pour la France de conserver ses colonies*] (48). Painting 'the mulattoes' as the most immediate threat to the colony allowed Moreau de Saint-Méry to discourage "miscegenation." Coupled with the much more detailed terminology he began to publish in the mid-1780s (Fabella, 2010, 54) and fully published in 1797 in his *Description*, Moreau de Saint-Méry implicitly encourages "white" men *not* to continually mate with women of color lest their degenerate offspring pass into "whiteness" completely, thereby threatening the "white" colonists not only with the financial ruin that would come from the loss of the colony, but with degradation.[15] 'We call them *Misallied*,' Moreau de Saint-Méry wrote, 'the White Men whose wives are not White Women. We must regard them as new intermediaries between

---

14 In 1789, the abbé Grégoire published a pamphlet entitled *Mémoire en faveur des gens de couleur ou sang-mêlés de St. Domingue, & des autres isles françaises de l'Amérique*. For more on Grégoire's pamphlet, see Florence Gauthier (2013). Raimond's response to Moreau de Saint-Méry (1791b), discussed in the introduction to the present volume, was directed at this pamphlet.

15 Other colonists, like the anonymous author of the *Histoire des désastres de Saint-Domingue* (1795), would link the 'tendency' of 'les blancs' to manumit their lovers and children of color directly to general rebellion. The author, very likely François Laplace (Benzaken, 262), writes that such manumissions were a 'giant step towards general emancipation,' and that even though the ability to manumit one's offspring had been designed to 'limit inconstancy and to attempt to prevent the wandering spirit of these men,' such attempts were 'futile because all they really did were to open the eyes of the mulattoes who were themselves owners of slaves' (1795, 308). Before Benzaken's discovery of an inscription on a version of the text housed at the Municipal Library of Grenoble that attributed the *Histoire* to 'Cit. Laplace,' the *Histoire* had been erroneously attributed to the naturalist Descourtilz or alternatively to the French intendant François Barbé-Marbois; David Geggus also speculated that the text had most likely been written by 'an obscure Dominguan coffee planter' who may have been a part of the Rotureau family in Limbé parish (Geggus, 2007b, 301).

the Whites and the people of color. Their marriages, however, align them with the latter' (1797, 1:99).[16] The depiction of the skin color and physical appearance of the children produced by these *misalliances*, too, becomes increasingly negative as the taxonomy continues. Moreau de Saint-Méry describes "quadroons" as 'a very pale yellow' and as having 'perhaps more than a white man, a need for a shelter from the sun, which burns his skin and also touches him with freckles' (1:76). He describes the 'Métis' as having 'markedly white skin,' but writes, 'his whiteness is not at all animated … [he] bears the climate badly, and has few children, if any' (1:77). 'One must have truly expert eyes,' Moreau de Saint-Méry continues, 'to distinguish these last mixtures from the pure whites … There exist some *Sang-mêlés* in Saint-Domingue who are derived from the fourth mixture of *Sang-mêlés*, always with the whites, to such a degree that they really only have in their veins *one five hundred and twelfth part* African blood' (1:79; italics in the original). Later, Moreau de Saint-Méry consoles his readers who might fear that people who were really '*Sang-mêlés*' could be walking amongst them unknown by suggesting that:

> The Mamelukes who are the product of a male Mameluke with a female Mameluke are perhaps so rare that one would probably not even find four of them in the whole colony, and no one would be surprised by this fact, if they have really paid attention to what I have said about the degeneration of the *Gens-de-Couleur* after the quadroon. (1:78)

Even though Moreau de Saint-Méry describes ascending and descending degrees of whiteness to the 'nth degree' (Garraway, 2005, 224), for him, the only "interracial" coupling that would not produce the sterility of "monstrous hybridity" was that of the *pure* 'Nègresse' and the *pure* 'Blanc,' which engendered the 'Mulâtre.' This is because Moreau de Saint-Méry, unlike Buffon or Jefferson, considered the "African race" to degenerate as it became increasingly "whitened." Moreau de Saint-Méry writes:

> Of all the combinations of whites and negroes, it is the *Mulatto* who derives the greatest physical advantages. Of all the crossings of the races, it is he who obtains the strongest constitution and is best suited to the climate of Saint-Domingue. To the soberness and strength of the negro, he joins the bodily grace and the intelligence of the white. (1:76)

16 Moreau de Saint-Méry would appear to have been influenced in these observations by Hilliard d'Auberteuil, who had earlier written: 'He who is base enough to forget his own morals, is even more capable of forgetting the laws of society; & we are right not only to scorn him, but to suspect the honesty of those who out of either convenience or oversight, have fallen far enough to *misally themselves*' (1776, 2:79, emphasis added).

Yet Moreau de Saint-Méry's attribution of 'strength' and 'intelligence' to 'mulattoes' should not be viewed in concert with Buffon's theory of 'hybrid vigor' (Sollors, 1997, 133) or Jefferson's more general idea of 'improvement of the blacks in the body and mind, in the first instance of their mixture with whites' (1982, 141).[17] Moreau de Saint-Méry is not saying that the primary instance of 'crossbreeding,' to use Buffon's word, would cause 'regeneration,' as Jefferson wrote in his 1787 *Notes on the State of Virginia* (1982, 141); the Martinican colonist is simply saying that the 'Mulatto' is not by him or herself a degenerate being (but not a super-hybrid being either). Moreover, Moreau de Saint-Méry's belief in the 'strength' and 'intelligence' of the 'mulatto' should be viewed in light of his other observations about 'Mulatto' men, namely that the majority were lazy and had a love of pleasure (1797, 1:90).

Unlike Buffon, who saw in successive generations of "interracial" children a paradoxical symbol of 'regeneration,'[18] Moreau de Saint-Méry merely wrote about such people as impending symbols of doom who might one day pass imperceptibly into "whiteness," unnoticed because their bodies would no longer be *marked*, though their minds would always be so. In fact, although Moreau de Saint-Méry appears to sanction the first instance of "interracial" coupling, such a belief was likely transcribed by him more for pragmatic reasons than as evidence of any kind of advocacy of "racial" mixing for its own sake.

Moreau de Saint-Méry implied that the French government and the French colonists were in favor of increasing the class of free people of color because they needed the increased tax revenue and needed the free men of color for soldiers (1797, 1:69). Garrigus writes of this, 'colonial administrators were willing to increase the free population of color, as long as this occurred in ways that made colonial society more manageable' (2006, 201). Whatever Moreau de Saint-Méry's reasons for promoting the development of more 'Mulattoes,' his broader beliefs about "mixed-race" degeneracy

---

17 Buffon's idea that "racial" mixing would eventually dispense with the logic of slavery would find much more ambivalent expression, not only in the work of Moreau de Saint-Méry, but in the works of Hilliard D'Auberteuil, who, in his *Considérations sur l'état présent de la colonie de Saint-Domingue* (1776), wrote of the long-term effects of "miscegenation:" 'when the natural and biological [*organique*] character of the negro race has been absolutely erased, there will no longer be any reason to support differences that no longer consist of anything real: it is an end beyond which we should not desire, or they [the differences] will become absolutely useless' (2:94).

18 The images of degeneration and regeneration could also be considered metaphors since, according to Mona Ozouf, 'regeneration' as it was connected to 'revolution,' was an obsession in French political discourse at the end of the eighteenth century. This kind of political rather than biological regeneration was associated with the desire to 'resuscitate' a languishing body politic after a revolution, for example (219).

"Monstrous Hybridity" in Colonial and Revolutionary Writing

remain important since, along with his "racial" taxonomies, Moreau de Saint-Méry's opinions about the effects of "racial mixing" would provide the standard vocabulary for nearly every representation of the Haitian Revolution published in the nineteenth-century Atlantic World. If Sollors has written that '[i]n the nineteenth and the first half of the twentieth century the belief that Mulattoes were "feeble" or unable to procreate themselves, or that their children would be impaired in fertility had so much political, scientific, and general intellectual support that it may be called the "dominant opinion" of the period' (1997, 132), likewise the idea that the degraded human issue of "interracial" couplings was responsible for the French loss of Saint-Domingue had so much 'general support' in the nineteenth century that it was without a doubt, as the following section of this chapter will show, almost the only explanation of the causes of the Haitian Revolution in the period.

In the end, what literary historian Doris Garraway, drawing on the works of Françoise Vergès and Lynn Hunt, has called Moreau de Saint-Méry's 'colonial family romance' or the powerful 'logic of filiation' that positioned "white" men as the fathers of all people of color in the colony (Garraway, 2005b, 224; Hunt, 1992, 199; Vergès, 4), also had the effect of discouraging "miscegenation" by suggesting that it would create degenerate, vengeful, and parricidal individuals exactly like the "monstrous hybrids" who abound in early descriptions of the Haitian Revolution. Myriad writers, functionaries, and private citizens across the Atlantic World would explicitly use this naturalistic language of "monstrous hybridity," and especially that of Moreau de Saint-Méry, to characterize the free people of color and "mulattoes" as ultimately the most destructive force and the biggest potential threat to the colony of Saint-Domingue. The inscrutability, instability, and incongruity conferred by their position as either the "racial" intermediaries between "blackness" and "whiteness" or as the political and social intermediaries between slavery and freedom, appears to have provided the impetus for such a trope to be used to explain not only the origins, but the epistemological problems of the Revolution. The "monstrous hybrids" of seventeenth- and eighteenth-century naturalist travel writing would consequently become easy scapegoats for the Haitian Revolution in late eighteenth- and nineteenth-century representations of these world-historical events.

*

The mostly biological degeneration described by Moreau de Saint-Méry coupled with descriptions of the more spiritual and psychic incongruity of such people to be found in the travel writing of Labat, Nicholson, Le Pers, Raynal, and Du Tertre, returns us to one of the central questions inflecting narrative descriptions of the Haitian Revolution: were people of "mixed race" and free "negroes" to be considered the allies or enemies of the colonists, and to whose side of any revolution would "mulattoes" or the *"affranchis"* belong—to the side of their slave-mothers or to the figurative and literal side of their father-masters?

Almost from the very start of the widespread troubles in Saint-Domingue, the trope of the "monstrous hybrid" came to be catalyzed in a vocabulary of blame, whereby an *omnium-gatherum* of people of color became responsible not only for the start of the insurrection in Saint-Domingue, but for its qualitatively violent and parricidal characteristics. In his *Rapport sur les troubles de Saint-Domingue* (1797), for example, Garran de Coulon quotes from the letter of a colonist named Barillon from Bordeaux, who addressed the colonial assembly on May 11, 1791. Barillon wrote that the free people of color constituted, 'Our tormenters, our murderers, the monsters, who have fertilized the earth with the bones of our brothers' (3:36). In his indignant 1797 response to the British planter Bryan Edwards's history of the early days of the insurrection in Saint-Domingue, the French planter Venault de Charmilly, too, explained why people of "mixed race" should be altogether scorned, feared, and despised. After describing 'these Mulattoes' as having 'passions always ready to be excited, because of the mixture of two such diverse types of blood circulating in their veins' (13–14), Venault writes:

> The Mulattos have generally more finesse and guile than the Negroes; they have above all a barbarous and ferocious character that is everywhere apparent. It is because of a thousand proofs that I can provide, that I advance that almost all of the atrocious actions that have taken place in Saint-Domingue since the Revolution were guided, ordered, and, more often than not, executed by the Mulattoes ... There are very few acts of kindness and humanity that one could attribute to them, as an exception to this fact, whereas we could cite plenty of them with respect to the Negroes towards their masters or towards the Whites. (57)

The Marquise de Rouvray, the wife of a famous French colonist and military leader in Saint-Domingue who was reputed for his extramarital affairs as well as his support of the free people of color, also painted the *"affranchis"* and the *"sang-mêlés"* as horrifically monstrous beings responsible for all the troubles of the colony. In a letter to her adult daughter dated May 29, 1793, the Marquise writes that, unlike her husband, she could never place her trust in the 'Mulattoes' whom she describes as 'a race of wimps, cowards, assassins, and thieves [*une race de poltrons, de lâches, d'assassins, de voleurs*]—in the end, the assemblage of every vice without a single virtue' (rpt. in Rouvray, 1959, 97); and in a subsequent letter dated August 13, 1793, the Marquise focused more squarely on the parricidal effects of slavery, "racial mixing," and revolution when she wrote, 'Everyone has their *mulâtresse* whom they have brought with them or whom they came here to find, and with whom they are going to produce a new generation of mulattoes and quadroons destined to slit the throats [*égorger*] of our children and our grandchildren' (rpt. in Rouvray, 1959, 102). Though he did not share his wife's disdain for the '*mulâtresse*,' the Marquis de Rouvray, also linked the potential destruction of the colony to the '*hommes de couleur*' when he wrote:

> necessity requires that you create a law that would make them more like your equals than your enemies, to have them sit at your table, give them seats in your assemblies. If they fight for a common homeland, nothing will equal their valor. Otherwise, they will turn this same valor against you, and having stained their hands with the blood of the slaves, they will stain them with yours, and your battles will be filled with parricide. (qtd. in Métral, 1818, 79)

It would seem that a great many Saint-Dominguans held opinions on the causes and effects of the revolutionary events in Saint-Domingue that were linked to ideas about "race" and parricide. The daughter of Théodore-Charles Mozard,[19] the famous publisher of the Port-au-Prince *La Gazette de Saint-Domingue*, for instance, penned her own memoir of the final days of her life in the colony, which she published in 1844 under the title *Mémoire d'une Créole de Port-au-Prince*. In this memoir, Laurette-Aimée Mozard Nicodami de Ravinet, who was only a child when she left Saint-Domingue, blamed the 'mulatto' for all the 'killing' in the colony: 'It is the *mulâtre* born of the *négresse* and the colonist who lit the fire, in order to assure their inheritance by killing and ruining the legitimate heirs' (21). Like the Marquise de Rouvray, Ravinet also more explicitly linked the loss of her father's livelihood, her own inheritance, and the ultimate destruction of the colony to 'the luxury and the immodesty of *les mulâtresses*, public women,' whom she accused of having created 'the bastards' who 'wanted to legitimate their blood by excessive force and acquire the rights of citizenship without obtaining it by way of the laws for which we strove with as much justice as generosity. Fire and assassinations would assure them of the scepter without liberating the slaves' (24).

Other French colonists blamed free people of color more directly for the insurrection of the slaves when they suggested that the "*affranchis*," who in

---

19 According to the prospectus for the *Gazette de Saint-Domingue*, Mozard had been associated with the prior Port-au-Prince based newspaper, *Les Affiches Américaines* for ten years before he started the *Gazette* (1790, 4). In 1789, Mozard also published a play set in Saint-Domingue and entitled *La répétition interrompue: divertissement national, en un acte, en prose et en vers, mêlé de chant, fait à l'occasion de la réunion des trois ordres de l'état*.

their minds owed their freedom to their "white" fathers in the first place, were ingrates who had ultimately betrayed their own family members.[20] Drouin de Bercy, who would call 'mulattoes' a 'hideous monument of the debasement of the whites,' wrote:

> the mulattoes forgot that they owed to the whites their existence and their fortunes, which their fathers had endlessly increased, all while peacefully searching for ways to improve their status. These means seemed too slow for those ambitious bastards … they wanted to control the whites themselves: the mulatto Ogé caused a revolt, and such discord sowed rage and vengeance in the hearts of the negroes, the mulattoes, and in all parts of this unfortunate Island. (8)

As Drouin de Bercy's summation indicates, many French people living in the colony at the time of the insurrection, like the colonist Gros discussed in the introduction to this volume, attributed the Revolution to individual free people of color like Ogé, Rigaud, or Raimond, whom they described as either having brought the French Revolution with them back to Saint-Domingue, or as having ultimately encouraged the slaves to revolt. To that end, in his 1802 *Des Colonies Modernes sous la Zone Torride, et particulièrement de celle de Saint-Domingue*, the colonist Barré de Saint-Venant wrote, 'Remember that a single man ['the *sang-mêlé* Raimond' (vi, ftn. 1)] was sufficient to raise the *Société des amis des noirs*, and lead you into the disarray which you now bemoan' (vi). Barré de Saint-Venant later asks, 'what will you do with this population? For what could it be beneficial? The 110,000 *affranchis* will intensify the plague that desolates you, for you have not forgotten that this is the caste which wrought havoc on everything' (210). He continues by sardonically asserting, 'Besides, do you believe that two such disparate peoples could fraternize and live together? For my part, I believe it to be impossible' (210).

As Barré de Saint-Venant's questions imply, not only did most of those who evoked the trope of "monstrous hybridity" have an opinion on the "racial" impetus for the insurrection and whether or not it was appropriate for "blacks" and "whites" to live together and fraternize in Saint-Domingue, ostensibly because they were different 'peoples,' but they also had opinions about what should be done with the free people of color, in general, and people of "mixed race" in particular. These opinions ranged from advocating

---

20 Moreau de Saint-Méry also expressed this idea in his *Considérations* when he wrote of the 'affranchis' 'They are free because of a concession that they have acquired based on our generosity [*munificence*]' (1791, 37). Raimond refuted this notion in his *Observations sur l'origine et les progrès du préjugé des colons blancs contre les hommes de couleur* by writing, 'the [free] men of color are not, as the planters eternally repeat, freed men who owe their liberty to the whites' (1791a, 13).

for manumission of all people with any proportion of "white" blood, to giving political and civic rights to the so-called "*affranchis*," to deportation of all free people of color over a certain age, to barring marriage between people of color and "whites," to the extermination of the entire population of people of color, often including the slaves.[21]

The Marquise de Rouvray penned a remarkably detailed outline for the total 'destruction or deportation' of the free people of color in a letter to her daughter in August of 1793. She wrote that a massacre of the "white" population of Saint-Domingue was generally unavoidable unless

> we succeed in creating another way of doing things which will entail the destruction or the deportation of all free men and women of color, after having marked them on both cheeks with the letter 'L' for *Libre*, so that they will never be tempted to come back to Saint-Domingue. (102)

According to Rouvray, these deportations would remain in effect *ex post facto* as well since 'those who were born subsequently' would at the age of 'seven years old' be branded and deported. 'If we held firm to this rule,' the Marquise writes, 'we would be able to rebuild our properties in Saint-Domingue' (102). Her plans for entirely ridding Saint-Domingue of the free people of color and especially those of "mixed race" continues as she proposes sterilization:

> One other measure may perhaps be more final than the one that I just described, which would be to render male and female children of color unable to reproduce [*mettre hors d'état de produire*] ... the men would be too weak to try anything against the whites and the women would no longer serve the latter. In the end, my dear girl, if we do not crush this caste, there will be no salvation for Saint-Domingue. (103)

The aforementioned colonist Barillon also made the case for 'crush[ing]' 'mulattoes' when he argued that the 'colonial system' desperately needed to 'deviate from the French constitution, by moving in the opposite direction' (qtd. in Garran de Coulon, 3:37). In order to perform this contradiction of French constitutional principles, Barillon suggested the 'extermination'

---

21 Many of these ideas were actually in circulation in pre-revolutionary Saint-Domingue as well. For example, Hilliard D'Auberteuil wrote that 'It should be forbidden with severe penalties for the *affranchis* and girls of color to marry Whites, or at least such marriages should become null, in a civil sense; the police and the laws of the colony do not have to admit of such unions' (2:80). Girod de Chantrans, like Hilliard D'Auberteuil (2:89), for his part, suggested manumitting or at least ceasing to sell as slaves 'all the people of color less black than the mulattoes.' He wrote, 'It is in reality time to declare them free' (204).

of 'mulattoes' or 'at least their deportation to the island of Ascension ... providing them with food for one year ... and giving them for a bishop *that troublemaker [coquin] Grégoire, and for a mayor that coward Brissot*' (qtd. in Garran de Coulon, 3:36, italics in the original).[22] Wary that the majority of the French might disapprove of his primary suggestion of exterminating the 'mulattoes' by way of the 'bayonette,' Barillon concludes that '*the first point is the deportation of the mulattoes, and the confiscation of their property in compensation [for the property] of the whites that were burned*' (qtd. in 3:36, italics in the original). According to Garran de Coulon, a group of sailors had also threatened to '*exterminate that execrable race of mulattoes. This is the expression used in a recitation signed by these sailors themselves*' (3:440, italics in the original).[23]

In his spirited response to the above-mentioned pamphlet that had been anonymously published by Moreau de Saint-Méry, Raimond would also speak in distinct terms of "racial" extermination. In contemplating Moreau de Saint-Méry's statement in his *Observations* that the colonists should '*Be wary of the* gens de couleur *who have just arrived from Europe*' [*Méfiez vous des gens de couleur qui vous arrivent d'Europe*] (qtd. in Raimond, 1791b, 7, italics in the original), Raimond wondered why Moreau de Saint-Méry had attributed Ogé's actions to the latter's connection to the Société des Amis des Noirs. Raimond argued that Ogé's rebellion could be easily explained by the fact that the former had in his pockets letters from the colonists that detailed their plans for massacring the free people of color, including Ogé. Raimond subsequently accused Moreau de Saint-Méry of remaining silent with respect to 'several facts that could naturally explain the insurrection of the mulattoes.' 'Why not still attribute [Ogé's] project of insurrection to his desire to avenge the death of his brother whom you had assassinated by one of his own slaves,' Raimond asks, 'in promising to him his liberty?' (32); and of Moreau de Saint-Méry in particular, Raimond wondered, 'Why did he not say that before the arrival of Ogé in Saint-Domingue many massacres of people of color had already occurred. Why pass over with silence the talk that was circulating in Saint-Domingue that you wanted to slaughter the *hommes de couleur* long before the atrocious scene at Saint-Pierre?' (33). Guy Joseph Bonnet, another former soldier of color from Saint-Domingue, also likened the aftermath of Ogé's revolt and punishment to a massacre of the

---

22 The French abbé (Henri) Grégoire was a well-known advocate of abolishing slavery in the late eighteenth and early nineteenth centuries. Jacques-Pierre Brissot, also known as Brissot de Warville, was a well-known Girondist and anti-slavery activist who in 1790 founded the Société des Amis des Noirs.

23 Garran de Coulon is quoting from the 'Addresse de l'équipage de *Jupiter* à la Convention nationale' (3:440).

free people of color in his memoir of the above events, when he wrote that the actions of the French colonists constituted 'a new Saint-Barthèlemy of the *hommes de couleur*' (xviii).

The number of times that exterminating the entire population of "mulattoes," free people of color, and eventually all "negroes" is alluded to in the literary history of the Haitian Revolution is astounding. This is likely what led André Rigaud to lament in his 1797 memoir that 'There exists (and this is not at all in doubt), there exists a faction that tends to want the total destruction of all the citizens of color in Saint-Domingue' (iii–iv). Such horrifying tendencies on the part of ordinary citizens, as well as public officials, mariners, and travel writers, *vis-à-vis* people of color suggests that the "racial" prejudices bolstered and encouraged by pseudoscientific debates about "race" not only supported the ends of slavery and contributed to widespread understandings of the Haitian Revolution, but could also be used to urge the implementation of modern policies of eugenics and what we now call ethnic cleansing. Indeed, revolutionary Saint-Domingue was a world in which the tropology of "monstrous hybridity" was so well accepted that a language that reeked of *genocidal imaginings* was fairly ubiquitous.

The French colonists and later French metropolitan writers like Pierre Victor Malouet and Pamphile de Lacroix, however, often attributed the basis for such genocidal thoughts and desire to deport the people of color on the part of the French to the fact that the colonists themselves felt threatened with extermination by the former slaves and free people of color. In his *Collection de mémoires et corréspondances officielles sur l'administration des colonies* (1802), the former French colonist Malouet writes that 'blacks' were the 'natural enemies' of Europeans (4:33) and asked his readers to consider what might be the ultimate outcome for Saint-Domingue with respect to the policies of 'equality' and 'fraternity' instituted in metropolitan France during the French Revolution. 'The colonists of our blood,' Malouet writes, 'will they be slaughtered until the last or subjugated by the blacks? For it is clear that such is the plan of the African chiefs, the horrible but unavoidable result of an equality of rights, the first doctrine of the first attempt at revolution' (4:33). Malouet's solution to 'the liberty of the blacks,' which he says could only lead to the 'domination' and 'massacre' of the 'whites' in Saint-Domingue (4:46), was initially to bolster what Hilliard d'Auberteuil had referred to as the 'intermediary class' of free people of color (Hilliard, 1776, 2:88). This would be accomplished by giving free people of color the same political rights as 'whites' in ostensible exchange for their help in subduing the slaves. Malouet writes:

> In all countries where slavery has been established, men of a free origin necessarily form the first class; but the freed, remaining in the second

one, must there find a community of interests with the first one, which renders them its auxiliaries; the height of absurdity is to place them at such a distance from the whites that they believe they have much to gain in becoming their enemies. That is what we have done. (4:10)

Malouet further explained the mistake the colonists had made with the free people of color when with 'an extravagant vanity' they 'ordered their degradation' (4:11). Malouet writes that although 'the class of free negroes and mulattoes ... have, by their color, which is the sign of inferiority in all countries, their share in the lowest ranks of society,' as property owners they should have had the privileges of the 'grands blancs.' He further said that 'an unreasonable prejudice had placed them below the last of the whites' (4:140), and therefore that the rebellion of the free people of color had been inevitable since 'no group of men will let themselves be degraded' (4:11). As a corrective, Malouet proposed a new 'colonial system,' which he represented as capable of restoring the erstwhile colony to France. He explains, however, that his 'colonial system,' in granting civic rights to most free people of color and freedom to all of those of "mixed race," should not be blindly based on the type of doctrine of absolute equality circulating in metropolitan France since 'the colonists are strangers on several points to [French] metropolitan community and identity' (4:13). Instead, for Malouet, colonial rights for the free people of color needed to be based upon the social parity that he believed should characterize those with similar property interests in slavery. Later in the text, Malouet clarifies that his system would not necessarily need to do away with color prejudice at all (4:141).

Nevertheless, by the second decade of the nineteenth century and in the wake of Haitian independence, Malouet's policy of containment or co-optation of 'mulattoes' in order to reinstate the slavery of 'blacks,' had become one of extermination of the latter. According to Baron de Vastey, Malouet's secret instructions to the three French spies—Dravermann, Lavayasse, and Medina—who had been sent to the northern kingdom of Haiti to retake the former colony in 1813, just before the Bourbon restoration, were inflected with the language of extermination. Vastey writes that on October 1, 1812 King Henry Christophe had received a letter from Malouet in which the latter insultingly addressed the Haitian sovereign with 'the epithet of the chief of the rebellious slaves' and spoke to him of 'the extermination of our race, which will be replaced by another, taken from the heart of Africa if we do not consent to once again become slaves' (qtd. in Vastey, 1815b, 8; Madiou, 5: 266–67). Vastey's interpretation of Malouet's desire to truly exterminate any free 'blacks' who would not consent to become slaves, or could not be compelled to do so, was not without merit. Malouet's sixth instruction to the three spies was 'Purge the island of all the blacks whom it would be inappropriate to admit among the free and whom it would be dangerous to leave among those who are engaged on the plantations' (rpt. in Vastey, 1819, Appendix: 58-69).[24]

The supposed desire to exterminate the 'whites' that was inherent in the discourse of "monstrous hybridity" and to which Malouet had alluded as early as 1802 became the *raison d'être* for thinking about ways to regulate, deport, or destroy the people of color of French Saint-Domingue and later independent Haiti, even after the failed project of Dravermann, Medina, and Lavayasse. In 1814, Drouin de Bercy painted General André Rigaud using the language of "monstrous hybridity" when he described him as 'the assassin of France and the Antilles' (8):

> The mulatto Rigaud, who at that time was in contact with the maniac Robespierre and the senseless friends of the blacks, found himself at the head of the mulattoes and the negroes of the southern part [of the colony] ... he had overtly declared: 'That the tranquility which had succeeded their departure [to France], was only a deceptive calm, that it would soon vanish, and that there would never again be peace in Saint-Domingue while a single white remained.' (10)

Drouin de Bercy concludes these thoughts by noting, 'Every mulatto or negro chief, from that moment on, avidly adopted this opinion' (10). Describing the free people of color, and particularly people who were considered to be of "mixed race," as responsible for all the problems of the former colony and as themselves desirous of exterminating 'whites' provided Drouin de Bercy with the basis for evoking a system of both terrorization and deportation. Drouin de Bercy spent ten pages describing how 'ambush,' starvation (53) and 'terror' should be 'the order of the day' (63) during any French attempt to retake the colony, sparing neither women, children, nor the elderly (59–60). Furthermore, Drouin de Bercy acknowledged that many French people of his era were of the opinion that 'the colony will never be tranquil if we do not destroy every last one of [the people of color].' Drouin de Bercy therefore proposed that 'all the leaders above the rank of corporal must disappear,' 'all of the black women ... who were mistresses and prostitutes ... should be subject to the disposition of the government which will send them wherever seems fit,' and as for the 'mulatto caste, as the most dangerous, the most restless, the cause and soul of all the insurrections of the negroes, they should be treated, if it is even possible, with more severity than the blacks'

---

24 A copy of these instructions, furnished by Haiti's Comte de Limonade, was printed in the appendix of the February 20, 1815 edition of *L'Ambigu*, a periodical that circulated widely in the early nineteenth-century francophone Atlantic (see, 'Appendix au No. 428,' 3-12).

(169–71). If those hardly vague propositions are not convincing enough, Drouin de Bercy concluded by unequivocally proposing that after this 'purg[ing]' the colony could be easily repopulated by a continuation of the slave trade:

> When the island has been completely conquered and purged of all of those who could cause trouble ... the government, one year afterward ... could send on its behalf ten old ships, provisionally armed [*armée en flute*], to traffic in Africa for as long as it sees fit in order to introduce blacks into Saint-Domingue. (171)

Lacroix also attributed thoughts of extermination to the Haitian revolutionaries as a way to justify the aggressions of the French colonists, but he focused on Augustin Rigaud, the brother of André Rigaud. Lacroix claimed to reprint a letter written by Augustin that was intercepted by the French colonists, quoting the elder Rigaud as having written:

> kill, ransack, burn, there is no longer any salvation ... I leap towards vengeance ... we will defeat these brigands who want to slaughter our caste and reduce us to slavery. Vengeance! Vengeance! I embrace it all: my last word is to take my revenge on these barbarians ... Long live liberty! Long live equality! Long live love!
>
> [*tuez, saccagez, brûlez, il n'y a plus de salut ... Je vole à la vengeance ... nous vaincrons les brigands qui veulent égorger notre patrie et la réduire à l'esclavage. Vengeance! Vengeance! Je vous embrasse tous: mon dernier mot est de me venger de ces barbares ... Vive la liberté! vive l'égalité! vive l'amour!*]. (qtd. in Lacroix, 1819, 1:194–95)

One cannot help but suspect that these accusations of a wish to exterminate the "white" colonists, which Drouin de Bercy attributes to André Rigaud and Lacroix attributes to Rigaud's brother, formed merely part of a horrific logic of murderous justification whose aim was to provide the basis for the French attempt to retake the colony. If, as Laurent Dubois has written, the Haitian revolutionary leaders justified the violence of their revolt against French colonial authority by evoking the violence of colonial slavery (L. Dubois, 2009, 111–12), the colonists, too, would use the violence of the revolutionists and the rebellious slaves to cover up the very forms of brutality that had occurred on their plantations and during the Revolution itself and to justify whatever violence they used to quell revolts and rebellions of all kinds. It is noteworthy that most of these writers fail to mention General Leclerc's own massacre of 'the 6th colonial demi-brigade' as well as various other populations of people of color (Girard, 2011, 215), about which the British author Leitch Ritchie wrote:

"Monstrous Hybridity" in Colonial and Revolutionary Writing

> From the forced deportation of Toussaint Louverture in 1802 down to the expeditionary army, and their expulsion in 1804, is a period of the most atrocious events. A war of extermination was waged against the ameliorated blacks and the people of colour, with a ferocity scarcely credible. Unsparing massacre, and the refusal of all quarter became the order of the renewed hostility on both sides;—but for the African and his descendants were reserved deaths the most horrible. Thousands were nightly carried out in their harbours and drowned, or they were thrown alive, men, women, and children, to bloodhounds, to be torn limb from limb and devoured. No torment was considered too excessive; no mode of destroying life too dreadful to be inflicted. (1833, 309)

According to Girard, Leclerc had in fact openly considered 'a general massacre of virtually the entire adult black population of Saint-Domingue' (2011, 220). Ritchie's report appears to confirm this:

> The atrocious [Leclerc] expedition at length arrived upon the shores of St. Domingo; a scene of blood and torture followed, such as history had never before disclosed, and compared with which, though planned and executed by whites, all the barbarities, said to have been perpetrated by the insurgent blacks of the north, amount comparatively to nothing. (1833, 310)

Ritchie was not the only nineteenth-century writer to express horror at the mass drownings that took place during the Leclerc expedition. General Jean-Pierre Ramel (*le jeune*), who served under Rochambeau in Saint-Domingue, also acknowledged these events with shock and revulsion:

> Who were the men whom we drowned in Saint-Domingue? blacks who had been captured as prisoners on the fields of battle? no; conspirators? even less so! Nobody was convicted of anything: because of a simple suspicion, a report, an equivocal word, 200, 400, 800, up to 1,500 blacks had been thrown into the sea. I saw this happen, and I complained about it [*J'ai vu de ces exemples, et j'en ai gémi*]. I saw three mulatto brothers undergo the same fate. On 28 *frimaire* they were fighting within our ranks, two of them were hurt; on the 29th we threw them into the sea, to the great astonishment of the army and the planters. They were rich and had a beautiful house that was taken over by the general two days after their death. (rpt. in Lamartine, 1998, 9)

Yet another purported eyewitness claimed in a letter entitled 'Picture of St. Domingo' (1803), which was published in *The Literary Magazine and American Register*, a magazine edited by Charles Brockden Brown, that in November of 1802, 'business' had called him to Port-au-Prince, where he 'had the opportunity of taking a near view' of Rochambeau's terrible 'intentions' (447). The anonymous author writes:

> The month of November, and the two succeeding ones, were destined to witness scenes the most horrid; scenes that bear the deepest tinge of barbarous atrocity. Seven or eight hundred blacks, and men of colour were seized upon in the streets, in the public places, in the very houses, and for the moment confined within the walls of a prison. Thence they were hurried on board the national vessels lying in the harbor, from whence they were plunged into eternity. (447)

The author continues by saying that this mass drowning was far from an isolated incident: 'These horrid scenes were repeated at Leogane, at Petit-Guave [sic], and in the whole circuit of Jeremie [sic]' (447–48). Later, in L'Anse à Veau, under the orders of 'the ferocious D'Arbois,' who was 'anxious to provoke a general insurrection in the south of the island,' 'several blacks and one white from Nantes, whose name I well remember was Billiard, were all carried on board the [ship] Adelaide for the purpose of being sunk in a watery grave' (448). As a result of all of this 'premeditated barbarity' (448), the writer concludes, '[t]he billows now washed these unfortunate victims to the shore, floating with their eyes, as it were, turned towards heaven, they seemed to demand vengeance on the author of their untimely death' (449).[25]

Many fiction writers who claimed that their works were based upon the kind of eyewitness account contained in *The Literary Magazine and American Register* also spoke of the massacres perpetrated under Leclerc's orders. Alexandre de Saillet is one such author who referenced these 'sinister events,' saying that they had produced 'immeasurable consequences.' In his *Lucile de Saint-Albe, épisode de la révolution de Saint-Domingue*, a novel inspired by the reportedly true events recounted in de Pallaiseau's *Histoire de Mesdemoiselles de Saint-Janvier: Les deux seules blanches conservées a Saint-Domingue* (1812),[26] de Saillet writes that after the capture of Toussaint Louverture and the subsequent defection of many of his former allies, '1,200 blacks and men of color' who were fighting on the side of the French,

> had remained on the fleet; the sailors and the soldiers only tolerated having among them these men who could turn into their most savage enemies (of which thousands of examples only provide too much evidence) with

---

25 Similar tales of the mass drowning of 'les noirs' and 'les hommes de couleurs' that occurred during the Leclerc/Rochambeau expedition are recounted by Vastey and Boisrond-Tonnerre as proof that violence could only meet violence and excess only excess in the state of revolution as it existed in French Saint-Domingue (Boisrond-Tonnerre, 1851, 69; Vastey, 1814a, 68–74).

26 Saillet's novella originally appeared in six installments in the *Moniteur de la mode* and was eventually reproduced in a volume of short stories in 1848. In the final version being examined here, Saillet changed the names of the Saint-Janvier sisters to Saint-Albe, as well as the first names of the two daughters (see also, Hoffmann, 2010, 26).

the utmost of repugnance. One day, in a time of trouble, a terrible shout was heard on board the French fleet: 'Kill all those who can kill us' [*tuons tout ce qui peut nous tuer*] and 1,200 defenseless men were slaughtered and thrown into the sea. (87)[27]

Notice that even while representing the actions of the French in this instance as truly abominable, de Saillet still quasi-justifies this "racial" massacre by noting that it was with a fully reasonable sense of paranoia (since 'thousands of examples only provide too much evidence') that the soldiers had decided to mitigate the ability of people of color to suddenly switch sides by defensively drowning 'all those who could kill us.'

For his part, Lacroix, from whom de Saillet clearly derived this portrayal, not only attributed such a desire to commit wholesale massacre to the free people of color of Saint-Domingue, without any mention of the widely reported drowning of these same people perpetrated on the orders of Leclerc and later Rochambeau, but he described early nineteenth-century independent Haitian citizens as the continuous 'usurpers' of metropolitan authority who had themselves tried to exterminate the French colonists. Such a claim helped Lacroix, as it had others before him, to justify his proposal for a French retaking of the colony, even as late as 1819 (2:326).[28] At the end of the final volume of his work, Lacroix first tries to admonish Haitian officials by calling on them to consult their blameworthy

---

27 The phrase 'Tuons ce qui peut nous tuer' comes directly from the work of Pamphile de Lacroix (1:238) and was widely repeated in accounts of this mass drowning of Saint-Domingue's people of color. See, for example, Ardouin's *Etudes* (5:299), and Eméric Bergeaud's novel *Stella* (1859), the latter of which contains the following rendition of the events: 'There was therefore a risk of death for the jailors, and their only counsel was their desperation. *Let us kill*, they cried, *those who can kill us* [*Tuons*, crièrent-ils, *ce qui peut nous tuer*]. The action was almost as rapid as the word. The tides of the sea opened up and closed upon twelve hundred cadavers' (220).

28 See also Dominique Du Pradt's *Pièces relatives à Saint-Domingue et à l'Amérique* (1818), wherein the author alludes to those who 'still think about reconquering St. Domingue,' and suggests that the troubles between Christophe and Pétion, coupled with the latter's late illness, might eventually lead the way toward the 'profits that we can still acquire there' (266). For an opposing perspective from the era, see Narcisse-Achille de Salvandy's *De l'Emancipation de Saint-Domingue* (1825), wherein the author writes, 'other than some young publicists … no one would want France to go and undertake an expedition two thousand leagues from its shores for a cause that is so evidently condemned by fortune. No serious man has proposed it' (37). In subsequent pages of the pamphlet, Salvandy goes on to propose that Haiti should become the equivalent of a protectorate of France since 'France … can live without Saint-Domingue; it has done so ever since [the colony] was lost … The Haitians have not been able to do so, because independence has been for them [a question] of land; the land, [a question] of life' (45).

consciences for the actions of Louverture, Dessalines, and Christophe (2:326–27), and later he threatens Haitians with the specter of total political, financial, and geographical destruction when he writes, 'It is for the Haitians to coldly calculate therefore that we will remain the masters of their legal existence' (2:330). This last iteration is an unmistakable allusion to the official recognition of Haitian independence, which no nation had yet been willing to give while France remained opposed to the idea. Lacroix wrote more explicitly that Haitians needed to seriously consider providing monetary compensation to the French colonists for all they had lost during the Revolution since, according to him, the French could return to Haiti and burn everything with abandon, especially because they were now not the ones whose property would be destroyed. Lacroix threatens, 'we would destroy more in a one day than they would be able to re-establish in a year. These are considerations rather than threats, which I submit to the Haitians themselves' (332).

The threat of a French take-over of Haiti was so apparently intertwined with the concept of "monstrous hybridity," and especially concerning the ideas of the purported "racial" divisions between "mulattoes" and "blacks" in nineteenth-century Haiti, that even as far out as 1856 the French literary critic Alexandre Bonneau wrote in the article 'Les Noirs, les jaunes, et la littérature française en Haïti' that if Haitians 'wanted to rise even higher, they must above all avoid the kind of bloody discord that has so many times divided them in the last 50 years, and take as a motto the conciliatory words of the poet [Jean-Baptiste Romane]:[29] "Blacks and yellows, be united."' Bonneau's comment encouraging the unification of the 'yellows' and 'blacks' of Haiti was much more than an insincere platitude. Bonneau actually menaced the Haitian people with a future French take-over if they did not rid their country of its characteristic 'murderous hatred of Europeans,' which had originally been encouraged, Bonneau believed, by Boisrond-Tonnerre (141). On that score, Bonneau concluded that:

> There is, in the end, a duty and decorum to forget the hatred that they have too often shown toward France. We could, even after the disasters of 1814, seize Saint-Domingue once again. No matter the bravery of the blacks, our soldiers have defeated enemies who were much more formidable. (155)[30]

---

29 Romane was a Haitian poet most famous for having published a lyrical poem called *L'Hymne d'Indépendance* in 1825. See, Christophe (1999).

30 Bonneau's works were at least somewhat known in nineteenth-century Haiti. Liautaud Ethéart referenced this article in his *Les Miscellanées* (1855, 122) and Louis Joseph Janvier mentioned Bonneau's later writing in *La République d'Haïti et ses visiteurs* (1883, 20, 73).

"Monstrous Hybridity" in Colonial and Revolutionary Writing

Bonneau's comment evokes the widely held belief that the "mulattoes" and "negroes" of Haiti had been and would always remain embroiled in a genocidal war of extermination. After all, it was Bryan Edwards who explained this as a *truth* in one of the first attempts to provide a history of the insurrections in Saint-Domingue. Edwards wrote:

> Between these two bodies, however, as the reader must have perceived, there existed the most inveterate and rancorous animosity, which had already manifested itself in many conflicts; and nothing but the presence of an invading enemy in the country restrained it, in any degree, from proceeding to that extremity of civil contest—a war of extermination—in which mercy is neither to be given nor accepted. (3:420)

The idea that the outside powers of Spain and England had prevented this 'war of extermination' apparently set the stage for an author like Bonneau to link such putatively natural "racial" enmities to a logic of conquest in which an occupying power could argue that it was saving Haiti from itself. This argument, that the so-called "racial" divisions between the 'yellows' and 'blacks' of nineteenth-century Haiti necessitated outside intervention, would become a primary focus of Baron de Vastey's critique of colonialism, as we will see in the following chapter.

In the end, recognizing the origins of "monstrous hybridity" first in naturalist travel writing and later in metropolitan debates about "race" has, I hope, served as the necessary basis for comprehending the way in which pseudoscientific ideas about "race" affected eighteenth- and nineteenth-century understandings of the Haitian Revolution as the events unfolded and in the decades after Haitian independence, and ultimately contributed to a widely disseminated narrative of "mulatto/a vengeance." This narrative became the primary way in which the Haitian Revolution would be understood up until at least the U.S. Civil War. The next two chapters, which tie the writings of various authors such as Baron de Vastey, Victor Hugo, Herman Melville, and Harriet Beecher Stowe to a literary genealogy of "monstrous hybridity," will further explain how such ideas, and the homicidal, parricidal, and, at times, bordering on genocidal, thoughts that the instability, incongruity, and uncertainty of "monstrous hybrids" appears not only to have evoked but justified in the context of Haiti, have been transmitted all across the Atlantic World in a variety of ways.

CHAPTER TWO

Baron de Vastey, Colonial Discourse, and the Global "Scientific" Sphere

'Haïti signifiait liberté, Saint-Domingue esclavage.'

—Eméric Bergeaud, *Stella* (1859)

'Malheureusement, chez ces hommes blancs, mulâtres, noirs, fermentaient des passions violentes, dues au climat, et à un état de société dans lequel se trouvaient les deux extrêmes: la richesse orgueilleuse et l'esclavage frémissant ... —On ne voyait dans aucune colonie des blancs aussi opulents et aussi entêtés, des mulâtres aussi jaloux de la supériorité de la race blanche, des noirs aussi enclins à secouer le joug des uns et des autres.'

—Georges Le Gorgeu, *Etudes sur Jean-Baptiste Coisnon et Toussaint Louverture* (1881)

While the European and U.S. American authors whose writings comprise a great deal of the literary history of the Haitian Revolution certainly dominated what scholar Nick Nesbitt has called the 'global discursive sphere' (2005, 29) when it came to writing about the Haitian Revolution, people of color, and especially those who would come to call themselves Haitians, hardly stood by in silence. Many free people of color in revolutionary Saint-Domingue, like André Rigaud, Toussaint Louverture, and Julien Raimond, as we have seen, contested the insulting terminology used to describe people of color as well as the monstrous characterizations of people of "mixed race" as vengeful "mulattoes" who were primarily responsible for the bloody quality of the Revolution. Post-independence Haiti, too, would see its fair share of authors who sought to contest the dominant image produced in European writing of "Africans" and all of their descendants as hopelessly inferior and degraded. Much of early Haitian literature and historiography was, in the words of Vèvè Clark, 'designed to reflect or radically alter political realities' by celebrating what Pierre Nora has called the 'lieux de mémoire' (Nora, 7) and by showcasing the 'other side of history' (Clark, 241). David Scott has called such a form of writing 'vindicationism' and defines the term as writing which describes the 'practice of providing evidence to refute a disagreeable or incorrect claim and a practice of *reclamation*, and, indeed, of *redemption* of what has been denied' (Scott, 83, italics in the original).

Baron de Vastey,[1] the secretary to King Henry Christophe, is perhaps the most noteworthy of the early nineteenth-century Haitian historians to have attempted to 'radically alter' the 'political realit[ies]' of slavery and colonialism by entering into what we might call a global "scientific" sphere in which his position as a person of color was supposed to have made him, not an interlocutor, but the subject of study itself. In his myriad writings, Vastey, one of the most oft-discussed Haitian historians of the Revolution in the nineteenth-century Atlantic World, addressed not only what he perceived to be the 'incorrect claim[s]' about Haiti that dominated in this European-American discursive public sphere, but the lack of competing voices capable of refuting those descriptions. Vastey wrote that he had authored his most sustained treatment of Haitian history, *Essai sur les causes de la révolution et des guerres civiles d'Hayti* (1819), precisely because 'Haiti lacks a general history written by someone indigenous to the country.' 'The majority of historians who have touched on the subject have been Europeans' (1), he said, who 'only had, to guide themselves materials created by whites' (2). As a result of the

---

1 Vastey, *né* Jean Louis Vastey according to his baptismal certificate (*Acte*), after acting as the assistant to André Vernet, became secretary to the northern Haitian leader Henry Christophe and was made a baron some time after Christophe crowned himself King of Haiti in 1811, and definitely before December 26, 1812 (see, Cheesman, 12). According to the 1814 edition of the *Almanach Royale d'Hayti*, Vastey was not only one of the many 'secretaries' of Christophe (12), in addition to being a member of the 'privy council of the king' (29), but was also the 'chief clerk' [*greffier en chef*] of the Sovereign Court of Justice [*Cour Souveraine de Justice*] (109) and one of the 'Amateurs' of Christophe's Théâtre Royale' (126). According to the 1816 *Almanach*, Vastey had also become by that time the 'précepteur' of the 'prince Royal' (12) and had been promoted to the rank of 'Chevalier' or knight on October 28, 1815 (29). Vastey's upward mobility would only appear to have continued, for aside from assuming the editorship of the *Gazette Royale d'Hayti* at some point between 1815 and 1816, an edict published in the *Gazette Royale d'Hayti* on December 28, 1818 also lists Vastey as member of the newly created Chambre Royale d'Instruction Publique (1), and the *Almanach* from 1820 lists Vastey as one of the chancellors of the king and describes in great detail his new duties, which included 'Keeping the register of the records of birth, marriage, death, and all of the other *actes* of the members of the Royal Family' as well as 'the safeguard and deposit of the archives of the Royal family' (40). Vastey published at least eleven different prose works that circulated throughout the Atlantic World, in addition to numerous short essays in *La Gazette Royale d'Hayti*.

inherent 'spirit of prejudice and bias' (1) in these works, which Vastey claimed had revealed that '*whites*' would never abandon their desire to compete with '*blacks*,' 'the scale has always tipped towards their side and not the other' (2). Vastey's proposal to daringly reveal the 'other side' of colonial history, the 'indigenous' side, if you will (1), offers a distinct challenge not only to a dominant European historical tradition, but to a prolific transatlantic "scientific" tradition that had sought to paint enslaved Africans as wholly simple and ignorant beings who were variously content with their condition or too brutish and violent to ever live in harmonious freedom with "whites."

While much of my prior work on Vastey is devoted to contextualizing and historicizing his rebuttals of European contributions to early Haitian revolutionary historiography, what is under examination in this chapter is the way in which the works of Christophe's erstwhile secretary fit into the discourse of a much wider, and wholly hostile, pseudoscientific sphere that had used the two Haitis of the early nineteenth century as the culminating example of "monstrous hybridity." In making the case that the radical poetics of anti-colonial slavery found across Vastey's works makes him the direct progenitor of much of what we now call postcolonial criticism and theory, my aim is to explore Vastey's pioneering position in this humanistic discourse that circulates around deconstructing the twin axes of "scientific" racism and European colonialism. Recognizing Vastey's œuvre as a vital precursor to those of later thinkers from the African diaspora like Aimé Césaire can help us to see how the philosophical contradictions of the early modern and nineteenth-century revolutionary Atlantic World were precisely that which created the stage for the modern violence of colonialism that we see in the early twentieth century.

It will perhaps appear ironic that in seeking to expose how the former colonists had used fears of "monstrous hybridity" to create political dissension and emotional scission among the people of color in Saint-Domingue and later Haiti, Vastey could not shake the violence of the very grammar that had encouraged and even created such discord. As the second section of this chapter will show, Vastey, who would exercise considerable influence over how the Haitian Revolution was discussed in the first half-century after independence, was not immune to the effects of the "racial" taxonomies of his day and the violent beliefs about people of color that such taxonomies sought to instill. By also examining Vastey's own adoption of the language of "monstrous hybridity," I hope to prove that his writings are an important part of the literary history of the Haitian Revolution not only because they provide crucial anticipations of modern postcolonial inquiry, but because they reveal how a racialized vocabulary sparked and encouraged by pseudoscientific debates about "race" permeated nearly every discussion of the Haitian Revolution in the nineteenth century.

Colonial Discourse and the Global "Scientific" Sphere

In the third and final section of this chapter, I outline how the three conflicting ways of reading Vastey's own "race" in the nineteenth century ("mulatto," "negro," and "white") has something to tell us about his subjugated position in contemporary Haitian revolutionary historiography. Baron de Vastey's *avant la lettre* deconstruction of colonialist print culture has been obfuscated in a vast array of works in which his name appears, usually in passing, across the disciplines of history, literature, cultural studies, anthropology, sociology, and the history of science. This is largely the result of the fact that in scholarship on the Caribbean and the Atlantic World as a whole, where Vastey is discussed at all, he is most often discursively referred to and even dismissed as an "ideologist," a "propagandist," or a mere "publicist." When conceived of as a "propagandist," "publicist," or "ideologist" (and thus on the side of state power) rather than a "black Jacobin" or a free-floating intellectual (and thus as politically aligned with the masses), Vastey's status as the apparently phenotypically "white" son of a slaveholder who argued that Haiti should be ruled by a "black" former slave has been troubling for those who would want to draw the same kind of strong lines in accounting for his intellectual and political identities that nineteenth-century reviewers of his works hoped to draw in accounting for his "racial" identities.

*

Jean Louis Vastey, Baron de (January 21, 1781–1820) (pronounced Vâtay) (Romain, 67) is best remembered as the acerbic secretary of early nineteenth-century Haiti's King Henry Christophe I and as the author of a scathing indictment of colonial slavery entitled *Le Système colonial dévoilé* (1814). Though he is largely unknown outside of academic circles today, in the early nineteenth century, Vastey was an international public figure well known for his anti-colonial writing. *Le Système colonial dévoilé*, Vastey's damning exposé of the inhumanity of the 'colonial system,' had so widely circulated in the nineteenth-century Atlantic World that upon its publication it was immediately reviewed in French, US, German, and British journals and newspapers (Daut, 2012, 60; Fanning, 70; Schuller, 40). In fact, Vastey's prose works were referenced, cited, or reprinted in the northern US press more frequently before the US Civil War than any other Haitian author throughout the rest of the nineteenth century, leading one early American periodical to dub him 'the Alpha and Omega of Haitian intellect and literature' ('Review of New Books').

In what is his most well-known work today, *Le Système colonial dévoilé* (1814) or *The Colonial System Unveiled*,[2] Vastey argued that 'white' Europeans,

---

2 For an English translation of this work, see Bongie (2014).

in general, and the French colonists, in particular, had published numerous versions of colonial history that had been designed to further subjugate people of African descent. To that effect, Vastey wrote that it was not just the telling of Haitian history that had been dominated by the colonial European point of view, but the meaning of "blackness" itself. He observed, 'the majority of historians who have written about the colonies were *whites, colonists* even.' For Vastey, the colonial discourse propagated by these particular *'whites,'* like the plantation violence it mirrored, had the effect of 'smother[ing]' the histories of the slaves through a strategy of endless discursive *denigration* that drowned in a sea of constant inscription any opposition to its narrative of Africans as uncivilized and practically inhuman:

> The friends of slavery, those eternal enemies of the human race have written thousands of volumes freely; they have made all the presses in Europe groan for entire centuries in order to reduce the black man below the brute; the small number of our unfortunate class have had a difficult time to throw even some small retorts against their numerous calumnies, having been compromised by the confluence of all the circumstances that smothered their voices. (1814a, 95)

Vastey suggested that these writers, 'the friends of slavery,' had enacted a kind of discursive violence against 'the black man' in the global "scientific" sphere, matched only by the physical violence the enslavers had enacted against them on the plantation. Vastey inferred that the endlessly grinding 'groans' [*gémissements*] (1814a, 65) of the European printing press that had painted 'the black man' as a 'brute' rather than as a human, were every bit as responsible for the continuation of the 'colonial system.' He inferred that his own writing represented one of the first examples of a Haitian author being able to use that same technology to provide a counter-narrative capable of dismantling the forms of knowledge irradiated in European colonial writing. 'Now that we have Haitian printing presses,' he said, 'we can reveal the crimes of the colonists and respond to the most absurd lies, invented by the prejudice and greed of our oppressors' (95).

Throughout his œuvre, Vastey's attention to the many racist distortions being produced in colonial discourse was aimed at contesting the dominant idea that Africans were a barbaric species, incapable of enlightenment, and that nineteenth-century Haiti could furnish the definitive proof for such beliefs. Vastey worked hard at the outset of *Le Système* to contest the link that some European colonists were making between putative African savagery and the supposed inability of Haitians to govern themselves in a civilized way. He writes, 'Our cruel enemies will continue to claim that the civilization of Africa is impossible; they will say that these savage people will massacre the missionaries, and that besides, the African having no aptitude at all for the sciences, [civilizing them] would be a fruitless enterprise' (1814a, 19–20). Vastey opposed the kind of exceptionalism that allowed European travel writers to use their experiences of isolated regions of Africa to develop an essential theory about all Africans. He wondered what would happen to beliefs about 'whites' if he were to employ the same logic that had been used to subjugate and enslave people of African descent. Vastey urged his audience, which comprised not only his own countrymen, but many U.S. and European readers, to consider that one might find 'some whites' in places like Kamatchatka and Greenland who would fit the exact same description of barbarity and degradation that Europeans had used to paint Africans.[3] In these places, Vastey writes, 'You have an infinite number of people of the white race who are corrupt [*abâtardis*] and degenerate.' 'Men of this species,' he continues, 'languish in the most profound, most complete ignorance, others of them are rude and cruel, and immersed in barbarism, even selling one another, and you never speak of this at all.' Instead, he writes, 'You spread lies about us, you degrade us, and you dare even to place us in the ranks of animals by refusing to recognize our intellectual faculties' (1814a, 22). Nesbitt has recently challenged Vastey's commitment to the tenets of universal emancipation partially on the basis of these statements: 'Such passages deploying the very logic they seek to critique rather than referring to any norm (such as liberty or justice) beyond the specificity of their iteration,' Nesbitt writes, 'undoubtedly reveal the limitations of Vastey's rhetorical invective' (2013, 178).

To be sure, however, Vastey's statement about 'some' of the degraded 'people of the white race' whom one might find in Greenland was meant to be read with irony. An ironic reading of this passage is supported by the very 'rhetoric' of universal justice that Vastey later espouses, even if still deploying, to a certain degree, the language of the pseudoscience of "race." In his later *Réflexions politiques*, Vastey asks why a state of mental or physical difference alone, even if understood as inferiority, would be reason enough to subjugate and enslave a person. He asks: 'are the physical and moral qualities specific to mankind prejudiced when it comes to differences in skin color? Strength, courage, virtue, and vice, good or bad habits, do they originate in the skin or rather in the heart[s] of men?' (1817b, 18). Seemingly answering his own question, Vastey writes, 'Well, if so, Scythian races, Mongolians, and Ethiopians, whites, yellows, and blacks, oppress one another! hate one another! because you are not of the same color! exterminate each other! those of the victorious [skin] color will exclusively control the universe' (18).[4] The

---

3 For Vastey's audience, see my article 'The Alpha and Omega of Haitian Literature: Baron de Vastey and the U.S. Audience of Haitian Political Writing.'

4 In his *Mémoire historique sur Toussaint* (1818), a former military officer from Saint-

inference that racism was wholly connected to genocidal imaginings exposes the intolerance of difference itself rather than the discovery of differences as the primary cause of the oppression, hatred, and extermination of the Other. Vastey appears to be rhetorically wondering why, if Africans were inferior to Europeans in some essential way that could be proven, this would be a valid reason to subjugate, dominate, and indeed terminate them. Thus, Vastey cannot be seen as 'deploying the very logic' as his colonialist interlocutors in this instance, since the ends of his statement about white inferiority is not to kill, enslave, rape, or steal from the 'whites' in Greenland, Kamatchka, or anywhere else.

Long after Vastey, Césaire would use the same rhetorical strategy of pointing out that it was the logical fallacies of "racial" prejudice that undergirded colonial slavery, rather than the conquest of the Americas itself (Césaire, 33), which had led to the slow and inevitable march towards modern genocide. 'The crowning barbarism that sums up all the daily barbarisms is Nazism,' Césaire wrote, 'before they [Europeans] were its victims, they were its accomplices ... they tolerated Nazism before it was inflicted on them' (36). '[A]t bottom, what he cannot forgive Hitler for is not *the crime* in itself,' Césaire concludes:

> *the crime against man*, it is not *the humiliation of man as such*, it is the crime against the white man, the humiliation of the white man, and the fact that he applied to Europe colonialist procedures which until then had been reserved exclusively for the Arabs of Algeria, the 'coolies' of India, and the 'niggers' of Africa. (36, italics in original)

Vastey's refutations of colonial writing about "race" gain new purchase when placed alongside Césaire's theory that the racism undergirding colonialism led directly to the genocide of the holocaust.[5] Vastey may very well have been the first writer of color from the Americas to employ the kind of discourse analysis that Césaire so adeptly uses in *Discourse on Colonialism* (1955) to

---

Domingue, Augustin Régis, also questioned why a difference of skin color or "race" between 'whites' and 'blacks' would seem to have *a priori* not only confirmed the inferiority of the latter but sanctioned their subjugation and enslavement by the former. In a passage in which he directly refutes Venault de Charmilly's claim that 'the blacks are not worthy [*digne*] of liberty,' Régis writes, 'they were not made for being slaves either, they come from the same branch of the human race [*souche de l'espèce humaine*], like all other men, and they come from the same father-creator: and because, finally, if blacks are of a different color than whites, that is not a reason to want to segregate them from the rest of society, nor is it a reason to place them within the ranks of animals' (16).

5 Colonialism itself was a system of genocide for some writers, like Tzvetan Todorov, who has written, 'the sixteenth century perpetrated the greatest genocide in human history' (1999, 4).

deconstruct and indeed discredit the disingenuous writing of Europeans on the subject of "race." In his *Réflexions sur une lettre de Mazères*, for example, Vastey uses Mazères's claim that Haitians were merely 'ignorant, overgrown, simple-minded children, who have neither energy of the mind or of the spirit [*qui n'ont de ressort ni dans l'esprit ni dans l'âme*]' (qtd. in 106), to demonstrate how such thinking actually debased Europeans: 'If Mazères were capable of logic, he would have recognized that he was reducing himself and the former colonists to the bottom rung of humanity; because, alas, these *overgrown, ignorant, simple-minded children ...*, defeated them in battle, loathe them, and have sworn an implacable hatred for them' (1816d, 106).

Vastey concluded that the will to prove the inherent intellectual inferiority and therefore bestiality of Africans on the part of travel writers as well as philosophers, which had been the *cause célèbre* of pseudoscientific debates about "race" for at least two centuries, was not the innocent, labored deduction of men who sought to unlock the origins of humankind. Much like the Trinidadian historian Eric Williams (1944), Vastey had determined that arguments about natural African inferiorities were in all reality the end result of a cruel and calculating monetary logic promulgated by those who stood to benefit both intellectually and materially from the economics of slavery. Before citing the planter and naturalist Edward Long's bizarre claim that 'negroes' were 'morally inferior' to Europeans because they 'eat wild cats,' Vastey writes that European writers who penned such absurdities were merely 'the embodiment of sophists [*archisophistes*], filled to the brink with prejudices' to the extent that 'in order to turn the black man into a material thing [*matérialiser l'homme noir*]' they gave recourse to the 'most puerile arguments and the most ridiculous stories' (1814a, 31). Directly addressing his European audience Vastey said, 'there is not a lie or an absurdity that you have not invented in order to justify your horrendous deeds and injustices' (1814a, 30). Vastey's utilization of a pseudoscientific vocabulary about the 'white race' therefore probably betrays less a paradoxical complicity with the very "racial" logic he sought to combat, than it reveals his keen ability to show that the rationalities that undergirded slavery had the effectiveness of performativity. That is to say, why should it matter at all if 'Africans' ate cats since certainly other people in the world might do so as well. Such a relativist and negative judgment about the meaning of eating cats can only be a reflection of the fact that since enslavers absolutely needed to prove that people of color were inferior, they turned what could have been narrated as merely cultural or social differences into facile evidence of inferiority that could then be used to justify slavery.

While such a circular logic may have been expected from the colonial planters of the West Indies who sought to claim and preserve for largely economic reasons a superior status as masters over their putatively inferior slaves, Vastey sharply rebuked his metropolitan European interlocutors for the contradictions inherent in their own philosophical treatises on the equal 'rights of man.' He wrote: 'history will be astonished that such a dreadful [colonial] system, whose very foundation was built upon violence, rape, plunder, and treachery ... has found zealous apologists among the enlightened nations of Europe' (1814a, 13):

> Posterity will never believe that in an age of Enlightenment, like ours, men who call themselves savants, philosophers, would have wanted to turn other men into animals, thereby contradicting the fact that primitive man has only one origin, solely in order to conserve their atrocious privilege of being able to oppress a part of humankind ... Where are we indeed in an era of Enlightenment in which all the great geniuses were born who have graced their countries with immortal works. (1814a, 30)

For Vastey, it was inconceivable that the French *philosophes* in particular could be such ardent advocates of the natural rights of man precisely as they supported divisive "racial" theories that would help to turn men and women into chattel through slavery. He complained that 'the French, who were at one time democrats, philanthropists, spreaders of liberty and equality, and ardent defenders of the rights of man, are now the unremitting supporters [*séctateurs*] of the slave trade, the enemies, the persecutors of the human race: Oh madness! Oh inconceivable infamy!' (1814a, vi).

Vastey's critique of Western rationalism thus prefigures in certain other ways Césaire's powerful and important *Discourse on Colonialism*, which also questioned the philosophical underpinnings of imperialism by asking us to consider what the word colonization means:

> what fundamentally, is colonization? To agree on what it is not: neither evangelization, nor a philanthropic enterprise, nor a desire to push back the frontiers of ignorance, disease and tyranny, nor a project undertaken for the greater glory of God, nor an attempt to extend the rule of law. (10)

Césaire answers his own question with his famous equation that 'colonization = "thingification"' (21) and argues that this system which continued to be upheld by many of those who considered themselves to be the advocates of human rights, represents one of the primary contradictions of Western civilization. Not only had Vastey already described the *thingification* encouraged by early modern colonialism as wholly the product of transatlantic slave trade—remember, the colonists had tried to *'matérialiser l'homme noir'*—but, like Césaire, who was writing in the midst of the falling empires of the twentieth century, Vastey, too, wanted to break the term colonialism of its associations with the transmission of civilization and instead define the concept, as it was being practiced by Europeans, as the racist, tyrannical domination of one group of people over another. Vastey's definition of the term 'colonial system' was, in fact, an immediate reference to the writing of the former French colonist Victor Malouet. In his *Collection de mémoires et correspondances officielles sur l'administration des colonies* (1802), Malouet explained that what he called the 'colonial system' was incompatible with the 'principles of liberty and equality' as they were being encouraged in France:

> Thus, experience has taught us that the doctrine[s] and principles of liberty and equality, transplanted to the Caribbean, can only produce there devastation, massacre, and combustion [*l'incendie*]. It is therefore necessary that a society composed of masters and slaves should be safeguarded by its founders of all political influence[s] capable of making the slaves want to slit the throats of their masters. (4:14)

'This principle,' he concludes, 'has been the fundamental basis of what I call the *colonial system*, I insist on the evidence, and I warn against all the reasons, all the arguments, by which one would wish to contradict it [*l'éluder*]' (4:14).

In his *Notes à M. le baron V.P. Malouet* (1814), Vastey directly addressed Malouet's claim that the eventual outcome of the French 'colonial system' as it was then being practiced (as opposed to the changes Malouet would institute) would be the inevitable destruction of 'whites.' Vastey quoted Malouet as having written: 'At last it is known, this secret full of horror: the liberty of the blacks means their domination! It means the massacre or enslavement of whites, the burning of our fields, of our cities' (qtd. in Vastey, 1814b, 14).[6] Vastey turned Malouet's understanding of the function of the 'colonial system' on its head when on the title page of *Le Système* he wrote: 'At last it is known, this secret full of horror: the Colonial System means domination by Whites, it means the Massacre and Enslavement of blacks.' Here, Vastey deftly undermines Malouet's claim that a 'new system of colonialism'—one which would ensure the elimination of all dangerous 'political influences'—was a necessary protection for 'white' society against 'black' society when he pronounced that such a statement was merely another sophism the planters had used in order to veil the brutalities of slavery for their own personal gain.

Vastey also anticipated Césaire's statement that 'no one colonizes innocently … no one colonizes with impunity' (39), when he wrote that the French colonists were more or less 'undistinguishable monsters': 'They have all committed, participated and contributed to the horrors [of slavery],' Vastey

---

6 See also, the original in Malouet (1802, 4:46).

wrote, and 'besides, the number of colonists who were kind and humane, is so small that it is not worthwhile to make an exception to the general rule' (1814a, 38). Such a statement effectively makes no distinction between what Albert Memmi would later come to call 'the colonizer who refuses' and the 'colonizer who accepts' (19). For Memmi, the main difference between these two kinds of inhabitant of the colonies is that the one 'who refuses' might have signed a petition or attended a protest to express his indignation and disapproval of colonialism while continuing to live and profit in the colony, while the one who accepts, 'endeavors to falsify history, he rewrites laws, he would extinguish memories. Anything to succeed in transforming his usurpation into legitimacy' (52). Though he outwardly condemned the latter kind of colonist in virtually all of his writings, in Vastey's mind, anyone who did not actively seek the end of the colonial system was not only guilty of its perpetuation, but was himself a monster.

Underlying Vastey's commentary about the monstrous nature of colonialism is also a subtly phrased argument that it was the 'ingenious barbary!' of color prejudice (1814a, 89), rather than "mulatto" or "negro" biology, which was responsible for the parricidal quality of the Haitian Revolution. In an apostrophized lamentation to these color prejudices, Vastey writes, 'oh, how your influence operates powerfully on the Heart[s] of men; it is you who causes him to disown his brother, to hate and persecute him; it is you who has been the spirit and motor of the ferocious colonist when he was unleashing his cruelty upon us' (1814a, 89). This evocation of fratricide allows Vastey to assert a belief that was widespread among the former free people of color from Saint-Domingue, that colonial life was dominated by vengeance *for* the free people of color. Vastey offers as evidence the fact that in colonial Saint-Domingue:

> A white person could strike a so-called free person with impunity, beat him with a baton, even kill him; [and] he would come off with a simple fine, that he never paid; and the unfortunate who would have pushed back by giving some blows of his own, would have his hand cut off, or he would have been hanged without mercy if the white person found himself hurt in the conflict. (1814a, 79)

As further proof of the 'deplorable' treatment of the free people of color, Vastey reprinted the French government's own 'Règlement des Administrateurs concernant les Gens de Couleur Libres' of June 24, 1773. The decree forbade free people of color from using the last names of their white fathers, from dressing like whites (including wearing shoes in some instances), and from occupying any public function or profession, such as priest, schoolteacher, surgeon, pharmacist, or doctor; Vastey also noted that free people of color were 'obliged to undertake forced labor [*corvées*]' of all types (1814a, 76–77).[7] Vastey concludes his gloss of the inhumane treatment of the free people of color by noting ironically that Haitians should be glad that colonial administrators had mistreated them since, 'Without the flaws of this administration, the revolution would never have taken place, and we would still be under the yoke of the colonists.' 'Oh! Give thanks to their injustices,' he adds, 'since that is what forced us to break the chains of tyranny forever!' (1814a, 86–87). Here, Vastey's writing prefigures that of yet another fierce twentieth-century opponent of colonialism. In 'Colonialism is a System,' Jean-Paul Sartre would also describe colonialism as unsustainable due to its very contradictions: 'the colonists themselves have taught their adversaries; they have shown the hesitant that no solution was possible other than force' (47). Likewise, Vastey inferred that the same violence that had been used constantly against the slaves by their masters and against the free people of color by the "white" colonists, provided all people of color in the colony with the education in resistance they needed to spark rebellion.

I will later return to Vastey's problematic statement that the injustices perpetrated against free people of color were what caused *them* to 'break the chains of tyranny forever'; for now, I would like to point out that this statement was written by a person who felt himself to have been hunted during the multiple scenes of mass drowning that took place during the Leclerc-Rochambeau expedition and that were discussed at length in chapter one of this volume. The very real threat of the final outcome of colonial color prejudice—genocide—seems to be what taught Vastey to be wary of the idea that with the end of slavery and colonialism in Saint-Domingue would come the end of racist aggression towards the people of Haiti and correspondingly the end of the need for both physical and discursive defenses of Haitians. In *Le Cri de la patrie* (1815), Vastey warned his contemporary readers against the fantasy that life for people of color in metropolitan France could be suddenly free of prejudice when he explicitly complained about racism there:

> If I had the need for proof in order to demonstrate to the Haitians that any concession of civil and political rights that we propose to concede to the people of color would only be a trap set up to attack with surprise their

---

7 The abbé Grégoire also noted that free men of color were forced to join the *maréchaussée*, a military brigade devoted to capturing runaway slaves; were forced into the military at the age of 17 (1820, 5); were forbidden from exercising a range of professions, including becoming a goldsmith (6), and practicing medicine or surgery (7). Grégoire further noted that free people of color were forbidden from 'using the same fabrics as whites' and 'eating with whites' (8). They were equally 'forbidden from entering France' (9) and excluded from holding 'any appointments & government posts, either in the judicial system or in the military' (9). See also L. Dubois (2004, 61–64).

good faith and their confidence, I would only have to let them see what is going on in France even with respect to the mulattoes and quadroons, who after having been employed in the service of the government in myriad capacities from the Revolution up until now, have just been expelled and dismissed with utter disdain. Therefore, if in France itself under the eyes of the king and the *philosophes*, these poor people are discharged and subjected to public affronts and reduced to poverty, what would it be like in a country of prejudices under the rule of people like Palissot, Mazères, and Drouin? (28)

This statement functions as a way to caution the Haitian people against any attempts at coercion by the former French colonists who continued to try to retake the colony throughout the first two decades of Haitian independence, as can be seen in the writings of Drouin de Bercy, le Borgne de Boigne, Malouet, and Mazères. Because of such threats, Vastey counseled Haitians to continue to guard their weapons and be ready for war when he wrote:

[s]ons of the mountains, inhabitant of the forests, cherish your weapons, those precious keys, preservers [*conservatrices*] of your rights, never abandon them, bequeath them to your children with a love of liberty and independence and the hatred of tyrants as the most beautiful inheritance [*le plus bel héritage*] that you could bestow. (1814a, 4)

If Vastey celebrates the legacy of the Haitian Revolution in *Le Système colonial devoilé*, in *Cri de la conscience* the ancestors suddenly appear not to mourn or to complain as elsewhere in Vastey's œuvre, but to commemorate the victories of the Haitian Revolution:

We have avenged the spirits of our brave companions who died gloriously for liberty and independence; the ghosts of our fathers, our mothers, our sisters, who were victims of the French, have arisen from the ashes of the pyres, from the depths of the seas, from the intestines of rapacious dogs, to applaud us and chant with us, vengeance! vengeance! (10)

Vastey's glee and celebration of both discursive and physical vengeance here may seem a far cry from (and may paradoxically appear to confirm) the kinds of deeply personal and parricidal "mulatto/a" vengeance narratives attributed to "monstrous hybrids" by the likes of Drouin de Bercy in the post-Haitian revolutionary Atlantic World. Yet Vastey's brand of vengeance was not motivated by the kinds of monstrous "racial" thinking attributed to people of "mixed race" in the work of someone like Drouin de Bercy. At least one of Vastey's early reviewers acknowledged the fact that the vengeance Vastey advocated had nothing to do with the supposedly innate barbarity of Africans or the propensity for "mulattoes" to want to kill their "white" fathers. Instead, it had everything to do with the kind of justice and 'imprescriptable right to resist oppression' (*Declaration*) ostensibly advocated by the radical Enlightenment thinkers who authored the *Declaration of the Rights of Man and the Citizen*.

The following review of *Colonial System* published in *The Antijacobin Review* in 1818 acknowledges the complicated relationship of the Haitian Revolution to vengeance:

> of the cruelties practised by the French in St. Domingo, Europe had, in a great measure, till now, been totally ignorant. The mask has, however, been withdrawn, by the liberty which the Haytians have given themselves, and perhaps the most signal vengeance they can now take of their ancient oppressors, is to give an impartial history. In reading over the tract before us we have doubted whether we were in the society of men or of wild beasts; but a little reflection easily convinced us that the brutes of the field could not act as the monsters we have been placed in company with. ('Système Colonial,' 1818, 243)

Unlike many of the writers who will be consulted in the final section of this chapter and who will characterize Vastey and his writing as monstrous, not only because he upset their notions about "race" and human identity, but because he advocated and defended the violence of the slaves against their masters, here, Vastey's writing causes the author of this article not only to doubt that blacks are 'wild beasts,' but to perform exactly the kind of subversion of categories that Vastey's writing urges when he asserts that it is the colonists who are 'the monsters.' What Vastey had ultimately succeeded in accomplishing, then, was to convince many of those in the Atlantic World who read his writings that the Haitian brand of 'vengeance' during the revolution (and Vastey's daring exposé of the monstrosity of the colonists afterwards) was wholly justified and even occasioned by the greater violence of colonialism.

*

As the nineteenth century progressed, Vastey's defense of post-independence Haiti would necessarily become more oriented towards dismantling the racist detractions of the independent northern kingdom, which Vastey believed to pose an additional threat to Haiti's independence. Despite some inconsistent support on the part of the U.S. and British governments, many Anglophone journalists, like their French counterparts, were quite critical of the two Haitis of the early nineteenth century. The Anglophone press was filled with articles that ridiculed the idea that Christophe had instituted a monarchy, writing, for example, that 'the black King of Hayti is as jealous of his royal titles, as any White Legitimate in any part of this world' (*Republican Farmer*, November 26, 1816). Another newspaper even described Christophe as a 'black emperor' who was 'imitating his white brother [Napoleon]' in committing 'robberies' against the United States (*The Evening Post*, May 25, 1810); a much later biographical sketch published after Christophe's death in *The Atheneum or Spirit of the English Magazines* on May 1, 1821, also mistakenly identified Christophe as an emperor, but this time Christophe was described as being of "mixed race": 'A more singular character than this mulatto emperor has not appeared in the political world for many centuries,' the author writes. 'The principles of morality were no guides to him, he had a command under General Leclerc, and betrayed him ... his ferocious disposition caused him to be dreaded' and '[l]ike Buonaparte,' whom the author claimed Christophe sought to emulate, 'everything must be military with him.'[8] Each of these judgments connects monarchy and empire to tyranny in some form, suggesting that there was a kind of hypocrisy, something monstrous even, in a former slave titling himself in the terms of European dynastic rule when it was dynastic kings who had subjugated him in the first place. The judgments above also cast aspersions on Christophe's character, linking his "blackness," of whatever degree, to the kinds of imitation, robbery, treachery, and jealousy to be found within the trope of "monstrous hybridity."

In at least one U.S. American periodical, this disdain turned to all out mockery when Christophe's entire court was ridiculed in the Baltimore-based *Niles Weekly Register* on November 9, 1816. The article referred to Vastey as the 'baroness Big Bottom,' to Christophe as 'king Stophel himself,' and to Limonade as 'Lime Punch.' The article further stated that the 'vast pomposity' of Christophe's court was being described for the 'benefit of all who desire to "*laugh and to be fat*", at the fools and knaves who applaud it—black or white.' The author of the *Niles* article even associated Christophe with primates, which had been a common 'leitmotif' in the sixteenth and seventeenth centuries (Hoffmann, 1973, 32):

---

8 In *La Vie de J. J. Dessalines, chef des noirs révoltés de Saint-Domingue* (1804), Dubroca also identified Christophe as a 'mulatto' filled with a desire to massacre 'whites.' Dubroca writes of Christophe: 'This mulatto chief first took up arms with Biassou and became distinguished in this school of carnage and horrors. It was him who in the month of June 1795, at the moment when the French commissioners had proposed to the insurgents an amnesty full and absolute [*une amnistie pleine et absolue*] and called for them to return to the flag of the Republic, penetrated the city of Cap, with one named *Macaya*, at the head of three thousand blacks [*noirs*], and committed there a horrible massacre [*carnage*] of whites, and terminated this bloody scene by setting fire to the city, which entirely destroyed it. On the strength of his crimes and his lowliness, Christophe became the secret agent of the tyrannical acts of Toussaint-Louverture' (63–64).

> Bonaparte once asked a West Indian how Christophe *aped royalty*—the newspapers can now inform him, for they give a long account of a set of black fellows at Hayti, the *quondam* grooms and scullions of the 'legitimate' days, disguised as gentlemen and ladies, riding in somber processions, acting royalty with about as much display of sense as is usual on such occasions; that is little or none at all.[9]

This passage renders the contemporary government in Haiti illegitimate by referencing the '"legitimate" days' when 'black fellows,' the 'scullions' or subservients of "whites," did not 'disguise' themselves as 'gentlemen and ladies.' The article also associates monarchy in Haiti with a nonsensical form of mimicry or 'ap[ing].' Even though the article in the *Niles Weekly Register* purportedly ridiculed anyone, 'black and white,' who applauded the monarchy of Christophe, the article took specific aim at Haiti in such a way as to narrate "monstrous hybridity," even poking fun at the king's personal physician: he was 'no ordinary physician, but a negro' who specialized in 'itch ointment.'

In both actual response to this kind of writing in the context of France,[10] and hypothetical response in the context of the U.S. and Great Britain (Vastey once acknowledged that one of the 'greatest regrets' of his life was that he had never 'learned English' [1816d, 56]), Vastey highlighted the idea that what was disturbing about Christophe's monarchy to the Atlantic World was decidedly the putative incongruity of:

> The crown on the head of a Black man! There you have what the French publicists, the journalists, the creators of Colonial Systems [*faiseurs de systèmes de colonisation*] cannot digest; one would say to hear them, that a black king is a phenomenon that has never been seen in the world! Who will therefore reign over the blacks, if the blacks cannot be kings? Is royalty such a privilege that it belongs exclusively to the white color? (1817b, 17)

Vastey's writing confronts the hypocrisy latent in critiques of Christophe's monarchy as a part of what the abbé Grégoire would later refer to as the

---

9 The article from *Niles Weekly* was published in response to *The Boston Palladium*'s reportage of a birthday party given for Christophe's wife, Queen Marie-Louise. Vastey had published a pamphlet detailing the event and parts of it appeared in translation in the Boston paper, and the article was reprinted in the *Daily National Intelligencer*, October 16, 1816.

10 Dauxion Lavayasse had actually written a letter to Napoleon Bonaparte in which he called Christophe 'un drôle de roi,' 'very burlesque ... who will have his generals, his doctors, and his favorites beheaded at the slightest whim of his bloodthirsty moods' (qtd. in Saint-Rémy, 1853, 127).

'aristocracy of the skin,' as inferred in the title of his 1820 *De la noblesse de la peau*. Yet even the abbé Grégoire found a monarchy created by people of color to be incongruous and inherently in conflict with the concept of democracy. According to Alyssa Goldstein Sepinwall, Grégoire was 'disgusted with the return of monarchy' in northern Haiti and for this reason he was an ardent supporter of Pétion. Grégoire was 'appalled that as much of the world was slowly adopting republican principles, the North of Haiti was abandoning them,' Sepinwall writes. 'He was especially incensed at the irony of blacks' creating a system based on arbitrary titles' (2000, 48). For Sepinwall, Grégoire's disdain and unwillingness to correspond with the northern kingdom derived from the fact that he viewed Haiti as a 'laboratory for republicanism' (2000, 48), and he saw Christophe's kingdom as an obstacle to spreading a republican message throughout the Atlantic World, just as he saw the U.S.'s continued slavery as a similar obstacle (see Grégoire, 1820, 86).

Vastey, however, was keen enough to recognize that while a monarchy in one part of Haiti and a republic in the other may have appeared to confirm Haiti's "monstrous hybridity" to many frightened European observers, others welcomed the "racial" enmity that such a division putatively represented. To that end, responding to the former French colonist le Borgne de Boigne's writing, in which the latter had suggested that the French should further encourage the dissensions already supposed to have been exemplified by the divisions of the 'mulattoes of the South' and 'Negroes of the north' (qtd. in Vastey, 1817b, 153), Vastey wrote: 'It is with this childishness, these injurious epithets, that our enemies count upon to divide us, what difference could exist between a man from the North, from the West, or from the South?' (1817b, 153). Like Vincent Ogé, who had also used the phrase 'injurious epithet' to describe the terminology applied to people of "mixed-race" in Saint-Domingue, albeit to quite a different end from Vastey,[11] the latter viewed as inherently insulting a vocabulary that, by virtue of its recourse to "racial" taxonomies, would segregate people into distinctly oppositional categories based upon skin color or "race."

One of Vastey's arguments in his *Essai*, in fact, was that revolutionary loyalties in Saint-Domingue, and later national loyalties in the two post-independence Haitis, were due to geography and not, as popularly

---

11 In his 'Lettre de M. Ogé le jeune au président de l'assemblée provinciale du Nord,' published on December 29, 1790 in *La Gazette nationale ou Le Moniteur universel*, Ogé denied that he had ever sought to raise the slaves against the colonists: 'When I asked the National Assembly for a decree that I obtained in favor of the American colonists formerly known under the *injurious epithet* of sang-mêlé, I did not include in my complaints the plight of blacks living under slavery' (741, italics added).

believed, due to skin color or "race." He wrote, 'in the civil wars [of Haiti], whether with whites or among ourselves, the people have taken sides in these wars in accordance with the regions in which they found themselves, rather than according to their own individual opinions or [skin] colors' (124–25). More than confronting what he considered to be a false statement on the part of le Borgne de Boigne, such a contestation of "monstrous hybridity" as characterized by the innate hatred of the 'negroes of the North' for 'the mulattoes of the South,' and vice versa, also allows Vastey to position those who would make such claims as outsiders incapable of writing about Haiti faithfully and with impartiality.[12] In the opening pages of his *Essai*, Vastey suggested that the works of those European historians who had devoted a few pages to Haitian history were filled with such errors precisely because these writers did not understand the inner workings of the country they observed. He wrote that to provide a *true* history, 'one must have a perfect understanding of the people and the affairs of the country about which he is writing ...; it is not surprising then,' Vastey writes, 'if [European] writers, who were otherwise of great talent, have made mistakes with respect to what they have written about Haiti, and have given some very defective portraits' (1819, 2).

Vastey not only considered as 'defective' the idea that Haiti was divided by 'mulattoes' and 'blacks' or the *light-skinned* and the *darker-skinned*, but seemed to celebrate as natural and desirable the diversity that was, for him, exemplified by people with lighter and darker skin living together in various regions of Haiti. He estimated, for example, that all three territories of Haiti—'the *North*, the *South*, and the *West*'—contained a population that was 'more or less' 'mixed.' By this Vastey meant that in all regions of Haiti the 'proportion' of 'blacks' to 'people of color' was the same and stood at around '*14/15ths black* [*quatorze quinzième de noirs*] and '*1/15th people of color* [*un quinzième de couleur*],' respectively (1819, 124, italics in original). Vastey urged his readers to believe that:

[i]n peacetime as in wartime, this mixture has always existed, and it cannot be otherwise, since it is nature that has formed these familial

---

12 The idea that 'mulattoes' possessed an innate hatred for 'pure blacks' and vice versa persisted throughout the nineteenth century and is intimately connected to post-revolutionary ideas about Haiti. Even as Caleb Cushing, a journalist and the future U.S. Attorney, praises the deceased Vastey's works as those of a 'regenerate African,' he questions whether the recent reunification of the northern and southern regions of Haiti under Boyer will endure, on the grounds that '[t]he total difference in their past modes of life, of education, and of government, is a powerful obstacle to the consolidation of the blacks and mulattoes under a republican chief; but a more insurmountable impediment is the hatred which the two casts [*sic*] have generally entertained for each other since the very beginning of their struggle for independence' (133).

ties, and that wants the mixing of the races; neither of these colors has ever separated from the other one in order to exclusively take one side or another. (1819, 124)

This statement does the work of absolving Haitians of the monstrous charge of being racist against one another, but it also attempts to transgress and indeed undercut the notion that people with lighter and darker skin hues could never live together in a compatible way.

Such a reversal of the terms of "monstrous hybridity" anticipates the mid-nineteenth-century work of the Haitian historian Joseph Saint-Rémy, who wrote in his introduction to Boisrond-Tonnerre's *Mémoire pour servir à l'histoire d'Haïti* (1804), '... there is a law instituted by nature, that the races only improve themselves by mixing' (1851, xxi). While Saint-Rémy's encouragement of "racial mixing," like Vastey's much more amorphous argument on this score, may seem self-serving when we consider that both men were considered to be of "mixed-race" themselves, we must also acknowledge that their celebration of Haiti's fruitful diversity was a narrative designed to encourage the familial, and in some ways, *deraced* model of the nation instituted by the first Haitian constitution. Article 3 of the Constitution of 1805 states, 'The citizens of Haiti are brothers amongst one another; equality, in the eyes of the law, is indisputably recognized'; while Article 14 mandates, 'All distinctions of color amongst children of the same family ... must necessarily cease.' Article 14 also declares that all of the inhabitants of the island of Haiti shall be called 'blacks.' These articles are politically complicated, as Sibylle Fischer has pointed out. Fischer writes that Article 14 in particular '[d]isrupts any biologistic or racialist expectations' by rendering '"black" a mere implication of being Haitian and thus a political rather than a biological category' (2004, 232). More than rendering 'black' a political (and nation-based) category, however, this article of the constitution also attempts to imbue language with new meaning. The word 'black' in this document does not designate skin color so much as it attempts to erase the notion of skin color and, therefore, deny that divisions based on outward appearance can any longer exist in Haiti. Like Vastey's discursive defenses of Haiti, these articles dismantle the project of pseudoscientific debates about "race" since, in Fischer's words, '[f]rom the taxonomic lunacy of a colony that had more than one hundred different terms to refer to different degrees of racial mixture and color we have moved to a generic denomination: black' (232).

Whatever we may think of Dessalines's attempt to render all Haitians 'black,' and thereby make "blackness" unmarked, normative, and dominant, or the metaphorical inference that all Haitians were actually 'mixed' in some way, as is found in Vastey and Saint-Rémy's writing, Vastey's objection to the notion of a Haiti divided by 'negroes' and 'mulattoes,' like Ogé's rejection of the term '*sang-mêlé*,' and Raimond and Bonnet's similar irritation with racialized terminologies, reminds us that the word "mulatto" and all of its hypothetical variants were meant to be demeaning to the people of color of Saint-Domingue. In questioning our assumptions about what Doris Garraway has called the 'productive paradox' (2005, 1) that "hybridity" as a metaphor offers us, therefore, the term 'mulatto,' which absolutely reeks of the pseudoscience of slavery, must be subjected at every turn to interpretive scrutiny.

This scrutiny even applies to Vastey himself, whose writings on Pétion absolutely demonstrate that he, like so many other contributors to the narrative of "mulatto/a" vengeance, employed the trope of "monstrous hybridity." Although, as his many writings indicate, Vastey sharply rebuked those who would maintain that any inherent animosity existed in Haiti between "blacks" and "mulattoes" or people of "mixed race," Vastey himself was not immune to the effects of pseudoscientific debates and the rampant language of "monstrous hybridity" that its advocates generated. In *Cri de la patrie*, although Vastey never specifically refers to Pétion as a "mulatto," he adopted the language of "monstrous hybridity" when he accused the former Haitian general of being 'more French than white Frenchmen themselves' (1815c, 15), and of being racially prejudiced against 'negroes' like Dessalines and Christophe (1815c, 5). In *Le Cri de la conscience* Vastey wrote that such claims on his part were not mere accusations, that he could provide proof that Pétion was 'an inveterate enemy of the blacks, and who harbored against them in his heart a profound and hidden hatred' (1815b, 88-89). Amongst his proof that Pétion was concealing "racial" prejudices against 'negro[es]' was the fact that Pétion had reportedly once told a deputy of color that he had 'taken up arms to overthrow Dessalines' due to the 'firm resolution' he had made to 'no longer be led by a negro' (1815c, 5).

As in all writing characterized by "monstrous hybridity," political ambiguity, incongruity, or uncertainty easily becomes racialized when Vastey links Pétion's stated duplicity, repulsive amalgamation, and uncanny heterogeneity to a figurative color wheel that allowed him to change his skin color depending upon the situation. Vastey wrote that Pétion was 'sometimes a republican, sometimes a slave, sometimes a *bonapartiste*, sometimes a royalist; black, yellow, or white; he puts on a mask according to convenience and circumstances.' Vastey also claimed that Pétion's political and "racial" loyalties were as variable as the wind: 'you see him change by turns his color and his shape in order to perpetuate this civil war … Nothing better describes the Machiavellian and diabolic character of Pétion than an amalgam of heterogeneous qualities that mutually repel one another' (1815c, 27).

In *Le Cri de la conscience*, Vastey continued to link what he considered to be the duplicitous and inexplicable behavior of Pétion to "monstrous hybridity" when he condemned a January 1815 article about Haiti that he suspected to have been authored by Pétion under the 'baroque name of Colombus.' Vastey wrote that the writing could not be 'reasonably attributed to a Haitian' since its contents were so 'anti-Haitian.' He was 'led to believe, therefore, that it was the product of a certain *quidam*, a mixed type, neither white, nor black, at times one and at times the other' (57), and ultimately he discovered that 'Colombus' was 'Pétion himself' (58). In the same work, Vastey used the word 'monster' at several junctures to describe Pétion: 'the deeper that I dig into Pétion's character, the more I find him to be an indescribable monster.' Vastey also refers to Pétion at one point as a 'unnatural monster' (69), and he uses the word 'monster' again when explaining that Pétion's loyalties could change depending on his 'ambitions' and the 'circumstances' in which he found himself. Vastey explicitly linked Pétion's political wavering to "monstrous hybridity" when he claimed that Pétion had been 'an aristocrat under Colonel Maudit, a democrat under the civil commissioners, a Jacobin under Hédouville, Leclerc, and Rochambeau, a Haitian despite himself under Dessalines, a republican in his revolt against the King, and at the same time, a Bonapartist; and royalist slave under Louis XVIII' and that now 'he is ready to become Haitian once again despite himself, or rather Bonapartist.' 'Such is the entire life of this monster of hypocrisy and dissimulation,' Vastey explained (1815b, 64). Vastey claimed, furthermore, that such characterizations of Christophe's nemesis were effectively incapable of approaching the reality of Pétion's perfidy and that perhaps there was no language to adequately describe the monstrous behavior of the Haitian president. He writes:

> Where is the artist skilled enough to be able to faithfully render the physiognomy of a hydra, of a pariah, on whose forehead one might see the imprint of an awful mixture of the fury of Moloch, the crimes of Robespierre and Marat, the betrayal and hypocrisy of Judas! upon the appearance of this odious monster, the frightened painter would have thrown his brush and recoiled in horror and dismay. (1815b, 88)

While "monstrous hybridity" had been used in much of colonial discourse on Haiti in attempts to prove the inherent degradations of "blackness," Vastey linked the grotesque character of Pétion to his "whiteness." He said that the three commissioners—Draverman, Medina, and Lavayasse—sent by the French government to spy on Christophe's kingdom in the hopes of reinstating French rule in the colony 'were specifically responsible for working with Pétion to place the black population into slavery [*parvenir à plonger la population noire dans l'esclavage*], and the majority of the yellows in degradation [*dans l'avilissement*].' This is because 'Pétion and some of his accomplices, whose color was nearer to white and who wanted to sully themselves with this abomination, were to become *white* by carrying the letters of *whites* [*lettres de blancs*], a worthy reward for their horrid service' (1815b, 7).[13] In other words, Vastey accuses Pétion of essentially trying to purchase "whiteness" by doing the work of "whites," which amounted to helping "whites" to retake the former colony.[14]

13 The phrase *lettres de blancs* refers to the idea that people of color could carry honorary "whiteness." Pierre Faubert explains that *lettres de blanc* 'served the same purpose for those who held them as the *lettres de noblesse* otherwise had for commoners; that is to say that with one of these titles, *a black or yellow man would be the equal, before the throne and before the law, and even in social circles, to the blondest man from Picardie*' (1856, 78). Faubert derived this explanation from Wallez, whom he cites in several places in the preface to *Ogé ou le préjugé de couleur* (1856). Faubert further elaborates on this in *Ogé* by saying that these were part of the instructions that Malouet gave to Dauxion Lavayasse (192). See also Wallez, *Précis historique des négociations entre la France et Saint-Domingue* (1826), wherein he writes that Dauxion-Lavayasse had proposed that 'by the *lettres de blancs* … an individual of whatever color' would be given 'the state of a white man' [*l'état d'un individui blanc*] (15).

14 The immediate context for Vastey's remarks was the capture of the French spy Franco Agoustine Medina by Christophe's government, whereby the French *espion*, who had entered Christophe's kingdom without authorization (Brière, 68), was found to have on his person letters containing 'secret instructions,' signed by Malouet himself. These instructions called upon the spies not only to encourage "racial" divisions in Haiti, but to inform the French government of the inner workings of the Haitian governments and their leaders. Under the orders of Christophe, Vastey had these instructions reprinted, thereby exposing Pétion's correspondence with various French colonists, which seemed to confirm the latter's complicity with the spies. Vastey took these letters as evidence that Pétion, 'whose color was nearer to white' anyway, was not an ardent defender of the independence of Haiti, but was instead a conspirator who, like the whites he resembled, sought to subject his own people to slavery. As a point of contrast, the Haitian historian and biographer of Toussaint Louverture, Joseph Saint-Rémy's description of Pétion's connection to such "whiteness" completely contradicts the portrait offered by Vastey. Saint-Rémy writes, in fact, that the 'virtuous Pétion' was the 'fils naturel' or illegitimate son of a *colon blanc* (1853, n. 128), who, like Christophe and Dessalines after him, was 'deployed in the service of the French with as much devotion and courage; but with one difference, he did not at all soak his hands in the blood of his compatriots, in order to please the whites, like these two generals.' Furthermore, Saint-Rémy says that, contrary to popular belief, Louverture and Pétion were not enemies, since Louverture, 'on the contrary valued Pétion for his capability and his bravery.' Saint-Rémy says that the feeling was not exactly mutual, however, since 'Pétion thought he saw in [Louverture], and with some reason, the apostle of the colonists, the enemy of liberty' (56). Consistent in Saint-Rémy's overarching admiration for Pétion is the Haitian historian's belief that Pétion's oscillating devotion between the side of the Haitian revolutionists and that of the French government was no different from that of Dessalines, Christophe, or even Louverture himself. In other words, Saint-Rémy paints Pétion as hardly an exception.

Operating at a much more implicit level in Vastey's description of Pétion's complicity with the former French colonists and the current French government is Vastey's belief in what we might now call a kind of ideological "whiteness," where "whiteness" is understood as a 'normative, dominating, unexamined power that underlies the rationality of Eurocentric culture and thought' and which 'serves to push to the margin' those 'defined as not-white' (Smith, 2004). For Vastey, this ideology of "whiteness" was materially linked to the desire to enslave, subjugate, and/or terminate people of color. In an edition of the *Gazette Royale* published on May 24, 1816, in recounting the assassination of General Delvare allegedly ordered by Pétion, Vastey wrote that Pétion had commanded that all of the documents pertaining to the affair be burned so as to hide all evidence of his criminality in having unjustly, in Vastey's opinion, executed Delvare.[15] Vastey writes, 'these papers were of the utmost importance, and they contained the proofs of Pétion's betrayal, which is nothing less than his desire to re-enslave the blacks and re-establish the prejudices of 1789' (3). Vastey had already written in *Le Cri de la conscience* that, in his connivance with the former colonists to restore Haiti to France, Pétion 'had wanted to steal the freedom of seven-eighths of the population and degrade the one-eighth that would remain, solely because of the difference of their skin color [*différence de leur épiderme*]' (1815b, 32). According to Vastey's descriptions there was, in the end, little to differentiate Pétion and his desires for Haiti from the desires of the "white" French colonists who also sought to subjugate Africans simply because of the color of their skin. That is to say that the desire to place others in subjection based on "race" was itself codified by Vastey as a European and, therefore, as a "white" desire. In *Le Système colonial dévoilé*, Vastey characterized 'les blancs' as the 'race of Cain': 'I find in them the same spirit of hatred, of envy and pride, that passion for riches which is spoken of in scripture, which leads him to sacrifice his brother, this is the same spirit that animates the traffickers of human flesh' (1814a, 31–32). In his *Notes*, Vastey sardonically pointed out that, contrary to the writing of Malouet, "blackness" was not an ideology of domination that would eventually lead to

---

In fact, he paints his shifting behavior as one of the wholly characteristic rules of the Haitian Revolution.

15 Although the article in question is unsigned, a subsequent publication of Vastey's, in which he refers to himself as having written these words in the *Gazette*, allows us to identify the baron as the author of the article from the *Gazette Royale* dated May 24, 1816. In his *Réflexions: adressées aux Haytiens de partie de l'Ouest et du Sud* (1816), Vastey begins by writing, 'In the *Gazette Royale* of May 24, I gave an account of the assassination of the unfortunate General Delvare …' (1). Incidentally, this detail also allows us to identify Vastey for the first time as the editor of the *Gazette Royale*, at least in the year 1816, since the May 24 article mentioned above was headed with the title, 'The editor of the Gazette Royale to his Compatriots' (1).

Colonial Discourse and the Global "Scientific" Sphere

the 'massacre of whites,' wondering why the French continued to 'disturb our peace' since when 'have blacks ever sailed the seas in order to invade, enslave, and destroy whites?' (1814b, 13).

Because nary a description of "monstrous hybridity" would be complete without a reference to extermination of some sort, Vastey likens Pétion not only to a racist "white" European, but to a genocidal colonist when he more explicitly charges him with the horrible ambition of wanting to exterminate his own countrymen. He writes, 'In every era, men have been guilty of all the crimes: deicide, regicide, homicide, etc. have terrified humankind; but never before has any monster stained himself with the type of crime as horrible as that of which Pétion is guilty, of the *assassination* of an entire people' (1815b, 52). This last statement encapsulates Vastey's belief that Pétion shared with the many European writers examined in the previous section of this book, a desire (and a plan!) to essentially kill all people of color in the former colony in order to restore its status as French. Ultimately, Pétion's monstrous "whiteness" is not only linked to an ideology of domination and subjugation, but to one of the genocide of an 'entire people.'

Vastey's characterization of Pétion as a "monstrous hybrid" who sought to ingratiate himself with "whites" and thereby become "white" by acting "white," suggests a certain level of internalization, on Vastey's part, of the implicit "racial" grammar undergirding discussions of Haiti. It is not the fact that Vastey represents Pétion as a traitor and a colluder that tells us Vastey had adopted the narrative of "mulatto/a" vengeance, but rather that he uses a language of "monstrous hybridity" to do that representing. Ultimately, what Vastey cannot stomach is what he considered to be Pétion's incongruous desire to operate with what he implied was a "white" frame of mind. To Vastey, Pétion's co-optation of "whiteness" itself entailed the domination, oppression, and extermination of people of color.

While continuous circulation of the trope of "monstrous hybridity" may have implicitly influenced the way in which Vastey wrote about Pétion, Haiti, and even himself, pointing out that Vastey used the narrative of "mulatto/a" vengeance may also present a danger for the modern reader. This is because he or she may be tempted to either shy away from these passages or to seize gleefully upon them precisely because they could be interpreted as affirming the idea that many light-skinned Haitians have been inherently prejudiced against darker skinned Haitians and vice versa. If in this section of the chapter, perhaps like Vastey, I have labored under an appropriate fear of 'stereotype threat,' which, according to Claude M. Steele, happens 'whenever we're in a situation where a bad stereotype about one of our own identities could be applied to us … We know that anything we do that fits the stereotype could be taken as confirming it' (5), it is precisely to prove the point that talking about "race" while living in wholly *raced* bodies and wholly *raced* worlds, forces us all to examine how we may end up unwittingly reaffirming "racial" stereotypes when we fail to question either what we have included and excluded in our discussions of "race" or the assumptions that undergird those choices. Talking and writing about "race" without implicitly adopting the racialized beliefs of those whom we study takes a great amount of reflection and reflexivity.

In his book *Whistling Vivaldi: How Stereotypes Affect Us and What We Can Do* (2011), Steele discusses the phenomenon of internalization of "racial" stereotypes when he writes, quoting at the outset Gordon Allport, 'the great mid-twentieth-century social psychologist,'

> 'One's reputation, whether false or true, cannot be hammered, hammered, hammered, into one's head without doing something to one's character'. The psyche of individual blacks gets damaged, the idea goes, by bad images of the group projected in society ... Repeated exposure to these images causes these images to be 'internalized', implicitly accepted as true of the group and, tragically, also perhaps of one's self. (46)

A. James Arnold, influenced by the writings of Maryse Condé, similarly observes that the narratives and idioms expressed in the folktales of some slaves and former slaves often reflect 'interiorization of the image their masters had of them.' Arnold writes, 'Through their own folktales, the slaves had incorporated and expressed others' stereotypes of them' (2006, 259).

By including what I believe to be Vastey's own internalization of the trope of "monstrous hybridity," I hope to show that this vocabulary was so readily available, accessible, and indeed metonymic that it could even be used by those who had historically been the primary targets of its tropology. That is to say that Vastey felt perfectly justified in utilizing the language of "monstrous hybridity" in an attempt to defame Pétion in two texts that were written primarily for and addressed to Haitians living under both governments, *Le Cri de la patrie* (1815) and *Le Cri de la conscience* (1815). This suggests that Vastey believed that he could count upon the immediate discursive purchase of the trope of "monstrous hybridity" to create a sense of fear, disgust, and violence that would in turn perform the function of making Pétion hated in the eyes of the Haitian president's own constituents, even though such a trope had been used against many of the very people whom Vastey addressed with his text. In essence, Vastey's writings serve as a reminder that as a latent weapon that encouraged fear, disgust, terror, division, and indeed extermination, "monstrous hybridity" provided such a ripe opportunity for defaming a person's (or a nation's) character that it was in operation in nearly every discussion of Haiti, and it could be used and understood by virtually anyone who had access to the 'global discursive sphere.'

Colonial Discourse and the Global "Scientific" Sphere

The mid-nineteenth-century Haitian historian Beaubrun Ardouin argued exactly that the trope of "monstrous hybridity" had been used as a superficial and pernicious explanation for political divisions since the time of Louverture and Rigaud. Ardouin also pointed out how many of the Haitian people had internalized these superficial beliefs, on the hand, and how certain Haitian leaders had capitalized upon these beliefs, on the other. In his *Etudes sur l'Histoire d'Haïti*, Ardouin wrote:

> It is a mistake on the part of foreigners to have believed that they saw in these two wars [of Louverture and Rigaud, and Christophe and Pétion, respectively] a quarrel of *castes*, a struggle of *colors*: this detestable question was not the real cause. Without a doubt, this talk, of *nègres*, of *mulâtres*, had been employed during these disastrous struggles; without a doubt barbaric actions had taken place that would contribute to the misleading opinion of superficial observers: Haitians themselves, often without thinking about it, and who were often not instructed on the real reasons for these internecine dissensions, also believed on faith what was publicly written about these ancient times, especially in the foreign realm, without considering that on both sides, men of both colors fought against one another in opposing ranks, and that they equally perished the victims of these terrible furies. (1:102–03)

Along these lines, it was Vastey himself who had actually evoked this 'talk, of *nègres*, of *mulâtres*,' when in the aforementioned article from the *Gazette Royale*, dated May 24, 1816, he accused Pétion of spreading the lie that it was Henry Christophe who was on a mission to kill all the 'men of color.' He wrote that Pétion was only pretending to

> empathize with the fate of the men of color, in saying that we had destroyed them all; whereas in private he told his confidants that there were many people of color in the North who were very attached to the King; I would like to see these scoundrels wiped out, every last one of them; for what have they to do there? Such were the political maxims of this vile brigand in those times, to excite insurrection, to cause harm, to do all of this in order to reap the benefits. ('L'Editeur de la Gazette,' 1)

It is perhaps the sourest of ironies that while Vastey sought to establish Pétion as the very embodiment of the "monstrous hybrid" whose continued existence was detrimental to independent Haiti, in the early literary history of the Haitian Revolution it would be Vastey himself—who utterly denied any whiteness when he apologized for his putative lack of eloquence in writing, 'I, who am neither white, nor a colonist' (1814a, 39)—who would become the primary symbol in the myriad narratives in which he appeared of the vengeful "mulatto" who was racially prejudiced and himself characterized by monstrous cruelty towards his own people. Exploring this topic at length, the final section of this chapter essentially provides a roadmap for thinking about how it was 'Haitian exceptionalism,' with its 'formula of banalization,' or the idea that, as an historian, Vastey was exceptionally biased and vengeful and, as a person, he was exceptionally prejudiced and even monstrous and, therefore, not 'really that important' (Trouillot, 1995, 96), which has led to the relative 'silencing' of his historical and theoretical works in the historiography of the Haitian Revolution. As we are about to see, Vastey's historical, theoretical, and philosophical challenges to the colonial memories produced in the European public sphere made him one of the most frequently referenced Haitian historians in the early nineteenth century and one of the most highly visible symbols of "monstrous hybridity" in the first three decades of the nineteenth-century literary history of the Haitian Revolution.

*

Early nineteenth-century travelers to Haiti who mentioned Vastey attempted to account for his "racial" identity and his political loyalties in a variety of ways. In these works, Vastey is variously described as a man of "mixed race" whose hybridity was related to his desire to seek vengeance against "whites," or alternatively as a "negro" whose efforts at writing, laudable though they may have been, were simple examples of mimicry that could never rise to the level of European writing, or even as a seemingly "white" man whose real "racial" identity was exposed by his savage personality. What these superficially different descriptions have in common is a reliance on the language of "monstrous hybridity."

William Woodis Harvey, a Methodist preacher who was sent to northern Haiti by the Methodist Church to encourage Protestantism throughout the kingdom (Findlay and Holdsworth, 266), described Vastey in his *Sketches of Hayti* (1827) as a 'mulatto' whose 'fierceness,' 'duplicity,' and 'meanness' rendered him 'at once despicable and odious,' and who entertained a hatred 'towards whites of all nations [that] rendered him sometimes an object of terror' (223). Harvey directly connected his assessment of Vastey's vengeful personality to the trope of "monstrous hybridity" when he wrote:

> Had the character of Vastey been as consistent, as his abilities were respectable, he would have deserved our admiration; but this unhappily was not the case ... [O]n one occasion, he was heard calmly to declare that if he were allowed to follow his own wishes, he would massacre every white man in the Island. The monster who had wantonly imbrued his hands in the blood of his nurse—for with this horrid crime was he

charged—and who, during the struggle for liberty, had coolly assisted in the massacre of thousands was alone capable of conceiving, and had he been permitted, of executing, so dreadful a purpose. In short, he was the very counterpart of Dessalines—an assemblage of all that was mean, and savage, and diabolical. (223–24)

Harvey then ties Vastey's fantastic monstrosity to the baron's own writing. For Harvey, it is the mutability of Vastey's character (demonstrated by his uncanny similarity to Dessalines), coupled with an 'assemblage' of 'diabolical' personality traits, that made his abilities as an author less 'respectable.' Moreover, according to Harvey, Vastey's actual 'countenance' was a 'correct index to the dark passions, and sometimes to the villainous purposes, of his soul,' which 'often revealed their workings, when he was most desirous of concealing them' (224). Harvey's description of Vastey's facial expressions as ultimately revelatory distinctly coincides with the idea that people of "mixed race" were imprinted with indelible physical traits that might, through close observation, betray their connection to "blackness." Harvey specifically demonstrates the anxieties provoked by both the instability of Vastey's "racial" identity and the specter of "monstrous hybridity" when he warns his readers that though Vastey was 'represented to be a kind and affectionate husband,' 'the savage himself is often found capable of the strongest conjugal affection' (225). Anxieties about "miscegenation" here operate in a space that marks Vastey's hybridity as a threatening attempt to conceal his innate savagery (after all, he is the 'counterpart' of Dessalines). Harvey consoles himself, in the end, by implying that though Vastey's interior savagery might have been temporarily concealed by exterior signs of kindness and affection, the native 'savage' in him, the 'insidious character he bore,' could be readily 'discovered in his countenance and conversation' (226).

The kind of beliefs about "miscegenation" found in Harvey's writings concerning the inability of 'mulatto' subjects to contain their interior and 'savage' blackness under exteriors of 'kind and affectionate' "whiteness" (and the inability of others to immediately recognize these traits) is made most apparent when Vastey is assumed to be a 'white man.' In the diaries of Frances Williams-Wynn, written over the first four decades of the nineteenth century and edited by Abraham Hayward in 1864 (seven years after her death), Williams-Wynn recorded her observations not of 'the writer's daily life,' but of the 'conversations and compositions which attracted her attention in the course of her daily intercourse with the most cultivated people and her assiduous study of curious books and manuscripts' (Hayward, v, vi). An author whom Williams-Wynn refers to only as Mr. Courtenay penned one of these 'curious' manuscripts. In it, Courtenay claims to have spent time in Christophe's palace in the company of Admiral Home Popham,[16] and mentions having known Vastey, whom he refers to as a 'clever, gentlemanly white man, educated in France'; he writes, 'I became acquainted with him and liked him much, though many of his countrymen assured me he was a perfect savage in disposition' (qtd. in Williams-Wynn 177). After Williams-Wynn's rendition of Courtenay's statement, Hayward intervenes with an editorial footnote clarifying that Vastey was actually a 'mulatto, and one of the most remarkable of the race' (177). The editor's intervention is supposed to contradict what Courtenay feels and knows using his own common sense—that Vastey is a 'white man' whom he likes very much, even though others characterize him as a common 'savage.' The conflicting statements about Vastey made by the editor and by Courtenay (by way of Williams-Wynn) distinctly reflect fears that were prevalent in the nineteenth-century Atlantic World about the consequences of "miscegenation" and the inability properly to know about a person's loyalties, personality, and ultimately, the merit of his or her works, based on perceived notions of "race." Vastey's identity as a 'white' man bewilders Courtenay exactly because Vastey's appearance of "whiteness," his French education and his likeability, do not match up with the identification of him as a 'savage.' The editor, then, appearing to sense Courtenay's own anxiety over such incongruity, provides the common-sense explanation that unwittingly links Vastey's savagery to the "black" 'race' (thus absolving *pure* "whiteness") and his 'remarkable' achievements to "miscegenation" (thus downplaying *pure* "blackness" and bolstering "whiteness").

The widely cited Englishman James Franklin, too, has something to say about Vastey's "race" in connection with his intellectual abilities, but he attributes Vastey's unreliability as an 'historian' neither to the fact that he was a 'mulatto,' nor to an idea of the baron as 'white,' but, in a third racialized scenario, to the fact that he was a 'negro.' In *The Present State of Hayti* (1828), Franklin, who viewed Haiti as 'a lasting monument of what may be expected from injudicious emancipation' (409), describes Vastey as a 'warm advocate for the genius and talents of his countrymen' (213). However, Franklin adopts the same skepticism about the merits of Vastey's writing that he maintains with respect to representations of Haiti as regenerated or

---

16 This detail allows us to identify the author as George W.C. Courtenay, who was a lieutenant on the *Iphigenia* when that vessel took Popham 'on a courtesy visit to Cap-Henry in May 1819' (Cole, 253); Courtenay would later serve as Britain's 'Consul General at Hayti from 1832 to 1842' (O'Byrne, 234). According to an entry in John Hearne's *Commonplace Book*, Courtenay also penned a 'Poetical Epistle' to his housekeeper and lover in Haiti. The entry to the poem is marked, 'Poetical Epistle— supposed to have been written by Captain Courtenay ... Consul in Hayti,--to his House Keeper in Port-au-Prince—Madame Celeste!' (157).

'improved.'[17] Franklin says that Vastey is 'no authority' on the cruelties of planters in Saint-Domingue '*before* the rebellion' (92, emphasis in original), since 'we have nothing from him but allegations and assertions, without proof to support them' (91). 'It is true,' Franklin admits, that Vastey 'puts forward some statements of cruelties inflicted on his negro brethren, but those were subsequent, even by his own account, to the revolt and to the emancipation.' Vastey is thus guilty of having 'forgotten that the first acts of cruelty and indiscriminate murder, were committed by his very brethren' (91–92). Franklin's only explanation for what to him were such obvious exaggerations and misrepresentations is: 'Vastey being a negro, it is natural that he should exhibit the worst side of the picture, without noticing its better one' (91). Even if Franklin's statement of "racial" determinism is meant primarily to underscore the exaggerated effects of "racial" partisanship, the fact that he believes that his own status as a European traveler makes him innately objective, authoritative, and therefore capable of explaining everything about Vastey, Haiti, and ultimately, "race," ties his works to the kind of 'narrative authority to represent the "Rest"' found not only in European travel writing (Smethurst, 1), but in pseudoscientific debates circulating in the Atlantic World. Franklin used this same self-prescribed authority to represent when he asserted that Vastey had vastly overstated the case for the regeneration of Haiti in his *Réflexions* when trumpeting the fact that 'we write and we print. Even in our infancy our nation has already had writers and poets who have defended its cause and celebrated its glory' (1816d, 84). Franklin claims, on the contrary, that the catalogue of Haitian writers and poets numbers only three writers, including Vastey, and only one poet, Juste Chanlatte, whom he characterizes as the composer of plays 'teeming with fulsome compliments to the monarch's virtue' and 'sonnets to the peerless beauty of the queen.' Franklin finishes his cynical assessment of Vastey's claims for literary regeneration by stating, 'unless the Baron de Vastey can adduce other proofs of Haytian capacities,' he must remain skeptical since 'at present but little of that improvement manifests itself which has been the subject of so much praise and admiration.' 'That the people of Hayti should improve,' he writes, 'I confess I wish may be realized, but at this moment it is very distant from it' (215).

17 In the book's preface, Franklin claims that 'the short delineation here attempted will, in all probability, suffice to shew that the accounts which have been given at different times of Hayti and its inhabitants have been much too highly coloured by the zealous advocates of negro independence' (vii). 'Experience,' the author continues, 'has convinced him that the representations so generally received of the improvement which it has made are greatly exaggerated, and he is not without the hope that the following sheets will convey more correct information on the subject, and thus prove useful to the merchant, if not interesting to the general reader' (viii).

From "Monstrous Hybridity" to Enlightenment Literacy

While Franklin uses Vastey and his works to make a broader claim about Haitian, and by implication 'negro,' *incapacities* for objectivity, historical writing, poetry, art, regeneration, and, in essence, civilization,[18] abolitionists, both in the 1820s and in ensuing decades, often celebrated Vastey as the very proof of "black" humanity and therefore 'regeneration,' citing him as having 'prove[d] how capable a black writer is of emulating his white brethren even on the score of literature.'[19] Many abolitionist writers used Vastey's works to muse upon the very idea that "negro" writing was a shockingly remarkable phenomenon that nonetheless refuted claims of inherent natural African inferiority and affirmed the belief that "blacks" and especially Haitians were capable of 'civilization.' The botanist William Hamilton's English translation of Vastey's *Reflexions on the Blacks and Whites* (1817), for example, demonstrates the remarkable interest of metropolitan writers in the ways in which Vastey and his writings could be used as a functional part of both transatlantic anti-slavery thought and pseudoscientific "racial" debates.[20] Citing Ignatius Sancho and Phillis Wheatley

---

18 The 'vaguely scientific' ideas espoused by Franklin would find more formal expression in the texts of mid-nineteenth-century "racial" thinkers like Thomas Carlyle and George Fitzhugh, who argued that Haitians had squandered both their liberty and the resources of what had once been one of the most lucrative colonies in the world. Harvey and Carlyle, for example, to differing degrees both promoted the idea that Haiti was a strange and disturbing country whose inhabitants 'were hardly sensible' of the prejudices and 'defects' in their literature (Harvey, 223) and where 'black Peter was exterminating black Paul' (Carlyle). Even more representative of such sentiments is the claim of U.S. pro-slavery apologist Fitzhugh, in *Sociology for the South* (1854), that the whole island had degenerated into 'a state of savage anarchy which invites and would justify another conquest and reduction of the inhabitants to that state of slavery for which alone they are fitted, and from which they so wickedly escaped' (277).

19 Ironically, this enthusiastic assessment is made in an editor's footnote (372) to the 1820 English translation of Jacques-François Dauxion Lavayasse's *Voyage aux îles de Trinidad...*, originally published in 1813, the year before Lavayasse led Malouet's secret mission to Haiti.

20 The translator of *Reflexions on the Whites and Blacks*, listed only as W.H.M.B., dedicates the translation 'to the philanthropists of every country' (3), while the publisher adds that the translator is 'an Englishman, of a liberal profession, resident in the Island' (5). However, several newspaper articles published in England allow us to identify for the first time 'W.H.M.B.,' the translator of three of Vastey's works, *Reflexions on the Whites and Blacks*; *Political Remarks on Some French Journals*; and *An Essay on the Causes of the Revolution and the Civil Wars of Hayti*, as William Hamilton, a British botanist who spent several years living in the West Indies. According to his application for a Radcliffe Travelling Fellowship, which was signed 'William Hamilton, M.B. *And corresponding Member of the Medico-Botanical Society for London*,' Hamilton was a 'Master of Arts and Bachelor of Medicine of the University of Oxford' (1832-35, 1). The first item that helps to identify *this* William Hamilton as Vastey's primary translator is an article

as among the relatively few earlier instances of 'African genius' (9), the publisher of the translation says that Vastey's work is important evidence of what 'Africans' or 'Negroes' might be capable of when 'unrestrained by those shackles which have hitherto depressed the minds, no less than the limbs, of the unfortunate natives of Africa' (10), and he concludes that Vastey's *Reflexions* is 'perhaps the first work by a Negro, in which the energies of the mind have been powerfully excited and have found a proper scope for action' (10). This last claim would be explicitly cited in a number of publications on both sides of the Atlantic,[21] and elaborated upon in many others. The Virginian abolitionist John Wright, for instance, made use of Vastey's works as a part of his argument for immediate emancipation of U.S. slaves. In his 1820 *Refutation of the sophisms, gross misrepresentations, and erroneous quotations contained in 'An American's' 'Letter to the Edinburgh reviewers'*, Wright quotes several passages from 'that able negro writer, the Baron de Vastey' (33), and then comments with amazement: 'These are the arguments used by a Haytian, a *negro!*' Vastey's writing, he concludes, might well convince naysayers that 'there is at least one of the negro race

entitled 'Original *and* Interesting State Papers,' from the Liverpool Mercury dated April 3, 1818. The author of the article states, 'We have been favoured by a most respectable and intelligent friend, Dr. William Hamilton, now residing at Cape Henry, with the following interesting proclamation, which has not, we believe, appeared before now in any British print.' After reprinting Hamilton's translation of Christophe's proclamation, the author inserts a 'Note of the translator,' which reads, 'Owing to the indisposition of Baron Vastey, preventing his attending to public affairs, a small error has crept into this proclamation ...' While this article allows us to identify Hamilton as having lived in Haiti, as well as having been interested in translating Haitian documents, in addition to having been aware of Vastey's writing, a letter printed from this same William Hamilton in volume 5 of *The Gardener's Magazine and Register of Rural and Domestic Improvement* (1829) in which the British botanist quotes from and translates *Réflexions politiques* of the 'late Baron de Vastry [sic],' provides further evidence which helps us to identify this Hamilton as the original translator of three of Vastey's works (1829, 100). Further cementing the connection, Hamilton would also reference Vastey as his 'talented and lamented friend' in his *Memoir on the Cultivation of Wheat in the Tropics* (1840), which was also signed William Hamilton, M.B. In this text, Hamilton translates yet another passage from *Réflexions politiques* (90). Hamilton's interest in Haitian affairs was deep and abiding, as evidenced by his moving preface to the translation of Vastey's *Essai* (which cross references Hamilton's earlier translations) and also by a letter that he had written to Baron Dupuy in his personal correspondence with Joseph Banks (see 'To Joseph Banks' and Howard et al.). I am writing about the connection between Hamilton and Vastey in much greater detail in a book-length work tentatively titled, *Baron de Vastey and the Origins of Black Atlantic Humanism*.

21 See, for instance, reprints of this statement in *The Liverpool Mercury*, April 3, 1818 ('Hayti'); *The City of Washington Gazette*, May 21, 1818 ('From a Late English Paper'); *The Philanthropist*, March 20, 1819 ('From a Late English Paper').

whose abilities and eloquence as a writer are in no way inferior' (35).[22] Wright uses Vastey's very own words to argue that Africans, and particularly Haitians, had reached a sufficient level of 'civilization' to disprove theories of inferiority. The way in which these kinds of arguments were framed—Vastey's works *are* or *aren't* proof of a whole host of ideas about "race"—reveals an anxiety about the legacy of the Haitian Revolution and its larger connection to pseudoscientific debates about "race" circulating in the nineteenth-century Atlantic World.

In at least one instance, the question of Vastey's "racial" identity provided the occasion for an acerbic professional and personal debate about the 'the Negro' 'Species' itself and, more specifically, about what constituted 'full-blooded negro' identity. In an article entitled 'The Negro—Not a Distinct Species' (1858), the last of a series of 'broadsides' about 'race,' John K. Ewcorstart, 'a Boston unitarist with abolitionist leanings' (Breeden, 251) argued that the works of American ethnologists, and Nott and Gliddon in particular, were filled with 'erroneous assertions … in which the negro is condemned' (Ewcorstart, 270). One of these 'erroneous assertions' was the idea that the 'pure negro' was incapable of writing anything worth 'remembering,' which had been maintained by Ewcorstart's adversaries, in part, to establish that the 'Negro' was a different species from the 'Caucasian.' Ewcorstart refutes this notion by maintaining from the first, 'it is a matter of history that Blumenbach collected a large library of books written by negroes,' and later, as further proof for his contrary position, Ewcorstart wrote, '[f]or the sake of argument, I beg leave to insert this page, written by a negro, which I believe is not only worth "remembering" but which shows what the negro can do with a fair field before him.' Before going on to insert a long passage from Vastey in English translation, Ewcorstart tells the reader that the passage was 'written by Baron de Vastry [*sic*], one of the counselors of Christophe, himself a pure negro, who published some reflections on

---

22 Abolitionist writers often strategically compared Vastey's works with those of pro-slavery advocates. One British journalist in 1820, identifying Vastey as the 'most distinguished political writer' in Haiti, stated that he had bested his nemesis the colonist Malouet with 'equal vehemence and vigour,' and that 'in point of style, energy of thought, and powerful eloquence the black is infinitely superior' ('History,' 73). In his *An Excursion through the United States and Canada* (1824), William Newnham Blane, commenting on the views of the Virginian John Taylor (an influential political thinker and associate of Jefferson's; see Sheldon and Hill, 2008), remarks that 'I have seen a work written by a native of St. Domingo, the Baron de Vastey, which both in style, composition, and just and proper feeling, so far surpasses the writings of Col. Taylor that most persons would suppose, that the Colonel, (always of course excepting his transcendent merit in being of a whitish colour,) had a much greater affinity to the baboon than the Haytian' (219).

the state of Hayti, about thirty-five years ago' (271).[23] Vastey's writings help Ewcorstart to conclude that Haiti

> is a practical demonstration of what the negro is capable of doing. I challenge the affirmative to show any portion of the Caucasian race which have been enslaved and made so great progress in so short a time, or who have ever gained and maintained their liberty by striking manfully with the sword. (272)

The medical doctor T.C. Rogers appears to have attempted to meet Ewcorstart's challenge. In a response to Ewcorstart's article, Rogers took issue with a number of the former's assertions, including the claim that Vastey stood as an example of a '*full-blooded negro*, who has written a page worthy of being remembered' (454). He writes, 'The example brought forward by Dr. E. of Baron de Vastry [*sic*], cannot be received into this discussion as evidence until his pedigree is satisfactorily proven.' Rogers not only doubted that Vastey was a 'pure negro' after all, but actually seemed to hint at the idea that the publication from which Ewcorstart quoted Vastey, Hamilton's English translation of *Réflexions politiques sur quelques journaux français concernant Haïti* (1817), may not have even existed. Rogers says, 'we also expect to be referred to what book or paper the extract given was taken from. While it stands exclusively on Dr. E's authority, though he be a gentleman of the strictest veracity, an instance so extraordinary cannot be satisfactory to scientific investigators' (454). Finally, Rogers suggests that even if Ewcorstart's evidence could be authenticated, 'It is somewhat remarkable that, although there are 4,000,000 of negroes in the United States, Dr. E. was obliged to go to Hayti for a solitary and ill-authenticated example of a negro who had "written a page worthy of being remembered". If he cannot furnish an illustration out of this great body of negroes in the U.S.,' Rogers concludes, 'he has certainly undertaken a hopeless cause; for it is well known that the negro intellect in this country, is far in advance of their African progenitors and African contemporaries' (454).

Before moving on to conclude that ideas about Vastey's "racial" identity have influenced ideas about his political identity, one additional mention of Vastey in 1844 right after the revolution that put an end to Jean-Pierre Boyer's decades-long (1818–43) presidency, inserts Vastey once again directly into

---

23 While the name Ewcorstart is one that will hardly be known even to specialists in the history of the science of race today, the medical doctor's works did exert at least some influence when it came to thinking about Haiti. In particular, the passage cited here was repeated verbatim, but without attribution, in an article entitled 'Toussaint Louverture and the Republic of Haiti,' published in *Chambers's miscellany of instructive & entertaining tracts* in 1872 (162).

formal pseudoscientific "racial" debates, but also raises important questions about literary genre. Edward Binns, a medical doctor and abolitionist, was the author of *Prodromus: Towards a Philosophical Inquiry into the Intellectual Powers of the Negro*, a tract published in 1844 in three installments in *Simmond's Colonial Magazine and Foreign Miscellany* and then later that year as a separate pamphlet.[24] Although, like Rogers and Ewcorstart, Binns participated more formally in "scientific" debates about "race" than many of the other writers hitherto examined, it is not the "scientific" dimension of his account of the 'intellectual powers of the negro' that primarily interests me here, but the way in which his uneasy comparison of Vastey to European writers showcases the inadequacy of generic literary categories to fully capture or explain that which might appear to be *different*, notably in the following passage:

> As an historian, when compared with Europeans, he cannot be ranked in the first class; but as a chronicler of events and occurrences, he is inferior to few writers. His work is more of a memoir than a history, and, doubtless, the facts that he relates are well founded, however highly colored. Viewed simply *as* an African, his learning and talents are highly respectable; and if we except some few faults of diction, and some acerbity of temper, we cannot refuse him the meed of literary homage. (39–40)

Binns's views on Vastey here demonstrate the specific cultural, historical, and "scientific" valence Vastey's works had in a nineteenth-century Atlantic World that put him on a par with today's more well-known writers from the early African diaspora, Phillis Wheatley and Ignatius Sancho. Yet Binns's unfavorable comparison of Vastey to 'first class' European historians also sounds curiously similar to Thomas Jefferson's remarks about Ignatius Sancho in *Notes on the State of Virginia*:

> Upon the whole, though we admit him to the first place among those of his own colour who have presented themselves to the public judgment, yet when we compare him with the writers of the race among whom he lived ... we are compelled to enroll him at the bottom of the column. (140)

Furthermore, Binns's assessment of Vastey as a (mere) 'chronicler,' and of his work as resembling 'more a memoir' than 'a history,' recalls Thomas Jefferson's famous phrase about the African American poet Phillis Wheatley: 'Religion, indeed, has produced a Phillis Whately [sic]; but it could not produce a poet'

---

24 Binns is probably most remembered today for his 1846 *The Anatomy of Sleep*, which at least one expert in the field has called '"the capstone of the prescientific era" of sleep research' (Wilse B. Webb, qtd. Finger, 244).

(140). As Bruce Dain has written of this passage, 'Jefferson had to dismiss a Wheatley' since 'one instance of substantial black reason or imagination would upset his whole scheme' (34), which was ultimately designed to deny blacks a 'fundamental humanity' (35).[25] With respect to Vastey, it is not only Binns's own inherent biases that are exposed (Vastey's facts are 'well-founded,' but 'highly coloured' from Binns's point of view, and while his 'talents are highly respectable,' Vastey's commitment is interpreted as 'acerbity of temper'), but the uneven ground on which the very comparison was posed. Binns's comparison between the 'African writer' and the European one relies upon a vocabulary (something Europeans call 'history' is inherently better than something else they call a 'chronicle') that is always already overdetermined by fantasies of true 'history' as unencumbered by political commitments and disengaged from its author's own life. Furthermore, the idea that a 'chronicle' or 'memoir,' if those terms are even adequate to describe Vastey's work (and even Binns is not sure that they are), does not reach the lofty level of 'history' is a completely subjective value judgment that relies upon arbitrary definitions of historical storytelling as linear, rational, and objective, rather than diversionary, expressive, and embattled.

The seemingly categorical yet equivocal, ambivalent yet unrelenting pronouncements about "race" *and* genre made by Binns and many of the other nineteenth-century writers who referenced Vastey likely cover up what Ann Laura Stoler has called in the context of colonial discourse 'epistemic anxieties' that register the 'uncommon sense of events and things' (2010a, 19). The instability of Vastey's "racial" and textual identity contained the power to upset the 'common sense' order that eighteenth- and nineteenth-century pseudoscientific debates about "race" sought to instill. If, as Michael Omi and Howard Winant write, 'race' as 'common sense' is 'a way of comprehending, explaining and acting in the world' (60), then the inability to properly *race* Vastey surfaces in confusions over how to understand, classify, and, in essence, *use* him and his works.

---

25 In a conciliatory letter to the abbé Grégoire dated February 25, 1809, Jefferson thanked the French priest for sending him a copy of his *De la littérature des Nègres* and seemingly acknowledged the epistemic anxieties present in his earlier assessment of "black" writing in *Notes*, stressing the 'hopeful advances' that they are making 'towards their re-establishment on an equal footing with the other colors of the human family.' According to Alyssa Goldstein Sepinwall, however, a few months after he penned this letter to Grégoire, Jefferson wrote another to a mutual friend in which he 'depicted Grégoire as simple-minded,' 'commented that he had given the Frenchman a "soft answer,"' and 'implied that whatever achievements had been achieved by those chronicled in *De la littérature*, it was only because they had some white blood' (Sepinwall, 2005, 174). For a recent account of the "racial" dimensions of Jefferson's *Notes* in relation to the Haitian Revolution, see Iannini (219–51).

From "Monstrous Hybridity" to Enlightenment Literacy

The nineteenth-century problem of how to read Vastey in terms of "race" and genre is distinctly linked to our contemporary difficulty over how to read Vastey politically. Such a quandary in contemporary Haitian historiography most often takes the form of identifying Vastey as, in the words of historian David Nicholls, the 'official ideologist and apologist of the kingdom' (1979, 43). At first, in his 1979 *From Dessalines to Duvalier*, Vastey's position as an intellectual revolutionary of "mixed race" who celebrated a "black" king's ascendance to the throne baffles Nicholls, who represents Vastey as an embodiment of the broader "racial" and political paradoxes of a nineteenth-century Haiti that was itself a "monstrous hybrid" to observers at the time precisely because it was part republic and part monarchy. In a later article, however, Nicholls substantially refined his earlier portrait of Vastey; but the quandary remained, as can be seen from his famous question: 'Into which category does Vastey fall: true radical—pointing to a firm foundation for a new national identity—or opportunistic spokesman of a new, self-serving elite?' Nicholls avoids entirely answering the question: 'as might be expected (in the case of a Haitian intellectual) the answer is complex' (1991, 108). Although not providing a definitive answer to a question that surely does not have one may appear to leave room for the kind of epistemological uncertainty that would allow for us to consider Vastey in light of multiple frames of political, authorial, and "racial" identity, Nicholls's parenthetical aside—that the answer should be 'complex' only in, or perhaps specifically in, the case of Haiti—belies a belief in what Michel-Rolph Trouillot has referred to as 'Haitian exceptionalism,' or the idea that Haiti is so strange that it is beyond comparison to other nations (1990, 8). In other words, Nicholls's appeal to complexity is made for the sake of painting Haiti and Haitians (especially Vastey) as exceptional rather than as complex in the mundane and obvious sort of way characteristic of every other nation and its citizens. In the end, the question that Nicholls seems to be asking is to whose side of the struggle against oppression did Vastey really belong: the side of the masses, on whose behalf he argues in *Le Système colonial devoilé*, or the side of the monarchical state power, on whose behalf many scholars believe virtually all of his writings are composed?

The populism of Vastey's *Le Système colonial devoilé* appears to have been overshadowed, in his day and in our own, by the spirited and paternalistic defense of monarchy maintained in many of his writings, including *Le Système colonial devoilé*, which begins with a dedicatory epistle 'To the King.' Chris Bongie writes that Vastey has likely been overlooked because in his works there is a 'complicity with political power' that is 'discomfiting' (2008, 235) since 'we in the humanities have been trained to recognize and valorize … "authentic" cultural producers whose philosophic or æsthetic ordering of the world might be imagined as taking place not *at* the side, but *to* the side, of men of state such as Christophe and Pétion' (32–33). Given that Vastey was both *at* the side of state power and *to* the side of larger state powers, I wonder if refraining from, in the words of Aiwha Ong, 'limiting public-sphere activities to "rational" critiques of the state or those critiques that are "free" of the state's penetrations,' might allow us 'to consider the various regimes of cultural normativity that have different relations to state power' (159). It is not so much the acknowledgement of the very real ties between Vastey's work and Christophe's government that should make us suspicious that 'Haitian exceptionalism' might be preventing us from reading the populist dimensions of Vastey's works. Instead, what ultimately renders historically anachronistic the idea that Vastey's connection to Christophe means he was not a true intellectual or even one of the founders of Haitian revolutionary historiography, is that it is hard to imagine using the term state-sanctioned publicity to describe the complex relationship between state power and revolutionary thought found in the writings of Thomas Jefferson, Benjamin Franklin, Condorcet, or Mirabeau.

Furthermore, the 'tension' apparent in Vastey's works between what Michael Hanchard refers to as 'state memory' and 'black memory' (or, more generally, 'collective memory' [62]), which begins in part as an opposition between 'statist' and 'nonstatist' forms of history (49), is not something we should ignore, disavow, or condemn; rather, it requires a study of its own. While 'state memory' is often codified by scholars as a kind of violence because it usually emphasizes 'the role of forgetting' for the sake of 'national unity' (46), 'black memory' or 'collective memory' has been praised for helping to 'keep alive the histories and peoples repressed or denied by the state' (46). Yet, as Hanchard points out, 'state memory' and 'black memory,' though not coterminous, are often not easily distinguishable either. He writes:

> While it has become chic in some circles to write and speak of diaspora populations—Africa, African descended, or otherwise—as communities defined by their traversal of boundaries, their seemingly borderless character, these same populations are nevertheless informed in some very critical and fundamental ways by the forces and consequences of nationalism. (61)

While Hanchard does not go as far as to suggest that 'state memory' and 'black memory' could ever exist without opposition to one another—indeed, he emphasizes that 'black memories and national memories do overlap, but they are not one and the same' (62)—the case of Baron de Vastey provides a fascinating example of a situation where these two forms of memory not only 'overlap,' but simultaneously collide, co-exist, and collaborate.

Thus, although I myself am indebted to earlier scholars for their studies on both Vastey and the Haitian Revolution, they too often appear to view a coherently defined radical intellectual sphere as clearly disengaged or even undermining a clearly defined conservative political sphere. If disquieting authors like Vastey and their disquieting texts are hard to read apart from the state power that both seemingly authorizes their existence and against which their texts appear to protest, it is at least partially related to the way that contemporary scholars, like their nineteenth-century counterparts, have been confused about how to read Vastey's "race," colonial status, and devotion to Christophe. It is also at least partially the result of the fact that the 'norms and values' of European literature have been 'equated with universal forms of thought' (Parry, 18) to the extent that it is difficult to recognize the overtly political and ideological nature of early Haitian publications as anything other than state-sanctioned propaganda.

If certain of Vastey's statements seem problematic or appear to provide evidence of propaganda or disingenuousness, then, as when he refers to the condition of the free people of color by saying, 'We will not make any distinction between these so-called free people [and the slaves], because … they suffered the same humiliations and the same outrages that the slaves did; we will consider them as such' (1814a, 74), I think it is because we tend to downplay the cumulative psychological costs of 'race-thinking' (Gilroy, 2000, 12). How else could we explain William Wells Brown, who had experienced both being a slave and a free person of color, making a similar case in *Clotel* (1853): 'The prejudice that exists in the Free States against coloured persons on account of their colour, is attributable solely to the influence of slavery, and is but another form of slavery itself' (2000, 171). In *Three Years in Europe* (1852), an autobiographical work that Brown published in London after escaping from slavery, the former fugitive slave expressed these sentiments again concerning his own experience with the effects of color prejudice:

> In the so-called Free States, I had been treated as one born to occupy an inferior position; in steamers, compelled to take my fare on the dock; in hotels, to take my meals in the kitchen; in coaches, to ride on the outside; in railways to ride in the 'Negro car'; and in churches, to sit in the 'Negro pew' (7).[26]

Although, unlike Brown, Baron de Vastey rarely made direct reference to his ancestry or personal life in his prose works, except to say that he was

---

26 See chapter ten of the present volume where Brown, in the context of revolutionary Saint-Domingue, with appeal to affect rather than to materiality, writes that 'the mulattoes *felt* their degradation even more keenly than the bond slaves' (1855, 5, emphasis mine).

Colonial Discourse and the Global "Scientific" Sphere

the child of an *Africaine* and therefore felt himself to be very 'African' (*ayant reçu le jour d'une africaine, je me crois très-identifié avec les africains*) (1816d, 31), in a rare autobiographical inscription from the 1815 pamphlet *À mes concitoyens*, Vastey movingly detailed why in the months after the kidnapping of Toussaint Louverture in June 1802—at a time when Leclerc began to advocate 'a genocidal policy aimed at killing virtually the entire black population,' even those who had been fighting on the side of France (Girard, para. 36)—he suddenly realized the qualified nature of his own liberty. In detailing why, after fighting against them, he suddenly took up the slaves' cause against the French, ostensibly some time in 1803, Vastey wrote:

> in order to avoid the death that our executioners were preparing for me, I fled into the woods to look for my salvation. Did I not find within the bosom of my maternal roots, fathers, mothers, brothers, friends who greeted me with transports of joy and the most pure friendship? Could I forget this moment when I threw myself into the arms of my brothers that I had unfortunately fought! What remorse did I not feel in their midst when instead of receiving the reproaches I believed I deserved, forgetting my ingratitude, or rather my error, they welcomed me among them with a truly paternal tenderness! From that moment forward I uttered an oath never to separate my cause from that of my fellow men, and I will perish in these sentiments. (1815a, 18)

This is one of the most remarkable passages in all of Vastey's œuvre not only because of the guilt expressed by Vastey, who admonishes himself for the errors of his past, but because his evocation of Leclerc's policy of wholesale extermination suggests to us that the "final solution" to the "race" problem in Saint-Domingue, at least as far as the colonists were concerned, always meant death for all free people of color regardless of social or economic status. That is to say that if one's color in the United States had always meant that he or she could be returned or turned into a slave, as Brown maintained in *Clotel*, in Saint-Domingue, being of color always meant that one could be exterminated. As the son and grandson of two extremely wealthy planters from Saint-Domingue—his maternal grandfather Pierre Dumas and father Jean Valentin Vastey—the future Haitian baron seems surprised to have found himself just as subject to Leclerc's policy of extinction as any other person of color. Tell me, what must it have felt like to have to try to live after having been persecuted, hunted down, and almost assassinated as a direct result of your skin color or "race?"

Vastey would try to tell us about the degrading effect of "racial" prejudices on his consciousness in his *Réflexions sur une lettre de Mazères*, a text which in its refutation of the arguments of the former colonist Mazères represents Vastey's most direct engagement with pseudoscientific debates about "race."

Vastey's sadness over the fact that he feels forced to use his words as political weapons overtakes him:

> if at this time I am experiencing intense regret, it is because I have been reduced to using my pen in order to redress these bloody outrages, and because I have not been able to find other arguments that would convince him [Mazères] even better than words that our type [*espèce*] is not inferior to his. (1816d, 5)

'I have been tempted twenty times to throw away my pen,' Vastey later writes,

> I feel humiliated, I am a man [*je suis homme*], I feel it to be so in all of my being, I possess all of the faculties, I have thought, reason, strength, I have every sense of my sublime existence, and I find myself obliged to refute puerile arguments, absurd sophisms, just to prove to men like me, that I am their equal [*leur semblable*]. (1816d, 15)

The dejected pathos inherent in these statements, far from suggesting that Vastey sought to paint free people of color as colonial victims in order to cover up their own colonial abuses, suggests that the ontological consequences of 'race-thinking' may have been far more collectively destructive for the then free people of Haiti than the immediately material consequences of slavery. A slave could be physically freed or could free himself, as William Wells Brown acknowledged when he arrived in England and suddenly felt, 'For the first time, I can say "I am truly free"' (1852, 9), but the future of the formerly enslaved mind was much more bleak, as the writing of Ngugi wa Thiong'o suggests. Ngugi tells us of the problem with 'decolonizing the mind':

> the biggest weapon wielded and actually daily unleashed by imperialism ... is the cultural bomb. The effect of the cultural bomb is to annihilate a people's belief in their names, in their languages, in their environment, in their heritage of struggle, in their unity, in their capacities and ultimately in themselves. (3)

In the context of nineteenth-century Haiti, who could say that the end of slavery had solved what Gina Ulysse would refer to as the 'image problem' (2012, 243), with which the Western world has absolutely bombarded Haiti since independence?

The morose but petulant self-justification to be found in Vastey's discursive defenses of Haiti, himself, and the *African race*, therefore, represents a crucial anticipation of the damaging psychological effects of what W.E.B. Du Bois would come to describe as 'double consciousness' in the early twentieth

Colonial Discourse and the Global "Scientific" Sphere

century.[27] For the post-revolutionary world in which Vastey lived, much like that of the post-Civil War U.S., was a world in which the 'problem of the color line' (Du Bois, 1986, 9) occasioned such pervasive existential anxieties, primarily because people of color and many of their allies understood that everything they did in the public sphere could be used as evidence in pseudoscientific debates about "race." Such an idea is wholly demonstrated by British abolitionist William Wilberforce's plea for Vastey's life after news of the death of the Haitian king had reached Europe. Wilberforce urged 'mercy' for Vastey by evoking the trope of "monstrous hybridity." He warned Haiti's new leader by writing, 'Often it has been confidently affirmed by those who would support the old prejudices ... that one of the proofs of [African] inferiority was the violence and cruelty with which they have been disposed to act towards each other.' 'An occasion has lately arisen among you,' he writes, 'for verifying or refuting the charge of which I have been speaking ... by letting the principles of your proceedings be manifest to the world' and allowing 'even guilty men' the 'benefit of a fair and impartial trial' (393). The effect of knowing that one was always being watched and judged by a derisive world—the result of what Du Bois would come to call 'twoness' or the 'sense of always looking at one's self through the eyes of others, of measuring one's soul by the tape of a world that looks on in amused contempt and pity' (12)—was keenly perceived by Vastey, who would make it his mission to combat the lugubrious image of Haiti being produced in the western European and U.S. literary and historical imaginations.

In the end, the condemnation of Vastey, without the kind of global transparency for which Wilberforce argued, is not most unfortunate because it may have confirmed ideas of Haitian and, by degrees, African 'inferiority,' but rather because in Vastey's death was lost a countrymen who understood and was perhaps better able to argue than any other writer of his era precisely how colonial racism had developed into a form of 'Haitian exceptionalism' whose proponents strategically placed Haiti on the margins of both history and humanity, and whose pronouncements many early Haitian authors believed had the capacity to forever distort their country's image in the minds of Haitians themselves.

---

27 Du Bois was actually familiar with at least one of Vastey's works since the English translation of Vastey's *Reflections on the Blacks and Whites* (1817) was listed in the former's *Some Notes on Negro Crime, Particularly in Georgia* (1904, 45).

CHAPTER THREE

Victor Hugo and the Rhetorical Possibilities of "Monstrous Hybridity" in Nineteenth-Century Revolutionary Fiction

'Ces hommes de couleur qui se multiplient avec une rapidité effrayante pourront être un jour bien funeste au repos de la colonie.'

—J. de Loyac, *Aventures de la famille Dolone* (1827)

'...the first moment we come ashore on St. Domingo, our souls shall swell like a sponge in the liquid element; —our bodies shall burst from their fetters, glorious as a curculio from its shell; —our minds shall soar like the car of the aeronaut when its ligaments are cut; in a word, O my brethren, we shall be free!—Our fetters discandied, and our chains dissolved, we shall stand liberated,—redeemed,—emancipated,—and enthralled by the irresistible genius of Universal Emancipation!!!'

—Uriah D'Arcy, *The Black Vampyre: A Legend of St. Domingo* (1819)

Up to this point in our exploration of the transatlantic print culture of the Haitian Revolution, we have focused our attention primarily on texts designed by their authors to be scientific, historical, or biographical. However, the late eighteenth to mid-nineteenth centuries also saw what can only be described as a deluge of representations of the Haitian Revolution that were meant to be fictional.[1] Before 1865, more than 100 novels and plays of the Revolution had been published or staged in the Atlantic World,

---

[1] The first attempt to directly fictionalize events from revolutionary Saint-Domingue in a novel comes in Pierre Anne Louis Maton de la Varenne's *Valdeuil; ou les malheurs d'un habitant de St. Domingue* (1795). An expanding bibliography of novels, poetry, and plays about the Haitian Revolution has been compiled by the author and is available at: www.haitianrevolutionaryfictions.com.

The Rhetorical Possibilities of "Monstrous Hybridity"

written by the well known and the obscure alike. In these fictions, the trope of "monstrous hybridity" continued to loom large, as people of "mixed race" were more often than not portrayed as either desiring of vengeance against the "whites" to whom they were related by birth or by whom they had been enslaved, and as hateful of other people of color and, especially, "negroes," who supposedly reminded them of their degradation.

The French novelist J.-B.C. Berthier published an inflammatory romance of the Haitian Revolution in 1801 entitled *Félix et Léonore; ou les colons malheureux*, in which "racial mixing" was described as not only completely unnatural—'there has never been an error more fatal in its consequences than that which has assimilated two species [*celle qui a assimilé deux espèces*] that are distinguished by the most essential of differences' (2:77)—but as the impetus for revolutionary parricide. Berthier consequently characterizes the free people of color in Saint-Domingue as both the unnatural children of their ostensibly "white" colonist-fathers and as the principle perpetrators of the violence of the Revolution: 'the men of color plunged their daggers into [their father's] breasts. They were the almost universal agents of the massacre of the whites' (2:182). Importantly, Berthier's novel was co-opted in an 1822 plagiarized adaptation published by M.E.V. Laisné de Tours under the title *L'Insurrection du Cap; ou la perfidie d'un noir*, leading to the further dissemination of this version of the "mulatto/a" vengeance narrative.

In *The Daughter of Adoption; A Tale of Modern Times* (1801), a novel that partially takes place in Saint-Domingue, British novelist John Thelwall also characterized 'Mulattoes' as inherently filled with the kind of vengeance that was as terrifying as it was awe-inspiring: 'Mulattoes: a set of people in whose composition vices the most atrocious, and virtues the most rare and disinterested, are frequently so confused and blended, that it is sometimes equally difficult to condemn them with sufficient abhorrence, or applaud them with sufficient ardour' (206). Thelwall, who likely culled the vast majority of his information about Saint-Domingue from the naturalist travel writing of Bryan Edwards and Baron de Wimpffen (Scrivener, Solomonescu et al., 22), uses this understanding of the "monstrous hybridity" of 'mulattoes' to tell us that a 'mulatto' planter's desire for revenge against Lucius Moroon, the 'white' Creole man who had slept with his wife, was the result of the 'unbridled passions of his cast [sic]' (210).[2]

In 1837, Louis Levrault published a short adaptation of German author Heinrich von Kleist's novella *Die Verlobung in Santo Domingo* (1811) or *Betrothal in Santo Domingo*. Levrault's translation/adaptation was called

---

2 For a reading of Thelwall within the context of British writing on the Haitian Revolution, see Hörmann (2010).

From "Monstrous Hybridity" to Enlightenment Literacy

'Tony La Mulâtresse: Légende Haïtienne.'[3] In this abbreviated tale, which was later translated into English and published in the *Yale Literary Magazine* in 1840, Levrault took his description of the perfidy of a 'mulâtresse' beyond simple revenge. Unlike Kleist's protagonist, Toni, who eventually regrets having seduced and then betrayed her 'white' lover, not only for the sake of the Revolution, but to avenge her mother's mistreatment at the hands of a European colonist, Levrault describes his Tony's unabashed 'hatred for all whites' as entirely inharmonious since she had 'a lot of white blood' (86). Levrault uses "monstrous hybridity" to explain both the physical and psychological incongruity of Tony's desire to kill the 'white man' who was her erstwhile lover:

> [h]alf the fanaticism of her race, half vanity, she arranged the death bed [*elle faisait le lit du mort*] of the young white man not only without experiencing any remorse or shame as a result of this atrocious betrayal, but with a sort of pleasure, and with the cruel innocence of a child who torments a poor bird in its cage. (89)

Finally, using a more obviously pseudoscientific angle, U.S. novelist and poet Herman Melville provided his own contribution to the image of "mulattoes" as "monstrous hybrids." In describing a 'mulatto' slave named Francesco, in his indirect representation of the Haitian Revolution, 'Benito Cereno' (1855),[4] Melville's Captain Delano enters into a debate about whether the effects of "miscegenation" were regenerative or degenerative. Delano declares:

> I am glad to see this usher-of-the-golden-rod of yours; the sight refutes an ugly remark once made to me by a Barbados planter, that when a mulatto has a regular European face, look out for him, he is a devil. But see, your steward here has features more regular than King George's of England, and yet there he nods, and bows, and smiles, a king, indeed—the king of kind hearts and polite fellows. (78)

---

3 Kleist's novella had been elsewhere translated into French in 1830 as 'Les Amours de Saint-Domingue.' See Hoffmann (2010, 39).

4 'Benito Cereno' was first published in serial form in 1855 in *Putnam's Monthly*, a respected Northern-based journal that was generally anti-slavery. Jean Fagan Yellin tells us, '*Putnam's* became the first important national magazine to take a stand against slavery,' and in the issues which carried Melville's story were articles against the spread of slavery to new territories as well as an essay that claimed that U.S. democracy would not be complete until slavery was abolished (Yellin, 216). For 'Benito Cereno' as it relates to the Haitian Revolution, see Eric J. Sundquist (1998); Beecher (2007); and Gillman and Gruesz (2011).

The Rhetorical Possibilities of "Monstrous Hybridity"

Melville's ironic characterization of Francesco, whose 'European face,' according to popular understandings of "race," should have made him a 'devil,' continues with Delano's observation that 'it were strange indeed, and not very creditable to us whiteskins, if a little of our blood mixed with the African's should, far from improving the latter's quality, have the sad effect of pouring vitriolic acid into black broth—improving the hue perhaps, but not the wholesomeness' (78). Although at first Delano believes in Francesco's feigned demonstration of politeness and kindness, and therefore that 'a little of our blood' 'improv[es] ... the wholesomeness' of Africans, the deposition included at the end of the tale, meant to authenticate the *true* version of events versus the *false* impressions created by Delano, was designed to remove all doubt for Melville's readers about Francesco's *real* character (and thus, potentially, about the *real* effects of "miscegenation"). The deposition seemingly confirms that the 'blood' of 'whiteskins' mixed with that of an 'African's' would, after all, create a 'vitriolic' combination when we find out that:

> the mulatto steward, Francesco, was of the first band of revolters, that he was, in all things, the creature and tool of the Negro Babo; that, to make his court, he, just before a repast in the cabin, proposed, to the Negro Babo, poisoning a dish for the generous Captain Amasa Delano. (99)

While Berthier, Thelwall, Levrault, and Melville painted people of "mixed race" in these tales as wholly vengeful because of the incompatibility of 'white blood' and 'black blood,' in other nineteenth-century fictions of the Haitian Revolution the monstrosity of hybridity, whether political or "racial", also provided opportunities for people of color to display 'spectacular resistance' (Bhabha, 1994, 172) to authority. Frances Hammond Pratt's *La Belle Zoa, or, The Insurrection of Hayti* (1854) provides such an example of the way in which the trope of "monstrous hybridity" unwittingly gave voice to a radical lexis that fictionalized revolutionaries could use to boldly defy colonial power. In Pratt's novel, all of the famous revolutionary leaders are described as people of "mixed race," including Toussaint Louverture, whose assumed duplicity, the author writes, was ultimately responsible for the success of the slaves: 'By gaining on their side the great Toussaint, a mulatto favored by France, an illegitimate, allied by blood to their nobility, their purpose was easily brought about' (71).

Pratt's characterization of Louverture as being related to the colonists 'by blood' was hardly an outlier since, according to Grégory Pierrot, Louverture was often read as a 'mulatto' in the early nineteenth-century British press: 'For years, articles in the *Times of London*,' Pierrot writes:

> seemed to use randomly the three racial markers of *black*, *negro*, or *mulatto* to characterize Toussaint. Whereas the two first terms were arguably

used indifferently to mean the same thing, the latter could not have been considered equivalent, especially in a context where much of the war opposed three categories referred to as whites, blacks, and mulattoes. (2008, 599)

Furthermore, Pierrot writes that in one such article 'Jean-Jacques Dessalines is mistakenly presented as a freeborn mulatto of a very brutal and ferocious disposition.' The 'mistaken' ideas of "race" presented in the *Times of London* leads Pierrot to conclude that such renderings of Louverture, in particular, approach the figure of the 'tragic mulatto' (599–600). Yet Pierrot's own summation of the descriptions contained in these articles actually brings to mind much more readily the trope of "monstrous hybridity" and the incongruity and instability that nearly always accompanied its evocation. 'When he was fighting the British,' Pierrot writes, 'Toussaint could be a mulatto sometimes because mixed bloods were supposed to be somewhat savage for being somewhat black; ferocious, cruel, and perverse for being mixed; but also intelligent for being somewhat white' (600).

In Pratt's novel, it is not only Louverture who emerges simultaneously as a violent person of "mixed race" and a noble revolutionary leader. The future king of Haiti, Henry Christophe is described by Pratt as both a vengeful 'mulatto' who had a 'deep and absorbing passion' to redress his mother's fatal beating at the hands of her "white" master (30) and as a cogent and inspirational leader capable of leading his people to freedom. In *La Belle Zoa*, the stigmatic vengeance of "mulattoes" often turns into an unwitting celebration of their persuasive intelligence and rhetorical power. The marriage of vengeance and liberation is on full display when Christophe explains the logic behind his revolutionary goals to Lord Briant, an Englishman whom Christophe has just discovered is his paternal uncle. The future king says that after his mother's death, 'I felt a burning thirst for vengeance, a thirst that has deepened with the years, and, modified by classical lore, has ripened into retaliation' (31). He continues to justify the Revolution on the more philosophical grounds of the Enlightenment, however, by stating, 'the laws of nature had not bound the negroes to degradation or stamped them as subjects of abuse.' Christophe even reverses the terms of pseudoscientific characterizations of people of color as degraded when he claims instead that it was, '[t]he French of Hayti [who] were enervated by dissipation, and [were] consequently a feeble race,' concluding that 'the recent oppression of the free mulattoes would enlist them in the cause of freedom' and 'that a war of extermination would be of short duration, and no doubt successful' (33–34).

Pratt's description of Christophe as a vengeful 'mulatto' revolutionary who evokes a 'war of extermination' in one breath and espouses a defiant counter to pseudoscientific debates about "race" in another, speaks to the ways in

The Rhetorical Possibilities of "Monstrous Hybridity"

which representing "monstrous hybridity" seems to have often provided a metaphorical podium for people of color to profess some of the most horrific justifications for murder and torture and some of the most profound rhetorical arguments against the repressions of slavery. The seemingly irreconcilable gulf between Pratt's two very different characterizations of Christophe reflects the ambivalence that is nearly always embedded in "racial" tropes.

There is perhaps no better description than the concept of the *tropicopolitan* for thinking through the ways in which the ambivalence of colonial tropologies and the "racial" stereotypes to which they refer provide opportunities for thinking about and/or imagining radical opposition on the part of the people these stereotypes and tropes describe. In his groundbreaking exploration of the imperial underside of early modern and eighteenth-century literary texts, Srinivas Aravamudan proposed 'the term tropicopolitan as a name for the colonized subject who exists both as a fictive construct of colonial tropology *and* actual resident of tropical space, object of representation *and* agent of resistance.' These 'tropicopolitans,' he writes, 'the residents of the tropics, the bearers of its marks—challenge the developing privilege of Enlightenment cosmopolitans' (4). For Aravamudan, the representation of rebellious colonial subjects, like the eponymous hero in Aphra Behn's *Oroonoko* (1688), who urges the slaves in Surinam to rebellion by telling them, 'we are bought and sold like apes or monkeys to be the sport of women, fools, and cowards, and the support of rogues, runagates, that have abandoned their own countries for rapine, murders, thefts, and villainies' (Behn, 58), presents the opportunity to glimpse the way that stereotyping and tropology work to unwittingly and often eloquently dramatize the many different kinds of opposition within which real world subalterns engaged to destabilize the authority of colonialism. That is to say that even a trope as inflammatory as "monstrous hybridity" allowed for a vocabulary that was capable of matching the rhetoric of the real-life 'agents of resistance' whose actions *did* challenge colonial slavery and racism. Those who used the narrative of "mulatto/a" vengeance to explain the "racial" motivations behind the Haitian Revolution often undermined the very stereotypes about people of color they anxiously sought to repeat by allowing their "monstrous hybrids" to couch their desires for revenge using the same kind of uber-rational challenges to the pseudo-science of "race" that a real-life revolutionary like Vastey had exposed as undergirding plantation slavery.

Drawing inspiration from Aravadmudan's theory, in the first section of this chapter, we will witness how the same kind of voicing of opposition to slavery and defenses of the Haitian Revolution, coupled with unwittingly eloquent and moving expressions of the interiority that accompanied such resistance, as we find in the works of Baron de Vastey, appeared with surprising similarity in the many radical speeches of fictionalized revolutionary people of color to be found in various fictions of the Haitian Revolution. The gloss of several less well-known fictionalized representations of the Haitian Revolution in the first part will set the stage for my argument in the second part, which is that the most poignant example of the confluence between radical justifications for revolutionary violence and monstrous "racial" thinking are presented in Victor Hugo's 1826 *Bug-Jargal*. In Hugo's novel, the speeches of "mixed-race" revolutionaries, who are always depicted as "monstrous hybrids," directly echo the unnervingly violent demand for liberty or death that we find in the revolutionary writing of revolutionaries like Baron de Vastey, Boisrond-Tonnerre, and Dessalines. I suggest that the transatlantic print culture of the Haitian Revolution was not only responsible for Hugo's adoption of the narrative of "mulatto/a" vengeance, but for the articulate language of protest to be found in the dialogue of the people of color who were portrayed as "monstrous hybrids." My interpretation of *Bug-Jargal*, using Stoler's tactic of reading 'along the archival grain' (Stoler, 2010a, 53) to pursue the function of "monstrous hybridity" in revolutionary fictions, will begin with Hugo's imaginative rendering of the real-life revolutionary Biassou, but will ultimately fall on the invented character of Habibrah. In essence, I argue that by giving us a glimpse into Habibrah's psychology, or the inner motivations of his mind, Hugo perhaps unintentionally allowed one of the most monstrous characters in the entire literary tradition of the Haitian Revolution to express the most humanity. My focus is on Habibrah, not only because most of the scholarship dealing with "hybridity" in the novel focuses on the eponymous hero (Bongie, 1998; Bonin, 2008; Grossman, 1986; Toumson 1990; Gaitet, 1997; Prasad, 2009), but because it is actually Habibrah rather than Bug-Jargal who passionately pleads for the recognition of his own human dignity using the language of the transnational abolitionist movement.

In the final section of this chapter, I turn to the problem of translating the "monstrous hybridity" turned radical rejection of slavery found in *Bug-Jargal* by looking at the British author Leitch Ritchie's abolitionist adaptation of the novel into *The Slave-King*. Here, I suggest that even abolitionist texts that betrayed distinct sympathies for slaves and other people of color often also betrayed latent beliefs in "monstrous hybridity" and the "mulatto/a" vengeance narrative of the Haitian Revolution that this trope supported.

As the many fictions under consideration in this chapter will reveal, anxieties about the righteousness of the Haitian Revolution most readily surface in the figure of the "monstrous hybrid," who was ambivalently portrayed as at once capable of the most outrageous crimes and the most daring displays of humanity, the most heinous justifications of parricidal revenge and the most moving rhetoric of revolution. The language of "hybridity," symbolized by the transitive nature of these curiously defamatory and celebratory descriptions of people of color, thus call forth the very incongruity, uncertainty, and ambivalence that characterized the events of the Haitian Revolution themselves.

*

In a 1795 'failed play' (L. Hunt, 173) entitled *Le Blanc et Le Noir*, the storied French playwright Charles Antoine Guillaume Pigault-Lebrun, who once said that this work had only 'aroused a desperate silence' (L. Hunt, 173), dramatizes the collision between the fictional revolutionaries' confrontation with Enlightenment logic and the slaves' potential for enacting revenge. In the preface to the 1796 published version of the play, Pigault-Lebrun implicitly evokes the literacy narrative of the Revolution: 'I read Raynal, and then I wrote this work' (7). This Raynalian frame, coupled with the "hybridity" implied by the play's title—'Black and White'—allows us to view the fictional slave Télémaque as a 'tropicopolitan' whose revolutionary rhetoric challenges the privileges Europeans had claimed for themselves by virtue of having been born "white." At the same time, the French playwright's portrayal evokes the kind of "monstrous hybridity" to be found in the "mulatto/a" vengeance narrative of the Haitian Revolution. Télémaque tells his master:

> Today I am still a degraded being [*un être dégradé*], even though my soul, great and proud, is at last independent ... a ray of light has been cast on my violated and ignored rights: I have yielded to the necessity of avenging my blood, which has just been flowing under a merciless whip. (21)

Despite the inhumanity of the 'merciless whip' to which he has recently been subjected, Télémaque reveals that his master's son, Beauval *fils*, who is an admirer of Raynal and Rousseau—he calls them 'those friends of virtue, the world's benefactors' (51)—'taught me how to speak, to think' (22). As a result of learning how to think and talk, Télémaque can phrase his opposition to slavery using the expression of one of the most famous 'tropicopolitans' in all of Western literature. After describing the wrongs of slavery, Télémaque repeats almost verbatim the words of Voltaire's 'Negro in Surinam' from *Candide* (1759): 'Europeans, it is at this price that you eat sugar' [*Européens, c'est à ce prix que vous mangez du sucre*] (Pigault-Lebrun, 25).[5]

---

5 One of the most famous passages in all of Voltaire's *œuvre*, the 'Negro in Surinam,' presents Candide with the opportunity to renounce Pangloss's Leibnitzian optimism when he sees a 'negro' slave hanging from a tree who has been tortured based on the rules for slave punishments set forth in Louis XIV's *Code noir*. The slave tells Candide: 'When we are working in the sugar refinery, and when the mill catches our finger, they cut off our hand; when we want to run away, they cut off our leg: I found myself in both

From "Monstrous Hybridity" to Enlightenment Literacy

Pointing out that Europeans had subjugated people of color in order to procure something as trivial (but culturally important) as sugar does the work of undermining the humanism that was supposed to have undergirded the Enlightenment. Yet, unlike Voltaire's 'negro,' who sighs his protest against slavery in a language of fatalist resignation, Télémaque more fully becomes the figure of the "monstrous hybrid" when he intermingles his desire for justice with a grammar of revenge. Far from surrendering to his fate, Télémaque tells the slaves, 'our ancestors, our friends, our women, our children, Africa at last, demand vengeance, and have not yet been avenged,' and he urges the slaves to rebel assuring them, 'I will lead you to vengeance and to liberty' (88). The blurred line between using violence to achieve slave liberation and using it to achieve personal vengeance against particular slaveholders causes Télémaque subsequently to reflect on the contradictions of the European Enlightenment's relationship to encouraging slave rebellion in the first place. At the end of the play, we find out that Télémaque's desire for vengeance has, indeed, been tempered by his recognition that the violence he has promoted in the name of liberty is opposed to the humanity he hopes to procure for people of color. The play essentially ends with Télémaque calling off the revolt:

> Brave companions, let us hasten to prove to our enemies that idleness, thievery, and injustice have not put these weapons into our hands ... Go back to the plain, fertilize the fields that we have just devastated, and perhaps the example of Beauval, by instructing the Colonists about their true interests, will force them to at last secure their fortunes with justice and humanity [*les determiner enfin à consolider leur fortune par la justice et l'humanité*]. (123)[6]

cases. It is at this price that you eat sugar in Europe [*C'est à ce prix que vous mangez du sucre en Europe*] ... The Dutch missionaries who converted me told me every Sunday that we were all children of Adam, whites and blacks ... Now you will have to admit that a person could not abuse his relatives in a more horrible manner' (123).

6 Similar scenes in which Enlightenment literacy is ultimately able to temper revolutionary vengeance abound throughout the literary history of the Haitian Revolution. One noteworthy example of this tendency to make a slave backtrack on his desire for liberty comes in volume three of Harvey Sinclair's *A Peep at the World: or, the Children of Providence, a novel*. In this work, a 'noble' slave named Marco draws inspiration for rebellious imaginings from the life of Toussaint Louverture. The narrator writes: 'The actions of Toussaint, the heroic black at St. Domingo, were filling all orders of men with wonder and admiration. Marco, though far advanced in years, prided himself in having led armies to the field. He had read as much as he could: a hero of *any* country excited his veneration; but the deeds of one of his own colour agitated him to a madness of enthusiasm which no bounds could control. The idea of pursuing the traces marked out by Toussaint employed his thoughts by day, his dreams by night. Hence then his sullen

The Rhetorical Possibilities of "Monstrous Hybridity"

By putting these words of revolutionary recantation into the mouth of a 'negro' slave, Pigault-Lebrun is able to write into his play the actual resistance that took place in Saint-Domingue and ostensibly justify its violent quality in the hopes of discouraging further slavery at the same time as he critiques such violence as being ultimately non-productive. The author's ambivalence about justifying slave violence comes to light when he appears to realize that representing a violent reality from the past for the purposes of didacticism in the present has a far different effect than prognosticating or seeming to encourage a violent reality in the present in order to produce a material change for the future. The effect of Pigault-Lebrun's ambivalence is made manifest when he has Télémaque challenge the logic of the very unpopular actual violence of the Revolution. The play suggests that though the slaves-turned-revolutionaries may have had justice on their side, it was they who were responsible for setting a more humane example for the inhumane colonists. The playwright's skepticism about the Revolution as a vehicle that could be used to produce humanistic changes is ultimately illustrated by his transformation of Télémaque from the figure of the "monstrous hybrid" into that other famous and ubiquitous figure to be found in nineteenth-century colonial literature—that of the 'bon nègre' or 'the good negro' (Hoffmann, 1973, 138) who patiently waits to be freed from slavery rather than violently freeing himself.

Pigault-Lebrun's oscillation demonstrates the very fact that even though the insurrection in Saint-Domingue was a justifiable event for many eighteenth- and nineteenth-century "philanthropists," its characteristic violence called forth a variety of ambivalent and often contradictory emotions for people who were less involved in anti-slavery activism. Such ambivalence and contradiction are summed up by Beauval *fils*'s desire to both help the slaves and to save the life of his father, who had reportedly been a cruel master. Beauval asks Télémaque if supporting the ultimate goal of the revolutionaries to free the slaves in Saint-Domingue would require him to become parricidal, concluding, 'Here I am, then, between my father and the blacks! ... Inspire me, my God,' he supplicates, 'my heart is innocent, but the only choices I have are crimes' (100).

"Monstrous hybridity," its crimes, and the irresolute nature of revolutionary violence are more explicitly on display in an 1824 play by Charles de Rémusat entitled *L'Habitation de Saint-Domingue*, which according to

deportment; hence his gloomy reserve. Mighty plans were resolving in his bosom; and a demeanour of humbleness could hardly be expected from the man, full of the big idea of rivaling the glories of the hero of St. Domingo' (3:155). The narrator tells us, however, that his slave, Marco, eventually '*dropped* the design' since 'His God, he said, would never prosper an action of ingratitude' (3:156).

Doris Kadish, was never staged or published during its author's lifetime (Kadish, 2008, xi). Rémusat portrays the behavior of a 'negro' slave named Timur as simultaneously vengeful and benevolent, heroic and atrocious. The play, which takes place on the Valombre plantation in Saint-Domingue, revolves around Timur's desire for revenge against Léon, his master's son, who raped Timur's love interest, a slave named Hélène. Timur's figurative hybridity is marked by his fellow slaves' accusation that although, in fact, described as a 'Congo black,' he had, perhaps, turned 'white in order to become a master' [*Es-tu un blanc pour être le maître*] (146) and was therefore not a 'good black, a pure one,' after all, since he refused to indiscriminately kill 'whites' (147).

Though Timur is filled with vengeance, when he justifies not immediately killing Léon by saying that he wants to force his rival to suffer first (147–48), Rémusat also allows Timur to express his indignation at the planters in a language reminiscent of the kinds of justification for revolutionary violence that we find equally in European Enlightenment thought, the culture of discursive resistance that sprung up in and around Saint-Domingue by people like Raimond, Rigaud, and Louverture, and in the nineteenth-century Haitian writing of Boisrond-Tonnerre, Vastey, and Dessalines. Timur challenges the numerical logic of slavery itself, for instance, when the budding revolutionary reminds his followers that the slaves vastly outnumber the colonists and that their enslavement could therefore only endure as long as they chose to remain in that condition: 'we are twenty against one,' Timur tells the slaves, 'It is they who are our prisoners, our slaves, our dogs' (51). Timur continues by confronting a logic of slavery that would liken people of color to domestic animals who were fated to serve "whites" rather than to wild animals whose only desire was to roam free: 'Timid animals born to serve, sleep, and die. You could have been the bison galloping through the savannas,' he argues:

> And yet you are only the ox who exhausts himself in labor, who grazes in the stable and nourishes with his own flesh the one who has kept him down! Look at what they've made you: your backs are made only for carrying a load, your arms only for swinging a pickaxe, and your shoulders only to feel the sting of the whip! So be it! Keep your shackles! In fact, pass them down to your children, to your African brothers, who, thanks to you, will keep coming, eternally, to replace you like a herd that the plague has devastated. (57)

Here, using a point of reference that carries the philosophical undertones of Jean-Jacques Rousseau, Timur challenges the slaves to alter their own conditions by suggesting that slavery was a choice the slave had to choose to *unmake*.

The Rhetorical Possibilities of "Monstrous Hybridity"

In his *Discours sur l'origine et les fondements de l'inégalité parmi les hommes* (1755), Rousseau claimed that human beings could never become slaves of any sort without their implicit consent. Freedom and the violent desire for its preservation was, for Rousseau, as natural to humans as it was to wild animals:

> As an unbroken steed bristles his mane, paws the ground with his hoof, and struggles violently at the mere approach of the bit, while a trained horse patiently endures the whip and the spur, barbarous man does not bow his head for the yoke that civilized man bears without a murmur, and he prefers the most stormy liberty to tranquil subjection ... when I see animals born free and abhorring captivity break their heads against the bars of their prison, when I see multitudes of utterly naked savages scorn European pleasures and brave hunger, fire, sword, and death, simply to preserve their independence, I sense that it is inappropriate for slaves to reason about liberty. (1992, 60)

Nevertheless, Timur makes himself exactly the kind of slave who 'reasons about liberty' when he tells his followers that he viewed his arrival on shore after a horrendous experience of the middle passage as a kind of 'deliverance,' since he 'thought of my brothers I would there find, who seemed to be waiting for me to help them wreak their vengeance' (58). There is an immediate way in which we can view both Pigault-Lebrun and Rémusat's portrayals of slaves, whose eloquent rhetorics of justice appear incongruous next to the physical violence offered by their desires for vengeance/freedom, as an interpretive legend that can teach us how to read the discursive opposition of *real-life* people of color like Vastey. It is precisely the *real-life* counter to colonialism and slavery mounted by Vastey that would end up being tropicalized into "monstrous hybridity" and therefore paradoxically serve rather than destroy the narrative of "mulatto/a" vengeance.

Later in the nineteenth century, similar ambivalences about the potential dangers of "monstrous hybridity" would surface in Alexandre Dumas's adventure novel *Georges* (1843).[7] In this text, Dumas's character of "mixed race," a free person of color named Georges Munier who comes from a prominent slave holding family in Ile de France (present-day Mauritius) at first attempts to use the Enlightenment's infinite perfectibility of man to achieve equality with the "white" French colonists. Once Georges fails there, he decides to turn that Enlightenment hermeneutic into a revolutionary discourse involving both violent revenge against the colonists who had discriminated against him and raising the slaves to rebellion, despite

---

[7] In the nineteenth century a lawsuit was brought against Dumas by those who claimed he had plagiarized *Georges* (1843) (see Racault, 142).

his own property interest in keeping them in a state of slavery. Dumas's portrayal of Georges led the 1903 English translator of the novel to refer to Dumas himself as an 'inspired mulatto' given that he faced 'every obstacle and insult with irrepressible energy and spirit' exactly like his character (qtd. in Hoffmann, 2003b, 10),[8] but there is a way in which such 'mulatto' inspirations always turned into evidence not of their unconquerable 'spirit' but of their unconscionable vengeance. In many ways, what Dumas's character Georges offers us is a repressed "mulatto/a" vengeance narrative of the Haitian Revolution symbolized by the incongruity of a former slaveholder leading a slave rebellion.

Both Patrick Girard and Wernor Sollors have suggested in passing mention of *Georges* that '[p]erhaps Dumas's île de France was a symbolic stand-in for another island to which the writer traced his own roots ... "Saint-Domingue" ... forever associated with the revolution undertaken by people of color in the name of liberty' (Sollors, 2007, xxi; Patrick Girard, 205), an observation that is strengthened by the fact that Dumas explicitly references Haiti and the Revolution at several different junctures in the text. The first overt reference to the Revolution comes when a former slave of Georges' named Laïza gives a speech to the maroons and slaves of other plantations in order to convince them that because of the Haitian Revolution liberty was not only something that they should try to attain, but something that they could attain. Laïza tells the slaves:

> once upon a time there was an island where all the slaves wanted to be free; together they rose up and they made it happen. This island used to be called Saint-Domingue; at this time, it is called Haiti ... Let's do what they did, and we will be free like them. (312)

Like many of the Haitian Revolution's other 'tropicopolitans,' Laïza attributes the freedom of slaves in Haiti to the slaves' 'will' to attain it, paralleling Christopher L. Miller's contention that 'the most important "abolitionists" in the French Atlantic were these slaves who freed themselves in massive numbers before anyone could "emancipate" them with a written decree' (2008, 86). Laïza tells Nazim that the slaves of Ile de France vastly outnumber the colonists and would therefore likely be victorious: 'There are twelve thousand of them and eighty thousand of us. And the day that we count, they will be lost' (144). What the slaves needed, therefore, was

---

8 Alexandre Dumas (1802–70) had direct ties to Haiti and was considered by many in the nineteenth century to be of "mixed race" since he was the grandson of the marquis Antoine-Alexandre Davy de la Pailleterie and a "black" slave from Trou-Jérémie in Saint-Domingue named Louise-Cessette Dumas. The marquis's son had reportedly been a celebrated general in the Napoleonic army.

The Rhetorical Possibilities of "Monstrous Hybridity"

a leader, a 'Black Spartacus" to awaken the masses and convince them of this truth. The passage in the novel where Georges implores his own father, Pierre Munier, to become the head of the slave militia bears the influence of the "Black Spartacus" imagery that has been so intimately associated with the Haitian Revolution, demonstrating the near-apocryphal status of this legend. Georges says, 'Father ... there they are, the Negroes, and they are awaiting a leader' (61).

While a certain uneasiness with the violence of the Haitian Revolution is what ultimately leads to fissures in the heroic portrayal of "monstrous hybrids" turned 'tropicopolitans' in the works of Pigault-Lebrun, Pratt, and Rémusat, it was the political divisions of nineteenth-century Haiti itself that provided the referential cracks *vis-à-vis* any justification for the Haitian Revolution in *Georges*.[9] A jealous slave named Antonio, mocking Laïza's reference to and reverence for Haiti, provides his own interpretation of the Caribbean island nation when he states with irony:

> Yes ... yes, Laïza has spoken the truth; I have heard tell that there is, beyond Africa, far, far away, where the sun sets, a big island where all the negroes are kings. But, on my own island just as on Laïza's island, in the kingdom of animals just as in the kingdom of men, there was an elected leader, but only one. (313)

Antonio's statement provides an implicit dig at Haiti's government by suggesting that the country could not be properly governed because all of its inhabitants believed that they were 'kings.' After Antonio's commentary, a debate ensues over who should be the leader of the revolt: the slaves or the free people of color.

This debate carries distinct undertones of popular Haitian revolutionary history concerning the rift between the generals André Rigaud (who had never been a slave) and Toussaint Louverture (who had been enslaved in Saint-Domingue). It is clear that Antonio wants to be the leader of the revolution when he states, 'He who is worthy of being our leader ... is the man who has lived with whites and with blacks; the man who possesses the

---

9 Though Dumas is not traditionally thought of as anti-slavery, and still less as an abolitionist, he did write a letter to the famous Martinican abolitionist and editor of the anti-slavery organ, *Revue des colonies*, to say, 'All of my sympathies ... are instinctively and nationally for the adversaries of the principals that the sirs of the *Revue coloniale* defend [the *Revue coloniale* was a pro-slavery organ to which the *Revue des colonies* was opposed]; that is exactly what I want everyone to know, not simply in France, but everywhere where I count brothers of race and friends of color' (qtd. in Hoffmann, 2003a, 477). This letter was previously printed in an English translation in *Five French Negro Authors* (1939), edited by Mercer Cook.

blood of the one and the other; the man who, being free, will sacrifice his liberty' (313). Antonio posits his status as a slave, as well as his experience with 'whites' and his blood connection to them as a traditional 'mulatto,' as that which will render him capable of understanding how best to defeat the colonists at their own game of domination. He is both shocked and dismayed when Laïza and the slaves nominate Georges, who has never been a slave, for the position instead. The seeds of Antonio's betrayal of the revolutionary cause are born at this moment and will ultimately lead to the failure of the colonial African version of the Haitian Revolution.

When Georges assumes leadership of the rebellion, the narrator tells us, 'only two days separated him from the catastrophe that would make of him another Toussaint Louverture or a new Pétion' (318). Hoffmann has written of this direct allusion to a 'black' and a 'mulatto' Haitian revolutionary leader, respectively:

> The allusion is clear: in the struggle for the independence of Haiti, Toussaint Louverture fails; having made the mistake of trusting Napoleon's word, he was sent to die in a dungeon of the Jura. Alexandre Pétion, on the other hand, was proclaimed president of the Republic (or more exactly of the southern part of the island) in 1807. (2003b, 496)

At the end of the novel, in any event, it is unclear whether we should view Georges as a Louverture or a Pétion (or even what it might mean to be one or the other) since he escapes from the island on a slave ship, of all things, and ultimately leaves his followers in a state of slavery. Even if Georges has obtained personal revenge against his enemies, he has done nothing to change the material condition of the slaves. What we can take away from the text may be the fact that the betrayals Georges experiences, first by Antonio, a supposed ally, then by his own brother, and next by his friend, Lord Murrey, reflect some of the larger epistemological problems of revolution, where genealogical affiliation, similar class, or even stated camaraderie and devotion did not often determine true allegiances. We might say that the plot of *Georges* essentially follows the kaleidoscopic complexities of the loyalties, allegiances, and motives of Haitian revolutionary figures like Toussaint Louverture, André Rigaud, Jean-Jacques Dessalines, Henry Christophe, and even Vincent Ogé.

*

While almost all of the plays and novels written by those whom Hoffmann might call the many 'scribblers' of the Haitian Revolution (2009, 341), were propelled into obscurity as the nineteenth century progressed, the

The Rhetorical Possibilities of "Monstrous Hybridity"

most sustained, influential, and widely read fictionalization of the Haitian Revolution in which the dynamic nature of "monstrous hybridity" is on display is undoubtedly Victor Hugo's novel, *Bug-Jargal* (1826). Hugo's novel tells the tale of a young French military captain, Léopold D'Auverney, who leads a battalion of soldiers during the early days of the insurrection in Saint-Domingue. The novel centers on his troubled relationship with the noble slave Pierrot, whom we later learn is actually Bug-Jargal (a fictional leader of the Haitian Revolution). At first, Léopold believes that Pierrot is an unfortunate slave who has become the victim of his uncle's ire, but later he comes to think that Pierrot has actually kidnapped and then raped his wife, Marie, not to mention that he also believes Pierrot has killed his uncle (Pierrot's master) and his baby cousin. It is only as the story unfolds that Léopold discovers that Pierrot is actually Bug-Jargal, that it is he who has saved the life of Marie and the baby, and that Pierrot/Bug has remained a loyal friend to him all along, having actually protected Léopold and preserved his life at several junctures. Ultimately, the fact that Bug-Jargal puts his life in danger to save Léopold provides the final catalyst for the novel's ending, when one of Léopold's soldiers mistakenly kills Bug.

Léopold recites these events to a fascinated audience of soldiers, along with a detailed account of his imprisonment by the revolutionary figures Biassou, Rigaud, and the deformed '*nain*' or dwarf Habibrah, all described as having varying degrees of "mixed blood." Léopold's captivity narrative provides this protagonist with the opportunity to recount his impressions concerning the "monstrous hybridity" of these "mulatto" revolutionaries. Léopold's confusion about both the identities and the loyalties of various people of color, especially "mulattoes," registers the kind of epistemic uncertainty that came from not knowing to which side of the Revolution any particular person might belong at any particular moment, coupled with the kind of instability provoked by popular ideas about people with "mixed blood" that Hugo had imbibed from his myriad sources. *Bug-Jargal* anxiously portrays people of color as capable of assuming multiple political identities, nations, languages, cultures, religions, and even "races." This ability to transform themselves according to the circumstances is coded as monstrous by Léopold, who is the primary character to suffer as a result of his inability to properly decode the political loyalties and identities of various people of color.

The language of prejudice used to describe the "mixed race" characters in *Bug-Jargal* has led Roger Toumson to refer to the novel as wholly 'anti-mulatto' (Toumson, 79). Chris Bongie appears to agree with Toumson's assessment when he writes, 'Hugo rigorously identifies all mixed-race characters in negative terms' (Bongie, 1998, 238). More recently, Pratima Prasad has touched upon the influence of pseudoscience on Hugo's 'negative' depictions of 'mulattoes' in maintaining that the 'questionable morality [of Habibrah and Biassou] stems directly from the indeterminacy of their race' (135). Not all of the critics who have discussed *Bug-Jargal* over the years have believed in the connection between "race" and the behavior of the "mulatto" characters, however. Hoffmann, whose writings on *Bug-Jargal* remain perhaps the most influential, agrees that all three of the demonic revolutionary figures in the novel are described as 'Mulattoes,' but he contends that we should not extrapolate too much about 'Mulatto' biology from these wicked portrayals. Hoffmann writes, 'In the end, if Hugo does not let us forget that in *Bug-Jargal* the ill-intentioned protagonists are Mulattoes, he does not discuss at length their physical appearance, and does not seem to directly impute their vices to their ethnotype' (1996, 7).[10]

Although, on the contrary, I do find that Hugo attributes the 'ill-intention[s]' of his 'protagonists' to their 'ethnotype,' the physiological fatalism that underlays Hugo's vision of 'Mulattoes' is actually not the most important function of "hybridity" in this text. Instead, the "hybridity" of Hugo's characters of "mixed race" marks the rhetorical possibilities of justifiable transgression with respect to the slaves as inherent to the trope of "monstrous hybridity" itself.

Despite their differing opinions on the meaning of the "mulatto" in *Bug-Jargal*, the question that no critic has yet asked is why, in a novel that many agree essentially makes all people of "mixed race" out to be evil, parricidal, and duplicitous, these are the characters whom Hugo has permitted to espouse the most moving revolutionary motifs and the most dejected anti-racism pathos. Even with all of the critical focus on the meaning of "race" in *Bug-Jargal*, what still has yet to be fundamentally examined is how the epistemological problems symbolized by these revolutionaries not only produced a distinct ambivalence about the simultaneously frightening and fascinating camouflage of "hybridity," but engendered some of the most unwittingly eloquent challenges to slavery. As Prasad observes in passing in what is actually a study of the character Bug-Jargal, 'in his grandiose rhetoric and his call to violent action, it is Biassou and not Bug-Jargal who comes closer to incarnating the "black Spartacus" whose coming was prophesied by eighteenth-century writers' (137). Chris Bongie, who focuses most of his energy on Biassou in his own study of the novel,

---

10 Many critics have also read *Bug-Jargal* as embodying some form of "racial" ambiguity, but mostly to positive effect. In *The Early Novels of Victor Hugo*, Catherine Grossman has argued that the character Bug-Jargal represents neither "blackness" nor "whiteness" but instead a utopian ideal, and that 'through his genuinely revolutionary goal of unity in diversity," he 'threatens those villains of either race who espouse an autocratic, hegemonic ideal' (105).

The Rhetorical Possibilities of "Monstrous Hybridity"

similarly argues that Habibrah's own speech can be read as an 'empowering act of self-representation, in which alienating "white masks" are once and for all dropped and the authentic decolonized "soul" makes itself visible, with the help of a little "necessary violence"' (1998, 257). Yet if these critics were able to recognize the relationship between the speeches and what we now call postcolonial thought, what we have not been told is why it is the seemingly unsympathetic characters of Biassou and Habibrah, rather than the nobly painted Bug-Jargal, who, in two of the most elegantly disturbing poetics of homicide, most effectively lament the psychological effects of slavery and racism. In other words, I am asking how it is that Hugo, whom we can hardly have claimed was an abolitionist or an anti-slavery activist at the time he wrote *Bug-Jargal*, was able to so forcefully mimic and, in some ways, even outmatch, the proto-postcolonial revolutionary writings of someone as artful and convincing as Baron de Vastey?

If, as many critics have shown, Hugo borrowed from several prominent histories of the Haitian Revolution to provide the historical backdrop for *Bug-Jargal*, I contend that the postcolonial-sounding content of the revolutionary monologues in question is likewise related to the representations and actual expressions of the *real-life* revolutionaries depicted in many of these same sources. The extensive research done by previous scholars on the historical sources of *Bug-Jargal*, especially the work of Jacques de Cauna, allows us to identify Hugo's known influences as some of the most ardent spreaders of the trope of "monstrous hybridity" and the narrative of "mulatto/a" vengeance it implies.[11] Hugo's rendition of the trope of "monstrous hybridity" as capable of producing rationalities for revolutionary violence also resembles many other representations of the Revolution from the period, even those Hugo almost certainly never read. The idea that rebellion was one of the monstrous, but logical, consequences of enslaving or mistreating the "mulatto" as a person who was genealogically related to both "whites" and "negroes," was constantly repeated in the nineteenth century, making tracing its genesis to any given source fraught with the problems of derivation that are practically inimical to the transatlantic print culture of the Haitian Revolution. It would probably be more accurate to say, then, that where the "mulatto" was concerned, Hugo's novel, like nearly all early nineteenth-century representations of the Haitian Revolution,

---

11 De Cauna's important article 'Les Sources historiques de *Bug-Jargal*' reveals that Hugo borrowed considerably from Bryan Edwards, Colonel Malenfant, Michel-Étienne Descourtilz, and Jean-Philippe Garran de Coulon (1985, 29). More recent research by Bongie acknowledges that in addition to Pamphile de Lacroix, certain passages of *Bug-Jargal* are directly linked to the writing of Antoine Dalmas (Bongie, 1998, 25), and possibly even the colonist Gros (Bongie, 2004, 153).

bears a much more fluid rather than constant relationship to the ideas about "race" in circulation in early nineteenth-century writing about the Haitian Revolution.

Understanding the meaning of Hugo's "mixed-race" revolutionaries requires much more than reading *Bug-Jargal* side-by-side with other works on the topic from the era. The historical works painstakingly identified as some of the sources for Bug-Jargal by Etienne, de Cauna, and Bongie were part of an ethos of the Haitian Revolution, which demands that this body of writing be read at the same time as the novel, not with an eye to plagiarism, but with an eye to dialogism.

Reading the works that make up the literary history of the Haitian Revolution as part of a larger conversation about "race" and revolution taking place within the Atlantic World produces not just a literary genealogy of *Bug-Jargal*, but a "racial" and revolutionary legend for understanding how the narrative of "mulatto/a" vengeance was experiencing an almost unprecedented level of textual simultaneity that we might call an 'imagined community' (Anderson, 1983, 7). This textual 'community' would be based not on a culture of romanticism, but on a culture of the Haitian Revolution. Recognizing Hugo's work less as a product of a French romantic imagination that was in many ways obsessed with 'miscegenation' (Prasad, 45), and more as part of transatlantic print culture of the Haitian Revolution, provides a detailed road map for understanding how the pseudoscientific understandings of "race" first found in naturalist travel writing moved from the relatively privileged world of the educated into the mainstream of the nineteenth-century Atlantic World *because* of the Haitian Revolution itself rather than solely because of writings that had been published about it. Thus, although pointing out the scenes in Hugo's novel that may have been directly influenced by earlier writing on the Haitian Revolution continues to provide new and intriguing information about the genesis of *Bug-Jargal*, what will be examined here is how the widespread understanding of "mixed-race" revolutionaries as degraded, vengeful and parricidal in one of the most widely read fictions of the genre aided the dissemination of the "mulatto/a" vengeance narrative.

Hugo explains that the term *griffe*, for example, used in *Bug-Jargal* to describe Habibrah, refers to the work of Moreau de Saint-Méry. In one of his extremely influential footnotes, Hugo writes that Moreau de Saint-Méry 'had arranged into generic types [*espèces génériques*] the different skin colors [*teintes*] that are present within the mixtures of the population of color.'[12]

---

12 Hugo owes the entirety of his formal vocabulary for his "racial" taxonomies to Moreau de Saint-Méry by way of Pamphile de Lacroix, who, as Bongie has observed, was Hugo's 'single most important source of information about Saint-Domingue' (2004,

The Rhetorical Possibilities of "Monstrous Hybridity"

Hugo further explained Moreau de Saint-Méry's "racial" classificatory system by writing that 'according to this system, all men who do not have eight parts of whiteness are said to be black' [*tout homme qui n'a point huit parties de blanc est reputé noir*] and,

> Going from this color to white, we can distinguish nine main stocks [*souches*], that have within them many varieties according to whether they have retained more or less parts of one or the other color. These main types are the *sacatra*, the *griffe*, the *marabout*, the *mulatto*, the *quadroon*, the *métis*, the *mamelouc*, the *octoroon* [*quarteronné*], and the *mixed-blood* [*sang-mêlé*]. (30)[13]

According to Hugo, Moreau de Saint-Méry had arrived at these classifications by 'elaborat[ing] upon the system of Franklin' (29). Although Sollors observes that he has 'not been able to find such a system' in the works of Benjamin Franklin (1997, 459), the American revolutionist did discuss the topic of 'molattoes' using a narrative of "monstrous hybridity." In a brief letter written to the editor of the *Pennsylvania Gazette* on August 30, 1733, Franklin wrote:

> It is observed concerning the Generation of Molattoes that they are seldom well belov'd either by the Whites or the Blacks. Their Approach towards Whiteness, makes them look back with some kind of Scorn upon the Colour they seem to have left, while the Negroes, who do not think them better than themselves, return their Contempt with Interest; And the Whites, who respect them no Whit the more for the nearer Affinity in Colour, are apt to regard their Behaviour as too bold and assuming, and bordering upon Impudence. As they are next to Negroes, and but just above 'em, they are terribly afraid of being thought Negroes, and therefore avoid as much as possible their Company or Commerce: and Whitefolks are as little fond of the Company of Molattoes.

Franklin signed this piece, in which he refers to '*Molatto gentlemen*' as 'monstrously ridiculous,' with the pseudonym 'Blackamore.' David Waldstreicher has written that such a moniker compares the 'self-identified author, a mechanic, with a happy slave, content to remain in a subordinate

---

302). Victor Hugo's brother, Jean-Abel, would reprint this passage verbatim in his *France pittoresque: ou description pittoresque, topographique et statistique des départements et colonies de la France* (1835, 3:293); and the passage was also repeated in translation several decades later in John Relly Beard's widely referenced *The Life of Toussaint L'Ouverture* (1853, 321–24).

13 Hugo directly lifted the majority of the language for this explanatory footnote from Lacroix's *Mémoire pour servir à l'histoire de la révolution de Saint-Domingue* (1819, ix–x).

position' and that the essay itself 'turned race into a metaphor for social order' (2004, 97–98). Elsewhere, Waldstreicher has argued that 'Mulattoes' were a 'metaphor for those of intermediate or mutating status: people putting on airs or missing their cues' (2011).[14] More than that, Franklin's description evokes the same "monstrous hybridity" of naturalist travel writing that would have "mulattoes" holding equal scorn for both "whites" and "blacks."

If Hugo's description of Habibrah bespeaks the same general disdain for the 'mutating status' of 'mulattoes' as Franklin's own, it also stirs up one of the archetypal stereotypes of "monstrous hybridity," namely, that "pure blacks" and those of "mixed race" had an innate hatred or animosity for one another. Hugo evokes such debates when he has the noble Bug-Jargal state, as if to explain the excesses of the slave Habibrah: 'How did I not predict such perfidy? That's not a black, it's a mulatto' (169). Bug's suggestion that the "mulattoes" were responsible for the ferocious character of the Revolution (153) not only 'scapegoats the mulatto' (Bongie, 2004, 215), but makes internal color prejudice among the Haitian revolutionists responsible for the violent quality of the Revolution rather than slavery and colonialism.

On that point, Bug argues that the cruelty of the "mulatto" revolutionaries was directly responsible for the wholesale violence of the colonists. 'How could you have stuck to these horrible retaliations?' Bug asks. 'Listen to me, Jean Biassou; it is these cruel acts that will lose for us our just cause ... Why these massacres that obligate the whites to use ferocity? Why still use these tricks [*jongleries*] in order to excite the furor of our miserable comrades, who are already far too exasperated?' (153). Not only is the brutality of the revolutionists transformed from being about liberty to being about revenge, but the genocidal reaction of the French colonists to the onset of revolution is characterized as the logical response to the characteristic callousness of the slaves of "mixed race" rather than as merely the slaveholder's further perpetuation of the depredations of slavery. More importantly, that Hugo makes these statements of blame come from the eponymous hero and not from Léopold, suggests to me that Hugo also 'scapegoats' Bug-Jargal.

Franklin and Moreau de Saint-Méry were hardly alone among Hugo's sources in deploying the kind of "racial" determinism that would end up finding its way into descriptions of "mulatto" revolutionaries in *Bug-Jargal*. In his history of the Haitian Revolution, for example, Lacroix puts the utmost importance into properly "racially" identifying people so as to properly reveal

---

14 Despite these unflattering descriptions of people of "mixed race," like his good friend Moreau de Saint-Méry, Franklin reportedly acknowledged that he had many of his own mistresses of color, and one of them was possibly Barbara, his 'servant,' sometimes called his 'slave,' who was also, by some accounts, allegedly the mother of Franklin's son William (see Reuter, 146; Ford, 13).

The Rhetorical Possibilities of "Monstrous Hybridity"

their personalities, behaviors, and political and personal loyalties. Lacroix opens his text with a very precise "racial" taxonomy of the colony, stating that in order to avoid any errors in "racial" classifications and 'to distinguish and immediately visually demonstrate [*montrer de suite à l'oeil*] the color of individuals, I have printed in CAPITAL LETTERS the names of the blacks, in *italics* those of the mixed-bloods [*sang-mêlés*], and as normal text the names of whites' (ix). According to Lacroix's typography, in which only "whiteness" was normative and unmarked, "race" or skin color was so importantly (but not necessarily apparently) operative in Saint-Domingue as to require altered script in order to prevent the reader from making the kinds of mistake in classification the original developers of "racial" taxonomies had anxiously sought to avoid. The frank certainty about "racial" categorization with which Lacroix's text was framed at the outset is, however, undermined by the ability of the 'sang-mêlés' to, in his own words, 'dissimulate and hate' (1:64).

The vengeance and dissimulation supposedly inherent to "mixed-race" people takes center stage in *Bug-Jargal* when Léopold describes the colonial confusion over the side of the Revolution to which the '*hommes de couleur*' were supposed to have belonged. The governor of the colony, Blanchelande, also a real-life figure, exhibits his belief that the free people of color are really on the side of reinstating French authority over the colony when he notes that he has given them a church for asylum. However, a planter who is himself described as a '*sang-mêlé*' paradoxically attempts to convince Blanchelande not to trust the 'mixed-bloods' in an attempt to distance himself from the *hommes de couleur* and to pledge his allegiance to the French. He tells Blanchelande, 'Do not do anything! ... The mixed-bloods are our worst enemies. They alone are for us to fear' (65). The planter's own duplicity is revealed, nevertheless, when after the revolutionaries capture him, he attempts to deny his "whiteness." The planter, in pleading for his life, cries, 'No, no! mister general, no my brothers, I am not white! That is an abominable lie! I am a mulatto, a mixed-blood like you all, son of a negress like your mothers and your sisters!' (126).

The kind of "monstrous hybridity" that led free "mulattoes" like the planter to opportunistically choose their political loyalties had long been characteristic of representations of the free people of color during the Haitian Revolution. In one of Hugo's known sources, Félix Carteau's *Soirées Bermudiennes* (1802), for example, we are treated to the following description of 'Mulattoes':

> They have drawn from their African blood, and probably from the climate as well, the particular vices of the Negroes, without possessing either the constancy, nor the drive, nor the strength of mind, nor the numerous advantages of the Europeans; I mean with respect to useful enterprises;

since as far as having the means to produce harm and do evil, that is the only thing that remains. (153)

Carteau further writes that 'mulattoes' were, '[o]f a proud and vindictive character, and yet naturally impetuous [*fougueux*], flighty, and violent; there is not a single consideration,' Carteau writes, which 'could halt the effect of these two fatal tendencies: thousands of reported deaths could not provide a brake. The need to avenge themselves, in relation to the depth of their pride, is with them a fury, a fanatic rage' (153). Dalmas provided a similarly vengeful illustration of the free people of color of Saint-Domingue when he described the 'nègres, mulâtres, ou quarterons libres' one generally calls 'les hommes de couleur' as a 'species of men, superior to the whites with respect to their physical aspects [*supérieure aux blancs sous les rapports physiques*],' but 'far beneath them in intellectual and moral qualities.' 'Fruits of a tolerated concubinage in this island because it is impossible to prevent it,' Dalmas continues, 'they represent a mixed caste, degraded and ungrateful, and groveling at birth, who like low-hanging ivy wrap themselves around the oak that provides them with support, intertwine themselves in all its branches, and finish by smothering it' (1:11–12).

If Hugo was able to derive support for his understanding of the demonic and unstable personalities of "mulattoes" as owing to their biology, what Hugo also likely derived from such texts was the idea that skin color or "race" could be considered a political legend for determining the *rightness* or *wrongness* of behavior during the Revolution. For example, while de Cauna observes that Hugo culls 'this conventional exoticism that confuses Africa with the Americas' from Descourtilz's *Voyage d'un naturaliste* (1809), Hugo also appears to derive from the naturalist's text the idea that skin color and "race" were concepts that could determine not just physical appearance, but behavior. Jeremy Popkin has written that Descourtilz's recitation of his captivity by various revolutionaries makes its author seem '[p]rofoundly self-centered' since 'Descourtilz judged those he encountered largely in terms of how they treated him personally' (2007, 272). Not only does Descourtilz either demonize or celebrate the revolutionaries of color he encounters based upon their treatment of him, but in many respects he also uses "racial" taxonomies as a key with which to interpret whether an individual's behavior was treacherous or generous. When describing the people of color involved in the captivity of the colonist Lachicotte,[15] whom the naturalist considered 'a faithful historian, who has relayed to me only the most exact details' (127), Descourtilz categorizes them as

---

15 For information pertaining to this prominent family in Saint-Domingue, see Sullerman-Hollerman (1995).

variously 'nègres' or 'noirs' if they were kind to Lachicotte and as 'mulatto' or 'hommes de couleur' if they treated Lachicotte cruelly. At one point, Descourtilz's describes Lachicotte as having been saved by an 'old free negro, filled with compassion' (129). Contrast this with the author's description of André Vernet, whom Descourtilz describes as an 'homme de couleur,' who eventually betrays Lachicotte by falsely promising the latter that his plantations would be saved (128). When Lachicotte arrives at his plantation, however, he finds that despite Vernet's promises,

> The workroom [*l'atelier*] of this plantation, which had until then been content, listening to the voice of barbarity, wanting to give in to the enemies of my color, stoked the fire of discord that the foreign evildoers, those destructive vampires [*les malfaiteurs étrangers, ces vampires désolateurs*] had just lit, with envious eyes that were filled with rage. (128)

Though Descourtilz does not specifically describe Vernet as one of these evildoing 'vampires,' the juxtaposition between his other descriptions of the perfidy of the 'hommes de couleur' with the general nobility and kindness of the 'nègres' provides a striking contrast throughout the text. While nearly all of the 'noirs' or 'negroes' with whom Lachicotte comes into contact, including Toussaint Louverture himself, end up helping him in some way and are described variously as 'brave negroes' (132, 136) or 'good negroes' (132), on the one hand; on the other, he needs to be saved from practically all of the 'hommes de couleur' or 'mulâtres.' Such is the case with 'Philippe, my father's bastard,' according to Lachicotte, who tells Descourtilz, 'this inexorable farmer, my sworn enemy, was furious to learn that I was still living, and had resolved to go to any length in order to become the sole inheritor of our vast properties' (131). Lachicotte also tells Descourtilz about another 'homme de couleur,' 'named *Pierre Michel* ... whose mother I had saved two times,' but who still 'openly declared himself my enemy' (133). Remarkably, according to Lachicotte, still another family member of "mixed race" also sought to destroy him. Lachicotte contends that 'prudence obliged me to ask for help from Saint-Louis Rossignol, the bastard of one of my relatives,' and he describes Rossignol as '[t]hat ambitious mulatto who had enjoined himself to the cause of the rebels and refused me any assistance' (136). Lachicotte further says that after escaping the 'mutins' who were constantly shooting at him, that Rossignol 'overtook me and put me in a dungeon in his house, in the hopes of causing me to starve to death' (137). While Rossignol seeks to starve him, Lachicotte says that he was 'fed during the five days my confinement lasted by some young negroes [*jeunes négrillons*] who, out of compassion for me, threw me some half ripened guavas' (137).

Although it is true that Descourtilz may have merely reported what Lachicotte, that 'faithful historian,' told him about the skin color of the people involved in his capture and release, Descourtilz's selection of these particular anecdotes (as opposed to some others) demonstrates his worldview, one where "race" was not only indicative, but performative; and where the term 'negro' could imply goodness, whereas any kind of "hybridity" would imply treachery and parricide. This same language of instability, duplicity, and parricidal vengeance would also become immediately associated with the idea of 'mulatto' slaves in *Bug-Jargal*.

The popular idea to be found all across the transatlantic print culture of the Haitian Revolution that the free people of color, and especially 'mulattoes,' would murder and betray those who seemed to support them, in some cases even their own family members, would find distinctive adaptation in *Bug-Jargal*. Like Descourtilz, Hugo portrays all of the slaves with 'mixed blood' as responsible for the most dangerous, duplicitous, and hateful parricide during the Revolution. Yet, unlike in Descourtilz's narration, the radical speeches Hugo puts into the mouths of these "mulatto" revolutionary actors provides one of the most illustrative models for understanding the ways in which representations of "monstrous hybridity" could exemplify all at once the epistemological problems of the Revolution, the horror of parricidal vengeance, and the profound righteousness of slave rebellion.

What John Quincy Adams once referred to as the orator's 'voice of eloquence' that would 'not be heard in vain' (27), provides Hugo's Biassou with a way to momentarily transcend the horrors of his hybridity by using his powers of persuasion to expose the depredations of slavery and colonialism. Biassou, whom Hugo portrays as a '*saccatra*' or a person with 'between eight and twenty-three parts of white blood' (Moreau de Saint-Méry, 1797, 1:86), encourages his fellow former slaves to revolt against their masters by telling them:

> For a long time we have been as patient as the lambs to whose wool the whites compare our hair; let us now be as implacable as the panthers and jaguars of the countries from which they have snatched us. Only strength can procure rights; everything belongs to the one who appears to be strong and without pity. (101)

In these speeches, which evoke the writing of Rousseau,[16] and which Bongie has characterized as 'eloquent performances' that allow Biassou to express an 'astonishing number of postcolonial concerns' (1998, 247), the former

---

16 In book one of *The Social Contract*, Rousseau suggested that the only thing that mattered was to 'act so as to become the strongest,' and later he wrote of slavery more specifically, 'it is an empty and contradictory convention that sets up on the one side, absolute authority, and, on the other, unlimited obedience.' Translation by Dutton (1913).

The Rhetorical Possibilities of "Monstrous Hybridity"

slave turned general also uses the power of oratory to remind his audience that the ties of consanguinity had not been respected by the colonists, those 'enemies of the regeneration of humankind,' and that therefore they need not be respected by the slaves either.[17]

With more overtly parricidal undertones, Hugo's Biassou encourages his followers to rebel when he commingles the narrative of "mulatto/a" vengeance with a narrative of humanly righteous rebellion:

> Congo blacks, Creole blacks ... vengeance and liberty! Mixed-bloods, do not allow yourselves to grow cool by the seductions of *los diablos blancos*. Your fathers are on their side, but your mothers are on ours. Moreover, oh, *hermanos de mi alma* [brothers of my soul], they have never treated you as a father would, but only as a master would; you were slaves just like the blacks. (102)

Biassou's call to arms provides a suasive challenge to a logic of plantation loyalties that would make all free people allies regardless of color by suggesting to the *hommes de couleur libres* that, as Vastey had written, they were free in name only. This challenge to the organization of colonial society and its distinctively "racial" rationalizations was intermixed with the unthinkability of parricidal violence that we find constantly in the trope of "monstrous hybridity." Biassou states:

> While a miserable loincloth hardly covered your limbs that had been burned by the sun, your barbaric fathers were strutting around with *de buenos sombreros* ... Cursed be those unnatural beings! But, as the holy commandments of *Bon Dye* forbid it, don't strike your own father. If you recognize him in the enemy ranks, who prevents you, *amigos*, to say to one another: *Tue papa mwen, mwen tue papa ou* [you kill my father, I will kill yours]! Vengeance, people of the king! Liberty for all men! (102)

Biassou's subsequent call for unrelenting massacre is reminiscent of that language of genocide, which representations of "monstrous hybridity" seem to incessantly call to mind. As Etienne has pointed out, this speech was influenced by Lacroix's statement that during the Haitian Revolution,

> The laws of morality and nature had been completely outraged by the war between the whites and the people of color; there were fathers who snuffed

---

17 Vastey had used this very language of regeneration to talk about the end of slavery in Saint-Domingue when he wrote that the 'regeneration of a large part of the human race has begun.' He further characterized the French as the primary obstacle to the regeneration of all of Africa when he wrote that they continued to 'shamefully' traffic in slaves and were thus the 'enemies' of the 'human race' (1814a, vi).

out the lives of their own sons, and sons who plunged their bloody hands into their father's breasts. In their reciprocal debauchery, they encouraged themselves by saying, you kill mine, and I will kill yours [*tue le mien, je tuerai le tien*]. (Lacroix, 196. See also Etienne, 133; Bongie, 2004, 122)

Biassou ratchets up the rhetoric of extermination, however, when tells his audience:

> No grace at all for the whites, for the planters! Massacre their families, devastate their plantations ... Shatter the earth so that it will swallow up the whites! Courage, then, my friends and brothers! Very soon we will fight and exterminate ... Victors, we will in turn enjoy all the pleasures of life. (103)

Hugo's description of people of "mixed race" as the cause of the volatility of personal relationships and political loyalties bears a clear relationship to the writing of Lacroix, but the vision that the slaves were actually gleeful about this vengeance bears an uncanny resemblance to several descriptions of free people of color in Antoine Métral's *Histoire de l'insurrection des esclaves dans le nord de Saint-Domingue* (1818), a work it is much less clear whether Hugo knew.[18] Métral summed up the paradoxes of "racial" instability and its connection to parricide when he wrote that after the non-ratification of the Treaty of Ouanaminthe, which was supposed to have provided 'political equality' (94) for the free people of color *vis-à-vis* the French colonists,

> The *affranchis*,[19] indignant at the refusal to ratify a treaty that was more useful to the planters than to themselves, avenged with perfidy the scorn

---

18 Prasad has actually speculated that Hugo may have read Métral's 1825 *Histoire de l'expedition des Francais a Saint-Domingue: Sous le consulat de Napoleon Bonaparte, 1802-1803* (129).

19 Métral clarifies that he uses the 'expressions' 'affranchis' and 'hommes de couleur' 'without distinction ... to designate the free people [*la classe des hommes affranchis*] whether by birth or by the will of their master, paying no mind to the nuances that exist between the black and the white' (76–77). Métral's usage of these two terms is not as racially innocent as his caveat would lead us to believe, however. Raimond, for one, pointed out that the term '*affranchis*' was itself a racist term used to further disenfranchise the free people of color because the majority of the people identified as '*affranchis*' in the late eighteenth century had never been slaves at all, but were rather born free—and therefore had not really been *freed* from slavery as the term indicates—either to parents of color who were free themselves or they had been manumitted upon birth by their own "white" fathers (1791b, 53–55). John Garrigus, explaining Raimond's quarrel with the term, says that in the early 1760s the French government undertook a project of systematically perpetrating abuses of color prejudice against the *hommes de couleur*, whom they began to refer to as '*affranchis*' around 1770 'as a way of saying that they were all ex-slaves, even those who were born free' (2006, 167).

of their worth and the ingratitude towards their benevolence: they handed over the city to the slaves who attacked it during the night. The colonists, errant and scattered in the streets, no longer recognized either their friends or their enemies; betrayal having mingled them. (96)

Furthermore, Métral had already lamented the treachery, betrayal, and parricide of revolutionary fighting, mostly on the part of 'mulattoes,' when he wrote:

How many fathers, children, wives perished at that time! ...
The slaves were committing parricide. They assassinated those who had given them life either in debauchery or in adultery, for having left them in slavery or for not having demonstrated enough affection towards them; it was without repentance and with pride that they delighted in these parricides; but it was for liberty. (23–24)

Unlike Lacroix or Métral, who could claim to be writing a history and therefore the *truth*, Hugo does not leave it up to the reader to decide if his fictional representation of Biassou as a parricidal "monstrous hybrid" wholly desirous of exterminating 'the whites' has any relationship to a reality that might be called *true*. Hugo intervenes with a footnote that not only translates the Creole phrase *'tue papa mwen ...'* into French for his audience, but also allows him to make a claim to empirical truth about the psychology of 'mulattoes' as generally parricidal. He writes, '[w]e have in fact heard mulattoes, struggling in a sense with parricide [*capitulant en quelque sorte*], pronounce these execrable words' (102).[20]

If there were no shortage of places in the early nineteenth-century Atlantic World where Hugo, who had never been to Saint-Domingue, might have *heard* such parricidal *truths* being espoused about 'mulattoes,' there were also more than a few places where he might have *heard* revolutionary justifications for such seemingly indiscriminate violence. There is a certain sense of intertextuality between the revolutionary logic expressed by Biassou and Habibrah in *Bug-Jargal* and other writings on the Haitian Revolution, which we have little clear evidence that Hugo may have read. Such intertextuality, rather than providing us with positive confirmation of influence, demonstrates exactly how widespread was the intermingling of "race," revolution, and the questions of knowing they invited in the minds of nineteenth-century writers.

Nowhere in *Bug-Jargal* does Hugo allow a person of color to expose the

---

20 Hugo's interest in parricide is well known. Jeanne Bem tells us, for example, that 'One finds constantly [in Hugo's works] the motif of the guillotine, the theme of parricide, and the law of the talion' or an eye for an eye, a tooth for a tooth (39).

inhumanity of slavery more fully than in the character of Habibrah. The *'griffe'* is introduced to us in the following way: 'that hideous dwarf was fat, short, pot-bellied, and moved with a curious rapidity on two spindly and weak legs that, when he sat down, folded under him like the arms of a spider' (30). Habibrah is further disfigured and even made monstrous when Léopold says that he was 'one of those beings whose physical constitution is so strange that they would appear to be monsters, if they didn't evoke laughter' (30). Finally, Habibrah is constantly referred to as a *'nain'* (43), whose 'face was always a grimace, and was never the same: bizarre mutability of features, which at the very least gave his ugliness the advantage of variety' (31). If *Bug-Jargal* 'can only be read as tremendously ambivalent,' as Kirsten Silva Gruesz and Susan Gillman have argued (239), part of the reason for this ambivalence is that this description of Habibrah as having almost the physical constitution of a 'monster' is undermined in certain ways by the sheer eloquence of this same character's protest against the prejudices he suffered under the domination of his master.

Our only insight into Habibrah's motives for killing his master comes when he uses his powerful 'voice of eloquence' to tell Léopold:

> Do you believe then, that because I am a mulatto,[21] a dwarf, and deformed, that I am not a man? [*Crois-tu donc que pour être mulâtre, nain et difforme, je ne sois pas homme*] Ah! I have a soul more profound and stronger than the one to whom I am going to deliver your feminine body [*corps de jeune fille*]! I was given to your uncle like a capuchin monkey [*sapajou*]. I served his pleasures, I put up with his scorn. He loved me, you say; I had a place in his heart, yes, between his female monkey and his parrot [*sa guenon et son perroquet*]. I have chosen another one with my dagger. (179–80)

Such a speech allows the heinously disfigured Habibrah to express his opposition to slavery and his desire for revenge not only in a language that appears to provide an 'empowering act of self-representation' (Bongie, 1998, 257) and might strike twentieth-century readers as a recognition of the 'dignity of blacks' and of their suffering (Hoffmann, 1996, 2), but in a language that is also more immediately phrased using the vocabulary of transnational abolition.

The striking cry for humanity apparent in Habibrah's rhetorical, 'Am I not a man?' resonates with the creation of the famous Quaker abolitionist motto, 'Am I not a man, and a brother?' Add to this question Habibrah's 'because I am a mulatto, a dwarf, and deformed,' and the query resonates beyond "race"

---

21 Here, Habibrah refers to himself as a 'mulatto,' demonstrating how Hugo attempts to make people of the color the ones who had politicized the "biological" category of the 'mulatto.'

as well, especially when we think about Habibrah as a disabled person who has been not only enslaved but mocked because of his physical limitations. In Habibrah's defense of his disability, he calls out as lacking in humanity those who would make his 'infirmities' a constant joke. He tells Léopold:

> If I walked into your sitting room, thousands of scornful laughs greeted me; my height, my deformities, my features, my pathetic outfit, the deplorable infirmities of my constitution, everything about me lent itself to the taunts of your obnoxious uncle and his detestable friends … I had to mingle my laughter with the laughter I aroused. Answer this: do you believe that such humiliations are the way to treat a human being? (180)

As with all "monstrous hybrids" who exhibit such 'spectacular resistance' to authority and challenge the logic of their enemies with their superior oratorical powers, Habibrah cannot shake the language of vengeance. He prefaces the above speech with a grammar of revenge when he tells Léopold, 'You have laughed at me enough, now you can tremble' (180). Once again, the marriage of vengeance and moving opposition to the prejudices and abuses of slavery are phrased with the same despondent pathos of dejection we saw in the writing of Baron de Vastey.

After all, it was Vastey who, in his *Réflexions sur une lettre de Mazères*, used the very language of humanity found in Enlightenment discourse to expose the 'excess of logic and malice [*déraison et méchanceté*]' inherent in attempts to prove that Africans were a different species than Europeans and thus fit for slavery. Vastey said that such an 'impious' and 'absurd' discussion 'forced me to doubt, for my part, that they [the Europeans] were human' (1816d, 15). Habibrah's own question, 'Am I not a man?' seems to reveal a repressed connection to Vastey's own insistence that 'I am a man [*Je suis homme*]; I feel it to be so in all of my being' (Vastey, 1816d, 15). Exactly like Vastey, Habibrah puts into doubt the logic of those who would argue that people of color were not 'men' and therefore not members of a human family who should be treated with dignity and respect regardless of their physical appearance.

It is not out of the realm of possibility to think that Hugo may have had some indirect, if not direct, familiarity with the works of Vastey, which were read in France simultaneously as part of the most 'eloquent' expression of 'dignified anger' (Métral, 1819, 528) and as a 'violent diatribe against the French, the ex-colonists, and any person who played a role in the events of Saint-Domingue' ('Civilisation,' 1819, 59). In 1819, Métral published an extremely influential article in two installments, 'De la littérature haïtienne,' in the liberal journal *La Revue encyclopédique*.[22] The

---

22 Métral's article would go on to be referenced and directly cited in a number of Anglophone reviews of Vastey's works and of Haitian writing more generally. An

first installment relied heavily on the works of Vastey to make the case that post-independence Haitian writing proved that Haitians were 'men,' much as the abbé Grégoire's *De la littérature des nègres* (1808) had done for 'Blacks' in general. Métral used the literary output of Haiti, starting with Dessalines and Christophe's constitutions, along with the writing of Juste Chanlatte, Jules Solime Milscent, Desrivières Chanlatte, and Vastey, as proof that Haitian 'minds' on both sides of the island 'had been elevated to the most sublime ideas of poetry and eloquence, and had even delved deeply into the most profound abstractions of metaphysics' (1819, 526–27). After referencing Juste Chanlatte's *Le Cri de la nature* as an 'admirably traced' recitation of the revolution in Saint-Domingue (527), Métral cited a long passage drawn from Vastey's *Réflexions politiques*, in which the Haitian baron had written:

> Force, courage, virtue, vice, do they derive their source from the skin or from the heart of man? Well, then, if that is so, if it is merely a difference of color that is a crime in your eyes ... arm yourselves, rise up against the vision of the Creator who is the one who wanted there to be different types of people on this earth. (qtd. in Métral, 1819, 528; Vastey, 1817b, 18–19)

Métral concluded his citation of this passage by acknowledging, '[t]hese objections are rich, ingenious with respect to their desired effect, without betraying in any way the artifice of education' (528).

If he was familiar with this article, Hugo, whom we know to have been a reader of *La Revue encyclopédique* since in 1822 he penned a letter to the periodical's editor contesting a review of some of his own poems (R. Bonnet, 327–28), would also have been treated to Métral's opinion that in Vastey's *Le Système* there is a

> profound melancholy that has overtaken the soul of this writer when he laments the deplorable calamities of which his country had been the theater; he puts before our eyes the horrible and bloody tableau of people who had been entirely exterminated and of whom we only find tombstones

---

article entitled, 'History, Literature, and Present State of Hayti' published in *The British Review, and London Critical Journal*, for instance, using only the lengthy passages quoted in Métral's article about Juste Chanlatte and Vastey, made the case that 'The Haytians express themselves with much force and meaning on moral and political questions.' Going on to refer to Baron de Vastey as 'the most distinguished political writer,' the reviewer states that his *Réflexions politiques*, 'abounds with deep and original views; and, in the most eloquent and glowing language, he contrasts the former degradation and stupidity of his countrymen with their present rapid progress in knowledge, and in the useful arts and sciences' (73). Bearing the more immediate influence of Métral, the British author notes that it was with 'sarcastic and impetuous eloquence' that Vastey refuted 'the assertions of those who maintained that it was impossible to civilize Africa' (74).

and ruins; then he represents his fellow citizens as having been threatened by the same fate, but saved by the strength of their own arms; he makes an invocation to these arms as a new kind of divinity, because these first exterminated people had not had access to their usage. (1819, 533; see Vastey, 1814a, 3–4)

Métral finishes his assessment of Vastey's justified vengeance by noting that the Haitian baron had also bested his nemesis, the colonist Claude Pierre Joseph le Borgne de Boigne: 'Whoever would impartially judge the works of these two writers,' Métral writes,

> will see exactly how much the black man had over the white man with respect to the tone of his style and the strength of this logic, and above all a decided eloquence. The white man writes with his mind, but the black man writes with his heart. He writes for liberty, and it is from liberty and from the heart that comes the great genius of inspiration. (534–35)

If Métral had seen within Vastey's works the expression of a 'black' man's soul, quite a different assessment of the Haitian baron's 'heart' might have reached Hugo in an 1819 review of Vastey's *Réflexions politiques* published in the *Bibliothèque universelle des sciences, belles-lettres, et arts*. The reviewer begins his assessment of Vastey's works by recommending that they be read as a 'violent diatribe':

> The two hundred-page volume that carries this title was written by a negro. The author is, as we might imagine, under the influence of an extreme rancor against the French nation in general, and against the writers who argue for the possibility of different order of things than that which exists today in the kingdom of Haiti. ('Civilisation,' 58–59)

Where Métral saw a 'thunderous eloquence' (Métral, 1819, 534) in Vastey's style, the reviewer from the *Bibliothèque universelle* saw merely 'errors of print, spelling, and language.' Indeed, he writes: 'While the style is far from being correct, it is hard to imagine that this work is that of a negro, and that he had undertaken his education since the people of Haiti became independent' (59). Before going on to quote extensively from the work under review, the writer claims that the most immediate goal of *Réflexions politiques* was to 'nourish in the heart of the young Royal Prince a vigorous hatred against all of those who would even try to bring back a system of oppression in the colony' ('Civilisation,' 1819, 59).[23]

---

23 For information about Vastey as the teacher of Henry Christophe's son, see chapter two of this volume.

From "Monstrous Hybridity" to Enlightenment Literacy

Much like Vastey's critic from the *Bibliothèque universelle*, who saw in the Haitian baron's writing not the dignity of mankind, but the 'negro's' faults of temper, Léopold's description of Habibrah as desiring of indiscriminate vengeance practically begs us to answer Habibrah's question about his humanity negatively if we use the criteria of the Enlightenment for which Hugo apparently had so much disdain. Although Habibrah's appeal to humanity might indicate to the contemporary reader that Hugo was able to 'make ... room, obliquely, for a postcolonial vision—of subaltern resistance and cultural hybridity' (Bongie, 2004, 37), it is not hard to imagine that for the nineteenth-century reader the poignancy of Habibrah's 'Am I not a man?' would have been in some ways offset by the revelation that, in an act of revenge, Habibrah has brutally murdered Léopold's uncle (and in fact took pleasure in doing it) as well as enslaved two small 'white' children. Léopold tells us that upon arriving in the revolutionary camp he sees 'two children clothed in slave pants [*caleçon des esclaves*], and each carrying a large fan of peacock feathers. These two slave children were white' (96).

The idea that former slaves would attempt to seek vengeance on the slaveholders by making their former masters—and worse, their former masters' children—into slaves was one of the principal nightmares of post-Haitian Revolution European society. Drouin de Bercy had written that in post-independence Haiti, reverse racism of this stripe was the order of the day: 'Dessalines had published a decree that forbade any man of color to take a white woman for a mistress,' but 'Christophe had taken this hatred even further, he made them slaves' (10). While it may be true that Habibrah's cry for humanity and wish to shame the French for their actions strikes some of the chords of Enlightenment righteousness, his words also paint a picture of "racial" revenge that undermines the idea of universal emancipation for all human beings that underwrote popular justifications for the Haitian Revolution.

Moreover, Habibrah's sympathetic and sentimental plea for justice and humanity is in many ways incongruous with Hugo's portrayal of this character's own lack of sympathy and humanity. Consider one of the final scenes in *Bug-Jargal*, in which Habibrah, like Biassou before him, perverts the discourse of pity as a sign of humanity promulgated principally by Rousseau, who claimed in his *Discours sur l'origine et les fondements de l'inégalité parmi les hommes* (1755) that it was pity or what we now call sympathy that marked the distinction between human beings and animals (2002, 31). In order to trick Léopold into saving his life, Habibrah, who has almost fallen over a cliff and hangs from a single branch, pleads:

> Master! ... don't go away, grace! in the name of *bon Dye*, don't let die an impenitent and guilty human creature whom you could have saved ... Will

you have no pity for your poor buffoon? He is very criminal; but wouldn't it prove to him that the whites are superior to the mulattoes, the masters to the slaves? ... could it be true that a human being could, seeing his fellow man in such a horrible position, be able to save him and not do it? (187)

When Léopold is moved by the 'impulse of pity' and overwhelmed by the 'lamentable' 'accent of terror and suffering' (187), he 'forgets all' and tries to save Habibrah. Nevertheless, when Léopold reaches out for Habibrah's hand, Habibrah tries to pull Léopold into the pit with him stating, 'I know that I could have saved myself with you, but I prefer for you to perish with me. I prefer your death over my life' (188). According to Habibrah's own logic, Léopold's demonstration of sympathy makes him a 'human being,' while Habibrah's lack thereof signals the fact that he truly is a 'monster' (189) and not human at all.

If there is a similarity between Habibrah's monstrous testimony and the writing of someone like Baron de Vastey, which Hugo absolutely could have encountered, I must still insist that whether he did or not is probably beside the point. For, as the research of Malick Ghachem has shown, much of the writing from Old Régime Saint-Domingue suggests that slave rebellions and their justifications were actually quite *thinkable* to the colonists. Ghachem writes that there was 'an anxiety about the retributive impulses of slaves as "the natural enemies of society" (to use Montesquieu's phrase)' (9), and '[l]ike manumission, the radical abuse of slaves by masters and overseers was alternately viewed as both an impetus for slave revolt and a necessary means of discouraging black insubordination' (11). The view of Garran de Coulon certainly seems to support Ghachem's interpretation:

> Putting aside even considerations of justice and morality, which would render such a state of affairs insupportable, it was impossible to think that [slavery] could have lasted forever, and that the negroes would not soon enough come to retake the freedom of which they had been deprived by violence. They had been attempting to do it almost since the establishment of the colony. (1:19)

If the idea that the slaves might desire to redress the abuses of slavery through revolution had been utterly *thinkable* to Garran de Coulon, there appears to have been something completely *understandable* about it as well. As we saw in the first part of this chapter, various novelists and dramatists who depicted the Haitian Revolution had no trouble imagining the many reasons why slaves might want to achieve revenge against their masters. The easy to imagine grievances of the slaves probably have something to tell us not only about why the complaints of Habibrah and Biassou bear a resemblance to the monologues of slaves in someone like Pigault-Lebrun's play, but also how Habibrah's desire for measured vengeance could possibly bear such a distinct similarity to a scene in Rémusat's never-performed play.

Hugo almost certainly never had access to *L'Habitation de Saint-Domingue* since, as far as we can tell, this piece was never staged or published in the nineteenth century. The scene is the one in which Timur argues that Léon should have to suffer before his death. Timur justifies his desire to torture his captives first by telling the slaves:

> Listen, my friends [*camarades*] ...What do you want? The death of those two whites? I thought that you hated them more than that? Tell me, did the whites kill us all at once? Tell me...How many hours, how many days, did they make us die by degrees? How long did each one of us spend rotting in the hold? how long in the jail? how long in the fields? working in the presses? I have died here every minute for four years already!... and I would kill them, just like that? all at once? [...] No, no ... They don't even deserve that. They have to wait, they have to suffer, they must die more slowly... (147-48).

Hugo's Habibrah attempts to justify his vengeance in a similar manner when he tries to convince Léopold that it is he who has been wronged and not he who perpetrates wrongs:

> Oh! for having suffered such a long time, my vengeance was so short! I could not even make last all the tortures that are reborn for me every moment of every day for my odious tyrant! for him to have been able to experience before his death the bitterness of wounded pride and to have felt the burning scars that are left behind by tears of shame and rage on a face that is perpetually condemned to laughter. Alas! it is very hard to have waited so long for the hour of punishment, and to have finished it with one stab of the dagger. (180)

While Rémusat's Timur insists that Léon understands who seeks to kill him and why—Timur states, 'I do not want to kill him without him knowing why ... to kill him, is nothing; I need to do better than that' (51)—Hugo's Habibrah laments that Léopold's uncle 'died without having recognized me' because Habibrah had 'struck with his dagger too quickly' (181). Habibrah makes certain to avoid the same error by revealing himself to Léopold precisely so that his enemy can 'clearly see' him. Habibrah rejoices that 'This time, at least [my vengeance] will be more complete' (181).

It is not hard to imagine that the narrative of "mulatto/a" vengeance and the biological fatalism it implied was an able distraction to the alternative of envisioning slaves who not only wanted to confront their masters with violent retribution, but to shame them in public with a catalogue of misdeeds. Ending the "miscegenation" that seemed so abhorrently responsible for the

Haitian Revolution probably seemed like a much more viable (and even desirable) option than ending the abuses of slavery through its abolition.

Yet, still, because the connection of the Haitian Revolution to the actual abuses of chattel slavery is often repressed in narratives of "mulatto/a" vengeance, people of color in *Bug-Jargal* are not the only ones to blame for the monstrous birthing of the Haitian Revolution. Hugo wrote that it was actually 'The *philosophes*' who had 'fathered the philanthropists, who,' in turn 'gave birth to the *negrophiles*, who produced the eaters of whites,' concluding, 'these purportedly liberal ideas of which we are intoxicated in France are a poison in the tropics' (68). This statement has been tied to the general hostility towards both abolitionism and the Haitian Revolution in early nineteenth-century France. In *Le Génie du Christianisme* (1802), René de Chateaubriand famously wrote of the inhumanity of the Haitian revolutionists:

> The sensible and religious tone in which the missionaries spoke of the blacks of our colonies ... rendered the masters pitiful, and the slaves more virtuous ... With philosophy, we have lost everything: we have even extinguished sympathy; for who would dare to plead the cause of the blacks after the crimes they have committed? (1:164)

This statement about the callousness of the slaves during the Haitian Revolution has been widely cited in scholarship on *Bug-Jargal* as evidence not only of an anti-abolition fervor that swept through early nineteenth-century France, but as indicative of Hugo's opinion on the Haitian Revolution (Etienne, 54; Hoffmann, 2009, 341). Because Hugo once stated that he desired to be 'Chateaubriand or nothing' (Bongie, 1998, 234), the above statement has also been taken as an indication that Hugo intended *Bug-Jargal* to provide a sharp indictment of the Haitian Revolution.

Given the magnitude of writing that characterized the Haitian Revolution as the monstrous outgrowth of disloyal slaves, parricidal free people of color, and misguided philanthropists, it is not clear to me why Chateaubriand's opinion more than myriad others that are more directly related to *Bug-Jargal* should stand as evidence of Hugo's opinion on the causes of the Haitian Revolution. Evoking the specter of a monstrous birth, Bryan Edwards, for instance, whose history of the Revolution had been translated into French in 1797, provided a tale of '"mulatto/a" vengeance' that is in accord with *Bug-Jargal*'s generally hostile attitude to both 'mulattoes' and the Enlightenment. He wrote:

> the mulattoes scorned to be outdone in deeds of vengeance, and atrocities shameful to humanity. In the neighborhood of Jérémie a body of them attacked the house of M. Séjourné and secured the persons of both him and his wife. This unfortunate woman (my hand trembles while I write!)

was far advanced in her pregnancy. The monsters, whose prisoner she was, having first murdered her husband in her presence, ripped her up alive, and threw the infant to the hogs. They then (how shall I relate it!) sewed up the head of the murdered husband in_____!!!![24]

Edwards concluded by lamenting, 'Such are thy triumphs, philanthropy!' (99).

Edwards's belief that the cruelty of the 'mulattoes' was one of the monstrous products of anti-slavery 'philanthropy' was shared by many European writers. Despite a great many disagreements with the British planter, in his response to Edwards, the French colonist Venault de Charmilly did appear to concur with the former when he also characterized the philanthropists of Europe as 'barbarians' 'who have bathed themselves in our blood' (13–14). He wrote: 'The supposed rights of man were absurd in Europe, but they are barbaric in the Colonies, they have put the sword and the firebrand in the hands of the Mulattoes, who put them afterward in the hands of the negroes' (50). Barré de Saint-Venant, too, echoed the belief that the European philanthropists who had urged universal emancipation were partially to blame for the troubles of Saint-Domingue:

> In effect, when by a philanthropic move either perfectly or poorly understood [*bien ou malentendu*], the national assembly of France declared that all the negroes were naturally free, and that no man had the right to buy another one, it destroyed all of the colonial properties ... Immediately, all work ceased, all matter of disorder, all kinds of crimes were committed. (498)

Bug-Jargal was part of the same concerted effort *not* to link the revolutionary project of the slaves to the goals of freedom and equality, but rather to link it to a kind of "mulatto/a" vengeance that was figured as the ultimate and undesirable effect of European philanthropy.

*

In the twentieth-century, *Bug-Jargal* was variously fêted as an abolitionist novel by André Marie Ntsobe, likely because of the very speeches of

---

24 A version of this story can also be found in the anonymously published *Histoire des désastres de Saint-Domingue* (1795), in which, linking the rebellion of the slaves to "mulatto/a" vengeance, the author writes that in the city of Jérémie the 'mulattoes' had happened upon the pregnant Madame Séjourné, whom they subsequently 'attached to a tree, opened up her belly, and fed her baby to the pigs, right before the eyes of the unfortunate dying woman' (212).

The Rhetorical Possibilities of "Monstrous Hybridity"

characters like Habibrah and Biassou who railed against slavery (Hoffmann, 1996; and Gewecke, 61), admonished as an example of negrophobia, probably because of the homicidal undertones of those same speeches (Toumson, 63), and characterized as 'painfully self-contradictory' (Bonin, 194). Yet if in nineteenth-century France the novel was received in contradictory and ambivalent ways (Toumson, 208), and in nineteenth-century England it enjoyed a popularity that might be characterized as extreme (Bongie, 2008, 3),[25] in the antebellum U.S., despite a general obsession with the Haitian Revolution, reviewers of *Bug-Jargal* actually seemed uninterested in the text and its translations. One U.S. review of *Bug-Jargal* noted that the novel 'did not affect to describe the manners of the day' and thus 'do[es] not belong to our subject' ('French Novels and French Morals,' 1836, 52); another mention of the translated version (Leitch Ritchie's *The Slave King*) acknowledged that Hugo 'stands confessedly at the head of the French novelists of the present day' ('The Slave King,' 1), but was similarly indifferent to the novel itself; and a review originally published in *The Select Journal of Foreign Periodical Literature* in January 1834 had this unflattering thing to say about *The Slave-King*:

> Hugo's second romance, *Bug-Jargal*, a tale of the insurrection in St. Domingo, was never much to our taste. The essential improbability of such a character as Bug Jargal, a negro of the noblest moral and intellectual character, passionately in love with a white woman, yet tempering even the wildest passion with the deepest respect, and sacrificing even life at last in her behalf and that of her husband, is too violent a call upon the imagination. (19)

While U.S. reviewers were often *blasé* about the work, at least one Haitian writer from the later nineteenth century took deep offense at Hugo's depictions of "monstrous hybridity." The ethnologist Antènor Firmin expressed effusive praise for the French poet as well as sincere criticism of *Bug-Jargal*'s representation of Habibrah as 'stamped with the mark of condemnation' (313). Firmin wrote in *De l'égalité des races humaines*—a work designed to refute the pseudoscientific racism of Comte de Gobineau—that Hugo's biases against the *griffe*, in particular, had obviously been derived from the 'prevailing ideas' of the poet's world:

> There is a striking example of this in the first literary production of one of the greatest thinkers of the nineteenth century, Victor Hugo. This poet, whatever might have been his genius, even because of his genius,

---

25 The novel was actually translated into English four separate times in the nineteenth century (1833, 1844, 1845, 1866) (Bongie, 2004, 3).

has always been the faithful reflection of the thought of his century ... In *Bug-Jargal*, Victor Hugo wanted to provide examples of the character of each of the human types represented by his heroes. He showed the generous white man [*blanc*], the poetically noble black man [*noir*]; but of the *griffe* he made the most hideous of beings. Habibrah, whom he presents as a *griffe*, is physically ugly and deformed; as for his morals, he is peevish [*grincheux*], cowardly, envious, and hateful. It is a work of adolescent youth, which only better highlights the influence that these prevailing ideas [*les idées ambiantes*] must have exercised on the *sublime child*, the future master of French poetry. (313)

The kind of ambivalence expressed in Firmin's refractory description of Hugo's first novel surfaces most readily when examining the heretofore mentioned Scottish novelist Leitch Ritchie's 1833 English translation of the text. Unlike Firmin, who celebrates the poet while acknowledging his errors, Ritchie, who clearly must have thought Hugo a worthy enough author to want to translate him, took a great many liberties with the plot of *Bug-Jargal* in order to, in Bongie's words, unapologetically 'conscript ... *Bug-Jargal* to the abolitionist cause' (2008, 122).

In a literary history about how ideas of "race" to be found in various kinds of portrayals of the Haitian Revolution were transmitted and in some ways translated across time and geography, it is perhaps fitting to end this chapter with a few brief remarks about *The Slave-King*. As Bongie has written, '*The Slave-King* has perhaps the most to tell us about the original text because, unlike all subsequent translations, it departs radically at points from its French model, demanding to be read not simply as a translation but as an *adaptation* of what Hugo wrote' (2008, 121).[26] Nevertheless, if Bongie has focused on the additions of the 1833 translation that make the text an integral part of the literary history of romanticism, I contend that because *Bug-Jargal* has historically been one of the more influential fictions within the literary

---

26 The idea that Ritchie had actually adapted rather than merely translated the original text was an opinion shared by some contemporary reviewers. One review of *The Slave-King* originally published in *The Albion, A Journal of News, Politics, and Literature* on August 3, 1833, for example, characterized the translation in an ambivalent, if enigmatic way: 'With some judicious variations from the original of Victor Hugo, this is a finely imagined and powerfully written romance ... We have rarely been so beguiled into the detail of a plot; but its intense and startling interest must plead our apology; or rather, we feel that no apology can be required' (81). A subsequent reviewer for a Spanish translation of a different French work published in *Brother Jonathan. A Weekly Compendium of Belle Lettres and the Fine Arts, Standard Literature ...* in January 1842, mentions *The Slave-King*, also noting that it was hardly faithful to the original: 'Leitch Ritchie's "Slave King" ... may be better called a story founded on Bug Jargal [*sic*] than a translation of it' (156).

The Rhetorical Possibilities of "Monstrous Hybridity"

history of the Haitian Revolution, what Ritchie did not so much *adapt* in *The Slave-King*, but translate in a particular way, has every bit as much to tell us about how the narrative of "mulatto/a" vengeance first found in pseudo-scientific debates about "race" reached a transatlantic reading public in the context of the Haitian Revolution.

Through his lexical choices, Ritchie, perhaps like the Polish translator of Joseph Conrad's *Heart of Darkness*, according to Ewa Kujawaska-Lis, 'exaggerated ... the ideological perspective of the original' (Kujawaska-Lis, 166). Kujawaska-Lis writes that a 'translator can transform the text because of two distinct, yet interconnected processes: initially as the source text reader who reconstructs its meaning; and as the target text producer.' She says: 'At times it is difficult to determine whether the ideological shift results from the translator's conscious decisions or his misunderstanding/misinterpretation of the original, on the one hand, or an attempt to produce a natural-sounding, contemporary target text, on the other' (167). We already know that at the 'macrostylistic level' (166), Ritchie turned the text into an abolitionist novel, an effect achieved primarily through his conscious addition of scenes that do not appear in the original and his fundamental rewriting of the novel's ending (Bongie, 2005b). At what Kujawaska-Lis calls the 'microstylistic level' (66), however, Ritchie almost always tried to be faithful to *Bug-Jargal* when translating passages having to do with 'the mulattoes' and the other '*sang-mêlés*.' Even so, at times the adjectives and verbs Ritchie selected, perhaps to render the text more readable in English, the way in which he interpreted and rewrote footnotes to make them more interesting for his own audience, and the supplemental material he provided at the end to historically frame the novel for British readers who may not have been as familiar with the history of Saint-Domingue/Haiti, had the effect of causing him to translate the text in a way that only intensified the trope of "monstrous hybridity."

If Ritchie's faithfulness to the original narrative of "mulatto/a" vengeance to be found in Hugo's novel says little about the translator's own ideas about "race," his additions and changes to Hugo's authoritative footnotes about people of "mixed race" reveals perhaps his own implicit skepticism of the transcendent possibilities of the trope of "monstrous hybridity." Recall that in Hugo's *Bug-Jargal*, after being captured by Biassou, the very planter, described as '*sang-mêlé*', who had earlier desperately denied his connection to the 'negroes,' suddenly claims his "African" heritage in pronouncing that he is a 'mulatto' or an 'homme de couleur' (119). When the planter states, using a method straight out of pseudoscience, that he can prove his "Africanness" owing to the 'black circle that you can see around my nails' (127), Hugo had intervened with a footnote designed to prove the essential verisimilitude of the scene by telling the reader, 'many of the *sang-mêlé* have at birth

From "Monstrous Hybridity" to Enlightenment Literacy

this sign, which fades with age, but resurfaces when their own children are born' (127). It is Hugo's André Rigaud who, at this point, echoing the protests of Raimond and Vastey which we saw in chapter two, signals to the planter that in using the word 'mulatto' to describe himself, the planter had ultimately revealed that he could not be trusted. Rigaud states, 'If you had been a mulatto, in fact ... you would not use that word' (127). In the footnote accompanying this statement, Hugo provided an additional authoritative detail that stressed for the reader the essential *truth* inherent in his representation of Rigaud's opposition to the word 'mulatto': 'we must remember that the men of color furiously rejected this qualification, invented, they say, by the scorn of whites' (127).

In *The Slave-King*, it is precisely in the footnote following Rigaud's protest of the planter's use of the word 'mulatto' that Ritchie makes Hugo's view of people of color seem even more monstrous than in the original. If we recall that Hugo had merely written that the men of color 'furiously rejected' [*rejetaient avec colère*] the appellation of 'mulatto,' Ritchie's decision to substitute the animalizing verb 'hoot' for the more literal translation, 'reject,' reveals a much more obvious disdain for 'mulattoes.' He writes: 'Men of colour *hoot* at the name of mulatto; a word, they say, [was] invented by the whites to signify their contempt for blacks' (157, emphasis added). The wild suggestiveness of a verb like 'hoot,' unlike the agency-granting verb 'reject,' does not convey any sense of righteousness or humanity on the part of the people doing the rejecting. Like the words 'mulatto' and 'negro' themselves, the verb 'hoot' has historically been used to dehumanize those to whom it has been ascribed, being one of the principle verbs used by Mary Rowlandson to characterize the speech of the 'Indians' in her 1682 captivity narrative.

In the eighth remove of *The Sovereignty and Goodness of God: Being a Narrative of the Captivity and Restoration of Mrs. Mary Rowlandson*, Rowlandson writes: 'Now the Indians gather their forces to go against Northampton. Over night one went about yelling and *hooting* to give notice of the design' (emphasis added). By characterizing the speech of this 'Indian,' and the language of her captors in general as a series of yells, hoots, 'hoops,' and loud noises, Rowlandson labors to dehumanize the 'Indians.' For these verbs do not recognize the sounds being made by the Wampanoags as anything resembling a human language. Rowlandson also uses a succession of dehumanizing adjectives and nouns, calling her captors 'ravenous beasts,' 'barbarous creatures,' and at one point even calling them wholly 'inhumane creatures.'

If, as Mark Dow has wryly observed, 'demeaning a people's language' is merely one 'element in dehumanizing the speakers' (2), then what does it mean to characterize the opposition of people of "mixed race" to a

The Rhetorical Possibilities of "Monstrous Hybridity"

terminology that was insulting to them in a way that completely divests these people of the eloquence, dignity, and *resistance* Hugo had originally (even if ironically or unconsciously) allowed his revolutionary speakers to convey? That is to say that the lack of dignity offered by the translator's choice of diction lies in sharp contrast to Biassou's earlier more respectable opposition to the words, 'Nègres et mûlatres,' which remarkably resembles Baron Vastey's own dispute with these terms in his *Essai* (see chapter two of the present volume). '[W]hat does that mean?' Hugo's Biassou sardonically asks, 'Did you come here to insult us with these odious names, invented by the contempt of whites? Here, there are only men of color and blacks, do you hear me, mister colonist?' (120). By devaluing in some sense Biassou and Rigaud's opposition, what the translator has done belies the pervasiveness of the trope of "monstrous hybridity" whose primary function was to make the Haitian Revolution a tale of "mulatto/a" vengeance.

Two additional passages reveal the translator's more distinctive role in exacerbating the trope of "monstrous hybridity" to be found in Hugo's original. The first of these passages appears in the explanatory footnote that follows the first usage of the word 'griffe' to describe Habibrah. Instead of attributing the racial taxonomy to Moreau de Saint-Méry, as does Hugo, in the interest of 'mak[ing] the English reader acquainted with the origin and names of the various classes,' Ritchie attributes this terminology first to Franklin and then to Hugo himself, with no mention at all of Moreau de Saint-Méry: 'According to the system of the exact Franklin, the colour of Habibrah was composed of twenty-four to thirty-two parts, and ninety-six to a hundred and four black. This colour Victor Hugo tells us, is called Griffe by the French' (11). Ritchie's elimination of the reference to Moreau de Saint-Méry is evidence that fiction carried the full authority of truth, even in matters of "racial" calculation. But after recasting the dizzying calculation of the possible ratios of 'white blood' and 'black blood' to be found in Habibrah's person, the translator adds his own claim to authority. Ritchie writes: 'the mulatto, it should be observed, is the result of the union of pure white and black blood, and is the least handsome both in feature and hair of all the combinations' (11). Why add that the 'mulatto' is the least handsome and insist that this 'should be observed?' What purpose does such an *observation*, indeed, an *intervention*, on the part of a translator serve when stated as incontrovertible fact, other than to inject the translator's own "racial" prejudices against 'mulattoes' into a text that exhibits enough of those prejudices on its own?

The final addition that reveals the translator's own contribution to the narrative of "mulatto/a" vengeance comes in the authenticating notes appended to the translation. Ritchie said that these notes were designed to provide a 'historical sketch' and had been culled largely from the experiences of a 'friend who has lately travelled in St. Domingo, and is in every way qualified to write on the subject' (viii). These notes, like the novel itself, revive the attendant stereotype in the trope of "monstrous hybridity" about an innate conflict between 'blacks' and 'mulattoes.' Ritchie has this to say about the War of the South:

> The contention that ensued between the distinctive races, the blacks and mulattoes, headed by the two leaders [Toussaint Louverture and André Rigaud], each claiming ascendant authority ... brought on the colony a conflict of most resentful passions, distinguished by the Haitians as a 'War of Colour,' the evil effects of which have not ceased to operate, even at this day. (303)

Here, Ritchie contends that it is Haitians (rather than his travelling friend) who called the Rigaud–Louverture conflict a 'War of Colour,' an argument that would be constantly repeated rather than proved throughout the nineteenth century and which we have already seen contested by the writings of Baron de Vastey.

Such a dynamic of racialized blame was echoed by Melville's character Delano, who mused on the topic of "black–mulatto" relations in 'Benito Cereno.' Melville writes of the leader of the ship rebellion, Babo, that he was 'not unconscious of [his] inferiority' when faced with the aforementioned 'mulatto' Francesco, and later, 'Captain Delano imputed his jealous watchfulness [of Francesco] to that peculiar feeling which the full-blooded African entertains for the adulterated one' (78). Delano's thoughts on the matter provide a prime example of the way in which the idea that prejudices emanated from people of color themselves had been spread all across the Atlantic World merely by its subtle inscription in various texts that were written about slavery in the Americas.

Ritchie pushes the implied belief that 'full-blooded African[s]' had a natural disdain for 'adulterated' ones even further when he claims that it is this 'War of Colour' that is responsible for the 'evil effects' of "racial" prejudice between the 'distinctive races' in the Haiti of his time, rather than the twin legacy of slavery and colonialism. Absent entirely in the historical gloss provided by Ritchie is any mention of the fact that the French colonists had actively sought to create, encourage, and maintain these 'distinctions' based on color, precisely in order to create a class of 'intermediarie[s]' who could help to preserve slavery. That former French colonists like Mazères, Malouet, le Borgne de Boigne, and Drouin de Bercy had actively sought to encourage in post-independence Haiti the maintenance of the much-longed-for "racial" divisions of colonial society is also never mentioned. Furthermore, by inserting the aside that his authority comes from Haitians themselves

The Rhetorical Possibilities of "Monstrous Hybridity"

(by way of the claimed first-hand experience relayed by his friend to him), Ritchie accomplishes exactly what Hugo before him and Melville after him had accomplished in making the assertion of enmity between 'blacks' and 'mulattoes' to come from people of color themselves. In so doing, the author once again absolves himself of the charge of color prejudice and makes it seem as if the very notion of "blacks" having prejudices against one another was so out of the realm of conceivable possibilities as to be monstrously responsible for the then present conditions of Haiti.

The larger point to take from the microstylistics of Ritchie's translational choices is that "monstrous hybridity" and the "mulatto/a" vengeance it conveys were not at all in apparent contradiction with the goals of abolition as the 'cause of humanity' (Ritchie, 179); just as Hugo's adoption of a language of dignified protest for "monstrous hybrids" did not in any way contradict a general disdain for either the Revolution or people of "mixed race."

To conclude, even though the translator may have taken pains to include additions that would allow Léopold to paint 'blacks' as 'my brothers of humanity' (Ritchie, 259), it is questionable whether this brotherhood also included the many "mulattoes" to be found in the text. It is perhaps, then, because a wholly deprecating trope like "monstrous hybridity" carried within it an utterly *thinkable* and understandably violent response to slavery and colonialism that involved both affect and logic that such a trope was not incompatible with the humanitarian cause of abolition. Perhaps, what we should be asking is what anti-slavery activists hoped to gain (or stood to lose) from attaching their movement not only to the Haitian Revolution, but by embedding their descriptions of this event within a grammar of racialized vengeance? As the next two sections of *Tropics of Haiti* will show, in many ways, the narrative of "mulatto/a" vengeance exposes a profound ambivalence on the part of abolitionists and other anti-slavery activists when it comes to the subjects of "race" and revolution.

PART TWO

Transgressing the Trope of the "Tropical Temptress": Representation and Resistance in Colonial Saint-Domingue

'Wendell Phillips says that he was once in Faneuil Hall, when Frederick Douglass was one of the chief speakers. Douglass had been describing the wrongs of the Negro race and as he proceeded he grew more and more excited and finally ended by saying that they had no hope of justice from the whites, no possible hope except in their own rights to arms. It must come to blood! They must fight for themselves. Sojourner Truth was sitting, tall and dark, on the very front seat facing the platform, and in the hush of feeling when Douglass sat down she spoke out in her deep, peculiar voice, heard all over the hall: "Frederick, is God dead?"'

—W.E.B. Du Bois, 'The Damnation of Women' (1920)

'I do not consider that we, as females, as individuals, are blamable for the faults of government. It is not for us to attempt assuming even a slight hold of the reins; our impotent hands could not without masculine force propel the wheels of the state.'

—Frances Hammond Pratt, *La Belle Zoa; or the Insurrection in Hayti* (1854)

'Am I not a woman and a sister?'

—motto adapted from the seal of the British Society for the Abolition of the Slave Trade, 1787

In her 1992 book *Haiti, History and the Gods*, Colin (Joan) Dayan writes of the lack of attention given to women of color in dominant histories of Haiti:

Transgressing the Trope of the "Tropical Temptress"

> What happened to actual black women during Haiti's repeated revolutions, as they were mythologized by men, metaphorized out of life into legend? It is unsettling to recognize that the hyperbolization necessary for myths to be mutually reinforcing not only erases these women but forestalls our turning to their *real* lives. (48)

Dayan's question about what happens to the '*real* lives' of women of color when they are filtered through the lens of what she calls the 'familiar conceit of the double Venus ... beneficent or savage, virginal or polluted' (48), reflects the fact that in much of eighteenth- and nineteenth-century writing from Saint-Domingue there persists an obvious tropology of women of color as highly dangerous "tropical temptresses." John Garrigus writes, in fact, that 'no account of Saint-Domingue was complete without an account of tropical temptresses' who supposedly lured white men with 'highly developed sexual skills' (2003, 77) and that 'such images of morally corrupt feminine desire dominated print discussions of race in Saint-Domingue' after a permanent printing works was established there in 1763 (Garrigus, 2006a, 154).

The figure of the "tropical temptress" was so apparently operative in the literary-historical imagination that she appeared with largely the same lexicon even in non-printed works that may not have publicly circulated in the era. An unedited manuscript dating from the early 1790s entitled *Les Trois Voyageurs ou légère incursion de l'île de Saint-Domingue*, attributed to a M. Levaigneur, provides the perfect example of the widespread characterization of the "tropical temptress." In the handwritten manuscript, the poet accuses a colonist named Verlan of trying to cement his position as a 'grand blanc' in procuring for himself:

> A Laïs, the color of café-au-lait
> That in these climates one calls a *mulâtresse*
> Charming brunette, with plump breasts,
> dark eyes, and graced with the limbs of a *gazelle*
> Slender waist, and genuine hips;
> Who, exposing him to many hazards,
> By the excesses of her libertinage
> Proudly maintains his household
> And populates it with the prettiest of bastards
> That he thinks are his own, as is the custom.
> (qtd. in Fouchard, 1955, 64)[1]

---

[1] Jean Fouchard writes that a 'suggestive' note on the flyleaf of the manuscript, which reads, 'M. Levaigneur, presently in Port-au-Prince, September 1791,' might permit us to identify the author of the *Les Trois voyageurs* as M. Levaigneur himself (1955, 60). Garrigus attributes the poem instead to Gabriel François de Brueys d'Aigalliers (2006a, 154). Having examined the document, which is housed at the Bibliothèque de Nantes,

Transgressing the Trope of the "Tropical Temptress"

The French colonist Gabriel François Brueys d'Aigalliers, whose private letters, which often included poems, were collected and published in 1805 under the title *Œuvres choisis de G. F. Brueys d'Aigalliers*, similarly described women of color both as the objects of treacherous seduction and as the signs of universal 'degradation [*avilissement*].' In a 1764 letter to a Mademoiselle Vicaire, Brueys d'Aigalliers notes that 'these creatures with black skin or rather more or less swarthy' were the objects of longstanding 'scorn [*méprise*]' precisely because of the 'libertinage that … reigns in women of this species, libertinage that does not defame them at all, and from which, on the contrary, they derive vanity' (1805, 48).

Levaigneur's poem about the perfidious power that women of color held over "white" men and Brueys d'Aigallier's linkage of that power to the wholesale 'degradation' of their 'species,' bolsters Doris Garraway's assertion that '[i]n narrative descriptions of Saint-Domingue by Creoles and metropolitans alike, the free mulatto woman stands as a privileged icon of colonial libertinage, embodying the very nexus of concupiscence, luxury, and consumption' (2005a, 191). As Garraway (2005a), Young (1995), Dayan (1995b), Garrigus (2006a), and Jenson (2011), have shown, many eighteenth-century travel writers who wrote about the colonies produced theories of "race" that tell this same story of corrupt female desire and degradation. The authors of these kinds of texts seemed intent upon proving the inferior, savage, and even inhuman nature of peoples of African descent by focusing almost exclusively upon the dangerously seductive qualities of women of color, and especially women of "mixed race," in their discussions of "miscegenation" and in their development of "racial" taxonomies.

Nearly everyone who has studied the figure of the "tropical temptress" cites the French writer Hilliard d'Aubertueil, who famously spoke of the woman of "mixed race" as the very sign of the libertine ways of the colony when he wrote in his *Considérations sur l'état présent de la colonie française de Saint-Domingue* (1776): 'Mulattas are in general much less docile than mulattoes because they have established over the majority of the whites an empire founded on libertinage … all of their movements are driven by pleasure' (2:77). Garraway has inferred that colonists like d'Aubertueil focused on the seductive power of women of "mixed race" in order to absolve themselves of guilt for doing what they described as repugnant: 'by imputing to this group the desires they refused to suppress in themselves,' Garraway writes, 'the whites sought to deny that they continued to do the prohibited thing' (2005a, 209). Moreover, as Hilary Beckles has argued,

---

I see little evidence pointing to authorship by Brueys d'Aigalliers, other than the fact that Brueys d'Aigalliers, like the author of *Les Trois voyageurs*, wrote of his experiences in Saint-Domingue simultaneously in prose and in verse.

such transference allowed the planters to continuously construct women of color in ways that bolstered their own power as part of a 'slave owning patriarchy, that understood a great deal about ideological representation, social authority, and economics' (1998, 137).

Despite the ubiquity of references to the seductive powers of the '*mulâtresse*' in much scholarship on Saint-Domingue, what we have not examined thus far is the connection between these super sexualized descriptions of all women of color in the colony and the "mulatto/a" vengeance that would be described as its most immediate consequence. If images of women of color as the very emblems of 'concupiscence' and 'corrupt feminine desire' dominated in the print culture of colonial Saint-Domingue, they are also ever present in the literary history of the Haitian Revolution. There is a distinct connection between the highly sexualized mythology of women of color found in colonial writing from Saint-Domingue and eighteenth- and nineteenth-century colonial European descriptions of these same women as not only degraded and corrupt, but violent and vengeful during the Haitian Revolution.

Of all the writers who wrote about the degradations of "racial mixing," the Martinican naturalist, lawyer, and statesman M.L.E. Moreau de Saint-Méry provides perhaps the best illustration of the ways in which such a discourse of corrupt feminine desire could be linked to the kind of specifically "mulatta" vengeance that would end up finding its way into the transatlantic print culture of the Haitian Revolution. Moreau de Saint-Méry had his own mistress, a free woman of color, with whom he had at least one daughter (a topic that will be explored in chapter four), but he still painted the '*Mulâtresse*' as the arbiter of colonial sexual corruption:

> The entire being of a *Mulâtresse* is given over to sensual pleasure, and the fire of this Goddess burns in her heart only to be extinguished with her life. This cult, behold its code, all its wishes, all its successes. There is nothing of which the most inflamed imagination could conceive that she has not sensed, divined, accomplished. Charming all of the senses, delivering them to the most delicious ecstasies, suspending them with the most seductive raptures: behold her unique study; and nature, which is in some ways the accomplice of this pleasure, has given her spells, charms, sensibility, and that which is the most dangerous of all, the faculty for experiencing, much better than he with whom she shares them, the sensual pleasures that even the codes of Paphos[2] could not contain. (1797, 1:92)

Earlier in the *Description*, Moreau de Saint-Méry had attempted to explain the inner motivations of 'the large class of women who are the fruit of the

---

2 The legendary birthplace of Aphrodite (Garrigus, 2006a, 155).

mixture of white men [*des blancs*] with female slaves' in writing that such women 'occupy themselves with vengeance, using weapons of pleasure, for having been condemned to degradation' (1797, 1:15). The French colonist here finds that women of "mixed race" not only derive from their 'degradation' a unique ability to experience pleasure and equally to seduce, but a drive towards procuring revenge against the 'white men,' who, in helping to create them, were ostensibly responsible for their subjugated positions.

Directly influenced by Moreau de Saint-Méry, in Thelwall's *The Daughter of Adoption*, the jealous musings of a 'Creole' woman named Miss Danae concerning 'mulatto women' are described using the same grammar of racialized vengeance:

> She beheld with a discerning eye, those attractive artifices by which the mulatto women, in defiance of all the disadvantages of complexion, and the opprobrium of 'relations on the coast,' eclipsed at once the more delicate charms and boasted accomplishments both of the European ladies, and the native whites. She beheld it at first, indeed, with surprise and indignation; but soon discerning the cause, with a spirit not very unlike that boasted virtue of patriotism, which has prompted so many noble and so many detestable actions, she determined to vindicate the honour of white and red, against the triumphant voluptuousness of the olive complexion and tawney-coloured votaries of the West-Indian Venus. (77)[3]

The 'charms' of these 'paphian goddess[es]' (Thelwall, 129) later appear to provide a curious contrast to the ire of 'mulatto men,' when the character Henry visits Port-au-Prince and expresses shock to find that 'the recent insurrections of the mulatto men were every now and then introduced with expressions of infuriated rancour that formed a curious contrast to the voluptuous admiration and infatuated devotion with which they talked of their mulatto women' (128). It is only later in the novel that one of Thelwall's characters will tie such descriptions more clearly to the vengeance *of* "mulattas" as opposed to desire coupled with vengeance *for* them by intimating that it was well known in the colony that 'the revenge and jealousy of a mulatto-woman are not to be trifled with' (211).

As in Thelwall's novel, S.J. Ducœurjoly's *Manuel des habitans de Saint-Domingue* (1803) also bears the direct influence of Moreau de Saint-Méry's

---

3 The 'Venus' reference likely came from Baron de Wimpffen, who weighed in on "mixed-race" women by telling us, 'these female mulattoes who dance so exquisitely, and who have been painted to you in such seducing colors, are the most fervent priestesses of the American Venus. They have reduced voluptuousness to an art, which they have carried to the highest point of perfection' (1817, 112).

reference to the 'mulâtresse' as driven to revenge by the 'codes of Paphos.' The ultimate purpose of Ducœurjoly's 'manual,' according to the unnamed author of the introduction to the work, was to furnish to those who wished to recover the colony, 'everything that is necessary for them to avoid making any missteps, and to preclude any notion of imprudence, whether it be in their preparations for the voyage, or in the manner in which they behave at the end of their mission' (iv). While in the main narrative Ducœurjoly focuses mainly upon the habits of 'negroes,' the causes of their skin color, and the production, climate, and geography of different regions of the colony, the author of the introduction states that he is going to furnish additional information necessary for comprehending 'the physical and moral aspects of the *Creoles* and the people of color, of both sexes' (1:cxxv). The author goes on to provide a description of the *'mulâtresse'* as a vengeful "tropical temptress":

> A *mulâtresse* appears to be a being imprinted and molded by sexuality; on the forehead of one of these priestesses of pleasure, one could engrave the famous verse that one of our most celebrated tragedians has taken from Horace: *C'est Venus toute entière à sa proie attachée.* Without pretending here to draw the degrading portrait of the celebrations of the *Paphos* of the Antilles, I am content with merely repeating, after a man who found himself well instructed in these odious mysteries, *There is nothing of which the most inflamed imagination could conceive that she has not sensed, divined, accomplished.* The excess of these *Laïs*, since 1770, especially, no longer knows any limits. (1:cxxxvii)[4]

This *'mulâtresse'* not only derived a distinct pleasure from causing harm to others, but her very sensualized existence inspired hatred in "white" women: 'This detail, highly abridged,' the author writes:

> is sufficient for imagining the atrocious torments that terrible jealousy and that outraged tenderness caused to grow in the hearts of the white Creoles; for it must be observed that the pleasures of the most charming *Mulâtresse* were the envy of nature, and her sweetest triumph, was to, by dint of her caresses and lechery, tear the young lover away from his charming, adored wife, who had once been the joy and felicity of his life, in order to attach him to her train and to humiliate his sensitive companion by making her feel the upper hand of her charms, the superiorities of her advantages, and by making a trophy out of her victory before the eyes of the entire colony. (1:xcccvii–iii)

---

4 The first italicized quote in the passage is from Jean Racine's *Phèdre* (1677). The second italicized quote is from Moreau de Saint-Méry's *Description* (1797, 1:92); the mention of a *Laïs* perhaps bears a cultural relationship to Levaigneur's poem.

Transgressing the Trope of the "Tropical Temptress"

It was not only the woman of "mixed race" who was linked to the trope of the "tropical temptress" through the purported jealousy, outrage, and vengeance that her very existence was capable of unleashing in herself or in others. At times in the literary history of the Haitian Revolution, as in much of eighteenth-century naturalist travel writing, all women of color were defined as being capable of inspiring or committing vengeful acts because of their "race." This is because the act of "miscegenation" itself was often viewed as responsible for the internal feelings that would inevitably lead to racialized vengeance. The Jamaican planter Edward Long, for example, whose three-volume *History of Jamaica* (1774) contains its own "racial" taxonomies, describes African women as joyfully preying upon the foolhardy 'paramours' who take African mistresses:

> the quintessence of her dexterity consists in persuading the man she detests that she is most violently smitten with the beauty of his person ... To establish this opinion which vanity seldom fails to embrace, she now and then affects to be jealous ... and by this stratagem, she is better able to hide her private intrigues and her real favourites. (2:331)

After describing how these African women eventually rob their lovers, Long muses upon the putative unnatural fact of "miscegenation": 'such is the mirror of almost all these conjunctions of white and black! two tinctures which nature has dissociated like oil and vinegar' (2:331). Note that it is the very *unnatural* act of the 'conjunctions of white and black' itself and not simply the resulting offspring, as in much of the trope of "monstrous hybridity," that provides a metaphor and vocabulary for linking "interracial" sex to vengeful and duplicitous behavior.

In his 1841 *Histoire de l'expédition militaire des français à Saint-Domingue*, Antoine Métral also characterized the 'African' women of Saint-Domingue as having used their *natural* attractiveness to perform sexual revenge against their masters:

> These African women found a method of mollifying their slavery, in the passions that they inspired in their masters; they skilled themselves in the arts of pleasure [*la volupté*]; they had a naturally touching and naïve manner, they mingled with their caresses tender refusals, delays, and looks filled with lascivious langor. They employed desperation and the powers of tears, without neglecting finery [*la parure*], nor dancing, nor scented baths. (16)

Aside from the fact that Métral is conflating the stereotypical portrayal of free women of color in Saint-Domingue with that of the slave women who would not ordinarily have had access to 'finery' and 'scented baths,' it is the act of "miscegenation" itself that has the power to inspire vengeance *for* "mulatto/as." According to Métral, it was the ostensibly "white" slave mistress who was 'Too often, proud and jealous ... [who] imposed upon them out of vengeance punishments filled with indecency and ignominy' (16).

Garrigus has suggested that the colonists invented such characterizations of women of color, and especially "mulattas," as a futile attempt to contain "miscegenation" in the colony (2003, 77). Historian Philippe Girard, however, who has also studied these highly sexualized descriptions of women of color, has questioned such conclusions on the part of historians, whom he views as 'dismiss[ing] Saint-Domingue's sensuous reputation, and particularly that of the *mulâtresses*, as a colonial construct.' Girard argues that we cannot completely 'cast aside' these accounts simply because they were written by people with 'an agenda' (2009, 64). According to him, 'primary sources amply back the claim that extramarital affairs were unusually common in Saint-Domingue before and during the Leclerc–Rochambeau expedition.' Thus, he concludes: 'A historian can accept these events as historical facts, even as they dissect the motives of the sexual partners who indulged in such affairs and of the writers who related them' (64–65).

Yet I would urge us to ask a completely different set of questions about these accounts; questions that would be less related to veracity or distortion and more attendant to interpretation and experience. I want to know whether, by focusing too much on those relatively brief passages in writings from colonial and later revolutionary Saint-Domingue in which women of color are painted as highly erotic sexual beings, we have become unable to read 'along the archival the grain' (Stoler, 2010a, 53) of these narrations to understand how an analysis that is much less dependent upon the experiences of the men doing the narrating could produce an alternative picture of these same women as obstinate, influential, radical, and even revolutionary? In other words, I am asking what picture of the woman of color might emerge if we read simultaneously in opposition to and in consultation with the dominant epistemology, recognizing that colonial discourse was always filled with both 'rival and reciprocal energies' (Stoler, 2010a, 53)?

As historian Barbara Bush has observed, much of '[h]istory has been written for men, by men and thus records only what men wish to see' (147). The result is that 'the woman's role in slave resistance ha[s] ... been obscured by over-emphasis on her sexual functions and the highly biased interpretation of these functions,' all of which 'ha[s] left a negative and distorted picture' (147). Late eighteenth- and early nineteenth-century writers did more than just create a narrative of "mulatto/a" vengeance that was nearly always juxtaposed with pseudoscientific theories of "race." They also, at times unwittingly, produced an enormously varied, uncertain, and unstable picture of women of color as radical and rebellious. That is to say that if one reading of the behaviors described above leaves us with a trace of the desire and disgust, seduction and sentiment that was reportedly inherent to living in proximity to these women of color, another reading of that same behavior could produce a record of radical rebellion against patriarchal authority and participation in anti-slavery activism on the part of these same women. In their writings, the colonists' obsession with the sexuality of women of color has often served to cover up an anxiety about the possibilities, real or imagined, for these women to transgress colonial authority and contribute to anti-slavery efforts.

The woman of color's myriad contributions to what Beckles has called in another context, 'broad-based ideological preparation' (137) of the Haitian Revolution, as portrayed in its literary history, brings to the surface deep anxieties about the kinds of actions that could be considered revolutionary in the first place. Witness a greatly suggestive anecdote from Justin Girod de Chantrans, the Swiss traveler, which has gone largely unnoticed in recitations of his descriptions of women of color. In his *Voyages*, Girod de Chantrans quite famously contended that women of "mixed race" in Saint-Domingue had erotic powers that charmed and corrupted 'whites': 'these women, who are naturally more lascivious than European women,' writes Girod de Chantrans:

> flattered by their power over whites, have gathered together, in order to conserve it, all the pleasures to which they themselves are susceptible. Pleasure has become for them an object of particular study, a well-researched and necessary art ... Immodest, without shame, they have acquired, without even trying, a decided superiority in libertinage. (181)

But only a few pages earlier in his narrative, he had recounted a brief story about an enslaved *'mulâtresse,'* whom he represented as having in her own way foreshadowed divine slave resistance: 'I am sending you an exact copy of a note that was surprisingly found in the last few days in the hands of a young *mulâtresse*, enslaved & ill-content with her master,' Girod de Chantrans writes, 'She had written it in her own blood, & I still have it.' The note said, according to Girod, 'I am leaving all vengeance to God; it belongs only to him' (qtd. in 170). While Girod de Chantrans presents this tale merely as one last piece of evidence concerning the danger of teaching slaves to read and write, there is a way in which we could and *should* interpret the fact that the letter was written in the slave woman's own blood as a much more immediate death threat rather than a providential one. For, as Bush has written of the relative lack of inscriptions about women of color in the largely male-authored archive that constitutes the basis of much of the historiography on slave rebellions, 'the influence and power certain black women held over slaves may have been ignored or overlooked by European men conditioned to believing in the total political and social subjugation of their own women' (156).

Perhaps the most striking example of the ways in which the participation of women of color during the Haitian Revolution can have been easily distorted and silenced—once by the sorts of repression of their *'real* lives', and a second time by excessive focus upon the more entertaining accounts of colonial women of color in their historical *afterlives*—comes from the much less consulted Colonel Charles Malenfant's 1814 *Des Colonies, et particulièrement celle de Saint-Domingue*. Malenfant led a battalion during the Leclerc expedition to restore slavery to Saint-Domingue and, according to the abolitionist James MacQueen, he later became a spy for the French government in Surinam (180). Malenfant writes that during a military campaign designed to attack 'a camp of negroes, in Fonds-Parisien, in the plain of Cul de Sac,' his troops captured a 'great Vaudou priestess' (217-18). According to the captured slave women whom Malenfant subsequently interviewed, this great priestess was responsible for placing myriad obstacles in the way of his troops in the hopes of thwarting their discovery of the revolutionists' camp. After capturing the great priestess, whom he describes as a 'very beautiful, well-dressed *négresse*,' however, Malenfant complains that his troops 'instead of listening to her and obtaining information about her plans ... cut her to pieces with the blade of their swords' (218–19). The colonel, for his part, claimed that if he hadn't been busy with the pursuit of the male revolutionists, he would have not have 'suffered for them to have massacred her, without at least having obtained ample information about her projects' (219). Though Malenfant highlights and indeed mocks the ineffectiveness of the efforts of this *'belle négresse créole'* to prevent his troops from finding the camp, he also rather ironically recognized that with her death a great deal of information about not only her involvement but the movements of the Haitian revolutionists themselves was lost forever.

Despite the fact that Malenfant surely wanted to 'interrogate' this powerful priestess in order to get her to reveal information that would have helped the colonists, the behavior of his troops, as precipitous as it was presumptuous, provides a metaphor for the ways in which the lives of women of color during the Haitian Revolution have often been dismissed as ancillary, unimportant, and, ultimately, disposable. Malenfant appears continuously stunned and bemused by the power and influence that 'Vaudou' priestesses wielded over adherents of their religion. Take, for example, Malenfant's description of another priestess from 'Arrada': 'the negroes and negresses do not hide their belief that no one could have any human power over her' (220). Malenfant's astonishment that the Haitian revolutionists believed in the power of these priestesses, in particular, and 'Vaudou,' in general, speaks to not only his biases as an outside observer, but to his complete disregard for the important roles of such women, whose military diversions have been well-documented by historians (Girard, 2009, 69–77). Moreover, according to Karol K. Weaver women of color also operated as *'hospitalières,'* 'infirmières,' midwives, herbalists, *'kaperlatas,'* and even *'commandeurs,'* leading Weaver to refer to such women as, 'medical revolutionaries' who 'forcefully and skillfully resisted slavery' and 'contributed to the revolution that ultimately freed Saint-Domingue from French control' (3, 7, 5, italics in original).[5]

In not taking for granted how to read the behavior of women of color described in the works of largely male authors, I believe we can uncover what Stoler has called '[s]ubjugated knowledge," or 'unsanctioned idioms, and disqualified practices [that] were not outside official knowledges but folded as preserved possibilities with them' (2010b, 212). Monique Allewaert says that 'transversal reading' of this kind does not require us to read 'against' an author's 'stated interests' (24), which I take to mean that reading *along with* the dominant colonial perspective, which was to pilfer, rape, enslave, and kill, may actually be the best way 'to access desires and fantasies' about revolutionary women of color 'that cannot be reduced to the more dominant interests that move through that same work' (Allewaert, 2013, 24). The opposite of *silencing* is to make noise, which is exactly what the women of the Haitian Revolution were described as having done by not only historians and other chroniclers of the period, but by the many novelists and poets whose imaginings populated the Atlantic World up through the middle of the nineteenth century.

In the three fictions of the Haitian Revolution that will be more fully elaborated upon in the chapters that make up Part Two of *Tropics of Haiti*, the same manifest tropologies of "racial" temptation inspired by the existence of women of color appear directly alongside representations of such women as fiercely benevolent in the protection of their kinfolk, often ardently anti-slavery when it came to the topic of abolition, and sometimes radically rebellious in the face of both the Haitian revolutionaries and the French colonists alike. These are women who are represented not only as having fully participated in the Revolution, but as also having been immediately defiant in the face of both colonial and broader patriarchal authority. We might say, therefore, that inherent in the "mulatto/a" vengeance narrative's

---

[5] Long before either Girard or Weaver, historians like Moitt and Bush stressed that women's roles during the Haitian Revolution were not limited to armed combat, even though 'armed revolt was an important dimension of women's resistance to slavery' (Bush, 148–53, 156, 159; Moitt, 126, 128, 132) since women often acted as go-betweens or emissaries (Bush, 159), engaged in 'marronage' (126), and 'transported weapons' and other goods (128).

trope of the "tropical temptress" is the same kind of ambivalence that could make a "monstrous hybrid" into a 'black Spartacus.'

Before moving on to the three fictions of revolutionary Saint-Domingue covered in Part Two—the anonymously published *La Mulâtre comme il y a beaucoup de blanches* (1803); *Zelica the Creole* (1820), attributed to Leonora Sansay; and 'Theresa, a Haytien Tale,' by an author who signs his or her name only 'S'—I want to make the case that it was not only through acts of physical violence that we find the women of color of the Haitian Revolution behaving heroically. Though, as Bush and Arlette Gautier have pointed out, female revolutionaries of color have not often been named in contemporary histories of the Haitian Revolution (Bush, 154; Gautier, 2010, 221), with the notable but usually cursorily mentioned exceptions of Sannite Belair, Marie-Jeanne Lamartinière, and Défilée Bazille or Défilée-la-folle (Braziel, 2005, 58),[6] who are each known and praised for having engaged in armed, violent acts, what we might call alternatively revolutionary female heroes appear with surprising frequency in the literary history of the Haitian Revolution.

Purported eyewitnesses, for example, tell us about benevolent women of color who defy the orders of both their masters and the male revolutionaries. In the *Histoire de Mesdemoiselles de Saint-Janvier, les deux seules blanches conservées à Saint-Domingue* (1812), an author known only as Mademoiselle de Palaiseau, who claimed to have collected this story from two "white" girls who witnessed the events described therein, describes a slave called 'La bonne Marie' as the 'protectrice' of the Saint-Janvier and Georges families.[7] 'La bonne Marie's' behavior is striking particularly because it is

---

6 Thomas Madiou writes that Sannite Belair was a young free woman of color who had married one of Louverture's lieutenants, Charles Belair. She was known as 'la brigande,' famous for, in Madiou's words, 'having slashed, with her own hands, a young white man [*avait de ses propres mains, sabré [un] jeune blanc*]' (Madiou, 2:362). Marie Jeanne Lamartinière is noteworthy for having 'led the *indigènes* in the extraordinary Battle of Crête-à-Pierrot' (Dayan, 1995b, 47), and Braziel Evans quotes sources who attribute Bazile's nom de guerre, Défilée, to the fact that she is thought to have 'order[ed] Dessalines's soldiers to march on into battle, crying, "DE—FI—LEZ!"' (qtd. in Braziel, 2005, 66). For more on Bazile and Lamartinière see Madiou (3:326). Other female revolutionaries include Cécile Fatiman, who assisted at the ceremony of Bois-Caiman and purportedly led a battalion at the important battle of Vertières (Madiou, 3:47).

7 De Palaiseau's narrative appears to have been the inspiration for an 1821 German drama entitled *Die Schwestern St. Janvier*, by playwright Johanna Franul von Weissenthurn. Susanne Kord describes the play as portraying 'the terror regime of General Dessalines and the attempt, by loyal and humane blacks, to save the sisters St. Janvier who stand symbolically as the last remnant of white ideology on the island' (2007, 13). Kord describes Dessalines's wife, whose name has been changed to Julia in this rendition, as accusing her husband of '*inhibiting* the cause of black emancipation

her own father who killed M. de Saint-Janvier during the Revolution. As if to punctuate the very ambiguity of "racial" lines of loyalty, de Palaiseau tells us that there was also 'another Marie, whom Mme. de Saint-Janvier had welcomed into her home out of sympathy. This last [Marie] was far from resembling the other, for she was hiding, under a very sweet exterior, an atrocious character' (21). The evil Marie tells the revolutionists, including la bonne Marie's father Jean-Baptiste, where the families are hiding (24), leading to the execution of Mme. Georges and her three daughters. Later, after the assassination of the Emperor Jean-Jacques Dessalines, Marie-Claire Heureuse (Dessalines's wife), procures a passage to New York for the two Saint-Janvier children, effectively saving their lives a second time.[8]

The tale of the Saint-Janvier sisters is a remarkable narration of the complications of female resistance in Saint-Domingue. As Jeremy Popkin has written: 'Five separate black rescuers—four of them women—played a role in the girls' survival' (2007, 364). Importantly, one of these rescuers, Marie-Claire Heureuse, protects the Saint-Janvier sisters from her own husband, the famed founder of Haitian independence, Jean-Jacques Dessalines. Heureuse therefore shirks patriarchal authority in a broad and complex way that defies horizontal understandings of resistance as "black" against "white," the enslaved against the free, here, pitting males against females and husbands against wives. Yet, even more importantly for our purposes, by naming one Marie 'good,' and the other evil, and depicting the benevolent behavior of the third Marie as an all too humane response to the untoward cruelty of Dessalines, the text once again forecloses our ability to view all three Maries as engaging in acts of revolution that made sense within the individual contexts and subjectivities in which these women found themselves. In other words, by inviting us only to view la bonne Marie and Marie-Claire Heureuse as 'good,' the text in essence makes invisibly treacherous the third Marie, who becomes almost a stock character or a foil meant primarily to reinforce the author's own anti-revolutionary ideological standpoint. It is up to us to read beyond the author's interpretation of this behavior if we want to get at a fuller picture of female radicality.

If, when we say revolution or resistance, we mean only that which is armed, physical, immediately violent, and can be clearly read as anti-slavery, then we 'forestall' learning about the many motives and perspectives of some

---

through revolution' (13). The tale also provided the inspiration for Alexandre de Saillet's *Lucile de Saint-Albe, épisode de la Révolution de Saint-Domingue.*

8 Heureuse also saved the naturalist Michel-Etienne Descourtilz when she hid him from her husband, in all places, under her bed, which Descourtilz wrote about in his *Voyages d'un naturaliste* (see also Girard, 2011, 125). For Marie-Claire Heureuse, see Dayan (1992, 47).

women of color who may have been ideologically on the side of the revolutionists, like Heureuse, but who perhaps could not agree with its bifurcated logic of 'liberty or death.' By foreclosing an expansion of the category of revolution beyond the violence-dominated, masculinist military sphere, we become blinded to the many other ways in which women (and men) were imagined as having held what we might interpret to be alternatively significant and powerful roles.

The future empress of Haiti was not the only male revolutionary's wife revered for her benevolence in saving the lives of various "white" colonists. In her *Mémoire d'un Enfant* (1867), Athénaïs Michelet (*née* Mialaret), the third wife of the famous French historian Jules Michelet, recounts how it was Suzanne Louverture (Toussaint Louverture's wife) who saved her father, Yves Mialaret, from the vengeance of the revolutionary general, not once, but at least twice, and possibly also a third time.[9] Athénaïs Michelet says that she penned this memoir at the behest of her husband, who had so often asked her to write this history. Having briefly sketched it once before in a short piece entitled 'L'Oiseau,' Michelet says that she had merely 'reconstructed the story' of her father's life out of 'a few letters' (172). She made it a 'point of duty,' she wrote, 'never to add a single word of my own to these often very incomplete documents' (172). The only difference between the early version penned by her and this later account was, according to Michelet, that 'In a former work ("L'Oiseau"),' she had 'inadvertently stated' that her father visited Louverture during his captivity at the Joux. 'This was impossible,' Michelet later wrote, 'as he was in America at the time' (173).

Female revolutionary benevolence enters into the memoir when Michelet recalls how her father had gone to Saint-Domingue at the age of 19 in the capacity of a school teacher (154) and would eventually provide private instruction to Toussaint Louverture's children. Michelet says that he was eventually taken captive, along with two others, by the Haitian general for five months. 'Forgotten in the deepest cells,' she writes, 'and scarcely fed, they were very near death. Toussaint ordered them out to be shot; but when the time came he had a misgiving, and doubtless appreciated the advantage that might accrue to himself from sparing one of the three prisoners.' However, according to Michelet, 'With negro superstition, he would not make the selection, but left it to Fate, or rather to female divination; and the French youths were brought before Madame Toussaint. "You require a teacher for your children," said he: "choose one of these three monkeys"' (161). Louverture's wife saved Michelet's father, and the other two prisoners were shot (161). Mialaret, who had only narrowly escaped certain death, was

---

9 All translations of this text are taken from Mary Frazier's 1868 translation of the original, *The Story of My Childhood*.

later arrested as a spy under the orders of Louverture, eventually having 'found himself once again within the tyrant's den' (167). Michelet writes that 'two things, however, insured my father's safety,—his evident loyalty (for he might contend openly, but never betray); and then too, he was beloved by Madame Toussaint, to whom he had always shown great respect' (167). In addition, in a more ambiguous passage that accounts for revolutionary benevolence towards Mialaret, possibly on the part of Dessalines's wife, after her father had the 'audacity to remonstrate' against the 'slave-trade,' Michelet says that Louverture, whom a 'blind fury began to absorb' threw her father into prison yet again (167). Milaret's daughter goes on to say that though it seemed to her father that finally his 'last hour was drawing near,'

> But a woman's heart was on the watch for his safety. One night whose morrow he was doubtless destined never to welcome, his sentinels were intoxicated and slept heavily. My father who was awake heard a rustling noise,—the sound of something moving against the wall. It was a ladder of ropes. He seized it, climbed up and descended on the other side. Two friendly negroes awaited him, with a horse for his use and a passport,—which I have yet,—made out for a tradesmen, and signed by Dessalines. (168–69)

There also exist accounts of less famous women of color who were celebrated for performing acts their authors viewed as extraordinary, both because of the revolutionary conditions under which they were performed and because of what these actions seem to signify about the ideologies of these women with respect to the Revolution. Elie-Joseph-Brun Lavainne, for example, whom Jeremy Popkin says 'must have been among the last living French witnesses to the Haitian Revolution' (2007, 329), recalls in his 1855 memoir of events that occurred in 1803, when he was just 12 years old, a 'black woman' who saved him from drinking contaminated water during the Revolution (Popkin, 2007, 20; 333). Bernard Barthélemi Louis Leclerc, a court official in Cap-Français in 1791, also claimed in his 1793 recitation of the events that a benevolent 'black woman,' his '"amie"' saved his life during an insurrection (qtd. in Popkin, 2007, 376). Antoine Métral, who published his *Histoire de l'insurrection dans le nord de Saint-Domingue* in 1818, for his part, claims that slave women often saved the lives of the white colonists whom they had nursed as babies and these lucky colonists thus 'escaped the shackles of the conspirators by a tenderness contracted in the cradle' (24). Marcus Rainsford, too, writes of a benevolent woman of color who provided a U.S. vessel commander captured by the Haitian revolutionaries and subsequently deprived of adequate subsistence, with 'a basket, containing the most delicate food, with the finest fruits.' Rainsford writes that this woman 'with a face most beautiful and of the finest symmetry' 'entreated him to receive them silently and to destroy any remnants, as a discovery would be fatal to her, and prejudicial to himself' (234–35). Rainsford had also described a different 'mulatto woman' whose loyalties also appear to have been divided when she provided, under unclear circumstances, information to the French military by conveying to the colonels Spencer and Chamilly the fact that the city of Léogâne had been 'evacuated' (187), information which allowed them to enter the city unchecked and unharmed. In a similar account, Venault de Charmilly spoke of a 'mulâtresse' who alerted the French military to the fact that Fort Bizoton had been abandoned, allowing them to take that route for refuge (151).

Other witnesses to slavery and revolution in Saint-Domingue describe the ways in which the complexities of family loyalties made acts of benevolence *vis-à-vis* slavery enormously fraught for some women of color. One of the only moments in which female resistance to authority is broached in Baron de Vastey's collection of slave testimonies, *Le Système colonial dévoilé* (1814), is a moving reference to his mother, Elisabeth 'Mimi,' 'fille naturelle' of 'Dumas, a planter from Marmelade, currently a property owner in France' (70–71).[10] After describing how 'Mimi' saved an infant slave named Laurent from being thrown into 'le four à chaux' by her own father (thus, Vastey's grandfather), eventually raising him as her own child so that the slave mother could return to work, Vastey writes: 'virtuous and kind Mimi, you are no longer! But you enjoy in our hearts eternal blessings as the reward for your good deeds; your friend here consecrates your name and your virtues for the veneration and the friendship of all kind and sensitive hearts' (71). Even though Mimi's resistance to her father's despotism likely took place long before the formal Revolution began, Vastey's brief and fleeting narration of her defiant behavior unwittingly provides a framework for thinking about benevolence as resistance, which will be the subject of chapter five of the present volume.[11] The bulk of Vastey's *Le Système* is devoted to explaining how all people of color, and

---

10 For Elisabeth 'Mimi' as Vastey's mother, see Daut (2014, 180).

11 Two advertisements for runaway slaves on the Dumas plantation listed in Jean-Pierre Le Glaunec's marronage database reveal both male and female slave resistance on Vastey's grandfather's plantation. The first advertisement reads: 'A negro named Charlot, without a brand, skin a little bit red, pock marked, big feet, ran away as a maroon on the 22nd of September last from the plantation of Dumas, in Marmelade. Those who recognize him, are pleased to arrest him and to give notice to M. Sorbier, Trader in Cap, or to M. Crabère, lawyer of the aforementioned plantation: there will be a reward.' The second reads: 'François, 27 years of age, & Jean-Baptiste, 28 years old, both from the Congo nation, stamped DUMAS; and a *Mulâtresse*, named Marinette, stamped DELISLE, 27 years old, escaped as maroons on the 19th of May; all three of them belonging to the Dumas plantation in Marmelade. Those who have any knowledge of them are pleased to arrest them & to give notice to M. Bertrand ...' See http://www.

especially women, were victimized by slavery and colonialism rather than emboldened. If slave resistance should be viewed as anti-slavery, as Beckles contends, opposing the violence of slavery in ways that produced material results was also anti-slavery. The slave in question not only lived, according to Vastey, but went on to produce a family, not of slaves, but of Haitian citizens: 'Laurent, which is the name of this child, is at the present time, forty-five years old, the father of a large family, an excellent manager, and one of the best Haitian farmers' (1814a, 71). Every moment of resistance and especially female resistance constituted a threat to the patriarchal slave-owning society of Saint-Domingue precisely because it contained the life-giving possibility to upset the entire colonial logic of "white" domination over "blacks," as well as the more general Enlightenment logic of male domination over females. It was a bold counter-move, then, on Vastey's part, to praise a woman of color for extraordinarily defying patriarchal authority, and in so doing, subverting the very colonial logic that supported slavery.

In his 1859 novel of the Haitian Revolution, Eméric Bergeaud, who is the subject of chapter nine of *Tropics of Haiti*, also represented women of color as having played various benevolent roles, some of them seemingly contradictory. In this novel, which Bergeaud contended should be read as 'history' (v), the historian turned novelist interpreted the following story as an example of the heroism of women of color:

> A woman and her husband were being taken to be hanged. The man turned pale at the sight of the rope; the woman, stoic and strong, put it around her own neck and encouraged her husband, by her example and her words, to sacrifice his life for liberty.

Bergeaud includes a further example of female revolutionary heroism when he recounts how '[a] mother, witnessing the dread of her two daughters whose sad fate she was about to share, said to them: "My children, do not cry; rejoice, rather, to die: our loins will not any longer produce slaves [*nos flancs ne porteront point d'esclaves*]"' (249). Nevertheless, Bergeaud writes that

> on the other side, the women of our country [*les femmes indigènes*], whose fathers, husbands, sons, and brothers were fighting under the flag of the insurrection, at the same time, performed in the cities the office of doctors and sisters of charity; they were taking care of sick Europeans with a generosity that is almost without example, and as such, they opposed to the rabid scourge that seemed to have been aroused by the powerful avengers of slavery, another scourge, that of humanity. (225).

marronnage.info/fr/lire.php?type=annonce&id=6576 and http://www.marronnage.info/fr/lire.php?type=annonce&id=11324.

The account of John R. Beard in *The Life of Toussaint L'Ouverture* (1853) closely matches Bergeaud's description of the revolutionary benevolence of women of color. Beard wrote:

> There were other benefactors. Sisters of charity, truly worthy of the name, went from street to street, and from bed to bed, ministering with tenderness and skill to the sick, the despairing, and the departing. Womanly love was almost the only virtue that maintained itself erect. When all other remedies had proved vain, that noble affection showed itself fertile in resources, nor was it the less respectable because in the extremity it resorted to fetish practices which had their origin in Africa. More simple and even more touching was that manifestation of it which compelled young women to follow their lovers to their graves. Amid the faithless only faithful found. It is terrible to think that some of these worthy women may afterwards have been repaid with slavery. (218–19)

In a different rendering of female revolutionary contributions, Edmond Bonnet, the son of Guy Bonnet (a former general and aide to André Rigaud who had been exiled to Santiago de Cuba [Girard, 2009, 149]), also describes female benevolence, but this time, towards the male revolutionists. Bonnet recalled an episode in which Dessalines was protected by a free woman of color named Madame Pajeot, who was the governess of a church in the parish of la Petite Rivière de l'Artibonite. Bonnet says that Pajeot, 'shared the concerns of the masses' (114), describing how on one memorable occasion, after serving Dessalines his coffee, Pajeot simulated the position of a person being arrested in order to signal to Dessalines and his ally Nicolas Saget that French troops planned to arrest the general immediately. Because of Pajeot's heroic actions, Dessalines narrowly escaped capture.

The conflicted language used by Métral in his description of women in combat in Saint-Domingue further demonstrates how different forms of benevolence could be variously celebrated or demonized all in one text based upon the gaze of the onlooker. Métral writes that under the Revolution:

> The weaker sex showed itself to be stronger: young women without expressing a single complaint ... went with pride before their punishment, and with the most touching example, encouraged those who were hesitant to die for liberty. We saw some of them with an even more surprising character smile in dying in the presence of their masters against whom they desired vengeance. (1818, 43)

This is the same Métral who had earlier in his text praised "black" female slaves for weeping over the corpses of their masters when they could not save them (23). Métral's statement that 'one sees great vice alongside great virtue' (1818, 22) thus becomes an unwitting microcosm of the paradoxes of female resistance in Saint-Domingue, where the meanings of virtue and vice were not nearly as clear as many nineteenth-century witnesses of the Haitian Revolution assumed.

It is only natural to be influenced to a certain extent by the authors of these texts in our interpretations of the benevolent (or disloyal) behaviors of the women described above. However, if we try for a moment to counter-intuitively decontextualize the portrayal of these women from the ideological standpoints of their authors, we might make room for understanding the complexities of revolutionary involvement without recourse to the binary of *good* versus *bad*, which is to say that no matter the author's point of view, what is important is that these women are being described as continuously breaking all kinds of rules, interrupting what we might call the 'voice-over' (Berlant, 1997, 223) of dominant narratives, and daring to challenge male authority. In several completely different kinds of personal tales of female revolutionary involvement, we see, on the one hand, women of color whose actions were demonized by those who inscribed them because they corresponded with the actions of the male revolutionists and, on the other hand, women of color whose actions were praised because they were viewed as having contributed to Haitian independence. Take, for example, what scholar Deborah Jenson has called the 'cryptic comment' (2011, 8) made by General Leclerc in a letter in which he claimed that the authorities had arrested 'one of the mistresses of Toussaint who had come here to assassinate me' (qtd in Jenson, 2011, 8). Clearly, Leclerc condemned this woman who sought to kill him, but his condemnation underscores the fact that the celebration of revolutionary behavior is wholly dependent upon the ideology to which not only the author subscribes, but also that to which the readers subscribe, and not necessarily that of the people who are being described. In other words, to the Haitian revolutionists, the woman trying to assassinate Leclerc was almost certainly a welcome ally, if not a direct agent, while to the French colonists, surely, she was a grave enemy, but her own motives are much less clear.

Malenfant's 1814 narrative, too, contains a second-hand account of female revolutionaries that further punctuates the idea that, in Simon During's words, 'representations are produced from certain points of view' (143). The colonel reported that the Haitian revolutionary leader, Hyacinthe, personally told him that the revolutionists often received ammunition from 'negresses who frequently visited the camps and lived in the city. These women received [ammunition] in exchange for the cabbage, carrots, and other vegetables they sold to white soldiers; and sometimes they received [ammunition] as the price of their favors' (Malenfant, 1814, 235). Hyacinthe, as one of the leaders of the revolt, even though he protected Malenfant on more than one occasion, viewed the actions of these female slaves as a heroic contribution to the Revolution, while Malenfant clearly viewed this behavior as treacherous.[12] On the flip side, many of the former Haitian revolutionists and their descendants tended to unquestioningly commemorate these same actions undertaken by women of color who fought on the side of the *indigènes* during the Revolution. The Haitian historian Thomas Madiou clearly spoke with approval and admiration of women of color who aided the revolutionary cause by hiding ammunition under their dresses (3:20), or who captured, arrested, and delivered for execution colonists who had escaped to the woods (3:18).

Dealing with descriptions of the sexuality of women of color provides perhaps the best examine of how practicing de-contextualization might be revelatory with respect to female revolutionaries. As Bush has observed, women of color using their sexuality in the context of the Haitian Revolution—no matter on which side that sexuality was deployed—has been treated with disdain by those who have inexplicably drawn the conclusion that women of color were more likely to betray their fellow slaves due to their putative involvement with colonial men (154). This conclusion bears the distinct influence of the many travel writers who in their writings on Saint-Domingue suggested that women of color, both slave and free, did not usually participate in the Revolution except to warn planters and other colonialists, with whom they were often in love, to the plans of rebellious slaves (A. Gautier, 1990, 154–55). Ducœurjoly, for one, claimed that:

> the *négresses* who lived with white men were ordinarily more attentive to their duties, they acquired a manner of thinking that distinguished them from the others. They revealed to their masters and their lovers the plots of the slaves; even though they were more attracted [*décidé pour ceux-ci*] to these here, they understood that they would be less happy with them if they remained submissive. (1:27)

Jean Casimir, writing about slavery in more general terms, has cautioned us about drawing the same conclusions found in the historical works we are studying: 'To speak of fugitives and deserters is to think like the slave trader and the planter. On no scientific basis can one favor their opinion and perceptions over the overt opposition of those they enslaved' (2009, xii). Similarly, to think of women of color as allies or enemies, traitors or devotees of the revolutionary cause, is to think like the 'slave trader and the planter,' because in doing so we ignore or discount the feelings and

---

12 Malenfant describes Hyacinthe as powerful and adored to the point of 'idolatry' by the 'blacks' of the colony. He writes: 'if he had wanted to, he could have become the chief of the colony, and more powerful than Toussaint L'Ouverture had ever been' (1814, 76).

Transgressing the Trope of the "Tropical Temptress"

perceptions of these women themselves, who may simply have been trying to survive—a form of resistance itself—in an oppressive logic where slavery and colonialism were not only certain kinds of spiritual deaths, but always had the capacity to occasion physical deaths. Rather than trying to focus only upon women of color whose ideology about the Revolution matches our own—ideologies which are certainly influenced by the fact that our opinions about the these events are hardly a matter of *life and death*, as they were for the people whom we study—I wonder if we better serve the interests of women's history by considering the roles of all of the women of the Haitian Revolution, even if we do not approve.[13]

A deeper consideration of the motivations behind the behaviors of women of color—both slave and free—described in an array of texts published about the Haitian Revolution, as well as an expansion of the term revolution to include the more controversial acts of benevolence towards "whites" and even counter-revolutionary behavior, can help us to comprehensively reassess the kinds of biases in 'existing analyses of the woman's role in slave resistance' that have contributed to the 'historical invisibility' of women of color (Bush, 147). As Rhoda E. Reddock has written, 'In the women's movement throughout the world, women have had to reexamine and reinterpret history and often rewrite it in order to make women visible' (127). Rewriting history to 'make women visible' does not require powers of invention. Rather, rewriting history calls for strategies of intervention that call into question the assumptions in dominant histories of war and revolution not only about what constitutes revolutionary acts and resistance to authority, but also what constitutes history itself. Seen within this frame, historical writing is much less the 'litany of the actual' (Allewaert, 150) than a complication of the perspectival: recognizing that what an author narrates is *true* for him or her, but perhaps not for us. Such perspectivism may be even more necessary when dealing with the histories of subjugated populations. This is because, in Elizabeth Colwill's words, the history of women of color during the Haitian Revolution is 'multiple rather than singular' and 'exists only as fragments, hidden with texts written by others and for other purposes' (2009, 138). If this is true, then like Moitt, who says that '[t]o get at the slaves' perception of their own condition, one can draw on some of the literary works on the French Caribbean that are an authentic representation of the Caribbean historical experience' (126), to get at the perspectives of female revolutionaries of color in the literary history of the Haitian Revolution, I examine

---

13 In his introduction to the 2006 L'Harmattan edition of *Adonis; ou le bon nègre*, Chris Bongie hints at this problem of judging the actions of the past from the safe distance of the present when he asks, 'Ultimately, among us, who would dare to pronounce these words: liberty or DEATH?' (2006, xxxvii).

the represented motives of these women, some slaves, some free, as described in three deliberately fictive accounts of the Haitian Revolution.

By turning primarily to more obviously fictionalized accounts, I continue to ask, influenced by Geoffrey Hartman's work on trauma narratives, whether there is a 'potentially literary way of knowing' (544). In such an analysis, I want to know if the historico-literary portrayals of women of color found in the myriad works covered in this section of the book constitute more than mere representations. Many of these overtly fictionalized accounts claim to be based upon or inspired by the *'real'* lives of women of color detailed in historical accounts of the Haitian Revolution. There are therefore a variety of ways in which we can view both the fictional and seemingly more historical accounts of the Haitian Revolution contained in Part Two of *Tropics of Haiti* as mere referents, even if deeply influenced by the individual subjectivities and ideologies of their authors, for the uncertainty and ambiguity experienced by women of color who were often portrayed as having grappled deeply with the questions of *right* and *might* called forth by the Haitian Revolution.

Ultimately, considering the portrayal of revolutionary women in fictions of the Haitian Revolution to be a vital component in the broader history of the Haitian Revolution allows us to transcend simply studying the disappointingly stereotypical image of the "tropical temptress" repeatedly found in the narratives of colonial European and U.S. American travelers to Saint-Domingue. We can now move to consider that of the more vexed and complicated "tropical temptress's" literary sisters, the female revolutionary, the benevolent resister, and the anti-slavery muse.[14] In the end,

---

14 Contemporary feminist historiographers of slave resistance in the Americas passionately make the case that female slave resistance should perhaps not be understood using dominant epistemologies. In the words of Moitt, 'what appears on the surface to be docility is often a very subtle, calculated and conscious form of resistance' (126). Moitt has in fact uncovered the ways in which female slaves in the Caribbean resisted the repressions of slavery by engaging in 'armed revolt, *marronage*, the use of poison, and work avoidance and withdrawal,' as well as more 'subtle forms of resistance, such as insolence and verbal altercations with the slaveholder' (126). In addition, Weaver discusses how women of color often participated in 'occupational sabotage by allowing malingerers to remain with the walls of the plantation hospital long after their "illnesses" had been cured,' where they could not only 'interfere with the productivity of the plantation,' but could plot to terrorize whites and gain access to important herbs that they used as poisons (2006, 59–60). Though 'scholars of the French Caribbean have paid little attention to these "subtle" acts of resistance on the part of female slaves, believing that they do not constitute the "most important" acts, what should be emphasized,' Moitt writes, 'is the variety of responses possible in the continuum along which resistance occurred from armed rebellion to acts of accommodation' (126). Similarly, a 'continuum' of responses to the repressions of slavery and the onset of revolution in

the ways in which revolutionary women of color negotiated the fraught positions of being the slaves, lovers, daughters, sisters, friends, and wives of "white" colonial men and "black" revolutionary men, is not all that clear to us. Oscillating between benevolence and resistance, spying and informing, stealing and providing, were simply some of the many kinds of response and engagement with revolution (and interpretations thereof) that we are continuing to uncover. With all of this uncertainty, what we can say for sure is that, given the surprising frequency with which female characters of color appear in radical and resistant roles in fictionalized accounts of the Haitian Revolution in the first half of the nineteenth century—and the similarity of these fictional accounts to the descriptions made by historians, purported eye-witnesses, and other contemporaries of these events—it is astonishing that more attention has not been devoted to addressing the representation of female revolutionaries of color in both fiction and nonfiction during the Haitian Revolution.[15] At the very least, the representations of the female revolutionaries who will be explored in the following analyses of *La Mulâtre, Zelica,* and 'Theresa' can act as reminders of the continuing 'historical invisibility' (Bush, 147) of the '*real*' lives' of black women during the Revolution, which we must continue to try to uncover, even if doing so means to approach the topic in unconventional ways.

Saint-Domingue is precisely what we find in the early literary history of the Haitian Revolution and especially in its portrayal of women.

15 A. Gautier (1985), Moitt (2001), and M. Ferguson (1992) have each written book-length works on women and slavery with chapters or large sections on women and revolts, and all lamenting that more attention has not been devoted to the subject, but there is to date no book-length work devoted solely to the topic of female revolutionaries during the insurrections in Saint-Domingue or the later events of the Haitian Revolution.

CHAPTER FOUR

Moreau de Saint-Méry's Daughter and the Anti-Slavery Muse of *La Mulâtre comme il y a beaucoup de blanches* (1803)

'I remember four women of my boyhood: my mother, cousin Inez, Emma, and Ide Fuller. They represented the problem of the widow, the wife, the maiden, and the outcast. They were, in color, brown and light-brown, yellow with brown freckles, and white. They existed not for themselves, but for men; they were named after the men to whom they were related and not after the fashion of their own souls.'

—W.E.B. Du Bois, 'The Damnation of Women' (1920)

'Je ne conseille point aux dames de lire l'Histoire de la catastrophe de Saint-Domingue: ici toute curiosité, même naturelle, doit cesser; leur âme serait trop péniblement affectée; il y aurait trop de danger pour elles à seulement parcourir cette longue série de crimes de lèse-humanité.'

—Jean-Baptiste Bouvet de Cressé, Préface, *L'Histoire de la catastrophe de Saint-Domingue* (1824)

'Est-il rien de plus accablant pour des pères, que la honte de donner l'être à des enfants incapables de remplir aucunes fonctions civiles, & condamnés à partager l'humiliation des esclaves.'

—Hilliard d'Auberteuil, *Considérations sur l'état présent de la colonie de Saint-Domingue* (2:79)

Scholars of Saint-Domingue have known for some time now that before he was married Moreau de Saint-Méry had a mistress, a free woman of color named Marie Louise La Plaine, with whom he lived for five years in Saint-Domingue. Some scholars have even speculated that La Plaine's child, Jeanne-Louise, 'called Aménaïde,' according to her baptismal record, might have been Moreau de Saint-Méry's daughter since he bequeathed three slaves to her in the 1778 act of dissolution from her mother which he filed with the courts in order to prepare for his marriage to a white Creole woman (Camus, 1960; Rogers, 2006, 87).[1] The fact that Moreau de Saint-Méry later became Aménaïde's 'legal guardian' has only added to the suspicion that the 'young quadroon, raised in France' was his child (Rogers, 2006, 87). The historian Michel Camus writes, 'this generosity on the part of Moreau de Saint-Méry in favor of a quadroon ... permits us to believe that Jeanne-Louise was his child.' The baptismal record 'reinforces this impression,' Camus writes, since Aménaïde's godfather was a powerful and well-known lawyer in Cap-Français (where Moreau de Saint-Méry worked and lived), while her godmother was the wife of a former attorney general of the king (Camus, 1960). Furthermore, according to an entry in the Notariat de Saint-Domingue dated May 30, 1788, Moreau de Saint-Méry had been named the 'legal guardian' of a young 'quadroon, raised in France' named 'Jeanne-Louise, called Aménoïde [sic].' Rogers, who was the first to acknowledge the existence of the document, has therefore concluded that since Aménaïde was the 'daughter of his previous *ménagère*, a free mulattress,' she was 'presumably' Moreau de Saint-Méry's child as well (2006, 87).

Much more than circumstantial evidence, however, allows us to confirm for the first time that Jeanne-Louise, 'called Aménaïde,' was indeed Moreau de Saint-Méry's daughter. As with much of what we know about Moreau de Saint-Méry's life, the corroboration of this fact comes directly from Moreau de Saint-Méry himself. In his *Voyage aux Etas Unis, 1793–1798*, a manuscript that was never published during his lifetime (Mims, v–vi), Moreau de Saint-Méry clearly states that he is traveling with his wife, his teenage daughter named Aménaïde,[2] his young son, and several other

---

[1] Moreau de Saint-Méry's wife was Louise Catherine Milhet, the daughter of an infantry captain from Louisiana. She and Moreau de Saint-Méry were married on April 18, 1781 (Elicona, 12). For scholars who have speculated about Moreau de Saint-Méry's daughter, see Garrigus (2006a, 155); Dubois (2004, 68); and Jenson (2007, 34–35).

[2] Though Moreau de Saint-Méry never mentions the age of his daughter in the *Voyages*, the fact that the shipmate Hollin, who admired Aménaïde on *La Sophie*, asks for her hand in marriage in April of 1794, permits us to assume that she was, as Gérard Gabriel Marion has written, 'of marital age' [*en âge d'être établie*] (17), that is just shy of her sixteenth birthday. On the contrary, if she had been born in 1782, the year after Moreau de Saint-Méry's marriage to Milhet (they married on April 18, 1781, she could not have been born earlier than January 1782 [Elicona, 12]), she would have been only 11 or 12 years old. Thus, it seems that the child called Aménaïde who was born on May 21, 1778 in Saint-Domingue (Camus, 1960) and over whom Moreau de Saint-Méry became the legal guardian some time in 1788, and the teenage daughter also called Aménaïde of the *Voyages*, who was old enough to be married in late 1793 when the ship *La Sophie*

family members and friends (1913, 8). Moreau de Saint-Méry also noted this affiliation in the entry dated September 8, 1807 in his *Notes historiques: états de Parme*: 'M. de Saint-Méry, *fils*' had arrived at Parma 'to pick up Madame la Comtesse Dall'Asta, his sister, and take her to France' (2003, 326). In the early 1800s, Aménaïde Moreau de Saint-Méry had married an Italian count named Pompeo Dall'Asta, with whom she later had two children (Peyrard, 23; le Comte, 264).[3]

That Moreau de Saint-Méry was 'connected to free people of color by a complex web of familial and social ties' (L. Dubois, 2004, 68) is unlikely to surprise anyone with even a cursory knowledge of colonial plantation sexual practices.[4] What will be more surprising perhaps is that Moreau de Saint-Méry, whose *Description de la partie française de Saint-Domingue* forms the epicenter of studies of colonial racism (Sollors, 1997, 120; Garraway, 2005b, 227; Garrigus, 2006b, 65; Dayan, 1995, 229; Rogers, 2006, 77), apparently raised his daughter to be considered "white," first in Saint-Domingue and then later in the United States, France, and Italy (Moreau, 1913, 47, 138, 402; Elicona, 215; Moreau de Saint-Méry, 2003, 220, 226). Such a revelation begs us to consider Moreau de Saint-Méry's writings in the *Description* about women of color in Saint-Domingue from an interpersonal dimension with renewed scrutiny.

After describing the 'Mulâtresse' as a 'Goddess' with a 'fire' that 'burns in her heart' (1797, 1:92), Moreau de Saint-Méry went on to write that, because of their natural concupiscence, '*Mulâtresses* are almost generally condemned, and ... are associated with the female slaves' (1:94). Robert Young's theory of the 'colonial desiring machine,' which circulates around an ambivalent axis of desire and aversion for "non-white" bodies (98), does much to explain Moreau de Saint-Méry's simultaneous attraction to and repulsion for women

embarked from Portland, England to the United States, are almost certainly the same person.

3 Aménaïde was known for her 'remarkable' paintings and musical scores. She had one son with an Italian count from Parma, Pompeo Dall'Asta (Lecomte, 264). Her son's name was Conte Edoardo Dall'Asta (1803–84), and he eventually became one of the most distinguished functionaries in Parma (Lecomte, 264).

4 It is possible that Moreau de Saint-Méry may have had a paternal relationship with some other children of color as well. He vaguely writes in a footnote to his *Considérations*, 'I have, at home [*chez moi*] in Paris, a *mulâtresse* who has never had any other wet nurse [*nourrice*] than her mistress [*maîtresse*]' (1791, 71). Moreau de Saint-Méry ostensibly suggests that his wife is breastfeeding a female baby of color since the Martinican colonist had used this footnote to prove that "white" women in France 'who have known only frivolous pleasures' had found ways to 'relieve the suffering of humanity' by nursing 'baby negro[es].' He writes, 'sometimes, this baby-negro [*cet enfant-nègre*] who was just deprived by death of a mother, suckles from a white breast [*presse un sein blanc*]' (1791, 71).

Moreau de Saint-Méry's Daughter and the Anti-Slavery Muse

of color.[5] However, it was his paternal relationship with the daughter whose death he once wrote would have the power to kill him (1913, 19)[6] that perhaps explains the following often ignored equivocation: 'One should not conclude either,' Moreau de Saint-Méry wrote, 'from what I am saying about the mores of Mulattas that there aren't any who know virtue. Yes, we do see some whose conduct deserves to be taken as a model ... but these exceptions are unfortunately rare' (1797, 1:94). The very rare virtuous 'Mulâtresse' would have to make many 'sacrifices' and undertake a fierce 'combat,' he said, in order to have 'the kind of courage' it would take to 'resist the example of [her] fellow women' and to 'triumph' over her naturally lascivious and degenerate nature (1:94).

Is it possible that Moreau de Saint-Méry was thinking of someone like his own beloved[7] daughter when he wrote each of these passages about women of "mixed race" which, we might say, 'proliferate with illegitimate meanings' (Holgersson-Shorter, 52)?[8] For as H. Holgersson-Shorter has

---

[5] Young borrowed the term 'desiring machine' from Deleuze and Guattari's *Anti-Oedipus* (1977) to express the idea that colonialism was 'not only a machine of war and administration ... it was itself the instrument that produced its own darkest fantasy—the unlimited and ungovernable fertility of "unnatural unions"' (Young, 98).

[6] In a passage of his *Voyages* marked February 4, 1793, Moreau de Saint-Méry refers to a frightening event one night when his daughter was almost knocked overboard by a wave. He stated that had Aménaïde died during this episode, her death would have 'killed him' (1913, 2:19). The event was so startling indeed that 'Our dear Aménaïde,' Moreau de Saint-Méry wrote, 'stayed for the rest of the night in our cabin with us' (2:19). The averted catastrophe of February 4 is only one of several instances in the *Voyages* in which Moreau de Saint-Méry references his daughter. He discusses her painting (27), love for music (138), the effect of her beauty upon one of the shipmates (49), and teaching her English (47).

[7] Moreau de Saint-Méry's voluminous correspondence with his daughter, whom he affectionately and variously calls 'ma chère cocotte' (March 9, 1806) and 'la chère Aménaïde' (March 19, 1806), is housed at the Archivio di Stato in Parma. Although there is nothing particularly striking about Moreau de Saint-Méry's terms of endearment for his daughter on their own, surely it means something that in box 9, marked 'Lettere famigliari ...,' nearly every letter is addressed to his daughter, 'Mme. La Comtesse Dall'Asta, née Moreau de Saint-Méry,' whom the Martinican patriarch at one point chides for not responding to his letters quickly enough (May 4, 1806). For more on the entire collection of items relating to Moreau de Saint-Méry in Parma see Emile Carra, *Gli Inediti di Moreau de Saint-Méry à Parma* (1954) and *L'Ossessione della Memoria: Parma settecentesca nei disegni del Conte Alessandro Sanseverini* (1997), published by the Fondazione Cassa di Risparmio di Parma.

[8] Dominique Rogers has shown that Moreau de Saint-Méry also had sympathies for other free women of color, like the woman of mixed race, Marie-Rose Ledoux (2006, 82), the two lyricists Minette and Lise, a 'wise woman' named Marie-Guérineau, and the widow Cottin, of whom he wrote: 'this venerable woman, this *mulâtresse* who silences

• 223 •

written of Thomas Jefferson's affair and child with a slave named Sally Hemmings, 'The more Jefferson tries to characterize himself as the author of *Notes on the State of Virginia* and, by extension, of the United States, the more the illegitimacy of the mulatta threatens his own legitimacy and authority' (52). Moreau de Saint-Méry's own 'authority' to write with what he calls 'certitude' about the past splendor of the colony (1797, 1:ix–xii) is similarly threatened by the 'illegitimacy' of his pseudoscientific claims about "interracial" degeneracy. Recall that Moreau de Saint-Méry describes the successive male children of "interracial" sex as effeminate, weak, and of questionable and savage morals, while the women become increasingly licentious, sexually dangerous, infertile and corrupt the nearer they are to "whiteness" (1797, 1:78). Could Moreau de Saint-Méry have truly believed the theory of successive degeneration he was espousing when these claims were undoubtedly refuted by the very existence of his own daughter? Perhaps, then, what Ann Laura Stoler has called 'loud asides in the imperative sense … wedged within those folds of truth claims' in colonial discourse (2010a, 23) applies to Moreau de Saint-Méry, who may have been thinking of this very same daughter when he qualified that he was simply writing about some of the 'most precocious mulattas' (1797, 1:92).

Although the fact that he had a daughter of "mixed race" begs us to question whether Moreau de Saint-Méry was being disingenuous in certain passages of the *Description*, Aménaïde Moreau de Saint-Méry's existence occasions even more questions about the silenced, invisible, and erased daughter who was written out of colonial history by her father's own elisions. I find myself endlessly wondering how Aménaïde might have read and responded to the passages in which her father paints such an unflattering portrait of women of color? Would she have agreed that she was the exception rather than the rule or might she have loudly objected to her father's portrayals of women like her, offering herself as a master in painting and music, a mother and a wife (Lecomte, 264; Moreau, 1913, 27, 138, 421; Gambara, 132), as the incontrovertible proof that women of color were capable of virtue by eighteenth- and nineteenth-century standards?[9] More importantly, perhaps, if Aménaïde Moreau de Saint-Méry had objected to her father's writings about women of color, what avenues might have been open to her, as the child of one of the most prominent figures of colonial Saint-Domingue, to refute the dominance of such portrayals?

Moreau de Saint-Méry's simultaneous embrace and repression of what

---

the prejudices of color and birth by her virtues' is 'charitable, hospitable, and she gives everything she makes to the unfortunate' (qtd. in Rogers, 2006, 83).

9 Aménaïde Moreau de Saint-Méry's portrait of her father is housed at the Galleria Nazionale di Parma in Italy. See page 240 below.

Moreau de Saint-Méry's Daughter and the Anti-Slavery Muse

Young has called, in another context, 'the mixed-race offspring that resulted from inter-racial sexual intercourse, the proliferating, embodied, living legacies that abrupt, casual, often coerced, unions had left behind' (25), provides us with an interpretive lens through which to reconsider the image of free women of color in Saint-Domingue. Though "black" female concupiscence seems to be by far the dominant image of free women of color in Saint-Domingue, the 'rare' and 'virtuous' free woman of color—the kind Moreau de Saint-Méry may have considered his daughter to have been—was also the subject of an anonymously published epistolary romance entitled *La Mulâtre comme il y a beaucoup de blanches, ouvrage pouvant faire suite au Nègre comme il y a peu de blancs*.[10] Throughout this chapter, I ask how our understanding of the role played by women of color in both the Haitian Revolution and the colonial Saint-Domingue abolitionist movement would change if we viewed the writings of a free woman of color named Mimi to be found in *La Mulâtre* as a form of autoethnographic writing designed to provide not only what the Haitian author Baron de Vastey might call a 'légitime defense' (Vastey, 1819, iii) for herself, but also a critique of slavery and color prejudice.

La Mulâtre tells the tale of a free woman of color named Mimi, who, like Aménaïde, was the daughter of a "white" Creole father. In a series of letters written back and forth between Mimi, her "white" Creole lover Sylvain, and her father, along with several other minor characters, Mimi's

---

10 The letters begin in March of 1773 and end in May of 1775, a period which, according to Julien Raimond, would have been the height of color prejudice in Saint-Domingue (1791b, 52). While most of the letters are from Mimi to Sylvain and vice versa, occasionally the reader glimpses letters from Mr. de B. (Sylvain's friend) to Sylvain or between Mimi and her sister Sylvie or her friend Saintie. There are also letters from Mimi's father, Mr. le G., to both Mimi and Sylvain, and at one point Mr. le G. also writes to Mimi's mother, Rosette. Though the last part of the novel's title refers to Joseph Lavallée's abolitionist adventure novel *Le Nègre comme il y a peu de blancs* (1789) or *The Negro, Equaled by Few Europeans*, the novel loosely follows the plot of Jean-Jacques Rousseau's *Julie; ou la nouvelle Héloïse* (1761). The novel differs from Rousseau's text in that the anonymous author of *La Mulâtre* only interjects his or her own thoughts into the story once to tell the reader that everything in the letters between Mr. de B. and Sylvain not concerning Mimi has been suppressed (1:34). Unlike Julie, who cedes her 'innocence' to her schoolteacher, Saint-Preux, in the first book of Rousseau's novel and near the beginning of the tale itself, Mimi does not consummate her relationship with Sylvain until the end of *La Mulâtre*. In addition, the reader is never entirely sure whether Sylvain raped Mimi or whether she slept with him *willingly*. Furthermore, while Julie responds in kind to Saint-Preux's declaration of love almost immediately, it takes Mimi over a year of novelistic time and half of the book to admit her love for Sylvain. Lastly, while Rousseau acknowledges the potentially offensive nature of his 'novel' in the preface (Rousseau, 1997, 3), the author of *La Mulâtre* left no preface for us to parse.

letters chronicle her attempts to resist Sylvain's persistent and coercive plot to seduce her. Though Mimi admits that she loves Sylvain, because he is already married to a woman named Fany, with whom he has two children, and because interracial marriage is outlawed in the colony,[11] Mimi refuses to merely become his mistress and thereby lose her 'virtue.' After Mimi and Sylvain end up consummating their relationship in a scene that is ambiguously narrated as a possible rape, Mimi subsequently commits suicide and Sylvain later follows suit.

Woven in between Mimi's simultaneous remonstrations and avowals of love for Sylvain, we find passionate deconstructions of the pseudoscientific theories of "race" made popular by travel writers and functionaries like Moreau de Saint-Méry. Mimi's representation of herself as capable of resisting the sexual corruption of life in the colony interrupts the dominant image of the free woman of color as a seductress put forth by multiple eighteenth-century travel writers like Girod de Chantrans and de Wimpffen, who, much like Moreau de Saint-Méry, complained about the dangerous, deviant, and singular sexual agency of women of color (Wimpffen, 112; Chantrans, 112). Mimi describes herself, much to the contrary, as a virtuous woman of color whose very existence could undermine the idea that there was anything inherently *blanche* about 'virtue.' Her letters thus expose pseudoscientific theories as primarily designed to affirm the kind of theories of "white" superiority that supported colonial patriarchy.

In many respects, Mimi's letters do more than simply deconstruct or react to colonial discourse. Mimi radically inserts herself into the civic life of the colony when she argues for non-violent reform of colonial laws rather than revolution, becoming what we might call a 'tropicopolitan,' after Srinivas Aravamudan, rather than a "tropical temptress." That is, Mimi stands as another example of the 'colonized subject who exists both as a fictive construct of colonial tropology,' and an 'actual resident of tropical space, object of representation *and* agent of resistance' (Aravamudan, 4). By arguing for reform rather than revolution, and utilizing a strategy of interaction with colonial discourse rather than contradiction of it, Mimi's letters provide the occasion to think about the various ways in which free women of color could resist the unflattering and dangerous images of them put forward in various kinds of writing, and also engage in forms of self-representation as resistance to this dominant discourse. In other words, I am much less suggesting the always plausible possibility that the author of *La Mulâtre* was a woman of color herself than I am suggesting that what is important is that the author,

---

[11] In 1778, the French government passed a law that forbade interracial marriages. The law was affirmed by an 1803 ministerial decree that 'banned marriage between blacks and whites' (Heuer, 515).

whoever he or she was, was able to *imagine* the way a woman of color might feel when faced with the abundance of writings circulating in the Atlantic World describing her as lascivious, seductive, and vengeful.

When read as a kind of first-person narrative, Mimi's letters emerge as a part of what Gillian Whitlock has called a 'tradition' of 'female life writing' in 'colonial space' that 'disrupts received forms of self-representation' (22). Reading Mimi's letters as a first-person account of life in Saint-Domingue is in keeping with the ways in which other anonymously or pseudonymously published female-centered narratives, particularly nineteenth-century epistolary romances, have been read. For example, Leonora Sansay's *Secret History; or the Horrors of Santo Domingo* (1808) is often taken to be indicative of the author's own experiences in the colony during the final days of the Revolution, and later as the mistress of Aaron Burr (Drexler, 2003, 184); while the back cover of the anonymously published epistolary romance *The Woman of Colour* (1808) unabashedly states that the author's 'letters recount *her* impressions of Britain and its inhabitants as only a black woman could record them' (emphasis added). Furthermore, as Lyndon J. Dominique, the editor of the new edition of *The Woman of Colour*, notes, 'If *The Woman of Colour was* written by a Caribbean woman of color, she would not have been the first to have published in England.' As Dominique tells us, a poem entitled '"Written by a Mulatto Woman" predates the novel by twelve years,' and though there is 'nothing within the body of the poem that suggests the [author's] race,' he writes, '[t]he race neutral approach taken by this "Mulatto Woman" poet presents the startling possibility that educated women of color like her and Olivia [the protagonist of *The Woman of Colour*] could have published many such anonymous poems, articles, etc. in eighteenth-century British texts.' This hypothesis allows Dominique to conclude that in early nineteenth-century England it may have been 'entirely acceptable, even desirable, to use a woman of color's own voice to promote personal religious crusades such as missionary work as well as political ones like the abolitions of prejudice and slavery' (2007, 212).

We find female authors using the voices of women of color to promote the abolition of both slavery and racism in the literary history of the Haitian Revolution, perhaps most famously in Claire de Duras's *Ourika* (1823), which briefly mentions the revolts in Saint-Domingue (as will be discussed in chapter five), but also in many other less well-known texts. E. Jouannet, under whose name *Zorada; ou la créole* appeared in 1801, for one, claimed to be publishing the personal journal of the eponymous woman of "mixed race." In her journal entries, Zorada, who says she is the daughter of a 'white colonist' and a 'négresse' (1:88), criticizes the planters for raping and otherwise 'corrupting' their slaves: 'The spectacle of their barbarity with respect to their poor slaves [*leurs pauvres noirs*], confronted me continuously, and justified in my eyes the aversion that I felt towards this inhuman caste' (1:91). Although at first Zorada appears to be hypercritical of the slaves' revolt too, she eventually assigns a cosmological rationality for revolutionary violence and even quasi-justifies the Revolution in remarking, 'These bloody scenes of devastation and destruction have proved that supreme justice sometimes allows one crime to be punished by another [*la suprême justice laissait agir quelquefois le crime, pour punir le crime*]' (2:27).

Later in the nineteenth century, under the title *Le Nègre et la Créole ou Mémoires d'Eulalie D**** (1825), Gabrielle de P*** purported to publish a narrative written by a "white" Creole woman from Saint-Domingue named Eulalie D*** as a corollary to Claire de Duras's *Ourika* (1:1). The author writes, 'It is the publication of the touching history of Ourika that helped me to decide to bring to light the adventures of Eulalie D***: the fate of this young Creole woman seems to have been made to contrast with that of the famous *négresse*' (1:1). Although this text does not provide a voice of authority and subjectivity for a woman of color, per se, in likening Eulalie's subject position to that of de Duras's 'brilliant Ourika' (1:25), the author evokes the same kind of repressed subjectivity of women of color in a colonial context. The soon to be orphaned Eulalie, the daughter of a slave trader who would herself eventually be transported from revolutionary Saint-Domingue to Africa and come to believe that she was African, never misses an opportunity to critique the depredations of slavery and the slave trade. She writes, 'Having myself experienced the unhappiness of exile and social subjugation [*déplacement social*], I felt that slavery was an error in the order of all things, and that all of the children of God were my equals' (1:39). Eulalie's thoughts on the Haitian Revolution also emerge as contrary to much of the writing of her time when she says (not without her own prejudices, of course) of the inhabitants of the island where she once lived, 'the indolent African had become the courageous citizen of Haiti' (1:89). Despite the bravery evinced in many of the critiques in which Eulalie uses her voice to criticize male authority, the repressed subject position in which she finds herself is still evident throughout the text, and is most readily glimpsed when she writes, 'I have not wanted to reveal all of my actions to the false judgments established by the decorum of society [*Je n'ai pas voulu livrer toutes mes actions aux faux jugements établis sur les convenances de la société*]' (3:170).

If, then, we read Mimi's letters as part of such a tradition of using the veiled voice of a woman of color to expose the interpersonal devastation wrought by slavery and color prejudice, a woman who must conceal her identity to avoid 'false judgments,' we allow her to be read as both a literary character who resists discursive domination, as well as a historical referent, a form of ventriloquation, for the difficult subject position of female agents of resistance in colonial Saint-Domingue. Mimi resists the non-personhood of colonial typology by writing herself into existence in a "white," male-dominated discursive world in which 'black people' in particular, as Henry Louis Gates, Jr. has written in another context, 'could become speaking subjects only by inscribing their voices in the written word' (1989, 130). In a novel without a narrator or even a named author, Mimi's letters, like the writing by Olaudah Equiano, which Gates Jr. discusses, exemplify the ultimate 'invisible speaking voice that can only write' (131). Mimi's voice that can only write, not only chronicles her eventual forced submission to Sylvain and subsequent suicide at the end of the narrative, but provides a powerful critique of color prejudice, slavery, and colonial despotism, challenging the conventional notion that women of color played no role in the Saint-Domingue abolitionist movement. Mimi's letters are therefore invaluable both for the divergent image they present of free women of color in Saint-Domingue and because they offer the possibility for a tradition of female self-representation as resistance.

Thinking about Mimi's letters as part of a ventriloquated scene of writing as resistance provides us with a few alternative possibilities for thinking about "non-white" female agency in revolutionary Saint-Domingue. It allows us to consider that all free women of color did not just submissively become the concubines of "white" men, nor did they purely aspire to this role, passively accepting the demonic characterizations of them produced in all kinds of colonial writing. Perhaps some free women of color actively resisted the characterization of themselves as 'tropical temptresses' (Garrigus, 2003, 81) or 'mad women in the attic' (Gilbert and Gubar, 2, 51), recognizing the many layers of coercion involved in colonial sexual relations. Perhaps they also expressed anti-slavery thoughts and contributed to the transnational abolitionist movement. For, if the historical record chronicles female slaves who engaged in poisoning their masters, infanticide, and abortion, in acts of 'self-justification ... just as horrific as [their] circumstances' (Aravamudan, 319), I am asking if there were also discursive acts of 'resistance' and 'self-justification' in which free women of color in Saint-Domingue may have been engaged in order to mitigate the horrors of slavery and colonialism.

*

As intriguing as it may be to imagine what Moreau de Saint-Méry's daughter, if she considered herself to have been of "mixed race" at all, would have thought of her father's writing, such a question does not really concern what Aménaïde Moreau de Saint-Méry Dall'Asta thought about the many defamations of people of color to be found in her father's work. Instead, such a question ultimately reflects the 'heavy silence' concerning free women of color in studies of colonial Saint-Domingue and the Haitian Revolution

(Cottias, 125). The now burgeoning scholarship about the subjectivity and agency of free women of color in Saint-Domingue usually relies upon notary records and other official government documents (Garrigus, 2006a, 197; Rogers, 2003, 40–42), or the writings of numerous male travel writers who 'transposed, reproduced, and intercepted' from a 'masculine point of view' the attitudes and habits of women of color (Cottias, 125). When the writing of women is consulted, it is often the writing of "white" women like Leonora Sansay or the Marquise de Rouvray (Dayan, 1995, 166, 187, 225; Dillon, 2007, 77–78; Drexler, 2003, 184). Reliance upon these sources has produced an 'archetype' of the colonial free woman of color in Saint-Domingue as a 'seductress' (Cottias, 135), an 'opportunist' who preyed upon the weaknesses of "white" men, but tells us next to nothing about the attitudes of these women themselves.

Because writing was not always an available option for free women of color (like slave women, many of them were illiterate [Socolow, 291; Rogers, 2006, 85]),[12] they very likely inscribed themselves in colonial space in alternative ways, either by creating new forms of self-representation or transforming old ones. In order to determine the precise shapes these inscriptions may have taken, scholars have resorted to analyzing the well-documented behaviors of women of color, both slave and free. More recent historiography, for example, details the participation of women of color in the revolutionary movement as spies, ministers of poison, and even as soldiers (Girard, 2009, 69–71; Geggus, 1996, 272). Other studies outline some of their more controversial forms of resistance, including using their bodies and their sexuality as resources to procure weapons, food, and other goods (Girard, 2009, 78; Ca. Charles, 45), refusing to work (Kafka, 49), performing abortions, committing infanticide (Geggus, 1996, 271; H. Trouillot, 1957, 22), and successfully bringing lawsuits against those who had defrauded them (Garrigus, 2006a, 77–78; Rogers, 2003, 46–47). Some historians have even connected the free woman of color's sexual 'license' in a libertine society to her economic agency and social mobility (Girard, 2009, 62, 67; Ca. Charles, 45; Socolow, 292), recognizing that 'women's empowerment may take different forms' (Ca. Charles, 44). Other scholars have been less eager to equate what looks like sexual 'freedom' and participatory revolutionary violence to agency (Geggus, 1996, 266; Jenson, 2007, 32) since colonial sexual practices, like revolutionary acts, involved complicated layers of coercion and consent.

---

12 Socolow has noted that many free women of color were only able to sign their names and that even for the most affluent, traveling to France to receive an education was 'exceptional' (291–92). Dominique Rogers says that illiteracy rates for free women of color were much higher than those for "white" women, somewhere in the range of 56–95% for free women of color, as opposed to 23% for white women (2003, 85).

One reason for such differing views of the agency of free women of color in Saint-Domingue is that we are dealing with 'a paucity of sources' created by women of color themselves (Girard, 2009, 63), and therefore we have not been permitted to penetrate deeply into the subjectivity behind their behaviors. Without a fuller understanding of the complicated ways in which women of color may have represented themselves, we cannot be certain how each of the forms of physical resistance outlined above translated into emotional agency for them. Yet, since, as Carolle Charles has written, we must think of 'resistance as the capacity to create something different, something that challenges the existing system of domination' (53), scholars, like the women whom they study, have had to be creative when exploring female forms of resistance in Saint-Domingue, where it may not have taken the forms we desire or expect. Deborah Jenson warns, in fact, that in 'privileging' the slave narrative as the 'gold standard of literary testimony,' 'we obscure the existence of genres other than the slave narrative that *were* produced through complex and mediated processes' (2011, 3). As a first step to uncovering the 'hopes and motives of female actors' (Girard, 2009, 63), Jenson has suggested that 'the black or colored courtesans of Saint-Domingue' whose poetry was transcribed by Moreau de Saint-Méry in his private journal were the authors of an oral Haitian Creole poetic tradition that can be regarded as a form of 'history from below.' In Jenson's reading, these women (who were often the concubines of their "white" slave masters or prostitutes) become 'the founders of a Creole discourse of sexual relations in a slave society' (2007, 30). Such a form of 'auto-representation,' which Jenson describes as a 'war of words reminiscent of rap' (27), was used by women of color to assert their presence in the 'civic arena' (47), make complaints about the police (48), ridicule their lovers or masters (44–47), and even critique the writing of Moreau de Saint-Méry (49).

These 'rare early inscription[s] of the experiences or perspectives of non-white women in slave holding societies' uncovered by Jenson (2011, 279) demonstrate at the very least that some women of color were acutely aware of their portrayal in the print culture of Saint-Domingue and that many of them actively questioned the essentialism behind the descriptions of colonial travel writers. The fact that most of these poems and songs circulated only in the private sphere under the cover of anonymity (Jenson, 2007, 49–50)—meaning that they were not printed in the newspapers of Saint-Domingue—only underscores the difficulty for women of color who sought to oppose the 'dominant narrative' inscribed by colonial men. Like the women of color whom Jenson describes in her study, Mimi's letters can be read as part of this same mediated history that *was* 'produced' by an anonymous author whose literary fiction of the Revolution, despite our lack of knowledge about his or her biographical identity, nonetheless forces us to recognize the complex ways in which women of color indirectly inscribed their own normally invisible, essentialized, and/or silenced voices in colonial spaces. Doris Garraway has perhaps best explained the benefits of reading literature for what it can reveal about interiority, which might be otherwise concealed. She writes, 'the particular contribution of literary criticism to the study of cultures lies in its ability to go where historians often do not tread.' For, 'on the basis of a close reading,' Garraway writes, we are permitted to imagine:

> what cannot be verified; to posit what could never have been documented in any historical archive; to recover fantasies, beliefs, mentalities, and silences in which the desires and anxieties of historical subjects may be lodged; to consider furthermore, the ways in which a text's form and structure provide as much insight into the cultural conditions of its production as the manifest narrative it contains. (2005a, xii)

Mediated through an anonymous author, then, the epistolary romance contained in *La Mulâtre* provides a rare and intimate portrait of the 'desires and anxieties' of one woman of color from Saint-Domingue who was adamantly anti-slavery, even as a slave owner, critical of color prejudice even while exhibiting her own, and who argued for colonial reform rather than revolution, but was unable to specify exactly what those reforms might entail.

The circumstances narrated in Mimi's letters are a stark reminder not only that subjectivity is always multiple, changing, and often ambivalently dependent upon immediate circumstances, but also that the free people of color did not form a 'singular and unique class' (H. Trouillot, 1957, 41). Mimi, like Aménaïde, has a metropolitan French education and owns her own slaves, but there the similarities between the two women end. While Aménaïde 'passed' for a white woman in France and enjoyed the privileges of marriage to an Italian count, Mimi has three options—a life of celibacy (thereby safeguarding her virtue), marrying a man of color and thus being 'relegated' to the 'abject class of sang-mêlé,' or giving herself to a 'brutal master,' a 'white man' who will eventually 'treat' her worse than his 'slaves' since her submission will have confirmed her baseness in his eyes (83). In her sexuality, therefore, Mimi finds a kind of prison, providing a stark contrast to the sorts of liberation described in historical works that detail the ways in which colonial women of color used their sexuality to attain power.

That some free women of color may have found their sexuality empowering is entirely possible, but as Hénock Trouillot reminds us, when discussing the free people of color, 'it is more a question of multiple reactions more or less different or contradictory' than a stable and universally shared attitude (1957,

41). Mimi's friend Saintie acknowledges such differing attitudes in writing, 'Mimi is far from resembling those women who prefer an honored vice that procures protection and fortune, to a suppressed virtue' (83). Saintie's words remind us that free women of color, like the colonists, likely approached their sexual 'choices,' and the consequences thereof, with vastly different strategies and outcomes.

The other women in *La Mulâtre* provide further examples of the complexities and nuances of women's lives in Saint-Domingue. Mimi's mother, Rosette, is described as an illiterate 'négresse' who has two children with Mimi's father. Rosette is apparently a 'kept woman' since Mimi's father continues to provide subsistence for the whole family, lending credence to the idea that some free women of color, while 'clearly not as prosperous as the most important white inhabitants of Cap Français … obtained a respectable level of wealth' through 'sexual liaisons' with "white" men (Socolow, 292). Mimi's friend Saintie, on the other hand, also has experience with "white" men, but she has not been nearly as 'successful' as Rosette. She tells Mimi the story of her own failed love affair in order to impress upon her friend the urgency of safeguarding her virtue. Saintie writes, 'although you were raised in France, you cannot give yourself any illusions about the deplorable obstacle that an accident of fate has placed between your condition and that of Mr. ***. You can only aspire to the humiliating success of being his mistress …!' (20). As if to combat the idea that women of color could use their sexuality as a marketable and expendable good, Saintie reminds Mimi that her 'virtue' is the only 'good' that she possesses as a free woman of color (79).[13] Again, Saintie writes, 'A virtuous woman, when she is of color, only has one prejudice against her; but there is one which is not less fatal; that is to be with a man without the permission of the law' (84). Mimi's sister Sylvie, who has not had the good fortune to be educated in France (though she is literate), has also been affected by colonial plantation sexual practices. This is evidenced by the fact that Sylvie tries to seduce Sylvain, purportedly in order to distract him from Mimi and thereby protect her sister from the fate that she (Sylvie) had already suffered when she fell prey to the advances of a "white" man.

---

13 This claim, which both Saintie and Mimi make, that a free woman of color only has her virtue and without that is twice cursed, provides another contrast with Rousseau's *Julie*. When Julie laments the loss of her virtue to her friend Claire, her friend responds by telling her, 'How many virtues do you still possess for one that has become tainted? Will that make you any less sweet, less sincere, less modest, less generous? Will you be any less worthy, in a word, of all our praises? … Ah! Believe me, you could lose a great deal before any woman purer than you could ever be found' (1:81); and, in fact, Julie achieves virtue through marriage, something that Mimi will never be able to do with Sylvain.

While it is clear that Mimi is surrounded by women of color who have not 'known virtue' (according to eighteenth-century standards), Mimi highlights her own individual virtue to emphasize the contradictions of judging an entire group of people based on the actions of a small sector of the population. Mimi places her virtues on display when she charges Sylvain with having the audacity to write a love letter to her simply because she is a woman of color. The outraged Mimi writes, 'What! Does the miserable prejudice against my color authorize you to think that I could be without virtue? If an opinion that is welcomed in these parts debases [*m'avilit*] me in your eyes, must I justify it by a conduct that you would scorn in your equals?' (6). Mimi contends that Sylvain only believes she is without 'virtue' because she is not 'white,' and that he expects her to engage in 'behavior' he 'would scorn' were she 'white.' There were thus two different standards for evaluating normative female behavior in the colony, and "non-white" women signaled their own lack of virtue merely by not being "white" in the first place.

Mimi argues that judging people using such a circuitous logic submits 'the virtuous and the vicious woman' to the same standards 'simply because they have a red or a black skin color!' while 'whites' who are 'criminals of the most heinous crimes can, by changing their location, aspire to recover the esteem of society and occupy an honorable place within it' (221). No such transformation was possible for people of color, for their dark skin marked them everywhere they went. She writes, 'It is because, slaves of a blind prejudice, you only treat us ordinarily according to this so-called law, and not according to what we individually merit' (186). This statement effectively recognizes that some women of color might 'know how to seduce' (37), as Sylvain's correspondent Mr. de B. notes, but that this did not mean that all women of color could be judged on this basis.

Mimi's argument is at heart a move away from the essentialism of colonial discourse, as well as the one-to-one reversals found in much of anti-colonial writing. Reverse essentialism in anti-colonial discourse is most readily demonstrated by Frantz Fanon's statement that 'to the expression: "All the natives are the same," the colonized reply, "All colonists are the same"' (1968, 49). According to Gloria Anzaldúa, such a coercive logic 'lock[s] one into a duel of oppressor and oppressed' where 'both are reduced to a common denominator of violence ... All reaction' to this violence, she says, is then 'limited by, and dependent on, what it is reacting against' (100). Mimi refuses to see herself in all free women of color and likewise refuses to defend or vindicate all free people of color from the charges leveled against them by the colonists. Mimi instead argues that women of color, like all people, should be judged upon their individual merits. She further resists the counter-productivity of racialism when she refuses to argue that all women of color are virtuous, maintaining only that she is virtuous and, therefore, that all women of color cannot be *not* virtuous. Ultimately, rather than vindicating or affirming essentialist claims by refuting them, Mimi opts instead to undermine the governing logic of the "racial" ideals that would assign a stable and universal metaphysics of degradation to all women of color.

Mimi upsets this metaphysics of color when she calls into question the assumptions of virtue that were unequivocally afforded to *'les blanches.'* Mimi disdains a certain Mme. de C. and claims that she is not even worthy of being called 'white' after she spreads a rumor that Mimi was pregnant with Sylvain's baby but had an abortion. Mimi writes that Mme. de C. is 'a white woman like so many others whose only advantage over us is their skin color' (171). She continues by noting that 'whites' who judge women of color indiscriminately 'are not even worthy of being so [i.e. white]' (180). If "whiteness" equals virtue then Mimi finds that some people whose phenotypes signified as "white" could not actually be considered "white" using the same colonial criteria that had been used to bar people of color (who often signified as "white" as well) from the category of "whiteness." In this way, Mimi does not provide a narrative designed to refute an incorrect historical record by producing a new one, which would align her with 'vindicationists' (Scott, 83) like Julien Raimond, who specifically refuted the writings of Moreau de Saint-Méry.[14] On the contrary, Mimi interacts within this framework of both colonial patriarchy and colonial racism by allowing for "whiteness" as a symbol of virtue. Mimi's point is less to prove that none of the "white" Creole women in Saint-Domingue were virtuous than it is to expose the fact that many other "white" women had lovers outside of marriage, but that this had not hurt public opinion of all "white" women or tainted the association of "whiteness" with virtue.

---

14 What David Scott has called 'vindicationism' was not just a feature of early Haitian writing (83). Moreau de Saint-Méry and Girod de Chantrans had themselves undertaken highly publicized defenses of the "white" Creoles. According to Yvonne Fabella, both men 'sought to redeem the reputation of white creoles by portraying them as imperfect yet virtuous men and women' (2010, 54). Of "white" Creole women, Moreau de Saint-Méry wrote, 'Charming sex! This is your prerogative, sweetness and goodness. It is for tempering the pride of man, for captivating him ... that nature made you' (qtd. and translated in Fabella 2010, 57). The utility and expediency of Moreau de Saint-Méry's writings was recognized both in Saint-Domingue and in France, where he was viewed as the only person 'capable of making appreciated in the metropole the importance of the colonies' (Silvestre, 10). Furthermore, the *Description* was highly praised by the colonists, according to an entry in Moreau de Saint-Méry's *Voyages* from November of 1798: 'My friend M. Regnaud de Villevert to whom I had sent my entire description of Saint-Domingue, has thanked me for it and speaks to me of the rights it has given me with respect to the appreciation of the Colonists' (402).

Mimi's interaction within this racialized discourse of femininity makes the title of the novel itself wholly ironic. Mimi is an example of a 'mulatto woman' who is just as virtuous as any 'white woman.' Yet 'white women' cannot be universally considered virtuous. The title is an ironic negation because there is no such thing as 'the white woman' or the 'mulatto woman'; there are only women who, regardless of their skin color, "race," class, age, or education, are all different from one another. Mimi therefore resists making totalizing claims at the same time as she exposes a power apparatus designed to uphold "white" femininity by juxtaposing it against already assumed "black" female concupiscence.

Even when travel writers seemingly turned their attention away from *les négresses* and *les mulâtresses* to acknowledge the libertine ways of *les blanches*, they often linked the behavior of the latter to the pernicious influence of free women of color. Moreau de Saint-Méry, for example, defended the honor of 'white women' in a backhanded fashion when he wrote, 'Who would believe, in any event, that the Mulattresses are often taken as models for the White women'; and later, 'We are also rather surprised to see that in their attitudes, their gait, and their gestures, a lot of the young Creoles concentrate on imitating the Mulattresses' (1797, 1:97). Yvonne Fabella writes that Moreau's characterization of "white" women is a

> far cry from the stereotypical white creole woman, lascivious and indolent yet capable of horrific brutality [since] the nurturing plantation mistress described by Moreau was a model of feminine virtue ... she put that virtue to work for the success of the plantation system, and in regaining control over her own temper she simultaneously asserted control over her own slaves. (2010, 57)

Baron de Wimpffen also observed that, from his point of view, women of "mixed race" were 'the envy and despair of the white ladies who aspire to imitate them' (114). In 1808, Leonora Sansay would add that in colonial Saint-Domingue, 'female virtue is blasted in the bud by the contagious influence of example' (96). Sansay describes women of "mixed race" as lacking in virtue because of their own biology, however, while "white" women lack it because of the influence of the cultural environment. Sansay went on to attribute the "mulatto" woman's 'life of pleasure' to her 'birth,' 'destiny,' and to 'nature,' while the "white" Creole woman's desire for 'pleasure' was attributed to the 'torrent of fashions' and had the effect of destroying her 'native simplicity' (96).

Mimi interacts with such causal theories by directly connecting the 'degradation' of "white" female sexuality to unbridled male sexuality instead of to "black" female concupiscence. She writes, 'It is very easy for white women to have lovers in a place where the men so masterfully make use of their slaves!' (90). There is an inextricable link in Mimi's mind between libertine "white" female sexuality, the predatory sexuality of the "white" male colonists, and slavery. Furthermore, while the image of the hypersexual "black" woman has historically been used to affirm "white" femininity, according to Mimi, it was also used to affirm patriarchy. Mimi argues that "white" male colonists had deliberately created an underclass of people who could serve both their economic needs and sexual desires, as well as better position them to be the only stewards of the colony.

Garraway has written that Moreau de Saint-Méry's writings in particular install a 'powerful logic of filiation,' whereby 'white men' became 'the real and symbolic fathers of the subaltern races in the colony' (2005a, 247). Mimi, for her part, ridicules and renders absurd this colonial society where "white" colonists created a sub-class of people—their own children—whom they could use to their own advantage, either as courtesans, mistresses, or slaves. She writes: 'isn't it amusing that the whites regard the class of men of color, which they degrade so much even though they are the source, as a nursery of qualified candidates destined to decorate their harems!' (119). Mimi's statement exposes 'whites' as the 'source' of free people of color, while simultaneously and sardonically accusing them of having created women of "mixed race" (their own daughters) in order to sleep with them. Raimond had also envenomed the source of free men of color by accusing the colonists of having created people of "mixed race" in order to enslave them: 'The father who creates an individual to make him his slave, is he not a monster?' (1791b, 56). Such sentiments were also shared by Mimi's other contemporary, Olympe de Gouges, who wrote in her *Déclaration des droits de la femme et de la citoyenne* (1791):

> The Colonists aspire to rule like despots over men to whom they are fathers and brothers; and disregard the laws of nature ... These inhuman colonists say: our blood circulates in their veins, but we cast it off ... It is in these places, which are closer to nature, that the father disregards the son. (21)

What Raimond called the '*manufacture des mulâtres*' (1791b, 58) or the creation of this 'underclass,' in Mimi's words, served to affirm patriarchy (and thus the subaltern status of "non-white" women), first by creating different standards of evaluation for male and female behavior—male sexual experiences were encouraged while female sexuality was muted (115–16). Second, it worked to make women, and especially free women of color, dependent upon "white" men, if not economically, then in the everyday jurisprudence of the colony. Nowhere is Mimi's indignation over women of color's lack of power more readily displayed in the letters than when her mother, Rosette, attempts to bring charges against a thief who has broken into her home. Since Sylvain is a 'white man,' a lawyer, wealthy, and of high standing in the community, he offers to help Mimi's mother attain justice. Instead of being grateful to Sylvain for his help, Mimi writes:

> There is still one remark that infinitely troubles me: it is that without the protection of some white man, would we always be the victims of others? We must therefore be right twice in order to obtain justice? ... How could our morals not become corrupted? How could girls of color not throw themselves as they have done into the arms of white men? (193)

Even if women of color could 'attain justice,' wealth, or other perks through their liaisons with "white" men, Mimi rejects such a utilitarian attitude and the supposed gratitude Sylvain wants her to feel precisely because rather than interrupting or changing the power structures at hand, in her mind this behavior would primarily serve to re-establish it.

For Mimi, colonial sexual practices not only made the colonists bad lovers and husbands to "non-white" women, but unnatural fathers who refused to resume their role as protectors of their own children.[15] Mimi writes, 'I admire ... [the] irresistible power [of color prejudice] over the whites in general; thousands of their children are the unfortunate victims, and not a single one dares to make a representation about their civic state, and to ameliorate their ignominious fate' (223). According to Mimi, the colonists often described themselves as powerless in the face of their desire for women of "mixed race," whose charms they found 'irresistible,' but simultaneously presented themselves as important and powerful colonial legislators. Mimi suggests that the "white" colonists' belief in the inferiority of people of color was therefore disingenuous, and solely used, in Mimi's words, to help 'prove' that white men were 'superior to others' (193).

Mimi also interacts with the language of patriarchy to expose how it was actually incommensurate with the color prejudice that affirmed it when she asks:

> Are we not born the same? What rights does one person really have over another? What faculties do whites have over blacks? If there exists a difference between them that places superiority on one side, shouldn't the mixed-bloods at least share the advantages since it is our fathers who would have them? (91)

---

15 This discourse surrounding fathering apparently sparked quite a debate with Moreau de Saint-Méry writing back to the abbé Grégoire in order to defend "white" colonists as good fathers and virtuous citizens (Garrigus, 2006, 242). For more on this kind of debate see also Miller (2008, 69–71) and Raimond (1793, 5).

Moreau de Saint-Méry's Daughter and the Anti-Slavery Muse

If men were supposed to be more powerful than women, fathers having more authority than mothers, Mimi asks why the children of "white" men do not benefit from both the "whiteness" and powerful masculinity of their fathers. In other words, Mimi wonders why it was that people of "mixed race" should inherit the degraded conditions of their "black" mothers if their "white" fathers were so omnipotent.

The author of *La Mulâtre* may have been influenced in this position by Jean-Jacques Rousseau, who is referenced in Chapter LVIII of the novel, and who, in his *Discours sur l'origine et les fondements de l'inégalité parmi les hommes*, had written:

> just as violence had to be done to nature in order to establish slavery, nature had to be changed in order to perpetuate this right. And the jurists, who have gravely pronounced that the child of a slave woman is born a slave, have decided in other words, that a man is not born a man. (1992, 62)[16]

Mimi was far from the only writer of color in the context of Saint-Domingue more specifically to have noticed the logical fallacy behind the idea that the child follows the condition of the mother as well as the illogical science behind theories of "miscegenation." Raimond, too, explicitly ridiculed and rendered suspect colonial prejudice by linking it to pseudoscientific theories of degradation in asking, 'is it possible for men to create a species that is inferior to their own?' (1791b, 57).

Such contradictions concerning the genealogies of slavery as a human condition and the supposed degradations of "miscegenation" bring us back to Moreau de Saint-Méry's daughter of color. Aménaïde's very existence permits us, as Mimi's own existence did for her, to question the sincerity of a man who once wrote that after the first instance of "miscegenation," resulting in the "mulatto," subsequent generations of "interracial" children, exactly like his daughter Aménaïde and his grandson Edoardo, would become increasingly 'pale,' sallow, and weak, ultimately culminating in wholesale degeneracy and infertility (1797, 1:76–77). Mimi interacts with this very theory of "mixed-race" degeneracy when she asks why "white" men should be 'so base as to degrade their own blood in such a way? ... Why doesn't their blood instead have the power to purify that of the negroes?' (222). In other words, if 'white blood' was so much purer than 'black blood,' why would white men like Moreau de Saint-Méry and Mimi's father be so 'base' as to 'dishonor' it by mixing it with that of the 'blacks?'

If Mimi's letters constitute one of the few first-person attempts to imagine "non-white" female subjectivity in Saint-Domingue, Aménaïde

16 Translation by Cress.

Transgressing the Trope of the "Tropical Temptress"

Aménaïde Moreau de Saint-Méry Dall'Asta, 'Ritratto del Padre' (1802),
oil on canvas.
Reprinted with permission from Parma Galleria Nazionale.

Moreau de Saint-Méry's Daughter and the Anti-Slavery Muse

Moreau de Saint-Méry's portrait of her father resting his elbow on volume I of the *Description de la partie française de Saint-Domingue*, gives us at least one insight into her thoughts about her father's storied career as one of the most famous naturalists of Saint-Domingue. In his portrait, the patriarch appears content, relaxed, and is nobly dressed. There is little in the painting to suggest anything other than admiration on the part of its artist. Even with the painting, however, the truth is that we will likely never precisely know what Moreau de Saint-Méry's daughter thought of her father's derogatory claims about women of color (which were so obviously undermined by her very existence).[17]

Yet the character of Mimi has at the very least permitted us to imagine that while "white" men like Moreau de Saint-Méry certainly had relationships with "non-white" women that were fraught with complexities—encompassing everything from hate, repulsion, disgust, and denial, to love, desire, admiration, and recognition—women of color like Aménaïde may have had equally fraught relationships with the "white" men who were their fathers. Mimi's phrase about her own father best sums up such complexities: 'What! My father who loves me so could also be subject to this odious and cruel prejudice' (221).

*

While the author of *La Mulâtre* left little to no indication of his or her identity, the novel's appearance in 1803 in Paris (the year that marked the failure of the Leclerc expedition), the setting of the novel in pre-revolutionary Saint-Domingue during the fraught years of 1773 to 1775, and its reference to one of the most popular abolitionist novels of the eighteenth

---

[17] Although H.W. Kent says that Aménaïde prepared a biography of her father before her death (240), it seems that she may have never finished it, if, indeed, she ever attempted to write such a work. The papers that Moreau de Saint-Méry Dall'Asta's daughter, Clelia Sorelle Monza, donated to the Archivio di Stato of Parma on December 31 of 1901 are, however, fully consultable, including the volume entitled *Materiali per la biographia di Moreau de St. Méry* (see Carra, 37). I have consulted these materials along with several other boxes of papers donated by Moreau de Saint-Méry's granddaughter. They include many of Moreau de Saint-Méry's awards and diplomas, as well as several volumes of personal letters that may be of interest to scholars (for a catalog of these items, including several interesting paintings of Moreau de-Saint-Méry, see Carra, *L'Ossessione Della Memoria*, 140–60). In fact, Moreau de Saint-Mérty Dall'Asta kept up a voluminous correspondence with her father, part of which is housed at the National Archives in Parma, Italy. These letters attest to a loving and devoted relationship between father and child. For the letters, see Box 9, *Lettere famigliari di M. Moreau de Saint-Méry* (see also Carra, 38).

century, provides a ripe field for speculation about the author's class, gender, race, education, and identity.

Garrigus, who is to date the only scholar to have provided an in-depth analysis of the novel, engages in such speculation over its authorship. In his first article on the novel, Garrigus suggests that *La Mulâtre* 'could be described as the first Haitian novel' (2003, 74). Despite such a spectacular and intriguing claim about a novel that, he says, constitutes a 'failed foundational fiction' because it imagines a 'mulatto solution' to the problem of slavery (2003, 82), in the introduction to the newly published L'Harmattan edition, Garrigus instead posits Moreau de Saint-Méry himself as a possible author of the text (2007a, xxv). Garrigus's later assertion is highly unlikely, however, since the author of *La Mulâtre* contests Moreau de Saint-Méry's very theories of "mixed-race" degeneration and espouses anti-slavery sentiments. In addition, as the previous analysis has shown, the author had clearly read and aligns him- or herself with the reform writings of Raimond, who very publicly opposed the writings of Moreau de Saint-Méry.

Because of the novel's contentious engagement with theories of "mixed-race" degeneration, it would be tempting to consider Raimond himself as a possible author. In his *Réponse aux considérations de M. Moreau, dit Saint-Méry, par M. Raymond, citoyen de couleur de Saint-Domingue* (1791), Raimond states that he is taking up the cause of the free men of color because numerous authors have already pleaded the case of the slaves. However, in just over 65 pages of text, Raimond does not so much refute the idea that women of color were corrupt as affirm it by blaming the "white" colonists. Not only did Raimond *not* publicly defend women of color against the charges of colonial detractors like Moreau de Saint-Méry, but, as Garrigus acknowledges, he seemed to focus more on the effect that corrupt colonial sexual practices were having on free men of color who found themselves legally and socially powerless to stop "white" men from preying upon their wives and daughters (Garrigus, 1996, 42; Garrigus, 2006a, 219).[18] Raimond was in many respects infinitely more concerned with defending free men of color and their virtues as citizen-soldiers than he was with vindicating women of color, whom he admitted had been corrupted by the French colonists who had 'forced them to prostitute themselves, by forbidding marriage with whites' (1791a, 14). Yet, like almost all of those who wrote about the insurrection in Saint-Domingue and later the Haitian Revolution, in his spirited attempt to dismantle the (il)logic of colonial racism, Raimond also adopted the language of pseudoscientific

---

18 The abbé Grégoire also refused to deny that free colored females were sexually immoral. He did point out, however, that "white" men were guilty of neglecting their children (Garrigus, 2006a, 241).

debates about "race." Sometimes Raimond's adoption of such a language operated merely in a descriptive way, as when he describes the 'mulatto' as the 'product of a white man with a black woman' (1791a, 1) and the 'gens de couleur ou sang-mêlés' as the 'product of the mulattoes among themselves or of the mulattoes with whites, and their different progenitors' (2).

At other times, the influence of the travel writing of the period on Raimond's own ideas about "race" becomes much more complicated and ambivalent. Raimond hardly disputed widespread reports of the licentiousness of women of color in the colony, and seemingly affirmed these accounts when he wrote: 'These whites reference the debauchery of the *mulâtresses*, whom they themselves have corrupted' (1791a, 14). While the above statement might appear to be a quasi-defense of women of color even as it confirms their corruption, Raimond's later statement paints the woman of color wholly as a "tropical temptress." He writes that by forbidding "interracial" marriage,

> The legislator, by way of this measure, moves them away from marriage, and pushes girls of color towards libertinage; because it is really clear that a girl, wanting to have children who will be considered white, would prefer to live in concubinage with a white man who will procure them for her, than to get married to a man of color, who would seem to degrade her. (1791a, 19)

In addition, while Raimond's own umbrage at being labeled a 'mulatto' demonstrates the injurious nature of the term in colonial Saint-Domingue (see the introduction to this volume), the passage in which he attempts to insult Moreau de Saint-Méry by insinuating that the colonist was himself of "mixed race" (with almost definite conscious irony) shows that, like Vastey, Raimond had to a certain extent internalized the racial prejudices of his day (1791b, 16).[19] Furthermore, the rights of citizenship (namely, participation

---

19 In his *Réponse aux considérations de M. Moreau de Saint-Méry*, Raimond insinuated that Moreau de Saint-Méry was himself technically a free person of color, when he wrote, 'M.M.—can he say all of this, and then go back to his forefathers, without having covered himself with all of the reproach that is worthy of a man who has scorned and betrayed the class from which he came? [*qui méprise et trahit la classe dont il sort*]' (16). The insinuation likely came from an '*avertissement* preceding an address to the society of the *Amis des noirs* to the national assembly,' dated April 4, 1791, where one member, Clavière, wrote of Moreau de Saint-Méry: 'We will completely undo *this colonist* (Moreau de Saint-Méry) *whose facial features and skin color* [*les traits du visage et la couleur de la peau*] *cause us to suspect a double betrayal*; that of the rights of man and *that of his brothers*, so to speak,' since, 'If *African blood* does not run through the veins of M. Moreau, which is *doubtful*, etc.' (qtd. in Ardouin, 1855, 1:79–80, italics in original). David Nicholls will later repeat as fact the idea that Moreau de Saint-Méry was a free person of color (1979, 73).

in the civic world) that Raimond so vehemently argued for in his *Mémoire*, would not affect women (1793a, 23).

Whoever the author of *La Mulâtre* was, Garrigus says that it is likely that he or she came from a wealthy class since the text was published in two volumes, each with elaborate frontispieces. Mimi is dressed in these frontispieces in the bourgeois attire of the early nineteenth century rather than the colonial attire of eighteenth-century Saint-Domingue (Garrigus, 2007a, xxiv). The novel was advertised in several different circulating libraries and even went into a second edition, which supports the idea that the author may have been a wealthy and well-connected free woman of color (like Aménaïde) who had been reticent about attaching her name to a simultaneously anti-slavery and anti-revolution novel.[20]

The year and place of *La Mulâtre*'s publication (1803 and Paris) coupled with the fictive time and location of the letters (the 1770s and colonial Saint-Domingue), provide us with perhaps the best clues as to why the author of the novel may have desired to remain anonymous. These temporal contexts mean that the novel must be understood not only in the context of colonial Saint-Domingue, but also in the contexts of late revolutionary Saint-Domingue and early nineteenth-century Napoleonic France. In the pre-revolutionary Saint-Domingue of Mimi's letters, it would have been dangerous for a woman of color to speak out against color prejudice and slavery. In the 1770s, many prohibitions limited the movements, occupations, and roles of free people of color in the colony.[21] Later, a colonial document

---

20 As Edward Jacobs has written of circulating libraries in England, they 'dealt *substantially* in contemporary fiction ... and they were patronized *disproportionately* by women and lower class readers' (603, italics in original). He adds that 'certainly throughout the eighteenth century, many authors remained anonymous for the sake of respectability' and that since 'writing could much more easily compromise a *woman's* honor,' overall, 'anonymous works were 2.5' times more likely to appear in circulating libraries than female-authored texts. For advertisements of *La Mulâtre*, see: *Journal général de la littérature de France ou répertoire méthodique*, Volume 6: 480; *Journal typographique et bibliographique* ..., Volume 6:286; *Nouveau dictionnaire historique des sièges et batailles mémorables* ..., Volume 6: lxxxix; *Catalogue des livres français italiens, espagnols, portugais, & c*: 200; *Catalogue de la bibliothèque centrale des salons littéraires de Donbernard*, 1809 (which lists the novel's publication date as 1809); *Catalogue des livres de lecture du Cabinet littéraire de Louis Knab*, 1809. These last two advertisements could have been simple errors or it could be that *La Mulâtre* also went into a second edition.

21 According to Girard, in Saint-Domingue, 'whites could not marry their slaves (after 1685) or free women of colour (after 1778),' (2009, 63) and there were several edicts published in the late eighteenth century that forbade people of color from entering certain social spaces, like cabarets and taverns, from accumulating property, from dressing or wearing their hair in the manner of whites, or from assuming the names of their white fathers (Peabody, 2005, 62). For reprints of these edicts, see Grégoire,

entitled 'Lettres des députés de Saint-Domingue ... Intercepté par un Mulâtre, communiqué, sous le secret,' dated August 12, 1789 and published in March of 1790 ordered 'that we arrest people under suspicion; that we seize all writings where the very word liberty is pronounced' and commanded the colonists to 'Lock up the free people of color. Do not trust those who have just arrived from Europe' (5–6).

Even though Garrigus has uncovered vast documentation of the economic influence and independence of free women of color in the colony, this financial agency, and perhaps even freedom, must be distinguished from the kind of power that comes not only from citizenship but from what Seymour Drescher calls 'the ability to hold formal power' within organizations (112). In other words, the relative economic influence and agency that free women of color may have enjoyed in colonial Saint-Domingue, appears not to have done much, if anything, to alter not only the kinds of colonial laws that made free people of color subject to being 'lock[ed] up' merely for having 'just arrived from Europe,'[22] or to disrupt the feelings of terror occasioned by such laws in early revolutionary Saint-Domingue.

If the author of *La Mulâtre* wrote anonymously in late revolutionary Saint-Domingue, fearing how such an anti-slavery reform text might be viewed on the 'eve of independence' (Garrigus, 2003), her fears of writing such a tale would have not been diminished in metropolitan France, where 'the meaning of freedom itself was increasingly circumscribed for all free people of color' (Peabody, 2005, 63). In 1778, a law was passed in metropolitan France that required all 'blacks' in the metropole to carry identification or risk being shipped back to the colonies (Peabody, 1996, 129). The *Police des Noirs*, as it was known under the *ancien régime*, was abolished in 1789 after the French Revolution, but was quickly re-established, along with slavery in the colonies, under Napoleon in 1802 (Peabody, 1996, 138). In addition, on May 29, 1802, a new law forbade free people of color from residing in Paris and in June of the same year another law forbade both 'blacks' and 'mulattoes' from even entering the country (Garrigus, 2007a, xxvii).[23]

Mémoire en faveur des gens de couleur ou sang-mêlés de Saint-Domingue (1789, 5–10); Baron de Vastey, *Le Système colonial dévoilé* (1814, 78–79); as well as Raimond's *Réponse*, wherein he charged whites with using color prejudice as a form of terror against the free people of color (1791b).

22 Such fears were not entirely unfounded for, in late 1802, as the situation in Saint-Domingue became increasingly perilous and total war seemed almost inevitable, Leclerc ordered 'the largest massacre [of the free people of color] to date' (Girard, 2011, 215). See also chapter one of this volume.

23 For documented cases of people of color living in France without the proper identification or who failed to register with the *Police des Noirs* and were sent back to the colonies, see Peabody (1996).

Furthermore, as Jennifer Heuer has noted, 'the abolitionist movement was weak in the early nineteenth century [in France] and had little public presence' (537). Doris Y. Kadish adds that 'the memory of violence [in Saint-Domingue] also produced a profound mistrust of anti-slavery writing and abolitionism ... abolitionism virtually disappeared in France in the early years of the nineteenth century (Kadish, 1995, 669–70).

As a subtle critique of color prejudice and the institution of slavery, *La Mulâtre* would have constituted exactly the kind of critique of his 'order' that Napoleon so feared in Germaine de Staël, who was eventually forced into exile, and in the writings of Olympe de Gouges, who had already been guillotined (Miller, 2008, 139). Catherine R. Montfort tells us that 'as far as literature was concerned, Napoleon wanted to promote or sponsor writers as long as they did not criticize the new order he was establishing' (98).[24] A woman of color, not to mention any woman in early nineteenth-century France under Napoleon Bonaparte's regime, was hardly at liberty to produce the kinds of critique of slavery and therefore state authority, whether direct or indirect, to be found in Mimi's letters.[25]

Indeed, Mimi associates her thoughts on the injustices perpetrated against both free women of color and the slaves with things that she should not publicly express. As the citation below makes clear, Mimi is perfectly aware of the precarious atmosphere in which her private letters are composed, as well as the dangers that their public exposure might present to her safety:[26]

---

24 The problems that women in the public sphere faced in France, however, began before Napoleon's ascension to power. Maximilien Robespierre closed the clubs in 1793, and declared that all women must wear the cockade in public (Landes, 94). Later, the Convention 'forbade all gatherings of women' (Montfort, 97). The closing of the clubs can be seen as a specific reaction against 'public women' since 'salon' culture was distinguished by its 'decidedly feminine character' (Landes, 40).

25 This last point about the number of women writing during pre-revolutionary France is the subject of some debate in the historiography of French women's writing. Carla Hesse (2001), for example, maintains that there were quite a substantial number of women writing and publishing successfully in the *ancien régime*. Miller has cautioned that although the position of women to speak was relatively better during the later years of the *ancien régime*, 'women authors, numbering perhaps a dozen in the revolutionary period, were subjected to an "excessive strictness"' (2008, 113).

26 Letter writing was, however, often not a completely secure or even private form of communication in the novel either. Take, for example, the scene after Mimi and Sylvain consummate their relationship. The way in which the knowledge of this consummated interracial romance is treated by the other characters in the novel presents this sexual act as though it were as seditious as the outbreak of revolution itself. When Mr. le G. writes to Rosette to tell her how Sylvain committed suicide in the forest, he begins his letter with 'read and burn my letter' (239), suggesting that merely being in possession of such an epistle could be dangerous to both his and Rosette's safety. Earlier in the novel,

> There are reflections that have come to me on this subject that I do not dare communicate. One should not openly quarrel [*rompre en visière*] with widely accepted customs. Doing so would be simply to scoff at them to no avail, and would reform them only in our own opinion while shocking that of the public without even altering it. Only a wise and natural legislation would be able to reconcile nature with the rules of society. Therefore, I must content myself with simply detesting them in my heart. (109)

Though Mimi suggests that she can only 'quarrel' with 'widely accepted customs' in the private space of a letter and in her 'heart,' the anonymous author nevertheless forces into the public sphere a ventriloquated voice of protest that Mimi would only dare utter in the private sphere. Mimi directly critiques slavery in one of her letters to Sylvain when she writes of the slaves:

> How could they not be endlessly fearful? They have only enemies around them and if they are met at night by detachments, they are mercilessly shot if they flee or whipped if they are captured. Mama and my sisters claim that I will get used to the wicked treatments that I see exercised against these miserable beings; in that case, I will surely change! For my heart bleeds just thinking about it. (165)

Although Garrigus reads *La Mulâtre* as ultimately silencing and stereotyping the slaves—Sylvain describes Mimi's slave Fédalie as 'this detestable *négresse*' 'with a dead heart that nothing could move,' 'constantly half asleep,' and monosyllabic (107)—and thus finds that the novel's 'abolitionism' is 'muted' (2003, 85), this judgment appears to arise from an inability to reconcile the fact that, as chapter ten of this volume will show, much of the transatlantic abolitionist movement could be deemed racist by today's standards, even though it would be hard to question the commitment to anti-slavery of most of its activists. That is to say that while racism is

---

we are told that a single letter from Sylvain to Mimi had been discovered and 'this letter started a war in the house' (187). The accounts of those who lived in revolutionary Saint-Domingue also bespeak a sense of surveillance, either by men or the larger colonial authority. The Marquise de Rouvray, for example, also cautioned her daughter about the dangers of letter writing when she wrote, 'Since your letters to me often arrived opened by [your father, le marquis de Rouvray], under the pretext of eagerness to hear your news, do not respond to anything that I tell you relative to him. On the contrary, overwhelm him with statements of friendship, which is very necessary to your own interests and will perhaps serve to stop him from the spending that always comes from the habitually bad morals and the immorality of his character, which Saint-Domingue does not restrain' (97). Garran de Coulon also suggested that the correspondence of free people of color was under surveillance when he wrote, 'all of the letters and packages addressed to the *hommes de couleur* were essentially opened' (1:121).

undoubtedly always inexcusable, it does not follow that anti-slavery thought was necessarily always anti-racist. As Miller has written of a later moment in the nineteenth century, 'To argue against slavery and the slave trade ... was to be a part of a certain, small elite movement; but to go further and militate against all prejudice based on skin color ... was a far lonelier position' (2008, 51). The most famous anti-slavery novel to be published in the entire Atlantic World, Harriet Beecher Stowe's *Uncle Tom's Cabin* (1852), provides perhaps the best example of the way in which a novel that was unequivocally against slavery, and even abolitionist, was filled with prejudices against the people whom it sought to defend and describe.

Like Stowe, who wrote over 50 years later, Mimi's own feelings against slavery were unequivocal. She insisted that slavery meant to inherently deprave, being 'a condition [that] degrades men and makes fools, traitors, and villains out of them' (223), even as she exhibited her own color prejudices. Also like the Stowe of *Uncle Tom's Cabin*, Mimi's answer to the totalizing violence of slavery was *not* the totalizing violence of revolution.[27] She wrote: 'if there is radical vice attached to a place, I can but see one method, that is reform' (203). As if to circumvent the very possibility of violence, Sylvain reminds Mimi that 'everything that carries with it the tint of blood is repugnant to my soul' (198). Mimi responds by writing, 'I do not have a more bloodthirsty soul than you, but I like for justice to be done' (203). That Mimi desires for 'justice to be done' suggests that she believes in more than just pecuniary punishments, one of the major complaints of the free people of color in Saint-Domingue (Vastey, 1814a, 79), but that she would not go so far as to argue for violent revolution.

Mimi's disdain for and critique of violent revolution also aligns her with some of the most famous French metropolitan women writers of her own day, such as Germaine de Staël, who referred to the Terror and the French Revolution, respectively, as 'that monstrous epoch,' and a 'terrible event' (1796, 7, 52) and who spoke of those 'compatriots who had been sacrificed in those days of blood' (1796, 6). Olympe de Gouges connected her own distaste for violent revolution more squarely to the Haitian Revolution in the preface to the 1792 edition of her play *De L'Esclavage des noirs* when she argued adamantly that the slaves and the free people of color were 'cruel' in their imitations of the 'tyrants,' whose actions they paradoxically 'justified' when they responded to the horrors of slavery with 'the invention of the most barbaric and atrocious tortures' (1792, 5).[28] While Miller says

---

27 For Stowe and violence, see Boyd (1994).
28 Perhaps, ironically, de Gouges was accused of having incited the insurrection in Saint-Domingue with her play *L'Esclavage des noirs, ou l'heureux naufrage*, which incidentally was the cause of a small riot in Paris when it re-opened on December 31,

that for authors like Staël and de Gouges, 'The violence of revolted slaves ... is a line of demarcation, a limit of sympathy' (2008, 131), the thought of violence does not preclude Mimi's sympathetic identification with the slaves. Instead, her moral quandary, and her inability to specify the 'legislative' reforms that could be put in place to do away with slavery and color prejudice, has to do with the anachronisms of novelistic time *vis-à-vis* the author's time.

Though the author of *La Mulâtre*'s thoughts on slavery and revolution may have been influenced by writers like de Gouges and Staël, unlike for these authors, the particular context in which our anonymous novelist wrote betrays the problem of arguing for the possibility of non-violent reform while a violent revolution was actually accomplishing the same goals. What would it have meant for a novelist to use the voice of a woman of color from Saint-Domingue to argue for reform as a method of change at the end of a very passionate and bloody revolution that had every appearance of being on the verge of securing independence and freedom for people of color? Would Mimi's non-violent stance have been viewed by the Haitian revolutionists as a kind of disloyalty, a way of 'forgetting Haiti' before it was even created (Miller, 2005, 247–48), in a burgeoning 'military society' where citizenship was being forged through violence and 'consolidated through the ties of freemasonry?' (Sheller, 254). Anthropologist Mimi Sheller has discussed the ways in which citizenship in Louverture's and later Dessalines's Saint-Domingue, as in post-independence Haiti, was constructed around the idea of the citizen soldier. According to Sheller, this left little opportunity for women of color to participate in the advent of a new society—'a republican fraternity in arms' (254)—'except as mothers of warriors' (255). Mimi's letters represent a brave interruption to the continuation of a patriarchal narrative that erased the involvement of women of color not only in the Revolution itself, but also erased their contributions to anti-slavery thought. At the same time, Mimi's reform argument precariously places her in the position of opposing, not necessarily the impending independence of Haiti, but the method by which that independence was achieved, and, more importantly, she appears in the suspect position of not being able to offer a viable alternative to violence.

Women of color living in revolutionary Saint-Domingue like Mimi were not the only people to experience conflict and fear, and to become ideologically suspect in the minds of others, with respect to revolutionary

---

1789 at the Théâtre des Nations (Striker, 76–77). In her preface to the printed edition of the play, written in 1792, Gouges wrote that people were 'blaming' and 'accusing' her of having 'encouraged this revolution, which I did not participate in at all except for the prophecy of it that I made' (2).

methods.[29] General Toussaint Louverture is often portrayed as a 'conciliator whose allegiances rested in a complicated and serpentine curve of tension and compression' (206). According to José Buscaglia-Salgado, who, without explicitly using the term, evokes the idea that "mulatto/a" vengeance stemmed not solely from literal interpretations of "race," but from incongruity, in general, writes of Louverture: 'He owed his authority both to his African father and to his European master ... he had to weigh and check the forces of both those loyalties all his life' (206).

Louverture has often been accused of failing to produce an independent nation exactly because of his refusal to enact the de-contextualized violence of revolution (all the colonists are the same) that characterizes the role of Dessalines, a fact that led C.L.R. James to conclude that, 'all his life [Louverture] strove for conciliation with enemies and peaceful settlements of all disputes' (168). Instead of suspecting their loyalties to anti-slavery, we might view both Louverture and Mimi as practicing an eighteenth-century form of what bell hooks has referred to in the twentieth century as 'feminist masculinity' (70). While 'patriarchal masculinity teaches men that their sense of self and identity, their reason for being, resides in their capacity to dominate others,' on the contrary, according to hooks, 'feminist masculinity teaches us all ... how to love justice and freedom in ways that foster and affirm life' (70–71). Mimi, like Louverture, appears to be caught between a vision of freedom inspired by the seemingly counterpoised ideas of 'justice and freedom,' since she desires revolution for the changes it will bring for people of color, but also fears it for the potential violence it will bring to the innocent.

In the end, Mimi's own suicide can be read just as ambivalently as the novel's relationship to the Haitian Revolution itself. It could be seen as the ultimate act of liberation, an effort to circumvent the very limits of self-representation imposed upon women of color by interacting within them, or perhaps, alternatively, as the ultimate re-inscription of the patriarchal view that female resistance amounts to madness, as in the tropes of the "tropical temptress" and the tragic "mulatta." In the first reading of Mimi's death, we can view her suicide as her refusal to live in a society that defies the possibility of virtue for all women of color regardless of individual

---

29 Kadish notes that it was 'widely perceived that the issue of slavery was a woman's issue, on the basis of women's humanitarian interests, their capacity for emotional response, their special concern for women and children, their ties with religion, and the like' (1995, 670). Miller, however, appears to take issue with this characterization when he acknowledges that although there may have been a greater 'proportion' of female abolitionist writers in the period, they were not 'necessarily more sensitive than everyone else' (2008, 107). For more on the role of women during the nineteenth-century transatlantic abolitionist movement see A. Gautier (1990, 153–61) and Goutalier (1990, 143–51).

circumstance and would indeed conspire to force them to submit even when they resisted. Mimi's madness would therefore become a conscious choice, making her like Toni Morrison's character Sethe, who 'deliberately' went 'mad' 'in order to not lose [her] mind' (qtd. in Gilroy, 1993, 221). Mimi's death would then signal the failure of revolutionary violence to produce liberation from the pressures of colonial sexual practices, as well as its failure to produce real liberation for women of color because of a lack of reform that might have enabled them to participate in both the civic and discursive spheres. Mimi's death would also be a powerful commentary on the failure of both the male revolutionists and "white" proto-feminists in France to upset the apparatus of power and domination that constituted both colonial patriarchy and colonial racism. In other words, "black" men achieved liberation while "white" women, in the words of Mamie E. Locke, writing in another context, 'remained on their pedestals, cherished positions to be revered and envied' (233), but women of color were largely forgotten.

In the other reading, Mimi's madness signals the author's own failure to imagine an ending in which Mimi could actuate what Jeanne Larabee has called, in the context of the writings of Mary Prince, an 'epistemology of resistance' (453) which could be used to undermine the maddening structure of patriarchal racism. Mimi describes her own death in maddening terms when she writes, 'An ardent fever is circulating in my veins … a fire that is destroying me, a poison that consumes me … Good Lord! my mind is gone' (236–37). In this reading of Mimi as ultimately tragic, she would become a typical tragic "mulatta" martyr when after her death a parade is thrown for her and her father states, 'What a lesson for women and for everyone!' Her death would provide a 'lesson' to women because it shows 'the evils' that a 'single instant of seduction and weakness' could engender (241). Mimi's death confirms not only that "miscegenation" is a tragedy, but that women writers who are forced to 'toil away in anonymity' eventually go mad and kill themselves, as Virginia Woolf once wrote of Shakespeare's imaginary sister (49).

Rather than choosing between one or the other reading, this essay embraces epistemological uncertainty and makes room for both interpretations. Here, free women of color enter into the discursive imaginary of the Haitian Revolution, at the same time as they are written out of post-independence society through Mimi's death, as they have been written out of the story of abolition and slave resistance in the context of the Haitian Revolution. In gesturing towards the double-voiced scene of writing presented by Mimi, who represents repression and failure, and the author of *La Mulâtre*, who represents relative privilege and agency, we gain new avenues for imagining and uncovering forgotten or invisible female revolutionary discourses in Saint-Domingue. For Mimi's letters, as both a fictional representation and a historical referent of female discursive resistance, ask us to consider that some free women of color living in Saint-Domingue may have resisted becoming 'more and more what they would need to be in the eyes of the white planters "in order to deserve their fate"' (Sartre, 52):[30] courtesans, traders, spies, and parricidal mothers. Mimi's ventriloquated speaking voice that can only write contests the limited role assigned to women in both the *résistance* and in a future independent society, a role that depended primarily upon what they could do with their bodies and not with their minds.

---

30 Jean-Paul Sartre has defined colonial racism as a system where 'the oppressors produce and maintain by force the evils which, *in their eyes*, make the oppressed resemble more and more what they would need to be in order to deserve their fate (Sartre, 52, italics in the original). Furthermore, as Philippe Girard has written, women who did participate in the revolution, either by using their sexuality to 'gain significant sway' with the colonists, or engaging in violence, 'obtained the equality of death,' receiving the 'same punishment earmarked for men' (2009, 77–78).

CHAPTER FIVE

'Born to Command': Leonora Sansay and the Paradoxes of Female Benevolence as Resistance in *Zelica; the Creole*

'Je connais, disait un vieux philosophe Anglais, deux choses qui portent dans la tête tout le délire de l'orgueil et de l'impudence: c'est l'encensoir entre les mains d'un homme, et l'écritoire entre celles d'une femme. J'espère que mon titre de femme et d'auteur me fera pardonner cette citation. D'ailleurs, pas un des intéressés ne croira pas la sentence sans appel.'

—Emilie J..t, *Zorada; ou la Créole* (1801)

'En cette occurrence, comme en bien d'autres, les femmes se montrèrent plus hommes que les hommes.'

—Victor Schoelcher, *Colonies étrangères et Haïti* (1843)

In 1808, Leonora Sansay (born Mary Hassal) anonymously published an epistolary romance which many literary critics and historians take to have been at least partially inspired by the time the author spent in Saint-Domingue during the latter years of the Leclerc-Rochambeau expedition (1801–03), *Secret History; or the Horrors of Santo-Domingo in a series of letters, written by a Lady at Cape François to Colonel Burr, Late Vice President of the United States, Principally during the Command of Rochambeau*. Historian Tessie Liu writes that the 'bits of complex life' described in *Secret History*, namely the author's affair with U.S. Vice President Aaron Burr, alluded to in the novel's title, 'suggest that *Secret History* is largely autobiographical' (394).[1] Elizabeth Maddock Dillon, for her part, points out that '[l]ike

---

[1] Hassal is known for having pursued an extra-marital affair with the U.S. statesmen Aaron Burr in the late eighteenth and early nineteenth century. According to Burr's memoirs, Hassal was called 'Leonora' by him and others and was 'too well known under

Mary's fictional sister, Clara, Sansay was married to a French colonial from Saint Domingue, Louis Sansay,' concluding that because the names Clara and Mary are used in *Secret History* and were two of the names Sansay used, 'the novel is loosely based on Leonora Sansay's experience in Saint-Domingue during the years 1802–03' (2007, 77–78). In addition, Colin (Joan) Dayan has convincingly argued that the 'source' for Sansay's epistolary 'book of horrors' was actually a letter Sansay penned to Burr on May 6, 1803, only a year after she had arrived in Saint-Domingue with her husband (1995, 167).[2]

In her letter to Burr, signed 'Leonora,' Sansay refers to herself in the third person, using one of the other names by which Burr often referred to her and which she would later give to one of the principal characters of *Secret History*: 'that Clara you once lov'd,' she writes, 'She came to St. Domingo about the time I did, and at first liv'd tranquilly enough with her husband—but you know she never lov'd him & he was jealous, and sometimes rendered her miserable' (rpt. in Drexler, 2008, 225). Sansay goes on to detail the 'effect quite miraculous' that the climate of Saint-Domingue has had upon 'Clara,' who, invited to all of the most important balls in the country, 'there began her empire like that of Venus rising from the waves' (225). After describing 'Clara's' numerous escapades, Sansay implores Burr to 'Answer me. I think this long letter deserves an answer. There's certainly matter enough in it to form a romance; but whose life has afforded so many subjects for a romance as that of its writer?' (230). Sansay's probable romanticization of herself in the form of 'Clara' in her letter to Burr lends great weight to Michael Drexler's argument in the introduction to the Broadview edition of *Secret History* that Sansay, 'no longer satisfied to be a satellite to influential men ... aimed to attract the admiration of the public at large' by using a 'self-representational strateg[y]' that was 'clearly adapted from her own experience' (2008, 32). Talking about herself in the third person was a 'representational strategy' that appears to have allowed Sansay to romantically detail her French libertine escapades

---

that name' (qtd. in Drexler, 2008, 27). Drexler tells us that 'almost everything we know about the life of Leonora Sansay comes from her sporadic appearance in the memoirs and private journals of Aaron Burr, where letters from her and about her surface over the course of twenty years' (27). It is precisely 'Leonora,' aka Mary Hassal's correspondence with Burr that ties Hassal definitively to the name Leonora Sansay (as well as a host of other names) and to *Secret History*. In addition, '[a] letter from Leonora to Burr that outlined *Secret History* (and told the story of "Clara's" escapades) was published in the appendix to a 19th century novel about Burr' (Van Bergen). See also Angela Vietto's entry, 'Leonora Sansay,' in the *Dictionary of Literary Biography* (330–36).

2 For more on the relationship between Sansay's letters to Aaron Burr and *Secret History*, see Vauthier (1970, 69–71).

while simultaneously distancing herself from them in a disapproving and Francophobic antebellum U.S. public sphere.[3]

By signing *Secret History* only with the moniker 'A Lady at Cape François,' Sansay allows herself to inhabit the sensory worlds of both Mary and her fictional sister, Clara, both Philadelphia and Saint-Domingue, and thus become at once an 'American' critic of colonial slavery and patriarchy *and* a pleasure-loving 'French' Creole coquette who defies the boundaries of decorum and propriety by taking many lovers.[4] After all, it is Clara, a native of the U.S. married to a French man, who adopts the libertine ways of the Creole colony, and Mary, the U.S. American outside observer, who both censures and disapproves. Mary writes:

> It is true Clara is said to be a coquette, but have not ladies of superior talents and attractions, at all times and in all countries been subject to that censure? ... when a woman, like Clara, can fascinate, intoxicate, transport, and whilst unhappy is surrounded by seductive objects, she will become entangled, and be borne away by the rapidity of her own sensations, happy if she can stop short on the brink of destruction. (153)

This literary strategy of what Monique Allewaert has called 'anabiography,' or autobiographical discontinuity, since 'Sansay passed under at least five names,' a fact which Allewaert says 'exceed[s] biographical criticism's drive to crystallize an identity or a personality' (151), also paradoxically allows Sansay/Hassal to be wholly bound neither to Clara or Mary at all. Instead she simply emerges as an innocent 'Lady at Cape François,' a revealer of, in the words of Gretchen Woertendyke, 'intimate secrets' of Saint-Domingue 'for the benefit of public history' (255).

Despite her attempt at relative anonymity, Sansay's first two known publications, *Secret History* and *Laura* (1809), signed respectively by a 'Lady at Cape Francois' and a 'Lady at Philadelphia,' were tied to Mary Hassal/Leonora Sansay in her own lifetime. According to Burr's memoirs, Mary Hassal was called 'Leonora' by him and others and was 'too well known under that name' (qtd. in Drexler, 2008, 27). Jennifer Van Bergen adds that 'Burr's biographer, Matthew L. Davis mysteriously referred to [Mary Hassal] as "Madame D'Auvergne, but better known as Leonora Sansay, the author of the Horrors of St. Domingo, &c.," and Burr referred to her by the names D'Auvergne and Clara' (Van Bergen). In addition, an 1809 issue of the Philadelphia-based periodical *The Port-Folio* identifies the author of Laura as

---

3 For Francophobia in the antebellum U.S., see A. Hunt (1988, 37).

4 In contrast, Sean Goudie has written that it is the character Clara who 'evolves into a figure of créolité—a creolized and creolizing West Indian goddess in the making' (210).

the 'same lady who published about a year ago a collection of stories written from St. Domingo' (qtd. in Lapsansky, 30). Because Sansay/Hassal was well known as the author of *Secret History*, the state of authorship behind this text may be operating as what Carla Peterson has referred to, in the context of some of Frances Ellen Watkins Harper's early pseudonymous publications, 'an open secret that refuses to conceal authorial identity' (2007, 192). Peterson writes of Harper:

> Neither Watkins's female identity nor the sketches' content thus compelled her to resort to the use of a pseudonym ... Instead, it invites readers to recognize the writer as one of their own for whom periodical publication has become a primary means of fostering the imagination of community among concerned black Americans. (192)

In *First Person Anonymous*, Alexis Easley explains such 'discontinuities in women's authorial identities' more broadly by writing that:

> rather than assuming individualized consistent authorial personae ... anonymity allowed women to appear and disappear in their work ... Likewise, it enables us to view pseudonymous publication as a strategy designed to complicate the authorial position, rather than a defensive means of obscuring an essential 'self' or 'voice.' (7)

In other words, rather than viewing pseudonymity or anonymity solely as repressive and coerced responses to male-dominated literary spheres, such strategies on the part of nineteenth-century female authors may have been used at times as a conscientious way of expressing multiple frames of identity in an Atlantic World public sphere that, at least for its female authors, often prized domesticity and dependence over worldliness and independence.

The author of the much less studied 1820 novel that was anonymously published in London, *Zelica; the Creole*, most often attributed to Sansay, takes what Joan de Jean has elsewhere called the 'privileges of anonymity' (884) a step further than either *Secret History* or the seemingly autobiographical *Laura*. The author of *Zelica* not only declines to use the epistolary form of *Secret History*, but forgoes even disclosing her sex when she signs the text with the gender neutral marker, 'An American.' Although this kind of anonymity may have allowed women to 'call into question the existence of a sexed body behind their literary texts' (Easley, 7), perhaps it also allowed Sansay—if, indeed, she is the author of *Zelica*—to further disassociate herself from the events described in her earlier narrative of Saint-Domingue. With *Zelica*, which takes in large part the plot and the majority of its protagonists from *Secret History*, the author simply becomes an anonymous 'American' among many others in an early nineteenth-century anti-slavery London, rather than a 'lady' writing at the place in which revolution to overthrow slavery was occurring. "Americanness" thus emerges as the distinct 'privilege' of an 'American' author radically disassociating herself not only from the gendered perspective of her past works, but the personal events of her past life, thus creating yet another, perhaps more authoritative, frame of identity for herself as the one who sees the Revolution rather than who is seen in it.

Despite the idea that Sansay may have wished to distance herself from the 'secret history' she detailed in her first known publication, *Zelica* was also, erroneously or not, linked to Sansay in her own lifetime. Though Leonora Sansay was only re-identified in 1993 as the author of *Zelica, the Creole* by Philip Lapsansky of the Library Company of Philadelphia, in 1821, the Boston-based periodical *The Atheneum, or Spirit of the English Magazines* ('Literary Report,' 128) and *The Edinburgh Review, or Critical journal* ('Quarterly List,' 1821, 266), identified a 'Madame de Sansée' [*sic*] as the author of *Zelica; the Creole*.[5] While Simone Vauthier and Michael Drexler have both expressed doubts that Sansay authored *Zelica* since, in Vauthier's words, 'the author of Zelica evinces a much greater comprehension of the Haitian situation and its political characteristics' (1970, 79), Allewaert, on the contrary, has concluded that because of these advertisements, 'the evidence strongly suggests that Sansay did in fact write Zelica' (152). However, I think what is more important than determining whether or not Sansay authored this third novel, is recognizing that because *Zelica* is based almost entirely on the purportedly *real* events disclosed in *Secret History*, the 1820 publication needs to be read as not only a quasi-historical novel, but as a quasi-biographical one.

If *Zelica* denotes a considerable expansion of *Secret History* by Sansay, or even if the text merely represents an appropriation of *Secret History* by someone else, the text constitutes a historical romance that makes fascinating use of Sansay/Hassal's interpretations of the events of the Haitian Revolution. Helen Hughes defines 'historical romance' as linked to both history and the novel, but she writes that what distinguishes the historical romance from either of these forms is that in order to create the 'verisimilitude' of a true story, the historical romance uses 'history itself …

---

5 If scholars have been all too certain that Leonora Sansay, aka Mary Hassal, is definitely the author of *Secret History* and *Laura*, the evidence tying Sansay to the authorship of *Zelica; the Creole*, *The Scarlet Handkerchief*, and the no longer extant *The Stranger in Mexico*, is a bit more vexed. The only thing linking Sansay to the publication of *Zelica* and the other texts are in fact the two above-mentioned advertisements that erroneously state her name as 'Sansee.' The title page of the three-volume *The Scarlet Handkerchief* identifies the author of that tale as the author of *Zelica* and numerous 1823 advertisements announce the forthcoming publication of *The Stranger in Mexico* as having been written by the same author of *Zelica* and *The Scarlet Handkerchief*.

to validate the story' (18). Hughes writes, 'If the narrative incorporates a good deal of historical details, the impression is given that this is the result of indefatigable scholarly research, and so—of course—true' (18). In Sansay/Hassal's case, with respect to *Secret History*, the impression given is not that the novel is the result of 'indefatigable scholarly research' on the part of its author, but rather that it is based on the author's incontestable 'evidence of experience' (J. Scott, 777). In *Secret History*, for example, Sansay/Hassal is able to connect what she has either personally seen or directly heard about in Saint-Domingue to the historical events that led up to the Haitian Revolution when she writes:

> When religion was abolished in France, the rage for abolition as well as that of revolutionizing reached this place, and the nuns were driven from the convent by Santhonax [*sic*], a name which will always fill every Frenchman's breast with horror: he caused the first destruction of the cape ... and actually set fire to the town. (94)

In *Zelica*, the narrator repeats the above passage from *Secret History* almost verbatim, but this time she successfully captures an air of historical authority when writing about the same details that were offered as a part of an autobiographical experience in *Secret History*. The narrator of *Zelica* writes: 'When religion was abolished in France, the rage for abolition extended itself with the revolution to St. Domingo, and the nuns were expelled from the convent by Santhonax [*sic*], a name that will be forever abhorred by the friends of piety and humanity' (2:220). Later in *Zelica*, the author expands upon this description by subtly giving a much more active role to Santhonax: 'It was Santhonax [*sic*],' the narrator tells us, 'who caused the first destruction of the Cape, by setting it on fire with his own hands' (2:221).

Zelica also repeats, again nearly verbatim, many of the scenes of "racial" revenge from *Secret History*, such as when the narrator describes a 'black chief' and his wife who were sentenced to death by Rochambeau after having 'committed the cruelest outrages in the island' (2:67). Sansay describes the chief's wife in both *Secret History* and *Zelica* as a 'fury in female form' (1820, 2:68; 2007, 92), who stabs her husband's former secretary 'with a penknife till he expired' (1820, 2:70; 2007, 92). Furthermore, both texts contain an infamous intimation that General Pierre Xavier Boyer, 'who had served under Bonaparte in Italy and Egypt' (Girard, 2011, 140), and General Leclerc's wife, Pauline (sister of Bonaparte) had an illicit affair. In *Secret History*, we are told that when Mary arrives at the Leclerc residence, Pauline Leclerc 'reclined again on the sofa and amused general Boyer, who sat at her feet, by letting her slipper fall continually, which he respectfully put on as often as it fell' (64). In *Zelica*, the narrator describes what was once a merely ridiculous situation in much more explicitly factual terms: Madame Leclerc is described as wearing

> the smallest slipper in the world, which appeared a world too wide for the prettiest foot in the universe, [which] fell at intervals on the carpet, and the indefatigable General Boyer replaced it with an air of as much triumph as he could have shown at planting his standard on the wall of a vanquished city. (1:165)

These details, when framed by a third-person narrator, capture an air of historical authority, even if clearly romanticized, that is patently different from that which we find in the first-person epistolary accounts of *Secret History*, which relied more on point of view and therefore *interpretation*, rather than on the *positivism* of omniscient narration.

The very different narrative effect created by the genre of *Zelica* as an historical novel and that of *Secret History* as an epistolary romance is what led Lorthrop Stoddard to dismiss the latter as a useful historical account of the Leclerc-Rochambeau expedition: in his words, it was too 'gossipy and personal in tone' (401). If the 'personal tone' used in *Secret History* has continued to provide the necessary 'evidence' for thinking about (and dismissing) that work as some kind of 'gossipy' romance rather than as history or even as a historical novel,[6] its author's 'personal' life romanticized into epistolary form for public consumption, the detached third person omniscient point of view in *Zelica* provides the authorial distance from these same eyewitness events necessary for thinking about the text as providing a romantic history of the life of another woman who was in every way different from Sansay; a woman of color, named Zuline.

In one of the most memorable scenes of *Secret History*, Sansay portrays 'a girl of colour' as having 'employed all her eloquence' (131) to save her U.S. American lover and a French colonist from the treachery of a 'ruthless mulatto' revolutionary. Sansay recalls how this 'girl,' whose name was Zuline, and who claimed not even to have known the French colonist she saved, says that she would have been willing to 'sacrifice' 'all her trinkets, which were of considerable value' (131), 'to save the life of an innocent person' (131). In order to save both men and ensure their safe passage to the U.S., however, Zuline must entertain the vows of love made by a 'mulatto' soldier, referred to only as 'this unrelenting savage.' According to Sansay, Zuline 'employed' the same ostensibly sexual 'eloquence,' as 'the means of saving many others.' Sansay concludes this rendition of the trope of the "tropical

---

[6] Vauthier has maintained that *Secret History* is difficult to read as 'pure fiction' (1970, 72), while Philippe Girard refers to the novel as a 'memoir ... *à clef* disguised as a romantic novel pretending to be a history' (2011, 141).

temptress" by telling the reader that she has personal knowledge that the events she recounts are *true*: 'the accounts I have heard of her kindness and generosity oblige me to think of her with unqualified admiration' (132).

There is almost certainly at least a figurative relationship between the admirable Zuline and the benevolent Zelica, the latter of whom is also described as a woman of color who saves, not her own lover, but Clara and her abusive husband, also named St. Louis, from revolutionary violence on several different occasions.[7] Zelica says to Clara: 'Remember that you are in a land of peril, encompassed by war and all its attendant horrors; and, when increasing dangers approach, or evils menace you, I will be near to shield and protect you' (1:177). If, indeed, the real life of Zuline was the inspiration for the fictional character of Zelica, then we might read the 1820 novel as based upon the represented life of not only Sansay/Hassal, but a woman of color herself. It is not just Zelica's desire to protect that might lead us to conclude that there is an intertextual, and therefore, an 'anabiographical' relationship between Zuline and Zelica. Like Zuline, who entertains with great 'horror' the possibility of a romantic relationship with the 'mulatto' revolutionary (132), Zelica is also immediately horrified by the idea that she could marry the revolutionary chief Henry Christophe, who would later become the king of the northern part of Haiti. The sexual threat posed by all men of color in *Secret History* as filtered through Mary's consciousness, but also in all probability drawn from the real fears of Sansay/Hassal, becomes an inseparable part of the fictional turned historical/autobiographical world of *Zelica*.

While scholars have acknowledged that the inspiration for the character of Zelica may have been the personage called Zuline in *Secret History*, as a whole, literary critics and historians have been much less interested in

---

7 According to Léon François Hoffman in *Le Nègre romantique*, in the eighteenth and nineteenth centuries 'Z' names were commonly given to slave characters and people of color because they seemed exotic (63). However, the name Zelica is likely more immediately linked to Thomas Moore's famous poem, *Lallah Rookh* (1817). In fact, volume 1, chapter 2 of Sansay's text quotes the following stanza about the beautiful and exotic Zelica from Moore's epic:

There's a beauty for ever unchangeably bright,
Like the long sunny lapse of a summer-day's light,
Shining on,—shining on, by no shadow made tender,
Till loves falls asleep in it sameness of splendour.
This was not beauty.—Oh nothing like this,
That gave to young Zelica such magic of bliss.

Owing to the popularity of Moore's epic oriental romance, Zelica became a common name in operas in the nineteenth century and led to several other *Lallah Rookh*-inspired novellas and short stories which also used the name Zelica. Zelica is also the name used in Samuel James Arnold's 1796 *The Creole; or The Haunted Island in Three Volumes*.

elaborating upon the implications of the intertextual relationship between the two publications. With the exception of Kimberly Manganelli, who explored the shift in 'genre and narrative structure from *Secret History* to *Zelica*' (33), we have not yet read the latter publication as immediately tied to Sansay's own autobiographical writing (and, therefore, to the literary history of the Haitian Revolution) through its repetition and expansion of the supposedly real-life events recounted in the former.[8]

The almost entirely derivative relationship between *Secret History* and *Zelica* holds an importance far beyond the connection between Zuline and Zelica. This autobiographical derivation means that the confusion found in *Secret History* over the meaning of revolutionary violence—exemplified by Mary's statement that 'Unfortunate were those who witness the first wild transports of freedom' (77)—is also repeated by the author of *Zelica*, who writes, 'It is lamentably true that the first wild transports of freedom in St. Domingo were accompanied by excesses shocking to humanity' (1:9). In fact, aside from borrowing all of its major characters from *Secret History*, and numerous descriptions of Creoles, "mulattoes," and the climate of Saint-Domingue that provide us with yet more evidence of the ubiquity of the narrative of "mulatto/a" vengeance, what ties *Zelica* most closely to Sansay's 1808 work is the expression of a conflicted disdain for the violence of the Haitian Revolution as a method of abolishing slavery. This disdain is only complicated by a similar contempt for slavery and an anxious recourse to pseudoscientific understandings about "race."

In *Secret History*, even though Sansay owns that slavery is a 'brutal state of subjection' (77), she continuously describes the 'black' slaves as 'brigands' (82–83), noting that they were 'inured to a savage life' (73) and 'rendered furious by a desire of vengeance' (77). In *Zelica*, "monstrous hybridity" is also

---

8 *Zelica* was published the very same year that King Henry Christophe died from a self-inflicted gunshot wound. The coincidence of these dates has led Manganelli to conclude, 'Sansay may have seen the death of Christophe as an opportunity to *refashion Secret History* into a new narrative that she could resell' (33). However, Christophe's death occurred late in the year in October of 1820. It is therefore unlikely that *Zelica*, which does not reference the death of Christophe at all but rather constantly labors to describe his increasing power over the island, was inspired by news of Christophe's death since that would have left the author only a little over two months to write and publish a daunting three-volume novel. Interestingly enough, *Zelica; the Creole* was actually later advertised in 1821 in several British periodicals under the erroneous title *Zelica; the Creole, or the death of Christophe*. See *The British Review and London Journal*, Vol. 17, 260; *The London Magazine*, Vol. 3, 347. These advertisements lead me to infer that it is these later entities, who had an interest in selling the novel, rather than the author herself, who may have linked *Zelica* erroneously to Christophe's death in the vein that Manganelli implies.

referenced by the author as any set of conflicting, incongruous, or epistemologically confusing understandings of the Haitian Revolution. On the one hand, Zelica seemingly sympathizes with the slaves when she repeatedly refers to the 'rights' of which they 'had so cruelly been deprived' (1:99); on the other, the narrator, Zelica, and the majority of the "white" colonists, repeatedly describe the slaves who had revolted against their masters as having been 'rendered ferocious by their sufferings' because they 'were intoxicated with a desire of vengeance' (1:9). Later in *Zelica*, the narrator even says that the revolutionaries are 'monsters ... who are covered with every crime at which humanity shudders' (1:221).

The conflict between the simultaneous anti-slavery and anti-revolutionary stance of both texts, makes *Zelica* and *Secret History* difficult to comprehend on purely ideological levels. Was the disdain for slavery expressed in both works sincere? Was the recourse to the narrative of "racial" revenge malignant evidence of their respective authors' own racism or blind repetition of the "mulatto/a" vengeance narrative of the Haitian Revolution that was in constant circulation in the Atlantic World? These tensions are further complicated in *Secret History*, especially, by the near-endless juxtaposition of "white" female powerlessness with "black" male agency. Along these lines, Drexler has concluded that *Secret History* cannot be 'an obvious reform novel,' precisely because its portrayals are 'neither abolitionist nor feminist' (2013, 145). Liu more forcefully questions the possibility of considering the text transgressive when she writes, '*Secret History* furthers a strong negrophobic agenda. The novel undermines a feminist abolitionist position, for it ultimately posits that the freedom of white women is incompatible with black power' (392).

Even if Liu is right that in *Secret History* it is 'black sovereignty' which is to be feared from Sansay's point of view rather than 'blackness itself' (416), I think we must pay more attention to the fact that this expansion of Sansay's Zuline episode in *Zelica* paradoxically celebrates the transformation of a woman of color from the stereotypical "tropical temptress" that Sansay describes in Letter X of *Secret History* as 'extremely beautiful' and 'destined from their birth to a life of pleasure' (95) into a distinctly sovereign female agent of resistance in her own right. For, importantly, Zuline's own safety is not the result of her own power, but rather she is saved from the 'mulatto' by the 'power of the American gentleman, who had great weight with Dessalines' (132). *Secret History* is in fact filled with scenes like this one that divest its female characters of agency. Mary laments her inability to protect Clara from her own husband: 'Alas! I never so deeply regret my own want of power as when reflecting that I am unable to be useful to you' (119). Sometimes, the absence of female agency is even more explicitly related to marriage, as when Mary writes to Burr in *Secret History*: 'How terrible is the fate of a woman thus dependent on a man' (115). At other times, this powerlessness is linked to the growing power of the slaves. Mary writes: 'How terrible was the situation of these unfortunate women, insulted by the brutal passion of a negro, and certain of perishing if they resisted or if they complied' (92).

In *Zelica*, in contrast, a woman of color suddenly becomes no longer merely the agent of a kind of dangerous sexuality that was ultimately threatening to "white" womanhood, nor is she simply an imperiled subservient, a victim of the sexual caprices of "white" colonial men as equally as of the Haitian revolutionists. Instead, she also becomes a formidable opponent in her own right. This powerful portrayal of Zelica as a woman of color with astonishing agency has led Caroll Smith-Rosenberg to call Zelica the text's 'one truly powerful and masterful character. It is she who understands and controls the movements of black and white armies, she who is able to thwart the plans of French generals and black "chiefs"' (2003, 454). However, it seems to me that because the trope of the "tropical temptress" is always doubly inflected with stereotypical portrayals on one hand and the utter transgression of those portrayals on the other, like Zuline from *Secret History*, none of the women in *Zelica* are horizontally powerful.

Female agency is complicated by the fact that women of color are simultaneously the ultimate symbols of female resistance to patriarchal authority and of inescapable sexual repression. Although Clara's slave, Madelaine, for example, is subject at any moment to the colonial culture of rape that plagued all slave societies in the Atlantic World, she is also described as a powerful and immortal sorceress whose life, 'already extended beyond the limits of mortality, was not to be destroyed by the power of man' (3:282).[9] Similarly, as a woman of "mixed race," Zelica represents the very product of colonial rape culture, but she, much like Madelaine, is described by the revolutionary Glaude as one who seems to have been 'born to command' (1:122). The description of the patriarchal perils attending Clara in *blackface*, too, would have resonated in the pro-slavery propaganda of the post-Haitian revolutionary period, where "white" female victimization at the hands of brutal "black" male revolutionaries became a powerful referent for female

---

9 Defining 'rape culture' in general, Joseph Dorsey has written that 'it is an acquired deviation from basic human instincts of sexual desire, a common display of a pathological behavior that is learned. It is evident in societies that essentialize masculine and feminine conduct,' he says, 'as an active/passive polarity. Women and men are vulnerable to rape in any group or community that predicates gender differentiation on oppositional formulas of male aggression and female docility.' Of rape in colonial societies, he adds, 'internal and external identities of sexual violence in slave-based societies from the perspective of patriarchy and the language that endorses it ... supports the position that rape constitutes a culture of its own' (295).

subjection. Nevertheless, Clara, who is painted as suddenly unprotected, vulnerable, and 'exposed to the gaze of the multitude' once the Revolution begins in earnest (1:31), is simultaneously all-powerful too when she is imagined by Glaude as being able to call forth with 'her voice' the 'force of her country ... to assist the blacks in their struggle for freedom,' and eventually become crowned the 'queen of the Island' (1:134). Thus, we might say that even in light in of the unusual and in many ways spectacular displays of female benevolence as a form of power to be found in *Zelica*, this power is ordinarily marked by the same ideological anxieties that keep us from pinning down the "racial" stance of the author of *Zelica*. Like so many fictional representations of the Haitian Revolution, *Zelica* resists being read as being completely anti-slavery by being both anti- and pro-revolution, and resists being read as completely anti-"miscegenation" by celebrating the actions of its heroine of "mixed race." Paradoxically, then, we might say that in *Zelica*, "non-white" women (and "white" women in *blackface*) embody a full spectrum of sexual and "racial" anxieties *and* revolutionary and radical possibilities.

Somewhat paradoxically, it is the agency-divesting language of the trope of the "tropical temptress," and the obvious face of "mulatto/a" vengeance it offers, which allows us to glimpse the shadowed or sublimated face of this figure as an agent of non-compliance and rebellion. In the first part of this chapter, therefore, I argue that recognizing Zuline, the putative real-life benevolent revolutionary woman of color from *Secret History* as a model for the tropicalized character of Zelica provides the occasion for us to glimpse how in *Zelica* female benevolence as resistance becomes the ultimate historical antidote to the masculinized violence of revolution and slavery. Indeed, "non-white" female benevolence is represented as the only path to liberation in a world where all men (be they characterized as "white" or "black") pose the same moral, physical, spiritual, and sexual threat. Yet, in the second section, by placing *Zelica* within a larger literary history of the Haitian Revolution, what emerges out of "non-white" female benevolence is not only a metaphor for thinking about the kind of subjection to patriarchal authority that confronts all of the female characters in *Zelica*, but also ambivalence about the meaning of the Haitian Revolution with respect to its characteristic violence, an ambivalence that was widely shared in the transatlantic literary history of the Haitian Revolution. In the third and final section, we will see that the language of uncertainty surrounding the implications of "miscegenation" becomes an easy cover through which to work through these anxieties about the meaning of the Haitian Revolution.

As surely one of the first "American" attempts to portray a heroine of "mixed race," *Zelica* has so much to tell us about the ideological work of writing about women of color and the Haitian Revolution and the ways in which such a project was always doubly relational, portraying these women in relationship to other "black" men and "black" women, on the one hand, and "white" women and "white" men, on the other. Ultimately, examining the vastly convergent relationships of various "non-white" women to ideologies of revolution as catalyzed by certain characters in the novel, allows us to explore some of the ways in which the narrative of "mulatto/a" vengeance, provided a vocabulary not only for eroticizing and demonizing women of color, but, paradoxically, for radicalizing and celebrating their behavior.

*

Zelica tells the tale of Clara St. Louis, a U.S. American woman who travels to Saint-Domingue with her French Creole husband Louis de St. Louis. St. Louis hopes to recover his property under the reign of Toussaint Louverture, but after insurrection breaks out, the St. Louis couple and their friends are forced to flee to the mountains to escape the violence. Accompanying them are a "white" Creole woman named Justine Sénat, who is having an affair with Clara's husband, a French soldier named Belmont, who eventually marries St. Louis's sister, Louise, and finally, there is Zelica, who is described as a beautiful woman of "mixed race" (this last fact is unbeknownst to them at first because she is ashamed of it), whose "white" father, de la Rivière, supports the insurrection. A very important detail is that de la Rivière has pledged the hand of his daughter to General Henry Christophe as a way to cement his support for the Revolution and to symbolically create a *rapprochement* between the former free people of color and the former slaves. Zelica, who is not without her own color prejudices, however, vows to die rather than marry Christophe, whom she considers to be kind, but despises because of his dark skin. In addition, Zelica is in love with a young French soldier named Lastour, whom she meets while studying in France, which provides her with yet another reason for dismissing Christophe as a potential suitor. Because of Christophe's love for her, Zelica holds remarkable influence over the male revolutionaries of color and she uses that influence to save the lives of Clara and her husband on several occasions.

Clara, for her part, is the inspiration for several jealousy-fueled disputes during the Revolution. A "mulatto" revolutionary named Glaude loves Clara almost to the point of folly. Clara's French tutor, Préval, also falls in love with her, while General Donatien Rochambeau (a real-life figure), who becomes the leader of the expedition to restore slavery in the colony of Saint-Domingue after the kidnapping of Toussaint Louverture and General Leclerc's eventual death, is also smitten with Clara and employs many treacherous measures, all of them eventually foiled, in order to possess her. Because of the interest in Clara displayed by these men, and especially Rochambeau, Clara's husband St. Louis eventually begins to display renewed interest in his wife, which invites the ire of the French general. Because he feels that his wife's chastity and loyalty to him are threatened by Rochambeau, St. Louis becomes abusive and locks Clara up. He deserts his military post, and will eventually be compelled to flee from the island disguised as a sailor in order to save his life.

While most of the "mixed-race" protagonists in the trope of the "tragic mulatta" end up dying when they cannot be with the objects of their love, in opposition to this trope, in *Zelica* it is actually the "white" woman Clara, who had been under Zelica's protection, who dies before reuniting with her husband. Zelica's father, de la Rivière, attempting to murder Glaude, who had kidnapped Clara, accidentally stabs Clara in the heart. Glaude in turn stabs de la Rivière and escapes from the scene unharmed. Afterward, the St. Louis' faithful and powerful slave, Madelaine, who is also a sorceress, entreats a priest to consecrate the dead bodies, and she correspondingly vows to stay on the island and watch over the corpse of her mistress forever. As for Zelica, after learning of Clara and de la Rivière's deaths, she plunges into the ocean in an attempt to commit suicide. With perhaps the utmost sense of irony, Zelica will ultimately be rescued by the very boat that contains both St. Louis and her lover, Lastour. The tale ends uncertainly when Zelica presumably travels to the United States on a vessel bound for the continent.

Using the image of powerless, subservient, or concupiscent "black" women as a way to contrast, heighten, or bolster the fraught sexuality and adumbrated power of "white" women has been a much-discussed phenomenon in Atlantic literary and cultural studies. As Sander Gilman has famously noted, in the eighteenth and nineteenth centuries, the image of the 'black' woman's supposedly lascivious nature injected into 'white' society in order to 'sexualize' it, was nearly 'ubiquitous' (209). T. Denean Sharpley-Whiting adds that overly sexualized portrayals of women of color in nineteenth-century French fiction cover up an authorial anxiety about 'race' and sexuality that 'allow[s] the [white] French writer to maintain a position of moral, sexual, and racial superiority' (7). Claire Midgley writes that in British women's fiction, 'The presentation of black women as passive victims is inseparable from the empowerment of white women' (134). Gilman, Sharpley-Whiting, and Midgley's attention to the anxiety surrounding descriptions of women of color in several realms of nineteenth-century discourse—art, literature, medicine, abolitionist thought—resonates with the usual analyses of "non-white" female presence in Sansay's *Secret History* and in *Zelica*. Emily Clark has recently written of Zuline, for example, that 'Succumbing to the temptations of the *mulâtresse* was evil, but she was, in the end, a woman susceptible to the mastery of any white man who could satisfy her taste for luxury' (53). Kimberly Manganelli, who discusses *Zelica* in *The Tragic Mulatta and the Tragic Muse* (2011), concludes that post-revolutionary fiction turns the woman of color into a figure subject to 'patriarchal authority' rather than 'revolutionary agency' (19). Yet, in a surprising departure from the usual way in which Sansay's works have been read, in *Zelica* I see powerful rather than powerless "black" female identity as undergirding both "white" female and "black" male agency.

The unusual way in which *Zelica* departs from the more prominent portrayals of women of color in fictions of the Atlantic World was captured in the only known full-length review of the novel from the nineteenth century, which was published in *The Independent; A London Literary and Political Review* on March 3, 1821. The reviewer appeared to find it curious that the author of *Zelica* chose to have a powerful woman of "mixed race" play the hero. After recounting the entire plot of *Zelica*, the reviewer writes:

> French intrigue dominates in these volumes. St. Louis is scarcely less detestable than the black Glaude; and for Zelica she seems a being capable of ubiquity—for we find her ever present when any difficulty occurs. This power is very useful to a novel writer, however the reader may think it comes in a very questionable shape.

The reviewer goes on to quote a lengthy passage from the novel in which Zelica's 'shape' is painted using the pseudoscientific vocabulary of the trope of the "tropical temptress":

> Zelica, whose large black eyes swim in melting languor, and who had not been deprived, by a long abode in France, of the gracefully indolent movements that are distinguishing characteristics of the creole ladies—formed by nature to fascinate, and furnished by education with all the powers of pleasing—was a perfect enchantress.

As if this passage were not evidence enough of the reviewer's claim, he goes on to cite Zelica's own statement: 'I love with all the ardour of the burning climes from which I derive my origin' (143). What seemed to be the astounding and contradictory 'shape' of the eponymous hero to this reviewer immediately reveals the way in which promoters of the trope of the "tropical temptress" were working hard to produce the woman of color as *only* a seductress.

At a more textual level, however, Zelica's position as an awesome woman of color, even as presented in the review, becomes an invariable reflection of the almost unbelievable way in which her radical consciousness was narrated in the novel. It is almost as if it is Zelica herself who is refusing to be entirely sublimated by what was in many ways the much more dominant colonialist epistemology that runs through the novel. In *Zelica*, whenever the beauty of the title character is described, it is portrayed as wholly inviting and seducing, and dangerous and powerful. Zelica is variously described as a 'beautiful sorceress,' 'irresistibly interesting,' an 'enchantress whose slightest motion enslaves' (1:55), and Belmont describes her as 'the fair, the fascinating Zelica—who combines the beauty of the houris with all the graces only to be acquired in Paris, and the irresistible languor created by this voluptuous climate' (1:55). Glaude, for his part, thinks that the 'power that Zelica possessed over Christophe was like resistless magic' (2:33). If we turn to the tale of female agency that is being simultaneously called forth with these descriptions, we can see how the language of the woman of color's powers of sexual seduction helped to tell a more redeeming tale about their revolutionary power. Part of what makes Zelica attractive to St. Louis, in this respect, is her uncanny ability to do what he, even as a man, cannot:

> Zelica protecting his wife from danger—Zelica, whom he had not seen since their separation on the mountain, but whom he had at times thought of as the most charming creature in the universe, occupied the volatile imagination of St. Louis more than the alarming attack of Glaude. There was something irresistibly interesting to him in the mystery that surrounded her, and he regretted not having been exposed to the dangers of a combat with Glaude to have enjoyed the pleasure of hearing her voice bid the combat cease. (2:58–59)

Remarkably, Zelica is perfectly aware of the power she possesses to 'bid the combat cease.' She says that she is the only person who might have the 'power of counteracting [Glaude's] designs at present' (1:178), and she does end up frustrating his revolutionary plans at several different junctures. She even prevents the execution of St. Louis, which had been ordered by Christophe. Other descriptions of Zelica seem to lend supernatural powers to the eponymous hero: 'Zelica, bounding like a fawn from cliff to cliff, appeared to consider the danger of the road very trifling compared to that from which it was leading them' (3:85).

It is not just Zelica who, in addition to displaying daring physical prowess, holds an amazing aptitude to impede revolutionary violence. The novel anxiously disputes the presumed unequivocal powers of patriarchy and male physicality by allowing all of the text's female heroes to easily thwart the plans of "black" male revolutionaries and "white" French soldiers alike. Madelaine, for example, spectacularly causes the failure of the 'designs of Clairvaux [a revolutionary of "mixed race"]'—to produce the 'destruction of all white men in existence'—when she has a male slave alert St. Louis to

Clairvaux's plans.[10] The narrator writes: 'The affrighted slave, who trembled before the being whom he considered as a mighty magician, hastened to the field, and told his master that Madelaine warned him of some threatening danger' (2:29). Zelica also assures Clara that 'Madelaine alone is faithful, and the reputation she has of being a sorceress has, I am convinced, preserved you from many dangers' (3:119). Later, Madelaine's powers are more fully described when the former slave performs an 'invocation to the powers she worshipped, praying them to avert her mistress from the evils that threatened her' (3:139). We are told, in fact, that Madelaine can protect Clara from the rebellious slaves because she 'was revered by them, and indeed by all the people of colour in the city, as being gifted with supernatural powers' (3:102).

"White" male power, in contrast, is so impotent in *Zelica* that it is Zelica and Madelaine who variously intervene to protect Clara and her sister-in-law Louise from all the men in the colony. Even though Clara tells Rochambeau that only her husband can protect her, it is actually Zelica who is the only person capable of protecting Clara in this revolutionary scenario. The narrator even tells us that Zelica thinks that the fact that her father betrothed her to Christophe might be a blessing in disguise since, as she tells Clara: 'I ought not to complain of a fate that gives me the power of being useful to you' (1:177). Zelica also uses her influence with Christophe and Glaude to such an extent that she is able to tell Clara, 'the most official power in the country protects you' (3:139), a reference to Christophe's ascent within the ranks of the revolutionary army. Furthermore, when Clara perilously travels to Rochambeau's 'fatal palace' (3:118), Zelica darkens her face with berries and assumes the habit of a slave in order to protect Clara from the treachery of the French general, telling her: 'Do not recoil from a disguise assumed for your preservation ... I stained my skin with berries whose effect Madelaine must be well acquainted with' (3:116). Zelica can best protect Clara when she is wearing *blackface* (notably, this action is authorized in the text by Zelica's evocation of the slave Madelaine), once again affirming that it is female "blackness" that is protective and liberatory and male "whiteness," like male "blackness," that imperils and threatens. Zelica tells Clara that 'staining [her] skin with the juice of a berry that turns it perfectly black' was a 'precaution absolutely necessary' (3:192) for both her and Clara's survival. Zelica explains to Clara that her own father also assures his safety by donning *blackface*: 'His colour, like that which now stains my own face, was assumed ... by a chemical preparation, [he] assumed the hue of those to whom he had devoted himself' (3:201).

10 The author probably refers to Augustin Clervaux, a 'light-skinned, French-educated officer' whom historian Philippe Girard describes as 'disinclined to fight his countrymen' (2011, s93).

Transgressing the Trope of the "Tropical Temptress"

Zelica's powers of protection and Clara's attempts at resistance[11] are only bolstered at every turn by the color black itself. In each scene in which Clara adopts resistant behavior, Zelica is present and often dressed as a slave wearing *blackface*.[12] In this way, it is actually "blackness" (in a very exaggerated form) and slavery that provide the needed contrast and authorization for Clara to oppose the 'tyranny based on sex', yet hers is the very same "blackness" and class position that makes one most subject to the 'tyranny based on color' (Raupach, 20). The surprising power of female agency in *blackface* is further put on display when the narrator describes a scene in which several "white" women escape the violence of the Revolution by painting their own skin black. The narrator tells us, 'The delicacy of their complexion and the beauty of their hands were concealed by tar; but the effeminacy of their persons and the timidity arising from their perilous situation, would have betrayed them to less acute observers' (3:232). "Blackness" provides the means of escape and thus both safety and transgression for "white" women, but it paradoxically also renders more apparent the 'delicacy' and fragility of "white" female status in Saint-Domingue.

The fact that "blackness"—like the Haitian Revolution—could be read as both threatening and protective shines through most clearly in this immediately arresting depiction of how "non-white" female power could also be deployed in service of the violent logic of revolution. It is actually Toussaint Louverture's wife, referred to only as Madame Louverture, who succeeds in convincing Christophe to adopt the binaristic logic of "black" violence against "white" violence that had often characterized portrayals of the Haitian Revolution. Madame Louverture tells Christophe:

> These monsters ... are resolved on your destruction, and you can only prevent it by destroying them; if you suffer them to remain on the island, they will employ all means to reduce you to the slavery from which you have escaped. To prevent it—to preserve your freedom, you have but one resource, and that is war—eternal war with white men ... let no proposals of peace allure you ... let your cry be ever, Liberty or death! (1:207)

---

11 Clara saves Préval from Rochambeau, she succeeds in convincing Rochambeau to cease using dogs to chase down the revolutionists, and she also prevents the closing of a convent, which is described in the text thus: 'never had a pious purpose been attained by more unhallowed means' (2:238).

12 Characters who wear *blackface* as a disguise are a well-seasoned theme in the literary history of the Haitian Revolution. *Blackface* escapes occur in numerous representations of the Haitian Revolution, including those of Berthier, Laisné de Tours, Picquenard, Beraud et al., Edmund Quincy, Pratt, Lamartine, Hugo, and in both the anonymously published *La Mulâtre* and *Oxiane*.

Inspired by the real life of a woman of color, this little passage rewrites the genealogy of Dessalines's April 28 proclamation, which is often interpreted as a mandate to exterminate the remaining French colonists. The proclamation is most often considered to be the handiwork of Dessalines's secretary Boisrond-Tonnerre, and Philippe Girard writes that Dessalines presented the 'massacre as a form of nation building,' urging the Haitian people to recognize, 'Your reconciliation had be sealed in the blood of your executioners' (qtd. in Girard, 2011, 322).[13] Later, *Zelica* directly alludes to the April 28 proclamation when the narrator says:

> On the third day after the evacuation, a proclamation was issued by Dessalines, in which every white man was declared an enemy of the Indigenes, as they call themselves; their colour alone, it was declared, was sufficient to make them be regarded as objects of hatred, and to devote them to destruction. (3:217)

By attributing the argument for the extermination of the French colonists and the unqualified hatred of "whites" often interpreted to be germane to the document, to the influence and sentiments of none other than the wife of Toussaint Louverture, the author of *Zelica* radically (even if unwittingly) inserts women of color into the history of the Haitian Revolution as powerful, influential, and necessary.

However, the author of *Zelica* clearly reproves Madame Louverture's exhortation to 'eternal war with white men' when the narrator suggests that the erstwhile general's wife had made an error in assuming that there could never be any 'peace' between these 'white men,' whom she calls, 'monsters,' and the revolutionists. The narrator undermines Madame Louverture's logic of 'Liberty or death!' by reminding the reader that even though Toussaint Louverture had been kidnapped and taken to France to suffer 'imprisonment, from which he was only freed by death' (1:207), Madame Louverture herself had, much to the contrary, been humanely treated: 'But a degree of mercy that this unfortunate woman did not expect from those whom she regarded as monsters, to whom every species of cruelty was sport, allowed her to follow her husband to France' (1:207). It is only in decontextualizing this portrayal of Madame Louverture from its author's point of view—which was to suggest that the French government had shown mercy

---

13 Girard attributes the following statement about the measures to be taken against the French colonists to Boisrond-Tonnerre: 'May they shudder when approaching our coasts ... because of the terrible resolution that we will take to kill all French born individuals' (qtd. in Girard, 2011, 319). In *Beyond the Slave Narrative*, however, Deborah Jenson makes a convincing case for not disavowing Dessalines's authorship of such proclamations since collaboration was and is a hallmark of governance (2011, 90–94).

to Madame Louverture even though she was hardly prepared to exhibit it towards them—that we can see her as a revolutionary woman who is being represented as having had an influence over the male revolutionaries that is not only unmatched by any other character in the text, but produces the most radical outcome of them all. In this reading, Madame Louverture becomes not simply the tragic widow of the Haitian Revolution's most tragic general, but the very author of the independent Haiti that constantly eluded her husband.[14] The key point is that the bodies of women of color and the varying rather than static kinds of influence they were capable of signifying during the Revolution, could allow an author to work through the problem of promoting freedom without promoting violence, of either the literal kind that had been used during the Revolution or the figurative kind that "miscegenation" represents in *Zelica*; at the same time, the actual effectiveness of violence as a way to liberation for slaves, especially in the context of Saint-Domingue, often unwittingly surges through these portrayals anyway.

*

The author of *Zelica*'s portrayal of what is in many ways presented as "non-white" female responsibility to protect people from the Revolution's 'excesses shocking to humanity' (1:9), marks an important strain in the genealogy of the literary history of the Haitian Revolution. Unlike Madame Louverture, in representations of the Haitian Revolution not all of people of color appear to be working for the side of the former slaves turned revolutionists. Often depictions of benevolent people of color who behaved in ways that seemed incommensurate with the totalizing and dichotomous violence of the Haitian Revolution—as "black" slaves against "white" masters—appear to betray the same anxieties about the ultimate meaning of the kinds of revolutionary violence that even while carrying the capacity to free, also had the capacity to be every bit as essentializing as the "racial" taxonomies that undergirded much of colonial writing. Just like Zelica and Zuline, who appear to have chosen sides when they go to great lengths to save their lovers, former masters, friends, and children from the male revolutionists, on the one hand, or from the "white" male colonists, on the other, we find

---

14 Even though in *Zelica* Madame Louverture's statement seems to carry the ideas set forth in the proclamation, later in the text the narrator hints at the more received version of this text's authorship as being that of Dessalines's secretary, Louis Félix Boisrond-Tonnerre: 'The author of this eloquent production, himself a white man, was the first victim sacrificed to a raging thirst for blood, which, like that of a tiger, became insatiable and increased in proportion to the number of victims it devoured' (3:218).

no shortage of such benevolent women of color in various kinds of writing about the Haitian Revolution.

Using "black" female benevolence towards "whites" as a way to critique or worry over the violent implications of revolution was a well-seasoned theme in histories of the Haitian Revolution. The nineteenth-century Haitian historian Joseph Saint-Rémy acknowledged as much when describing Dessaline's wife, Marie Claire Heureuse's often evoked protection of "whites." Saint-Rémy noted that by recounting her story, historians of the Haitian Revolution had provided not only an interesting detail for the reader, but a convenient way to soften the mostly terrifying events recorded in such narratives. Saint-Rémy writes, 'this godly woman whom we always find in the bloody epics of Saint-Domingue, in order to diminish the horror, one night saved numerous victims. She saved above all for France a great naturalist, M. Descourtilz' (1853, 58). Importantly, these 'godly' women of color to be found in the 'epics of Saint-Domingue' are ordinarily described in fictions of the Haitian Revolution as being *des négresses* rather than *des mulâtresses*.

In one of the first novels of the Haitian Revolution, the French writer Jean-Baptiste Picquenard's *Adonis; ou le bon nègre* (1798), for example, a *négresse* named Zerbine confides revolutionary secrets to a noble slave named Adonis, who uses the information, not to further the goals of the Revolution, but to save his master's family. The novel celebrates Zerbine's behavior as a 'return to virtue' (76)—she had previously been the lover of the ruthlessly represented revolutionary Biassou—and rewards her by allowing her to marry the noble Adonis and eventually escape to the United States. Similarly, in Picquenard's second novel of the Haitian Revolution, *Zoflora; ou la bonne négresse* (1800), which Chris Bongie calls a 'muted version of the colonial "family romance"' (2008, 104), the eponymous hero is not only willing to defy male revolutionaries like Biassou, but to sacrifice her own life to reunite a virtuous "white" man named Justin with a "white" Creole woman named Amicie, who happens to be the daughter of Zoflora's own master. Thinking of her love for Justin, Zoflora says, 'yes, ... I will sacrifice the love that I have for you, to the love that you have formed for the daughter of my master ... Zoflora will die for you' (208). Both *Adonis* and *Zoflora* are examples of the ways in which the image of women and men of color as benevolent protectors could provide a gentle salve for "white" metropolitan readers who were becoming accustomed to reading more terrorizing accounts about the Haitian revolutionists.

Even though Picquenard, drawing upon an ardent *négrophile* tradition[15] in

---

15 Picquenard was not the only abolitionist to utilize the noble savage for 'the cause of humanity' (76). According to Ardelle Striker, since the eighteenth century French playwrights, particularly those with anti-slavery goals, had sought to counter depictions

Transgressing the Trope of the "Tropical Temptress"

France, was anti-slavery and appears to decry the violence of the Revolution in both *Adonis* and *Zoflora*, according to Chris Bongie, it would be hard to describe him as a pacifist, given the fact that the motto of the newspaper he established in Saint-Domingue in 1794, *L'Ami de l'Egalité*, was unequivocally, 'La liberté ou LA MORT' (2006, xxxvii). Bongie writes that *Adonis* and *Zoflora* encapsulate the very large *décalage* or gap between revolutionary thought and revolutionary actions, which, for Bongie, is really a question about whether there is a 'possibility of social justice' without recourse to 'revolutionary violence' (xxxviii). In Picquenard's portrayal, the totalizing violence of the Revolution is further called into question when we learn that the kind of pity exemplified by Zerbine and Adonis could supposedly make even the most ardent revolutionists shirk the "racial" binaries of slave rebellion. At first, in *Adonis*, Picquenard describes Biassou as having been capable of 'resist[ing] the tears of so many thousands of families' and 'repell[ing] with severity the touching pleas of a crowd of young women, tender mothers, and respectable old men' (39). However, as hardened as the heart of Picquenard's Biassou may have been, when confronted with the suffering of children, he was ultimately unable to completely resist 'the first cry of nature, the innocence of humanity.' Unlike Hugo's Habibrah, who has no problem applying to children a binary logic that would turn slaves into masters and masters into slaves, Biassou opts to save two "white"

of Africans as savage brutes by producing a counter-stereotype that drew from the long tradition of the noble savage. Striker has written, to this effect, that at the end of the eighteenth century, 'négrophile' playwrights and novelists presented black characters in 'simple but positive terms.' Such a 'négrophile' tradition was also prominently featured in the literary history of the Haitian Revolution. One example comes from Joseph Lavallée's 1789 adventure novel *Le Nègre comme il y a peu de blancs*, set in pre-revolutionary Saint-Domingue, where the author makes his 'négrophile' intentions clear from the outset. Lavallée writes in the preface to the text: 'I am only tasked with making the Blacks loved' (xiii). In this tale, Lavallée will indeed make a hero out of the noble African Itanoko, who is eventually transported to and then enslaved on the island of Saint-Domingue. In fact, Lavallée promotes 'love' for the 'blacks' in general by singing the particular praises of the heroic Itanoko. The author even cautions lest anyone believe that Itanoko constitutes an exception to the rule when it comes to 'Negroes': 'If anyone reproaches me for having only written a novel, I will respond: the actions of my Hero comprise the separate traits of individual Negroes ... It is not therefore exactly a novel; it is the history of a national character that I am offering in the character of a single man' (xiii). Of his abolitionist intentions in telling this tale, Lavallée writes, 'O Blacks! [the universe] will not forget you then. I sense that a novel is not made to operate this grand revolution; but a novel is read by the whole world' (xii). Lavallée's comments suggest that this novel of heroic "black" actions and "interracial" love has the power to shape opinion and perhaps to create political and material change in the form of a 'revolution' of the mind with respect to color prejudice and slavery.

children named Joseph and Paulin from capture and execution. Picquenard writes: 'his heart had been moved, perhaps for the first time in his life; sobs oppressed him, and abundant tears flooded his face' (39). Picquenard's description of Biassou's transformation in this instance into a 'feeling' 'savage,' utterly exemplifies not only the humanitarian problem of revolutionary violence, but the epistemological uncertainty about both identity and ideology that plagues so many literary accounts of the Haitian Revolution.

Many other benevolent "black" women as portrayed in literary fictions of the Haitian Revolution appear to provide the necessary backdrop for critiquing the Haitian Revolution, when they perform acts of kindness towards "whites," not because they are completely disloyal to the revolutionary cause of anti-slavery or even because they are anti-violent, but because they are bound by the ties of kinship. As Carolle Charles writes,

> kinship is more than a list of biological relatives: it is a system of categories and statuses that often contradicts genetic relationships. It determines obligations, genealogical status, lineage, names, rights of inheritance, forms and patterns of conjugality and mating, norms and conventions governing sexuality, as well as people in concrete social relationships. (46)

In short, kinship is a way of feeling about others that might make us approach them in a manner we might ordinarily reserve for our genealogical family members. Take, then, Alexandre de Saillet's portrayal of a slave woman named Marie in *Lucile de Saint-Albe, épisode de la Révolution de Saint-Domingue*. Marie appears to favor the ties of kinship over those of genetics when she chooses to perform the counter-revolutionary biddings of her "white" 'foster sister' [*sœur de lait*] (115), Lucile, over joining the revolutionary efforts of her "black" father, Jean-Baptiste. By exploiting Marie's feelings of kinship, Lucile encourages a woman whom she views as an 'inferior being …' (116), to commit her loyalties to her 'foster' family and the very one that enslaved her. Lucile tells Marie that the two of them are invariably linked by more than just mutual love and devotion for one another since, 'you are my sister by the milk of your mother, which was my first nourishment' [*tu es ma sœur par le lait de ta mère, qui fut ma première nourriture*] (120). Lucile tries to make of Marie more than just one of her 'milk sisters' when she finishes by asking her slave to go and save 'our father' (120), referring to M. de Saint-Albe, a "white" colonist, in defiance of Marie's own "black" father. In this novel, the complicated entanglements of family life on the plantation altogether disrupt, forge, sever, and merge biology with kinship in a variety of intricate and contradictory ways. The behavior of Marie, when read not as betrayal against her actual biological father and therefore against the Revolution, but instead as one part of a set of endless possible responses to the interpersonal limits, pressures, and epistemological quandaries generated by colonialism, slavery, and revolution, calls into question the meaning of a revolution that in the blink of an eye could turn one's own child into one's own foe.

That all of this female transgression occurs in the context of various kinds of interpersonal relationship only punctuates the complications engendered by a revolution whose aims (abolition of slavery) and methods (violent rebellion) seemed clear enough, in theory, but whose praxis was deeply troubling for those who had to live through and, afterward, *with* the individual consequences. The seemingly unstable ideologies of many of the people of color we find in the literary history of the Haitian Revolution appear to reflect the ambivalence of an Enlightenment public sphere that continuously sought to reconcile the fact of revolution with the logic of revolutionary thought, which, in the context of the Haitian Revolution, meant coming to terms with the fact that being anti-slavery in post-independent Haiti bore a distinct and often unequivocal relationship to violent revolution that was for many abolitionists and anti-slavery thinkers, as for many family members, still quite unthinkable.

To that end, in the Boston abolitionist Edmund Quincy's 'Two Nights in Santo Domingo' (1843), originally published in the Boston Female Anti-slavery Society's annual abolitionist yearbook, *The Liberty Bell*, edited by Maria Weston Chapman,[16] a woman of color named Stéphanie arises as a fierce but conflicted female revolutionary, whose benevolent actions appear to contradict the fact that ideologically she remains in favor of the Haitian Revolution rather than against it. Stéphanie simultaneously wields astonishing authority and influence over "black" male revolutionary figures *and* saves her former masters from the vengeance of the revolutionists. Quincy ascribes this seemingly contradictory behavior to Stéphanie when he writes that she helps to plan and execute this 'holy insurrection' (92), but still found a way to save her foster sister, Mme. de Mirecourt, and her

---

16 *The Liberty Bell* was published in 15 volumes beginning in 1839. It contained poetry, essays, biographical entries, and fiction, including short stories and drama. According to Junius P. Rodriguez, 'The sale of these books provided both fund-raising and moral suasion opportunities for the society' (199). Chapman, who traveled to Haiti with her husband, an experience she wrote about in a short story called 'The Young Sailor' (1853), also wrote a brief history of the 'second American Republic' entitled simply 'Haïti,' which was published in the 1842 issue of *The Liberty Bell*. The 1842 issue is noteworthy because it contained several poems by William Lloyd Garrison who, like Quincy, was a regular contributor to the volume, as well as Lydia Maria Child's influential 'The Quadroon's Tale.' Other famous contributors to *The Liberty Bell* included Harriet Martineau, James Russell Lowell, Wendell Phillips, Henry Wadsworth Longfellow, Placido (a Cuban ex-slave executed in 1844 after having sparked insurrection there), Frederick Douglass, and Thomas Clarkson.

husband from 'the terrible vengeance which I fear the husbands, fathers, and brothers of the outraged slave women *will* wreak on the wives, daughters, and sisters of their tyrants' (94). Quincy's description of Stéphanie's motives also unwittingly connects the vengeance of the revolutionists to "racial mixing" by implying that it is the male kin of these 'outraged slave women' who will in due course seek to obtain revenge for the implied rape of those who were 'wives, daughters, and sisters.' Such a characterization of Stéphanie's ability to be simultaneously in favor of the Haitian Revolution and against the depersonalized violence that characterizes the 'vengeance' of the male characters alluded to above marks Quincy's own alignment with the anti-violent Boston Female Anti-Slavery Society—which itself aligned with the anti-violent rhetoric of William Lloyd Garrison (Rodriguez, 199)— in whose volume Quincy's work appeared.[17] However, Quincy does seem to equivocate a little on the question of violence when Stéphanie reminds her master of the reasons she is capable of benevolence while many of her fellow revolutionists are not: 'It is to that tenderness ... that foolish tenderness, that you will owe your life, indeed if it can yet be saved. It is an unwhipped slave that would save you and yours a faint taste of those horrors which your race has so long heaped upon mine' (91).

As the works of Picquenard, de Saillet, and Quincy suggest, using the body of "black" women in the vein of the '*bonne nègresse*' to explore the many human consequences of revolutionary violence was apparently common enough in the eighteenth and nineteenth centuries; what was much less common was to portray women of "mixed race" in the role of espousing such anti-Haitian Revolution abolitionism.[18] *Zelica* represents an important

---

17 The preamble of the 1835 constitution of the Boston Female Anti-Slavery Society reads: 'Believing slavery to be a direct violation of the law of God, and productive of a vast amount of misery and crime; and convinced that its abolition can only be effected by an acknowledgement of the justice and necessity of immediate emancipation,—we hereby agree to form ourselves into a Society to aid and assist in this righteous cause as far as lies within our power.' Garrison's wife, Helen, was a member of the society (D. Hansen, 1993, 4).

18 The '*bon nègre*' was, naturally, also an extremely widespread trope in abolitionist fictions, but was perhaps especially so in writing about the Haitian Revolution. For example, in Anna Maria Mackenzie's *Slavery, or the Times* (1792), a character called Adolphus writes a letter in which he comments upon the 1791 insurrection of the slaves in Saint-Domingue: 'Blind and undistinguishing, these wretched negroes advert but to a terrible revenge. It is enough that they are offended. It is enough that they can grasp the means of retaliation. Mercy, compassion, even justice, cannot make their claims good where the voice of revenge is only to be heard. How pitiable to reflect that innocence can offer no plea strong enough to secure itself, but, involved in one fate with the cruel and unjust, sinks before the death-dealing conquerors' (2:98). In *Memoir of Pierre Toussaint, Born a Slave in Santo Domingo* (1854), after describing Pierre Toussaint

first in the literary history of the Haitian Revolution, then, in that it is very likely the first intentionally fictional attempt to portray a woman of "mixed race" as dignified, virtuous, and benevolent in order to critique the violence of the Haitian Revolution.[19]

Even so, *Zelica* could not sum up any better the way in which an author could call forth the narrative of "mulatto/a" vengeance while still being anti-slavery and pro-Haitian independence than when Zelica says of the Haitian revolutionists: 'though their advocate, I am not their admirer; and, whilst I think that they have an indisputable right to the freedom they are struggling to obtain, I feel an involuntary sensation of horror at the sight of a black, and never behold one without shuddering' (85). Smith-Rosenberg argues that Zelica 'is unable to project a coherent political persona' precisely

as 'bearing no other connection' to Toussaint Louverture 'other than accidentally arises from similarity of name, color, country, and being both born in slavery, and on the same river' (6), Hannah Farnham Sawyer praises the subject of her memoir for being against the sort of revolutionary violence that had come to be associated with much of the abolitionism of her day. Sawyer says of her Toussaint, 'We cannot doubt how highly he prized liberty for the slave, yet he was never willing to talk on the subject. He seemed to fully comprehend the difficulty of emancipation, and once, when a lady asked him if he was an Abolitionist, he shuddered, and replied, "Madame ils n'ont jamais vu couler le sang comme moi," "They have never seen blood flow as I have"; and then he added, "They don't know what they are doing"' (85). Pierre Toussaint is the ultimate admirable 'negro,' in Sawyer's portrayal because, having witnessed the Haitian Revolution, he understood that the ends ostensibly did not justify the means. She writes of him, 'He was a true negro, such as God had made him, and he never strove to be any thing else. The black men represented as heroes in works of fiction often lose their identity, and cease to interest us as representatives of their race, for they are white men in all but color. It was a striking trait in Toussaint, that he wished to ennoble his brethren, by making them feel their moral responsibility as colored men, not as aping the customs, habits, and conversation of white men. He never forgot that he "lived in a black house", nor wished others to forget it' (98). Sawyer seems to find comfort in the fact that this *real* 'black man' was anti-slavery, but not an abolitionist, or worse, a revolutionist. For other portrayals of the '*bon nègre*' within the context of revolutionary Saint-Domingue, see *Selina, a novel founded on facts* (1800, 3:95–96); Anne Trelawny, *Offspring of Mortimer; or, Memoirs of the Straford family, a domestic novel* (1808, 4:71–79).

19 Though Jean Fagan Yellin has written that Lydia Maria Child's *Hobomok* (1824) can be considered the first U.S. novel to represent "miscegenation" at length (1989, 71), as Simone Vauthier has pointed out, it is actually *Zelica* which may represent a number of 'firsts' in U.S. American literary production. Vauthier writes, 'To our knowledge, *Zelica* is the first attempt in a [U.S.] American novel to provide a significant place for historical black characters, displayed not only with a profound comprehension of their motives and their actions, but even with real admiration for their power [*énergie*], and a certain sympathy for their struggle' (1970, 95). In addition to portraying 'black characters,' *Zelica* may be the first heroine of "mixed race" in the U.S. literary tradition.

because she is the 'colored celebrant of personal liberty who shudders at the sight of blacks' (2003, 463). Indeed, for Smith-Rosenberg, touting individual liberties is just about the only coherent thread that runs through the text, leading her to conclude: 'What a striking move—celebrating women as the only virtuous republicans in a novel deeply informed by classical republicanism, a political discourse that resolutely proclaimed women incapable of civic virtue' (453). The author's likening of slavery to a father's ability to 'dispose' of his daughter's hand to a man of color and therefore to perpetuate the horrors of "racial mixing," nevertheless sacrifices the capacity of *Zelica* to present a coherent critique of either patriarchy or the actual chattel slavery to which the above passage refers by brimming with fears about the implications of "miscegenation."

The reader is treated to a major insight into Clara's distinct disgust over "racial" mixing when she thinks, 'to be loved by a half-civilized negro, who had sufficient cause to pursue, with unmitigated hatred, all those whose colour she bore, was appalling' (1:148). In her inner musings, Clara is able to recognize that Glaude, that 'half-civilized negro,' had 'sufficient' reasons for hating those of her 'colour,' but at the same time she remains unable to imagine without trepidation becoming the lover, let alone the wife, of such a 'negro.' Like the cruelty that was represented as an innate part of the Revolution in *Zelica*, any "white" woman's sexual association with a "black" man is treated as a fatal monstrosity that is quite literally unthinkable. Zelica even pleads with her father to help her save Clara from Glaude, imploring, 'aid me to counteract [Glaude's] designs to save—to protect her from his violence. Oh! Let not that angelic woman become the prey of a monster' (2:213). Zelica's proposed marriage to Christophe, too, is horrifying mostly because Christophe is phenotypically "black" and Zelica is phenotypically "white." De la Rivière even chides Zelica for harboring her own color prejudices when he tells her, 'you have no objection to make to the man I have chosen for you ... but his colour ... believe me, the childish repugnance you feel will yield to the influence of time and habit' (2:207). The wish to read a certain radicality into de la Rivière's accusation of color prejudice and remonstration of Zelica's fears of "racial" mixing must be tempered by the fact that, by all accounts, de la Rivière is portrayed as an insensible and insensitive father who simply desires his own brand of patriarchal control over both his daughter and the island. Like Mimi in *La Mulâtre*, Zelica accuses her father of refusing to assume his paternal responsibilities of protection over his daughter: 'You, who would risk your life to relieve the oppressed and to avenge the wrongs of the injured, are you only insensible to the pains you create; must all receive from you support and protection, except her who has not but you to protect and support her?' (2:206).

Zelica even equates her impending marriage to Christophe not simply with the 'violation' of her body and mind, but with slavery itself. Zelica says of her father, 'He has broke the chains that bound a people, yet despotically disposes of my hand; he is an enthusiast for liberty, yet leaves his wretched daughter no choice between that most abhorred slavery, mental bondage—and death' (3:202). Sharon Block writes that in early America, 'Marriage set up a fiction of the invisibility of a woman's ability to consent to individual sexual acts, which allowed a husband to define her consent for her' (21). In this case, it is Zelica's own father who seeks to define the consent of his daughter by essentially commanding her to marry Christophe under the threat of great bodily violence. He tells her, 'that the slightest attempt to escape from the island would destroy the confidence reposed in her, and give her entirely into [Christophe's] power' (2:205). If *Zelica* delimits her father's demand that she marry Christophe to primarily a form of sexual and emotional bondage that could be equated with the physical and spiritual bondage of slavery and the frightening specter of "miscegenation," then what shape does desirable rather than undesirable resistance to patriarchal and colonial despotism take on under such a metaphor? For when marriage is likened to not just a *form* of slavery, but to the brutality of the very chattel slavery that precipitated the Revolution (and the "miscegenation" that was often identified as its catalyst), female resistance to marriage suddenly transforms into slaves defying their masters by starting a revolution and children of "mixed race" defying their "white" parents in acts of violence (even if only inflicted upon the self).

Before vowing to 'seek no refuge from my horrible fate but the grave,' Zelica claims that her father's obstinacy represents proof that 'the votaries of freedom have ever steeled themselves against the voices of nature' (2:212). Zelica implies with this statement that she recognizes that for her father "racial mixing" was positively linked to the project of freedom: he shouts at one point, 'Liberty! that is the flame that consumes every private feeling—that is the sublime pursuit to which all other feelings must be sacrificed' (2:209)—but for Zelica, there was something just as unnatural and horrifying about "miscegenation" as there was about the Haitian Revolution. Just before her attempted suicide, she exclaims, 'I could not obey the orders of my father and live—therefore I spare him the regret of having sacrificed his child in immolating myself' (3:286).

*

If we have been focusing on the face of the "tropical temptress" that can be read as rebellion and transgression, and was used as a way to critique the violence of the Haitian Revolution, we must not forget that the other face of this figure is still desire and disgust, or a very palpable ambivalence about identity that always accompanies the narrative of "mulatto/a" vengeance.

As we have seen, the Haitian Revolution wavers between being portrayed as the same fatal monstrosity or generative possibility in *Zelica* as "racial mixing." In many respects, we can also read the simultaneously repulsive and attractive qualities of the Haitian Revolution as reflecting the simultaneously repulsive and attractive qualities of the kind of "miscegenation" that had produced Zelica in the novel and the Revolution in the transatlantic print culture of the Haitian Revolution. The uneasy characterizations of people called, 'whites,' 'Creoles,' 'quadroons,' and 'negroes,' and 'mulattoes' punctuates the difficulty in determining a person's "race" based on his or her outward appearance and of determining a person's political or social status based on perceptions about his or her "race." In a revolution in which, as Michelle Burnham has written about *Zelica*'s sister text, *Secret History*, 'agents and victims of power often rapidly change places' (196), the fact that "white" people could be on the side of the slaves and "black" people could be on the side of the colonists only further confused viewing the Haitian Revolution (and the "miscegenation" that was often blamed for being its catalyst) in the unequivocal terms of right and wrong, or desirable and undesirable. *Zelica* is a text in which free "mulatto" revolutionaries disguise themselves as "black" slaves, "white" women and "white" men put on *blackface* to escape revolutionary violence, powerful Vodou priestesses thwart the goals of the Revolution, once-powerful "white" planters disguise themselves as low-ranking soldiers, and former slaveholders join the revolutionary cause. These confusions are precisely what lead Clara to conclude: 'everything in this country is false—everything delusive' (1:200).

Such epistemological problems or problems of knowing with certainty are overtly discussed in the text when the narrator tells us, 'No one knew by whom they were betrayed, or from whom they were to defend themselves' (2:11). In addition, after the capture and impending death of Belmont, we are told, 'in the universal astonishment that prevailed, no one knew how to act,—what to believe,—or what to apprehend' (3:173). Justine, in fact, characterizes Zelica's father as one of these betrayers who made everything difficult to comprehend when she remarks that 'his name will be handed by the inhabitants of St. Domingo to the execration of posterity ... to acquire the reputation of a philanthropist, [he] assisted the negroes to break their chains and regain their liberty' (2:138). Later, the narrator exclaims of de la Rivière's partiality to the Revolution: 'Oh! how could a man,—a Frenchman, submit to be the instrument of such horrible tyranny?' (3:177). Along the same lines, it is exactly the mistaken idea that Zelica's father has defected from the side of the Haitian revolutionists to that of the colonists that precipitates his death when Glaude shouts, 'traitor!' (3:293) and stabs him. However, Glaude was incorrect in his belief in de la Rivière's defection. It is true that de la Rivière considered Dessalines's behavior to be 'an act of cruelty that will be forever condemned—that has deformed the image of Liberty, for which we fought and will eternally stain the annals of those people, even if they should rise into the grandeur that they are capable of attaining' (3:264). Still, despite these doubts about the future of the island under "black" rule after 'the oceans of blood that have deluged their country' (3:264), the narrator tells us that de la Rivière has not at all changed sides, for he was 'devoted to Christophe—his engagements with him were not of a nature to be broken—he could not retract without betraying the cause of freedom, which he was pledged to support with all the powers of his soul' (3:288). What a tortured projection of the political conflicts of the Revolution masquerading as "racial" ones, which were never—forgive the pun—as black and white as the familiar dichotomy of the "white" colonists versus the "black" slaves and the racial taxonomies that supported these understandings would have us believe!

The shifting lines of loyalty in Saint-Domingue were so puzzling (and dangerous) even that at one point Clara worries out loud that Zelica, like her father, might eventually be influenced by the revolutionists and turn against her "race." Believing that Zelica is "white" herself, Clara asks her if, by consenting to live with Christophe in order to save her (Clara), she will 'not finally adopt the views of those you abhor ... since you abandon the people of your own race, and fix your abode among these monsters?' (1:181). Though Zelica is, in the parlance of the colony, a "quadroon," in the scene described below, her father, like so many other characters in the novel, relates and refers to her as he would a "white" woman. De la Rivière explains to Zelica that her marriage to Christophe might have the capacity to lessen the hatred of the former slaves for the white color: 'Christophe, in offering you his hand, has conquered the aversion he more justly feels for your colour—a colour that forever recalls to him images of injustice and oppression' (2:207). Furthermore, the narrator tells us that Zelica's skin is so 'white' that even Glaude, who is himself described as a 'mulatto,' believes that Zelica is a 'white' woman. In recalling Zelica's 'sweetness' and 'firmness,' we are told that Glaude feels conflicted since he 'abhorred all the race to which, from her colour, he concluded she belonged' (1:122). The other characters in *Zelica* also treat with utter hysteria the plausibility of Zelica's marriage to a "black" revolutionary because of their perceptions of her "whiteness." When Zelica reveals her fate to Clara, the latter hyperbolizes, 'can a father doom his child to perish?' (3:204). Moreover, St. Louis remarks that the proposed marriage between Zelica and Christophe is nothing but 'folly' (2:139), and considered the arrangement to be so outrageous that he proposed to 'speak of it to the colonial prefect, and procure a decree that will annul this preposterous testament and restore Zelica to her rights' (2:140).

Justine, who is aware of Zelica's *true* 'colour,' feels very differently about the proposed marriage: 'Her fate is less fair than her face ... There is nothing so revolting in the idea [of her marriage to Christophe] ... the enchantress will only return to her native colour, which all the water of the oceans would not wash out of her veins' (2:139). While Justine's comment reflects theories of "racial mixing" like Moreau de Saint-Méry's, which precariously (and with much authorial ambivalence) link it to successive degeneration, Zelica's father's scheme to marry his daughter to Christophe, precisely in order to ensure the success of Haitian independence, reflects those theories common in pseudoscientific debates about "hybridity" by natural historians like Buffon,[20] who, much like Sophie Doin and Lydia Maria Child would go on to do, proposed "miscegenation" as a way to create a *rapprochement*, and therefore possible regeneration, between people of different skin colors. We might say, therefore, that discussions surrounding the implications of Zelica's "race" bounce between the same ideas of regeneration and degeneration that had been used historically to discuss both "racial mixing" and Haitian independence. The debate is over whether Zelica could easily and more appropriately 'return' to "blackness" than she could pass imperceptibly into "whiteness." Zelica tells Clara that her father promised her hand to Christophe precisely in order to 'cement the union that had been formed between him and the black chiefs' (3:129). Zelica, for her part, links the 'folly' of "racial mixing" that her proposed marriage to Christophe represents to the kind of "racial" degeneration that subsequent generations of people of "mixed race" who procreated with *pure* "blacks" were supposed to have unleashed: 'The ardour of my father in the cause he had embraced,' Zelica says, '*degenerated* to madness, and, to cement the union that had been formed between him and the black chiefs, he promised to bestow on them his vast estates, and the hand of his daughter' (3:129, emphasis added). The choice of the word 'degenerated' here is particularly interesting given its specific valence in pseudoscientific debates about "race" and its relationship to ideas about the Haitian Revolution. According to Sean Goudie, the Caribbean and the United States constituted twin poles of *créolité* in the New World, one of which was 'a creole regenerate U.S.,' the other 'a creole degenerate West Indies' (10). Like the writings by Benjamin Franklin that Goudie discusses, we might say that *Zelica* opposes the type of *créolité* that would lead further into "blackness" precisely because the entire text labors to mythologize what Goudie might call a '*creole regenerate* Anglo American empire in North America formed in opposition to—according to eighteenth-century stereotype—the *creole degenerate* West Indies' (37). To that end, Zelica urges Clara away from Haiti, to 'hasten with your husband to that happy clime that gave you birth, and that has never been stained with the crimes that here make humanity shudder' (3:190).

20 See chapter one of this volume.

If we think about the romantic concepts of Creole regeneration and degeneration with respect to the United States, more specifically now, it is easy to see why the ending of *Zelica* can have been read quasi-heroically by scholars who suggest that 'Zelica, fusing black and white and refusing to admit that fusion, embod[ies] America in its racial and ideological complexity' (Smith-Rosenberg, 2000, 266). At the end of the novel, Smith-Rosenberg writes, 'together, the brave white soldier as virtuous republican and the quadroon as white "lady" will quite literally embody future Americans' (266). In some ways, Smith-Rosenberg's interpretation is quite plausible. In the final pages of the novel, we find Clara—who claims that her fate depends on her husband—stabbed to death, not by the 'monster' Glaude, but by Zelica's own father, Madelaine only retaining the power to protect, as she vows to stay on the island and watch over the 'grave of the fair and unfortunate Clara' (3:309). Zelica, in contrast, survives the Revolution, and we would be forgiven for believing that she eventually seeks 'asylum' in the United States, as suggested by Clara (3:207), and achieves the refugee's dream of being folded into the U.S. body politic.

Like everything relating to the Age of Revolution, however, reading Zelica as a metaphor for 'future' American identities is not without its own problems. Although, the U.S. comes to symbolize a place of refuge that is repeatedly referred to as the 'land of liberty' (1:134), and a place where 'all the rights of man [were] respected' (1:31), at the time *Zelica* was published, the U.S. was quite literally a land of *unfreedoms* for people of color like Zelica. It was not just the continuation of chattel slavery on U.S. shores that could bind Zelica to an uncertain future of slavery in 'America,' but ideas about "race" and the color prejudices that usually follow. Zelica herself tells us that upon her birth, she became bound to a slave mother, 'descended from the African race' (3:125), who in giving birth to her, gave birth not only to a genealogical slave, but to a spiritual one. Zelica tells Clara: 'To begin at the very source of my misfortunes, they proceeded from the beauty of my mother' (1:75), and she later explains her family history more fully:

> My mother, an amiable and beautiful woman, was descended from the African race, and was, consequently, marked with the stigma that attended those people. My father, captivated by her beauty, and won by her merit, had resolution enough to combat the prevailing prejudices of his country, and married her. This union, that formed [my father's] happiness, has devoted me to indefinable misery. (3:125)

This ancestry of 'indefinable misery' connected to both slavery and the "miscegenation" that produced Zelica, is a history that escaping to the United States will not erase. Justine, to that effect, reminds St. Louis that

Zelica might indeed be 'celebrated for her extraordinary beauty,' but that her mother, who was 'but one degree removed from black,' was 'still a slave' (2:138). Justine's remonstration of St. Louis's desire for Zelica serves as a reminder that wherever Zelica goes, her mother will always have been 'still a slave,' and even if no one else recognizes this fact, Zelica (and her body) will always remember it. What St. Louis refers to as the 'line of her ancestors from the creation' (2:139), then, is a lineage of slavery that Zelica cannot remove simply by landing upon U.S. shores, a place where rampant anti-"miscegenation" laws[21] contained the distinct possibility to foil her plans for marriage to Lastour and where fears of French *émigrés* would have made both Lastour and the ever-melancholy Zelica immediately suspect upon their arrival anyway (see A. White, 2010, 190). As Manganelli acknowledges:

> If the ship carrying Zelica and her betrothed Lastour had docked in New Orleans in 1804, the couple ... might not have been allowed to disembark immediately. Like many other refugees from Saint-Domingue who immigrated to New Orleans, Zelica and Lastour might have been forced to stay on board as officials inspected the ship 'in order to preclude the "illicit entrance of negroes and colored people."' (qtd. in Manganelli, 37)[22]

Finally, what are we to do with the fact that at the end of the novel Zelica is practically unconscious and unable to enjoy the freedom that has so anxiously been bestowed upon her? After all, Zelica had tried to commit suicide and was saved against her own wishes by many of the very men she had sought to escape.

Given all of the uncertainty about the possible fates awaiting Zelica both on her journey to the U.S. and upon landing on its shores, the ending of the novel seems to me to merely punctuate the anxiousness of non-violent attempts to espouse abolitionist thought, which were wholly complicated not simply by the material facts of slavery and revolution themselves, but by the vastly divergent gendered and "racial" identities through which anti-slavery and revolutionary ideas could be narrated. The conflicts of identity and politics experienced by nearly all of the characters in *Zelica* are perhaps less surprising when we consider the original problem I identified at the outset of this chapter in terms of locating the ideology of this tale, along with determining its genesis, and the identity of its author. These complications

---

21 For example, in 1662 Virginia outlawed interracial 'fornication,' and in 1664 Maryland followed suit by legally banning interracial marriage. In 1691, Virginia explicitly forbade interracial marriage, being careful to include "mulattoes" in its legislation (Shipley, 103).

22 Manganelli quotes from Jennifer M. Spears (2009, 192).

of classification are undergirded by the triple historical context of *Zelica*: the revolutionary Saint-Domingue and independent Haiti, which together comprise its setting, the anti-slavery London world in which the text was first published, and the antebellum slave-holding U.S. from which the author presumably came—or, perhaps, we cannot presume this last assertion at all. If Lydia Maria Child also signed her first novel *Hobomok* (1824) with the appellation 'An American' as a 'subversive' move that allowed her to 'assum[e] a masculine place as a representative American,' meaning a U.S. writer (Dolata, 44), the author of *Zelica* seems even to be resisting attaching any kind of stability to this idea of 'An American' read as a U.S. identity. For example, the French Creole St. Louis corrects General Rochambeau's mistaken conflation of the term 'American' with the inhabitants of the U.S. when he says, 'you know, general, that we are all here Americans.' Rochambeau accedes and corrects his error: 'Very true; but I mean a native of the United States' (2:174). This passage invites, nay, practically begs of us, to suspect that the author of *Zelica* was actually not from the U.S. at all, but was precisely what she or he claimed to be, 'An American.'

In the end, *Zelica*'s anxiety about nearly everything having to do with the people of the Haitian Revolution and their position in the Americas and to people ever uncertainly called 'Americans' is emblematic of the epistemological problems engendered by the issues of revolution, "race," and slavery. Nearly all of the texts found in the literary history of the Haitian Revolution, as various kinds of responses to the revolution in Saint-Domingue and the fact of Atlantic World slavery itself, were beset with problems of knowing that made giving recourse to tropologies of "race" both attractive and functional. In the case of *Zelica*, the trope of the "tropical temptress" as a universally understood sign for the degradations of "miscegenation" is fractured by these inconsistent and contradictory portrayals of Zelica's "racial" identity and by her failure to adhere to the stereotypical portrayal of such a character as a dangerous seductress. We would be unable to unequivocally describe Zelica as wholly a victim of "miscegenation"—a tragic "mulatta," if you will—nor could we describe her as having the kind of negative agency to seduce and coerce found in natural history's trope of the "tropical temptress." While the character of Zelica is neither tragic nor treacherous in the received ways, she is also only partially a romantic heroine of the Revolution—a female revolutionary. Because of Zelica's lack of a distinct position on the project of emancipation and her own color prejudices, she is not a distinctly liberating 'agent of resistance,' but one who is even at times an agent of compliance.

The contradictions of *Zelica* remain a large part of the reason why the text has been understudied, particularly in comparison to its sister text, the already relatively understudied *Secret History*. It has been hard enough for scholars to recognize and acknowledge women who are revolutionary in the received way. It is easy to see how women who are behaving in ways we do not want or expect would be further castigated, made unimportant, and indeed made invisible by a history of triumphalism that wants all revolutionaries to be Toussaint Louverture, whose position in the Haitian Revolution was not nearly so simplistic and un-conflicted as many of the earliest romances of his life made it seem.

CHAPTER SIX

'Theresa' to the Rescue! African American Women's Resistance and the Literary History of the Haitian Revolution

'All the women are white, all the blacks are men, but some of us are brave.'

—Gloria T. Hull, Patricia Bell Scott, and Barbara Smith (1982)

'What if I am a woman …?'

—Maria W. Stewart, 'Mrs. Stewart's Farewell Address to Her Friends in the City of Boston, Delivered September 21, 1833'

'And woman's voice is heard amid
   The accents of that warrior train
And when has woman's voice e'er bid
   And man could from its hest refrain?'

—George Vashon, 'Vincent Ogé' (1854)

While in some respects 'Theresa, a Haytien Tale' (1828) is quite conventional in its portrayal of a free woman of color living in revolutionary Saint-Domingue, Madame Paulina, who seeks to preserve the virtue of her daughters at all costs, in other respects, the serialized short story is quite radical in its suggestion that this same woman's daughter, Theresa, was ultimately responsible for the independence of Haiti. While *Zelica* uses female revolutionaries of color largely to critique the violence of the Haitian Revolution and to express anxieties about "miscegenation," 'Theresa' uses what is described by its author as the very 'agency' (644) of its eponymous female protagonist of color in order to enter into a conversation about the place of "non-white" women in both the Haitian Revolution and the pre-Civil War project of "racial" uplift in the United States. As one of the first two short stories written in publication outlets designed primarily for writers of color, and both of which are set in Saint-Domingue, 'Theresa' punctuates the interest and relevance of Haiti for the antebellum African American community;[1] but by portraying its heroine, Theresa, as *the* hero of the Haitian Revolution and thus as responsible for the subsequent independence of Haiti, the tale fills a lacuna in writing about the Haitian Revolution circulating in the U.S., as well as in the broader Atlantic World, which often remained silent on the subject of female revolutionaries who fought on the side of the Haitian revolutionists.

As an anonymously published short story that takes a heroic woman of color as its primary protagonist and was published in a primarily African American venue, 'Theresa' is probably one of the least well-known nineteenth-century representations of the Haitian Revolution. Because of its content and the circumstances under which it was published, however, it is also perhaps one of the most important. 'Theresa' was serialized in four installments, signed only with the initial 'S,' in the first African American newspaper, *Freedom's Journal*, on January 18, January 25, February 8, and February 15, 1828. Frances Smith Foster, who first brought renewed attention to the text in 2006 when she republished it in the 'Forgotten Manuscripts' section of the *African American Review*, says, '"Theresa" had been highly anticipated by readers of *Freedom's Journal* since its existence was advertised before it actually appeared and the editors even apologized for its delay on two separate occasions' (2006, 637).[2] In *The Origins of African American Literature* (2001), Dickson Bruce, who was probably the first contemporary critic to mention the text, claims African descended authorship for 'Theresa' in arguing that the short story 'represents one of the first attempts to confront the Haitian revolution and perhaps the first attempt by an African writer to create a black romantic heroine' (173).[3] Foster appears to agree with Bruce's assessment when she suggests that although *Freedom's Journal* did often print articles by "white" authors that had already been printed in other newspapers, journals, or magazines, the fact that 'Theresa' was titled an 'Original Communication' permits us to

---

1 Prior to the recovery of 'Theresa,' most scholars considered the Louisiana-born Francophone author Victor Séjour to have published the first African American short story when 'Le Mulâtre' appeared in 1837 in *La Revue des Colonies*, which was the 'first French serial directed by and produced for people of color' (Bryant, 251). Séjour's short story is the subject of chapter seven of the present volume.

2 The first advertisement/apology came on January 11, 1828, when the editors wrote: '*Haytien Tale* by S. is necessarily laid by till next week, for want of room.' Again, on February 1, 1828, the editors noted that '*Haytien Tale* by S. is unavoidably delayed till our next, for want of room.'

3 'Theresa' was mentioned much earlier in twentieth-century literary criticism by Lorenzo Dow Turner in his 1929 article, 'Anti-Slavery Sentiment in America Prior to 1865,' published in *The Association for the Study of Negro Life and History* (408).

'reasonabl[y] conclude,' that it, like the other 'texts not otherwise attributed to non-African American sources but identified as being produced 'for' *Freedom's Journal* were created by African Americans' (2006, 636). Jean Lee Cole, who has written about 'Theresa' more recently, also argues that the text was likely written by an author of color precisely because the 'Original Communications' section in which the story appeared was 'reserved for pieces written by African Americans' (160).

While scholars appear to be in agreement about the apparent "race" of the author of what may for now be considered the first African American short story, making an exact identification of the author has presented more complicated problems. Foster's speculation over the authorship of this text and the circumstances surrounding its anonymous publication, for example, also extends to thinking about whether the writer was a man or a woman. But Foster dismisses the idea that the author's apparent wish to remain anonymous might tell us anything about the gender of its writer. She writes that because many of the articles in *Freedom's Journal* were published anonymously or pseudonymously, we might assume that 'the paper's readers either knew who the writer[s]' of such articles were, or, in her words, 'didn't care' (2006, 636). Foster concludes that because *'Freedom's Journal* was edited and dominated by men ... "S" was probably a man,' though she acknowledges that '[g]ender is the single most important element' in 'Theresa' (637). Nevertheless, Foster's suppositions over this text's authorship do not end there, for she even suspects that the author of 'Theresa' was the famous black orator Prince Saunders, 'a New England teacher of African descent who moved to Haiti after the Revolution to organize an education system (and to convert Haitians to Protestantism)' (636).[4] While Cole has little to say about the possible gender of the author of 'Theresa,' Bruce has also inferred that the writer was most likely a man. Bruce even offers a 'teenage James McCune Smith' (172) as the potential author of the piece, probably because another article on the subject of 'African genealogy' that appeared in *Freedom's Journal* in December of 1828 and that has been linked to Smith (Dain, 239–40) was signed only with the initial 'S' (Bruce, 167).

If both Foster and Bruce offer Saunders and McCune Smith, respectively, as potential candidates for the authorship of 'Theresa' primarily because

---

4 According to Leslie Alexander, Saunders 'first traveled to Haiti in 1815 after British abolitionist William Wilberforce encouraged him to help establish schools there. Shortly after his arrival, Henri Christophe the ruler of Northern Haiti, appointed Saunders as the Minister of Education' (59). Saunders was the author of a compendium of texts that he called *The Haytian Papers* (1816), which was subtitled 'A collection of the very interesting proclamations and other official documents; together with some account of the rise, progress, and present state of the kingdom of Hayti,' and it was designed to encourage free black migration to Haiti (Alexander, 59).

these men had names beginning with the letter 'S,' had written or would later write about Haiti, and were African American, northern, free, and male, and would therefore ostensibly have had access to publishing in the 'male dominated' *Freedom's Journal*, I wonder why we could not similarly assume or suspect that a text which, Cole says, 'participates in debates about black womanhood' (173, ftn. 9), could not have been authored by a female of color? That is to ask, after Mary Helen Washington, 'Why is the fugitive slave, the fiery orator, the political activist, the abolitionist always represented as a black man?' (xvii–xviii). I am asking, in the much same vein, why the writer of revolutionary tales—not to mention the revolutionaries themselves—is always assumed to be male?

The Connecticut-born Maria W. Stewart (1803–79), whom Beverly Guy Sheftall calls an 'abolitionist' with 'feminist impulses' (3), was also a free person of color living in the northern U.S., she had a name that began with the letter 'S,' and she also might have had access to *Freedom's Journal* through her connection to its Boston agent, David Walker (Richardson, 6), who was her 'close friend' and 'role model' (Peterson, 1995, 57, 17).[5] In addition, like both Saunders, who exhibited a deep and abiding interest in Haitian independence in his preface to the *Haytian Papers* (1816), and McCune Smith, who gave a sketch of Toussaint Louverture in his 1841 *A Lecture on the Haitian Revolutions*, Stewart also mentioned Haiti directly in the course of her career as an orator and author. In her 1832 'An Address, Delivered before the Afric-American Female Intelligence Society of Boston,' later printed in the prominent abolitionist William Lloyd Garrison's *The Liberator* on April 28, 1832, Stewart spoke out against international non-recognition of Haiti and praised the Haitian Revolution: 'the Haytians, though they have not been acknowledged as a nation, yet their firmness of character, and independence of spirit have been greatly admired, and highly applauded.' The author of 'Theresa' similarly praised its eponymous hero for risking her life to ensure an independent Haiti: 'Oh Hayti!—be independent and let Theresa be the unworthy sacrifice offered to that God, who shall raise his mighty arm in defence of thy injured children' (643). Also like Stewart, who begged God to 'Grant that we may soon become distinguished for our moral and religious improvement, that the nations of the earth may take

---

5 Walker is listed as an 'authorised agent' of *Freedom's Journal* in an issue dated March 16, 1827 as well as in several subsequent issues. Walker's speeches and remarks were also occasionally printed in *Freedom's Journal* before his mysterious death in 1830. See 'Original Communication,' dated April 25, 1828, and 'Address' in the December 19, 1828 edition. According to Stewart's biographer, Marilyn Richardson, Walker's 1829 *Appeal to the Colored Citizens of the World* was considered so inflammatory by pro-slavery southerners that 'a group of men in Georgia offered ten thousand dollars to anyone who would capture him alive; one thousand dead' (8).

knowledge of us' ('Religion'), the author of 'Theresa' asks God to intervene on behalf of the Haitian people, their revolution, and their subsequent nation-building project when Theresa implores the Lord to 'Be near to the Haytiens in their righteous struggle' and to

> Raise up some few of those, who have been long degraded—give to them dominion, and enable them to govern a state of their own—so that the proud and the cruel may know that thou art alike the Father of the native of the burning desert, and of the more temperate region. (642)

If not Stewart, might not the author of 'Theresa' have been one Sarah Louise Forten, the daughter of Charlotte and James Forten, who published approximately a dozen poems and essays between 1831 and 1837 (Dunbar, 104) and who also has a name that begins with an 'S'? Sarah Forten's father is well known for having had a longstanding interest in Haiti, which his biographer, Julie Finch, says 'nothing could efface' (220). According to Finch, the elder Forten became a manager of the Haytian Emigration Society and maintained an active network of correspondents who 'could keep him apprised of conditions in Haiti' throughout his life (218). Like Stewart, Sarah Forten herself almost certainly alluded to the Haitian Revolution when she used Louverture's famous expression about the 'tree of liberty' in her most well-known essay, 'The Abuse of Liberty,' published in *The Liberator* on March 26, 1831.[6] After asking about slaves, 'Is it because their skins are black that they are to be deprived of every tender tie that binds the heart of man to earth?' Forten makes the following prophecy:

> can you think He, the great spirit who created all men free and equal— He who made the sun to shine on the black man as well as on the white, will always allow you to rest tranquil on your downy couches? No,—He is just and his anger will not always slumber. He will wipe the tear from Ethiopia's eye; He will shake the tree of liberty, and its blossoms shall spread over the earth. (48)

Sarah Forten's premonition of a God who acts as the 'Black Spartacus' aside, with the knowledge of Haiti that was in constant circulation in the nineteenth-century Atlantic World and especially in communities of color in the United States, the author of 'Theresa' could have been almost any woman with access to the world of publishing. This is especially true if we believe

---

[6] Subsequent to being captured by the armed forces of General Leclerc, Toussaint Louverture reportedly said, 'In overthrowing me, you have only knocked down one trunk of the tree of the liberty of the blacks; but it will grow again from the roots, because they are deep and numerous' (qtd. in Barskett, 382).

that, as Michael Drexler and Ed White have written, 'following its dissemination throughout the U.S. in the fall of 1801, Toussaint's Constitution became the most widely read piece of literature authored by an African American and may have remained so until the publication of the *Narrative of the Life of Frederick Douglass* in 1845' (59). Indeed, in the nineteenth century the Haitian Revolution intricately tied the culture of the erstwhile French colony of Saint-Domingue to an emergent African American literary tradition in the United States. The pioneering work of Phillis Wheatley, the first African American author to publish a book of poetry, was also linked to the Haitian Revolution when the anonymous translator of Joseph Lavallée's adventure novel set in Saint-Domingue, *Le Nègre comme il y a peu de blancs* (1789), appended the U.S. English-language edition of the text, *The Negro Equaled by Few Europeans* (1801), with an entire body of poems by Wheatley.[7] This intricate linking up of African American with both Afro-Caribbean and French colonial history lends credence to the notion that, as Maxwell Whiteman has observed, 'To the American Negro of the nineteenth century ... no subject was more engrossing than the history and uprisings of St. Domingo,' but it also emphasizes the significance of a Franco-Haitian revolutionary lexicon whose inattentions to the complications of gender needs to be examined much more as a crucial part of early African American literary history.

In this chapter, by juxtaposing the revolutionary life and writings of Maria W. Stewart, Sarah Forten, and other early nineteenth-century U.S. women writers of color with the radical Franco-Haitian grammar of 'Theresa,' I do not mean to imply that Stewart, Forten, or anyone else mentioned here themselves actually wrote this representation of the Haitian Revolution, but merely that they or any other radical women of color like them in the early nineteenth-century antebellum U.S. could have. Identifying the author of 'Theresa' as female would be a significant discovery for American literary traditions though, if only because the events narrated in 'Theresa' represent a radical departure, not only from other literary representations of the Haitian Revolution circulating in the Atlantic World, but from virtually all of the male-authored texts about Haiti published in the "black" press of the 1820s and '30s. The biblical references exhibited in the passages quoted above, the desire to protect and defend the virtues of women of color, and the representation of marriage and domesticity as secondary to the goal of freedom to be found within the pages of 'Theresa,' have much in common with early "black" female writing in the antebellum U.S.

---

7 Lavallée's novel had first been translated and published in London by J. Trapp, A.M. in 1790 before going on to be translated yet again and published anonymously in Philadelphia in 1801.

Transgressing the Trope of the "Tropical Temptress"

Yet, still, in this chapter, by linking 'Theresa' to what can only be termed an emergent understanding of nineteenth-century African American female print culture,[8] my intention is less to proffer a particular female author of color—or even a female at all—as the writer of 'Theresa,' than to point out how constant assumptions about male authorship are intimately linked to the constancy of assumptions about the role of women of color (or lack thereof) in revolutionary discourses and movements, and indeed, in violent revolutions themselves. In other words, the rejection of the very notion that 'Theresa' could have been authored by a woman is, to my mind, merely another part of a grand historical elision that created the myth of the "tropical temptress" as only an agent of dangerous seduction and not of revolution, thereby writing women of color out of the revolutionary history of Haiti. If it is true that, as Bassard writes, 'archival work acts a "form of counter-memory"' (5), then it seems to me that the recovery of 'Theresa' has helped us to recuperate a short story that places women's involvement in the Haitian Revolution front and center in early nineteenth-century "black" nationalist culture. Early African American culture, like the dominant U.S. culture against which it was often set, excluded or circumscribed the experiences and voices of women of color in various ways. 'Theresa,' however, seems to suggest that women of color could not have been ancillary to the projects of freedom and independence in Haiti in the way they had been represented in dominant histories that circulated throughout the Atlantic World.

Establishing the place of 'Theresa' within the broader literary history of the Haitian Revolution as well as the basis for the anonymous publication in the antebellum U.S. of a text like 'Theresa,' requires also examining the state of African American male and female authorship in the 1820s and very early 1830s. Of particular interest to this analysis will be those texts related to the Haitian Revolution or Haitian independence. With the exceptions of the case of Stewart's friend David Walker, whose, *Appeal to the Colored Americans of the World* appeared in 1829, one year after the publication of 'Theresa,' and

---

8 Though much has been written on African American women's history, literary, cultural, and otherwise, since Carla Peterson's 1995 *Doers of the Word*, I think that the following statement from Peterson is still largely true of the state of the African American women's studies: 'so much of our history has yet to be recovered, we are not in a position to theorize in totalizing fashion about black literary production, either by constructing a literary canon of masterpiece texts; by formulating a black aesthetic based on the cultural matrix of the blues, the vernacular, or folk expression; or more narrowly, by insisting upon the existence of a transhistorical black feminist aesthetic' (4). In *Spiritual Interrogations* (1999), Katherine Clay Bassard adds, 'given the violence enacted against black women's histories, bodies, and texts, the archives will remain incomplete and inadequate sources for an empirically complete counternarrative of black women's literary production' (5).

that of the emergent African American female literary societies of the 1830s, before which Maria Stewart would appear as an orator, this examination of 'Theresa' as a part of early African American print culture in the U.S. will focus mostly on writings about Haiti that appeared before the publication of 'Theresa.' In so doing, I suggest that 'Theresa' not only implicitly questions the ideologies of gender to be found in earlier representations of the Haitian Revolution within the pages of *Freedom's Journal*, but also juxtaposes the vital roles played by women of color in Haitian independence and in the struggle for freedom and equality taking place in the United States. In many ways, 'Theresa' actually presents an argument for the idea that it was not just men who were revolutionary, but that women of color could also be revolutionaries in their own way and thus, in the words of Theresa, 'be made useful to the cause of freedom' (642).

It bears repeating, however, that by establishing a parallel history between the content of 'Theresa' and the life and writings of nineteenth-century U.S. women writers of color, and Maria Stewart in particular, including the censure Stewart suffered for her infamous challenge to African American men during an appearance at the all-male African Masonic Hall (also printed in *The Liberator* on May 4, 1833), I do not wish to suggest that any of these women actually wrote the text.[9] Instead, I hope to continue to highlight the connection between the gendered dimensions of historical portrayals of the Haitian Revolution in the Atlantic World and the gendering of (anonymous) revolutionary writing. 'Theresa' is a vital part of the literary history of the Haitian Revolution and a vital part of the literary history of the antebellum U.S. precisely because it is, if not the first, surely one of the first African American short stories, the content of which allows us to imagine the place of "non-white" female revolutionaries during the Haitian

---

9 In the speech, 'An Address Delivered at the African Masonic Hall,' Stewart directly questioned the masculinity of the men in her audience: 'If you are men, convince them that you possess the spirit of men; and as your day, so shall your strength be.' Yet even more daring, perhaps, was the sharp reprimand she had for the men in her community whom she viewed as shirking their duties: 'Had those men among us, who have had an opportunity, turned their attention as assiduously to mental and moral improvement as they have to gambling and dancing, I might have remained at home, and they stood contending in my place.' This speech was so unpopular that, according to her contemporary and vice president of the Massachusetts General Colored Association, William C. Nell, Stewart 'encountered an opposition even from her Boston circle of friends, that would have dampened the ardor of most women' (qtd. in Richardson, 27). Peterson says that Stewart's 1833 speech before the all-male society was a 'fatal miscalculation' because '[a]lthough devoted to community racial uplift work as well as to the antislavery cause, black Freemasonry, like its counterpart in the dominant culture, nonetheless constituted a distinctly male space in which black men, particularly of the middle class, sought to work out gender and class roles' (68).

Revolution, on the one hand, and on the other, to imagine the bravery it must have taken for a writer like the author of 'Theresa' to dare to enter the masculine enterprise of publication in a culture which 'officially excluded' and 'restrict[ed] the role of black women in the articulation of racial uplift programs' (Peterson, 1995, 17).

*

'Theresa' tells the tale of a family of three free women of color, Madame Paulina, who upon the arrival in Saint-Domingue of the Leclerc expedition sent by Napoleon Bonaparte to reinstate French rule over the colony from 1802 to 1803, finds herself 'left a widow, unhappy—unprotected and exposed to all the horrors of the revolution' (639), and her two daughters, Amanda and Theresa, 'who in the morning of life, were expanding, like the foliages of the rose into elegance and beauty' (640). The women are described as having lived in the 'once verdant plains' of the town of St. Nicholas (639). Upon the arrival of Napoleon's troops, however, Madame Paulina resolves to 'depart from the endeared village of her innocent childhood' and, 'like the pious Aeneas,' lead her daughters out of all 'the horrors, in which St. Nicholas was now involved' (639, 640).[10] In order to save herself and her daughters, whom she had kept 'long concealed from the knowledge of the enemy,' and ostensibly from the physical and sexual threats of the arriving French troops, which would lead to 'the mother's wretchedness, and the daughter's shame and ruin' (640), Madame Paulina dresses herself as a French captain and her children in the attire of 'prisoners,' and flees to the woods. However, when the women encounter a French battalion, the reader is told that in her performance as a French soldier Madame Paulina 'must either act well her part or be reconducted by the foe to St. Nicholas, and there … receive a cruel and ignominious death' (641). Although initially feigning inattentiveness, because of her keen abilities of observation, Theresa overhears the French lieutenant who took Madame Paulina 'for what she was so well affected to be,' tell her mother 'many military schemes, which were about being executed, and if successful, would, in all probability, terminate in the destruction of the revolutionists, and, in the final success of the French power in this island' (642). In a panic about what would become of her family under the continuation of French rule, while her mother and sister are sleeping, Theresa, 'like an heroine of the age of chivalry' (643), embarks upon a seemingly ill-fated mission to alert Toussaint Louverture to the French plot.

When Theresa eventually succeeds in alerting Louverture and the other Haitian revolutionists to Leclerc's designs, we are told of her heroism that

---

10 In Virgil's representation in the *Aeneid*, Aeneas was the legendary founder of Rome.

'the important services she had rendered her aggrieved country and to the Haytien people—the objects which prompted her to disobedience, induced her to overstep the bounds of modesty, and to expose to immediate dangers her life and sex' (644). For her efforts, Louverture himself gives Theresa 'all the distinctions due her exalted virtue' (644), but she hardly has time to celebrate because when she returns to the spot where she left her mother and sister and finds them gone, she believes that the price of freedom for her people has come at the expense of her family. Believing that her actions were responsible for their deaths, Theresa exclaims, 'Oh! God! forgive this matricide! Forgive Theresa, who to save her country, sacrificed a mother and a sister' (645). According to the narrator, by this time the remaining French troops had 'retreated with precipitance, leaving their baggage with their gasping friends, on the spot where victory perched on the standard of freedom' (645). After all of this, much to Theresa's surprise, Amanda and Madame Paulina are discovered hiding in one of the French troops' bags by Captain Inginac, and the story ends when the reader is told, 'joy succeeds sorrow—the lost ones are regained ... the mother and sister of the unhappy THERESA' (645).

Even though as a literary text of just under 4,500 words, 'Theresa' may not seem to require the same kind of sustained and in-depth literary engagement as either *Zelica* or *La Mulâtre*, the importance of the text within the broader literary history of the Haitian Revolution in the Atlantic World should not be underestimated. 'Theresa' stands as one of the most important representations of the Haitian Revolution before 1865 in that it represents a radical departure from both male- and female-authored fictions that featured female protagonists of color and were set in revolutionary Saint-Domingue. Other fictional female revolutionaries of color, for example, were almost always either censured for their contributions to the Revolution, as was Madame Louverture in *Zelica*, or praised for their sympathy and benevolence for the "whites" with whom they were in combat. In such tales, more often than not, women of color whose sympathies and even revolutionary actions were once on the side of the revolting slaves, do an about-face when they fall in love with "white" European men, as is the case in the German Heinrich von Kleist's *Betrothal in Santo Domingo* (1811).[11]

In Kleist's rendition of the Revolution, which Seán Allan refers to as a broad commentary on a lack of 'human decency' (11) written in the 'aftermath of the post-Revolutionary Terror in France' (10), the revolutionary 'quadroon' Toni's entire purpose during the Revolution is to lure "white" men into her home with the help of her mother, Babekan (described as a

---

11 Translations of the title and citations are taken from Ronald Taylor's translation of the novella 'Die Verlobung in Santo Domingo' in *Six German Romantic Tales* (1993).

'mulatta'), and seduce them so that male revolutionaries can come in and enact their vengeance before the relationship can be consummated.[12] Toni's own "mulatto/a" vengeance is, however, tempered when she falls in love and sleeps with the Swiss soldier Gustav von der Reid. Though Toni no longer harbors revolutionary sentiments after falling in love with Gustav, in true tragic fashion, Gustav (who has also fallen in love with Toni) eventually comes to believe that his lover is 'base' and 'cold-blooded' (83). Because he does not know that Toni has defected from the Revolution, he ends up shooting her and later commits suicide when he realizes his error.

Kleist's tale, even if primarily meant to underscore the human tragedy and epistemological problems involved in violent revolutions, presents female revolutionaries of color with the judgment of bifurcated terms as variously demonic or pitiful. Clearly, Kleist, 'whose interest in these events was aroused evidently by his having been temporarily imprisoned in the same Fort Joux in France where Toussaint l'Ouverture had been held captive and died' (McGlathery, 224), wants us to sympathize with Toni, whose adoption of the virtues of monogamous love coincides with her defection from the totalizing violence of the Haitian Revolution, on the one hand, and, on the other, to condemn Toni's mother Babekan, who uses her sexuality and that of her daughter to facilitate the brutal violence of the male revolutionaries. By opposing the actions of women of color in such a markedly horizontal way—good versus bad, right versus wrong—the text precludes the consideration that women like both Toni and Babekan could have been and likely were female revolutionaries who behaved and responded to events based on a complex set of personal and subjective experiences and beliefs. As we saw in *Zelica*, there is room for accepting, without the kind of judgment that usually circumscribes descriptions of the lives of women of color, the fact that

---

12 Aside from Kleist's novella and Franul von Weissenthurn's drama, several other literary representations of the Haitian Revolution circulated in Germany. See, for example, Friedrich Döhner's 1792 'Des Aufruhrs schreckliche Folge oder: die Neger. Ein Original-Trauerspiel in fünf Aufzügen,' which Susanne Zantop translates as *The Terrible Consequences of the Rebellion; or the Negroes* (145); Johann Gottfried Herder's *Negro Idylls* (1796); August von Kotzebue's *Die Negersklaven* (1796); Theodor Körner's play, an adaptation of Kleist's novella (Zantop, 1997, 145), entitled *Toni* (1812); as well as Caroline Auguste Fischer's serialized short story, 'William der Neger,' according to Zantop, published in five installments from May 19 to May 24, 1827 in *Zeitgung für der elegante Welt* (1997, 145). Fischer's text appears to have been first published in her 1818 collection, *Kleine Erzählungen und romantische Skizzen*. Zantop writes of these portrayals of the Haitian Revolution: 'All of these texts—even those whose obvious purpose is abolitionist and whose topic only marginally touches on the revolutionary events in the Caribbean—renegotiate the relationships between race, class, and gender within a colonial context. Or rather, they rewrite the colonial love stories as they are turned, literally, upside down by the revolutionary conflicts (1997, 145).

historically "black" female revolutionaries could be utterly ruthless towards their captors and shamelessly benevolent, and everything in between.

In contrast to *Betrothal in Santo Domingo*, 'Theresa' is marked both by an utter lack of sentimentality and the total absence of a marriage plot, as if to say that women living under the repressions of slavery and revolution had more pressing concerns than the kind of domesticity associated with marriage in the nineteenth century. The lack of romance and sentiment in 'Theresa' implies a disavowal of romantic love and affection as the driving motives in life. Instead, the text offers duty to one's countrymen or one's national family (even above that of genealogical family) and the will of God as supreme. Theresa demonstrates such a prioritizing of the good of the nation over that of the family and of working towards the divinely sanctioned right of people of color to achieve emancipation from slavery over other personal considerations when she realizes that she may have to sacrifice her sister and mother to help ensure the freedom of people of color. Theresa 'saw with her mind's eye the great services which might be rendered to her country,' but 'Her absence ... she was confidently assured ... would probably terminate the already much exhausted life of her dear mother, and complete the measure of Amanda's wretchedness' (643). 'Theresa' further exhibits the quandary of thinking about revolutionary engagement as a choice between the national family and the genealogical family when the narrator says:

> The salvation of her oppressed country ... was an object of no little concern; but she also owed a duty to that mother, whose tender solicitude for her happiness, could not be surpassed by any parent, and a sister too, whom she tenderly loved, and whose attachment to her was undivided. (643)

The pitting of family concerns against national concerns in 'Theresa' evokes the idea of the Haitian Revolution as a tragic family romance. This brief tale has resonance with Louverture's own family conflict and the trope of the tragic "mulatto/a," placing 'Theresa' in a much broader transatlantic tradition of representing the Haitian Revolution as a series of individual family conflicts—rather than metaphorical ones—which will be taken up at length in Part Three of *Tropics of Haiti*. In 'Theresa,' unlike in Alphonse de Lamartine's portrayal of Louverture in his play *Toussaint Louverture* (1850) as a man who had to fatally choose between his devotion to the nation or to his own children, for example, the anonymous author of 'Theresa' shows us less the tragedy of its heroine's choice between the family and the nation than it celebrates the fact that Theresa was able to choose at all.

Importantly, when Theresa believes that her mother and sister are dead, she does not seek or even contemplate romantic love as a way of procuring safety and protection for herself. Her thoughts instead center on joining her national family. We are told that she sought to find 'her way back to the camp of the kind Toussaint L'Ouverture to claim his fatherly protection, and seek a home in the bosom of those, to whom she had rendered herself dear by her wisdom and virtue' (645). The implicit disavowal of marriage and the attention to what Bassard calls, in another context, *'performing* community' (9), in concert with Theresa's remarkable bravery and agency, points to the anonymously authored short story as a distinct precursor of a tradition of questioning the Victorian ethic of '"true womanhood", which stressed piety, chastity, submissiveness, and domesticity' (Sheftall, 1), to be found in African American women's writing from Maria Stewart to Harriet Jacobs to Anna Julia Cooper.[13] Notably, Theresa assumes that she will be pardoned for 'her disobedience' and for having 'overstepped the bounds of modesty' (644) associated with femininity in first having defied the authority of her mother, and second, for having dared to believe that she could contribute something to the Haitian Revolution. The narrator writes, 'She felt that her conduct was exculpated, and self-reproach was lost in the consciousness of her laudable efforts to save St. Domingo' (644).

One of the other ways in which 'Theresa' patently differentiates itself from other fictions of slavery with "black" female protagonists that are either set in Saint-Domingue or mention the Haitian Revolution, lies not only in its lack of sentimentality with respect to marriage, but in its lack of sentimentality about the violence of the Haitian Revolution. In 'Theresa,' for instance, there is no lamenting of the horrible necessity of revolutionary violence and its disastrous meaning for humanity, such as we saw in the works of Sansay and in *Zelica* and which we find equally in the works of two other nineteenth-century women's novels, Emilie J...t's, *Zorada; ou la créole, publiée par Emilie* (1801) and Claire de Duras's *Ourika* (1824).[14] Léon

---

13 Stewart asked what is 'more neglected than the proper education of females?' in her 'Address to the Female Literary Association of Philadelphia,' and she urged free women of color less to focus on finding somebody to marry—though she did not condemn marriage—than to start their own businesses, educate themselves, and help one another. Harriet Jacobs, too, expressed ambivalence about marriage when she famously wrote in her *Incidents in the Life of a Slave Girl* (1861), 'reader, my story ends with freedom; not in the usual way, with marriage' (302). Writing much later, Anna Julia Cooper, urged that 'marriage was not the only route to self-actualization' (Sheftall, 24) when in *A Voice from the South* she wrote: 'I grant you that intellectual development, with the self-reliance and capacity for earning a livelihood which it gives, renders woman less dependent on the marriage relation for physical support (which, by the way, does not always accompany it). Neither is she compelled to look to sexual love as the one sensation capable of giving tone and relish, movement and vitality to the life she leads. Her horizon is extended. Her sympathies are broadened and deepened and multiplied. She is in closer touch with nature' (68-69).

14 Although there appears to be some confusion over the authorship of *Zorada*

François Hoffman writes of *Zorada* that it was probably the first attempt by a French author to describe a "mixed-race" character who was faced with the 'problems posed to her by the consciousness of her identity and her role in a society plagued by the contradiction between the organization of its economy and the moral principles that she claims' (1973, 138). Zorada is the daughter of a "white" man and a "black" female slave and says, therefore, that she is 'destined' by her birth 'to find herself among the slaves ... to suffer the fate of my mother' because of the 'laws that reigned in the colony of Saint-Domingue' (1:87–88). Though Zorada finds herself attracted to a "white" colonist named James, due to all of the cruelty against black slaves to which she is a witness, she cannot imagine 'except in horror the notion of marrying one of their executioners' (1:92). However, once the Haitian Revolution begins, Zorada loses some pity for the slaves and ultimately flees to France, where, in true tragic "mulatta" fashion, she subsequently dies of sadness after discovering that the Frenchman with whom she had fallen in love and with whom she had an affair while in Saint-Domingue, has married a "white" woman.

Duras's *Ourika*, too—which was loosely based 'on the true story of a black child brought to France from Senegal shortly before the [French] Revolution' (Dejean and Waller, viii) and was likely influenced by *Zorada*, with whose plot it has much in common—contains elements of tragic sentimentality that allow the writer to simultaneously muse upon what Duras presents as the disastrous consequences of the Haitian Revolution and the unrequited love of a "black" woman for a "white" man in a racially intolerant and slave-holding society. *Ourika* recounts the doomed life of an African woman, Ourika, brought to Paris by the "white" governor of Senegal, whose sister, Madame de B., subsequently adopts her. The *unnaturalness* of Ourika's position as a "black" woman within a "white" society is only matched by Ourika's own opinion of the Haitian Revolution as an *unnatural* tragedy. This once again implicitly conflates a metaphor of "racial mixing" as *unnatural*, represented by Ourika's presence in France and her

(Hoffmann lists the author only as 'Emilie J ... T,' which is the name listed on the title page, and Kimberly Manganelli lists the publisher, François Vatar-Jouannet, as the author, the title of the work, the 'avant-propos,' and the introduction to volume one point to a female author. One telling passage of the introduction reads: 'I know, said an old English philosopher, two things that bring to mind all of the delirium of pride and impudence: it is the thurible in the hands of a man, and the inkwell in those of a woman. I hope that my title of woman and of author will pardon me this citation' (vi–vii). Moreover, in the introduction, the author, ostensibly the Emilie who claims to have edited the diaries, refers to herself in the third person as a 'she' when recounting a conversation *she* had had with the mistress of the home where Zorada had once lived in Nantes.

love for a "white" man, with ideas of the Haitian Revolution as *unnaturally* violent, and both situations as therefore tragic. One of the most famous lines in *Ourika* comes from Madame de B.'s friend, a marquise who observes, 'Ourika has flouted her natural destiny. She has entered society without its permission. It will have its revenge' (14). The sense of tragedy that others feel with respect to Ourika's "race" is only matched by the sense of tragedy that she herself feels when Madame de B.'s son, Charles, the man with whom Ourika has fallen in love, marries a "white" woman named Anaïs and subsequently has a child with her. Yet, as with Zorada, it is when the Haitian Revolution begins that Ourika loses all sense of pity for the slaves of Saint-Domingue of whom she says, 'The Santo Domingo massacres gave me cause for fresh and heartrending sadness. Till then I had regretted belonging to a race of outcasts. Now I had the shame of belonging to a race of barbarous murderers' (21). The Haitian Revolution provides a distinct moment for Ourika (and thus the ambivalently abolitionist Duras),[15] to further meditate on the destructive nature of violence, and especially of "black" on "white" violence, when Ourika continues, 'Sometimes I used to tell myself that, poor negress though I was, I still belonged with all the noblest spirits, because of our shared longing for justice. The day when decency and truth were victorious would be their day of triumph, and mine' (23). In Duras's rendition, the Haitian Revolution ultimately marks Ourika as a member of a race of 'barbarous murderers' since she bears the 'stain' (27) of those who know no social justice.

Another short story of the Haitian Revolution, Louis Levrault's 'A Haytian Legend,' which was 'translated, with alterations from the French'[16] and published in *Yale Literary Magazine* in 1840, utilizes a more common version of the "interracial" romance within the context of the Haitian Revolution to unequivocally demonize the actions of its "mixed-race" revolutionary heroine, Lucile, who was 'so handsome, yet so perfidious' (17).[17] Like Kleist's Babekan, Lucile's mother, Doralice, urges her daughter to use her

---

15 Partially because he says that 'Duras covers up the horrors of the Atlantic crossing' (2008, 167), Christopher Miller wonders what is precisely the message that *Ourika* sends with respect to slavery. In *The French Atlantic Triangle* (2008), he asks 'is *Ourika* abolitionist in any sense?' and 'Does Duras actually condemn slavery?' (170).

16 Levrault's tale was actually called 'Tony La Mulâtresse: Légende Haïtienne,' and consists mostly of a translation and adaptation of Kleist's earlier novella. Levrault's tale was published in the fourth volume of *La France Littéraire* in 1837 (81–96). See chapter three of this monograph for a discussion of Levrault's version.

17 *Yale Literary Magazine*, which hails itself as the 'the first undergraduate magazine,' was founded in 1836. According to Helen Phillips, it is 'the oldest existing publication at Yale and … the oldest literary review in North America.' For more information about the magazine, including a link to Phillips's article see http://www.yale.edu/ylit/.

sexuality and her position as a woman of "mixed race" to seduce and then kill French soldiers. Lucile is described as 'a handsome girl' whose 'complexion was not much darker than that of a Spaniard. Indeed she prided herself on having much English blood in her veins, and this it was that prevented her from entertaining violent hatred towards the whites' (14). Lucile's mother tells her, however:

> don't you know that men are willing prisoners to beautiful girls? I expect you to entertain this fine Monsieur, and when he is no longer on his guard, we will have some ropes ready, and leave him bound hand and foot to await the arrival of Marc Anthony. We shall in this way obtain honor, and contribute our share to the destruction of this race of tyrants. (13)

Sentimentality operates in a negative fashion in this U.S.-produced version of Levrault's tale for the reader is told:

> During the scenes of carnage which signalized this revolution our young mulattress soon became familiar with the ideas of treachery and murder. In her view, as in that of all the insurgents, any means which promised to rid them of their enemies, appeared proper. As the whites had not pitied them, they could not, of course, expect pity *from* them; and in this deadly struggle, women, and even children took part. (16, italics in the original)

Lucile can feel no sympathy because she has been treated with no sympathy. She therefore participates both in the 'sentiment of hatred toward whites,' which she 'imbibed' from her mother (who assassinated her own master in his bed [15]), and in the 'fanaticism of her race' (16). Doralice's main motive in seeking vengeance against "whites" is precisely the fact that Lucile's 'white father,' only one of Doralice's 'former lovers,' eventually not only abandoned her, but 'compelled [her] to work as a slave after having reigned like a sultaness [*sic*]' (15). Doralice and Lucile not only lack 'pity' but they are motivated by a desire for revenge, marking this tale as a distinct part of the "mulatto/a" vengeance narrative of the Haitian Revolution circulating in the Atlantic World.

In Frances Hammond Pratt's *La Belle Zoa, or, The Insurrection of Hayti* (1854), a much less obvious narrative of "racially" driven sentimentality, this time a positive version, reverses the putative unequivocally violent goals of the Revolution for the tale's "mixed-race" female hero. Adelle, who is the 'yellow' 'waiting maid' (8) of the titular character of the story, is actually portrayed as a revered and powerful sorceress who is also one of the central leaders of the first insurrection in Saint-Domingue. The male revolutionists even chant 'vive Adelle' again and again after the sorceress puts a curse on a dead body (12) and Pratt refers to her as 'the heroine of the insurrection' (14).

However, Adelle soon rethinks the vengeance that is described as motivating the Revolution and wonders, 'Can revolutionized Hayti prosper while the laurels of victory are so deeply dyed in the blood of helpless innocence?' (52). As a result, like Sansay's Zuline, Adelle eventually devotes the rest of her life to saving "white" families like Zoa's from the vengeance of cruel insurrectionists.

According to Pratt's portrayal, Adelle is open to the possibility of benevolence and to revealing revolutionary secrets precisely because she is a woman of "mixed race" and, therefore, supposedly closer to "white" femininity. Before prodding Adelle for information about the pending insurrections, we are told that Zoa's master, 'Monsieur Docou whirled his gold headed cane, as if an important idea had passed through his mind; He knew that but a small portion of negro blood ran in her veins' (23). In essence, it is the conflict of Adelle's skin color, her "racial" instability that also allows her to be ambivalently tropicalized into not only a rare female revolutionary but a rare, virtuous woman of color. The fact that Adelle's overt resistance to colonial authority becomes muted into a moderate, sympathetic, and humanistic identification with the colonists once again defines (and perhaps confines) female revolutionary behavior to the sphere of sentimentality; but perhaps Adelle's 180 degree about-turn also reflects Pratt's own conflicted sense of the Revolution as having noble goals, but insupportable methods.

Though we could hardly accuse Pratt of being pro-slavery or anti-abolitionist, she does seem to have had a marked disdain for the violence of the Haitian Revolution. In the apologia that precedes *La Belle Zoa*, Pratt writes, 'That slavery is a sin, a curse to the slaveholder, is sure; but where is the individual, or who are the class of individuals, endowed with wisdom, will and power sufficient to eradicate the evil with justice to all parties?' In the same author's note, Pratt claimed that the events described in her novel were based on the testimony of her French tutor's grandmother, Mrs. Potts, who 'witnessed so much of the exterminating war' and is 'now beyond the reach of the black man's rage' (3). Pratt's reading of the Haitian Revolution as an 'exterminating war' developed out of 'black' 'rage,' rather than the slave's yearning for freedom, specifically calls forth the narrative of "mulatto/a" vengeance when we recall that, as I wrote in chapter three of this volume, all of the "black" male revolutionaries in her tale are presented as "mulattoes."

Unlike in *Ourika, Zorada*, or the numerous other tales of the Haitian Revolution published after 'Theresa,' where women of color are painted as utterly paralyzed by both their tragic, unrequited love for "white" men and the senseless violence of the Haitian Revolution, or utterly demonized like in Levrault's tale as a result both of their "mixed race" and their unfailing devotion to the Haitian Revolution, 'Theresa' seems to support an unqualified view of revolutionary violence as a positive and generative method of change without a single mention of how skin color might affect one's allegiances. In fact, gradations in skin color are ultimately unimportant in the tale. Though being a woman with *lighter* skin hue clearly affords Theresa's mother the opportunity to pass as "white," the fact that she passes her daughters off as her own prisoners suggests that they may have actually had *darker* skin than their mother. Nonetheless, variations in skin color seem to operate more as a way to invest in situational performances that might provide opportunities for freedom (for people with light and dark skin alike) rather than as the driving motives for seduction, self-hatred, or revolution itself.

Although presenting heroines of color who could *pass* for "white" would soon become one of the abiding conventions of early African American literature, in 'Theresa' the differential skin color of its heroes and heroines alike has little do with the plot itself and has much more to tell us about the sweeping essentialism to be found in cultures of slavery, whereby all people of color may not have been slaves, but all people of color were certainly subject to color prejudice. Theresa implores God to help banish color prejudice when she asks:

> O, my god! Hast thou suffered thy creatures to be thus afflicted in all thy spacious earth? Are we not too thy children? And didst thou not cover us with this sable exterior, by which our race is distinguished, and for which they are condemned and ever been cruelly persecuted! (642)

Note how Theresa experiences no internal, psychological conflict about being a person of color and especially not about being of "mixed race," as in the tropes of both the "tropical temptress" and the tragic "mulatto/a." There is also no wondering about which side of the Revolution she should belong to, as in the case of Lamartine's female hero of "mixed race," Adrienne, nor are we presented with the kinds of epistemological problems that will lead Victor Séjour's Alfred to eventually assassinate his own "white" father, as we will see in chapter seven of this volume. 'Theresa,' on the contrary, is probably the first, and may indeed be the only, fictional representation of the Haitian Revolution published before 1865 that presents a sustained portrayal of a female revolutionary of color in unequivocal radical and "racial" terms.

There are only two other brief examples of which I am aware of female revolutionaries portrayed as unapologetically revolutionary and, perhaps rather suggestively, they are both drawn from mid-nineteenth-century African American writing. The first of these examples comes in William Wells Brown's 1854 speech turned pamphlet, 'St. Domingo, its Revolutions and its Patriots.' Narrating the ephemeral and obviously metaphorical history of a female slave named 'Vida,' or life, and her lover, 'Lamour,' or love, Brown writes:

> Another gang of these savages was commanded by a woman named Vida. She was a native of Africa, and, like Lamour, had been ruthlessly torn from her native land. Her face was all marked with incisions and large pieces had been cut out of her ears. Vida kept a horse, which she had caught with her own hands, and had broken to the bit. When on horseback, she rode like a man. On arriving at places too steep to ascend, she would dismount, and her horse would at once follow her. This woman, with her followers, met and defeated a battalion of the French, who had been sent into the mountains. Lamour and Vida united, and they were complete masters of the wilds of St. Domingo;—and, even to the present day, their names are used to frighten children into obedience. These two savages came forth from their mountain homes, and made war on the whites wherever they found them. (29)

The second example comes to us from the African American poet George B. Vashon, who emigrated to Haiti in the nineteenth century and was friends with William Lloyd Garrison (Hanchett, 206). Much as we saw with Madame Louverture in *Zelica*, he also used the image of a famous Haitian revolutionary mother and wife in his literary contribution to the Haitian Revolution's archive. In his poem 'Vincent Ogé' (1854), Vashon spoke of women as having an immediate 'power' over the Haitian revolutionaries who were their children, spouses, lovers, and siblings: 'Hers is the power o'er his soul/That's never wielded by another,/And she doth claim this soft control/ As sister, mistress, wife, or mother' (lines 204–07). The poet continues by telling the reader that the influence of these women could be covert as when 'So sweetly doth her soft voice float/O'er hearts by guilt or anguish riven/It seemth as a magic note/Struck from earth's harps by hands of heaven' (lines 208–11); or overt, as when he attributes Ogé's exhortation to rebellion to the influence of his mother:

> And there's the mother of Ogé,
> Who with firm voice, and steady heart,
> And look unaltered, well can play
> The Spartan mother's hardy part;
> And send her sons to battle-fields,
> And bid them come in triumph home,
> Or stretched upon their bloody shields,
> Rather than bear the bondman's doom.
> 'Go forth,' she said, 'to victory';
> Or else, go bravely forth to die! (lines 212–21)

As the poem further develops, in a passage clearly influenced by Martineau's *The Hour and the Man*,[18] Ogé's mother is in many ways more obstinate in her counsel than was Louverture's wife in *Zelica*, for she tells her sons, 'But if your hearts should craven prove,/Forgetful of your zeal—your love/For rights and franchises of men,/My heart will break; but even then,/Whilst bidding life and earth adieu,/This be the prayer I'll breathe for you' (lines 230–35). Mrs. Ogé's 'prayer' is pretty astonishing with respect to the role of women of color in the literary imagination of the Haitian Revolution when we consider the fact that she warns her sons not to disregard her advice lest she disavow them. She tells them, 'Passing from guilt to misery,/May this aye for your portion be,–/A life, dragged out beneath the rod–/An end, abhorred of man and God–/As monument, the chains you nurse–/As epitaph, your mother's curse!' (lines 236–41). The fact that both of these fleeting and unequivocal portrayals of revolutionary women of color are also to be found in the African American literary tradition lends further credence to the idea that mid-nineteenth-century African American protest culture was still distinguished by a largely Franco-Haitian grammar in which 'Theresa' had helped, at least genealogically, to place the idea of revolutionary women of color at the center.

It is not just her skin color or her allegiances to the revolutionary cause that present no inner conflict for Theresa; the narrator of this tale also exhibits no ambivalence about the violence of the Haitian Revolution. By way of contrast, the narrator clearly condemns the violence not simply of slavery, but of the French soldiers sent to Saint Domingue to attempt to subdue the rebellious former slaves:

> The French in this combat with the Revolutionists, suffered much, both from the extreme sultriness of the day, and the courage of those with whom they contended; disappointed and harassed by the Islanders; they thought it a principle of policy, to resort to acts of cruelty; and to intimidate them, resolved, that none of them should be spared; but that the sword should annihilate, or compel them to submit to their wonted degradations. (639)

The narrator continues by reversing the famous trope of the "white" baby impaled on a spike by "black" revolutionaries recounted most famously in Bryan Edwards's *Historical Survey of St. Domingo* (1797) in stating that 'All the natives were doomed to suffer; the mother and the infant that reposed on her bosom, fell by the same sword, while groans of the sick served only as the guides which discovered them to the inhumanity of the inexorable,

---

18 Martineau's character Papalier, a slave-owning colonist, describes Madame Ogé, the mother of the real-life Haitian revolutionary figure Vincent Ogé, as having 'hoped to hear that her race had risen and were avenging her sons on us' (1: 49).

at whose hands they met a miserable death' (639).[19] Such descriptions of the barbarous and inhumane way in which the French treated the rebellious slaves and their families counters the many portrayals of the Haitian Revolution circulating in the Atlantic World in which the slaves are the ones being described as inhumane and cruel. The narrator proceeds to connect any cruelty the French experience at the hands of the revolutionists to the primary cruelty of the French. In this configuration, the French are responsible for the cruelty of the revolutionists, and thus the behavior of the slaves is marked as providential and justified by God. The success of the Haitian revolutionists is, for the author of 'Theresa,' not only 'righteous' but humane. 'S' writes that the information Theresa is the able to transmit to the revolutionists 'would not fail to give success to Haytian independence, disappoint the arch-enemy, and aid the cause of humanity' (642). In addition, even if the narrator of 'Theresa' does say that the 'sons of Africa' had been 'provoked to madness' by 'French barbarity' (639), he or she does not appear to view this 'madness' as being at odds with either humanity or with the will of God. On the contrary, Theresa has her own violent imaginings:

> with a prophetic eye she saw the destruction of the French, and their final expulsion from her native island. She entreated the Creator, that he would bless the means, which through her agency, he had been pleased to put in the possession of her too long oppressed countrymen, and that all might be made useful to the cause of freedom. (644)

Remarkably, Theresa asks for God's blessing for this violence, which in theory would upset the very tenets of what may very well be the most important non-violent reform movement in U.S. history, abolitionism.

Many adherents of the non-violent abolitionist movement led by William Lloyd Garrison distinctly believed that human violence could not be justified for any reason—Garrison once wrote of the *Liberator* that '[i]ts objects are to save life, not destroy it' (132)—and Garrison and most of his followers believed that violence was actually contrary to the will of God. To that

---

19 See, for example, a famous story about a 'white infant' 'recently impaled on a stake' during the 1791 insurrection in Saint-Domingue that was widely reprinted from volume three of Bryan Edwards's *Historical Survey of St. Domingo* (1797). The famous line reads that M. Odeluc, a plantation owner, upon returning to his 'estate' 'found all the negroes in arms on the side of the rebels and (horrid to tell!), *their standard was the body of a white infant whom they had recently impaled on the stake!*' (3:75; italics in original). The *Edinburgh Magazine* reproduced an excerpt of the tale in 1797 ('Insurrection,' 412), which would subsequently be reproduced and circulated in publications all across the Atlantic World until 1865 and beyond. The image also starts to appear in novels around the turn of the century, as in volume three of *A Winter in Dublin* (1808, 3:90–99). For the genealogy of this story, see L. Dubois (2009, 111).

'Theresa' to the Rescue!

end, in the 1833 official 'Declaration of the Sentiments of the National Anti-Slavery Convention,' Garrison would declare that society's rejection of 'the use of all carnal weapons for deliverance from bondage,' and he implied that abolitionists, though not necessarily slaves,[20] should 'rely ... solely upon those [means] which are spiritual, and mighty through God to the pulling down of strong holds.' In 'Theresa,' however, the violence of the slaves is the spiritual method of 'pulling down of strong holds,' for it is 'through God' that Theresa possesses the 'agency' and knowledge required to help the slaves defeat the French.

Ultimately, by juxtaposing the virtually unequivocal way in which female revolutionaries are treated in 'Theresa' with the quivering equivocations about revolutionary violence or direct demonization of revolutionary acts to be found in other fictions of the Haitian Revolution circulating in the Atlantic World, I hope to have demonstrated the way in which this 1828 text defied the literary conventions of its time by both portraying a female hero of color and not apologizing for or sentimentalizing the violence of the Haitian Revolution. In the broader tradition of writing about the Haitian Revolution to be found in the Atlantic World, celebrating the violence of the revolutionists was a tricky endeavor, not only for "white" abolitionists like Garrison, but for "non-white" authors and orators in general.

*

While the setting of 'Theresa, a Haytien tale' is, indeed, Haiti, it is painfully obvious that the writer of this brief tale had little or no first-hand knowledge or experience of either Haiti or Saint-Domingue, or even the vicissitudes of Haitian revolutionary history. For example, the names of the characters in 'Theresa' are all anglicized—we have Paulina instead of Pauline, Amanda instead of Amandine, and Theresa instead of Thérèse. Furthermore, I have not been able to locate the city of Cape Marie (where Madame Paulina's brother resides) on any maps of Saint-Domingue,[21] and

---

20 Horace Seldon recalls Garrison's criticism of Stowe's unflinching attitude toward non-violent responses to slavery on the part of slaves themselves, as he believed it was expressed in *Uncle Tom's Cabin*: Garrison wondered, 'whether Mrs. Stowe is a believer in the duty of non-resistance for the white man, under all possible outrage and peril, as well as for the black man; whether she is for self-defense on her own part, or that of her husband or friends or country, in case of malignant assault, or whether she impartially disarms all mankind in the name of Christ, be the danger or suffering what it may be' (qtd. in Seldon, 'Garrison on Violence').

21 There was, however, a parish in the jurisdiction of Jérémie called Notre Dame du Cap Dame Marie. See *A Guide to the Jeremie Papers*, http://web.uflib.ufl.edu/spec/manuscript/guides/jeremiefull.htm.

the author repeatedly refers to 'Hayti' and the 'Haytiens' to describe the contemporary moment of 1802 even though these terms were certainly not in use in revolutionary Saint-Domingue, and especially not in the reign of Toussaint Louverture, who declared in his 1801 Constitution that he and all the inhabitants of Saint-Domingue would die 'free and French.' This brings me to perhaps the most blatant of the text's historical anachronisms. There is no mention of the fact that Louverture was no longer in Saint-Domingue at the time of Haitian independence (which occurs at the end of the narrative), having, in reality, been kidnapped along with his family by Bonaparte's troops and taken captive to France, where he died alone in a dungeon in 1803. Furthermore, even though Jean-Jacques Dessalines is responsible for declaring the independence of Haiti, aside from Louverture, the only other *real life* Haitian revolutionary leader whose name comes up in the tale is that of a 'captain Inginac' (645). The Inginac mentioned in the tale is most likely meant to refer to Joseph Balthazar Inginac, who actually served as a general under Dessalines and would more than likely have been known to free people of color in the U.S., not as a revolutionary hero, but as the Haitian secretary of state under Jean-Pierre Boyer who encouraged and promoted U.S. African American emigration to Haiti.[22]

Jean Lee Cole views these historical anachronisms less as questions of ignorance than perhaps ones of expediency and utility for its author. Cole explains that historical accuracy in 'Theresa' was likely not the goal since, 'Rather than represent the experience of a specific individual or an actual event, "Theresa" ... rendered experience in fictive terms—that is, as representative of a class or type of people: black revolutionary women' (159). She adds that by using the medium of fiction, the author was 'Freed from the need to demonstrate the absolute "truth" or "authenticity" of Theresa's ... experience (a fundamental preoccupation of most, if not all, slave narratives)' and was 'thus able to imagine possibilities—what could happen, what might be possible' (159). Cole concludes that by focusing upon Madame Paulina and Theresa's heroic actions over those of Louverture or any of the other male revolutionaries mentioned in the text, 'Theresa' gains the status of instructional myth: 'These fictionalized aspects of the story allow it to transcend, if incompletely, the historical moment; it approaches the level of myth, which

22 Incidentally, according to Léon Dénius Pamphile, as a part of colonization efforts aimed at sending free people of color to Haiti, which President Boyer wholly supported, in June of 1824, Inginac approached Thomas Paul of the First African Baptist Church in Boston (where Maria Stewart was also a worshipper [Peterson, 1995, 19]) 'for twelve men to work his coffee plantation, to join the five men he had already received' (41). Paul, for his part, had earlier traveled to Haiti as a missionary and, like many free blacks in the 1820s, for whom 'Haitian emigrationism' was an 'essential element' of 'black nationalism,' supported the emigration of free blacks to the country (Dixon, 2000, 3).

both removes the story from history and enables readers to apply its lessons to blacks living in the United States of 1828' (161).

But what was the lesson that the "black" readers of 'Theresa' were to take from the text? While Cole considers it one which encourages 'young, defenseless wom[e]n' to 'embrace the cause for black civil rights' and 'stand up for liberty' (161), I view the didacticism of 'Theresa' also as a call to antebellum U.S. men of color to remember the important (even if largely unrecognized) role that women of color had played in the Haitian Revolution. As such, the text also served as a reminder for African American men to not forget the crucial role that African American women were then playing in the early nineteenth-century movement for civil rights and would continue to play in the project of "racial" uplift designed to combat slavery. 'Theresa's' female-driven plot challenges the popular historical role assigned to women in revolutionary history as traitors or passive observers of revolutionary movements and the idea that women of color could play or would only play marginal or sporadic roles in the abolition of slavery. More immediately, 'Theresa' provides a counterpoint to the many previous articles about Haiti published in the short-lived *Freedom's Journal* that had made virtually no mention of women at all and the many general articles about women of color that not only circumscribed their experiences, but censured and censored them.

Two free men of color, John Russworm and Samuel Cornish, edited the inaugural issue of *Freedom's Journal*, published in March of 1827.[23] Cornish was a former pastor of New York's First Colored Presbyterian Church, while Russworm (who was born in Jamaica and educated in Quebec and Maine [Bacon and Jackson, 2010a, 167]) was a graduate of Bowdoin College, where he was the first African American student ever admitted (Bacon, 2010, 82; Bacon and Jackson, 2010a, 167). When Cornish resigned six months after the first issue of the journal, Russworm took over until 1829, when he decided to leave the U.S. for Liberia (Bacon, 2010, 82–83). Foster says that the journal was always a 'diasporic medium,' and 'from the first issue ... had promoted a Pan-African identity that connected the fate and fortunes of those living in the United States with others of the African diaspora' (2006, 635). According to Jacqueline Bacon and Maurice Jackson, the journal, whose motto was 'We wish to plead our own cause,' 'had fairly wide distribution for its time and was distributed to black and white readers in the North and in parts of the South as well as in England, Canada, and Haiti' (2010b, 16). Bruce adds:

---

23 Foster says that the journal was actually founded 'by a diverse group of African Americans from several cities' (2006, 632) and included as editors Richard Allen and Thomas Paul, founder of the Black Baptist Church in Boston (634).

As had been traditional since Wheatley's time, much that appeared in the [*Freedom's*] *Journal* was intended to emphasize the importance of a distinctive black perspective on issues of color and authority. Its columns followed tradition in presenting, for example, poems and brief pieces capturing the sorrow of the enslaved, expressing a pain in slavery that only a black voice could portray. (172)

More often than not, the diasporic, 'black voice' was represented as male.

Although the Haitian Revolution was an important topic and popular enough that it was often written about in the paper, its leaders and heroes were almost always described as men. Take, for example, a series of articles published about Louverture in *Freedom's Journal*. The first article in the series was published on May 4, 1827 and began, 'There are very few events on record which have produced more extraordinary *men* than the Revolution in St. Domingo' (emphasis added).²⁴ A continuation of the same sketch, published in *Freedom's Journal* on May 11, 1827, evoked the trope of the "tropical temptress" in writing of Louverture: 'he was particularly attentive to the means of reforming the loose and licentious manners of the females … His maxim was that women should always appear in public as if they were going to church.'²⁵ The final installment of 'Toussaint Louverture' was

---

24 This passage was reprinted from an article first published in the United States in *The Monthly Review*, but the original source for the quotation may have been Sir James Barskett's *History of the island of St. Domingo* (1818). The line was also reprinted in *Galignani's Magazine* and *Paris Monthly Review*. Additional reprints can be found in *Oriental Herald and Journal of General Literature*, *The Quarterly Review*, and *Chartist Circular* edited by W. Thomson. The writer for *Freedom's Journal*, however, attributes the sketch to *The Quarterly Review*.

25 The author appears to have derived this claim from the French author Pamphile de Lacroix's *Mémoires pour servir à l'histoire de la Révolution de Saint-Domingue* (1819), wherein Lacroix writes of Louverture: 'He wanted the women, and above all the white ladies, to be dressed as if they were going to church and for them to have their chests entirely covered. He has been known to, while averting his eyes, send them away and cry out that *he could not conceive of the way in which honest women could lack such decency*. We saw him another time, throw his handkerchief over the breast of a young woman, saying in a severe tone to her mother, *that modesty should be the prerogative of her sex*' (401, emphasis added). Later in the nineteenth century, the Haitian historian Joseph Saint-Rémy would describe Louverture as having had entirely 'monastic morals,' especially when it came to women. As one example, Saint-Rémy writes: 'Was he not seen to, having one day entered one of the cathedrals of the island, questioned on their catechism the little white girls, the daughters of the colonists—and, in seeing one of them, whose bodice, in this holy place was,—the reader will excuse the word,—it is a part of the language of the time in question and is appropriate to the situation,—alluring [*désinvolturé*]; did he not suddenly throw his handkerchief upon her chest and say to this poor girl, who was perhaps as innocent as an angel, "Cover yourself?"' (1850, 395)

published on May 18, 1827, and anachronistically attributed the ensuing independence of Haiti to Louverture himself in proudly proclaiming: 'Such was the man to whom the island was indebted for its posterity.'

Other articles reprinted in *Freedom's Journal* or originating from the journal itself, continued to assume that all revolutionaries were necessarily men and to elide or circumscribe the experiences of women. To that end, an article published on November 30, 1827, reprinted from *The Genius of Universal Emancipation*, refutes the idea that common slaves in the United States could not ever carry out the kind of revolutions that had taken place throughout world history, including in Haiti: 'Who ... were the Generals that commanded the armies of the Republic, in the days of Cromwell?' the author asks. 'From what grade of society, did France during the Revolution procure her Marshals, was it not from the common people? Who was Toussaint, Dessalines, and a number of other generals who acted so prominent a part in the Revolution of Hayti—were they not domestic slaves?' ('From the Genius'). A subsequent article from *Freedom's Journal* published on April 6, 1827 further evoked the idea that the Haitian Revolution had been carried out by ordinary slaves, 'men' who 'were of little education—of still less experience in military affairs, and more expert in the use of the hoe and the spade, than in wielding a sword or leveling a musket.' The author continued by referring to the Haitian Revolution as an unprecedented display of masculinity on the part of 'African slave[s]': 'The man who could think it possible that the African slave would take up arms in defense of his birthright and spend his heart's blood for its possession, would have been regarded as a madman, and his reflections branded as the dreams of a visionary.' 'But times have changed,' the author continues, 'the revolution of St. Domingo, which taught the world that the African, though trodden down in the dust by the foot of the oppressor, yet had not entirely lost the finer sensibilities of his nature, and still possessed the proper spirit of feelings of a man' ('For the Freedom's Journal. Haytien Revolution'). The author of another article published as part of a serialized column entitled *Scrapbook of Africanus*, which appeared in the May 4, 1827 edition of *Freedom's Journal*, directly evoked masculinity as the *sine qua non* of revolutionary actions: 'I conceive, that many who then took up arms [after Ogé's failed revolt] in the defence of all that is dear to everyone who *thinks himself a man*, never laid them down until the recent and partial acknowledgment of the island' ('For the Freedom's Journal. Hayti No. III,' emphasis added).[26] Finally, in an additional essay from the *Scrapbook* (June 29, 1827), the author

26 According to Elizabeth Rauh Bethel, *The Scrapbook of Africanus* was a serialized column that appeared in *Freedom's Journal* in 1827 and was designed to present a 'richly textured narrative of Haytian history and culture' (1997, 156).

praises the establishment of '[a] Military Academy' in Port-au-Prince and the education of Haitian men: 'in Hayti, where many expect nothing but ignorance, we find men skilled in the different arts and sciences, who would be an honour to any country' ('For the Freedom's Journal ... V).

Masculinity was also evoked in the name of defending unfair descriptions of Haiti and Haitians in the U.S. press by an article published in the first edition of *Freedom's Journal* on March 16, 1827. In this article, the author or authors, who were more than likely the editors of the journal, directly linked attacks on Haiti to 'umanly' behavior when they warned:

> We caution the dissatisfied and envious in this country, who are continually forging 'News from Hayti' to desist from their unmanly attacks upon a brave and hospitable people. Were our readers as well acquainted with their motives for venting their spleen as we are, they would give as little credit to their fabrications. ('By a Late Arrival')

One of the goals of *Freedom's Journal*'s reportage about Haiti was, in fact, to refute fabrications about Haitian history and to point out mischaracterizations of Haiti's new government. Cornish and Russworm declared in this same issue that since 'the relations between Hayti and this country are become daily more interesting, it is highly important that we have correct information.' They continued: 'Our readers may depend on our columns, as we shall never insert any news whatever, of a doubtful nature concerning that island.'

Bacon, who has examined a variety of different kinds of articles about Haiti to be found in the short-lived *Freedom's Journal*, writes that 'manhood was part of the drive for freedom that inspired the heroes of the Haitian Revolution ... ideals of masculinity for African Americans were not merely reflected in personal behavior or character; they were linked to citizenship and freedom and had political and communal implications' (2010, 85). She continues: 'To be worthy of being called "a man", then, required resistance to oppression such as was demonstrated by the slaves of Saint-Domingue' (85).[27]

---

27 Columns about Haiti or slavery in the early African American press were not the only places where masculinity ruled the day or in which "black" female identity was almost completely elided, ignored, or downplayed. James Oliver Horton has written that 'Gender ideals of black society were heavily influenced by middle-class black males through the pages of black newspapers ... These newspapers instructed men, in terms not unlike those applied to other American males, in the ways of manhood' (56). In the pages of *Freedom's Journal*, for example, there are articles (both original and reprinted from elsewhere) instructing men to be temperate, so as to pay attention to the duties of providing for their families ('Intemperance'); there are also articles cautioning young men against being idle in the streets, dressing poorly, or smoking ('Propriety of

'Theresa' to the Rescue!

Bacon argues even so that 'although they appeared less frequently, female heroes of the Haitian Revolution were featured as well in *Freedom's Journal's* columns, enabling contributors to link discourses of womanhood to those of nation and race in important, empowering ways' (86). In any case, 'Theresa' is Bacon's first and only example of female revolutionaries portrayed in *Freedom's Journal*, making the short story less an example of one of the broad tendencies to be found in the journal's articles than a distinct outlier.

When one famous Haitian woman—King Henry Christophe's wife—is mentioned prior to the publication of 'Theresa,' it is hardly to attach her name to the legacy of Haitian independence. On the contrary, this particular mention of Queen Marie-Louise punctuates the idea that women of color were usually portrayed in the context of Haiti as people to be protected, saved, defended, and even pitied. In an article entitled 'From the (Boston) Columbian Centinel. Madame Christophe,' reprinted in *Freedom's Journal* on May 11, 1827, the author refutes an inflammatory account of Madame Christophe that had first been published in the *New York Enquirer*. Ardent racist Mordecai Manuel Noah (Bacon, 2010, 90) had described Madame Christophe as 'a fat, greasy wench, as black as the ace of spades, and one who would find it difficult to get a place as a Cook in this city. So much for royal taste.' The author of the refutation first published in the *Boston Centinel* defends Madame Christophe against 'this calumny': 'We are induced, from a personal acquaintance with Madame Christophe for many years previous to and after she was elevated to the rank of Queen of Hayti, to bear testimony against the above illiberal and unjust representation.' The author continues by stating, 'We particularly regret that such misrepresentations should originate in the United States, as it must have a tendency to injure Americans in the estimation of the black population of Hayti; who have been, and continue to be the friends of all friendly foreigners, especially the Americans' ('From the (Boston) Columbian').[28]

Conduction'), and there are abolitionist tracts designed to encourage "black" men to have 'manly courage' in the face of slavery ('People of Colour').

28 Another series of articles entitled 'Madame Christophe' was also published in *Freedom's Journal* on June 27, July 4, and July 11, 1828. In this series, the author spies the former Queen Marie-Louise eating at a 'trattoria' with her daughter in Pisa, Italy, where the former was then residing. The writer describes the former queen as having the appearance of 'a poor deserted black woman, eating her macaroni in a miserable "Trattoria" an object of derision to the vulgar, and of curiosity to all' ('Madame Christophe' [b]). In the conclusion to the series, however, the author defends the former queen, whose life he says was saved by Baron Dupuy, one of Christophe's ministers and primary interpreter, writing that all the 'Ex-Emperors, Kings, Queens, Princes, and Princesses, and more particularly their Ex-Ministers and Ex-Courtiers' should 'take an example from this uneducated black woman, and instead of vainly clinging to the

If the author of 'Theresa' was inspired to write a short story with a female heroine of color as a response to the masculinist tone of writing about Haiti in the U.S. press, *Freedom's Journal* would not have been the only place where the Haitian Revolution and "black" masculinity were overtly conflated. Although the 'black press,' inaugurated by the establishment of *Freedom's Journal*, was 'an important forum for keeping the memory of the Haitian Revolution alive and interpreting its significance for African Americans' (Bacon and Jackson, 2010b, 16), it was not the only medium for African Americans to do so, and was thus not the only way in which the connection between masculinity and the Haitian Revolution circulated in the African American community. In his 'Memoir presented to the American Convention for Promoting the Abolition of Slavery and Improving the Condition of the African Race' (December 11, 1818), Saunders conceives of men as the especial creators of government, reprinting a letter from Joseph Banks, one of the 'privy counselors' of the King of England. Banks had written: 'I hold the newly established government of Hayti in the highest respect. It is without doubt, in its theory, I mean the Code Henri, the most moral association of men in existence; nothing that white men have been able to arrange is equal to it' (qtd. in Saunders, 1818b, 18).[29] Saunders interpreted Banks's statement about the *Code Henri* in distinctly masculinist terms when he evoked the fraternity he hoped Christophe's laws might encourage with respect to the reunification of the northern and southern governments of Haiti. Having praised 'the men who have destroyed or driven away' the 'hostile troops' of France, Saunders wrote, 'Perseverance ... in the line of conduct laid down in the Code Henri cannot but in due time conquer all difficulties, and bring together the black and white varieties of mankind under the ties of mutual and reciprocal equality and brotherhood' (19). In addition, in the preface to his *Haytian Papers*, Saunders refuted the idea that Europeans had an overwhelming influence upon the writings which emanated from the government of Haiti by pointing out (and seeming to praise) the fact that all of the secretaries of Christophe's government were 'black men, or men of colour' (iii).

phantom of power they once had, instead of throwing away the realities of happiness they still possess, for the shadow of their former state, which they can never possess again, they would do well to follow Madame Christophe's example, lay aside the titles and honours they now so zealously and ridiculously exact, and endeavour to find tranquility, if not happiness, in competency and retirement' (July 11, 1828). This article had originated in the British *New Monthly Magazine and Literary Journal* ('Madame Christophe' [d], 481–85).

29 Saunders also mentioned Haiti in his 'Address Delivered at Bethel Church, Philadelphia: on the 30th of September, 1818, Before the Pennsylvania Augustine Society for the Education of People of Colour' (1818a, 4).

While Saunders can hardly be faulted for pointing out that Christophe's government contained only men, the fact that neither he nor any of the other male writers of his time who discussed post-independence Haitian society paid attention to the role of women (or lack thereof) within this new society and its government, suggests that, as Francis Wigmoore has written of their nineteenth-century Caribbean male counterparts, these 'thinkers who could discern the class, race, and colonial dynamics of the classist, racist, and imperialist societies in which they flourished could not similarly discern the patriarchal structures of those same societies' (117). This lack of discernment on the part of the leaders who created independent Haiti is linked directly to the same oversight of male abolitionists and civil rights leaders like Frederick Douglass, who later in the nineteenth century argued that the woman question was subordinate to the question of citizenship and participation for men of color (M. Locke, 231). In the U.S., such exclusions of women from government offices and preclusion of their voting rights had disastrous consequences. According to Mamie E. Locke, 'Passage of the Fifteenth Amendment elevated African-American men to a political status that thrust them into the patriarchal world' while 'African-American women had once again been omitted from the cornerstone of American democracy, the Constitution of the United States' (233). Mimi Sheller writes similarly that in post-independence Haiti, 'women were indeed marginalized from the public sphere, and thus largely absent from the archives which were written by men, for men, and mostly about men' (2012, 147).

Men of color like Saunders who had direct experience with Haiti were not the only orators to take an interest in the topic. While Russworm would write a number of articles that directly discussed Haitian society in *Freedom's Journal*, prior to that, the commencement speech he gave at Bowdoin College in 1826, entitled 'The Condition and Prospects of Hayti,' attracted widespread attention and would subsequently be excerpted in many of the major newspapers and journals of the nineteenth century (W. James, 24).[30] According to Russworm's biographer, Winston James, it was the research conducted for a previous 22-page essay written in Russworm's hand, entitled 'Toussaint L'Overture [sic], the Principal Chief in the Revolution in St. Domingo,' which 'provided the platform for his later, more analytical

---

30 On October 12, 1827 and again on July 13, 1827, Russworm expressed disillusionment within the pages of *Freedom's Journal* that President Boyer had 'agreed' to pay an indemnity to France in exchange for recognition of Haiti's independence' (qtd. in Jackson and Bacon, 2010a, 64). Portions of Russworm's speech were reprinted in the *Argus, Boston Courier*, the *Boston Centinel*, the *Boston Commercial Gazette*, the *Norwich Courier*, and the *National Philanthropist*, in addition to the Baltimore-based *Genius of Universal Emancipation* (W. James, 24).

argument so forcefully presented in "The Conditions and Prospects of Hayti'" (132). In the essay Russworm would adopt the rhetorical form common in African American writing of this time, and also demonstrated in 'Theresa,' of using Toussaint Louverture as a metonym for Haitian independence. Russworm praised Louverture for the 'talents and virtues' that 'entitle him to the grateful recollections of his liberated countrymen' and noted that 'his character exhibits many of those qualities which have distinguished the most illustrious governors and commanders' (131–32). In his commencement speech, Russworm not only linked Haitian independence once again to the famous Toussaint Louverture, but more directly connected Haitian independence to masculinity when he said of Louverture and a host of other male figures associated with the Revolution:

> Such were its effects upon the Haytians—men who in slavery showed neither spirit nor genius:—but when Liberty, when once Freedom struck their astonished ears, they became new creatures:—stepped forth as men, and showed to the world, that though Slavery may benumb, it cannot entirely destroy our faculties. Such men were Toussaint L'Ouverture, Dessalines and Christophe! (168)

For Russworm, becoming independent had everything to do with becoming a man, much the same way that Frederick Douglass's own violent, physical resistance of his master, Covey, had everything to do with how he 'was made a man' (1960, 50).

Each of the speeches, articles, and pamphlets discussed above found widespread circulation in the early nineteenth-century U.S. press and would likely have been noticed by many African American readers. Even so, if the "non-white" female readers of *Freedom's Journal* were paying just as much attention as the men to the writing about Haiti to be found in the northern U.S. press, the avenues open to them for speaking about or publishing their own responses to and interpretations of the Haitian Revolution—particularly interpretations that may have countered, opposed, or complicated the idea that the Haitian Revolution was the ultimate and *manly* defeat of colonial authority and slavery—were either non-existent or vexed. According to Carla Peterson, 'black women' 'were officially excluded' from 'black national institutions' like the American Moral Reform Society, 'through which men of the elite came together to promote public civic debate on practical issues of racial uplift as well as those more theoretical considerations of black nationality' (1995, 17). Horton adds that in the first quarter of the nineteenth century, although women were to play some key roles in the "black" churches that had been established in places like Boston, Philadelphia, and New York, the leadership of organizations like the African

Baptist Church of Boston was overwhelmingly male (55). As far as literary societies went, the Gilbert Lyceum, which was the 'first and only [literary] society, which admitted individuals of both sexes' was not established until 1841 (Porter, 568). Horton writes of this: 'The separation of black male groups from those of black females served to underscore gender divisions common in nineteenth-century America' (66). 'All women were expected to defer to men,' he writes, 'but for black women deference was a racial imperative. Slavery and racism sought the emasculation of black men. Black people sought to counter such an effect.' As such, '[i]t was seen as a black woman's duty to allow black men to "feel tough and protective"' (70).

Judging by the myriad articles published in *Freedom's Journal* on the topic of female behavior, not speaking out publicly and being 'bashful' and 'modest' was one of the ways in which a 'black woman' was supposed to defer to a 'black man.'[31] Take, as one example, an article published on October 26, 1827, written 'For the Freedom's Journal' and signed only with the initial 'J': 'We hope the time may never come, when the gentler virtues shall be banished for bolder more masculine manners,' the author writes. 'Nothing sooner lessens our respect for a woman, than when we notice in her any want of that delicacy which seems to be her peculiar attribute. In the garb of modesty we hope to ever see her arrayed' ('For the Freedom's Journal. Observer. No. VII'). Another article, also signed by 'J', argued that women should watch their verbosity: 'There is one thing in woman, which, be she old or young, handsome or ugly, wife or maid, I do loath and abhor. A babbling tongue is the "object of my implacable disgust"' ('For the Freedom's Journal. Observer. No. V').

Naturally, not all women followed the mandate to keep silent, be modest, and appear to be delicate in public. Letters to the editor and a handful of poems tell us that some women of color did indeed access, patronize, and contribute to *Freedom's Journal*. A letter published in the August 10, 1827 issue, by a woman who signed her name only 'Matilda,' contained the following challenge in the form of a rhetorical question:

---

31 Women were urged by various articles in *Freedom's Journal* to be 'bashful,' 'modest,' 'virtuous,' and to avoid all 'vulgarity' ('For the Freedom's Journal. Observer. No. VII'). An article entitled 'Duties of Wives' (February 21, 1829) cautioned women about the 'absolute necessity of making and keeping that house really a home,' urging that 'it never can be a woman's interest to cross even the foibles of her husband, when they are harmless.' There were also entries arguing for 'female tenderness' ('For the Freedom's Journal. Female Tenderness'), female fragility—'a small touch may wound and kill it' ('Varieties' [b])—and which claimed that 'the Christian doctrine assigns woman to the man as the partner of his labours, the soother of his evils, his helpmate in perils, his friend in affliction' ('Varieties' [b]), and one article comically instructed men by way of allegory on how to 'tame a shrew' ('Persian Mode of Taming a Shrew').

> Will you allow a female to offer a few remarks upon a subject that you must allow to be all-important. I don't know that in any of your papers, you have said sufficient upon the education of females. I hope you are not to be classed with those, who think that our mathematical knowledge should be limited to 'fathoming the dish-kettle', and that we have acquired enough of history, if we knew that our grandfather's father lived and died. ('Messrs. EDITORS')

'Matilda' was not the only woman who sought to contribute to the journal. The editors mention an 'Amelia,' 'whose poetical lines' 'we cannot insert, being too personal' as well as a poet named 'Rosa,' 'of our sister city' ('To Correspondents').[32]

Though *Freedom's Journal* was perhaps one of the only outlets for publication available to African American women writers in the 1820s, by the 1830s things had begun to change rapidly. In her article on 'negro literary societies' from 1828 to 1846, Dorothy B. Porter describes a flourishing of African American female literary societies in the early 1830s after the establishment in Philadelphia of the all-male Reading Room Society (558–59). The Female and Literary Society of Philadelphia, for example, was founded in 1831 (559); the Minerva Literary Association, also in Philadelphia, was organized in October of 1834 (561); and Porter notes that the Afric-American Female Intelligence Society was already well organized by 1832 (569), leading her to conclude that 'women took the lead in the organization of literary societies in Boston' (569). In contrast, at the time of the publication of 'Theresa,' not only were all the female African American literary societies above not yet established, but according to Peterson, there was truly no 'national network of black women leaders that would allow them as a group to enter into the arena of civic debate and engage in sustained written production' (1995, 19). This meant that women who sought to enter the masculine domain of publishing and oration in the 1820s and very early 1830s, like Maria Stewart, who was probably the first woman of color to ever appear before and address a 'promiscuous assembly' (Peterson, 1995, 58), and the women of color who published anonymously or pseudonymously in the 'Ladies Department' of Garrison's *The Liberator* as well as in the pages of *Freedom's Journal*, would still have to do so in primarily male venues.

Garrison, for his part, often published the poems, essays, and other works

---

32 On March 23, 1827 the editors did, however, publish a decidedly un-personal poem by 'Amelia' entitled 'By A Late Princess.' A poem by 'Rosa' entitled 'For the Freedom's Journal. Lines on Hearing of the Death of a Young Friend' was published on October 26, 1827. Additional poems by 'Rosa' were published on October 26 and November 30, 1827, and February 8, 1828. A response to one of Rosa's poems, 'To Rosa,' published in the journal on March 21, 1828 was signed only 'FRERE.'

'Theresa' to the Rescue!

by members of the 'all-black' Female Literary Society of Philadelphia. He was reportedly so enamored with the group that 'he took with him several of the compositions by these ladies with the idea of publishing them, not only for their merit, but with the hopes that other ladies living in other cities would organize into similar groups' (Porter, 559). Porter writes, however, that 'For the most part these writings were signed with just a forename, pseudonym, or simply by "A Lady of Color". This makes the identification of the authors difficult, if not impossible' (560). Like 'Theresa,' the writings and oration of such women provide a direct challenge to the idea that revolutionaries had been and would always be male and that women would play a subordinate role in the abolitionist movement and "racial" uplift programs of the United States. In an 'Address to the Female Literary Association of Philadelphia,' which was published in *The Liberator* on June 9, 1832, the anonymous author writes:

> It is nothing better than affectation to deny the influence that females possess; it is their part to train up the young mind, to install therein principles that may govern in maturer years; principles that influence the actions of the private citizen, the patriot, the philanthropist, lawgivers, yea, presidents and kings. (91)

Notably, 'Matilda,' too, writing for *Freedom's Journal*, addressed the issue of the female sphere of influence when she wrote:

> We possess not the advantages with those of our sex whose skins are not colored liked our own, but we can improve what little we have ... The influence that we have over the male sex demands, that our minds should be instructed and improved with the principles of education and religion, in order that this influence should be properly directed. ('For the Freedom's Journal')

In an additional piece published in *The Liberator* on October 13, 1832 entitled, 'For the Liberator: Address to the Female Literary Association of Philadelphia, on their First Anniversary, By a Member,' after directly alluding to the yellow fever then sweeping through Philadelphia, the author expresses revolutionary sentiments when she writes: 'dare to tell our enemies, that with the powerful weapons of religion and education, we will do battle with the host of prejudice which surround us, satisfied that in the end, we shall be more than conquerors' (162).[33]

---

33 Later in the nineteenth century, Garrison would also report on the lectures of Oneida Debois, a 'colored female lecturer,' who, having escaped from slavery in Alabama, emigrated to Haiti. Debois, who was called a 'French Zambo' by the *Hartford*

Stewart also had a history of publication within the pages of *The Liberator*, both anonymously and under her own name.[34] One of the hallmarks of Stewart's writing and oration is the fact that, like the author of 'Theresa,' she saw women of color not as passive observers and thus mere beneficiaries of revolutions, but as revolutionaries and 'conquerors' in their own rights. Stewart argued, to that end, that women had been important for revolutionary movements throughout history and she called on women of color to fulfill their historical and providential roles to intervene on behalf of the oppressed. In her 'Farewell Address to Her Friends in the City of Boston, Delivered September 21, 1833' Stewart challenged the dominant idea of women of color as non-revolutionary, defiantly exhorting:

> What if I am a woman; is not the God of ancient times the God of these modern days? Did he not raise up Deborah, to be a mother, and a judge in Israel? Did not queen Esther save the lives of the Jews? And Mary Magdalene first declare the resurrection of Christ from the dead? Come, said the woman of Samaria, and see a man that hath told me all things that ever I did, is not this the Christ?

Stewart continued by not only reminding her audience that such revolutionary women continued to exist, but by prophesying that they would play a sacred role in the abolition of slavery and in the ideological combat against color prejudice:

> If such women as are here described have once existed, be no longer astonished then, my brethren and friends, that God at this eventful period should raise up your own females to strive, by their example both in public and private, to assist those who are endeavoring to stop the strong current

---

Post, apparently went on a speaking tour of the northern U.S. in the early 1860s whose object was to 'acquire means for establishing a school for girls in Gonaïves, Hayti and to disabuse the public mind of some of the prevailing prejudices that the African race is capable of any high degree of civilization' (qtd. in Garrison, 'A Colored Female Lecturer,' 59).

34 She published a poem in *The Liberator* in 1831 without attribution: the same poem that appeared at the end of the 1835 volume of the *Productions of Mrs. Maria W. Stewart*. Richardson cautions, however, that this poem may not have been written by Stewart (75). In any event, Stewart's 'Address Delivered before the Afric-American Female Intelligence Society' appeared in the *Liberator* on April 28, 1832; her 'Lecture Delivered at the Franklin Hall, Boston' appeared on November 17, 1832; and her 'Address Delivered in the African Masonic Hall' appeared on May 4, 1833. There were also a handful of advertisements for Stewart's work published in Garrison's magazine. Stewart's pamphlet, *Religion and the Pure Principles of Morality* was advertised on March 31, 1832; *The Productions of Mrs. Maria W. Stewart* was advertised on September 12, 1835; and her *Meditations*, was also advertised in the journal on several different dates.

of prejudice that flows so profusely against us at present. No longer ridicule their efforts, it will be counted for sin. For God makes use of feeble means sometimes, to bring about his most exalted purposes.

The passage above directly places Stewart in a radical feminist tradition of not simply inserting her presence as an equal, but questioning the assumptions behind the idea of casual sexism that pervaded 1830s Boston, and ultimately left Maria Stewart as one of its casualties, for 'Why cannot we become divines and scholars?' she would ask.

By the early 1830s, Stewart, along with the anonymous black female writers publishing elsewhere in the African American press, had good reason to push back against the idea that men would be the ones to lead African Americans and, especially, slaves out of oppression, and therefore to suspect that under the leadership of these men, many of whom saw women of color as variously helpless, treacherous, or even contemptuous, a new patriarchal society would simply be constructed upon the heels of the old one. In his 1829 *Appeal*, David Walker, for example, assumed that the 'person' to lead the U.S. equivalent of the Haitian Revolution would be male, because in this time period persons were almost always grammatically referenced as men:

> Read the history particularly of Hayti, and see how they were butchered by the whites, and do you take warning. The person whom God shall give you, give him your support and let him go his length, and behold in him the salvation of your God. God will indeed, deliver you through him from your deplorable and wretched condition under the Christians of America. I charge you this day before my God to lay no obstacle in his way, but let him go. (23)

Furthermore, and with far more dire implications for women, Walker blamed female slaves and, by extension, all women of color for the lack of revolutionary prowess to be found among the slaves in the United States. Walker told the tale of a '*servile*' 'black' slave woman who gave in to her '*natural fine* feelings' when she helped a white slave-driver escape certain death at the hands of escaped slaves (28, italics in original). Walker concludes:

> But I declare, the actions of this black woman are really insupportable. For my own part, I cannot think it was any thing but servile deceit, combined with the most gross ignorance: for we must remember that humanity, kindness and the fear of the Lord, does not consist in protecting devils. (29)

Peterson says of Walker's rendition of this story that 'in Walker's text it is the black woman who serves as the emblem of black disunity' (1995, 65). That 'disunity' seems precisely to derive from her status as a woman and her resulting 'fine feelings,' a line of thought that was wholly in keeping with the way in which women of color had been portrayed in the nascent nineteenth-century African American press as compliant, but stands in opposition to much of the transatlantic print culture of the Haitian Revolution, where this kind of 'disunity' with the revolutionists would often be portrayed as benevolence rather than betrayal. As Horton writes, 'Black newspapers were clear in their support of the place reserved for the female sex in American society. In their pages were countless stories of the dire consequences that awaited those who did not accept and conform to the pattern, within the limits of their ability' (56). For the militant Walker, however, woman's position as a member of the 'gentler sex, naturally more moral, more loving, more caring than men' was not the virtue or ideal that it would appear to be throughout the majority of the early black press (Horton, 55); instead, these gendered distinctions were nothing more than a weakness that made 'black' females obstacles to freedom rather than allies. The characterization of this 'servile' 'black woman' whose innate weepy sentimentality is portrayed as having compelled her to let a horrible slaveholder go, was part of a broad myth concerning women's (in)ability to participate in the necessarily depersonalized violence of the Revolution. Maria Stewart not only understood this, but dared to refute it.

Walker's judgment of this slave woman's actions as a form of betrayal is consonant with the trope of the "tropical temptress" and the way in which its overt face covers up female revolutionary potential if it does not match preconceived notions of what that should look like. Even though Stewart counted Walker among her closest of friends and once referred to him as 'the most noble, fearless, and undaunted David Walker' (qtd. in Hinks, 114), she could not have failed to notice the way in which masculinity was linked to revolutionary ideas and the way in which women were explicitly written out of the discourse of abolition and "racial" uplift. Stewart not only believed in the kind of violent revolution supported by Walker—she said at her 'Address Delivered at the African Masonic Hall' in 1833, 'where is the man that has distinguished himself in these modern days by acting wholly in the defence of African rights and liberty? There was one, although he sleeps, his memory lives'—but she believed that this 'man' might actually turn out to be a woman. This belief is particularly apparent in Stewart's 'Lecture Delivered at the Franklin Hall' (Boston, September 21, 1832) in which she said, 'Me thinks I heard a spiritual interrogation—"Who shall go forward, and take off the reproach that is cast upon the people of color? Shall it be a woman?" And my heart made this reply—if it is thy will, be it even so, Lord Jesus!'[35]

---

35 Stewart would not only receive censure for the daring challenge to masculinity found in her speech before the African Masonic Hall, in consequence of which she

Like Stewart, who wondered who that female revolutionary might be, a question that has resonance with the famous 'Black Spartacus' passage in the abbé Raynal's historic compilation *Histoire des deux Indes* (1770-1780), the character Theresa also wonders who would convey back to the revolutionists the 'invaluable discoveries' that were related to her mother by the French troops. She wonders, 'In what manner she must act?' (643) and, thinking more directly about the crucial information in her possession, the narrator writes of her: 'Important as they were to the cause of freedom, by whom shall they be carried. Who shall reveal them to the Revoluists [*sic*]' (642–43). Thus, although Srinivas Aravamudan has wondered in *Tropicopolitans*, 'if Toussaint L'Ouverture had been a woman, which passage in the *Histoire des deux Indes* might she have chosen as a point of departure?' (315), and subsequently offers a virtual female reader who examines the Medea passage of the *Histoire* and is consequently inspired to poison her master and commit infanticide in acts of resistance like Diderot's Medea in the *Histoire*, both the story of 'Theresa' and the writing of Stewart complicate the idea that women revolutionaries may have been differently inspired from their male counterparts. Both Stewart and Theresa found themselves presented with the same kind of prophetic question associated with the 'Black Spartacus' passage—'Where is he, this great man whom nature owes to her vexed, oppressed, and tormented children? Where is he?' (Raynal, 6:206–08). Unlike the author of the 'Black Spartacus' passage, however, the author of 'Theresa,' just like Stewart, seems to ask, might this revolutionary not be a *woman*?

Anonymity may have freed the writer of 'Theresa' from having to submit the literary heroes of her text to the cult of domesticity and the 'fine feelings' of benevolence as markers of true humanity or concrete evidence of the biological weakness of females. Such anonymity may therefore have also protected her from the judgment of her male allies, whose response to 'Theresa' could not have been predicted for, clearly, Stewart felt shocked and betrayed by the response to her speech before the African Masonic Hall. Stewart said in her 'Farewell Address,' 'I was misrepresented, and there was none to help.' The anonymous writer of the June 9, 1832 'Address to the Female Literary Association of Philadelphia' also understood the precariousness of the forum in which she sought entrance when, after exclaiming

---

would be practically banished from African American society in Boston, but she also appears to have been at odds with her one-time patron Garrison, whose feelings about violent revolution were ambivalent and who supported colonization efforts, which Stewart opposed (Richardson, 25). Yet Stewart did not believe that violence was the only way to freedom. In 'Religions and Pure Principles of Morality,' Stewart wrote: 'Far be it from me to recommend to you, either to kill, burn, or destroy. But I would strongly recommend to you, to improve your talents.' For Stewart's opposition to colonization, see her speech before the African Masonic Hall, February 27, 1833.

that one day indeed 'may the female character be raised to a just stand' (91), she wrote, 'At some future period I may explain more particularly my reasons for thinking as I do, although it should elicit the exclamation of—"thou art beside thyself, thy great zeal hath made thee mad"' (91).

If using Haiti and the Haitian Revolution as her setting rather than the antebellum U.S. provided a way to make revolutionary women less invisible in the U.S. public sphere and to avoid the charge of madness, such a setting may also have provided the author of 'Theresa' a veil through which to subtly enter and critique a masculinist public sphere that failed to recognize the contributions and possibilities of women of color in its own backyard. Therefore, although Foster writes that she is 'hard pressed to call this story feminist,' I hope that the above examination of the text has shown that 'Theresa,' like the writings of other women of color in the antebellum U.S. (much of which was anonymously published), was wholly radical for its time, and dare I say it, even feminist, even as it conformed in many ways to the strict definitions of femininity, virtue, and domesticity that often restricted the voices and movements of "white" and "non-white" women alike.

My ultimate wish, then, is that the landscape provided by the above gloss of early African American print culture and transatlantic revolutionary thought might provide a way to understand the reasons why the author of 'Theresa,' whether "black" or "white," male or female, may have sought to remain anonymous. 'Theresa' was and is a dangerous tale in the sense that it defies the gender conventions of revolution in the Atlantic World by portraying a lone woman of color on a quest to 'give success to Haitian independence' (642); it also defied the gender conventions of an early African American print culture that often viewed all men of color as potential revolutionaries and all the women of color as potential people to be saved, potential wives, or potential threats to the revolutionary cause, but rarely as unequivocal allies.

By way of offering some final thoughts for this section, it is perhaps unsurprising at this point that the three fictional representations examined in Part Two of *Tropics of Haiti* have vexed authorship in common. 'Theresa' appears to have been published under the same kinds of simultaneous repressions and privileges of anonymity that I have suggested characterize the authorship and publication of both *Zelica* and *La Mulâtre*. As T. Denean Sharpley-Whiting has written, 'The precarious position of being seen and simultaneously not seen, of invisibility, or seen invisibility... is one with which black women are all too familiar' (3). Anonymity may have been one way in which women writers turned that invisibility into speaking voices and literary presence for themselves, while paradoxically insuring that they would never receive credit for these works and, as a consequence, remain both unseen and disembodied in perpetuity. In the absence of concrete evidence leading to the identity of the author of 'Theresa,' I want to ask if by unwittingly adopting the paternalist attitudes and structures of reference found in these masculine historical works that dominate Haitian revolutionary history (namely, by assuming male authorship of revolutionary texts), do we also, in the words of Wigmoore, writing on 'black' masculinity in the Caribbean, 'reinscribe ... by default, a subjugated womanhood, en route to [our] vision of a black world?' (118). Beverly Guy Sheftall tells us that early nineteenth-century African American women writers like Stewart 'were aware of their own erasure from the annals of history' (24). Such erasures were also unwittingly recognized by an anonymous piece published in *Freedom's Journal* on April 13, 1827. The clearly male author of the piece writes:

> With the holy name of woman I associate every soft, tender, and delicate affection ... Can I look down on her tomb without affection? Man has always done justice to his memory—woman never. The pages of history lie open to the one; but the meek and unobtrusive excellencies [sic] of the other sleep with her unnoticed in the grave. In her may have shone the genius of the poet, with the virtues of the saint, the energy of the man, with the tender softness of the woman. She too may have passed unheeded along the sterile pathway of her existence, and felt for others and I now feel for her. ('Varieties' [c])

In this chapter I have argued that it is precisely because of the pervasiveness of such obvious historical erasures that the author of 'Theresa' willfully opposes both the *scientist* and masculinist histories of Haiti that dominated antebellum U.S. African American print culture and the transatlantic print culture of the Haitian Revolution. In so doing, the author unwittingly provides what may be the only unequivocal portrayal of a fictional Haitian female revolutionary hero in the entire Atlantic World,[36] a female hero of color whose actions in creating the circumstances for an independent Haiti rivaled those of Toussaint Louverture, making women less the historical beneficiaries of male bravery and heroism than some of its primary enablers.

---

36 It is worth mentioning that, according to Léon-François Hoffmann, celebrating the Haitian Revolution was so rare in nineteenth-century French print culture that Lamartine's *Toussaint Louverture* 'constituted the century's only literary justification [in France] for the Haitian fight for independence' (2009, 343).

PART THREE

The Trope of the Tragic "Mulatto/a" and the Haitian Revolution

'Is incest worse than parricide!—or does that jealous and avenging power (whom in my cups I have so often laughed at while I trembled), decree me just scope enough for crimes to damn me; but nothing to delight?'

—John Thelwall, *The Daughter of Adoption* (1801)

'The mixed race thus sprung up, as it is now doing at the South, numerous and hated, attracting, yet repelled,—often educated, yet shut out from all the prizes of life,—rich, yet despised—free, yet oppressed,—the sons of the whites, yet unacknowledged in civil and social existence—the son of blacks, yet aspiring to a more honorable position, and therefore ashamed of their parental stock;—ever in a false position, and suffering all the agonies of a wounded spirit.'

—Maria Weston Chapman, 'Haiti'

'Dans toutes les colonies, ces derniers sont toujours regardés avec mépris par les blancs, tandis qu'ils se croient fort au-dessus des nègres. On les appelle les *gens de couleur* libres; mais les colons ne peuvent leur pardonner leur origine. Placés entre les deux races, ils en forment une troisième en butte à la haine des autres, et ne savent pour qui prendre justement parti.'

—Gabrielle de P****, *Le Nègre et la Créole ou Mémoires d'Eulalie D**** (1825)

The kind of "interracial" family drama that had the potential to muddle Theresa's decision to press forward with her revolutionary convictions is explicitly connected to the development of one of the most prominent

The Trope of the Tragic "Mulatto/a"

"mixed race" tropes in all of Atlantic literary history: the tragic "mulatto/a." The tragic "mulatto/a" is normally characterized as a "mixed-race" person who finds him- or herself depressed, suicidal, fratricidal, and/or patricidal due either to his lack of identity or to her innate, biological corruption (see Sollors, 1997, 240). According to the stereotype, these individuals are often confused about whether they are more "white" or more "black," and they are often made to choose between their dual identities, passing either into "whiteness" (one of the most familiar presentations) or into "blackness." Those characters who choose "whiteness," even summarily so, are normally punished with death or worse, as in William Wells Brown's *Clotel; or the President's Daughter* (1853), while those who choose "blackness" are usually praised and esteemed, as in Frances Ellen Watkins Harper's *Iola Leroy, or Shadows Uplifted* (1892). Other figurations of the tragic "mulatto/a" present these characters as sexually depraved, weaklings, or even homosexuals, as in William Faulkner's *Light in August* (1932) and *Absalom, Absalom!* (1936), inevitably returning to the idea that they were somehow degenerate, corrupt, and, therefore, condemned to die in a tragic way because of their "mixed race," as in the portrayal of Cora in *The Last of the Mohicans* (1826).

Sterling Brown, who first called attention to the trope in 1937, has suggested that the stereotype or myth of the 'tragic mulatto' emerged because 'mulatto' characters lent themselves more easily to the theme of tragedy. 'The Negro of unmixed blood is no theme for tragedy,' he writes, 'rebellion and vindictiveness are to be expected only from the mulatto' (1982, 77). Eve Allegra Raimon, however, has suggested that with this designation Brown had wrongly given the trope a 'masculinist appellation' (Raimon, 5). Raimon argues instead that 'the very tragedy of the figure's fate depends upon her female gender' precisely because 'the sexual vulnerability of a female light-skinned slave is essential to propel the plot forward and to generate the reader's sympathy and outrage' (5). Theresa Zackodnik, who is also critical of Brown's 'definition' of the 'tragic mulatto' as a male figure (xv), adds that the trope was created by 'white female abolitionists' (xi), more specifically Lydia Maria Child (xiv), and was designed to 'function … in post-Civil War American literature as a sensationalized figure of ruined womanhood' (xi).

The literary history of the Haitian Revolution puts into immediate contestation not only the idea that 'tragic Mulattoes tend to be mulattas' (Peel, 231), but that such a figure was created in U.S. American fictions of the nineteenth century. As the many texts under examination in Part Three of *Tropics of Haiti* will attest, the theme of tragedy and the "mixed-race" character, whether male or female, far predates the mid-nineteenth-century work of U.S. authors like William Wells Brown and Lydia Maria Child, who are often credited with creating the figure (Raimon, 9, 26; Sollors,

1997, 231–34; S. Brown, 74–75; Zackodnik, xi–xiv).[1] The female incarnation of this figure appears to a great extent, for example, in both Emilie J...t's *Zorada; ou la Créole* (1801) and the anonymously published *La Mulâtre comme il y a beaucoup de blanches* (1803), as well as in Alphonse de Lamartine's *Toussaint Louverture* (1850). Moreover, the tragic male "mulatto" not only appears with some regularity in nineteenth-century French fiction, as in Anthony Thouret's *Toussaint, Le Mulâtre* (1834), Honoré de Balzac and A. de Poitevin de l'Egreville's *Le Mulâtre* (1824),[2] or Alexandre Dumas's *Georges*, but is actually more common than the female version, appearing in well over half of the Francophone fictional representations of the Haitian Revolution published in the Atlantic World. Building from the productive assertion of Jennifer Devere Brody that William Thackeray's Rhoda Swartz in *Vanity Fair* (1848) is a 'tragic mulattaroon' (27), I think we can only view the association between tragedy and "miscegenation" as a distinct part of an Atlantic, rather than a purely U.S., literary culture.

Léon-François Hoffmann has explained the appearance of the 'mulatto' in early nineteenth-century French fictions, in general, by suggesting that while 'blacks' were often portrayed as noble savages and 'good negroes' (1973, 138), the theme of '*batârdise*' haunted the 'mulatto' in Romantic French literature. This is because 'mulattoes' were associated with illegitimacy in nineteenth-century France, where being a 'bastard' was considered to have been the 'source of social malaise' and to have 'engendered a revengeful complex of envy' (1973, 235). This cycle of 'envy' and 'malaise' is precisely what leads the 'mulatto' towards the tragedy of parricide rather than towards mere monstrosity in fictions of the Haitian Revolution.

Although it may be true that 'mulattoes' in U.S. literature do not often 'play the role of martyr,' as Nancy Bentley has argued, and may not commit suicide as often as their female counterparts, in the context of the Haitian Revolution their tragic natures stem from the same rebellious and putatively 'natural desire for vengeance' as that to be found in the U.S. version (Bentley, 507–08).[3] Penelope Bullock explains this desire for revenge in the U.S. context by suggesting that the 'tragic mulatto' is usually:

---

1 Anne duCille contests the idea that the light-skinned female protagonists in Brown's *Clotel; or The President's Daughter* (1853) are even tragic at all: 'Brown didn't invent the tragic mulatta. Nor are his colored heroines strictly or even primarily tragic ... Instead of pining away for her daughter or lapsing into a neurasthenic swoon over her lost love, Clotel, through ingenuity and determination, thrice escapes from slavery, traveling hundreds of miles to rescue her child before she is cornered on that fateful bridge in the nation's capital' (455).

2 Published under the pseudonym of Aurore Cloteaux.

3 See also Berzon (1978, 74).

the son or daughter of a Southern white aristocratic gentleman and one of his favorite slave mistresses. From his father he has inherited mental capacities and physical beauty supposedly superior to that of the white race. Yet despite such an endowment, or rather because of it, his life is fraught with tragedy ... Suffering the degrading hardships of bondage, he becomes miserable and bitter. The indomitable spirit of his father rises up within him, and he rebels. (79)

In the male figure, rebellion often takes the shape of what Heather Hathaway has called an 'oedipal confrontation,' whereby the son seeks both to reverse the structure of power and domination imposed upon him by his own father and to get revenge for his father's non-recognition. Hathaway has observed that in many of fictions of the 'mulatto,' 'the violation of identity caused by miscegenation' exacerbates a desire for patricide in the son, who seeks to dismantle 'the alliance between "the father" as lawmaker, as ruler, ... by transforming *him* into the vulnerable, victimized role that the mother and son once occupied' (154, 165). It is precisely the "mulatto's" justification for and fulfillment of bloody revenge that makes him just as capable as a "mulatta" of generating both 'sympathy and outrage' (Raimon, 5), two sentiments which comprise the core of the powerful image of the tragic "mulatto/a" in the transatlantic print culture of the Haitian Revolution.

The image of the tragic "mulatto/a" can be also traced to late eighteenth- and early nineteenth-century French colonial writing, where the trope surfaced in conjunction with the idea of colonial plantation rebellion as an Oedipal family conflict. In 1785, Justin Girod de Chantrans recounted the characteristic parricidal consequences of "miscegenation" and incest that characterize descriptions of tragic "mulattoes":

> I will end this letter with an example of libertinage ... that is known all throughout the colony. An unmarried white man of about 50 years old or thereabouts, the father of numerous mulattoes and mulattas, had within his ranks a daughter with whom he fell in love ... he urged her every day to submit to his desires; everyday he was refused. At first, he tried to seduce her, but unable to, in this manner, conquer the repugnance of his daughter, he tried threats and eventually resorted to cruelty. (158)

Girod de Chantrans describes the woman's brothers as 'witnesses to the horrors of which she had been the victim,' and he says that they became so 'overtaken with pity and indignation [that] they strangled the father in his bed.' The brothers were soon thereafter arrested and executed, 'along with the sister, who was in on the plot.' Girod de Chantrans calls this situation a veritable 'catastrophe,' an example of 'cruelty armed with despotism and the most unbridled debauchery' (159). The utter calamity that this tragic family drama presented lay in the dual tragedies of incest and patricide that eventually led to the obliteration of a family. The kind of destruction of the family wrought by aggressive and/or incestuous "miscegenation" eventually became a stock narrative in the literary history of the Haitian Revolution.

In *Le Système colonial dévoilé*, Baron de Vastey also represented incestuous "miscegenation" as not only appallingly common in Saint-Domingue, but as one of the causes of the tragedy of plantation parricide. He wrote that the colonists refused to 'respect the laws of nature with respect to their illegitimate daughters [*filles naturelles*]' (1814a, 89) and elsewhere found that there were a 'great number of planters who were guilty of incest and other crimes against nature' (1817b, 100). For Vastey, suicide and infanticide were the logical consequences, even if still tragic reactions, to what he called the 'crapulous debauchery' of colonial rape and incest (1814a, 89). He asked:

> Is it shocking if we were susceptible to suicide and poisonings; if our wives closed off their hearts to the tender feelings of motherhood with cruel pity by causing the deaths of the dear and sad fruits of their love? In essence, how do you bear life when it reaches the ultimate depths of degradation and misery? When you must die a thousand times for one, in the cruelest of torments, when you are relegated to this deplorable situation without any hope of escaping from it; loving life, is it not a sign of cowardice? Oh, why give life to such unfortunates, who will be condemned for their entire lives to lead a frail existence in reproach and torment, in a long web of death without end, to snuff out such an odious life, was that such a great crime? It was compassion, humanity!!! (1814a, 71–72)

The miscegenated "interracial" drama of slavery that would inevitably lead to parricide, infanticide, and suicide, as described to differing effects in the works of Girod de Chantrans and Vastey, were also more explicitly associated with the events of the Haitian Revolution.[4] Antoine Métral wrote that parricide of the stripe described by Girod de Chantrans was the natural consequence of "miscegenation" in the revolutionary context of Saint-Domingue: 'Nature shudders when one thinks about the fact that the victors were the children of the blood of their masters mixed with that of the slaves; but a most unfortunate vengeance had filled their hearts, and left the colonists only with the choice of escaping or dying' (1818, 92–93). We also find similar characterizations of people of "mixed race" as exceptionally vulnerable to vengeful parricide in various other kinds of writing from revolutionary Saint-Domingue. Consider the following lines from a poem

---

4 The suicides of slave women from Saint-Domingue also appear in one fictional genealogy of a slave from Saint-Domingue. See Samuel Jackson Pratt's *Family Secrets: Literary and Domestick* (1797, 4:123).

published anonymously in the *Moniteur Général de la partie française de Saint-Domingue* on November 15, 1791, entitled 'Ode à la philanthropie': 'But what horde of rebels/Rushes maddened to carnage:/In his cruel hands, the Slave/Carries the torch and death./Stop, tool of parricide' (qtd. and trans. in Popkin, 2003, 514).

This word 'parricide' was used continuously in writing about the Haitian Revolution all across the Atlantic World, and it describes exactly what this very racialized revolution meant for many of those who lived through it or wrote about it afterward: it was a potentially deadly conflict between family members. The Marquis de Rouvray, for example, although not nearly sharing his wife's disdain for "mulattoes" and the '*affranchis*,' also linked the potential destruction of the colony to the parricidal consequences of "racial mixing." On that score, he urged the French colonists to grant the free people of color their rights in order to stave off a revolution, arguing:

> necessity requires that you create a law that would make them more like your equals than your enemies, to have them sit at your table, give them seats in your assemblies. If they fight for a common homeland [with you], nothing will equal their valor. Otherwise, they will turn this same valor against you, and after having stained their hands with the blood of the slaves, they will stain them with yours, and your battles will be filled with parricide. (qtd. in Métral, 1818, 79)

The cruel crime of parricide, when represented as the logical outgrowth of a corrosive combination of "miscegenation" and revolution, provided a rationale for viewing people of "mixed race" as responsible for both the Haitian Revolution's excesses and the annihilation of the family. As Susan Zantop has written of early nineteenth-century German representations of the Haitian Revolution, '[w]hen submissive women turn into man-eating hyenas, the family, clearly, is in deep trouble' (145); all the more so when these 'man-eating hyenas' are the children of those men they are described as seeking to 'eat.'

The parricidal Haitian revolutionary imaginings that resulted from thinking about the children of slave women and their masters as characters in a fatalist "interracial" family conflict was one of the primary ways in which the narrative of "mulatto/a" vengeance was spread throughout the nineteenth century. This is perhaps best demonstrated in the U.S. context by Harriet Beecher Stowe's best-selling novel *Uncle Tom's Cabin* (1852), arguably the most famous anti-slavery novel to have ever circulated in the Atlantic World (Parfait, 152). In Stowe's novel—which many contemporary critics have accused of contributing to the "racial" types found in the minstrel show (Lott, 222; Lhamon, 140; Fiedler, 400; Meer, 261) and about which the novelist James Baldwin once wrote, 'Here, black equates with evil and white with grace' (17)—a New Orleans planter by the name of Augustine St. Clare connects the possibility for a slave revolt in the United States to both Haiti ('San Domingo') and the children produced by "racial mixing." St. Clare states:

> there is a pretty fair infusion of Anglo-Saxon blood among our slaves now ... There are plenty among them who have only enough African blood to give a sort of tropical warmth and fervor to our calculating firmness and foresight. If ever the San Domingo hour comes, Anglo-Saxon blood will lead on the day. Sons of white fathers, with all our haughty feelings burning in their veins, will not always be bought and sold and traded. They will rise and raise with them their mother's race. (392)

Stowe's Augustine seems to have bought into the idea that during the Haitian Revolution people of "mixed race" had been parricidal owing precisely to the mixture of 'Anglo-Saxon' with 'African blood.' According to Bruce Dain, Augustine's comments also provide evidence that fears of 'Haitian-style race war ... had taken on complex racial overtones, based on American readings of the racial complexities of Haitian society, before, during, and after the revolution there' (82). In Stowe's rendition, the Haitian Revolution had little do with the literacy of the slaves involved, the European Enlightenment, or the French Revolution, but instead had everything to do with the concept of "racial mixing" and in all probability Stowe's own fears of such contact.[5] Her character's statement also more explicitly evokes pseudo-scientific debates about "race" by suggesting that 'Anglo Saxon blood' would operate powerfully on the ostensibly docile 'negroes' to produce the kind of 'haughty feelings' that would make a life of slavery unlivable, and therefore a repeat of Saint-Domingue's "racial" revolution on U.S. shores almost inevitable. Stowe's text thus demonstrates how the idea of the parricidal "mulatto" son, and the "racial" tropologies it revived, came to be practically indistinguishable from the idea of the Haitian Revolution. The conflation of the fact of the Haitian Revolution with the idea of the "mulatto" provided a powerful vocabulary with which to argue both for and against "miscegenation," abolition, and, ultimately, revolution.

One of the characteristics that distinguishes the inherent criminality of the tragic "mulatto/a" from that of the "monstrous hybrid" is the sense of regret and impending doom, or the psychological effect that committing sinful patricide was imagined to have produced in these 'sons of white

---

5 Stowe's novel also advanced a colonization thesis that would supposedly preclude "white" and "black" contact through the removal of freed slaves to either Haiti or Liberia (Stowe, 1852, 609-626).

fathers.' These sons were described as having been constantly pitted against their own family members by a logic of both revolution and family lineage that should have made all "blacks" slaves, all "whites" masters, all children the same *color* as their parents, and therefore all revolutionists "black" and all colonists "white." The way in which the "interracial" family produced a confusion of every idea of "race" and political loyalties, along with a tormented psychology of outraged leniency towards colonist-fathers, is featured in Métral's subsequently published *Histoire de l'expédition militaire des français à Saint-Domingue* (1841). Métral quotes a revolutionary of "mixed race" and former free man of color named Ferrand Ferrou as having chastised the French colonists for the mass drowning of the free people of color, so often evoked with horror in the literary history of the Haitian Revolution.[6] According to Métral, Ferrou ordered the guilty colonists to be rounded up for punishment, but instead of killing them he lamented, 'How has it benefited us to be connected to you by the most tender and sacred ties of nature, since our women are also your wives and your mothers; and without fear of being parricidal, you soak your hands in their blood.' Ferrou continued by reminding the colonists that those they had killed had been 'brothers, spouses, companions, loyal friends in servitude, in war, in liberty.' Ferrou showed ultimate mercy, however, by commanding the colonists in question to immediately leave the colony: 'Even though a justified resentment would beg of us to sacrifice you, go, cross that bloody ocean, and rejoin your own kind, and see in us your enemies, but not your executioners' (qtd. in Métral, 1841, 194–95).[7]

Ferrou's presentation of the relationship of the free people of color to the colonists as wholly familial, and his wish to avoid the revenge of further parricide, extends Doris Garraway's description of the sorts of 'colonial family romance' common in 'white Creole ideologies of desire and reproduction in French Caribbean slave societies' (2005a, 34), to include thinking about how the actual families produced out of such 'desire' would respond in the 'San Domingo hour.' In other words, the logic of 'desire and reproduction' constantly narrated in colonial writing oscillates between vengeance and clemency in the context of slave revolts and rebellions, especially where the family was concerned. That is to say that in revolutionary Saint-Domingue, the familial logic undergirding representations of "white" and "non-white"

---

6 Although detailed information about his involvement in the Haitian Revolution is hard to come by, General Ferrand Ferrou was reportedly at the head of a troop of soldiers made up of Polish defectors who fought for the side of the revolutionists during the wars in Saint-Domingue (see Pachoński and Wilson, 1986, 211).

7 John Relly Beard quotes from this passage verbatim (using his own translation) in his *The Life of Toussaint L'Ouverture* (1853, 260–61).

relationships formed not only an 'incestuous family romance' (Garraway, 2005a, 34), defined as a 'society in which white men placed themselves within the position of symbolic fathers of all the races ... while at the same time erecting a cult of desire around mixed-race woman and fantasizing their sterility' (34), but an "interracial" family drama characterized by tortured musings about the interpersonal consequences of revolutionary loyalties.

That "miscegenation" on the plantation, and the constant rape and incest it called forth, might make "black" sons want to kill their "white" fathers and vice versa in the revolutionary hour constitutes one of the primary tropes of the Haitian Revolution in late eighteenth- to mid-nineteenth-century writing. Within this particular discourse of writing about the Haitian Revolution, the "interracial" family drama, which has all the elements of classic Greek tragedy, including mistaken identities, *quiproquos*, unrequited love, suicides, infanticides, patricide, and all sorts of fratricide, those of "mixed race" were often depicted as being principally responsible for the bloody quality of the Revolution precisely because of their natural susceptibility to the twin passions of vengeance and parricide, as much as because of the epistemological problems created by plantation "miscegenation" and the onset of colonial revolution.[8] If the 'colonial family romance' can be used at the *macrolevel* as a metaphor to retrospectively describe colonial plantation sexual relations in the French Caribbean, the "interracial" family drama focuses on the *microlevel* of "interracial" relationships of various kinds, as they were imagined and portrayed to have existed during the Haitian Revolution and to have been affected by the broken, unknown, or artificially forged ties of kinship on the plantation.

Tragic figures of "mixed race" in the literary history of the Haitian Revolution act, in many ways, as much more than symbols for the fact that revolutionary loyalties and family ties were not nearly as clear-cut or as *commonsense* as plantation logic might at first suggest. In the chapters that make up Part Three of the present volume, we will see that forms of kinship on the plantation, which were nearly always portrayed as "miscegenous" in some way, were imagined to have complicated, severed, or destroyed the actual, rather than purely metaphorical, relationships of people narrated as being some kind of "interracial" family. In this section, then, I seek to

---

8 Sollors has argued that in critical literature the term 'tragic mulatto' 'seems to carry the sense of violent action, sentimentality, and denouement in an unhappy ending,' rather than suggesting the relationship between abolitionist fiction and the tragedies of Sophocles and Aeschylus (1999, 242–43). Here I use 'tragic' to denote both the 'unhappy ending' and the epistemological problems found in Greek tragedy that contribute to the tragic nature of the dramas of Sophocles and Aeschylus and many representations of the Haitian Revolution.

The Trope of the Tragic "Mulatto/a"

understand how "white" fathers were imagined to have treated their "black" sons and daughters during the Revolution, whether or not these children were biological. Similarly, I want to know how slave-mothers related to their children who had been freed and vice-versa, how did extended family members deal with being on different sides of the Revolution, and how were husbands and wives in "interracial" relationships imagined to have chosen sides? I propose to examine these questions not in the *big meta* sense of the generalities that we might find in the works of Moreau de Saint-Méry, but in the *little meta* sense of actual parent to child, sibling to sibling, spouse to spouse, extended family member to extended family member, and father-master to slave-son that we glimpse in the many histories, biographies, novels, short stories, plays, and poems of the Haitian Revolution.

A few examples drawn from various kinds of texts from within the literary history of the Haitian Revolution demonstrate how we might move from the realm of thinking about the more metaphorical sense of the "interracial" family common in political discourse (to be further explored in chapter eight) to that of the living family as represented in the more personalized tales of the Haitian Revolution that inform the corpus under study in this section. In the anonymously published novel *Oxiane; ou la Révolution de Saint-Domingue* (1828), the eponymous "mixed race" hero is described not only with a language of biological incongruity that recalls the trope of "monstrous hybridity," but with the vocabulary of tragedy, rampant in the trope of the tragic "mulatto/a." We are told that as a 'mulatto,' 'Oxiane had been born proud, sensitive, and generous. He possesses the qualities and defects of his double origin: he was susceptible to ardent passions, easily irritated, even more easily disarmed: a word, a gesture, a glance sufficed to dispel his anger' (1: 91). This sensitivity and generosity, derived from his 'double origin,' are precisely the characteristics that leave Oxiane open to becoming a tragic character. He remains uninterested in participating in the Revolution exactly because of his loyalty to a 'white' slave owner, M. Dubreuil, whom we later learn is Oxiane's father. We are told that Oxiane

> did not dare to evaluate at what point the revolt was legitimate [for the slaves]. His attachment to M. Dubreuil, his gratitude, an even more tender feeling, gave him a compelling reason to espouse the cause of the whites [*lui faisaient une loi impérieuse d'épouser les intérêts des blancs*]; but the affection of the negroes and the people of color for him, caused him to be regarded by them as the natural leader of their party (1:92)

Oxiane's biological connection to "whiteness" and his affection for his master provide him with the rationale for ultimately rejecting rebellion as the way to produce liberty for the slaves. He says: 'No, if I must begin by

The Trope of the Tragic "Mulatto/a"

becoming a murderer and an arsonist in order to become a liberator, I do not want this sad glory at all [*je n'envie point cette triste gloire*]' (2:197). Such a sentiment is shared by the character Domingue in a 1792 short drama about the early days of the insurrection entitled *La Mort du Colonel Maudit, ou les Anarchistes à Port-au-Prince*. In declaring that he would die for the 'whites,' Domingue says, 'It would be better to leave the black men slaves than to make of them thieves and assassins' (7). Nevertheless, in *Oxiane*, when John Dubreuil (the man we later learn is Oxiane's half-brother) succeeds in forcing Oxiane's love interest, a "white" Creole woman named Clara, to agree to marry him (John) in order to save Oxiane's life, the Oedipal drama and the kinds of epistemological problems it symbolizes surface once again. Oxiane eventually becomes filled with a desire for personal vengeance against John. Upon John's death, Oxiane learns that he has unwittingly precipitated the death of the man who turns out to be his own brother. The narrator tells us, 'The truth was at last known; [Oxiane] was the son of M. Dubreuil, and he had caused the death of his brother' (3:29). The tragedy of this 'fatal secret' (3:126) is summed up with the following description of Oxiane's feelings after his brother's death: 'disgust with his existence overtook him ... the future filled him with fear, the present weighed on his soul.' The narrator continues by writing that for Oxiane there was no longer a 'single moment in which this memory was not a torment' (3:29). The kinds of epistemological uncertainty that characterize both understandings of "race" and revolutionary loyalties are further called forth when Clara mistakenly believes that Oxiane has also murdered her father, who turns out to be alive in the end. The narrator tells us, 'she reproached her love [for Oxiane] like a parricidal thought [*elle se reprochait son amour comme une pensée parricide*]' (2:213). Oxiane's anxiety about having caused the death of his own brother, and Clara's anguish about being in love with the man she believes has killed her father, form part of a larger discourse of "miscegenation" circulating in the Atlantic World that associated both figurative and literal "racial hybridity" with the epistemic uncertainties of choosing sides during the Haitian Revolution, especially when those sides were marked not merely by political lines, but by familial ones.

There are also plenty of examples of how the tragedy of these "interracial" family dramas did not necessarily depend upon the idea of "biological" families of "mixed race," but could also characterize the kinds of families that were described as having been the result of coercive kinship on the plantation, which often forced the contact between slaves and their masters to become familial.[9] Though the eponymous character of Baron Roger's

---

9 For example, this kind of kinship inflected patricide occurs in the *Histoire des désastres de Saint-Domingue* (1795), wherein the author recounts the following tale: 'An

Kelédor, histoire Africaine (1828) is not a "mulatto" in the calculated sense of "racial" taxonomies, the trope of the tragic "mulatto" as an Oedipal family drama is performed in this narrative too, propelled by Kelédor's view of his slave master as his surrogate father. When Kelédor returns to the Spanish side of Saint-Domingue after serving in the *maréchaussée* in French Saint-Domingue,[10] he finds his wife Mariette unwillingly in the arms of their master's son, Don Manuel. Kelédor subsequently strikes Manuel to the ground and believes that he has killed him (we later learn that Manuel is actually alive). A combination of remorse and fear immediately sets in for Kelédor, who thinks of his master's family as his own and therefore of his master's son as a kind of brother, even if a romantic rival. In an attempt to process the consequences of his actions, Kelédor immediately thinks about the betrayal of the father-figure that his actions represented. '[W]hen I dared to think about it,' Kelédor laments, 'in what an abominable pit of sorrow and despair did I not find myself? I, a murderer! murderer of the son of my master, my benefactor!' (160–61). He continues by saying to himself, 'I am a madman, an assassin! Jésus, Mahomet,[11] I no longer have any God! the heavens and the earth both reject me' (161). Kelédor concludes these thoughts by musing on the successive loss of his first family at the hands of the slave-traders who captured him and the subsequent loss of his adopted family because of the entanglements of aggressive "miscegenation" that characterized plantation life. 'Stolen from my parents,' Kelédor bemoans, 'from my country, by circumstances, the chilling memory of which fills

---

inhabitant of Limbé, called *Châteauneuf*, had raised under his roof a black child, who was born on his plantation, kindness and habit caused him to cherish the child as if he were his own son. *Adonis*, reaching the age of 15, became the right-hand man [*la domestique de confiance*] of his master. He abused this position one day: Châteauneuf [*sic*] punished him and sent him to the garden to work; but soon enough, overcome with affection for his pupil, he called him back and he was back in his master's good graces. The passing of several years led to the entire forgetting of this fault on the part of the master, but the punishment never left the memory of the proud slave. The insurrection exploded: the unfortunate old man, aged 80, was taken by the rebels. His virtues and his humanity found grace for him before their eyes and they left him free within their camp, requiring only that he promise never to try and escape. At the end of several days, Adonis appeared; the sight of his master recalled to him the offense that he had received ten years before: that furious tiger threw himself upon his victim and immolated him.' The author punctuates the tale with irony by claiming to have seen the 'will of Châteauneuf' who like a good father, 'left to Adonis liberty, his wardrobe, and ten thousand pounds' (196).

10 For the *maréchaussée*, see chapter two of this monograph.

11 In his native Senegal, Kelédor had been a devoted Muslim. He reluctantly converts to Catholicism at the behest of Mariette, who makes Kelédor's baptism the *sine qua non* for their marriage.

The Trope of the Tragic "Mulatto/a"

me with horror, I was losing, by an even more cruel catastrophe, a second family' (162). The family drama of plantation rebellion in *Kelédor* that seemingly pitted fathers against sons and brothers against brothers became immediately symbolized by the very idea of "racial mixing." Importantly, it was the image of his own "black" wife in the arms of a "white" man that Kelédor could never shake and that caused him to fly into an inconsolable rage and ultimately 'give in to my vengeance' (159).

While some of the texts in the literary history of the Haitian Revolution attempt to preclude "interracial" romances before they could even occur, as in *Kelédor*, suggesting that these relationships could only produce feelings of rebellion (and, therefore, the possibility of parricide), many anti-slavery writers narrated "interracial" coupling as the way to create a *rapprochement* between the "races" (and, thus, the preclusion of revolution). "Interracial" romances depicting "white" men with "black" women in the context of Saint-Domingue and/or the Haitian Revolution were especially common in various kinds of abolitionist fiction set in Saint-Domingue.[12] For instance, one of the central intimate relationships in Joseph Lavallée's abolitionist adventure novel *Le Nègre comme il y a peu de blancs* (1789) occurs between a French man named Dumont and an African woman, and the majority of the story revolves around the African Itanoko's desire to marry their "bi-racial" daughter, Amélie, which he eventually does. Lavallée's text celebrates both the valiant actions of Itanoko and "interracial" marriages as proof that color prejudice against "blacks" has no natural, and therefore rational, basis.

Although less common, there were also abolitionist texts in which "interracial" relationships featured "white" women with men of color.[13]

---

12 See also Jean-Baptiste Radet and Pierre-Yon Barré's play *La Négresse; ou le pouvoir de la reconnaissance*, first performed in 1787. The play promotes "interracial" marriage by depicting an African maiden and her "white" French lover being urged to marry by the young man's father. The father tells the youngsters: 'Let's go my children, let us leave. Come, come to France and demonstrate a model of benevolence and humanity' (qtd. in Striker, 77 [my translation]).

13 The French author Adèle Daminois's novel *Lydie; ou la créole* (1831), set in Saint-Domingue, depicts an "interracial" romance between Lydie, a 'white' Creole, and a 'mulatto' slave named Astolfe. Daminois's abolitionist tale of "interracial" love between a "white" female and a "non-white" male is unusual in that most of the "interracial" romances of the Haitian Revolution depict "white" males with "black" females, especially for the purposes of encouraging abolition. A note in Daminois's preface proves how shocking such a story would likely have been to most nineteenth-century readers. She writes of the character Astolfe, who eventually marries Lydie: 'a slave; a mulatto! They will exclaim in reading my work; is it possible to attract the attention of delicate readers to such a being, and above all women readers who, finding with some reason their own color very pretty, cannot view without horror those who do not have the good fortune to resemble them' (vi). Daminois demonstrates that her aims were primarily to destroy

In an anti-slavery short story by Sophie Doin[14] a harmonious "interracial" relationship between a '*noir*' and a '*blanche*' in Saint-Domingue is put on display for the purposes of promoting abolition and an end to color prejudice. In the tale 'Blanche et Noir,' published in 1828, we see "interracial" love depicted as the cure to both slavery and feelings of violent rebellion.[15] Doin narrates the story of a 'black' character named Domingo who was ultimately unable to reconcile his anti-slavery goals with the violence of the impending Haitian Revolution. Referencing the Enlightenment literacy narrative of the Revolution, Doin writes of Domingo:

> But in enlightening himself, his thoughts were turned to the subjugated blacks, his unfortunate brothers; soon enough, he found himself shuddering while contemplating the degradation of the species [*la dégradation de l'espèce*], and the fatal effects of sanguinary power. This kind of natural philosophy was really dangerous in that era, where pride of caste sought to destroy everything. (2)

Even though the incongruity of Domingo's condition as a slave who is educated inspires him to rebellious thoughts, these thoughts lead him just short of committing the corresponding violent actions of the rhetoric of 'liberty or death' that would come to be considered germane to the logic of both the Haitian Revolution and Haitian independence. Doin describes the effects and limitations of Domingo's awakening as such: 'Domingo, elevated above the common fate of the slaves by … the knowledge [*les connaissances*] he had acquired, dared to think, and began to feel developing within him all the feelings of a free man' (4).

Doin's portrayal reveals complicated ideas about the connection between revolutionary aims and "interracial" love, however, when the narrator tells us that Domingo was not interested in participating in a bloody rebellion, because of a different sort of 'feeling.' Doin writes that, like other rebellious

---

color prejudice when she writes in the preface: 'There is something crazy and absurd in believing that one is a privileged being because one possesses a rosy skin and long hair, and given that three quarters of the globe is populated with men of the negro race, it is probable that this major segment cannot reasonably be consecrated to scorn nor to abjection and just because some Europeans have said so' (1:xiii).

14 Doris Kadish has written of these tales, 'Doin's works assign important roles to women that, although not equivalent to those partially played by men, indicate the moral and intellectual significance, if not superiority, she attributed to women and the degree to which their authority is envisioned as central to the future of Haiti' (1995, 114).

15 In the corresponding tale, 'Noire et Blanc' (1828), a 'black woman' named Nelzi saves her 'white' master from the impending insurrection, and "interracial" coupling is proclaimed a success when the character Eugénie exclaims, 'oh, how beautiful is this love here, white and black!' (8).

slaves, Domingo 'could have let himself become lost in the desire for vengeance; but love elevated him above color prejudice, love had taught him clemency' (5). More properly, it is Domingo's love for a 'white' woman that 'elevates' him, not above his slavery or even his "color," but above violent revolution. In fact, once Domingo and his lover, Pauline, get 'married' they are compelled to go hide and live in the woods in seeming perpetuity because of what their "interracial" relationship might mean during the Revolution and later in independent Haiti. Doin writes that it was only '[t]welve years later, when the Republic of Haiti had been gloriously seated on solid ground,' that 'we were able to glimpse, by accident, deep in a thick forest, a flawlessly constructed cottage. A black man and a white woman lived there; they lived off of the hunt and wild fruit; we admired the love and the sweet manners of the two spouses' (6).

This ending generates troubling questions about the relationship of "interracial" love to "black" freedom since while Domingo is hiding in the forest away from the 'scenes of carnage' of the Revolution, the revolutionaries are busy fighting for the liberty that will also eventually benefit Domingo and any subsequent children he may have with Pauline. The text therefore begs questions about the kind of "miscegenation" that is being promoted in 'Blanche et Noir' since "interracial" love is presented as a liberating salve to both slavery and the violence that produced Haitian independence.

An "interracial" romance is also central, perhaps more surprisingly, in the French planter H. Furcy de Bremoy's decidedly apologetic *Evrard; ou Saint-Domingue au dix-neuvième siècle* (1829). The pro-slavery romance of *Evrard* demonstrates the utter ambivalence that resulted from talking about and representing "racial mixing" in the context of the Haitian Revolution, whether for ill or for good. In a text whose author wrote that emancipation had produced 'the sad effect' of 'condemning' the colonists 'to be forever legally dispossessed' (viii), not only is an "interracial" romance sanctioned by a marriage in a church, but "interracial" children are allowed to prosper and thrive. The "white" Pauline and the "black" Valentin's marriage and creation of an "interracial" family in *Evrard* stands in stark and immediate contrast to the works of Daminois, Lavallée, and Doin, in which successive "miscegenation" is still precluded by the fact that "interracial" children are never born out of the amorous romances driving the central plot in these tales.

The Victorian abolitionist author Harriet Martineau's *The Hour and the Man* (1841) provides perhaps the most haunting vision of the ways in which even fiction writers with anti-slavery aims could be much more ambivalent when it came to the topic of the "interracial" family than their portrayals of "interracial" romances and "black" revolutionary heroes might at first suggest. Martineau's three-volume novel follows the family of Toussaint Louverture and his rebel chiefs Dessalines, Christophe, and Jean Biassou, along with some "white" planters whom Louverture protects. One of these planters is a man named Papalier who has an infant with a slave woman named Thérèse. Thérèse is described as a 'young negress' (1: 52) possessed of a 'beauty which was celebrated all over the district—a beauty which was admitted as fully by the whites as by people of her own race' (1:57). Despite his admiration for Thérèse's beauty and education, which he claims rivals Toussaint's own (1:72), we are told by the narrator that Papalier 'habitually and thoroughly' 'despised the negroes' (1: 69). Yet Papalier is unwilling to part with Thérèse, whom he tells: 'I cannot spare you, my dear' (1: 81). The one being whom Papalier can and does 'spare,' however, is his child with Thérèse. During a secret night march, the baby is on the verge of crying when Papalier rips the child out of Thérèse's arms and smothers it, effectively writing it and the revolutionary possibilities of both further "miscegenation" and patricide out of the story.

As these various iterations of the tragic "interracial" family drama that "miscegenation" could unleash attest, parricidal actions became a dominant ethos of early nineteenth-century attempts to narrate the Haitian Revolution. In the vast majority of fictions of the Revolution under consideration here, "interracial" mixing was considered to have produced the Revolution itself, reflecting and creating an ambivalence about "miscegenation" that became mediated through the variously demonized, enchanted, or tragic portraits of "mulatto/a" figures that populate nineteenth-century representations of the Haitian Revolution across the Atlantic World. The uses of the "mulatto/a" and "miscegenation" as either examples of peril or promise in various kinds of fiction about Saint-Domingue contain striking parallels to the uses of the Haitian Revolution in the literary history of the Atlantic World. As we will see in the works of Victor Séjour, Alphonse de Lamartine, and Eméric Bergeaud, whose works form the primary focus of Part Three of this study, in the nineteenth-century Atlantic World, the image of the "interracial" family was used both to encourage and discourage abolition, to exalt and to defame slave rebellion, and to celebrate and lament the work of various kinds of philanthropic and intellectual movements associated with the Enlightenment.

The binaries between celebrating and demonizing revolution, and vaunting and decrying "racial mixing" represent one of the primary reasons for which the two images—that of the Revolution and that of the tragically rebellious "mulatto/a"—were so closely interconnected in the nineteenth century. Depending upon the individual's optic, the "mulatto/a," like the Revolution, abolition, and Enlightenment thought, could be celebrated as the harbinger of *rapprochement* or demonized as the symbol of corruption and degradation. As the many fictions discussed in the three chapters that make up Part Three of *Tropics of Haiti* will show, the images of both the Haitian Revolution and the tragic "mulatto/a" became central and often interchangeable referents in the transatlantic anti-slavery movement.

CHAPTER SEVEN

"Black" Son, "White" Father: The Tragic "Mulatto/a" and the Haitian Revolution in Victor Séjour's 'Le Mulâtre'

'Perhaps the first chapter of this history, which has begun in St. Domingo, and the next succeeding ones, which will recount how all the whites were driven from all the other islands, may prepare our minds for a peaceable accommodation between justice, policy and necessity; and furnish an answer to the difficult question, whither shall the colored emigrants go? and the sooner we put some plan under way, the greater hope there is that it may be permitted to proceed peaceably to its ultimate effect. But if something is not done, and soon done, we shall be the murderers of our own children.'

—Thomas Jefferson to St. John Tucker (August 28, 1797)

'So it's the miscegenation, not the incest, which you can't bear.'

—William Faulkner, *Absalom, Absalom!* (1936)

In this chapter, through a reading of Louisiana-born author Victor Séjour's representation of the Haitian Revolution in 'Le Mulâtre' or 'The Mulatto,' originally composed in French and first published in Paris in 1837,[1] I consider the conflation of the literary history of the tragic "mulatto/a" with the literary history of the Haitian Revolution in one of the first short stories written by an American author of African descent. Séjour's

---

1 'Le Mulâtre' was first published in *La Revue des Colonies* by the radical anti-slavery journalist Cyrille Bissette. *The Revue* was a short-lived publication, running only from 1834 to 1842. For more on the *Revue*, see Brickhouse (2004, 89–94) and Bongie (1998, 266–79). For a full English translation of 'The Mulatto,' see Victor Séjour, 'The Mulatto,' trans. Philip Barnard, in *The Norton Anthology of African American Literature*, ed. Henry Louis Gates Jr. and Nellie Y. McKay (New York: W.W. Norton and Co., 1997): 287–99.

role in the development of the important and controversial figure of the tragic "mulatto/a" is crucial because, as David O'Connell has observed, '"The Mulatto" was Séjour's personal contribution to the French and U.S. American antislavery movements' and was thus 'not simply ... a blow struck for the cause of abolition in the French colonies, but ... also one of the first manifestations of a "literature of combat" written by an American black' (O'Connell, 1972, 61). Yet, even more importantly, with this story, Séjour—a man whose father was born in Saint-Domingue, but who lived the majority of his own life in metropolitan France[2]—once again links the U.S. African American literary tradition to a Francophone origin and ultimately to the literary history of the Haitian Revolution. The contribution of 'Le Mulâtre' to the same transatlantic print culture of the Haitian Revolution that had posthumously claimed Phillis Wheatley as its poet laureate thus suggests that a Franco-Haitian grammar of resistance to slavery continued to be one of the most abiding ways that the Atlantic hemisphere's people of color turned references to the Revolution into a trans-historical language for the political aspirations and frustrations of their own days.

In 'Le Mulâtre,' the primary vehicle for transmitting Séjour's post-Haitian emancipation anti-slavery message remains not simply a slave rebellion in colonial Saint-Domingue but the tragic "mulatto/a," who, in this story represents the more psychological, rather than purely biological, corruption of the family caused by plantation "miscegenation." Séjour's tale suggests that colonial plantation sexual practices would inevitably lead both the slave and the master, fathers and their sons, to a kind of dehumanization and degradation that was ultimately worse than slavery itself. Importantly, the deprivations of plantation "miscegenation" are not necessarily linked to acts of "interracial" sex proper, nor to the births of actual people called "mulattoes," but to acts of rape that are portrayed as being the locus of "interracial" sex on the plantation and therefore of all "interracial" (read:

---

2 Victor Séjour was born Juan Francisco Louis Victor Séjour Marcou-Ferrand on June 12, 1809 in New Orleans. He was said to be a 'quadroon' (Davidson, 1869, 501) and was the son of Juan Francisco Louis Victor Séjour Marcou (a 'mulatto' and a native of St. Marc, Haiti, who had fled to New Orleans during the Haitian Revolution) and a free woman of color named Cloïsa Philippe Ferrand (O'Connell, 1972, 60). Both the elder Séjour and his young son were members of a literary group called La Société des Artisans, in which various writers presented their poetry and other written works. With the passage of an 1830 anti-sedition law in Louisiana, however, which proscribed 'imprisonment at hard labour' or death for any person who made 'use of language' in public that could produce 'discontent' or 'excite subordination among the slaves,' these kinds of literary groups were severely stifled. The elder Séjour sent his son away because he was 'convinced that the teenager possessed exceptional writing ability and [was] anxious that he escape the onus of race prejudice in Louisiana' (Bell, 1997, 94).

plantation) families. 'Le Mulâtre' is primarily a tragic tale, then, because of the sexual violence that is presented as being germane to the development of the estranged and disaggregated "interracial" families that come to symbolize all human interactions on the colonial plantation. In this way, the social and emotional rape of both the bodies and minds of individual slaves, in addition to those of their family members, surfaces as the inherently tragic genesis of not only the "mulatto," but of all people of color on the plantation.

The plot of 'Le Mulâtre' is, in fact, wholly determined at the outset by the predominance of sexual assault. The tale is narrated by an old former slave named Antoine, who recounts the early days of the Haitian Revolution to an unnamed traveler. Antoine's *kont* takes place on a remote plantation in the hills of Saint-Domingue. It is the tale of a 'mulatto' slave named Georges, whose mother, Laïsa, was raped by her master, Alfred.[3] Georges remains unaware that Alfred is his father until directly after he kills him at the end of the story. When Laïsa dies, Alfred believes that his secret has also perished, and Georges becomes one of his favorite slaves; but when Georges attempts to alert Alfred to an impending assassination attempt at the hands of some of Alfred's own slaves, Alfred paradoxically begins to doubt his slave's loyalties, believing instead that Georges may have been a co-conspirator. Alfred soon after recognizes his error and ends up saving Georges from almost certain death at the hands of those same slaves. The story takes a turn towards rape again when Georges's wife Zélie (a 'mulatta') receives the punishment of death for raising her hand against Alfred after he attempts to rape her, too. Distraught and angry over his wife's death, Georges takes their two-year-old son and runs away to join the 'maroons' in the mountains of Saint-Domingue, vowing to return to his master's plantation to exact revenge when the moment is right. Revenge is exactly what Georges enacts years later when he kills Alfred's new wife and child and then beheads his former master. Just as Georges's hatchet strikes his head, however, Alfred has enough time to murmur that he is Georges's father. Believing that someone who has killed his own father is 'cursed,' Georges commits suicide and emerges as the very embodiment of the tragic "mulatto" stereotype.

Séjour's exposure of the sexual aggressions that arguably lay at the heart of all plantation "miscegenation" involving masters and their slaves brings

---

3 In Haitian Creole, the verb for story-telling is *tire kont*, which literally means to turn out a story. The names Georges and Laïza will also be used by Alexandre Dumas in his tale of rebel slaves on Ile de France (present-day Mauritius). In Dumas's *Georges* (1843), the protagonist is also a young man of color named Georges who befriends a slave named Laïza. Aside from using the same names, the two works contain a lot of similarities in theme and narration, which is perhaps not surprising given the authors' acquaintance with one another in France and their positions as men of color with origins in Saint-Domingue living in the metropole.

troubling questions to bear on the kind of celebratory notions of cultural hybridity or 'fusion' as to be found in the works of Séjour's friend, Cyrille Bissette. In 'De la fusion des deux races aux colonies et des causes qui la retardent' (1834), Bissette had written that eventually the 'white and the black populations in the [French] colonies' could:

> fraternize and join together, in everybody's best interests, to work the land in common, their shared homeland of today, in which a better organization of labor and the development of an eminently social feeling for the fraternity of man will turn it into a homeland that is for all of them as beloved as it is free, industrious and prosperous. (qtd. and translated in Bongie, 1998, 275)

Chris Bongie has written that for Bissette the 'formation of a creole society' was 'characterized not by the disappearance of the old racial identities ... but by a productive restructuring of relations between the three classes': "mulattoes," "whites," and "blacks" (1998, 274–75). 'Le Mulâtre,' however, functions as an ardent critique of the ability for the sort of "racial hybridity" or 'fusion' that had grown out of the violence of colonial slavery to actualize such a post-emancipation vision of freedom and prosperity. Indeed, when juxtaposed with Séjour's story, Bissette's rhetoric of productive rather than destructive "interracial" interactions might 'strike us' as not only 'painfully naïve' (Bongie, 1998, 275), but as discursively violent, especially for a person who had seen first-hand the kinds of relationships that were generated by slavery as a slave owner in Martinique. Bissette could hardly have been a stranger to the fact that 'fusion' on the plantation had always been an arm of power for plantation owners. In the words of Alicia Arrizón, '[m]assive miscegenation was facilitated by [the] social condition' of exploited classes in the colonial context, and it was the 'position of power' enjoyed by the colonists that made it possible for those in the ruling class to 'exploit women' (2006, 6). In short, using the concept of 'fusion' as a metaphor for the creation of a just society is inherently problematic since a much more literal "racial" 'fusion,' laden with subjugation, was being practiced at the very moment Bissette wrote these words. The kind of 'fusion' occurring on the colonial plantation is shown by Séjour, then, not only to have been the consequence of what James Arnold has called 'aggressive heterosexual desire' (1995, 25), but to have been, precisely at the moment in which Séjour was writing, occasioning the infinitely tragic destruction of the very kind of social organization that in 'Le Mulâtre' might have made the ever-dreadful life of the slave still worth living: the family.

Unlike in some of the more celebratory romances of Doin, Lavallée, or Daminois, in which "interracial" romances remain illustrative of constructive connections between "whites" and people of color, reproductive sex in 'Le Mulâtre' does not create radiating systems of kinship, but endless organisms of alienation. Séjour's tale does not offer opportunities for dynamic or fruitful relationships of any kind between people of different "races." The power structures instituted by slavery prevent *real* contact from occurring between "non-whites" and "whites," just as it prevents *real* contact from taking place between parents and their children. The vision of freedom through "interracial" love in Séjour's narrative, therefore, is merely chimerical, a distraction from the more material sexually coerced "interracial" sex taking place on actual plantations. Importantly, Georges obtains his liberty through the rebellion of *marronage* and not through any feeling of kinship developed out of the "interracial" sex between his father-master and his slave-mother. This representation of "interracial" love as destructive rather than productive challenges certain portrayals of "racial mixing," notably by Lydia Maria Child, as capable of leading to the success of non-violent abolitionism. Like a good naturalist character who is 'pushed far from the route of virtue' by some force outside of his own control, Georges is driven by narrative inevitability to use his self-actuated freedom to take the lives of his own "white" family members, including his father and half-brother, unknowingly destroying his own "interracial" family along with slavery. The message appears to be that the family—"white," or "black," or both—cannot thrive under the repressive social and legal conditions of the plantation.

What is most striking about Séjour's utilization of the trope of the tragic "mulatto/a" to narrate the familial consequences of slavery is precisely the fact that 'Le Mulâtre' weds the Oedipal structure of revolutionary thought with the Oedipal fantasies of the colonial plantation. Ronald Paulson writes that in the Oedipal model of the French Revolution, 'the son kills, devours, and internalizes the father, becoming himself the authority figure, producing a rational sequence of events' (8). In representations of the Haitian Revolution, this 'rational sequence of events' was very often imagined to mean that slaves would become masters and masters slaves, a reversal that contradicts a revolutionary project whose most popular narrative today centers on its desire to produce liberty for everyone. Georges's murder of his father-master, much to the contrary, relies less upon his desire to physically enslave Alfred than upon his desire to make his master know how it *feels* to be a slave. Contrary to William Wells Brown's assertion that during the Revolution, 'mulattoes took the lives of their white fathers, to whom they had been slaves, or who, allowing them to go free, had disowned them; thus revenging themselves for the mixture of their blood' (1855, 25), Georges initially wants to take his master's life not to avenge the 'mixture of his blood,' but in order to avenge the social structure of the plantation that prevented the slave from having a family of his own. Georges accomplishes this primarily by making Alfred experience the murder of everyone he loves. In this way, Georges forces his father into the role of emotional and social degradation that had once been his own province as the unrecognized slave-son of his master. Moreover, he compels his father to experience the same sense of social alienation, even if only fleetingly, that Séjour describes as being germane to every slave's life.

It is important to recognize that the main difference between the patricide of the tragic "mulatto/a" as it is represented in 'Le Mulâtre' and the way in which it is imagined to be the result of "monstrous hybridity" in *Bug-Jargal* is that in Séjour's short story the patricide is considered to be an actual consequence of an epistemological problem in the vein of Sophocles's *Oedipus* rather than a metaphor for the eventual outcome of a slave's (like Habibrah's) relationship to his master. The only reason Georges is even capable of literally rather than merely figuratively killing his father is because he cannot recognize Alfred's paternity and therefore cannot purposely avoid killing him, as Hugo's Biassou suggested one might have an imperative to do in the revolutionary context (see chapter three of this volume). What makes Georges appear tragic rather than purely despicable in this regard is that he does not set out to kill his father or to commission others to do it for him, but rather becomes unwittingly entangled in the web of secrecy and lies that forms the epicenter of slavery's "miscegenated" histories.

The plantation system was characterized by hidden and often-denied webs of kinship between "white" father-masters like Alfred and the children they produced out of relations with slave women like Laïsa. These secret webs of affiliation meant that in the revolutionary hour a father could not only be mistaken for an enemy by his son, but might actually have been the enemy of his son. If patricide is the Christian sin Hugo's Biassou claimed it to be, then a revolution could pose dire problems for both father-masters and slave-sons, whose "racial" loyalties placed them on opposite sides of the revolution's binary, but whose family ties should have precluded them from waging war against one another. Therefore, if 'Le Mulâtre' has both 'psychoanalytic significance and revolutionary relevance' (Vauthier, 1980, 91), in the pages that follow I want to explore how the narrative lamentation over the consequences of Georges's parricide makes him one of the wholly tragic "mulattoes" of the transatlantic print culture of the Haitian Revolution rather than one of its ardent 'political rebel[s]' (Sollors, 1997, 167).

*

Like Hugo, Séjour had a long-standing interest in the idea of parricide (Bem, 39–51). J. John Perret and M. Lynn Weiss each tell us, for example, that in his theatrical works, Séjour had 'a proclivity for having parents directly or indirectly cause the death of the progeny' (Perret, 188; Weiss, xxi). Yet Séjour's first literary effort depicted the opposite problem: patricide. In 'Le Mulâtre,' Séjour depicts plantation "miscegenation" as the ultimate impetus for such plantation patricide, not necessarily because "racial mixing" might cause physiological degeneration (as in the trope of "monstrous hybridity"), but rather because of the conscious and unconscious spiritual and psychological torments occasioned by being born as the tragic result of rape. Anna Brickhouse has written that 'Georges's murder of his master and father more generally represents the violent, patricidal inevitability of slave revolt' (2004, 118), but I would here like to link the fatalism of this patricidal narrative not solely to the slave rebellion described therein, but to the plantation "miscegenation" that is represented as its origin and that one finds incessantly narrated as the cause of the Haitian Revolution in the literary history of these events. Sollors has written that

> the son's search for the name of the father and of the father-son conflict culminat[es] in a lurid, unknowingly committed patricide in an interracial family structure in which a modern Oedipus or Job endures the loss of his mother and his wife, and has to make the agonizing discovery that the tyrant and villain he has decapitated in revenge is his own father. (1997, 167)

I am asking that we now consider the effect of this 'inevitability' and 'agonizing discovery' upon the son-slave, for whom this patricide represents a 'curse' and not the fulfillment of righteous vengeance. The accident of killing his father denies Georges both his coveted family and the pleasures of revenge when he learns that the man he has murdered is the very man he has sought his whole life; for, as much as Georges had desired revenge, he had desired a father more.

Throughout the narrative, Georges is plagued with a distinct longing to know the identity of his father and the origins of his birth. The narrator tells us: 'Georges had grown up without ever having heard the name of his father; and he tried at times to pierce the mystery that enveloped his birth, [but] he found his mother inflexible and mute to his questions.'[4] Moreover, we are told that Georges 'would have given ten years of his life to have known the name of his father.' Of this scene, Brickhouse writes: 'The withheld paternal name ... denies the slave his complete selfhood, his full capacity as a speaking subject within the colonial order' (2004, 122). This scene also turns on one of the central tenets of the tragic "mulatto/a" trope in the literary history of the Haitian Revolution precisely because of the epistemological

---

4 All quotations for this text taken from the web version established at: http://www.centenary.edu/french/textes/mulatres.html.

problems Georges encounters: he does not actually know the identity of his father nor that of any other sibling he might have, which, in the 'San Domingo hour,' leaves him open to the possibility of committing endless and unknowable levels of parricide, reflecting the larger existential as well as epistemological consequences of the Haitian Revolution.

The incessant representation in fictions of the Haitian Revolution of people of "mixed race" as having not only tortured biologies and psychologies, but convoluted genealogies which leave them open to parricide, coincides with the kinds of problems of knowing that W. Maurice Shipley contends the existence of "mixed-race" people posed for the American South:

> How was this mulatto individual to be treated? Was he Black or white? What laws were applicable to him or her? Would not the product of miscegenation serve to raise questions in regard to Southern mores and morality? Were not mulattoes a genuine threat to either an erosion or total collapse of the existing rules of separation of the races? (102–03)[5]

These questions are similar to those posed by the French colonists in the context of revolutionary Saint-Domingue: did "mulattoes" belong to the side of the white colonists or to the side of the black slaves? Were they the biggest threat to sustaining the colony under French rule?[6] And, perhaps most important, what was a "white" father's paternal duty towards his "black" child during a slave rebellion or revolution, and vice versa?

These questions can only be partially answered, or rather they can only be answered ambivalently, by analyzing 'Le Mulâtre.' The narrator sets us up to believe that Georges's initial affection for his master meant that he would indeed save him during any kind of slave rebellion. The narrator says of Georges's feelings for Alfred that it was '[a]s if nature was leading Georges to Alfred; he loved him, as much as it was possible for him to have loved a man.' Even though Georges's 'love' was not entirely reciprocated by Alfred—the slave owner merely evinces some 'esteem' for his son—Georges still attempted to alert his master to the assassination that some runaway slaves, described as a 'horde of brigands,' were preparing for the slave owner. If Georges's duty as a loyal slave or the *bon nègre* was to try to alert his master, who is described as 'perhaps good, humane, loyal even towards his

---

[5] Writing of "miscegenation" in the U.S. American plantation context, Paul H. Outka argues: 'The historical facts of sexuality on the plantation, and beyond, powerfully undermine our ability to keep the slave definitionally different. Suddenly we find out that the Other may not be so other' (311).

[6] See Philibert François Rouxel de Blanchelande, 'Proclamation,' in *Supplément au numéro 91 de La Feuille du jour* (March 31, 1792), 1–2; Garran de Coulon (1792), 15–17; and Popkin (2007), 112.

equals; but without a doubt, a severe and unkind man towards his slaves,' to the impending slave insurrection, the benefit of the doubt would only later be reciprocated. After initially suspecting that Georges had betrayed him, Alfred finally assumes his paternal duty when he flies to the aid of his son, who, being 'covered with wounds,' suddenly found himself 'saved by the very man who had accused him of betrayal.'

Given the stated 'love' and 'esteem' shared by these two men, only one of whom is aware of their genealogical relationship, it is worth thinking about how these confused and entangled affections between a slave and his master would eventually become muddled to the point of driving Georges to kill Alfred. Despite a description of the 'haughty and tenacious habits' [*volontés hautaines et tenaces*] that Georges derived from his 'oriental compositions,' and that would inevitably seem to lead him down the 'fearless path of crime,' the origins of Georges's Oedipal rebellion appear to lie much more in his desire to avenge his master's complete abuse of his paternal authority as a slave master than in his "mulatto" biology. The filial duty of the slave, like the filial duty of the son, becomes disfigured in 'Le Mulâtre' by the father-master's social transgressions of his own paternal duties.

In the colonial context, a father-master's paternal duty had, of course, to be differentiated from his legal duty. His legal duty, according to both Southern and French colonial law, was to treat the child as a slave, but in French Saint-Domingue, as in antebellum Louisiana, many fathers often defied this legal duty in favor of what they saw as their paternal duty. In his influential *Description ... de la partie française de Saint-Domingue*, for example, Moreau de Saint-Méry imputes the father-master's manumission of his slave-children to both 'paternal affection' for them and to his own 'self-respect,' highlighting the idea that being the father of a slave or otherwise non-free person was not a respectable position precisely because a master should not have 'affection' for his slaves and a father should not enslave his own sons (1797, 1:68). Girod de Chantrans attributed what he viewed as a tendency towards manumission of "mixed-race" children to the suggestion that "white" colonists who took women of color for mistresses became kinder slave masters who were able to temper their overall prejudices because 'it is not natural to mistreat she who procures and shares with us the most grand of all the pleasures' (185). Even though there were certain social and practical considerations for seeking to differentiate people of color from "whites" *tout court*, what Carolyn Vellenga Berman has called the 'French colonial tendency' of Louisiana Creoles to create "mixed-race" families confounded the U.S. American understanding of property inheritance and ultimately the domestic in the nineteenth century because it allowed those of "mixed" descent to claim property rights and even reverse the terms of the slave system by owning their own slaves (338). Carolyn Cossé Bell adds:

'In some instances, the offspring ... inherited considerable wealth upon the death of their white father' (112).

The literary history of the Haitian Revolution incessantly describes the consequences of a proliferation of people of color living on the plantation who were often *in* the house, but were certainly not considered to members *of* the house, and who were very likely *in* the family, but not necessarily considered to be members *of* the family. Slave-holding families were often narrated as having been threatened by the presence of these illegitimate children, who, depending upon the situation, might have found themselves in a position to claim the rights of inheritance.[7] The very idea that a slave master's recognized son and unrecognized son might eventually find themselves embroiled in a fratricidal combat over inheritance is wholly demonstrated in *Oxiane; ou la révolution à Saint-Domingue*, for example, when John Dubreuil seeks to destroy his 'mulatto' half-brother precisely in order to avoid having to share his father's property with him. Before we know that Oxiane is John's brother, Folbert, a French soldier under John Dubreuil's command, describes Oxiane as his superior's potential rival. Folbert tells John that Oxiane has essentially become 'the adopted son' of M. Dubreuil (63), and Folbert says that one day Oxiane may even become the elder Dubreuil's inheritor since 'the old man has not forgiven you for your adventures' (63).[8] Even though, unlike Séjour's Alfred, M. Dubreuil treated Oxiane as his 'adopted son,' like Alfred he did not want to publicly acknowledge that Oxiane was actually his biological son. Oxiane's father even destroyed the papers that would have proven that he had been legally married to his son's mother, Zaïde, and thus that Oxiane was a 'fils légitime' (2:104). According to Simone Vauthier, such denials of the genealogical ties between planters and their slave children allowed slave masters to uphold the idea that a distinct separation existed between the "races" and therefore to affirm the 'opposition white/non-white' (1980, 88). Vauthier writes: 'The planter may scatter his seed indiscriminately as long as he refuses to acknowledge his offspring, he can keep his blood-line pure and his dynastic order working' (1980, 84).

In 'Le Mulâtre,' the image of the slave-master who does not acknowledge the existence of his offspring and even enslaves them, not only produced material consequences for the master-father's children, but was painted as having spiritual consequences for him as well, namely, in the form of the

---

7 Brickhouse writes: 'As a mulatto in the French West Indies, Georges occupies a racial and cultural position of liminality, lying unstably between the "most miserable shack" of the slave and the educated gentleman that Georges has the legal and social potential to become in later adulthood, if his paternity is acknowledged' (2004, 117).

8 John Dubreuil *fils* had been accused of rape while living in France (1:22–23).

"Black" Son, "White" Father

dishonor that this behavior could potentially bring to his non-slave family. Alfred's sense of dishonor over his personal history of "racial mixing" is illustrated in 'Le Mulâtre' when the slave owner refuses to formally recognize that Georges is his son and therefore has both the child and the mother sent away from his sight immediately after Georges's birth. Alfred's shame and embarrassment is highlighted by the fact that he forbids Laïsa ever to speak of him as Georges's father. Consequently, Laïsa tells Georges: 'You don't know then that he has forbade me to speak to you of him under the threat of hating you ... and don't you see, Georges ... the hatred of this man, that's death.' Laïsa's warning, in essence, prepares us for understanding how in 'Le Mulâtre' the total 'natal alienation' (Patterson, 5) of the slave from his own father, who would kill him in order to continue to deny any *filiation*, was the primary cause of the son's rebellion in the revolutionary hour.

Such images of familial alienation caused by embarrassed colonial fathers and the threats of physical violence on both sides that they carried, were widespread in fictions of abolition (for example, in *Clotel, or the President's Daughter* [1853]), and they also appear with some regularity in the literary history of the Haitian Revolution. In Lamartine's 1850 play *Toussaint Louverture* the "white" colonist father of Adrienne, Louverture's niece of "mixed race," 'swears' 'never, had I been intimate with this abject race/ ... /that no child of the slave, during that dishonorable journey,/had received from me, along with the light of day, shame' (lines 1909–12). In order to keep this entirely undignified secret from General Leclerc, Salvador commissions one of his minions to kill his own daughter, whom he had previously sold into slavery along with her mother. As with Séjour, it is the non-recognition of paternity itself that allows Adrienne to join the side of the revolutionaries and sets up her potential to commit patricide.

This kind of 'natal alienation' not only made the father the 'natural enemy of his son' (or daughter), as we see in William Faulkner's own indirect representation of the Haitian Revolution, *Absalom, Absalom!* (1936, 83), but always set up revolutionary violence to become patricidal and infanticidal. For we must not forget that the slave, too, was often conceived of as the 'natural enemy' of his master. Orlando Patterson's writing about the ways in which the slave master's relationship with his slave necessarily existed upon a tendentious authority that depended upon diffusing the natural animosity of the slave for the master, is illuminating in this respect: 'In all slaveholding societies the slave posed grave moral and spiritual dangers,' Patterson writes:

> The master's task, then, had both a negative and a positive aspect. On the negative side, he had to diffuse the potential physical and spiritual threat posed by his slave's presence. And on the positive side, he had to secure

extracoercive support for his power. Both were achieved by acquiring the thing we call authority. (36)

On the plantation, although 'brute force' was almost universally considered to be 'indispensible' (Patterson, 3), it was hardly ever used as the only method of acquiring such authority. While whipping was one of the many material tools slave masters used to cement their authority, other conceptual and, arguably, more socially effective tools, including naming, clothing, and particular living arrangements that were all designed to keep the slave in his or her place, so to speak, by creating a sense that it was 'normal' for some to be masters and others to be slaves (Patterson, 8).

Is not this naming, adorning, housing, and punishing the same way in which a parental figure creates his authority over a child as natural and unquestionable? What makes Alfred's authority much more difficult to bear than any despotic father's remains his most effective 'extracoercive support': the persistent threat to disrupt the ties of kinship between a mother and her son, a sister and her brother, a husband and his wife. The planter's ability to disrupt the ties of kinship, a fate that was perhaps worse than physical death because it condemned one to live a life of what Patterson calls 'social death' (Patterson, 8), is immediately illustrated in 'The Mulatto' when the narrator says, 'Here, one sells the husband without the wife; there, the sister without the brother; over there, the mother without the children.' Like most novels of slavery, the slave master's ability to punish his slaves by selling or killing their family members creates a sense of psychological and emotional terror that constitutes a symbolic whip. Not only is there the omnipresent threat that Alfred might kill or sell Laïsa's son if she revealed his secrets, but Alfred denies Laïsa the possibility of a relationship with her own brother, Jacques Chambo, when he mistakenly believes that the two are carrying on a love affair. Alfred is also responsible for the death of Georges's wife, totally disrupting his son's attempt to construct a family in the void left by Alfred's denial to him of an ancestral family, including his uncle. Patterson calls all of this a 'social death' because, he says, 'slaves differed from other human beings' (5), not only in that they were 'natally alienated' (6), but in that 'they were not allowed freely to integrate the experience of the ancestors in their lives, to inform understandings of social reality with the inherited meanings of their forbears, or to anchor the living present in any conscious community of memory' (5).

There has been much debate in the historiography of slaveholding societies about whether or not the kind of 'authority' and repression of memory and community sought by Alfred could ever have been fully achieved by a master, on the one hand, and whether, on the other, this 'authority' truly had the kind of existential and ontological consequences of 'social death' described by Patterson.⁹ It is not necessary to enter into this debate here. What is important is that even if this 'authority' or total 'social death' cannot have been fully achieved because, aside from sparking slave rebellion, we now know that slaves created communities and complex systems of communication as well as diverse, alternative webs of kinship, this is not so in Séjour's short story. Séjour represents Alfred as having the kind of total 'authority' that Patterson describes, most likely because of the widespread way in which the narrative of "mulatto/a" vengeance, as the inevitably violent response to the authority of father-masters, was so successfully transmitted across the transatlantic print culture of the Haitian Revolution both before and after Séjour's time.

Europeans who traveled to Saint-Domingue often understood the slave master's authority as being total and absolute, and they almost always depicted it as such. The British planter and travel writer Bryan Edwards, for example, wrote in his widely reprinted historical survey of Saint-Domingue:

> In countries where slavery is established, the leading principle on which government is supported, is *fear*; or a sense of that absolute coercive necessity, which, leaving no choice of action, supersedes all questions of *right*. It is in vain to deny that such actually is, and necessarily must be, the case in all countries where slavery is allowed. (3:36)¹⁰

Furcy de Brémoy similarly wrote in 1833: 'If after one has resided in the colonies, one acknowledges that a lot of the inhabitants treat their slaves with too much inhumanity, one would be forced to admit also that in order to be obeyed by the slaves, one has to manage them with the utmost severity' (qtd. in Hoffman, 1973, 58).¹¹ Such information easily and incessantly found its way into fictional descriptions of the Haitian Revolution as well. In M.M. Baignoux et A***'s 'Augustin, ou la révolte des noirs' (1843),¹² a slaveholder named M. Brianchet tells his son Augustin, who has recently returned to the colony from France and is subsequently horrified by the Italian overseer Pernetti's constant 'mistreatment' (294) of the slaves on his

---

9 For challenges to Patterson's argument, see Morgan (1998), Turner (2004), and V. Brown (2008).

10 This passage is also quoted in Dayan (1995, 207).

11 Originally from H. Furcy de Brémoy, *Le Voyageur poète* (1833).

12 In 1843, Pierre Philippe Baignoux et M.A.***, published a collection of stories entitled *Amélina, Godefroy et Augustin ou les trois époques d'Haïti*. The last of these stories, 'Augustin, ou la révolte des noirs,' was published anonymously. Although the final story was written by Alexandre Duboy, who 'removed the anonymity' when in 1846 he published *Godefroy et Augustin, ou deux épisodes de l'Histoire de Saint-Domingue, avec une notice sur la découverte de cette île*, it has most often been attributed to Baignoux. The story 'Amélina' was signed by Baignoux, and 'Godefroy' was signed by M.A.***.

father's plantation, 'in order to impose upon the slaves, you must know how to look them in the eye [*il faut savoir les regarder en face*], and in order to be obeyed, we must use a language other than sweetness' (302), a reference to Pernetti's endless whippings.

Moreover, Séjour would have only had to take a look at Louis XIV's *Code noir* (enforced in both the French Caribbean and French Louisiana) to derive the idea that the legal status of the master was designed to produce both total 'authority' and the 'social death' of the slave. Although the *Code noir* strictly outlawed excessive brutality against slaves, because it did not 'permit the slave to play any role in the arena of law and right,' it set slaves up to 'exist legally only insofar as they disobey[ed]' (Dayan, 1995b, 209). As Dayan has pointed out, while these codes were often 'heralded as defining and prohibiting brutality,' 'the Code's most rational language makes no sense' because it 'allowed planters to hide behind legality,' and thus the *Code's* 'commitment to protection [became] a guarantee of tyranny' (210, 207). This is because 'owners were barely punished,' if at all, for harming their slaves, but slaves were punished harshly if they harmed their masters or ran away: 'for maroons, branding with a *fleur-de-lis*, cutting the hamstring, or, after the third escape, death' were merely a few of the gruesome punishments that the *Code* sanctioned (C. Miller, 2008, 28). The pseudonymous Gabrielle de P***'s Eulalie recognized as much when she wrote, 'there had been made for the colonies, under the title of the *Code noir*, a collection of laws that in appearance gave negroes certain guarantees, but so weak and so ill respected was it, that it is almost ridiculous to even mention it' (1:40). Furthermore, Eulalie says that the rights supposedly granted to the slaves by the *Code noir* were undermined by an attempt to render them into objects rather than persons. She writes, 'an act put forth in Châtelet in 1705,' had 'declared blacks to be the *merchandise* [*meubles*] of their masters, like the livestock of the cattle ranch, to whom they had been compared' (1:43). Finally, in 1771, Louis XVI issued an edict that Dayan says 'reduced humans to proprietary objects' (1995b, 213). The edict read:

> It is only by leaving to the masters a power that is nearly absolute, that it will be possible to keep so large a number of men in that state of submission which is made necessary by their numerical superiority over the whites. If some masters abuse their power, they must be reproved in secret, so that the slaves may always be kept in the belief that the master can do no wrong in his dealing with them. (qtd. in Goveia, 44)[13]

Séjour is not alone in the nineteenth-century anti-slavery transatlantic literary tradition in representing the master as having the complete social

---

13 Original in Pierre de Vaissière, *St. Domingue, 1629–1789* (1909).

and legal 'authority' described in so many accounts of colonial Saint-Domingue. In the U.S. context, Wells Brown also described the master as having 'power ad infinitum over another' when he argued that slavery was a system 'where we find one man holding unlimited power over another' (2006, 4). We might say, then, that in the mid-nineteenth century, it was not yet necessary to demonstrate all of the ways in which slaves found methods of subverting that 'authority' in order to create a distinctly "black" American identity and culture, and therefore to mitigate, reduce, or eliminate the effects of 'social death.' Creating a distinctly "black" American identity would become a project of later nineteenth-century African American novels like *Iola Leroy*, where the slave's complex system of communication is demonstrated and where the ties of broken kinship are reinstated during Reconstruction. In Séjour's tale, much to the contrary, it was not the slave's methods of communication or his recovered family ties that contained the liberating possibility to subvert the authority of the master, it was rebellion, and rebellion alone. This is because it was only revolution that contained the possibility to disrupt the master's own 'belief,' and overturn the law's attempt to legally perform into existence such beliefs, that the master could 'do no wrong.'

Being privy to the ending of the story, we know that at some point Alfred's total authority breaks down. Interestingly enough, this authority is not broken down by the initial slave rebellion. The impetus for this breakdown is instead the refusal of one of his female slaves to share his bed. When Zélie refuses Alfred, it is as if her refusal creates recognition or awareness that it was actually possible to transgress or at the very least resist this authority. It is perhaps ironic that the catalyst for Alfred's loss of authority over his plantation stems from his sexual exploits, since his sexuality constitutes one of the things he uses to procure total authority in the first place. By creating sexual relationships with slave women based upon terror and fear, Alfred attempts to ensure that any progeny resulting from these relationships will share that same terror and thus reproduce a psychology of "white" dominance over "black" submission. Patterson writes:

> From the community at large, authority came with the institutionalization of the slave relationship. It was achieved by incorporating it into the normative order ... Those who were not directly involved with the relationship—though indirectly influenced by it—had to come to accept it not just grudgingly, but as the normal order of things. (36)

In the plantation economy, Alfred represents both father and master, and as a son and a slave Georges should have submitted to his master's authority—'the normal order of things,' in both instances. Zélie's rebellion and Alfred's inhuman treatment of her, however, teaches Georges that there was nothing 'normal' about slavery nor about Alfred's attempt to force a woman to sleep with him against her wishes. It is certainly Georges's complicated genealogy as both son and slave of his master—or, in Sollors's terms, 'neither black nor white yet both'—that sets him up to play the tragic "mulatto," but also ties Séjour's narration of the grievances of the slaves more formally to the tragic terms of the "interracial" family drama.

*

If his untenable position as the son and the slave of his own father is in some ways narrated as being more responsible than his biology for the feelings of rebellion that would eventually lead Georges to commit patricide, the threat of rape and incest on the plantation only served to heighten these feelings. Our combination of the treacherous father-master becomes a figuration of the haunting father-rapist when Antoine narrates Alfred's total assault on the will of Georges's mother: 'he ran his indecent hands over the powerful, half-naked breasts of the beautiful African ... I will not tell you all that he did to possess her; because she was almost raped.' As a female slave, Laïsa is legally powerless to repel her new master's touch since, in Saidiya Hartman's words, a slave woman's very status as a non-person on the plantation 'presume[s]' that she is 'always willing' (1996, 539). In concert with this idea, we are told that Laïsa eventually began to 'share her master's bed.' Even though the narrator tells us that she had been 'almost raped,' meaning that she did not fully resist, Laïsa was still a victim of an unwanted sexual relationship precisely because her status as a slave precluded the very notion of resistance.

The complicated way in which rape becomes narrated, or specifically un-narrated, by the voided legal ability to resist, is a direct function of the slave woman's complicated relationship to agency. For example, in Baron Roger's *Kelédor*, when Kelédor discovers his wife in her master's arms, he is not quite sure if Mariette was a willing participant or not. The narrator writes, 'I enter into Mariette's bedroom, and what do I see? Oh, Righteous God, who did not see fit to mitigate my anger just then! It was Don Manuel holding Mariette in his arms, Mariette in tears, but not pushing him away! [*mais ne le repoussant pas*]' (159). Because Mariette does not outwardly appear to resist by pushing Don Manuel away, Kelédor is momentarily confused. Was her submission the result of her own desire for her master or the result of Don Manuel's total abuse of his power over her? Kelédor ultimately decides that the latter is the case and concludes, 'Don Manuel, abusing all the influence of his family, all of the authority that his position gave him, without a doubt had betrayed her trust and assaulted her candor [*violenté sa candeur*]' (161).

The resistance of slave women is similarly complicated in 'Le Mulâtre' because it is shown to have involved making vexing compromises that might better position one to survive. When Laïsa is being sold in the slave markets, she asks the vendor: 'and if he [Alfred] doesn't please me [as an owner]?' The vendor replies: 'My goodness, that would be unlucky [for you] because [the sale] is complete.' In many respects, Laïsa's attempt to have a say in who would become her next master can be viewed as a part of the 'intricate bargaining that preceded the final deal' in slave markets, a bargaining in which slave traders often had 'to rely on the slaves to sell themselves' to buyers (W. Johnson, 8, 16), but also in which slaves like Laïsa often attempted to resist being sold to masters they feared.[14] The narration of the sale provides a description of Laïsa's attempt to exercise her own will by resisting being sold to Alfred and later by resisting his sexual advances. The narrator even provides an account of all the things that Alfred had done, which the narrator finds too horrible to name, in order to fully 'possess' Laïsa. Since Laïsa's status as a slave woman made her will negligible, if not non-existent, she eventually does sleep with Alfred. Because we have already been told that she finds Alfred repulsive and dangerous when he purchases her in the slave market, the *kont* suggests and we are permitted to believe that her perceived willingness is that which preserves her life, as with Linda Brent in Harriet Jacobs's *Incidents in the Life of a Slave Girl* (1861). In other words, Laïsa's eventual *consent*, a reversal of her initial 'insolence' towards Alfred, may reflect an attempt on her part to use her will to transgress the depravity of physical death by consenting to live a life of 'social death.' This bold attempt to assert a compromising will is ultimately as complicated as Linda Brent's *decision* to sleep with Mr. Sands rather than Dr. Flint in Jacobs's tale (Jacobs, 85).

Although Laïsa was in many ways powerless to oppose the sexual advances of Alfred, Georges's 'mulatta' wife, Zélie, 'the virtuous slave, full of noble indignation,' was able to 'repel him in a last effort, but so briskly, and so powerfully, that Alfred lost his equilibrium and hit his head in falling down.' Zélie suddenly understands the implications of injuring her master for a woman in her position. Antoine tells us that Zélie, 'at this sight ... pulled out her hair in desperation, and cried with rage, for she understood, the poor woman, the death that awaited her for having made blood flow from such a vile being.' If we agree with Hartman that a slave is perhaps not, as Patterson argues, a 'socially dead' person, but is rather a 'bifurcated subject' under the intense weight of being both 'person and property,' then we can understand

---

14 A similar attempt to narrate the depredations and negotiations of the slave market in Saint-Domingue occurs in volume two of Elizabeth Anne Le Noir's novel, *Clara de Montfier* (1808).

the dilemma for every slave woman: legally she 'could neither give nor refuse consent' for sexual relations, and therefore could never be raped or have other crimes perpetrated against her, but she could be the perpetrator of crimes herself and be punished (Hartman, 1996, 538, 540).[15] Zélie's 'desperation' and tears therefore reflect her recognition that she cannot legally resist her slave master, and that in forcefully doing so, she has committed a capital offense, for which the punishment would be hanging.

The sexual politics of "miscegenation" are here all caught up in the Oedipal structures of revolution and its epistemic violence. When Georges begs Alfred to save Zélie's life, he reminds him: 'you and I alone know that she is innocent.' Georges's statement returns to the idea that "racial mixing" was an embarrassment in the United States as well as in the French colonies (women of color were good enough to sleep with, but not good enough to become wives), yet it also reminds Alfred that he is the father of a slave-son and that he has attempted to commit either figurative or literal incest with his own daughter, since he is effectively 'desiring the woman who is structurally, and very likely also biologically, his daughter' (Brickhouse, 2004, 124). What is even more striking, if that is possible, than thinking about Alfred as having attempted to rape his own daughter (and Georges as having potentially married his own sister) is that we must now consider that Zélie was actually the first to attempt to commit the unhallowed patricide that unrecognized ties of kinship could always make possible in the context of slave rebellion, for Alfred is either her father, her father-in-law, or ... both.

Zélie's bold martyrdom may make her a tragic "mulatta," but it also makes her the heroine of the tale. Zélie's refusal to do Alfred's will is what placed the surety of his power as a master into question and threatened to disrupt his total authority over the plantation, in much the same way that the Haitian Revolution and its attending creation of an independent nation-state greatly populated by former slaves threatened the entire system of Atlantic slavery. When Georges reminded Alfred of his sexual exploits, the narrator tells us: 'At this last speech of the mulatto, blush began to rise in Alfred's face and anger in his heart.' Alfred's anger at being reminded of his 'libertinage' and inability to assault Zélie sexually causes him to send Georges away and out of his sight, just as he had when Georges was first born. When Alfred tells Georges to leave, Georges explains to him the unnatural nature of the sequence of events leading to Zélie's arrest: 'I say

---

15 In his study, Patterson refuses to treat slaves conceptually as property since, 'to define slavery only as the treatment of human beings as property fails as a definition, since it does not really specify any distinct category of persons. Proprietary claims and powers are made with respect to many persons who are clearly not slaves' (21), by which he meant primarily children and spouses.

that you are a scoundrel ... she will die because she did not prostitute herself to you ... to you because you are white ... to you because you are her master ... infamous corrupter.' The logic of slavery's sexual, racial, and legal politics is laid bare in this passage. Georges explicitly notes that Alfred believes that he is sexually entitled to slave women who are legally forced to sleep with him, or be punished with death; he thus calls Alfred's virility into question (why does he have to force women to sleep with him?), and he also blames "white" men, rather than women of color, for the disastrous and corrupting effects of "miscegenation"—an important reversal.

Importantly, if Georges now wants to rebel against his father-master, this is presented to us as the logical response to his suffering at the hands of that same father-master, rather than a physiological reaction resulting from the mixture of his father's "white" blood with his mother's "black" blood. It is Alfred's excessively sexual and decidedly non-paternal attitude towards his son's wife that creates a desire within Georges to break free from the chains of slavery (we find out that he has run away to join the maroons in the mountains of Saint-Domingue), but it also produces a desire for revenge in Georges. He wants to institute what the French call the *loi du talion* or 'an eye for an eye, a tooth for a tooth.' He therefore vows to wait and kill Alfred at the 'moment where precious and dear ties attach him to this world.' Georges wants to wait until a physical death detaches Alfred from all of the things that make him socially alive, namely a wife and a child, which Georges, as a slave, or a 'socially dead' person, will forever be denied.

At the very beginning of 'Le Mulâtre,' Antoine describes the way in which the sexual, social, and legal politics of the plantation inevitably created a psychology of rebellion in the slaves despite being designed to create a psychology of defeat:

> a negro is as vile as a dog ... society repels him; men detest him; the laws curse him ... Ah! that is a truly unlucky being, who does not even have the consolation of being always virtuous ... If he is born good, noble, generous; if God gives him a loyal and grand soul, despite all of that, more often than not, he goes into the tomb with his hands tainted with blood, and his heart still greedy for vengeance because more than one time he saw his young man's dreams destroyed; because experience taught him that his good actions did not count, and that he should not love his wife, nor his sons, for one day, the first will be seduced by her master, and his blood sold far way despite his desperation.

In this passage, by contending that slavery prevents 'negro[es]' from loving their wives and children, Séjour predates African American women authors like Harriet Jacobs, who argue in their works that slavery prevented women of color from remaining 'pure' and virtuous (119). Séjour also once again predates Wells Brown, who said something similar in his speech before the female anti-slavery society:

> A Slave is one that is in the power of an owner. He is a chattel; he is a thing; he is a piece of property. A master can dispose of him, can dispose of his labor, can dispose of his wife, can dispose of his offspring, can dispose of everything that belongs to the Slave, and the Slave shall have no right to speak; he shall have nothing to say. The Slave cannot speak for himself; he cannot speak for his wife, or his children ... Slavery is a system that tears the husband from the wife, and the wife from the husband; that tears the child from the mother, and the sister from the brother; that tears asunder the tenderest ties of nature. (2006, 4)

Antoine's own speech helps to bring to life precisely the ways in which the knowledge that his wife can be raped and his children sold at any time causes the slave to dampen his human feelings towards his own family. Slavery and "miscegenation" as the yin and yang of the "interracial" family are figured as unnatural, then, exactly because they put "whites" and "blacks," the free and the enslaved, into unsustainable social relations with one another (one is alive and the other is dead), but they also put slaves into indefensible social relations with each other (all of them are 'socially dead').[16] Because slaveholders had the power to separate slave families and commit adultery with, and even rape, women of color, the slave family remains non-existent or 'socially dead'. Séjour describes revolutionary actions as almost inevitable for a slave under these conditions, as Antoine tells his young listener: 'If he lives, it is for vengeance; for soon enough he will awaken ... and, the day he shakes off his servility, it would be better for the master to hear a starved tiger screaming next to him, than to meet him face to face.' Séjour's inclusion of this revolutionary logic places him squarely within the tradition of abolitionists who often sought to use the Haitian Revolution as a dire example of what happens when slavery's excesses meet the slave's recognition that the only way to transcend the non-personhood of his social death was through rebellion. In this light, Antoine's comments more immediately link the revolutionary project to "mulatto/a" vengeance and to Paulson's Oedipal structures of revolution, rather than explicitly to liberty. Antoine's observation that the awakened slave contains more ferocity than a 'starved tiger' stereotypically connects revolutionary violence to the concept

---

16 Patterson poses the problem as such: 'Although the slave might be socially dead, he remained nonetheless an element of society. So the problem arose: how was he to be incorporated? Religion explains how it is possible to relate to the dead who still live. It says little about how ordinary people should relate to the living who are dead' (45). Inexplicable here is how the dead relate to those who are also dead.

of cannibalism, but in so doing it suggests that this awakening is the logical and inevitable consequence of being an enslaved human being who must witness the depravities of plantation "miscegenation," and it is not the result of being a person who could be classified as a "mulatto." The idea is that chattel slavery, with its attending sexual and moral depredations, could only breed 'ugly passions in man,' to use a phrase from Melville's 'Benito Cereno' (77). This is because it would inevitably lead to a desire in figurative and biological slave-sons for total usurpation of the father-master's authority and its potential reversal of the power structure, but it would not necessarily produce liberty.

Even the famous 'Black Spartacus' passage of Raynal's *Histoire* connected the idea of rebellion not only to freedom through absolute and total carnage, but also to the pleasures of revenge. In the *Histoire*, the paragraph following the 'Black Spartacus' passage reads:

> Spanish, Portuguese, English, French, Dutch, all of these tyrants will become the prey of the rod and the flame. The fields of the Americas will quickly become drenched with the blood that has been inevitable for such a long time, and the bones of the unfortunate people that have been piling up for so long will flutter with joy. (1780–84, 6:221)

It is this final word 'joy' that suggests revenge rather than purely liberty for, according to Raynal, the earthly remains of the slaves that 'have been piling up' will finally rejoice in being avenged.

Ultimately, if Georges is a tragic "mulatto" it is because the narrative suggests that at first he is compelled (and even delighted) to kill his master in order to avenge the rape of his mother and the death of his wife Zélie, completing the 'oedipal triangle' (Hathaway, 163), but also to avenge the 'social death' of the slave. Georges does not seek to obtain revenge simply against his father-master-rapist, but against Alfred's whole family (a family that turns out to be his too). Like the little white children who laughed 'gaily' at the death of Zélie, Georges shows no pity or sympathy for his former owner. After killing Alfred's wife and baby (his own half-brother), Georges says: 'Now that she is dead, it is your turn, master.' Georges's human sympathies have been smothered by the system of slavery. To his master's pleas for 'Pitié ... pitié ...' and 'grâce ... grâce,' Georges replies: 'I believe my vengeance worthy of yours ... I would have sold my soul to Satan, if he had promised me this moment.' This passage remains powerful precisely because it answers the excesses of slavery with the excesses of the Haitian Revolution, showing how one engendered the other. In transcending his social death (by joining the maroon community, he is able to imagine a situation other than servility), Georges loses what eighteenth-century philosophers like Jean-Jacques Rousseau and Thomas Jefferson considered to be the overriding evidence of humanity: pity, or what we now call sympathy.[17] Georges's powerful claim that 'he would have sold his soul to Satan' in order to kill Alfred, in effect, mirrors Habibrah's pleasure in killing Léopold's uncle in *Bug-Jargal*, but it also suggests that the real tragedy of slavery and revolution—and the "miscegenation" that both came to imply—remains that in the end they made tragic monsters of both slaves and their masters, fathers and their sons.

The poverty of pity exhibited equally by the revolutionists and the colonists, and its terrible consequences for the family during the Haitian Revolution, was lucidly captured by the abbé Jacques Delille in several stanzas of his poem *Le Malheur et la Pitié, poëme en quatre chants* (1804):

> Oh, fields of Saint-Domingue; oh, horrifying scenes!
> Ah! flee, save yourself, poor families!
> The tigers are on the loose; from the African sun
> Every fire burns at the same time in their breast.
> For you their cruel art will paint suffering;
> Robespierre, himself, drunk of their vengeance.
> There, children impaled with the tip of a dart
> Their dark battles form the standards;
> Here, the son falls with his throat slit on the father
> The brother on the sister, the daughter on the mother.
> ...
> What are the causes of this disastrous scourge?
> Some abuses of rights that you perpetrated against them?
> Their hatred remembers it; and the black deception [*imposture*]
> In their ulcerated hearts embitters this insult.
> Ah! if both parties could hear the voice of Pity,
> That between the two colors would rebirth friendship.
> Avoiding that an excess of severity, of indulgence,
> Will only encourage audacity, and arm vengeance;
> And this earth in the end, soaked with their sweat;
> Will no longer be tinged with blood and bathed in their tears. (13–14)

The same kind of poetics expressed by Delille of the 'excess of severity' on the part of masters that had 'arm[ed]' the slaves to 'vengeance' and contained the capacity to dehumanize all involved, and thus to tear 'poor families' apart, appears with some regularity in nineteenth-century abolitionist writing, especially where slave revolts and rebellions enter the conversation. Consider that the staunchly abolitionist abbé Grégoire in his *De la Noblesse*

---

17 Jefferson once declared 'I feel: therefore I exist' (1959, 2:567). For Rousseau and pity, see chapters one and two of this volume.

de la peau (1826) talked of how slavery corrupts both slaves and masters by extinguishing all sense of sympathy. Grégoire wrote, 'It is therefore true that greed and pride extinguish sympathy, smother the most sacred inspirations of nature in men,' concluding, 'slavery and color prejudice corrupt equally the masters, the slaves, and the free people of color' (51–52). In *The Daughter of Adoption* (1801), John Thelwall had written similarly of slavery, using a much more directly fraternal metaphor: 'Thus is all sympathy exterminated by the excess of sufferance! Man ceases to feel for man, and brother for brother; and human nature is degraded below the brute!' (131).

Séjour's contribution to this conversation about the relationship between pity and humanity, slavery and degradation, revolution and the family, was that enslavement created a cycle of revenge, whereby masters like Alfred continued to exercise and even augment their total authority over slaves, further alienating themselves from their own slave-children, in order to anticipate and prevent rebellions, but that these cruel actions caused the 'awakened' slave to seek even more disastrous kinds of revenge. Acts of insubordination were a threat because they created awareness that subordination was possible, but also awareness that it was the slave's belief in the master's total authority, rather than the 'normal order of things,' that rendered him submissive and fearful. This premise is illustrated in one of Toussaint Louverture's speeches in Lamartine's 1850 play of the same name: 'Are you afraid of the whites?' Louverture says, 'You, afraid of them! and why?/ ... /Where does this great distance between their [whites and blacks] fates come from:/Why does one obey and the other command? ... /From where the difference between them? ... In fear/The more cowardly of the two is the inferior being' (lines 2274; 2305–306; 2314–315).[18] Louverture's speech also approaches the ideas of Rousseau, who wrote in his chapters on 'Right of the Strongest' and 'Slavery,' in Book One of *The Social Contract* (1762), that slavery—as 'a metaphor for the condition of man in *modern* (which means European) society' (C. Miller, 2008, 7)—was a result of the strongest unnaturally and immorally instituting their will over the weaker. Rousseau suggested that 'if the strongest is always in the right, [then] it is only a question of behaving so that one may be the strongest,' and he argued that 'it is an empty and contradictory convention that sets up, on the one side, absolute authority, and, on the other, unlimited obedience.'[19] In other words, both in finding their courage (to use Raynal's term) and in recognizing the impossibility for a human being to truly 'renounce being a man,' the slaves could overthrow the unnatural system of slavery.

---

18 This speech is similar to one found in Charles de Rémusat's play (see chapter three of this volume).

19 All translations taken from Cole (1913).

In 'Le Mulâtre,' nevertheless, overthrowing slavery would not cure, and would indeed be presented as having certainly augmented, the familial problems wrought by the plantation system. When Georges realizes that Alfred is his father, in the act of murdering him, the tragic cycle of slavery's "miscegenated" Oedipal drama promises to continue for this family. Georges takes his own life in an attempt to ensure that none of Alfred's progeny will survive, but this act also ensures that Georges will pass down the curse of this same "miscegenated" genealogy to his own surviving child: the child will grow up deprived of his family because of slavery.

At the end of 'Le Mulâtre,' it is Georges's son who will necessarily be made to suffer the spiritual and psychic price of colonial plantation sexual practices. Of Georges's revelation that Alfred is his father, the narrator tells us, 'Georges believed that he had misheard, but the word *father*, like the death knell, chimed in his ear; but to assure himself of this, he opened the fatal bag ... [and cried] I am cursed.' We are told that the next day Georges's dead body was found next to Alfred's. Even if we permit ourselves to believe that Georges's son might never discover the reasons why he had been alienated in every way from both of his parents and all of his ancestors, and therefore might never consciously seek to avenge their deaths or his own 'social death,' the ancestral rape from which he came was inscribed upon his very body, if not in his very mind, as a result of what Toni Morrison evoked with the term 'rememory.' In *Beloved* (1987), Sethe explains 'rememory' when she tells her daughter Denver, 'What I remember is a picture floating around there outside my head. I mean, even if I don't think about it, even if I die, the picture of what I did, or knew, or saw is still out there' (43).

Du Bois's recollection in *The Souls of Black Folk* (1903) of his thoughts upon seeing his son born with bluish eyes and golden hair provides perhaps a more material example of the way in which the rape of slave women was inscribed upon the bodies of people of color in seeming perpetuity, even long after the end of slavery:

> I came to love the wee thing, as it grew strong; as its little soul un-folded itself in twitter and cry and half-formed word, and as its eyes caught the gleam and flash of life. How beautiful he was, with his olive-tinted flesh and dark gold ringlets, his eyes of mingled blue and brown, perfect little limbs, and the soft voluptuous roll which the blood of Africa had moulded into his features! I held him in my arms, after we had sped far away from our Southern home,—held him, and glanced at the hot red soil of Georgia and the breathless city of a hundred hills, and felt a vague unrest. Why was his hair tinted with gold? An evil omen was golden hair in my life. Why had not the brown of his eyes crushed out and killed the blue?—for brown were his father's eyes, and his father's father's. And thus in the Land of the Color-line I saw, as it fell across my baby, the shadow of the Veil.

"Black" Son, "White" Father

> Within the Veil was he born, said I; and there within shall he live,—a Negro and a Negro's son. Holding in that little head—ah, bitterly!—the unbowed pride of a hunted race, clinging with that tiny dimpled hand—ah, wearily!—to a hope not hopeless but unhopeful, and seeing with those bright wondering eyes that peer into my soul a land whose freedom is to us a mockery and whose liberty a lie. I saw the shadow of the Veil as it passed over my baby, I saw the cold city towering above the blood-red land. I held my face beside his little cheek, showed him the star-children and the twinkling lights as they began to flash, and stilled with an even-song the unvoiced terror of my life. (102–03)

The 'unvoiced terror' of a 'hunted race' that was in Du Bois's estimation passed down from generation to generation, much like genes for blue eyes and golden hair, proves to be the most poignant tragedy of Séjour's narrative. For, can we not imagine a literary genealogy in which the now fatherless son of Séjour's Georges grows up to be Faulkner's Charles Bon from *Absalom, Absalom!* (1936) 'trying to revenge his mother' (216), and his father, in Séjour's case, and ending by creating a nearly endless cycle of tragic "mulatto/as?" Would these tragic "mulatto/as" be condemned to live lives of endless suffering as they rail against the twists of racialized fate that had made them part of both a 'hunted' and a 'haunted' race? Faulkner makes a ghost of Jim Bond (the son of Charles Bon) when he explains his disappearance and tells us that although '[t]hey couldn't catch him,' 'nobody ever seemed to make him go very far away, he just stopped howling for a little while. Then after a while they would begin to hear him again' (301). It is Faulkner's Shreve, however, who connects this 'howling' to the kind of "racial" and sexual conquest that had been the stuff of nightmares for the nineteenth-century Atlantic World:

> I think that in time the Jim Bonds are going to conquer the western hemisphere. Of course it wont quite be in our time and of course as they spread toward the poles they will bleach out again like the rabbits and the birds do, so they wont show up sharp against the snow. But it will still be Jim Bond; and so in a few thousand years, I who regard you will also have sprung from the loins of African kings. (302)

Such fantastic plantation "miscegenation," with its ability not only to occasion parricide, but to invite incest, has involved the whole human family in not only Faulkner's representation of the Haitian Revolution, but also in John Thelwall's, who tells us, 'the sins of the fathers have involved the children' (439). Yet if in Thelwall's *The Daughter of Adoption*, the 'incest threat' (Scrivener, Solomonescu et al., 27) could be narrowly avoided, at least in the European metropolis, by the fortuitous revelation of common parentage, the threat of incest after life on a West Indian plantation—like the traumatic inscription of rape onto generations of "black" bodies—was an eternal possibility, impossible to mitigate since slavery had meant that many ties of kinship not only stood unacknowledged, but were unknown. Such family ties were therefore as impossible to trace as Jim Bond. In 'Le Mulâtre,' the only antidote capable of mitigating the 'incest threat' wrought by the tangled family connections of plantation life is parricide. When Georges commits both patricide and fratricide, he eliminates Alfred's ability to forcibly procreate with the slave women on his plantation, who might have been his own daughters, and he eliminates the once very real likelihood that Alfred's child with his legitimate wife might grow up to commit incest with one of the slave owner's many other unrecognized slave children and grandchildren. Of course, this threat has in reality only been lessened by Georges's actions since there is probably no way to know how many other women on his plantation Alfred had raped.

'Le Mulâtre' demonstrates some of the ways in which the "interracial" family became an acceptable vehicle onto which to unload not only the anxieties of "miscegenation," but also fears about the long-term psychological effects of slavery and the shortcomings of revolution to reverse or ameliorate those effects. While the Haitian Revolution has often been celebrated in our contemporary moment as the triumph of the disempowered over the empowered, Georges's final lament reminds us that many people in the nineteenth century who agreed with the Revolution's ultimate goals continued to question the meaning and enduring human (or family) cost of the violence of revolution that had been necessary to do away with the violence of slavery.

In closing, it must be said that even though in many respects 'Le Mulâtre' labors to produce revolutionary violence as the result of the social, legal, and sexual repressions of life on the plantation, rather than the physical or biological corruptions imagined to have been produced by "miscegenation," it is hard not to wonder if nineteenth-century readers would have been able to see beyond the pseudoscientific resonance of the word 'mulâtre' to get to the very real grievances of the slaves that are narrated within the tale. After all, the nineteenth-century France in which 'Le Mulâtre' was published and read was very much the same Atlantic World that in 1845 would allow Eugène de Mirecourt to produce the following review of Séjour's contemporary Alexandre Dumas:

> The physical appearance of M. Dumas is rather well-known: stature of a drum major, arms like Hercules with all the extension possible, prominent lips, an African nose, fuzzy hair, tan skin. His origin is written from one end to the other of his person; but it reveals itself much more even in his

character. Scratch the surface of M. Dumas and you will find a savage. He takes after the negro and the marquis all together. However, the marquis hardly goes farther than the skin. Remove some of the makeup [*Effacez un peu le fard*], rip off the scruffy suit, don't make too much out of certain habits of regency, turn a deaf ear to a language of the streets, get rid of any remaining traits of civilization [*aiguillonnez un point quelconque de la surface civilisée*], pretty soon the negro will show you his teeth. The marquis acts his part in public, the negro betrays himself in intimacy [*le nègre se trahit dans l'intimité*]. (37)

In 1856, Alexandre Bonneau was even more insistent about calculating and musing upon the implications of Dumas's "mixed-race" identity:

M. Alexandre Dumas belongs to the African race of Haiti ... our ingenious writer only owes 32 parts of his physical and moral composition to Saint-Domingue, whereas he owes 96 parts to the *gaulois* or *francs*;[20] he is a quadroon. His son only owes to Haiti 16 of these parts, he is a *métis*, and if by means of generation, he perpetuates his race in our European world, this last offspring, as a *mamelouk*, will only owe to blackness eight parts of his being. (137)

Bonneau continued by using this "racial" calculation to evoke the century-old pseudoscientific argument about literacy as proof of humanity:

Haiti follows with love all of the doings of Messieurs Alexandre Dumas [*fils* and *père*]. They are seriously asking over there, if the author of *Monte-Cristo* owes his genius to the African stock [*levain sudanien*] or to the French stock [*levain français*]. The Haitians without out any question have proclaimed themselves for the former hypothesis; permit us to be inclined towards the latter, for it alone gives us hope that the talent of M. Alexandre Dumas *fils* will one day equal that of his father. (1856, 137–38)

If the remarkable output of Dumas helped Bonneau to resolve the question about whether or not Dumas was a French or a Haitian writer, today's critics have at times used a similar grammar to question Séjour's position as an 'African American writer,' wondering about the place of a light-skinned Francophone man (who seemed to them to be more concerned with foreign affairs) in what was once seen as a largely Anglophone and U.S.-centric literary tradition of African American writing. According to Frances Smith Foster, such critics 'questioned whether he could be said to represent or to have influenced "the" African American literary tradition'

---

20 Moreau de Saint-Méry's racial taxonomy had 128-parts (see chapter one of this volume; and Sollors, 1997, 133).

(2006, 632).[21] This kind of desire to classify and quantify "blackness" and even "Americanness" based on arbitrary signifiers like language, skin color, and narrative setting is ahistorical. Séjour's friends considered him to be an 'American' writer of color,[22] and the U.S. press happily reported upon his literary and theatrical accomplishments in France.[23] Upon his death, several obituaries and announcements even ran in U.S. newspapers.[24] Séjour was also included in an 1869 edition of *The Living Writers of the South*, and in 1943 the *Atlanta Daily World* described him as one of the 'New Orleans group of French-speaking mulattoes … of Negro descent, American birth, and one of the most popular playwrights of the nineteenth century' ('Work of Victor Séjour,' 3). This is just to say that Séjour's contemporaries and literary historians for a long time after his death did not question either his importance or his place within the African diaspora, and particularly within a U.S. tradition of African American writing. Such skepticism remains problematic precisely because it imposes one litmus test for "blackness" and another for "Americanness," both of which reflect all at once nineteenth-century racialism and contemporary U.S. American politics of identity. These are the very structures of inclusion and exclusion that the Haitian revolutionists had hoped to destroy along with plantation slavery.

---

21 In her essay "Creative Collaboration: As African American as Sweet Potato Pie," originally published in 2006, Foster more directly contests the idea that Séjour was not a *real* or *representative* African American in writing: 'Accepting Séjour as an African American seems appropriate since he was born in New Orleans, his father was a free mulatto from Santo Domingo and his mother was a Louisiana native of African ancestry. Moreover, Séjour grew up in a larger African American community than many African Americans of the eighteenth-century colonies did' (2009, 91).

22 See Davidson (501); [Anon.], 'Editorial Notes,' *The Independent … Devoted to the Consideration of Politics, Social and Econ*, August 19, 1869, 4; [Anon.], 'The Drama,' *The Critic*, February 12, 1881, 41.

23 See 'Brief Notes,' *New York Times*, June 28, 1874, 10; 'Rehearsal of the Coming Syrian Drama,' *The Albion: A Journal of News, Politics and Literature*, January 26, 1861, 41; 'Our Special Paris Correspondence,' *Spirit of the Times; A Chronicle of the Turf, Agriculture, Field Sports, Life*, April 7, 1855, 81; *Cincinnati Daily Gazette*, October 4, 1872.

24 See 'Obituary,' *New York Times*, September 22, 1874; 'The Rich Harvest of Death,' *New York Evangelist*, 46.2 (January 14, 1875), 8; *Philadelphia Inquirer*, September 22, 1874; *The Daily Times Picayune*, October 18, 1874; *The Sunday Times*, November 1, 1874.

CHAPTER EIGHT

Between the Family and the Nation: Lamartine, Toussaint Louverture, and the "Interracial" Family Romance of the Haitian Revolution

'Où trouver ailleurs une patrie, s'écriaient la plupart d'entre eux les larmes aux yeux, l'esclave en retrouve une dans la vaste Afrique, le maître dans les trois autres parties du monde, et nous enfants de cette terre, espèce nouvelle d'hommes, nulle part.'

—Antoine Métral, *Histoire de l'insurrection des esclaves dans le nord de Saint-Domingue* (1818)

'Es-tu fou? puis-je l'empêcher d'être mulâtre? puis-je lui donner un père, une mère, en faire un enfant légitime?'

—*Oxiane; ou la révolution de Saint-Domingue* (1828)

Ronald Paulson, Lynn Hunt, and Françoise Vergès have described many literary, visual, and political inscriptions of revolution as having had the kind of inherently Oedipal representational structures that we have seen in Victor Séjour's 'Le Mulâtre.' Lynn Hunt has written that Oedipal metaphors of revolution were abundant in the early modern world because 'most Europeans in the eighteenth century thought of their rulers as fathers and of their nations as families writ large' (xiv). In the mind of the populace of *ancien régime* France, she suggests, the French Revolution necessarily entailed overthrowing the father-king, much the same way that for those who wrote about the Haitian Revolution, a slave rebellion metaphorically and often literally entailed overthrowing the father-master. Hunt calls these Oedipal fantasies of rebellion against the state, 'family romances,' and tells us that they were essentially 'metaphors for political life, metaphors that developed in response to changing events ... but also metaphors that drove the revolutionary process forward' (199).

Vergès, like Garraway after her (2005a, 224), borrows the term 'family romance' from Hunt to describe the Oedipal significations of colonial revolutions. According to Vergès, it was Sigmund Freud who had used the term 'family romance' to evoke 'the fiction developed by children about imagined parents,' whom they imagine replacing their own parents (Vergès, 3; see also Freud, 2003, 39). In Vergès's adaptation of both Freud and Hunt's usage of the term, what she calls the 'colonial family romance' in Africa and the Caribbean, helped government officials to create a 'fable' about France being 'La Mère-Patrie' and the slaves being her colonized, rebellious, and ungrateful children (4). This was 'a romance created by the "colonial parents,"' she says, who positioned themselves as the benevolent ("white") fathers of both the slaves and the free people of color so that when both 'rejected her, it was their ingratitude, rather than her tyrannical "love" that explained their behavior' (Vergès, 5). 'It is a colonial family romance,' Vergès continues, 'because French colonial rhetoric filled the tie between France and its colony with intimate meaning,' but since 'it wanted to be a republican romance, it both suffused the colonial relation with familial metaphors and offered the grounds to challenge French colonialism' (5–6). In other words, because the language of 'colonial domination' was itself inherently Oedipal, so, too, was the language of colonial rebellion.[1]

The myriad metaphors of family life occasioned by the existence of the colonial plantation in Saint-Domingue similarly provided not only a language for the erstwhile colonists to imagine retaliating against their unruly colonial 'children,' whom the former planters had claimed merely wanted to usurp their natural authority, it also provided those rebellious 'children' with a grammar of violated rights with which to challenge the authority of their self-stated colonial parents. In the literary history of the Haitian Revolution, these longings for rights would be phrased with a much more distinctly racialized vocabulary of the 'colonial family romance,' what we might call an "interracial" family romance. In many representations of the Haitian Revolution, this "interracial" family romance is paradoxically represented as having offered the slaves an emotive vocabulary to justify not only eradicating the abuses of the colonial powers, but replacing colonial power entirely. If the 'colonial family romance' narrates the rebellion of colonized children who seek to replace their colonizer parents with less despotic ones, then the "interracial" family romance of the Haitian Revolution, called forth most distinctively by writings about the life of Toussaint Louverture, is a story about "black" and "mulatto" children who agonize over their desire to

---

[1] Colonial rebellions and revolutions appear also to have been Oedipal for one of the most important philosophers in the psychoanalytic tradition, Jacques Lacan, who, in 1968, under pressure from radical students, admitted that 'the Oedipus complex was a colonial imposition' and not the other way around (Mirzeoff, 17).

replace their "white" parents with "black" ones or their "black" parents with "white" ones.

Paulson, for his part, has asked an important question about such interpretations of revolution as being naturally tied to metaphors of the Oedipus complex. Paulson asks if a revolution 'appear[s] to be oedipal because it *is* always an oedipal conflict or because we tend to "represent" it in the Freudian sense of regressing to such scenes for equivalents?' (8). Paulson's rhetorical question calls upon us to consider not only why such a regression into the abyss of Oedipal territory provided one of the most common metaphors of the Haitian Revolution, but how and why that metaphor became infused with popular ideas about "race," namely the rampant narrative of "mulatto/a" vengeance. What did the trope of the tragic "mulatto/a," with its manifest relationship to ideas about children of color unwittingly or reluctantly killing their "white" parents and vice versa, offer to both readers and writers as they tried to understand the meaning of the Haitian Revolution? That is to say, what is it that made the image of Toussaint Louverture and his family caught up in an international romance of parricide one of the most widely told stories of the Haitian Revolution?

The many biographers, journalists, novelists, poets, playwrights, memoirists, and historians who would tackle the subject of Louverture's life in the nineteenth century almost always painted his conflict with France as intimately connected to this sort of "interracial" family romance. This was a romance that inevitably forced Louverture to choose between his ("black") sons and his ("white") nation, on the one hand, and that required his sons to choose between their ("black") father and their ("white") nation, on the other. The language of "mulatto/a" vengeance, as both vengeance *of* and *for* "mulattoes," which supposedly made "black" children want to kill their "white" fathers, was used to describe not only the relationship between Toussaint Louverture and Napoleon Bonaparte, but the relationship between Louverture and his own children. The "interracial" family romance found in descriptions of the dilemma faced by the Louverture children with respect to their father was also imagined to have been responsible for the potentially fratricidal scission between two of Louverture's sons, Isaac and Placide (one usually described as "black" and the other as "mulatto"). These racially inflected descriptions became some of the most often repeated stories about the fabled family of Toussaint Louverture, the man whom William Wordsworth would call in his 1803 poem named for the revolutionary hero, 'the most unhappy man of men' (Wordsworth, 1803).

There are basically two poles in the literary imagination of the Haitian Revolution that associated the life of Louverture with a tragic, Oedipal "interracial" family romance of "miscegenation," revolution, and revenge. The first strain of representing Louverture in these tragic "racial" terms was promulgated, in part, by the memoirs of Louverture as they were published and read in the nineteenth century. In *Mémoires du général Toussaint-Louverture écrits par lui-même*,[2] published and edited by the Haitian historian Joseph Saint-Rémy in 1853, Louverture paints himself as the loyal, but unjustly dishonored son of 'la mère-patrie' (88), who had been betrayed by his metaphorical *brother*, Leclerc, all because of his 'color.'[3] Louverture accused Leclerc of having behaved towards him 'with methods which have never been used even with respect to the greatest criminals. Without a doubt I owe this treatment to my color,' he wrote, 'but my color ... my color, has it ever prevented me from serving my country [*ma patrie*] with diligence and devotion? The color of my body, does it compromise my honor and my bravery? [*La couleur de mon corps nuit-elle à mon honneur et à ma bravoure*]' (85). Going on to use a familial metaphor of the nation, Louverture admonished the French government, and Bonaparte particularly, for not having fairly resolved the dispute between he and Leclerc, his *brother* in nation. Louverture asked, 'If two children are fighting one another, does not their mother or their father have a duty to prevent them from doing so, to find out which one of them is the aggressor, and punish

---

2 I refer here and throughout this monograph to the 1853 version established by Saint-Rémy because that is the version with which nineteenth-century readers would have been familiar. However, there are actually four versions of Louverture's memoirs, which all have their own slight variants. According to Daniel Desormeaux, who recently republished the memoirs with an insightful introduction, the four versions are as follows: 'an entire manuscript written by the hand of Toussaint (which represents the original), a second written in French by someone else, but under the dictation of Toussaint, which contains several crossed out sections and annotations in the margins by Toussaint, a third written completely by someone else that also contains several sections that are crossed out and a note from Toussaint at the end, a fourth impeccably recopied by someone but with the same note at the end (which permits us to say that this one represents the final version that had been officially submitted to the First Consul' (Desormeaux, 2011, 16, translation mine). For more on the different versions, see also Walsh (2011, 88–105). For an English translation of Saint-Rémy's memoirs that had been published in 1863 by John Redpath as a part of an historical compilation of writings about Louverture, see *Toussaint L'Ouverture: A Biography and Autobiography* (1863).

3 Saint-Rémy writes that he first learned of the existence of the memoirs when several excerpts from them were published in 1845 in the French newspaper *La Presse* (1853, 18). He goes on to write that a colleague transmitted to him a copy of one of the memoirs and that later he found the handwritten memoirs themselves in the Archives Générales de la France. The French abolitionist and historian Victor Schoelcher also mentioned the handwritten memoirs in his 1889 *Vie de Toussaint Louverture* (see Desormeaux, 2011, 19). However, Desormeaux, who has studied each of the different versions of the memoirs, notes that even though Saint-Rémy claimed to be publishing a 'version intégral' or the complete version of the text, the 1853 publication 'was missing entire paragraphs that Toussaint had added in the third and fourth versions of the Memoirs' (2011, 12)

him or punish them both in the case that they are both wrong?' (88). Instead of censuring Leclerc's actions, however, Louverture claimed that he himself was unjustifiably punished by Bonaparte (his national father) as the guilty party, without a trial, and subsequently imprisoned 'in a dungeon,' while 'General Leclerc enjoys his liberty' (89).

The second strain of a narrative of Toussaint Louverture that connects his life to the trope of the tragic "mulatto/a" focuses on the "interracial" conflict between Louverture and two of his sons: an adopted child named Placide—who was reportedly the son of Louverture's second wife, Suzanne, and a 'mulatto' named Séraphin or Jean-Marie Clère (Gragnon-Lacoste, 15; de Cauna, 1997, 1874–75; Donnadieu and Girard, 57)—and Isaac, Louverture's first biological child with Suzanne Louverture (see Isaac Louverture, 229; Girard and Donnadieu, 50).[4] Most nineteenth-century historical accounts of Louverture's relationship to these sons suggest that he sent them to the metropole, not only to be educated, but as quasi-hostages whose presence in France was supposed to provide evidence of their father's allegiance to Bonaparte. This is the version of the story that would be told by Josephine Bonaparte herself in the *Mémoires historiques et secrets de l'impératrice Joséphine* (1820), edited by Marie Le Normand. The empress writes that she had urged

4 Isaac Louverture contested the idea that Placide had ever been formally adopted by his father, according to a letter with the date May 12, 1821 given to the nineteenth-century historian Georges Le Gorgeu by Thomas Prosper Gragnon-Lacoste, author of *Toussaint Louverture, général en chef de l'armée de Saint-Domingue, surnommé le premier des noirs. Ouvrage écrit d'après des documents inédits et les papiers historiques et secrets de la famille Louverture* (1877). Isaac wrote of Placide, 'Having learned that my half-brother [*mon frère utérin*] ... wishes to get married under the title of the adopted son of Toussaint Louverture, I thought it was my duty, being the only legitimate son of Toussaint Louverture, to oppose this singular pretention and to prevent you from it. I declare ... that [Placide] is not the adopted son of Toussaint Louverture, and I present in support of my claim an affidavit dated November 11, 1815 ... It is nowhere said in this document that my half-brother is the adopted son of my father. If I have tolerated that this half-brother uses the name of Louverture, which he assumed in Paris at the Collège de la Marche, where my father permitted, at my request, that he should be raised with me, I can no longer, however, consent for him to use the title of the adopted son of Toussaint Louverture in his marriage documents, a title that does not belong to him, and which it will be very easy for me to prove, not only with this affidavit that I have had the honor of presenting before you, but with the statements of several people from both here and Saint-Domingue' (rpt. in Le Gorgeu, 41–42). A note from Gragnon-Lacoste accompanying the copy of the letter that he transmitted to Le Gorgeu gave recourse to the "science" of "race" in order to corroborate in some senses Isaac Louverture's account of the family's genealogy: 'It should be remembered,' Gragnon-Lacoste writes, 'that Toussaint Louverture and Jeanne Baptiste, his [first] wife, had been black, whereas Placide Clère was a light-skinned mulatto [*mulâtre clair*]; and *two blacks can only create a black*' (qtd. in Le Gorgeu, 43). See also Gragnon-Lacoste (15).

her husband not to send Leclerc to Saint-Domingue since in her mind such a decision constituted a 'fatal move' that 'would forever take this beautiful colony away from France.' Instead, Bonaparte's wife counseled the First Consul to 'Keep Toussaint Louverture there. That is the man that you require in order to govern the Blacks.' '[W]hat complaints could you have against this leader of the Blacks?' Bonaparte's wife asked. 'He has always maintained a correspondence with you; he has done even more, he has given you, in some sense, his children for hostages' [*il vous a remis en quelque sorte ses enfants en otages*] (1:356).⁵ As the story goes, in the course of their pseudo-captivity, Placide and Isaac were educated at the Collège de La Marche, along with the children of André Rigaud and Boisrond-Tonnerre; but Louverture's children were supposedly privileged by Bonaparte, who would go on to use them as pawns in an attempt to force their father to surrender during the Leclerc expedition.⁶

The most popular ending to this tale is the version in which the children's 'précepteur,' the abbé Coisnon, brings the teenagers to the Louverture plantation in Ennery with a letter from Leclerc insinuating that Isaac and Placide were *de facto* wards of the French government whose destinies depended upon the surrender of their father. According to popular history, Placide ended up fighting on the side of the revolutionists, while Isaac (who wrote in his own memoir that he was the one who had carried that fateful letter from the First Consul to his father), preferred to stay on one of the family's plantations in Ennery with his mother until the whole family was captured and exiled to France (see, for example, I. Louverture, 305–09).

With some variation, the above is the version of the family conflict that would be lucidly dramatized using the trope of the tragic "mulatto/a" by Alphonse de Lamartine in his 1850 verse drama *Toussaint Louverture*. While most of the other stories that will be examined here are about how Louverture chooses between his "black" sons and the "white" colonial order—what I describe as a choice between the family and nation—in Lamartine's play, Louverture's sons and his niece are asked to demonstrate either their devotion to their biological fathers by choosing sides during the Revolution or they are asked to figuratively and literally replace their

---

5 In his *Histoire de Toussaint L'Ouverture, chef des insurgés* (1802), Cousin d'Avallon, who culled much of his information from Dubroca, tells us that 'In order to remove all suspicion, [Louverture] sent his sons to France; we no longer doubted the good faith and the sincerity of the father when we saw him abandon the destiny of his family to France' (40, ftn.).

6 Le Gorgeu writes, however, that it was actually Josephine Bonaparte who entertained the children and especially Isaac, since Bonaparte, 'did not like blacks, and he has proven so. The sight of Toussaint Louverture left him with a most disagreeable impression' (21).

biological fathers by turns with national fathers. As a result of this kind of alternative conflict between the family and the nation, in Lamartine's play, Louverture's sons, one described as '*le noir*' and the other as '*le mulâtre*' (line 1774), take turns accusing each other of disloyalty to both their national family (France) and their genealogical family (Toussaint Louverture). It is Louverture's oldest son, called Albert in the play,[7] who scolds his younger brother by evoking the now familiar metaphor of parricidal vengeance, this time against the nation: 'Why such old anger against the whites' [*Pourquoi contre les blancs ces anciennes colères*], he asks. 'All prejudice aside, these tyrants are our brothers' (lines 2053–54). While Albert/Placide's language evokes the fratricidal implications that were always a possibility during a revolution, it is Louverture whose language more specifically resembles that found within the trope of the tragic "mulatto/a." The play turns the Oedipal "interracial" family drama, which can be distinguished by its fatalist narration in the work of Séjour, into a tragic "interracial" family romance where characters are forced to consciously choose between a "black" identity and a "white" one, when Louverture tells his sons that they must, 'Choose without hesitation between the whites and me' (line 2595).

It is no surprise that Lamartine employed the language of the "interracial" family romance that the trope of the tragic "mulatto/a" invites when we consider the fact that *Toussaint Louverture* bears the influence of some of the most ardent chroniclers of the narrative of "mulatto/a" vengeance, especially the works of Pamphile de Lacroix and Isaac Louverture, as published by Antoine Métral.[8] As we shall see, their influence can be most clearly discerned in Lamartine's attempt to make into a racialized Oedipal romance Louverture's sons' decisions to stay with their father in Saint-Domingue or to remain loyal to France. Lamartine's play and its attempt to render Louverture's life into an "interracial" family romance is merely a part of a long genealogy of writing on the Haitian revolu-

---

7 Lamartine changed the names and situations of many of the real-life actors of the Revolution in his drama, added other characters, and omitted some people altogether. Notably, Lamartine omitted Saint-Jean, the youngest of Louverture's sons with his second wife, Suzanne, and in *Toussaint Louverture*, Albert and Isaac share the same father, but have different mothers. Lamartine also changed the name of Louverture's niece from Louise Chancy to Adrienne, and the name of the preceptor of his sons from Coisnon to Salvador. Notably, in the play, Placide/Albert chooses to fight with the First Consul rather than with his father.

8 Lamartine claimed, for his part, that he wrote from memory and that he owed the historical details presented in the play to the 'unedited notes of General *Ramel*, which one of my colleagues ... in possession of these important memoirs, wanted to transmit to me [*veut bien me communiquer*]' (5). Le Gorgeu also cites the *Mémoires inédits de général Ramel* (see Lamartine as reprinted in Hoffmann, 1998, II; and Le Gorgeu [1881]).

tionary hero which, by the early to mid-nineteenth century, had in many ways succeeded in irrevocably linking the image of Toussaint Louverture to the narrative of "mulatto/a" vengeance. Analyzing nineteenth-century writing about Louverture from authors as various as Louverture himself, his son, Isaac, Lamartine, Métral, Lacroix, and Saint-Rémy, reveals how the resonant association of the "mulatto/a" with tragedy became explicitly attached to ideas not only about the connection between "racial mixing" and the Haitian Revolution, but about the failures of Toussaint Louverture to create an independent nation. The trope of the tragic "mulatto/a" not only appears to have provided those living in the nineteenth-century Atlantic World with an immediately understandable metaphor for connecting the personal and political heartbreak of the Louverture family to ideas about the corrupting and calamitous effects of "racial mixing," but for linking the causes and putative "failures" of the Haitian Revolution itself to the kind of unthinkable parricidal violence called forth by the narrative of "mulatto/a" vengeance.

*

The personal and political conflicts that would turn the lives of the Louvertures into a tragic "interracial" family romance for an author like Lamartine had been of significant interest to readers in the Atlantic World throughout the nineteenth century, evidenced by the myriad biographies, histories, and fictions that sought to bring Toussaint Louverture back to figurative life. Between his death in 1803 and 1865, not counting the thousands of reprints and translations in various venues of Wendell Phillips's famous speech, 'Toussaint L'Ouverture' (1861) (Clavin, 211–14, ftn. 46), at least 60 memoirs and biographies in English and French alone were specifically devoted to describing the life of Louverture.[9] This is not to mention the hundreds of newspaper and magazine articles published in France, the United States, Great Britain, and Haiti/Saint-Domingue that made significant attempts to contribute to the biography of Louverture, nor does this take into account a substantial number of dictionary and encyclopedia entries devoted to the sketching of his life or the countless eulogies penned in Louverture's honor after his death. Interest in the life of Toussaint Louverture appears

---

9 Clavin writes that the source of Phillips's remarkable popularity was likely the abolitionist press and, in particular, John Redpath, who later published 'a book-length edition of Phillips's lectures,' which included 'Toussaint L'Ouverture' under the title of *Speeches, Lectures, and Letters* in 1863. The book saw multiple editions and, according to Clavin, 'newspapers reported the sale of nearly one thousand copies a week between September and October' (212, ftn. 46).

to have retained its caché throughout the second half of the nineteenth century. In his 1881 study, *Etudes sur Jean-Baptiste Coisnon and Toussaint-Louverture*, which was dedicated to Thomas Prosper Gragnon-Lacoste's own 1877 biography of Louverture, Le Gorgeu wrote that Louverture's capture remained one of the most 'fateful dates in the history of France.' '[T]he year 1802,' Le Gorgeu wrote, 'will remain in certain respects, for us French people, a painful time ... History, Poetry, Engraving [*la Gravure*] have been dedicated to his memory' (5).

To put mentions of Louverture into transatlantic perspective, according to Michel Fabre, the Haitian revolutionary hero was mentioned in the nineteenth-century 'black' U.S. press, at least as frequently as such other notable figures as Pushkin and Alexandre Dumas, all of whom Fabre calls 'black beacon[s]' or crucial icons in the international 'lieux de mémoire' of the free northern U.S. 'black' community (Fabre, 1994, 123–24). The interest, influence, and importance of nineteenth-century writing about Louverture is perhaps best understood in the kind of relative terms towards which Fabre's study gestures. Between 1777 and 1839, which is about the same time span considered for writings about the life of Louverture, not counting reprints and subsequent editions, there were roughly 80 biographies published in the Atlantic World about George Washington—that other revolutionary hero whose life has been similarly mythologized, romanticized, and dramatized.[10] Unlike with Louverture, however, this number *does* include bibliographic, encyclopedic, and dictionary entries (see Baker, 1889, 1–77).[11] It is almost a certainty, therefore, that if we took into account all mentions of Louverture, including the many, many letters he wrote to French newspapers in which he attempted to shape his own image (Jenson, 2011, 45–50), the number of published texts about his life would far surpass those concerning the life of George Washington, the man 'whose life history,' according to William

---

10 The comparison with Washington is especially apt since Louverture was often favorably compared in abolitionist writing and speeches to the first president of the United States. See Phillips and Beard, for example. The most interesting of this genre, however, comes in Ralph Waldo Emerson's 1844 essay on 'Character,' in which the U.S. writer amorphously juxtaposes the image of Louverture with Washington in writing, 'Suppose a slaver on the coast of Guinea should take on board a gang of negroes, which should contain persons of the stamp of Toussaint L'Ouverture: or, let us fancy, under these swarthy masks he has a gang of Washingtons in chains.' For a reading of Emerson's essay, see Brickhouse (2004, 20). Emerson mentioned Louverture and the Haitian Revolution again in his 1844 'Emancipation in the British West Indies.' For a reading of the latter, see Belasco (2000, 185).

11 According to Baker, who notes that he 'does not necessarily claim [his study] to be exhaustive,' but certainly 'sufficient' (x), there were no French biographies of Washington published during this time.

Spohn Baker, 'has been written so often and has appeared in so many forms, from the slight sketch to the ponderous quarto, from the schoolbook of a single volume, to the finished production of many, that but few are aware of the number and how constantly it has been added to' (xii).

If 'constantly' rewritten, supplemented, and embellished biographies of Washington created the image of a larger than life and insanely moral revolutionary hero who could supposedly never tell a lie (Lengel, 156), the rewriting, supplementation, and embellishment of the life of Louverture found in biographies performed a quite similar function with respect to Louverture's goodness. If Washington's honesty is the most time-honored myth of the American revolutionary hero, Louverture's humanity was the most commonly retold tale about the Haitian revolutionary hero. Nineteenth-century sources widely reported that during the Revolution, Louverture had not only 'prevented the destruction' of his master's plantation, but that in order to save his master's life he had 'secretly conveyed' the whole Bréda family to a ship that was bound for Baltimore (Child, 44). This is precisely the tale that Lydia Maria Child would recount in her 1865 sketch of Louverture published in *The Freedman's Book*, whose purpose was to provide newly 'freedmen' with 'fresh strength and courage from this true record of what colored men have accomplished, under great disadvantages' (iv). Child's entry on 'Toussaint L'Ouverture' is by far the longest (50 pages), greatly surpassing her entries in the book on two other well-known, popular, and important Atlantic figures, Frederick Douglass (19 pages) and Phillis Wheatley (seven pages). Child's portrayal of Louverture, in which a literate and pious ex-slave consistently refuses to adopt the indiscriminate logic of a revolution that would pit all the former slaves and free people of color against all the "white" French colonists, demonstrates the way in which, by the time of the U.S. Civil War, Louverture had become one of the most salient symbols in the Atlantic World of remaining humane, rather than vengeful, under even the most oppressive of circumstances.

Phillips's 1861 speech, 'Toussaint L'Ouverture,' which Matthew Clavin has said 'testifies to a Civil War culture that revolved around the memories of the Haitian Revolution' (89), provides a particularly striking case in point of the way in which Louverture's 'charity and his patriotic virtue' not only became 'proverbial' (Le Gorgeu, 10), but set up Louverture to play the star role in one of the most tragic dramas of the *bon nègre* in the Atlantic World. Phillips would claim of Louverture that, like 'all of the leading negro generals,' he 'saved the man under whose roof he was born, and protected the family' (476). Phillips urged his audience to believe at the outset that Louverture's humanity towards his figurative father-master was precisely the result of his 'unmixed' status, being a 'negro' 'with no drop of white blood in his veins' (468). He began his speech by saying, in fact, 'If anything …

that I say of him to-night moves your admiration, remember, the black race claims it all,—we have no part or lot in it' (476). Philips's desire to stress Louverture's *pure* "blackness" runs against the grain of the conclusion drawn by Karen Sanchez-Eppler, who has written that 'the problem of anti-slavery fiction [in the United States] is that the very effort to depict goodness in blackness involves the obliteration of blackness,' suggesting that this is why more positive traits were associated with "mixed-race" figures in nineteenth-century U.S. literature (102). However, in the literary history of the Haitian Revolution, we might say that the exact opposite was the case. Many authors who contributed to the transatlantic print culture of the Haitian Revolution sought to stress the goodness of 'blackness' by 'obliterating' the idea that such goodness emanated from a connection with "whiteness." This is to say that if the 'mulatto' was a 'complex' figure in nineteenth-century France (Hoffmann, 1973, 230), it was equally so in the United States, where tales of "mulatto/a" vengeance, especially those written by abolitionists, began to dominate the genre of writing about the Haitian Revolution towards the middle of the nineteenth century. As one example, Louverture's humanity was immediately juxtaposed in Phillips's speech with a description of the 'mulatto' Rigaud, 'who worked only by blood and massacre' (474). Like nearly all writing on the Haitian Revolution, Phillips's celebrated speech had the added effect of promulgating a distinctive discourse of "mulatto/a" vengeance that took Haiti, its revolution, and its revolutionary heroes as prime examples.

Phillips's speech is hardly an outlier in the genre of Louverture writing. Nearly all renditions of Louverture's tragic life, whether meant to be fictional, historical, or biographical, are flanked by the narrative of "mulatto/a" vengeance in some way, if not in the body of the work itself, then through the editorial footnotes, introductions, and appendices that often accompany such works. One of the best examples of the way in which Louverture's life would be made to match this narrative by the work of editors occurs in the memoirs of his son, Isaac Louverture. Isaac Louverture's memoirs, which Philippe Girard and Jean-Louis Donnadieu have recently referred to as 'tainted recollections' (42),[12] were first published as a part of Antoine Métral's 1825 *Histoire de l'expédition militaire des français à Saint-Domingue, Sous Napoléon Bonaparte. Suivi Des Mémoires Et Notes D'I. Louverture Sur*

---

[12] Surprisingly, Alexandre Bonneau was much less severe in recording the purported biases of Isaac Louverture's memoir: 'The book is written in a style that calls for neither praise nor criticism. The son places his father on a pedestal that is in our opinion much too elevated; but a child is permitted to see his father's actions only through a flattering prism, and God forbid that we reproach Isaac for his filial piety. Besides, his *Mémoires*, despite their numerous errors, are important for the history of his country' (1856, 142).

La Même Expédition Et Sur La Vie De Son Père. Importantly, in the body of the memoir itself, Isaac Louverture never mentions "race" at all. In fact, when he tells the reader that his brother Placide, 'is a son from Madame Toussaint Louverture's first marriage' [*un fils du premier lit de madame Toussaint-Louverture*] (229), Isaac does not call his half-brother a "mulatto," and he does not refer to his brother's purported "race" or skin color in the later version published by Gragnon-Lacoste either. Instead, in this later version, Isaac continues to refer to Placide as his 'half-brother [*frère utérin*],' saying that for a long time his brother had also used the name Louverture. According to Isaac, it is because of this that Placide 'was considered to be the oldest son of the general-in-chief,' even though Isaac viewed himself as the Haitian general's eldest biological son (I. Louverture, rpt. in Gragnon-Lacoste, 287).[13] In addition, in neither of the versions does Louverture's son ever bring up what the nineteenth-century African American writer William Wells Brown would refer to as the 'war of color' (1855, 17) between Rigaud and the revolutionary hero; a conflict that had been consistently portrayed in the transatlantic print culture of the Haitian Revolution as the result of inherent hatred for "mulattoes" and "negroes" and vice versa, a prime example of which exists in Bryan Edwards's *The History, Civil and Commercial, of the British Colonies in the West Indies* (3:430). Moreover, Isaac Louverture does not even mention color prejudice as having been the primary obstacle standing in the way of a *rapprochement* between 'the first of the Blacks' and the 'first of the Whites.'

Isaac Louverture's recollections of the life of his father had been 'tainted,' indeed, but not necessarily by him. Despite Isaac's profound silence on the question of "race," the events described by him were implicitly racialized at the outset by Métral's historical writing. The historical part of the work written by Métral, which precedes the memoir and makes up the bulk of the publication, contains this summation of the "interracial" family romance that had been associated with the Haitian Revolution for two decades: 'Blacks and whites seem to come from the same family, of which the people of color, children of the one, and of the other, form the parental links' (1825, 103). These 'parental links,' Métral offers, had been forged primarily by women of color themselves, whom he characterized as so many "tropical temptresses" who were studied in 'arts of seduction' (17). Métral more explicitly alluded to the pseudoscientific debates that undergirded such beliefs about "racial mixing" when he wrote, '[f]rom the mixture of white and black blood, is born a new race of man [*une nouvelle espèce d'homme*] designated by the

---

13 A slightly different version of the memoirs would be published by Gragnon-Lacoste as part of his 1877 biography of Toussaint Louverture under the title 'Manuscrit de M. Isaac Louverture' (see Gragnon-Lacoste, 287–348).

name of people of color; these were the *affranchis* who found themselves between servitude and liberty' (17). He goes on to specifically narrate the relationship of this 'new race of man' to revenge, as the kind of vengeance *for* "mulattoes" that was ubiquitous in the literary history of the Haitian Revolution when he writes, '[t]heir fathers, half smothering the cry of nature, left them in this middling servitude [*servitude moyenne*] that was not any less filled with shame' (17). Such unnatural births could only breed the kinds of unnatural death found in narratives about vengeance *of* "mulattoes." Métral ultimately evokes the Oedipal language of the "interracial" family romance when he writes that these 'children, abandoned by their parents,' would become the 'most cruel enemies' of their own fathers (18). Because of the absence of any other framework with which to understand Isaac Louverture's contextually nondescript writing about his own father, by flanking the memoir with the language of "mulatto/a" vengeance, and thereby associating the Haitian Revolution with the consequences of "racial mixing," Métral conditions readers of the memoir to link not only the Haitian Revolution to a parricidal conflict among "white" fathers, "black" mothers, and "mulatto" children, but to the life of Louverture. That is to say that by the mere juxtaposition of Métral's history with Isaac's memoir, Louverture's life is marked by the same sort of "interracial" family romance of the Haitian Revolution that for Métral could only lead to parricide. The ultimate effect of Métral's peritextual annotations, asides, and additions is that the family history of the Louvertures became once again intimately associated with a distinctive vocabulary of "mulatto/a" vengeance that made the literary history of Toussaint Louverture also a part of the literary history of the trope of the tragic "mulatto/a."

If Toussaint Louverture's relationship to his sons was implicitly racialized in the memoir of Isaac Louverture by way of Métral's history, Saint-Rémy's edition of Toussaint Louverture's own memoirs probably has the most to tell us about how the life of Louverture came to be distinctly associated with the kinds of tropologies of "race" found within the palimpsestic literary history of the Haitian Revolution. Saint-Rémy much more directly racialized Louverture's life through the introduction, copious footnotes, and other documentation he provided as context for the 1853 publication. In the memoirs of Toussaint Louverture as they were published by Saint-Rémy in the nineteenth century, the Haitian general, like his son, never mentions "racial mixing" or even uses the word "mulatto." In addition, also like his son, Louverture remained obviously, and, in some ways, painfully silent on both the widely reported conflict with his children and the War of the South.[14]

14 Saint-Rémy accused Louverture of having purposely made no mention of his conflict with Rigaud out of shame: 'L'Ouverture seems to have been ashamed of

The Trope of the Tragic "Mulatto/a"

In great contrast, in both the introduction and footnotes to Louverture's memoirs, Saint-Rémy, like Pamphile de Lacroix, who was the Haitian author's dear friend—Saint-Rémy wrote of him, 'I regret the death of this good man who honored me with his friendship and promised to provide a more complete version of his memoirs of Saint-Domingue' (1853, ftn. 318)—labors to consistently identify the "race" of nearly every person whom Louverture mentions. For example, Saint-Rémy identifies the Haitian writer Hérard Dumesle as a 'griffe' because he was the son of a 'mulatto' and a 'negro' (24), and after Louverture mentions 'Gabart, leader of the 4th demi-brigade and the *chef de bataillon* Pourcy' (52), Saint-Rémy offers a footnote not only telling us the full names of these men, but identifying them both as 'mulattoes' (52). Once again, after Louverture's mention of General Charles Belair, the editor adds a note identifying the general as a 'young and handsome black man' who was Louverture's nephew (70). Such explanations by Saint-Rémy seem, at first glance, to want to encourage us to read Louverture's memoir with all of the biases of "racial" determinism suggested by the pseudoscientific terminology that is being deployed. However, we must proceed carefully. Even though by placing these kinds of seamless editorial footnotes, in which people are identified as 'blacks' or 'mulattoes,' Saint-Rémy seemingly mimics the practice of Lacroix in suggesting that skin color was so important to the interpretation of behavior that it needed to be observed, acknowledged, and recorded at all times, Saint-Rémy includes such information precisely to prove the opposite. For Saint-Rémy including the skin colors or "race" of nearly every person whom Louverture mentions in the memoir proves that extraordinary crimes and extraordinary virtues were characteristic of 'negroes' as equally as 'mulattoes.' Saint-Rémy is ultimately saying that if we want to properly contextualize the meaning of the Haitian Revolution with respect to "race," we *need* to know about how the skin colors of all of the people with whom the Haitian general came into contact ultimately reveals nothing in advance about what they would or would not do, and to whom they would or would not be loyal. He wrote that Louverture treacherously treated the '*anciens libres*, negroes and mulattoes, whom he always embraced, with the same proscription' (19). Saint-Rémy's description here revels in the language of "monstrous hybridity," but to a much different and, we might even say, paradoxical effect. In Saint-Rémy's mind, it was precisely

---

himself here: everything is silence, just like when under the Spanish flag he fought the principle of general liberty that Republican France had proclaimed' (1853, 23). Contemporary historians, however, have been much more forgiving of Louverture's silences. Desormeaux writes, for example, that Louverture, whom he refers to as the 'first of the black memorialists,' is no different from other memorialists who 'never speak of an episode that does not show them in a glorious or loyal light' (2011, 31).

Louverture's capacity for extraordinary 'virtue' as well as extraordinary 'crime' that made him the equal of the "whites" to which people of African descent had been constantly compared. Saint-Rémy writes, 'that which proves that there are no races that are better or worse than any another is that Toussaint Louverture went too far in his crimes as well as in his virtues' [*exagéra le crime comme la vertu*] (18). This is all to say that while Louverture stated that he was penning these memoirs solely in order to counter the fact that 'the most atrocious of lies have been spread about me' (86), his writing was made to perform a vastly different function by Saint-Rémy, one that was consonant with a redemptive narrative of discursive revenge that co-opted much of the language of the "mulatto/a" vengeance narrative.

Saint-Rémy, 'whose editing,' Arthur Saint-Aubin says, 'encourages the reading of the narrative as a literary text rather than as a historical document' (2011, 107), made Louverture into both a tragic "racial" figure and an ardent "race man" who took his revenge with the pen and not the sword from the very first page. This was partially achieved by Saint-Rémy's decision to place on the title page, along with an engraving of Louverture, the Haitian general's aforementioned poignant question, 'The color of my body, does it compromise my honor and my bravery?' The quotation and the image with which it appears frames the entire memoir within the terms of vindicationist responses to the pseudoscience of "race" found in the works of other nineteenth-century writers in the Black Atlantic, like Olaudah Equiano in *The Interesting Narrative of the Life of Olaudah Equiano* (1789), Baron de Vastey with his *Réflexions sur une lettre de Mazères* (1816), and, later, Theodore Holly's *A vindication of the capacity of the Negro race for self-government, and civilized progress, as demonstrated by historical events of the Haytian Revolution* (1857).

An activist tradition of abolition tied to "racial" uplift was more immediately linked to the memoirs by Saint-Rémy when he dedicated the text to the U.S. abolitionist 'Mistress Harriet Beecher Stowe, author of the philosophical novel *Uncle Tom's Cabin*' (Saint-Rémy, 1853, 5). In his dedication, Saint-Rémy said to Stowe that her novel would help the United States to 'succeed in defeating the monster' of slavery because the abolitionists had 'truth' and Stowe herself—'daughter of the heavens' [*fille du ciel*]—on their side (6). Saint-Rémy subsequently pointed to color prejudice as ultimately a family tragedy when he asked Stowe, 'isn't it shameful, madame, that in the nineteenth century of Christianity, the diversity of skin colors can still serve in some countries as the mark of separation [*proscription*] between different branches of the human family?' (6). Both the quotation from Louverture pulled out of its original context and the question to Stowe make it seem as if it will be Louverture in his capacity as a memoirist rather than Saint-Rémy in his capacity as an editor who will systematically dismantle the idea of African inferiority in the way that Saint-Rémy viewed *Uncle Tom's Cabin* as having done. In reality, it is Saint-Rémy and decidedly not Louverture who will address the pseudoscience of "race," both in his introduction to the text and by way of the explanatory footnotes found throughout the volume.

In his introduction, after condemning the colonists for having 'invoked SCIENCE against us,' Saint-Rémy writes, '[i]n the eyes of history, all the races have mixed, have merged, and so in our eyes all men have mixed' (15–16). The broader purpose of his engagement with the proponents of 'SCIENCE,' who had sought to prove that 'the angles of the face so often invoked'[15] could 'legitimate the oppression of races,' was to dismantle the abundance of theories linking a presupposed African indisposition to literacy to African inferiority. One of Saint-Rémy's goals was to use Louverture's memoirs as proof that Africans were 'men' capable of literary output. This stands in stark opposition to the goal of Louverture as he wrote the memoirs themselves. Louverture went out of his way to depoliticize possible interpretations of his motives by saying that he merely wanted 'to provide to the French government an exact account of my conduct ... even if it is used against me' (29). The memoirs are made to perform the function of revenge, albeit a much more discursive one since Louverture was evidently not in a position to take physical or political revenge after being kidnapped by Leclerc, when Saint-Rémy presents Louverture as a writer defying the "racial" hierarchies of his time and the political failures of his life. Saint-Rémy wrote that Louverture had been a 'stranger to all instruction except for that which comprises meditation'; having hardly 'come out of slavery' (26), but that his memoirs 'will serve above all to prove that the intelligence of the negro can rise to the heights of the greatest knowledge [*peut s'élever à la hauteur de toutes les connaissances*]' (24).

Desormeaux has written that notwithstanding his obvious admiration for

---

15 Anatomical arguments about 'blacks' designed to support slavery had become increasingly popular during the Enlightenment (Curran, 215). The most famous proponent of the phrenological argument was probably Georges Cuvier, who is best known today for having exploited a woman named Saartije Baartman, often referred to pejoratively as the 'Hottentot Venus.' Baartman had been captured by European enslavers from South Africa and subsequently taken to Europe only to suffer the humiliation of being used as a living display by Cuvier and others (Samaan, 628–29). In his *Tableau élémentaire de l'histoire naturelle des animaux* (1797–98), Cuvier said of the 'race' that he had elsewhere referred to as 'Caucasian' (1817, 1:99), 'The white race, with its oval face, long hair, prominent nose, to which belong the civilized peoples of Europe, and which seems to us to be the most beautiful of them all, is also superior to the others by the force of its genius, courage, and activity' (71). As for 'Africans,' Cuvier would write in *Le Règne Animal Distribué D'après Son Organisation* (1817), 'the negro race ... is black, its hair curly, its skull compressed and its nose flat, its protruding face [*museau saillant*] and thick lips make it significantly like monkeys; the tribes of which it is composed have always remained barbaric' (1:99).

'La couleur de mon corps nuit-elle à mon honneur et à ma bravoure?' from Joseph Saint Rémy's *Mémoires du Général Toussaint-L'Ouverture, écrits par lui-même* (1853). Courtesy of the John Carter Brown Library at Brown University.

Louverture, Saint-Rémy, who said that Louverture was 'a man who would have honored any nation' (1853, 17), only succeeds in 'vainly combating' the science of race because he himself 'remains blinded by racial and political prejudices' (2011, 57). Desormeaux further suggests, '[e]xiled and without support in France,' Saint-Rémy's editing of the memoirs, 'reveals more of his own political "interests" … It is in fact, his intellectual "interests" that will eclipse the original work of Toussaint [Louverture] itself' (2011, 54). Whether or not Saint-Rémy's own 'racial and political prejudices,' whatever those may have been, caused him to 'eclipse' or obscure the original intent of the memoirs, is perhaps not as meaningful as the story about Louverture and "race" that is being told through Saint-Rémy's editorial choices. Much like Leitch Ritchie, whose translation of *Bug-Jargal* into *The Slave King* (see chapter three of this volume) only served to exacerbate the trope of "monstrous hybridity" found in Hugo's original text, Louverture's own feebly expressed idea about "race" as having been one the causes of his conflict with France was indeed exacerbated and even bolstered by the fact that Saint-Rémy wants Louverture's memoirs to tell a very different story, but a no less tragic one, about the independence of Haiti.

This story about national independence, one that presents the capability of a former slave to achieve literacy as evidence of his humanity, also offers the literate slave turned into a flawed (because human) leader as the true hero of Haitian independence. In Saint-Rémy's rendition, Louverture *had* absolutely tried to usurp the authority of his national father when he attempted to replace Bonaparte's authority with his own, a move that was supposedly evidenced by Louverture's 1801 Constitution. In the footnote accompanying mention of this document, Saint-Rémy says that for Louverture to declare himself 'general for life' in the Constitution with the right to name his own successor, 'was to have, in fact, proclaimed the independence of Saint-Domingue' (1853, 87). Saint-Rémy also quotes from Napoléon Bonaparte's *Mémoires*, in which the First Consul imagined Louverture having, by way of the Constitution, declared war against him: 'Toussaint knew very well,' Bonaparte writes, 'that in proclaiming his constitution, he had thrown away his mask and had drawn his sword out of its sheath forever' (qtd. in 1853, 87).

The problem with this story—one in which a rebellious (and literate) ex-slave seeks to replace a head of state—is that it is not really in Louverture's memoirs. Louverture argued that he had not at all sought to replace Bonaparte with his Constitution, but had merely wanted to 'offer some laws, based on local customs' that would take into account 'the character and morality of the inhabitants of the colony' (87). He further writes, '[t]he Constitution was designed to have been submitted for approval to the [French] government, which, alone, had the right to adopt it or reject it' (87). Louverture went on to accuse Bonaparte of never having even entered into a dialogue about the document, of having sent Leclerc to the colony instead. All of these explanations and vindications of his behavior allow Louverture to consistently paint himself as the honorable—rather than vengeful—ex-slave, even when he was still suffering under the dishonorable position of slavery. Louverture wrote: 'I was a slave, I dare to admit it; but I never suffered the reproach of any of my masters [*J'ai été esclave, j'ose l'avouer; mais je n'ai jamais essuyé des reproches de la part de mes maîtres*]' (90).

The omission of any mention of his children as a factor in his decision to ultimately demonstrate his stated loyalty to Bonaparte by ending the war with Leclerc, in some respects, complicates the widely circulated notion that Louverture's political position had been compromised by his love for his children. In his *Vie de Toussaint L'Ouverture* (1850), Saint-Rémy had repeated the popular story about Louverture and his children as locked into the "interracial" family romance that had dominated portrayals of Louverture's life for around half a century. Saint-Rémy, for example, pre-empted the silences in Louverture's memoirs concerning these events when he explained that when faced with the choice between his children or rebelling against the authority of Bonaparte, 'L'Ouverture was especially amazed that one would want to make his children the price of his surrender' (1850, 349). Saint-Rémy continues:

> Challenging, in the midst of this moment of supreme emotion, the free will of his children, he proposed to them the choice between staying by his side or going back to join the whites. Isaac Louverture declared that he would never fire against France; while Placide, he declared that he would die at the side of his father. (349)

Saint-Rémy makes a point of telling the reader how this situation upsets standard ideas about "racial," not to mention political and familial loyalties, when he writes, 'nevertheless Isaac was a negro, the true son of Louverture, and Placide was a mulatto, his adopted son.' Going on to explicitly reference the work of Lacroix and repeat this "interracial" family romance as a conflict that was tinged with the possibility of fratricide, Saint-Rémy evokes the works of 'General Pamphile,' who 'said that the next day these two fellows, brothers [*deux frères congénères*], fought in opposing ranks, that is to say that Placide was with Louverture and Isaac with Leclerc' (349). This fact alone seemed to prove to Saint-Rémy that injustices had been done to the former free people of color, who had been painted by many historians as treacherous traitors to the cause of the former slaves. Saint-Rémy writes, 'It is you, then, Placide ... it is you who offered the last consoling smile to the hero of our race, the sigh of filial benediction. I thank you in the name of all of the people of color' (391).

The Trope of the Tragic "Mulatto/a"

The exiled nineteenth-century Haitian historian is hardly the origin of the inference that the dilemma between Louverture and his children was one of "race." Nor was Saint-Rémy the origin of the idea that Placide and Isaac Louverture had found themselves embroiled in a fratricidal as well as a patricidal conflict. As we are about to see, Saint-Rémy's biography, which bears the influence of both Isaac Louverture (Desormeaux, 2011, 23) and Pamphile de Lacroix, as well as Alphonse de Lamartine, merely demonstrates the way in which writing about the Haitian Revolution was itself a palimpsest that over time allowed the tragedy of Toussaint Louverture to become indelibly linked to a tragic family romance of "miscegenation." The "interracial" family romance of the revolutionary hero that we find constantly in the literary history of the Haitian Revolution provides a particularly apt example of the ways in which the narrative of "mulatto/a" vengeance would influence for generations to come some of the most popular ideas about both Haiti and "race," including the abiding trope of the tragic "mulatto/a." In many ways, the narrative of the familial tropology of the tragic "mulatto/a" was put into motion through writings about the life of Toussaint Louverture.

*

Almost from the beginning of attempts to write his life, the story of Louverture and his children having fallen out of favor with Bonaparte had been considerably sentimentalized in a way that set up the Haitian general to become the kind of tragic hero found in Greek drama and that undergirds the very idea of the tragic "mulatto." That is to say, in the literary history of the Haitian Revolution, Louverture would become *the* hero of the revolution who was ultimately ruined by his own *hamartia* or the very trait that made him noble, his honor, whether codified as owing to his national loyalties or his paternal, filial, and "racial" devotions.

One of the first attempts to provide a biography of the Haitian general, the anonymously published *Buonaparte in the West Indies, or the History of Toussaint Louverture, the African Hero* (1803), which was anonymously published by British author James Stephen, immediately dramatizes the conflict between the family and the nation as a question of honor, sentiment, and heroism. The scene in which Louverture must decide between his children and the Revolution is presented in the language of the theater. In part three of the biography, after recounting the conflict between Louverture and his children, Stephen writes, '[l]et us now proceed to the last act of the illustrious life of Toussaint' (3:10). In explaining the events that preceded this 'last act,' Stephen had referenced the Louverture children's preceptor, Coisnon, whom he calls a 'miscreant' (2:10), as having written in his report to the French ministry in 1802 that upon seeing one another, '*The father and the two sons threw themselves into each other's arms. I saw them shed tears,* and WISHING TO TAKE ADVANTAGE OF A PERIOD WHICH I CONCEIVED TO BE FAVORABLE, *I stopped him at the moment where he stretched out his arms to me*' (2:10). What Stephen reads as Coisnon's rebuke of Louverture's attempt to show gratitude to the tutor of his young children provides the occasion for the British historian to admonish the French character and exalt the English one: 'Englishmen, here you have a striking picture of French feelings!' (2:10). Stephen continues by discussing Louverture's reaction upon reading the letter in which Leclerc demanded the surrender of Louverture, 'the African hero.' In Stephen's estimation:

> the tears of the mother and her boys, and their sobbing entreaties, pour anguish into the hero's bosom. He still remains silent. The conflict of passions and principles within him may be seen in his expressive features, and in his eager, glistening eye. But his tongue does not attempt to give utterance to feelings for which language is too weak. Awful moment for the African race! Did he hesitate? perhaps he did. It is too much for human virtue not to stagger in such a conflict. It is honour enough not to be subdued. But why do I speak of *human virtue?* The strength of Toussaint flowed from a higher fountain, and I doubt not that at this trying moment he thought of the heroism of the cross, and was strengthened from above. (2:12)[16]

Stephen continues:

> Coisnon saw the struggle, he eyed it with a hell-born pleasure, and was ready in his heart to cry out "victory," when the illustrious African suddenly composed his agitated visage, gently disengaged himself from the grasp of his wife and children, took the envoy into an inner chamber, and gave him a dignified refusal. "Take back my children," said he, "since it must be so. I will be faithful to my brethren and my God!"

Stephen concludes by evoking the idea of the universal literary hero:

> Most of my readers, I fear, are but badly versed in history, and have read

---

[16] In contrast, in his 1804 *Mémoire pour servir à l'histoire d'Haïti*, one of the first histories of the Haitian Revolution to be published in the Atlantic World, the secretary of Jean-Jacques Dessalines, Louis Félix Boisrond-Tonnerre, hardly remarked upon Louverture's children—saying of them only that Louverture's 'two sons, employed in the French army, who had been sent back to him during the first negotiations, fought with their father and no longer enjoyed the type of consideration that had been given to them during their voyage' (52).

little of those who were called Heroes in ancient times. I am sorry for it because they will therefore have only my word for it, that there is nothing in history to be compared with this conduct of Toussaint. (2:12)

Nearly a decade later, in *The History of Toussaint Louverture* (1814), Stephen, this time under his own name, tried to more explicitly historicize what he had earlier romanticized when he continued to paint Louverture as having tragically sacrificed his sons in the name of liberty. The 1814 edition of Stephen's biography was dedicated to 'his imperial majesty, the Emperor of all the Russias,' and its preface provides an explanation for the author's motive for producing the earlier 1803 version. The editor tells us that the first iteration had been created 'with a view chiefly to its probable influence on the minds of the lower classes of the English readers,' and that it had also been, 'designed to counteract the false impressions which many of them had received of the character of Bonaparte; exhibit him not as friendly, but irreconcilably hostile' (vii). According to the preface of the 1803 edition, however, the original text also seems to have been designed at least in part to refute the portrayal of Louverture by the French journalist Louis Dubroca (Stephen, 1803, 1:13). Nevertheless, the publisher of the 1814 version said that the newer edition had only been very slightly altered from its original to 'omit ... many familiar expressions and allusions which might offend the tastes of his polite readers.' Equally omitted were 'some passages and terms, which, in the altered state of our relations with France, could not now be used without impropriety' (vii–viii). Notable in its absence from the 1814 version is the memorable insult:

> Everybody has heard of Toussaint, the famous Negro general. Who does not know that it was he who fought so bravely for the freedom of the poor blacks in St. Domingo, and who also defended the island for France during the whole of the last war. In this, by the by, he did no more than his duty as a Frenchman ... He has been basely requited for all his services by that same slavish republic. (Stephen, 1803, 1:2)

Also missing is the equally unforgettable barb concerning the kidnapping of Louverture: 'I shall write it with shame as well as indignation; for though I thank God I am not a Frenchman, I am a White man, and a native of Europe' (3:10).

The absence of overt rancor in the later version on the part of the historian, who remonstrates against the treatment of a 'black man' by a 'White man,' seems to coincide with Mike Goode's assertion that in the eighteenth century the romantic historian strove to be a 'chivalric man of feeling' rather than the man of scientific ideas that he would become in the Victorian era (5). To that end, in Stephen's later account, the family conflict of the Louvertures, while still containing many of the elements of sentimentality, appears in much less melodramatic terms. Stephen writes that the children were 'hostage youths, so beloved and so worthy of [their father's] affections' (42), but the 'cold-blooded Coisnon' told Louverture:

> You must submit ... or my orders are to carry my pupils back to the Cape. You will not, I know, cover yourself with infamy, by breaking faith and violating a safe conduct. Behold, then, the tears of your wife; and consider that, upon your decision, depends whether the boys shall remain to gladden her heart, and yours or be torn from you both forever. (42)

Stephen writes that Louverture ultimately chose to fight with his compatriots rather than to save his sons, and subsequently repeats the passage from the earlier version, that Louverture 'gently disengaged himself from the grasp of his wife and children,' and then cried out, 'Take back my children ... since it must be so. I will be faithful to my brethren and to my God' (43–44).

A very different reading of these events comes to us from Louis Dubroca in his *La Vie de J.J. Dessalines* (1804). Dubroca, whose sympathies certainly did not lie with the Haitian general, wrote:

> If you recall, the French government had sent to Toussaint Louverture his two children in order to try to remind him of his duties by attacking the feelings of his heart: here is the manner in which this barbaric father sought to turn this circumstance into a situation that could profit his perfidy. (80).

Dubroca continues by affirming, in some sense, Stephen's account of the events when he writes that Coisnon attempted to prevent Louverture from embracing his sons amidst all the 'tears that were flowing.' Dubroca's Coisnon does this, however, not to rebuke Louverture's gratitude but to check his loyalties. Coisnon says to Louverture, 'Is it really Toussaint ... is this really the Friend of France that I am about to embrace?' (80). After affirming his loyalty to France and sending his sons back to the French government with a letter in which he asked for Leclerc to 'suspend the attack' in order to provide him with more time to pacify the 'other black leaders,' Dubroca says that Louverture betrayed the 'armistice of four days' that he had asked for in the letter by 'ordering the massacre of all the whites in the colony' (82–84). Louverture's stated duplicity had, for Dubroca, something to tell us about the qualities of Louverture as a father. The French historian represents Louverture as having perilously, and seemingly without regard for their welfare, sent his sons directly into the eye of the storm, knowing full well that his betrayal might have cost them their lives (84).

In 1817, Baron de Vastey would repeat the idea found in the works of

Stephen, that Louverture's decision regarding his children was a heroic, if tragic, declaration of his fraternal loyalty. Vastey provides the following description of the encounter between Louverture and his newly returned French-educated children in his *Réflexions politiques*:

> During the Leclerc expedition, the French wanted to use the children of the general [Louverture] as instruments to separate the father from the cause of his brothers; [Leclerc], therefore, sent back two of his children with M. Coisnon, their preceptor. During the meeting that took place in Ennery, between the general Toussaint, his children, and the preceptor, national love was put into opposition with paternal love [*l'amour de la patrie fut mis en prise avec l'amour paternel*]. This unfortunate father was placed by the barbaric French in the cruel position of having to choose between the salvation of his brothers and his country or the life of his own children; after much struggle and indecision, this unhappy father nobly made the sacrifice of his children for the salvation of his fatherland [*patrie*]. (3)

In Vastey's version, Louverture's choice is precisely between his genealogical family and his national family, leaving the door open for the revolution to take on the same quality of the "interracial" family romance with all of the parricidal implications we saw in the works of Dubroca, albeit much to the credit of the general in Vastey's version.

Perhaps unsurprisingly, it was Pamphile de Lacroix, whose text was one of the most influential nineteenth-century histories of the Haitian Revolution, who not only further sentimentalized, but explicitly racialized the above events in the immediately melodramatic terms recognizable to students of the trope of the tragic "mulatto/a." Lacroix's romanticization of Louverture's refusal to submit to the authority of France is so telling with respect to its author's ideas about "mulatto/a" vengeance that it is worth quoting at length. In the scene presented below, Lacroix describes Louverture as 'irritated' by the ultimatum that Leclerc sent with Isaac and Placide:

> [Louverture] told his children that *he left them free to choose between their country and their father* [leur patrie et leur père]; *that he did not blame them for their attachment to France, which was responsible for their education; but that between him and France there was his color, whose future he could not compromise by placing it at the mercy of an expedition in which were prominently figured several white generals, as well as* Rigaud, Pétion, Boyer, Chanlatte, etc., *all of his personal enemies; that the order to continue fighting before the negotiations meant that France had put more confidence in its weapons than in its rights ... and that, if they did not know how to co-exist with the blacks while* [the blacks] *still had some power, what would it be like when he and his men did not any longer have any?* (2:125; emphasis original)

Between the Family and the Nation

Lacroix uses the kinds of idea about "race" found in the narrative of "mulatto/a" vengeance both when he suggests that all of Louverture's 'personal enemies' were people of "mixed race," indicated by their names appearing in italics (reverse italics in this instance because the dialogue itself is italicized) and that the problem between Louverture and France was one of 'color.'[17] Lacroix goes on to portray Louverture as having been forced to choose between his ("black") children and the France that had educated them, on the one hand, and his ("black") brothers and the liberty he had promised them on the other.

In describing the aftermath of Louverture's tragic decision that the good of the many, the slaves, outweighed his paternal affections or the good of the few, Lacroix writes, 'His sons threw themselves into his arms, their caresses could not move him; inflexible, he incessantly responded to them by saying: *My children, pick your side, whichever it is, I will always cherish you*' (2:126). By including his entreaty to his children, Lacroix's Louverture places the onus of choosing between the family and the nation back onto the revolutionary hero's own sons, who must now choose between their ("black") father, Louverture, and their ("white") nation, France. Lacroix goes on to write, 'Their tears and their supplications not leading to any change, ISAAC all of a sudden detached himself from the arms of his father: "Well then!" he said, "see in me a faithful servant to France, who could never bring himself to bear arms against her"' (2:126). Placide, on the other hand, whom Lacroix describes as a '*griffe de couleur*, half-brother [*frère utérin*] of ISAAC,[18] professed as much indecision with his eyes as with his conduct: TOUSSAINT LOUVERTURE, petrified, blessed ISAAC even as he walked away' (2:126). This version of the "interracial" family romance, where a "black" biological son (indicated to the reader by his name appearing in capital letters) turns his back on his "black" father, reaches its tragic conclusion when Lacroix tells us that it was Placide, the adopted son of "mixed race," with all of his indecisiveness, who ultimately

---

17 Recall that Lacroix uses all capital letters to denote those figures who are "black" and italicizes the names of all "mulattoes" or people of "mixed race." See chapter three of the present volume.

18 As far as I can tell, the first usage of the very distinct term 'frère utérin' to describe the genealogical relationship of Isaac and Placide Louverture was in a 'lettre ministerielle' dated January 3, 1817 in which the latter is referred to as the 'frère utérin d'Isaac' (qtd. in Schoelcher, 1889, 435). The phrase was picked up by Lacroix and then seems to have been repeated by Isaac Louverture in the 1821 letter that he penned to contest the desire of his 'frère utérin' to use the name Louverture. Later, the phrase would be repeated in the version of Isaac Louverture's memoirs published by both Métral and Gragnon-Lacoste, as well as in the historical works of the Haitian Revolution by Schoelcher (1889, 436) and Poyen-Bellisle (120).

• 397 •

chose to denounce France forever: '*Placide*, subdued by his influence [*dompté par son ascendant*], threw himself sobbing around his father's neck and said to him: *I am yours, my father: I fear the future, I fear slavery; I am ready to fight with you to oppose it; I no longer know France*' (2:126). Ultimately, Lacroix's account of the difficult decision the Haitian general and his sons had to face concerning the fate of the latter demonstrates the utility of the trope of the tragic "mulatto/a" to cover up a host of anxieties about "racial" loyalties not matching perceived "racial," familial, or political identities. Here, a 'black' biological father and son reject each other, while a 'griffe' adopted son is unexpectedly loyal. The anxieties about "race" on display in such a portrayal of the life of the Louvertures as an Oedipal "interracial" family romance (and all of the epistemological uncertainty it invited) would find further expression in mid-nineteenth-century French theater.

Before going on to consider the way in which the trope of the tragic "mulatto/a" unfolds in the theatrical work of Lamartine, it is worth acknowledging that after Lacroix, the single biggest influence on Lamartine's play was the memoir of Isaac Louverture. Louverture's son referenced his captivity only by saying that at the time of the arrival of the Leclerc expedition, 'Toussaint-Louverture found himself in Santo-Domingo' and that:

> at last, after having retained Coison and two of his students on board for several days, against their will, Leclerc said to them ... *I have the greatest hope of coming to an agreement with Toussaint-Louverture ... it is necessary for you to take him this letter from the First Consul.* (236)

The middle child of Suzanne and Toussaint Louverture also wrote that after he and Placide were reunited with their father it was their younger brother, Saint-Jean, who would go on to be kept a hostage upon the orders of Leclerc. Moreover, according to Isaac, the *benjamin* of Louverture's children with Suzanne was 'not the only member of the family' 'who was, during this war [in Gonaïves], under the power of general Leclerc.' Isaac Louverture writes, 'General Paul-Louverture, his uncle, *le colonel de dragons*, Jean-Pierre Louverture, his brother ... the *chef de bataillon* Chancy, his cousin,' were also under the thumb of Leclerc and, 'his mother, a woman who was truly cherished and venerated in her country, had just missed being taken by general Rochambeau' (291–92). In addition, while Lacroix, Stephen, and Vastey had described Louverture as having chosen the side of the Revolution over loyalty to France and his children, in Isaac's memoir, when Louverture finally reaches an agreement with Leclerc to put down his arms and submit to the authority of France, Isaac describes his father using a language that suggests that, at least in his mind, he had indeed chosen his children over the Revolution. Isaac Louverture writes, '[i]t seemed that everything was competing [*Il semblait que tout eut concouru*] during this meeting to make us see in this one man the heart of a father, of a husband, of a warrior defending the interests of his country [*patrie*] and his comrades in arms' (293). Moreover, although Lacroix had represented Isaac Louverture as having chosen France over his father, the son seemingly refuted such an assertion by representing himself as the always devoted and indeed the *true* child of the Haitian general. After Toussaint Louverture was arrested and initially placed on board a ship called the *Créole* for deportation, the memoir reports, 'Isaac-Louverture, who thought that he no longer had a father, wanted to die also' (304–05).[19]

In the version of these events dramatized in *Toussaint Louverture*, Lamartine's Isaac similarly states that he, unlike his brother Albert, will remain loyal to his family because, 'Me, I love my parents' (line 1359). Even though many critics have observed that Lamartine gets Isaac Louverture's "race" wrong, so to speak, I think that the story that emerges from what may have been a simple error is far more important to our understanding of the play than has been previously acknowledged. With this portrayal of Isaac as the "mulatto" son who chooses Haiti after having been forced to choose between a "white" identity and a "black" identity, symbolized by France and Haiti, respectively, Lamartine frames the entire text within the parameters of the trope of the tragic "mulatto/a" with one important difference. In Lamartine's play, the thematic of the vengeful "mulatto" becomes that of the *avenging* "mulatto" who righteously fights for national rather than personal aims. Isaac's "mulatto" dilemma, as he decides to become an *avenging* "mulatto," is only one of the text's such engagements with this differently operating tragic tropology of "race." Lamartine's portrayal of Louverture's niece, Adrienne, as a woman of "mixed race" prepared to commit literal patricide, poises her to become one of Dessalines's famed *avengers of the Americas* as well. Lamartine's portrayal of Louverture's son Albert, who is also prepared to commit figurative patricide as an *avenger of France*, further epitomizes the tragic "interracial" family romance that was called forth by ideas about the conflict between the family and the nation in connection with the Haitian Revolution.

*

The most sustained and well-known portrayal of the family conflict of the revolutionary hero as principally about "race" comes from the French poet, playwright, and politician Alphonse de Lamartine. In the preface to the

---

19 Louverture and his family would eventually be taken on board a different ship called *L'Héros*, which was bound for France (rpt. in Girard, 2014, 134).

The Trope of the Tragic "Mulatto/a"

1850 published version of *Toussaint Louverture*, Lamartine claimed to have begun writing the play in 1840, but he said that 'Diverse circumstances and various more urgent political problems caused me to lose sight of this sketch' (4).[20] Lamartine also explained that if the play seemed unpolished and was guilty of historical inaccuracies or inconsistencies, this was because he had lost the original manuscript during a journey to the Pyrénées. Regardless, Lamartine wrote that he was aiming to be more activist than literary with *Toussaint Louverture*: 'I did not at all design this feeble sketch for the Théâtre Français,' he wrote. 'I wrote it for the melodramatic theaters of the *boulevard*. I conceived of it more for the eyes of the masses than for the ears of the elite with their refined tastes' (4). The play had apparently been originally conceived by Lamartine as a drama promoting the abolition of slavery in the French colonies: 'I have not at all hidden any of its numerous imperfections; it was only my intention to provide a speech in verse and acting in favor of the abolition of slavery' (10). Nevertheless, the play enjoyed an initial run of 24 performances after it opened to mixed reviews on April 6, 1850 at the Théâtre de la Porte Saint-Martin in Paris (Hoffmann, 1998, xxviii–xxviii), before going on to be published by Michel Lévy in the same year.

Though the play would not actually be staged or published until after the general emancipation of all French slaves and the permanent abolition of French slavery in 1848, with which Lamartine's name was directly associated (Lamartine, 1998, 10), the action of the play begins just before the arrival of the Leclerc expedition, when Louverture sends his sons to France as proof of his allegiance to the metropole. Louverture's sons are eventually sent back to Saint-Domingue by Bonaparte, initially without their father's knowledge, and are held as hostages by Leclerc. The generals Leclerc and Rochambeau subsequently reveal their plan to keep Louverture's sons in captivity if the general does not consent to compel the revolutionists to surrender. When confronted with a choice between the sons he has raised from birth and the people he is trying to lead towards liberty, Louverture describes the conflict in the same terms of indecision, tragedy, and parricidal consequence that ideas about the Haitian Revolution as an "interracial" family conflict seem to have incessantly called forth: Louverture says, 'At last! I give birth to a people and, cursed on this earth,/Alone, I have no child who calls me his father!/Liberty of my race, is this your price?/ That to save my people, I must lose my sons?/ ... /To save my sons, I must lose my race?' (lines 2336–40). In the face of Louverture's ambivalence, a priest by the name of Father Antoine shows up and urges Louverture to fight for Haiti,[21] saying, 'If you

---

20 I quote here and throughout from the version edited and established in 1998 by Léon-François Hoffmann with Exeter University Press.

21 Although, in 1802, the French colony was still known by the name of Saint-

lose your children, your people will replace them' (line 846). Consequently, Louverture and his "mixed-race" niece, Adrienne, whom we later learn is the daughter of Salvador, a "white" French colonist, decide to wage war if the French return to the island. Meanwhile, Louverture's sons, Albert and Isaac, have been having a heated debate with Salvador (who is their guardian and preceptor), about whether they will be loyal to their national father, Bonaparte, or to their genealogical father, Louverture. Albert chooses Bonaparte and France in an act that suggests a figurative patricide, while Isaac vows to 'love' his father and Haiti always. With one son on the side of the Revolution and the other on the side of the Leclerc expedition, the play sets up the possibility for the many different kinds of parricide—infanticide, fratricide, and patricide—that characterize the "interracial" family romance of the Haitian Revolution.

While French writers of Lamartine's own era, like Théophile Gautier, criticized the play as much as they praised it (Hoffmann, 1998, xxvii; Harris, 209), nineteenth-century Haitian authors who mentioned Lamartine tended to venerate the famous French poet unequivocally. Such is the case in the fleeting reference to Lamartine in the works of Antènor Firmin (575) as well as in the more substantial mentions of the French poet in the works of Demesvar Delorme and Pierre Faubert. In the preface to Faubert's play *Ogé; ou le préjugé de couleur*, first performed in 1841 for students of the Lycée National de Port-au-Prince, of which Faubert was the director, the Haitian playwright says that Lamartine, 'whose impartiality, with respect to his historical interpretations, is recognized even by his enemies,' was a 'great writer, who was also, as no one denies, one of the most ardent of the modern abolitionists' (31). In his *Les Théoriciens au pouvoir* (1870), Delorme, for his part, wrote that Lamartine was 'the poet of poets, who will end up proving to us that the culture of literature and sentiment is not at all incompatible with the governance of societies, and that the most ethereal of poetry itself is not in contrast with politics and government' (1:606). Ostensibly addressing Lamartine's critics, Delorme went on to write that the French poet, 'preaches not only, as you have said, dreams and illusions. He preaches reason, rights, the truth, and all that is just, all that is good, all that has to be, all that can be' (1:610). The nineteenth-century Haitian playwright Liautaud Ethéart, who was the editor of a volume entitled *Les Miscellanées*, also heaped excessive praise on Lamartine for *Toussaint Louverture*, calling the French poet an 'eminent dramaturge' (qtd. in Bonneau, 1856, 136). Saint-Rémy more explicitly discussed the play when with similarly effusive acclamation he wrote in his introduction to *Vie de Toussaint L'Ouverture*

Domingue, throughout the play, Lamartine's characters will use the name of independent Haiti.

(1850) that Lamartine, 'A white man,—a great poet and great politician,—has just made tremble the ashes of the illustrious negro capitan,—a great poet and politician also. Lamartine has sung Toussaint Louverture.—Glory to the bard [*chantre*] and to the hero' (vii). Finally, Beaubrun Ardouin expressed his unending esteem for Lamartine and, particularly, for the latter's *Histoire des Girondins* (1847), when he wrote that this work, in which Lamartine 'had pleaded the cause of the blacks,' meant that 'Lamartine should remain forever honored by all Haitians' as the 'greatest single person' to have contributed to the 1848 emancipation of all slaves in French colonies (1855, 2:261).

The admiration and even adoration that many nineteenth-century Haitian writers felt for Lamartine was apparently mutual. In a letter addressed to Ardouin dated May 20, 1853, and reprinted by Ethéart in *Les Miscellanées*, Lamartine wrote:

> Monsieur,—I thank you for the kind regard that you had to think of me when you wrote your history of Haiti. It is the history of our faults and of our reparations. *No one other than you* could have been better suited to properly retell the history of our turmoils, excesses, and the triumphs of the human race that you have so intimately encouraged. No one is more interested in this story than I am, because Providence reserved for me the unexpected fortune to have written my name on the documents upon which the birth of liberty was penned. (rpt. in Ethéart, 122, emphasis in original)

If many of the play's most ardent advocates in the nineteenth century focused upon *Toussaint Louverture*'s heroic portrayal of a "black" leader as evidence of its author's understanding of the ontological consequences of ideas about "blackness," the same could be said of more contemporary criticism. The former Senegalese President, Léopold Senghor, claimed, for example, that *Toussaint Louverture* was a masterpiece because it 'argues in favor of racial equality, stigmatizes slavery, and spreads new ideas about the condition of blacks.' Senghor further added that Lamartine's 'generous ideas ... make him, rightfully, the precursor of the struggle for négritude' (68–69). Vèvè Clark seconded the opinion that Lamartine was *avant la lettre* by arguing that in *Toussaint Louverture*, 'the phenomenon of double-consciousness' is performed 'in 1848 well before W.E.B. Du Bois invented the term' (245).

Not everyone who has focused on the play's engagement with "blackness" has been so happy with Lamartine's efforts. While Yves Bénot weakly praised the play, which he thought was aesthetically 'mediocre,' for its veneration of Toussaint Louverture (41), David O'Connell has charged that with respect to "race," Lamartine merely 'cynically exploits the black hero theme for his own personal advantage' (1973, 527). Arthur Saint-Aubin tends to agree that the real subject of the play is not "blackness" when he makes the case that it was 'not about Haiti, black men in general, nor, ultimately, Toussaint L'Ouverture specifically.' Saint-Aubin finds instead that *Toussaint Louverture*, which he says, 'avoids staging miscegenation proper' (2007, 345), is about 'white masculine subjectivity and agency' (333).

In spite of some relatively renewed interest in the relationship of *Toussaint Louverture* to "race" from these twentieth-century literary critics and historians, little attention has been paid to the romance of "miscegenation" that makes this text important for understanding the *longue durée* of the literary history of the Haitian Revolution. *Toussaint Louverture*, for good or for ill, may not only have something to tell us about Lamartine's personal and political ideas about "blackness" or, more broadly, "race"; we might also view the text as revealing the way the "interracial" family romance of the life of Toussaint Louverture found its way into the popular realm, as well as the different ends to which this version of the narrative of "mulatto/a" vengeance could be put to use. I would suggest, in fact, that the kind of 'staging' of the trope of the tragic "mulatto/a" and therefore "miscegenation" that we absolutely do find within Lamartine's portrayal of Toussaint Louverture's children as confronted with the myriad potentialities of parricide, is precisely what makes the play an immediately crucial component for understanding how pseudoscientific ideas of "race" were being used in concert with the Haitian Revolution as a tool for exploring the moral, spiritual, and psychological consequences of revolutions in general.

Although the troping that could be accomplished through the body of the "mulatto" as a symbol of revolutionary ambivalence seems to set the stage for understanding the fact of being in the position to choose between one's family and one's nation—Salvadore tells us, 'uncertainty casts in the mind the same disquiet [*inquiétude*]./The officer is pensive, the soldier discontent;/ The mulatto, undecided, floats; the black waits' (lines 1515–18)—*Toussaint Louverture* is a play whose "racial" complexities cannot be understood merely in terms of "blacks," "whites," and "mulattoes." It is in using a vocabulary of "mixed-race" identity, in addition to characters who are portrayed as being of "mixed race," that the play poignantly dramatizes the anxiety that was called forth by not being able to count upon "race" or family connection to determine political loyalties. The true tragedy of this version of Louverture's life, then, is that neither "race" nor family nor political loyalty will matter in the end anyway, especially not in a context in which one who was portrayed as noble and good could suffer exactly because he was noble and good.

As in Séjour's 'Le Mulâtre,' in *Toussaint Louverture*, having genealogical ties to both "whiteness" and "blackness" is shown to be an inherently tragic condition because of the epistemological and ontological problems these "interracial" identities might occasion during the revolution. Adrienne remains depressed about her dual origins throughout the play, and she is the one character who most literally finds herself in the conflicted position of having to choose between a "white" parent and a "black" parent. In act I, scene II, for example, we are told that Adrienne is the product of the union between a 'négresse' and a 'colon.' She laments this dual heritage to her friend Lucie while they are discussing the revolution, explaining how it is that she came to be raised by Toussaint Louverture, 'You know the circumstances of my birth, my dear Lucie!/ ... /From the sister of Toussaint I was born,/The free blood of whites, the blood of slavery,/Are warring in my heart just as on my face/And I feel they have once again come to life in me, in different instincts/The race of slaves and that of the tyrants' (lines 163–69). Adrienne is at this point unaware that her father actually raped her mother—Isaac later tells us of Salvador's relationship with Adrienne's mother, 'Lover, persecutor, and executioner, one by one,/More than one beautiful slave, from her mother he has ravished/Lost in his arms honor and then life./One day one of these raptures produced a baby:/When he had to flee the triumphant Haiti,/He sold, as he left, the baby and the woman' (1318–1323)—and so she notes that it is difficult to hate the 'whites' because in hating these 'tyrants,' she would actually have to hate a part of herself.

Unlike Séjour's Georges, Adrienne consciously realizes that a "racial" revolution may mean that she will find herself in the tragic position of having to 'hate' the man who gave her life based on the fact that he is a colonist and therefore the enemy of the Revolution she supports. Adrienne paints her dilemma in the traditional language of the tragic "mulatta" when she laments, 'the blood remembers its source,' saying, '[t]he image of this white man pursues me night and day;/In vain to my country do I owe all of my love!/My memory, chasing this stubborn image,/Refuses to hate he, from whom I was born' (lines 178, 180–84). Adrienne's brand of 'double-consciousness,' if you will, stems from the fact that though she cannot consciously remember her father, her 'blood' can. What complicates these 'warring' 'blood' memories, which might in another plantation culture have presented merely the comparatively benign possibility of incest, is the fact of the Revolution itself. Tying her loyalties to the Revolution means for Adrienne that she might be called upon not only to hate, but to strike her own father.

The children born of "interracial" sexual relations in *Toussaint Louverture* are thus presented as tragic both because of the inherent violence that had produced them and the unnatural violence their positions might occasion. Even so, rather than being swept up in the torrent of events and circumstances that characterize naturalist characters like Séjour's Georges and Zélie, Lamartine's more realist Adrienne consciously pledges her allegiance to Louverture with a full understanding of the kind of patricidal consequences that could result. Adrienne's decisiveness sets her up to become a tragic hero of her own making rather than the fatalist subject of nature's whims. Adrienne consents to the possibility of committing patricide when she vows to fight to the death for Louverture and, in so doing, replaces her biological "white" father, Salvador, with her "black" uncle, Louverture. Adrienne tells Louverture that from this point forward he and her country will be one and the same. She asks, 'My uncle and my country, are they not the same thing?/ Are not you all that of which it is composed?' (lines 966–67), and later she tells Louverture, 'Oh! I will be your daughter, and that's enough!' (line 1019).

In rejecting her biological father, Adrienne, as Isaac will later do, chooses a "black" identity over a "white" one, but in so doing, in true tragic "mulatta" fashion, she ultimately chooses death. At the very end of the play, the stage direction maintains that after Adrienne hoists the black flag alerting all the revolutionaries to begin war against the Leclerc expedition: 'At the first firing of a gun, one saw Adrienne, exposing her body to all the bullets, bend and fall having been struck with a fatal blow to the heart; she tottered and fell into the folds of the flag' (146). The fact that Adrienne dies wrapped in the flag of the Haitian revolutionaries, actively 'exposing herself' to danger, completes her position as a martyr for Haitian independence. Louverture had even told her that, unlike his sons, she had demonstrated that she was 'worthy of the blood of Toussaint, at last!' (line 2415).

Adrienne's decision to fight on the side opposing her own biological father, and thus to replace him with Louverture as a national father, underscores the idea that the logic of kinship as based on biology or genealogy could not be relied upon to signify or reveal political loyalties or, even more confusingly, family ones. The complicated way in which biological and/or genealogical kinship is openly disavowed in the play is only punctuated by Adrienne's foreshadowing of the great tragedy she sees in the making for the Louverture family when she says:

> Toussaint, forcing the father to concede to the politician,
> Will swear false fidelity to the republic,
> And in order to better deceive her, into her triumphant arms,
> As hostages to the victors he will hand over his children
> 'Let France, he says, from now on be their mother,
> And if I betray her let them detest their father!'
> Liberty witnesses this horrendous holocaust
>   [*La liberté reçut cet holocauste affreux*];
> In sacrificing his sons, he will sacrifice himself for them. (lines 250–57)

At the very outset, Adrienne's confused vision is recognition of the fact that Louverture's statement that he was 'a father above all' (line 848) would necessarily complicate his desire to lead the Haitian people to independence. Louverture had told his followers, 'You were merely a herd [*troupeau*], I am making you a nation! [*je vous fais nation!*]' (line 876), but even he implicitly foreshadows the complete reversal of this standpoint when he mentions that it was he who had given Bonaparte the only tool to defeat him, 'the day where the thought occurred to me/To confide my blood to this offending race' (lines 744–45). Even though Louverture had seemingly cast off Albert because of the latter's loyalty to France—the last thing Louverture said to his oldest son was 'Well, leave then! I no longer know you! ... /Pardon me, oh, my country! this cry of nature' (2616–17)—once he learns that Albert's life depends on his capitulation, he does an about face in surrendering himself.

If Adrienne had presciently described Louverture as incapable of the potential infanticide it would take to lead the Haitian people to freedom, the very real threat of such an unthinkable action is presented to us by Adrienne's father, Salvador. For him, there could be no question over which tie is more important, that of family or of nation. Salvador orders Adrienne to be killed in order to keep the secret of her birth from his superiors. Salvador's repudiation of his own daughter in this way, coupled with Adrienne's disavowal of her own father, disrupts the idea that biology determines paternity, but also that biology necessarily determines kinship.

The denial of biology in determinations of political and even familial loyalties remains important because Salvador will seek to convince Louverture's sons that biological paternity is not as relevant during a revolution as the symbolic paternity of the nation-state, and thus Salvador will urge them not only to symbolically kill their father, but to take up against him the arms that had the potential to physically kill him. Since Saint-Domingue is at this time a part of France, Salvador essentially tells Isaac and Albert that if they fight on the side of their father, they will be betraying their nation, France, or rather, their true family, in any event, the only family that matters. Salvador tells Isaac of Albert's choice to fight for France:

> Be aware, my friend, that the man to whom one owes his life
> Is less than the man to whom one owes his country.
> Chance provides a father, one does not choose him,
> ...
> We are men, my friend, we are no longer sons or brothers!
> For me, if the consul was fighting with my father,
> I would rip out my heart if it seemed uncertain. (lines 1403–05, 1411–13)

Isaac immediately understands the parricidal ramifications of this sermon, crying out, 'This man speaks horrors!' (line 1414).

While Isaac remains skeptical and even properly horrified by Salvador's patricidal remonstrations against biological paternity, Albert completely buys into Salvador's argument. Albert's decision to remain loyal to Bonaparte is what sets up, in addition to the horrid possibilities of patricide and infanticide, the tragedy of fratricide. Albert had told his brother that Bonaparte was their 'adopted' father when he admonished Isaac for seeming to forget the latter's benevolence: 'What! From the first of the whites little blacks adopted,' Albert says, 'Allied to the French, to be free like them,/ To receive lessons from their famous teachers; … /*Voilà* that which your mouth calls slavery! … /Go! you are only a child! … /Go! you are only a savage! …' (lines 1193, 1197–98, 1211–12). During a subsequent quarrel with Isaac, Albert displays his preference for France even more fully when he cries out, 'Bonaparte is my God!' (line 1342), to which his brother replies, 'Bonaparte is a white man!' (line 1343). The quarrel between the two brothers redirects the potentially fratricidal conflict from merely political and familial terms to at once "racial" and even biblical terms. Alfred has effectively said that his God (and therefore his father in a much more metaphysical sense) is a "white" man. Albert continues by arguing that he must go off to fight for Napoleon because, 'though my father made me a man, yes, but [Napoleon] made me free' (line 1380). Albert's interpretation is that the French have given him a new father, a new God, his freedom, and therefore a relationship to "whiteness" that goes beyond mere "race" or phenotype. Alfred ardently tries to deracialize his decision by tying it to ideas about a national family rather than a "racial" one. Louverture, for his part, does not appear to buy his son's logic. He accuses his son of forgetting that he is "black." After Albert tries to convince his father to reconcile with Bonaparte, Louverture tells his oldest son, 'Stop! Between us I see my entire race./Be true to your blood, my son, before I can embrace you!' (lines 2561–62).

It is Albert's choice in choosing the French nation over his Haitian family, or "whiteness" over "blackness," in his father's eyes, that Lamartine privileges as accomplishing the destruction of Louverture, resonating with those racialized Oedipal metaphors that seem to incessantly plague representations of the Haitian Revolution. The only way for Louverture to see his sons again is to promise Rochambeau that he will not wage war against the Leclerc expedition. Now, the same scene earlier described has become about symbolic patricide rather than about possible infanticide. When Louverture agrees to capitulate to Bonaparte's demands in order to save Albert, he acknowledges that his sons have been his downfall. The fact of being a father and having human feelings is all to the credit of the revolutionary hero, whose honor is, nevertheless, shown to have tragically accomplished his erasure as the founder of liberty and independence in Haiti. Louverture wonders, 'must I divest myself of every human feeling,/To be nothing more, Lord, but an instrument in your hand' (2342–43). Later, Lamartine's Louverture concludes that he is not willing to sacrifice 'every human feeling' even for a revolution that is characterized as being a part of the plan of the 'Lord.' In choosing his children over the Revolution, Louverture says, 'I no longer see myself as a leader, I am only a father,/Father more weak, at last! than the weakest mother' (lines 2380–81).

Toussaint Louverture suggests that the revolutionary hero's downfall is the direct result of the fact that he puts his sons above the cause of the Revolution, allowing them in effect to figuratively kill him. Once again, Louverture's *hamartia* or his honor, joined together with his paternal devotion is the dominant representation that leads us towards viewing him as the figure of literary tragedy. Lamartine's play anxiously suggests that human sentiments are incompatible with the great heroism required to effectuate radical change. However, the fact that Louverture was unable to disavow his children for the sake of general liberty only made him more heroic according to the pathos of the play. Louverture laments that in the pages of history it will be said of him that 'Toussaint was leading his people to the promised land,/But he would never see the fruits of his conquest! … /Alone, he would have been a king! … but he had sons!' (lines 2590–92). Louverture's final words put into stark relief the text's ambivalence about the more metaphysical meanings of nation building when Louverture turns to the audience and says, 'Oh! these great founders had neither sons nor wives!/ … /But me! … You win, oh whites! … I had a heart!' (lines 2599–61).

The myriad representations and biographies of Louverture circulating in the nineteenth-century Atlantic World which had painted Louverture as a father tragically betrayed by the son of his own "race," had the effect of merely reinforcing and in some ways institutionalizing the trope of the tragic "mulatto/a." As *Toussaint Louverture* demonstrates, it was layer upon layer of literary history that had produced the idea that the Louverture family's decision about whether or not to remain loyal to France or to each other could be best understood in terms of the "interracial" family. The "interracial" family romance registered by Lamartine's play was apparently so strong that in an 1850 parody of *Toussaint Louverture* written by Charles Varin and Eugène Labiche, entitled *Traversin et Couverture: parodie de Toussaint Louverture en 4 actes: mêlés de peu de vers et de beaucoup de prose*, Traversin (a stand-in for Louverture) is described using the language of the "mulatto." Couverture says of Traversin, 'Politics causes him lot of worry! … and you know the color of worry! … He has caught yellowness [*la jaunisse*]' (5). If the 'yellowness' of the "mulatto" was a disease that was catching, later, the same character refers again to Traversin/Louverture using an equally demeaning language of ideas about "mixed-race" identities. Couverture implies that being anything less than a "pure" 'black' was shameful when she says of Traversin/Louverture, 'He has not stopped being black ... but he is a ... lemon black' [*c'est un noir ... citron*] (5).

Such ideas of people of "mixed race" as diluted or impure in some way (and also sour like lemons), inevitably leads to a conversation about the ability for "mulattoes" to wear the mask of simulated kindness that we saw within the trope of "monstrous hybridity" and that also characterizes Séjour's Alfred's questions about the meaning of the 'smile' of the 'mulatto': 'was it one of joy, or of anger?' But if Séjour's Georges was not aware of the inability of his father-master to read his expressions, Lamartine's Louverture knows exactly how to dissimulate. He tells Adrienne of his plan to spy on Leclerc in order to uncover the latter's motives: 'I must change my attire, my profession, my language:/I know how, when I want, to transform my face,/I know how, without even placing a blindfold over my eyes,/To feign playing the part of the blind' (lines 1038–41).

In Varin and Labiche's play, Père Antoine, whose name Varin and Labiche did not even bother to change, similarly advises Traversin to dissimulate in the face of the 'whites' who are coming to shore (presumably the Leclerc expedition), not so that he might better discover their motives, but so that he might better ambush them: 'you let the whites come close,' he tells Traversin, 'you greet them ... you blow them kisses ... you sing to them: Little white, my good brother ... and when they are very close ... Pif! Paf! Pan! ... burn, slaughter, massacre! ... it will all be very nice' (10). A cynicism about the life of Toussaint Louverture as a tragic revolutionary hero shines through in this narration of the heroic 'black' general turned the indecisive color 'yellow' and the easily contrived vengeance that made him want to 'burn, slaughter, and massacre' at the urgings of a man of God.[22] This cynical tone is further punctuated by the son of Traversin, Albert (as in Lamartine's play), who remarks, 'This cracked voice [*Cette voix fêlée*] ... this is the cry of my conscience' [*c'est le cri de ma conscience*] (37), an immediate reversal of Lamartine's statement, in his preface to the published version of the play, that the drama was 'a cry of humanity in five acts and in verse' (2).[23]

---

22 The fact that Lamartine had portrayed Louverture as compelled to action by a 'white' priest was also criticized in a review in 1851 of the British edition of *Toussaint Louverture*, published in London. The reviewer writes that *Toussaint L'Ouverture* [sic] is a 'bad play,' in part because '[t]he feeble lachrymose personage who weeps for the responsibility imposed upon him, and in the most important and decisive moments moves but at the prompting of another's will, bears but little resemblance to the extraordinary man whose fierce and fiery energy, promptitude and decision, even more than his superior intelligence, raised him among his countrymen to an authority that has been compared to that of the most despotic sovereigns of Asia' ('Toussaint-L'Ouverture,' *The Westminster and Foreign Quarterly Review*, Oct.–Jan. 1850–51: 237).

23 Students of Haitian literature and historiography will undoubtedly recognize that

In many respects, even with its racist representations of the indecisiveness of "mulattoes" and the weakly inferred inhumanity of Louverture, Varin and Labiche's play calls into question some of the larger humanitarian questions about the Haitian Revolution that were implicitly evoked by *Toussaint Louverture*. As much as Lamartine's drama is characterized by a romantic pathos of tragedy that would make the audience or reader sympathize with Louverture, the play also uses, rather overtly at times, the same vocabulary of "monstrous hybridity" that had made the Haitian Revolution one of the most frightening symbols of "racial" extermination in all of the Atlantic World. In so doing, the play at times equivocates about the revolutionary violence that had secured the independence of Haiti. At one point, Lamartine's Louverture describes himself as experiencing a kind of physiological chaos with respect to making a decision about the Revolution when he says, 'The black man [*Le noir*], the citizen, the leader, the former slaves,/United in a single man creates such chaos/That his flesh and his blood are fighting with his bones,/And in questioning himself he could not say/If the cry that he elicits is going to be a blessing or a curse' (lines 1701–05).

The 'humanity' demonstrated in the end by Lamartine's painting of Louverture as a 'Spartacus' who still refuses to occasion the death of his own children in the name of the Revolution suggests to us that this reversal of the usual "interracial" family romance of the Haitian general's life—since here Louverture chooses his children over his nation—may have been merely one of the most useful visual and instantly referential ways to open up a very real dialogue about the consequences of revolutions and wars, and whether or not the ostensibly peaceful ends always justified the immediately violent means. As Lamartine's play—and the parody of it—dramatizes these issues, the problem with revolutions is that they involve a person's mother, brother, sister, father, and children. But the logic of an extremely violent revolution, and especially one that was phrased as the only solution to the problem of slavery, tells us that the only thing that matters is which side you are on: the slaves or the masters. Of course, it was not so simple for those who lived during the era of the Haitian Revolution, as they tried to decide whether all of the violence would be worth it, in the end, and whether not only their own lives, but the lives of their children were worth it.

The most eloquent phrasing of the problem of perhaps being ideologically on the side of a revolution's attempt to produce freedom for the oppressed but having trouble with the many implications of its indiscriminate violence, comes to us from the Algerian-born French writer Albert Camus, who once

---

the phrase 'cri de ma conscience' closely resembles the title of Baron de Vastey's 1815 *Le Cri de la conscience*, a text in which Vastey would proclaim of his descriptions of what he interpreted as Pétion's betrayal of Haiti's independence, '*c'est le cri de ma conscience!*' (85).

evoked the problem by saying, 'It's easy to be anti-colonialist in the bistros of Paris or Marseille ... I have to denounce blind terrorism in the streets of Algiers, which might one day strike my mother or my family. I believe in justice,' he wrote, 'but I'll defend my mother before justice.' Later in his career, at a press conference after his receipt of the Nobel Prize, Camus reportedly stated, 'If I had to choose between justice and my mother, I would choose my mother' (qtd. in Prochaska, xvii). Judging from the near-constant portrayal of the life of Louvertures as an "interracial" family romance in the literary history of the Atlantic World, the violence in Saint-Domingue seems to have called forth similar kinds of anxieties about the implications of arguing for a kind of justice that might one day mean being forced to choose between one's parents and one's politics, or between the family and the nation.

CHAPTER NINE

A 'Quarrel between Two Brothers': Eméric Bergeaud's Ideal History of the Haitian Revolution

'[T]he mulatto general Rigaud arrived at Philadelphia from France on the 7th ... attention is anxiously drawn towards him, by a report that he was lately in this state ... It is not for the sake of persecuting an individual that we introduce this article, but the safety of this and the southern states imperiously requires that he should be expelled, if he has really entered them, and that at any rate his motions should be closely watched.'

—*'Look Sharp!' Federal Republican & Commercial Gazette*, March 28, 1810

'What are all these comforts and splendors compared with the rescue of my country, and the redemption of an oppressed race? What is my life, compared with the life of this Republic? Say, dearest, that you will give me willingly to this righteous cause.'

—Lydia Maria Child, *A Romance of the Republic* (1867)

'The revolution, like Saturn, devoured its own children.'

—William Wells Brown, *The Black Man, his Antecedents and his Genius* (1863)

If historical, editorial, and biographical racializations of the life of Louverture by writers like Lacroix and Métral influenced Alphonse de Lamartine in his portrayal of the downfall of the revolutionary hero as a tragic "interracial" family romance, Eméric Bergeaud's narration in *Stella* (1859) of the divisions between two fictional revolutionaries as a shameful 'quarrel between brothers' (137) was influenced by some of the same tropologies that made Louverture's struggle with his children appear Oedipal. Instead of using the "interracial" family romance and its language of patricide to describe Toussaint Louverture and his children, in *Stella*, Bergeaud focuses on what he paints as an unfortunate, but in the end redemptive, fratricidal conflict between two brothers with different skin colors, Romulus, whose skin color could be 'compared to the blackest of ebony,' and Rémus, whose skin Bergeaud said was the 'pale shade of mahogany' (8). Bergeaud, for his part, wrote that he had used the names of these Roman figures 'less with the thought of establishing a one-to-one analogy between them and the historical twins, but because they were brothers' (20).[1] In fact, Bergeaud wants us to read his rendition of Romulus and Rémus, who, because of the meddling of Rémus's "white" colonist father, 'even forgot that they were brothers' (139), as initial stand-ins for the internecine fighting that had ensued between Toussaint Louverture and André Rigaud during the War of the South from 1799 to 1800. This version of a 'quarrel between brothers' that eventually resulted in the founding of a country would not result in the death of Bergeaud's Rémus, as it had his Roman counterpart. Instead, the conflict would be resolved when the two brothers eventually united against the *Colon*, Rémus's father, during Haiti's war of independence. Metaphorically speaking, then, Romulus and Rémus are, by turns, not only Louverture and Rigaud, neither of whom were present at Haiti's founding, but Dessalines and Pétion, as well. To that end, Bergeaud noted in his preface that he had actually borrowed the 'details' for his two main characters, whom he said were less individuals than 'collective beings'— 'properly speaking they have no individuality at all' (vi)—from the lives of the four revolutionaries who for him 'personified' both the 'excess and the glory' of the Haitian Revolution: Louverture, Rigaud, Dessalines, and Pétion (vi). Bergeaud would credit these men, when all was said and done, with not only having united together to defeat the French colonists, but with having managed the 'laborious birthing of a new society' (vi).

Stella, which has most often been attributed to the pen of Eméric Bergeaud, spans the years 1789–1804, or the beginning of the French Revolution until Haitian independence.[2] The narrative revolves around

---

1 In Roman mythology, Romulus and Remus, who were credited with the founding of Rome, were the twin sons of Mars, the god of war. When Romulus 'divide[d] the new city with two parts for himself and one for his brother,' the resulting enmity between the brothers ended in the eventual slaying of Remus by Romulus (Bierlein, 192–94).

2 In his *Bibliographie générale et méthodique d'Haïti* (1941), Ulrick Duvivier wrote that Bergeaud, who was born in Cayes, Haiti in 1818, had been the secretary of General Borgella, his uncle, and a commissioner of public instruction before being exiled to St. Thomas. Duvivier also quotes an intriguing suggestion from an unnamed source, who apparently wrote that Bergeaud's wife was ' ... as well educated as her husband ... [and] contributed to the authorship of *Stella*' (qtd. at 230). Duvivier may have borrowed such

The Trope of the Tragic "Mulatto/a"

Romulus and Rémus's desire to exact revenge upon the *Colon*, Rémus's "white" father, who beats their mother Marie, or 'L'Africaine,' to death after he overhears her describing to her sons the nature of Rémus's birth. It turns out that Rémus was the product of the *Colon*'s rape of Marie after she was captured in her native Africa by European enslavers and forcibly taken by them to Saint-Domingue. The memory of the fatal beating of Marie at the hands of the *Colon*, as described below, haunts the two boys throughout the tale and provides them with the inspiration necessary to lead the Haitian Revolution:

> Right away the terrible whip resounded; a scene of horror commenced, the details of which will make you tremble. To the multiplying noise of the blows were mingled sharp, heart-rending cries that weakened little by little until they descended into a moan. The whip hits, hits for two hours. The victim jumped, writhed, grated her teeth. Her mouth foamed, her nostrils flared, her eyes came out of her head. There was no more life, but her body was still quaking and the whip was still striking, stopping at last on an inert cadaver. (19)

The *Colon*'s brutality against their mother effectively performs the same role for Romulus and Rémus that Zélie's death performed for Séjour's Georges. The two brothers become not only filled with a desire for the pleasures of vengeance—Bergeaud writes, 'To kill their enemy with their hands and to feel him die would have been almost an orgasm for them' [*eut été pour eux presqu'une volupté*] (34)—but they become awakened to the popular notion expressed by many of the 'tropicopolitans' of the Haitian Revolution's literary history, that they had only been enslaved because they had allowed it. Rémus describes the effects of this awakening when he tells his brother: 'Do you know that we were ridiculous for believing for such a long time that our master was a giant? Fear alone has the power to magnify objects to such a degree. I am really ashamed of it; this purported giant is a *man* like us' (23, italics in the original). In order to exact their revenge on this mere '*man*,' 'the assassin of the *Africaine*' (66), the boys first run away from

---

an inference from the Haitian novelist Frédéric Marcelin, who in an article entitled 'D'Ignace Nau à *Stella*' published in *Mercure de France* in 1923, stated as a matter of fact that *Stella* was the work of 'Mme. Eméric Bergeaud,' who 'threw herself into writing this historical novel, and recounted, symbolically at least, the fierce struggles that destroyed slavery's version of the Bastille in Saint-Domingue [*la Bastille esclavagiste de Saint-Domingue*] and created the first black country [*patrie*], Haiti (1804)' (220–21). Louis Morpeau, directly influenced by Marcelin (since he was responsible for the publication of the former's article in *Mercure de France*), wrote in *La Revue Mondiale* 15 April 15, 1922 that the first Haitian novelist 'to date, is a female novelist [*romancière*], Mme. Eméric Bergeaud, who was so modest that her husband signed her work *Stella*' (1922, 45).

the plantation and later return to burn down the *Colon*'s house. Though the *Colon* escapes their immediate vengeance, in the course of the struggle the two brothers capture a young woman whom they initially believe to be the *Colon*'s daughter since she was living on his plantation. The beautiful blonde woman is the eponymous Stella, and Romulus and Rémus later learn that she was not the *Colon*'s daughter, but a native of France. She had been kidnapped by the *Colon*, who had taken her to the colony with the hope of marrying her. When Stella refused to become his wife, the *Colon* had her locked away in a tower, where she was residing at the moment Romulus and Rémus discovered her existence.

The young blonde woman, whom Bergeaud refers to in his preface as merely an 'abstraction' (vi), serves not simply as the symbol of the transmission of Enlightenment thought to Haiti from France, but, like Marie, whom the author similarly calls an 'ideal' (vi), Stella provides the broad inspiration, motivation, and support that the brothers will need to defeat the *Colon*. Stella even offers to fight with them because, as she says, 'though I am a woman, I can still be useful' (61), and it is she who leads the brothers into their initial war with the *Colon*, crying out, 'Aux armes, aux armes!' (62). Bergeaud describes Stella as such a fierce revolutionary in her own right that at one point she is able to save the lives of both Romulus and Rémus: 'She diverted the shot that would have taken down Rémus,' and 'Romulus was going to be shot from behind while he had his hatchet raised upon his enemy; [but] the young girl prevented the shot of the soldier ... and shoved her sword into his throat' (64). Though in many ways Stella's behavior makes her consonant with the kind of transgressive female revolutionaries seen in Part Two of this volume, her most obvious narrative function as an 'abstraction' is to offer the voice of didactic reason by reminding the brothers not only to forever 'banish discord,' but to 'hate oppression so as to never suffer in the future from oppressors, and to never become one of them' (306).

Though the brothers are urged by Stella to believe that 'discord is a violent and dolorous state that exhausts individuals and ruins societies' (198), the *Colon* eventually succeeds in sowing uncertainty in Romulus and Rémus concerning whether they should recognize one another as 'an enemy or a friend' (198). The *Colon* creates the epistemological uncertainty of "mulatto/a" vengeance when he convinces Romulus that Rémus feels superior towards him because of his skin color: 'You differ from your brother by the color of your skin,' the *Colon* tells Romulus, 'the shade of your skin is darker than his: there you have it, the reason for which he believes you are morally below him, and suffers at length that you are in command of him' (133). As a result of Romulus's belief in the central tenets of this lecture, we are told that the country became 'a wide open arena for Romulus and Rémus, who descended upon it filled with anger and passion, without there being anyone there to get between them to stop this fratricide' (153). After a long series of baleful fighting during which Romulus unites with the *Colon* and the French commissioners land in Haiti and attempt to recruit the rebellious former slaves to fight in the French army against the British, the brothers eventually realize the error of their discord. They subsequently reunite to execute the *Colon* and claim independence for Haiti, 'the most beautiful country upon which the sun has ever shone' (323).

Bergeaud's vision of Haitian revolutionary history as 'beautiful' is extraordinarily divergent from the way in which these events had been represented in European-produced histories by pro-slavery apologists and abolitionists alike. Bergeaud's tone of nostalgia for this glorious past of the Revolution stands in sharp contrast to the sentiments of the French abolitionist Victor Schoelcher, for instance, who had lamented having to tell the story of the Revolution in his 1843 *Colonies étrangères et Haïti*, 'what a terrible history to tell' (2: 141). If portraying the Haitian Revolution as an incomprehensible and unredeeming 'war of extermination' between 'blacks' and 'whites' and/or 'mulattoes' and 'blacks' as in *Oxiane; ou la révolution de Saint-Domingue* (2:91), or as a 'general massacre' as in 'Augustin, ou la révolte des noirs' (386), can be said to characterize the vast majority of fictions of the Haitian Revolution, in great contrast, Bergeaud explained that with *Stella* he was merely putting 'into relief some of the most beautiful features of our national history' (v). Thus, his entire description of the Haitian Revolution is determined at the outset by his view of the transcendent sublimity rather than the exceptional brutality of the wars of independence. Bergeaud even made the case that fiction rather than the history book proper was the perfect medium for retelling this triumphant history precisely because the novel lent itself more easily to describing that which was already 'beautiful': '[i]n surrounding these facts with the ornaments of fiction, our intention was to not add anything to history; that which is beautiful does not need to be embellished' (vi). In evoking the form of the novel as merely a 'beautiful' 'ornament' that might dress up but not necessarily embellish an already 'beautiful' story, Bergeaud sets up the reader of *Stella* to become the recipient of what we might call an 'ideal history.'

Doris Sommer has referred to early national Latin American writing of this type as 'foundational fiction' and has explained that for many nineteenth-century writers,

> there could be no clear epistemological distinction between science and art, narrative and fact, and consequently between ideal history and real events ... In the epistemological gaps that the non-science of history leaves open, narrators could project an ideal future ... The writers were encouraged both by the need to fill in a history that would increase the

legitimacy of the emerging nation and by the opportunity to direct that history towards a future ideal. (1993, 7)

Contrary to the vast majority of the early nineteenth-century Haitian authors whose works will be examined in this chapter alongside *Stella*, Bergeaud's vision of Haitian history as 'ideal' in this way even extended to colonial Hispaniola, which he describes as 'a favored land, the heart of nature's charms, abounding in its most precious gifts [*prodigue de ses dons le plus précieux*]' (1). Later, Bergeaud would see in the second independent nation of the American hemisphere a garden of Eden, 'where the first man had lived' (324). Bergeaud's unfailing and in some ways uncanny optimism about the kind of place Haiti was both before colonialism and after independence also characterizes his portrayal of the conflict between Romulus and Rémus—or Rigaud and Louverture—which Bergeaud describes as a bitter but necessary moment in Haitian history. This is because the 'great compensation' of this 'fraternal' struggle was the country's eventual liberty and independence. Bergeaud writes:

> Stella was dreaming for her protégés of a future that even they could not have foreseen. The goal was far away. She took it upon herself to guide them towards it along this rough path, painful, but inevitable ... They needed to walk for a long time, to have their feet torn, and to stain with their blood the brambles in their path. They had to get lost in the darkness, make enemies of one another, fight each other, and later reconcile in order to regret their errors and weep over their wounds. (73)

Bergeaud's view that the Romulus-Rémus (or Rigaud-Louverture) conflict had been an essential detour on the way to a pre-ordained or cosmological Haitian independence stands in stark contrast to the opinion of the Haitian historian Joseph Saint-Rémy, whose historical works will in some ways provide the key to my reading of *Stella*. Saint-Rémy called the 'civil war' between Rigaud and Louverture 'one of the most bleak [*lugubre*] phases in the history of St-Domingue' (1850, 217). The Haitian historian also blamed what he called, the 'sacrilegious and implacable war that had exploded between [Louverture] and Rigaud' for having 'cut down [*moissonna*] all of the country's virtues, talents, [and] heroism,' and he further said that the conflict 'seemed only to have spared the wicked' (1850, 19). In *Stella*, because the quarrel between Romulus and Rémus could be essentially relocated as a fraternal squabble rather than a purely "racial" one, instead of providing the primary evidence of Haiti's tragic "hybridity," this conflict was merely one of the 'painful' and 'laborious' consequences of nationhood. Nevertheless, the novel envisages the reconciliation that needed to happen between Romulus and Rémus as marked by the simple kind of forgiveness that might occur

The Trope of the Tragic "Mulatto/a"

among siblings who may bicker, but who always love each other in the end. Bergeaud's novel narrates the actions of two revolutionary brothers who are willing not only to forget their differences, but to 'ignore' that their 'peril might be imminent' (209) for the sake of abolishing slavery and creating an independent Haiti. In narrating the suffering caused by the struggle between Romulus and Rémus, Bergeaud suggests that understanding the cosmological meanings of this history would only result in an increase of 'love' for Haiti on the part of its citizens. He wrote: 'No, one's country is not the place where one is well; it is often the place where one has suffered the most, and it is for this reason, perhaps, that we love it even more' (72).

The meaning of the nation for Bergeaud as a place where people both suffer and sacrifice, closely matches that which would come to define the concept for more modern historians. In his famous lecture 'What is a Nation?' (1882), Ernest Renan wrote, 'A nation is ... a large-scale solidarity, constituted by the feeling of the sacrifices one has made in the past and of those that one is prepared to make in the future' (19). '[T]he essence of a nation,' Renan explained, 'is that all individuals have many things in common, and also that they have forgotten many things. No French citizen knows whether he is a Burgundian, an Alan, a Taifale, or a Visigoth, yet every French citizen has to have forgotten the massacre of Saint Bartholomew' (11).[3] Bergeaud, too, wants his readers less to remember whether they are "mulattoes" or "negroes," words the Haitian author takes care never to use, or whether their ancestors had fought with Louverture or Rigaud, and instead to consider each other as 'brothers and sisters in nation' (292). By narratively performing the forgiveness, forgetting, and fraternal *love* that brought Romulus and Rémus (or Dessalines and Pétion) back to one another to create Haiti after their history of dissension, Bergeaud suggests that the origins of the nation could be marked by ("racial") reconciliation rather than ("racial") division. Bergeaud's description of Haitian revolutionary history as a fraternal romance, then, rather than an unfortunate "interracial" drama of "monstrous hybridity," projects not only an altogether *idealist* future for Haiti, but an almost entirely *raceless* one.

Within the pages of Bergeaud's novel, we find the character Stella counseling Romulus and Rémus to forever be united. She does so with the memorable lines:

> I only have one more thing to tell you: that is to always help one another, to lean upon one another, and to live together as if you were made of one sole being. Everything in nature that is fertile is double. The

---

[3] All quotations are taken from the version translated by Martin Thom and published in Homi Bhabha's *Nation and Narration* (1990).

combination of two different colors that characterizes Haitian society can only be favorable to its prosperity. It has already produced *liberty* and *independence*. (96)

By arguing for the fecundity rather than the sterility of Haiti's *doubleness*—people with lighter and darker skin hue—*Stella* directly addresses many of the nineteenth-century assumptions about the "racial mixing" that had produced the idea of the vengeful "mulatto/a" found in the texts of myriad journalists, pro-slavery apologists, and even abolitionist writers in the Atlantic World. These writers, often irrespective of their political persuasions, painted "miscegenation" as the catalyst of not only revolutionary violence in Saint-Domingue, but of the later division of independent Haiti into two separately governed states. *Stella* refuses this seemingly un-redemptive narrative of Haiti as a tragic "hybrid" republic by refuting popular nineteenth-century ideas about the "mulatto" on the one hand, and by rebuking the hatred inspired by the fact of Haiti's existence on the other.

It is precisely Bergeaud's rejection of a *commonsense* discourse of "race" about Haiti that had turned "mulattoes" and "blacks" into fierce enemies who banished themselves to separate parts of the island, in favor of his embrace of a memory of the Haitian Revolution in which everyone ended by calling each other 'brother and sister,' regardless of skin color, that makes this text an important one in the literary history of the Haitian Revolution. That is to say that I do not agree that it would be 'foolish,' in the words of Léon-François Hoffmann, to argue that *Stella* 'deserves to stand' alongside the works of 'Victor Hugo and Heinrich von Kleist, Alphonse de Lamartine and William Wordsworth' (1999, 226). The commanding place owed to *Stella* within this literary genealogy derives precisely from Bergeaud's description of Haitian revolutionary history as unequivocally glorious and fruitful rather than hopelessly tragic and sterile. Rather than presenting the country's ongoing political problems as the direct result of the same inherent "racial" divide between "negroes" and "mulattoes" that had supposedly occurred during the Haitian Revolution and had putatively led to an unproductive post-independence Haiti, Bergeaud rejected the very vocabulary of the debate. That is, its grounding in pseudoscientific "racial" terminology. Bergeaud seems to have taken to heart the idea that, as Baron de Vastey had written, the terms 'mulatto' and 'negro' themselves were merely 'injurious epithets, which our enemies count upon to divide us' (1817b, 153). Bergeaud represents Haiti's essential diversity and the unification of people with light and dark skin (never "mulattoes" and "negroes") into a heterogeneous citizenry called Haitians as the generative process responsible for the country's independence, thereby dismantling the "mulatto/a" vengeance narrative of the Revolution and the pseudoscientific vocabulary that supported it. The novel ultimately offers much more than a political, historical, and "racial" *roman à clef* for the Haitian Revolution. With *Stella*, Bergeaud attempted to both historically explicate and politically exculpate the Haitian Revolution, turning the war for Haiti's independence into a useful and instructive lesson in nation-building rather than a harmful and deleteriously divisive event of world history.

*

While the author of *Stella* may have hoped that his interpretation of the road Haitians had taken to independence as *ideal* would become a mainstay in Haitian historiography, *Stella*'s co-optation of what Hoffmann has referred to as the tenets of the 'Romantic school' (1999, 217)—that the poet was a 'visionary, capable of piercing the mystery of the world and explaining it through symbol and allegory' (217)—has invited scrutiny and as well as sharp critique from many a literary critic of the twentieth century. Historically, critics have found that *Stella* is divorced from the Haitian literary tradition because Bergeaud does not, as Jean Price-Mars would contend that all properly Haitian writers should, 'draw the material of their works from the milieu where they live' (Price-Mars, 1983, 178). Along these lines, in *Autour de deux romans* (1903), the famous Haitian novelist Frédéric Marcelin directly critiqued *Stella*:

> I could have, in enveloping myself in the veils of fiction, instead of producing *Thémistocle-Epaminondas Labasterre* [1901], have produced a conventional novel, just like that author who celebrated Toussaint L'Ouverture and André Rigaud under the bizarre denominations of Romulus and Rémus ... I could have showed you a young, pure, impeccable, sparkling [*pur, impeccable, foudroyant*], Haiti—according to the accepted formula ... I wanted something else. (27)

Nearly two decades later, Marcelin's unfavorable opinion of the novel had hardly changed. In a 1923 article published in *Le Mercure de France*, he wrote that the author of *Stella* had been unduly '[i]nfluenced by the theories of Jean-Jacques Rousseau on natural man and the fundamental goodness of primitive man'; he said that Bergeaud was 'allegorical like Fénelon, historical like Walter Scott with the elementary psychology of a Dumas, père.' Marcelin concluded his mostly unfavorable assessment of the book by saying that:

> *Stella* is a badly composed novel that, to be precise, is sometimes in conflict with history [*rivalise avec l'histoire parfois*] and where among the improbabilities and mumbo jumbo [*fatras*] flourish some beautiful phrases. A

little of the poetry of Bernardin de Saint-Pierre did grace this little corner of Haitian culture. (221)

The idea that *Stella* was a formulaic example of what Price-Mars called 'bovarysme collectif' (8), or the imitation by Haitian writers of European forms, has contributed to both the under study and under theorization of early nineteenth-century Haitian literature, and especially of the first Haitian novel.

Though later in the twentieth century, Dieudonné Fardin would claim the role of visionary for Bergeaud when he wrote, 'Bergeaud's *Stella* is the ancestor of the marvelous realism of which Jacques Stéphen Aléxis dreamt' (8), Léon-François Hoffmann remains the only twentieth-century scholar to have undertaken a serious and in-depth study of what he refers to as primarily a 'historical novel' (1984, 113).[4] Despite his relatively unfavorable assessment of *Stella*'s position in Haitian revolutionary literary history, Hoffmann has called for more attention to be paid to *Stella*, which he described as 'more than a literary curiosity,' because it 'eloquently articulates the basic obsession of all Haitian writers: a passionate affirmation of Haiti's originality and dignity, and an anguished fear that the sequels of colonization ... may prove stronger than patriotic efforts to eliminate them' (1999, 226). Still, unlike the works of Frédéric Marcelin, Fernand Hibbert, and Justin Lhérisson, considered to be the triumvirate of early Haitian novelists, in the words of Jean Jonassaint, *Stella* has 'never really [been] accepted as a "true Haitian novel" by contemporary Haitian criticism ... because it is a not a realistic account' (2002, 214). Yet I would argue that what Robert Cornevin has called the 'romanced history of the wars of independence' found in *Stella* (112) is precisely what makes the text 'a Haitian novel.' Early Haitian authors like Bergeaud grounded their 'works in the socio-political realities of the country' (Hoffmann, 1983, 19) precisely by engaging in the making of Haitian history and, more broadly, Haitian literature. For many early national Haitian authors, as for many early national U.S. authors, Haiti's image was a contemporary problem whose only remedy was imagined to be in the creation of a national literary and historical tradition.

The problem of the United States' national image had been of immediate concern for some time after U.S. independence too, as evidenced by the work of the Massachusetts politician Fisher Ames. In an 1803 essay entitled

---

4 This is beginning to change. Lesley Curtis and Christen Mucher have prepared an English translation of the novel to be published by NYU Press in 2015, in which, presumably, they will provide an interpretive introduction. Anne Marty also provided a brief introduction in the French-language version of the text she published with Editions Zoé in 2009.

'American Literature,' Ames wrote, 'Few speculative subjects have exercised the passions more or the judgment less, than the inquiry, what rank our country is to maintain in the world for genius and literary attainments. Whether in point of intellect we are equal to Europeans, or only a race of degenerate creoles' (458). Ames worried that the lack of an established and unique national literary tradition was harmful to U.S. credibility on several accounts since, despite the fact that 'nobody will pretend the Americans are a stupid race,' the country had not produced 'one great original work of genius.' He asked, '[i]s there one luminary in our firmament that shines with unborrowed rays?' (460). Likewise, we might say that it was precisely because of the kinds of "racial" meanings that had been attached to the idea of national literatures, and to which Ames alludes, that the revision of the historical understanding of the Revolution and the desire to create a specifically Haitian historical and literary tradition represents the primary engagement of nearly all early nineteenth-century Haitian authors.

The nineteenth-century Haitian poet, journalist, and historian Emile Nau (1812–60), for example, urged his compatriots not to worry about Haiti's literary future when he prophesied that Haiti would eventually find its own Edgar Allen Poe and James Fenimore Cooper (2003, 156) and that over time, contrary to the claims of Alexandre Bonneau, who had maintained that 'Haitian thought can only be formulated in the French language' (Bonneau, 1856, 117), Haitians would create their own national language, 'a little bit darkened' [*quelque peu brunie*] (Nau, 2003, 155). 'What a great day it will be,' Nau said, 'when in every genre Haiti has its own original artists' (2003, 155). Although Haiti's earliest writers had already been accused of imitating Lamartine and Hugo (Bonneau, 1856, 119; 'Mulatto Literature [a],' 326), it is hard to deny the profuse way in which, almost from the very moment of independence, Haitian writers boldly forced their entry into what one nineteenth-century U.S. magazine contributor referred to as the 'empire of literature' ('Mulatto Literature [a],' 326). They forced this entry primarily through what might be described as a deluge of national contributions to the literary history of the Haitian Revolution.

The Haitian Revolution and/or Haitian independence furnished the immediate material and subject matter for virtually all of Haiti's first published works of literature. The colonial history of Saint-Domingue, the Haitian Revolution, and the wars of independence were chanted by all of Haiti's first published poets, including Juste Chanlatte, Antoine Dupré,[5] Jean-Jacques Romane, and E. Sègny Vilevolex (Christophe, 1999), as well as Jules Solime Milscent, whose voluminous poems can be found

---

5 Joseph Saint-Rémy said of Dupré, 'He is in Haiti what Béranger is in France; the one just as the other, is well esteemed and popular' (1837, 471).

in Haiti's first review, *L'Abeille Haytienne* (1817–20), founded by Milscent himself. The Revolution and the immediate post-independence period were also the subject of the country's first operas, all written by Chanlatte in Haitian Creole: *Nehri* (c. 1812), 'an anagram of Henri' (Jonnaissant, 2008, 211; Fischer, 2004, 256), *L'entrée du roi dans sa capitale* (1818), and *La Partie de chasse du roi* (1820). The first of Haiti's plays to be printed and published also took up the topic of post-independence Haiti, slave rebellion and/or colonial revolution, respectively, with *Le Philosophe-Physicien* (1820) published in *L'Abeille Haytienne*,[6] Liautaud Ethéart and his *Le Génie de l'enfer* (1856), and Pierre Faubert's *Ogé; ou le préjugé de couleur* (1856), first performed in 1841.[7] The Haitian revolutionary past was also the subject of what may very well be Haiti's first sustained published works of fiction: Hérard Dumesle's epic prose poem, *Voyage dans le nord d'Hayti* (1824), and Ignace Nau's novella *Isalina; ou une scène créole* (1836). We also find the events of the Revolution fictionalized in two of the earliest Haitian short stories of which we are aware: Ignace Nau's 1836 'Un épisode de la révolution' and 'Le Lambi,' published in 1837. Moreover, in the first 50 years of Haitian independence, the country's history had already been treated by Louis-Félix Boisrond-Tonnerre in *Mémoire pour servir à l'histoire d'Haïti* (1804), Chanlatte in *Le Cri de la nature* (1810),[8] by Julien Prévost (Comte de Limonade) in his *Relation des glorieux événements qui ont porté leurs majestés Royales sur le*

---

6 Hoffmann, H. Trouillot, and Christophe Charles have each attributed this unsigned play to Juste Chanlatte (Hoffmann, 1995, 143; H. Trouillot, 1962, 41, 49; Charles, 53), while other scholars have assumed that the drama was written by the editor of *L'Abeille Haytienne* himself, J.S. Milscent, in order to 'denounce Haitian superstitions' (Ndiyae, 179; Vaval, 242). It is worth mentioning, however, that no contemporaneous mentions of the play name its author as either Chanlatte or Milscent, and a long review of the piece published in *La Revue encyclopédique* actually puts these later claims of authorship into serious question. The reviewer writes that the play was written by a 'dramaturge of 17 years old' who experienced 'great success in Port-au-Prince,' so much so in fact that the government believed that it needed to 'alert the public to the danger of his ruses [*jongleries*], in a brochure that was very well written and came from the government press' ('Bulletin Bibliographique,' 597). An additional but brief review of the play was published in *Annales de la littérature et des arts*, which happens to mention that the play was performed in Port-au-Prince and was 'very well received by Haitians' [*très goutée*]' ('Nouvelles Scientifiques et Littéraires,' 130). Further contemporary mentions of the work can be found in volume nine of the *Revue encyclopédique* (1821) ('Bulletin Bibliographique,' 536) and in *Mercure de France* (vol. 166), which mentions the play with a date of 1817 (248).

7 An additional unsigned play published in *L'Abeille Haytienne* in December of 1820, written in the style of Molière, was called *Le Prix de la vertu* (see Hoffmann, 1995, 143).

8 Chanlatte's text would later be republished as a part of Jean-Baptiste Bouvet de Cressé's *Histoire de la catastrophe de Saint-Domingue* (1824).

trône d'Haïti (1811), and by Baron de Vastey in at least 11 works published between 1814 and 1819.⁹

As a complement to nineteenth-century Haitian fictional production, the middle of the nineteenth century would see a flourishing of Haitian historical production. Thomas Madiou published his eight-volume *Histoire d'Haïti* between 1847 and 1848, and later in the nineteenth century, Saint-Rémy took up the genre of biography with his *Vie de Toussaint-L'Ouverture* (1850) and *Pétion et Haïti* (1854). Next, there was Ardouin, who, having already published a textbook of Haitian history entitled *Géographie de l'île d'Haïti: précédée du précis et de la date des événemens les plus remarquables de son histoire* (1832),¹⁰ would during the years 1853–60 go on to devote 11 volumes to the study of Haiti's past in his *Etudes sur l'histoire d'Haïti*. There was also Emile Nau, who sought the vocation of historian as well when he published his *Réclamation par les affranchis des droits civiles et politiques* (1840), and later he penned a history of the conquest of Hispaniola entitled *Histoire des Caciques* (1855).

Given the specific engagement with the history of Saint-Domingue, the Revolution, and the immediate post-independence period of all of Haiti's most eminent nineteenth-century authors, that the country's first novelist takes up these topics as well should hardly come as a surprise. *Stella* is not only genealogically connected to the five or six decades of the transatlantic print culture of the Haitian Revolution that preceded its appearance, but it is also connected to a more specifically Haitian literary tradition through its concern with the effect on Haiti's future of historical distortions found in writing on the topic. Correcting the assumptions of the past, one of the abiding hermeneutics of early nineteenth-century Haitian writing, was the self-stated goal of the author of *Stella*. This is why in the preface to the novel, Bergeaud insisted that *Stella* should not be read as merely a fictionalized account of the Haitian Revolution, but as a corrective historical account. He wrote in the *avertissement* that 'this book, in order to produce some good, will only take from the novel its form. The truth must come out of it [*Il fallait que la vérité s'y trouvât*] … that is the reason why we have taken so much care not to distort history' (vii). If we want to understand how a

---

9 Hoffmann is much more cynical in his assessment of the preoccupation of early Haitian writers with the Revolution, which he refers to as an 'obsession:' 'The first generation of Haitian writers celebrated the birth of their nation almost obsessively and with near mystical fervor. Practically every succeeding issue of the first Haitian periodicals contains, couched in pompous neoclassical verse an ode to Freedom, a sonnet to Dessalines or Toussaint, a denunciation of Bonaparte or a dithyramb to the fallen heroes' (1994, 366).

10 In this work, Ardouin would also characterize the War of the South between Louverture and Rigaud as 'between brothers' (18).

novel like *Stella*, its fictive status implied by the genre, can purport to correct history—to force an ostensibly buried truth to come out of the book itself—not just in concert with the literary conventions of the time, but with the pressing urgency of nation-building in mind, we must first understand the kinds of histories that the novel seems to emulate and those from which it seems to deviate.[11]

In 1804, Boisrond-Tonnerre penned the first post-independence history of Haiti written by a member of the new nation, *Mémoire pour servir à l'histoire d'Haïti*. In the *Mémoire*, the former secretary of Dessalines purported to offer an impartial account of the events from his personal, unbiased perspective. 'One will not accuse this pen of vengeance,' he said, 'for it will not be guided by partiality; all of the facts that this memoir contains must enter into the domain of history, which will contribute to our posterity' (14). In Boisrond-Tonnerre's rendition of the *truth* of Haitian history, Dessalines emerged as a hero rather than an 'assassin' (Levasseur, 6), standing in stark opposition to more popular portrayals of the founder of Haitian independence as an 'homme-tigre' (Levasseur, 30)[12] or a 'monster, covered with blood and crimes' (Dubroca, 1804, 6–7). While General Louverture had most often been written about as *the* revolutionary hero, Boisrond-Tonnerre offered General Dessalines as *the* founder of Haiti, whose image needed only to be retold from a national perspective in order to make his heroism broadly understood. Boisrond-Tonnerre felt that this could best be accomplished by comparing Dessalines to Louverture. He wrote:

> Toussaint owed his success [during the war against Rigaud] to this general [Dessalines] alone, which would have meant the death of his

---

[11] *Stella* also bears the influence of the ubiquitous Pamphile de Lacroix. For example, before describing the excesses of Romulus and Rémus during the war of independence of 1802–04, the narrator describes the crimes of the colonists, who had drowned nearly 800 free people of color by borrowing from and directly citing the work of Lacroix: 'We have borrowed this story from a pen that has been hardly susceptible to exaggeration, the pen of a general and officer who, having been a part of the French expedition, would have been more likely to have wanted to downplay rather than highlight the true colors of this frightening act' (219). In a footnote to the above passage, Bergeaud mistakenly lists Lacroix's name as 'Paul' instead of Pamphile (219).

[12] Levasseur's memoir was originally published under the title *Notice historique sur les désastres de St. Domingue pendant l'an XI et l'an XII. Par un officer français, détenu par Dessalines*. According to Deborah Jenson, '[a]long with Adjutant Commander Urbain Devaux, Levasseur was one of two hostages provided by General Rochambeau to guarantee French adherence to the emerging negotiations for the French retreat, and to facilitate communication with Dessalines' (2012, 620-21). In addition, Jenson tells us that 'Levasseur spent at least two years in Saint-Domingue, and he spoke Kreyòl well enough to transcribe and translate an extended quote by Dessalines' (621).

troops without the discipline that Dessalines introduced among them and without the example he gave to them by throwing himself into their ranks to lead them in combat. (17)

Boisrond-Tonnerre continued to exalt Dessalines above all the other revolutionary heroes by describing him as '[w]ithout ambition, modest, and blindly obedient to the orders of his leader.' '[H]e seemed to have been born for war,' the secretary adds, 'it made him a happy soldier and ended by making him a hero [*la faisait en soldat heureux et la terminait en héros*]' (17).

Though Boisrond-Tonnerre notably promotes the image of Dessalines as the kind of 'great man' who was a national hero rather than a national disgrace, one of the alternative effects of his memoir is that it combats those narratives produced by colonial writers who often portrayed pre-revolutionary Saint-Domingue as having been populated with idyllic slaves and benevolent masters whose peaceful lives had been disrupted by monstrous revolutionaries like Dessalines. In his 1799 adventure novel *Zoflora; ou la bonne négresse*, for instance, the French author Jean-Baptiste Picquenard refers to Saint-Domingue before the Revolution as 'a new El Dorado' (vii). Picquenard goes on to describe how the main character, Justin, felt about pre-revolutionary Saint-Domingue: '[t]he old country of Haiti was for him the island of felicity; or rather he believed he was making his entry into an antique Eden' (48).

In Boisrond-Tonnerre's description, Saint-Domingue had certainly never been an 'El Dorado'; nor had it been an 'Eden,' or a place whose flora and fauna needed to be meticulously studied, recorded, and published about. On the contrary, Boisrond-Tonnerre describes the desecration of the land, widespread bloodshed, rape, and murder of the *hommes de couleur* and the slaves by the colonists themselves as the true 'scenery' of the colonial period. For him, nature provides only a backdrop to describe violence, economics serves simply to illustrate colonialism's excesses, and the French language and expressions are primarily used to expose barbarity rather than to conceal crimes. Boisrond-Tonnerre tells us the tale of 'forests turned into hanging grounds,' of 'ships turned into jails,' of 'hundreds of blacks and mulattoes being led to their deaths daily' (70):

> women and children were the prey of rapacious soldiers who, with the utmost inhumanity, ripped their ears off simply to obtain the earrings; a necklace, a handkerchief became the price of saving one's self from a gunshot, and if it so happened that a scared farmer got lost in the woods, he would have been immediately shot or tied up and sent to Saint-Marc to be put to death. (39)

In addition, Boisrond-Tonnerre described in immediately cerebral terms the way in which the French language itself had facilitated the cruelty of the colonists: 'To arrest, to drown, or to hang, all signified the same thing [to the French],' he said:

> Those barbarians had created a new vocabulary. To them, drowning 200 individuals was a national glory; to hang someone meant to obtain a promotion; to be eaten by dogs was to descend into the arena;[13] to shoot someone was to put him into a heavy sleep ... What a horrible language! (75)

Like Boisrond-Tonnerre, Baron de Vastey tells us that it was with a cloak of euphemistic language that colonial writers were able to most effectively conceal the crimes of colonialism. Vastey would repeat the above passage verbatim and without attribution in his *Essai sur la causes de la révolution et des guerres civiles d'Hayti* (1819, 28); and in *Le Système colonial dévoilé*, Vastey had already discussed European discursive strategies for disguising the barbaric behavior that was an inherent part of colonial slavery and attempts to record colonial history. Vastey wrote that the majority of European writers:

> entered into the smallest of details on the production, the climate, the rural economy, but they took much care not to reveal the crimes of their accomplices; very few had the courage to speak the truth, and even in saying it, they looked for ways to disguise or attenuate with their expressions the enormity of these crimes. (1814a, 39)

Vastey, who had also argued that Haitians were the ones who needed to write Haitian history, made a point of highlighting that with his own 'unveiling' of the 'secret' history of colonial Saint-Domingue, 'It is not a novel that I am writing, it is an exposé of misfortunes, long sufferings and unheard of tortures' (1814a, 39). He went on to argue that the novel could never offer an adequate medium to describe the violence of colonialism since, '[f]lowers and adornments suit those paintings of which man does not have to be ashamed.' However, 'for such a somber subject to sink into a cesspool of crimes, they are useless. I will do nothing but retell' (40). If fiction is merely another way to 'attenuate' the 'cesspool' of colonialism, then like Bergeaud's Stella, who asks the dueling brothers, Romulus and Rémus, 'What could kindness [*bienveillance*] do for you? ... You evidently attach too much esteem to a sterile sentiment' (43), Vastey's account of slavery in *Le Système* rejects

---

13 L. Dubois has explained the expressions referred to by Boisrond-Tonnerre: 'Fond of euphemisms for the horrors he was inflicting, Rochambeau referenced the practices of ancient Rome in calling the punishment of being eaten alive by dogs "descending into the arena"' (2004, 292).

the benevolent rhetoric of sentimental abolitionism or what Marcus Wood calls 'the promiscuous emotional dynamics of sentimental empathy' found most readily in abolitionist fiction (2002, 13).

In spite of bearing the influence of both Boisrond-Tonnerre and Vastey *vis-à-vis* the idea that only historiography written by Haitians could properly vindicate Haitian revolutionary heroes and reveal the real crimes of 'the colonial hydra' [*le hydre colonial*], an expression used by both Bergeaud (73) and Vastey (1819, 6), Bergeaud believed that it was precisely because of its flowery language and use of metaphor that the genre of the novel had the ultimate power to properly disseminate the redemptive meanings of Haitian history to the masses. Bergeaud would seem to echo implicitly the claim of the abolitionist author Joseph Lavallée that novels are of inherent importance to convey crucial messages because they are 'read by the whole world' (Lavallée, xii). Bergeaud wanted his novel not only to tell Haitian history, but to serve as a stand-in for the history book itself, particularly for 'those who would not be able to apply themselves to a thorough study of our annals' (v). In some ways, Bergeaud believed that the form of the novel was superior to the form of the history book, and he somewhat paradoxically wrote that this was because the novel could provide the best medium to uncover truths that might otherwise remain buried. He wrote that '[h]istory is a river of truth that pursues its majestic course all throughout the ages,' but the 'novel is a lake of lies [*lac menteur*] whose expanse is concealed under the earth; calm and still on the surface, it sometimes hides within its depths the secret destinies of peoples' (19). One of the 'secret destinies' that could be revealed through a novel about the Haitian Revolution was that Haitians were the 'regenerated men' (102) of whom Vastey had dreamed when he wrote in his *Réflexions ... Mazères* that the proof that post-independence Haitians were becoming regenerated was that already 'we write and we print. Even in our infancy our nation has already had writers and poets who have defended its causes and celebrated its glory' (1816d, 84).

If Bergeaud's attempt to reconstruct Haitian history for the purposes of revealing the *regeneration* of Haiti had been influenced in the sense of abstract genealogy by the works of its predecessors, Boisrond-Tonnerre and Vastey, in the more immediate sense, Bergeaud's idea that the novel had the power to transcend history and to prove the humanity of the Haitian people was influenced by the nineteenth-century Haitian historian Beaubrun Ardouin. According to the pithy foreword Ardouin provided to the first edition of *Stella*, he himself was the one who had seen to it that the text would be published, 'when I found an opportune moment' (viii). He also offered a brief description of how the novel came to be in his possession. He explained that Bergeaud 'had devoted the sad leisure of a long exile [in Saint-Thomas] to the publication of this book,' and that in 1857, having been struck with a health problem that put his life in danger, he came to Paris to seek the aid of medicine ... Being almost certain of his recovery, he had brought his manuscript with him in order to have it published; but not having obtained an immediate cure, he confided it to me. (vii)

According to Ardouin, upon Bergeaud's return 'to the country in which he was residing, he ended up dying' (vii). Ardouin wrote that in seeing to it that the novel would be published posthumously, 'I am fulfilling today the promise that I made to my sincerely regretted friend' (viii). The Haitian historian went on to describe Bergeaud's motives for writing the novel by saying that he

> sought to console himself for the harshness of his status [*des rigueurs de sa position*] and for the boredom he experienced far from his native land, from that country [*patrie*] which his venerable father had nevertheless contributed to founding for an entire race of men who had been oppressed for centuries! (vii)

Ultimately, Bergeaud's dear friend tells the reader of *Stella* that this text was an important one for Haiti since it would 'result in the sincere union of her children' (viii).

Ardouin's influence over *Stella* was likely not confined solely to the realm of the novel's physical publication. Bergeaud's own preface to *Stella* echoes a number of Ardouin's claims about the utility of history in general and Haitian history in particular. Bergeaud wrote, '[a] novel, without having the severe gravity of history, could be a useful book' (v), and concluded that by writing this novelized history of the Haitian Revolution, he was 'paying homage to the country' (vi). Ardouin had similarly written in the first volume of his *Etudes sur l'histoire d'Haïti* that 'in writing these pages, my goal is to excite in my compatriots ... the desire to understand under their true lights the events that brought the defenders of our rights to create a country for us' (1:5). In various places in the *Etudes*, which Ardouin admits were heavily influenced by another ardent disseminator of the narrative of "mulatto/a" vengeance, Garran de Coulon (1:4) and which bear the clear influence of Lacroix in several passages (see, for example, Ardouin, 5:299), the Haitian historian also argued that he was animated by the desire to ensure that Haitian history would not become distorted or disfigured by documents and statements that were 'sometimes dishonest' [*quelquefois mensongers*] (1:4). Creating an honest Haitian history, Ardouin implied, was of crucial importance to avoiding the risk that Haitians would either repeat the past or of have a harmful opinion of it since, 'the past is the regulator of the present as it is for the future' (1:2). Ardouin even anticipated Michel

Foucault's twentieth-century statement that 'if one controls people's memory one controls their dynamism' (1976, 25):

> the future of a people often depends upon the manner in which their past is presented to them. If they bear a false judgment about the facts of their annals, about the principles that have guided their predecessors, their politicians, they will suffer in spite of themselves, the influence of this error, and they will be vulnerable to deviating from the route they must follow in order to arrive at their prosperity. (Ardouin, 4:132)

In publishing these volumes, Ardouin claimed that he had no aim other than to examine Haitian history 'from the point of view natural to a Haitian, and in opposition to the myriad foreign authors who have themselves considered this history from their point of view' (1:1). Ultimately, Ardouin believed, like historians Boisrond-Tonnerre and Baron de Vastey before him, that Haitian history written by Haitians was critical to the development and 'prosperity' of independent Haiti. That is to say that only Haitian historians had the capacity to prevent a harmful historical framework from being imposed upon independent Haiti; a colonial framework that would perhaps, in Foucault's words, show people 'not what they were, but what they must remember having been' (1976, 25).

Thomas Madiou also worried about the possible effect of not having a national history on Haitians:

> It is impossible to steer a society towards the way of progress, to help them to avoid all of the pitfalls into which have fallen so many inexperienced peoples [*de jeunes peuples*], if we do not meditate on the events of the past of the entire world and in the country we would like to regenerate. (1:i)

For Madiou, it was both the study of and the making of history that would help Haitians, as it had helped 'the Greeks,' the 'Romans,' and even 'Jesus Christ' to found a 'lasting society' (1:ii).

Bergeaud, too, was immediately concerned with the way the absence of a people's recorded history, its 'nonhistory,' in Glissantian terms (1989, 62), could seem to erase the very fact of a people's existence. When retelling the history of the conquest of the island of Hispaniola by Christopher Columbus in the chapter entitled 'Haïti,' Bergeaud writes that the island's first inhabitants had been 'a gentle people, harmless, and hospitable' (1859, 309), but had been 'soon enough attacked, subjugated by force, and condemned to homicidal labor,' before being completely exterminated. Bergeaud lamented, '[w]hat became of these primitive people? How did they come to this island? To what branch of the human family did they belong? How did they become separated?' He mourned the lack of any answers to these questions when he wrote, '[n]o one knows; their history is completely unknown; we only know of their deplorable demise' (310).

Even though Emile Nau had published his *Histoire des Caciques* in 1855, four years before *Stella*, what Bergeaud considered to be a general ignorance about the history of the indigenous population of the island was less the result of a total absence of historical writing on the topic than of a lack of historical writing by the people in question. Whether or not his assessment is entirely accurate, Bergeaud wrote of Hispaniola's former inhabitants: 'They left behind neither history nor chronicle, nor tradition ... nothing survived, except for a few words passed down to the present inhabitants of the island' (1859, 310). Then, bearing the influence of Nau's *Histoire des caciques*, Bergeaud wrote that it was precisely because they had wanted to at least try to preserve something of the memory of Haiti's first inhabitants that

> the heroes of 1803 had restored the country to its first name, the name that had been given to it by the Indians, and of which they became the inheritors, independently of any kind of similar origins [*communauté d'origine*] ... they called the country Haiti in memory of these same Indians who had there enjoyed at one time independence and happiness. (317)[14]

Perhaps ironically, histories written by their subjects was the very reason Nau gave for taking up the topic of the 'grand and heroic' first inhabitants of Haiti who had been completely 'slaughtered' by the Europeans (15). Nau wrote that even though Haitians were not the 'descendants of the aborigines of Haiti,' either culturally or "racially," nineteenth-century Haitians and the original indigenous population of the island had been linked to one another by the chains of slavery and the suffering to which it bound them equally: 'The African and the Indian gave one another their hands in chains. It is through this communal fraternity of misery [*confraternité de malheur*], through their communal suffering, that their futures were bound together' (14). Because of this shared history of suffering, the lives of the indigenous population of Haiti needed to be inscribed by a Haitian since, 'the fact of inhabiting today the country where they had lived, requires us, more than anyone else, to inquire into the history of our predecessors ... the companions in servitude of our first ancestors on this soil' (15). Nau congratulated himself and other Haitian historians when he wrote that now that a 'national writer' had undertaken the project of 'recounting the era of colonization with his *Histoire*, *voilà*, all of Haitian history built by Haitian hands.' 'It is assuredly very honorable for our country,' Nau continued, 'that all of its annals have been preserved and written by its own citizens' (12).

---

14 For a historiographical account of the naming of Haiti, see Geggus (2002).

While Nau had little to say about the color prejudice that undergirded the extermination of the 'caciques' of Haiti, Bergeaud would link the enduring prejudices of colonial slavery to the conquest of the island using the same metaphor of slavery as a 'chain' of suffering. In the same chapter in which he offers a sad resumé of indigenous history, Bergeaud wrote that in addition to the physical chains of slavery, captivity, and conquest, there was also 'another chain, invisible, untouchable,' a 'chain of prejudice' (1859, 315). Bergeaud would go on to say that it was this 'chain of prejudice' that was responsible for all of the suffering of the colonial period: 'Prejudices are like the miasma of slavery, they vitiate the air of the colonies. In order to thrive there, you must raise up your head and breathe in a more elevated atmosphere' (1859, 316). In many ways, the final part of Bergeaud's statement provides a necessary precursor for understanding Bergeaud's contribution, in *Stella*, to dismantling pseudoscientific theories of "race" and the prejudices they incessantly inscribed onto the physical bodies and the body politic of the Haitian people. In *Stella*, some of the most dominant ideas of "race" as biological are contested, ideas that had been circulating in the political, historical, literary, and increasingly, *scientific*, spheres of the Atlantic World for centuries.

*

By the mid-nineteenth century, both "miscegenation" and the Haitian Revolution had become central and often interchangeable metaphors in the Atlantic World for the problems of slavery and slave rebellion. One reason for this is that, as Georges Fouron has written, 'many European and US intellectuals used the black nation as a negative referent to express their racist ideology,' and these racist 'prevarications' were 'accepted without question and repeated with complacency even, or especially, by the most educated elites of these societies' (72). An influential essay, 'The Mulatto a Hybrid—probable extermination of the two races if the Whites and Blacks are allowed to intermarry' (1843) by the medical doctor Josiah C. Nott, provides the perfect example of the way in which ideas about "race" first found in naturalist travel writing from the early modern world became widely accepted, repeated, subsequently proffered as truth, and then continuously attached to the Caribbean. Nott cites Edward Long's position on hybridity in order to prove that 'mulattoes,' because they were actually a 'hybrid' species, could not reproduce themselves and were therefore actually sterile:

> I have said that the Mulatto is a *Hybrid*. By this term is understood the offspring of two distinct species—as the mule from the horse and the ass.

> Hybrids, when bred together, have a tendency to run out and change back to one of the parental stocks. This has been remarked of the Mulattos in the West Indies. (254)

Nott took his analysis of 'mulatto' degeneration even further than either Long or Moreau de Saint-Méry when he wrote, 'the Mulatto or Hybrid is a degenerate, unnatural offspring, doomed by nature to work out its own destruction.' 'Mulattoes are much shorter lived,' he concluded, 'and it is a common subject of remark in the Southern States, that they are more liable to be diseased and less capable of endurance than the whites or blacks of the same condition' (255). Nott's comments represent the widely held belief among pro-slavery advocates in the mid-nineteenth-century United States (Sollors, 1997, 132) that "racial mixing" would result in 'degenerate,' infertile offspring who, since they had been 'produced by a violation of nature's laws,' would only become 'more degenerate in each successive generation' (Nott, 255).

On the French side of the Atlantic, Joseph Arthur, Comte de Gobineau, too, in his *Essai sur l'inégalité des races humaines* (1854-55), had remarked upon the results of "racial mixing," and not to Haiti's credit. Unlike Nott, Gobineau expressed a theory of "mulatto" regeneration and explicitly referenced Haiti rather than the West Indies in general in connection with that theory. Gobineau wrote that the island of Haiti was 'split into two factions that were separated less by the incompatibility of their politics than by the color of their skin; the mulattoes stay on one side, the negroes on the other.' He went on to say, 'to the mulattoes belong, without a doubt, more intelligence, a mind that is more open to ideas ... European blood has modified the nature of the African, and these men could, if they were to find themselves lost in a mass of whites ... become otherwise useful citizens' (1:180). The inutility of the 'mulattoes' of Haiti had everything to do with their actual geographical and physical connection to the 'negroes' of Haiti. Gobineau explained that in Haiti the 'negroes' far outnumbered the 'mulattoes,' which was 'unfortunate' in his mind since the 'supreme joy' of 'negroes' was 'laziness; their supreme reason for being, murder' (1:80–81).[15] Gobineau more fully painted Haiti's specific brand of hybridity—'negroes' living together and procreating with 'mulattoes'—as having had dire and even murderous consequences:

> The history of Haiti, of democratic Haiti, is nothing more than a long recitation of massacres: massacres of mulattoes by negroes, whenever they have been stronger, of negroes by mulattoes when the power has been in

---

15 Gobineau derived much of his information about the differences between 'mulattoes' and 'negroes' and the tendency for the latter to want to exterminate the former from Bryan Edwards (3:420–30).

the hands of the latter. Their institutions, as philanthropic as they purport to be, cannot accomplish anything; they exist powerlessly on the paper upon which they have been written ... In concert with the natural law that has come to us from above, the black species [*la variété noire*], belonging to the branch of human beings who are least susceptible to becoming civilized, encourages the deepest horror for all other races; as a result, we see the negroes of Haiti energetically expelling whites and forbidding them to enter their territory; they would even like to exclude the mulattoes and look towards their destruction. (1:49)

The result of the inherent "hybridity" of Haiti was not only the vengeance of these 'negroes' *for* 'mulattoes' and vice versa, but infertility, isolation, and lack of productivity.[16] Gobineau writes:

The hatred of outsiders is the principle motive of all local politics [in Haiti]. Thus, as a consequence of the inherent laziness of the species [*l'espèce*], agriculture has been annihilated, manufacturing only exists in name, trade is diminishing day by day, poverty, in its deplorable progression, prevents the population from reproducing, while the continuous wars, revolts, and military executions have succeeded in constantly diminishing it. The inevitable result and not far off conclusion will be that this country, whose fertility and natural resources had at one time enriched generations ... will end up as a desert. (1:49)

Gobineau's argument about the tragic sterility of post-independence Haiti and the total separation between 'negroes' and 'mulattoes' he envisioned as potentially restorative (1:82–83), became so popular that in an article that appeared in 1859 in the pro-slavery organ *Debow's Review*, W.W. Wright of New Orleans used Gobineau's work not only to argue for the 'hatred existing between blacks and mulattoes' (549), but for his final conclusion about the emptiness of Haitian independence. Wright's assessment of Haiti

---

16 The idea that Haiti offered a tragic case study for the effect of 'negro' independence on the economic productivity of a region was a feature of earlier writing about Haiti as well. One other good example of this kind of claim comes in the anonymously published, *The South Vindicated from the Treason and Fanaticism of the North* (1836), wherein the author writes, 'If it be not wished that a fate similar to that which has befallen Hayti should overtake the colonies, that they should be rendered wholly unproductive to the revenue of the country, and that the property invested in them should be preserved from destruction, the advisers of the crown must pause before they listen to the ill-judged suggestions of enthusiasts; for they must banish from their minds the idea that the work of cultivation can be made productive by means of free labor. Such a thing appears to me to be impossible. The negro, constituted as he is, has such an aversion to labor, and so great a propensity for indulgence and vice, that no prospect of advantage can stimulate him; and as for emulation it has not the slightest influence over him' (120).

was that '[t]he fruits of freedom in that island since its independence, in 1804, are *revolutions, massacres, misrule, insecurity, irreligion, ignorance, immorality, indolence, neglect of agriculture*, and indeed an actual renewal of slavery under a different shape' (531, emphasis in original).

One of the astounding things we learn by studying the connection between Haiti and pseudoscientific debates about "race" is that European and U.S. writers had been conjuring up the same narrative of "mulatto/a" vengeance for decades. This fact did not go unnoticed by nineteenth-century Haitian writers. In *La République d'Haïti et ses visiteurs* (1883), Janvier traced the genealogy of this idea of Haiti as a tragic "hybrid" republic as far back as Dubroca:

> This is a tactic that has been more or less followed since 1800 by an entire horde of malicious pamphleteers and ignorant writers since Dubroca ... paltry [*piètres*] historians and intellectuals who, *en vrais moutons de Panurges*,[17] had all copied one another and toiled to make people believe that Haitians, mulattoes and blacks, still wanted to rip each other to pieces. (154)

Moutons de Panurge, indeed! The connection between the 'mulatto/a" vengeance narrative of Haiti and pseudoscientific ideas about "race" was so entangled in the minds of nineteenth-century writers that an 1853 article published in *The Albion* about Haitian literary production was presented under the title 'Mulatto Literature,' which must have seemed to its author as so entirely descriptive of and appropriate to Haiti that he felt no need to use the words Haiti or Haitian. In the article in question, the author writes that the apparently amusing and unfit for 'high culture' 'literary state' of the 'negro or mulatto empire of Hayti,' was chiefly due to the fact that 'the negro is a pleasure-loving being, of warm blood; and the Mulatto ... his brother, differing from him mainly in a lighter-coloured skin' was 'sprung from two volatile sources.' 'The French-Haytian Mulatto,' this writer continued, was actually the 'embodiment of volatility, the like of which perhaps few countries can exhibit' (326).

In 1860, Benjamin Hunt would also link ideas about "race," and the "mulatto" in particular, directly to Haiti. In his *Remarks on Hayti as a Place of Settlement for Afric-Americans; and on the Mulatto as a Race for the Tropics,* Hunt not only references the disgust for "racial mixing" that he says found its 'strongest advocates among the slaveholders and other readers of *De Bow's Review*,' but he cites Moreau de Saint-Méry's theory of 'mulatto'

---

17 This is a French expression meaning 'to follow the herd.' The expression comes from Rabelais's *Gargantua*, wherein a character named Panurges makes a flock of sheep follow him into the water and drown.

degeneration (albeit to disagree with it) before adding his own contribution to these pseudoscientific debates. Hunt, whose work would originally have been bound with several other works by the same publisher under the title of *Hayti and the Mulatto* (1860),[18] appears to be all in favor of 'Mulattoes':

> This race, if on the white side it derives its blood from either the English or the French stock, possesses within itself a combination of all the physical and mental qualities necessary to form a civilized and progressive population for the tropics, and it is the only race yet found of which this can be said. (36)

Hunt continued: 'I have no wish to undervalue the blacks of Hayti … [they] can furnish a solid base for a population for the tropics, but not the population' (36). In other words, 'blacks' were only necessary to create 'mulattoes.' It is not just because of his ridiculous adoption of the theory of 'mulatto exceptionalism' that we must ultimately read anything written by Hunt with skepticism, but also because he derived his idea about the political problems between the 'blacks' and 'mulattoes' of Haiti, which kept him from recommending the 'removal' of 'Afric-Americans' to the country (20), from none other than Pamphile de Lacroix, one of the most influential disseminators of the narrative of "mulatto/a" vengeance. Hunt calls Lacroix 'an able French historian' (31), and Hunt's own work bears the same arm of "white" supremacy that undergirds all "racial" taxonomies. The "racial" supremacist ideas that support the kinds of positive expressions about "racial mixing" to be found in the work of Hunt are best encapsulated in Captain Amasa Delano's words from Melville's amorphous representation of the Haitian Revolution, *Benito Cereno* (1855): 'it were strange indeed, and not very creditable to us whiteskins, if a little of our blood mixed with the African's should, far from improving the latter's quality, have the sad effect of pouring vitriolic acid into black broth—improving the hue perhaps, but not the wholesomeness' (78). That is to say that undergirding all theories about "miscegenation," whether of the regenerative or degenerative ideology, is an attitude of "white" supremacy.

The "white" supremacy hiding under the surface of all theories of the "mulatto" is almost too apparent in an 1856 article published in *La Revue Contemporaine* entitled 'Les Noirs, les jaunes et la littérature française en Haïti.' In this article, which promised to provide a distinct account of the literature of Haiti, Alexandre Bonneau advanced the idea that what Haiti

---

18 Hunt's work was bound with William Wells Brown's previously published speech turned pamphlet 'St. Domingo, its Revolutions and its Patriots' (1855) and James Theodore Holly's own widely read *A Vindication of the capacity of the Negro race for self-government and civilized progress* (1857).

really needed was to do away with its special relationship to 'fusion.' That is, Haitians needed to accept that 'fusion between the Europeans and the Africans had been going on for more than three centuries' and 'had produced the mulatto species [*la variété mulâtre*] whose intelligence and remarkable aptitude could not be contested.' This kind of 'fusion' lay in stark contrast with the kind of "hybridity" that was being produced by the 'mulattoes' and 'blacks' of Haiti together. Bonneau went on to say that he hoped 'the black race would cease to exist by transforming itself' (152) with the kind of "racial" mixture he viewed as having led to the success of Carthage, Rome, Babylon, and Greece. Bonneau offers a bleak picture of Haiti's future 'if it stays black, in a word.' He says that if Haiti did not 'attract ... Asian emigrants, be they Indian or Chinese,' with whom they might mix (noticeably, he does not encourage further mixture with Europeans), 'their political future will not be long since they have neither the necessary knowledge to govern themselves, nor the administrative aptitude, nor the feelings of nationality [*le sentiment de la nationalité*]' (153).[19] Bonneau would go on to use the country's literature against the Haitian people through his claim that Isaac Louverture and the Haitian journalist Félix Darfour, were the only 'blacks of Haiti' who could be properly recognized as a 'littérateurs' (1856, 115), concluding that 'All of the other Haitian examples, in the domain of literature as in the domain of business, come from the class of the *métis*' (115).

Moreover, Bonneau declared that it was the French language that had offered the lexicon necessary for the slaves to seek their liberty in the first place:

> One might ask first whether the French language was not the most powerful instrument of this emancipation, driven by the energy of the mulattoes who had been raised in our schools and instructed with our literature ... the French spirit is responsible for the birth of liberty on Haitian shores, and it is under the influence of our language that this feat was accomplished. (108)

Bonneau's attribution of Haiti's revolution to 'mulattoes' and to the French (by way of their language) was not merely a sophomoric and self-serving interpretation from one who may have been entirely unaware of the number of slave rebellions that had been taking place in Saint-Domingue since 1719, particularly in the Sud-de-Cap region (Debien, 1996, 109), nor was it a simple

---

19 Ethéart had actually praised as 'impartial' Bonneau's review of Ardouin's histories in an article in *Les Miscellanées* (122), but this was before Bonneau's publication of the incendiary 1856 piece on Haiti in *La Revue contemporaine*. In *La République d'Haïti et ses visiteurs*, Janvier would, for his part, ardently criticize Bonneau for precisely this passage (1883, 155).

example of his enduring color prejudice; Bonneau's comments perniciously invite among the 'blacks' and 'mulattoes' of Haiti the very dissensions that he appeared to admonish. He wrote, for example, that the 'blacks' of Haiti needed to let themselves be 'governed by the *hommes de couleur*':

> Those of the blacks who can think, can also glean from the annals of Haiti valuable insights about the behavior they must undertake in the interest of their country. The only men who have adopted, in their governing of the nation, a grand and productive politics have belonged to the class of mulattoes. (153)

Bonneau's comments patently echo the actions of the French colonists during the Revolution who, as many nineteenth-century Haitian authors had sought to prove, tried to encourage divisions between Louverture and Rigaud during the insurrection in Saint-Domingue in order to preserve their own colonial power over the island. Bonneau's comments also bespeak the claims for Haiti's "monstrous hybridity" made by many of the former French colonists, like Venault de Charmilly, Mazères, Malouet, and Drouin de Bercy (see chapter one of this volume) who, by stoking the fires of discord between Pétion and Christophe, designed policies aimed at restoring the erstwhile colony to France. Therefore, we might say that the brand of "mulatto/a" vengeance created by people like Bonneau and Gobineau, which masqueraded as theories of 'mulatto exceptionalism,' had been designed solely to encourage the same kinds of division that had occurred at the behest of the French colonists during the Revolution.

Finally, so intertwined with ideas about "race," and "racial mixing" in particular, was Haiti, that the specter of the Haitian Revolution as a "race war" was evoked in the 1863 spoof pamphlet in which the term "miscegenation" itself was coined. In the pamphlet, which was published anonymously during the U.S. Civil War, the authors (later identified as David Goodman Croly and George Wakeman)[20] infamously claimed to advance an argument for what they would go on to call 'miscegenation,' or "racial mixing." The full title of the pamphlet was *Miscegenation: The Theory of the Blending of the Races, Applied to the American White Man and the Negro*. In this pamphlet, the authors conjured up the history of the Haitian Revolution with irony:

> It will be a sad misfortune if this war should end without a battle being fought by a black general in command of a white or mixed body of troops. We want an American Toussaint L'Ouverture, to give the black his proper position in this continent, and the day is coming. (56)

---

20 Carter (2013) identifies the two New York journalists as the authors of the 'anti-Republican propaganda' pamphlet (71).

A 'Quarrel between Two Brothers'

The evocation of Haiti in a pamphlet about the essential dangers of 'miscegenation,' was meant to further provoke fears that the South would eventually be 'subdued by a black soldier' and that 'the negro' would subsequently find himself in 'supreme control' (57). What all of these examples of the juxtaposition of Haiti with arguments about 'miscegenation' clearly suggest is that there was an immediate and direct association of Haiti, its revolution, its government, and its culture with the negative effects of 'the blending of various races of men' (1).

Of all the Haitian writers of the nineteenth century who responded to this kind of racist writing about their country circulating in the Atlantic World, Bergeaud unquestionably provides, in *Stella*, the most creative response to the narrative of "mulatto/a" vengeance. *Stella* refuses the association of Haiti with a tragedy of "monstrous hybridity"—here, the idea that the country's independence had been rooted in a horrible "race war" between "mulattoes" and "blacks"—by using the image of the Haitian flag itself as the ultimate symbol of the country's unity and prosperity rather than the symbol of its unending vengeance. Bergeaud wrote that the origin of the red in the flag of Haiti could be located in Romulus and Rémus's deceased mother's blood-soaked dress, described as a 'somber flag whose bloody creases the breeze unfolds' (213). If the red in the flag was a reminder of Marie's brutal suffering at the hands of the *Colon*, the addition of the color blue was a reminder of the work of national healing. Bergeaud writes:

> Later, another color, borrowed from the azure of our sky, was placed next to the one which had harbored the vengeance, maybe to soften the sinister reflection, maybe to recall the duality of the work of Haitian independence, accomplished by the common devotion of individuals of two different skin colors, and that Providence has blessed by creating yet another society under the auspices of liberty. (213)

With this description, Bergeaud revises the longstanding legend of how the Haitian flag was created by Dessalines. According to Colin (Joan) Dayan, the legend goes:

> On May 18, 1803 at the Congress of Arcahaie, General-in-Chief Dessalines ripped the white out of the French tricolor ... Trampling it under his feet, he commanded that the red and blue—symbolizing the union of the mulatto and black—be sewn together as the new flag and that *'Liberté ou la Mort'* (Liberty or Death) replace the old inscription, *'R.F.'* (*République Française*). (1995b, 52)

Bergeaud's modification of the flag's origins not only subdues the idea that this standard was the symbol of Haitian vengeance—or *Liberté ou la Mort*—

by making it the work of fraternal unity between people with lighter and darker skin hue or in pseudoscientific terms, "mulattoes" and "blacks," but it attempts to heal the violent sexual past of the country that might have made Dessalines want to trample the original French flag.

Though the weaving of the blood of Marie's murder into the Haitian flag suggests the kind of problematic but 'productive paradox' that Garraway says marks transculturation in the French Caribbean (2005, 1), Bergeaud's celebration of Haiti's duality comes in spite of rather than because of his acknowledgement that the origins of the difference in skin color between Romulus and Rémus often lay in violent rape. Because he appeared to be entirely conscious of this contradiction, Bergeaud's vision actually required a willful rather than an incidental transformation of thinking about the sexual violence that lay at the heart of all colonial plantation sexual practices. For good or ill, *Stella* proposes a rereading, or rather an intertextual revision, of the origins of the many different gradations in skin color that one might find in Haiti in order to produce a discourse that is anti-race. Although we have already been told that Rémus was the product of the *Colon's* rape of Marie, Bergeaud explains that it was actually '[d]ue to a whim, a picturesque game of nature, [that] the youngest [of the brothers] ... had the pale hue of mahogany, whereas the older could have been compared to the darkest ebony' (9). We might say that Bergeaud would like us to believe that the human beings produced by such "mixing," because it was through no fault of their own, did not have to be reminders of what W.E.B. Du Bois would come to call the 'the unvoiced terror' of the 'black' man's life (1965, 102; see chapter seven of this volume). By erasing (or subduing) rape as the origin of the contrasting skin colors of Romulus and Rémus, Bergeaud locates a new myth about "race" or skin color that, as Saint-Rémy had described in his *Vie de Toussaint-L'Ouverture*, was based upon a reading of phenotypical differences as simply as haphazard as the wind and therefore ultimately as politically and historically meaningless. Saint-Rémy had written, 'in essence, skin color [was] nothing more than accident of nature, [since] an evil spirit can animate equally the body of a negro, a mulatto, or a white man' (1850, 239).[21]

---

[21] This is actually quite a remarkable and understudied passage, especially when we consider that it constitutes a rare pre-1900 acknowledgement of Haitian Vodou by a writer of color from Haiti. Not only that, but the passage fundamentally uses the cosmology of Haitian religious perspectives and spiritual practices rather than a solely European or U.S. American Judeo-Christian conception of the world. West Indian religious practices were most often demonized in colonial writing and early Haitian writers therefore often remained silent on the subject. Monique Allewaert has accounted for the rare inscriptions of these beliefs in colonial writing by saying, 'The inhabiting of a body by an external force might seem to replicate the colonial Anglo-European belief

The idea that the Haitian flag could incorporate the symbol of the *Colon*'s murder of Marie, a woman he had previously raped, *and* the symbol of the fraternal love that had created Haiti, and thus be transformed into a metaphor for Haitian nationalism, turns the tragic fact of colonialism's coercive hybridity into a sublime narration of accepted national diversity. Not without its own pitfalls. In so doing, Bergeaud implicitly denounces the suggestion of an author like Victor Séjour, who had in many ways inferred with the utmost fatalism that "mulatto/a" vengeance was the incurable and inevitable result of plantation "miscegenation." *Stella* interrupts this kind of pessimistic outlook by offering in its place an idealistic, even if paradoxical, vision of acceptance of diversity—here, people with dark skin and lighter skin finding a way to live together as a harmonious national family—as the answer to the problems of color prejudice and slavery, not just in Haiti, but everywhere in the world.[22]

*

If understanding Haiti's image in the hyper "racialized" literary and historical milieu of the Atlantic World is necessary in order to understand *Stella*'s defensive posture about the long-term philosophical implications of the Revolution, acknowledging the relationship of the plot of *Stella* to the work of Saint-Rémy is equally essential for understanding how the Haiti of the independence period could become the primary model for a new world that was imagined to be devoid of "race." Out of all the Haitian historians whose works either implicitly or explicitly influenced Bergeaud, it is Saint-Rémy's *Vie de Toussaint-L'Ouverture*, from which Bergeaud almost entirely derived the idea that Louverture and Rigaud had been engaged in a fratricidal conflict, which provides an essential key

---

that black persons were weak or half-formed humans, or perhaps exchangeable objects, who could be moved by the will of masters. However, although the phenomenon of possession might seem to confirm the idea that black persons are empty ciphers who could be claimed by superior forces, it instead shows precisely the opposite; it emphasizes that a person is not an emptiness but an assemblage' (138). In Saint-Rémy's commentary, not only does the black body represent an assemblage that is open to co-optation and 'disaggregation,' but so, too, and remarkably, does the 'white' body. It is this openness and this *sameness*, not at all dependent upon one's belief in the concept, which provides Saint-Rémy with evidence that 'blacks' and 'whites' were equals.

22 According to Susan Gillman, the Cuban writer José Martí made a similar argument by positing that after Cuba's 'First War of Independence, 1868–1878,' there were '"no races" in Cuba' and that 'the question of race [wa]s necessarily both unnecessary and divisive, because the issue was resolved during the First War of Independence' (2002, 147).

to understanding *Stella*'s engagement with both history and the narrative of "mulatto/a" vengeance.

In *Vie de Toussaint-L'Ouverture*, in great contrast to most European writers, like Bryan Edwards, Pamphile de Lacroix, and Marcus Rainsford, who had blamed Rigaud for the War of the South, Saint-Rémy uses a grammar of "mulatto/a" vengeance to describe Sonthonax as the one who had 'sown the seeds of the most impious war, the war of color, that would soon bloody the unfortunate land of my country!' (205). Later, Saint-Rémy would also blame one of Louverture's most trusted confidants, General Etienne Laveaux, in addition to Sonthonax, for the conflict between Rigaud and Louverture and therefore, 'all the blood that flooded the fields of Saint-Domingue' (303). Saint-Rémy also believed that Hédouville was another European who had tried to foment color prejudice between 'blacks' and 'mulattoes' in Saint-Domingue (1850, 206). Saint-Rémy's judgment about the causes of the split between Rigaud and Louverture appears on the surface to match one eyewitness version of the role played by outsiders in the War of the South. In his *Mémoire historique sur Toussaint-Louverture* (1818), Augustin Régis, who referred to himself as an 'homme de couleur' and 'former major-general' [*ex-officer d'état-major-général*] of the 'former military of Saint-Domingue' (see front matter), explained, 'it is within my knowledge that the civil war between brigadier General *Rigaud* and General-in-Chief *Toussaint Louverture* had been solely provoked and ensured by a letter from the general of division *Marie Gabriel-Théodore Hédouville* ... in which he ordered *Rigaud* to disobey the orders of Toussaint' (30).[23] Régis concluded, then, that the 'War of the South between *Rigaud* and *Toussaint* was the work of General Hédouville before his departure from the colony for France' (38). There is, however, one subtle and previously unrecognized difference between Saint-Rémy's account of the events and that of a bystander like Régis. Even while acknowledging the role of Hédouville, Sonthonax, and Laveaux in encouraging strife between the two revolutionary leaders, Saint-Rémy insisted upon referring to the conflict between Louverture and Rigaud as, 'the war of color because we must call things by their name.' He asked:

do you know what it means, this war? It means that you only need to have black skin for the mulatto to often doubt the sincerity of your feelings;

---

23 The belief that the conflict between Rigaud and Louverture had been deliberately contrived can be seen in an 'Extract of the letter from General Maitland to Lieutenant Colonel Grant,' as published in Jacques Nicolas Léger's *Haiti, son histoire et ses détracteurs* (1907). According to the document, on June 17, 1799 Maitland had written to Grant, 'the grand objective of your purpose in Saint-Domingue consists in trying to ... prevent any friendly *entente* between Rigaud and Toussaint' (rpt. in Léger, 379).

it means that you only need to have a yellow skin for the negro to often doubt in turn the sincerity of your feelings! (235–36)[24]

In essence, Saint-Rémy believed that it was color prejudice, or racism, rather than "race" itself, that was at the root of the problems between Rigaud and Louverture, who had both been dishonorably embroiled in 'the fratricidal war that had demolished the south' (1850, 275). Even so, Saint-Rémy did believe that the majority of the blame could be placed upon Louverture himself. This position stands in stark contrast to the vast majority of historians who had written on the topic and assigned most of the blame to Rigaud. Saint-Rémy, citing as proof of his divergent conclusion the fact that Louverture did not mention this conflict with Rigaud in his *Mémoires*, writes, 'Let no one come to tell us that Rigaud was the aggressor, no! … The civil war was the work of Toussaint Louverture' (1850, 235). Saint-Rémy furnished as proof the fact that:

> in a long memoir written in his hand, going back to the Château de Joux … in which he explains his life and his conduct, [Louverture] takes care, perhaps out of remorse, not to speak of this war [with Rigaud]; it seems as though the recollection of it frightened him and that he wanted to erase it from his memory. (1850, 235)

If *Stella* also alludes to the divisions between Louverture and Rigaud and later between Pétion and Dessalines as ones of color, it is only to prove that all of those divisions were the work of the French colonists, in concert with Saint-Rémy's reading, *and* that they no longer existed in the post-independence period. Without any mention of the words "mulatto" or "negro," Bergeaud portrayed the *Colon* as 'the poisonous fig tree [*le figuier maudit*], who had abused the trust he had too easily acquired' since it was he who had 'persuaded' Romulus that 'Rémus was an enemy he needed to seek to destroy' (132). The *Colon* instigated this dissension when he introduced what Bergeaud refers to as '[a] horrible question, the most horrible question that has ever been raised among men, is without contradiction the question of what is vulgarly called *color*' (133–34). Bergeaud's thoughts on the implications of this 'horrible question' of '*color*' are so eloquent that they are worth quoting at length:

---

24 The idea that Hédouville had been principally involved in encouraging the War of the South seems to have been popular in nineteenth-century Haiti. Saint-Rémy wrote: 'Haitians have spoken so often [about Hédouville's 'secret instructions'], in which, according to them, he attempted to divide the inhabitants of Saint-Domingue along the lines of color' (1850, 206).

The Trope of the Tragic "Mulatto/a"

> It contains a proposal of which the simple enunciation is absurd, and it is consequently useless and even ridiculous to discuss it. The rationales for slavery and the prejudices that hideously form its *cortège* are well known. They come solely from insatiable greed. To torture the miserable Africans without remorse, the masters [*les maîtres*], veiling their crimes with sophistry, have purported that they were inferior to all the other individuals of the human race, and only because they were *black*. Many of them, not even having been slave owners,—without a doubt to their chagrin,—have also said this and *written* it. But this inferiority is so little proven that we are convinced that even those who have espoused it do not even really believe that it exists. Is there a color that is privileged in nature? Where is the animal who can be judged based on the appearance of its fur? (134–35)

Bergeaud continues by asserting that '[p]rejudices based on skin color are malicious nonsense. The hatred of color is an insidious lie,' he contends, 'we hate in someone else—because we know how to hate—their achievements, their virtues, the things they have that we do not; we do not hate someone's color' (134). This sermon on the evil absurdities of color prejudice concludes with Bergeaud's counsel to his readers to '[c]urse at every instance these diabolical inventions made credible by the Machiavellianism of the colonists, which were fatal to their own authors' (134). If we recall that Gobineau had written that the hatred of other "races" was natural to Africans and therefore to the 'negroes of Haiti,' then Bergeaud's argument that these prejudices had been contrived by the colonists opposes the idea that the struggle between Romulus and Rémus, or Louverture and Rigaud, was an inevitable consequence of the "racial mixing" that had produced "mulattoes" in the first place.

In Saint-Rémy's reading of the successful way in which the colonists had been able to turn Louverture and Rigaud against one another, the Haitian historian actually absolved Louverture of the charge of color prejudice, suggesting that his usage of the narrative of "mulatto/a" vengeance was merely pragmatic:

> I believe in the good sense of Louverture. I believe that this extraordinary man only wanted to feel as if he were alone on this island, and that he wanted to rid himself of all those who would resist his power; I will not insult him by thinking that he really believed what he said about mulattoes; I would prefer to believe that in seeking to destroy the legitimate and salutary influence that these men had ... he wanted only to find himself without a competitor. (239)

In turn, in *Stella*, Bergeaud also portrayed Romulus, or the darker-skinned brother, as being haphazardly responsible for the majority of the conflict with his lighter-skinned brother, Rémus. Bergeaud writes, 'Romulus put into place the obstacles that had been communicated to him by his *faux amis*: he became suspicious and defiant' (135). Rémus, on the other hand, 'assumed an air of great disdain and confronted *le Colon* who was hiding behind his brother' (135). Bergeaud goes on to represent Rémus as having barely tried to defend himself against the 'violent, murderous shock' of Rémus's behavior. For what happens next, however, Bergeaud does not need the historian.

The mystery of Rémus's (or Rigaud's) failure to defeat Romulus (or Louverture) can be better explained by cosmology than history: 'This is what history has not been able to tell,' Bergeaud writes, 'It has clearly determined that the probable causes of the events of which Rémus fell victim were his own fault; but the error has remained unexplained ... History can only say that which it knows.' Bergeaud continues, '[i]ts view, limited by the horizon of the natural world [*choses naturelles*], grasps with difficulty the truth that shines beyond. The marvelous is not in its domain. It relegates the realm of mystery to the novel ...' (146). In one of the most fascinating passages of *Stella*, Bergeaud then attempts to use precisely the extra-historical capacities of the novel, its 'marvelous' domain, to pierce the mystery of Rémus/Rigaud's downfall when he portrays a mysterious giant in the forest as responsible for Rémus's perceived capitulation. The kind of fratricide that marked the Haitian Revolution in the literary imagination will be narrowly avoided. The spirit, whom Bergeaud refers to in the novel as 'le génie de la patrie' or the 'spirit of the nation' (152), is described as preventing Rémus from acting upon his desire to raise his arm against his brother, even in self-defense. 'Le génie de la patrie' tells Rémus, '[b]eware of aspiring to a glory for which you must sacrifice the most tender sentiments of nature, a glory that can only be acquired through the price of your brother's blood!' (150). Subsequently, 'the spirit' asks Rémus for his total 'abnegation' (151), and the youngest of Marie's children promptly complies.

Hoffmann has written of this scene that the 'mystery' of Rigaud's failure during his war with Louverture 'had baffled historians,' but that Bergeaud explains Rémus's (or Rigaud's) failed attempt to defeat his rival through the symbol of the giant and his historical visitation. 'This kind of explanation,' Hoffmann writes, 'is obviously meaningless for a historian ... Bergeaud chose to give his country a symbolic interpretation. The reader is free to choose whether or not to accept it, whether or not to enter into the novel's universe' (1999, 219). Bergeaud wants his reader to believe, nevertheless, that it was not only in the universe of his imagination that Romulus or Louverture was the guilty party, but that this was a truth that had been written in the cosmos. Bergeaud alludes to Louverture's eventual kidnapping, deportation, and lonely death in France as the work of divine retribution when, using a metaphysical explanation, he discursively punishes Romulus's betrayal of his brother:

> The lesson in store for Romulus would be instructive for an entire people; that is why Providence wanted it to be eloquent, severe, and grand. The oldest son of the African abused his powers against his brother; France will in turn abuse its powers against him. He will become the victim of his own injustices and his disunity against nature, he will learn that equality is a law from God that we are never permitted to transgress, and that only unity offers to members of the same family the firm guarantees of peace and existence. (170)

At this point in the novel, Romulus becomes Dessalines and Rémus becomes Pétion, which allows the two brothers to engage in a *rapprochement* that would become the inspiration for the Haitian national motto: '*l'union, c'est la force*' or 'union is strength' (203).

Importantly, 'Le génie de la patrie' will surface again in the character Stella's final speech, which drips once again with references to God and to Stella herself as not only the 'virgin of the mountain,' but the 'virgin' Mary (301, 308). Stella notes that the driving element behind the forceful union of Romulus and Rémus was the promise Rémus made before 'the supernatural being,' who 'counseled' him to refrain from engaging in a war with Romulus, promising that he would be eternally compensated for his actions (308). Stella implies that the independence of Haiti resulting from the union of Romulus and Rémus meant that 'le génie de la patrie' had kept his promise of making Haiti forever independent. The reader is meant to believe, therefore, that Haiti's liberty was the work of this supernatural force, whose description by Bergeaud bears an uncanny resemblance to Guillaume Guillon-Lethière's 1822 painting 'Le Serment des ancêtres,' which also depicts Haitian independence as the work of God.

The famous painting, which was badly damaged during the 2010 earthquake in Port-au-Prince and has only recently been repaired, depicts an Almighty ("white") God reuniting Dessalines and Pétion under the law.[25] As Helen Weston has written, in the painting we see Pétion and Dessalines swearing an oath to unite against Napoleon Bonaparte. Weston

---

25 Guillon-Lethière was purportedly the child of a 'white' colonist and 'black' slave from Guadeloupe (Simonetta and Arikha, 87). According to Weston, the painting was brought to Haiti by one of Guillon-Lethière's sons in March of 1823. It was subsequently hung in a cathedral, where it escaped notice until 1991, when it was restored. Before the 2010 earthquake that nearly destroyed Port-au-Prince, the painting was hanging in the Presidential Palace of Haiti (Weston, 176). For more on the painting's restoration and second return to Haiti from France, see (S.Wood).

writes that the '[b]roken chains of slavery can be seen at the feet of the two military leaders. The oath is sworn over the tablets of the law and these are blessed by the hands of Jehovah ... The outlines of a liberty bonnet can be seen above the writing on the tablets and the words, "Liberté", "Loix", and "Constitution" are clearly discernible' (176). Bergeaud's narrative description of this union most clearly resembles that found in the painting when Stella famously tells the two brothers that it was the unification of the two sides of the Haitian family—not "mulatto" and "black," but lighter and darker—'that had already produced liberty, and independence' and that 'would produce civilization once again by incorporating the seed of life contained in this divine exhortation: Love each other as I have loved you [*Aimez-vous les uns les autres*]' (97). By this statement, Haitian independence is rendered not only the work of natural law, as in Stella's earlier supplications, but the work of divine law, as in Guillon-Lethière's painting. The will of God is evoked in *Stella* itself by the quoted phrase '*Aimez-vous les uns les autres*,' borrowed of course from the gospel of John (15:12).

It is not only a modification of the 'Liberty, Equality, and Fraternity' of the French Republican motto, along with its divinely sanctioned racialization of the Haitian national motto that 'l'union fait la force,' that is evoked by both Guillon-Lethière's painting and Bergeaud's novel, but the Constitution of 1805 of Dessalines. It is with the word 'Law' that Guillon-Lethière's painting renders official and juridical the idea that Haitians of whatever skin color could no longer be divided, which is exactly what Dessalines had hoped to accomplish with his constitution. If you recall, Article 14 of the 1805 Constitution of Dessalines had not only declared that all of the inhabitants of the island of Haiti shall be called 'blacks,' but that 'all distinctions of color amongst children of the same family ... must necessarily cease.' If Dessalines had sought to prove that all Haitians were 'black' and therefore were 'of the same family,' regardless of skin color, in *Stella*, Bergeaud labors to prove that all Haitians were actually "mixed," but not in the biological sense offered by naturalist travel writers and other proponents of pseudoscientific theories of "race." Haitian society was "mixed," that is to say diverse, because one could find people of various skin colors even in the same family, like Romulus and Rémus. The diversity of these mixtures—people with different skin colors all living together—was precisely what made the country beautiful. Unlike for Dessalines, the recognition of difference was not a problem for Bergeaud.

Bergeaud appears to be illustrating through his novel a theory of difference that George Lipsitz might call 'inter-ethnic anti-racism,' a form of '[s]olidarity' based not on 'identity,' but 'identities.' Lipsitz writes that '[s]olidarity based on identity is limited; solidarities based on identities are unlimited.' This is because, for Lipsitz, it does not follow that recognizing difference leads to inequality, nor that promoting 'sameness,' as Dessalines

The Trope of the Tragic "Mulatto/a"

Guillaume Guillon-Lethière, 'Le Serment des ancêtres' (1822), oil on canvas.

can be interpreted as having done, was to promote equality. Lipsitz concludes that '[p]eople who have to see themselves as exactly the same in order to wage a common struggle' are poorly positioned for understanding modern racism. This is because 'racialized groups' who 'suffer from racism' (14) have 'coasted on the solidarities of sameness for too long' which has led such peoples to 'misread their circumstances' through an inability to 'see power from more than one perspective' (15).

Glissant's theory of *'relation'* reminds us that any social justice movement that is predicated on the solidarity of the 'rhizome' is itself a ploy for power. Glissant writes that '[s]ameness is sublimated difference; diversity is accepted difference,' where 'diversity' is defined as 'neither chaos nor sterility,' but the 'human spirit's striving for a cross-cultural relationship, without universalist transcendence' (1989, 98). In *The Womb of Space*, Wilson Harris also railed against the 'homogeneity' of common origins, saying that such beliefs originated as a 'biological hypothesis that relates all mankind to a basic or primordial ancestor,' but that 'as a cultural model, exercised by a ruling ethnic group, it tends to become an organ of conquest and division because of *imposed* unity that actually subsists on the suppression of others' (xviii). If the cultural and perhaps even "racial" homogeneity argued for by Dessalines closed off a potentially fruitful conversation about difference because the erstwhile Haitian general viewed that kind of recognition as tending towards 'division' and 'suppression' rather than unity and inclusiveness, in *Stella* it was the kind of 'cultural heterogeneity,' which Harris found could open up 'ceaseless dialogue' and that tended towards building 'arcs or bridges of community' (Harris, xviii), that Bergeaud's ideal history calls to mind.

The idea that Haiti was at the outset a diverse, heterogeneous society is an interpretation that is not entirely incompatible with the 1805 Constitution's desire to make all Haitians 'brothers.' Recall, again, that articles 3 and 14 of the 1805 Constitution had made into law the concept that all those born in Haiti were brothers 'of the same family for which the head of the state is the father.' Bergeaud appears to be referencing this very article of the Constitution when he writes that Haiti's independence had meant that 'from now on all orphans will have a mother' (293). This understanding of the nation as one's family, which had been used for the pernicious purposes of encouraging patricide by Salvador in Lamartine's *Toussaint Louverture* (1850), is transformed into a fraternal romance by the author of *Stella*, who at the end of the novel tells us, 'Touching scenes were taking place in the streets. People encountered one another, they recognized each other, they kissed each other, they cried, they laughed, they gave one another the gentle names of brothers and sisters ... brothers and sisters in nation' (292). The metaphor of the heterogeneous, not "interracial," family offered by Bergeaud does not require the kind of 'sameness' that Dessalines had promoted—the Haitian family must be "black"—nor did it require the kind of "racial" labeling and calculating found in pseudoscientific discourses of "race." Here, the diversity of the human family could be acknowledged and celebrated simply by the passing recognition that Romulus and Rémus happened to be brothers with different skin colors. Bergeaud's evocation in certain ways of a metaphor of Haiti as *métis* or as "mixed," then, does not refer to 'marked bodies' like "negroes" or "mulattoes," but rather to what José Buscaglia-Salgado has called 'mulataje' or a 'history of subversion of race as a marked category' (xvii). If everyone is "mixed"—in Bergeaud's universe there are no "negroes" or "mulattoes"—then it follows that there are no "races" in the first place. In other words, Haiti's diversity signifies the potential ability of the country's *doubleness* not only to erase racial difference, but to erase the idea of "race" itself.

Bergeaud's imagining of Haiti's identity as non-"racial" and his attempt to divinely sanction the *rapprochement* between people with light and dark skin brings us back to the notion of the role of memory in nation-building. *Stella* shows that for Romulus and Rémus to come together to build this *raceless* state, they must not only abide by the laws of nature and the laws of religion in not engaging in fratricidal combat, but they must abide by the unwritten laws of nation-building. Building on Renan's idea that the inhabitants of modern nation-states have 'forgotten many things' (11), contemporary literary theorist Homi Bhabha adds to the list of requirements for the self-conscious construction of a nation by noting that not only have the members of nation-states forgotten many things, but they have 'remembered to forget' them:

> It is this forgetting—the signification of a minus in the origin—that constitutes the *beginning* of the nation's narrative … the identity of part and whole, past and present, is cut across by the 'obligation to forget' or forgetting to remember. The anteriority of the nation, signified in the will to forget, entirely changes our understanding of the pastness of the past, and synchronous present of the will to nationhood. (1994, 230)

This forgetting in order to remember the nation is a willed forgetting whose primary goal is to create one memory of the nation's origins that stresses unity and continuity even if it has the effect of changing people's lived memories of the past.

While forced forgetting has been characterized in scholarship on the nation as a form of violence by the state against the people (Hanchard, 46, 49), as Simon During has written, 'cultural nationalism' and collective memory of this sort probably takes on a different meaning in the postcolonial state, where it might be developed as 'a mode of freedom … against imperialism' (139). To that effect, long before either Renan or Bhabha had theorized the concept of forgetting as the first step towards national unity, Baron de Vastey and Julien Prévost had already quasi-theorized the utility and value of the kind of 'forgetting to remember' which they viewed as necessary to unify Haiti. In his *Essai sur les causes de la Révolution et des guerres civiles en Haïti* (1819), Vastey writes that Julien Prévost, the count of Limonade, had at one point sent four of Christophe's ministers to Pétion, offering the following conditions for an end to the divisions: '1. the total forgetting of the past; and 2. a frank and sincere reunion.'[26] The performative 'total forgetting of the past' offered by Vastey and Prévost in order to promote the 'reunion' of the northern and southern states of Haiti is exactly what Bergeaud describes as occurring during the immediate post-independence period between Romulus and Rémus or Dessalines and Pétion. Romulus tells Rémus: 'Brother, I have insulted and abused you; forget about it; I repent it all!' Rémus responds: 'Brother, I have forgotten everything ... On your part, forget all the wrongs that I have perpetrated against you. Love me, let's love each other always' (199).[27] When both brothers agree to forget the past in order to love their nation by loving one another, they unite against the *Colon* and finally succeed in defeating him. The text demonstrates, in the end, that Haitians must unite against outsiders who wish to re-enslave them if they want to be a prosperous nation, but it also suggests that Haitians must forget certain aspects of the nation's origin story, namely, those aspects that are likely to promulgate resentment and division, not towards the colonists, but towards one another.

The idea that it was the founders of Haitian independence who had been tasked with forgetting certain parts of Haitian history—importantly, they

---

26 A copy of the original document that had been addressed to Pétion on February 10, 1815 was published later that year under the title of 'L'Olivier de la Paix.' It was signed by the 'Comte de Limonade' (Julien Prévost) and printed by P. Roux.

27 Bergeaud had also spoken of 'forgetting' the Haitian Revolution in an article published in the Port-au-Prince-based newspaper *Le Temps* on November 10, 1842. In the article, which was entitled, 'Insurrection d'Ambouille Marlot,' which referred to the case of a free person of color who had been implicated in the Moïse affair (see also Ardouin, 1855, 4:266), Bergeaud began by saying that the War of the South, 'The civil war, that horrible fire lit by a perfidious hand and nourished by the ardent rivalry of two powerful leaders, that bloody, deadly war, whose consequences have so disastrously influenced the future of our country, had at last ended' (1). He goes on to note that, in order to 'encourage public confidence,' Louverture hastened to appear before the public in *Cayes* to 'sing a *Te Deum*, after which he gave a speech from the pulpit that was full of kindness and generosity; he proclaimed the total forgetting of the past [*l'oubli total du passé*], the renunciation of all vengeance, and the abdication of any rancor, and even offered to give passports to whomever desired to go and live elsewhere: but *woe betide those who attempt anything further from this point on!* [*malheur à ceux qui s'agiteront désormais!*]' (1, emphasis in original).

were not to forget the suffering they had all experienced under colonialism—constitutes the major break of Bergeaud from the influential work of Saint-Rémy. Saint-Rémy insinuated that writing about the civil war between Rigaud and Louverture was painful but necessary for him:

> I myself would have liked to have ripped [this page] out of the book of history, but no!—we must conserve this page so that our nephews, blacks and yellows, can read in it about the errors of their fathers, and learn to live in the communal happiness that unity and peace always bring. (1850, 236)

Whereas Bergeaud wholly downplayed the historical significance of those divisions for the sake of unity, Saint-Rémy concentrates on them and their pernicious effects in order to provide a lesson about how *not* to act. This is because Saint-Rémy's vision of Haiti's past is ultimately pessimistic. Saint-Rémy could only vaguely gesture towards the kind of fruitful contact among the "races" and nations of the world that he thought could be a radically new way forward for Haiti when he wrote, 'there is a law made by nature, that the races only ameliorate themselves in mixing, that well-being only increases by free commerce, that understanding is only enriched by the exchange of ideas, that populations only become more civilized by coming into contact with others' (1851, xxi); but ultimately he could not see beyond the violence of the Haitian Revolution. In other words, the Haitian Revolution had not operated either the 'exchange of ideas' or the kind of fruitful 'coming into contact' for which Saint-Rémy longed.

In his introduction to Boisrond-Tonnerre's *Mémoire*, Saint-Rémy would even blame what he called Boisrond-Tonnerre's 'politics of exclusion' of 'whites' from Haiti for all the 'antagonisms of class, race, of public misery, and tears we have seen flow' (1851, xix–xx). He further accused the secretary of Dessalines of having a hatred for 'whites' that, 'pushed to the extent of its consequences, would eternally divide the human race into stupid and savage categories' (xx).

Saint-Rémy's critique of what he viewed as Boisrond-Tonnerre's inherently violent disposition and Louverture's acquired violence is part of the historian's general attitude towards what he viewed as an unnecessary and incomprehensible aggression—both physical and political—against "whites" in both the revolutionary and the post-independence period. Saint-Rémy never justified the massacres sanctioned by the government of Dessalines and blamed such inhumanity almost entirely on Boisrond-Tonnerre. That is to say that for Saint-Rémy, the ends of the Haitian Revolution, Haitian independence, never justified some of the means. In a moment of rare praise for Dessalines, Saint-Rémy reveals that he considered Dessalines 'more wise and more moderate' than Christophe because he knew that 'it is necessary for conquerors to have pity as well as clemency' (1850, 270). In Saint-Rémy's estimation, 'there is magnanimity in keeping the peace' (1850, 46), and the ultimate tragedy of Louverture's own life, as he had seen it, was that at the height of his power he was no longer the 'so good, so pious, so humane' revolutionary hero of 1791, but had become a blindly violent and viciously ambitious man, in whose name Saint-Rémy would evoke a metaphor of matricide to describe the transformation of the extraordinary revolutionary hero into an ordinary assassin (250). Saint-Rémy wrote:

> After so many acts of barbarity committed under the administration of L'Ouverture, I no longer recognized the so good, so pious, so humane Toussaint of the year 1791; it is true that Nero[28] in his youth, believed that he was avenging the Gods [*il est vrai que Néron dans sa jeunesse, croyait outrager les Dieux*] in signing a death decree, and that later he slit the throat of his own mother! (1850, 250).

While Saint-Rémy's ambivalence about the violence of the Haitian Revolution shines through in his various praises and rebukes of Louverture, Rigaud, Dessalines, Biassou, and other revolutionary figures (see chapter ten of this volume), Bergeaud was able to reconcile the violence of the Haitian Revolution in much less ambivalent terms. Stella, whose disdain for despotic violence was clear from her critique of the French Revolution, tells the brothers that the war she has encouraged them to undertake against the colonists is both 'necessary and just' (210). At every turn, the novel accomplishes the justification of the violence of the Haitian Revolution by pointing to slavery as a 'state of exception,' or what Giorgio Agamben might call a place that exists so far outside of 'juridical-constitutional grounds' (2005, 1–2) as to render its victims into a '*conditio inhumana*' (2000, 35). It was this 'state of exception' that turned human beings into what Agamben has elsewhere called 'bare life' (1998, 83), or in Ewa Ziarek's words, 'damaged life, stripped of its political significance' (2012), that had first occasioned and later sanctioned the war. These justifications allow the pious and virginal Stella to both explicate and exculpate the gruesome actions of Romulus and Rémus almost without apology.

It is with his usage of the language of parental wounding that one can almost see Bergeaud quietly and carefully tiptoeing into this dance of celebrating the Haitian Revolution but not seeming to take glee from describing the wholesale massacre of human beings, especially "white" ones. In the metaphor used by Bergeaud below, French liberty becomes the mother of impending Haitian liberty, making the Haitian Revolution,

---

28 The Roman emperor Nero is infamous for having executed his own mother, among other atrocious deeds.

or France's attempt to smother it, a parricidal conflict between mother and child, and thus, the ultimate 'state of exception.' Bergeaud writes:

> This liberty, born from France, that is to say from her revolution, sanctioned by decrees, is legitimately her daughter. Attempting to destroy it is to commit parricide. One would never have thought France capable of it. But she has recently published a law that promotes the slave trade and maintains slavery in all of the colonies of which she has reclaimed possession since the peace; she has re-established slavery in Guadeloupe. Here [in Haiti] the persecutions organized by the *Colon*, his Confidence, his joy, announce clearly what is brewing. (208)

If in Saint-Rémy's metaphor, Louverture horrifically killed his own mother, then in Bergeaud's she deserved it. Parental wounding surfaces again in the following matricidal passage in which Romulus tells the *Colon*:

> You bring war to me. France is an unnatural mother [*mère dénaturée*] who wants to kill her own child. So be it! We will have a war! I fear no one. If I must perish, I will perish with honor, I will die as a soldier, and God will take care of my vengeance! (173)[29]

Further images of parental wounding and the retribution it inspires, nay invites, on the part of the 'wounded child,'[30] are called forth when we remember that the *Colon* is in reality fighting against his own son. Rémus desires to kill his father with his own hands and to take pleasure in doing so. Bergeaud tells us that one of the 'strange effects of their hatred' for the *Colon* was that

---

29 Cousin d'Avallon had used this very familial metaphor in his *Histoire de Toussaint* when he wrote, 'The colonies are the daughters of the nations that have formed them. They are united by the same ties that link mothers to their children. They have the right to all of her tenderness and all of her care [*sollicitudes*]. The metropole owes them a very particular protection' (iv). D'Avallon also reproduces a letter written by Napoleon Bonaparte and addressed to Toussaint Louverture in which the First Consul speaks of Louverture's conduct as potentially causing Saint-Domingue to become the 'theater of an unfortunate war where fathers and sons will slit each other's throats [*s'entr'égorgeraient*]' (rpt. in D'Avallon, 114).

30 I borrow this phrase from Ann Wierda Rowland, who uses the term to discuss Wordsworth's poem 'Vaudracour and Julia.' Rowland writes that the poem 'narrates a crisis of violence committed by and against children which culminates in the mysterious death of Vaudracour's illegitimate son, a death' which, she contends, is 'an obscured scene of infanticide' (679). Rowland finds that the notion of the 'wounded child' and the metaphor of 'infanticide' became the 'central image[s]' of Wordsworth's personal and political narrative of France and the French Revolution' (679).

if someone at this very hour had wanted to take the life of the *Colon*, they would have been immediately opposed, and they would have defended the life of their enemy to the peril of their own; this devotion by another name was merely the consequence of the right to punish him which they believed they alone possessed, to inflict upon him the formidable death of the law of the talion. (25)

By describing the conflict between *la mère patrie* and her wounded children, or the *Colon* and his figurative and literal slave-sons, as the result of a parent's desire to commit infanticide, meaning that all reaction represents self-defense on the part of the child, Bergeaud justifies patricide and matricide as natural, ordinary—and even necessary—consequences of independence; slaves must overthrow their masters, even if it means ("black") sons must kill their ("white") fathers (and mothers).

The behavior of Romulus and Rémus is justified with even more apology when Bergeaud describes how after the defeat and deportation of Rochambeau the brothers take out into the ocean and drown 800 French soldiers who were being treated in a hospital.[31] Still, even while expressing mitigated horror, Stella seems to want to excuse this behavior when she explains of Romulus and Rémus:

> They had barely deviated from the state of nature; untamable passions were bullying them; they had under their eyes the pernicious example of enlightened men who did not know how to lead; their wounds were still bleeding, they [the French] had been too unjust with them, they had suffered too much. (298)

Of the impending 'holocaust of the enemy' (318) sanctioned by the decree read by Rémus (supposed to be the April 28 proclamation of Dessalines), Stella would conclude, as a matter of fact, 'Thus was accomplished the revolution of Saint-Domingue, inaugurated by a torture—the torture of Ogé, Chavannes, and other martyrs—and finished with a massacre' (322). We might say that for Bergeaud, the ends did justify the means, which is perhaps the true tragedy of slavery: that it made a violent revolution, portrayed as a conflict between mother and child and father and son, not only seem to be, but perhaps actually be, the only way out of slavery and colonialism in Saint-Domingue. Bergeaud writes, '[d]espite all the crimes that have soiled this path with blood, this revolution was greater than any other. The people it emancipated can today feel glorified: they should even reference it often in their mind in order to learn not to deviate from the past' (322).

---

31 Here, Bergeaud may have here borrowed and then elaborated upon a detail found in Schoelcher's *Colonies étrangères et Haïti* (2:141).

The Trope of the Tragic "Mulatto/a"

The one part of the past that both Bergeaud and Saint-Rémy agreed Haitians should try to deviate from was the famous law of 'white' exclusion first instituted by Dessalines's 1805 Constitution. Article 12 had maintained that 'no white person, whatever his nation, can set foot on this territory as a property owner, and can never here acquire any property.' Of this law, which was not officially off the Haitian law books until the U.S. occupation in the early twentieth century, Saint-Rémy wrote, '[t]his system, in continuing a fatal antagonism among members of humanity—who are all unified among one another—will retard the moral and intellectual development of men who have a black face [*un front nègre*] like me' (1851, xii).[32] Bergeaud alluded to the infamous law in quite similar terms when he said, '[c]ivilization is not exclusive; it attracts rather than repels. It is through [contact] that the great unification of humankind will take place' (324).

It is important to recognize that Haiti's policy of 'exclusivism' (Saint-Rémy, 1853, xx), interpreted as evidence of color prejudice, insularity, and incivility on the part of Haitians themselves by a writer like Saint-Rémy, was not, as it had popularly been represented, unequivocally supported in either of the two post-Dessalines Haitis. Baron de Vastey, one of Christophe's most important statesmen, had used the metaphor that all of humankind was one great family in his *Réflexions sur une lettre de Mazères* when he wrote, '[w]ho doubts today, except the ex-colonists, that all men are brothers and that they are linked together through their origins to the same family?' (1816d, 12); in his *Essai*, Vastey more directly argued that the fact that Pétion had retained Dessalines's property exclusion in his own constitution meant that the Haitian president had *de facto* 'sanctioned' 'color prejudice.' Vastey wrote that this law, 'excluding all whites in general ... was so far from being reasonable, that it was also unjust, impolitic, inconsequential, and contrary to the laws of all civilized nations' (1819, 319). Nevertheless, though it is true that article 38 of Pétion's constitution states, '[n]o white person whatever his or her nationality can set foot on this territory as a property owner' (rpt. in Vastey,

---

32 Saint-Rémy had perhaps good reason to believe that the law was harming Haiti's image abroad. In July of 1822, Haitian Secretary of State Joseph Inginac invited the United States to be 'the first New World republic' to recognize Haitian independence. President James Monroe responded to the request during a session of the U.S. senate on February 26, 1823. He said that formal recognition of Haiti was out of the question since it was a land where 'provisions ... prohibit the employment in the government of all white persons who have emigrated there.' He continued by noting that there were also provisions that prohibited the 'acquisition by such persons of the right of citizenship or to real estate in the island ... [which] evinces distinctly the idea of a distrust of other nations' (qtd. in Baur, 325). The law was also cited by Bonneau and Gobineau as evidence of Haiti's insularity and lack of civilization.

1819, 317),[33] we should not necessarily interpret this law as evidence of a desire on the part of the citizens of Pétion's republic for unequivocal isolation and/ or postcolonial protectionism disguised as defensive nationalism, either. In an 1817 article published in *L'Abeille Haytienne*, 'Suite Aux Considérations,' Jules Solime Milscent, one of Pétion's own confidants, similarly used the romance of the great human family in arguing that global trade, rather than colonialism, was not only the best way for human beings to have contact with one another, but could itself become a gentle salve for the wounds of the past:

> Trade forms the chain that connects various peoples. It is [trade] that calms the great quarrels of men and urges them towards reconciliation. The inhabitants of a country who are deprived of it fall into poverty ... They can only reach with difficulty towards a perfect civilization, a stable prosperity. Because they accept few foreigners, their customs and their manners become conspicuous. Their corner of the earth is almost always dangerous because they prefer violent methods rather than peaceful connections [*Leur voisinage est presque toujours nuisible, parce qu'ils préfèrent les moyens violents aux relations pacifiques*]. (7)

In the end, one cannot help but see in the passages quoted above from Vastey, Saint-Rémy, Bergeaud, and Milscent the germs of an understanding of 'nations' as 'second-best to world unity' (Hobsbawm, 31) that characterizes much of what we might be inclined to call Black Atlantic humanistic thought. In his *Discourse on Colonialism*, the Martinican poet Aimé Césaire famously wrote, 'I admit that it is a good thing to place different civilizations in contact with each other; that it is an excellent thing to blend different worlds ... that for civilization exchange is oxygen.' He then asked, 'has colonization really *placed civilization in contact*? Or, if you prefer, of all the ways of *establishing contact*, was it really the best? I answer *no*' (33). Like Césaire and many other twentieth-century writers from the African diaspora, many of the early nineteenth-century Haitian writers whose works we have been examining saw themselves as creating a new world based on a notion of a communal or fraternal love imagined to reside in humanistic nationhood rather than the domineering parental love that had been likened

---

33 Vastey thought that a more reasonable law would have maintained: 'No French person whatever his color can set foot on this territory for any reason at all until the French government has recognized the independence of Haiti' (1819, 318). For a provocative justification of the constitutional article barring 'whites' from property ownership, see Ardouin's *Réponse ... à Isambert*, wherein Ardouin writes that the law was a protection against certain 'amis voyageurs' or 'traveling friends' who came to 'encourage discord' and 'give bad advice' to the Haitian government (1842, 16).

to despotic colonialism. In this new world, there would not be any "races" at all. In a passage that evokes the kind of anti-'race-thinking' that Paul Gilroy has likened to a 'planetary humanism' (2000, 2), Bergeaud wrote, 'soon there will be neither blacks, whites, or yellows on this earth, neither Africans, Europeans, Asians, or Americans, there will just be brothers' (324). Such a statement underscores the prescient cosmopolitanism of nineteenth-century Haitian discourses on "race," whose creators were, in many ways, the progenitors of the kind of world envisioned by more contemporary humanists, like Gilroy and Césaire, the latter of whom would eventually argue that the end of the tyranny of colonialism could only be operated through a 'humanism made to measure the world' (73).

PART FOUR
Requiem for the "Colored Historian"; or the 'Mulatto Legend of History'

'Haiti is in its infancy; and the population, formed out of discordant materials, is precisely in the state that might be anticipated by any one at all conversant with the history of mankind.'

—Charles Mackenzie, *Notes on Hayti, made during a Residence in that Republic* (1830)

'Haïti! ce nom seul résume tout le mal que les ennemis de l'abolition disent de la race africaine.'

—Victor Schoelcher, *Colonies étrangères et Haïti* (1843)

'Haïti est un argument ... qui gêne et qui déplait.'
—Louis Joseph Janvier, *La République d'Haïti et ses visiteurs* (1883)

In his *Haïti: ses progrès et son avenir* (1862), which would incidentally appear with the same publisher (E. Dentu) as *Stella*, the nineteenth-century French literary critic Alexandre Bonneau listed Éméric Bergeaud's novel in his bibliography of works about Haiti that his readers might consult for additional information about the country. Bonneau's bibliography, which contained just over 55 works by travel writers, former French colonists, and Europeans as well as Haitian historians and memoirists,[1] comprised in the mind of its author the most 'essential, important, or interesting' works on the subject of Haiti. Bonneau explained that this list, in any case, was not meant to be exhaustive, since '[t]he bibliography of Haiti would fill an entire volume if we wanted to cite all of the works relating thereto' (165).

---

1 Among Haitian writers, the list also includes works by Boisrond-Tonnerre, Vastey, Dumesle, Inginac, Madiou, Saint-Rémy, Nau, Saint-Amand, Ardouin, and Pradine.

Requiem for the "Colored Historian"

While many of Bonneau's entries contain no annotations at all, the brief note he included after mentioning Bergeaud's novel explained that *Stella* is 'a historical and political novel about Haiti' wherein 'the author personifies the black race [*race noire*] under the name of Romulus, and the mulatto class [*classe de mulâtre*] under the name of Rémus' (172). This description comes in spite of the fact that, as we have seen, Bergeaud never once uses the term 'mulatto' or any other "racial" taxonomic marker in his novel of over 300 pages. Bonneau's wish to supply what in his mind must have been the missing pseudoscientific term 'mulatto' to describe that 'class' of people represented by Bergeaud's portrayal of Rémus, provides not simply more evidence of the way in which Haitian revolutionary history has been inevitably linked to a tropics of "race," but Bonneau's insertion is also wholly representative of a series of "racial" (mis)readings of Haitian literature and historiography that, I argue, directly led the twentieth-century historian David Nicholls to believe in what he called the 'mulatto legend of history.' That is to say, even when pains are taken to specifically divest the history of the Haitian Revolution from its manifest association with "racial" revenge and, specifically, the supposed inherent "racial" contest between "blacks" and "mulattoes" that so often plagues the historiographic as well as the political spheres of Haitian discourse, critical practices of reading and interpretation can render null authorial attempts to disengage from this version of the narrative of "mulatto/a" vengeance.

At the outset of *Tropics of Haiti* we discussed how "race," as it was biologically understood in the eighteenth century, was viewed as having produced considerable feelings of unrest and rebellion among the free colored population of colonial Saint-Domingue and how resulting ideas about such people, who were often generically referred to as "mulattoes," came to affect popular understandings of the role played by nineteenth-century Haitian historians in the making of Haitian revolutionary historiography. We ended with the premise that what Michel-Rolph Trouillot once referred to as 'Haitian exceptionalism'—the resonant idea of 'Haiti's apartness' or that it is 'unlike any other country in the world—period' (1990, 3)—was linked to both scholarly and popular understandings of the contributions of Haitians to historical discourse about their country through the nineteenth-century trope of the "colored historian," or its modern-day iteration in the 'mulatto legend of history.' The trope of the "colored historian" derives from the words that accompanied an image of the former U.S. slave William Wells Brown in the 1882 edition of *The Rising Son; or, the Antecedents and Advancement of the Colored Race*. Although the term was likely meant to convey simply that Brown was a historian of "color," because the phrase is doubly inflected—the historian is not only person of "color," but his history is "colored" as well—I believe that it also has something to tell us about how the "color" of Haitians

Requiem for the "Colored Historian"

WM. WELLS BROWN, M.D.

The Colored Historian.

'The Colored Historian,'
from William Wells Brown's *The Rising Son; or, the Antecedents
and Advancement of the Colored Race* (1882).
Manuscripts, Archives, and Rare Books Division, Schomburg Center
for Research in Black Culture, The New York Public Library,
Astor, Lenox, and Tilden Foundations.

historians has affected not only the way in which the Haitian Revolution has been (mis)read as a "racial" revolution, but the way in which the works of nineteenth-century Haitian authors themselves have been (mis)read as evidence of an intrinsic enmity of "blacks" for "mulattoes" and vice versa.

Based on Trouillot's argument in *Silencing the Past* concerning the hidden or occluded agendas of western ontological epistemologies, I have argued that many contemporary scholars who discuss nineteenth-century Haitian historians, despite their otherwise remarkable erudition and overwhelming 'political generosity' (Trouillot, 1995, 106), still continue to mirror if not directly mimic the overtly racialist (and sometimes racist) views of the otherwise well-meaning abolitionists like John Beard, who was the first to develop the notion that history could have a "color," on the one hand, and Victor Schoelcher, who first made the case that such biased histories could be used for legendary purposes, on the other, as well as the more subtle racialism of twentieth-century radicalists like C.L.R. James, who ushered the trope into the twentieth century with his writing on Saint-Rémy. I have pointed to statements from Léon-François Hoffmann, Philippe Girard, and Chris Dixon which resemble Grant Farred's unqualified declaration in his study of James's *The Black Jacobins* that the 'light skinned mulattoes' of Saint-Domingue were a 'deeply prejudiced and racist class,' who 'resented the black slaves and the authority they gained from the Revolution and they sought to undermine, and where possible, invalidate those achievements' (1997, 239), as evidence that the idea of an inherent split between "mulatto" and "black" Haitian historians has never been fully deconstructed in scholarship and has consequently gained both a mythological and performative status. Ultimately, I have suggested that the argument made by Nicholls (and evoked by Farred above, and many, many other scholars),[2] that there was 'a group of mulatto historians in the mid-nineteenth century [who] developed

---

2 Acceptance of Nicholls's "color" thesis, in the sense that the theory is repeated as *truth* rather than as an argument that might need to be analyzed, examined, and deconstructed, appears to varying degrees in Forsdick (2012, 158); Geggus (2002, 70); Largey (2006, 74); Bongie (2008, 227-28); Sheller (2000, 101). Many of these works present groundbreaking research for their respective fields, and because the evocation of the 'mulatto legend of history' or its corollary in so-called "*noirisme*" is often located in mere pithy asides, I do not mean to detract from the contributions of these authors to their fields. The point of including this list by a rather diverse array of scholars, for all of whom I have nothing but immense respect, is to point out simply that Nicholls's thesis has gone largely unquestioned; that is, it has been accepted as being *a priori* true, and thus enjoys an ever-widening circle of influence. In essence, I am arguing that the validity and plausibility as well as the ideological, and material consequences of Nicholls's theory need to be analyzed, examined, and questioned, just like any other historical thesis.

an elaborate legend of the past which was calculated to strengthen the position of the ruling class and to legitimate its ascendancy' (1974, 16), constitutes a form of racialism, or evidence of a pervasive and problematic belief that 'there are heritable characteristics, possessed by members of our species, that allow us to divide them into a small set of races, in such a way that all the members of these races share certain traits and tendencies with each other that they do not share with members of any other race' (Appiah, 1990, 5). It is my contention that it is this brand of racialism—which tells us that we can understand Haitian historical writing based on the skin color of the writer—that has been uncritically repeated in many academic works and is the dominant form in which the "mulatto/a" vengeance narrative—as vengeance *of* and *for* "mulatto/as"—continues to surface in scholarly discourse today.

The purpose of the three chapters that will make up this final section of *Tropics of Haiti* is to re-examine the popularity of the nineteenth-century trope of the "colored historian," or the enduring stereotype that "blacks" and "mulattoes"—because they were "blacks" and "mulattoes"—created competing narratives of Haitian history that reflected not only the supposedly longstanding divisions between these two groups in colonial society and, later, in independent Haiti, but that were designed to produce the domination of one group over the other. Before turning more fully to the development of the trope of the "colored historian" in mid-nineteenth-century writing, we must first outline some of the general inconsistencies and fallacies inherent in its twentieth-century iteration, the 'mulatto legend of history.' Doing so will help us to more fully understand how Nicholls's theory reflects both the epistemological problems of "racial" taxonomies and the epistemological anxieties occasioned by not being able to *know* about ideology based on color or "race." As we have seen, these problems of *knowing* lay at the heart of all narratives of "mulatto/a" vengeance. By drawing attention to the nineteenth-century origins of Nicholls's own brand of what we might call, drawing on the works of Paul Gilroy, historiographical 'raciology' (2000, 11), we will come to appreciate that Nicholls did not invent the concept, the vocabulary, or the stereotypes, and certainly not the anxiety that accompanies his thesis concerning the 'mulatto legend of history.' What Nicholls did do was take the idea out of the realm of nineteenth-century abolitionist discourse and place it front and center in the modern scholarly realm, where its acceptance into the received understanding of the politics undergirding Haitian-produced historiography has largely gone unquestioned.

Unlike the 'mulatto legend of history,' whose authority has hardly ever been doubted, the way in which Nicholls viewed all of Haiti's political history through the lenses of 'race' and 'colour,' which the late British historian was at pains to reconcile with class, as Anthony Maingot observed in his 2002

Requiem for the "Colored Historian"

David Nicholls Memorial Lecture (9–14), has actually received a healthy amount of criticism from fellow historians and political scientists.[3] Nicholls's *magnum opus* on Haiti caused some historians to raise their eyebrows at his view of the importance of skin color to interpretations of Haitian politics almost as soon as it hit the shelves. For example, in his 1981 review of *From Dessalines to Duvalier*, our own living giant of Haitian revolutionary history, David Geggus, wrote that Nicholls's 'color-conflict approach certainly seems in some places of dubious validity.' Geggus went on to support this comment with reference to Nicholls's own explanations:

> the regime of the dark-skinned president Geffrard was Francophile and pro-mulatto, and yet favored black immigration and employed ministers inherited from the black Emperor Faustin [Soulouque] (who 'relied to a considerable extent upon mulattoes'), only to be overthrown by the populist Sylvain Salnave, who was 'generally associated with the *noiriste* tradition' but almost white. (1981, 416)

Nicholls's inconsistent usage of the terms 'mulatto' and 'black' and, in the case of Geffrard, the wholly pseudoscientific term 'griffe' (1979, 93),[4] to explain political ideologies and allegiances rather than purely "racial" ones, seems to have further confused the matter for Geggus. This is because Nicholls was forced to confront the fact that many of the people he considered to have been "mulattoes" did not fit the color molds—either phenotypically or ideologically—that he so carefully sought to craft. To that end, as Matthew Smith wrote in his 2007 article *'From Dessalines to Duvalier Revisited: A Quarter-Century Retrospective,'* 'some of the book's more

---

3 Although in a new collection of essays devoted to understanding the legacy of Nicholls's work, *Power and Politics in Haiti* (2013), the editors Kate Quinn and Paul Sutton refer to Nicholls as 'the most well-informed academic in the United Kingdom on the political history of Haiti' (1), they, too, acknowledge 'the controversies that his work on Haiti and the Caribbean occasioned' (2). They observe that the central foci of these controversies has usually revolved around Nicholls's uneasy understanding of the relationship between "color" and class in Haiti, and his attempt, but ultimate failure, to separate the idea of skin color or phenotype from the idea of "race."

4 Nicholls's completely unselfconscious usage of the pseudoscientific term *'griffe'* is particularly suspect since, as the nineteenth-century Haitian ethnologist Antènor Firmin has written, 'If the black man has always been looked down upon by the white race, if the mulatto has remained in their eyes for a long time a monstrous being, the *griffe*, was he not at the end of the day the scapegoat for all of these theories that have been born out of this prejudice, that owing to Enlightenment contradiction, have finally found their way into contemporary science? Also we must not forget the systematic scorn that was professed therein for the pure African, thus, the *griffe*, even less fortunate, still contains the mark of condemnation' (313).

fascinating sections are weakened by Nicholls's persistent over-reliance on ideological battles' (32), specifically related to the lines of color upon which Nicholls viewed these 'ideological battles' as having been drawn.

Nicholls's writing about Haitian historians is beset by the same kind of historical, interpretive, and even "racial" inconsistencies that can be found in his political theories. Nicholls describes the Haitian historian Thomas Madiou as an outlier in his broader theory when he argues that Madiou was a 'mulatto' writer who not only failed to adhere to the 'mulatto legend' or to any of the various 'mulatto cliques,' but did not usually align himself with 'mulatto' politicians either. 'Although a mulatto,' Nicholls writes, 'Madiou was never totally committed to the mulatto clique or cliques, as his association with the regimes of Soulouque and Salomon will indicate' (1979, 88). Rather than constituting an exception to the rule, upon closer examination, Nicholls's characterization of Madiou as a 'mulatto' historian whose works were 'never simply an elaboration of the mulatto version of Haitian history' (88) is exemplary of the general way in which Nicholls's theory of 'deep divisions' in Haitian history based on 'colour distinctions' begins to fall apart when the individual trajectories of Haitian historians, rather than collective generalizations about them, enter the political and historical frame.

Madiou is hardly the only 'mulatto' historian or Haitian writer with light skin, in Nicholls's estimation (which is to say nothing about how Nicholls knows that Madiou is precisely a 'mulatto'), who does not fit into the proper color mold of 'mulatto' and *noiriste* histories. Nicholls would seem to contradict his own argument that the 'principle exponents' of the 'mulatto legend,' Ardouin and Saint-Rémy, sought to create historical works that would legitimate the rule of the 'mulattoes' who were in power when he acknowledges that while Ardouin remained faithful to Boyer to the end, Saint-Rémy, along with three of the other 'mulatto' historians whom Nicholls also accused of generally adhering to the 'mulatto legend,' were actually anti-Boyer. Nicholls writes, '[Dumai] Lespinasse, [F.E.] Dubois,[5] and Saint-Rémy ... having supported the opposition [to Boyer] in the period before 1843, were less concerned to picture Boyer as the legitimate successor to Pétion; they saw rather the spirit of the founder as inspiring the liberal and democratic movements of 1843' (100).[6] Nicholls does appear to be at least

---

[5] F.E. Dubois was, incidentally, the cousin of Beaubrun Ardouin, but the two apparently had a highly visible political squabble in 1839 that was played out in the Port-au-Prince-based newspaper *Le Télégraphe* (see Ardouin, 1840, 4–5). Dubois, who had been the 'officier de l'état civile' in Jérémie (1840, 4), would later become Secretary of State under Fabre Geffrard, who was president of Haiti from 1859 to 1867.

[6] For the abuses of the Boyer regime and the way in which it led to a revolution mounted against him in the name of the people, see Bellegarde (1953, 141–46).

a little conscious of the fact that the arguments about Haitian historians he was supporting were far from absolute, and to that end he wrote:

> The outline of the mulatto legend as presented here is expressed in very general terms; as well shall see, there have been mulatto writers who disagreed with particular aspects of the picture. Also I am not at all suggesting that the judgments made by these writers were uniformly false; much of what they said about the Haitian past could well be accepted by historians who were less committed to practical politics than these men were. (1979, 91)

Such qualification provides unexpected confirmation that, as Dupuy has observed of the "racial" ideologies in Nicholls's political theories, 'the fluidity of these categorizations and the difficulty of drawing a clear cut-off line between mulatto and black makes them just as arbitrary and socially and politically contingent as the distinctions between whites and blacks' (46). Nicholls's comment also reveals that he does not necessarily disagree with the content of the writing, but rather his main issue is with its "color."

Indeed, operating under the assumptions of the "colored historian," as Nicholls asks us to do in order to understand Haitian history, makes quasi-racial taxonomers of us all. It requires us to calculate a person's "color" or "race" based on what he or she looks like, and then to use that predetermined calculation to interpret his or her writing or, even more curiously, it might ask us to use the writing itself to produce an idea of the person's skin color, or, at the very least, an idea of the "color" of the person's ideology. Yet, in the literary history of the Haitian Revolution, examples abound of the way in which phenotype was not determinative or at any rate representative of historical ideology, at least partially because judgments about the lightness or darkness of skin color were and are wholly subjective. The difficulty in determining the shade of "blackness" at which a person could no longer be considered a "mulatto" in terms of "color" rather than in terms of genealogy—i.e. by having some "white" ancestry—or at what point a person should be regarded as a "mulatto" owing to the political ideology expressed in his works, regardless of "color," is symptomatic of the epistemological problems inherent in the narrative of "mulatto/a" vengeance.

In order to prove that "mulatto" and "black" writers nearly always preferred to exalt the achievements of people of their own skin color, Nicholls refers to the 1842 *Manifeste de Praslin*[7] as particular evidence that in nineteenth-century Haiti, "mulatto" revolutionaries were overwhelmingly

---

7 The *Manifeste de Praslin* was the document that had laid the groundwork for the institution of the eventual provisory government of Charles Hérard, which took effect after the revolution of 1843 had unseated Boyer.

• 466 •

praised in public discourse to the detriment of their "black" counterparts. However, in his critique of the document Nicholls makes pronouncements about the "race" or "color" of the Haitian revolutionary actors mentioned therein that do not appear to have aligned with the way that the very Haitian historians accused of adhering to the 'mulatto legend' had viewed them. For example, Nicholls saw in this document evidence for the 'mulatto legend of history' because, according to him, Wagnac and the 'mulattoes' Geffrard, Vancol, and Magny had been referred to at a certain dinner as the 'illustrious founders of our Haitian independence,' while there was no mention of Dessalines, Christophe, or any of the other 'black' leaders. According to Madiou and Pradine, nevertheless, even though Wagnac would later serve as a general in Pétion's army (Pradine, 1886, 1:244), he was not a 'mulatto,' but 'noir' (Madiou, 2:424). In addition, like the Martinican abolitionist Cyrille Bissette, Saint-Rémy considered Magny to be 'nègre' (Saint-Rémy, 1850, 353; Bissette, 8). Moreover, while Nicholls describes Hérard Dumesle, one of the signatories of the document, as a 'griffe' who was aligned with the 'mulattoes,' for Saint-Rémy, Dumesle's skin color made placing him in a distinctive "racial" or "color" category entirely dependent on context. When presumably abiding by the laws of the 'calculus of color,' Saint-Rémy describes Dumesle as the 'son of a mulatto and a negro, that is to say a griffe' in his introduction to Louverture's *Mémoires* (24), but when trying to prove the merits of the 'black race' in his *Vie de Toussaint L'Ouverture*, Saint-Rémy had called Dumesle 'a negro [*nègre*] whose wisdom and intelligence was possessed by few whites' (313).

The gap between individual opinions about the phenotype of various revolutionary actors and the purported ideologies they were meant to represent in the works of the authors in which their names appear, is further illustrated by the U.S. abolitionist William Wells Brown's description of Haitian president Jean-Pierre Boyer, the man Nicholls considered to be unequivocally a 'mulatto.' Brown writes: 'Though called a mulatto, Boyer was nearly black and his long residence in Europe gave him a polish in manners foreign to the island. He was a brave man, a good soldier, and proved himself a statesman of no ordinary ability' (1863, 204). The pseudoscientific "racial" terminology of Saint-Domingue stands in tension here with individual subjectivity[8] since for Brown, Boyer's 'black' skin color does not match either what he perceives to be the Haitian president's political ideology or his "racial" category. The conflict between individual subjectivity and categorical phenotypical

---

8 Such a tension is encapsulated by one article about Haitian literature published under two separate racialized titles, three years apart in the *National Anti-Slavery Standard*; first, in 1853 under the title 'Mulatto Literature,' and again in 1856, under the title 'Negro Literature.'

taxonomy is illustrated with even more irony by Saint-Rémy's description of Pétion as 'black.' In *Pétion et Haïti* (1864), Saint-Rémy describes the former Haitian president as 'born of the natural union of M. Pascal *Sabès, blanc,* and Dame Ursule, *mulâtresse.*' However, 'even though he was a *quadroon,* a type of *mixed-blood* [*sang-mêlés*], whose skin is ordinarily white,' Pétion 'came into this world so black [*si noir*] that with his straight hair he could have been taken for an Indian.' Saint-Rémy writes that it was because of 'the black skin [*la peau noire*] of the newborn' that Pétion's father 'doubted his paternity' and 'refused to give him his name' (23–24). Finally, Baron de Vastey's rival from Pétion's southern republic, Noël Colombel, for his part, had protested against Vastey's characterization of him as having practically 'white' skin and therefore as behaving with the attitude of domination of 'whites.' Colombel wrote in his *Examen d'un pamphlet*:

> This text has wonderfully served [Vastey] in his efforts to rail against me and to tear me apart with his beautiful teeth [*me déchirer à belles dents*]. According to the honest M. Vastey, I am nothing more than an infidel, a traitor, a perfidious creature, in a word the fiery student of S. Exc. le Président Pétion, schooled in his principles; and there is nothing Haitian about me, even my skin color, because he claims that I am more white in color [*il pretend que ma couleur se rapproche le plus de la blanche*], another thing I did not know and that M. Vastey took it upon himself to teach me; I have always thought, up until the present time, that the tint of my skin color was somewhat brownish, like that of my principles and that of my feeling that I am Haitian and absolutely, Haitian. (23)

It is hardly my contention, in any event, that we should be concerned with the theory of the 'mulatto legend of history' simply because, like the nineteenth-century writers who developed the trope of the "colored historian," Nicholls uses arbitrary "racial" and color distinctions to describe Haitian revolutionary actors. The much more serious problem is that if Nicholls's determinations of phenotype were just as vexed as the "racial" taxonomies from which he culled his vocabulary, as the final three chapters of *Tropics of Haiti* aim to show, his theory was also every bit as hierarchical, essentialist, and therefore as Haitian exceptionalist as the nineteenth-century writings upon which they were based. Moreover, a theory like Nicholls's—which could lead to the conclusion that in early nineteenth-century Haiti, 'Divided to the vein, blacks and mulattoes tore their country apart in search of an ethnic advantage that would prove mutually self-destructive' (Beckles, 1996, 502)[9]—subsumes the fact that the Haitian

---

9 Worse yet, in an extremely poorly researched article by Lisa Macha Saye, the author, a professor of 'public administration,' drawing upon Nicholls's statement that

politicians and historians under accusation in Nicholls's theory did not so much create nineteenth-century Haiti, but were rather products of what Paul Farmer has called 'expansionist European empires.' For Farmer, this means that nineteenth-century Haiti was a 'quintessential Western entity' (1994, 50). For us, it confirms that "mulatto/a" vengeance was an anxious projection of the Atlantic imagination designed, in part, to occlude the very epitome of the kinds of color prejudices that continued to uphold slavery throughout most of the first half of the nineteenth-century, if not in England, then in the United States, and in the colonies of Spain and France. In other words, the "racial," political, and class divisions almost certainly present in nineteenth-century Haiti, as they were across Europe and the Americas, were divisions that had been folded into the law, science, and even into the family in an entanglement of ways throughout the colonial period. To expect that they miraculously evaporated after Haitian independence is just as absurd as to believe that the end of the U.S. Civil War solved all of the United States' problems with racism. The obsession with pointing out the prejudices of nineteenth-century Haitians in the transatlantic print culture of the Haitian Revolution was thus a mirror that reflected and deflected the legacy of the color prejudices that had been instituted there under imperial rule and were absolutely rampant in those ruling empires themselves.

One other feature of the 'mulatto legend' that must be recognized as an absolutely untenable essential principle, on precisely the grounds that it covers up the role of 'expansionist empires' in not only perpetuating color prejudices (and the slavery it was designed to uphold) in their own countries, but in helping to create that very reality in Haiti, is that "mulatto" historians were the singular promoters of color prejudice in nineteenth-century Haiti who simultaneously argued that color prejudice was not a feature of nineteenth-century Haiti (Nicholls, 1979, 91). The Haitian historian Louis Joseph Janvier, whom Nicholls viewed as one of the promoters of the 'black legend' (1979, 89), argued in his 1883 *La République d'Haïti et ses visiteurs*, 'As for the prejudice of caste, it ceased to exist in Haiti in 1804' (157). Even though Nicholls says that those who subscribed to the 'mulatto ideology' tended to blame the French colonists for any remnants of color prejudice in Haiti, the

---

governance in Haiti was 'something alien' (qtd. in Saye, 71; Nicholls, 1979, 245), states that '[p]erhaps one of the first dysfunctions concerning the newly liberated Haitians and the administration of the newly independent Haitian government was the institutionalization of skin color as a determination of status,' before ultimately concluding, 'this researcher agrees with Nicholls' assertion in 1979, and posits anew that in the body of literature and terminology associated with discussion and research on developing countries, Haiti is indeed something alien' (Saye, 2010, 83).

supposedly *'noiriste'* Janvier clearly believed this to be the case when he wrote in *Les détracteurs de la race noire d'Haïti* (1882):

> in Haiti the subtle distinctions of color and caste that had been carefully established for political ends by the French colonists and maintained with Machiavellianism by agents from the metropole in the former Saint-Domingue—by the agent Hédouville, among others—these childish, petty, and absurd distinctions of color and caste have almost completely disappeared. (341)

The fact that Janvier made the exact same argument as Ardouin (1:102–03) about the near non-existence of color prejudice in nineteenth-century Haiti and about the role of the French in encouraging color prejudices, does seem to contradict Nicholls's claim that '[t]he mulatto version of the past, then, has certain definite features which fit into a wider ideology' (1979, 101).[10]

The idea that 'distinctions based upon family and colour' (Nicholls, 1985, 31) could not entirely explain Haitian political history was precisely the point made by Janvier when he complained about the kind of "racial" misinformation being spread about Haitian political divisions:

> Above all, do not say, I beg of you, that one finds in the parliament of Haiti a yellow side and a black side; do not say, either, that there is a mulatto opposition. That is not so. There are in Haiti two parties,[11] whereas in other countries, there might be many more. On one side, I see men who want to have the power, and on the other side, men who have it and do not want to give it up. That is the truth. Both sides are right. Power is very precious here as in every country in the world. Blacks and mulattoes are in one party; blacks and mulattoes are in the other party. That is the truth. (1883, 156)

The example that Janvier would later use as evidence of his larger argument is that of a pre-emptive strike undertaken by the government of Emperor Faustin Soulouque I of Haiti against the bourgeois opposition to his rule on April 16, 1848.[12] In response to the fact that this event was widely reported

---

10 Another of Nicholls's *'noiriste'* historians, Antènor Firmin, also seemed to acknowledge the role outsiders had played in encouraging color prejudices in Haiti when he wrote in *De l'Egalité des races*, 'The doctrine of the inequality of the races engenders the most idiotic prejudices [*enfantent les plus sots préjugés*], creating one of the most harmful antagonisms among the diverse elements that make up the Haitian people ...' (xiv).

11 Later, Janvier will explain that these two parties are the 'parti national' and the 'parti libéral' (160).

12 As Murdo J. MacLeod has explained, the opposition to Soulouque's presidency

in the U.S. and European press as a 'massacre' of 'mulattoes' only on the part of the 'black' Soulouque government, Janvier writes :

> Let me also reiterate that the bourgeoisie which had opposed Soulouque was composed of blacks and mulattoes and that among the victims of the 16th of April there were also blacks ... The day of April 16, 1848 was the result of pure politics and was not at all an event occasioned by the question of color prejudices. (1883, 247)

Janvier concludes, 'Nothing is more frustrating than to watch the ignorant insert [*mêler*], into all sorts of political acts in Haiti with which they have most often been entirely unfamiliar [*le plus souvent étrangère*], this irritating question of *color prejudices*' (1883, 247, italics in original). For many later nineteenth-century Haitian authors like Janvier, the kind of illogical, disjointed, and even unintelligible ramblings about color prejudice that characterized writing about Soulouque in the mid-nineteenth-century U.S. and European public spheres (for examples, see Dayan, 1995b, 12; Brickhouse, 2004, 224–30) and which Janvier ardently attacked in his own work, were able distractions from the fact that, as Frédéric Marcelin would write concerning his childhood recollection of the 'massacre' of April 1848 in *Au Gré de Souvenir* (1913), 'Every tyranny, whether it is white or black, ends the same' (26)—presumably, in violence.[13] This kind of confusion, ambivalence, and uncertainty about divisions based on 'color' or 'race,' rather than divisions based upon class, economics, and the timeless desire for power, would lead Nicholls to constantly qualify his own assertions, as when he writes that in 'April 1848 [Soulouque] took vigorous steps to eliminate actual or potential opponents, *most* of whom were mulattoes' (1979, 82, italics added).[14]

---

came primarily from the 'mercantile and intellectual classes of Port-au-Prince and the other cities, people generally considered to be the elite ... Whether they were plotting against him or not is unknown,' MacLeod says, but '[i]t would be strange given their growing dissatisfaction with him if they were not' (40). In any event, Soulouque crowned himself emperor only two days after the 'massacre.' Ironically, later in his reign, Soulouque would be accused of 'being too close to the elite community' (42).

13 For a different reading of the role of Soulouque in nineteenth-century Haiti as connected to the valorization of what is popularly called the 'Vodou' religion, see Kate Ramsey (2011, 79–80).

14 Nicholls comes closest to putting forth the idea that class might matter more than "race" in Haiti when he writes, 'colour lines tended to coincide in general with class lines, reinforcing economic and social distinctions in the country' (1979, 71). Although, of course, he is not strictly right about this either, as he hesitates to acknowledge when he writes that Ardouin and Madiou both ascribed to 'the principle that "all poor mulattoes should be considered as blacks, and that all rich blacks should be considered

Perhaps unsurprisingly, Nicholls's writing, hesitations and all, can be immediately linked to the racialism of the nineteenth-century transatlantic abolitionist movement. In the chapters that follow, we will see that it is actually in the writing of Haiti's abolitionist allies from the nineteenth century rather than in the country's pro-slavery detractors, that we find the origins of the "colored historian." The trope of the "colored historian," as it was developed in the nineteenth century by famous abolitionists like Victor Schoelcher, John Beard, William Wells Brown, and James Redpath, not only contains a similar language and political vocabulary as that to be found in the twentieth-century theory of the 'mulatto legend of history,' but it invites the same ideological inconsistencies that would trap Nicholls inside a prison of epistemological problems from which he could never write his way out.

Constantly working backwards, then, it is now time to unfold another page of the palimpsest of Haitian revolutionary writing as we turn more fully to the influence of nineteenth-century abolitionist texts about Haiti on the development of the idea that history could have a "color" and even a "race." It is only after examining the origins and impetus for the creation of this racialized legend in the first place that we will be able to more fully evaluate the strength of the contention that Saint-Rémy and Ardouin's mid-nineteenth-century historical writings make them the 'principle vindicators of the traditional mulatto elite version of the Haitian past' (Nicholls, 1979, 89). By exposing the series of "racial" (mis)readings that led these two writers in particular (Saint-Rémy in chapter ten and Ardouin in chapter eleven) to be offered as the primary 'exponents of the mulatto legend' (Nicholls, 1979, 90), I believe that we will come to appreciate how adopting the practices of reading associated with the nineteenth-century idea of "mulatto" and "black" histories themselves—practices that ask us to read with an *a priori* idea of what we will find in an author's historical work based on ideas about his or her skin color or "race"—continues to prevent us from reading the radically transformative way in which many nineteenth-century Haitian authors were the progenitors of the kind of Black Atlantic humanism briefly discussed at the end of chapter nine of *Tropics of Haiti*. Ultimately, it will be in chapter twelve, though, that we will

---

as mulattoes'" (1979, 78); and again later, when he says, 'it is interesting to see how black politicians from the middle and upper classes have consistently used the colour issue to divert attention from the question of economic class, and to convince the black masses that their interests are the same as those of the leaders themselves' (1979, 87). See also Nicholls's *Haiti in Caribbean Context* (1985), wherein the historian seemed to contradict his earlier "color" thesis in writing 'economic and social class based upon achievement, particularly, upon wealth, is perhaps the most significant category for understanding the social and political structure of Haiti today' (31).

see at work the way in which past and present critiques of Pierre Faubert's play *Ogé, ou le préjugé de couleur* (1856) offer particularly salient case studies for understanding how the trope of the "colored historian" has prevented us from seeing the 'new narratives' (Ulysse, 2015) of Haiti offered by many nineteenth-century Haitian writers.

CHAPTER TEN

The Color of History: The Transatlantic Abolitionist Movement and the 'Never-to-be-Forgiven Course of the Mulattoes'

'*Vive le roi! Vive la France, à bas les mulâtres*, et reprenons Saint-Domingue!'

—M.D.A.L.F., *La vérité sur Saint-Domingue et les mulâtres* (1824)

'… the Haytian Revolution is also the grandest political event of this or any other age.'

—James Theodore Holly, *A vindication of the capacity of the Negro race for self-government, and civilized progress, as demonstrated by historical events of the Haytian Revolution* (1857)

'Although the whites and the free colored men were linked together by the tenderest ties of nature, there was, nevertheless, a hatred to each other, even stronger than between the whites and the blacks. In the earlier stages of the revolution, before the blacks under Toussaint got the ascendency, several attempts had been made to get rid of the leaders of the mulattoes, and especially Rigaud. He was hated by the whites in the same degree as they feared his all-powerful influence with his race, and the unyielding nature of his character, which gave firmness and consistency to his policy while controlling the interests of his brethren.'

—William Wells Brown, *The Black Man, His Antecedents and His Genius* (1863)

In 1853, the British abolitionist and Unitarian minister John R. Beard[1] published what would become one of the most widely adapted biographies

---

1 Biographical information about John Relly Beard (1800–76), a Unitarian minister and a prolific author, can be found in McLachlan (1935, 1–20).

of Toussaint Louverture to circulate in the nineteenth-century Atlantic World, *The Life of Toussaint L'Ouverture: The Negro Patriot of Hayti*. At the time of its publication, following upon the abolition of slavery in the French colonies in 1848, the almost singular focus of the transatlantic abolitionist movement had become the abolition of slavery in the United States. For a British anti-slavery activist like Beard, the goal of abolition in the U.S. was plainly connected to the history of the Haitian Revolution and, more specifically, to the life of Toussaint Louverture. In the opening pages of the biography Beard wrote:

> THE life which is described in the following pages has both a permanent interest and a permanent value. But the efforts which are now made to effect the abolition of slavery in the United States of America, seem to render the present moment specially fit for the appearance of a memoir of TOUSSAINT L'OUVERTURE. A hope of affording some aid to the sacred cause of freedom, specially as involved in the extinction of slavery, and in the removal of prejudices on which servitude mainly depends, has induced the author to prepare the present work for the press. If apology for such a publication were required, it might be found in the fact that no detailed life of TOUSSAINT L'OUVERTURE is accessible to the English reader, for the only memoir of him which exists in our language has long been out of print. (v)

Beard's statement connects the noble goals of the abolition of slavery and the erasure of color prejudice in the United States to bringing broader attention in the Anglophone world to the life of Louverture in the void left behind, presumably, by James Stephen's *The History of Toussaint Louverture* (1814) going out of print. Yet even though Beard states that he also hoped to help with the 'removal of color prejudices' by publishing this biography, his own work inevitably contributed to the transatlantic circulation of the "mulatto/a" vengeance narrative of the Haitian Revolution. Beard's biography contains immediate referents to all three of the tropologies of "race" that I have so far elaborated upon as being the constituent elements of "mulatto/a" vengeance: "monstrous hybridity," the "tropical temptress," and the tragic "mulatto/a." Beard's most original contribution to the discourse of "mulatto/a" vengeance, however, was the language he supplied for the fourth and final trope: the "colored historian."

Beard's biography of Louverture, unlike that of his Anglophone predecessor Stephen, was not based on either personal experience or original research. It was essentially a compilation of prior attempts to write the history of the Haitian Revolution by people like Pamphile de Lacroix, John Candler, W.W. Harvey, Joseph Saint-Rémy, Harriet Martineau, Alphonse de Lamartine, Antoine Métral, and Isaac Louverture. Despite the fact that his biography is entirely dependent upon these earlier histories, Beard begins with a terse lamentation of the biases of previous authors who had written about the life of Louverture. According to Beard, these biases could be identified based on the nationality, "race," or 'caste' of the author in question and, more particularly, whether that author was either French or a 'mulatto.' Beard writes, 'The sources of information on this subject are found chiefly in the French language. To several of these the author acknowledges deep obligation.' However, '[t]he tone taken on the subject of negro freedom in Hayti, by reviews, is partial and unjust,' Beard says. 'Possibly this may be attributable to a mulatto pen,' since '[t]he blacks have no authors.'[2] Beard continues by lamenting that the

> [c]ause [of the blacks], consequently, has not yet been pleaded. In the authorities we possess on the subject, either French or mulatto interests, for the most part, predominate. Specifically predominant are mulatto interests and prejudices, in the recently published Life of Toussaint L'Ouverture, by SAINT REMY, a mulatto: this writer obviously values his caste more than his country or his kind. (v–vi)

Leaving aside for the moment an evaluation of Beard's claim about Saint-Rémy's 'mulatto' biases, Beard's general pronouncement about the 'authorities' of previously published histories of the Haitian Revolution probably makes him the first Anglophone writer to offer the idea that not only people, but historical discourse itself, could take on the actual quality of a "racial" identity.

Beard may have found inspiration for this racialized theory about the color of history, in part, from a statement made by fellow British traveler John Candler in his *Brief Notices on Hayti* (1842). Candler had traveled to Haiti during the reign of Christophe, and he wrote that he sought to publish his observations of life in the northern kingdom in order to 'bring ... before the public a view of the present state of Hayti.' Candler wrote that in so doing, 'it seemed desirable to prefix to the narrative a brief sketch of the history of the island. The Author had intended to prepare such a sketch,'

> but upon examining those works, both French and English, which are considered as authorities, he found so many discrepancies and counter

---

2 Only a few years later, in 1856, Alexandre Bonneau would second the idea that the 'blacks have no authors' when he wrote that the only literary or historical text published 'by a black' from Haiti was Isaac Louverture's *Mémoires d'Isaac-Louverture* (1856, 141). Although Bonneau had considered Isaac Louverture to be a 'black' Haitian writer (1856, 142), Beard probably discounts the memoir of Louverture's son because it had actually been published in Paris, where its author had resided since 1802.

statements, involving the character of several of the leaders in the revolution, that he abandoned the attempt in despair. The history of Hayti has yet to be written, nor can it be written impartially, so as to establish the truth and the whole truth, till the present generation have passed away. (iii)

Candler narrowly intimates that 'the history of Hayti' could not be written with impartiality by anyone other than a Haitian when he adds:

> The present Secretary of State of Hayti, General Inginac, who is now advanced in age, and who was engaged in the wars of the revolution, almost from his boyhood, has prepared a narrative of the passing events of the period, both civil and military, which is intended for publication at his decease. This narrative, when published, will, no doubt, illustrate many circumstances that are now obscure, and serve to unfold more clearly the character and motives of some remarkable men, his contemporaries. (iii–iv)[3]

Although Candler was looking to Inginac's future work to perhaps remedy the problem he had identified, he was not unaware that several nineteenth-century Haitian writers had already written historical works about the Revolution. Of Baron de Vastey, for example, Candler wrote that he was 'a mulatto, a man of respectable literary acquirements, as his history of Hayti shows, but of a base and dishonourable disposition' (37). As we saw in chapter two of *Tropics of Haiti*, Candler would hardly be the first or the last writer to banalize Vastey's writings by suggesting, either explicitly or implicitly as above, that Vastey's "race," coupled with his devotion to Christophe, meant he was incapable of providing an 'impartial history.' Still, if in 1842 Candler was looking to the near future of Haitian authorship to partially remedy the problem of impartial history, in 1853 Beard had only to look to a biography of Louverture written by one such Haitian author who did not live during the Revolution, that of Joseph Saint-Rémy, to decide that Haitian authorship was not the answer to the problem, but was the problem itself.

It was Saint-Rémy's *Vie de Toussaint-L'Ouverture* (1850), and this work alone, that confirmed for Beard an idea he seemed to have already formed in his mind: that 'mulattoes' could not be trusted to write the history of the Haitian Revolution any more than could the French. Beard's subsequent inference that 'mulatto interests and prejudices' 'predominate' in Saint-Rémy's works *because* of the author's status as a 'mulatto' only hints at the biographer's disdain for what he later calls those of the 'bastard and degenerate race' of 'mulattoes' (60). Indeed, the biggest problem with Beard's

---

3 In 1843, Inginac would indeed publish his history of Haiti under the title *Mémoires de Joseph Balthazar Inginac ... Depuis 1797 jusqu'à 1843*.

idea that Haitian history could had a "color" is that it presupposes a similar language and ideological viewpoint with respect to the relationship between "race" and both revolutionary Saint-Domingue and independent Haiti as many of Haiti's most unabashedly racist detractors. As we are about to glimpse, even though Beard would offer himself as a friend of Haiti, his biography of Louverture is characterized by a rather adamant narrative of "mulatto/a" vengeance, which only barely manages to disguise its generally racist outlook concerning all people of color. This is because the "racial" tropologies to which Beard is beholden, perhaps largely as a result of his sources, helped to establish social, "racial," and geographic hierarchies that not only continued to define some people as natural slaves and others as natural masters, and some people as the historians and others as the subjects of history, but that defined certain types of people (namely, abolitionists) as friends to slaves, and certain others (namely, "mulattoes"), as their enemies.

Consider, to that end, the following passage that Beard included about the 'men of mixed blood' (195) during the years that led up to the Revolution:

> Their pride of blood was the more intense, the less they possessed of the coveted and privileged colour. Haughty and disdainful towards the blacks, whom they despised, they were scornful toward the petits blancs, whom they hated, and jealous and turbulent toward the planters, whom they feared. With blood white enough to make them hopeful and aspiring, they possessed riches and social influence enough to make them formidable. By their alliance with their fathers they were tempted to seek for every thing which was denied them in consequence of the hue and condition of their mothers. The mulattoes, therefore, were a hot-bed of dissatisfaction, and a furnace of turbulence ... Unable to endure the dominion of their white parents, they were indignant at the bare thought of the ascendancy of the negroes; and while they plotted against the former, were the open, bitter, and irreconcilable foes of the latter. If the planters repelled the claims of the negroes' friends, least of all could emancipation be obtained by or with the aid of the mulattoes. (21–22)

Here, the abolitionist Beard starts to resemble many pro-slavery apologists, like Comte de Gobineau, George Fitzhugh, and Alexandre Bonneau, who had produced or would later also produce 'negroes' and 'mulattoes' as indomitable 'foes.' The idea that 'mulattoes' were brazen obstacles to the emancipation of the slaves, unlike the abolitionists who were the 'negroes' friends,' also embodies the very essence of Chris Bongie's argument in *Friends and Enemies*. Drawing on what Régis Debray had called '*frères enemies*,' or in modern popular parlance, the *frenemy*, Bongie has written that 'the existence of two rival Haitis' in the period following Haitian independence, one ruled by 'the "mulatto" Alexandre Pétion' and the other by 'the "black"

Henry Christophe,' 'troublingly replicates the binary between friends (the colonized) and enemies (the colonizers) upon which the world-historical outcome of the Haitian Revolution depended' (2008, 25). The "racial" tropologies and hierarchies in operation in abolitionist works like Beard's, nevertheless, also disrupt this seemingly uncompromising binary. Through his own writing Beard tries to produce abolitionists as the indisputable 'friends' of the slaves, but by virtue of his adoption of the "mulatto/a" vengeance narrative, and thus the very color prejudices that were upholding slavery, he actually reveals himself to be the ontological *frenemy* of the very people he said he sought to uplift.

The fact that many abolitionists in the mid-nineteenth-century were themselves espousing color prejudices in their discussions of Haiti did not go unnoticed by nineteenth-century Haitian writers. In his four-part epistolary response to the French abolitionist Victor Schoelcher, "Lettres à M. Victor Schoelcher relativement à son livre sur Haïti," which appeared in the Haitian newspaper *La Sentinelle de la Liberté* from November 9, 1843 to December 28 of the same year, Saint-Rémy essentially asked what was next for Haiti if even the country's "friends" used the racism of colonial categories to paint 'mulattoes' and 'negroes' as indelibly involved in an eternal "race war." Saint-Rémy went on to accuse Schoelcher of being a 'négrophile' who argued on behalf of the 'negro,' instead of being a 'philanthropist' who argued on behalf of humankind.[4] Saint-Rémy wrote in his letter of November 9, 'it is comforting to think that the barriers of the nations are going to be broken, that the diversity of skin colors is going to be erased, and that one day the only supremacy that will exist among men will be that of virtue, intelligence, and merit.' Saint-Rémy consequently called on abolitionists, 'the missionaries of the sainted universal emancipation,' to seriously consider the kind of tone used in their works with respect to "race." He wrote, referring to the Virgin Mary, 'she knows no caste, she knows only man; she is not a negrophile, she is a philanthropist' ('Lettres,' November 9, 1843).[5]

The problem with the kind of 'négrophile' that Saint-Rémy viewed Schoelcher to be is precisely that a *négrophile* was often, if not always, a person who essentialized "blackness" or "Africanness" by purporting to love and celebrate it as if "blackness" were a thing one could grasp. Even if, as

4 Ardouin also appeared to draw a distinction between the *négrophile* and the philanthropist in his *Réponse à Isambert* (8) and he accused Isambert of not really having been the friend of Haitians when he wrote 'Oh! Monsieur, if you were really the friend of the Haitians [*l'ami des haïtiens*], without distinction of color ...' (90).

5 Saint-Rémy's critique of the *négrophile* as not really the 'ami des noirs' predates the wholly negative association with which this term would come to be associated in the twentieth century. See, for example, Petine Archer Straw's *Interplay Negrophilia: Avant-Garde Paris and Black Culture in the 1920s* (2000).

Doris Kadish has written, 'la littérature négrophile' often presented 'black characters ... as possessing heroic qualities' (2014, 1), this heroism often quickly devolved into the same kinds of essentialist thinking to be found in works that are much more deliberately racist.[6] This is because many *négrophile* abolitionists, like Beard and Wendell Phillips, rather overtly demonized people of "mixed race" when they exalted heroic figures like Louverture for being *pure* "blacks," and suggested that this spoke to the merits of "blackness" in general, but used the idea that supposed traitors like Rigaud were of "mixed race" to disparage "mulattoes" as a whole, and unwittingly encourage "racial" separatism. Because the prerequisite of hating the "mulatto" is actually having a veiled ambivalence about (and often a barely concealed derogatory opinion of) "blackness," in so doing, such *négrophile*s actually reified the very color prejudices they claimed to abhor. This kind of contradiction was practically inherent to the strand of Enlightenment thought that had contributed to the development of both the "racial" taxonomies found in the narrative of "mulatto/a" vengeance and the transatlantic abolitionist movement.

Such contradictions did not go unnoticed in the U.S. sphere, either. Saint-Rémy would hardly be alone in the sentiment that some of the self-professed 'friends of the blacks' were practically indistinguishable in their beliefs about "race" from some of most their most obvious enemies. In his *A Vindication of the Capacity of the Negro Race for Self-Government, and Civilised Progress* (1857),[7] James Theodore Holly also identifies how it was in uncritically adopting racialist perspectives that were shot through with evocations of "white" supremacy, that many nineteenth-century abolitionists ended up betraying the same color prejudices that would in the end actually make them the enemies of the people of color on whose behalf they claimed to argue. In his speech, which would go on to be published as a pamphlet, Holly, much like Éméric Bergeaud, never uses the distinctive terminology of naturalist "racial" taxonomies like "mulatto," and he points out that the ideas of "negro" inferiority latent in the works of the supposed friends of the slaves of the United States were actually antithetical to the philanthropic project of abolition:

> Yes, I say, we may add a large number of the noisy agitators of the present day, who would persuade themselves and the world, that they are really Christian philanthropists, to that overwhelming crowd who openly

---

6 For more on *la littérature négrophile*, see also Maurice Jackson (2009, 168).

7 The title page of the publication notes that the contents were first given as a lecture 'before a Literary Society of Colored Young Men, in the City of New Haven, CT, after my return from Hayti in the autumn of 1855; and subsequently repeated in Ohio, Michigan, and Canada West during the summer of 1856' (3).

traduce the negro; because too many of those pseudo-humanitarians have lurking in their hearts a secret infidelity in regard to the real equality of the black man, which is ever ready to manifest its concealed sting, when the full and unequivocal recognition of the negro, in all respects, is pressed home upon their hearts. (5)

If after digesting the hierarchies ever present in the narrative of "mulatto/a" vengeance, which will be unfolded in this chapter through Beard's abolitionist writing about Louverture, we may be tempted to ask, after Ann Laura Stoler, 'How could racism serve such a wide spectrum of political agendas at the same time?' (2010b, 159), the cases of William Wells Brown and James Redpath, both of whom would go on to reproduce Beard's work under their own names with differing degrees of co-optation, will likely not provide any answers. For what are we to make of the fact that the ideology of "racial" supremacy that is undoubtedly expressed in Beard's work was also parroted, repeated, and revised by one of the most famous nineteenth-century abolitionists in the Atlantic World, who, as a former slave himself, arguably suffered in the worst way from the material effects of pseudoscientific "racial" discourse? Moreover, how do we account for the fact that Redpath, in translating Saint-Rémy's edition of Louverture's *Mémoires*, would do more to bring awareness of nineteenth-century Haitian writing than any other U.S. author since the time of Baron de Vastey *and* that he would simultaneously have an almost unmatched influence in spreading the narrative of "mulatto/a" vengeance in the United States?

These are questions that I can raise, but cannot purport to fully answer in a study like this without engaging in the fool's errand of psychoanalysis. The best I can do is suggest that the kinds of ideas of "race" reproduced in Beard's biography, and in the broader transatlantic abolitionist movement, should remain of enduring interest in every study of the Haitian Revolution, and not just because such writing provides the basis for understanding the way in which the narrative of "mulatto/a vengeance" circulated almost continuously in the nineteenth-century public sphere. The continuous circulation of the same repeated ideas about revolutionary Saint-Domingue and later independent Haiti also gives rise to questions about who can and cannot be considered an author and who can and who cannot speak, when we are dealing with what Meredith McGill has called 'a culture of reprinting' (14). The deep involvement of Beard, Brown, and Redpath in this particular mid-nineteenth-century transatlantic 'culture of reprinting' reveals an idea of "race" as *commonsense* to be the central problematic of the literary history of the Haitian Revolution, whose mid-nineteenth-century corpus is almost entirely made up of texts whose ideas, if not entire thematic framework, had been copied from prior authors.

Examining the problems occasioned by the constant reprinting, copying, and paraphrasing of Haitian history exposes what Said has called the 'self-containing, self-reinforcing character of a closed system [of representation], in which objects are what they are *because* they are what they are' (70, emphasis in original). For our purposes, such a discursive tautology means that the incessant and incestuous ideas about "race" to be found in the late eighteenth-century literary history of the Haitian Revolution were often repeated as commonsense *truths* by nineteenth-century writers because their authors had derived their sources from people whose works were considered to be reliable and *true*. Even when the historical *facts* of various works about the Haitian Revolution came under scrutiny, the tautology of this 'closed system' of "racial" representation made Saint-Domingue a place that was populated unquestioningly by people called "negroes" who had to be "slaves" because they were "negroes" and people called "whites" who had to be "masters" because they were "white"; but the people called "mulattoes" did not quite fit. They threatened to disrupt the binary of the first two systems because it could not be easily determined on the basis of the word "mulatto" alone to which of the first two categories ("white"/ master and "negro"/slave) such individuals belonged. The theory of the "colored historian" is the ultimate extension of such colonial authority and the attendant anxieties that had produced this 'closed system' in the first place, since it was this trope that allowed an author to determine that historical writing could be reliably judged, and therefore disregarded, on the basis of an author's "race." If "mulattoes" and "negroes" were represented as having been out for revenge against the intedeterminancy of their own identities during the Haitian Revolution, they would now be represented as using history as the arm of their post-Haitian independence vengeance against their purported political impotence.

The first part of this chapter will trace the development of the trope of the "colored historian" in Beard's works, paying special attention to the way in which the claim that Haitian revolutionary historiography was plagued with distinct biases that could be characterized as "racial" in nature was itself reliant on the "white" supremacist hierarchies that were always present in the broader narrative of "mulatto/a" vengeance. In the second and third sections, I suggest that Beard's ideas were most influential when it came to this trope precisely because his exact words concerning "mulatto" history would make their way into several of the constantly circulated and revised publications of the U.S. abolitionist and former fugitive slave, William Wells Brown, including his 1853 novel *Clotel*, as well as into the still referenced studies of the widely influential James Redpath. In the fourth and final section, focusing on how Beard's opinion of Saint-Rémy influenced nineteenth-century receptions of the latter's work by Redpath and others, I engage in an unprecedented examination of Saint-Rémy's writing with the goal of discovering what merit, if any, there was in Beard's designation (and later, in C.L.R. James and David Nicholls's reformulations) of the Haitian historian as the primary example of the problem with "mulatto" histories.

To use a spatial metaphor, marking Haitian authorship as singularly vexed by "racial" politics has relegated it to what David Theo Goldberg has called *'periphractic* space.' According to Goldberg, relegating people to *'periphractic* space' 'does not require the absolute displacement of persons to outside the city limits, to the literal margins of urban space. It merely entails their circumscription in terms of location and their limitation in terms of access—to power, to (the realization of) rights, and to goods and services.' The 'dislocation, displacement and division' that is always a feature of such 'spatial circumscription,' Goldberg says, is the 'primary mode by which the space of racial marginality has been articulated and reproduced' (188). In much the same way, what we might call the discursive circumscription of Haitian authorship by nineteenth-century historians from Europe and the United States, who marked Haiti's historians as prejudiced, biased, and even incompetent, repeatedly relegates Haitian authorship to the kind of "racial" margins invoked in Goldberg's spatial metaphor, where it could be easily policed, contained, and *'silenced.'*

*

Beard first demonstrates his wholesale subscription to "racial" classification schemes when he attempts to calculate the degree of 'white' and 'black' blood to be found in the 'mulatto,' 'quarteroon,' 'tierceroon,' and 'metif' (21). To these descriptions are appended the oft-reprinted passage from the work of Lacroix about Moreau de Saint-Méry having created his "racial" taxonomy based upon the 'system of Benjamin Franklin' (Beard, 321; see also chapter three of this volume). In the ensuing biography, Beard will do much more than use the terms 'negro,' mulatto,' etc. to demonstrate his adherence to the "racial" tropologies of the transatlantic print culture of the Haitian Revolution. Throughout the body of the text, Beard brings together a virtual microcosm of the entire narrative of "mulatto/a" vengeance and each of its tropes. The following statement by Beard regarding colonial Saint-Domingue pretty well encapsulates his studied adherence to all of the stereotypes contained within the narrative of "mulatto/a" vengeance:

> On that land of servitude there were on all sides masters living in pleasure and luxury, women skilled in the arts of seduction, children abandoned by their fathers or becoming their cruelest enemies, slaves worn down by toil, sorrow and regrets, or lacerated and mangled by punishments. Suicide,

abortion, poisoning, revolts and conflagration—all the vices and crimes which slavery engenders, became more and more frequent. (22)

Five decades of writing about the Haitian Revolution had clearly been able to canonize and in some ways immortalize the kinds of "racial" beliefs about "mulattoes" and "blacks" found in eighteenth-century naturalist travel writing and in the earliest accounts of the Haitian Revolution. While these tropes probably appear collectively to varying degrees in nearly every work written about the Revolution since 1804, they are rarely seen together with the kind of imagist force with which they consistently emerge in Beard's work.

Beard brings together all of the major thematics of the trope of the "tropical temptress," for instance, with its attending scenes of seduction and repulsion, desire and disgust, transgression and rebellion, when he writes:

> From the mixture of black blood and white blood arose a new class, designated *men of colour*. On the part of the planters, passion and lust were subject to no outward restraint, and rarely owned any strong inward control. African women sometimes possess seductive attractions. If in any case these were employed to mitigate the penalties of servitude, the blame must chiefly be imputed to the degraded condition in which the system held them; and if when they had obtained power over their paramours, they, in pride and jealousy, inflicted on them humiliating punishments, they did but serve as effectual ministers of well-merited retribution. Content to live in a state of concubinage, the proprietors could not expect the peaceful and refining satisfactions of a home; and alas! only too readily took the consequences of their licentious course in imperious mistresses, and illegitimate offspring. But vice is its own avenger. From the blood sprung from this mixed and impure source, came the chief cause of the troubles and ruin of the planters. (19)

At the end of this description of how 'African women' sometimes used their 'attractions' to 'inflict ... humiliating punishments' on their lovers, Beard links this 'licentious course' to the origins of the Revolution itself, as so many of his predecessors had done. The vengeful revolutionary 'blood sprung from this mixed and impure source' would be subsequently characterized by Beard using the language of the tragic "mulatto/a."

In Beard's rendition, even though the 'mulatto' was the 'chief cause' of the 'troubles and ruin of the planters,' he was ultimately unable to effect revolutionary change on his own due to the inherent tragedy of being 'mixed,' a condition which had both physiological and psychological consequences:

> The mulatto, to the qualities of pride and meanness, adds singular strength of muscle and impulse of passion. Conscious of power, he also feels within

him boiling emotions. If victory depended on a dash, he would be master wherever he dwells. But the very exuberance of his nature precludes caution and banishes prudence, and in the impetuosity of his rush he incurs as much peril as he occasions. Impatient of delay, he pays for momentary advantages by speedy and irretrievable defeat. Yet the same unbridled will which brings disaster nourishes vindictiveness; he is therefore ever prepared, if not panting, for revenge. The fight, consequently, is renewed, but without a change of result; and so life passes away in extravagant and disappointed efforts. (110)

This description poises Beard to rehearse essentially every claim about the monstrosity of 'mulattoes' to be found in the literary history of the Haitian Revolution. In narrating the tragic futility of the 'mulatto' to obtain parricidal revenge against his 'criminal parents' (60), Beard evokes the trope of "monstrous hybridity." It is with the idea that the incongruity occasioned by "racial mixing" made "mulattoes" and "blacks" inherently despise one another, on the one hand, and that "mulattoes" were equally rejected by the "whites" whom they similarly deplored, on the other, that we can most readily glimpse the way in which Nicholls's entire theory about the 'deep divisions of colour' present in Haitian society since the time of independence was in all reality merely a rehearsal of the longstanding "mulatto/a" vengeance narrative of the Haitian Revolution. The trope of the "colored historian," from which the 'mulatto legend of history' was in great part derived, was inextricably dependent upon the tropics of Haiti found within the narrative of "mulatto/a" vengeance.

Beard lays the pseudo-scientific basis for the trope of the "colored historian" when he writes that the 'mulattoes,' 'whites,' and 'negroes' of Saint-Domingue naturally hated one another: 'on every side the grossest injustice prevailed; crime was repaid with crime; vengeance followed vengeance; the civilised master degraded himself no less than the neglected slave; between the two stood the mulatto, the enemy of both, and prepared to sacrifice either for his own aggrandizement' (66). Later, despite the fact that he was wholly influenced by the works of Saint-Rémy (which he attempted to discredit even as he drew information and quoted from the latter's own biography of Louverture [see Beard, 77, 118), Beard would refer to the War of the South as a 'war of the skin' (21) between Rigaud and Louverture, arguing that it was the result of natural 'mulatto' hatred for 'blacks' and vice versa. Beard writes:

> On their part the men of colour were displeased at seeing the supreme command settled in the hands of an African of pure blood, and flocked around the standard of Rigaud. The blacks, under the protection of the Government and Toussaint, beheld the gathering clouds not without

excitement, yet in confidence; nor were they unwilling, after so many victories, to try a last fall with their special foe. (110)

Post-independence Haiti, for Beard, merely offered a continuation of the same theme of divisive color prejudices between these 'special foe[s].' Beard makes a statement that recalls the work of Gobineau, among other pro-slavery advocates:

> Conscious of that individual superiority which ensues from a share in the influences of civilization, the mulattoes of Hayti despised the untaught and the rude crowd of black labourers by whom they were surrounded, and felt, that in submitting to their sway, they put themselves under the domination of a majority, whose authority lay exclusively in their numbers. Their natural position, they believed, was at the head of the Haytian government. (304)

The 'blacks,' for their part, were not without their own prejudices against 'mulattoes,' according to Beard:

> Not without reason ... they look[ed] with suspicion and jealousy on all attempts at political elevation which were made by mulattoes. It is even to be feared that the blacks, under their distrust and fears, were much averse to the culture which education gives, and of which the mulattoes, who possessed some tincture of European civilization, were, in their eyes, the representatives. Thus, the progress of the island, in those arts and attainments on which the good of society consists, was materially retarded, and the way paved for a renewal of strife and bloodshed, with their demoralizing effects. (304)

The post-independence effects of such paranoia, insecurity, and hatred on the part of the 'blacks' was that they became 'averse' to 'education' and 'culture' and by extension to the 'European civilization' that 'mulattoes' supposedly symbolized. This claim closely echoes that of the former British Consul to Haiti, Charles Mackenzie, who wrote in his own travel narrative that Haiti was composed of a 'discordant' populace (1:xii) marked by its internal 'prejudice,' which was crucial to recognize because of the 'importance' of these "racial" divisions 'in determining the political concord of the republic' (1:26).

Beard's judgments also echo the claims of many avowed "racial" supremacists from the Anglophone world like Thomas Carlyle, who had implied that such a combination of incompatible "black" people living together had produced little since independence (see chapter two). The myriad claims about "race" found in Beard's biography resemble in plenty of other ways the self-professed "racial" supremacy of some of the most ardent pro-slavery apologists from both sides of the Atlantic. One such apologist whose ideas Beard approached was George Fitzhugh, who would write of Haiti in his *Sociology of the South* (1854), 'History furnishes but a single instance where negroes have been well governed without masters, and in that instance the rule was ten times more rigorous than that of the master.' Fitzhugh continued, 'Tousaint [sic], the president of Hayti, by a strict military surveillance, kept them at work on separate farms, and punished them capitally for the third offence of quitting the farm without a written permit.' The problem with post-Louverture Haiti for Fitzhugh was that '[s]ucceeding administrations have relaxed the government till the whole island is in a state of savage anarchy which invites and would justify another conquest and reduction of the inhabitants to that state of slavery for which alone they are fitted, and from which they so wickedly escaped' (276–76).

This kind of ideology was much more directly linked than Fitzhugh's commentary reveals to the discourse surrounding the former French colonists' desire to reconquer their erstwhile colony, a topic that was being publicly debated in France throughout at least the first three decades of Haitian independence. In 1824, a former property owner from Saint-Domingue, who signed his name only with the initials M.D.A.L.F., published a pamphlet entitled *La Verité sur Saint-Domingue et les mulâtres*, in which he argued that since independence, the 'mulattoes' of Haiti had only been able to compel the 'blacks' to work by 'force,' 'and the obligation to work by force is really slavery' (3). He went on to say that rather than accepting as the price of recognition the proposed indemnity from the Haitian government to the French government, which was being ardently discussed in Parisian newspapers like *Le Constitutionnel* (Brière, 127), it would be better to simply reconquer 'Saint-Domingue,' since 'there is nothing resembling culture there' and the 'commerce of Saint-Domingue,' without France, 'will never be anything like what it once was.' This entire argument is permeated with the same recourse to the *frenemy* that we find incessantly evoked in the trope of the "colored historian," as when the author writes that 'the black slaves' of Saint-Domingue 'had been treated worse by the *ancien libres* negroes and mulattoes than by the Europeans!' (30). This argument could apparently be used to justify the idea 'that the interest of the blacks even more than that of the whites, requires the restitution of their former properties to the white colonists, and there will be nothing easier to do than to retake Saint-Domingue with an army of blacks' (2).

While the 'conscious political motives,' to use Michel-Rolph Trouillot's words (1995, 106), of Beard's assessment of Haiti's progress since independence were obviously at odds with those of these pro-slavery apologists from France and the United States, the 'exercise of power' (Trouillot, 1995, 160) exhibited in these discussions of "race" in Haiti is quite the same. Just as with Fitzhugh and the pseudonymous French planter, Beard's judgments about Haiti's lack of 'civilization,' 'culture,' and 'progress' since independence allows him to disengage from his own civilization's contributions to the problems he is describing. This blindness is what allows Beard to conclude that it was the aforementioned divisions between 'mulattoes' and 'blacks' that had created Haiti's problems rather than the legacy of colonialism and slavery from which he was the inextricable beneficiary by virtue of being a free person who was *not* of color living in England.

The kind of racism expressed in Beard's biography of Louverture was not merely an unfortunate aberration by one anti-slavery writer. The transatlantic anti-slavery movement was in many ways predicated on the very pseudoscientific categories of "racial" organization that supported slavery and that made the Haitian Revolution appear to be a vengeful "race" war rather than a righteous struggle for freedom. Being beholden to the naturalist "racial" taxonomies that had created the terms "negro" and "mulatto" themselves almost always leads to the kinds of hierarchical thinking inherent in these terms. The "mulatto"-hating *négrophile* can almost always be revealed to be the proponent, even if unwittingly, of "white" supremacy. As Andrew S. Curran has written, many Enlightenment thinkers who were also associated with the abolitionist movement 'continued to portray the *nègre* as a highly degenerate being whose corporeal and moral liabilities were, alas, both considerable and undeniable.' '[F]rom their point of view,' Curran explains, there 'was no contradiction between lecturing in compassion and lecturing one's readers about the brutal realities of race' (Curran, 166). Thus, Beard's status as an abolitionist begins to matter less and less when assessing his views about "race," since from his perspective "black" people still emerge as inferior to "white" people, and the "mulattoes" of Haiti stand only as the most obvious obstacle for the argument of "racial" separatism that undergirded much of abolitionist writing and stood as the most obvious putative proof of the supremacy of "whiteness."

In one of the most highly referenced and circulated works from the eighteenth century in which a detailed discussion of what we now recognize as "white" supremacy appears, Thomas Jefferson had made of the "mulatto" a metonym for the transcendent value of "whiteness." In *Notes on the State of Virginia* (1787),[8] Jefferson famously wrote, '[t]he improvement of the blacks

---

[8] The "racial" theories expressed in *Notes on the State of Virginia* had been derived for the most part from eighteenth-century naturalist travel writing, as Christopher Iannini has shown: 'The majority of his "evidence" for the innate racial inferiority of New World blacks,' Iannini writes, 'is derived more or less directly from [Edward] Long, including his discussion of the "reticular membrane" as the permanent location of black skin color, his observation on black perspiration, body odor; and tolerance for heat … and his consideration of writings by African American and Afro-British authors such as Phillis Wheatley and Ignatius Sancho as specimens of black intellectual capacity' (231–32).

in body and mind, in the first instance of their mixture with the whites, has been observed by every one, and proves that their inferiority is not the effect merely of their condition of life' (141). Even so, Jefferson was decidedly not an advocate of "racial mixing." He wrote of the slave, '[w]hen freed, he is to be removed beyond the reach of mixture' to avoid the possibility of 'staining the blood of his master' (1982, 143). Beard, too, wrote with great ambivalence and contradiction about the special powers of "racial mixing" to encourage 'African' 'improvement,' even in the context of slavery:

> Before the sixteenth century, the African races were little known in the Christian world. Since then they have been brought into close contact with white men. A fusion has ensued. That fusion in Hayti has gone far to render pure African blood somewhat rare. A similar result is rapidly taking place in the United States. In this intermingling of two diverse streams, Providence seems to intend the improvement of both. The union involves the personal freedom and the social elevation of the blacks. It will also in time issue in a higher moral culture on the part of the whites. We shall learn to do justly by the weak; they will be aided to rise out of an existence little more than sensuous; while, in cases in which the two streams flow together in the same veins, the black may obtain nerve and hardihood, and the white may be enriched and mellowed. (317)

Although Beard seems to imply that such "racial" 'fusion' could benefit both 'whites' and 'blacks,' his statement that 'whites' may experience some level of 'moral' elevation—in contrast with 'blacks,' who will not only be socially elevated but will finally be able to transcend their 'weak' and 'sensuous' 'existence'—has only to do with the fact that if such 'fusion' were to occur, the living products of these 'two diverse streams,' in his mind, would no longer be subject to the passions of slaveholders. This is because they would suddenly find themselves to be the singular beneficiaries of the kind of 'personal freedom' that such a 'union' with "whiteness" involves. As such, it is not because 'blacks' are equals that they deserve freedom, in Beard's estimation, but because their 'union' with 'whites' will require it. This is quite a different thing from arguing that it was because all human beings were equal that they deserved freedom. The concept of 'fusion' suggested by Beard seems to necessarily involve the 'disappearance' of "blackness" as a condition of 'ris[ing] out' of a slavery, at the same time that its author appears to fear the effects of "mulattoness."

The idea of 'fusion' in the literary history of the Haitian Revolution, however, was often evoked to much more consciously pernicious ends than in the work of Beard. Such 'fusion' would also be referenced by Alexandre Bonneau in order to disparage Haitian independence within the context of a larger argument about African inferiority. Bonneau's idea that the 'blacks' of Haiti could take a lesson from the history of 'fusion' and help to facilitate their own disappearance through "racial mixing" (1856, 154) was prefaced by the following gloss:

> The fusion between the Europeans and the Africans has been going on in our colonies for more than three centuries, where it has produced the mulatto variety, whose intelligence and remarkable aptitudes cannot be contested. The population of mulattoes will constantly increase in America and in the Caribbean; they will one day be dominant in the majority of tropical regions … This is how the black race will eventually cease to exist in becoming transformed … it will clear the land [*défrichera la terre*] in order to enrich the world, and in undertaking this extraordinary project, it will cast off its black skin [*dépouillera sa vieille peau*] and its ancient instincts to itself benefit from the fruits of its work in a new form and with perfected faculties, which will permit it to take an active role in the great march of civilization [*grand mouvement de la civilization*]. (1856, 152–53)

As Beard moves further away from what Bongie has called the 'painfully naïve' (1998, 265) idealism of the kind of 'fusion' expressed in Cyrille Bissette's contributions to transatlantic abolitionist discourse, and closer to the unequivocal racism of "white" supremacy to be found in the work of writers like Bonneau, Beard's inherently derogatory opinion of 'negroes' becomes ever more apparent:

> In looking back on the series of events of which I have spoken, I am impressed with the necessity of guarding against two extremes. Of these, the one degrades the African to the level of the brute; the other sets him on an equality with the Caucasian. The negro is a man; equally is it true that the negro race is inferior to the highest style of man. Individuals belonging to that race have risen very high in the scale of civilized life. Toussaint L'Ouverture commands our respect and admiration. But the race at large cannot be accounted equal to some others, if only because as yet it has no history. (316)

Beard not only demonstrates here beyond doubt that he believes in the inferiority of 'negroes,' but in concert with his earlier idea that there were no *pure* "blacks"' in Haiti anymore anyway, he effectively ensures that the lack of a ("black") Haitian revolutionary history can never be written because hardly any of its representatives still exist. Beard 'silences' Haitian-produced histories on the grounds that they could never be 'black' enough to be impartial, but he also implies that the 'inferior' 'negro' actually 'has no history,' or 'culture.' These two enduring problems in Beard's tautology, being impossible to eradicate, would prevent the 'rare' 'negro' of 'pure African blood' from rising to the highest scales of civilized life. This argument itself represents one of the hallmarks of eighteenth- and nineteenth-century expressions of "white" supremacy. In perhaps the most famous expression of "white" supremacy in the U.S. context, Jefferson wrote:

> never yet could I find that a black had uttered a thought above the level of plain narration; never see even an elementary trait of painting or sculpture. In music they are more generally gifted than the whites with accurate ears for tune and time, and they have been found capable of imagining a small catch. Whether they will be equal to the composition of a more extensive run of melody, or of complicated harmony, is yet to be proved. Misery is often the parent of the most affecting touches in poetry.—Among the blacks is misery enough, God knows, but no poetry. Love is the peculiar oestrum of the poet. Their love is ardent, but it kindles the senses only, not the imagination. (1982, 140)

What Beard's work, read in concert with Jefferson's own, demonstrates is that believing in the concept of "race" itself almost always devolves into essentialist arguments for "racial" supremacy and the corresponding hierarchies that such ideas imply. A point of view in which "race" is considered to be *real* is what permits the very same hierarchies that supported slavery to pervade not only the works of the infamous enemies of Haiti like Jefferson,[9] Gobineau, Fitzhugh, Carlyle, and Bonneau, but the work of someone like Beard, a man who professed to be a friend to Haiti when he wrote that he fervently hoped 'Hayti will gradually, if slowly, rise to take a position among the first nations of the earth' (317), but who proved himself to be more the country's *frenemy* when he suggested that there was not yet and perhaps there could never be a reliable "colored historian."

*

In many ways, it is by examining the writing of William Wells Brown, the former slave turned anti-slavery activist, that we can most readily glimpse the problems occasioned by the near constant printing and reprinting of texts about the Haitian Revolution that characterized this particular transatlantic print culture. Brown's history of reprinting and revising large sections of Beard's biography of Louverture under his own name spans three decades of the nineteenth century. These constantly circulated passages would not only help to spread many of the tropologies of "race"—and therefore, the narrative of "mulatto/a vengeance"—to be found in Beard's works, but

---

9 In a letter to Aaron Burr dated February 11, 1799, Jefferson famously referred to Haitians as 'the cannibals of the terrible republic' (1950, 31:32). For more on Jefferson's views relating to Haiti, see Zuckerman (1993); and Iannini (2012, 249).

Brown's publications would in different ways help to keep alive the trope of the "colored historian."

On May 16, 1854, Brown, a former fugitive slave from Lexington, Kentucky,[10] who believed that he was the son of his master's brother (Brown, 1970, 13; 1863, 12), gave a speech in London at the Metropolitan Athenaeum that was almost entirely derived from Beard's biography of Louverture. The speech was entitled 'St. Domingo, its Revolutions and its Patriots,' and in it Brown not only repeated nearly verbatim and without any attribution much of the historical particulars to be found in Beard's biography, but he also repeated, revised, and adapted Beard's ideas about the "racial" and political divisions between the "mulattoes" and "blacks" of Haiti in the colonial period and beyond. For example, Brown adapted from Beard the ideas found in the passage below and copied without modification the italicized portion:

> Owing to the amalgamation of whites with blacks, there arose a class known as mulattoes and quadroons. This class, though allied to the whites by the tenderest ties of nature, were their most bitter enemies. Although emancipated by law from the dominion of individuals, the mulattoes had no rights; shut out from society by their color, deprived of religious and political privileges, they felt their degradation even more keenly than the bond slaves. The mulatto son was not allowed to dine at his father's table, kneel with him in his devotions, bear his name, inherit his property, nor even to lie in his father's graveyard.[11] *Laboring as they were under the sense of their personal and social wrongs, the mulattoes tolerated, if they did not encourage, low and vindictive passions. They were haughty and disdainful to the blacks, whom they scorned, and jealous and turbulent to the whites,*[12] *whom they hated and feared.* (5; see also Beard, 21–22, emphasis mine)[13]

---

10 Brown had successfully escaped from slavery in 1834. In 1849, he traveled to Europe as a delegate for the American Peace Society and moved to London. Because of the passage of the Fugitive Slave Act in 1850, Brown had to stay in Europe until 1854, when some of his British friends purchased his freedom (Elder, 2611).

11 The un-italicized portion of Brown's speech was directly derived from Beard as well. Beard had written, 'Thus the son was unable to take his food at his father's board, kneel beside his father in his devotions, bear his father's name, lie in his father's tomb, succeed to his father's property,—to such an extent were the rights and affections of nature reversed and confounded. The disqualification pursued its victims, until during six consecutive generations the white blood had become purified from its original stain' (21).

12 Beard's text reads 'petits blancs' here instead of 'whites.'

13 Brown also repeats this passage in the chapter entitled 'Toussaint L'Ouverture' in his later publication, *The Black Man, his Antecedents and His Genius* (94), and again in *The Rising Son; or the Antecedents and Advancements of the Colored Race* (143).

Like Beard before him and Nicholls after him, Brown attributes nineteenth-century Haiti's political problems, not to the legacy of slavery and colonialism, but to the legacy of color prejudice supposedly created by "mulatto/a" vengeance itself. Citing the idea that the 'mulattoes' had initially 'joined the planters in a murderous crusade against the blacks, who were the slaves,' Brown concludes, '[t]he never-to-be-forgiven course of the mulattoes in fraternizing with the whites to prevent the slaves getting their liberty, created an ill feeling between these two proscribed classes, which a half a century has not been able to efface' (14). Also like Beard, Brown would go on to use a combination of the tropes of "monstrous hybridity" and the tragic "mulatto/a" to paint people of "mixed race" as even more hateful of their 'white fathers' than they were disdainful of their ostensibly "black" slave mothers. Evoking the parricidal effects of "monstrous hybridity," Brown writes:

> Mulattoes took the lives of their white fathers, to whom they had been slaves, or who, allowing them to go free, had disowned them; thus revenging themselves for the mixture of their blood. So frightful was this slaughter, that the banks of the Artibonite were strewed with dead bodies, and the waters dyed with the blood of the slain. (25)

Brown offered this speech again at St. Thomas's Church in Philadelphia on December 20, 1854 in anticipation of its publication as a pamphlet that would appear in Boston in 1855. Brown's 'St. Domingo' would subsequently be reprinted in myriad publications across the Atlantic World, where it would be bound with works like Theodore Holly's *A Vindication of the capacity of the Negro race for self-government, and civilized progress* (1857) and Benjamin Hunt's *Remarks upon Hayti as a Place of Settlement for Afric-Americans* (1860). Passages copied from the 1854 speech—and therefore, from Beard's biography—would find additional expression in some of Brown's later nineteenth-century works, such as in his 1863 *The Black Man, his antecedents and his Genius* and his 1873 *The Rising Son; or the Antecedents and Advancements of the Colored Race*. These publications added to the continuous circulation of the "mulatto/a" vengeance narrative of the Haitian Revolution in the nineteenth-century Atlantic World.

Long before he began to formally write about Haiti, however, as several scholars have acknowledged, Brown 'clearly had its history on his mind' (Brickhouse, 2004, 25), as evidenced by his insertion of several phrases from Beard's biography into his first novel, *Clotel; or the President's Daughter* (1853). Geoffrey Sanborn writes:

> It is no secret that William Wells Brown did not write everything that appears under his name in *Clotel*. Since 1969, when William Edward Farrison published an edition of *Clotel* with extensive notes on Brown's

sources, scholars have known that Brown lifted passages from Lydia Maria Child's 'The Quadroons,' John Reilly [sic] Beard's *The Life of Toussaint L'Ouverture*, Bishop William Meade's *Sermons Addressed to Masters and Servants*, and Theodore Weld's *Slavery As It Is*. (65)

What has not been fully acknowledged is the fact that it was exactly because Brown could count upon Beard's ideas about "race" to be considered generally *true* that he was so easily able to transpose them, not only into his speech about the Haitian Revolution, but into his own first novel, composed largely of excerpts and adaptations of reprinted works,[14] and which on the surface had nothing to do with Haiti.[15] Reading together for the first time several of the many passages from *The Life of Toussaint L'Ouverture* that Brown adapted to an antebellum U.S. context in the 1853 version of *Clotel*, as well as his mingling of *Clotel* with 'St. Domingo,' suggests that ideas about Haiti and ideas about "race" were often one and the same thing in his literary imagination.[16] That is to say that to talk about Haiti in the antebellum U.S. was, for Brown, to talk about "race," and in many ways to talk about "race" for him was to talk about Haiti. It is the twinning of these ideas that ultimately reveals the way in which the material practices of power that had created "racial" taxonomies as *true* were part of the same discursive practices of power that led to the development and institutionalization of what we are calling the trope of the "colored historian." In other words, the discourse that had established "race" and "color" as "scientific" *truths*, was functionally the same discourse that had

---

14 As Geoffrey Sanborn has written in a recent article about Brown, 'Almost all of chapters four and eight and part of chapter twenty-three are taken from [Child's] "The Quadroons"; the opening of chapter twenty-three and ten sentences in chapter twenty-four are taken from *The Life of Toussaint L'Ouverture*; eight paragraphs in chapter six are taken from Meade's collection; and four sentences from Weld's introduction appear in chapter sixteen. Elsewhere…Brown recycles some of his own previously published material, reprints a poem by Grace Greenwood without identifying her as the author, and incorporates newspaper articles without citing their actual sources. In the latter cases, Brown does not actually represent the work of another writer as his own; at most, he simply leaves open the possibility that he composed the passages. …the total amount of the plagiarism in *Clotel* [is] eighteen passages, or 4,781 words, derived from eight different sources' (65).

15 Brown would go on to publish three additional versions of the novel, each with a slightly different title: *Clotelle: A Tale of the Southern States* (1864); *Clotelle; or the Colored Heroine* (1867); and a more altered version of the novel under the title *Miralda; or, The Beautiful Quadroon*, which was serialized in the *Weekly Anglo-African* in 1860–61 (Ernest, 28). For a history and analysis of these different editions, see Levine (2000, 309).

16 For a reading of *Clotel* together with 'St. Domingo' in the context of fears about yellow fever in the United States, see also Wisecup (2008).

established the authority that "race" was the key to reading the Haitian Revolution, Haitian independence, and, ultimately, Haitian revolutionary historiography. The casual but deliberate effort by transatlantic abolitionists to exclude nineteenth-century Haitian participation in the making of the *true* history of the Haitian Revolution on the grounds that such participation itself was racist, is only the most fervent expression of a *tropics of Haiti* that will be repeated in the works of Brown.

Thinking about the perhaps endless implications of Brown's own hapless participation in this 'exercise of power' throughout his œuvre, given his copying and reprinting from sources with vastly different ideologies about "race," is much more complicated than we will have time to fully examine here. On this account, Geoffrey Sanborn has generously written that the difficulty of attributing to Brown without qualification the ideas in any of his works that 'associate blackness with a migrating instability,' constitutes 'the most promising' 'basis' of Brown's 'abolitionist consciousness' since 'the 'he' to whom I am assigning this attraction to breaks and flows is impossible to locate with any certainty' (69). Paying attention only to the ideas about "race" found in *Clotel* that Brown derived from *The Life of Toussaint L'Ouverture*, then, I want to ask (but perhaps, not to answer) how we should think about Brown's relationship as an author to the ideas of "racial" supremacy that he would invariably imply and even seem to endorse in both *Clotel* and 'St. Domingo.' These are ideas that may have begun as the result of his copying from Beard, but that Brown would continue to develop into the nineteenth century and even to repeat with unequivocal force in *The Rising Son*, the text in which Brown most clearly alludes to the trope of the "colored historian."

The impossibility of locating Brown's ideas about "race" with any fixity surfaces from the first page of *Clotel*, when the author explicitly connects feelings of insurrection among the slaves in the United States to the narrative of "mulatto/a vengeance:" 'With the growing population of slaves in the Southern states of America, there is a fearful increase of half whites, most of whose fathers are slave owners and their mothers slaves' (81).[17] Echoing a statement made by Augustine St. Clare in *Uncle Tom's Cabin*, which had been published the year before *Clotel*, about the likelihood that slaves with 'Anglo-Saxon blood' would one day 'rise and raise with them their mother's race' (Stowe, 392), Brown writes that these 'half whites' were to be feared because:

---

17 Frederick Douglass similarly wrote in his *Narrative of the Life* (1845): 'Every year brings with it multitudes of this class of slaves. It was doubtless in consequence of a knowledge of this fact, that one great statesman of the south predicted the downfall of slavery by the inevitable laws of population' (27).

The infusion of Anglo-Saxon with African blood has created an insurrectionary feeling among the slaves of America hitherto unknown. Aware of their blood connection with their owners, these mulattoes labor under the sense of their personal and social injuries, and tolerate, if they do not encourage in themselves, *low and vindictive passions*. (2000, 201; italics added)

The phrase 'low and vindictive passions' comes directly from Beard's biography of Louverture and, as we have seen, would later be repeated by Brown in 'St. Domingo.' Yes, indeed, before Brown was talking about Haiti, he was thinking about Haiti, and through his transposition of Beard's work into *Clotel*, he was even writing about Haiti. But what would be the ultimate effect of overlaying the causes of the Haitian Revolution as they had been expressed in the narrative of "mulatto/a" vengeance with the history of slave revolts and rebellion in the United States? Could it be that Brown, that otherwise seemingly ardent detractor of the "racial" supremacy expressed in the works of writers like Thomas Carlyle (Brown, 1852, 217–19; see also Blackett, 156) would evoke and even appear to sanctify nearly all of the tropologies of the narrative of "mulatto/" vengeance whenever he explicitly or implicitly evoked Haiti?

The phrase about 'low and vindictive passions' from *The Life of Toussaint L'Ouverture* was not the only one Brown reprinted in *Clotel*. He also copied the following statements (indicated with italics) from Beard:

The evils consequent on slavery are not lessened by the incoming of one or two stray rays of light. If the slave becomes conscious of his condition, and aware of the injustice under which he suffers, if he obtains but a faint idea of these things, he will seize the first opportunity to possess himself of what he conceives to belong to him. (2000, 201, emphasis mine)[18]

The fact that in Brown's mind the problems of slavery and color prejudice facing the antebellum U.S., and the link between "miscegenation" and slave rebellion, were the same problems that had faced Haiti and led to the Haitian Revolution, meant for him that a rebellion of the U.S. slaves against their condition was not only possible, but inevitable. In demonstration of this point, in *Clotel*, when describing Nat Turner's slave rebellion in

---

18 Beard had written: 'The evils consequent on slavery are not lessened by the incoming of one or two stray rays of light. If the slave becomes conscious of his condition, and aware of the injustice under which he suffers, if he obtains but a faint idea of these things; and if the master learns that a desire for liberty has arisen in the slave's mind, or that free men are asserting anti-slavery doctrines, then a new element of evil is added to those which before were only too powerful' (19).

The Color of History

Southampton, Virginia in 1831, Brown directly lifts Beard's description of Dessalines to describe one of the 'runaway negroes,' Picquilo, who had joined the 'revolters' in the Dismal Swamps (201). Brown describes Picquilo in the following manner (the italicized phrases indicate the portions plagiarized from Beard):

> He was *a bold, turbulent spirit*; and *from revenge imbrued his hands in the blood* of all the whites he could meet. *Hunger, thirst, fatigue, and loss of sleep he seemed made to endure as if by peculiarity of constitution. His air was fierce, his step oblique, his look sanguinary.* (2000, 202)[19]

So convergent was the history of slave rebellion in the United States with that of Haiti in the literary imagination of Brown that he would even describe the punishment of the Southampton revolters with language borrowed from Beard's description of Rochambeau's usage of dogs to hunt down the Haitian revolutionists (Beard, 194, 265). Brown writes that after the capture of Turner,

> *Without scruple and without pity*, the whites *massacred all blacks* found beyond their owners' plantations: the negroes, in return, set fire to houses, and put those to death who attempted to escape from flames. *Thus, carnage was added to carnage*, and the blood of the whites flowed to *avenge* the blood of the blacks. These were the ravages of slavery. *No graves were dug* for the negroes; their *dead bodies became food for dogs and vultures, and their bones, partly calcined by the sun, remained scattered about, as if to mark the mournful fury of servitude and lust for power.* (203, emphasis mine)

The original text from Beard, however, reads:

> Without scruple and without pity they massacred the herds of blacks whom the fate of war had thrown into their hands; two hundred they immolated at the fort of Mount Nolo; a little further on, six hundred fell beneath their murderous hands. Thus carnage was added to carnage, and black blood flowed to avenge white blood. The savage and torn sides of Mount Cahos, the odorous banks of the Artibonite, offered the spectacle of barbarity opposed to barbarity, and war was only prolonged assassination. These are the horrible devastations of slavery. No graves were dug, no mounds were raised for sepulture. Dessalines had prohibited interment,

---

19 Beard had written of Dessalines, 'That chief, who had the west under his command, was of a bold, turbulent, and ferocious spirit; now from revenge, now from ambition, he imbrued his hands in the blood of both white men and black men. Hunger, thirst, fatigue, and loss of sleep he seemed made to endure as if by a peculiarity of constitution. His air was fierce, his step oblique, his look sanguinary' (167).

in order that the eyes of his assailants might see his vengeance even in the repulsive remains of carnage. It is said that the monster slew a mother for having buried her son. The French, carried away by the movements of the war, gave no attention to the religious duty of burial, so that the dead bodies became food for dogs, vultures and crocodiles; and their bones, partly calcined by the sun, remained scattered about, as if to mark the mournful fury of servitude and lust of power. (193-94)

Note that Brown virtually obliterates the idea of "black" savagery that could have been indicated in the minds of his readers by Beard's description of Dessalines. In Brown's account, while dogs still eat the remains of the poor slaves who had dared to usurp the authority of their masters, Beard's 'monster,' Dessalines, who would in turn kill a woman for defying his orders when she buries her child, is nowhere to be seen. We might say, then, that in this instance Brown actually encounters difficulty with neatly transferring Beard's descriptions of revolutionary Haiti into his own descriptions of a slave revolt in the antebellum United States and, more particularly, in an antebellum print culture of the Haitian Revolution where Dessalines was a most threatening specter.

If, in *Clotel*, Brown had not desired to completely associate Turner's revolt with the infamous tales about Dessalines circulating in the antebellum U.S., in 'St. Domingo,' he would try once again to associate the life of Nat Turner with events in Haiti. This time, though, it was towards a more acceptable figure, Toussaint Louverture, that Brown would look for a comparison in saying, 'Although the French had all the strongholds in the island, they found that they were not masters of Hayti. Like Nat Turner, the Spartacus of the Southampton revolt, who fled with his brave band to the Virginia swamps, Toussaint and his generals took to the mountains' (23).[20] If making a 'Spartacus' out of Dessalines was still largely unthinkable in the mid-nineteenth-century transatlantic abolitionist movement, as a revolutionary hero, Louverture—the 'Black Spartacus'—was practically

---

20 As Alfred Hunt has written, 'there is no direct evidence connecting Nat Turner's short-lived but bloody revolt in 1831 with the Haitian Revolution' (120). However, this lack of 'evidence' apparently did little to change the association of the two events in the minds of those living in the Atlantic World. According to Hunt, a 'New Yorker who was not in Virginia at the time' named Samuel Warner would write after describing the events, 'Such were the horrors that attended the insurrection of the Blacks in St. Domingo.' Going on to connect the Haitian Revolution to Turner's revolt, Warner continues, 'similar scenes of bloodshed and murder might our brethren at the South expect to witness, were the disaffected slaves of that section of the country but once to gain the ascendancy. In a "General Nat", they might then find a wretch not less disposed to shed innocent blood, than was the perfidious Dessalines' (qtd. in A. Hunt, 121).

irreproachable. Even so, after Dessalines, that "monstrous hybrid" who 'imbrued his hands in the blood of both white men and black men' (Beard, 167), revolutionaries of "mixed race" were still the almost uniform scapegoats for the recriminations of both slavery and revolution. Brown told of the vengeance that "racial mixing" could supposedly produce in the hearts of the "racially mixed" when he wrote of Rigaud, Pétion, and Boyer that '[t]hese three were mulattoes, were haters of the blacks, and consequently had become the dupes and tools of Bonaparte, and were now on their way to assist in reducing the land of their birth to slavery' (1855, 20).

If the "mixed-race" revolutionaries who populate Brown's 1854 speech are vengeful as a result of their 'blood,' Brown describes their desires for "racial" revenge as only having been exacerbated by the pseudo-slavery in which they found themselves, even as free people of color. Brown will go on to link what was to him the inherent immorality of "racial mixing," first described in *Clotel*, to colonial Saint-Domingue. In 'St. Domingo' Brown suggests that the treatment of the free people of color in Haiti was more degrading than 'bond slavery' (5). In *Clotel*, Brown had expressed a similar sentiment when he wrote, '[t]he prejudice that exists in the Free States against colored persons, on account of their color, is attributable solely to the influence of slavery, and is but another form of slavery itself' (2000, 171). Brown's thoughts on the 'immorality' of 'amalgamation,' as he called it in *Clotel*, also immediately influenced his thoughts on the "mixed-race" population of Haiti. Brown prefaced his remarks in 'St. Domingo' about the 'low and vindictive passions' of 'mulattoes' that caused them to rebel against colonial authority, for instance, with the following statement: '[a]s in all countries where involuntary servitude exists, morality was at a low stand' (5).[21] The immorality of racial "miscegenation" alluded to in his speech was actually a favorite topic of Brown, according to Angelyn Mitchell, who calls him a 'moral propagandist' (11). Implying that some of Brown's characterizations might have been more the result of pragmatism than passion, Mitchell says:

> It is clear that Brown saw no dichotomy between art and propaganda ... Any device that would damage the 'peculiar institution' of slavery ... was

---

[21] While Beard's text does not contain this exact statement, chapter three of *The Life of Toussaint L'Ouverture* is entitled 'The diverse elements of the population of Hayti—The blacks, the whites, the mulattoes; immorality and servitude.' Brown would include a variation of this same sentence in *The Black Man, his Antecedents and His Genius*: 'Like the involuntary servitude in our own Southern States, slavery in St. Domingo kept morality at a low stand. Owing to the amalgamation between masters and slaves, there arose the mulatto population, which eventually proved to be the worst enemies of their fathers' (92).

employed. In light of this purpose, the sexual licentiousness of the slave owner and the control he and his family wielded over Black women receive particular attention. (11)

Indeed, '[f]or Brown, illegitimacy, the result of the ravaging of Black women and the inevitable destruction of the family structure, is a corrupt principle upon which slavery is founded' (Mitchell, 11). Brown's seeming disdain for "racial mixing" as it was to be found in a slaveholding society surfaces through the character of Henry Morton in *Clotel*, who states that because of the persistence of "racial mixing," New Orleans is doubtless the most immoral place in the United States' (179). As evidence for this, Brown uses not the 'licentiousness of the slave owner,' but the contradictions of U.S. law. He tells us that in Louisiana '[t]he most stringent laws have been passed in that city against negroes, yet a few years since the State Legislature passed a special act to enable a white man to marry a coloured woman, on account of her being possessed of a very large fortune' (179). While nearly everything that Brown lifted from *The Life of Toussaint L'Ouverture* relates to the narrative of "mulatto/a" vengeance in some way, Brown has more often been accused of being a 'colorist' in the U.S. context because some readers have felt that his novels portray the most virtuous and undeserving slaves as 'near-white' female heroines, on the one hand, and 'the worst slaves' as 'the "real Negroes"' (Gilmore, 1997, 749), on the other. Yet the passage directly cited above from *Clotel* is actually much more in keeping with the more complicated defamation of "mulattoes" to be found in the literary history of the Haitian Revolution. In fact, in nearly all of the passages borrowed from Beard and inserted into *Clotel*, the narrative of "mulatto/a" vengeance seems ever apparent.

Brown's description of himself as a person of 'mixed blood' (1863, 6), whose 'fair complexion was a great obstacle to my happiness, both with whites and blacks, in and about the great house' (18), only further obscures whatever idea we might want to derive about the contradictory representations of people with light skin as virtuous in *Clotel* and treacherous in 'St. Domingo.' As in the vast majority of the literary history of the Haitian Revolution, Brown's simple recitation of "mulatto/a" vengeance across his œuvre turns the anti-racist abolitionist into a colluder with the ideas of "race" undergirding "white" supremacy. In his preface to *The Black Man*, which also contains many of the same plagiarized passages from *The Life of Toussaint L'Ouverture*, Brown writes:

> I admit that the condition of my race, whether considered in a mental, moral, or intellectual point of view, at the present time cannot compare favorably with the Anglo-Saxon. But it does not become the whites to point the finger of scorn at the blacks, when they have so long been

degrading them. The negro has not always been considered the inferior race. (29)

Though Brown intends to offer several of the Haitian revolutionists, including Louverture, Dessalines, Rigaud, Christophe, Boyer, and Pétion, as proof for his claim that the inferiority of 'negroes' was only temporal or even relational, we cannot help but to note that this was precisely the argument that Beard had made at the end of his biography of Louverture. Once again, while the politics and motives and even the "racial" consciousness of the authors might be different, is the effect on the hierarchical thinking of "racial" supremacy any different when 'negroes,' for whatever reason, are considered to be 'inferior?'

I pose this question particularly because by the time we see Brown publishing *The Rising Son* in 1873, he was still directly quoting from and adapting the "racial" tropologies and, especially, evoking the trope of "monstrous hybridity," found in *The Life of Toussaint L'Ouverture*. Writing of Haiti in *The Rising Son*, Brown says that 'seventy-nine years' had not been able to 'efface' the 'ill-feeling between the two proscribed classes' in Haiti (147), and he described 'the mulattoes of Hayti' as having 'despised the uneducated black laborers' in the post-independence period (177), adding, '[t]he mutual hatred between the mulattoes and the blacks was so deeply rooted, that neither party could see anything good in the other' (178). In borrowing the *tropics of Haiti*, or the idea of "racial" revolution, found all across the transatlantic print culture of the Haitian Revolution, Brown much more directly expresses an ideology of "white" supremacy. In the same work, Brown makes a pronouncement that would seem to imply that he actually believed that 'mulattoes' were superior to *pure* 'blacks': 'as a people, the mulattoes were endowed with greater intelligence' (155). This statement performs a *racial tropics* consistent with readings of Brown as a 'colorist,' yet the statement also presents a contradiction. In 'St. Domingo' we saw the "colored historian" critique simulateneously what he called the 'War of Colour' between the 'blacks' and 'mulattoes' of revolutionary Saint-Domingue and the attitude of superiority that he felt was germane to a person's position as a 'mulatto,' and to do so by suggesting that the 'never-to-be-forgiven course of the mulattoes' was the result of their 'haughty and disdainful' feelings towards the 'blacks, whom they scorned' (1855, 5). Moreover, in *Clotel*, Brown had critiqued the very idea that that slaves with lighter skin felt themselves to be superior to those with darker skin:

> There is, in the Southern States, a great amount of prejudice amongst the negroes themselves. The nearer the negro or mulatto approaches to white, the more he seems to feel his superiority over those of a darker hue. This

is, no doubt, the result of the prejudice that exists on the part of the whites towards both mulattoes and blacks. (135)

Although Brown seems to critique the idea of "mulatto" superiority here in *Clotel* and in some places in 'St. Domingo,' later in the speech Brown would say of the 'mulattoes:' 'The habits of the mulattoes, their intelligence, energy, and boldness, naturally pointed them out as the leaders of the slaves' (1855, 9). Will the *real* William Wells Brown please stand up?

Although it is doubtful that we could ever purport to discover any unified, stable, and noncontradictory evidence of Brown's *real* ideas about "race," perhaps it is in the gap between the *lived experience* of racism and slavery and the *intellectual experience* of writing about racism and slavery to which we should now turn in order to understand how Brown could have *represented* many of the very same racist ideas that upheld the system of slavery from which he had so injudiciously suffered and so unceremoniously escaped.

If, in the words of Robert S. Levine, Brown's appropriations, modifications, and transformations of the works of others in *Clotel* and beyond 'presses his readers to rethink their assumptions about race, gender, and slavery by teaching them how they might better read cultural texts and scripts' (2000, 4), Brown's own particular practice of reading and copying from the literary history of the Haitian Revolution not only caused him to perhaps unwittingly express ideas consonant with "white" supremacy, but to contribute to the development of the trope of the "colored historian." In 'St. Domingo,' on the subject of impartial history, Brown writes, '[n]o revolution ever turned up greater heroes than that of St. Domingo. But no historian has yet done them justice' (33). In *The Black Man, His Antecedents and His Genius*, he similarly states, '[w]hen impartial history shall do justice to the St. Domingo revolution, the name of Toussaint L'Ouverture will be placed high upon the roll of fame' (105). It would be hard not to see Brown's dismissal with a sloppy sleight of hand of half a century of writing on the topic of the Haitian Revolution, including those works by Haitian authors themselves like Vastey, Boisrond-Tonnerre, Dumesle, Chanlatte, Madiou, and Ardouin, as an extension of the same 'exercise of power' that made European writers like Beard feel that they could determine what constituted history, what was and was not *true*, and who could and could not speak. However, there is a way in which we could view Brown's involvement in the 'silencing' of the Haitian Revolution as the result of his failure to fully acknowledge that, as a former slave and a fugitive one at that, a subaltern in the body politic of the United States, if you will, he only possessed the most tendentious historical authority.[22]

---

22 At the time he wrote his own biography, Brown was still technically a slave, having

Brown most fully elaborated upon the idea that the "subaltern" slaves of the United States could not speak—first expressed in his 'Lecture Before the Female Anti-Slavery Society of Salem' (1847)—in his 'Speech Delivered at the Horticultural Hall, West Chester, Pennsylvania' on October 23, 1854, an idea that would find expression again in 1988 by Gayatri Spivak in her famous article, "Can the Subaltern Speak?" In this speech Brown told the audience:

> We cannot tell the evils that exist in the southern States. Like the painter who stands idle by the side of his picture, waiting for the crow to go out before lifting the screen from the canvas, for fear of frightening his visitors with the unfinished work, so we must wait and let the future historians complete the picture. (248)

He continued by acknowledging that coming from a former slave, such a statement might seem strange: 'I know that, after having spent twenty years as a slave,' he said, 'one would suppose that I might relate the evils that I witnessed. And so I might. I might stand here for hours and tell you what I saw, and felt, and know, but now is not the time' (248). Although Brown says that he 'might' one day tell of the full range of his experiences as a slave, in his earlier 1847 speech he had implied that conveying such information might be largely impossible. After stating, '[s]lavery has never been represented. Slavery can never be represented,' he would go on to tell his audience that such silences and lack of representation were the source of great pain for a former slave like himself:

> When I begin to talk of Slavery, the sighs and the groans of three millions of my countrymen come to me upon the wings of every wind; and it causes me to feel sad, even when I think I am making a successful effort in representing the condition of the Slave. (110)

Still, Brown told the audience in Philadelphia:

> I think I have a right to speak of the shortcomings of the people of this country. I stand here as the representative of the slave to speak for those who cannot speak for themselves, and I stand here as the representative of the free coloured man who cannot come up to this convention. (248)

In the end, if, in the words of Said, '[t]here is nothing mysterious or natural about authority' since 'it is virtually indistinguishable from certain

---

escaped from his master's plantation in early 1834, but his freedom was not purchased until 1854. Brown provides a detailed account of how he escaped from slavery in chapters VII–XI of his *Narrative* (68–108).

ideas it dignifies as true, and from traditions, perceptions, and judgments it forms, transmits, reproduces' (1979, 20), in the case of Brown, what he borrowed from Beard was not only a history of Haiti, and a biography of Louverture, but a narrative of "mulatto/a" vengeance that was filled with the kind of language of "racial" supremacy that might allow one to believe that he did have the authority to speak *for* his subjects, an inverted position of power that stands in great conflict with many of Brown's other writings.

*

In 1863, James Redpath, a Scottish-born U.S. abolitionist who had become one of the most famous publishers of anti-slavery tracts in the Atlantic World would, by virtue of his revisions of Beard's biography, help to spread not only the "mulatto/a" vengeance narrative of the Haitian Revolution, but help to further develop the vocabulary for the trope of the "colored historian." Redpath, who had at one point employed William Wells Brown as one of his book agents (Redpath, 1861, 9; Boyd, 175),[23] is most well known for having revised and then republished, in Boston, Beard's biography along with the first English translation of Saint-Rémy's 1853 edition of Louverture's memoirs, under the title *Toussaint L'Ouverture: A Biography and Autobiography*.[24] Redpath's republication of Beard's biography, which was advertised in William Lloyd Garrison's *The Liberator* and was widely reviewed in the nineteenth-century U.S. press (Clavin, 82, 109), would essentially cement the idea that histories of Haiti always had a "color."

Redpath traveled to Haiti in 1859 in order to gather information, 'geographical, political, and historical' (1861a, 10), which might encourage free Americans of color to emigrate there. Redpath was not only an ardent supporter of "black" emigration to the country (see Clavin, 50; A. Hunt, 177–78; Boyd, 171), but he eventually became the official agent of the Haytian Bureau of Emigration located in Washington, D.C. In 1861 Redpath published

---

23 Redpath was also connected to Brown in other ways. In 1864, Redpath would publish Brown's *Clotelle: A Tale of the Southern States* as a part of his dime novel series, *Books for the Camp Fires* (Greenspan, xxxiii). For more on this connection see also Cox (2000, 222). Brown's 'St. Domingo' also appeared in two installments (June 15, 1861 and August 31, 1861) in the *Pine and the Palm*, which was also edited by Redpath.

24 According to Alfred Hunt, Haitian President Fabre Geffrard asked Redpath to act as an agent for black U.S. emigration to Haiti: 'Redpath attacked his new position with vigor: he established the Haytian Bureau of Emigration in Boston to facilitate recruitment in the Northeast, he published *A Guide to Hayti* to promote life on the island, and he founded a newspaper, the *Pine and the Palm*, to publicize his project in the antislavery community' (177). In *The Rising Son* (1873), Brown wrote that he had visited Haiti 'thirty years ago' (140).

his *A Guide to Hayti*. This travel book was basically comprised of a collection of essays on various topics that Redpath thought would be of interest to visitors and migrants to Haiti alike. For example, there were essays on the soil of Haiti, its vegetation, governmental structure, revolutionary history, the amount of available vacant land, etc. The essays were written by Redpath himself, British travelers like W.S. Courtenay,[25] and Haitian officials like F.E. Dubois, Beaubrun Ardouin, and Auguste Elie.

It is immediately noticeable in the *Guide* that neither Redpath nor any of his contributors ever once use any pseudoscientific terms like "mulatto" to describe the population of Haiti. In his essay 'The People of Hayti,' Redpath attempts to skirt the authority of the pseudoscientific discourse that had always inevitably determined the tone and tenor of descriptions of Haiti when he describes Haitians as being, '[a]s in all the Republics of the tropics and Central and South America ... divided into two distinct parties, the enlightened class and the uneducated mass' (129). Moving into greater detail about these two classes, Redpath explains, '[t]he enlightened class may be described in three words: They are Frenchmen. All the distinguishing traits of the Parisian gentleman are reproduced in the educated Haytian.' As for the 'uneducated class,' what Redpath call 'les habitants,' these

> have the characteristics that are attributed to inland Irish; they are hospitable, superstitious, of a never-failing good nature, thoughtless of the morrow, with a quaint and prompt mother-wit, polite and sociable, but without ambition, and with little disposition to regular work. Their vices are contentment, petty theft, and a tendency to polygamy. (129)

While Redpath is here working hard to avoid using the "racial" taxonomies of naturalist travel writing (albeit in a manner that manages to disparage the Irish), it is his stance on the purposes of "black" emigration to Haiti that betrays the probably unconscious "racial" supremacy that undergirds his work.

In his essay 'A Parting Word,' Redpath reveals a "racial" separatist ideology that has everything to do with his belief in the "color" of history. In imitating the 'voice of God,' which was for him 'the voice of history,' Redpath encouraged free 'black' Americans, God's 'persecuted children in the States,' he said, to 'COME OUT OF HER, MY PEOPLE' (171).[26] Redpath explains his position on emigration to Haiti by making implicit

---

25 George W.C. Courtenay was a lieutenant on the *Iphigenia* when that vessel took Admiral Hope Popham 'on a courtesy visit to Cap-Henry in May 1819' (Cole, 253); Courtenay, who spent some time in Christophe's palace, would later serve as Britain's 'Consul General at Hayti from 1832 to 1842' (O'Byrne, 234).
26 This phrase comes from the Book of Revelation 18:4.

reference to a belief in climatology, which included the intimation that the "mixing" of people with different "racial" identities, from different parts of the world and with different 'missions,' should be discouraged. Redpath writes:

> There is a profound significance in the fact of the diversity of the races,— far deeper than many of our sages know. It was for wise and grand purpose that the European and the African have for a time become different in destiny and in physical capacity; and it belongs to the same blind and false philosophy that disputes about the relative superiority of the sexes, to inquire whether the Black man or the White is the more capable of a glorious future. Their missions in the world are different; and, until these are fulfilled, their identity must be preserved. (171)

It is at this point in *The Guide* that the "racial" separatist ideology of Jefferson's *Notes on the State of Virginia* emerges as the *urtext* of one of the most prominent nineteenth-century movements for "black" emigration to Haiti. Jefferson had rather famously argued that the day of the emancipation of slaves in the U.S. would be the day when the separation of the "races" would be definitively required in order to avoid a "race war." He wrote:

> Deep rooted prejudices entertained by the whites; ten thousand recollections, by the blacks, of the injuries they have sustained; new provocations; the real distinctions which nature has made; and many other circumstances, will divide us into parties, and produce convulsions which will probably never end but in the extermination of the one or the other race. (138)

Belief that this kind of "racial" violence was inevitable led Jefferson to ask, 'What further is to be done with them?' His response was unequivocal: 'When freed, [the slave] is to be removed beyond the reach of mixture' (143).

After the onset of revolution in Saint-Domingue, answering the question, 'whither shall the colored emigrants go?' as Jefferson had written to St. John Tucker in 1797,[27] had become a much more practical rather than a merely

---

[27] Jefferson was a proponent of St. John Tucker's colonization scheme. Tucker was a fan of Jefferson too and had even referenced Jefferson's *Notes* in his 1796 *A Dissertation on Slavery* (see chapter 15, document 6). By quoting from one of Jefferson's letters to him, Tucker further links the U.S. president's fears in *Notes* about "white" and "black" contact directly to Haiti: 'The recent scenes transacted in the French colonies in the West Indies are enough to make one shudder with the apprehension of realizing similar calamities in this country. Such probably would be the event of an attempt to smother those prejudices which have been cherished for a period of almost two centuries' (qtd. in A. Hunt, 1988, 122).

theoretical question. Jefferson answered by referring to the "mulatto/a" vengeance narrative with all its parricidal undertones:

> Perhaps the first chapter of this history, which has begun in St. Domingo, and the next succeeding ones, which will recount how all the whites were driven from all the other islands, may prepare our minds for a peaceable accommodation between justice, policy and necessity ... if something is not done, and soon done, we shall be the murderers of our own children. (1854, 196)

Once Louverture was seen as having almost complete control of the colony in 1801, Jefferson was finally able to conceive of a much more concrete potential answer to his question. He wrote to James Monroe on November 24, 1801, that the free 'colored' population of the United States could be transported to

> the island of St. Domingo, where the blacks are established into a sovereignty de facto, and have organized themselves under regular law and government. I should conjecture that their present ruler might be willing, on many considerations, to receive even that description which would be exiled for acts deemed criminal by us, but meritorious, perhaps, by him. (1854, 4: 421)

Two decades later, in a letter to Jared Sparks written on February 4, 1824, Jefferson would be much more certain that 'St. Domingo' was the proper location for "black" emigration. Jefferson told Sparks, who would eventually serve as the president of Harvard College:

> In the plan sketched in Notes on the State of Virginia, no particular place of asylum was specified; because it was thought possible that in the revolutionary state of America ... events might open to us some one within practicable distance. This has now happened. St. Domingo has become independent; and if the public papers are to be credited, their chief offers to pay their passage, to receive them as free citizens, and to provide them employment. (1854, 10:292)

Christopher Iannini writes that precisely because of such a statement we should see *Notes on the State of Virginia* as itself intimately linked to the Haitian Revolution, especially since in the first two decades of Haitian independence, 'commentators from across the political spectrum had begun to appropriate the language and imagery of *Notes* in their accounts of the insurrection [in Haiti]' (242). Iannini has, therefore, read Jefferson's Haiti letters, many of which were published in 1854, as revisions of his original 'meditations on slavery' in *Notes* (223). The events of the Haitian Revolution, in this light, merely allowed Jefferson to offer 'new evidence' to readers of the *Notes* 'for his hypothesis of inevitable racial violence absent a plan for colonization' (Iannini, 249).[28]

The repressed Jeffersonian origins of the mid-nineteenth-century "black" emigrationist movement surfaces most apparently in Redpath's works when the abolitionist explains, '[t]o preserve the African race in America, emigration from it is the first condition' (1861c, 171). This is because as far as the African in the United States is concerned, '[h]is future is *annihiliation*. There is no other possible result—whether slavery or freedom shall prevail' (1861c, 172). Going on to echo the precise claims of Jefferson, Redpath wrote, '[e]verything conspires to promote it. Pride of race, self-respect, social ambition, parental love, the madness of the South, the meanness of the North, the inhumanity of the Union ... all say to the Black and the man of color, seek elsewhere a home and a nationality' (1861c, 172).

The only hope of destroying this color prejudice for Redpath would have been an 'insurrection, successfully conducted' in which the 'millions now enslaved' could 'exhibit their equality, in courage, and in arms, with their masters.' The only problem with this was that, in Redpath's mind, the 'Africans' in the United States were not likely to win such a contest, on the one hand, since, '[t]he Saxon race is a race of fighters' (1861c, 172), and because these Anglo-Saxons had the 'physical majority,' on the other. Redpath likened the result of such an unequal contest to 'trying to drive back an ocean, which ... will throw up the bodies of your children, after a generation or two, pale and unrecognizable, on its Saxon shores!' (1861c, 174).

Jefferson, too, had at one point been supremely confident in the United States' ability to defeat the former slaves of Saint-Domingue if they were ever to present themselves on American shores for the purposes of freeing

---

28 Jefferson is not the only U.S. president who has been intimately linked to the Haitian emigration movement. According to James D. Lockett, after the creation of the American colonization society in 1816, 'Most of the American presidents supported the efforts of the American Colonization Society; other outstanding members were John Marshall, Chief Justice of the United States, Henry Clay, Speaker of the House, and the "Great Pacificator," Daniel Webster, the great orator, Rufus King, the leader of the Federalist party, Patrick Henry ("give me liberty or give me death"), and William Harris Crawford of Georgia, presidential candidate in the election of 1824' (Lockett, 429). Lockett writes that it was Abraham Lincoln, who 'fully agreed with the thesis of the colonizations,' and who was 'probably the most ardent and eloquent spokesman for the cause' (Lockett, 430). In fact, Lincoln supported the creation of a U.S. colony of free people of color on Ile-à-Vâche, a tiny island off the coast of southern Haiti, which had been leased by a lawyer from the United States named Bernard Kock. See Kock's 'To his excellency, Abraham Lincoln, President of the United States. Washington, D.C. 1862.' According to Lockett, the experiment ended in apparent disaster when Kock refused to pay the emigrants from the United States and he was forced to flee (439-40).

U.S. slaves. In the same letter to Monroe of November 24, 1801, Jefferson boasted:

> The possibility that these exiles [to St. Domingo] might stimulate and conduct vindictive or predatory descents on our coasts, and facilitate concert with their brethren remaining here, looks to a state of things between that island and us not probable on a contemplation of our relative strength, and of the disproportion daily growing; and it is overweighed by the humanity of the measures proposed, and the advantages of disembarrassing ourselves of such dangerous characters. (421)

Only two years after he published *The Guide*, Redpath's ideas about the inutility and ineffectiveness of violence on the part of the slaves of the U.S. to produce the abolition of slavery in the Union had completely changed. That is to say that Redpath would seem to have become much less skeptical of what Matthew Clavin has referred to as the 'second coming of the Haitian Revolution' (75) by the time he republished Beard's *Toussaint L'Ouverture* in 1863. In his introduction to the biography, Redpath offers to use the life of Louverture to answer the question: 'Are Negroes fit for Officers?' Going on to provide that answer, Redpath writes:

> We are entering on that debate now. The Life of Toussaint may help to end it. What Toussaint, Christophe, Dessalines did,—'plantation-hands' and yet able warriors and statesmen, all of them,—some Sambo,[29] Wash, or Jeff, still toiling in the rice-fields or among the sugar-canes, or hoeing his cotton-row in the Southern States, may be meditating to-day and destined to begin tomorrow. (1863, vi)

At the end of the work, Redpath's ambivalence about Louverture, that most famous of 'black soldiers' (1863, 218), emerges when Redpath cautions his reader about the kinds of moral lesson one might draw from the life of 'the Haytian patriot.' He writes:

> I do not intend to paint the Haytian patriot as a perfect man. Moral perfection once appeared on earth. It is not likely to have appeared a

---

29 This seems to be a case where Redpath may have more directly borrowed from William Wells Brown. In 'St. Domingo' Brown had warned that should the slaves of the United States 'be obliged to shed rivers of blood; should we, to preserve our freedom, be compelled to set fire on seven-eighths of the globe, we shall be pronounced innocent before the tribunal of Providence, who has not created men to see them groan under a yoke so oppressive and so ignominious. Who knows but that a Toussaint, a Christophe, a Rigaud, a Clervaux, and a Dessalines, may some day appear in the Southern States of this Union?' (1855, 32).

second time among the slaves of Hayti. Toussaint has been accused of harshness and cruelty. I am not prepared to affirm that the charges are without foundation. But it is equally true that his enemies have done their utmost to point out stains in his character. Unfortunately, the means for a thorough investigation are wholly wanting. (1863, 288)

Redpath's closing argument provides the frame for understanding his own contribution to the development of the trope of the "colored historian." If Redpath ended the biography by casting doubt on prior attempts to write the life of Louverture by suggesting that such works had been penned by Louverture's 'enemies,' Redpath began the biography by recognizing Saint-Rémy as one of those potential 'enemies.'

Redpath introduced Beard's biography by inserting the latter's statement about 'mulatto' and French biases that had culminated in the idea that Saint-Rémy was more interested in his 'own caste' than in objectively narrating the life of Louverture. Our only clue to Redpath's own thoughts about these claims comes in the form of the footnote that followed their recitation, where Redpath wrote:

> With this work the editor has taken the liberty of making a few verbal and other changes in the text of the opening chapters; of erasing the two elaborated guesses as to Toussaint's Scriptural studies and readings in the Abbé Raynal's philosophy; and of omitting the entire Book IV, which gave a sketch of the history of Hayti from the death of Toussaint to the reign of the late Emperor Soulouque. The alterations in the first chapters referred chiefly to statements respecting modern Hayti, with which the editor's travels and his official relations to its Government had made him more familiar than the author. Book IV was erased because it was deemed an inadequate presentation of the history of an independent negro nationality,—not unfair, indeed, nor essentially inaccurate, but too meagre for publication in the United States where its statements would necessarily be weighed in the scales of party. It is hoped that a full and impartial history of Hayti will, erelong, be presented to the American people. (1863, iv)

Redpath's apparent disagreement with Beard's assessment of the divisions based on "race" in post-independence Haiti is evidenced by his deletion of Book IV of *The Life of Toussaint L'Ouverture*, which contains virtually all of the passages that I identified in the earlier section of this chapter as expressing ideas of "white" supremacy.[30]

Redpath's apparent disagreement with many of Beard's ideas about "race"

---

30 Tellingly, Redpath left unedited Beard's judgments about "mulattoes" and "blacks" throughout the history of the Haitian Revolution.

was not only relegated to the realm of contemporary Haiti. Redpath explains that while '[i]n the historical record of Dr. Beard, no changes have been made' (1863, v), except to the 'notes and illustrations' that had been originally supplied,[31] '[t]his fact does not imply a uniform concurrence of judgment. For it is but justice to say, that, although "the blacks have no authors," they have found in Dr. Beard not a friend only, but an able and zealous partisan.' Beard's own partisanship was confirmation in Redpath's mind that:

> There have been three versions of Haytian history,—the white, the black, and the yellow: the white representing the pro-slavery party, the black that of the negroes, and the yellow that of the mulattoes. The abolitionists of England and America have adopted the negro standard,—refusing equally to pay any homage to Pétion, the idol of the mulatto historians, whom they call the Washington of Hayti, or to regard Toussaint as the *bête noir* [sic] of the revolution, or otherwise than as Hayti's hero. (1863, v)[32]

[31] Redpath wrote that instead of including Beard's notes, he had appended 'more interesting and pertinent' ones to the biography. Redpath's version contained large sections from his own *Guide to Hayti* and there are also appended excerpts from Harriet Martineau's *The Hour and the Man*, a reprint of Wordsworth's famous poem about Louverture, a description of a visit to the prison of Louverture at the Chateau de Joux penned by John Bigelow, as well as an advertisement for a reprint of Wendell Phillips's speech 'Toussaint L'Ouverture.'

[32] Interestingly, abolitionists from both sides of the Atlantic had worked fairly hard to try to paint Toussaint Louverture instead as actually much better than George Washington. Beard wrote, for example, 'Does the reader think of Washington, who, when he might possibly have become a king, became a private citizen? We are not sure that Washington's means for establishing a throne in the midst of the high-minded republicans of the Anglo-Saxon race were equal to those which Toussaint possessed among the uncultured and recently liberated Haytians, whom nature made fond of parade, and custom had habituated to royalty. The greater the opportunity, the greater the temptation; nor can he be accounted the inferior man who overcame in the severer trial. Nor must it be forgotten, that while Washington could, with confidence and safety, leave his associates to their own well-tried and well-matured powers of self-government, L'Ouverture had, in comparison, but children to deal with and provide for' (142). Wendell Phillips much more explicitly favored Louverture to Washington when he wrote, 'I would call him Washington, but the great Virginian held slaves. This man risked his empire rather than permit the slave trade in the humblest village of his dominions' (1884, 494). Brown similarly wrote, 'Toussaint's career as a Christian, a statesman, and a general, will lose nothing by comparison with that of Washington. Each was the leader of an oppressed and outraged people ... Toussaint's government made liberty its watchword, incorporated it in its constitution, abolished the slave-trade, and made freedom amongst the people. Washington's government incorporated slavery and the slave-trade, and enacted laws by which chains were fastened upon the limbs of millions of people. Toussaint liberated his country-men; Washington enslaved a portion of his, and aided in giving strength and vitality to an institution that will one day rend

Even as he implies that Beard is guilty of having created a 'white' 'Haytian history,' taking the germ planted by Beard for the "colored historian" from the stage of fertilization to seedling, Redpath ends up still implying that 'mulatto historians' idolized Pétion and regarded Louverture as the 'bête noir [*sic*] of the revolution.' This judgment, coming from Redpath, who, like Beard, fails to offer any proof to support it, begins to look like simply another extension of the exercise of self-constituted authority that historians in the nineteenth century had established for themselves in part by denying that authority to Haitian writers like Saint-Rémy. Nevertheless, Redpath did not fail to notice and comment upon Beard's statement about Saint-Rémy. He wrote: 'It is from the "*Mémoires de la Vie de Toussaint L'Ouverture*," edited by the M. Saint Remy, whose partisan spirit Dr. Beard reproves, that the Autobiography of the great General and Statesman is taken' (1863, v).

While Redpath may have failed to defend Saint-Rémy against the unsubstantiated charges with which the Haitian historian had been faced (at least by the lack of evidence to be found in Beard's work), a nineteenth-century reviewer of Redpath's *Toussaint L'Ouverture* for the *North American Review* seemed to have read between the lines of Redpath's veiled critique. The reviewer minced no words when he pointed out some of Beard's own biases, especially as they related to 'mulattoes.' The reviewer argued that most of the books that had been written about Haiti were characterized by a general tendency to castigate 'mulattoes': 'Mr. Beard's chapter upon the subsequent history of Hayti is meager,' the reviewer writes, 'and partly because it slurs the merits and genius of the great mulatto governors of that island. This is indeed the fault with all the books that have been written about Hayti ... The unfairness to the mulatto is but one of the results of a defective method of treatment' (595–96). So influential was the idea of the "colored historian" that we find it repeated in many less well-known texts of the Haitian Revolution. In a sketch of Louverture published in Fred Tomkins's *Jewels in Ebony* (c. 1866),[33] the author writes, echoing Beard by way of Redpath, whom he mentions along with Martineau, Phillips, and Wordsworth, '[f]or a long while great injustice was done to the memory of Toussaint L'Ouverture, and also the blacks who fought so fiercely in

---

asunder the UNION that he helped to form' (1855, 37). For both positive and negative U.S. reactions to Louverture's association with George Washington, see Clavin (3, 89).

33 While the date of publication is notably absent from the title page of this work, some of the author's statements reveal that it was published some time after 1863 and either during or immediately after of the Civil War. The author writes, for example, 'James Redpath has recently published in Boston a biography of Toussaint L'Ouverture' (59).

resistance of slavery, for the histories of St. Domingo were written by prejudiced French writers, or by equally prejudiced mulattoes' (59).

This kind of exceptional claim of biases is also repeated in *The Lesson of St. Domingo: How to Make the War Short and the Peace Righteous* (1861). The unnamed author writes, on the one hand, that the works of 'the principal English writers,' Rainsford and Edwards, are 'warped to suit an intensely pro-slavery philosophy' and that the writings of Lacroix and Malenfant exhibit 'prejudices, if they had any,' that were certainly 'not in favor of the negro' (3–4). The works of the French abolitionist Victor Schoelcher, on the other hand, along with those of the Haitian historian Beaubrun Ardouin, appear to the writer of *The Lesson of St. Domingo* to let in the 'clear and cloudless sunshine of a consistent and natural story' (4). No matter the stated reasons, these much less apparently racialized biases, which are just as erroneous as the overtly racialized ones, tend towards proving that even the determination of who was and who was not biased was on the whole not merely subjective, as are all judgments, but actually random. It should now be clear that it is probably impossible to truly believe in any one account of the Haitian Revolution over any other, regardless of the purported merits of its sources and the stated intentions of its author. Every history, after Michel-Rolph Trouillot, has its own political, textual, and interpretive encumbrances, and many, many instances of 'inclusion' and 'exclusion' (Trouillot, 1995, 48).

It is now time to ask the question that has been hovering in the background of *Tropics of Haiti* ever since we recognized the nineteenth-century origins of the 'mulatto legend of history.' We must now assess Beard's claim that 'mulatto' writers had been uniformly 'unjust' in their opinions of independent Haiti and, specifically, that Saint-Rémy, the only 'mulatto' historian from Haiti whom Beard appears to have read, was 'biased' because of his 'caste.' That is to ask, can we determine if there was any merit in Beard's argument that Saint-Rémy 'valued his caste more than his country or his kind?' By the same token, was C.L.R. James on solid ground when he unequivocally dismissed Saint-Rémy as a 'mulatto' who 'hated L'Ouverture like poison' (388)? I'm afraid the only way to find out is to actually read Saint-Rémy rather than merely rely upon the historical conclusions drawn by nineteenth-century abolitionists and other anti-slavery writers who clearly had their own "racial" agendas.

*

Even though Nicholls argued that in Saint-Rémy's works, 'Toussaint in particular was accused of having become a tool of the whites and of harbouring a passionate hatred of mulattoes' (1979, 91), the twentieth-century British historian still found a way to acknowledge that Saint-Rémy's

Requiem for the "Colored Historian"

Vie de Toussaint-L'Ouverture was 'full of both admiration and condemnation' for the Haitian leader (1979, 97). Despite the very real criticism of Louverture that we saw Saint-Rémy offer in chapter eight of *Tropics of Haiti*, the Haitian historian does sing Louverture's praises, particularly in his biography of the Haitian general, where he writes:

> Toussaint really opened up every social destiny for my race; despite his faults, his mistakes, his crimes, if you will, he elevated, in the eyes of Europeans, a black race that had been so maligned; he showed that the graces of God had not been distributed to men according to the whiteness of their skin. (1850, 112)[34]

In Saint-Rémy's mind, chanting homage to the great service that Louverture had performed for the 'black race,' in spite of his flaws, only proved the very insignificance of his skin color. Moreover, Saint-Rémy would write that Louverture, though subject to the virtues and vices of ordinary men, 'was still superior to any of the blacks and any of the mulattoes of his time' (1850, 315). Ultimately, Saint-Rémy concludes that it was precisely Louverture's tragic humanity, his capability to choose wrongly, his realism in broad literary terms, or his "monstrous hybridity" in the terms of the "mulatto/a" vengeance narrative of the Haitian Revolution, that made him a great man:

> He was one of those characters that the heavens [*ciel*] cast down upon the earth in certain eras in order to shake up humanity and to whom for this revolutionary mission it sometimes gives weakness, sometimes power, sometimes benevolence, sometimes cruelty, sometimes success, and sometimes the reverse, for it is with all of these antitheses that a man

---

[34] Saint-Rémy's own works would go on to serve the same purpose of proving the humanity and capability of "negroes" for some in the Atlantic World, judging by an 1859 mention of Saint-Rémy's works in an article entitled 'The Genius and Prospect of Negroes.' The article, published in the British journal *Meliora, a Quarterly Review of Social Science* reads, 'In reading the earnest, eloquent pages of M. Saint-Rémy, we see sufficient proofs of the identity of his race with our own. The same ambition and jealousies, and too often the same corruptions which disgrace us, harass and disgrace the Haitians. But individual heroisms, of which we are justly proud, do them also honour; and the people, so often misled, as among ourselves, for the most part take a correct view of things, because, in Haiti as here, the people must be disinterested.' The author concludes that 'at this early period of its annals to have produced three authors so eminent as M. de Pradine, M. Ardouin, and M. Saint-Rémy constitutes an irresistible claim to our respect, and justifies the strongest hopes of what may come hereafter from the general cultivation of the African mind. Nor is it less to the honour of France to have produced a community of negroes and coloured men capable of establishing an independent state like Haiti, and, so soon after its establishment, writers like these to grace its literature' (264–65).

The Color of History

can transform the world [*secoue le monde*] and force it to take a new path, forever beneficial to posterity. (1850, 408)

While I think that we can plainly see that Saint-Rémy hardly 'hated L'Ouverture like poison,' since he considered him to be the most important of Haiti's revolutionary heroes, Louverture was not the only great "black" revolutionary hero in Saint-Rémy's mind. Far from arguing that it was the '*affranchis*' who had led the struggle against colonial oppression and were 'the true pioneers of liberation and independence' (Nicholls, 1979, 95), Saint-Rémy also praised Boukman, referring to him as 'the first Spartacus of the black race' (1850, 22). Moreover, Saint-Rémy represented Biassou, Jean-François, and Jeannot as 'the three men who had determined the course of the insurrection after the death of Bouckman' (1850, 24). Saint-Rémy later described Jeannot as detestable because of his unnatural cruelty—he said of him, '[w]e saw him command the shooting of his coachman, his relative, his friend, for having delayed for a few minutes the execution of his orders'—but he also writes that Jean-François and Biassou 'shuddered at the idea of the crimes of Jeannot' and ultimately executed their fellow revolutionary as a result of his horrific behavior (31). Saint-Rémy continued to praise Jean-François and Biassou by arguing that, in this instance, 'humanity like political necessity [*l'humanité comme la politique*] inspired them to rid the world of this monster that dishonored it' (31). Biassou and Jean-François's justified retribution, as evidence of their 'humanity,' is only outdone by Louverture's own humanity, which Saint-Rémy linked to the general's literacy. Saint-Rémy writes of Louverture before his governorship of the colony:

> Literacy was truly humanizing [*Les lettres humanisaient réellement*]; it was the art of reading and writing that Toussaint possessed over his kind, which helped him to make his way without having soiled his hands with the murder of any of his fellow beings and without having dishonorably pillaged; two crimes, whose examples he had only too often before his eyes. (1850, 25)

If Saint-Rémy's praise for Jean-François and Biassou is eventually tempered by the same force of ambivalence that characterizes his praise for Louverture— for example, Saint-Rémy calls Biassou 'abrupt, proud, ill-tempered, violent, angry, [and] vindictive,' while Jean-François will later be described as 'unmotivated [*peu entreprenant*], uncouraged, having owed his leadership only to his superior intellect' (1850, 23)—the same kind of ambivalence also surrounds Saint-Rémy's portrayal of André Rigaud. Saint-Rémy writes that Rigaud was a 'mulatto' in the 'true sense of the term' because he had a 'white' father and a 'négresse' for a mother (1850, 82). Hardly seeming to prefer Rigaud because he considered him to be a 'mulatto,' though, Saint-Rémy went on to variously demonize (1850, 37), criticize (1850, 219), and praise (1850, 82–84) him as the one 'who would play such a large role in the history of the colonies' (1850, 82). Saint-Rémy describes Rigaud as a man who 'terrified Pétion,' and reveals that Pétion liked neither Rigaud nor Louverture. Saint-Rémy's ambivalence about the character of both Rigaud and Louverture shines through when the Haitian historian quotes and appears to agree with the assessment of the French General François-Marie Périchou de Kerverseau, who had written:

> I very much fear the exalted ambition, the hot head [*la tête effervescente*], the ill-tempered character, the attitude of domination of General Rigaud; but I do not fear any less the clever genius, the moderate hypocrisy, the hidden ambition, the devious plans of Toussaint: these are two men who only have despotism in mind. (qtd. in Saint-Rémy, 1850, 265)

Kerverseau continued his unfavorable judgment of the two revolutionary heroes by more fully evoking the epistemological uncertainty of "monstrous hybridity": '[b]oth of them are fake and secretive [*artificieux et dissimulés*],' Kerverseau wrote, 'but Toussaint is so by nature, and Rigaud has only become so through his dealings with men' (qtd. in Saint-Rémy, 1850, 265–66).

Even in finding that Saint-Rémy had imputed the majority of the blame for the War of the South to Louverture, as we recognized in chapter eight of *Tropics of Haiti*, it is still pretty safe to say that on the whole his portrait of Rigaud is filled with far less 'admiration' than his portrait of Louverture. It is of Louverture that Saint-Rémy would write, '[t]his man has proven by the heights of his intelligence, by his genius, that in giving the skin of human beings a black or white color, God had only wanted to diversify his work, and not to establish hierarchies and dependencies' (1850, viii). Saint-Rémy, in fact, reserves some of his most spirited criticism for people who were called 'mulattoes.' He calls the revolutionary André Vernet, who would eventually become secretary to Dessalines 'a mulatto with a weak and suspicious mind, two faults which seem irreconcilable; unmotivated, he only showed bravery through emulation [*il n'acquérait de bravoure que par l'émulation*]' (1850, 84). Saint-Rémy's portraits of the tragically faulted heroes of the Revolution, like his portraits of Louverture, Rigaud, Biassou, and Jean-Francois, do not extend to the 'mulâtre,' Julien Raimond, either, for according to our historian, Raimond was unfortunately stricken with a 'weak character' [*faiblesse de caractère*] (1850, 310). Moreover, in a footnote he added to Louverture's *Mémoires*, Saint-Rémy spoke briefly of 'a camp under the orders of a mulatto, Aignan, one of the most cruel men of whom we have retained memory' (1853, 53). Elsewhere in his footnotes to Louverture's *Mémoires*, Saint-Rémy says that Clerveaux, 'a mulatto' who was born in 'Marmelade in 1763,' was 'one of the traitors, who, on 16 *frimaire* in year 11 (December 6, 1793), delivered his city to the Spanish' (1853, 60). One of the most surprising stories that Saint-Rémy tells about a 'mulatto' comes in another footnote in the *Mémoires* where Saint-Rémy details the proposed purchase of Louverture by Jean-Baptiste Lapointe, a 'mulâtre' soldier who 'was in charge in l'Arachaye' in the aftermath of general emancipation in 1794. Saint-Rémy says that 'reliable witnesses [*témoignages honorable*]' recalled that Lapointe 'did not believe that liberty would endure' and these witnesses said therefore that Lapointe had offered to buy Louverture from the Comte de Bréda 'in order to raise his spirits' (1853, 90–91).

Throughout both his biography of Louverture and his introduction and edition of Louverture's memoirs, Saint-Rémy offers much praise for people he calls 'mulatto' or 'black' when he finds them worthy. My point is simply that this praise or scorn does not appear to have been doled out based on Saint-Rémy's ideas about a person's skin color or "race." A perfect example of this is when Saint-Rémy writes that under the rule of Louverture, 'General Dessalines [was] wiser and more moderate' than Christophe since 'he knew how to recognize courage wherever he saw it, [and] calmed vengeance, in taking under his protection all of the unfortunates. He knew that with civil unrest, the victors must have pity and clemency' (1850, 270). While Saint-Rémy was willing to praise Dessalines for his 'moderation' and 'clemency' towards Louverture's army, in a footnote in the *Mémoires*, he also calls Dessalines, 'the principal instrument of the cruelties of L'Ouverture' (1853, 99). We might say that far from a being a decided partisan, then, Saint-Rémy's driving hermeneutic, like that of many contributors to the narrative of "mulatto/a" vengeance, is actually ambivalence and uncertainty. These two characteristics cause him to offer a portrait of the Haitian Revolution and Louverture that might be called bravely nuanced or deeply disturbing depending upon what the reader wants to believe about the Haitian Revolution or the life of Louverture.

This sense of ambivalence is likely the result of the fact that much of Saint-Rémy's recitation of the events of the Haitian Revolution is reliant upon the work of Pamphile de Lacroix. Saint-Rémy's dependence on one of the most storied narrators of "mulatto/a" vengeance also leaves him open to narrating racism, just as Brown and Redpath's reliance on Beard (and Beard's reliance on the transatlantic print culture of the Haitian Revolution) left them open to expressing ideas of "racial" supremacy. In other words, the vocabulary Saint-Rémy used to describe the epistemological problems of the Haitian Revolution, problems that were most immediately symbolized for him (as they had been for Lacroix) by the life of Louverture would also be beholden to the same grammar of "monstrous hybridity" that we have seen in use throughout the literary history of the Haitian Revolution. To say that Saint-Rémy contributed to the "mulatto/a" vengeance narrative of the Haitian Revolution, particularly in his portrayal of Louverture as having vengeance *for* mulattoes, is qualitatively different than saying that he created a 'mulatto legend of history' designed to uphold 'mulatto' rule in post-independence Haiti.

If we now return to the quarrel with history that makes up the bulk of the claim that Saint-Rémy's bias towards "mulattoes" was *legendary*, it should now at the very least be questionable which works of the Haitian historian Beard, James, and then Nicholls were reading (if they fully read him at all). Despite the obvious influence of European histories and methodologies on his biography, in his *Pétion et Haïti*, Saint-Rémy actually credits four Haitian historians with having had the most influence on his own works. Saint-Rémy writes:

> As for my method, four writers, of whom I declare myself to be the tributary, four of the fathers of our national history, necessarily served as the benchmarks for me [*devait nécessairement me servir de jalons*], Toussaint L'Ouverture with his *Mémoires*, Boisrond-Tonnerrre with his own, M. Hérard Dumesle with his *Voyage dans le nord d'Hayti*, M. Ardouin with his *Géographie*. (19)

Saint-Rémy's praise for Boisrond-Tonnerre stands out in this pantheon of Haitian historians due to the fact that Saint-Rémy had sharply criticized the secretary of Dessalines both in the preface to Louverture's memoirs—where he wrote that Boisrond-Tonnerre tried to defame Louverture with 'with false and malignant claims' (1853, 23)—as well as in the preface to Boisrond-Tonnerre's *Mémoire pour servir à l'histoire d'Haïti*, where he had accused Boisrond-Tonnerre of having been 'more deadly than useful [*plus funeste que utile*]' (1851, vii). Saint-Rémy had even characterized Boisrond-Tonnerre as one of the *ancien libres* who had attached himself to Dessalines because 'he loved blood' and was 'vicious like him,' and, was furthermore, 'full of vanity, creepy,' and 'filled with treachery' (1851, x–xi). Nevertheless, Saint-Rémy said that despite Boisrond-Tonnerre's inaccuracies and venomous personality, he was still able to understand the cultural value of a work like his *Mémoire*. In his introduction to Boisrond-Tonnerre's memoirs, Saint-Rémy would call him, 'the first who thought to record the proceedings of the struggles we waged against the conqueror of Europe [Napoleon Bonaparte]' (1851, vii). This recognition of Boisrond-Tonnerre as a pioneer in Haitian historiography suggests that Saint-Rémy was capable of at least a little balance in his assessments of the work of people with whom he disagreed at the level of history, politics, and/or personality.

The Color of History

Another example of Saint-Rémy's often admirably balanced attempts to evaluate the works of his academic rivals comes in his writing about fellow Haitian historian Thomas Madiou. In *Vie de Toussaint-L'Ouverture*, Saint-Rémy heavily criticized Madiou:

> the entire book of M. Madiou is nothing but a web of erroneous facts and false judgments. This national writer, to whose patriotic efforts we must at least show sincere homage, was never in a position to provide a proper history; original documents having not been available to him [*n'a jamais été dans les conditions d'une bonne donnée historique; les documents originaux lui ont manqué*]. (1850, 18)[35]

Yet, in *Pétion et Haïti*, that same ambivalence to be found in Saint-Rémy's descriptions of Louverture, the driving force of his hermeneutic, would surface once again when Saint-Rémy acknowledged that Madiou's works, despite what he viewed as their profound methodological problems, had been useful to him:

> even the *Histoire d'Haïti* by M. Madiou was useful to me at times. Thus, Seneca, *the philosopher*, was right to say that we always learn something from a book no matter what it is; and it is true that thanks to the publication of three of Madiou's volumes, I was better able to think about certain events [*envisager certains événments*] and certain characters. (1854, 1:19)

Similarly, though Saint-Rémy did not mention Baron de Vastey in his gloss of Haitian historians who had influenced him, probably because he considered the latter to be 'one of the two flatterers of the monster [Christophe], who only doled out pompous praise for him in their writings in order to save their own lives [*deux courtisans du monstre, qui en font dans leurs écrits de pompeux éloges, pour mettre à l'abri leurs jours*]' (1854, 5:48), Saint-Rémy apparently thought that at least some of Vastey's historical ideas had merit. On at least a couple of occasions Saint-Rémy used Vastey's *Essai* as a source in *Vie de Toussaint-L'Ouverture* (407) and in *Pétion et Haïti* (5:154, 280).[36]

---

[35] Nicholls believes that we should see this criticism itself as part of the 'mulatto legend' of the past: 'It is against the background of Madiou's three-volume history that we must see the historical writings of Aléxis Beaubrun Ardouin and Joseph Saint-Rémy, who emerged as the principle vindicators of the traditional mulatto elite version of the Haitian past' (1979, 89).

[36] Strangely enough, in *Vie de Toussaint*, Saint-Rémy quotes from the English translation of Vastey's *Essai*, perhaps as a result of his exile in France, which is to say that Saint-Rémy may not have had access to the original French edition for one reason or another.

If Saint-Rémy's characterizations of people with light and dark skin up to this point have been utterly ambivalent, his nearly unqualified praise and admiration for Pétion appears hyperbolic and characterized by an almost total lack of ambivalence. Pétion is referred to in *Vie de Toussaint-L'Ouverture* as 'the most philanthropic man of his kind' (37), and in a footnote he added to Louverture's *Memoires*, Saint-Rémy similarly said of Pétion, 'No one was greater, before or after, in the annals of America' (125). Importantly, however, even though Saint-Rémy uses the vocabulary of pseudoscientific debates about "race" when he describes Pétion as a 'quadroon' (1854, 23), he continuously writes about the leader of the Southern Republic of Haiti as 'a man who belonged to the African race' (1854, 21). Along the same lines, in his various works, Saint-Rémy sometimes calls himself 'black' and sometimes refers to himself as a 'mulatto' or even more generically as a man of color. In his tribute to Lamartine, which appears in the introduction to his *Vie de Tousssaint-Louverture*, Saint-Rémy wrote of himself, 'Mulatto, I am accomplishing today a duty, in the name of my distant homeland, to thank Lamartine for having raised up and surrounded with a flood of his poetry the memory of the hero who made my race famous [*qui a illustré ma race*]' (viii). In his introduction to Boisrond-Tonnerre's *Mémoires*, though, Saint-Rémy said that he had a 'black face [*front nègre*]' (xxi). In still another instance, Saint-Rémy referred to himself as an 'homme de couleur,' using the language of colonial Saint-Domingue rather than that of independent Haiti. To add another contingency to Saint-Rémy's practices of self-identification, in praising Placide Louverture for remaining faithful to his father during the Leclerc expedition, Saint-Rémy referred to himself more in terms of his actual phenotype when he said that Louverture's son Placide 'wore the same skin as me' (1850, 390–91).

In spite of Saint-Rémy's mostly unnuanced portrait of Pétion—he refers to the former president of the Southern republic of Haiti as 'almost a God to his citizens' (1854, 12)—it is not clear to me why we should view Saint-Rémy's unending reverence for the former general turned president, no matter how strange, surprising, or incomprehensible it may seem to us today, as being any more about skin color or "race" than Baron de Vastey's similarly hyperbolic admiration for Henry Christophe. Vastey dedicated *Le Système colonial dévoilé* to the king of Haiti, writing:

> YOUR MAJESTY is the only Sovereign, the only black prince, indeed the only man of our color who can effectively raise his voice in order to make himself heard and plead before the Sovereigns of Europe and the Tribunals of the Nations, the cause of our Oppressed Brothers. Destined, by Divine Providence, to lend a final hand [*à porter la dernière main*] to the regeneration of the Haitian People and to place them within the ranks

of independent peoples; one of our first Founders of liberty, the most noble and the most ardent defender of the rights of man, it is YOUR MAJESTY; one of the first among Haitian heroes who brought down the axe of Slavery and of colonial Despotism, having forcefully contributed to its upheaval, it is YOUR MAJESTY who extracted the final roots. (1814a, iii–iv)

Boisrond-Tonnerre's own explicit admiration of Jean-Jacques Dessalines as the *real* revolutionary hero was filled with similar superlatives:

Haitians, for whom the courage of a hero has lifted forever the anathema of color prejudice, in reading these memoirs you will measure with your eyes the abyss from which he has saved you. And you, slaves of every country, you will learn by this great man that liberty is naturally in man's heart and that the keys to this [liberty] are in his hands. (95)

Moreover, if we really wanted to talk about the partisanship of a Saint-Rémy, a Vastey, or a Boisrond-Tonnerre, where would that leave us when considering the writing of Juste Chanlatte, secretary to Henry Christophe, in whose *Le Cri de la Nature* (1810) the name of Dessalines is not mentioned once?

To borrow the rhetorical questioning style of Saint-Rémy himself, then, is it because Vastey, Boisrond-Tonnerre, and Chanlatte, who were reported to be of very light skin, had admiration for men who reportedly had very dark skin, that we find their allegiances to be devoid of color prejudices? At the same time, is it because Saint-Rémy, who self-identified at times as a 'mulatto,' admired a man whom he sometimes identified as a 'mulatto' and other times as a 'quadroon' despite his 'black skin,' that we find this Haitian historian's admiration for a historical figure to be a matter of color or "race?" For, to arrive at the conclusion that Saint-Rémy praises "mulattoes" at the expense of "blacks," we need to read with the utmost postmodern cynicism. That is, we need to read with the belief that everything positive Saint-Rémy said as about "blackness" or "black" people was either disingenuous or a lie and, consequently, we need to dismiss or discount as not serious any criticism he offered of "mulattoes." We must now seriously ask, then, what kind of bias must a reader already have in mind in order to derive the idea that Saint-Rémy 'regarded Toussaint as the bête noir [*sic*]' of the Revolution— Saint-Rémy said of Louverture's memoir, 'I will praise the heavens if his work more than mine can lift up the race to which I belong in the eyes of the civilized world' (1853, 27)—or that Saint-Rémy, who barely mentions Ogé in his biography of Louverture, promoted a 'mulatto legend' that 'was, if anything, even less balanced in [its] discussion of the role of the *affranchis* in colonial Saint-Domingue than was Ardouin' (Nicholls, 1979, 96); and I think it would take the most selective of (mis)readings of them all to arrive at

C.L.R. James's utterly myopic conclusion that Saint-Rémy hated Louverture 'like poison.'

It is only by disavowing (dare I say, 'silencing') a great deal of what Saint-Rémy actually wrote, as opposed to what he has been accused of writing, that we can accept the hasty judgments of Beard, Redpath, James, and Nicholls. After all, we are talking about a man who directly addressed the idea that would be put forth by the French abolitionist Victor Schoelcher (1843, 2:228) and later by Nicholls, that "mulattoes" like him only wanted to see other "mulattoes" in power when he wrote, 'Why would I, a mulatto, want to be commanded and governed by a mulatto, if I have a negro, an uncle,[37] indeed who is more capable of bringing about the happiness and the glory of my country?' (1850, 245–46).

The cynical reader who is determined to find something to condemn in Saint-Rémy might better focus on the fact that he believed, much like Beard, Redpath, Brown, James, and Nicholls, that even if owing primarily to their skin color rather than to their "races," there were categories of people in the world who could be broadly described as "white," "mulatto," or "black." In other words, Saint-Rémy's problem might not be that he loved "mulattoes" and hated "blacks," but that he believed that there were "mulattoes" and "blacks" in the first place. Even so, at the risk of sounding like an apologist, I would like to state after Kwame Anthony Appiah that 'Racialism is not, in itself, a doctrine that must be dangerous, even if the racial essence is thought to entail moral and intellectual dispositions.' This is true, Appiah says, only so long as 'positive moral qualities are distributed across the races' (1990, 5). Thus, even though I, too, believe that, 'unlike most Western educated people,' 'racialism is false,' the racialism of Saint-Rémy does not make of "racial" or phenotypical differences a 'moral' problem (Appiah, 1990, 5). With Saint-Rémy, the problem stops at the recognition of difference and the assignation of that difference to a broad category of identity and does not devolve into either hierarchical or negative essentialist thinking. That is to say that for Saint-Rémy skin color could serve very well as an organizing principle, at the very least for the purposes of generally classifying different phenotypes or referring to family genealogies, but it did not lead him down the path of the racism of "racial" supremacy, as it did for Beard, Redpath, and even Brown. Much to the contrary, Saint-Rémy remained throughout his life a passionate detractor of all ideas of "racial" superiority, which is to say that while he may have pointed out difference (such as saying that

---

37 In a footnote after his usage of the words 'un *oncle*,' Saint-Rémy explains, 'this expression is a mark of deference accorded in Haiti by mulattoes to black men [*Cette expression est une marque de déférence accordée en Haïti par les mulâtres aux hommes noirs*]' (1850, 245).

"mulattoes" were people who generally looked a certain way or had certain genealogical claims to people described as "white"), he does not make statements defining *essential* personality, intellectual, political, or physiological traits (beyond the color of their skin) of the people whom he identifies as "mulatto" or "black." As we shall see in the next chapter, Schoelcher's racialist arguments about 'l'imagination jaune' or the 'yellow imagination' of Boyer-era Haitian writers, much to the contrary, fall into the category of what Appiah calls 'extrinsic racism' because, unlike Saint-Rémy, Schoelcher believes that a person's 'color' 'entails certain morally relevant qualities' that explain, if not '*warrant*,' the 'differential treatment' (Appiah, 1990, 5) they continuously receive.

CHAPTER ELEVEN

Victor Schoelcher, 'L'imagination Jaune,' and the Francophone Genealogy of the 'Mulatto Legend of History'

'La révolution de Saint-Domingue semble n'avoir effrayé personne. Il existe en France des colons qui croient toujours pouvoir recouvrer leurs biens dans cette île. Les journaux font même circuler en ce moment le bruit d'un projet de conquête et de recouvrement.'

—Mme Gabrielle de P****, *Le Nègre et la Créole ou Mémoires d'Eulalies D**** (1825)

'Thy coming fame, Ogé! is sure!/Thy name with that of L'Ouverture.'

—George B. Vashon, 'Vincent Ogé' (1854)

'… personne ne songeait à se demander si la nuance de l'héroïsme est noire, blanche ou jaune, pas plus que si *les organes qui le servent*, quand il excite notre admiration, justifient tel système d'anthropologie plutôt que tel autre.'

—Pierre Faubert, *Ogé, ou le préjugé de couleur* (1856)

While Beard, Brown, and Redpath may have all, in their own ways, ensured the transatlantic circulation of the trope we have come to recognize as the "colored historian," continuing to trace the genealogical relationship of this nineteenth-century trope to the 'mulatto legend of history' and, specifically, to the part of Nicholls's claim that involves discussing how 'mulatto histories' were *legendary* because they could 'explain and justify the predominant position of the mulatto elite' (1979, 86), leads us to the world of the French abolitionist, Victor Schoelcher. Like the Anglophone abolitionists studied in the previous chapter, Schoelcher was one of the most visible contributors to the literary history of the Haitian Revolution in the nineteenth-century Atlantic World. Through his discussions of Haiti in his *Colonies étrangères et Haïti* (1843), Schoelcher would play an enormously prominent role in the dissemination of the trope of the "colored historian." In fact, Schoelcher was probably the first of the nineteenth-century contributors to the literary history of the Haitian Revolution to suggest that Boyer-era Haitian writers had created a *legendary* history designed to legitimate their *own* rule. If you recall, Nicholls had defined the histories created by Ardouin and Saint-Rémy as *legendary* because this 'version of the past,' he said, had been presented for its 'exemplary value' in the present. Nicholls explained that the 'mulatto histories' of Ardouin and Saint-Rémy could be called *legendary* precisely because, 'The past is being used as a weapon in the present' (1979, 86). As we are about to see, however, the great majority of the constitutive claims concerning the 'mulatto legend of history' in Nicholls's *From Dessalines to Duvalier* are nearly identical to the claims made by Schoelcher with respect to what the latter called 'l'imagination jaune.' Indeed, Nicholls's entire theory of the 'mulatto legend' appears to have been directly influenced by (if not directly copied from) the work of Schoelcher. The problem with finding the roots of the trope of the "colored historian" in the works of Schoelcher is that, even though Schoelcher presented himself as a 'friend to the blacks,' his writing about "race" in Haiti was, particularly where "mulattoes" are concerned, every bit as vexed as that of Beard, Redpath, and Brown. That is to say that Schoelcher's writings were not unencumbered by his own color prejudices, a form of hierarchical thinking that helped to cover up his own personal role, however inadvertent, in the "racial" problems he was describing.

Schoelcher had briefly traveled to Haiti in the 1840s in order to observe the effects of emancipation. He would write up his impressions of the current state of the country in the second volume of a controversial work entitled *Colonies étrangères et Haïti* (1843). In this travelogue/history, Schoelcher described the aim of his desire to visit Haiti using the following self-reflexive rhetorical questions: 'Will I find [in Haiti] what I have just been told in many contexts in the French colonies: disorder and barbarity? Will the Haitians provide the proof for those who say that they are uncivilizable?' 'Their condition,' he asked, 'will it be able to shake my faith in the perfectibility of the human races? This island, where emancipation had its most terrible and its most beautiful triumphs, what will it tell me?' (2:171). With these questions at hand, Schoelcher sought to paint himself as an innocent and objective explorer who, possessed with the abolitionist's singularly unprejudiced 'faith' in humankind, was merely out on a quest to discover, by visiting Haiti, the *truth* about 'the perfectibility of the human races.'

While Schoelcher may have thought of his project as relatively harmless, in his often discussed and much disputed[1] writing on mid-nineteenth-

---

[1] Cyrille Bissette, the Martinican abolitionist and editor of the radical anti-colonial

century Haiti's political problems, especially in an infamous chapter entitled 'La faction jaune,' Schoelcher would make his own contribution to the problematic brand of racialism we have previously identified in the works of Beard, Redpath, and Brown. For example, Schoelcher depicted many of Haiti's most prominent writers of the 1840s, including Emile Nau, Beaubrun Ardouin, Pierre Faubert, and Hérard Dumesle, as having in their own ways contributed to a 'mulatto' desire to 'intellectually assassinate the black race' (2:239). In Schoelcher's estimation, these proponents of 'the yellow imagination' had sought to all but remove 'black' revolutionary leaders like Toussaint Louverture from the Haitian Revolution's pantheon of heroes. This was a political move, Schoelcher said, whose aim was to legitimate the despotic and sanguinary rule, first, of Pétion, then, of Boyer (2:239):

> The care that has been taken to diminish the role of the black men and to establish, despite the truth, the yellow men as the principal leaders of the insurrection, tends to lend a kind of merited legitimacy to having a preponderance [in the government] of these people here over those people there, and this perfidious method has only had too much success in the midst of a people who know nothing [*au milieu d'un peuple qui ne sait rien*]. In all of the countries in the world, it is in Haiti that Toussaint Louverture is the least honored!! (2:226)

To say nothing of the hierarchical thinking expressed in Schoelcher's claim that Haitians are 'a people who know nothing,' going on to describe in great detail the primary features of this colorful history that had been propagated by the 'yellow men' in the 'interest of caste' (2:225), Schoelcher explains that in putatively ignoring the historical contributions of Louverture, 'The mulattoes who could not defeat him, they, whom he overpowered and humiliated, they with whom he was forced to sever ties, because they were defiantly revolting against the authority of *an old negro*, have very unfortunately succeeded in tarnishing his reputation in his own country' (2:226). Instead of Louverture, Schoelcher said,

---

journal *La Revue des colonies* (1834–42), was one of the loudest and most ardent critics of the work of Schoelcher. In his *Réfutation du Livre de M.V. Schoelcher Sur Haïti* (1844), Bissette accused Schoelcher of 'denaturing history' so as to 'transform every idea that we had about Haiti up until this day' (3). Bissette was not the only journalist to take issue with Schoelcher's characterization of Haiti as a land of color prejudice. Writers from *Le Courrier de la Martinique* were also avowed opponents of Schoelcher's work, and specifically of his writings about both Haiti and Martinique. The newspaper's longstanding feud with the French abolitionist is documented at length in Charles Gaumont's *Abrégé des calomnies du Courrier de la Martinique contre M.V. Schœlcher* (1850). For two different interpretations of the war of words between Bissette and Schoelcher, see Bongie (1998, 279) and Brickhouse (2004, 91).

Francophone Genealogy of the 'Mulatto Legend of History'

> Ogé and Chavannes have become, under the reigning faction, the greatest celebrities of the country; their names are on everyone's tongue, and from one end of the republic to the other the deliverance is never mentioned without first naming Ogé and Chavannes. Hidalgo and Allende, the two heroes of Mexican independence, have not been more celebrated ... than Ogé and Chavannes in Haiti. (2:219)

'As for Pétion,' Schoelcher adds, 'whom all the mixed-bloods, regardless of the party to which they belong, agree is the Haitian *par excellence*, there is certainly in this judgment a whole lot of predilection of color' (2:228). Moreover, Schoelcher says that the kind of history encouraged by Boyer's 'yellow' historians, who would make of Pétion *'the founder of liberty'* (2:226) rather than Dessalines, had been promoted, first, to cover up the fact that 'It has only been too true for a long time that the men of color rejected any solidarity with the slaves' (2:225); and second, to legitimate post-independence 'mulatto' rule over the 'black' population since the death of Christophe. In Schoelcher's mind, the actual populace of Haiti had always been mostly 'black' rather than 'yellow,' 'but it is the people of color who are in power, hence their glorification to the detriment of the others' (2:235).[2]

Yet, just as Nicholls was forced to clarify that there was not one 'mulatto' political party in the Boyer era, but at least two, Schoelcher was also forced to acknowledge that under Boyer's rule, 'the yellow faction' had actually been divided. The division, according to Schoelcher, was between an older generation aligned with Boyer, which included Ardouin, and a younger generation that was a part of the opposition to Boyer's rule, which included Nau and Dumesle. Schoelcher read this intra-caste division as partially manifested in the willingness, or not, of Haiti's early historians to recognize at least some merit in the idea of offering Louverture as one of Haiti's revolutionary heroes. Schoelcher sourced what he interpreted as Ardouin's characterization of Louverture as an 'inept executioner' [*inepte bourreau*] who was merely the tool of the 'white' colonists (2:226–28) to the fact that Ardouin was 'the writer of the ruling faction.' On the other side of the 'mulatto' aisle, 'M. Emile Nau, who belongs to the young generation,' Schoelcher said, and 'who counts among his enemies the government of M.B. Ardouin, does not have the bad faith to make of Toussaint a tool of the Creoles' (2:227). Other opponents of Boyer's government, like Hérard Dumesle, Schoelcher said, also 'knew how to show [Louverture] some justice' (2:228).

---

2 Schoelcher supported this belief with the following statistic: 'The population of this country is unfortunately composed of two very distinct classes: the people of color, who have about 60–100,000 people; [and] the negroes, who have about 5 or 600,000' (1843, 2:235).

It should now be immediately apparent to the attentive student of Nicholls's *From Dessalines to Duvalier* that the 'mulatto legend of history' owes its direct genealogy, if not its entire argumentative framework, to Schoelcher's *Colonies étrangères*. This is a problem since Schoelcher's discussion of "racial" or "color" divisions in Haiti revels in the same kinds of hierarchical thinking, a distinct feature of all theories of "white" supremacy, that we found in the works of Gobineau, Bonneau, and Fitzhugh. In this French abolitionist's version, however, the target of derision and disgust would be the "mulatto" rather than the "negro."

Chris Bongie has acknowledged Schoelcher's 'anti-mulatto prejudice,' which he says, 'affects the choice and interpretation of the textual sources through which Schoelcher filters Haitian history and supplements the account of his own experiences there' (1998, 281). However, Bongie tends to downplay and even affirm the most problematic consequence of these prejudices when he writes that 'in drawing attention to the distortions involved in the production of what David Nicholls has referred to as the "mulatto legend" that, along with its noiriste mirror-image, dominated nineteenth-century Haitian politics and culture, Schoelcher is on extremely solid ground' (284). As we will see, it is not possible to separate the insupportable 'anti-mulatto prejudice' of Schoelcher from the tropology of the 'mulatto legend of history,' since believing that historians who share the *same* skin color or "race" might also, by virtue of their skin color or "race," share the same attitudes or politics necessarily implies that one has adopted certain tenants of racialism. As Ariela J. Gross has written, 'black people cannot simply be people with a "shared history", because you need biology or morphology to define the group who "share" the history' (183, ftn. 315). Similarly, "mulattoes" cannot be people with a shared politics any more than they could be described as people with a "shared" vision of history without, in essence, reverting to ideas consonant with the pseudo-science of "race."

Not only does Schoelcher repeat the precise language of the pseudo-science of "race," with all its hierarchies understood, that had justified the implementation of chattel slavery, but his general theory about 'the yellow faction,' which he had to constantly revise to include *yellow factions*, in the plural, was so often qualified and equivocal that it reveals itself to have been based upon a cynical practice of constant (mis)readings. At least, this was the charge of the Martinican abolitionist Cyrille Bissette, who had called Schoelcher's virtual obsession with defaming 'mulattoes' an 'idée fixe' that Schoelcher had used to argue that 'everywhere the *yellow faction* oppresses the blacks' (1844, 7). In his *Réfutation du livre de M.V. Schoelcher sur Haïti* (1844), Bissette forcefully documented a regular litany of Schoelcher's misreadings of history and "race." For Bissette, these misreadings included Schoelcher's improper designation of certain Haitian revolutionaries like Fabre Geffrard,

Francophone Genealogy of the 'Mulatto Legend of History'

Etienne Magny, and Jean-Baptiste Riché as 'mulattoes' when they were really 'blacks' (8–10), which Bissette argued caused Schoelcher to 'draw false conclusions' about their behavior (9). Bissette also said that Schoelcher's history of the Haitian Revolution contained frequent errors in dating various key events (15), and that Schoelcher was guilty of having suppressed certain facts that did not fit the picture of "mulatto/a" vengeance he sought to paint. Bissette observed, for example, that in his condemnation of the execution of the Haitian journalist Félix Darfour, whose voice Schoelcher said had been silenced not only because he spoke out against Boyer but because he was an 'African' (1843, 182–83), Schoelcher conveniently forgot to mention that 'the citizens Laborde, Béranger, Saint-Laurent, and Saint-Martin [who were also executed] were mulattoes.' This fact alone allowed Bissette to conclude that 'it is not the issue of caste that divides Haitians in all of their undertakings, but rather the issue of political parties, regardless of color, because these parties are always equally composed of blacks and mulattoes on both sides' (1844, 15).

It is Schoelcher's description of the unfortunate Riché (Jean-Baptiste Richet),[3] whom the French abolitionist had, in Bissette's eyes, wrongly painted as a 'mulatto,'[4] and whom Schoelcher had accused (apparently falsely) of having killed his own 'mulatto' wife and children out of pure vengeance during the Haitian Revolution (Bissette, 12), which represents Bissette's strongest argument for the idea that Schoelcher had sought to use "race" or skin color as the explanatory linchpin for everything. Bissette recounts how Schoelcher's claim that Riché/Richet's 'mulatto' treachery was so horrific that he had killed his own 'mulatto' wife and children took on a *legendary* status of its own since, 'It seems as though several newspapers from the United States have taken M. Schoelcher's book seriously, like the newspapers of Paris. One of these leaflets, having provided a review of the book, repeated the infamous act attributed to Riché' (Bissette, 13; see also Schoelcher, 1843, 153; Richet, 'Le général Jean-Baptiste Richet,' 1843, 3). As Bissette would go on to acknowledge, Riché/Richet had refuted this very charge in a letter to the Haitian newspaper *Le Manifeste* (1841–44) on September 24, 1843. Riché/Richet wrote, 'I read a work in which was attributed to me the terrible crime of having killed my wife and my children':

---

3 In a letter to *Le Manifeste*, 'Riché' signed his name Richet ('Le Général Jean-Baptiste Richet au rédacteur du *Manifeste*,' 3). Richet would become Haitian president after a brief and successful *coup d'état* unseated Jean-Louis Pierrot. He would only rule for a few months, however, dying suddenly on February 27, 1847. Soulouque assumed power in Haiti after Richet's death (MacLeod, 37–38).

4 To the chorus of amateur "racial" taxonomers who would try to determine the precise skin color or "race" of Riché (Richet), Beard adds, 'Riché was what is called a griffe—that is, though he had white blood in his veins, he was, in appearance, in no way distinguished from a black' (315).

I must protest against this abominable lie, no, no, I have not ever committed a crime so terrible; I would not have been able to survive it. I know that General *Charles Charlot* had been accused of committing that crime in Limbé ... I was married in 1809, and I have had the good fortune up until now, to still have a wife who is alive and who is enjoying, at this very moment, perfect health in Cap [Haïten]. (qtd. in Bissette, 13; see also, Richet, 3)[5]

In his memoirs, originally published in 1843, Joseph Balthazar Inginac, a former general of the Haitian Revolution and Secretary of State under Boyer, also denied that 'Riché' had committed such a crime. Inginac said, 'General Charles Charlot,' had 'put to death a young woman of color with whom he was living and their two children, which has been attributed to General Riché' (53). It was primarily errors of identification like this one, then, that led Bissette to conclude of Schoelcher's 'history' that it was composed of mere *'stories, tales, puff pieces [puffs], and fiddlesticks'* (54).

Even though in reading the above passages, Bongie has criticized Bissette for 'reinscribing the absurd colonial distinctions that ought to have no place in post-colonial Haiti' (1998, 283), I think Bissette was actually being much more consciously ironic than Bongie is giving him credit. That Schoelcher did not 'know how to distinguish what is yellow from what is black' (qtd. in Bongie, 1998, 283; see also, Bissette, 112), was probably a useful and effective point of focus for someone like Bissette, who sought to dismantle the French abolitionist's dichotomized "racial" theory of Haitian political divisions, especially since the French Atlantic world to which Bissette's writings were addressed was one that for the most part took such binaries to be unquestionably *true*. Proving that Schoelcher had made "mulattoes" out of people who were not generally considered to be so in order that he might more easily defame them, rather than providing some sort of surprising evidence that Bissette also believed in "race" (it would have been more surprising if he had not), quite effectively makes the case that these 'errors' reveal an intentional 'malice' on the part of Schoelcher, whose 'calculation[s], in as much as they were errors served his *idée fixe* and the prejudices of the colonists' (Bissette, 7).[6] In other words, what is much more important for our purposes than whether or not the people in question were *really* "mulattoes" or "blacks" is the fact that Bissette's critique goes a long way towards proving that Schoelcher's entire theory was based on an *a priori* idea about "mulattoes"

---

5 According to Madiou, both 'Jean-Baptiste Riché and Charles Charlot were noteworthy for their cruelties' (5:153).

6 In his *Abrégé des calomnies du Courrier de la Martinique contre M.V. Schœlcher* (1850), Gaumont contested the idea that Schoelcher universally presented 'mulattoes' in a negative light (15).

as evil and degraded, an idea that helps to explain how and why the term "mulatto" has become a wholly pejorative means to convey much more about a person's psychology and behavior than his or her phenotype.[7]

The patient reader of *Tropics of Haiti* will not fail to notice that Schoelcher's derogatory opinions about Haitians he considered to be 'mulatto' or 'yellow' resembles the vast corpus of writing about colonial and revolutionary Saint-Domingue that has been under examination here and that was unfailingly populated with images of "monstrous hybrids," "tropical temptresses," and "tragic mulattoes." Schoelcher's co-optation of this widely accepted "racial" grammar to describe post-independence Haiti is precisely that which allowed him to write with such authority about the "color" of Haitian revolutionary history. Borrowing the omniscient language of naturalist travel writers, in using what Mary Louise Pratt has called the voice of 'the monarch-of-all-I-survey' (201), helped lend a kind of authority to Schoelcher's writing, without requiring him to provide the sort of evidence valued in the tradition of modern historiography. As we are about to see, neither Schoelcher nor Nicholls after him offer any convincing proof that the names of 'Ogé and Chavannes' were being celebrated throughout nineteenth-century Haiti to the detriment of Louverture and Dessalines. While Schoelcher might have been able to isolate certain instances in which Ogé and Chavannes were mentioned with celebration in Haiti, none of his *evidence* comes anywhere close to proving that such celebrations were *legendary* or even common among nineteenth-century Haitian historians, and especially not in the works of Ardouin or Saint-Rémy. Schoelcher, in fact, can only name two Haitian writers, Ardouin and Pierre Faubert, in connection to his assertion that the 'mulattoes' of Haiti sought to 'offer Ogé as the *first martyr of independence*' (2:226). Yet Schoelcher actually presents very little evidence that could support the claim that Ardouin believed Ogé to be the 'first martyr of Haitian independence,' and what evidence he produces to support this same accusation against Faubert is the direct result of what I will show in the final section of this chapter to have been a form of cynical (mis)reading.

---

7 See, for example, Rubens François Titus's decidedly non-scholarly *Roadmap to Haiti's Next Revolution: A Plan for Diaspora Haitians to Contribute to a Peaceful Turnaround Universe* (2012) in which the telecommunications executive states, 'Let us define a Haitian mulatto. The term "mulatto" in my definition does not relate to the skin complexion of a racially mixed individual, nor does it compare with the official use of the term during French colonial times … Haitian mulattoes may or may not be of a mixed breed; they are self-conscious of their own privileged status in Haitian society and, worst of all, are willing to take the necessary social and political actions to protect the aforementioned privilege at all costs while blocking any type of equal access to literary education to the rest of the Haitian population' (12).

Somewhat paradoxically, it is probably the fact Schoelcher's work is replete with the kinds of ambivalence, contradiction, and misreadings that are germane to the colonial archive that his account could have been accepted so authoritatively by Nicholls. For, the only proofs Nicholls provides for his similar claims against Saint-Rémy and Ardouin come in the form of four historical documents, all of which remain of dubious relevance to the claim at hand, which is that celebration of Ogé and Chavannes had become *legendary* in mid-nineteenth-century Haitian history.[8] It is in the fissure

---

8 Although Nicholls repeatedly describes Ardouin and Saint-Rémy as the 'principal exponents of the mulatto legend' (1979, 90), there is very little in the published works of either man that suggests, as he claims, that these Haitian historians believed that the '*affranchis*' had been the 'true pioneers of liberation and independence' (1979, 95). In fact, when I followed the footnotes that were linked to this *particular* claim, I found only four sources cited and none that had anything to do with either Saint-Rémy or Ardouin. The first text is the previously mentioned *Manifeste de Praslin* of September 1842. The *Manifeste* was the document that had laid the groundwork for the institution of the eventual 'provisory government' of Charles Hérard, which took effect after the Revolution of 1843 had unseated Boyer. Nicholls interpreted this manifesto as having omitted Louverture, Christophe, and Dessalines from among the heroes of Haitian independence in favor of Ogé and Chavannes, and he therefore saw the document as providing evidence for the *legendary* status of the "mulatto" version of history. Even if we do read this document as slighting "black" revolutionary heroes, it hardly follows that the works of Saint-Rémy and Ardouin, who had nothing to do with the publication of the *Manifeste*, were a part of a larger "mulatto" history. The second piece of evidence used by Nicholls in support of the idea that the "mulatto" version of history was 'legendary' is F.E. Dubois's *Précis historique de la revolution de 1843* (1866), a text that is as pithy as it is minor when compared to the lengthy and richly documented works of Madiou, Saint-Rémy, Ardouin, and Vastey. Nicholls focuses on the fact that in Dubois's *Précis*, at one particular political event, 'toasts were drunk "in memory of Ogé and Chavannes, these first martyrs of liberty", but no mention was made of the black leaders' (Nicholls, 1979, 96; see also F.E. Dubois, 1866, 46). The problem with producing this document as evidence for a *legendary* history of Haiti is that the 'toasts' referenced by Nicholls were made by individuals, as Nicholls acknowledges, and not by the Haitian collectivity (for example, this was not a refrain chanted in a parade of thousands or even hundreds of people). More importantly, Ardouin and Saint-Rémy do not seem to have been present and are not mentioned anywhere in the work. The third document that Nicholls cites, Emile Nau's *Réclamation par les affranchis des droits civiles et politiques: Ogé et Chavannes* (1846), is similarly offered by Nicholls as proof of a *legendary* history. While Nicholls does not directly quote from this document, his reference does point us to page 46, where we find a phrase about Ogé and Chavannes having been 'the first defenders of our rights and our first liberators' who had a 'superior spirit than ours' (45–46). The problem is that this statement is entirely out of context here. The aptly named historical text of Nau (a text that is hardly well known today and was rarely referenced in the historiography of the nineteenth-century Atlantic World), offers to present the history of Ogé and Chavannes as merely men who with non-violent goals

between what had been claimed and what could ultimately be proven on the basis of *empirical* evidence that the *commonsense* narrative of "mulatto/a" vengeance emerges as what "colored" Schoelcher's own vision of Haiti. The *truths* about "mulatto" motivations, attitudes, and politics carried within the narrative of "mulatto/a" vengeance itself, having an authority that had been ardently contrived across two centuries of discourse, filled the lacunae between history and interpretation. As we are about to glimpse, this is true not only of the argument that Ogé had become a *legendary* 'martyr' for Haitian independence in the nineteenth century, but is also particularly true of Schoelcher's attempt to make any criticism of Toussaint Louverture by Haitians proof of the powers of the *legendary* 'yellow imagination.'

*

In evaluating the claim for the supposedly 'legendary' status of Ardouin's "mulatto" history, it seems to me that it is to his 1832 *Géographie d'Haïti* that we should look. This is first because at the time of the publication of Schoelcher's *Colonies étrangères*, Ardouin had not yet published any of the eleven volumes of his *Etudes*; and second, because it is Ardouin's geography, with its pithy 50-page history of the country, rather than the voluminous *Etudes*, that would become the standard geography textbook throughout nineteenth-century Haiti (see Redpath, 1861, 25; D. Ramsay, 1881). In the *Géographie*, while Ardouin's praise for Pétion for having, 'showed every concern for the happiness of his country,' does stand in sharp contrast to

in mind sought to force the recognition of their rights as citizens of France, rights they viewed as having been recognized by the revised decree of March 28, hardly an original claim. The final document cited by Nicholls, with respect to the legendary status of free people of color like Ogé and Chavannes, is H.A. Brouard's 'Histoire: Affaire du Fonds Parisien,' published in two installments in the Haitian newspaper *L'Union* on August 24 and 31, 1837. In the first installment, Brouard claims that the 'movement of 92' in Saint-Domingue 'was preceded by the affair of Fonds parisien,' in addition to that of the 'unfortunate Chavannes and Ogé.' Going on to say that his brief history will only concern the first of these events, Brouard writes, 'the memory of this affair has been religiously conserved among the families who were the actors and victims, and it is from them that we culled everything' ('Histoire,' 24 August 1837, 2). It is unclear to me exactly what Nicholls took issue with in this portrayal since Brouard very clearly represents these free men of color as having in mind the goal of achieving liberty and equality for the free people only and not for slaves. Furthermore, nowhere in the story does Brouard present these men as the true founders of independence or as having had anything to do with sparking slave insurrection. Instead, he suggests that this event contributed to the general feeling of unrest, dissatisfaction, and rebellion that had been brewing in the colony for years. Madiou's portrayal of this affair is practically identical to Brouard's (Madiou, 1:65–67).

his portrayal of Henry Christophe as 'savage' and having created a 'bloody throne' (26), it does not follow that he bolsters the importance of Ogé over that of Louverture. Nor does it follow that Ardouin 'presents Alexandre Pétion as the *founder of Haitian liberty*' (Schoelcher, 1843, 2:226). On the contrary, Ardouin pretty quickly passes over the history of Ogé, 'that courageous citizen,' with relatively little commentary. In what commentary he does offer, Ardouin merely acknowledges that Ogé had demanded that the French colonists respect the rights ostensibly granted to the free people of color (because they were property owners) by an article adopted by the National Assembly on March 28. Ardouin subsequently recounts in the space of two paragraphs the brief revolt, escape, extradition, and execution of Ogé and his accomplices, referring to their punishments as simply 'those atrocious murders' (14). This is all to say that it is a struggle to find the idea that Ogé was one of the first martyrs of independence rather than a victim of revolutionary political fervor in one of the standard textbooks of Ardouin's day. Even if we were to find such a claim there, the idea that Ogé's revolt and punishment were connected in some way to the independence of Haiti would hardly have been the product of a 'yellow imagination.'

The idea that the brief insurrection led by Ogé was intimately linked to the formal start of the slave rebellion in August of 1791 was the almost universally uniform opinion of the French colonists. Not only had the colonists Gros and Mahy de Cormeré made this argument (see the introduction to this volume), but a work signed by the colonist known as Chôtard *aîné* entitled *Précis de la révolution de Saint-Domingue: depuis la fin de 1789, jusqu'au 18 juin 1794* (1795) insinuated that Ogé had intended to occasion more than simply 'rights for his class' since, according to Chôtard, Ogé 'had his eye on the throne itself' and wanted his 'insurrection' to be 'embrace[d] by the entire colony' (51). The French colonial government, understanding this very well, according to Chôtard (who clearly disapproved), sought to 'envelop the testimony of Ogé' in the utmost 'secrecy.' Chôtard writes, 'The government felt that the publication of this document would have raised the entire colony [*soulevé la colonie entière*]' (52). In addition, the anonymous author of the *Histoire des désastres de Saint-Domingue* (1795), whom Jean-Charles Benzaken has recently revealed was actually the Citoyen Laplace (262), much more clearly and unequivocally blamed Ogé. A footnote that appears after the author's mention of Ogé as a 'Creole quadroon' who was dissatisfied with the colony and therefore sought to occasion an insurrection reads, 'French men! here is the real source of all the misfortunes of Saint-Domingue' (161). This same anonymous author did not just connect the revolt of Ogé to the general insurrection of Saint-Domingue, but also linked Ogé's punishment to the devastation of the colony, as well as to genocidal imaginings. Laplace writes, 'It seems that the northern section alone had been devoted to total extermination ... in order to avenge the soul of Ogé [*les mânes*] and expiate the horrible punishment the leader had undergone' (201). In an anonymous work published the next year, *Réflexions sur la colonie de Saint-Domingue* (1796), which drew heavily on the *Histoire* cited above and whose front matter mentioned that it had been penned by the same hand, the author elaborates on what he viewed as Ogé's connection to the general insurrection of Saint-Domingue, saying that 'the unfortunate Ogé' was the most 'fanatical' of the 'protégés' of Brissot, Grégoire, and Raimond, who sought to bring the revolution from France to the colony. For this author, the result of Ogé's efforts and his subsequent punishment had led to the 'simultaneous raising of the slaves and the men of color in the northern section, the richest, the most populated, and the most flourishing' (1:101-102).

The letters of the Marquise de Rouvray to her daughter, the Comtesse de Lostanges, spanning from 1791 to 1796, and collected in *Une Correspondance familale au temps des troubles de Saint-Domingue*, stand as particularly relevant examples of the tendency of the French colonists to blame the so-called "*affranchis*" for the general insurrection of the colony. In a letter dated August 13, 1793, de Rouvray blames the Haitian Revolution not on Ogé, but on another free person of color, Julien Raimond, of whom she asks, 'What are we going to do with that scoundrel Raimond, the mulatto or quadroon who brought with him back from France the terrible Revolution of Saint-Domingue? Will he escape the reprisal that his crimes merit?' (1959, 105). In 1802, Barré de Saint-Venant also imputed the start of the Revolution to 'Raymond' (vi). Venault de Charmilly, in his *Lettre à M. Bryan Edwards ... en refutation de son ouvrage, intitulé Vue Historiques de Saint-Domingue* (1797), blamed both the 'mulattoes' and 'Nègres creoles' (13–14, 50); while in *De l'utilité des colonies* (1814), the colonist Mazères referred to the 'mulattoes' as the primary motor of the insurrection: 'There is essentially no doubt about the origin of the misfortunes of Saint-Domingue. The black population was the instrument, the mulattoes the instigators ...' (79). As some contemporary historians have argued, before, during, and after his trial, many of the French colonists of Saint-Domingue would much more formally accuse Ogé and other free people of color of having wished to raise the slaves in order to discredit the claims of the landed free people of color for civil equality (Garrigus, 2010, 35–37).

Early nineteenth-century British memoirists like Bryan Edwards and Marcus Rainsford were also under the impression that the "mulattoes" and other free people of color had desired to instigate a slave rebellion. Both, in their respective works, reprinted a document that had been published in Philadelphia in 1793, and which U.S. refugees from Saint-Domingue had mistakenly identified as Vincent Ogé's confession (Garrigus, 2010, 22).[9] The document that Edwards and Rainsford refer to as the *'Testament de Mort d'Ogé'* (Edwards, 1793–1801, 4:205; Rainsford, 1805, 383–86) had actually been written by Vincent Ogé's brother, Jacques. The 'testament' contained not only a confession signed by Ogé's brother, but a detailed summary of his entire interrogation by French officials. Part of that interrogation had to do with the behavior of Jacques Lucas, one of the free people of color who had been identified as having participated in the 1790 revolt. The minutes of the interrogation reveal that, according to Jacques Ogé, 'Lucas had a plan to raise the negro slaves against the whites, and to slit the throats of the latter with the former; that is the proposition that he made to Vincent Ogé, brother of he who is accused.' Jacques Ogé told the French colonial officials that he and his brother had been opposed to such a 'horrible and cannibal crime.' Nevertheless, Lucas and some of his followers had tried to arouse the slaves, and upon their arrest, they 'declared in court that it was him, the accused, who had such a design' and 'said prisoners took him, the accused, for said Lucas' (rpt. in Rainsford, 1805, 389).

The fact that Lucas was not executed while Chavannes and both Ogé brothers were, tells us, I think, at least a little something about whose side of the argument the French colonial officials believed. That French officials had wanted to believe (or at least had wanted to make others believe) that Ogé sought to either inspire or directly bring about a slave rebellion was also the conclusion drawn by Edwards. Edwards also believed that the 'testament' constituted Vincent Ogé's confession, and he wrote that the document 'detail[ed] at large the measures which the coloured people had fallen upon to excite the negroes slaves to rise into rebellion.' According to Edwards, it was Vincent Ogé who 'declares that the ringleaders still maintained the same atrocious project, and held their meetings in certain subterranean passages, or caves, in the parish of La Grande Riviere, to which he offers, if his life might be spared, to conduct a body of troops so that the conspirators might be secured' (1793–1801, 52).

Later nineteenth-century historians like Lacroix, whose history of Haiti was published in 1819, and, it bears repeating, had an almost unmatched influence on the development of the transatlantic print culture of the Haitian Revolution, also connected the punishment of Ogé to the subsequent Revolution. Lacroix writes, 'The execution of Ogé and his companions separated once and for all the class of *mixed-bloods* from that of the Creoles:

---

9 That the 'confession' was first published in Philadelphia is unsurprising when one considers the fact that, as David Geggus has written, 'the printers and polemicists who fled the colony [of Saint-Domingue] to Philadelphia in the mid-1790s' created a 'new, refugee press' upon arriving in the U.S. (2007a, 80).

despite the fact that nature continued to reunite them by affiliation, and that their interests as property owners were the same, hatred and vengeance broke these bonds forever' (64). All of this simply means that if, when perusing nineteenth-century Haitian newspapers, one is bound to find an article here or there that makes of Ogé, along with Louverture, Dessalines, Christophe, and Pétion, one of 'that multitude of martyrs who cemented with their blood the emancipation of this land' ('Les morceaux suivants,' 1844), it is hardly as though there were no historical precedents for deriving such a conclusion. It is one of the hallmarks of 'Haitian exceptionalism' to criticize Haitian authors, politicians, and citizens, in general, for things that are passed over with little notice, mention, or care in other situations. Demonizing certain nineteenth-century Haitian historians for their often principled (rather than *ad hominem*) criticism of Louverture certainly falls into this camp.

It is true that, as Schoelcher points out, Ardouin and Emile Nau, much like Boisrond-Tonnerre and Vastey before them, and Saint-Rémy after them, criticize Louverture, primarily for what they viewed as his blind allegiance to the French government and overly close relationship to the French colonists. However, once again, it does not follow that by pointing out what they viewed as Louverture's faults, these Haitian historians sought to bolster, in the words of Schoelcher, 'in every illogical mind, [*pour tout esprit un peu logique*], the idea that the black men were perfectly incapable of holding the reins of the government, and that consequently they needed to let themselves be governed by the yellow men' (1843, 2:227). With particular attention to this last claim, Schoelcher offers little evidence that any of the 'mulatto' writers of Haiti whom he mentions ever argued that "mulattoes" like Pétion should naturally dominate "blacks" like Dessalines, or that they used the history of Louverture to make that case. Boisrond-Tonnerre, who is well known for having criticized Louverture, argued that Dessalines's eventual rule over Haiti was not only the natural conclusion to the Revolution, but the inevitable one, since it was Dessalines 'alone' upon whom the revolutionaries had been relying in the months before the kidnapping of Louverture. 'We had nothing more to fear from Toussaint L'Ouverture,' Boisrond-Tonnerre writes, 'it was easy to see that he was not the soul of the country's army and that we only looked to Toussaint without Dessalines as the simulacra of a commander in chief' (45).

In an article published in the *Gazette Royale d'Hayti* (August 27, 1816), Baron de Vastey would offer much more pointed criticism of Louverture:

Toussaint had virtues, genius, and a talent for governing; but he lacked the experience that we have acquired with time and through the revolutions we have experienced: still imbued with the prejudices of the old regime and the fanaticism the priests had inculcated within him, he could not detach himself from that odious yoke; he had conserved a particular predilection for our tyrants; circumvented and dominated by them in all of his actions, they led him into error after error, and they led him even to death; this predilection, I say, that he had for our tyrants, became injurious to his citizens, and led them into, at various epochs, the greatest of prejudices ... Toussaint Louverture was so impotent that he was never able to do anything great for his country [*était dans l'impuissance de ne pouvoir jamais rien faire de grand pour le pays*]; and if he had not been the unfortunate victim of his own credulity, under him, we would have still been languishing without glory, in a state very near to prejudice and slavery, under the yoke of the ignominious French [*et s'il n'avait pas été la malheureuse victime de sa crédulité, sous lui, nous eussions toujours langui sans gloire, dans un état voisin des préjugés et de l'esclavage, sous le joug ignominieux des Français*]. ('Suite du coup,' 1)

Discussing further what life was like under the 'inept' Louverture, in the same article Vastey writes, 'there existed only the specter [*ombre*] of liberty; but the ex-colonists did not even want this specter, which offended them and prevented them from having the power to torture us and to take away our lives at their will, as in 1789' (2).

In contrast to writers like Boisrond-Tonnerre and Vastey (both considered to have been "mulattoes," in the parlance of their days), who argued that Dessalines and Christophe respectively were the proper men to rule independent Haiti, many nineteenth-century writers from France, as we saw in chapter nine with Bonneau and Gobineau, often made precisely the argument that we find Schoelcher accusing Ardouin and Faubert of having maintained: that it was "mulattoes" who should rule in independent Haiti. Are the proponents of Haitian exceptionalism thus working hard to separate the argument—that 'yellow men' should rule 'black men'—from its origin in "white" supremacist thinking and displace it onto Haitians, and more specifically, onto the image of the "mulatto?"

The only piece of evidence Schoelcher offers that could even remotely suggest that what may have been Ardouin's derogatory opinion of Louverture was widely shared in mid-nineteenth-century Haiti comes in a source for which Schoelcher provides no citation, but I have located in Ardouin's 1842 *Réponse du Sénateur B. Ardouin à M. Isambert*. Schoelcher quotes Ardouin as having 'said again' of Louverture, 'only a few months ago' that there was a 'cry of universal horror and disapproval that we hear *everywhere* proffered in Haiti against the memory of *this instrument of the colonists*, whose duplicity was the end, however unjust and criminal, of this famous black man [*dont la duplicité a été la cause de la fin, toutefois injuste et criminelle de ce noir célèbre*]' (qtd. in Schoelcher, 1843, 226). Schoelcher takes this statement of Ardouin as the proof that 'yellow' writers, not having been able to exact physical revenge on Louverture, were now taking discursive revenge by defaming him throughout the country.

There is a sense of irony, however, in what was actually a question posed by Ardouin to François André Isambert, who was the founding member of the Société Française Pour L'Abolition de l'Esclavage, that does not come through without reading the entire pamphlet of Ardouin and without understanding the historical context of Ardouin's disagreement with this French abolitionist. The immediate occasion for Ardouin's *Réponse ... à Isambert* had nothing to do with creating a history of Haiti and everything to do with responding to what he perceived as various calumnies about Boyer circulating in France. In his insightful *Haïti et la France, 1808–1848: le rêve brisé* (2008), Jean-François Brière has minutely detailed the way in which Isambert and Schoelcher were engaged in a negative publicity campaign against Boyer in the late 1830s and early 1840s. Isambert, in particular, had apparently written an inflammatory article in the French newspaper *Le Constitutionnel* on July 5, 1841, just after Schoelcher had returned from Haiti. In this article, which Brière calls 'violently hostile to the Boyer regime,' Isambert accused the Haitian president of having 'established in Haiti the tyranny of the mulattoes over the blacks' (274).[10] In Brière's estimation, '[t]his open confrontation' between the Haitian government and French abolitionists like Isambert, who had proclaimed their friendship to Haiti,

> illustrated that it was even before the publication of Schoelcher's testimony (which dates from 1843), that the relationship had deteriorated between the myriad French abolitionists from the metropole and the regime of Boyer. On both sides, the feeling of having been deceived, betrayed by an old ally, produced an extreme rancor. Isambert accused the mulattoes of having created a situation in Haiti that weakened the arguments for those who sought to defend the black race. (275)

On the other side of the affair, 'The message of the Boyerist[11] writers to the

---

10 Isambert was most well known for having defended Cyrille Bissette against the charges of treason brought against him in 1824. Isambert had also 'represented Boyer before the French tribunal' in 1827 (Brière, 274). For Isambert's account and defense of the charges brought against Boyer, see *Mémoire pour S. Ex. le président de la république d'Haïti* (1827).

11 Brière's designation of Ardouin as a 'Boyerist' writer is much more appropriate than calling him an adherent of the 'mulatto legend' or calling him a 'mulâtrist' and perhaps provides a model for how to refer to the political allegiances of Haitian authors without taking recourse to ideas about "race." Brière is right to speak more specifically of pro-Boyer authors as having a quarrel with Isambert since some other Haitian authors who have been accused of adhering to the 'mulatto legend,' like Saint-Rémy, but

abolitionists of France was clear: they needed to concern themselves only with that which directly involved them, that is to say, with the liberation of the black slaves' (Brière, 275–76). Ardouin had reminded Isambert, in this respect, that 'the black population of Haiti has no masters: it is in Martinique, in Guadeloupe, in Bourbon, and in Cayenne that there are masters and slaves. The population of Haiti has weapons, Monsieur,' Ardouin said, 'to defend itself and to preserve its liberty; no one could ever bring slavery back here!' (1842, 23). Ardouin then sarcastically implied that rather than turning their attention to the restrictions and repressions they viewed as having been a distinct part of nineteenth-century Haiti, Isambert and Schoelcher might do well to focus on the restrictions and repressions of nineteenth-century France.[12] Referring specifically to Isambert's critique, in a personal letter that he had written to Ardouin on November 18, 1841, of the elimination of a jury trial in Haiti for certain capital crimes such as treason, Ardouin noted that France had recently instituted some suspicious laws concerning jury trials, such as trying an accused who was not present (1842, 8). Ardouin asked Isambert, then, 'Why are you therefore so impassioned, so ardent when it comes to Haitians, and so cold, so reserved when it comes to the French?' (1842, 8). Furthermore, Ardouin accused the French abolitionists of having ultimately betrayed Haiti, first when France had attempted to reinstate slavery in Saint-Domingue during the Leclerc expedition and in so doing turned Louverture against his own people, then in France's repeated attempts to re-conquer the island throughout the first two decades of independence, and finally in its extortion of 150 million francs in 1825 as the price of recognition for Haitian sovereignty. With respect to this last issue, Ardouin had wondered where the friends of Haiti were at that time. He asked, 'Why did you not persuade your Charles X and your ministers,

---

unlike Ardouin, actually continued to admire the French abolitionist. Saint-Rémy even dedicated the first volume of *Pétion et Haïti* to Isambert, calling the French abolitionist 'one of the most noble, most devoted to my race.' Saint-Rémy said to Isambert, 'This public offering is as much a feeble marker of personal esteem as it is of a debt that Africa and America have contracted with you, and in the name of their children, I have here tried to fulfill it in my capacity as a black man' (1854, 3).

12 Though Ardouin does not go into great detail about the specific abuses of nineteenth-century France, according to Robert Justin Goldstein, the July Monarchy (1830–48) under the leadership of Louis Philippe was seen as having betrayed 'the reforms that the martyrs of the "glorious days" of the July Revolution had died for.' This betrayal was 'symbolized by the absurdly minute expansion of the suffrage in April 1831 (from the 0.3 percent of the population eligible to vote under the Restoration to 0.5 percent of the population),' and by the fact that this government instituted a 'massive crackdown of the press' (119). In addition, Goldstein wrote, 'the July Monarchy turned an especially deaf ear to the crushing poverty of the vast majority of the population' (120).

you, the friend of Haiti, to recognize our independence without demanding an indemnity?' (1842, 10).

Ardouin's deconstruction of Isambert's 'Haitian exceptionalism' reaches a tipping point when the Haitian historian turns his attention to the fact that Isambert had accused the 'mulattoes' of Haiti of providing the former colonists with evidence that 'blacks' are not 'susceptible to civilization.' Isambert wondered, 'how should we respond to these opponents of the abolition of slavery?' (qtd. in Ardouin, 1842, 18). To this, Ardouin replied:

> What could you say to the adversaries of the abolition of slavery? Show them the blacks of Haiti, who having shaken the odious yoke that weighed them down for two centuries ... without assistance from any other power, have achieved the independence of their country, and having consolidated this independence with institutions whose positive influence, despite what their detractors say about them, has produced happiness amongst the greater portion of them ... in spite of all of the foreign intrigues and after the internal discord whose alleged politics announced its eternal continuation. (1842, 18)

Ardouin continued, '[t]ell them to compare the situation of Haiti with that of the other republics of the new world, so that they will really be able to judge if the blacks are not susceptible to civilization' (18). When Isambert wrote that the Haitian government was behaving so poorly that he couldn't even talk about it any more—'We are really ashamed of what has happened in Haiti, that we dare not speak of it any longer, and we fear the revelations of the press' (qtd. in Ardouin, 1842, 19)—Ardouin sarcastically responded, '[y]ou do not dare to speak of Haiti any longer? Since when? Since the fifth of July 1841? After this shocking publication on the part of a former friend of Haiti, do we really have any reason to fear the revelations of the press?' (1842, 19).

Beyond the actual politics of this dispute, Ardouin does seem to be on to something when he questions Isambert's friendship for Haiti. After all, Isambert had also counseled the Haitian citizens to destroy any remnants of Pétion in saying, 'only one thing remains for you to do, burn the bust of Pétion' (qtd. in Ardouin, 1842, 19). Later in the letter Ardouin quotes Isambert as even having written, '[a]nd if one day you are destroyed by the storm that you have unleashed, what would we be able to say in your defense, or as an excuse for you?' (qtd. in Ardouin, 1842, 23). Unsurprisingly, just as in the works of Beard, Brown, and Redpath, hierarchical thinking was also a feature of Isambert's thinking about Haiti, which did not go unnoticed by Ardouin. Ardouin quotes Isambert as having written, '[a]h! who would not groan to see that the friends of the black race, *those who by the mixture of their blood with the European race* seemed called to serve as a model and an example to the friends of humanity, wanted to merely become tyrants!' (qtd. in Ardouin, 1842, 17).

The background of Ardouin's dispute with Isambert allows us to see that it was in the context of his sarcastic response to the Haitian exceptionalist arguments being put forward by Isambert that Ardouin referenced Louverture as the 'instrument of the colonists.' Ardouin reminded Isambert that 'your good friend, Mr. Schoelcher' had never missed an opportunity to disparage Pétion' (1842, 20). Here are Ardouin's exact words (in my translation):

> I am amused to see the disagreement between you and your friend with respect to our hero; I also enjoyed finding in your publication of 1841 your appreciation for the *wise administration of Pétion*; but I would be curious to find out if you also differ in your opinion with Mr. Schoelcher on Toussaint-Louverture, whose administration [Schoelcher] wanted to represent as the essence of greatness, moderation, humanity, despite the universal cry of horror and disapproval the voyager had heard everywhere proffered in Haiti, against the memory of that instrument of the colonists whose duplicity was the end, however unjust and criminal, of this famous black man. (1842, 20)[13]

Interestingly, in this passage Ardouin is actually referencing something he thinks Schoelcher ('the voyager') has *heard*—that everywhere in Haiti people remonstrate against the memory of Louverture, that 'instrument of the colonists'—which means that Ardouin is not discussing something that he himself necessarily believes, but something he believes about Schoelcher's visit to Haiti. Schoelcher, therefore, has not only taken Ardouin's words out of context, but he has actually misquoted the Haitian historian. Schoelcher accomplished this by changing the tense of the verb *entendre* (to hear) from past (*a entendu*) to present (*entend*) and by replacing Ardouin's usage of the specific subject, 'ce voyageur,' to the often self-implicating pronoun 'on' (which can mean, we, they, or even I). In other words, Ardouin had used the past tense when he said that 'the voyager had *heard*,' while Schoelcher had employed the present tense when he quoted Ardouin as saying, 'du cri universel d'horreur et d'improbation que *l'on* entend *partout* proférer en

---

13 It seems particularly useful to have the original French in this instance: 'J'aime à trouver ce dissentiment entre vous et votre ami, à l'égard de notre héros; j'aime à trouver dans votre publication de 1841 l'appréciation de *la sage administration de Pétion*; mais je serais curieux de savoir si vous différez aussi d'opinion avec Mr. Schoelcher, sur Toussaint-Louverture dont il a voulu nous représenter l'administration comme le type de la grandeur, de la modération, de l'humanité, malgré ce cri universel d'horreur et d'improbation que ce voyageur a entendu proférer en Haïti, contre la mémoire de cet instrument des colons dont la duplicité a été la cause de la fin, toutefois injuste et criminelle, de ce Noir célèbre.'

Haïti contre la mémoire de *cet instrument des colons* ...' The footnote that follows this statement puts the ethics of Schoelcher's (mis)reading of this passage of Ardouin's *Réponse* into even further question. Ardouin wrote:

> Lots of French people relish in exalting the administration of Toussaint-Louverture, of celebrating his *virtues*, whereas they do not accord any merit to Dessalines: Mr. Schoelcher is one of them. The reason is quite simple;—Toussaint gave the colonists back their properties and told the former slaves to go back to work,—whereas Dessalines took the *axe* [*la hache*] to this evil race [*race maudite*]. (1842, 20)

In an earlier footnote, Ardouin had also gestured towards the idea that it was the French who had denatured the history of the Haitian Revolution:

> The French flatter themselves sometimes in saying that they were the first to give liberty to the blacks [*les noirs*], in citing the decree of the Convention of February 5, 1794; but the *fact* is that this decree had only formalized the general liberty which had been proclaimed in Saint-Domingue by Sonthonax and Polverel, and these agents *had been forced* into this measure by the insurrection of *les noirs*, who by taking up arms with their own hands, made of it a *political necessity*. As such, it would be more correct to say that *les noirs* achieved liberty with their own hands. (17, emphasis in original)

Given the backdrop of these hostilities between the Haitian government and French abolitionists with respect to the rule of Haiti and to the facts of the Revolution, it makes sense that in his *Réponse* to Isambert, Ardouin's tone would be harshest where Louverture was concerned. As Ardouin had acknowledged, Louverture was undergoing a distinctive revival and recuperation in the France of the 1830s and 1840s for several different reasons. For one thing, Louverture's perceived moderate attitude towards revolutionary violence was attractive to abolitionists who hoped to end slavery in the French colonies without a repetition of the "horrors" of either the French Revolution of 1789 or the Haitian Revolution. For another thing, the romantic vision of Louverture reading Raynal had appeal for abolitionists and other philanthropists in the nineteenth century who wanted to believe that abolition was the natural outgrowth of the French Enlightenment. The Enlightenment literary narrative of the Haitian revolutionary hero only helped to bolster Louverture's reputation as an iconic, noble, but necessarily rebellious "black" leader whose wholesale power and European education had prevented him from needing to use indiscriminate violence like Dessalines. Within this version of the literacy narrative, Louverture could serve as the model of Enlightenment benevolence, improvement, and justice.

The tragedy of (and guilt over) Louverture's death and separation from his wife and children only added to Louverture's 'appeal ... to a contemporary romantic sensibility which affixed value to the exceptional individual' (Ferguson, 398). In the words of James Ferguson, 'Whether depicted in the most pejorative or positive of terms, or represented as an example of both virtue and vice, Toussaint is never seen as mediocre or uninteresting' (398). Louverture was not, however, the only object of a veritable nineteenth-century transatlantic cult of commemoration; the entire Louverture family was thus venerated. Writing from Paris, Louverture's own son Isaac captured with the utmost sentimentality his family's tragic deportation from Saint-Domingue. He writes of his mother:

> You would have to have the heart of a rock not to have been moved by the tears and groans of the women, men, and children who were present and who deplored her fate, when she was about to leave her country, a part of her family, and her home, which was that of charity and hospitality. These men, these women, these children, in an excess of grief, expressed their fears and their regrets with the utmost sensitivity: Madame, they cried at first addressing her, you are leaving? We will never see you again! Then to the commander of the regiment, ah! at least, Monsieur, do not kill her, do not kill her children. They thought that Toussaint Louverture was already dead. (309)

When seen within the context of both a romantic France that loved to exalt a (tragic) hero and an abolitionist France that was wary of more revolutionary violence, Isambert's and Schoelcher's interest in recuperating Louverture as completely anti-Bonaparte and unequivocally on the side of the slaves was hardly politically innocent or merely benevolently intended to help the Haitian people themselves. In an atmosphere of French abolitionism where anti-royalist and anti-revolutionary sentiment was common, making the life of Louverture itself *legendary* (since he died, in the eyes of abolitionists and other liberals, as laudably anti-royalist, anti-violence, as well as anti-Napoleon)[14] also meant that in some ways French abolitionists needed to ignore or make excuses for a Dessalines, who was not only famous for having massacred "whites," but who crowned himself an emperor; disavow a Christophe who had made himself a king; turn their backs on a Pétion and a Rigaud who had continuously refused to abide by the laws of republicanism; and make a contemporary enemy out of a Boyer who had sealed

---

14 As Sudhir Hazareesingh has written, the most ardent and famous liberals of the nineteenth century, Germaine de Staël, Benjamin Constant, François Guizot, and Alexis de Tocqueville, showed general 'hostility to the memory and legacy of Napoleon' (747–48).

Francophone Genealogy of the 'Mulatto Legend of History'

the loss of Haiti as a French colony forever, and who had thus betrayed the Haitian Revolution from the perspective of abolitionists (see Ardouin, 1842, 16). Louverture was, on the flip side, much easier to recover for abolitionists since he could easily be painted as a sympathetic but loyal victim of French colonial treachery in a way that Christophe, Dessalines, and Rigaud, in particular, could not.

Unlike Louverture, who would ardently deny in his *Mémoires* that he had ever sought to usurp Bonaparte's powers, and who declared in his 1801 Constitution that he would die 'free and French,' practically all of the other Haitian revolutionaries had been depicted in the literary history of these events as having at some point dared to constitute their own authority against France. These subalterns turned revolutionaries turned statesmen, along with Ogé, had flaunted their 'diva citizenship' (Berlant, 223), if you will, in the face of the French colonists whose power and authority they had dared to contest in multiple arenas to which they were not supposed to have had access. Ardouin is perfectly aware that one of Isambert's problems with Boyer, for whom he had initially served as legal counsel, was that the Haitian president had refused to take the French abolitionists' advice on certain matters, particularly on the question of the indemnity (1842, 10, 22). Ardouin quotes Isambert complaining that the Haitians 'did not want to follow the political direction he had charted for them' (22). Seeming to suggest that Isambert's criticism was a form of political revenge for the fact that Haitians had not only 'dared to be free,' but dared to govern themselves, and that this was the heart of Isambert's break with Boyer, Ardouin writes:

> Because it has pleased you to believe yourself so capable, as a politician, of giving our government advice about the way in which a country you have never even visited should be governed, does it please you now, Sir, to tell us that we have missed all of your warnings? What is this mania, by which certain figures in Europe are possessed, for believing that they alone must and can think for Americans in general. As for us, poor Haitians who have for so long seen the intellectual faculties of our race questioned, none of this will be shocking to us:—why would not a French lawyer, an enlightened jurist, be the most proper person to manage the affairs of Haiti, sitting in his office in Paris, rather than we politicians who have lived through the storms of our bloody revolutions? (24)

Ultimately, then, even though Schoelcher wants to use the 1842 text of Ardouin as the most apparent proof of the Haitian historian's dogmatic defamation of Louverture, because Ardouin wrote the *Réponse* for and to the French, in the particular context described above, it can ultimately tell us very little about what he wanted Haitians to believe about their own history. It is once again towards Ardouin's *Géographie* that we must return if we want to know how his historical ideas might have been able to frame widespread thought on the Revolution in Haiti. In his *Géographie d'Haïti*, Ardouin does criticize Louverture for his leadership of the colony, saying that the general was cruel and even at times 'tyrannical' (19). However, at the moment of the Leclerc expedition, rather than portraying Louverture as a traitor to the 'indigènes,' if anything, Ardouin portrays him as having himself been betrayed by his own ideals and devotion to France. Ardouin writes, 'the defection of general Toussaint was produced as much by his irresolution in this decisive circumstance, as by the hope that we had generally placed in the protective arms of France' (1832, 20–21). Even if we were to find that Ardouin was too severe in his judgment of Louverture as having been a faulted and even 'oppressive' leader (1832, 19) who did not rise to the occasion when presented with the opportunity to liberate the future Haitian people, Schoelcher's charge that this was a part of a 'yellow imagination' designed to bolster the rule of 'yellows' over 'blacks' contains little merit, especially when juxtaposed with the similar criticisms of Louverture offered by Boisrond-Tonnerre and Vastey, who could hardly be considered to have been under the influence of Boyer's 'yellow imagination.' Moreover, Schoelcher's claim that Ardouin accused Louverture of having wanted to reinstate slavery in the colony seems to be without teeth. In the *Géographie*, Ardouin absolves Louverture of the charge that he had ever sought any kind of continuation of slavery, saying that while one could find in the national archives of Santo Domingo lists of slaves who were sold into slavery on the Spanish side of the island by Jean-François and Biassou, 'Toussaint had always defended himself against this charge.' Ardouin continues by seeming to agree with Louverture's self-assessment when he writes, 'everything tends towards proving that Toussaint Louverture, whose intelligence was above that of Jean-François and Biassou, did not really contribute to the selling of these slaves' (178).

Schoelcher may have unconsciously realized that he was making an unnuanced argument about Ardouin that could not be fully supported by the entire corpus of the Haitian historian's writing. This ambivalence about being able to prove his own argument leads Schoelcher down the path to another kind of (mis)reading when he infers by mere juxtaposition that Ardouin *had* actually accused Louverture of selling slaves. For example, in one of his many 'hesitant asides' (Stoler, 2010a, 23), Schoelcher writes that, unlike Ardouin, Emile Nau admirably presented Louverture as having always had emancipation and independence in mind. Schoelcher did take issue, though, with Nau's statement that with his Constitution of 1801, Louverture 'tied the slaves to the glebe, re-establishing in some ways a kind of slavery' (qtd. in Schoelcher, 1843, 227). It is from this comment of Nau, rather than from anything Ardouin wrote, that Schoelcher concludes, 'Yes, Toussaint Louverture … is represented here … always ready to re-establish slavery' (227). In the paragraph that directly follows this claim, Schoelcher suddenly and without warning circles back to Ardouin in saying, 'Let us hasten to say, nevertheless, that Mr. Ardouin's ridiculous idea of Toussaint Louverture is not that of educated Haitians, even from his class' (227–28).

As for Dessalines, though in the *Géographie* Ardouin certainly prefers Pétion, he unequivocally refers to the former, and not the latter, as the '*Liberator of Haiti*' (22), Ardouin also argues that it was precisely because Dessalines had 'guided' the country 'in this immortal conquest' that he deserved this 'glorious title' (1832, 22). Ardouin's later criticism of Dessalines for the cruelty of his rule over post-independence Haiti and for the April 28 proclamation (1832, 23–24) is hardly different than Schoelcher's own criticism of Dessalines on both counts (Schoelcher, 1843, 2:142–44). Moreover, it is not as though Ardouin never similarly criticizes anyone he considers to be a 'mulatto.' For example, in describing Louverture's conflict with Rigaud, Ardouin writes, '[w]ar broke out again; but this time it was between two brothers ... Oh! they were both guilty for having let themselves be led astray' (1832, 18). He further writes, '[h]ow many evils would Toussaint and Rigaud have spared their country, if they had known how to unite their influence and the forces over which they commanded, to proclaim at that time this precious Independence without which there would not exist in Haiti either liberty or happiness!' (1832, 18). Ardouin, whom Schoelcher would later call a 'great admirer of Rigaud' ('Toussaint-Louverture,' 1892), almost certainly faults Rigaud for this conflict more than Louverture when he contends that 'impartial history will bring together the facts in order to verify whether or not Toussaint had seen through the *machiavelisme* of their common enemies, if he had not sensed the necessity of this great and important measure' (1832, 18). The ambiguity of this statement is only cleared up by the one that follows. Ardouin implies that regardless of what 'impartial history' may one day uncover about Louverture, '[e]ither way, this disastrous dissension to which Rigaud succumbed occasioned great misery' (1832, 18–19).

The major casualty of viewing Haitian historical writing within the frames of "mulatto" and "black" *legends* of history is that it circumscribes our interpretive capacities in such a way that we become unable to see, imagine, or theorize any of the other potentially endless reasons why Louverture, Rigaud, and Dessalines may have been unpopular revolutionary figures in post-independence Haiti when compared to Christophe and Pétion. If we were to undertake a systematic evaluation of Louverture's image in nineteenth-century Haiti through its newspapers using the 'yellow imagination'/'the mulatto legend of history' as a research question, for example, we would necessarily be limiting the scope of our interpretation at the outset. The problem is in the question itself, which begins with the premise that such an exploration would either prove or disprove Schoelcher's—and Nicholls's—theory. This has the effect of reducing all of Haitian history to a narrow question of "color" or "race" rather than opening it up to broader question of politics and class.

What is being denied to Ardouin, nevertheless, when we view any negative statements he might have made about Louverture, Christophe, or Dessalines as proof of the 'mulatto legend of history,' is the nuance of the historian. In short, it is to silence Ardouin to require him to constantly and unequivocally exalt the *legendary* conduct of Louverture despite the many conflicting reports of the revolutionary general's goals and desires before and during the Revolution that we find in eyewitness accounts, Louverture's letters themselves, and other historical records. The vastly different portrayals of Louverture that we find across the political spectrum of writing about this revolutionary leader in the nineteenth century suggests to me one thing: Louverture was a complicated revolutionary figure, subject to the political and ideological whims of representation, much more so than many nineteenth-century abolitionists like Schoelcher had wanted to believe. To deny Ardouin the freedom to explore that complexity, contradiction, and nuance is the essence of 'Haitian exceptionalism.' It is to say that the Haitian historian is not allowed to be an historian; he cannot be viewed as having an *unbiased* argument like other historians because he must always be a "colorist," which is to say that he must be an unabashed partisan of his own "color," merely creating history for the sake of dominating the other "color." When the Haitian historian has been sufficiently proved to be a partisan in this way or that (in contrast with the Western historian, who always finds a way to be objective), he becomes much easier to render banal or even erase. That is equally the formula of 'Haitian exceptionalism' and for 'silencing of the past' (Trouillot, 1995, 96).

As a writer from France, the nuanced voice of the historian was apparently perpetually open for Schoelcher. The French abolitionist's descriptions of 'black' revolutionaries like Dessalines and Christophe, the latter of whom he describes at one point as 'black Caligula' (2:152),[15] are presented with at least some of the complexity that their individual histories require. Schoelcher quasi-defends Christophe's creation of a monarchy in northern Haiti when

---

15 It is possible that Schoelcher derived this description from Saint-Rémy, who had written in his *Essai sur Christophe, Général Haïtien* (1839), that the Haitian king had been a 'second Caligula' (16). With the ambivalence that is wholly characteristic of his work, Saint-Rémy had also written, 'History does not perhaps offer any person who is more difficult to judge than general Christophe; on one side, the testimony of honorable people places him among the ranks of the greatest of men; on the other, commendable voices [*des voix recommendables*] in various accounts leave us only with a cry of anathema against him' (1839, 3).

he acknowledges with irony that the Haitian king himself had something to say about those who would make fun of his court:

> having learned that people were making fun of his princes of Marmelade and his dukes of Limonade (two districts of the island that he had made into fiefs), Christophe slyly said that he could completely understand how such a thing could cause laughter among those who had their own *Prince de Poix* (prince of Peas) and *Duc de Bouillon* (duke of Bouillon). (1843, 2:151)

In addition, of Dessalines's purported massacre of all the "white" inhabitants on the island in April of 1804, Schoelcher had this to say:

> Under the rule of the negro called *the liberator of Haiti*, it was enough to be white in order to deserve death, just as under the rule of the whites, it had been enough to be black in order to deserve slavery; it is not clear to me in which of these lay the greater savagery [*c'est un doute pour moi de savoir où est la plus grande férocité*]. (1843, 2:142)

If Schoelcher might have been able to pardon Dessalines's 'savagery' because of the latter's personal history with slavery—'he had been repeatedly and violently whipped; his body carried the scars of these vile punishments' (Schoelcher, 1843, 2:142)—on the contrary, "mulatto" revolutionaries in Schoelcher's descriptions, much of which were derived from spurious colonial sources like Lacroix, Garran de Coulon, Mazères, and Malenfant,[16] are presented in an uncompromisingly negative light.

Schoelcher rarely says anything positive about any revolutionary he considered to have been of "mixed race." For example, he evoked his special powers of seeing to determine that 'mulattoes' alone were 'responsible' (*coupables*) for the 'scission' between the 'yellows' and 'blacks' of Haiti (1843, 2:237). His primary and only example rests in the history of internecine strife between Louverture and Rigaud. Yet while the vast majority of Haitian writers had written that it was Hédouville who had divided Louverture and Rigaud by encouraging color prejudices and 'discord' between the two revolutionaries (see Boisrond-Tonnerre, 94; H. Christophe, 1814, 3; Vastey, 1819, 124–25; J. Chanlatte, 1824, 40–41; Dumesle, 166–67), Schoelcher

---

16 Bissette also quite correctly accused Schoelcher of having 'copied' for his history from the 'pamphlets and memoirs of Page, Brulley, Thomas Millet, Daugy, and other colonists from Saint-Domingue, the most fiery adversaries of the blacks and the *hommes de couleur*, their executioners in those times' (28). Reliance on these pamphlets is problematic in more ways than one. Raimond pretty convincingly showed through a side-by-side comparison in his *Lettres de J. Raimond, à ses frères les hommes de couleur* (1794) that Page and Brulley had distorted his own words in order to defame the free people of color (7–8). On Schoelcher's copying, see also Bongie (1998, 281).

unequivocally demonizes the 'yellow' general in contending that 'Rigaud alone is responsible':

> Here is the source of this war of color that tore apart the island and whose consequences still threaten it ... It was him, who in order to maintain himself against a superior rival, was obliged to give recourse to the passions of caste, it was him who, in accusing Toussaint of wanting to get rid of the yellow men, provoked the deadly recriminations of the black leader, for whom it was all too easy to recall the affair with the 300 *suisses*,[17] as well as the aid the mulattoes had, until the final moment, given to the colonists in order to preserve slavery. (1843, 2:122–23)

The blame that Schoelcher heaps upon Rigaud reaches a state of morbid hyperbole I have struggled to find expressed with such grotesque intensity in any other text, when he concludes:

> It would have been a great fortune for Haiti if Rigaud had never been born.[18] A soldier, full of valor, he tarnished his glory by unpardonable faults. He was a man of merit, without a doubt, but flawed [*incomplète*] ... Pawn [*acteur*] in a revolution of helots [*ilotes*], he did not know how to smother in his heart the prejudices that he combatted in others, and it is to him that can be traced the shame of having divided negroes and mulattoes to the point of hatred. (1843, 2:124)

As for Pétion, Schoelcher describes him as a 'bad patriot' (1843, 2:230) for having defected to the side of the French before and during the Leclerc expedition (even though Schoelcher represents Christophe and Dessalines

---

17 Schoelcher refers to the infamous deportation of a troop of slaves turned revolutionaries whose nickname was 'les Suisses' because they were willing to fight on the side of the *anciens libres* without pay, as had Swiss soldiers for the French Royal Army (Popkin, 2011, 45). According to Popkin, 'the abandonment of "the Swiss" by the leaders of the free men of color created a lasting distrust between them and the rest of the black slave population and was remembered with bitterness even after Haiti gained its independence' (45). In the nineteenth century, this contest was often written about less in terms of a division between the free people of color and the slaves, as in Schoelcher's writings, than as a problem between "mulattoes" and "blacks." Saint-Rémy took issue with these kinds of racialized characterization when he asked in his characteristic style, 'What does it matter if Beauvais voted for the deportation of the *Suisses*? Lambert, who was a negro, did he not also vote in favor of this deportation?—And Rigaud and Pétion, who were mulattoes, were they not opposed to it? ... Among the black slaves were there not also mulatto slaves?' (1850, 185).

18 The closest thing I have found that approaches Schoelcher's desire for Rigaud to have 'never been born,' is in Prince Saunder's collection of *Haytian Papers*, in which he calls Rigaud 'a man who was born evidently for the ill luck of his country' (89).

as having, at one point, done the same); and he says that it was only after Dessalines had himself turned against the French army that Pétion followed suit. In addition, Schoelcher says of Pétion's subsequent reign over the southern part of Haiti during the post-independence era:

> the one whom the mulattoes dare to call the Washington of Haiti, having *allowed himself* to be elected the temporary president three consecutive times, finished by *accepting* the presidency for life. In permitting himself to be allowed this omnipotence, he violated the fundamental principle of any republican government. A president for life is only a king in disguise, and soon enough he will acquire all of the vices of royalty. (1843, 2:233)

Schoelcher reserves his harshest judgment of Pétion for the moment when he describes the former Haitian president as having been a regular megalomaniac who loved power merely for the sake of having power rather than because he actually thought he was the best person to govern Haiti. To illustrate this point, Schoelcher writes that at the end of his life, Pétion, 'exhausted by his own indolence, tired of the plots with which he was obsessed, fell into a bitter skepticism, he died mysteriously at the age of 48, taking advantage, they say, of a mild illness and in order to escape from the acrid boredoms of his existence, let himself die of hunger' (1843, 2:233–34). Such an ineffective and useless coward was Pétion in this portrayal that he could hardly stand to live any longer a life of such listless ineptitude and pointless fury.

Ardouin's *Réponse* having been published in 1842, Schoelcher was no stranger to the kind of criticism that would be offered by Bissette, who would eventually write that *Colonies étrangères* was a dangerous book since it 'could do more harm than good by dividing Haitians, whom the author deigns to describe with the terms, the *black party* and the *yellow faction*' (4), nor would he have been a stranger to the kind of insults launched by Richet (Riché), who referred to Schoelcher as a 'malevolent person' (3). Anticipating Bissette's argument that his only goal, referring to 'blacks' and 'mulattoes,' was 'to divide us, and to make us slit each other's throats' (1844, 69), Schoelcher tried to make the case that unlike the 'mulattoes' of Saint-Domingue, he was the friend of the former slaves, just as, unlike the Haitians of the nineteenth century, he was a friend to the current slaves of Martinique and Guadeloupe, for whose freedom he was passionately advocating (1843, 242–44).[19] Directly responding to Ardouin, who had

---

19 Schoelcher had criticized the Haitian people, rather than the Haitian government, for not doing more to help end slavery in either the French colonies or the United States. He noted that Haiti did not even have its own abolitionist society and claimed that the majority of the country's writers stayed silent on the issue. He wrote, 'Is it not a shame

apparently accused Schoelcher of having tried to create divisions there based on color during his visit to Haiti, Schoelcher writes:

> Without respect for his title of president of the senate, he had the childishness [*simplicité*] to insinuate that I was, me, an agent of the colonists and of the French ministry, sent there in order to encourage the divisions of old Saint-Domingue, in order to more effectively reestablish slavery there. (1843, 2:224)

Schoelcher reacted to this type of criticism, in general, by making yet another comparison between his behavior and that of the 'mulattoes' of Haiti. He asserted that unlike the 'mulattoes,' who, 'far from being the friends of the blacks ... were, on the contrary, their most bitter enemies' (1843, 2:225), he was the friend of the 'blacks' of Haiti precisely because he was an abolitionist. Schoelcher ultimately defended himself by writing:

> Why, because I am, myself, a devoted abolitionist, decidedly against the *machiavélisme* of the government, have I been presented, has it been possible ... to present me as an agent of discord come to encourage the divisions between the two castes? You recognize two castes, then? You have committed the crime. (2:238)

While it seems doubtful that Schoelcher had deliberately tried to sow the seeds of political division in Haiti with his writing, or was a spy sent by the French government to help re-conquer the island, he absolutely expressed 'extrinsic racism' when he adopted a narrative of "mulatto/a" vengeance that was tinged with the pseudoscientific "racial" taxonomies that had been used by the former colonists of Saint-Domingue to stratify plantation society in order to better uphold the system of slavery. Schoelcher's view of 'mulattoes' as monstrous is particularly apparent when he writes that they were 'a *mixed race* issued from the debauchery of white men with their female

---

that you have not taken any in the efforts of Europe for emancipation, that you have not even sent any statement of solidarity or sympathy to the friends of emancipation, and that in this republic of emancipated slaves, there is not even a society of abolition? Is it egoism, is it indifference? (1843, 2:242–43). Janvier would later disagree with this idea, inferring that the mere threat of slaves overthrowing their masters, as had occurred in Haiti, and the impending independence of the country, was the biggest contribution Haiti could have made to the abolitionist movement. He wrote, 'It is the independence of Haiti that led to the emancipation of the slaves in the English colonies, to the foundation of Liberia, and to the emancipation of the slaves in Martinique and, later, in the United States ... it was the independence of Haiti and the sovereignty of Haiti that put an advantageous pressure on certain governments and that led to the emancipation of slaves in Puerto Rico and in Brazil' (1883, 56).

slaves' (1843, 2:90; emphasis added), a description that had been used by naturalist travel writers for at least three centuries to prove the superiority of "whiteness" as much as to justify keeping that *'mixed race'* in slavery with their mothers. Likewise, even though Schoelcher acknowledged that the term 'mulâtre' 'in the mouth of the whites' was an 'injurious term' (1843, 2:109), he admonished those Haitians who would want to do away with the divisive and racist terminology of the colonists. Schoelcher observes, '[i]n perishing, the colonists bequeathed color prejudice to this unfortunate land.' Consequently, 'the insurgents of Saint-Domingue, so proud in battle, blushed after their victory because of the shame that the former masters had attached to their names' (1843, 2:236). Schoelcher had apparently determined that the injurious history of these terms was hardly an argument to stop using them, to say nothing of his disregard for the shame felt by the people to whom these terms referred. He wrote:

> Instead of forcing the world to have respect for these names ... they wanted to hide them; and today it is to offend this population of negroes and mulattoes to call them *negroes* and *mulattoes*! They call themselves blacks and yellows, because they have preserved, with respect to these old titles, the same scorn the whites had. (1843, 2:236)

Schoelcher's belief that it was he who should decide what the people of Haiti should call themselves, and his stake in insisting that they refer to themselves using the "racial" taxonomies of colonialism, supports Bissette's claim of Schoelcher's colonial hubris: 'I went, I saw, and I *wrote*' (2).

In the end, both Bissette and Pierre Faubert will look to find evidence of Schoelcher's own racism and betrayal of the anti-slavery cause in a letter that the abolitionist published in the *Revue de Paris* in 1830. Both of Schoelcher's opponents point out that here Schoelcher argued for gradual rather than immediate emancipation, and both focus on the following passage as proof. Schoelcher asked, *'What shall we do with the emancipated negroes?'* 'For whomever has seen them *up close*,' he said, 'this question is *impossible* to resolve. Negroes who have left the hands of their masters with the ignorance and all the vices of slavery *will be good for nothing*, not for *society, not even for themselves*' (qtd. in Bissette, 46–47; italicized in original; see also, Faubert, 1856, 185–88). Schoelcher completes the letter with a statement that rightly horrified both Bissette and Faubert for its "racial" fatalism, if not for its unequivocal assertion that abolishing slavery was God's work rather than a human being's:

> *I do not see any longer with anyone else the necessity to INFEST present society,* which is already *bad enough,* with several *thousand brutes* decorated with the title of citizens, who would ultimately [*en définitive*] be *only* a vast

incubator [*pépinière*] of beggars and proletariats. As for that, *leave it to the great master* to do it. (qtd. in Bissette, 47; emphases in original)

As Faubert acknowledged 'out of fairness' (1856, 186), Schoelcher later deeply regretted what he wrote in that letter, as evidenced by the apology he would publish in 1849 in his *La Vérité aux Ouvriers et Cultivateurs de la Martinique*, where he said:

> How ... I myself could have attached to them the name of brutes, I would only know how to explain by my inexperience (I was writing for the first time and I was 25 years old); with that exaggerated style common in young people who do not yet know how to restrain their pen [*pas encore contenir leur plume*]. (qtd. in Faubert, 1856, 187; see also Schoelcher, 1849, 49)

Schoelcher finished the 1849 letter by stating, '[t]he project accuses much of the author's youth, but does not in the least bit reflect upon the friend of abolition' (qtd. in Faubert, 1856, 188). As the direct descendent of a famous revolutionary leader (Morpeau, 59), Faubert was perhaps less willing to accept this error of youth than we might be today. Nevertheless, the ideas of "racial" supremacy expressed in this letter of Schoelcher's 'youth' pales in comparison to one of his much more unforgivable final comments about 'la faction jaune' in *Colonies étrangères*.

Schoelcher's final paragraphs of Chapter V reveal much more about the danger inherent in his ideas about "race" than what he wanted us to believe was a youthful mistake with respect to his thoughts on immediate emancipation. In the paragraphs below, Schoelcher makes his most inflammatory comment yet about 'yellow men,' the consequences of which, pushed to its logical extreme, could only result in the perpetual domination of a "racial" majority over a "racial" minority, not merely in Haiti, but everywhere in the world. Schoelcher writes:

> Yellow men, have therefore the courage to abandon the reins, since it is impossible for you to drive the chariot. *Remember that you will never be able to do anything good, and that any aggressive action you would like to take in order to raise up the degraded black people* [pour relever le peuple noir avili] *will be considered by them as an act of oppression by the mulatto aristocracy, and will lead them to revolt.* (1843, 2:241)

In Schoelcher's mind, not only would any and every 'aggressive action' undertaken by 'mulattoes' be interpreted as an 'act of oppression,' regardless of the actual politics at hand, but Haiti was ultimately doomed if it did not find a way to have a 'black' leader. To that end, Schoelcher prognosticated:

As long as the permanent government of Haiti, a government of the majority, that is to say a black government, has not been established, the republic will live a precarious life, false, wretched, and suspicious. Let a negro come and everything will change [*Laissez venir un nègre et tout change de face*]. (1843, 2:241)

Taken to the final extent of its logic, Schoelcher's idea about Haiti needing to be ruled by a 'nègre,' in the pseudoscientific sense, would force everyone everywhere to become a true believer in "racial" taxonomies, unless of course rule by "racial" majority was only for Haiti. After all, who could be 'nègre' enough to rule in Haiti? Forty years after independence, how could it be determined who still had enough "white blood" to be considered one of the 'yellow men?' Or was it skin color rather than ancestry and genealogy that mattered? The more 'nègre' the better for Schoelcher, apparently. Never mind the fact that using Schoelcher's logic about the relationship of "race" or skin color to political rule means that the government of France will and should always be headed by "whites," since "whites" there vastly outnumbered "blacks." In effect, the argument of this French abolitionist, whom Nick Nesbitt has recently referred to as maintaining an 'unyielding and effective fidelity to a radical conception of universal human rights, one he inherited from the architects of the Haitian abolition of slavery' (2013, 85), justifies an immediately threatening world order that is based on the idea of rule by numerical "racial" majority, and therefore rule by "racial" supremacy. Using this logic, a "colored" man, even less one who is considered to be of "mixed race," would never have and should never have been able to become president of the United States.

*

Perhaps the best evidence which tends towards proving that Schoelcher had adopted the cynical practice of (mis)reading that is inherent to the trope of the "colored historian," is his discussion of Pierre Faubert's play *Ogé, ou le préjugé de couleur*. Coming now to Faubert's own defense of his play, which has hardly received the critical attention it deserves, as well as to the play's portrayal of Ogé, I suggest that it is precisely the cynical practice of (mis)reading everything in Haiti through the lenses of "race" and "color" that has led to the present obscurity of the play and to the obfuscation of the radical new humanism it espouses.

In 1841, Pierre Faubert,[20] who was the director of the Lycée National de

---

20 Pierre Faubert was from Cayes in southern Haiti, and was the son of a famous general of the Haitian army (Morpeau, 59). According to Faubert himself, his mother had sent him and his siblings to Paris to be educated at the Collège de France (1856, 1).

Port-au-Prince from 1837 to 1851, staged his play *Ogé, ou le préjugé de couleur* in order to, in his words, 'inspire noble sentiments' in the minds and hearts of his students and to 'make them see at the same time everything that is absurd or odious about color prejudice' (12). Victor Schoelcher, however, who had seen it in Haiti when he visited the country in 1841, accused Faubert of having encouraged color prejudice and national discord with the play.[21] This is because, in Schoelcher's interpretation, Faubert had presented Ogé as someone who 'only had general liberty in mind and died for it.' Schoelcher writes, '[e]ven better, [Ogé] leads his troops into combat against the whites, in 1790, with the black and red flag of Haiti that had only been created by Dessalines in 1803' (219). Schoelcher said that this historical inaccuracy on the part of Faubert, who had chosen to represent the life of Ogé over that of Louverture, must have been an indication that the play had been written 'under the influence of color prejudice.' Schoelcher would be even more earnest in his criticism of the Haitian playwright when he accused Faubert of having 'wanted to contribute to a falsified history of the country that is being spread here in the interest of caste' (1843, 2:225). For Schoelcher, Faubert's portrayal of Ogé was wholly disingenuous and politically motivated rather than merely ill-informed or ignorant since,

> M. Faubert, who knows very well, because of his status as an educated man, what truth there is in all of this, has nevertheless remained faithful

---

Faubert would later become 'Aide de camp et Secrétaire particulier' for President Boyer (F.E. Dubois, 1867, 183), whose daughter, Josephine (Fine) Laraque, he had married ('Decret,' 3). He became the director of the Lycée National de Port-au-Prince in 1837. During the presidency of Faustin Soulouque, who named himself Emperor of the island in 1849, Faubert, like many of the 'puissants' (the powerful) or writers, were, as he says, 'retained in prison.' Faubert eventually fled; first to Kingston, Jamaica, and later to Paris, where he would publish *Ogé* (Morpeau, 59–60; Faubert, 1856, 14). In 1857, Faubert's son Fénélon would win the Prize of Honor at the Sorbonne in Paris, which would be widely reported in the abolitionist U.S. press in order to prove the abilities of 'Africans,' in general, and Haitians in particular. For Fénélon Faubert's prize at the Sorbonne, see *Discours à trois jeunes Haïtiens, récemment couronnés au grand concours de la Sorbonne* (1858). For Fénélon Faubert's prize as reported upon in the U.S. press, see 'Our Special Contributors,' *The Independent*, 30 September 1858: 1; 'Later from Hayti,' *Chicago Press and Tribune*, 24 September 1859: 2; 'Speech of Dr. John S. Rock,' *Liberator*, 3 February 1860: 19; F.W. Chesson, 'Selections,' *Liberator*, 4 March 1859; 'Article 2,' *Littel's Living Age*, 7 May 1859: 344; 'Extract from "A Letter from Paris,"' *Liberator*, 8 October 1858: 162; 'Article 2,' *The African Repository*, December 1858: 381; 'Louis Napoleon and the Haytiens in Paris,' *Liberator*, 24 December 1858: 206; 'Haytiens in Paris,' *Friends' Review*, 11 December 1858: 222. For additional biographical details about Faubert, see Raphaël Berrou and Pradel Pompilus (1975).

21 For some documentation of Victor Schoelcher's visit to Haiti and all of the people with whom he met and visited, see Madiou (7:360–62).

to the order of the day, and sacrificing his integrity as an historian to his political passions, he presents the episode of Ogé in the agreed upon light. (1843, 2:219)

Using the trope of the "colored historian," Schoelcher subsequently claimed that it was historians working for the regime of Boyer that constantly sought 'in imitation of Pétion' to defame the 'black' revolutionary heroes and in so doing defame the 'black' race (1843, 2:239), and that it was devotion to this 'political passion' that was responsible for Faubert's rendition of Ogé's rebellion.

Schoelcher's next move against Faubert raises to new heights what Bongie has called, in another context, Schoelcher's 'unwarranted sense of his own detachment from the situation that he was describing' (1998, 279). Schoelcher writes that one day, when 'the students who performed the piece and those who enthusiastically applauded it demand the historical truth,' they will be able to find that truth in *Colonies étrangères* (1843, 2:219–20). Schoelcher thus offers to present for them the 'real' history of Ogé. According to this representation, Ogé 'was agitating [for political emancipation], but never for that of the abolition of slavery' (1843, 2:220). Schoelcher's proof for the claim that 'Ogé, in effect, did not fight for the slaves,' but only 'for the political franchise denied to his race,' and 'for his wounded pride, but not for liberty' (1843, 2:222), rests primarily upon two historical documents. The first document referenced by Schoelcher is Ogé's speech given before the Club Massiac on September 7, 1789. In this famous speech, eventually published as the 'Motion Faite par M. Vincent Ogé, Jeune à l'Assemblée des Colons, Habitants de St.-Domingue, à l'Hotel de Massiac, Place des Victoires,' the most relevant section of which I have included below, Ogé wrote that he believed that liberty and equality were for all people of color, slaves and free, and said that such liberty was likely inevitable unless the colonists took preparations to ensure that it would only happen in due time and on terms that were favorable to the planters.

Ogé began his speech by immediately identifying his interests as the same as those of the planters before whom he appeared: 'I have no other goal other than to contribute … to the conservation of our Properties, & to prepare for the disaster that is threatening us' (1789, 1). Ogé subsequently intimated that he had some ideas about how the impending 'disaster' could be prevented, and he offered to present those ideas to the colonists at a later date. He wrote:

Messieurs, this Liberty, a word we do not pronounce without enthusiasm, a word which brings with it the idea of happiness, if only because it seems to help us forget all the ills that we have suffered for centuries; this liberty, the greatest, the most valuable of goods, was it made for all men? I believe so. Must it be given to all men? I believe even that. But how should it be given? What are the best eras and conditions? There we have it, Messieurs, the greatest, the most important of all the questions; it involves America, Africa, France, all of Europe, & it is the principle reason for which I have determined, Messieurs, to ask for your ears. (1789, 5)

The speech, made before a pro-slavery society, would take on the much more evocative quality to be found in many nineteenth-century abolitionist premonitions about the consequences of the continuation of slavery when Ogé warned the colonists:

> If we do not take the most immediate, the most effective measures; if firmness, courage, constancy do not motivate us all; if we do not very quickly unite in one body [*en faisceau*] all of our intelligence, all of our means, all of our efforts; if we fall asleep for an instant on the edge of the abyss, let us tremble upon our awakening! Behold the blood that will run, behold our lands invaded, the objects of our industry ravaged, our homes burned, behold our cousins, our friends, our wives, our children slaughtered and mutilated, behold the slave who is raising the standard of revolt [*voilà l'esclave qui lève l'étendard de la révolte*], the islands will be nothing more than a vast and fatal conflagration; Commerce will be destroyed, France will have received a mortal wound, & a multitude of honest citizens will be impoverished, ruined; we will lose everything. (1789, 6)[22]

Most contemporary historians and literary critics have been inclined to take Ogé at his word when he said in this speech that 'liberty' was 'made for all men,' particularly, since he found himself before a pro-slavery society and would have had every reason to want to conceal such a belief. However, it would be all too hasty to conclude that this believer in the eventuality and practical necessities of universal emancipation was an abolitionist. John Garrigus has written of Ogé's speech that while

> [t]here is no evidence that Ogé was yet in contact with abolitionists ... when he appeared at the Hotel Massiac on September 7th he was naïve

---

[22] An example of such premonitory abolitionist writing also appears in William Wells Brown's speech 'St. Domingo, its Revolutions and its Patriots,' where Brown wrote that in the event of a revolution like Haiti's in the United States, 'the indignation of the slaves of the south would kindle a fire so hot that it would melt their chains, drop by drop, until not a single link would remain; and the revolution that was commenced in 1776 would then be finished ... and our government would no longer be the scorn and contempt of the friends of freedom in other lands, but would really be the LAND OF THE FREE AND HOME OF THE BRAVE' (1855, 38).

enough to inform these planters that he believed liberty should eventually be given to all men. It was a dangerous subject, he acknowledged. He claimed to have a plan that might tame 'the storm that rumbles over our heads', and if they accepted him in their group and approved this idea, he promised to return to Saint-Domingue immediately to carry it out. (27)

Bongie, too, interprets Ogé's speech as having 'unequivocally called for an end to slavery' (1998, 285). Regardless, while Ogé's belief that 'liberty had been made for all men' may hardly be in dispute now, for some historians of the nineteenth century, as Anna Brickhouse has written, 'Ogé had traditionally been an icon of *mulâtre* elitism, a revolutionary who agitated for equal rights on behalf of Saint-Domingue's *gens de couleur libres* though not for extending such rights to its almost entirely *noir* population of slaves' (2004, 230). The perspective pointed to by Brickhouse pretty fairly encapsulates Schoelcher's interpretation of Ogé's speech and Faubert's play.

Schoelcher finds the references to slavery in Ogé's speech 'timid and dubitative on liberty' and 'accompanied' by what he viewed as 'that immediate corrective, *behold the slave who is raising the standard of revolt*,' rather than, ostensibly, the free people of color. Schoelcher viewed Ogé's vision that it would be the slaves, rather than someone like Ogé, who would create an insurrection as proof that Ogé 'hardly merits, it seems to us, the honors that they would like to give to him today' (1843, 2:221). Later, Schoelcher seemed to derive a kind of grotesque pleasure from thinking about how Ogé's gruesome punishment might have been a form of bad karma earned because Ogé had never been an abolitionist:

> This man, for whom we cannot plead in the least because he did not plead for the slaves, perhaps only died in his undertaking for not having wanted to have the negroes at all by his side, indicating with this, that he had separated his cause from that of the slaves. (1843, 2:224)

Schoelcher's second piece of evidence for his accusation that Ogé was throughout his life the 'incontestably avowed' 'enemy' of 'general emancipation' (1843, 2:222) was a letter he wrote in 1790 to the provincial assembly of the north in Saint-Domingue. In this letter, the erstwhile revolutionist seemed to confirm, at least as far as Schoelcher was concerned, that he had never made an argument for general emancipation in the first place. The letter implores the colonists to

> come to duly appreciate the purity of my intentions. When I solicited of the National Assembly the decree I obtained in favor of our American colonists, known under the hitherto *injurious* epithet of the *sang-mêlés*, *I never comprehended in my claims the negroes in a state of slavery*. You and

my adversaries have poisoned my proceedings with this, to destroy *my estimation in the minds of the honest planters*. No, no, Messieurs, *we have only demanded concessions for a class of free men*, who have endured the yoke of your oppression for two centuries. We only desire the execution of the decree of March 28 (qtd. in Schoelcher, 1843, 2:223, italics original).

This letter provides Schoelcher with the evidence he needs to conclude with these harsh words, 'Ogé, of a passionate and irritable character, devoted himself energetically to the triumph of his caste, we must recognize this. He was one of the first victims of the struggle undertaken by the people of color against the whites, but not of general independence, of which he never thought' (1843, 2:222).

The fissures in Schoelcher's claim for Ogé's status as a celebrity in nineteenth-century Haiti first begin to appear when he weakens his own argument about the uniformity of 'yellow' opinions about Ogé. With a rather 'loud aside' (2010a, 23), to use another of Stoler's terms, Schoelcher writes, 'We are not the first to have judged Ogé as he must be judged,' since, 'Juste Chanlatte, a mulatto general attached to the service of King Christophe,' had formed the same opinion. Schoelcher's judgment of Ogé is, in any case, based on a fundamental misreading of the relationship between the two documents to which he refers. That is to say that his reading of the 1790 letter as confirmation that Ogé had wanted to keep the slaves in slavery exhibits a confusion between Ogé's immediate *demand* that he and the other free people of color be given rights, according to the way in which they interpreted the Colonial Assembly's 'decree of March 28,' which he clarifies had nothing to do with the slaves in the 1790 letter, and Ogé's *beliefs* about slavery and emancipation as expressed before the Club Massiac in 1789, his philosophical cause, which had everything to do with the slaves. In other words, Schoelcher confused Ogé's demands for his beliefs. Similar (mis)readings led Schoelcher to likewise mischaracterize some of the claims made in the text of Chanlatte. For, while Chanlatte does criticize Ogé for his 'false step that can only be explained by his prideful enthusiasm or by the refined politics of those who put him into motion,' Chanlatte does not say that Ogé was the enemy of general emancipation, nor does he accuse Ogé of having wished for the continuation of slavery. As far as the idea that Ogé's revolt and punishment were connected in any way to the ensuing independence of Haiti, Chanlatte appears to agree. Chanlatte connects the persecution of Ogé directly to the independence of Haiti when he writes, 'But this punishment became an altar, and august liberty had to one day become connected to it, and soon enough to fix before it, her dear daughter, independence' (1824, 34).

It may very well be the case that Ogé never had any intentions to himself lead a slave rebellion when he returned to the colony of Saint-Domingue with the hopes of forcing the "white" planters to recognize his belief that the National Assembly had granted civil rights to the free people of color, as John Garrigus has argued in a recent article based on 'the often-ignored transcript of Ogé's January 1791 interrogation in Cap Français' (see Garrigus, 201, 33–35 and 22). It does not logically follow, however, that Ogé did not believe that general emancipation should not eventually take place or that he was the 'incontestable' 'enemy' of that principle. Quite the contrary, since Ogé stated in absolutely uncompromising terms that he believed that liberty 'was made for all men' and should be 'given' to all. The question of when and how that liberty was to be achieved, which for Ogé was the most important question of the era, provided the focus for Faubert's defense of his play, as well as his response to Schoelcher's criticism.

In the introduction to the 1856 printed version of the play, which Faubert claimed was exactly the same version Schoelcher had seen (a claim that will be examined in the following chapter), Faubert explains that he was a reluctant playwright, having merely sought to find an age-appropriate play for his students as a reward for having finished their exams (1856, 12). Faubert writes that while teaching his students a little history he wanted to entertain them, and that this was his only motive for having taken up the pen of the playwright. According to Faubert, despite his aims with the play,

> some time after it was performed at the *lycée*, a French abolitionist who had assisted in the distribution of the prizes, published a work on Haiti in which this piece was represented as having been the execution of an order given by the government, and as a piece that was written under the influence of color prejudice. (1856, 13)

Faubert defended himself against such a charge by writing, 'Certainly, in seeking as I had done, to guard my students against this color prejudice, it would have been difficult for me, it must be observed, to have foreseen a judgment of this nature' (1856, 13). He said that the charges were entirely without merit since no one in Boyer's government or the Haitian president's family had ever even seen the play performed, to his knowledge, and they certainly had never seen the manuscript before it was published (1856, 15). Faubert is confident, therefore, that in reading the play for themselves, his readers will reach the conclusion that 'the person who wrote it, and who in his youth, had the good fortune to see the abbé Grégoire often and to receive the marks of his benevolence, has not expressed a single idea, any sentiment that this venerable apostle of abolition would have condemned' (1856, 14–15).

Before presenting the play to the public, Faubert includes a lengthy introduction in which he earnestly defends his portrayal of Ogé on literary, historical, and political grounds. In Faubert's mind, his portrayal of Ogé was pretty consistent with the idea that Ogé was fighting only for the rights of the free people of color, but believed that liberty had to be given to the slaves as well, as stated in the 'Motion.' Nowhere in the text does Faubert present Ogé as having argued for the liberty of the slaves, though at least a couple of fictional characters do complain about the condition of the slaves and the color prejudices against them. Moreover, the trial of Ogé and his accomplices is nearly the only point at which Faubert allows Ogé to enter the revolutionary drama in a meaningful way. When Ogé is captured and eventually tried as a traitor, the Procureur-Général reads from portions of Ogé's Club Massiac speech in order to support his claim that Ogé's designs were for the liberation of the slaves all along. The Procureur-Général tells the court:

> Indeed, this matter has to do with the three leaders of the revolt who were taken with arms in their hands, whose intention, known to all of the world, was the extermination of the colonists, and the freedom of the slaves. I know that we have purported, on the strength of some false letters they have written, that their revolt had as its aim only the amelioration of the lot of the free people of color: but can we have so soon forgotten the discourse that the mulatto Ogé, the principal accused in this matter, imprudently undertook at the Club Massiac? Here, sirs, are his own words, 'This liberty, a word we do not pronounce without enthusiasm, and which brings with it the idea of happiness; this liberty, the greatest, the most valuable of goods, is it made for all men? I BELIEVE SO. Must it be given to all men? I STILL BELIEVE SO'. (102)

The Procurer-Général follows up this recitation of Ogé's words before the Club Massiac by evoking the idea that the sentiments expressed by Ogé in the 1790 letter had been disingenuous: 'and if the author of this speech said, after these words, that the slaves only needed to be emancipated gradually,' 'his only goal was, without a doubt, to conceal from the colonists his real motives' (103).

Faubert's creative and ironic usage of Ogé's 'Motion' is consistent with his defense of his portrayal of Ogé as a *believer* in gradual emancipation whose *aims* in 1790 were solely to force the colonists to recognize the rights he believed had been encoded into law on March 28. Faubert argued that there was nothing at all ahistorical in this portrayal. He said that it was exactly the same as Alphonse de Lamartine's, who in his *Histoires des Girondins* had called Ogé a 'Spartacus' (qtd. in Faubert, 1856, 34; see also Lamartine, 1847, 1:324). Before quoting a long passage from Lamartine's *Histoire*, to that effect, Faubert reminds his readers that he could not be accused of having copied from Lamartine since, 'I do not think it would be useless to remind you that he published his *Girondins* a long time after the year 1841, when this piece was first performed at the Lycée de Port-au-Prince' (1856, 31).

As far as Ogé's revolt having been in some way connected to the later Haitian Revolution, an argument to be found in countless versions of the Haitian Revolution published in the Atlantic World, Faubert's Ogé merely makes the following prophecy before being put to death on the infamous wheel:

> Very well, colonists, take advantage of this moment, satiate your animal passions! Go ahead even, contribute to our martyrdom and savor the last cry of our agony! But listen to me also, a prophet whom death illuminates. I am going to make a prediction: only a little more time, and the arm of Liberty will destroy your tyranny; only a little more time, and the vengeance of the oppressed will make you disappear from this land that you have stained with so many crimes! (1856, 111)

Faubert's portrayal of Ogé's revolt as foretelling the rage of the impending Revolution and eventual massacre of the French population is hardly exceptional, much less a *legendary* "mulatto" history, when compared to many other historical portrayals of Ogé in the transatlantic print culture of the Haitian Revolution. Faubert's account of Ogé's arrest and execution falls in line with the vast majority of eighteenth- and nineteenth-century writing about Ogé, particularly with Garran de Coulon's reproductions of the historical documents pertaining to Ogé's arrest, from which Faubert derived the language for the Procureur-Général—Faubert said that he had 'deleted only some insignificant words and modified one or two phrases' (1856, 109).

As far as historiography was concerned, Faubert explained that his methodology was a mix of oral history, personal memory, interviews with relevant individuals, and consultation of the works of writers he considered to be impartial historians. He said that he was uniquely positioned to tell the story of Ogé, 'since several of my relatives were contemporaries of Ogé; in such a way that since my youth, I was, I can say it, accustomed to consider him in the way that I have represented him' (25). He further wrote:

> I would add that my view of things was only strengthened by the conversations that took place in my presence, at the home of the abbé Grégoire, during these difficult times; and if my memory is correct, the members of the *Société des Amis des Noirs*[23] who saw Ogé often had to moderate his

---

23 According to Carolyn Fick's description of the events, Faubert's argument may have some merit: 'Even the Société des Amis des Noirs,' she writes, 'the one group that did advocate for the immediate abolition of the slave trade ... found it more politically judicious to pose its arguments on humanitarian and moral grounds. For to directly

ardent sympathy for his brother slaves; they all thought, and they told him so, that any premature or illegal [*irrégulier*] actions could only hurt their cause, in providing an attack plan [*beau jeu*] for the enemies of emancipation, who were strong and numerous, against the abolitionists, who were subject to hatred and the most violent lies. (1856, 25–26)

Faubert's representation of what he believed to be the complicated perspective of Ogé is pretty similar to the version that Thomas Madiou would tell in his *Histoire d'Haïti*. According to Madiou, Ogé visited both the Club Massiac and the Société des Amis des Noirs in order to propose to them his policy of gradual emancipation. Madiou said that at the Club Massiac Ogé wanted to propose a policy that would have avoided a bloody conflict, but would also have gradually freed the slaves and compensated slaveholders (1:72).[24] According to Madiou, despite the fact that Ogé was 'coldly' received at the Club Massiac and not even permitted to fully espouse his theory on the merits of gradual emancipation (1:73), on March 28, 1790 the National Assembly produced a series of addendums to their original decree of March 8, one of which declared that all property owners over the age of 25 should have equal rights in the colony. Consequently, Ogé rushed home to see the effects of the decree upon life in Saint-Domingue. Madiou documents the obstacles Ogé faced when attempting to return to Saint-Domingue.[25] He points out that the Club Massiac had orchestrated an elaborate plan to prevent 'mulattoes' who had been 'enlightened' [*éclairés*] in Paris from returning to the colonies, fearing that they would 'propagate the ideas of liberty in the colonies that the European *philosophes* were spreading with much enthusiasm' (1:75). Madiou says that, ultimately, it was Julien Raimond who had 'calmed' the 'revolutionary ardor' of Ogé, convincing him that

---

attack the economic foundations of these issues would be to attack the legitimacy of key sectors of the national economy and formidable sources of the nation's wealth' (1997, 52).

24 Alphonse de Lamartine, who agitated for an end to slavery in French colonies in the 1840s, also believed that slave-holders would need to be compensated monetarily by the government to avoid financial ruin for the country and personal ruin for the planters. Lamartine discusses this in the preface to the first printed edition of his play *Toussaint Louverture* (1850) (republished in the 1998 version), where he credits himself with the abolition of slavery after the French Revolution of 1848 (1998, 2–11).

25 The troubles Ogé had reportedly faced when attempting to return to Saint-Domingue are also documented by the author of the *Histoire des désastres de Saint-Domingue*, who writes, 'His project was not such a secret that interested persons in France were unaware of it, and certain measures were put into place in all of the ports in order to prevent him embarking and arriving at his destination. Stubborn in his demands and braving all of the difficulties put in his way, he found a way to get to London, from there to North America, and finally to Saint-Domingue, where he arrived undetected and disguised on an Anglo-American ship' (161).

'time would bring the ameliorations that all men desire who are friends of humanity' (qtd. in Madiou, 1:74)

While Faubert does not go so far as to portray Ogé as needing to be calmed down by any of the other revolutionaries with respect to raising the slaves, or as having ever argued for immediate emancipation, referring to the actual written documents cited by Schoelcher, Faubert writes that the few statements Ogé made regarding slavery and slaves, 'do not prove anything against him' (1856, 30). This is because, in Faubert's interpretation, Ogé was a proponent of gradual rather than immediate emancipation, a position Faubert believed to be that of the majority of abolitionists at the end of the eighteenth century (1856, 26). Faubert writes that nearly all of the abolitionists of 1790 were 'generally in favor of gradual emancipation [*l'émancipation preparée*]' (1856, 27), including the abbé Grégoire (1856, 36).[26] Faubert's opinion was shared by Madiou, who said, 'you would have to be completely misled by passion or completely ignorant of the facts to submit that in 1789, 1790, 1791, and 1792 ideas of general liberty had been completely formed in their minds, be it of the blacks, be it of the *hommes de couleur*' (1:335). Faubert, for his part, adds that even the abbé Grégoire could not find fault with Ogé's idea of gradual emancipation, since 'if Ogé is guilty ... so are all of us' (qtd. in Faubert, 1856, 36).

Saint-Rémy, too, in one of the 1843 letters he published as a response to Schoelcher's *Colonies étrangères*, presents Ogé as the product of his era.[27] Far

[26] Interestingly, according to Garrigus, initially Grégoire was not interested in abolitionism at all, since before 1789 he was primarily known for being an 'advocate of Jewish assimilation' in eastern France (2006, 239). Raimond, however, convinced Grégoire to become an advocate of the free people of color, but not necessarily the slaves, when he traveled to the metropole just before the French Revolution. In fact, Garrigus tells us that Grégoire's sudden argument for immediate emancipation startled Raimond, who thought that this position might harm the free people of color's attempts to achieve equal rights and representation (2006, 240).

[27] In Nicholls's interpretation of this exchange, Saint-Rémy blames 'Schoelcher's own people, the whites' for having 'armed the mulattoes against the blacks' during the Haitian Revolution and vice versa (1979, 95). Nicholls says that in the letters to *La Sentinelle*, Saint-Rémy even accused Schoelcher himself of 'attempting once more to divide blacks from mulattoes in the interests of the whites,' and argued that '[i]t was Schoelcher's own people, the whites, who were "the source of all the evils" of Haiti' (1979, 95). However, my reading of the letters is that the dispute was more a philosophical disagreement between the two men. Saint-Rémy viewed his argument with the French abolitionist as one between a 'philanthropist' (Saint-Rémy) and a 'négrophile' (Schoelcher), on the one hand, and between someone who had access to documents that could prove the truth (Saint-Rémy) and someone who had relied upon a false colonial archive (Schoelcher), on the other. In the first letter, Saint-Rémy reveals that he had actually met Schoelcher during the latter's visit to Haiti and that though he

from arguing that Ogé was the true hero of the Haitian Revolution, the founder of Haitian independence, or the champion of the abolition of slavery, Saint-Rémy acknowledged, 'in fact, no one—neither the white planters, nor the *petits blancs*, nor the free negroes, nor the *sang-mêlés*—no one thought to attend to the raising of the minds [of the slaves].' This did not, however, mean that Ogé or any other free person of color did not believe that slavery was wrong, even though many of them had benefited from it in the past. Citing Ogé's various statements on the abolition of slavery, his contribution to the *Cahier des doléances*, as well as several anti-slavery statements made by Raimond in March of 1791, in the same letter Saint-Rémy argued that although the *anciens libres*, those with both light and dark skin, did initially see their cause as separate from that of the slaves, many of them came to view emancipation as inevitable, purposeful, and necessary. However, at the moment of the October 1790 rebellion, Saint-Rémy writes, 'Ogé did not believe that the moment had come to raise the workers [*les ateliers*]' ('Lettres,' 14 December 1843).

Bissette had also provided an 'apology' for the late eighteenth-century advocates of 'gradual emancipation,' but he would accuse Schoelcher of having been the ultimate Haitian exceptionalist on that point. Bissette reminded his readers that the venerated French abolitionist had himself once been an advocate of eventual emancipation. Discussing Schoelcher's criticism of Faubert, Bissette writes:

> M. Schoelcher would have wanted Ogé to speak, in 1789, of the liberty of the slaves as we speak of it *today*; that is to say as he did not even speak of it himself, in 1830, when he wrote in the *Revue de Paris* that 'those who wanted the immediate and spontaneous abolition of slavery were wasting their time' [*ceux qui veulent l'abolition de l'esclavage actuelle et spontanée font du sentiment en pure perte*]. (qtd. in Bissette, 31)[28]

had tried to help the French traveler by furnishing him with 'voluminous documents' related to 'the study of the causes of color prejudice,' Schoelcher disregarded them all. In Saint-Rémy's mind, it was this failure to consult the Haitian archive that had resulted in the 'thousands of errors' to be found in *Colonies étrangères et Haïti*, especially by one whom Saint-Rémy acknowledged 'preached against prejudices' ('Lettres,' 9 November 1853). Nevertheless, it should also be acknowledged that while it is true that in his letters to *La Sentinelle*, Saint-Rémy takes issue with many of the 'facts' put forth in Schoelcher's history of Haiti and blames the French colonists for any color prejudice there, in a much later letter to the editor published in the radical French republican journal *La Réforme*, on January 25, 1849, Saint-Rémy actually defends Schoelcher for his contributions to the abolition of slavery even while maintaining much of his earlier criticism of the French traveler turned historian.

28 Incidentally, it seems that Bissette, who had actually owned slaves in Martinique, had also at one time been a proponent of gradual emancipation. Brickhouse writes,

Francophone Genealogy of the 'Mulatto Legend of History'

Even Baron de Vastey, speaking ostensibly of the free people of color of which he had once been a part, had argued in an article written for the *Gazette Royale d'Hayti* on August 27, 1816 that:

> As for us, we were content to enjoy the specter of liberty [granted by the decree of 1792]; we allowed ourselves to be peacefully led under the rule, so to speak, of the ex-colonists; no idea of independence had yet entered into our minds, and the thought had not yet come to any of us that we could be both free and independent. ('Suite du Coup,' 2)

Contemporary historians have in some senses confirmed the idea that hardly anyone was to speak of emancipation in the era of Ogé, which is to say in the early 1790s. David Geggus has written, for example, that even in the documents signed by former slaves turned rebel leaders, Jean-François and Georges Biassou, '[w]e are a long way from the language of rights,' for, '[a]ddressing the concerns of the free men in the rebel camp, the[se documents] do not really support the contention of certain historians that the slave leaders demanded "full political rights"' (2007b, 312). I think it is safe to conclude that as far as the charge of having 'falsified history' goes, Faubert was no more guilty than any other writer of the era. In other words, we could hardly say that he had contributed to a kind of history that was anymore *legendary* than anyone else's. Moreover, the kind of worldview that would allow Schoelcher to critique Ogé for an opinion he himself had once shared, is the very rock upon which the 'Haitian exceptionalism' of the trope of the "colored historian," and its modern-day expression in the 'mulatto legend of history,' has been built.

'Initially adopting what historians of slavery have termed a gradualist approach to the emancipation of slaves, Bissette here writes from the tautological assumption that the abolition of slavery is fundamental to the promotion of liberty, and thus a noble goal, while nevertheless treating the issue as a "great question" to be considered not in absolute terms but in relation to the "general good"' (2004, 92).

CHAPTER TWELVE

'Let us be Humane after the Victory': Pierre Faubert's 'New Humanism'

'Faites-vous français, allemand ou américain. C'est le seul moyen d'être respecté et protégé sur le sol d'Haïti ... Faites-vous donc étranger, et Haïti deviendra pour vous un délicieux paradis ...'
—Justin Lhérisson, *La Famille des Pitite-Caille* (1905)

'Monde noir, ai-je dit? Cela aussi est un péché de rhétorique, car même la couleur de leur peau s'en allait se différenciant du brun chocolat, du chocolat clair au noir d'ébène ou au rouge brique.'
—Jean Price-Mars, *La Vocation de l'élite* (1919)

'Tout cet africanisme m'ennuie. Je peux bien aussi chanter mes ancêtres blancs.'
—Carl Brouard, 'Thibaut de Champagne'

An epistemological practice of (mis)reading that involves *a priori* judgments about the political ideologies operating in a text based on the perceived "race" or skin color of the author involved, whose origins I have located in claims Victor Schoelcher made about 'l'imagination jaune' of nineteenth-century Haitian historians, is directly linked to the relative critical silence surrounding the published version of Pierre Faubert's play *Ogé, ou le préjugé de couleur*. Despite the fact that Faubert was internationally known for his poetry and drama in the nineteenth-century Atlantic World (Bonneau, 1862, 14; St. John, 310–11; Vapereau, 967; Viau, 1861, 4; Schoelcher, 1893), the printed version of *Ogé*, which appeared in Paris with C. Maillet-Schmitz in 1856, has been largely overlooked, dismissed, or discounted in twentieth-century literary criticism. Bearing the broad influence of the trope of the "colored historian," when Faubert's drama has been mentioned in contemporary accounts of nineteenth-century Haitian literary culture, it is usually only within the peritext of a larger argument about "mulatto" biases (Garrigus, 2010, 20; Hoffmann, 1994, 366; Bongie, 1998, 284). As such, interpretive readings of the actual content of the play, with the notable exception of the chapter 'Transamerican theatre: Pierre Faubert and L'Oncle Tom' in Anna Brickhouse's *Transamerican Literary Relations and the Nineteenth-Century Public Sphere* (2004), have ordinarily been subordinated to ancillary footnotes or asides.

One example of the way in which preconceived notions about the political ideology behind Faubert's play have inhibited attempts to interpret it on literary grounds involves the inference and often the direct claim that Faubert had significantly revised his play after being forced into exile in 1851 in order to make it appear to be about combating color prejudice. Faubert's own statements concerning the genealogy of the play directly contradict the notion that his declared anti-racism position had been contrived as a defense against Schoelcher's critique. In the introduction to the play, Faubert wrote that *Ogé* had always been about combating color prejudice and urging unity among all sectors of the Haitian population. He said that he had only written the play in order to show his students 'all that is absurd and odious in color prejudice,' and that this alone was the 'the origin of the piece that I am publishing today' (1856, 13).

Importantly, Faubert, who would eventually act as the Haitian ambassador to the Pope at the request of Haitian President Fabre Geffrard ('Later from Hayti'; Morpeau, 59), remarked that in the 15-year interlude between the play's staging and its publication, he had only made some 'minor modifications' to the story. While he may fall short of providing a list of everything he might have changed, Faubert did make a deliberate point of underscoring the fact that these 'modifications' 'only concern a few details of staging [*mis en scène*] and style and a few ancillary developments that would not have been appropriate in a work intended for pupils [*élèves d'un collège*]' (37).

Faubert's claim that the play had always been about dismantling color prejudices rather than staging (and falsifying) history might be most strengthened by the consideration that he could have changed one of the most controversial elements of the play for publication and did not: the scene in which in the autumn of 1790, Ogé carries Dessalines's bi-color flag of 1803. Not only does Faubert leave the controversial scene intact, but he defends his choice on the grounds of literature and politics, rather than history, as he had done with most of Schoelcher's other objections. Invoking artistic license, Faubert directly addressed Schoelcher's criticism of the fact that in *Ogé* the erstwhile revolutionary carries the blue and red flag that had been created by Dessalines in the spring of 1803 rather than the red, white, and blue tricolor that would have been carried by the French army in 1790 (1856, 17–18). Faubert accused Schoelcher of double standards in his criticism of Haitian literature and art, with respect to his inference that the Haitian director had 'sacrifice[d] historical probity for his political passions' (Schoelcher, 1843, 219). Faubert pointed out that he was hardly alone among playwrights in merging different moments in history for the purposes of a storyline. After quoting a stanza of poetry from the French poet Boileau to prove his point ('Maigres historiens suivront l'ordre des temps' [18]), Faubert said that he could 'cite several examples of such literary anachronism that would be easy to call forth in the memory of anyone who is cultivated in literature [*lettres*]' (1856, 18).

Appearing to sense that this explanation would hardly satisfy his most fervent critics, Faubert turned to politics. He explained that at the time he wrote *Ogé*, a play that had been intended only for his students and their parents, 'and so to speak, in the family' (1856, 18), he also had a more pragmatic reason for presenting Ogé with the bi-color flag of the War of Independence: 'My audience was composed largely of veterans of the war of independence; and the tricolor flag had been that of the fateful expedition which was symbolized in our country by so much excess.' The three colors of the French flag, therefore,

> were a reminder to these proscribed victors of another time, of memories that were therefore too painful for it to have been used on our stage; I had to think about that even more after the [French] revolution of 1830,[29] when they were displayed outside the French Consulate in Port-au-Prince, and more than one of our veterans said to me: 'When I see this flag again, I think about having witnessed the drowning and hangings which took place under general Rochambeau.' So I thought that in a work that was not at all designed to go beyond the realm for which it was produced, I would rather expose myself to the reproach of not having been absolutely *factual* [*exact*] ... than that of having encouraged old enmities that we must try on the contrary to quell. (1856, 18–19)

At the present time, other than Schoelcher's equivocal and itself necessarily biased account of the play, there is little evidence that there was any marked difference between the version Faubert created for the students of the *lycée* in 1841, which he continued to stage throughout the rest of the decade, and the version he offered to the public in 1856 while living in exile in Paris.[30] Until

---

29 Faubert refers to the July of 1830 Revolution in France that resulted in the implementation of a constitutional monarchy under Louis Philippe. See Gildea (2008).

30 Schoelcher's opening comments about *Ogé* in *Colonies étrangères* in some ways support Faubert's account concerning his own motives. In a passage of *Colonies étrangères* that is ordinarily not referenced *vis-à-vis* Schoelcher's writing about *Ogé*, Schoelcher

such time as further evidence in the way of earlier drafts of the play might be uncovered, or we have access to first person descriptions made by some other nineteenth-century observers, it would be disingenuous and even cynical in a Haitian exceptionalist kind of way, for us to refuse to even acknowledge Faubert's claims that he only made very minor changes to the body of the play. (Mis)reading in this way, refusing to allow for evidence that might help to provide us with clues about a text's literary history—even though acknowledging the history of the play might ultimately do little to help us in our interpretations of *Ogé*—when we do not have evidence to support our disbelief, is once again to imply that we know better. Such intuitive and ever-skeptical *knowledge*, while it may be useful in certain kinds of historiography, operates to quite a different effect in critical interpretations of literary fictions.

The contemporary study of literary criticism perhaps inevitably results in a certain familiarity with and training in the methodology and theories of New Critics like W.K. Wimsatt and Monroe C. Beardsley. For these theorists, the kind of authorial intent implied by Faubert's account of his motives for writing *Ogé* would have needed to be treated as ambiguous, irrelevant, or irrecoverable with respect to the interpretation of what his

stated of the play, 'This piece, which has no action [*cette pièce sans action*], just like all of those [plays] written by people who are unaccustomed to the theater, [is] well written and in good taste' (2:219). Schoelcher goes on to describe the subject matter of the play as, 'the taking to arms of Ogé and Chavannes,' and he said that the drama was both 'national and designed to encourage every sympathy' (2: 219). The idea that the play had been designed to occasion 'sympathy' rather than the kind of dissensions of which Schoelcher would later accuse it of promoting seems to contradict Schoelcher's claim that Faubert had deliberately 'falsified history' to validate 'yellow' domination. That is to say that Schoelcher gives with one hand and takes away with the other. For his statement makes of Faubert both an unwitting and a deliberate participant in a 'mulatto legend of history.' Incidentally, Ardouin had accused Isambert of a similar sort of backhanded generosity when, after the French abolitionist completely lambasted the Haitian government of Boyer, Isambert wrote that he was pointing out the wrongs of the Haitian government because he was the 'uncontestable friend of a long-oppressed race' and was 'shedding tears over the extraordinary blindness' of Boyer's government, 'and the strange spectacle that you are putting on for the entire world,' and that he was only saying these things, 'because I believe in the purity of your intentions.' To this, Ardouin wrote, '… please permit me to tell you, Sir, the final words of your letter are in complete contradiction with the entire *ensemble* of the accusation that you have set out. In effect, how can you say that you *believe in the purity of our intentions*, when you have just spoken of us in such unequivocal terms about our supposed tyranny over the black race, our military despotism that, according to you, we have created in order to remove all guarantees of innocence, to take away the political and civil liberty of our citizens, etc. etc.?' (1842, 23, emphases in original).

literary work *does*. In Wimsatt and Beardsley's theory, relying upon the external motivations of an author for the purposes of explicating a work of literature is called the 'intentional fallacy.' They explain that the problem with trying to interpret or decipher the meaning of a poem in this way, based on ideas about the author's intent, is problematic because it 'begins by trying to derive the standard of criticism from the psychological *causes* of the poem and ends in biography and relativism' (21). Unlike the modern-day reader of Ogé, at the time he wrote *Colonies étrangères*, Schoelcher did not have access to Faubert's own expression of his motivations for writing the play. To get at Faubert's motives, Schoelcher used his own interpretation of the play as revelatory of Faubert's psychology at the moment that he envisioned the Haitian school director composing the play. According to Wimsatt and Beardsley's method, this would be called the 'Affective Fallacy,' or 'confusion' between the work and 'its *results*,' which they say is a 'special case of epistemological skepticism' (21). Using this frame of reference, we might observe that Schoelcher mistook his interpretation of what the play was *doing*—in his estimation, the 'falsification of history' and/or the encouragement of color prejudice—for a revelation of Faubert's *true* motives in creating the play: to legitimatize the political domination of "mulattoes" over "blacks." We might then conclude that Schoelcher believed that the 'psychological causes' of the play were revealed in the content of the play itself. The inability of Schoelcher to distinguish between what he believed to have been the *effects* of the play and what he believed to have been the political *mindset* of the author at the moment he wrote it constitutes 'epistemological skepticism' because it relies upon a longstanding critical habit of cynically (mis)reading everything to do with Haiti through the lens of "racial" domination. This form of cynicism has led directly to a phenomenon in contemporary literary criticism whereby scholars almost without fail offer seemingly *commonsense*, but fairly unsupported, judgments about not only the content of the play, but its literary genealogy. Despite the lack of evidence to prove Schoelcher's claims, Faubert's avowals concerning the literary genealogy of the piece have hardly been regarded with seriousness by either historians or literary critics, who have tended to infer, if not directly claim, that Faubert must have significantly revised the play in the 15-year gap between its first staging and its first publication.

With respect to the scene in *Ogé* in which the Procureur-Général recites a portion of Ogé's speech before the Club Massiac, it may be reasonable to interpret the 'absence of a source in the notes' as indicative of the 'fictional status of Ogé's speech, which is rendered in the same style as the play's numerous other quotations from historical documents such as the Code Noir' (Brickhouse, 2004, 232), and thus infer that with this play Faubert '[e]xploit[s] the imaginative similarities between history and fiction' by

'Let us be Humane after the Victory'

'report[ing Ogé's] words as if excerpted from an official document while tracing the official accounts of his proslavery stance to a pretense on the part of the planters themselves' (Brickhouse, 2004, 232). Yet a glimpse at the historical archive available to Faubert leads us to a vastly different conclusion. As I pointed out in chapter eleven of the present volume, the excerpted portion of Ogé's speech in Faubert's play closely matches the published version of that same speech that had circulated in the late eighteenth-century Atlantic World and would also be reprinted in volume one of Thomas Madiou's *Histoire d'Haïti* (1848), its printing in the latter suggesting that the document was still in circulation in the mid-nineteenth century. Perhaps, then, the absence of a footnote in *Ogé* indicates that Faubert believed that the speech was still a part of common knowledge (and therefore that a footnote was hardly necessary) in a mid-nineteenth-century French Atlantic World where Madiou and the famous French historian Jules Michelet were part of the same intellectual and historical circles.[31]

The idea that Faubert only imagined the speech tends to unwittingly lend legitimacy to Schoelcher's unproven claim that nineteenth-century Haitian writers invented Ogé as a hero in order to create a *legendary* history that could be used for the purposes of political and "racial" domination. It is, in fact, the latter of the *commonsense* claims mentioned above—that Faubert must have significantly rewritten or reconstituted *Ogé* in the interval between its first performance in 1841 and its publication in 1856—that much more directly serves the pervasive idea of the 'mulatto legend of history.' Garrigus, in particular, has unwittingly evoked the trope of the "colored historian" in wanting to see the 1856 version as having been deliberately 'transformed' by Faubert to become a self-conscious 'statement about the absurdity of color prejudice' (2010, 20). This conclusion can be reached, primarily, it seems, because the published edition of the play is rather overtly anti-color prejudice and does not make heroes of Haitian independence out of Ogé, Chavannes, or Pétion (who does not even appear in the play). Garrigus writes that Schoelcher 'saw Faubert's play during a visit to Haiti and described it as an example of mulatto prejudices against darker-skinned Haitians' (2010, 20). In the absence of anything that would confirm Schoelcher's reading and therefore affirm the trope of the "colored historian," the seemingly reasonable conclusion has been that the version of the play that Faubert ultimately published in 1856 must not have been the same version that he staged throughout the 1840s in Port-au-Prince. This kind of judgment about

---

31 Michelet and Madiou apparently kept up a friendly correspondence and held each other in mutual admiration. Their friendship is documented along with reprints of several of Michelet's important letters to Madiou and other Haitian historians in Hoffmann (1985, 10–12).

the play's literary history, which would make Faubert an erstwhile part of the 'nearly thirty years of mulatto oligarchy' under Boyer (Garrigus, 2010, 20), has meant that the almost singular critical focus on the play continues to be on the kind of ideological statement Faubert putatively *desired* to make with *Ogé*, rather than on the myriad interpretive (and unintentional) meanings that we might be able to derive from various readings of the *effects* of the play.

Trying to interpret the play primarily in terms that are consonant with the trope of the "colored historian" or the 'mulatto legend of history' has been to invite what is the most negative consequence of both affective and intentional fallacies. That is, that the 'poem itself,' or the play, in this case, 'as an object of specifically critical judgment, tends to disappear' (Beardsley and Wimsatt, 21). Sacrificing reading the substance of the play in favor of (mis)reading the "color" of the play has meant that the aesthetics of *Ogé* has hardly ever been considered as a subject of interpretation. Not only that, but what we might call Faubert's contribution to a proto-*critical race theory*, which is elaborated upon in the play itself as well as in the supporting documents that accompanied its publication, has been entirely overlooked. Most importantly, operating under the assumptions of the "colored historian" has further meant that the larger philosophical claims of the play with respect to violence as a method of political change have all but been ignored.

This is where the New Critics and I must part ways, nevertheless. For although Beardsley and Wimsatt's skepticism of authorial intent has been useful in some contexts of a literary history like this one, unlike them, I believe that the world in which the text was created (which is to say the world in which the author lived as opposed to our beliefs about the 'psychology' of the author him or herself) intimately matters to our interpretation of a work of literature because the author's world intimately mattered in the creation of the literary text itself. In other words, this literary history seeks to expose the often unconscious, and therefore at times unintentional, interplay between ideas about "race" in circulation in the Atlantic World and ideas about the Haitian Revolution. While the text may have something to tell us about the author's world, so, too, might the world of the author have something to tell us about the life of the text. From this perspective, when viewed as merely one more text within a broader transatlantic print culture of the Haitian Revolution, the entire corpus of which is just as subjective, historically idiosyncratic, and wholly open to interpretation as *Ogé*, it hardly matters whether Faubert's play can be considered historically *accurate* or not. Even less important is the fact that the play was written by a person whom many may have been considered to be, and who may have considered himself to have been, a "mulatto." Much more important for understanding the place of *Ogé* in the literary history of the Haitian Revolution is the way in which the tropologies of "race" circulating in the Atlantic World are reflected in the representation of revolutionary events in the play and consequently the relationship of the play's attempt to dismantle a "mulatto/a" vengeance narrative of the Haitian Revolution that had been used to justify continuing international aggression against Haiti in the global political sphere.

The poetics that emerges in the printed edition of *Ogé* once the shadow of the "colored historian" has been appropriately removed, is one of a text that reflects deep awareness of how the narrative of "mulatto/a" vengeance had been immediately informed by a dual discourse of exceptionalism. This was a discourse that involved ideas not only about "race" in Haiti, but about "race" in the United States. In his introduction to *Ogé*, Faubert seems to have understood presciently that, as Elizabeth Maddock Dillon and Michael Drexler have recently written, 'Haitian exceptionalism has its double in American exceptionalism' in so far as 'one [is] superlatively negative and the other superlatively positive.' Yet, whereas Dillon and Drexler locate the difference between these 'twin exceptionalisms' in our current moment of U.S.–Haitian relations, where Haiti has become a place that is 'conceptually far, far away' to U.S. Americans (forthcoming, n.p.), Faubert positioned nineteenth-century Haitians and U.S. Americans as uniquely close. As one of Haiti's Atlantic neighbors and the only other independent nation of the American hemisphere, the writings collected in *Ogé, ou le préjugé de couleur*[32] acknowledge and even make the case that events taking place in the United States had every relevance for Haitians. This was especially true where "race," slavery, and color prejudice were concerned. Faubert argued that attempts to locate color prejudice as an exceptional feature of life in Haiti were merely attempts to render less visible the fact that it was the United States, which Faubert situated as Haiti's potentially imperial enemy and its potentially friendly sovereign *double*, that was the quintessence of an exceptional land of color prejudice. Faubert wrote about U.S. slavery as that which made 'Americans' wholly unqualified to speak of color prejudice in the land of universal freedom he viewed Haiti to be.

If much of Faubert's introduction and at least one of the 'fugitive poems' that he appended to the published volume of *Ogé* are directly concerned with explicating the differences between the kind of color prejudice found in the United States, which was then supporting slavery, and the kind that was often reported to be a feature of mid-nineteenth-century Haiti, the body of the play offers quite a different commentary. Delphine and Alfred, two

---

32 The 1856 edition contained a dedication to Faubert's mother, a short 'Avertissement,' the introduction to the play, the play itself, a collection of 18 'Fugitive Poems,' and a lengthy collection of supporting historical documents, which included a short story about a 'maroon' slave named Marcio, which Faubert said he had penned at the age of 22 (166).

of the play's fictional characters, in the sense that they have no corollary to actual historical figures of the Haitian Revolution, separately and together offer philosophies of political revolution and juridical retribution that do not involve violence. Both of these characters prove to be fairly unyielding in their remonstrations against color prejudice as well as in their conceptions of universal humanity or what we might today call global human rights. This uncompromising attitude towards the functional inutility of violence (as well as the ills of color prejudice) seems to have had much less to do with criticizing the events of the Haitian Revolution or making historical claims about the life of Ogé than with the 'irruption' into political 'modernity' (Glissant, 1989, 100) caused by the military and political successes of the slaves during the Haitian Revolution.

The revolutionary logic endorsed by the most ardent avenger of the slaves in Saint-Domingue, Jean-Jacques Dessalines, had encouraged defensive violence as the singular answer to the political non-existence of both the slaves and the free people of color. Dessalines's revolutionary rhetoric also encouraged post-independence Haitians to view violence as the continuous key to their sovereignty. In his 'Proclamation at Gonaïves' addressing the citizens of the newly formed Haiti, Dessalines reminded the populace that liberty had only been won by the price of 'your blood':

> remember that you have done nothing, if you do not provide to the nations of the world a terrible but righteous example of the vengeance that must be exercised by a people who are proud of having restored their liberty and are wary when it comes to protecting it; let us frighten anyone who would dare to attempt to take it once again: let us begin with the French … Let them tremble in approaching our shores, if not from the memory of the cruelties they have committed here, at least from the terrible resolve that we are going to make, to condemn to death anyone born French who would defile, with his sacrilegious foot, the territory of liberty. (rpt. in Boisrond-Tonnerres, 1851, 4–5)

Such unqualified and perhaps perpetual violence against the French is here justified by the 'memory of the cruelties' perpetrated by the colonists and becomes the means to induce the birth of the Haitian citizenry, first, as physical beings rather than as property, and later the birth of their sovereign lives. However, for many political commentators in the Atlantic World, the end of slavery, or the end of 'bare life,' which has been lucidly defined in the context of slavery, as 'damaged life, stripped of its political significance' (Ziarek), should logically have meant the end of violence. In other words, if 'slavery was a continuation of the state of War' (Fischer, 2007, 6), then the end of slavery in Saint-Domingue should have meant the end of the 'state of War.'

'Let us be Humane after the Victory'

Constant French threats to Haiti's independence throughout the nineteenth century, however, kept alive the perpetual 'state of War' ostensibly called for by Dessalines. This was particularly the case after the government of Christophe captured (and executed?)[33] Franco Medina, one of the three agents sent by France to independent Haiti in order to pave the way for France's plan to retake the former colony. In his attempt to justify the gruesome punishment of Medina, Baron de Vastey observed that even

> the least clairvoyant know without a doubt that the French want to plunge us back into slavery or to destroy us; convinced of this great truth, we hear everywhere in all parts only cries to arms! the elderly, women, children are asking for weapons; already the brave soldiers of the mountains ... have outfitted themselves with huge and long swords and pikes in order to fight the French; we hope that this example will be followed throughout the kingdom; we only hear one shout: *Because the French must come, let them come only once! the more who come, the more we will kill!* ('Royaume d'Hayti,' 4)

After the "deal" struck in 1825 by France's Charles X with Haitian President Jean-Pierre Boyer to pay off an illegitimate debt to the tune of 150 million francs as the price of French recognition of Haitian independence, and with Boyer subsequently out of power in 1843 after what was considered a repressive regime, many Haitian authors began to speak once more of the country's 'regeneration.' This word implied both that the 'state of War' between Haiti and France had finally come to an end, and that with Boyer out of power, Haitians could finally achieve democracy (see 'République Haïtienne'; 'Au Héros de la régénération haïtienne'; *Le Manifeste*; 'Installation de l'assemblée'). In 1843, Haitian officials even began to sign their documents with the phrase, 'the 40th year of the independence of Haiti, and the 1st of its regeneration' ('Programme'). This 'regeneration' involved an almost constant reconsideration and renegotiation of Haiti's relationship to the international world and, specifically, entailed endless debates about the constitutional principle that had banned "whites" from owning property in Haiti, first included in Article 12 of Dessalines's 1805 Constitution (see, for

---

33 Contrary to the claims of Saint-Rémy, in his *Réflexions politiques*, Vastey, who was intimately involved in the Medina affair, wrote that the French spy had not been executed: 'Franco Medina is still alive,' Vastey writes, 'for more than four years we have been keeping this spy as living proof of [Pétion's] loyalty to the French cabinet' (145). According to Jean Brière, Laffont de Labédat had also affirmed in 1815 that Medina had not been executed by Christophe's government. Nevertheless, the family of Medina, who never returned either to France or to Santo Domingo, where his relatives were living, eventually received a pension from Louis XVIII (Brière, 68).

example, 'Fait Divers'; 'Citoyens Constituants'). It was not just the property exclusions and the enmity towards the French, which were considered to be a form of violence by many Haitian authors (and a form of "mulatto/a" vengeance by outside observers), and therefore, an obstacle for 'regeneration,' that now needed to be reconsidered. The 'regeneration' of Haiti also centered on a debate about how the country should best be governed and by whom. The regeneration of Haiti referenced above was intimately linked to the promise that many writers saw in the provisory government of Charles Hérard, whose mission was seen to be 'not simply revolutionary, but *régénateur*' in the sense that it would eventually develop into a permanent government whose head of state would be chosen by the people.

An untitled article published in *Le Manifeste* on October 1, 1843 explicitly discussed how every Haitian leader up until Hérard had been a dictator of some kind. The article states:

> Is it not to dictatorship that we owe all of the misfortunes, vices, and the deep corruption in which the country has been submerged? From Dessalines up until this day, what have we had here?—dictatorship, nothing but dictatorship: The country was Dessalines [*Le pays c'était Dessalines*], was Pétion, was Boyer.[34]

The author subsequently warned that the 'regeneration' of Haiti was being halted once again by the fact that Hérard had been encouraged 'to be again a sovereign and a dictator.' 'He should protest against this dictatorship,' the author writes, 'because it was out of hatred for dictatorship that the revolution [against Boyer] had taken place,—to accept a dictatorship, would be to betray the revolution, would be to perpetuate that which [the revolution] was understood to have forever sacrificed.'

Faubert was writing, staging, and then publishing *Ogé* after ostensibly having witnessed not only the opposition to Boyer, but the eventual violent overthrow of Hérard, who did indeed become a dictator, and then the same violence of *coup d'état* against Guerrier and Pierrot, along with the mysterious death of Richet/Riché, which was followed by the ascension to power of Soulouque, under whose reign Faubert would be banished to exile. When we consider the fact that between the ousting of Boyer in 1843 and the assumption of the Haitian presidency by Fabre Geffrard in 1859, Haiti had seen seven rulers in only fifteen years, it is not hard to imagine that many Haitians were frustrated that both the government and citizenry of Haiti were abusing their power. *Ogé* is thus being performed and published

---

34 The phrase 'Le pays c'était Dessalines ...' seems to be a play on the famous phrase attributed to Louis XIV, 'L'état, c'est moi.' See Rowen (1961, 83–98).

in a milieu in which the sentiment was being expressed, as demonstrated by the article in *Le Manifeste*, that Haiti's government had been merely one long chain of dictators. If frustrations about the utility and meaning of violence come to the surface in *Ogé*, therefore, they may very well have been the exasperated expressions of an era. In *Ogé*, the salve for the violence of the past emerges as pacification in the present. Consequently, the play puts forward not only a program of human rights built on the idea of biblical or *agape* love for one's enemies as human beings, but a philosophy of non-violent resistance that makes Faubert a forerunner in a tradition of Atlantic World humanism that has been most famously associated with the works and life of Martin Luther King, Jr.

*

Faubert's introduction to *Ogé* comprised not only his spirited response to Schoelcher, but also a savvy rebuttal of what would come to be called 'Haitian exceptionalism.' Not content to merely defend Haitians like himself against the charges of being singularly racist, charges that were mainly being launched from abroad by people like Schoelcher, Faubert repositions the "racial" lens that had been placed over Haiti's portion of the map to fall upon the United States. Faubert's criticism of the way in which "race" operated in the U.S. versus the way in which "race" was supposedly no longer in operation in Haiti rested on the distinction Faubert drew between the political divisions of Haiti that might have involved people with light and dark skin—whom Faubert calls 'yellows' and 'blacks'—and the kind of color prejudices that had supported slavery in Saint-Domingue and that were still reinforcing slavery in the United States. Faubert's critique of the proto-concept of 'Haitian exceptionalism' reveals the actual face of '*le préjugé de couleur*' to be located in American exceptionalism. Where American exceptionalism is understood as the idea that the U.S. embodies the 'purest form of political liberty and democracy' (Drexler and Dillon, forthcoming, n.p.), Faubert makes the opposite claim: that the U.S. was exceptional because of its status as a slaveholding nation that believed itself to have been the creator of the 'purest form of political liberty and democracy.' In Faubert's mind, when compared to Haiti, the U.S. was actually rather singularly devoid of the kinds of political and social freedoms enjoyed by all of the citizens of his country.

The (in)comparability of the kinds of freedom to be found in Haiti versus the United States, where Faubert viewed citizenship to be circumscribed by skin color, is established in his internationally recognized poem 'Aux Haïtiens,' which appeared at the end of the 1856 edition of *Ogé*.[35] In this

---

35 'Aux Haïtiens' had been reprinted a few times in the nineteenth-century Atlantic

poem, Faubert addresses the fact that Europeans and U.S. Americans who had in every way institutionalized the very color prejudices that they perceived as inherent to Haitian society were now turning around and accusing Haiti of being a singular land of color prejudice. Faubert therefore sets up a comparison between the kind of freedoms enjoyed by the citizens of Haiti and the unconscionable deprivation of those freedoms encountered by people of color in the U.S. For Faubert, U.S. criticisms of the supposed prejudices to be found in Haitian society were symptomatic of the same prejudices that supported slavery and segregation in the United States.[36] In other words, criticizing Haitians for their color prejudices was merely another extension of U.S. racism.

Faubert's poem is addressed 'to Haitians,' though, and not to 'Americans.'[37]

World. An excerpt appeared in James Redpath's *The Pine and the Palm* on December 7, 1861, and another excerpt appeared in the Parisian journal *La Fraternité* on April 25, 1893. In addition, the African American writer Jessie Redmon Fauset, who is associated with the Harlem Renaissance, quoted and translated a portion of the poem in an article about Haitian literature written for *The Crisis* magazine in September of 1920. See Fauset (1995, 355–60).

36 While many U.S. politicians had criticized Haiti for what they viewed as restrictions on the freedom of the press, particularly, under the government of Soulouque (see Brickhouse, 2004, 230), parts of the antebellum United States also had strict laws prohibiting the publication and distribution of seditious materials, particularly where slavery was concerned, effectively limiting the freedom of the press. For instance, in 1830 a Louisiana state law restricted written materials that might have a 'tendency to produce discontent among the free coloured population.' The law stated that any person who made 'use of language' in public that would produce 'discontent' or 'excite subordination among the slaves therein, or whosoever shall knowingly bring into this state, any paper, pamphlet or book, having such tendency as aforesaid, shall on conviction thereof ... suffer imprisonment at hard labour or death' (qtd. in Bell, 94). According to Bell, Louisiana newspapers often used 'gruesome images of the slave revolution in Saint-Domingue' to prove that the 1830 law was justified (Bell, 92).

37 Faubert does address at least one 'American' with his writing, as Brickhouse pointed out in an engaging article in which she details the 'transamerican' ties between *Ogé*, which was dedicated to Harriet Beecher Stowe, and her *Uncle Tom's Cabin* (1852). Faubert had referred to the novel as 'the little volume that moved the two worlds' (1856, 37). According to Brickhouse, Faubert's engagement with Stowe shows that he intended his work to gain not just the attention of Europeans and Haitians (he published the work in Paris), but the attention of the world. Haitian writers like Faubert and Saint-Rémy were not the only writers in the Atlantic World to conceive of *Uncle Tom's Cabin* as intimately connected to Haiti in some way. Hannah Farnham Sawyer, in her *Memoir of Pierre Toussaint, Born a Slave in St. Domingo* (1854), quotes from an article in the *Evening Post* in order to link the life of her subject, Pierre Toussaint, to Stowe's novel: 'UNCLE TOM NOT AN APOCRYPHAL CHARACTER.—A correspondent suggests to us, that the aged black man, Pierre Toussaint, who came to this city nearly sixty years

It asks the Haitian people to consider the trivial nature of Haitian political divisions when the United States, which was figuratively next door, was much more critically divided along lines of "color" or "race." The immediate consequences of such divisions in the United States were chattel slavery and the same kind of political disenfranchisement that had plagued the free people of color of Saint-Domingue. Faubert writes: 'What! divided when so close to your shores,/Mulattoes and blacks are proscribed!/When this Republic, burdened with slavery,/Dreams, greedily, of your flourishing fields' (161). Setting aside for the moment Faubert's perhaps unintentional recognition that perhaps there was enmity and division between 'Mulattoes' and 'blacks,' his reference to the United States as 'this Republic burdened with slavery' that was 'so close' to Haitian 'shores,' almost certainly reflects recognition of the fact that if, as Brickhouse has written, 'Haiti was a virtual obsession in the nineteenth-century United States' (2004, 227), the U.S. was an almost obsessive point of reference for Haitian governance as well. Having a slaveholding country so close consistently acted as a *chiaroscuro* for Haitian freedom in the country's political discourse.

F.D. Chanlatte's 'Vues politiques sur le sort des personnes libres, mais non blanches qui se trouvent aux Etas-Unis d'Amérique ou ailleurs,' published in *Le Télégraphe* on August 4, 1822, stands as a particularly salient example of the tendency of many Haitian political writers to posit post-revolutionary Haiti as the fulfillment of the kind of radical liberty and equality that had failed in the post-revolutionary United States. Chanlatte describes the founders of the United States as having 'expressed the most noble and most sublime feelings possible for a free and humane people.' However, he notes that while every state in the U.S. 'recognizes the rights of man and of the citizen; they have not included men of color [*les hommes de couleur*] in these privileges' (2). After describing the forced deportations of some free people of color from states like Louisiana, Chanlatte laments, 'We cannot do anything to improve their fate, except to invite them to come live among us, because they are rejected by their fellow citizens of a color other than their own, and of whom they are the children.' Chanlatte ultimately invites free people of color from the United States to come to Haiti, where 'they will find the political happiness that is principally attached to the enjoyment of the rights of man and of citizen' (2).

In 1824, Haitian president Jean-Pierre Boyer echoed the idea that Haiti could offer *real* freedom and liberty when he wrote in his 'Instructions au Citoyen J. Granville,' which was also aimed at encouraging and even

---

ago from St. Domingo, and last week closed a long, useful, and blameless life, might, if Mrs. Stowe could have been supposed to have known him, have sat as the original of the portraiture to which she gave the name of Uncle Tom' (qtd. in Sawyer, 116).

Requiem for the "Colored Historian"

facilitating emigration from the United States, that Haiti was the U.S. without slavery and color prejudice. Writing to his U.S. agent, Boyer said that he, like all Haitians, was immediately sympathetic to

> the situation that you have just alerted me to regarding the descendants of Africans who find themselves in the United States of America, and who are obliged to leave it, because far from enjoying there any of the rights of free men, they have there only the most precarious of existences and are showered with humiliations.

The realities of color prejudice in the U.S. only bolstered the image of Haiti as a paragon of freedom for people of color in the U.S. since, in Boyer's estimation, 'I have often asked myself why Haiti, whose sky is so gentle, and whose government is analogous to that of the United States, was not the preferable place of their refuge' (rpt. in Edouard, 1888, 8:27).

In the earlier mentioned *Manifeste de Praslin* of 1842, Charles Hérard also alluded to the notion that Haiti was the epitome of liberty itself for 'Africans' who were still suffering under slavery when he wrote:

> Brothers and friends! On our native land, the land of liberty, the hydra of slavery dares once again to show its hideous face, when in foreign lands, in the land of slavery, the African race dreams about the liberty and happiness to be found under the shade of the branches of the palm trees in Haiti. (rpt. in 128)

Later in the mid-nineteenth century, independent Haiti, with its unequivocal constitutional clauses banning slavery forever and proscribing the recognition of "racial" difference, continued to surface in Haitian political discourse as a 'flourishing field' when compared to the soul-killing and barren desert of slavery still to be found in the United States. The idea that Haiti was a refuge for freedom would be behind the Geffrard government's role in the publication of James Redpath's *Guide to Hayti* (1861), which was 'authorized by the government of Hayti' (11).

The official 'Call to Emigration' that appeared in English in the *Guide* was written by Haitian Secretary of State F.E. Dubois, and it reads (in Redpath's original English translation):

> Men of our race dispersed in the United States! Your fate, your social position, instead of ameliorating, daily becomes worse. The chains of those who are slaves are riveted; and prejudice, more implacable perhaps, than servitude, pursues and crushes the free. Everything is contested with us in that country in which, nevertheless, they boast of liberty; they have invented a new slavery for the free, who believed that they had now no

· 582 ·

masters; it is this humiliating patronage which is revolting to your hearts. (Redpath, 1861, 97)

After positing the U.S. as the precise opposite of its image as positively politically 'exceptional,' Dubois would go on to offer Haiti as the kind of land of salvation that the U.S. would eventually embody in the popular imagination. Emma Lazarus, whom Shira Wolosky has written was 'among the first poets specifically to assert ethnic voice in America' (139), is regularly quoted as having said, 'Give me your tired, your poor, your huddled masses yearning to breathe free' (qtd. in Wolosky, 151). Before Lazarus, there was Haiti's F.E. Dubois, who rang the same bell of emigrationist idealism when he told people of color in the United States, 'Come, then, to us! the doors of Hayti are open to you.' Dubois subsequently explained, as Boyer had done in 1824 (rpt. in Edouard, 1888, 8:25–26), that all of the rights and privileges of citizens would follow any person 'of African blood,' upon landing on Haitian shores. 'You will have power, also, freely to exercise your religion,' he assures, before writing:

> I have spoken here only of the members of the African race, who groan in the United States more than elsewhere, by reason of the ignoble prejudice of color; but our sympathies are equally extended to all those of our origin who, throughout the world, are bowed down under the weight of the same sufferings ... The hour of the reunion of all the children of Hayti is sounded! Let them be well convinced that Hayti is the bulwark of their liberty! (Redpath, 1861, 99)

The Haitian government's corrective for the fact that those who had become their citizens had been treated as property by the French colonists was to deny property to anyone foreign to the country. It is precisely this wrinkle in the narrative of Haiti as the 'bulwark of liberty' or universal freedoms that, rather than disrupting Dubois's wish to swap the associations that would become consistent with popular ideas about American and Haitian exceptionalisms, actually bolsters it. As Charles Ogletree, Jr. has written, the United States' 'enthusiasm for newcomers has historically been tempered by its skeptical view of outsiders of a different race, ethnicity, economic status, religion, or political affiliation' (755). That is to say that contradictions of the kind to be found in a country that would exalt its liberties and freedoms at the same time (and usually in the same breath) that it denied them to certain kinds of 'others,' had never been in opposition to the positive version of American exceptionalism, but was always germane to it. If slavery and color prejudice threatened to unravel the tightly bound narrative of (U.S.) American exceptionalism in the eyes of many Haitian writers and politicians, for many nineteenth-century European and U.S.

writers, it was Haiti's property exclusions that provided the fodder for arguing that Haitians themselves were destroying their country's image as the bastion of freedom in the Atlantic World.

Even if the property exclusion clause for foreign "whites" meant that Haiti was not entirely free of color prejudice, surely, it was hard for Faubert, who would later become a member of the Geffrard government, to imagine how anyone from the United States, daring to describe Haitians as unconscionably prejudiced, could think that there was anything more dire than the kind of color prejudice that was supporting antebellum U.S. slavery. In the passage below taken from Faubert's introduction to *Ogé*, the playwright specifically discusses how the form of color prejudice to be found in the United States was so literally dehumanizing as to virtually eclipse the kind of prejudices one might find in a place with a historical legacy of slavery rather than a continuous reality of it. With much irony, Faubert compares the situation of people of color in the United States unfavorably to the situation enjoyed by all Haitians by virtue of the fact that Haitians lived in a society where everyone was considered to be of color:

> in my opinion, the mulatto and the black [in Haiti] are, whatever the case may be, entirely unified in all that concerns this color prejudice; since both the one and the other equally experience it. In fact, even if you are virtue and genius incarnate, if you have a black or a yellow skin, go to a country where color prejudice reigns, for example, certain parts of the United States in North America: the lowest of white emigrants, whom you probably would not even have wanted for your lackey in Europe, and to whom you would have given alms, but still refused to employ in your service, would blush to find himself seated next to you in the theater: due to the sole privilege of his color … were his skin color even whiter than that of the whites themselves, if he is of a suspect origin, he is a pariah like the blackest of the blacks; he is, under the law and in fact, above any man who cannot claim to belong, without a single atom of African mixture, to the Caucasian race. (1856, 22)

Redpath's account of color prejudice in the United States would appear to confirm Faubert's impressions. In 'A Parting Word,' which was published at the end of his *Guide to Hayti*, Redpath would say that despite the many accomplishments of free 'blacks,' 'two words' foretold their future in the United States: "*Damned niggers.*" He wrote that the image of inferiority conjured by the idea of "blackness" would probably never be erased since, '[h]ave you not already produced eminent men,—able writers, physicians, and orators? And yet, what has their genius hitherto availed them? I once heard a distinguished lecturer, who, refused a seat in a first-class car, paid his passage as freight, and was charged by his weight' (173). I am reminded

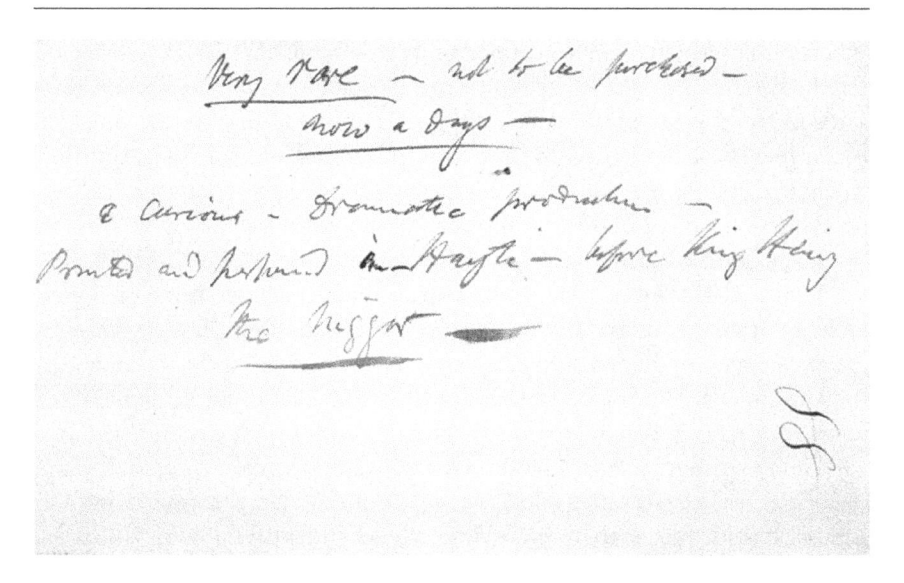

Flyleaf inscription from Juste Chanlatte's *La Partie de chasse du roi* (1820).
Reprinted with permission from the Lilly Library
at the University of Indiana, Bloomington.

by Redpath's comments of Frantz Fanon's poignant statement, 'You will never make colonialism blush for shame by spreading out little known cultural treasures under its eyes' (1968, 223). Theories of African inferiority did not 'blush for shame' either after nearly fifty years of sovereign rule in Haiti. This is a point illustrated with some particular poignancy by a handwritten inscription on the inside of a copy of the Comte de Rosiers, Juste Chanlatte's, 1820 opera, *La Partie de chasse du roi*, held at the Lilly Library at the University of Indiana, Bloomington. The inscription, which likely dates from 1852, reads: 'Very rare—not to be purchased—now a days—a curious—frantic production—Printed and Performed in Hayti—before King Henry the Nigger.'[38]

If the negative way in which Soulouque had been written about in the U.S. press, which 'widely' reported on his actions throughout his presidency, was also any indication (see Brickhouse, 2004, 230), Haitians like Faubert and Dubois (seconded by Redpath) were right to believe in the constancy of the color prejudices of the United States. The nineteenth-century U.S. public

---

38 Chanlatte's play forms part of the Bernardo Mendel Collection of the Lilly Library at the University of Indiana Bloomington. It is not clear who wrote the inscription, but it appears to be written in the same hand as a date, 1852, scribbled on a preceding page. For information about the Mendel Collection, see http://www.indiana.edu/~liblilly/etexts/mendel/.

sphere never seemed to miss an opportunity to demonstrate a willful disregard for the merits of a "black" head of state like Soulouque, whom journalists loved to represent as an illiterate buffoon. According to Brickhouse, one U.S. newspaper even 'undermin[ed] the very possibility of Haitian authorship' when it disputed the idea that Soulouque could have composed an 1851 proclamation aimed at the unification of the entire island of Hispaniola (2004, 224). The ridicule attached to the presidency of Soulouque in both the U.S. and European nineteenth-century public spheres finds its double today in attempts to formally render illegitimate and even shockingly mock the presidency of Barack Obama, who has been constantly racialized by the U.S. media. U.S. radio personality Rush Limbaugh, for example, often refers to him as 'Obama, "the magic Negro"' (qtd. in Ehrenstein), and in a 2008 book written by Ann Coulter, Obama was a part of a list of 'half-black celebrities' the conservative author would accuse of 'representing himself as simply "black",' rather than 'half-white,' thereby identifying with the 'black father' who 'ditched' him rather than the 'white mother' who 'struggled to raise' him (Coulter, 7). The idea that there was a difference between the psychological experience of being "black" in the West Indies and being "colored" in the United States was eloquently captured by George Lamming in the twentieth century in his *The Pleasures of Exile*. Lamming wrote, 'No black West Indian, in his own native environment, would have this highly oppressive sense of being Negro … The West Indian, however black and disposed, could never have felt the experience of being in a minority. For the black faces vastly outnumber the white' (33).

It was not only the 'sense of being Negro' that might have been different in Haiti for Faubert, but the material consequences of being designated as "colored." Faubert's description of color prejudice in the United States draws a distinction between that lingering color prejudice supposedly found among the 'blacks' and 'Mulattoes' in Haiti and the kind that Faubert saw as having undergirded the strict dividing line between "whites" and "blacks" or the slaves and the free in the United States, a color prejudice that ascribed to the spurious biological theory of the "one-drop" rule. Faubert's statement that even a person who was designated as "black" but was phenotypically "white" would in the United States be treated as "colored," implies that every "non-white" could arguably have been subjected to slavery. Even if there were divisions between the 'Blacks' and 'Yellows' of Haiti (and Faubert seems to be willing to say that there might be when in 'Aux Haïtiens' he writes, 'Blacks and Yellows, be united!' [161]), this would still not be the same kind of color prejudice that threatened all people of color with a life of endless servitude in the United States. For the antebellum U.S. was a place where a person's genealogy or dark skin always meant that he or she could eventually become a slave, as attested to by Solomon Northrup's moving account in *Twelve Years a Slave* of how he, a free man, was kidnapped in Washington D.C. and sold into slavery for over a decade.

In many ways, Faubert's comments on "race," consciously or unconsciously, captured a certain amount of angst about "racial" divisions within Haiti, even as he vigorously sought to defend his country from the kinds of maniacal "racial" stereotypes that had produced the trope of the "colored historian" and could be found in the charges of seemingly well-meaning abolitionists like Schoelcher. In addition to exposing the contradictions inherent in a transatlantic abolitionist movement that, because it never became itself devoid of color prejudices, continued to uphold the very system of inequalities that supported slavery and which it purportedly sought to destroy, in his introduction Faubert performs a kind of "racial" solidarity that might have the potential to salve any lingering divisions in the Haitian populace, be they "racial," political, or class-based. In this way, Faubert's anti-racist ideology may have been unwittingly directed as much to Haitians as it had been to Haiti's detractors. By performing "racial" solidarity rather than "racial" division, Faubert tried to will into existence the kind of world in which he wanted to live rather than perhaps the kind of world in which he actually lived.

Calling racism a 'materialist prejudice' because its only goal was to produce slaves or to conquer territory,[39] in short, to uphold the domination of one group over another, Faubert writes that

> to appreciate the proper merit of this materialist prejudice that reduces man to a few accidents of biological constitution [*de l'économie organique*], in subordinating the faculty that makes them think, feel, and desire: when an unfortunate person comes to me and I soothe him, I feel myself to be

---

[39] In a stanza of the poem 'Aux Haïtiens,' Faubert alludes to the United States' imperial designs on Cuba: 'Hatred, dissension, and this rapacious vulture/Hovering over your skies already/To further perpetuate the ills of your race/Prepares to swoop down upon Cuba' (1856, 145). Later in the nineteenth century, Janvier would also comment on the United States' expansionists projects when he said that the American 'only has one fault: that of believing that all of the Americas should only be a vast colony or branch of the United States' (1883, 105). Both Faubert's and Janvier's comments support the idea that from the early nineteenth century up until the U.S. occupation of Haiti (1915–34), many Haitian writers expressed horror at the thought of U.S. intervention or becoming a U.S. protectorate. Bellegarde-Smith tells us that in the mid-nineteenth century, 'American hegemony, which replaced that of France,' was threatening to overtake Haiti since the U.S. government 'sought to expand its commerce through the 'acquisition' of territory, markets, and resources' (269). In fact, the U.S. had already intervened directly in Cuba, Puerto Rico, Panama, the Dominican Republic, and the Danish West Indies, while at the same time trying to control 'Haitian customhouses whose collections were virtually the sole source of revenue for the Haitian government' (270).

a part of a human family like anyone else, despite all of the denials of the world; because for me the characteristic sign of being a man is the ability to sympathize with my fellow men, and to relieve them as much as it is possible to do so: *miseris succerrere*.[40] That is the profession of my faith with respect to color prejudice. (1856, 20)

Despite Faubert's adherence in this passage to certain Enlightenment beliefs promoted by Rousseau, most notably that he was a 'man' because he could feel sympathy for others, many nineteenth-century abolitionists, as we saw with Beard, Redpath, and Schoelcher, were either unaware or unwilling to acknowledge the relationship between the Enlightenment discourse they often cited in the name of promoting liberty and equality, and the "science" of race, which was one of the Enlightenment's most immediate exercises of power, to put things in Foucauldian terms. In other words, if Foucault said that the 'Enlightenment' had discovered the 'liberty' as well as 'invented' the disciplines of torture and surveillance (1995, 222), here we have an Enlightenment that led equally to the development of the transatlantic abolitionist movement and to the racialism that undergirded slavery and eventually "racial" separatist ideologies. The "racial" taxonomies relied upon in abolitionist thought were the direct result of Enlightenment-produced *knowledges*, which in turn led to the harmful and spurious "one-drop" rule. These same *knowledges* were also behind beliefs in 'mulatto exceptionalism' (Gilmore, 59-60) and behind its opposite in "monstrous hybridity." We also find the "racial" grammar of the Enlightenment hiding behind the varying agendas of the African colonization movements promoted most notably by abolitionists in the U.S., whose direct aims were often, as with Redpath, to preclude "miscegenation."

Attacking the part of Enlightenment thought that had to do with "racial" taxonomies and beliefs in the supremacy of "whiteness" by underscoring that it was the idea of wanting to *know* itself that had undergirded slavery, was for Faubert to attack the very heart of the institution of slavery. To that end, Faubert evokes the absurdity of "racial" science: 'I demand it before all hearts that have been lifted up, all those who are intelligent ... is it not deeply regrettable that we must only consider a man according to certain physical attributes? [*d'après certaines apparences matérielles*]' (1856, 22). Faubert then specifically denied the validity of "racial" taxonomies themselves:

Would these beholders of all biological phenomena please tell me if they have yet measured in a precise manner the facial angle of this devotion of which I have just spoken, and determined the shade of skin of a friend, of a brother, of a mother whose feelings justify these sacred titles? (1856, 22)

40 A reference to Virgil, and which means 'to help those in need.'

While true believers in the idea of "race" held that they could determine everything about a person given their 'shade of skin color,' according to Faubert, the "racial" determinism of the colonial era was no longer a threat to Haitians since it could never again be instituted in independent Haiti. This was because, 'Men of both skin colors, as I said above, are, in all that concerns this prejudice, unified by the will of God; that is to say that this solidarity is one of those indestructible facts which defies all sophisms' (1856, 23).

Ultimately, even if Faubert does admit to a certain level of division in nineteenth-century Haiti, in his mind, this was not and could not have been constituted by the same kinds of "race" or "color" prejudices that would have been familiar to those living in the United States. For Faubert, "race" and "color" were the elements that had unified all Haitians, ostensibly across the divides of class and politics. He writes, 'Finally, besides these undeniable truths, the two condemned colors, have they not always been united one to the other through sacred bonds of kinship [*liens sacrés de parenté*], the most powerful feelings that are above everything?' (1856, 22). Faubert's contention that as far as prejudice and racism themselves were concerned, Haitians of 'both colors' were united, especially through their shared genealogies in slavery, actually anticipates the claims of writers from the twentieth-century *négritude* movement, who would insist that it was the experience of suffering under the twin repressions of slavery and color prejudice that united the various peoples of the African diaspora across the globe.

*

Paying attention almost exclusively to the trope of the "colored historian" or the 'mulatto legend of history' when reading nineteenth-century Haitian literary production has usually meant overlooking Faubert's very acute and in some ways *avant la lettre* explanation of the contradictions inherent in U.S. American and European discourse, where Haitians appeared as singularly color prejudiced. The same over-reliance on the theory of the 'mulatto legend of history' has also meant that what I have called Faubert's *new humanism*, drawing on Fanon's phrase (1968, 7), or the idea that after decolonization it was possible to effect revolutionary change both without violence and without the kinds of ineffective and passive sentimentality often found among the adherents of non-violence in the transatlantic abolitionist movement (see Stanley, 22; Festa, 199), has been completely missed by scholars.

While the introduction to the play is overtly and primarily concerned with defending Haitians and the playwright himself from the charges of color prejudice, the body of the play is much more concerned with making a commentary about the place of violence in revolutionary movements. The play, then, has something to tell us not solely about the 1790 revolt of Ogé, but it also invites commentary and reflection on the kind of violent regime change that had been a feature of Haitian politics since the assassination of Dessalines. It is this veiled critique of the violence of the contemporary Haitian political sphere that not only allows Faubert to offer what I am calling his 'new humanism' to his international audience, but comprises that which I think Faubert is most likely to have 'modified,' to use his own words, in the interval between 1841 and 1856.[41] As the director of the Lycée National de Port-au-Prince under several different Haitian leaders, Faubert would hardly have been in a position to offer the kind of overt critiques of state authority to be found in *Ogé*, especially in front of his students.

Although the play is entitled *Ogé*, it must be said that the plot of the drama actually revolves around a fictional character named Alfred and his "white" Creole love interest, Delphine, the daughter of one of the cruelest planters in Saint-Domingue (Le Vicomte de Laferrière), who had recently returned to the colony from France. Other fictional additions to the dramatization of these historical events include a planter named Le Marquis de Vermont, his son Arnold, who is Alfred's rival for the affections of Delphine, and various other minor characters who act as foils, such as Delphine's nurse, a slave named Annette.

The play begins with the knowledge that both Alfred and Delphine have recently returned to the colony after being educated in France. Although they both admit to being aware of the kinds of prejudice that have always existed in Saint-Domingue, they exhibit astonishment at the attitudes of the "white" planters towards both their slaves and the free people of color. Alfred tells Delphine:

> our beautiful days have passed, and the time of trials will soon begin for us. Despite the frightful picture of color prejudice that was given to me in Paris, which should have prepared me for all that I see here, what a painful shock I am experiencing! What! It is really delusional of me to have thought that I was the equal of a white man! (1856, 54)

---

[41] According to Brickhouse, other material that Faubert may have added to the play includes the final scene in which Delphine pleads with her father for the lives of the revolutionaries, which Brickhouse has referenced in connection with what she calls Faubert's 'revisionist' strategy (241). Brickhouse likens Delphine to Eva from *Uncle Tom's Cabin*, a text which Faubert references at the beginning of the introduction, but which had not yet been written when *Ogé* was first performed. Brickhouse also argues that Faubert is responding to the idea expressed in *Uncle Tom's Cabin* that Haiti was 'effeminate' and 'worn out.' Brickhouse writes, '[i]t is this pronouncement about Haiti throughout Stowe's popular novel, to which Faubert's play most movingly responds' (426).

Alfred goes on to reveal that he is planning to rebel against the color prejudices of the planters, telling Delphine that he will 'repay the oppressors of my race scorn for scorn' and 'these arrogant men will then know how to show me respect!' (1856, 54).

Though Delphine is disheartened at the treatment of the slaves like her nurse Annette, and sympathetic to the color prejudices of which Alfred complains, she still believes that violence has no place in remedying these problems. She states, 'Here, the most wholesome and the most generous ideas, as soon as it becomes a matter of color prejudice, are treated as chimerical; and intelligence, character, and education are nothing, if people lack what is called purity of origins' (1856, 55). Delphine demonstrates her rigid reproach of Alfred's desire for violent insurrection as a way to end these prejudices by attempting to force her lover to recognize a contradiction between all of the beautiful things of the world about which he learned through his formal education in France and the violent grammar couched in the revolutionary thought he was expressing. She says:

> you who used to love the arts so much and who aspired only to the happiness of cultivating them far from any commotion: you, the enemy of bloody battles, because of the cruel passions that always accompany them, it is you, Alfred, who have been able to throw yourself into such a desperate decision! Goodbye, then, to your dear illusions, and to that love of a glory that is devoid of human blood! Goodbye to noble pleasures and to the study of their fertile inspirations! Goodbye also to poetry and to music, once so powerfully operative in your heart! (1856, 57–58)

Delphine's belief that revolutionary violence had the power to counter the pacifying influence of poetry and music upon Alfred causes her to reflect upon what she perceives as the relationship between the complaints of the French revolutionists against the crown and the complaints of the free people of color against the colonists. Delphine compares the color prejudices to be found in Saint-Domingue to the kinds of prejudice of noble birth that had been found in *ancien régime* France and had led to the very French Revolution to which she alludes above. Delphine tells Alfred that color prejudice 'is the downfall of the happiness of the men of this country, just as it was once before for the powerful men of Europe who believed that birth could take precedence over merit' (1856, 55). As if taking her next comment straight out of a romance novel, Delphine essentially begs Alfred to allow her to love to mitigate the 'miseries of the society of which we are unfortunately a part.' She says, '[b]ut, whatever the opinions of men might be, the truth, could it ever stop being what it is, that is to say the expression of that over which the wisdom of God prevails? Let us therefore strengthen our courage,' she pleads, 'and, you, cease to believe that a prejudice which, in my eyes, is the most unjust of them all, could ever reach me' (1856, 55).

While both Alfred and Delphine likely witnessed first-hand the violence of the French Revolution of 1789 since they have only just returned from Paris in October of 1790, the star-crossed lovers seemed to have drawn very different lessons from the events in France. Instead of holding on to the 'dear illusion' that perhaps the "white" colonists would eventually recognize the equality of the free people of color (and in the meantime, Alfred could simply enjoy the beautiful scenery and the love of a beautiful woman), Alfred says that his 'project' is 'that of forcing our oppressors to recognize our rights' (1856, 56–57). He notes that doing so is precisely what will prove 'to my oppressors that I do not belong to a weak race! [*une race sans énergie*]' (1856, 56). Alfred subsequently entreats Delphine to '[r]espect my convictions, because they are sacred [*saintes*]' (1856, 58). Evoking the sentiment behind the radical revolutionary phrase *liberté ou la mort!* Alfred then states, 'do not try to deter me from certain death, because here life is only purchased with shame' (1856, 58). He continues by telling Delphine that the revolutionary vocation has come to him from above since, 'when you feel deeply in your soul that you are the equal of others, can you suffer a humiliating yoke to be imposed upon you? And must you not try any method in order to overcome it?' (1856, 56–57).

It is important to remember that in the play this revolutionary rhetoric, which resembles in many ways the language of Dessalines in his 'Proclamation of Gonaïves,' comes from Alfred and not Ogé. In fact, while the words of Ogé, the historical figure, will take center stage for a moment during the trial, throughout most of the rest of the play, Ogé, the fictional character, only plays the most auxiliary of roles. This is true both of scenes in which the revolutionaries plot the insurrection and in the fictional scene that occurs just before Ogé, Alfred, Chavannes, and the rest of the conspirators are condemned to death. Before the punishment of Ogé and company, for example, the revolutionists catch several of the colonists, including Arnold and his father, and Delphine's father, whom Alfred had earlier promised not to harm when he told Delphine, 'do not worry … your father, no matter the injustice of his opinions, will always be sacred for me' (1856, 56). Making good on his promise to Delphine, subsequent to the capture of these planters, Alfred and company ultimately decide to do the exact opposite of what we see the revolutionists doing in Victor Hugo's *Bug-Jargal* (1826). Recall that in *Bug-Jargal*, after Biassou and Habibrah capture several planters and members of the French military, they hold an inquest designed to force their captives to admit all of the atrocious things they have done to their slaves. This is in addition to mocking and debasing them before putting most of them to perfidious and cruel deaths.

In *Ogé*, Alfred and his followers perform the same kind of inquest, in which it is discovered that one of the captives, Donnabert, used vicious dogs specifically trained to hunt down and kill slaves who had either escaped or gotten lost (1856, 72); another planter was well known for placing oranges on the heads of his slaves and then attempting to shoot them, often missing and killing the slave instead; still worse, it is revealed that the Vicomte de Laferrière, Delphine's father, enjoyed cutting the tendon at the back of the knee of slaves he considered subordinate. Lastly, we find out that Arnold, Alfred's rival for the affections of the lovely Delphine, has the distinct honor of being infamous for deflowering young free women of color and thus bringing dishonor on their homes (1856, 76).

All of these testimonies, which, in certain ways, recall the slave punishments and sexual coercion attested to by Baron de Vastey in *Le Système colonial dévoilé* (1814), as well as those described by Dessalines in the 'Proclamation' and by Christophe in his *Manifeste du Roi* (see also Jonassaint, 2008, 212), tend towards proving the absolute horrors of slavery. As such, this testimony supports Alfred's earlier reflection that for people of color in Saint-Domingue, whether slave or free, having an actual 'life' had in many ways been forbidden. According to Alfred, 'Even the most pure pleasures of family life, that the heavens always provide for even the most unfortunate of men as a way to soften their misfortunes' had been denied to people of color. He sighs, 'Oh, how many amongst us have not cursed the day where they conceived of the idea to have a family!' (1856, 64). With these statements, and the gruesome recitations of all the ways in which the slaves had been utterly dehumanized by their masters, the patient reader of Haitian literary history would naturally expect the insurgents to execute their captives. However, the revolutionists prefer to show clemency. It is Alfred, importantly, who convinces Ogé and Chavannes, who are actually hell-bent on revenge in this portrayal, that showing humanity would only promulgate the noble cause of the free people of color, which is here phrased as a desire to achieve equality and 'civilization.' Alfred states:

> a generous pity for a defeated enemy can only benefit our noble cause. Yes, let us prove our strength [*énergie*] in combat, but let us be humane after the victory: this is what characterizes, in general, civilized peoples … At present, our friends in Europe think that our race is just as capable of civilization as any other: let us show them, from the start, that they are not mistaken. (1856, 81)

Rather than providing more evidence of the 'mulatto legend of history,' Faubert's depiction of the generosity shown to the colonists by the free people of color who participated in Ogé's revolt may have been derived from the eyewitness accounts of this event given by people like the colonist Mazères in *De l'Utilité des colonies* (1814). Recalling his involvement in the very events of the 1790 revolt that would be portrayed in Faubert's play, Mazères says that after the 'assassins' shot a white colonist named Sicard, he found himself confronted with Ogé. 'At this moment, Ogé, having stayed behind to give some orders, appeared in front of me like a guardian angel, he tore me from the hands of the assassins who had already seized me, and I was miraculously saved' (78). Mazères says that subsequently,

> I was taken to their headquarters, where I was able to tenderly acknowledge in Ogé a sweet man, simple and humane [*humain*]. I questioned him, I asked him about the goal of the frightful scene of horror to which I had just been subjected; he responded to me in these terms: 'It was against my orders that they killed M. Sicard; the whites refuse to acknowledge the decree which provides us with political rights; I have come here to compel them to do so, I have orders; I am not alone. The men of color from three provinces are acting in concert with me. You all have wanted this, mister white men! Oh well, then! we will die and you will die with us.' (78)

Mazères goes on to describe the followers of Ogé as '300 assassins without a plan, without resources of any kind, without having foreseen the least obstacle, but filled with the pride of the approval [*assentiment*] of Condorcet and Brissot' (79). Ogé himself was an exception, however, for Mazères says, 'Despite his horrible entourage, what I saw of him seemed to prove to me the purity of his intentions' (79). Mazères concludes of Ogé, '[a]t the very least, he showed me justice, and he even said to me, when I was confronted again with him: *Oh, monsieur, if all the whites had treated me like you did in their depositions, I would not have so much to fear about my fate*' (77). Mazères's description of Ogé as rather tame is seconded by Bryan Edwards, who wrote:

> Ogé himself, with all his enthusiasm, was naturally mild and humane: he cautioned his followers against the shedding of innocent blood; but little regard was paid to his wishes in this respect; the first white man who fell in their way they murdered on the spot: a second, of the name of Sicard, met the same fate; and it is related that their cruelty towards such persons of their own complexion as refused to join in the revolt was extreme. (1793–1801, 3:47)

This moderate and hapless revolutionary Ogé also appears in Emile Nau's *Réclamation par les affranchis des droits civiles et politiques* (1849). Nau describes Ogé as having released two young '*dragons*' who had been captured by his forces in the hope that they would transmit a letter to the Assembly that might bring about peace (33); in the end, Nau describes Chavannes and Ogé as only reluctantly resorting to violence (46–47).

What all of these accounts of the *humane* Ogé as opposed to the *vengeful* Ogé share is the idea of European 'Radical enlightenment,' which, according to Jonathan Israel, '(ususally) disavowed violence but openly embraced the principle of revolution if not necessarily in the sense of a general uprising then certainly in the sense of a general transformation of values, attitudes, and institutions' (745). Nau's characterization of Ogé as a humane revolutionary, in particular, seems to stem less from a desire to redeem "mulattoes," and more from a desire to condemn a version of Enlightenment revolution that would affirm and encourage non-violence, even for slaves. Nau's narration, while painting Ogé as some sort of hero, also likens him to a "vanishing Indian" who had to make way for the progress and, indeed, the violence that modernity necessarily entailed for Haitians. Going on to evoke the idea that it was the punishment of Ogé and Chavannes, and not their rebellion itself, that awakened the justified vengeance of the slaves, Nau writes:

> The justice of history had finally come for you. You may complain today about the blindness of the colonists, but how bright is the glory of our martyrs. And besides, did not the subsequent events sufficiently betray the wildest hopes [*les folles espérances*] of those first ones, in exciting the avengers of Ogé and Chavannes? (45)

Subsequently alluding to the idea that it was the failure of Ogé and Chavannes that had taught the slaves that violence was the only way, Nau writes, '[o]ther times, other men; grand events, grand souls. They had faith in the force of the law and not in the right of force [*Ils avaient foi dans la force du droit et non dans le droit de la force*]' (46).

Recent archival findings by Garrigus are in many ways coincident with the accounts of Ogé's radically *enlightened* (said with a full sense of irony) conduct given by Mazères, Nau, and Edwards, at least as far as Ogé's desire to lead a violent uprising is concerned. Garrigus writes, 'although it made no difference to the colonists ... the evidence contained in Bocquet's interrogation [of Ogé] strongly suggests that Ogé did not want an outright revolt, or at least prolonged combat' (2010, 37). For Garrigus, the Spartan sentence of Ogé, which required him to be 'broken on the wheel,' was more likely the result of the 'inconclusiveness' of the aims of the revolt itself and the ambiguous way in which it took place, rather than a result of any specific evidence against Ogé that pointed towards his desire to cause a slave rebellion. According to Garrigus, the French colonists 'sought to inflict a gruesome public death on Ogé and his lieutenants,' and it was '[t]his execution, far more than the revolt itself, [which] pushed Parisian revolutionaries, colonial free people of color, and perhaps enslaved people of color to a new level of hostility against the plantation regime' (2010, 22).

Given the severity of the retribution, it is not hard to believe that Ogé's gruesome punishment provided the necessary fuel and inspiration for broader slave rebellion. The official mandate of Ogé's sentence read that he and Chavannes should have their

> arms, legs, thighs, and backs broken alive on the scaffold that will be erected for this purpose, and subsequently be put by the executioner of this sentence on wheels, their faces turned towards the sky, to stay that way as long as it pleases God to spare their lives; afterwards, their heads shall be cut off and exposed on posts … : that of the aforementioned *Vincent Ogé* jeune on the great road that leads to Dondon, and that of the aforementioned *Jean-Baptiste*, called *Chavanne* [*sic*], on the road to Grande-Rivière, across from the Poisson plantation. (qtd.in Lacroix, 64)[42]

Although in real life, so to speak, Ogé's political motives and position in colonial society might have been 'deeply ambiguous' (Garrigus, 2010, 22), in Faubert's play, Alfred's encouragement of clemency for the colonists seems designed to perform a very particular political function that has very little do with revealing anything at all about the actual life of Ogé.

The statement 'let us be humane after the victory' seems to speak to two different but interrelated political problems that had everything to do with independent rather than revolutionary Haiti. First, the statement resonates with the play's implicit critique of the violence of Dessalines against the French colonists in the spring after Haitian independence. This reading is supported by three statements made by Faubert in the introduction to *Ogé*. He wrote:

> The principles I have set out in examining the essence of color prejudice necessarily entail its radical and absolute condemnation; I must state, therefore, in order to remain true to my logic [*conséquent avec moi-même*], that I could not approve of it against whites any more than against yellows and blacks. (1856, 23)

Evoking his earlier metaphor that all human beings were 'brothers' (1856, 25), Faubert also wrote, '[t]he principles I have outlined above relative to this color prejudice, speak to the fact that in my drama I did not think to be biased against the whites any more than the yellows and blacks' (1856, 37). Faubert's final prefatory remark, too, seems to have been designed to mitigate any feelings of hostility that his French readers might feel in

---

42 The Poisson plantation is significant because Poisson was a free man of color who had been involved in a brief revolt by three free men of color in 1790 called the 'affaire du fonds Parisien' (see chapter eleven of this volume for more context).

perhaps imagining themselves reflected in the treachery of the colonists in the play. Faubert wrote, 'besides, when undertaking my studies in Paris, I had as classmates young colonists who made me forget altogether about color prejudice: I could not therefore be motivated by any hostile feeling against the white race' (1856, 37)

The second political function served by the idea of 'being humane after the victory,' would have been the ongoing contemporary project of pursuing broad "racial" uplift, in which many of Haiti's nineteenth-century intellectuals saw themselves as immediately involved. This project of "racial" uplift not only required arguing for the abolition of U.S. slavery, but also appeared to necessitate that Haitians prove to the world by their own example that people of African descent were both capable of civilization and being human(e). This sentiment is captured in 'Aux Haïtiens' when Faubert tells the Haitian people that although they had won their freedom, which was 'crowned by a powerful and just God,' and may have proven that 'black and yellow' would be the 'equals of the whites,' the 'task of 'completing your glory' was still 'immense.' Faubert writes, 'Alas! how many brothers/Does this iniquity still oppress! Very well, you will dry so many bitter tears by honoring liberty' (1856, 144). Specifically referring to the question of violence in post-independence Haiti, Faubert concludes that this liberty could be honored in the following way: 'Yes, do not forget, my friends: your heroism/ is half that which you made you Conquerors [*Vous a fait à moitié vainqueurs*]/ From now on your virtues and your intelligence/Will better combat your oppressors' (1856, 144). Turning his gaze directly on to contemporary Haiti, then, he tells his compatriots that changing their country's image in the world's mind would have everything to do with abolishing slavery, on the one hand, and disarming themselves, on the other. This is because proving Haiti's ability to be non-violent and therefore 'civilized' could prove the worthiness of freedom for all people of color:

> ... up until this day implacable discord
> Unnerves you still, beautiful land;
> And your enchanted soil, inexhaustible goldmine
> Showers your sons with blood.
> Oh, my beautiful island, I only have in this moment
> The blessed eloquence of my heart!
> All of us, soon to be disarmed in the name of our country,
> Will groan of such an error
> ...
> Haitians, tighten your ranks!
> Eternal anathema to internecine war,
> Scourge of every nation!
> Rather, cry from above: Union!

God himself said it to us; Our Lord, that in man he esteems
The soul only, and not the color. (1856, 144–46)

That Haiti and Haitians could be involved in spreading something called 'civilization' to areas of the world that had been deeply damaged by contact with Europe was as old as Haitian independence itself (see Vastey, 1814a, vi, 18). The idea that non-violence was the key to this 'civilization,' however, was something new. As Laurent Dubois has written, 'the course of the Revolution was influenced in profound ways by representations of violence,' where 'political projects for the future' had been 'justified through evocations of past atrocities.' Indeed, '[t]he revolution generated new structures of violence, and its leaders often spoke of vengeance for old brutalities they had suffered as they justified new ones against their enemies' (L. Dubois, 2009, 112). As we have already seen in the works of Boisrond-Tonnerre, Vastey, and Ardouin, threatening the international world, and specifically France, with violence was often evoked in Haitian writing not only as a protection against any further French attempts to retake the colony, but as a willful guarantee of Haiti's broader sovereignty in a slave-holding Atlantic World.

Faubert appears to be calling for an end to the violent grammar of social and political revolution in independent Haiti. As if to drive home this novel argument for pacifism, which bears a relationship to both the past of the Age of Revolution of the characters' worlds and the present of Faubert's Age of Slavery world, in *Ogé*, Alfred tells his audience, 'we have other things to do besides exercising vengeance: we must rehabilitate an entire race of men unjustly deposed in the estimation of the world' (1856, 82). Alfred's statement calls forth the idea that Haitians needed to make good on the promise of their image as the 'beacon' of freedom for those still suffering under slavery, as the abbé Grégoire had written in *De la Noblesse de la peau* (1826, 81), through creating a non-violent (non-vengeful) 'civilization.' Haitians could most effectively live up to their status as exceptionally free and 'civilized' people by creating a stable society that would become known not for the violence of its origins,—'let us show them from the start'—or the instability of its governments—'implacable discord'—but for the humanity and generosity of its populace—'your virtue and your intelligence will better combat your oppressors.'

A subsequent statement by Alfred more directly voices the idea that the immediate satisfaction of obtaining revenge against a political opponent was ultimately counterproductive precisely because of the essentialist way in which the behavior of even the smallest group of people of color had always been metonymic for all people of color. Alfred says that the satisfactions of pursuing vengeance against the colonists would be short-lived and dearly bought: '[a]nd for the pathetic satisfaction of punishing several cruel men,'

Alfred states, 'we would deprive our brothers and our children of the inheritance of such a virtue,' alluding to the damage to their international image as humane and civilized (1856, 81). Alfred's desire to 'return scorn for scorn,' then, has suddenly changed into a desire to achieve "racial" as well as political reform while still having respect for what to him was the providential mandate of civilization: being humane in the face of victory.

From another perspective, in refusing to use the kind of revolutionary violence that has formed the basis of modern-day critiques of the 'Enlightenment Project' (Israel, 1), Alfred attempts to avoid forcing entry with aggressive physical action into the arena of rights, constitutions, and representation to which people of color had been ardently excluded through slavery, conquest, and colonialism. In Alfred's mind, violence was a method that would ultimately only confirm his inferiority in the eyes of his oppressors. His reluctance to take his merited revenge is recognition that for many nineteenth-century observers in the U.S. and Europe, as we have seen, the Haitian Revolution stood as evidence of the archetypal barbarity and inhumanity of all people of African descent, and especially of the vengeance of "mulatto/as."

That in the wake of independence, nineteenth-century Haiti had experienced its share of political problems only served as further evidence for those looking to disparage the new country and prove its inability to become "civilized." The play's subtextual argument for humanity in both the Haitian political sphere and the global political sphere, as opposed to simply the past of the revolutionary sphere, seems to be symptomatic of a feeling that violently forcing the recognition of Haitian freedom had meant that the Haitian revolutionists needed to commit the same violations of human rights they deplored in their oppressors. The difference was, of course, that the violence against the slaves had been sanctioned by the state, which is to say that it was justified as 'purposeful, right and inevitable' (Robbins, 190–91), while that of the revolutionists was taken as an unthinkable transgression of state authority and therefore as proof of the barbarity and lack of 'civilization' of "Africans." By the same token, almost continuous threats to Haiti's sovereignty in the first half-century of independence kept alive the more than rhetorical idea that violence would protect and preserve the country's independence from France and the United States.

It is this logic of violence as evidence for inhumanity and simultaneously as the means to achieving humanity that ultimately provided the obstacle to the very arena of 'civilization' to which the Haitian revolutionists had desired entry. This is to say that the actions of the colonizing powers—France, Great Britain, Spain, and eventually the United States—had forced both the colonized slaves and the free people of color in Saint-Domingue to take actions that would make them increasingly resemble the uncivilized barbarians that naturalist travel writers had spent more than two centuries trying to make them out to be. As Jean-Paul Sartre has written of colonialism:

> the oppressors produce and maintain by force the evils which, *in their eyes*, make the oppressed resemble more and more what they would need to be in order to deserve their fate. The colonist can absolve himself only by systematically pursuing the 'dehumanization' of the colonized, that is by identifying a little more each day with the colonial apparatus ... The machine runs smoothly; impossible to distinguish between idea and *praxis* ... The system wants the death and the multiplication of its victims at the same time. (Sartre, 52, italics in the original)

This paradox of using violence to achieve humanity is in some ways what makes the Haitian Revolution appear to be 'both a grandiose success and failure' by forcing it to 'restructure the debate on human rights' ironically through 'absolute violence' (Nesbitt, 2005, 38). If, in referring to the twentieth century, Nesbitt has asked, 'why must Haitians again and again assert their radical insurgency against "constituted power" in the face of a seemingly unending and total state of crisis?' (2005, 10), it seems to me that in the nineteenth century, *Ogé* seems to be calling upon us to ask why Haitians had to constantly prove their humanity—i.e. that they were not a 'weak' and inferior 'race,' in Enlightenment terms—through violent insurrection? If Faubert presents an Alfred who tries to end this vicious cycle of using violence to disrupt 'constituted power' when he argues for the revolutionists to show mercy, it is his own eventual punishment and Delphine's rebuke of the violent actions of the colonists that underscores the complications inherent in the philosophy of non-violence being put forward by Faubert.

Closely matching the description contained in the official punishment of Ogé cited by Lacroix, the futility of the early revolutionists' universal humanity is fully underscored by the utterly inhumane treatment they receive when they themselves become captives. When Alfred and his followers are captured, the "white" colonists do not exhibit the least mercy for them. Le Vicomte, in fact, proposes 'the torture of the wheel, inflicted in the manner that will produce the most terror possible' (1856, 100). The play's reversal of the "white" equals humanity, "black" equals savagery binary opposition becomes evident: it is the French colonists who are inhumane since they have no respect for the lives of their 'fellow men.' The colonists exhibit no sympathy precisely because they have dehumanized the people of color to such an extent that, as Annette says specifically of the slaves, 'a slave is not a person: it is a household animal [*c'est une bête de la maison*] that never doubts what it sees or what it hears' (1856, 50). If the free people of color and later the slaves would use violence to counter what the play suggests, rightly or wrongly, is their shared non-personhood, the colonists' logic of analogous violence would serve as the basis for the punishment of both groups.

Alfred's wish to achieve humanity and 'civilization' for all people of color by demonstrating it to those who were persecuting him suggests that it was only by becoming martyrs rather than victors that people of "African" descent could be considered human in the eyes of the world. They had needed to lose the Revolution in order to continue to be the sympathetic slaves who were worthy of the world's pity. To that end, before his capture and death on the infamous 'wheel,' Alfred says, '[f]riends, it is the foundation of a new society that we are constructing in this moment: let us try to give it as a base the most social of all the virtues, humanity' (1856, 81). Alfred's final word to the revolutionists pretty well encapsulates the contradictions between human rights at the state level or as a constitutional right, and human rights as an intrinsic, intuitive, and philosophical, or global principle. After the colonists decide that the punishment for Ogé and company must be 'terrible; since we have never seen a more audacious revolt' (1856, 88), Delphine pleads with her father to spare their lives by reminding him:

> Isn't it true that it was the humanity of one of these insurgents that saved your life? Would you respond to this generous action with a severity that will forever remove from you any chance of salvation, if the sad circumstances in which you found yourselves is reproduced once more? (1856, 97)

The last part of Delphine's statement suggests the cyclical nature of war. As William Faulkner wrote in *The Sound and the Fury*, '... no battle is ever won ... They are not even fought. The field only reveals to man his own folly and despair, and victory is an illusion of philosophers and fools' (76). Delphine, who loves her father though she disagrees with him, is rightly worried that whatever punishments are meted out to Ogé and company would only inevitably be returned on the 'folly' of the battlefield, the nature of revolution, like that of civil war, being potentially endless.

Despite Delphine's pessimism about the war ever reaching an end if the cycle of revenge were to merely keep repeating itself, certain characters in the play seem to posit with perhaps the utmost optimism (or naiveté) that the revolutionists did not need to continuously assert their humanity through aggression. In essence, that the cycle could be broken, and that it could be broken by the Haitian people. If we are reading contrapuntally, we might say that the play asks for Haitians to be the first to break the cycle of violence that had been ensured by the conquest of the Americas, escalated by the institution of chattel slavery, and further stoked when the Haitian revolutionists had decided to end their enslavement through violence. Because the violence of the Haitian Revolution had culminated in the freedom of the slaves as well as the citizenship desired by the free people of color and the creation of the sovereign state of Haiti, the play seems to be asking for non-aggression only 'after the victory' as the key to the recognition of Haitian personhood. Yet this rebuke of violence in the lexicon of Haitian governance comes despite the fact that the United States was still at that point refusing to formally recognize Haitian political sovereignty, which meant in many ways that they had failed to recognize Haitians *as a* people and *as* people.

In the end, as a country that is now without an army, Haiti paradoxically stands as the quintessential example of non-aggression towards other states. The country also stands as a prime example of what the effects of aggression from other states looks like. To the international community it is Haiti that has failed to respect the human rights of its citizens and therefore it is Haiti that must be perpetually open to (both political and spiritual) international intervention in the name of human rights. As long as the United States and the UN embed their desires to politically intervene in Haiti within a language of human rights, anything is permissible, including encouraging 'international financial institutions such as the WTO, the IMF, and the World Bank to essentially strip' Haiti of 'real economic autonomy and political sovereignty' (Braziel, 2006, 129). To take just one example, Tracy Kidder has written of how the IDB (Inter-American Development Bank) blocked aid to Haiti supposedly in order to protest the '2000 electoral process' that brought former Haitian president Jean-Bertrand Aristide to power (5). However, as Kidder convincingly shows, the blocking of aid had less to do with desiring that Aristide 'improve security and the administration of justice,' than with his 'preaching and criticisms of the United States' (4–5).

In *Specters of the Atlantic*, Ian Baucom said, 'the trouble with human rights discourse' as it is currently maintained by individual 'states,' 'is not that they fail ... to indict sovereign violence,' but that the language individual states use to uphold human rights is 'borrowed from the language' of totalitarianism (192). Violence is permitted from one state against another as long as it is embedded in the language of 'human rights.' For Baucom, speaking this language of 'human rights' means that the moment 'a state or extrastate body gives itself the responsibility to care globally for bare human life,' it can do anything to preserve global 'human life,' even using violence itself.[43] This is because if global 'human rights' means '[t]aking the care of life (as life) into its own hands,' then the state 'affords itself the power to regulate, evaluate, normalize, produce, or end the life' of not only its own citizens,

---

43 Baucom borrows the concept of 'bare life' from Agamben, who in *Homo Sacer: Sovereign Power and Bare Life* describes biological human life as simultaneously the embodiment of the political realm and outside of it (1998, 83).

but the citizens of the world (Baucom, 190). It is the consequences of this contest between the right to life as maintained by state power (represented in *Ogé* by the planters) and respect for life as a metaphysical principle that transcends the constituted authority of the state (represented in *Ogé* by the revolutionists) that was lucidly captured by Faubert in the final scene of the play, when Ogé and his followers are brutally executed.

Even though some Haitian intellectuals like Faubert, Baron de Vastey, Saint-Rémy, and, undoubtedly, many other people in the Haitian populace whose names we may never know, viewed the idea of the Haitian government's non-aggression in the international political sphere as a demonstration of humanity and as a measure of goodwill (they were unwilling to meddle 'in affairs outside of our island', as Baron de Vastey put it [1816d, 36]), the cycle of punishing the Haitian people for having 'dared to be free,' in the words of Dessalines, has never quite ended. I suppose that living in an era of endless war as we do, we should hardly be surprised that the 'new policy founded on respect for people and cultures' (77), called for by Aimé Césaire when he asked for a 'humanism made to measure the world' (73) has not yet been created. Césaire wrote that it was not a 'dead civilization that we want to revive,' but a completely 'new society' that we should imagine (52). I would like to think that this new world is still to come.

CODA:
Today's 'Haitian Exceptionalism'

'Violence can always destroy power; out of the barrel of a gun grows the most effective command, resulting in the most instant and perfect obedience. What never can grow out of it is power. In a head-on clash between violence and power, the outcome is hardly in doubt ... Rule by sheer violence comes into play where power is being lost.'

—Hannah Arendt, *On Violence* (1969)

'At the end of the eighteenth century, the large maroon community in Haiti lent its support to the general slave revolt that drove out the European occupiers and brought about the formation of an unstable, violence-prone black-and-mulatto republic.'

—Frederick B. Pike, *The United States and Latin America: Myth and Stereotypes of Civilization* (1992)

'In a situation of occupation or domination, the occupier, the dominant power, has to justify what it's doing. There is only one way to do it—become a racist. You have to blame the victim. Once you've become a raving racist in self-defense, you've lost your capacity to understand what's happening.'

—Noam Chomsky, *The Prosperous Few and the Restless Many* (2002)

The problem with 'Haitian exceptionalism' and all of the various tropologies and narratives that form its powerful and influential discourse is not only the fact that it perpetuates the old prejudices of "mulatto/a" vengeance, but that it keeps us from creating 'new narratives' about Haiti (Ulysse, 2015). This is partly because we must be ever-watchful to destroy the old ones as they continue to resurface in new ways, and partially because the forceful vocabulary of such a narrative has confused reality with representation to such an extent that we can no longer be sure which is which. While the "colored historian" is the most persistent of the tropologies to be found in today's scholarship about Haiti, in the popular media, "monstrous hybridity" prevails. Indeed, Haiti remains the punching bag for those looking for easy examples of "racial" prejudice even though they might better concentrate on the ones undoubtedly to be found in their own countries. Haiti also serves as a case study for the dangers of religious and linguistic hybridity as well as of political incomprehensibility (what Nicholls referred to as *la politique de doublure* [1979, 79]) in both U.S. and international political discourse. The Haitian language and the Haitian religion—taken as some of the most extreme measures of the country's "monstrous hybridity" and tropical sensuality in nineteenth-century representations of the Revolution, notably by Victor Hugo in *Bug-Jargal* (1826) and the anonymous author of *Idylles et Chansons* (1804)—still serve today to accentuate the strangely violent and dangerously exotic nature of Haiti and its "hybrid" people.[1]

Virtually all of the "racial" tropologies of the nineteenth century, which had never completely gone away anyway, surfaced with a vengeance in the popular media storm that followed in the wake of the January 2010 earthquake that practically destroyed the Haitian capital Port-au-Prince. In the article 'The Underlying Tragedy,' which was written for the *New York Times* twelve days after the earthquake, David Brooks, arguably the worst of the new offenders, essentially blamed the Haitian people and their 'progress-resistant culture,' in which 'responsibility' for the effects of the earthquake 'is often not internalized':

> Haiti, like most of the world's poorest nations, suffers from a complex web of progress-resistant cultural influences. There is the influence of the voodoo religion, which spreads the message that life is capricious and planning futile. There are high levels of social mistrust. Responsibility is often not internalized ...

---

[1] I refer to the 1821 edition of *Idylles et Chansons ou essais de Poésie Créole*, which relies upon the 1804 original rather than the 1811 reprint and wherein we find the following description of the Creole spoken in Saint-Domingue: 'The Creole language is a type of jargon that the Negroes, Creoles, and the majority of the colonists from the islands of America speak. It is corrupt, bastardized French, but suitable for gentle purposes ... This language has ... an infinity of *sweetness* [*mignardises*], an extreme gentleness ... that renders it proper to express with delicacy, and above all with a certain naiveté, feelings of love, with the same character that this passion takes on in the hearts of the sensual and voluptuous inhabitants of the Torrid Zone ... The Creole language nevertheless is not suited to poetry' (3).

> We're all supposed to politely respect each other's cultures. But some cultures are more progress-resistant than others, and a horrible tragedy was just exacerbated by one of them.

Brooks is quite obviously playing the blame game here by asserting both that the earthquake was 'man made'—he wrote, 'This is not a natural disaster story. This is a poverty story'—and therefore that it was essentially the fault of the Haitian people who, unlike U.S. Americans, are 'progress-resistant.' This claim that Haiti's 'poverty' and 'culture' were responsible for the devastation allows Brooks to deny the United States' extensive history of tampering with political and financial affairs in Haiti that are in great measure to blame for Haiti's economic conditions (see Farmer, 1994, 77–78). At the same time, Brooks's statement affirms some of the central tenets of U.S. 'culture': that 'voodoo' more than Christianity spreads the message that 'planning is futile'; that 'social mistrust' and lack of 'responsibility' are inherent to the Haitian people, but surely not to U.S. Americans; and, above all, that U.S. citizens are successful because their culture is inherently progress-receptive. Brooks's implied message is that U.S. society has succeeded precisely because it is everything that Haitian society is not. Brooks therefore taps into the quintessential U.S. American narrative of progress towards 'civilization' that has been used to justify everything from 'Indian Removal' to slavery to wars, occupations, and imperialism (Zinn, 629).

Brooks, who, to my knowledge, had never even been to Haiti before his article appeared, seems to have relied for these cultural judgments on works that are filled with various kinds of beliefs that could be labeled as the essence of 'Haitian exceptionalism.' Brooks's editorial in fact closely echoes the claims of Robert Rotberg in *Haiti: The Politics of Squalor* (1971), which was 'written with the collaboration of a psychiatrist deeply versed in Haitian studies' (Heinl and Heinl, 6), as well as upon the work of Nancy and Robert Heinl in *Written in Blood: The Story of the Haitian People*.[2] Heinl and Heinl believe that nearly all of Haitian history can be explained by one phrase, which is in their view, as in that of 'Foreigners long in the country,' or so they say, *'pa fot mwen'* or 'It's not my fault.' This Haitian Creole phrase is cited in the interest of providing a microcosm for all of Haiti's problems:

---

[2] The only source that Brooks actually names with respect to information about Haiti is Lawrence E. Harrison's *The Central Liberal Truth*, a work filled through and through with the kind of racialism always inherent in statements exhibiting 'Haitian exceptionalism.' One particular gem from Harrison's book reads, '[t]he array of fundamental problems that we associate with underdevelopment was, I believed, deeply rooted in the minds of Latin Americans. I found these same problems in particularly high profile in Haiti, which is not really a Latin American country, but an African American country' (xii).

lack of personal responsibility. Heinl and Heinl quote Rotberg's observation of Haiti, 'the unusual extent to which paranoia, well-systematized delusions of persecution and/or grandeur, the elaborations of which are logically construed on false premises seem to afflict peasants and elite alike' (Heinl and Heinl, 6). 'There is paranoia in Haiti, no doubt about it,' Heinl and Heinl write,

> Moreover there are deep feelings of insecurity and inferiority, rarely acknowledged, that typically appear in the people's reluctance if not inability to recognize, let alone accept, the Haitian situation as it really exists. They rarely acknowledge Haiti's national incompetence or the fact that this poor black country, no matter why, in almost two centuries of freedom has little to show but interrupted failure. (6)

Such judgments of the Haitian past lead Heinl and Heinl to conclude with irony that '[i]t is indeed not Haiti's fault. Haiti is imprisoned by its past' (6).

Imprisoned by its past, perhaps, but not in the way that Heinl and Heinl want to make out. I think it does 'matter why' Haiti is in 'dreadful shape,' to quote Tracy Kidder (2). If the legacy of slavery and almost continuous international and, especially, U.S. intervention did not matter, then people like Rotberg and Heinl and Heinl would not be so concerned with 'isolat[ing] the reasons why Haiti—once the most glorious colony in the world—had fallen upon such hard times' (Rotberg, ix). I can almost hear Michel-Rolph Trouillot whispering in my ear—'Haitian exceptionalism:' 'Deep in the psyche of Haiti ... lies a violence that goes beyond all violence' (Heinl and Heinl, 6)—acts as 'a shield that masks the negative contribution of the Western powers to the Haitian situation' (1990, 7).

If we think about the long and deep influence of the *tropics of Haiti* in determining opinions about the country, the reasons for blaming Haitians themselves for the effects of the 2010 earthquake become increasingly clear. Pat Robertson would locate the origins of the quake in providential revenge for the Haitian Revolution when in a broadcast of his show *The 700 Club*, he attributed the natural disaster to a 'pact to the devil' supposedly made by the slaves during the Haitian Revolution. Robertson said that as a result of this putative pact, 'You know, the Haitians revolted and got themselves free. But ever since, they have been cursed by one thing after the other.'[3] Robertson's

---

3 Elizabeth McAlister has called this narrative part of the evangelical 'Spiritual Mapping movement' and she says that it had been 'working actively for twenty years to promote this story. Robertson,' she says, 'had absorbed the idea through his affiliation with the movement and repeated it on the broadcast' (189). 'Pat Robertson says Haiti Paying for "Pact to the Devil."' CNN, January 13, 2010. http://articles.cnn.

implied message is that, in contrast, U.S. Americans succeeded after their revolution because they made a pact with God.[4] Once again, Haiti exists to, in the words of Paul Farmer, 'serve the powerful' (1994, 46), by providing a foil for the special properties of "whiteness," reassuring Christians of the transcendent value of their religion, and convincing the U.S. public not only of the exceptional nature of U.S. American democracy and culture, but that they deserve to be prosperous in the face of the suffering of others. After all, it was not they who made a pact with the devil (read: dared to violently usurp the authority of their masters).[5]

Robertson's attempt to link the Haitian Revolution to a natural disaster was hardly original. As Anna Brickhouse has written, in 1866, after devastating fires virtually destroyed the Haitian capital Port-au-Prince, the U.S. press, specifically the *New York Times*, blamed the Haitians themselves not simply for the devastation, but for the actual fires (2007, 1099). Moreover, the Haitian Revolution had been connected to an earthquake before. In 'Augustin, ou la révolte des noirs' (1844), the anonymous author immediately juxtaposed a narrative of "mulatto/a" vengeance with a devastating earthquake that hit Cap Haïtien in 1842. The author wrote that after the failure of the Leclerc expedition, '[a] great many of the inhabitants took to the coast in order to take refuge with the governor in the vessels; but a troop of mulattoes cut off their retreat and committed a horrid butchery' (386). The author then writes that his 'work had not yet been finished, when we learned that an earthquake on May 7, 1842 had almost completely destroyed Cap Haïtien, and that more than 4,000 inhabitants were buried under its ruins' (387). It was not just in vague juxtapositions like this, however, that Haitians would be blamed in some way for the earthquake or its aftermath. In his *Hayti, or the Black Republic* (1886), the infamous Spencer St. John, whose beliefs in 'negro inferiority,' are quite well known (St. John, 131–32; see also, Plummer,

com/2010-01-13/us/haiti.pat.robertson_1_pat-robertson-disasters-and-terrorist-attacks-devil?_s=PM:US

4 In *Courting Disaster: How the Supreme Court is Usurping the Powers of Congress and the People*, Robertson misquotes John Adams as having said: '[t]he highest glory of the American Revolution is this; it connected in one indissoluble bond the principles of civil government with the principles of Christianity' (38). The phrase actually first appeared in John Wingate Thornton, *The Pulpit of the American Revolution* (1860) and was not specifically attributed to Adams.

5 It goes without saying that there is absolutely no proof that Haitians ever made a 'pact' with the devil. But Robertson's claim actually tells us more about his own religious beliefs, fantasies, and fears than it ever could about Haitians who serve the gods or who practice what is commonly referred to as *Vodou*. For in the *Vodou* pantheon, there is no 'the devil,' this figure being a distinctive feature of Christianity. For Haitian Vodou, see Karen McCarthy Brown (1991).

39), wrote that seeing the ruins of the earthquake in Cap Haïtien proved to him 'how little energy is left in a people who could leave their property in such a state' (11).

It is perhaps a little unfair to single out Brooks and Robertson, then, since, as the studies of such 'bad press' by Plummer (1990), Lawless (1992), and Farmer (1994) suggest, these twenty-first century journalists are hardly the first or the last offenders. European and U.S. American journalists have historically been quick to blame the problems of Haiti on the "races," languages, religions, and cultures of Haitians. Mark Dow, for example, has pointed to several instances of the way that such belittling still manages to disparage Haitian culture. In his study, Dow writes of one journalist as referring to Haitian Creole as 'French or whatever' and another stating that in 'Haitian Patois' 'justice can mean revenge' (qtd. in Dow, 3). The U.S. Department of State (supposedly providing information to potential travelers to Haiti) also sneers at Haitian society in noting that the dominant religion of the country is Roman Catholicism. The consular information sheet also makes sure to include a sentence warning that 'much of the population also practices vodou (voodoo)' and that 'Haitians tend to see no conflict in these African-rooted beliefs coexisting with Christian faith.'[6]

I could go on and on about the manifold ways in which the trope of "monstrous hybridity" continues to be deployed against Haiti in the contemporary public sphere, but I do not want to give any more attention to these ugly narratives than I already have. For I have often found myself distressed in retelling these stories about the land that gave me my mother. While Haiti may have fulfilled Herbert Gold's desire for a titillating nightmare or may have been Graham Greene's idea of a dark comedy, for the people in my family who lived through Duvalier, and his son, and Aristide, and the occupation in the 90s, and floods, and misery, and then Aristide again, and more occupation, and MINUSTAH, and *goudougoudou*, and then more misery (to say nothing of my unknown revolutionary ancestors), there is nothing terrifically providential or fantastic in all of this. Haitians do just what everyone else in every other place does when faced with destruction and loss: they work through grief, try to find a way to rebuild, continue to live life, and ultimately move on. This is precisely the sentiment captured by Haitian writer Demesvar Delorme, who as a young child lived through what he described as the utterly terrifying 1842 quake. Delorme wrote, '[w]hen the terror had somewhat subsided, we gradually resumed our lives. Just as the worried people of the Middle Ages did, after in the year 1000 they watched come and go the time assigned by the popular prophets for the end of the world' (Delorme, 1942, 24).

---

6 See http://www.state.gov/r/pa/ei/bgn/1982.htm

If by connecting the late eighteenth- to mid-nineteenth-century versions of the St. Johns, the Brooks, the Robertsons, and the Heinl and Heinls all together, I have resurrected an unpleasant narrative, then it is only to show the ways in which the narrative of "mulatto/a" vengeance still exists today, even if mostly outside of the scholarly realm, in much the same way that it existed in the nineteenth century. It might often masquerade as a critique of culture, religion, politics, or language, where the Haitian people have purportedly bastardized French and do not understand that their own 'African-rooted' practices are in conflict with Christianity, but the conclusion is always the same. The Haitian people were not meant for *civilization*. Believing this makes it okay to also believe that they are simply a violent people who are deserving of (or at least responsible for) their fate since even their language makes no distinction between justice and revenge.

Though I am no longer naïve enough to believe that 'Haitian exceptionalism' will go away anytime soon without some kind of revolution of the mind, I am still optimistic enough to hope that what I have done in this literary history, other than reviving narratives that are likely to be the source of great pain for people who, to quote Saint-Rémy, 'have a black face like me,' is to open up a conversation about the other kinds of narratives we might be able to discover about Haiti. While I have here studied, alongside the "racial" tropologies of Haiti in circulation in the nineteenth-century Atlantic World, the ways in which nineteenth-century Haitian authors were manifestly engaged with narratives of "mulatto/a" vengeance, I am completely cognizant of the fact that many Haitian writers of the nineteenth century, as they do today, wrote about other interesting things, including philosophy, art, literature, the beauty of flowers and sunsets, raising children, pain, both physical and emotional, caring for the aging and dying, grief, love, romance, heartbreak, passion, excitement, education, and desire. It is in the diversity of the tales Haitian writers told, some of them having to do with the most important events and problems of their era, and some of them that might seem to us trivial or mundane now, it is in the kinds of poetry they innovated, in the colors of their often distinctive paintings, and in the soul shaking rhythms of the musical forms that they have created, co-opted, adapted, modified, and disseminated throughout the world, that we can find the new narratives we seek. *Se vye chodye ki kwit bon manje.*

Bibliography

'A Colored Female Lecturer.' *Liberator* 8 April 1864: 59–60. Print.
A Guide to the Jérémie Papers. Web. <http://www.library.ufl.edu/spec/manuscript/guides/jeremie.htm>. Accessed 10 September 2013.
Acte de Baptême, Jean Louis Vastey, 29 March 1788, Paroisse de Plaisance, Saint-Domingue (Haiti). Copy in possession of État-Civil de Saint-Domingue. Archives Nationales d'Outre-Mer, Aix-en-Provence, France.
Adams, John Quincy. *An Inaugural Oration, delivered at the author's installation, as Boylston Professor of Rhetorick and Oratory* ... Boston: Munroe and Francis, 1806. Print.
'Address to the Female Literary Association of Philadelphia.' *The Liberator*. Ed. William Garrison. 9 June 1832: 91. Print.
'Address to the Female Literary Association of Philadelphia, on their First Anniversary, By A Member.' *The Liberator*. Ed. William Lloyd Garrison. 13 October 1832: 162. Print.
A***. 'Augustin, ou la révolte des Noirs.' *Amélina, Godefroy et Augustin: ou les trois époques d'Haiti, par M.M. Baignoux et A****. Tours: Pomin, 1843, 1846. Print.
Adler, Joyce Sparer. '*Benito Cereno*: Slavery and Violence in the Americas.' *Critical Essays on Herman Melville's 'Benito Cereno.'* Ed. Robert E. Burkholder. New York: G.K. Hall. 1992. 76–93. Print.
Adorno, Theodor. 'Commitment.' *Aesthetics and Politics: The Key Texts of the Classic Debate within German Marxism*. Ed. Ernst Bloch. New York: Verso, 1997. 177–95. Print.
Agamben, Giorgio. *Homo Sacer: Sovereign Power and Bare Life*. Palo Alto: Stanford UP, 1998. Print.
—. *Means without Ends: Notes on Politics*. Tr. Cesare Casarino and Vincenzo Binetti. Minneapolis: U. of Minnesota P., 2000. Print.
—. *State of Exception*. Chicago: U of Chicago P, 2005. Print.
Alexander, Leslie M. '"The Black Republic": The Influence of the Haitian Revolution on Northern Black Political Consciousness, 1816–1862.' *African*

Americans and the Haitian Revolution: Selected Essays and Historical Documents. Ed. Jacqueline Bacon and Maurice Jackson. New York: Routledge, 2010. 57–79. Print.

Allan, Seán. *The Stories of Heinrich Von Kleist: Fictions of Security.* Rochester: Camden House, 2001. Print.

Allewaert, Monique. *Ariel's Ecology: Plantations, Personhood, and Colonialism in the American Tropics.* Minneapolis: U of Minnesota P, 2013. Print.

Almanach Royale d'Hayti pour l'année bissextile 1814, Onzième de l'indépendance, et la troisième du règne de sa majesté, présenté au roi, par P. Roux. Cap-Henry: P. Roux, 1814. Print.

Almanach Royale d'Hayti pour l'année bissextile 1815, Douzième de l'indépendance, et la quatrième du règne de sa majesté, présenté au roi, par P. Roux. Cap-Henry: P. Roux, 1815. Print.

Almanach Royale d'Hayti pour l'année bissextile 1816, Treizième de l'indépendance, et la cinquième du règne de sa majesté, présenté au roi, par P. Roux. Cap-Henry: P. Roux, 1816. Print.

Almanach Royale d'Hayti pour l'année bissextile 1820, Dix-septième de l'indépendance, et la neuvième du règne de sa majesté, présenté au roi, par Buon. Sans-Souci: Imprimerie Royale, 1820. Print.

Ames, Fisher. *The Works of Fisher Ames, compiled by a number of his friends.* Oxford UP, 1809. Print.

Anderson, Benedict. *Imagined Communities: Reflections on the Origin and Spread of Nationalism.* London: Verso, 1999. Print.

'Anecdote of Naimbana.' *The Anti-Slavery Record* 1.11 (November 1835): 129. Print.

Anonymous. *La Mulâtre comme il y a beaucoup de blanches.* 1803. Ed. John D. Garrigus. Paris: L'Harmattan, 2007. Print.

Anonymous. *La Mulâtre comme il y a beaucoup de blanches; Ouvrage pouvant faire suite au Nègre comme il y a peu de blancs.* Paris: Marchand, 1803. Print.

Anonymous. *The Woman of Colour.* Ed. Lyndon J. Dominique. Ontario: Broadview, 2007. Print.

Antier, Benjamin et al. *Bugg, ou les Javanais: mélodrame en 3 actes, à grand spectacle.* Paris: Quoy, 1828. Print.

Antigua and the Antiguans, A Full Account of the Island and its Inhabitants. London: Saunders and Otley, 1844. Print.

Anzaldúa, Gloria. *Borderlands/La Frontera: The New Mestiza.* San Francisco: Aunt Lute Books, 2007. Print.

Appiah, Kwame Anthony. 'Race.' *Critical Terms for Literary Study.* Ed. Frank Lentricchia and Tom McLaughlin. Chicago UP, 1989. 274–87. Print.

—. 'Racisms.' *Anatomy of Racism.* Ed. D.T. Goldberg. U of Minnesota P, 1990. 3–17. Print.

—. 'Is the Post- in Postmodernism the Post- in Postcolonial?' *Critical Inquiry* 17.2 (Winter 1991): 336–57. Print.

Bibliography

Araujo, Ana Lucia. 'Introduction.' *Politics of Memory: Making Slavery Visible in the Public Space.* Ed. Ana Lucia Araujo. New York: Routledge, 2012. 1–14. Print.

—. 'Transnational Memory of Slave Merchants: Making the Perpetrators Visible in the Public Space.' *Politics of Memory: Making Slavery Visible in the Public Space.* Ed. Ana Lucia Araujo. New York: Routledge, 2012. 15–34. Print.

Aravamudan, Srinivas. *Tropicopolitans: Colonialism and Agency, 1688–1804.* Durham: Duke UP, 1999. Print.

Ardouin, Beaubrun. *Géographie de l'ile d'Haïti: précédée du précis et de la date des événements les plus remarquables de son histoire.* Port-au-Prince, 1832. Print.

—. *Réponse du Sénateur B. Ardouin à un écrit anonyme intitule, Apologie des destitutions pour opinions politiques, ou dogme d'obéissance passive prêché aux fonctionnaires publics.* Port-au-Prince: Pinard, 1840. Print.

—. *Réponse du Sénateur B. Ardouin à une lettre de M. Isambert, Conseiller à la cour de Cassation de France, Membre de la Chambre de Députés.* Port-au-Prince: Pinard, 1842. Print.

—. *Études sur l'histoire d'Haïti; suivies de la vie du général J.-M. Borgella*, 11 vols. Paris: Dezobry et E. Magdeleine, 1853–60. Print.

Arendt, Hannah. *On Violence.* New York: Harcourt, Brace and World. 1969, 1970. Print.

Arnold, James. 'The Gendering of Créolité: The Erotics of Colonialism.' *Penser la créolité.* Ed. Maryse Condé and Madeleine Cottenet-Hage. Paris: Éditions Karthala, 1995. 21–67. Print.

—. 'Animal Tales, Historic Dispossession, and Creole Identity in the French West Indies.' *Monsters, Tricksters, and Sacred Cows: Animal Tales and American Identities.* Ed. A. James Arnold. Charlottesville: U of Virginia P, 2006. 255–68. Print.

Arrizon, Alicia. *Queering Mestizaje: Transculturation and Performance*: Ann Arbor: The U of Michigan P, 2006. Print.

'Article 2.' *Littel's Living Age* 7 May 1859: 344. Print.

'Article 2.' *The African Repository* December 1858: 381. Print.

'Au Héros de la régénération haïtienne.' *La Sentinelle de la liberté* 2 November 1843: 4. Print.

Audin, Louis. *Discours à trois jeunes Haïtiens, récemment couronnés au grand concours de la Sorbonne.* Paris: Moquet, 1858. Print.

Bacon, Jacqueline. *Freedom's Journal: The First African American Newspaper.* Lanham, MD: Lexington Books, 2007. Print.

—. '"A Revolution Unexampled in the History of Man": The Haitian Revolution in *Freedom's Journal*, 1827–1829.' *African Americans and the Haitian Revolution: Selected Essays and Historical Documents.* Ed. Jacqueline Bacon and Maurice Jackson. New York: Routledge, 2010. 81–92. Print.

Bacon, Jacqueline, and Maurice Jackson. *African Americans and the Haitian*

Revolution: Selected Essays and Historical Documents. Ed. Jacqueline Bacon and Maurice Jackson. New York: Routledge, 2010a.

'Fever and Fret: The Haitian Revolution and African American Responses.' *African Americans and the Haitian Revolution: Selected Essays and Historical Documents.* Ed. Jacqueline Bacon and Maurice Jackson. New York: Routledge, 2010b. 9–23. Print.

—. 'Introduction.' *African Americans and the Haitian Revolution: Selected Essays and Historical Documents.* Ed. Jacqueline Bacon and Maurice Jackson. New York: Routledge, 2010c. 1–6. Print.

Baker, William Spohn. *Bibliotheca Washingtoniana: A Descriptive List of the Biographies and Biographical Sketches of George Washington.* Philadelphia: Robert M. Lindsay, 1889. Print.

Balzac, Honoré de. *Z. Marcas.* Paris: Alexandre Houssiaux, 1853, 1840. Print.

Barré Saint-Venant, Jean. *Des colonies modernes sous la zone torride, et particulièrement de celle de Saint- Domingue.* Paris: Brochot, 1802. Print.

Barskett, James. *History of the Island of St. Domingo, from its first Discovery by Columbus to the Present Period.* London: Archibald Constable, 1818. Print.

Barthélémy, Gérard. 'Le Rôle des Bossales dans l'émergence d'une culture de marronage.' *Cahier d'études africaines* 3.148 (1997): 839–62. Print.

Bassard, Katherine Clay. *Spiritual Interrogations: Culture, Gender, and Community in Early African American Women's Writing.* Princeton, NJ: Princeton UP, 1999. Print.

Baucom, Ian. *Specters of the Atlantic: Finance Capital, Slavery, and the Philosophy of History.* Durham: Duke UP, 2005. Print.

Baur, John. 'Faustin Soulouque, Emperor of Haiti.' *The Americas* 6 (1949): 131–66. Print.

Bay, Mia. *The White Image in the Black Mind: African-American Ideas about White People, 1830–1925.* Oxford: Oxford UP, 2000. Print.

Beard, John Relly. *The Life of Toussaint L'Ouverture, the Negro Patriot of Hayti: Comprising an Account of the Struggle for Liberty in the Island, and a Sketch of Its History to the Present Period.* London: Ingram, Cooke, 1853. Print.

Beckles, Hilary. "Divided to the Vein: The problem of race, Colour and Class Conflict in Haitian Nation-Building, 1804–1820. *Caribbean Freedom: Economy and Society from Emancipation to the Present.* Ed. Hilary Beckles and Verena Shepherd. Princeton, NJ: Markus Wiener Publishers, 1996. 494–502. Print.

—. 'Taking Liberties: Enslaved Women and Anti-Slavery in the Caribbean.' *Gender and Imperialism.* Ed. Clare Midgley. Manchester: Manchester UP, 1998. 137–57. Print.

Beecher, Jonathan. 'Echoes of Toussaint Louverture and the Haitian Revolution in Melville's "Benito Cereno"' *Leviathan* 9.2 (2007): 43–58. Print.

Behn, Aphra. *Oroonoko; or the Royal Slave.* Web. <http://ebooks.adelaide.edu.au/b/behn/aphra/b420/>. Accessed 15 January 2013.

Bibliography

Belohlavek, John M. *Broken Class: Caleb Cushing and the Shattering of the Union.* Kent, OH: Kent State UP, 2005. Print.

Belasco, Susan. 'Harriet Martineau's Black Hero and the American Anti-Slavery Movement.' *Nineteenth-Century Literature* 55.2 (September 2002): 157–94. Print.

Bell, Caryn Cossé. *Revolution, Romanticism, and the Afro-Creole Protest Tradition in Louisiana, 1718–1868.* Baton Rouge: Louisiana State UP, 1997, 2004. Print.

Bell, Madison Smartt. *All Souls' Rising.* Vintage, 2004. Print.

—. *Toussaint Louverture: A Biography.* New York: Pantheon Books, 2007. Print.

Bellegarde, Dantès. *Histoire du peuple haïtien, 1492–1952.* Port-au-Prince, 1953. Print.

Bellegarde-Smith, Patrick. 'Overview of Haitian Foreign Policy and Relations: A Schematic Analysis.' *Haiti: Today and Tomorrow: An Interdisciplinary Study.* Ed. Charles Foster and Albert Valdman. Lanham: UP of America, 1984. 265–81. Print.

Bem, Jeanne. '*Châtiments*, ou l'histoire de France comme enchaînements de Parricides.' *La Revue des Lettres Modernes* 693–97 (1984): 39–51. Print.

Bénot, Yves. 'Lamartine et la nuit du Bois-Caïman.' *Europe* 66.715–16 (November–December 1988): 30–45. Print.

—. 'Diderot, Pechméja, Raynal et l'anticolonialisme,' *Europe; revue littéraire mensuelle* 41 (January–February 1963): 137–53. Print.

Bentley, Nancy. 'White Slaves: The Mulatto Hero in Antebellum Fiction.' *American Literature* 65.3 (1993): 501–22. Print.

Benzaken, Jean-Charles. 'Who was the Author of *L'Histoire des désastres de Saint-Domingue*, published in Paris in the Year III?' *Society for the Study of French History.* 23 March 2009. 261–67. Web. <http://fh.oxcofrdjournals.org>. Accessed 27 March 2014.

Béraud, Louis François Guillaume, and Joseph De Rosny. *Adonis ou, Le bon nègre, mélodrame, en quatre actes, avec danses, chansons, décors et costumes créoles.* Paris: Glisau, etc. 1798. Print.

Bergeaud, Eméric. 'Insurrection d'Ambouille Mort.' *Le Temps* 40 (10 November 1842): 1–2. Print.

—. *Stella.* Paris: E. Dentu, 1859. Print.

Berlant, Lauren. *The Queen of America Goes to Washington City: Essays on Sex and Citizenship.* Durham: Duke UP, 1997. Print.

Berman, Carolyn Vellenga. 'Creole Family Politics in *Uncle Tom's Cabin* and *Incidents in the Life of a Slave Girl.*' *Novel* 33.3 (Summer 2000): 328–52. Print.

Bernardin de Saint-Pierre. *Paul et Virginie.* Paris: Flammarion, 1996. Print.

Berrou, Raphaël and Pradel Pompilus, *Histoire de la littérature haïtienne illustrée par les textes.* 3 vols. Port-au-Prince: Édition Caraïbes, 1975–77. Print.

Berthier, J.-B.C. *Félix et Léonore, ou les colons malheureux.* 2 vols. Paris: Maradan, 1801. Print.

Berzon, Judith R. *Neither White nor Black: The Mulatto Character in American Fiction*. New York: New York UP, 1978. Print.

Bethel, Elizabeth Rauh. *The Roots of African American Identity: Memory and History in Free Antebellum Communities*. New York: St. Martin's Press, 1997. Print.

Beverly, John. 'The Margin at the Center: On *Testimonio* (Testimonial Narrative).' *De/Colonizing the Subject: The Politics of Gender in Women's Autobiography*. Ed. Sidonie Smith et al. Minneapolis: U of Minnesota P, 1992: 91–114. Print.

Bhabha, Homi K. *Nation and Narration*. London: Routledge, 1990. Print.

—. *The Location of Culture*. London: Routledge, 1994. Print.

Bierlein, J.F. *Living Myths: How Myth Gives Meaning to Human Experience*. Toronto: Ballantine Well Spring, 1999. Print.

'Biography of Remarkable Characters Recently Deceased.' *The Atheneum; or Spirit of the English Magazines* 1 May 1821. Print.

Binns, Edward. *Prodromus: Towards a Philosophical Inquiry into the Intellectual Powers of the Negro*. London: John Churchill, 1844. Print.

—. Excerpt from *Prodromus*. *Colonial Magazine and East India Review* 2 (May–August 1844). 154–84. Print.

Bissette, Cyrille A. *Réfutation du livre de M.V. Schoelcher sur Haïti*. Paris: Ebrard, 1844. Print.

Blackburn, Robin. *The Overthrow of Colonial Slavery, 1776–1848*. New York, Verso, 1988. Print.

—. *The Making of New World Slavery: From the Baroque to the Modern 1492–1800*. New York: Verso, 1997. Print.

Blackett, R.J.M. *Building an Antislavery Wall: Black Americans in the Atlantic Abolitionist Movement, 1830–1860*. Baton Rouge: Louisiana State UP, 1983. Print.

Blanchelande, Philibert François Rouxel de. 'Proclamation.' *Supplément au numéro 91 de La Feuille du jour* 31 March 1792. 1–2. Print.

Blanckaert, Claude. 'Of Monstrous Métis? Hybridity, Fear of Miscegenation and Patriotism from Buffon to Paul Broca.' *The Color of Liberty: Histories of Race in France*. Ed. Tyler Stovall and Sue Peabody. Durham: Duke UP, 2003. Print.

Blane, William Newnham. *Travels through the United States and Canada*. London: Baldwin and Company, 1828. Print.

Block, Sharon. *Rape and Sexual Power in Early America*. Chapel Hill: U of North Carolina P, 2006. Print.

Blum, Carol. *Rousseau and the Republic of Virtue: The Language of Politics in the French Revolution*. Ithaca: Cornell UP, 1990. Print.

Blumenbach, Johann Gottfried, *Contributions to Natural History*. Ed. Thomas Bendyshe. London: Garrison and Morton, 1865, 1806. Print.

le Borgne de Boigne, Claude Pierre Joseph. *Le Nouveau système de la colonisation*. Paris: Dondy Dupré, 1817. Print.

Bibliography

Boisrond-Tonnère, Louis Félix. *Mémoires pour servir à l'histoire d'Haïti.* Ed. Joseph Saint-Rémy. Paris: France, Libraire, 1851. Print.

Bongie, Chris. *Islands and Exiles: The Creole Identities of Post/Colonial Literature.* Stanford: Stanford UP, 1998. Print.

—. 'Introduction: Bug-Jargal, 1791: Language and History in Translation.' *Bug-Jargal.* Tr. and Ed. Chris Bongie. Ontario: Broadview Press, 2004. 9–47. Print.

—. '"Monotonies of History": Baron de Vastey and the Mulatto Legend of Derek Walcott's *Haitian Trilogy*.' *Yale French Studies: The Haiti Issue: 1804 and Nineteenth-Century French Studies* 107 (2005a): 70–107. Print.

—. 'Victor Hugo and "The Cause of Humanity": Translating *Bug-Jargal* (1826) into *The Slave King* (1833).' *The Translator: Studies in Intercultural Communication* 11.1 (2005b): 1–24. Print.

—. 'Introduction.' *Adonis; ou le bon nègre: anecdote coloniale.* 1798. Ed. Chris Bongie. Paris: L'Harmattan, 2006. Print.

—. *Friends and Enemies: The Scribal Politics of Post/Colonial Literature.* Liverpool: Liverpool UP, 2008. Print.

—. *The Colonial System Unveiled.* Tr and Ed. Chris Bongie. Liverpool: Liverpool, UP, 2014. Print.

Bonin, Kathrine. 'Signs of Origin: Victor Hugo's Bug-Jargal.' *Nineteenth-Century French Studies* 36.3–4 (Spring–Summer 2008): 193–204. Print.

Bonneau, Alexandre. 'Les Noirs, les Jaunes, et la littérature française en Haïti.' *Revue contemporaine et Athenaeum Français* (1 December 1856): 107–55. Print.

—. *Haïti:ses progrès, son avenir.* Paris: E. Dentu, 1862. Print.

Bonnet, Guy. *Souvenirs historique de Guy Joseph Bonnet, général de division des armées de la République d'Haiti ... Documents relatifs à toutes les phases de la révolution de Saint-Domingue recueillis et mis en ordre.* Paris: Auguste Durand, 1864. Print.

Bonnet, Raoul. 'Victor Hugo et la "Revue Encyclopédique"' (1822).' *Revue d'Histoire littéraire de la France* 21.2 (1914): 326–30. Print.

Bonniol, Jean Luc and Jean Benoist. 'Hérédités plurielles. Représentations populaires et conceptions savantes du métissage.' *Ethnologie française* 14.1 (1994): 58–69. Print.

Botelho, Keith M. '"Look on this picture, and on this": Framing Shakespeare in William Wells Brown's "The Escape."' *Comparative Drama* 39.2 (Summer 2005): 187–212. Print.

Boulle, Pierre. 'In Defense of Slavery: Eighteenth-century Oppositions to Abolition and the Origins of a Racist Ideology in France.' *History from Below.* Ed. Frederick Krantz. Oxford: Basil Blackwell, 1985, 1988. 219–46. Print.

—. *Race et esclavage dans la France de l'Ancien Régime.* Paris: Perrin, 2007. Print.

Boyd, Willis D. 'James Redpath and American Negro Colonization in Haiti, 1860–1862.' *The Americas* 12 (1955): 169–82. Print.

Braziel, Jana Evans. 'Re-membering Défilé: Dédée Bazile as Revolutionary Lieu de Mémoire.' *Small Axe* 9.2 (September 2005): 57–85. Print.

—. 'Haiti, Guantánomo, and the "One Indispensable Nation": U.S. Imperialism, "Apparent States", and Post-colonial Problematics of Sovereignty.' *Cultural Critique* 64 (Fall 2006): 127–60. Print.

Breedon, James O. 'In the Beginning(s): A Chapter in Antebellum American Ethnology.' *Transactions & Studies of the College of Physicians of Philadelphia* 45.4 (April 1978): 227–61. Print.

Brennan, Timothy. 'The National Longing for Form.' *Nation and Narration*. Ed. Homi Bhabha. New York: Routledge, 1990. 44–70. Print.

Brickhouse, Anna. *Transamerican Literary Relations and the Nineteenth-Century Public Sphere*. Cambridge: Cambridge UP, 2004. Print.

—. 'L'Ouragan de Flammes (The Hurricane of Flames): New Orleans and Transamerican Catastrophe, 1866/2005.' *American Quarterly Review* 59.4 (2007): 1097–1128. Print.

'Brief Notes.' *New York Times* 28 June 1874: 10. Print.

Brière, Jean. *Haïti et la France: Le rêve brisée, 1804–1848*. Paris: Editions Karthala, 2008. Print.

Brody, Jennifer DeVere. *Impossible Purities: Blackness, Femininity and Victorian Culture*. Durham: Duke UP, 1998. Print.

Brooks, Linda. 'Testimonio's Poetics of Performance.' *Comparative Literature Studies* 42.2 (2005): 181–222. Print.

Brooks, David. 'The Underlying Tragedy,' *New York Times* 14 January 2010. Web. <http://www.nytimes.com/2010/01/15/opinion/15brooks.html>. Accessed 27 January 2011.

Brown, Charles Brockden. 'On the Consequences of Abolishing the Slave Trade to the West Indian Colonies.' *The Literary Magazine, and the American Register* 4.26 (November 1805): 375–81. Print.

Brown, Gordon S. *Toussaint's Clause: The Founding Fathers and the Haitian Revolution*. Oxford: U of Mississippi P, 2005. Print.

Brown, Karen McCarthy. *Mama Lola: A Vodou Priestess in Brooklyn*. Ed. Claudine Michel. Berkeley, CA: U of California P, 2011. Print.

Brown, Sterling. 'Negro Character as Seen by White Authors.' 1933. *Callaloo* 14/15 (February–May 1982): 55–89. Print.

Brown, Vincent. *The Reaper's Garden: Death and Power in the World of Atlantic Slavery*. Cambridge, MA: Harvard UP, 2008. Print.

Brown, William Wells. *Three Years in Europe; or Places I have Seen and People I have Met*. London: Charles Gilpin, 1852. Print.

—. *St. Domingo, its Revolution and its Patriots. A Lecture Delivered before the Metropolitan Athenaeum, London, May 16, and at St. Thomas' Church, Philadelphia, December 20, 1854*. Boston: B. Marsh, 1855. Print.

—. *The Black Man, His Antecedents, His Genius, and His Achievements*. New York: Thomas Hamilton, 1863. Print.

—. *The Rising Son; or the Antecedents and Advancement of the Colored Race.* Boston: A.G. Brown and Company, 1882. Print.
—. *Narrative of William W. Brown, Fugitive Slave.* New York: Johnson Reprint, 1970. Print.
—. *Clotel; or the President's Daughter.* Ed. Robert Levine. Boston: Bedford/St. Martin's, 2000. Print.
—. 'A Lecture Delivered Before the Female Anti-Slavery Society of Salem. Nov. 14, 1847.' *The Works of William Wells Brown: Using His 'Strong, Manly Voice.'* Ed. Paula Garret and Hollis Robbins. Oxford: Oxford UP, 2006. 3–18. Print.
Bruce, Dickson, Jr. *The Origins of African American Literature, 1680–1865.* Charlottesville: UP of Virginia, 2001. Print.
Brueys d'Aigalliers, Gabriel François. *Œuvres choisis de G.F. Brueys d'Aigalliers, ancien major du régiment d'Angoumois, membre des Académies de Nismes, de Caen, des Arcades de Rome, et des Ricoverati de Padoue.* Nîmes: Imprimerie de la veuve Belle, 1805. Print.
Bryant, Kelly Duke. "Black but Not African: Francophone Black Diaspora and the *Revue Des Colonies*, 1834-1842." *The International Journal of African Historical Studies* 40.2 (2007): 251-282.
Buck-Morss, Susan. *Hegel, Haiti, and Universal History.* Pittsburgh: U of Pittsburgh P, 2009. Print.
Buffon, Georges Louis Leclerc, Comte de. *Œuvres complètes de Buffon, précédes d'une notice historique et ...* Vol. 2. Paris: F.D. Pillot, 1838. Print.
—. *Histoire naturelle générale et particulière, avec la description du cabinet du roy. Buffon@Web.* Web. <http://www.buffon.cnrs.fr/?lang=>. Accessed 18 February 2011.
—. *De l'Homme.* Ed. Michèle Duchet. Paris: Bibliothèque d'Anthropologie François Maspero, 1971. Print.
'Bulletin Bibliographique. Livres Étrangères.' *Revue encyclopédique, ou analyse raisonnée* 9 (January 1821): 536–94. Print.
Bullock, Penelope. 'The Mulatto in American Fiction.' *Phylon (1940–1956)* 6.1 (1945): 78–82. Print.
Burnham, Michelle. 'Female Bodies and Capitalist Drive: Leonora Sansay's *Secret History* in Transoceanic Context.' *Legacy* 28.2 (2011): 177–204. Print.
Burrows, Simon. *French Exile Journalism and European Politics, 1792–1814.* Rochester: Boydell Press, 2000. Print.
Buscaglia-Salgado, José F. *Undoing Empire: Race and Nation in the Mulatto Caribbean.* Minneapolis: U of Minnesota P, 2003. Print.
Bush, Barbara. 'Defiance or Submission? The Role of the Slave Woman in Slave Resistance in the British Caribbean.' *Immigrants & Minorities* 1.1 (1982): 16–38. Print.
Butler, Judith. *Gender Trouble.* Routledge, 2006. Print.
Buxton, Sir Thomas Fowell. *Letters on the Slave Trade.* London: John W. Parker, 1838. Print.

'By a Late Arrival from Port-au-Prince.' *Freedom's Journal* 16 March 1827. Print.

Cagidemetrio, Alide. '"The Rest of the Story"; or, Multilingual American Literature.' *Multilingual America: Transnationalism, Ethnicity, and the Languages of American Literature*. Ed. Werner Sollors. New York: New York UP, 1998. 24. Print.

Callanan, Laura. 'Race and the Politics of Interpretive Disruption in Harriet Martineau's *The Hour and the Man* (1841).' *Women's Writing: The Elizabethan to Victorian Period* 9.3 (October 2002): 413–32. Print.

Cambeira, Alan. *Quisqueya la Bella: The Dominican Republic in Historical and Cultural Perspective*. New York: M.E. Sharpe, 1997. Print.

Camus, Michel. 'Une fille naturelle de MOREAU de SAINT-MÉRY?' *G.H.C. Bulletin* 93 (May 1997): 1960. Web. <http://www.ghcaraibe.org/bul/ghc093/p1960.htm>. Accessed 2 February 2013.

Candler, John. *Brief Notices of Hayti*. London: Thomas Ward and Co., 1842. Print.

Carey, Brycchan. *British Abolitionism and the Rhetoric of Sensibility: Writing, Sentiment, and Slavery, 1760–1807*. Basingstoke: Palgrave Macmillan, 2005. Print.

'Carl Ritter's Researches in the Island of Hayti.' *The Foreign Quarterly Review* 20.39 (October 1837): 73–97. Print.

Carpentier, Alejo. *The Kingdom of this World*. Tr. Harriet de Onis. New York: Farrar, Straus, and Giroux, 2006, 1961. Print.

Carlyle, Thomas. 'Discourse on the Nigger Question.' The New School. Web. <http://cepa.newschool.edu/het/texts/carlyle/odnqbk.htm>. Accessed 18 February 2011.

—. 'Occasional Discourse on the Nigger Question.' *The Collected Works of Thomas Carlyle*. Vol. 13. London: Chapman and Hall, 1864. 1–28. Print.

Carra, Emilia. *Gli inediti di Moreau de Saint-Méry à Parme*. Parma: Fresching, 1954. Print.

Carteau, Félix. *Soirées Bermudiennes, ou, Entretiens sur les évènements qui ont opéré la ruine de la partie française de l'isle Saint-Domingue*. Bordeaux: Pellier-Lawalle, 1802. Print.

Carter, Greg. *The United States of the United Races: A Utopian History of Racial Mixing*. New York: New York UP, 2013. Print.

Casimir, Jean. 'Prologue: From Saint-Domingue to Haiti: To Live Again or to Live at Last!' *The World of the Haitian Revolution*. Ed. David Patrick Geggus and Norman Fiering. Bloomington: Indiana UP, 2009. xi–xvii. Print.

Castera, Justin Emmanuel. *Bref coup d'œil sur les origines de la presse haïtienne*. Port-au-Prince: Imprimerie Henri Deschamps, 1986. Print.

Castronovo, Russ. *Fathering the Nation: American Genealogies of Slavery and Freedom*. Berkeley: U of California P, 1995. Print.

Césaire, Aimé. *Discourse on Colonialism*. Tr. Joan Pinkham. New York: Monthly Review. 1972, 2000. Print.

Bibliography

—. *Toussaint Louverture: La Révolution française et le problème colonial.* Paris: Présence africaine, 2000. Print.

—. *La tragédie du roi Christophe.* Présence Africaine, 2000. Print.

Chanlatte, F.D. (François Desrivières). 'Vues politiques sur le sort des personnes libres, mais non blanches qui se trouvent aux Etats-Unis d'Amérique ou ailleurs.' *Le Télégraphe* 32 (4 August 1822): 1-3. Print.

Chanlatte, Juste, *Le Cri de la nature, ou hommage Haytien, au très-vénérable abbé H. Grégoire...* P. Roux: Cap-Haïtien, 1810.

—. *Histoire de la catastrophe de Saint-Domingue (par J. Chanlatte), avec la correspondance des généraux Leclerc, ... Henry Christophe, Hardy, Villon, etc. ... publiées par A.-J.-B. Bouvet de Cressé.* Paris: Librairie de Peytieux, 1824. Print.

—. *La Partie de chasse du roi, opéra, en trois actes. Paroles de Son Excellence M. le Comte de Rosiers, Musique de M. Cassian, haytien. Représenté pour la première fois devant LEURS MAJESTES, au Cap-Henry le Ier Janvier 1820, l'an 17ème de l'Indépendance.* Sans-Souci: Imprimerie Royale, 1820. Print.

Chapman, Maria Weston. 'Haïti.' *The Liberty Bell.* Boston: Massachusetts Anti-Slavery Fair, 1842. 164–204. Print.

—. 'The Young Sailor.' *The Liberty Bell.* Boston: Massachusetts Anti-Slavery Fair, 1853. 195–209. Print.

Charles, Carolle. 'Sexual Politics and the Mediation of Class, Gender, and Race in Former Slave Plantation Societies: The Case of Haiti.' *Social Construction of the Past: Representation as Power.* Ed. George C. Bond. London: Routledge, 1994. 44–56. Print.

Chateaubriand, René de. *Le Génie du Christianisme.* 2 vols. Paris: Garnier-Flammarion, 1966. Print.

Cheesman, Clive. Ed. *The Armorial of Haiti: Symbols of Nobility in the Reign of Henry Christophe.* London: College of Arms, 2007. Print.

Child, Lydia Maria. 'Toussaint L'Ouverture.' *The Freedman's Book.* 1865. Rpt. New York: Arno Press, 1968. Print.

Choiseul-Gouffier, Sophie de. *Le Polonais à St. Domingue; ou, La jeune Créole.* Varsovie: Zawadzki et Wecki, 1818. Print.

—. *Polak w St. Domingo, czyli Młoda Mulatka.* Tr. Joanna Widulińska. Zawadzkiego i Węckiego, 1819. Print.

—. *Der Pole auf St. Domingo oder die junge Creolin.* Tr. Theophil Landmesser Pfarrer. 2 vols. Bromberg: Louis Levit, 1858. Print.

Chôtard, aîné. *Précis de la Révolution de Saint-Domingue, Depuis la fin de 1789, jusqu'au 18 Juin 1794.* Philadelphia: Imprimerie de Parent, 1795. Print.

—. *Origine des malheurs de Saint-Domingue, développement du système colonial, et moyens de restauration.* Bordeaux: Imprimerie de Dubois et de Coudert, 1804. Print.

Christophe, Charles. *Les Pionniers de la littérature haïtienne: textes choisis.* Port-Au-Prince: Editions Choucoune, 1999. Print.

Christophe, Henry. *Manifeste du roi.* Cap-Henry: P. Roux, 1814. Print.

Cincinnati Daily Gazette, 4 October 1872. Print.

'Citoyens Constituants,' *La Sentinelle de la Liberté* 23 November 1843: 4. Print.

'Civilisation—Réflexions politiques sur quelques ouvrages et Journaux français concernant Hayti, par le Baron de Vastey, Secrétaire du Roi, Chevalier de l'ordre royal et militaire de Saint-Henry, Précepteur de Son Altesse Royale Monseigneur le Prince Royal d'Hayti, etc. A Sans-Souci, de l'Imprimerie royale, année 1817, quatorzième de l'indépendance.' *Bibliothèque universelle des sciences, belles-lettres, et arts*. Genève: Imprimerie de la Bibliothèque universelle, 1819. Print.

Clark, Emily. *The Strange History of the American Quadroon: Free Women of Color in the Revolutionary Atlantic World*. Chapel Hill, NC: The U of NC P, 2013.

Clark, Vèvè. 'Haiti's Tragic Overture: (Mis) Representations of the Haitian Revolution in World Drama (1797–1975).' *Representing the French Revolution; literature, historiography and art*. Ed. James A.W. Heffernan. Hanover: Dartmouth UP, 1992. 237–60. Print.

Clavin, Matthew. 'Race, Revolution, and the Sublime: The Gothicization of the Haitian Revolution in the New Republic and Atlantic World.' *Early American Studies* 5.1 (Spring 2007): 1–29. Print.

—. *Toussaint Louverture and the American Civil War: The Promise and Peril of a Second Haitian Revolution*. Philadelphia: U of Pennsylvania P, 2010. Print.

Cohen, Henry. 'Lamartine's *Toussaint Louverture* (1848) and Glissant's *Monsieur Toussaint* (1961): A Comparison.' *Studia Africana* 1.3 (Fall 1979): 255–69. Print.

Cole, Hubert. *Christophe: King of Haiti*. London: Eyre & Spottiswoode, 1967. Print.

Cole, Jean Lee. 'Theresa and Blake: Mobility and Resistance in Antebellum African American Serialized Fiction.' *Callaloo* 34.1 (Winter 2011): 158–75. Print.

Colombel, Noël. *Examen d'un pamphlet, ayant pour titre: Essai sur les causes de la révolution et des guerres civiles d'Haïti*. Port-au-Prince: Imprimerie royale, 1819. Print.

Colwill, Elizabeth. 'Sex, Savagery, and Slavery in the Shaping of the French Body Politic.' *From the Royal to the Republican Body: Incorporating the Political in Seventeenth and Eighteenth-century France*. Ed. Sara E. Melzer and Kathryn Norberg. Berkeley: U of Calif. Press, 1998. Print.

—. '"Fêtes de l'hymen, fêtes de la liberté": Marriage, Manhood, and Emancipation in Revolutionary Saint-Domingue.' *The World of the Haitian Revolution*. Ed. David Patrick Geggus and Norman Fiering. Bloomington: Indiana UP, 2009. 125–55. Print.

Constant, Fred. Foreword. *The Color of Liberty: Histories of Race in France*. Ed. Tyler Stovall and Sue Peabody. Durham: Duke UP, 2003. ix–xii. Print.

Cook, Mercer. *Five French Negro Authors*. Washington, D.C.: The Associated Publishers, 1943. Print.

Bibliography

Cooper, Anna Julia. *A Voice from the South*. Xenia: Aldine Printing House, 1892. Web. <http://docsouth.unc.edu/church/cooper/cooper.html>. Accessed 5 February 2013.

Cordier, Alphonse. *Voyage de la France à la Guadeloupe (etc.), hôpitaux militaires, prisons, et esclaves. L'Université catholique, recueil religieux, philosophique, scientifique, et littéraire*. Paris: Bureau de L'Université Catholique, 1854. Print.

Cornevin, Robert. *Haiti*. Berkeley: U of California P, 1982. Print.

Correspondence with the British Commissioners, at Sierra Leone, the Havana, Rio de Janeiro, and Surinam: relating to the slave trade, 1835: presented to both Houses of Parliament by command of His Majesty. London: William Clowes and Sons, 1836. Print.

Corzani, Jack. 'De l'Aliénation révolutionnaire: A propos de *L'Adieu à la Marseillaise de J. Brierre*.' *Mourir pour les Antilles—Indépendance nègre ou esclavage (1802–1804)*.' Ed. Michel L. Martin and Alain Yacou. Paris: Edition Caribéennes, 1991: 50–67. Print.

Cottias, Myriam. *La séduction coloniale. Damnation et stratégies. Les Antilles, XVIIème–XIXème siècles. Séduction et sociétés: approches historiques*. Ed. Cécile Dauphin et Arlette Farge. Paris: Seuil, 2001. 125–40. Print.

Coulter, Ann. *Guilty: Liberal 'Victims' and Their Assault on America*. New York: Crown, 2009. Print.

Cousin d'Aval[lon, Charles Yves]. *Histoire de Toussaint-Louverture chef des noirs insurgés de Saint-Domingue; précédée d'un coup d'œil politique sur cette colonie, et suivie d'anecdotes et faits particuliers concernant ce chef des noirs, et les agens directoriaux envoyés dans cette partie du Nouveau-Monde, pendant le cours de la révolution*. Paris: Pilot, 1802. Print.

Cox, Randolph. *The Dime Novel Companion: A Source Book*. Westport, CT: Greenwood, 2000. Print.

Croly, David Goodman and George Wakeman. *Miscegenation: The Theory of the Blending of the Races, Applied to the White Man and the Negro*. New York: H. Dexter Hamilton and Co., 1864. Print.

Curran, Andrew S. *The Anatomy of Blackness: Science & Slavery in an Age of Enlightenment*. Baltimore, MD: The Johns Hopkins UP, 2011. Print.

Cushing, Caleb. 'Article VI—Reflexions Politiques sur quelques Ouvrages et Journaux Français.' *The North American Review and Miscellaneous Journals* 3.1 (January 1821): 112–34. Print.

Cushing, William. *New and Complete Index to the North American Review: Volumes I–CXXV (1815–1877)*. Cambridge, MA: John Wilson & Son, 1878. Print.

Cuvier, Georges. *Tableau élémentaire de l'histoire naturelle des animaux*. Paris: Baudouin, 1798–99. Print.

—. *Le Règne animal distribué d'après son organisation*. 4 vols. Paris: Deterville, 1817. Print.

Daily Times Picayune, The. 18 October 1874. Print.
Dain, Bruce. *A Hideous Monster of the Mind: American Race Theory and the Early Republic.* Cambridge: Harvard UP, 2002. Print.
Dalleo, Raphael. *Caribbean Literature and the Public Sphere: From the Plantation to the Postcolonial.* Charlottesville, VA: U of Virginia P, 2011. Print.
Dalmas, Antoine. *Histoire de la révolution de Saint-Domingue: depuis le commencement des troubles, jusqu'à la prise de Jérémie et du Môle S. Nicolas par les Anglais; suivie d'un Mémoire sur le rétablissement de cette colonie.* Paris: Chez Mames Frères, 1814. Print.
Daminois, Adèle. *Lydie; ou la créole.* Paris: Leterrier, 1824. Print.
Dane, Joseph. *The Myth of Print Culture: Essays on Evidence, Textuality, and Bibliographical Method.* Toronto: U of Toronto P, 2003. Print.
Dash, J. Michael. *Haiti and the United States: National Stereotypes and the Literary Imagination.* New York: St. Martin's, 1988. Print.
—. 'Nineteenth-Century Haiti and the Archipelago of the Americas: Antènor Firmin's Letters from St. Thomas.' *Research in African Literatures* 35.2 (Summer 2004): 44–53. Print.
Daut, Marlene L. 'Un-Silencing the Past: Boisrond-Tonnerre, Vastey, and the Re-Writing of the Haitian Revolution.' *South Atlantic Review* 74.1 (Winter 2009): 35-64.
—. 'The "Alpha and Omega" of Haitian Literature: Baron de Vastey and the U.S. Audience of Haitian Political Writing.' *Comparative Literature* 64.1 (2012): 49–72. Print.
—. 'From Classical French Poet to Militant Haitian Statesman: The Early Years and Poetry of the Baron de Vastey.' *Research in African Literatures* 43.1 (Spring 2012): 35–57. Print.
—. "Monstrous Testimony: Baron de Vastey and the Politics of Black Memory," *The Colonial System Unveiled.* Tr. and Ed. Chris Bongie. Liverpool University Press, 2014. 173–210. Print.
Davidson, James Wood. *The Living Writers of the South.* New York: Carleton, 1869. Print.
Davies, Carole Boyce. 'Beyond Unicentricity: Transcultural Black Presences.' *Research in African Literatures* 30.2 (1998): 96–109. Print.
Davis, Arthur. 'Introduction.' *Clotelle: A Tale of the Southern States.* North Haven, CT: Archon Books, 1969. Print.
Davis, David Brion. *Inhuman Bondage: The Rise and Fall of Slavery in the New World.* London: Oxford UP, 2006. Print.
—. 'Declaring Equality: Sisterhood and Slavery.' *Women's Rights and Transatlantic Antislavery in the Era of Emancipation.* Ed. Kathryn Kish Sklar and James Brewer Stewart. New Haven: Yale UP, 2007. 3–18. Print.
Dayan, Joan (Colin). 'Codes of Law and Bodies of Color.' *New Literary History* 26.2 (Spring 1995[a]): 283–308. Print.
—. *Haiti, History, and the Gods.* Berkeley: U of California P, 1995b. Print.

Bibliography

Dean, Bradley P., and Ronald Wesley Hoag. 'Thoreau's Lectures after "Walden": An Annotated Calendar.' *Studies in the American Renaissance* (1996): 241–362. Print.

Debien, Gabriel. 'Marronage in the French Caribbean.' *Maroon Societies: Rebel Slave Communities in the Americas*. Ed. Richard Price. Baltimore, MD: The Johns Hopkins UP, 1979, 1996. 107–34. Print.

Debray, Régis. *Le scribe: Genèse du politique*. Paris: Grasset, 1980. Print.

Declaration of the Rights of Man and the Citizen. Web. <http://avalon.law.yale.edu/18th_century/rightsof.asp>. Accessed 10 September 2013.

'Decret.' *Feuille de Commerces, petites affiches et annonces de Port-au-Prince* 14 May 1843: 3. Print.

De Cauna, Jacques. 'Les Sources Historiques de *Bug-Jargal*: Hugo et la Révolution Haïtienne.' *Conjonction* 166 (June 1985): 1–14. Print.

—. 'La famille et la descendance de Toussaint-L'Ouverture.' *Généalogie et histoire de la Caraïbe* 90 (February 1997): 1874–75. Print.

DeJean, Joan. 'Lafayette's Ellipses: The Privileges of Anonymity.' *PMLA* 99.5 (October 1984): 884–902. Print.

DeJean, Joan, and Margaret Waller. 'Introduction.' *Ourika: The Original French Text*. Ed. Joan Dejean and Margaret Waller. New York: MLA, 1995. vii–xxii. Print.

De Kock, Leon. 'Interview with Gayatri Chakravorty Spivak: New Nation Writers Conference in South Africa.' *Ariel: A Review of International English Literature* 23.3 (July 1992): 29–47. Print.

Deleuze, Gilles, and Félix Guattari. *Anti-Oedipus: Capitalism and Schizophrenia*. Minneapolis: U of Minnesota P, 1983, 1977. Print.

—. *A Thousand Plateaus: Capitalism and Schizophrenia*. Minneapolis, U. of Minn. P, 1987. Print.

Delille, Jacques (abbé de). *La Pitié, poëme en quatre chants*. London: A. Brunswick, 1804. Print.

Delorme, Demesvar. *Les Théoriciens au pouvoir. Causeries historiques*. Paris: H. Plon, 1870. Print.

—. *Francesca; ou les jeux de sort*. Paris: E. Dentu, 1872. Print.

—. *1842 au Cap: Tremblement de terre*. Ed. Jean M. Lambert. Cap-Haïtien: Imprimerie du progrès, 1942. Print.

De Pauw, Cornelius. *Recherches philosophiques sur les américains ou Mémoires intéressants pour servir à l'histoire de l'espèce humaine*. London: A. Berlin, 1771. Print.

Deschamps, Michel-Hyacinthe. *Etudes des races Humaines: méthode naturelle d'ethnologie*. Vol. 2. Paris: Leiber et Comelin, 1859. Print.

Descourtilz, Michel Etienne. *Voyage d'un naturaliste et ses observations faites sur les trois règnes de la Nature, dans plusieurs ports de mer français en Espagne, au continent de l'Amerique septentrionale, à Saint-Yago de Cuba, et à St.-Domingue, où l'Auteur devenu le prisonnier de 40,000 Noirs révoltés, et par suite mis en* liberté par une colonne de l'armée française, donne des détails circonstanciés sur l'expédition du général Leclerc. Dédiés à ... le Comte de Lacépède. 3 vols. Paris, Dufart, 1809. Print.

Deslozières, L.-N. Baudry. *Les égarements du négrophilisme*. Paris: Migneret, 1802. Print.

Desormeaux, Daniel. 'The First of the (Black) Memorialists: Toussaint L'Ouverture.' *Yale Nineteenth-Century French Studies: The Haiti Issue* 107 (Spring 2005). 131–46. Print.

—. *Mémoires du général Toussaint Louverture*. Paris: Classiques Garnier, 2011. Print.

Dessalines, Jean-Jacques. 'Proclamation à Gonaïves.' *Panorama de la littérature haïtienne de 1804 à 2004*. Ed. Christophe Philippe Charles. Port-au-Prince: Editions Choucoune, 2003. 42–46. Print.

'Devonport Meeting.' *The Friends of Africa* 9 (1 July 1841). Print.

Diderot, Denis, and Jean le Rond d'Alembert. *Encyclopédie; ou dictionnaire raisonné des sciences, des arts, et des métiers. ARTFL Encyclopédie Project*. Web. <http://www.lib.uchicago.edu/efts/ARTFL/projects/encyc/searchform.html>. Accessed 18 February 2011.

Dillon, Elizabeth Maddock. 'The Secret History of the Early American Novel: Leonora Sansay and Revolution in Saint Domingue.' *Novel* 40.1–2 (Fall 2006–Spring 2007): 77–103. Print.

Dillon, Elizabeth Maddock and Michael Drexler. 'Introduction: Haiti and the Early United States, Entwined.' *The Haitian Revolution and the Early U.S.: Histories, Textualities, Geographies*. Ed. Elizabeth Maddock Dillon and Michael Drexler. Philadelphia: U of Pennsylvania P (forthcoming). Print.

Dixon, Chris. *African America and Haiti: Emigration and Black Nationalism in the Nineteenth Century*. Westport: Greenwood Press, 2000. Print.

—. 'Haiti.' *Nations and Nationalism: A Global Historical Overview*. Vol. 1. Ed. Guntram H. Herb and David H. Kaplan. Santa Barbara, CA: ABC-CLIO, 2008. 332–43. Print.

Doin, Sophie. *La Famille Noire ou la traite et l'esclavage*. Paris: H. Servier, 1825. Print.

—. *Blanche et Noir*. Web. <http://slavery.uga.edu/texts/literary_works/blanchenoir.pdf>. Accessed 25 March 2013.

—. *Noire et Blanc*. Web. <http://slavery.uga.edu/texts/literary_works/noireblanc.pdf>. Accessed 25 March 2013.

Döhner, Friedrich. 'Des Aufruhrs schreckliche Folge oder: die Neger. Ein Original-Trauerspiel in fünf Aufzügen.' *Theatralische Sammlung*. Vienna, 1792. 3–94. Print.

Dolata, April Michelle. 'The White Heroine and the Native Man: A Radical Writing of the Frontier Romance and a Revisionist View of America, Lydia Maria Child's *Hobomok*.' *Exit 9: The Rutgers Journal of Comparative Literature* 5 (2003): 43–52. Print.

Bibliography

Dominique, Lyndon J. 'Introduction.' *The Woman of Colour*. Ontario: Broadview, 2007. Print.

Dorsey, Joseph. '"It Hurt Very Much at the Time": Patriarchy, Rape Culture, and the Slave Body-Semiotic.' *The Culture of Gender and Sexuality in the Caribbean*. Ed. Linden Lewis. Gainesville, FL: UP of Florida, 2003. 294–322. Print.

Douglass, Frederick. *Narrative of the Life of Frederick Douglass, an American Slave*. Cambridge: Belknap Press, 1960. Print.

—. 'What to a Slave is the Fourth of July?' 1852. *The Heath Anthology of American Literature*. 5th ed. Vol. B. Ed. Paul Lauter et al. Boston: Houghton Mifflin, 2006. 1946–64. Print.

—. 'What To the Slave Is the Fourth of July?' 1852. *The Oxford Frederick Douglass Reader*. Ed. William L. Andrews. New York: Oxford UP, 1996. 108–30. Print.

Douthwaite, Julia V. *The Wild Girl, the Natural Man, and the Monster: Dangerous Experiments in the Age of Enlightenment*. Chicago: U of Chicago P, 2002. Print.

Dow, Mark. 'Occupying and Obscuring Haiti.' *New Politics* 5.2 (Winter 1995). Patterson University. Web. <http://www.wpunj.edu/newpol/issue18/dow18.htm>. Accessed July 2009.

'The Drama.' *The Critic* 12 February 1881: 41. Print.

Drachman, Edward R. *Presidents and Foreign Policy: Countdown to Ten Controversial Decisions*. Albany, NY: SUNY Press, 1997. Print.

Drescher, Seymour. 'Women's Mobilization in the Era of Slave Emancipation: Some Anglo-French Comparisons.' *Women's Rights and Transatlantic Antislavery in the Era of Emancipation*. Ed. Kathryn Kish Sklar and James Brewer Stewart. New Haven: Yale UP, 2007. 98–120. Print.

Drexler, Michael. 'Brigands and Nuns: The Vernacular Sociology of Collectivity after the Haitian Revolution.' *Messy Beginnings: Postcoloniality and Early American Studies*. Ed. Malini Johar Schueller, Edward Watts. Rutgers UP, 2003. 175–202. Print.

—. 'Introduction.' *Secret History or the Horrors of Santo Domingo*. Ed. Michael Drexler. Ontario, Canada: Broadview Editions, 2007. Print.

—. 'Leonora Sansay's Anatopic Imagination.' *Urban Identity and the Atlantic World*. Elizabeth A. Fay and Morzé Leonard Von. New York: Palgrave Macmillan, 2013. 143–73. Print.

Drexler, Michael and Ed White. 'The Constitution of Toussaint: Another Origin of African American Literature.' *A Companion to African American Literature*. Ed. Gene Andrew Jarrett. Wiley-Blackwell, 2013. 59–74. Print.

Dreyfuss, Joel. 'The Phrase.' *The Haitian Times* 4 December 1999. Web. <http://www.webster.edu/~corbetre/haiti-archive/msg01471.html>. Accessed 9 December 2013.

Drouin de Bercy. *De Saint-Domingue, de ses guerres, de ses révolutions, de ses ressources*. Paris: Chocquet, 1814. Print.

'Du Cap, le 22 novembre.' *Gazette Officielle de l'Etat d'Hayti* 23 November 1809. 187–88. Print.

Dubois, F.E. 'Call for Emigration by F.E. Dubois, Secretary of State.' *A Guide to Hayti*. Ed. James Redpath. Boston: Haytian Bureau of Emigration, 1861. 97–99. Print.

—. *Précis historique de la Révolution haïtienne de 1843*. Paris: Imprimerie de P.-A. Bourdier et Cie., 1866. Print.

—. *Deux ans et demi de ministère*. Paris: Imprimerie de P.-A. Bourdier, 1867. Print.

Dubois, Laurent. *Avengers of the New World: The Story of the Haitian Revolution*. Cambridge: Harvard UP, 2004. Print.

—. 'Avenging America: The Politics of Violence in the Haitian Revolution.' *The World of the Haitian Revolution* (2009): 111–24. Print.

Du Bois, W.E.B. *Some Notes on Negro Crime, Particularly in Georgia*. Atlanta, GA: Atlanta UP, 1904. Print.

—. *W.E.B. Du Bois: Writings: The Suppression of the African Slave-Trade, The Souls of Black Folk, Dusk of Dawn, Essays and Articles*. New York, NY: Library of America, 1986. Print.

—. 'The Damnation of Women.' Web. <http://www.web-books.com/Classics/ON/B1/B1115/09MB1115.html>. Accessed 13 April 2010.

Duboy, Alexandre. *Godefroy et Augustin: ou deux épisodes de l'Histoire de Saint-Domingue, avec une Notice sur la découverte de cette île*. Tours: R. Pornin, 1846. Print.

Dubroca, Louis. *La vie de Toussaint-Louverture, chef des noirs insurgés de Saint-Domingue; contenant Son origine, les particularités les plus remarquables de sa jeunesse, sa réunion aux fameux Biassou, Bouckmant, et Jean François, les atrocités de la guerre qu'il fit aux français sous les drapeaux de l'Espagne, sa perfidie en abandonnant les intérêts de cette puissance, ses attentats nombreux envers les agens de la république française, les actes de son independanë, et les premières horreurs qui ont accompagné sa résistance au gouvernement français*. Paris: Dubroca, Librairie, 1802. Print.

—. *La vie de J.J. Dessalines: chef des noirs révoltes de Saint-Domingue, avec des notes très détaillées sur l'origine, le caractère, la vie et les atrocités des principaux chefs des noirs, depuis l'insurrection de 1791*. Paris, France: Dubroca [et] Rondonneau, 1804. Microform.

Duchet, Michèle. *Anthropologie et histoire au siècle des lumières: Buffon, Voltaire, Helvétius, Diderot*. Paris: Bibliothèque d'Anthropologie François Maspero, 1971. Print.

—. 'Introduction.' *De l'Homme*. By Georges Louis Leclerc Buffon, Comte de. Ed. Michèle Duchet. Paris: Bibliothèque d'Anthropologie François Maspero, 1971. Print.

duCille, Ann. 'Where in the World is William Wells Brown? Thomas Jefferson, Sally Hemmings, and the DNA of African American Literary History.' *American Literary History* 12.3 (Fall 2000): 443–62. Print.

Ducœurjoly, S.J. *Manuel des habitans de Saint-Domingue*. 2 vols. Paris: Arthus-Bertrand, 1803. Print.

Bibliography

Ducrest, Georgette. *Mémoires sur l'impératrice Joséphine, ses contemporains, la cour de Navarre et de la Malmaison*. 3 vols. Paris and London: Colburne, 1828. Print.

Dumas, Alexandre. *Georges*. 1843. Ed. Léon-François Hoffmann. Paris: Gallimard, 1974. Print.

Dunbar, Erica Armstrong. *A Fragile Freedom: African American Women and Emancipation in the Antebellum City*. New Haven, CT: Yale UP, 2008. Print.

Du Pradt, Dominique. *Pièces relatives à Saint-Domingue et à l'Amérique pour faire suite à ses ouvrages sur l'Amérique*. Paris: Béchet, 1818. Print.

Dupuy, Alex. 'From François Duvalier to Jean-Bertrand Aristide: The Declining Significance of Color Politics in Haiti.' *Politics and Power in Haiti*. Ed. Kate Quinn and Paul Sutton. New York: Palgrave Macmillan, 2013. 43–64. Print.

Durand, Oswald. 'Tournée littéraire II.' *Haïti littéraire et sociale* (20 September 1905). 403–04. Print.

Duras, Claire de. *Ourika*. Tr. John Fowles. New York: MLA, 1994. Print.

During, Simon. 'Literature—Nationalism's Other? The Case for Revision.' *Nation and Narration*. Ed. Homi K. Bhabha. London: Routledge, 1990. 138–54. Print.

Du Tertre, Jean-Baptiste. *Histoire générale des Antilles habitées par les Français*. 4 vols. Paris: T. Iolly. 1667–71. Print.

'Duties of Wives.' *Freedom's Journal* 21 February 1829. Print.

Duvallon, Berquin. *Recueil de poesies d'un colon de Saint-Domingue*. Paris: Désenne, 1802. Print.

Duviver, Ulrick. *Bibliographie Générale et Méthodique d'Haïti*. Vol. 2. Port-au-Prince: L'Imprimerie de l'état, 1941. Print.

Easley, Alexis. *First-Person Anonymous: Women Writers and Victorian Print Media, 1830–70*. Burlington: Ashgate, 2004. Print.

Edgeworth, Maria. 'The Grateful Negro.' *The Literature Network*. Web. <http://www.online-literature.com/maria-edgeworth/tales-novels-vol2/8/>. Accessed 10 July 2009.

'Editorial Notes.' *The Independent ... Devoted to the Consideration of Politics, Social and Economic Tendencies, History, Literature, and the Arts* 19 August 1869: 4. Print.

Edouard, Emmanuel. *Recueil général des lois et actes du gouvernement d'Haïti: depuis la proclamation de son indépendance*. Vol. 8. Paris: Pedone-Lauriel, 1888. Print.

Edwards, Bryan. *An Historical Survey of the French Colony in the Island of St. Domingo*. London: Stockdale, 1797. Print.

—. *The History, Civil and Commercial, of the British Colonies in the West Indies*. 3 vols. London: John Stockdale, 1793–1801. Print.

Egerton, George. 'Politics and Autobiography: Political Memoir as Polygenre.' *Biography: An Interdisciplinary Quarterly* 15.3 (Summer 1992): 221–42. Print.

Ehrenstein, David. 'Obama the "Magic Negro": The Illinois senator lends himself to white America's idealized, less-than-real black man.' *Los Angeles Times* 19 March 2007. Web. <http://www.latimes.com/news/opinion/commentary/la-oe-ehrenstein19mar19,0,3391015.story#axzz2sqoFhTZ3>. Accessed 5 January 2014.

Elder, Arlene. 'William Wells Brown, 1815–1884.' *Heath Anthology of American Literature*. 5th ed. Vol. B. Ed. Paul Lauter et al. Boston: Houghton Mifflin, 2006. 2610–11. Print.

Elicona, Anthony Louis. *Un colonial sous la révolution en France et en Amérique: Moreau de Saint-Méry*. Paris: Jouve, 1934. Print.

Elkins, Stanley M. *Slavery: A Problem in American Institutional and Intellectual Life*. 1968. 3rd ed. Chicago: U of Chicago P, 1976. Print.

Emerson, Ralph Waldo. 'Character.' *Essays and English Traits*. The Harvard Classics. 1904–1914. Web. <http://www.bartleby.com/5/111.html>. Accessed 15 September 2014.

—. 'Emancipation of the British West Indies.' *The Complete Works*. 1904. Web. <http://www.bartleby.com/90/1104.html>. Accessed 15 September 2014.

Enz, Molly Krueger. 'The Mulatto as Island and the Island as Mulatto in Alexandre Dumas's *Georges*.' *The French Review* 80.2 (December 2006). 383–94. Print.

Esterquest, Ralph T. 'L'Imprimerie Royale d'Hayti (1817–1819). A Little Known Royal Press of the Western Hemisphere.' *The Papers of the Bibliographical Society of America* 34 (January 1940): 171–84. Print.

Ethéart, Liautaud. *Les Miscellanées*. Port-au-Prince: Imprimerie J.H. Courtois, 1855. Print.

Etienne, Servais. *Les sources de 'Bug-Jargal', avec en appendice Quelques sources de 'Han d'Islande'*. Bruxelles, Belgium, 1923. Print.

Ewcorstart, John K. 'The negro – not a distinct species.' *Medical and Surgical Reporter* 11 (1858): 264–72. Print.

'Extract from "A Letter From Paris."' *Liberator* 8 October 1858: 162. Print.

Eze, Emmanuel Chukwudi. 'Introduction.' *Race and the Enlightenment: A Reader*. Ed. Emmanuel Chukwudi Eze. Malden: Blackwell Publishing, 1997. Print.

Fabella, Yvonne. 'Redeeming the Character of the Creoles: Whiteness, Gender, and Creolization in Pre-Revolutionary Saint-Domingue.' *Journal of Historical Sociology* 23.1 (2010): 40–72. Print.

Fabre, Michel. *From Harlem to Paris: Black American Writers in France, 1840–1980*. Urbana: U of Illinois P, 1991. Print.

—. 'International Beacons of African American Memory: Alexandre Dumas Père, Henry O. Tanner, and Josephine Baker as Examples of Recognition.' *History and Memory in African-American Culture*. Ed. Geneviève Fabre and Robert G. O'Meally. New York: Oxford UP, 1994. 122–29. Print.

'Faits Divers,' *Le Progrès* 21 March 1844: 4. Print.

'Falsehood in Support of Slavery (From the Boston *Atlas and Daily Bee*).' *Liberator*, published as the *Liberator* 30.3 (20 January 1860). 10. Print.

Bibliography

Fanning, Sara C. 'The Roots of Early Black Nationalism: Northern African Americans' Invocations of Haiti in the Early Nineteenth Century.' *Slavery & Abolition* 28.1 (2007): 61–85. Print.

Fanon, Frantz. *Black Skin, White Masks*. Tr. Charles Lam Markham. New York: Grove Press 1967. Print.

—. *The Wretched of the Earth*. Tr. Constance Farrington. New York: Grove, 1963, 1968. Print.

Fardin, Dieudonné. *Histoire de la littérature haïtienne*. Port-au-Prince: Editions Fardin, 1967. Print.

Farmer, Paul. *Aids and Accusation: The Geography of Blame*. Berkeley: U of California P, 1993. Print.

—. *The Uses of Haiti*. Monroe: Common Courage, 1994. Print.

Farred, Grant. 'First Stop, Port-au-Prince: Mapping Postcolonial Africa through Toussaint L'Ouverture and his Black Jacobins.' *The Politics of Culture in the Shadow of Capital*. Ed. Lisa Lowe and David Lloyd. Durham, NC: Duke UP, 227–47.

Faubert, Pierre. *Ogé; ou le préjugé de couleur*. Paris: Librairie de C. Maillet-Schmitz, 1856. Print.

—. 'Aux Haïtiens.' *The Pine and the Palm*. Ed. James Redpath. 7 December 1861. Print.

Faulkner, William. *The Sound and the Fury: The Corrected Text*. Vintage, 1991. Print.

—. *Absalom, Absalom!* Vintage, 1991. Print.

Fauset, Jessie Redmon. *The Chinaberry Tree: A Novel of American Life & Selected Writings*. Boston: Northeastern UP, 1995. Print.

Ferguson, James. 'Le Premier des Noirs: The Nineteenth-Century Image of Toussaint Louverture.' *Nineteenth-Century French Studies* 15.4 (1987): 397–406. Print.

Ferguson, Moira. *Subject to Others: British Women Writers and Colonial Slavery 1670–1834*. London: Routledge, 1992. Print.

Ferrer, Ada. 'Talk about Haiti: The Archive and the Atlantic's Haitian Revolution.' *Tree of Liberty: Cultural Legacies of the Haitian Revolution in the Atlantic World*. Ed. Doris L. Garraway. Charlottesville: U of Virginia P, 2008. 21–40. Print.

Festa, Lynn. *Sentimental Figures of Empire in Eighteenth-Century Britain and France*. Baltimore: Johns Hopkins UP, 2006. Print.

Feugère, Anatole. *Un précurseur de la révolution, l'abbé Raynal, 1713–1796: documents inédits*. Angoulême: L'Imprimerie Ouvrière, 1922. Print.

Fick, Carolyn. *The Making of Haiti: The Saint-Domingue Revolution from Below*. Knoxville: U of Tennessee P, 1990. Print.

—. 'The French Revolution in Saint-Domingue: A Triumph or a Failure?' *A Turbulent Time: The French Revolution and the Greater Caribbean*. Ed. David Geggus. Bloomington: Indiana UP, 1997. 51–75. Print.

Fiedler, Leslie A. *Love and Death in the American Novel*. 1966. New York: Stein and Day, 1992. Print.

Finch, Julie. 'Sarah Forten's Anti-Slavery Networks.' *Women's Rights and Transatlantic Antislavery in the Era of Emancipation*. Ed. Kathryn Kish Sklar and James Brewer Stewart. New Haven: Yale UP, 2007. Print.

Finger, Stanley. *Origins of Neuroscience: A History of Explorations into Brain Function*. Oxford: Oxford UP, 1994. Print.

Finlay, George Gillanders and William West Holdsworth. *The History of the Wesleyan Methodist Missionary Society*. Vol. 2. London: Epworth Press, 1921. Print.

Firmin, Antènor. *De l'Egalité des races humaines: anthropologie positive*. Paris: Librairie Cotillon, 1885. Print.

Fischer, Caroline Auguste. 'William der Neger.' *Zeitgung für der elegante Welt* (19 May–24 May 1827). Print.

—. 'William der Neger,' *Kleine Erzählungen und romantische Skizzen*. Posen; Leipzig: Johann Friedrich Kühn, 1818. 26–73. Print.

Fischer, Sibylle. *Modernity Disavowed: Haiti and the Cultures of Slavery in the Age of Revolution*. Durham: Duke UP, 2004. Print.

—. 'Haiti: Fantasies of Bare Life.' *Small Axe* 23 (June 2007). 1–15. Print.

Fitzhugh, George. *Sociology For The South Or The Failure of Free Society*. Richmond: A. Morris, 1854. Print.

Flaubert, Gustave. *Madame Bovary*. Tr. Frances Steegmuler. New York: Random House, 1957. Print.

Fliegelman, Jay. *Prodigals and Pilgrims: The American Revolution against Patriarchal Authority, 1750–1800*. Cambridge UP, 1982. Print.

'For the Freedom's Journal. Haytien Revolution.' *Freedom's Journal* 6 April 1827. Print.

'For the Freedom's Journal. Hayti, No. III.' *From the Scrapbook of Africanus' Freedom's Journal* 4 May 1827. Print.

'For the Freedom's Journal. *From the Scrap-Book of Africanus*. Hayti V.' *Freedom's Journal* 29 June 1827. Print.

'For the Freedom's Journal. Female Tenderness.' *Freedom's Journal* 27 July 1827. Print.

'For the Freedom's Journal. Observer.-No. V.' *Freedom's Journal* 5 October 1827. Print.

'For the Freedom's Journal. Observer.-No. VII.' *Freedom's Journal* 26 October 1827. Print.

'For *The Liberator*: Address to the Female Literary Association of Philadelphia, on their 'First Anniversary, By a Member.' *The Liberator* 13 October 1832. Print.

Ford, Paul Leicester. *Who was the Mother of Franklin's Son?: An Historical Conundrum Hitherto Given Up—Now Partly Answered*. Private printing: Brooklyn, NY, 1889. Print.

Bibliography

Foreman, P. Gabrielle. '"Reading Aright": White Slavery, Black Referents and the Strategy of Histotextuality in *Iola Leroy.*' *Yale Journal of Criticism* 10.2 (Fall 1997): 327–54. Print.

Forsdick, Charles. 'Toussaint Louverture and Haitian Historiography: A Pigmentocratic Approach.' *Cultures of Colour: Visual, Material, Textual*. Ed. Chris Horrocks. Berghahn Books, 2012. 154–66. Print.

Foster, Frances Smith. 'Forgotten Manuscripts: How Do You Solve a Problem Like Theresa?' *African American Review* 40.4 (2006): 631–45. Print.

—. 'Creative Collaboration: As African American as Sweet Potato Pie.' *African-American Poets*. Vol. 1. Ed. Harold Bloom. New York: Infobase Publishing, 2009. 87–102. Print.

Foucault, Michel. 'Film and Popular Memory.' *Radical Philosophy* 11 (1976): 24–29. Print.

—. *Language, Counter-Memory, Practice: Selected Essays*. Tr. Donald F. Bouchard. Ed. Donald F. Bouchard. Ithaca: Cornell UP, 1977. Print.

—. *Discipline and Punish: The Birth of the Modern Prison*. Tr. Alan Sheridan. New York: Vintage Books, 1995. Print.

Fouchard, Jean. *Les Marrons du syllabaire: Quelques aspects du problème de l'instruction et de l'éducation des esclaves et affranchis de Saint-Domingue*. Port-au-Prince: Deschamps, 1953. Print.

—. *Plaisirs de Saint-Domingue; notes sur sa vie sociale, littéraire et artistique*. Port-au-Prince: Imprimerie de l'état, 1955. Print.

—. *Langue et Littérature des aborigènes d'Haïti*. Port-au-Prince: Editions Henri Deschamps, 1988. Print.

Fouron, Georges. 'Theories of "Race" and the Haitian Revolution.' *Reinterpreting the Haitian Revolution and its Cultural Aftershocks*. Ed. Martin Munro and Elizabeth Walcott-Hackshaw. Mona, Jamaica: U of West Indies P, 2006. 70–85. Print.

Foutz, Scott David. 'Ignorant Science: The Eighteenth Century's Development of Scientific Racism.' *Quodlibet Journal* 1.8 (December 1999). Web. <http://www.quodlibet.net/foutz-racism.shtmlhttp://www.quodlibet.net/foutz-racism.shtml>. Accessed 11 November 2009.

Frank, Luanne T. 'Heidegger's Hermeneutics and Parmenides.' Web. <http://proyectohermeneutica.org/pdf/ponencias/frank%20luanne%20t.pdf>. Accessed 1 December 2013.

Franklin, Benjamin. 'Letter to the Pennsylvania Gazette.' *Pennsylvania Gazette* 30 August 1733. Print.

Franklin, James. *The Present State of Hayti*. London: John Murray, 1828. Print.

Franklin, John Hope. *The Militant South, 1800–1861*. Cambridge: Belknap Press of Harvard UP, 1956. Print.

Franul von Weissenthurn, Johanna. *Die Schwestern St. Janvier; Schauspiel in fünf Aufzügen. Nach einer wahren Begebenheit, aus den Schreckenstagen auf St. Domingo*. 1821. Print.

'French Novels and French Morals.' *The Museum of Foreign Literature, Science and Art* (July 1836): 47. Print.

Frere. 'To Rosa.' *Freedom's Journal* 21 March 1828. Print.

Frieze, Henry S. and Walter Denison. *Virgil's Aeneid: with Explanatory Notes*. Ann Arbor: Scholarly Publishing Office, U of Michigan Library, 2006. Print.

Freud, Sigmund. *The Uncanny*. Tr. David McLintock. New York: Penguin Group, 2003. Print.

'From a Late English Paper.' *City of Washington Gazette* 3.165 (21 May 1818): 2. Print.

'From the Boston Columbian Centinel. Madame Christophe.' *Freedom's Journal* 11 May 1827. Print.

'From the *Christian Watchman*, Hayti, No. 1., From the Scrapbook of Africanus.' *Freedom's Journal* 20 April 1827. Print.

'From the *Genius of Universal Emancipation*. Slavery.' *Freedom's Journal* 30 November 1827. Print.

Furcy de Brémoy, H. *Evrard; ou Saint-Domingue au dix-neuvième siècle*. Paris: Pillet Aîné, 1829. Print.

—. *Le Voyageur poète*. Paris: Furcy, 1833. Print.

Fuss, Diana. 'Corpse Poem.' *Critical Inquiry* (August 2003): 1–29. Print.

Gaitet, Pascale, 'Hybrid Creatures, Hybrid Politics, in Hugo's *Bug-Jargal* and *Le Dernier jour d'un condamné*.' *Nineteenth-Century French Studies* 25.4 (Spring–Summer 1997): 251–65. Print.

Gambara, Lodovico et al. *Palazzi e casate di Parma*. Parma: La nazionale tip. editrice, 1971. Print.

Garran de Coulon, J. P. *An Inquiry into the Causes of the Insurrection of the Negroes in the Island of St. Domingo, to Which are added Various Observations of M. Garran de Coulon*. London: Johnson, 1792. Print.

—. *Rapports sur les troubles de Saint-Domingue*. Paris: Imprimerie nationale, 1797–99. Print.

Garraway, Doris. *Libertine Colony: Creolization in the Early French Caribbean*. Durham: Duke UP, 2005a. Print.

—. 'Race, Reproduction and Family Romance in Moreau de Saint-Mery's Description … de la partie francaise de l'isle Saint Domingue.' *Eighteenth-Century Studies* 38.2 (Winter 2005b): 227–46. Print.

—. 'Introduction.' *Tree of Liberty: Cultural Legacies of the Haitian Revolution in the Atlantic World*. Ed. Doris L. Garraway. Charlottesville: U of Virginia P, 2008a. 1–17. Print.

—. '"*Légitime Défense*": Universalism and Nationalism in the Discourse of the Haitian Revolution.' *Tree of Liberty: Cultural Legacies of the Haitian Revolution in the Atlantic World*. Ed. Doris L. Garraway. Charlottesville: U of Virginia P, 2008b. 62–90. Print.

Garrett, Paula, and Hollis Robbins. *The Works of William Wells Brown: Using His 'Strong, Manly Voice.'* New York: Oxford UP, 2006. Print.

Bibliography

Garrigus, John. 'Catalyst or Catastrophe? Saint-Domingue's Free Men of Color and the Savannah Expedition, 1779–1782.' *Review/Revista Interamericana* 22 (Spring–Summer 1992). 109–25. Print.

—. 'Redrawing the Colour Line: Gender and the Social Construction of Race in Pre-Revolutionary Haiti.' *Journal of Caribbean History* 30.1–2 (1996): 28–50. Print.

—. '"Sons of the Same Father": Gender, Race and Citizenship in French Saint-Domingue, 1760–1792.' *Visions and Revisions of 18th century France*. Ed. Christine Adams et al. University Park: Penn State P, 1997. 137–53. Print.

—. 'Race, Gender and Virtue in Haiti's Failed Foundational Fiction: *La Mulâtre comme il y a beaucoup de blanches* (1803).' *The Color of Liberty: Histories of Race in France*. Ed. Tyler Stovall and Sue Peabody. Durham: Duke UP, 2003. 73–94. Print.

—. *Before Haiti: Race and Citizenship in French Saint-Domingue*. New York: Palgrave Macmillan, 2006a. Print.

—. 'Moreau de Saint-Méry et le patriotisme créole à Saint-Domingue.' *Moreau de Saint-Méry ou les ambiguïtés d'un créole des lumières*. Ed. Dominique Taffin. Fort-de-France: Société des Amis des archives de la recherche sur le patrimoine culturel des Antilles. 2006b. 64–75. Print.

—. 'Introduction.' *La Mulâtre comme il y a beaucoup de blanches*. Paris: L'Harmattan, 2007a. vii–xxviii. Print.

—. 'Opportunist or Patriot? Julien Raimond (1744–1801) and the Haitian Revolution.' *Slavery and Abolition* 28.1 (April 2007b): 1–21. Print.

—. '"Thy Coming fame, Ogé! is sure": New Evidence on Ogé's 1790 Revolt and the Beginnings of the Haitian Revolution.' *Assumed Identities: The Meanings of Race in the Atlantic World*. Ed. John Garrigus and Christopher Morris. College Station, TX: Texas A & M UP, 2010. 19–45. Print.

Garrison, William Lloyd. 'Declaration of Sentiments of the National Anti-Slavery Convention.' *Selections from the Writings of W. L. Garrison*. Boston: R.F. Wallcut, 1852. Web. <http://utc.iath.virginia.edu/abolitn/abeswlgct.html>. Accessed 5 February 2013.

—. 'A Colored Female Lecturer.' *The Liberator*. Ed. William Lloyd Garrison. 8 April 1864. Print.

Gates, Jr. Henry Louis. *The Signifying Monkey: A Theory of African-American Literary Criticism*. Oxford: Oxford UP, 1989. Print.

—. *Loose Canons: Notes on the Culture Wars*. Oxford UP, 1993. Print.

—. *Black in Latin America*. New York: NYU Press, 2011. Print.

Gaumont, Charles. *Abrégé Des Calomnies: Du Courrier de La Martinique Contre M.V. Schoelcher*. Paris: Imprimerie de Soye et Cie, 1850. Print.

Gautier, Arlette. 'Le Rôle des femmes dans l'abolition de l'esclavage.' *Les Femmes et la Révolution française: actes du colloque international, 12–13–14 avril 1989*. Toulouse: Université de Toulouse-Le Miral Press, 1990. 143–51. Print.

—. *Les Sœurs de Solitude: Femmes et esclavage aux Antilles du XVIIe au XIXe siècle*. Rennes: Presses universitaires de Rennes, 2010. Print.

Gauthier, Florence. *L'aristocratie de l'épiderme: Le combat de la Société des Citoyens de Couleur, 1789–91*. Paris: CNRS Éditions, 2007. Print.

—. 'Au cœur du *préjugé de couleur* dans la colonie de Saint-Domingue. Médéric Moreau de Saint Méry contre Julien Raimond. 1789–91.' Web. <http://www.lecanardrépublicain.net/spip.php?article356>. Accessed 31 March 2013.

Geggus, David. 'Review of From Dessalines to Duvalier, by David Nicholls.' *Americas* 37.3 (1980): 415–16. Print.

—. 'Unexploited sources for the history of the Haitian Revolution.' *Latin American Research Review* 18 (1983): 95–103. Print.

—. 'Haiti and the Abolitionists: Opinion, Propaganda and International Politics in Britain and France, 1804–1838,' *Abolition and its Aftermath: The Historical Context, 1790–1916*. Ed. David Richardson. London: Cass, 1985. 114–40. Print.

—. 'Slave and Free Women of Color in Colonial Saint-Domingue.' *More than Chattel: Black Women and Slavery in the Americas*. Ed. David Barry Gaspar and Darlene Clark Hine. Bloomington: Indiana UP, 1996. 259–78. Print.

—. 'The Naming of Haiti.' *New West Indian Guide* 71 (1997): 43–68. Print.

—. 'The Caradeux and Colonial Memory.' *The Impact of the Haitian Revolution in the Atlantic World*. Ed. David Geggus. Columbia: U of South Carolina P, 2001: 231–46. Print.

—. *Haitian Revolutionary Studies*. Bloomington: Indiana UP, 2002. Print.

—. 'Print Culture and the Haitian Revolution: The Written and the Spoken World.' *Liberty! Egalité! Independencia! Print Culture, Enlightenment, and Revolution in the Americas, 1776–1838*. Ed. David S. Shields. American Antiquarian Society, 2007a. 79–96. Print.

—. 'Print Culture and the Haitian Revolution: The Written and the Spoken Word.' Proceedings of the American Antiquarian Society, 2007b. 299–316. Print.

—. 'Saint-Domingue on the Eve of the Haitian Revolution,' *The World of the Haitian Revolution*. Ed. David Geggus and Norman Fiering. Bloomington: Indiana UP, 2009. 3–20. Print.

—. 'Haiti and its Revolution: Four Recent Books.' *Radical History Review* 115 (Winter 2013): 195–202. Print.

Gewecke, Frauke. 'Victor Hugo et la Révolution haïtienne: Jacobins et Jacobites, ou les ambiguïtés du discours négrophobe dans la perspective du roman historique.' *Lectures de Victor Hugo: colloque franco-allemand de Heidelberg*. Ed. Mireille Calle-Gruber and Arnold Rothe. Paris: Nizet, 1986. 53–65. Print.

Gilbert, Sandra M. and Susan Gubar. *The Madwoman in the Attic: The Woman Writer and the Nineteenth-Century Literary Imagination*. New Haven: Yale UP, 2000. Print.

Gildea, Robert. *Children of the Revolution: The French, 1799–1914*. Cambridge: Harvard UP, 2010. Print.

Bibliography

Gillman, Susan. 'The Squatter, the Don, and the Grandissimes in Our America.' *Mixing Race, Mixing Culture: Inter-American Literary Dialogues.* Ed. Monika Kaup and Debra J. Rosenthal. Austin, TX: U of Texas P, 2002. 140–60. Print.

Gillman, Susan and Kirsten Silva Gruesz. 'Worlding America: The Hemispheric Text-Network.' *The Blackwell Companion to American Literary Studies.* Ed. Robert S. Levine and Caroline Levander. Blackwell, 2011. 228–47. Print.

Gilman, Sander L. 'Black Bodies, White Bodies: Toward an Iconography of Female Sexuality in Late Nineteenth-Century Art, Medicine, and Literature.' *Critical Inquiry* 12.1 (Fall 1985): 204–42. Print.

Gilmore, Paul. '"De Genewine Artekil": William Wells Brown, Blackface Minstrelsy, and Abolitionism.' *American Literature* 69.4 (December 1997): 753–80. Print.

—. *The Genuine Article: Race, Mass Culture, and American Literary Manhood.* Durham, NC: Duke UP, 2001. Print.

Gilroy, Paul. *The Black Atlantic: Modernity and Double Consciousness.* Cambridge, MA: Harvard UP, 1993. Print.

—. *Against Race: Imagining Political Culture beyond the Color Line.* Cambridge, MA: Harvard UP, 2000. Print.

Girard, Patrick. 'Le Mulâtre littéraire, ou le passage du blanc.' *Le Couple interdit: Entretiens sur le racisme; la dialectique de l'altérité socio-culturelle et la Sexualité; actes du colloque tenu en mai.* Ed. Michèle Duchet. Paris: Mouton, 1980. 191–213. Print.

Girard, Philippe. '*Rebelles* with a Cause: Women in the Haitian War of Independence, 1802–04.' *Gender & History* 21.1 (April 2009): 60–85. Print.

—. 'The Ugly Duckling: The French Navy and the Saint-Domingue Expedition, 1801–1803.' *International Journal of Naval History* 7.3 (2010). Web. <http://www.ijnhonline.org/2010/12/01/the-ugly-duckling-the-french-navy-and-the-saint-domingue-expedition1801-1803/>. Accessed 12 January 2013.

—. *The Slaves who Defeated Napoleon: Toussaint Louverture and the Haitian War of Independence, 1801–1804.* Tuscaloosa: U of Alabama P, 2011. Print.

—. 'The Haitian Revolution: History's New Frontier: State of the Scholarship and Archival Sources.' *Slavery & Abolition* (November 2012): 1–23. Print.

—. *The Memoir of Toussaint Louverture.* Ed. Philippe Girard. New York: Oxford UP, 2014. Print.

Girard, Philippe R. and Jean-Louis Donnadieu, 'Toussaint before Louverture: New Archival Findings on the Early Life of Toussaint Louverture.' *The William and Mary Quarterly* 70.1 (January 2013): 41–78. Print.

Girod de Chantrans, Justin. *Voyage d'un Suisse dans les Colonies d'Amérique pendant la derniere guerre.* Neuchatel: Imprimerie de la Société Typographique, 1785. Print.

Ghachem, Malick W. *The Old Regime and the Haitian Revolution.* New York: Cambridge UP, 2012. Print.

Glinel, Charles. *Alexandre Dumas et son œuvre: notes biographiques et bibliographiques*. Geneva: Slatkine Reprints, 1967. Print.
Glissant, Edouard. *Monsieur Toussaint*. Paris: Gallimard, 1961. Print.
—. *Caribbean Discourse: Selected Essays*. Tr. J. Michael Dash. Charlottesville: UP of Virginia, 1989. Print.
—. *Introduction à une poétique du divers*. Paris: Gallimard, 1996. Print.
Gobineau, Arthur (Comte de). *Essai sur l'inégalité des races humaines*. Vol 1. Paris: Librairie de Firmin Didot Frères, 1853. Print.
Goddu, Theresa. *Gothic America*. New York: Columbia UP, 1997. Print.
Gold, Herbert. *Haiti: Best Nightmare on Earth*. New Brunswick, NJ: Transaction Publishers, 2001. Print.
Goldberg, David Theo. *Racist Culture: Philosophy and the Politics of Meaning*. Cambridge: Blackwell, 1993. Print.
Goldstein, Robert Justin. *Censorship of Political Caricature in Nineteenth-century France*. Kent, OH: The Kent State UP, 1989. Print.
Goode, Mike. *Sentimental Masculinity and the Rise of History, 1790–1890*. Cambridge UP, 2009. Print.
Goudie, Sean. *Creole America: The West Indies and the Formation of Literature and Culture in the New Republic*. Philadelphia: U of Pennsylvania P, 2006. Print.
Gouges, Olympe de. *L'Esclavage des noirs, ou l'heureux naufrage, drame en trois actes, en prose*. Paris: la veuve Duchesne, la veuve Bailly et les marchands de nouveautés, 1792. Print.
—. *Les Droits de la Femme*. Les archives de la Révolution française; 9.4.147. Gallica bibliotheque numerique. *Bibliotheque nationale de France*. Web. <http://gallica.bnf.fr/ark:/12148/bpt6k426138>. Accessed 10 July 2009.
Gouraige, Ghislain. *Histoire de la littérature haïtienne de l'indépendance à nos jours*. Port-au-Prince: Imprimerie Theodore, 1960. Print.
Goutalier, Régine. 'Les Révoltes dans les Antilles françaises: Turpitude des îles et ses conséquences dans les comportements féminins.' *Les Femmes et la Révolution française: actes du colloque international, 12–13–14 avril 1989*. Toulouse: Université de Toulouse-Le Miral Press, 1990. 143–51. Print.
Goveia, E.V. *The West Indian Slave Laws of the Eighteenth Century* (Barbados: Caribbean Universities P, 1970. Print.
Gragnon-Lacoste, Thomas Prosper. *Toussaint Louverture, général en chef de l'armée de Saint-Domingue, surnommé le premier des noirs. Ouvrage écrit d'après des documents inédits et les papiers historiques et secrets de la famille Louverture*. Paris: A. Durand et Pedone-Lauriel, 1877. Print.
Greene, Graham. *The Comedians*. New York: Penguin Books, 2005, 1976. Print.
Greenspan, Ezra. Ed. *William Wells Brown: A Reader*. Athens, GA: U of GA P, 2008. Print.
Grégoire, abbé de. *Mémoire en faveur des gens de couleur ou sang-mêlés de Saint-Domingue, & des autres isles francaises d'Amérique, addressé a l'Assemblé Nationale*. Paris: Belin, 1789. Print.

Bibliography

—. *De la littérature des Nègres, ou Recherches sur leurs facultés intellectuelles, leurs qualités morales et leur littérature*. Paris: Maradan, 1808. Print.

—. *On the Cultural Achievements of Negroes*. Tr. Thomas Cassirer and Jean-François Brière. Amherst: U of Massachusetts P, 1996. Print.

—. *De la Noblesse de la peau*. Paris: J. Millon, 1996, 1820. Print.

Griggs, Earl Leslie and Clifford H. Prator. *Henri Christophe and Thomas Clarkson: A Correspondence*. New York: Greenwood Press, 1968. Print.

Gros. *An historick recital, of the different occurrences in the camps of Grande-Reviere, Dondon, Sainte-Suzanne, and others, from the 26th of October, 1791, to the 24th of December, of the same year*. Baltimore: Samuel and John Adams, 1792. Print.

Gros, Ariela J. 'Litigating Whiteness: Trials of Racial Determination in the Nineteenth-Century South.' *Yale Law Journal* 108 (1998): 109–88. Print.

Grossman, Catherine. *The Early Novels of Victor Hugo: Towards a Poetics of Harmony*. Geneva: Droz, 1986. Print.

Hall, Stephen G. *A Faithful Account of the Race: African American Historical Writing in Nineteenth-Century America*. Chapel Hill: U of North Carolina P, 2009. Print.

Hamilton, William. Unsigned letter. 'To Joseph Banks.' Banks Correspondence. British National Museum. 160–162. 1819. Print.

—. 'Vines within the Tropics.' *The Gardener's Magazine and Register of Rural and Domestic Improvement*. Ed. John Claudious Loudon. Vol. 5. (July 1829). 98–100. Print.

—. Application for Doctor Radcliffe's Traveling Fellowship. Kew Botanical Library and Archives. Director's Correspondence. Vol. 5. English Letters H.-L. 1832–35. Print.

—. *Memoir on the Cultivation of Wheat within the Tropics*. Plymouth, England: Henry H. Heydon, 1840. Print.

Hanchard, Michael. 'Black Memory vs. State Memory: Notes toward a Method.' *Small Axe* 26 (June 2008): 45–62. Print

Hanchett, Catherine M. 'George Boyer Vashon, 1824–1878: Black Educator, Poet, Fighter for Equal Rights, Part One.' *The Western Pennsylvania Historical Magazine* 68.1 (July 1985): 205–19. Print.

Hansen, Debra Gold. *Strained Sisterhood: Gender and Class in the Boston Female Anti-Slavery Society*. Amherst: U of Mass. P, 1993. Print.

Harris, Cheryl. 'Whiteness as Property.' *Harvard Law Review* 106.8 (1993): 1707–91. Print.

Harris, Ethel. *Lamartine et le peuple*. Paris: Librairie Universitaire, 1932. Print.

Hartman, Geoffrey. 'On Traumatic Novels and Literary Study.' *New Literary History* 26.3 (Summer 1995): 537–63. Print.

Hartman, Saidiya. *Scenes of Subjection: Terror, Slavery, and Self-Making in Nineteenth-Century America*. Oxford: Oxford UP, 1997. Print.

—. 'Seduction and the Ruses of Power.' *Callaloo* 19.2 (1996): 537–60. Print.

Harvey, William Woodis. *Sketches of Hayti: From the Expulsion of the French to the Death of Christophe*. London: Christophe. L.B. Seely and Son, 1827. Print.

Hathaway, Heather. '"Maybe Freedom Lies in Hating": Miscegenation and the Oedipal Conflict.' *Refiguring the Father: New Feminist Readings of Patriarchy*. Ed. Patricia Yeager and Beth Kowaleski-Wallace. Carbondale: Southern Illinois UP, 1989: 153–67. Print.

'Hayti.' *Liverpool Mercury* 5 May 1818. Print.

'Haytiens in Paris.' *Friends' Review; a Religious, Literary and Miscellaneous Journal* 11 December 1858: 222. Print.

Hayward, Abraham. 'Prefatory Notice.' *Diaries of a Lady of Quality from 1797–1844*. 2nd ed. Ed. A. Hayward. London: Longman, 1864. v–ix. Print.

Hazareesingh, Sudhir. 'Napoleonic Memory in Nineteenth-Century France: The Making of a Liberal Legend.' *MLN* 120.4 (2005): 747–73. Print.

Healy, Mary Aquinas. 'The Contributions of Toussaint L'Ouverture to the Independence of the American Republics, 1776–1826.' *The Americas* 9.4 (April 1953): 413–51. Print.

Hearne, John. *Commonplace Book, 1820–1849*. Ms. Yale Center for British Art.

Heidegger, Martin. *Parmenides*. Tr. André Schuwer and Richard Rojcwicz. Indianapolis, IN: Indiana UP, 1992. Print.

Heinl, Nancy and Robert Heinl. *Written in Blood: The Story of the Haitian People, 1592–1995*. Lanham: UP of America, 1996. Print.

Helme, Elizabeth. *The Farmer of Inglewood Forrest*. London: J. Clements, 1841. Print.

Herder, Johann Gottfried. 'Neger-Idyllen.' *Briefe zu Beförderung der Humanität*. Riga, Hartknoch, 1797. Print.

Hesse, Carla. *The Other Enlightenment: How French Women Became Modern*. Princeton UP, 2001. Print.

Heuer, Jennifer. 'The One-Drop Rule in Reverse? Interracial Marriages in Napoleonic and Restoration France.' *Law and History Review* 27.3 (2009): 515–48. Print.

Higman, B.W. *General History of the Caribbean*. Vol. 6. London: Unesco Publishing, 1999. Print.

Hilliard d'Auberteuil, Michel René. *Considérations sur l'état présent de la colonie française de Saint-Domingue: Ouvrage politique et législatif; présenté au ministre de la marine*. Paris: Grangé, 1776. Print.

Hinks, Peter P. *To Awaken My Afflicted Brethren: David Walker and the Problem of Antebellum Slave Resistance*. University Park: Pennsylvania State UP, 1997. Print.

'History, Literature, and Present State of Hayti'. *The British Review, and London Critical Journal* 15.9 (March 1820): 45–78. Print.

Hoagland, Sarah Luci. 'Resisting Rationality.' *Engendering Rationalities*. Ed. Nancy Tuana, Sandra Morgen. Albany: State University of New York P, 2001. 125–50. Print.

Bibliography

Hoffmann, Léon-François. *Le Nègre romantique*. Paris: Payot, 1973. Print.

—. *Essays on Haitian Literature*. Washington D.C.: Three Continent's Press, 1984. Print.

—. 'Lamartine, Michelet, et les Haïtiens.' Web. <http://webcache.googleusercontent.com/search?q=cache:NSUNn8Q9OCUJ:classiques.uqac.ca/contemporains/hoffmann_leon_francois/lamartine_michelet_haitiens/lamartine.html+&cd=2&hl=en&ct=clnk&gl=us>. Accessed 10 July 2009.

—. 'Victor Hugo, John Brown et les Haïtiens.' *Nineteenth-Century French Studies* 16.1–2 (1987–88): 47–58. Print.

—. *Haïti: Lettres et l'être*. Toronto: Éditions du Gref, 1992. Print.

—. 'Haitian Sensibility.' *A History of Literature in the Caribbean*. Ed. A. James Arnold. 3 vols. Amsterdam & Philadelphia PA: John Benjamins, 1994. Vol. 1:365–78. Print.

—. *Histoire littéraire de la francophonie. Littérature d'Haïti*. Vanves: EDICEF, Agence universitaire de la francophonie, 1995. Print.

—. 'Victor Hugo, les noirs et l'esclavage.' *Francofonia* 16.30 (1996): 47–90. Print.

—. *Haitian Fiction Revisited*. Pueblo, CO: Passeggiata Press, 1999. Print.

—. Documents. *Georges*. Ed. Léon-François Hoffmann. Paris: Editions Gallimard, 2003a. 474–87. Print.

—. 'Dumas et les Noirs.' *Georges*. Ed. Léon-François Hoffmann. Paris: Editions Gallimard, 2003b. 7–23. Print.

—. 'Notes.' *Georges*. Ed. Léon-François Hoffmann. Paris: Editions Gallimard, 2003c. 487–96. Print.

—. 'Representations of the Haitian Revolution in French Literature.' *The World of the Haitian Revolution*. Ed. David Patric Geggus and Norman Fiering. Bloomington: Indiana UP, 2009. 339–51. Print.

—. *Haïti: Regards*. Paris: L'Harmattan, 2010.

Holgersson-Shorter, Helena. 'Authority's Shadowy Double: Thomas Jefferson and the Architecture of Illegitimacy.' *Masters and Slaves: Plantation Relations and Mestizaje in American Imaginaries*. Ed. Alexandra Isfahani-Hammond. Gordonsville: Palgrave Macmillan, 2005. 51–66. Print.

Holly, Theodore. *A vindication of the capacity of the Negro race for self-government, and civilized progress, as demonstrated by historical events of the Haytian revolution: and the subsequent acts of that people since their national independence*. New Haven, CT: William H. Stanley, 1857. Print.

Hörmann, Raphael. 'Representations of the Haitian Revolution in British Discourse, 1791 to 1805.' *Human Bondage in the Cultural Contact Zone. Transdisciplinary Perspectives*. Ed. Raphael Hörmann and Gesa Mackenthun. Munster, Germany: Waxman, 2010. 137–70. Print.

hooks, bell. *Feminism is for Everybody: Passionate Politics*. Cambridge: South End, 2000. Print.

Horton, James Oliver. 'Freedom's Yoke: Gender Conventions among Antebellum Free Blacks.' *Feminist Studies* 12.1 (Spring 1986): 51–76. Print.

Howard, Richard A. et al. 'WILLIAM HAMILTON (1783–1856) AND THE PRODROMUS PLANTARUM INDIAE OCCIDENTALIS (1825).' Web. <http://biostor.org/reference/61820.text>. Accessed 10 March 2014.

Huggins, Nathan I. 'The Deforming Mirror of Truth: Slavery and the Master Narrative of American History.' *Radical History Review* 49 (1991): 25–46. Print.

Hughes, Helen. *The Historical Romance*. London: Routledge, 1993. Print.

Hugo, Jean-Abel. *France pittoresque: ou description pittoresque, topographique et statistique des départements et colonies de la France*. Vol. 3. Paris: Delloye, 1835. Print.

Hugo, Victor. *Bug-Jargal. Bug-Jargal / Victor Hugo and Tamango / Prosper Mérimée: Histoires d'esclaves révoltés*. 1826. Ed. Gérard Gengembre. Paris: Pocket Classiques, 2004. Print.

'Bug-Jargal.' *Le Conservateur Littéraire, édition critique*. Vol 2. Ed. Jules Marsan. Paris: Librairie Hachette, 1922. Print.

Hull, Gloria T. *All the Women are White, All the Blacks are Men, But Some of Us are Brave*. Ed. Gloria T. Hull, Patricia Bell Scott, and Barbara Smith. Old Westbury, NY: The Feminist Press, 1982. Print.

Hulme, Peter. 'Hurricane in the Caribees: The Constitution of the Discourse of English Colonialism.' *1642: Literature Power in the Seventeenth Century*. Ed. Francis Barket et al. Proceedings of the Essex Conference on the Sociology of Literature. Essex UK: University of Essex Press, 1981: 55-83. Print.

Hunt, Alfred N. *Haiti's Influence on Antebellum America: Slumbering Volcano in the Caribbean*. Baton Rouge: Louisiana State UP, 1988. Print.

Hunt, Benjamin. *Remarks on Hayti as a Place of Settlement for Afric-Americans; and on the Mulatto as a Race for the Tropics*. Philadelphia: T.B. Pugh, 1860. Print.

Hunt, Lynn. *The Family Romance of the French Revolution*. Berkeley: U of California P, 1992. Print.

Hurbon, Laënnec. *Voodoo: Truth and Fantasy*. London: Thames and Hudson, 1995. Print.

Hurtado, Aída. 'Strategic Suspensions: Feminists of Color Theorize the Production of Knowledge.' *Knowledge, Difference, and Power: Essays Inspired by Women's Ways of Knowing*. Ed. Nancy Rule Goldberger, Jill Tarule, Blythe McVicker Clinchy, and Mary Field Belenky. New York: Basic Books, 1996. 372–92. Print.

Hutton, Clinton A. *The Logic and Historic Significance of the Haitian Revolution and the Cosmological Roots of Haitian Freedom*. Kingston, Jamaica: Arawak, 2005. Print.

Iannini, Christopher. *Fatal Revolutions: Natural History, West Indian Slavery, and the Routes of American Literature*. Chapel Hill, NC: U of North Carolina P, 2012. Print.

Inginac, Joseph Balthazar. *Mémoires de Joseph Balthazar Inginac ... Depuis 1791 jusqu'à 1843*. Kingston, Jamaica: J.R. de Cordova, 1843. Print.

Bibliography

'Installation de l'assemblée' *Le Manifeste* 24 September 1843: 2–3. Print.

'Insurrection of the Negroes in August 1791 at Cape François. From Edwards's Historical Survey of St. Domingo.' *The Edinburgh Magazine or Literary Miscellany* (June 1797): 411–15. Print.

'Intemperance.' *Freedom's Journal* 23 March 1827. Print.

Israel, Jonathan. *Radical Enlightenment: Philosophy and the Making of Modernity, 1650–1750*, Oxford: Oxford UP, 2001. Print.

J. 'For the Freedom's Journal. Observer-No. V.' *Freedom's Journal* 5 October 1827. Print.

—. 'For the Freedom's Journal. Observer-No. VII.' *Freedom's Journal* 26 October 1827. Print.

Jackson, Maurice. *Let This Voice Be Heard: Anthony Benezet, Father of Atlantic Abolitionism*. Philadelphia, PA: U of Pennsylvania P, 2009. Print.

Jacobs, Edward. 'Anonymous Signatures: Circulating Libraries, Conventionality, and the Production of Gothic Romances.' *ELH* 62.3 (Fall 1995): 603–29. Print.

Jacobs, Harriet Ann. *Incidents in the Life of a Slave Girl, Written by Herself. Electronic Edition*. Ed. Lydia Maria Child. Chapel Hill, NC: Documenting the American South, 1861. Web. < http://docsouth.unc.edu/fpn/jacobs/jacobs.html>. Accessed February 2013.

Harriet Jacobs. *Incidents in the Life of a Slave Girl: Contexts, Criticism*. Ed. Nellie Y. McKay and Frances Smith Foster. New York: W.W. Norton, 2001. Print.

James, C.L.R. *The Black Jacobins: Toussaint L'Ouverture and the San Domingo Revolution*. New York: Vintage Books. 1963, 1989. Print.

James, Winston. *The Struggles of John Brown Russwurm: The Life and Writings of a Pan-Africanist Pioneer, 1799–1851*. New York: New York UP, 2010. Print.

Janvier, Louis Joseph. *Les Détracteurs de la race noire et de la république d'Haïti*. Paris: Marpon et Flammarion, 1882. Print.

—. *La République d'Haïti et ses visiteurs, réponse à M. Victor Cochinat (de la petite presse) et à quelques autres écrivains*. Paris: Marpon et Flammarion, 1883. Print.

—. *Une Chercheuse*. Paris: C. Marpon, E. Flammarion. 1889. Print.

Jefferson, Thomas. *The Writings of Thomas Jefferson: Being His Autobiography, Correspondence, Reports, Messages, and Other Addresses, Official and Private*. 9 vols. Ed. H.A. Washington. Washington D.C.: Taylor and Maury, 1854. Print.

—. *The Papers of Thomas Jefferson*. 33 vols. Ed. Julian P. Boyd, Charles T. Cullen, John Catanzariti, Barbara B. Oberg, et al. Princeton: Princeton UP, 1950. Print.

—. *The Adams-Jefferson Letters: The Complete Correspondence between Thomas Jefferson and Abigail and John Adams*. Ed. Lester J. Cappon. 2 vols. Chapel Hill: U of North Carolina P, 1959. Print.

—. *Notes on the State of Virginia*. 1781. Ed. William Peden. Chapel Hill: U of North Carolina. 1787, 1982. Print.

Jenson, Deborah. 'Fétichisme de la marchandise: La poésie créole des courtisanes noires de Saint-Domingue.' *Relire l'histoire et la littérature haïtiennes*. Ed. Christiane Ndiaye. Presses nationales d'Haïti, 2007: 27–56. Print.

—. 'Toussaint Louverture, Spin Doctor? Launching the Haitian Revolution in the French Media.' *Tree of Liberty: Cultural Legacies of the Haitian Revolution in the Atlantic World*. Ed. Doris L. Garraway. Charlottesville: U of Virginia P, 2008. 41–62. Print.

—. *Beyond the Slave Narrative: Politics, Sex, and Manuscripts in the Haitian Revolution*. Liverpool: Liverpool UP, 2011. Print.

—. 'Jean-Jacques Dessalines and the African Character of the Haitian Revolution.' *William & Mary Quarterly* 69.3 (July 2012): 615–38. Print.

Johnson, Sara E. *The Fear of French Negroes: Transcolonial Collaboration in the Revolutionary Americas*. Berkeley, CA: U of California P, 2012. Print.

Johnson, Walter. *Soul by Soul: Life inside the Antebellum Slave Market*. Cambridge: Harvard UP, 1999. Print.

Jonassaint, Jean. *Des Romans de tradition haïtienne: sur un récit tragique*. Paris: L'Harmattan, 2002. Print.

—. 'Towards New Paradigms in Caribbean Studies: The Impact of the Haitian Revolution on Our Literature.' *Tree of Liberty: Cultural Legacies of the Haitian Revolution in the Atlantic World*. Ed. Doris L. Garraway. Charlottesville: U of Virginia P, 2008. 200–22. Print.

—. 'Pour un projet de sauvegarde et d'édition critique d'œuvres haïtiennes'. *Littératures au Sud*. Ed. Marc Cheymol. Paris: Éditions des archives contemporaines, 2009. 197–207. Print.

Jouannet, Emilie. *Zorada, ou la Créole, publiée par Emilie J....t*. 2 vols. Paris: Imprimerie de Vatar-Jouannet, 1801. Print.

Kadish, Doris Y. 'The Black Terror: Women's Responses to Slave Revolts in Haiti.' *The French Review* 68.4 (March 1995): 668–80. Print.

—. 'Haiti and Abolitionism in 1825: The Example of Sophie Doin.' *1804 and Nineteenth-Century French Studies*. Yale French Studies 107 (2005): 108–30. Print.

—. 'Introduction.' *The Saint-Domingue Plantation, Or, The Insurrection: A Drama in Five Acts*. Tr. Norman Shapiro. Ed. Doris Kadish. Baton Rouge, LA: Louisiana State UP, 2008. xi–xxiv. Print.

—. 'LITERATURE OF SLAVERY: FRENCH LITERATURE.' Web. <http://slavery.uga.edu/docs/research/Literature%20of%20slavery.pdf>. Accessed 10 January 2014.

Kafka, Judith. 'Action, reaction, and interaction: Slave women in resistance in the South of Saint-Domingue, 1793–94.' *Slavery & Abolition* 18.2 (1997): 48–72. Print.

Kaisary, Philip. *The Haitian Revolution in the Literary Imagination: Radical*

Bibliography

Horizons, Conservative Constraints. Charlottesville: U of Virginia P, 2014. Print.

Kant, Immanuel. 'An Answer to the Question: What is Enlightenment?' Web. <http://www.english.upenn.edu/~mgamer/Etexts/kant.html>. Accessed 10 July 2009.

—. *Grounding for the Metaphysics of Morals.* 1785. 3rd ed. Tr. James W. Ellington. London: Hacket, 1993. Print.

Kaplan, Cora. 'Black Heroes/White Writers: Toussaint L'Ouverture and the Literary Imagination.' *History Workshop Journal* 46 (1998): 32–62. Print.

Kaplan, Sidney. 'Herman Melville and the American National Sin: The Meaning of "Benito Cereno."' *Critical Essays on Herman Melville's 'Benito Cereno.'* Ed. Robert Burkholder. New York: G.K. Hall, 1992. 37–47. Print.

Kent, Henry W. 'Encore Moreau de Saint-Méry.' *Bookmen's Holiday: Notes and studies written and gathered in tribute to Harry Miller Lydenburg.* Ed. Deoch Fulton. New York: New York Public Library, 1943. Print.

Kerby, Anthony. 'Hermeneutics.' *Encyclopedia of Contemporary Literary Theory: Approaches, Scholars, Terms.* Ed. Irene Rima Makaryk. Toronto: U of Toronto P, 1993. 91–93. Print.

Kidder, Tracy. 'The Trials of Haiti.' *The Nation* 27 October 2003. Print.

Kleist, Heinrich von. 'Betrothal in Santo Domingo.' Tr. Ronald Taylor. *Six German Romantic Tales.* Chester Springs: Dufour Editions, 1993. 71–103. Print.

Kock, Bernard. *To his excellency, Abraham Lincoln, President of the United States. [Washington, D.C. 1862].* Web. <http://memory.loc.gov/cgi-bin/query/h?ammem/rbpebib:@field(NUMBER+@band(rbpe+20406700))>. Accessed 10 November 2013.

Kord, Susanne. 'Defining Cultural Exchange: Of Gender, the Power of Definition, and the Long Road Home.' *Cultural Exchange in German Literature.* Ed. Eleoma Joshua and Robert Vilain. Rochester, NY: Camden House, 2007. 7–26. Print.

Körner, Theodor. *Toni: ein Drama in drei Aufzügen.* 1812. *Theodor Körners sämmtliche Werke.* Stuttgart: A.F. Macklot, 1818. Print.

Kotzebue, August von. *Die Negersklaven.* Leipzig: 1796. Print.

Krantz, Frederick (ed.). *History from Below: Studies in Popular Protest and Popular Ideology.* Oxford: Basil Blackwell, 1988. Print.

Kristeva, Julia. *Powers of Horror: An Essay on Abjection.* New York: Columbia UP, 1982. Print.

Kujawaska-Lis, Ewa. 'Turning *Heart of Darkness* into a Racist Text: A Comparison of Two Polish Translations.' *Conradiana* 40.2 (2008): 165–78. Print.

Kukla, Jon. *A Wilderness so Immense: The Louisiana Purchase and the Destiny of America.* New York: Alfred A. Knopf, 2003. Print.

Kutzinski, Vera M. *Sugar's Secrets: Race and the Erotics of Cuban Nationalism.* Charlottesville: UP of Virginia, 1993. Print.

'L'Editeur de la Gazette Royale à ses concitoyens.' *Gazette Royale d'Hayti* 24 May 1816: 1–4. Print.

L'ossessione della memoria: Parma settecentesca nei disegni del conte Alessandro Sanseverini. Parma: Fondazione Cassa di risparmio di Parma e Monte di credito su pegno di Busseto, 1997. Print.

La Liberté générale ou les Colons à Paris: Comédie en un acte et en prose. Au Cap Français: P. Roux, 1794. Print.

Labat, Jean-Baptiste. *Nouveau voyages aux îles de l'Amérique.* 4 vols. Paris: Théodore le Gras, 1742. Print.

Lacroix, Pamphile, Lieutenant-Général Baron de. *Mémoires pour servir à l'histoire de la Révolution de Saint-Domingue.* 2 vols. Paris: Pillet Aine, 1819. Print.

Lafleur, Gérard. *Les Caraïbes des Petites Antilles.* Editions Karthala, 1992. Print.

Laisné de Tours, M.V. *L'insurrection du Cap, ou La perfidie d'un noir.* Paris : A. Fleuriau, 1822. Print.

Lamartine, Alphonse de. *Histoire des Girondins.* Vol. 2. Brussels: Meline, Cans, et Compagnie, 1847. Print.

—. *Toussaint Louverture.* 1850. Ed. Léon-François Hoffmann. Exeter: U of Exeter P, 1998. Print.

Lamming, Georges. *The Pleasures of Exile.* Ann Arbor, U of Mich. P, 1991. Print.

Landes, Joan G. *Women and the Public Sphere in the Age of the French Revolution.* Ithaca: Cornell UP, 1988. Print.

Lanusse, Arnold. 'A Marriage of Conscience.' *L'Album Littéraire* 15 August 1843. 132–35. Print.

[Laplace, François]. *Histoire des désastres de Saint-Domingue, précédée d'un tableau du régime et des progrès de cette colonie, depuis sa fondation, jusqu'à l'époque de la Révolution française.* Paris: Garnery, 1795. Print.

—. *Réflexions sur la colonie de Saint-Domingue ou, Examen approfondi des causes de sa ruine, et des mesures adoptées pour la rétablir; terminées par l'exposé rapide d'un plan d'organisation propre à lui rendre son ancienne splendeur; adressées au commerce et aux amis de la prospérité nationale.* 2 vols. Paris: Garnery, 1796. Print.

Lapsanksy, Phillip. 'Afro-Americana: Rediscovering Leonora Sansay.' *Annual Report of the Library Company of Philadelphia for the Year 1992.* Philadelphia: Library Company of Philadelphia, 1993. 29–46. Print.

Largey, Michael. *Vodou Nation: Haitian Art Music and Cultural Nationalism.* Chicago: U. of Chicago Press, 2006.

Laroche, Maximilien. *L'Avènement de la littérature haïtienne.* Port-Au-Prince: Editions Mémoire, 2001. Print.

Larrabee, Mary Jeanne. 'I Know What a Slave Knows: Mary Prince's Epistemology of Resistance.' *Women's Studies: An Interdisciplinary Journal* 35.5 (2006): 453-473. Print.

'Last Days of Christophe, The.' *Littell's Living Age* 48.618 (29 March 1856): 799–804. Print.

Bibliography

'Later from Hayti.' *Chicago Press and Tribune* 24 September 1859: 2. Print.

Laurent, Gérard. Ed. *Toussaint à Travers sa Correspondance (1794–1798)*. Madrid: Industrias gráficas España, 1953. Print.

Lavallée, Joseph. *Le Nègre comme il y a peu de blancs*. Paris: Buisson, 1789. Print.

—. *The Negro Equaled by Few Europeans*. 2 vols. Tr. J Trapp. London: Printed for the Author, 1790. Print.

—. *The Negro Equalled by Few Europeans, To Which are Added, Poems on Various Subjects, Moral and Entertaining; By Phillis Wheatley, Negro Servant to Mr. John Wheatley, of Boston, New England*. 2 vols. Philadelphia: William W. Woodward, 1801. Print.

Lavayasse, Jean-François Dauxion. *A Statistical, Commercial, and Political Description of Venezuela, Trinidad, Margarita, and Tobago*. London: G. & W.B. Whittaker, 1820. Print.

Lawless, Robert. *Haiti's Bad Press*. Rochester: Schenkman Books, 1992. Print.

Le Constitutionnel. Journal du commerce, politique et littéraire 126 (5 July 1841). Print.

Le Gorgeu, Georges. *Etude de Jean-Baptiste Coisnon: Toussaint-Louverture et Jean-Baptiste Coisnon*. Paris: Pedone-Lauriel, 1881. Print.

Le Manifeste 1 October 1843: 1. Print.

Le Pers, J.-B. *Histoire de l'Isle espagnole ou de Saint-Domingue*. Ed. Pierre-François Xavier de Charlevoix. 2 vols. Paris: François Barois, 1731. Print.

Lecomte, Jules François. *Parme sous Marie-Louis*. Vol. 1. Paris: Hippolyte Souverain, 1845. Print.

Lee, Hannah Farnham Sawyer. *Memoir of Pierre Toussaint, Born a Slave in St. Domingo*. Boston: Crosby, Nichols, and Company, 1851. Print.

Lee, Harriet and Sophie Lee. *Canterbury tales for the year 1805*. Vol. 5. London: Printed for G.G. and J. Robinson, 1805. Print.

Léger, Jacques Nicholas. *Haïti, son histoire et ses détracteurs*. New York: The Neale Publishing Company, 1907. Print

Lemonnier-Delafosse, Jean-Baptiste. *Seconde campagne de Saint-Domingue … précédée de Souvenirs historiques et succincts de la première campagne*. Le Havre: Imprimerie de Brindeau, 1846. Print.

Lettre des députés de Saint-Domingue à leurs commettants, en date du 12 août 1789, interceptée par un mulâtre, communiquée, sous le secret, à M. le comte de Mirabeau … 1790. Print

'Les morceaux suivants' *Le Progrès* 15 February 1844: 2. Print.

The Lesson of St. Domingo: How to Make the War Short and the Peace Righteous (from the *New York Times* of May 27, 1861). Boston: A. Williams and Co., 1861. Print.

Le Noir, Elizabeth Anne. *Clara de Montfier: a moral tale: with original poems: respectfully inscribed to the Right Hon. Lady Charlotte Greville*. Reading: A. M. Smart and Co, 1808. Print.

Le Vaillant, François. *Voyage de M. Le Vaillant dans l'intérieur de l'Afrique, par le Cap de Bonne-Espérance, dans les années 1780, 81, 82, 83, 84 et 85.* 2 vols. Paris: Leroy, 1790. Print.
Le Vaillant, *Travels from the Cape of Good Hope.* 2 vols. Tr. Elizabeth Helme. London: William Lane, 1790. Print.
Lengel, Edward G. *Inventing George Washington: America's Founder, in Myth and Memory.* New York: Harper Collins, 2011. Print.
Lenormand, Marie-Anne. Ed. *Mémoires historiques et secrets de l'impératrice Joséphine Marie-Rose Tascher-de-Pagerie, première épouse de Napoléon Bonaparte.* 2 Vols. Paris: Chez L'Auteur, 1820.
Levaigneur, M. *Les Trois voyageurs, ou légère incursion sur les habitants des Etas-Unis d'Amérique et de l'île de Saint-Domingue.* 1790. Bibliothèque de Nantes. Print.
Levasseur, Armand. *Evènements qui ont précédé et suivi l'évacuation de Saint-Domingue, publiés par un officier de l'état-major de l'armée.* Paris: Deprez, 1804. Print.
Levine, Robert S. 'Sources and Revisions.' *Clotel; or the President's Daughter.* Ed. Robert S. Levine. New York: Bedford/St. Martin's, 2000. Print.
Levrault, Louis. 'A *Haytian Legend*: Translated, With Alterations, From The French Of Louis Levrault.' *The Yale Literary Magazine. Conducted by the Students of Yale University (1836–1851)* 5.1 (November 1839): 10–19. Print.
—. 'Tony La Mulâtresse: Légende Haïtienne.' *La France Littéraire* 4 (1837): 81–96. Print.
Lewis, R. B. *Light and Truth, Collected from the Bible and Ancient and Modern History, Containing the Universal History of the Colored and the Indian Race from the Creation of the World to the Present Time.* Boston: Benjamin F. Roberts, 1844. Print.
Lhamon, W.T., Jr. *Raising Cain: Blackface Performance from Jim Crow to Hip Hop.* Cambridge, MA: Harvard UP, 2000.
Limonade, Comte de. *Le machiavélisme du cabinet français.* Cap-Henry: P. Roux, 1814. Print.
Lipsitz, George. 'Ethnic Studies at the Crossroads.' *Kalfou: A Journal of Comparative and Relational Ethnic Studies* (Spring 2010): 11–16. Print.
'Literary Intelligence.' *The Museum of Foreign Literature, Science, and Art* 8.47 (May 1826): 480. Print.
'Literary Report.' *The Atheneum or Spirit of the English Magazine* 9.3 (1 May 1821): 128. Print.
Liu, Tessie. 'The Secret beyond White Patriarchal Power: Race, Gender, and Freedom in the Last Days of Colonial Saint-Domingue.' *French Historical Studies* 33.3 (2010): 387–416. Print.
Locke, Mamie E. 'From Three-Fifths to Zero: Implications of the Constitution for African American Women, 1787–1870.' *Women Transforming Politics: An Alternative Reader.* Ed. Cathy J. Cohen, Kathleen B. Jones, and Joan C. Tronto. New York: NYU Press, 1997. 377–86. Print.

Bibliography

Lockett, James D. 'Abraham Lincoln and Colonization: An Episode That Ends in Tragedy at L'Ile à Vache, Haiti, 1863–1864.' *Journal of Black Studies* 21.4 (June 1991): 428–44. Print.

Lokke, Carl Ludwig. 'Malouet and the St. Domingue Mulatto Question in 1793.' *Journal of Negro History* 24.4 (October 1939): 381–89. Print.

Lombard, Charles. *Lamartine*. New York: Twayne, 1973. Print.

Long, Edward. *The History of Jamaica. Or, General Survey of the Ancient and Modern State of that Island with Reflections on its Situation, Settlements, Inhabitants, Climate, Products, Commerce, Laws and Government*. 3 vols. London: Lowndes, 1774. Print.

'Louis Napoleon and the Haytiens in Paris.' *Liberator* 24 December 1858: 206. Print.

Louverture, François Dominque Toussaint. *Mémoires du général Toussaint-L'Ouverture, écrits par lui-même*. Ed. Joseph Saint-Rémy. Paris: Pagnerre, 1853. Print.

Louverture, Isaac. *Mémoires et notes d'Isaac Louverture, sur la même expédition, et sur la vie de son père. L'Histoire de l'expédition militaire des Français à Saint-Domingue, sous Napoléon Bonaparte*. Ed. Antoine Métral. Paris: Fanjat aîné, 1825. Print.

Lovejoy, Arthur O. *The Great Chain of Being*. Cambridge, MA: Harvard UP, 1936.

Mackenzie, Anna Maria. *Slavery, or, the times. In two volumes*. Vol. 2. London: G.G.J. and J. Robinsons; and J. Dennis, 1792. Print.

Mackenzie, Charles. *Notes on Haiti, Made during a Residence in that Republic*. London: Henry Colburn and Richard Bentley, 1830. Print.

MacLeod, Murdo J. 'The Soulouque Regime in Haiti, 1847–1859: A Reevaluation.' *Caribbean Studies* 10.3 (October 1970): 35–48. Print.

MacQueen, James. *The West India colonies: The calumnies and misrepresentations circulated against them*. London: Baldwin, Cradock, and Joy, 1824. Print.

'Madame Christophe' [a]. *Freedom's Journal* 14 (27 June 1828): 106. Print.

'Madame Christophe.' [b]. *Freedom's Journal* 15 (4 July 1828): 116. Print.

'Madame Christophe.' [c]. *Freedom's Journal* 16 (11 July 1828): 124. Print.

'Madame Christophe.' [d]. *British New Monthly Magazine and Literary Journal*. Part. 1. London: Henry Colburn, 1828. 481-85. Print.

Madiou, Thomas. *Histoire d'Haïti, Tome I, 1492–1799*. Port-au-Prince: Editions Deschamps, 1989. Print.

—. *Histoire d'Haïti, Tome III, 1803–1807*. Port-au-Prince: Editions Deschamps, 1989. Print.

—. *Histoire d'Haïti, Tome VII, 1827–1843*. Port-au-Prince: Editions Deschamps, 1989. Print.

Maffly-Kipp, Laurie F. *Setting down the Sacred Past: African-American Race Histories*. Cambridge, MA: Harvard UP, 2010. Print.

Maingot, Anthony. *Class, Color, and Pluralism in David Nicholls' Caribbean*.

Oxford: David Nicholls Memorial Trust. 2002. Web. <http://www.dnmt. org.uk/dnmt/images/docs/dnmlecture_2002.pdf>. Accessed 3 January 2014.

Mahy de Corméré, G.F. *Histoire de la révolution, de la partie française de St. Domingue. Développement exact des causes et principes de cette révolution.* Baltimore: Samuel and John Adams, 1794. Print.

Mahul, Alphonse Jacques. *Annuaire nécrologique* 2 (1821): 322. Print.

Malenfant, Charles. *Des colonies: et particulièrement de celle de Saint-Domingue ... exposé ... des causes et un précis historique des guerres civiles qui ont rendu cette ... colonie indépendante ... des considérations sur les moyens de la rattacher à la metropole.* Paris: Audibert, 1814. Print.

Malouet, Pierre Victor. *Collection de mémoires sur les colonies, et particulièrement sur Saint-Domingue.* 5 vols. Paris: Baudouin, 1802. Print.

Manganelli, Kimberly Snyder. *Transatlantic Spectacles of Race: The Tragic Mulatta and the Tragic Muse.* New Brunswick: Rutgers UP, 2012. Print.

'Manifeste de Praslin.' *Recueil général des lois & actes du gouvernement d'Haïti.* Vol. 7. Ed. Emmanuel Edouard. Paris: Pedone-Lauriel, 1888. Print.

Marcelin, Frédéric. *Thémistocle-Epaminondas Labasterre: petit récit haïtien.* Port-au-Prince: Editions Fardin, 1976, 1901. Print.

—. 'Lettres Haïtiennes: D'Ignace Nau à Stella—de Frédéric Marcelin à 1920.' *Mercure de France* 1.4 (1923): 220–24. Print.

—. *Au Gré de Souvenir.* Paris: Augustin Challamel, 1913. Print.

—. *Autour de deux romans.* Paris: Imprimerie Kugelmann, 1903. Print.

Marcellesi, Laure. 'Louis-Sébastien Mercier: Prophet, Abolitionist, Colonialist.' *Studies in Eighteenth-Century Culture* 40 (2011): 247–73. Print.

Marion, Gérard Gabriel. *Moreau de Saint-Méry, un colon rapatrié.* Web. <http://www.univ-ag.fr/modules/resources/download/default/doc_fac_droi_eco/Espace_informations_et_telechargements/Plans_de_cours_et_documents_TD/Plans_de_cour_Fac_Eco-Droit/Histoire_du_droit/Plans_cours_LS6/L%20S6%20instant%2005-Marion%20_G%20G_%20MSM%20un%20colon%20orapatrié%2040p.pdf>. Accessed 18 May 2012.

Marsollier des Vivetières, Benoît Joseph. *La mort du colonel Maudit, ou les anarchistes au Port-au-Prince; fait historique, En un Acte, et en Prose.* Paris: Cailleau, 1799. Print.

Martineau, Harriet. *The Hour and the Man, a Historical Romance.* 3 vols. London: Edward Moxon, 1841. Print.

Marty, Anne. 'Préface.' *Stella.* Geneva: Editions Zoé, 2009. Print.

Matilda. 'For the Freedom's Journal. Messrs. EDITORS.' *Freedom's Journal* 10 August 1827. Print.

Maupertuis, Pierre Louis Moreau de. *Vénus Physique.* Paris, 1745. Print.

Mazères, colon. *De L'Utilité des colonies, des causes intérieures de la perte de Saint Domingue et des moyens d'en recouvrer la possession.* Paris: Renard, 1814. Print.

McGlathery, James M. 'Heinrich von Kleist.' *Dictionary of Literary Biography:*

Bibliography

German Writers in the Age of Goethe. 90 vols. Ed. James Hardin and Christopher E. Schweitzer. Detroit: Gale, 1989. 216–29. Print.

McGill, Meredith. *American Literature and the Culture of Reprinting.* Philadelphia: U of Pennsylvania P, 2002. Print.

Ménégault, A.P.F. *Le Robinson de Faubourg Saint-Antoine, Ou, Relation des aventures du général Rossignol, et de M.A.C***, son secrétaire. Déportés en Afrique à l'époque du 3 nivôse.* Paris: Ménard et Desenne Fils, 1818. Print.

Milton Mayer, 'The Issue Is Miscegenation.' (1959). Rpt. in *White Racism: Its History, Pathology, and Practice.* Ed. Barry N. Schwartz and Robert Disch. New York: Dell, 1970. 211. Print.

Maynard de Queilhe, Louis de. *Outre-Mer.* 2 vols. Paris: Renduel, 1833. Print.

McAlister, Elizabeth. 'From Slave Revolt to a Blood Pact with Satan: The Evangelical Rewriting of Haitian History.' Division II Faculty Publications. Web. <http://wesscholar.wesleyan.edu/cgi/viewcontent.cgi?article=1112&context=div2facpubs>. Accessed 4 January 2014.

McClellan, James. *Colonialism and Science: Saint-Domingue in the Old Regime.* Baltimore: Johns Hopkins, UP, 1992. Print.

McCloy, Shelby. *The Humanitarian Movement in Eighteenth-century France.* Lexington, KY: U of Kentucky P, 1957. Print.

McCune Smith, James. *A Lecture of the Haytian Revolution with a Sketch of the Character of Toussaint L'Ouverture.* New York: Daniel Fanshaw, 1841. Print.

McLachlan, H. *Records of a Family, 1800–1933: Pioneers in Education, Social Service and Liberal Religion.* Manchester: Manchester UP, 1935. Print.

M.D.A.L.F., *La vérité sur Saint-Domingue et les mulâtres.* Paris: Marchand Du Breuil, 1824. Print.

Meer, Sarah. *Uncle Tom Mania: Slavery, Minstrelsy, and Transatlantic Culture in the 1850s.* Athens, GA: University of Georgia Press, 2005. Print.

Melville, Herman. 'Benito Cereno.' *Bartelby and Benito Cereno.* New York: Dover, 1990. Print.

Memmi, Albert. *The Colonizer and the Colonized.* Boston: Beacon Press, 1991. Print.

Menonville, Thierry de. *Traité de la culture du nopal, et de l'éducation de la cochenille dans les colonies françaises de l'Amérique; précédé d'un Voyage à Guaxaca.* 2 vols. Cap-Français: Herbault, 1787. Print.

Mercier, Louis-Sébastien. *L'an deux mille quatre cent quarante. Rêve s'il en fût jamais.* London: 1771. Print.

Métral, Antoine. *Histoire de l'insurrection des esclaves dans le nord de Saint-Domingue.* Paris: F. Scherff, 1818. Print.

—. 'De la littérature des nègres.' *La Revue encyclopédique, ou analyse raisonné des productions les plus remarquables dans la littérature, la science, et les arts … pour l'année 1819.* 2 vols. Paris: Au Bureau de la Revue Encyclopédique, 1819. Print.

—. *Histoire de l'expédition des Français à Saint-Domingue: sous le consulat de Napoléon Bonaparte (1802–1803).* Paris: Fanjat aîné, 1825. Print.

—. *Histoire de l'expédition militaire des français à Saint-Domingue sous Napoléon Bonaparte*. Paris: Edme et Alexandre Picard, 1841. Print.

Michelet, Madame Jules. *The Story of My Childhood*. Tr. Mary Frazier Curtis. Boston: Little, Brown, 1867. Print.

Midgley, Clare. 'Anti-slavery and the Roots of 'Imperial Feminism.' *Gender and Imperialism*. Ed. Clare Midgley. Manchester: Manchester UP, 1998. 161–79. Print.

—. 'British Abolitionism and Feminism in Transatlantic Perspective.' *Women's Rights and Transatlantic Antislavery in the Era of Emancipation*. Ed. Kathryn Kish Sklar and James Brewer Stewart. New Haven: Yale UP, 2007. 121-39. Print.

Migne, Jean-Paul (abbé de). 'Ethiopique.' *Nouvelle encyclopédie théologique* Vol. 42. Paris: J.-P. Migne, 1851–59. Print.

Mill, John Stuart. 'The Negro Question.' Web. <http://cepa.newschool.edu/het/texts/carlyle/millnegro.htm>. Accessed 10 July 2009.

Miller, Christopher L. 'Forget Haiti: Baron Roger and the New Africa.' *The Haiti Issue: 1804 and Nineteenth-Century French Studies. Yale French Studies* 107 (2005): 39–69. Print.

—. *The French Atlantic Triangle: Literature and Culture of the Slave Trade*. Durham: Duke UP, 2008. Print.

Milscent, Jules Solime. *L'Abeille Haytienne: journal politique et littéraire* 7 July 1817. Print.

—. 'Suite Aux Considérations.' *L'Abeille Haytienne: journal politique et littéraire* 16 August 1817. Print.

Mims, Stewart L. 'Introduction.' *Moreau De St. Mery's American Journey (1793–1798)*. Garden City: Doubleday, 1947. Print.

Mintz, Sidney. *Sweetness and Power: The Place of Sugar in Modern History*. New York: Viking, 1985. Print.

Mirecourt, Eugène de. *Maison Alexandre Dumas et Compagnie*. Paris: Chez Tous Les Marchands de Nouveautés, 1845.

Mirzeoff, Nicholas. *The Right to Look: A Counterhistory of Visuality*. Durham, NC: Duke UP, 2011.

Miscegenation: The Theory of the Blending of the Races, Applied to the American White Man and Negro. New York: H. Dexter Hamilton & Co, 1864. Print

'Miscellaneous and Literary Intelligence.' *North American Review* 1.1 (May 1815): 126–40. Print.

Mitchell, Angelyn. 'Her Side of His Story: A Feminist Analysis of Two Nineteenth-Century Antebellum Novels—William Wells Brown's "Clotel" and Harriet E. Wilson's "Our Nig."' *American Literary Realism, 1870–1910* 24.3 (Spring 1992): 7–21. Print.

Moitt, Bernard. *Women and Slavery in the French Antilles, 1635–1848*. Bloomington: Indiana UP, 2001. Print.

Bibliography

Mollien, Gaspard Théodore. *Haïti ou Saint-Domingue*. 2 vols. Paris: L'Harmattan. Print.
Montesquieu, Charles Secondat de. *The Spirit of the Laws*. Tr. Thomas Nugent. Cambridge: Harvard UP, 1900. Print.
Montfort, Catherine R. 'French Women Writers and the Revolution: Preliminary Thoughts.' *The French Revolution of 1789 and its Impact*. Ed. Gail M. Schwab et al. New York: Hofstra UP, 1995. 95–104. Print.
Moore, Thomas. *Lalla Rookh, An Oriental Romance*. London: Longman, Brown, Green, 1856. Print.
Moreau de Saint-Méry, Médéric-Louis-Elie. *Observations d'un habitant des Colonies sur le Mémoire en faveur des gens de couleur adressé à l'Assemblée nationale par M. Grégoire*. 1789. Print.
—. *Considérations présentées aux vrais amis du repos et du bonheur de la France : a l'occasion des nouveaux mouvemens de quelques soi-disant Ami des Noirs*. Paris, 1791. Print.
—. *Description topographique, physique, civile, politique et historique de la partie française de l'isle Saint-Domingue. Avec des observations générales sur sa population, sur le caractère & les mœurs de ses divers habitans; sur son climat, sa culture ... accompagnées des détails les plus propres à faire connaître l'état de cette colonie à l'époque du 18 octobre 1789; et d'une nouvelle carte de la totalité de l'isle. Par M. L.-E. Moreau de Saint-Méry*. 2 vols. Philadelphia: Chez L'Auteur, 1797. Print.
—. Moreau de Saint-Méry to Mme. La Comtesse Dall'Asta, née Moreau de Saint-Méry. 9 March 1806. Lettere famigliari di M. Moreau de Saint-Méry. Archivio di Stato di Parma.
—. Moreau de Saint-Méry to Mme. La Comtesse Dall'Asta, née Moreau de Saint-Méry. 10 May 1806. Lettere famigliari di M. Moreau de Saint-Méry. Archivio di Stato di Parma.
—. *Voyage aux États-Unis de l'Amérique, 1793–1798*. New Haven: Yale UP, 1913. Print.
—. *Notes historiques: états de Parme*. Reggio Emilia: Diabasis, 2003. Print.
Morgan, Jennifer. *Laboring Women: Reproduction and Gender in New World Slavery*. Philadelphia: U of Pennsylvania P, 2004. Print.
Morgan, Philip D. *Slave Counterpoint: Black Culture in the Eighteenth-Century Chesapeake and Lowcountry*. Chapel Hill: U of North Carolina P, 1998. Print.
Morpeau, Louis. 'Romanciers Haïtiens.' *La Revue mondiale* 147 (15 April 1922): 451. Print.
—. *Anthologie d'un siècle de poésie haïtienne, 1817–1925*. Paris: Editions Brossard, 1924. Print.
Morrison, Toni. *Playing in the Dark: Whiteness and the Literary Imagination*. New York: Vintage, 1993. Print.
—. *Beloved*. New York: Vintage, 2004. Print.

Mould, Michael. *The Routledge Dictionary of Cultural References in Modern French*. Milton Park, Routledge, 2011. Print.

Mozard, Charles-Théodore. *La répétition interrompue: divertissement national, en un acte, en prose et en vers, mêlé de chant, fait à l'occasion de la réunion des trois ordres de l'état*. Port-au-Prince: l'Imprimerie de l'auteur, 1789. Print.

—. 'Prospectus.' *Gazette de Saint-Domingue, politique, civile, économique et littéraire. Affiches, annnonces et avis divers*. Ed. Charles-Théodore Moazard. Port-au-Prince: Imprimerie de Mozard, 1790. Print.

'Mulatto Literature [a].' *The Albion, A Journal of News, Politics, and Literature* 9 July 1853: 326. Print.

'Mulatto Literature [b].' *National Anti-Slavery Standard* 11 (6 April 1853): 44. Print.

Murdock, John. *The Triumphs of Love; or, a Happy Reconciliation: a comedy. In four acts*. Philadelphia: R. Folwell, 1795. Print.

Muthu, Sankar. *Enlightenment against Empire*. Princeton: Princeton UP, 2003. Print.

N*****, 'A Haytian Legend.' *The Yale Literary Magazine* 5.1 (November 1839): 10–17. Print.

'N. 23—Constitution Impériale d'Haïti.' *Recueil général des lois & actes du gouvernement d'Haïti*. Vol. 1. Ed. S. L'Instant. Paris: Auguste Durand, 1851. Print.

'The Namesakes.' *Baltimore Patriot* 19 (May 1815): 2. Print.

'The Namesakes.' *Niles Weekly Register, supplement to Volume VIII* (March–September 1815): 172. Print.

Nau, Emile. 'Un épisode de la révolution.' *Le Républicain. Recueil scientifique et littéraire* 15 December 1836: 2–7. Print.

—. 'Le Lambi.' *L'Union. Recueil Commerciale et littéraire* 20 April 1837: 2–3. Print.

—. *Réclamation par les affranchis des droits civils et politiques*. Port-au-Prince: Bouchereau, 1840. Print.

—. 'Littérature.' *Panorama de la littérature haïtienne de 1804 à nos jours*. Ed. Christophe Charles. Port-au-Prince: Editions Choucounes, 2003. 152–56. Print.

Ndiyae, Christiane. 'La Caraïbe.' *Introduction aux littératures francophones: Afrique, Caraïbe, Maghreb*. Ed. Christiane Ndiyae. Montréal: Les Presses de l'Université de Montréal, 2004. 141–96. Print.

'Negro Literature.' *National Anti-Slavery Standard* 20 December 1856. Print.

Nelson, John Herbert. *The Negro Character in American Literature*. Lawrence, KS: Department of Journalism Press, 1926. Print.

Nesbitt, Nick. 'Troping Toussaint, Reading Revolution.' *Research in African Literatures* 35.2 (Summer 2004): 18–33. Print.

—. 'The Idea of 1804.' *Yale French Studies. The Haiti Issue: 1804 and Nineteenth-Century French Studies*. Ed. Deborah Jenson. 107 (2005): 6–38. Print.

Bibliography

—. *Universal Emancipation: The Haitian Revolution and the Radical Enlightenment.* Charlottesville, VA: U. of Virginia P., 2008. Print.
—. *Caribbean Critique: Antillean Critical Theory from Toussaint to Glissant.* Liverpool: Liverpool UP, 2013. Print.
Newman, Simon P. 'American Political Culture and the French and Haitian Revolutions.' *The Impact of the Haitian Revolution in the Atlantic World.* Ed. David Geggus. Columbia, SC: U of SC P, 2001. 72-89. Print.
Ngugi wa Thiong'o. *Decolonizing the Mind: The Politics of Language in African Literature.* London: Heinemann, 1986. Print.
Nicholls, David. '"A Work of Combat": Mulatto Historians and the Haitian Past, 1847–1867.' *Journal of Interamerican Studies and World Affairs* 16.1 (February 1974): 15–38. Print.
—. *From Dessalines to Duvalier: Race, Colour and National Independence in Haiti.* Cambridge: Cambridge UP, 1979. Print.
—. *Haiti in Caribbean Context: Ethnicity, Economy and Revolt.* New York: St. Martin's Press, 1985. Print.
—. 'Pompée Valentin Vastey: Royalist and Revolutionary.' *Revista de Historia de América* 109 (January–June 1990): 129–43. Print.
Nicholson, J.B.M. *Essai sur l'histoire naturelle de l'isle de Saint-Domingue, avec des figures en taille-douce.* Paris: Gobreau, 1776. Print.
Niles, Blair. *Black Haiti: A Biography of Africa's Eldest Daughter.* New York: Grosset & Dunlap, 1926. Print.
Nora, Pierre. 'Between Memory and History: *Les Lieux de Mémoire.*' *Representations* 26 (Spring 1989): 7–24. Print.
Nott, Josiah C. 'The Mulatto a Hybrid—probable extermination of the two races if the Whites and the Blacks are allowed to intermarry.' *American Journal of the Medical Sciences* 6.11 (July 1843): 252–56. Print.
'North American Review, The.' *The Literary Gazette; or Journal of Criticism, Science, and the Arts* 1.7 (17 February 1821): 100–05. Print.
'Nouvelles Scientifiques et littéraires (1).' *Annales de la littérature et des arts* 3.29: 130. Print.
'Obituary.' *New York Times* 22 September 1874. Print.
O'Byrne, William R. *A Naval Biographical Dictionary.* London: John Murray, 1849. Print.
O'Connell, David. 'Victor Séjour: Écrivain américain de langue française.' *Revue de Louisiane* 1.2 (1972): 60–61. Print.
—. 'The Black Hero in French Romantic Fiction.' *Studies in Romanticism* 12.2 (Spring 1973). Print.
Offen, Karen. 'How (and Why) the Analogy of Marriage with Slavery Provided the Springboard for Women's Rights Demands in France, 1640–1848.' *Women's Rights and Transatlantic Antislavery in the Era of Emancipation.* Ed. Kathryn Kish Sklar and James Brewer Stewart. New Haven, CT: Yale UP, 2007. 57–81. Print.

Ogé, Faubert. 'Motion Faite par M. Vincent Ogé, jeune à l'Assemblée des Colons, Habitants de S.-Domingue, à l'Hotel de Massiac, Place des Victoires.' Paris, 1789. Print.

—. 'Lettre de M. Ogé le jeune au président de l'assemblée provinciale du Nord.' *La Gazette nationale ou Le Moniteur universel* 29 December 1790. Print.

Ogletree Jr., Charles. 'America's Schizophrenic Immigration Policy: Race, Class, and Reason,' *Boston Law Review* 41.4 (1 July 2000): 755–70. Print.

'Ordonnance du Roi.' *Gazette Royale d'Hayti* 28 December 1818. Print.

Ott, Thomas. *The Haitian Revolution, 1789–1804*. Knoxville, TN: U of Tennessee P, 1973. Print.

Omi, Michael and Howard Winant. *Racial Formation in the United States: From the 1960s to the 1990s*. New York: Routledge, 1994. Print.

Ong, Aihwa. *Flexible Citizenship: The Cultural Logics of Transnationality*. Durham, NC: Duke UP, 1999. Print.

'Original and Interesting State Paper.' *Liverpool Mercury* April 1818. Print.

'Our Continental Correspondence.' *American Literary Gazette and Publishers' Circular* 15 December 1865: 126. Print.

'Our Special Contributors.' *The Independent ... Devoted to the Consideration of Politics, Social and Economic* 30 September 1858: 1. Print.

'Our Special Paris Correspondence.' *Spirit of the Times; A Chronicle of the Turf, Agriculture, Field Sports, Life* 7 April 1855: 81. Print.

Outka, Paul. H. 'Whitman and Race: ("He's Queer, He's Unclear, Get Used to It").' *Journal of American Studies* 36.2 (2002): 293–318. Print.

Oxiane; ou la Révolution de Saint-Domingue. 3 vols. Paris: Crobet, 1826. Print.

Ozouf, Mona. 'La Révolution française et l'idée de l'homme nouveau.' *French Revolution and the Creation of Modern Political Culture*. Ed. Colin Lucas. New York: Pergamon, 1988. Print.

Quérard, Jean-Marie. *La France littéraire*. Vol 10. Paris: Firmin Didot frères, 1839. Print.

Quevilly, Laurent. 2012: 'Le baron de Vastey'. Web. <http://laurent.quevilly.pagesperso-orange.fr/>. Accessed 10 October 2011.

—. *Le Baron de Vastey*. Paris: Books on Demand, 2014. Print.

P., Gabrielle de (Gabrielle de Paban). *Le Nègre et la Créole: ou, Mémoires d'Eulalie D***: par Mme Gabrielle de P****. 3 vols. Paris: Boulland, 1825. Print.

Pachonski, Jan and Reuel K. Wilson. *Poland's Caribbean Tragedy: A Study of the Polish Legions in the Haitian War of Independence 1802–1803*. Boulder, CO: East European Monographs, 1986. Print.

Palaiseau, Mlle. de. *Histoire de Mesdemoiselles de Saint-Janvier. Les deux seules blanches conservées à Saint-Domingue*. Paris: J. Blaise, 1812. Print.

Pamphile, Léon Dénius. *Haitians and African Americans: A Heritage of Tragedy and Hope*. Gainesville: UP of Florida, 2001. Print.

Parry, Benita. 'Problems in Current Theories of Colonial Discourse.' *Oxford Literary Review* 9.1–2 (1987): 27–58. Print.

'Past and Present State of Hayti.' *The Quarterly Review* 21.42 (April 1819): 430–60. Print.

'Pat Robertson says Haiti Paying for "Pact to the Devil."' *CNN* 13 January 2010. Web. <http://articles.cnn.com/2010-01-13/us/haiti.pat.robertson_1_pat-robertson-disasters-and-terrorist-attacks-devil?_s=PM:US>. Accessed 31 January 2011.

Patterson, Orlando. *Slavery and Social Death: A Comparative Study*. Cambridge: Harvard UP, 1982. Print.

Paulson, Ronald. *Representations of Revolution (1789–1820)*. New Haven: Yale UP, 1983. Print.

Peabody, Sue. *'There are no Slaves in France': The Political Culture of Race and Slavery in the Ancien Régime*. Oxford: Oxford UP, 1996. Print.

—. Rev. of *Democracy after Slavery: Black Publics and Peasant Radicalism in Haiti and Jamaica*, by Mimi Sheller. *H-Caribbean*. October 2002. Web. <http://64.233.167.104/search?q=cache:6mk7qinHrzMJ:www.h-net.org/reviews/showpdf.cgi%3Fpath%3D225101039174715+%22Haitian+national+archives%22+protect&hl=en&ct=clnk&cd=7&gl=us>. Accessed 12 October 2012.

—. 'Négresse, Mulâtresse, Citoyenne: Gender and Emancipation in the French Caribbean, 1650–1848.' *Gender and Slave Emancipation in the Atlantic World*. Ed. Pamela Scully and Diana Paton. Durham: Duke UP, 2005. 56–78. Print.

—. 'Free Soil in the Indian Ocean: French Slave Law on the Eve of Emancipation.' *Proceedings of the 10th Annual Gilder Lehrman Center International Conference, Slavery and the Global Trade in the Indian Ocean and Arab Worlds: Global Connections and Disconnections, New Haven, Yale University, November 7–8, 2008*. 1–35. Print.

Péan, Leslie J.-R. *Haïti, économie politique de la corruption: De Saint-Domingue à Haïti, 1791–1870*. Paris: Maisonneuve & Larose, 2003. Print.

Peel, Ellen. 'Semiotic Subversion in "Desiree's Baby."' *American Literature* 62.2 (June 1990): 223–37. Print.

Peltier, Jean Gabriel. 'Sur quelques ouvrages relatifs aux colonies françaises, et particulièrement à l'isle de Saint-Domingue.' *L'Ambigu: ou Variétés littéraires, et politiques* 46 (1814): 755–65. Print.

'People of Colour.' *Freedom's Journal* 23 March 1827. Print.

Perret, J. John. 'Victor Séjour: Black French Playwright from Louisiana.' *The French Review* 57.2 (December 1983): 187–93. Print.

Périn, René. *L'Incendie du cap, ou, Le règne de Toussaint-Louverture, où l'on développe le caractère de ce chef de révoltés, sa conduite atroce depuis qu'il s'est arrogé le pouvoir, la nullité de ses moyens, la bassesse de tous ses agens, la férocité de Christophe, un de ses plus fermes soutiens, les malheurs qui sont venus fondre sur le Cap, la marche de l'armée française, et ses succès sous les ordres du capitaine général Leclerc*. Paris: Marchand, 1802. Print.

'Persian Mode of Taming a Shrew.' *Freedom's Journal* 20 July 1827. Print.
Peterson, Carla. *'Doers of the Word': African-American Women Speakers and Writers in the North* (1830–1880). New York: Oxford UP, 1995. Print.
—. 'Literary Transnationalism and Diasporic History: Frances Watkin's Harper's "Fancy Sketches", 1859–60.' *Women's Rights and Transatlantic Antislavery in the Era of Emancipation*. Ed. Kathryn Kish Sklar and James Brewer Stewart. New Haven: Yale UP, 2007. 189–208. Print.
Peyrard, Christine et al. *L'administration napoléonienne en Europe: adhésions et résistances*. Aix-en-Provence: Publications de l'Université de Provence, 2008. Print.
Philadelphia Inquirer 22 September 1874. Print.
Philip, Maxwell. *Emmanuel Appadocca, or Blighted Life, A Tale of the Buccaneers*. 2 vols. London: Charles J. Skeet, 1854. Print.
Phillips, Helen. 'Yale Literary Magazine vs. Yale University.' Web. <http://www.yale.edu/ylit/history.pdf>. Accessed 5 February 2013.
Phillips, Wendell. *Speeches, Lectures, and Letters*. Boston: Lee and Shepard, 1884. Print.
—. *Toussaint L'Ouverture*. 1861. Rpt. Stamford: Overbrook Press, 1963. Print.
Piacentino, Ed. 'Seeds of Rebellion in Plantation Fiction: Victor Séjour's "The Mulatto."' *Southern Spaces*. Web. <http://southernspaces.org/2007/seeds-rebellion-plantation-fiction-victor-s%C3%A9jours-mulatto>. Accessed 6 January 2014.
Picquenard, Jean-Baptiste. *Zoflora; ou la bonne négresse: anecdote coloniale*. Paris: Didot, 1799. Print.
—. *Adonis; ou le bon nègre*. 1798. Ed. Chris Bongie. Paris: L'Harmattan, 2006. Print.
'Picture of St. Domingo.' *The Literary Magazine and American Register for 1803–4*. Vol. 1. Philadelphia: John Conrad and Co., 1804. 446–50. Print.
Pierrot, Grégory. '"Our Hero" Toussaint Louverture in British Representations.' *Criticism* 50.4 (2008): 581–607. Print.
Pilgrim, David. 'The Tragic Mulatto Myth.' *Jim Crow Museum of Racist Memorabilia. Ferris State University*. Web. <http://www.ferris.edu/news/jimcrow/mulatto/>. Accessed 4 June 2009.
Pigault-Lebrun, 'Le Blanc et le Noir.' *Œuvres complètes de Pigault Lebrun*. Vol. 11. Paris: J.-N. Barba, 1824. Print.
Plummer, Brenda Gayle. *Haiti and the Great Powers, 1902–1915*. Baton Rouge: Louisiana State UP, 1988. Print.
—. *Haiti and the United States: The Psychological Moment*. Atlanta: U of Georgia P, 1992, 2003. Print.
'Politics: Black Empire of Hayti.' *Military Register* 8 November 1815. 570–71. Print.
Pompilus, Pradel. *Manuel illustré de la littérature haïtienne*. Port-au-Prince: Editions Henri Deschamps, 1961. Print.
Popkin, Jeremy. 'Facing Revolution: Captivity Narratives and Identity in the

Bibliography

Saint-Domingue Revolution.' *Eighteenth-Century Studies* 36.4 (2003): 511–33. Print.

—. *Facing Racial Revolution: Eyewitness Accounts of the Haitian Insurrection.* Chicago: U of Chicago P, 2007. Print.

—. *A Concise History of Haiti.* Hoboken, NJ: Wiley-Blackwell, 2011. Print.

Porter, Dorothy. 'The Organized Educational Activities of Negro Literary Societies, 1828–1846.' *The Journal of Negro Education* 5.4 (October 1936): 555–76. Print.

Poyen-Bellisle, *Histoire militaire de la Révolution de Saint-Domingue.* Paris: Berger-Levrault, 1899. Print.

Pradine, L'Instant de. *Recueil général des lois et actes du gouvernement d'Haïti: depuis la proclamation de son indépendance.* Vol. 1. Paris: A. Durand, 1886. Print.

Prasad, Pratima. *Colonialism, Race, and the French Romantic Imagination.* New York: Routledge, 2009. Print.

Pratt, Frances Hammond. *La Belle Zoa, or, The Insurrection of Hayti.* Albany: Weed, Parsons, 1854. Print.

Pratt, Mary Louise. *Imperial Eyes: Travel Writing and Transculturation.* London: Routledge, 1992. Print.

Pratt, Samuel Jackson. *Family Secrets: Literary and Domestick.* Vol. 4. London: T.N. Longman, 1797. Print.

'Preamble of Constitution of the Boston Female Anti-Slavery Society (1835).' *Society for the Study of American Women Writers.* Web. <http://www.lehigh.edu/~dek7/SSAWW/writBoston%20FASS.htm>. Accessed 5 February 2013.

Prévost, Antoine François (abbé). *Histoire générale des voyages ...* 25 vols. Paris: Didot, 1747–80. Print.

Prévost, Julien (comte de Limonade), *L'Olivier de la Paix.* Cap-Haïtien: P. Roux, 1815. Print.

Price-Mars, Jean. *So Spoke the Uncle.* Tr. Magadaline W. Shannon. Washington, D.C.: Three Continents Press, 1983. Print.

Pritchard, Hesketh. *Where Black Rules White: A Journey across and about Hayti.* Westminster: Archibald Constable & Co., 1900. Print.

Prochaska, David. *Making Algeria French: Colonialism in Bône, 1870–1920.* New York: Cambridge UP, 1990. Print.

'Programme,' *Le Manifeste* 24 September 1843: 2. Print.

'Propriety of Conduction.' *Freedom's Journal* 13 July 1827. Print.

'Quarterly List of New Publications.' *The Edinburgh Review, or Critical Journal* March 1821: 266. Print.

Quincy, Edmund. 'Two Nights in St. Domingo, "An Ower True Tale."' *The Liberty Bell.* Boston: Massachusetts Anti-Slavery Fair, 1843. 71–110. Print.

Quinet, Edgar. *Merlin, l'enchanteur.* Paris: Michel Lévy frères, 1860. Print.

Quinn, Kate and Paul Sutton. 'Introduction: Duvalier and After.' *Politics and Power in Haiti.* Ed. Kate Quinn and Paul Sutton. New York: Palgrave Macmillan, 2013. 1–26. Print.

Rabelais, *The Works of Rabelais, Faithfully Translated From the French, with Variorium Notes and Numerous Illustrations*. Tr. Sir Thomas Urquhart and Peter Antony Motteux. Ed. Gustave Doré. Derby: Moray Press, 1894. Print.
Racault, Jean-Michel. 'Mimétisme et Métissage: sur *Georges* d'Alexandre Dumas.' *Métissages: Littérature, histoire comparée*. Ed. Jean-Claude Carpanin Marimoutou and Jean-Michel Racault. Paris: L'Harmattan, 1992. 141–50. Print.
Radet, Jean-Baptiste and Pierre-Yon Barré. *La Négresse; ou le pouvoir de la reconnaissance; comédie en un acte, en prose et en vaudevilles, mêlée de divertissemens*. Paris: Brunet, 1787. Print.
Raimon, Eve Allegra. *The 'Tragic Mulatta' Revisited: Race and Nationalism in Nineteenth-Century Anti-Slavery Fiction*. New Brunswick: Rutgers UP, 2004. Print.
Raimond, Julien. *Observations sur l'origine et les progrès du prejuge des colons blancs contre les hommes de couleur*. Paris: Belin, 1791a. Print.
—. *Réponse aux considerations de M. Moreau, dit Saint-Méry, député à l'Assemblée nationale, sur les colonies, par M. Raymond*. Paris: Imprimerie du patriote français, 1791b. Print.
—. *Mémoire sur les causes des troubles et des désastres de la colonie de Saint-Domingue*. Paris: Imprimerie du cercle royale, 1793a. Print.
—. *Réflexions sur les véritables causes des troubles et des désastres de nos colonies, notamment sur ceux de Saint-Domingue; avec les moyens à employer pour préserver cette colonie d'une ruine totale*. Paris: Imprimerie des patriotes, 1793b. Print.
—. *Lettres de J. Raimond, à ses frères les hommes de couleur. En comparaison des originaux de sa correspondance, avec les extraits perfides qu'en ont fait MM. Page et Bruelly, dans un libelle intitulé: Developpement des causes, des troubles, et des désastres des Colonies françaises*. Paris: Imprimerie du cercle social, 1794.
Rainsford, Marcus. *An Historical Account of the Black Empire of Hayti: Comprehending a View of the Principal Transactions in the Revolution of Saint Domingo; with its Ancient and Modern State*. London: Albion Press, 1805. Print.
Ramsay, David. *The History of the American Revolution in Two Volumes*. Vol. 1. Bedford, MA: Applewood Books, 1789. Print.
Ramsey, Kate. *The Spirits and the Law: Vodou and Power in Haiti*. Chicago: UP of Chicago, 2011. Print.
Raupach, Kirsten. '"When We with Magic Rites the White Man's Doom Prepare": Representations of Black Resistance in British Abolitionist Writing During the Era of Revolution.' *Monuments of the Black Atlantic: Slavery and Memory*. Ed. Joann Braxton and Maria Diedrich. New Brunswick: LT Verlag Munster, 2004. 19–28. Print.
Ravinet, Laurette Aimée Mozard Nicodami de. *Mémoires d'une Créole du Port-au-Prince (Ile Saint-Domingue)*. Paris: Librairie-Papeterie, 1844. Print.
Raynal, Abbé Guillaume-Thomas. *Histoire philosophique et politique des établissemens et du commerce des Européens dans les deux Indes*. 3rd ed. 10 vols. Geneva: Jean-Leonard Pellet, 1780–84. Print.

Bibliography

—. *A Philosophical and Political History of the Settlements and Trade of the Europeans in the East and West Indies*. 4 vols. Tr. J. Justamond. London and Edinburgh: T. Caddell and J. Balfour, 1776. Print.

Redpath, James. *Echoes of Harper's Ferry*. Boston: Thayer and Eldridge, 1860. Print.

—. 'The People of Hayti, Their Character, Origin, Language, Industry, and Numbers.' *A Guide to Hayti*. Ed. James Redpath. Boston: Haytian Bureau of Emigration, 1861a. 120–37. Print.

—. 'Editor's Introduction.' *A Guide to Hayti*. Ed. James Redpath. Boston: Haytian Bureau of Emigration, 1861b. 9–11. Print.

—. 'A Parting Word.' *A Guide to Hayti*. Ed. James Redpath. Boston: Haytian Bureau of Emigration, 1861c. 171–75. Print.

—. *Toussaint L'Ouverture: A Biography and Autobiography*. Ed. James Redpath. Boston: James Redpath, 1863. Print.

'Rehearsal of the Coming Syrian Drama.' *The Albion: A Journal of News, Politics and Literature* 26 January 1861: 41. Print.

Régis, Augustin. *Mémoire historique sur Toussaint*. Paris: F. Scherff, 1818. Print.

Reinhardt, Catherine A. *Claims to Memory: Beyond Slavery and Emancipation in the French Caribbean*. New York: Berghan Books, 2006. Print.

Rémusat, Charles de. *L'habitation de Saint-Domingue: ou, L'insurrection*. Paris: CNRS, 1824. Print.

'Researches in Hayti.' *The Museum of Foreign Literature, Science, and Art* 32 (March 1838): 333. Print.

'Review 2—No Title: "To the Academy of Marseilles."' *The Select Journal of Foreign Periodical Literature* 2.1 (July 1832): 8. Print.

'Review 3—No Title.' *The Select Journal of Foreign Periodical Literature* 3.1 (January 1834): 19. Print.

'Review 3—No Title.' *Brother Jonathan. A Weekly Compend of Belles Lettres and the Fine Arts, Standard Literature, and General Intelligence* (4 January 1842): 156. Print.

Renan, Ernest. 'What is a Nation?' *Nation and Narration*. Tr. Martin Thom. Ed. Homi K. Bhabha. London: Routledge, 1990. 8–22. Print.

'République Haïtienne,' *La Sentinelle de la liberté* 19 October 1843: 3. Print.

Reuter, Edward Byron. *The Mulatto in the United States: including a study of the role of the mixed-blood races throughout the world*. New York, NY: Haskell House Publishers, 1918. Print.

'Review of New Books.' *The Literary Gazette; or Journal of Criticism, Science, and the Arts* 17 February 1821. Print.

'The Rich Harvest of Death.' *New York Evangelist* 46.2 (14 January 1875): 8. Print.

Richardson, Marilyn. *Maria W. Stewart: America's First Black Woman Political Writer*. Bloomington: Indiana UP, 1987. Print.

Richet (Riché), Jean-Baptiste. 'Le général Jean-Baptiste Richet, au rédacteur du Manifeste.' *Le Manifeste*. 24 September 1843: 3–4. Print.

Rigaud, André. *Mémoire du Général de Brigade André Rigaud, en Réfutation des écrits Calomnieux contre les citoyens de couleur de Saint-Domingue.* Aux Cayes: L'Imprimerie de Lemery, 1797. Print.

Ritchie, Leitch. *The Slave-King: From the Bug-Jargal of Victor Hugo.* London: Smith, Elder, and Company, 1833. Print.

Ritter, Karl. *Naturhistorische Reise nach der westindischen Insel Hayti.* Stuttgart: Hallberger, 1836. Print.

Robbins, Richard. *Cultural Anthropology: A Problem-based Approach.* Itasca: Peacock Publishers, 1997. Print.

Robertson, Pat. *Courting Disaster: How the Supreme Court is Usurping the Powers of Congress and the People.* Brentwood, TN: Integrity Publishers, 2004. Print.

Rodriguez, Junius P. *Slavery in the United States: A Social, Political, and Historical Encyclopedia.* Vol. 2. Santa Barbara: ABC-CLIO, 2007. Print.

Roger, M. le Baron. *Kelédor: histoire africaine.* Paris: Moreau, 1828. Print.

Rogers, Dominique. 'Réussir dans un monde d'hommes: les Stratégies des Femmes de Couleur du Cap-Français.' *Journal of Haitian Studies* 9.1 (Spring 2003): 40–51. Print.

—. 'Entre "Lumières" et préjugés: Moreau de Saint-Méry et les libres de couleur de la partie française de Saint-Domingue.' *Moreau de Saint-Méry et les ambigüités d'un créole des Lumières.* Ed. Dominique Taffin. Fort-de-France: Sociétés des Amis des archives et de la recherche sur le patrimoine culturel des Antilles, 2006. 77–93. Print.

Rogers, T.C. 'The Negro-A Distinct Species.' *Medical and Surgical Reporter* 11 (July 1858): 448–58. Print.

Rotberg, Robert. *Haiti: The Politics of Squalor.* Boston: Houghton Mifflin Company, 1971. Print.

Rosa. 'For the Freedom's Journal. Lines on Hearing of the Death of a Young Friend.' *Freedom's Journal* 26 October 1827. Print.

—. 'For the Freedom's Journal. Music.' *Freedom's Journal* 26 October 1827. Print.

—. 'For the Freedom's Journal. Stanzas.' *Freedom's Journal* 30 November 1827. Print.

—. 'For the Freedom's Journal. LINES.' *Freedom's Journal* 8 February 1828. Print.

Rousseau, Jean-Jacques. *The Social Contract: or Principles of Political Right.* tr. G.D.H. Cole. New York: E.P. Dutton and Co., 1913. Web. <http://web.archive.org/web/20080718103110/http://etext.lib.virginia.edu/toc/modeng/public/RouSoci.html>. Accessed 10 March 2014.

—. *Discourse on the Origins of Inequality.* Tr. Donald A. Cress. Indianapolis: Hackett, 1992. Print.

—. *Julie, or the New Heloise.* Tr. Philip Stewart and Jean Vaché. Ed. Roger D. Masters and Christopher Kelly. Hanover: Dartmouth UP, 1997. Print.

Bibliography

—. *Discours sur l'origine et les fondements de l'inégalité parmi les hommes.* 1755. ed. Jean-Marie Tremblay. Chicoutimi, Québec: 2002. Web. <http://eet.pixelonline.org/files/etranslation/original/Rousseau%20JJ%20Discours%20sur.pdf>. Accessed 24 May 2014.

Rouvray, Laurent François Le Noir de. Ed. *Une correspondance familiale au temps des troubles de Saint-Domingue.* Paris: Larose, 1959. Print.

Rowen, Herbert H. '"L'Etat c'est à moi": Louis XIV and the State.' *French Historical Studies* 2.1 (Spring 1961): 83–98. Print.

Rowland, Ann Wierda. 'Wordsworth's Children of the Revolution.' *SEL* 41.4 (Autumn 2001): 667–94. Print.

Rowlandson, Mary. *Narrative of the Captivity and Restoration of Mrs. Mary Rowlandson.* Web. <http://www.gutenberg.org/files/851/851-h/851-h.htm>. Accessed 15 September 2013.

'Royalty.' *Niles Weekly Register* 11.271 (9 November 1816): 168. Print.

'Royaume d'Hayti.' *Gazette Royale d'Hayti* 6 (19 November 1814): 1–4. Print.

Rudé, Georges. *History from Below: Studies in Popular Protest and Popular Ideology in Honour of Georges Rudé.* Ed. Frederick Krantz. Montréal: Concordia University, 1985. Print.

Russworm, John Browne. 'The Condition and Prospects of Haiti.' *African Americans and the Haitian Revolution: Selected Essays and Historical Documents.* Ed. Jacqueline Bacon and Maurice Jackson. New York: Routledge, 2010. 167–69. Print.

S. 'Theresa; a Haytien Tale.' *Freedman's Journal* January–February 1828. Print.

S. 'Theresa; a Haytien Tale.' *African American Review.* 40.4 (2006): 641-645. Print.

Said, Edward. *Culture and Imperialism.* New York: Vintage Books, 1993. Print.

—. *Orientalism.* New York, NY: Vintage, 1979. Print.

Saillet, Alexandre de. *Lucile de Saint-Albe, épisode de la Révolution de Saint-Domingue.* Paris: P.C. Lehuby, 1848. Print.

Saint-Aubin, Arthur F. 'Editing Toussaint Louverture's Memoir: A Profile in Black.' *Journal of Haitian Studies* 17.1 (Spring 2011): 106-122. Print.

—. 'Alphonse De Lamartine's Toussaint Louverture and the Staging of White Masculinity.' *Nineteenth-Century French Studies* 35.2 (Winter 2007): 333–51. Print.

Saint-Rémy, Joseph. *Essai sur Henri Christophe, Général Haïtien.* Paris: Imprimerie de Félix Malteste et Cie, 1839. Print.

—. 'Esquisse sur les hommes de lettres d'Haïti.' *Revue des Colonies. Recueil Mensuel de la politique, de l'administration, de la justice, de l'instruction et des mœurs* 11 (May 1837): 469–72. Print.

—. 'Lettres à M. Victor Schoelcher Relativement à son livre sur Haïti: Première Lettre.' *La Sentinelle de la Liberté* 9 November 1843. Print.

—. 'Lettres à M. Victor Schoelcher Relativement à son livre sur Haïti: 2è lettre, Vincent OGE.' *La Sentinelle de la Liberté* 14 December 1843. Print.

—. 'Lettres à M. Victor Schoelcher Relativement à son livre sur Haïti: 3è lettre, *affaire des suisses.*' *La Sentinelle de la Liberté* 21 December 1843. Print.

—. 'Lettres à M. Victor Schoelcher Relativement à son livre sur Haïti: 4è lettre; Toussaint et Rigaud.' *La Sentinelle de la Liberté* 28 December 1843. Print.

—. No title. *La Reforme* 25 January 1849. Print.

—. *Vie de Toussaint-L'Ouverture.* Paris: Moquet, 1850. Print.

—. 'Foreword.' *Mémoire pour servir à l'histoire d'Haïti.* Louis-Félix Boisrond-Tonnerre. Paris: France, Libraire, 1851. Print.

—. 'Introduction.' *Mémoires du général Toussaint-L'Ouverture écrits par lui-même.* Paris: Pagnerre, 1853. Print.

—. *Pétion et Haïti, étude monographique et historique.* Vol. 1. Paris: Chez l'auteur, 1854. Print.

—. 'Contre la proscription des blancs et pour le mélange des races.' *Panorama de la littérature haïtienne de 1804 à 2004.* Ed. Christophe Philippe Charles. Port-au-Prince: Editions Choucoune, 2003. 234–36. Print.

Salles, Catherine. *Spartacus et la révolte des gladiateurs.* Brussels: Editions Complexe, 1990. Print.

Salvandy, Narcisse-Achille de. *De l'Emancipation de Saint-Domingue, dans ses rapports avec la politique intérieure et extérieure de la France.* Paris: Ponthieu, Delaunay Dentu, 1825. Print.

Samaan, A.E. *From a Race of Masters to a Master Race: 1948 to 1848.* Charleston, SC: CreateSpace, 2013. Print.

Sanborn, Geoffrey. '"People Will Pay to Hear the Drama": Plagiarism in *Clotel*.' *African American Review* 45.1 (2012): 65–82. Print.

Sanchez-Eppler, Karen. 'Bodily Bonds: The Intersecting Rhetorics of Feminism and Abolition.' *The New American Studies: Essays from Representations.* Ed. Philip Fisher. Berkeley: U of Calif. P, 1991. 60–92. Print.

Sansay, Leonora. *Zelica; the Creole.* 3 vols. London: William Fearman, 1820. Print.

—. *The Scarlet Handkerchief.* 3 vols. London: A.K. Newman and Co., 1823. Print.

—. Letter from Leonora Sansay to Aaron Burr, 6 May 1803. *Secret History or the Horrors of Santo Domingo.* Ed. Michael Drexler. Ontario: Broadview Press, 2008. 223–31. Print.

—. *Secret History or the Horrors of Santo Domingo* and *Laura.* Ed. Michael Drexler. Ontario, Canada: Broadview Editions, 2007. Print.

Sartre, Jean-Paul. 'Colonialism is a System.' *Colonialism and Neocolonialism.* Tr. Azzedine Haddour. Ed. Azzedine Haddour et al. London: Routledge, 2001. 30–55. Print.

Saunders, Prince. *Haytian Papers: A Collection of the Very Interesting Proclamations, and Other Official Documents; together with Some Account of the Rise, Progress, and Present State of the Kingdom of Hayti.* London: W. Reed, 1816. Print.

—. 'Address Delivered at Bethel Church, Philadelphia: on the 30th of September,

1818, Before the Pennsylvania Augustine Society for the Education of People of Colour.' Philadelphia: Rakestraw, 1818a. Web. <http://www.samanthagibson.net/Project/archive/files/prince-saunders,-to-augustine-society_ae12aed854.pdf>. Accessed 5 February 2013.

—. *Memoir Presented to the American Convention for Promoting the Abolition of Slavery, And Improving the Condition of the African Race, December 11th, 1818.* Philadelphia: Dennis Heartt, 1818b. Print.

Sawyer, Hannah Farnham. *Memoir of Pierre Toussaint, Born a Slave in Saint-Domingue.* Boston: Crosby, Nichols, and Company, 1854. Print.

Saye, Lisa Macha. "The Haitian State: Something Alien." *Journal of Third World Studies* 27.2 (Fall 2010): 71-88. Print.

Scarry, Elaine. *The Body in Pain: The Making and Unmaking of the World.* Oxford: Oxford UP, 1987. Print.

Schiebinger, Londa. *Plants and Empire: Colonial Bioprospecting in the Atlantic World.* Cambridge, MA: Harvard UP, 2007. Print.

Schiffman, Joseph. 'Critical Problems in Melville's "Benito Cereno."' *Critical Essays on Herman Melville's 'Benito Cereno.'* Ed. Robert Burkholder. New York: G.K. Hall, 1992. 29–36. Print.

Schoelcher, Victor. *Colonies étrangères et Haïti: résultats de l'émancipation anglaise.* Paris: Pagnerre, 1843. Print.

—. *La vérité aux ouvriers et cultivateurs de la Martinique: suivie des rapports, décrets, arrêtes, projets de lois et d'arrêtés concernant l'abolition immédiate de l'esclavage.* Paris: Pagnerre, 1849. Print.

—. 'Toussaint-Louverture et Rigaud'. *La Fraternité* ([September 01, 1892]; Issue 52). *Slavery and Anti-Slavery.* Gale Web Resources. Web. <http://find.galegroup.com/sas/infomark.do?&source=gale&prodId=SAS&userGroupName=acd_sas&tabID=T003&docPage=article&searchType=&docId=IW2500874218&type=multipage&contentSet=LTO&version=1.0&relevancePageBatch=&docLevel=FASCIMILE>. Accessed 10 January 2014.

—. 'Ce qu'on disait en 1855.' *La Fraternité* 25 April 1893. Print.

—. *Vie de Toussaint Louverture.* Paris: Editions Karthala, 1982. Print.

Schüller, Karin. 'From Liberalism to Racism: German Historians, Journalists, and the Haitian Revolution from the Late Eighteenth to the Early Twentieth Centuries'. *The Impact of the Haitian Revolution in the Atlantic World.* Ed. David Geggus. Columbia: U of South Carolina P, 2001. 23–43. Print.

Scott, David. *Conscripts of Modernity: The Tragedy of Colonial Enlightenment.* Durham: Duke UP, 2004. Print.

Scott, Joan W. 'The Evidence of Experience.' *Critical Inquiry* 17. 4 (Summer 1991): 773–97. Print.

Scott, Rebecca J., and Jean M. Hébrard. 'Rosalie of the Poulard Nation: Freedom, Law and Dignity in the Era of the Haitian Revolution.' *Assumed Identities: The Meanings of Race in the Atlantic World.* Ed. John Garrigus and Christopher Morris. 116–44. Print.

'Séance du 25 séptembre—Lundi.' *Le Manifeste* 29 October 1843: 1. Print.
'Séance du 29 séptembre.' *La Sentinelle de la Liberté* October 5, 1843: 4. Print.
'Secours aux réfugiés et colons spoliés. XIe siècle.' Archives Nationales de la France. Sous-série F/12 (Commerce et industrie). Ed. Christiane Demeulenaere-Douyère. Volume 1. Web. <http://www.archivesnationales.culture.gouv.fr/chan/chan/pdf/colons-spolies-A-K.pdf>. Accessed 17 June 2014.
Seeber, Edward. *Anti-Slavery Opinion in France during the Second Half of the Eighteenth Century*. Baltimore: Johns Hopkins UP, 1937. Print.
Séjour, Victor. 'Le Mulâtre.' *Revue des Colonies* March 1837: 376–92. Web. <http://www.centenary.edu/french/textes/mulatres.html>. Accessed 10 January 2014.
—. 'The Mulatto.' Tr. Philip Barnard. *The Norton Anthology of African American Literature*. Ed. Henry Louis Gates Jr. and Nellie Y. McKay. New York: W.W. Norton and Co., 1997. 287–99. Print.
—. *The Fortune-Teller*. Trans, Norman Shapiro. U of Illinois P, 2002. Print.
Seldon, Horace. 'Garrison on Violence, Nonviolence, and the Use of Force.' *The Liberator Files*. Web. <http://www.theliberatorfiles.com/garrison-on-nonviolence-violence-and-the-use-of-force/>. Accssed 15 March 2014.
'Selections.' *Liberator* 4 March 1859: 1. Print.
Senghor, Léopold Sédar. 'Lamartine, homme de pensée et d'action.' *Centenaire de la mort d'Alphonse de Lamartine, Actes du Congrès III*. Mâcon: Comité permanent d'Études Lamartiniennes, 1969. Print.
Sepinwall, Alyssa Goldstein. 'Exporting the Revolution: Grégoire, Haiti and the Colonial Laboratory, 1815–1827.' *The Abbé Grégoire and His World*. Ed. Richard Popkin and Jeremy H. Popkin. Boston: Kluwer Academic, 2000. Print. 41-69.
—. *The Abbé Grégoire and the French Revolution: The Making of Modern Universalism*. Berkeley: U of California P, 2005. Print.
—. 'Still Unthinkable? The Haitian Revolution and the Reception of Michel-Rolph Trouillot's *Silencing the Past*.' *Journal of Haitian Studies* 19.2 (Fall 2013): 75–103. Print.
Sharpley-Whiting, T. Denean. *Black Venus: Sexualized Savages, Primal Fears, and Primitive Narratives in French*. Durham: Duke UP, 1999. Print.
Sheftall, Beverly Guy. *Words of Fire: An Anthology of African-American Feminist Thought*. New York: Norton, 1995. Print.
Sheldon, Garrett Ward, and Charles William Hill, Jr. 2008: *The Liberal Republicanism of John Taylor of Caroline*. Madison, NJ: Fairleigh Dickinson University Press.
Sheller, Mimi. 'Sword-Bearing Citizens: Militarism and Manhood in Nineteenth-Century Haiti.' *Plantation Society in the Americas* 4.2 (1997): 233–78. Print.
—. '"The Haytian Fear": Racial Projects and Competing Reactions to the First Black Republic.' *Politics and Society* 6 (1999): 283–303. Print.

Bibliography

—. *Democracy After Slavery: Black Publics and Peasant Radicalism in Haiti and Jamaica*. Gainesville, FL: UP of Florida, 2000. Print.

—. *Citizenship from Below: Erotic Agency and Caribbean Freedom*. Durham: Duke UP, 2012. Print.

Shelton, Marie-Denise. *Image de la société dans le roman haïtien*. Paris: L'Harmattan, 1993. Print.

—. *Haïti et les autres: la révolution imaginée*. Paris: L'Harmattan, 2011. Print.

Shields, David S. 'Civilization.' *Keywords for American Cultural Studies*. Ed. Bruce Burgett and Glenn Hendler. New York: NYU Press, 2007. 44–49. Print.

Shipley, Maurice W. 'The Mulatto in American Literature.' *Reflections on Multiculturalism*. Ed. Robert Eddy. Yarmouth: Intercultural, 1996. 101–13. Print.

Shockley, William. *On Eugenics and Race: The Application of Science to the Solution of Human Problems*. Washington D.C.: Scott-Townsend, 1992. Print.

Silvestre, Augustin François. *Notice biographique sur M. Moreau de Saint-Mery: lue à la séance publique de la Société royale d'agriculture, le 18 avril 1819*. Paris: Imprimerie de Madame Huzard, 1819. Print.

Simonetta, Marcello and Noga Arikha. *Napoleon and the Rebel: A Story of Brotherhood, Passion, and Power*. Palgrave Macmillan, 2011. Print.

Sinclair, Harvey. *A Peep at the World; or, the Children of Providence, a novel*. Vol. 3 London: Printed for Parson and Sons, 1804. Print.

Singh, Nikhil Pal Singh. 'Liberalism.' *Keywords for American Cultural Studies*. Ed. Bruce Burgett and Glenn Hendler. New York: NYU Press, 2007. 139–45. Print.

Small, Curtis Jr. '"Cet homme est une nation": The Leader and the Collectivity in Literary Representations of the Haitian Revolution.' Diss. New York U, 2001. Thesis.

Smethurst, Paul. 'Introduction.' *Travel Writing, Form, and Empire: The Poetics and Politics of Mobility*. Ed. Julia Kuehn and Paul Smethurst. New York: Routledge, 2009. 1–20. Print.

Smith, James McCune. *A Lecture on the Haytien Revolutions; with a Sketch of the Character of Toussaint L'Ouverture*. New York: Daniel Fanshaw, 1841. Print.

Smith, Matthew J. '"From Dessalines to Duvalier" Revisited: A Quarter-century Retrospective.' *Journal of Haitian Studies* 13.1 (Spring 2007): 27–39. Print.

Smith, Phil. 'Whiteness, Normal Theory, and Disability Studies.' *Disability Studies Quarterly* 24.2. (Spring 2004) Web. <www.dsq-sds.org>. Accessed 15 April 2013.

Smith-Rosenberg, Carroll. 'Black Gothic: The Shadowy Origins of the American Bourgeoisie.' *Possible Pasts: Becoming Colonial in Early America*. Ed. Robert Blair St. George. Ithaca, NY: Cornell UP, 2000. 243–69. Print.

—. *This Violent Empire: The Birth of an American National Identity*. Williamsburg: U of North Carolina P, 2003. Print.

Socolow, Susan. 'Economic Roles of the Free Women of Color of Cap Francais.' *More than Chattel: Black Women and Slavery in the Americas.* Ed. David Barry Gaspar and Darlene Clark Hine. Bloomington: Indiana UP, 1996. 279–97. Print.

Sollors, Wernor. *Neither Black Nor White Yet Both: Thematic Explorations of Interracial Literature.* Cambridge, Harvard UP 1999, 1997. Print.

—. *Multilingual America: Transnationalism, Ethnicity, and the Languages of American Literature.* New York: New York UP, 1998. Print.

—. 'Introduction.' *Interracial Literature.* New York: New York UP, 2004. Print.

—. 'Introduction.' *Georges.* Tr. Tina Kover. New York: The Modern Library, 2007. xvi–xxv. Print.

Sommer, Doris. *Foundational Fictions: The National Romances of Latin America.* Berkeley: U of California P, 1993. Print.

Sonenscher, Michael. *Before the Deluge: Public Debt, Inequality, and the Intellectual Origins of the French Revolution.* Princeton, NJ: Princeton UP, 2009. Print.

Spears, Jennifer M. *Race, Sex, and Social Order in Early New Orleans.* Baltimore: Johns Hopkins UP, 2009.

The South Vindicated from the Treason and Fanaticism of the Northern Abolitionists. Philadelphia: H. Manley, 1836. Print.

'Speech of Dr. John S. Rock.' *Liberator* 3 February 1860: 19. Print.

St. George Tucker, 'A Dissertation on Slavery,' in Blackstone's Commentaries. 2: App. 31–32, 35–43, 54–55, 68–69, 74–81 (1803).' *The Founders' Constitution.* 1.15. Document 56. Chicago: U of Chicago P. Web. <http://press-pubs.uchicago.edu/founders/documents/v1ch15s56.html>. Accessed 10 January 2014.

St. John, Spencer. *Hayti; Or, The Black Republic.* London: Smith, Elder, and Company, 1884. Print.

Staël, (Anne-Louise) Germaine de. *De l'Influence des passions sur le bonheur des individus et des nations.* Lausanne: Jean Maurer Librairie, 1796. Print.

—. 'Mirza.' *Œuvres complètes de madame la baronne de Staël-Holstein. Œuvres posthumes de madame la baronne de Staël-Holstein, précédées d'une notice sur son caractère et ses écrits.* 2 vols. Paris: Firmin Didot, 1871. Print.

Stanley, Amy Dru. *From Bondage to Contract: Wage Labor, Marriage, and the Market in the Age of Slave Emancipation.* Cambridge, UK: Cambridge UP, 1998. Print.

'State of Hayti.' Rev. of 'La [*sic*] Système colonial dévoilé—Par le Baron de Vastey.' *The Port-Folio* 7.4 (April 1819): 315. Print.

Steele, Claude M. *Whistling Vivaldi: How Stereotypes Affect Us and What We Can Do.* New York: W.W. Norton, 2010. Print.

[Stephen, James.] *Buonaparte in the West Indies; or, The history of Toussaint Louverture, the African hero.* London: J. Hatchard, 1803. Print.

Stephen, James. *The History of Toussaint L'Ouverture.* New ed. London: J. Hatchard, 1814. Print.

Bibliography

Stephens, Michelle. *Black Empire: The Masculine Global Imaginary of Caribbean Intellectuals in the United States, 1914–1962*. Durham, NC: Duke UP, 2005.

Stewart, Maria. 'An Address Delivered at the African Masonic Hall, Boston, Feb. 27, 1833.' *Productions of Mrs. Maria W. Stewart presented to the First Africa Baptist Church & Society, of the City of Boston: a machine-readable transcription*. New York: The New York Public Library. Web. <http://digilib.nypl.org/dynaweb/digs/wwm9722/@Generic__BookView>. Accessed 1 February 2013.

—. 'An Address, Delivered Before the Afric-American Female Intelligence Society, of Boston.' *Productions of Mrs. Maria W. Stewart presented to the First Africa Baptist Church & Society, of the City of Boston: a machine-readable transcription*. New York: The New York Public Library. Web. <http://digilib.nypl.org/dynaweb/digs/wwm9722/@Generic__BookView>. Accessed 1 February 2013.

—. 'An Address, Delivered Before the Afric-American Female Intelligence Society, of Boston.' *The Liberator* 28 April 1832: 66–67. Print.

—. 'Lecture, Delivered at the Franklin Hall, Boston, Sept. 21, 1832.' *Productions of Mrs. Maria W. Stewart presented to the First Africa Baptist Church & Society, of the City of Boston: a machine-readable transcription*. New York: The New York Public Library. Web. <http://digilib.nypl.org/dynaweb/digs/wwm9722/@Generic__BookView>. Accessed 1 February 2013.

—. 'Lecture, Delivered at the Franklin Hall, Boston, Sept. 21, 1832.' *The Liberator* (17 November 1832): 183. Print.

—. 'An Address Delivered at the African Masonic Hall, Boston, Feb. 27, 1833.' *The Liberator* 4 May 1833: 72. Print.

—. 'Mrs. Stewart's Farewell Address to her Friends in the City of Boston, Delivered September 21, 1833.' *Productions of Mrs. Maria W. Stewart presented to the First Africa Baptist Church & Society, of the City of Boston: a machine-readable transcription*. New York: The New York Public Library. Web. <http://digilib.nypl.org/dynaweb/digs/wwm9722/@Generic__BookView>. Accessed 1 February 2013.

—. 'Religion and the Pure Principles of Morality, The Sure Foundation on Which We Must Build.' *Productions of Mrs. Maria W. Stewart presented to the First Africa Baptist Church & Society, of the City of Boston: a machine-readable transcription*. New York: The New York Public Library. Web. <http://digilib.nypl.org/dynaweb/digs/wwm9722/@Generic__BookView>. Accessed 1 February 2013.

Stoddard, Lorthrop. *The French Revolution in San Domingo*. Boston and New York: Houghton Mifflin, 1914. Print.

Stoler, Ann Laura. *Race and the Education of Desire: Foucault's History of Sexuality and the Colonial Order of Things*. Durham: Duke UP, 1995. Print.

—. *Along the Archival Grain: Epistemic Anxieties and Colonial Commonsense*. New Brunswick: Princeton UP, 2010a. Print.

—. *Carnal Knowledge and Imperial Power: Race and the Intimate in Colonial Rule*. Berkeley, CA: U of California P, 2010b. 2nd Edition. Print.

Stone, Kate. *Brokenburn: The Journal of Kate Stone, 1861–1868*. Ed. John Q. Anderson. Baton Rouge, LA: Louisiana State UP, 1995. Print.
Stowe, Harriet Beecher. *Uncle Tom's Cabin; or Life among the Lowly*. New York: Penguin, 1986. Web. Electronic Text Center. University of Virginia Library. Web. <http://web.archive.org/web/20110212020813/http://etext.lib.virginia.edu/etcbin/toccernew2?id=StoCabi.sgm&images=images/modeng&data=/texts/english/modeng/parsed&tag=public&part=all>. Accessed 10 January 2014.
Straw, Petine Archer. *Interplay Negrophilia: Avant-Garde Paris and Black Culture in the 1920s*. London: Thames and Hudson, 2000. Print.
Striker, Ardelle. 'Spectacle in the Service of Humanity: The Negrophile Play in France From 1789 to 1850.' *Black American Literature Forum* 19.2 (Summer 1985): 76–82. Print.
'Suite du Coup d'œil Politique sur la Situation actuelle du Royaume d'Hayti.' *Gazette Royale d'Hayti* 27 August 1816. Print.
The Sunday Times 1 November 1874. Print.
Sullivan-Hollemann, Elizabeth and Isabel Hillery Cobb. *The Saint-Domingue Epic: The de Rossignol des Dunes and Family Alliances*. Bay St. Louis, MS: The Nightingale Press, 1984. Print.
Sundquist, Eric. *To Wake the Nations: Race in the Making of American Literature*. Cambridge, MA: Harvard UP, 1993. Print.
—. 'Slavery, Revolution, and the American Renaissance.' Web. <http://www.unl.edu/Price/dickinson/sundquist.html>. Accessed 10 July 2009.
'Système Colonial Dévoil[é], Le'. *The Antijacobin Review; True Churchman's Magazine; and Protestant Advocate* 55.246 (November 1818): 242–51. Print.
Tinker, Edward Larocque. *Les Ecrits de langue française en Louisiane au XIXe siècle*. Paris: Librairie Ancienne Honoré Champion, 1932. Print.
'The Genius and Prospects of Negroes.' *Meliora* 1.2: 259–76. London: Partridge & Co, 1859. Print.
'The Horrors of San Domingo.' *The Atlantic Monthly* 11.68 (June 1863): 768–85. Print.
'The Slave King.' *The Albion, A Journal of News, Politics and Literature* 3 August 1833: 243. Print.
'The Slave King.' *Eastern Argus* 29 November 1833. Print.
The South Vindicated from the Treason and Fanaticism of the Northern Abolitionists. Philadelphia: H. Manly, 1836.
Thelwall, John. *The Daughter of Adoption: A Tale of Modern Times*. Ed. Michael Scrivener, Yasmin Solomonescu et al. Ontario, Canada: Broadview Press, 2013.
Thornton, John Wingate. *The Pulpit of the American Revolution*. Boston: D. Lorthrop and Co., 1860. Print.
'To Correspondents.' *Freedom's Journal* 2 November 1827. Print.
Todorov, Tzvetan. '"Race," Writing, and Culture.' *'Race,' Writing, and Difference*. Ed. Henry Louis Gates, Jr. Chicago: U of Chicago P., 1992. 370–80. Print.

Bibliography

—. *Conquest of America: The Question of the Other.* U of Oklahoma P, 1999. Print.

Tomkins, Fred. *Jewels in Ebony.* London: S.W. Partridge, c. 1866. Print.

Toumson, Roger. *La Transgression des couleurs: littérature et langage des Antilles.* Paris: Editions Caribéennes, 1990. Print.

'Toussaint L'Ouverture.' *Freedom's Journal* 4 May 1827; 11 May 1827; 18 May 1827. Print.

'Toussaint L'Ouverture.' *The Westminster and Foreign Quarterly Review* October–January 1850–51. Print.

'Toussaint L'Ouverture: a Biography and Autobiography.' Review. *The North American Review.* 98. 202 (1864): 595-602.

'Toussaint L'Ouverture and the Republic of Hayti.' *Chambers Miscellaney of instructive & entertaining tracts* 19 (1872): 132–64. Print.

Trouillot, Hénock. *La Condition de la femme de couleur à Saint-Domingue.* Port-au-Prince, Haiti: N.A. Théodore 1957. Print.

—. *Les Origines sociales de la littérature haïtienne.* Port-au-Prince, N.A. Théodore, 1962. Print.

'Translated for the *Boston Palladium*, Cape Henry (Hayti) Aug. 20.' *Daily National Intelligencer* 4.118 (16 October 1816): 2. Print.

Trouillot, Michel-Rolph. *Haiti: State against Nation: The Origins and Legacy of Duvalierism.* New York: Monthly Review Press, 1990. Print.

—. 'The Odd and the Ordinary.' *Cimarrón* 2.3 (1990): 3–12. Print.

—. *Silencing the Past: Power and the Production of History.* Boston: Beacon Press, 1995. Print.

Turner, Lorenzo Dow. 'Anti-slavery sentiment in American literature prior to 1865.' *The Journal of Negro History* 14.4 (October 1929): 371–72. Print.

Turner, Richard Brent. *Islam in the African-American Experience.* Indianapolis, IN: Indiana UP, 1997. Print.

Ulysse, Gina Athena. 'Writing, Performing and Pluralizing Haiti.' 21st Annual Haitian Studies Association Conference. Indiana University-Bloomington. 2009. Presentation.

—. 'Why Haiti Needs New Narratives More than Ever.' *Tectonic Shifts.* Ed. Mark Schuller and Pablo Morales. Sterling, VA: Kumarian Press, 2012.

—. *Why Haiti Needs New Narratives: A Post-Quake Chronicle.* Middletown, CT: Wesleyan UP, 2015.

Van Bergen, Jennifer. 'Introduction for *Another World is Possible.*' Web. <http://www.a-w-i-p.com/index.php/2010/01/03/reconstructing-leonora-sansay>. Accessed 4 February 2013.

Vandercook, John W. *Black Majesty: The Life of Christophe King of Haiti.* New York: Harper, 1928. Print.

'Varieties.' [a] *Freedom's Journal* 13 April 1827. Print.

'Varieties.' [b] *Freedom's Journal* 20 July 1827. Print.

'Varieties.' [c] *Freedom's Journal* 13 April 1827. Print.

Varin, Victor and Eugène Labiche. *Traversin et Couverture, parodie de Toussaint Louverture en quatre actes mêlés de peu de vers et de beaucoup de prose.* Paris: Michel Lévy frères, 1850. Print.

Vaissière, Pierre de. *St. Domingue, 1629–1789.* 1909. Qtd. and Tr. E.V. Goveia, *The West Indian Slave Laws of the Eighteenth Century* (Barbados: Caribbean Universities P, 1970. 44. Print.

Vapereau, Gustave. *Dictionnaire universel des littératures* ... Paris: Librairie Hachette, 1876. Print.

Varenne, P.A.L. (Pierre Anne Louis) Maton de la. *Valdeuil; ou les malheurs d'un habitant de St. Domingue.* Paris: L'éditeur, 1795. Print.

Vashon, George Boyer. 'Vincent Ogé.' Auburn, NY: Alden, Beardsley and Co., 1854. Print.

Vastey, Baron de. *Le Système coloniale dévoilé.* Cap-Henry: P. Roux Imprimerie du Roi, 1814a. Print.

—. *Notes à M. le Baron de V. P. Malouet, Ministre de la Marine et des Colonies, de Sa Majesté Louis XVIII, et ancien administrateur des Colonies et de la Marine, ex-colon de Saint-Domingue, etc., en réfutation du 4ème volume de son ouvrage, intitulé: Collection de mémoires sur les colonies, et particulièrement sur Saint-Domingue, etc.* Cap-Henry: P. Roux, 1814b. Print.

—. *A Mes Concitoyens.* Cap-Henry: P. Roux, imprimeur du Roi, 1815a. Print.

—. *Le Cri de la conscience.* Cap-Henry, P. Roux, 1815b. Print.

—. *Le Cri de la patrie, ou les intérêts de tous les Haytiens.* Cap-Henry: P. Roux, 1815c. Print.

—. *Réflexions adressées aux Haytiens de partie de l'Ouest et du Sud, sur l'horrible assassinat du Général Delvare, commis au Port-au-Prince, dans la nuit du 25 Décembre 1815, par les ordres de Pétion.* Cap-Henry: P. Roux, 1816a. Print.

—. *Communication officielle de trois lettres de Catineau Laroche: ex-colon, agent de Pétion; imprimées et publiées par ordre du gouvernement.* Cap-Henry: P. Roux, imprimeur du Roi, 1816b. Print.

—. *Translation of an Official Communication From The Government of Hayti, Dated 29 February 1816.* Tr. Marcus Rainsford. Bristol: John Evans Company, 1816c. Print.

—. *Réflexions sur une lettre de Mazères, ex-colon français, ... sur les noirs et les blancs, la civilisation de l'Afrique, le Royaume d'Hayti, etc.* Sans Souci: L'Imprimerie Royale, 1816d. Print.

—. *Réflexions on the Blacks and Whites: Remarks upon a Letter Addressed by M. Mazères, a French Ex-Colonist, to J.C.L. Sismonde de Sismondi* ... Tr. W.H.M.B. London: J. Hatchard, 1817a. Print.

—. *Réflexions politiques sur quelques Ouvrages et Journaux Français Concernant Haïti.* Sans Souci: L'Imprimerie Royale, 1817b. Print.

—. *Essai sur les causes de la révolution et des guerres civiles d'Hayti, faisant suite au Réflexions politiques sur quelques ouvrages et journaux français concernant Hayti.* Sans-Souci, Haïti: L'Imprimerie Royale, 1819. Print.

Bibliography

Vauthier, Simone. 'A Propos de l'image du noir aux Amériques dans la première moitié du dix-neuvième siècle.' *Recherches anglaises et américaines* 3 (1970): 67–98. Print.

—. 'Textualité et stéréotypes: Of African Queens and Afro-American Princes and Princesses: Miscegenation in *Old Hepsy*.' *Regards sur la littérature Noire américaine*. Ed. Michel Fabre. Paris: Publication du Conseil Scientifique de la Sorbonne Nouvelle, 1980. 65–107. Print.

Vaval, Duraciné. *Histoire de la littérature haïtienne: ou, 'L'âme noire.'* Imprimerie A. Héraux, 1933. Print.

Vergès, Françoise. *Monsters and Revolutionaries: Colonial Family Romance and Métissage*. Durham, NC: Duke UP, 1999. Print.

Venault de Charmilly, Pierre François. *Lettre à M. Bryan Edwards ... en réfutation de son ouvrage intitulé Vues historiques sur la colonie française de Saint-Domingue*. London: T. Baylis, 1797. Print.

Viatte, Auguste. *Histoire littéraire de l'Amérique Française des origines à 1950*. Paris: Presses Universitaires de France, 1955. Print.

Viau, M.H. 'The Poets and Poetry of Hayti.' *The Pine and Palm*. 7 December 1861: 4. Print.

'Victor Hugo: "The Grandfather of Humanity."' *The Literary World; a Monthly Review of Current Literature* 3 June 1882: 181. Print.

Vietto, Angela. 'Leonora Sansay.' *Dictionary of Literary Biography: American Women Writers to 1820*. Ed. Carla Munford, Angela Vietto, and Amy Winans. Detroit: Gale Research, 1999. 330–36. Print.

'Voici, sur Toussaint Louverture.' *Gazette nationale ou le moniteur universel* 20 nivôse, an 7. 448–49. Print.

Voltaire, François Marie Arouet de. *Candide*. Ed. Michelle Béguin and Jean Goldzink. Paris: Larousse-Bordas, 1998. Print.

—. *Essais sur les mœurs*. Web. <http://www.voltaire-integral.com/Html/11/04 INT_10.html#i2>. Accessed 5 May 2008.

Walcott, Derek. *The Haitian Trilogy: Plays: Henri Christophe, Drums and Colours, and The Haytian Earth*. New York: Farrar, Straus, and Giroux, 2002. Print.

Waldstreicher, David. *Runaway America: Benjamin Franklin, Slavery, and the American Revolution*. New York: Farrar, Straus, and Giroux, 2004. Print.

—. *A Companion to Benjamin Franklin*. Malden, MA: Wiley-Blackwell, 2011. Print.

Walker, David. *Walker's Appeal, in Four Articles; Together with a Preamble to the Coloured Citizens of the World, but in Particular, and Very Expressly, to Those of the united States of America*. Academic Affairs Library: UNC-Chapel Hill, 2001. Web. <http://docsouth.unc.edu/nc/walker/walker.html>. Accessed 24 January 2013.

Wallez, Jean Baptiste (Guislain). *Précis historique des négociations entre la France et Saint-Domingue; suivi de pièces justificatives, et d'une notice biographique sur le général Boyer, président de la république d'Haiti*. Paris: Ponthieu, 1826. Print.

Walsh, John Patrick. 'Toussaint Louverture at a Crossroads: The Mémoire of the "First Soldier of the Republic of Saint-Domingue."' *Journal of Haitian Studies* 17.1 (Spring 2011): 88–105. Print.

—. *Free and French in the Caribbean: Toussaint Louverture, Aimé Césaire, and Narratives of Loyal Opposition*. Bloomington, IN: Indiana UP, 2013. Print.

Ward, William S. 'American Authors and British Reviewers 1798–1826: A Bibliography.' *American Literature* 49.1 (March 1977): 1–21. Print.

Washington, Mary Helen. *Invented Lives: Narratives of Black Women 1860–1960*. Garden City, NY: Anchor Press, 1987. Print.

Weaver, Karol K. *Medical Revolutionaries: The Enslaved Healers of Eighteenth-Century Saint Domingue*. Urbana: U of Illinois P, 2006. Print.

Web, Frank J. *The Garies and their Friends*. 1857. Web. <http://www.gutenberg.org/cache/epub/11214/pg11214.html>. Accessed 3 January 2014.

Weiss, M. Lynn. 'Introduction.' *The Jew of Seville*. Victor Séjour. Tr. Norman R. Shapiro. Urbana and Chicago: U of Illinois P, 2002. xxi–xxii. Print.

West, Cornel. *The Cornel West Reader*. New York: Civitas Books, 1999. Print.

Weston, Helen.' Oath of the Ancestors by Lethière.' *An Economy of Colour: Visual Culture and the Atlantic World, 1660–1830*. Ed. Geoff Quilley and Kay Dian Kriz. Manchester and New York: Manchester UP, 2003. 176–95. Print.

Whipple, Charles K. 'Falsehood in Support of Slavery (From the Boston Atlas and Dailey Bee).' *Liberator, published as the Liberator* 30.3 (20 January 1860): 10. Print.

White, Ashli. *Encountering Revolution: Haiti and the Making of the Early Republic*. Baltimore: The Johns Hopkins UP, 2010. Print.

White, Charles. *An Account of the Regular Gradation in Man, and in Different Animals and Vegetables*. London, 1799. Print.

White, Hayden V. *Tropics of Discourse: Essays in Cultural Criticism*. Baltimore: Johns Hopkins UP, 1978. Print.

Whiteman, Maxwell. 'Introduction.' *St. Domingo, Its Revolution and Its Patriots*. William Wells Brown. Boston: B. Marsh, 1977. Print.

Whitlock, Gillian. 'Exiles from Tradition: Women's Life Writing.' *Re-siting Queen's English: Text and Tradition in Post-colonial Literatures*. Ed. Gillian Whitlock and Helen Tiffin. Atlanta: Rodopoi, 1992. 11–24. Print.

Whittaker, John R. 'Images of Exile and Racial Conflict in Lamartine's *Toussaint Louverture*.' *Mots Pluriels* 17 (April 2001): 1–9. Web. <http://www.arts.uwa.edu.au/MotsPluriels/MP1701jw.html>. Accessed 10 January 2014.

Wigmoore, Francis. 'Nineteenth- and Early-Twentieth-Century Perspectives on Women in the Discourse of Radical Black Caribbean Men.' *Small Axe* 7.1 (March 2003): 116–39. Print.

Wilberforce, William. *1840: The Correspondence of William Wilberforce*. Ed. Robert Isaac Wilberforce and Samuel Wilberforce. Volume 1. London: John Murray. Print.

Bibliography

Williams, Eric. *Capitalism and Slavery*. Chapel Hill: U of North Carolina P, 1944. Print.

Williams-Wynn, Frances. *Diaries of a Lady of Quality from 1797–1844*. 2nd ed. Ed. A. Hayward. London: Longman, 1864. Print.

Wimpffen, Alexandre-Stanislas, baron de. *A Voyage to Saint Domingo, in the Years 1788, 1789, and 1790*. Tr. J. Wright. London, 1817 [i.e. 1797]. Print.

—. *Voyage à Saint-Domingue, pendant les années 1788, 1789 et 1790*. 2 vols. Paris: Chez Cocheris, 1797. Print

Wimsatt, William K. and Monroe C. Beardsley, 'The Affective Fallacy.' *The Verbal Icon: Studies in the Meaning of Poetry*. Lexington, KY: U of Kentucky P, 1954. 21–40. Print.

Winant, Howard. 'Race and Race Theory.' *Annual Review of Sociology* 26 (August 2000): 169–85. Print.

Wisecup, Kelly. '"The Progress of the Heat Within": The West Indies, Yellow Fever, and Citizenship in William Wells Brown's *Clotel*' *The Southern Literary Journal* 41.1 (2008): 1–19. Print.

Woertendyke, Gretchen. 'Romance to Novel: A Secret History.' *Narrative* 17.3 (October 2009): 255–73. Print.

Wolosky, Shira. *Poetry and Public Discourse in Nineteenth-Century America*. Palgrave Macmillan, 2010. Print.

Wood, Marcus. *Blind Memory: Visual Representations of Slavery in England and America*. New York: Routledge, 2000. Print.

—. *Slavery, Empathy, and Pornography*. Oxford: Oxford UP, 2003. Print.

Wood, Susan. 'Saving a National Icon: Guillon-Lethière's Oath of the Ancestors.' Web. <http://www2.oakland.edu/oujournal/files/19_haitian.pdf>. Accessed 10 October 2013.

Wordsworth, William. 'To Toussaint L'Ouverture.' *The Morning Post*. 2 February 1803.

'Work of Victor Séjour is Described in New Phylon.' *Atlanta Daily World* 8 February 1943: 3. Print.

Wright, John. *Refutation of the sophisms, gross misrepresentations, and erroneous quotations contained in 'An American's' 'Letter to the Edinburgh reviewers.'* Washington, D.C.: Printed for the Author, 1820. Print.

Wright, W.W. 'Free Negroes in Hayti.' *De Bow's Review* 27 (1859): 526–49. Print.

Yellin, Jean Fagan. *The Intricate Knot: Black Figures in American Literature, 1776–1863*. New York: New York UP, 1972. Print.

—. *The Abolitionist Sisterhood: Women's Political Culture in Antebellum America*. Ithaca: Cornell UP, 1994. Print.

Young, Robert. *Colonial Desire: Hybridity in Theory, Culture, and Race*. New York: Routledge, 1995. Print.

Youngquist, Paul and Grégory Pierrot. 'Introduction.' *An Historical Account of the Black Empire of Hayti*. Ed. Paul Youngquist and Grégory Pierrot. Durham: Duke UP, 2013. Print.

Yudell, Michael. 2011: 'A Short History of the Concept of Race'. *Race and the Genetic Revolution: Science, Myth, and Culture.* Ed. Sheldon Krimsky and Kathleen Sloan. New York: Columbia UP. 13–30. Print.

Zackodnick, Theresa C. *The Mulatta and the Politics of Race.* Jacksonville: UP of Mississippi, 2004. Print.

Zamora, Margarita. 'Historicity and Literariness: Problems in the Literary Criticism of Spanish American Colonial Texts.' *MLN* 102.2 (March 1987): 334–46. Print.

Zanger, Jules. 'The Tragic Octoroon in Pre-Civil War Fiction.' *American Quarterly* 18.1 (Spring 1966): 63–70. Print.

Zantop, Susanne. *Colonial Fantasies: Conquest, Family, and Nation in Precolonial Germany, 1770–1870.* Durham: Duke UP, 1997. Print.

'*Zelica, the Creole, a novel by an American. 3 Vols.*' *The Independent, a London Literary and Political Review* 9 (3 March 1821): 141–43. Print.

Ziarek, Ewa. 'Bare Life.' *Impasses of the Post-Global: Theory in the Era of Climate Change.* Ed. Henry Sussman. Vol. 2. Web. 15 September 2012. <http://quod.lib.umich.edu/o/ohp/10803281.0001.001/1:11/--impasses-of-the-post-global-theory-in-the-era-of-climate?rgn=div1;view=fulltext>. Accessed 5 December 2012.

Zuckerman, Michael. 'The Power of Blackness: Thomas Jefferson and the Revolution in Saint-Domingue.' *Almost Chosen People: Oblique Biographies in the American Grain.* Berkeley: Berkeley UP, 1993. 175–218. Print.

Index

abolitionism 3, 37, 42–43, 481, 491–504, 513, 522, 558n22, 587
Adams, John Quincy 176
Afric-American Female Intelligence Society 320
Agamben, Giorgio 453, 602n43
Alexander, Leslie M. 290n4
Aléxis, Jacques Stéphen 421
Allan, Seán 297
Allen, Richard 311n23
Allewaert, Monique 207, 255, 257, 440–41n21
Allport, Gordon 134
Ames, Fisher 421–22
Anzaldúa, Gloria 234
Appiah, Kwame Anthony 20, 26–27, 28, 46, 64, 522–23
Aravamudan, Srinivas 49–50n1, 157–58, 226, 325
Ardouin, Beaubrun 20, 21, 29, 42, 107n27, 135, 402, 424, 428–30, 437n19, 457n33, 465, 470, 472, 479n4, 505, 513, 525
   depiction of Haitian history 526
   dispute with Isambert 539–45
   Géographie d'Haïti 533–34, 545–47
   Résponse 551
Arendt, Hannah 605
Aristide, Jean-Bertrand 602, 610
Arnold, A. James 134
Arnold, James 348
Arnold, Samuel James 260n7
Arrizón, Alicia 348
Arthaud, Charles 65

Baartman, Saartije 388n15
Bacon, Jacqueline 311, 314–15
Baignoux, Pierre Philippe 357n12
Baker, William Spohn 381–82
Baldwin, James 334–35
Balzac, Honoré de 331
Banks, Joseph 316
Barbé-Marbois, François 92n15
Barillon 99–100
Barré, Pierre-Yon 341n12
Barré Saint-Venant, Jean 75, 98–99, 188, 535
Barskett, James 312n24
Bassard, Katherine Clay 294n8, 300
Baucom, Ian 602–3
Beard, John Relly 22–23, 41–42, 47, 53, 60n13, 63, 171n12, 214, 462, 472
   biography of Toussaint Louverture 474–75, 476–78, 481, 493–94, 496
   use of racial tropes and hierarchies 479–80, 483–91, 493, 497–98, 502, 510–11, 517
Beardsley, Monroe C. 571–72, 574

• 679 •

Beckles, Hilary 199–200, 205, 213
Behn, Aphra 157
Belair, Charles 208n6, 386
Belair, Sannite 208n6
Bell, Carolyn Cossé 353–54
Bell, Madison Smartt 67n19
Bem, Jeanne 179n20
Benniol, Jean-Luc 7
Benoist, Jean 7
Bénot, Yves 402–3
Bentley, Nancy 331
Benzaken, Jean-Charles 534
Bercy, Drouin de 49
Bergeaud, Eméric 30n20, 41, 107n27, 110, 213–14, 344, 430–32
  non-use of racial taxonomies 480
  Stella 412–19, 424–25, 428–29, 439–56, 459–60
Berlant, Lauren 33
Berman, Carolyn Vellenga 353
Bernardin de Saint-Pierre 420–21
Berthier, J.-B.C. 153, 155, 270n12
Bethel, Elizabeth Rauh 313n26
Bhabha, Homi K. 7, 38, 450–51
Biassou, Georges 8, 124n8, 158, 515, 516, 546, 567
Biassou, Jean 343–44
Bigelow, John 511n31
Binns, Edward 144
Bissette, Cyrille A. 345n1, 348, 467, 490, 525–26n1, 539n10
  critique of Schoelcher 528–29, 530–31, 551, 553–54, 566–67n28
Blanckaert, Claude 76
Block, Sharon 280
Blumenbach, Johann Friedrich von 86n9
Boisrond-Tonnèrre, Louis 17, 31–32, 108, 128, 158, 162, 271n13
  Mémoire pour servir à l'histoire d'Haïti 423–24, 425–26, 428, 452, 502, 518, 520–21
Bonaparte, Josephine 377–79n6
Bonaparte, Napoléon 37, 54, 377–78, 390–91

Bongie, Chris 15, 30n20, 54n5, 146–47, 167, 168–69n11, 170, 176–77, 190, 217n13, 273–74, 348, 490, 528, 557, 559
  criticism of Bissette 530
  Friends and Enemies 66, 478–79
Bonneau, Alexandre 108–9, 371, 383n12, 422, 436–38, 456n30, 476n2, 478
  comments on "racial mixing" 489–90
  Haïti: ses progrès et son avenir 459–60
  theories of "white" supremacy 528
Bonnet, Edmond 214
Bonnet, Guy Joseph 18, 100–101, 128–29, 214
le Borgne de Boigne, Claude Pierre Joseph 122, 126, 127, 183, 194
Boukman, Dutty 515
Boulle, Pierre 7, 64
Bouvet de Cressé, Jean-Baptiste 220, 423n8
Boyer, Jean-Pierre 68, 127n12, 143–44, 310, 317n30, 467, 577
  ruling of Haiti 527, 581–82
Brantlinger, Patrick 71–72
Braziel, Jana Evans 208n6
Brickhouse, Anna 30n20, 351, 354n7, 559, 566n28, 569, 580–81n37, 590n41, 609
Brière, Jean-François 539–40n11
Brockden Brown, Charles 105–6
Brody, Jennifer Devere 331
Brooks, David 1, 606–7, 610, 611
Brouard, Carl 568
Brouard, H.A. 532–33n8
Brown, Sterling 330
Brown, William Wells 41–42, 150, 305–6, 349, 359, 363–64, 384, 412, 436n18, 460, 461i, 467, 472, 474
  abolitionist writing 481, 491–504, 558n22
  Clotel 148–49, 330–31, 331n1, 355, 482
  The Rising Son 501

Index

Bruce, Dickson 289–91, 311–12
Brueys d'Aigalliers, Gabriel-François 23, 198–99n1
Buffon, Comte de, Georges Louis Leclerc 86, 88–89, 91n13, 93–94n17
Bullock, Penelope 331–32
Burnham, Michelle 281
Burr, Aaron 227, 253–54n1, 255, 262–63, 491n9
Buscaglia-Salgado, José 10–11, 67, 71, 250, 450
Bush, Barbara 204, 205–6, 207n5, 208, 216

Camus, Albert 410–11
Camus, Michel 221
Candler, John 475
  Brief Notices on Hayti 476–77
Carlyle, Thomas 60, 140n18, 486, 491, 496
Carteau, Félix 173–74
Casimir, Jean 47, 216–17
Césaire, Aimé 112, 116, 119–20, 457–58, 458, 603
  Discourse on Colonialism 116–17, 118
Chanlatte, F.D. 182, 581
Chanlatte, Juste 17, 139, 182, 422–23n6, 502, 521, 560, 585
Chapman, Maria Weston 276, 329
Charles, Carolle 231, 275
Charles, Christophe 423n6
Charlevoix, Pierre Francois Xavier de 65n17
Charlot, Charles 530n5
Charmilly, Venault de 96, 116n4, 188, 438, 535
Chateaubriand, René de 187
Chavanne, Mark 58
Chavannes, Jean-Baptiste 22
Child, Lydia Maria 60, 276n16, 278n19, 283, 286, 330–31, 349, 412, 493–94
  writing about Louverture 382
Choiseul-Gouffier, Sophie de 44n21
Chomsky, Noam 605

Christophe, Henry 8, 23, 24, 31, 37, 66, 68, 78, 102, 123–26, 343–44, 478–79
  trope of 'black legend' 22
Clark, Emily 266–67
Clark, Vèvè 110–11, 402
Clarkson, Thomas 276n16
Clavin, Matthew 380n9, 382, 509
Clay, Henry 508n28
Coisnon, abbé 378, 392–93
Cole, Jean Lee 290, 291, 310–11
Colombel, Noël 468
colonialism 119–21
  Césaire 116–17, 118
  Oedipal significations of colonial revolution 373–76
  Vastey 111–51, 430, 451, 519, 567
Colwill, Elizabeth 217
Condé, Maryse 134
Conrad, Joseph 191
Constant, Benjamin 85–86, 544n14
Constant, Fred 46
Cooper, Anna Julia 300n13
Cooper, James Fenimore 422
Cordier, abbé Alphonse 76n2
Cornevin, Robert 421
Cornish, Samuel 311, 314
Coulter, Ann 586
Courtenay, George W.C. 137–38n16, 505n25
Cousin d'Avallon, Charles Yves 55, 70n20, 378n5, 454n29
Crawford, William Harris 508n28
"creole" 6, 22–23, 177, 281
Croly, David Goodman 438
Curran, Andrew S. 7, 488
Curtis, Lesley 30n20, 421n4
Cushing, Caleb 127n12
Cuvier, Georges 388n15

Dain, Bruce 11n11, 145, 335
Dalmas, Antoine 169n11, 174
Daminois, Adèle 341–42n13, 343, 348–49
D'Arcy, Uriah 152
Darfour, Félix 437, 529

• 681 •

Dash, J. Michael 30n20
D'Auberteuil, Hilliard 49, 83, 93n16, 94n17, 199, 220
Dauxion-Lavayasse, Jacques-François 125n10, 131n13, 140n19
Davis, Matthew L. 255
Dayan, Colin (Joan) 30n20, 77, 199, 254, 358, 439
  Haiti, History and the Gods 197–98
de Cauna, Jacques 169n11, 170, 174
de Gouges, Olympe 246, 248–49n28
de Jean, Joan 256
de Kock, Leon 44
de Loyac, J. 152
de Pauw, Cornelius 88
de Saillet, Alexandre 106–7, 275–76, 277
de Wimpffen, Baron Alexandre-Stanislaus 81–82, 226, 236
Debois, Oneida 321n33
Declaration of the Rights of Man 4, 9, 10n8, 11, 118
Défilée-la-folle (Défilée Bazille) 208n6
Delille, abbé Jacques 366
Delorme, Demesvar 401, 610
Descourtilz, Michel Etienne 39, 82, 92n15, 169n11, 174–76, 209n8, 273
Desormeaux, Daniel 30n20, 376n2, 385–86n14, 388–90
Dessalines, Jean-Jacques 8, 17, 31–32, 37, 68, 128–29, 158, 162, 184, 209, 214, 310, 343–44
  revolutionary rhetoric 576
  symbol of 'negro' savagery 84–86
  trope of 'black legend' 22
Dillon, Elizabeth Maddock 253–54, 575
Dixon, Chris 26, 462
Doin, Sophie 283, 342–43, 348–49
Dominique, Lyndon J. 227
Donnadieu, Jean-Louis 51–52, 383
Dorsey, Joseph 263n9
Douglass, Frederick 197, 276n16, 317, 318, 382, 495n17
Dow, Mark 192–93, 610

Drescher, Seymour 245
Drexler, Michael 254, 257, 262, 292–93, 575
Drouin de Bercy 66, 73, 77, 98, 103–4, 122, 184, 194, 438
Du Bois, W.E.B. 150–51, 197, 220, 402, 440
  The Souls of Black Folk 17, 368–69
Du Tertre, abbé Jean-Baptiste 57, 78–80, 95–96
Dubois, F.E. 465n5, 505, 532n8, 582–83, 585
Dubois, Laurent 9, 10n8, 21n16, 47, 104, 427–28n13, 598
Duboy, Alexandre 357n12
Dubroca, Louis 52–53, 54n7, 55–56, 69–70, 124n8, 435
  portrayal of Louverture 378n5, 394, 395
duCille, Anne 331n1
Ducœurjoly, S.J. 201–2
Dumas, Alexandre 163–65n8, 331, 347n3, 370–71, 381, 420
Dumas, Pierre 149
Dumesle, Hérard 386, 423, 467, 502, 526
  opposition to Boyer's rule 527
Dupré, Antoine 422–23
Dupuy, Alex 20, 466
Duras, Claire de, *Ourika* 227, 300–302, 304
During, Simon 215, 450
Duvalier, François 610
Duvalier, Jean-Claude 610
Duvivier, Ulrick 413–14n2

Easley, Alexis 256
Edgeworth, Maria 60
Edwards, Bryan 14, 58n9, 59n12, 70, 71, 82, 96, 109, 153, 169n11, 187–88, 307–8, 357, 384, 433n15, 442, 513, 535–36, 594, 595
Elie, Auguste 505
Equiano, Olaudah 229, 387
  The Interesting Narrative of the Life of Olaudah Equiano 17

Index

Esterquest, Ralph T. 56n8
Ethéart, Liautaud 401, 402, 423, 437n19
Etienne, Servais 170, 177–78
Ewcorstart, John K. 142–44

Fabella, Yvonne 235, 236
Fabre, Michel 381
Fanon, Frantz 33–34, 234, 584–85, 589
  Peau Noire, Masques Blancs 17
Fardin, Dieudonné 421
Farmer, Paul 469, 609
Farred, Grant 462–63
Farrison, William Edward 493–94
Fatiman, Cécile 208n6
Faubert, Fénélon 556n20
Faubert, Pierre 22, 30n20, 42, 131n13, 401, 423, 472–73, 524, 526, 553–54
  Ogé, ou le préjugé de couleur 555–67, 568–603
Faulkner, William 330, 601
  Absalom, Absalom! 345, 355, 369
Fauset, Jessie Redmon 580n35
female literary societies 320–21
Female Literary Society of Philadelphia 320–21, 325–26
Ferguson, James 544
Ferguson, Moira 219n15
Ferrer, Ada 2
Fick, Carolyn 9, 563n23
Finch, Julie 292
Firmin, Antènor 189–90, 401, 464n4, 470n10
Fischer, Sibylle 2, 128
Fitzhugh, George 140n18, 478, 491
  Sociology of the South 487–88
  theories of "white" supremacy 528
Forten, James 292
Forten, Sarah Louise 292–93
Foster, Frances Smith 289–91, 311n23, 326, 372n21
Foucault, Michel 429–30
Fouchard, Jean 198–99n1
Fouron, Georges 45, 432

Francis, Wigmore 30n20
Frank, Luanne T. 34
Franklin, Benjamin 171–72, 283, 483
Franklin, James 138–40
Freedom's Journal 289, 290, 291, 311–14, 317–19n30
Furcy de Brémoy, H. 84–85, 343, 357

Garran de Coulon, Jean-Philippe 17–18, 87–88, 96, 100, 169, 185, 246–47n26, 429, 549, 563
Garraway, Doris 30n20, 77, 129, 199, 232, 237, 336, 373–74, 440
  The Libertine Colony: Creolization in the Early French Caribbean 16
Garrigus, John 13, 15, 19, 58n9, 77, 94, 178n19, 198, 199, 558–59, 561, 573, 595
  analysis of *La Mulâtre* 242, 244–45, 247
Garrison, William Lloyd 276n16, 277n17, 291, 306, 308–9n20
  The Liberator 320–23n34, 504
Gate, Henry Louis Jr. 229
Gauthier, Florence 33
Gautier, Arlette 208, 219n15
Gautier, Théophile 401
Geffrard, Fabre 464, 465, 504n24, 528–29, 569, 578, 582
Geggus, David 2, 92n15, 464, 567
Ghachem, Malick 185
Gillman, Susan 54n5, 180, 441n22
Gilman, Sander 266
Gilmore, Paul 47
Gilroy, Paul 458, 463
  Against Race 33–34
Girard, Patrick 164
Girard, Philippe 2, 9, 24, 51–52, 68–69, 71, 105, 204, 207n5, 244–45n21, 252n30, 259n6, 271n13, 383, 462
Girod de Chantrans, Justin 205, 226, 235, 332–33, 353
Gliddon, George R. 142
Glissant, Edouard 430, 449

• 683 •

Gobineau, Arthur (Comte de) 57,
    189–90, 433–34, 456n30, 478,
    486, 491
  theories of "white" supremacy 528
Gold, Herbert 1, 610
  Haiti: Best Nightmare on Earth 48
Goldberg, David Theo 483
Goldstein, Robert Justin 540n12
Goldstein Sepinwall, Alyssa 26
Goode, Mike 394
Goudie, Sean 255n4, 283
Gragnon-Lacoste, Thomas Prosper
    377n4, 381, 384, 397n18
Great Britain 3
Greene, Graham 610
Greenwood, Grace 494n14
Grégoire, abbé Henri 100n22, 121n7,
    125–26, 145n25, 238n15, 242n18,
    366–67, 561, 565n26
"griffe" 4, 17–18, 89–90, 170–71,
    189–90, 193, 386, 397, 398,
    464n4, 529n4
Gros, M. 27–28n18, 39, 98, 169n11
Gross, Ariela J. 528
Grossman, Catherine 168n10
Gruesz, Kirsten Silva 54n5, 180
Guillon-Lethière, Guillaume
    446–48n25
Guizot, François 544n14

Haiti
  2010 earthquake 606–7, 608–9
  first Haitian constitution 128
  Haitian 'exceptionalism' 136, 146,
    151, 436, 460, 537, 548, 605–11
  Haitian Revolution 1–2, 24–25, 43
  contribution of women 288,
    319–20
  "Enlightenment literacy
    narrative" 4–5, 9–10n8, 36,
    50–53
  fictionalised accounts 152–95
  "mulatto/a vengeance narrative"
    4–5, 9–10, 15–17, 29, 32–33,
    34, 36, 67–68, 97–98, 281–82,
    475–76, 611

Oedipal significations of colonial
    revolution 373–76
  revision of historical accounts
    2–4, 11–13, 110–12, 128
  subject of Haiti's first works of
    literature 422–23
  witness accounts 29–30
  origin of national flag 439–40, 441,
    556, 569–70
  regeneration of 577–78
  replication of "racial" divisions in
    independent Haiti 28–29,
    194–95, 486
Hamilton, William 140–41n20
Hanchard, Michael 147
Harper, Frances Ellen Watkins 256, 330
Harris, Wilson 449
Harrison, Lawrence E. 607n2
Hartman, Geoffrey 218
Hartman, Saidiya 360, 361–62
Harvey, William Woodis 136–37, 475
Hathaway, Heather 332
Hayward, Abraham 137–38
Hazareesingh, Sudhir 544n14
Hearne, John 138n16
Hédouville, General Marie Gabriel-
    Théodore 442–43n24, 549–50
Hegel, Georg Wilhelm Friedrich 27
Heidegger, Martin 34
Heinl, Nancy 607–8, 611
Heinl, Robert 607–8, 611
Helme, Elizabeth 83n4
Hemmings, Sally 223–24
Henry, Patrick 508n28
Hérard, Charles 466n7, 532n8, 578, 582
Hesse, Carla 246n25
Heuer, Jennifer 246
Heureuse, Marie-Claire 209–11n8, 273
Hibbert, Fernand 421
Hilliard d'Auberteuil, Michel-René 14
Hoffmann, Léon-François 8, 24–25,
    26, 30n20, 166–67, 168, 260n7,
    300–301n14, 327n36, 331
  analysis of Haitian writers 424n9
  study of Bergeaud's *Stella* 419, 420,
    421, 445

• 684 •

Index

Holgersson-Shorter, H. 223–24
Holly, James Theodore 387, 436n18, 474, 480–81, 493
Horton, James Oliver 314n27, 318–19, 324
Hughes, Helen 257–58
Hugo, Jean-Abel 170–71n12
Hugo, Victor 109, 158–95, 270n12, 419, 422
   Bug-Jargal 39, 158–95, 274–75, 350, 366, 390, 592, 606
Hull, Gloria T. 288
Hulme, Peter 5n4
Hunt, Alfred 85, 498n20, 504n24
Hunt, Benjamin 435–36, 493
Hunt, Lynn 95, 373–74

Iannini, Christopher 44, 488n8, 507–8
Inginac, Joseph Balthazar 310, 456n32, 477, 530
Isambert, François André 538–45
Israel, Jonathan 595

Jackson, Maurice 311
Jacobs, Edward 244n20
Jacobs, Harriet 300n13, 363
   Incidents in the Life of a Slave Girl 361
James, C.L.R. 9, 42, 250, 462, 483, 513, 521–22
   The Black Jacobins 49, 52–53, 55, 57, 62–64, 65, 66, 462
James, Winston 317–18
Janvier, Louis Joseph 435, 437n19, 459, 469–71, 552n19, 587n39
Jean-François 515, 516, 546, 567
Jeannot 515
Jefferson, Thomas 86, 87, 93, 94, 144–45, 223–24, 345, 365–66
   "racial" separatist ideology 488–89, 491n9, 506–9
Jenson, Deborah 30n20, 85, 199, 215, 231–32, 271n13, 425n12
   Beyond the Slave Narrative 16
Johnson, Sara 30n20
Jonaissant, Jean 421

Jouannet, Emilie, *Zorada* 227–28, 300–301n14, 304, 331

Kadish, Doris 161–62, 246, 250n29, 342n14, 479–80
Kaisary, Philip 30–31n20
Kent, H.W. 241
Kerby, Anthony 34
Kerverseau, François-Marie Périchou 516
Kidder, Tracy 602, 608
King, Rufus 508n28
Kleist, Heinrich von 39, 153–54, 297–99, 302–3, 419
Kock, Bernard 508n28
Kord, Suzanne 208–9n7
Kujawaska-Lis, Ewa 191

La Mulâtre comme il y a beaucoup de blanches 40, 208, 219, 225–52, 297, 331
La Plaine, Marie Louise 220–21
Labat, Jean-Baptiste 74, 76n2, 81, 95–96
Labiche, Eugène 408–10
Lacan, Jacques 374n1
Lacroix, Pamphile de 49, 54n5, 55–56, 85, 101, 104, 107–8, 169n11, 170n12, 172–73, 177–78, 312n25, 412, 425n11, 436, 442, 475, 483, 513, 517
   writing about Louverture 379, 380, 386, 392, 396–99, 549
   writing about Ogé 536–37, 600
Lamartine, Alphonse de 299, 331, 344, 392, 419, 422, 475, 520
   Histoires des Girondins 562–63
   Toussaint Louverture 41, 327n36, 355, 367, 378–80, 398, 399–410, 412, 449, 564n24
Lamartinière, Marie-Jeanne 208n6
Lamming, George 586
Laplace, François 92n15
Lapsansky, Philip 257
Larabee, Jeanne 251
Lavainne, Elie-Joseph-Brun 211

· 685 ·

Lavallée, Joseph 225n10, 273–74n15, 293, 341, 343, 348–49, 428
Laveaux, Etienne 52–55n7, 55, 61, 442
Lazarus, Emma 583
le Glaunec, Jean-Pierre 212n11
le Gorgeu, Georges 54n7, 110, 377n4, 378n6, 381
Le Normand, Marie 377–78
Le Pers, Jean-Baptiste 57, 64–65, 74–75, 76n1, 95–96
Le Vaillant, François 82–83
Leclerc, Bernard Barthélemi Louis 211
Leclerc, General Charles 37, 59, 68, 84, 104–7, 121, 124, 149, 206, 215, 245n22, 376, 395
Leclerc, Pauline 258–59
Ledoux, Marie-Rose 223–24n8
Leger, Jacques Nicolas 442n23
Lemonnier-Delafosse, Jean-Baptiste 75–76
Levaigneur, M. 198–99, 202n4
Levasseur, Armand 84, 425n12
Levine, Robert S. 502
Levrault, Louis 153–54, 155
  'A Haytian Legend' 302–3n16, 304–5
Lhérisson, Justin 421, 568
Limbaugh, Rush 586
Lincoln, Abraham 508n28
Linné, Carl von (Linnaeus) 86n9
Lipsitz, George 447–49
Literary Society of Philadelphia 320
Liu, Tessie 253, 262
Locke, Mamie E. 317
Lockett, James D. 508n28
Long, Edward 86–87, 117, 432–33, 488n8
  History of Jamaica 203
Longfellow, Henry Wadsworth 276n16
Louverture, Isaac 37, 375, 377–79n4, 391, 392, 475, 544
  memoirs 383–84, 398–99, 476n2
Louverture, Jeanne Baptiste 377n4
Louverture, Placide 37, 375, 377–79n4, 384, 391, 392, 520

Louverture, Suzanne 210, 271–72, 377, 398
Louverture, Toussaint 8, 9, 37, 41–42, 47, 53i, 149, 162, 343–44, 374–80, 389i
  characterisation as 'black legend' 22, 498–99, 526, 527–28, 537, 547–48
  conflict with Rigaud 413, 441–43, 485–86
  described in racialized terms 69–71
  family genealogy 377n4, 397n18
  impact of enslavement 16, 68
  reading of Raynal's 'Black Spartacus' passage 49–54n3, 60–61, 543
  subject of biographies 474–76, 545
  used as symbol of Haitian independence 318, 543–44
  writings as person of color 17, 29, 30, 110, 376
Lowell, James Russell 276n16

McAlister, Elizabeth 608n3
McClellan, James 8, 11, 65n18, 80
McCune Smith, James 290–91
McGill, Meredith 3n3, 481
Mackenzie, Anna Maria 277n18
Mackenzie, Charles 459, 486
MacLeod, Murdo J. 470–71n12
MacQueen, James 206
Madiou, Thomas 208n6, 216, 424, 430, 464, 467, 502, 519
  Histoire d'Haïti 564–65, 573
Magny, Etienne 467, 528–29
Maingot, Anthony 463–64
Malchow, H.L. 4, 10n9, 46n23, 68
Malenfant, Colonel Charles 169n11, 206–7, 215–16, 513, 549
Malouet, Victor 14, 75, 122, 131n13, 142n22, 194, 438
  proposal for new 'colonial system' 101–3, 119
Manganelli, Kimberly 261, 267, 300–301n14

Index

Marcelin, Frédéric 413–14n2, 420–21, 471
Marion, Gérard Gabriel 221–22n2
Marshall, John 508n28
Martí, José 441n22
Martineau, Harriet 276n16, 512–13
The Hour and the Man 60–62, 65, 66, 307, 343–44, 475, 511n31
Marty, Anne 421n4
Mazères, M. 122, 194, 438, 535, 549, 593–94, 595
Meade, Bishop William 493–94
Medina, Franco Agoustine 131n14, 577
Melville, Herman 109, 154–55, 194–95
'Benito Cereno' 154n4, 194, 365, 436
Memmi, Albert 120
Menonville, Thierry de 64–65n17
Mercier, Louis-Sébastien 49–50n1
Métral, Antoine 69, 71, 83, 178–79n19, 181–83, 203–4, 211, 214–15, 333, 336, 412
  writing about Louverture 373, 379–80, 383–84, 384–85, 397n18
Mialaret, Yves 210–11
Michelet, Athénaïs 210–11
Michelet, Jules 25, 210, 573
Midgley, Claire 266
Milhet, Louise Catherine 221n1
Miller, Christopher L. 164–65, 246, 248–49, 250n29, 302n15
Milscent, Jules Solime 182, 422–23n6, 457
Minerva Literary Association 320
Mirecourt, Eugène de 370–71
"miscegenation" 4–5, 8, 38, 45–46n23, 57, 76–77, 94n17, 137, 199, 203–4
Mitchell, Angelyn 499–500
Moitt, Bernard 207n5, 217–18n14, 219n15
Monroe, James 507, 509
Montfort, Catherine R. 246
Moore, Thomas 260n7
Moreau de Saint-Méry dall'Asta, Aménaïde 220–25, 229, 239, 241n17

Moreau de Saint-Méry, M.L.E. 4, 15n14, 19n15, 23–24, 49, 55, 61n14, 62, 87, 90–95, 98n20, 231, 235, 240i, 242, 243n19
  characterizations of women 235, 236, 237, 238n15
  classification system 170–71, 172, 193, 226, 371n20, 483
  relationship with daughter 220–25, 239, 241n17
  writing about "racial mixing" 200–201, 223–24, 283, 338, 353, 433, 435–36
Morpeau, Louis 413–14n2
Morrison, Toni 251, 368
  Playing in the Dark 16–17
Mozard, Théodore-Charles 97
Mucher, Christen 30n20, 421n4
mulâtresse
  bias of male-authored descriptions 205–6, 230, 231
  female benevolence as resistance 207–11, 264–73, 304–5
  as female revolutionaries 215–16
  overly sexualised portrayals 200, 205, 222–23, 266–67
  participation in Haitian revolution and anti-slavery activism 206
  racial characterizations 204–5, 218–19, 222–23
  'rape culture' 263–64
  theories about revenge motivations 200–202
"mulatto" 4–7, 9, 10–11, 16, 32–33, 68–70, 78
  characterization of 'mulattoes' 74–77
  creation of 'mulatto legend' 22, 41–42
  social distinctions 13–15
  term of subjugation 17–19, 21n16, 192
"mulatto"; *see also* race, racial tropes, *mulâtresse*
"mulatto/a vengeance narrative" 4–5, 9–10, 15–17, 29, 32–33, 34, 36, 67–68, 97–98, 281–82, 475–76, 611

• 687 •

Nau, Emile 422, 424, 526, 532n8, 546–47, 594–95
  Histoire des Caciques 431–32
  opposition to Boyer's rule 527
Nau, Ignace 423
"negro" 4, 6, 12–14, 16, 18–19, 20–21, 27, 33–34, 46, 47, 57, 63–64, 88, 113, 281
  narrative of 'negro' savagery 57, 75, 82–85
Nelson, John Herbert 60n13
Nesbitt, Nick 9, 10n8, 30n20, 110, 115, 555, 600
Newman, Simon P. 3–4
Ngugi wa Thiong'o 150
Nicholls, David 37–38, 41, 42, 243n19, 460, 483
  "color" theory 462–66, 469–71, 472, 485, 493, 527, 528, 532n8, 548
  From Dessalines to Duvalier 19–25, 26, 41, 146, 464
  influence of Schoelcher 525
Nicholson, J.-B.-M. 80–81, 83, 95–96
Nightingale, Florence 60
Niles Weekly Register 124–25
Noah, Mordecai Manuel 315
Nora, Pierre 110–11
Northrup, Solomon 586–87
Nott, Josiah C. 87n10, 142, 432–33
Ntsobe, André Marie 188–89

Obama, Barack 586
O'Connell, David 345–46, 402–3
"octoroon" 4, 63, 171
Oedipal significations of colonial revolution 373–76
Ogé, Jacques 58n9, 536
Ogé, Vincent 22, 28n18, 29, 37, 43, 58n9, 61, 98, 100, 126, 128–29
  Club Massiac speech 557–60, 562, 572–73
  role in Haitian independence 534–36, 560–66
Ogletree, Charles Jr. 583
Omi, Michael 145
Ong, Aiwha 147

Outka, Paul H. 352n5
Oxiane; ou la Révolution de Saint-Dominque 338–39, 354, 373, 416
Ozouf, Mona 94n18

Pajeot, Madame 214
Palissot, M. 122
Pamphile, Léon Dénius 310n22
Patterson, Orlando 355–57, 359, 361–62
Paul, Thomas 311n23
Paulson, Ronald 36–37, 349, 364–65, 373, 375
Peabody, Sue 7–8n6
Perret, J. John 350–51
Peterson, Carla 256, 294, 318, 320, 323–24
Pétion, Alexandre 21–22, 24, 28, 31, 37, 66, 68, 78, 129–36, 478–79, 516, 550–51
  representation as the founder of liberty 527
Phillips, Helen 302n17
Phillips, Wendell 60, 197, 276n16, 480, 512–13
  1861 speech 'Toussaint L'Ouverture' 380, 382–83, 511n31
Picquenard, Jean-Baptiste 270n12, 273–75, 277, 426
Pierrot, Grégory 50n2, 57, 155–56, 578
Pigault-Lebrun, Charles Antoine Guillaume 159, 161, 163, 165, 185–86
Pike, Frederick B. 605
Poe, Edgar Allen 422
Polverel, Etienne 37
Popham, Admiral Hope 505n25
Popkin, Jeremy 2, 12n12, 209, 211
Porter, Dorothy B. 320, 321
Pradine, L'Instant de 467, 514n34
Prasad, Pratima 8–9, 167–68, 178n18
Pratt, Frances Hammond 155, 156–57, 165, 197, 270n12, 303–4
Pratt, Mary Louis 90, 531
Prévost, abbé Antoine François 73–74

Index

Prévost, Julien 423–24, 450–51n26
Price-Mars, Jean 420, 421, 568
Prichard, Hesketh 47–48n24
Prince, Mary 251

"quadroon" 4, 17–18
Quincy, Edmund 270n12, 276–77
Quinn, Kate 464n3

race
    calls for manumission of free people of color 98–100
    classification system 62, 63–64, 483, 529n4
    critical race theory 42, 457–58, 486–87
    lettres de blancs 131n13
    "miscegenation" 45–46n23, 57, 76
    naturalist racial taxonomies 4–9, 20–21, 23–24, 33–34, 57–58, 77–78, 88–89, 192, 436, 481, 482, 553
    pseudoscientific terminology 7–8, 11, 20, 57, 63–64, 505, 606
    pseudoscientific theories 86–88, 91n13, 226, 387–88, 419–20, 432, 435, 555, 589
    racial hybridity 4–5, 8–9, 11, 15, 158–59, 432–33
    racial tropes 5–6, 35–44
    "colored historian" 35, 37, 41, 460–73
    "monstrous hybridity" 35, 37, 38–39, 58, 59–60, 66, 73–74, 136–37, 158–59, 475
    tragic "mulatto/a" 35, 37, 266–67, 329–44, 346–47, 475
    "tropical temptress" 35, 37, 39–40, 198–219, 266–67, 280, 475, 484–85
    usage of double quotation marks 45–46
    'reprinting' of racial taxonomies 482–83, 517–18, 579
    social or biological interpretation 11–14, 15–16, 18–19

stereotyping 38, 40
themes of sexual aggression 347–48
thingification 118–19
types of racism 28n19
use of *blackface* as literary device 269–70
vocabularies used in Haitian writing 5–9, 23–24, 31–32, 33–34, 110–11
Racine, Jean 202n4
Radet, Jean-Baptiste 341n12
Raimon, Eve Allegra 330
Raimond, Julien 15n14, 16, 27, 30n20, 51, 61n14, 98, 128–29, 162, 178n19, 225, 235, 237, 516
    role in Haitian revolution 535, 564–65
    writings as person of color 17, 18, 19n15, 31, 242–44
Rainsford, Marcus 50n2, 56–57n8, 65, 66, 211–12, 442, 513, 535–36
    An Historical Account of the Black Empire of Haiti 49, 50–51, 52, 57–61
Ramel, Jean-Pierre 105
Ravinet, Laurette-Aimée Mozard Nicodami de 97
Raynal, abbé Guillaume-Thomas 49–50n1, 76n1, 87, 95–96, 159, 510
    Histoire des deux Indes 49–51, 52–53, 55, 60–61, 325, 365
Reddock, Rhoda E. 217
Redpath, James 24, 41–42, 60n13, 472, 579–80n35
    abolitionist writing 481, 482–83, 504–13, 582, 584
Redpath, John 376n2, 380n9
Régis, Augustin 115–16n4, 442
Reinhardt, Catherine A. 30n20
Rémusat, Charles de 161–62, 163, 165, 186
Renan, Ernest 418, 450–51
Richardson, Marilyn 29n5
Riché, Jean-Baptiste 528–30n3, 551, 578

• 689 •

Rigaud, General André 18, 22, 31, 37, 59, 62, 68, 70, 98, 101, 103–4, 110, 162, 383, 515–16
conflict with Louverture 413, 441–43, 485–86
Rigaud, Augustin 104
Ritchie, Leitch 104–5, 158, 189, 190–91n26, 193–94, 194–95, 390
Robertson, Pat 608–9n4, 610, 611
Rochambeau, General Donatien-Marie-Joseph de 105–6, 107, 121, 265
Rodriguez, Junius P. 276n16
Roger, Baron, *Kelédor* 339–41, 360
Rogers, Dominique 221, 223n8, 230n12
Rogers, T.C. 143–44
Romane, Jean-Jacques 422–23
Rotberg, Robert 607, 608–9
Rousseau, Jean-Jacques 12n13, 83n5, 159, 162–63, 176–77, 225n10, 233n13, 239, 365–66, 367, 420
Rouvray, Marquise de 96–97, 99, 230, 247n26, 334, 535
Rowland, Ann Wierda 454n30
Russworm, John 311, 314, 317–18n30

"saccatras" 4
Saget, Nicholas 214
Said, Edward 36, 482, 503–4
Orientalism 33, 68
St. John, Spencer 609–10, 611
Saint-Aubin, Arthur 387, 403
Saint-Domingue *see* Haiti
Saint-Rémy, Joseph 20, 21, 22, 29, 31–32, 42, 65–66, 128–29, 131–32n14, 273, 387–88, 417, 465, 472, 603
attention to racialized terms 479–80, 513, 611
Vie de Toussaint L'Ouverture 63, 312n25, 376, 385–87, 389–91, 401–2, 440, 441–43, 452–56, 467, 477, 504, 514–23
Sanborn, Geoffrey 493–94n14, 495
Sanchez-Eppler, Karen 383

Sancho, Ignatius 140, 144, 488n8
Sansay, Leonora (Mary Hassal) 39, 227, 230, 253–87
characterizations of women 236, 304
Laura 255–56
Secret History 253–58, 259, 261–63, 286–87
Zelica; the Creole 40, 208, 219, 256–87, 288, 297, 300–301
Sartre, Jean-Paul 121, 252n30
Saunders, Prince 290–91n4, 316–17, 550n18
Sawyer, Hannah Farnham 277–78n18, 580–81n37
Saye, Lisa Macha 468–69n9
Schoelcher, Victor 22–23, 42, 84n7, 253, 376n3, 416, 459, 462, 472
abolitionist writing 513, 522, 587
characterization of Louverture 527–28
Colonies étrangères et Haïti 524–26, 528, 554, 565–66, 570–72n30
critique of Faubert 556–57, 568–70, 579
cynical misreading of historical works 531–32, 542–43, 546–49, 559–60, 568
perceived 'anti-mulatto prejudice' 528–29, 538–39, 551–55
use of racialized terms 479, 526–27, 531
Scott, David 111, 235
Scott, Patricia Bell 288
Scott, Walter 420
Séjour, Victor 289n1, 305, 344, 346n2, 363–64
'Le Mulâtre' 40–41, 345–72, 379, 403–5, 409, 414, 441
theme of parricide 350–51
Seldon, Horace 309n20
Senghor, Léopold 402
Sepinwall, Alyssa Goldstein 126, 145n25
Sharpley-Whiting, T. Denean 266, 326

Index

Sheftall, Beverly Guy 291, 327
Sheller, Mimi 249, 317
Shipley, W. Maurice 352
Sinclair, Harvey 160n6
slavery 3
  abolition 3, 37, 42–43
  code noir 358
  creation of power structures 349–72
  manumission of "mixed-race" children 353
slavery; *see also* abolitionism; Haiti, Haitian Revolution
Smith, Barbara 288
Smith, Matthew 464–65
Smith-Rosenberg, Caroll 263, 278–79, 284
Socolow, Susan 230n12
Sollors, Werner 7, 11, 63–64, 77, 87n9, 95, 164, 171, 337n8, 351, 360
Sommer, Doris 416–17
Sonthonax, Léger Félicité 37, 442
Soulouque, Faustin 464, 465, 470–71, 556n20, 578, 586
Sparks, Jared 507
Spivak, Gayatri 44, 503
Staël, Germaine de 246, 248–49, 544n14
Steele, Claude M. 133–34
Stephen, James 54n7, 392–95, 398
  The History of Toussaint Louverture 475
Stephens, Michelle 5n4
Stewart, Maria W. 288, 291–92, 294–96, 300n13, 320, 322–25
Stoddard, Lorthrop 259
Stoler, Ann Laura 21, 23, 145, 158, 207, 224, 481, 560
Stone, Kate 60n13
Stowe, Harriet Beecher 109, 248, 309n20, 334–35, 387–88, 495, 580–81n37, 590n41
Striker, Ardelle 273–74n15
Sutton, Paul 464n3

Taylor, John 142n22
Thackeray, William 331

The Liberty Bell 276n16
The Woman of Colour 227
Thelwall, John 153, 155, 329
The Daughter of Adoption 201, 367, 369–70
'Theresa, a Haytien Tale' 208, 219, 288–327
  analysis of story 296–300, 316, 329–30
  historical anachronisms 309–11
  question of authorship 289–96
Thouret, Anthony 331
Titus, Rubens François 531n7
Tocqueville, Alexis 544n14
Todorov, Tzvetan 116n5
  The Conquest of America 34
Tomkins, Fred, *Jewels in Ebony* 512–13
Toumson, Roger 167
Trouillot, Hénock 232–33
Trouillot, Michel-Rolph 19, 29–31, 146, 460, 487, 513, 608
  Silencing the Past 1–3, 25–26, 27, 462
Truth, Sojourner 197
Tucker, St. John 506–7n27
Turner, Lorenzo Dow 289n3

Ulysse, Gina 45, 150
Van Bergen, Jennifer 255
Varin, Charles 408–10
Vashon, George B. 288, 306–7, 524
Vassière, Pierre de 82
Vastey, Jean Louis, Baron de 13, 14, 16, 22–23, 31, 56, 102–3, 109, 111n1, 157, 162, 177, 225, 423–24, 577, 603
  commentary on colonialism 111–51, 430, 451, 519, 567
  criticism of Louverture 537–38
  Le Cri de la conscience 122, 129–30, 134
  Le Cri de la patrie 121–22, 134
  Le Système colonial dévoilé 38–39, 113–15, 122, 123, 146–47, 212–13, 244–45n21, 333, 427–28, 520–21, 593
  portrayal of Louverture 395–96, 398

Réflexions politiques 115–16
Réflexions sur une lettre de Mazères
117, 149–50, 181–82, 428, 456–57
use of racialized vocabulary 112, 117–18, 193, 387, 419–20, 468
writings as person of color 17, 30, 33, 111–51, 158, 185, 477, 481, 502
writings on Pétion 129–36
Vastey, Jean Valentin 149
Vatar-Jouannet, François 300–301n14
Vauthier, Simone 257, 259n6, 278n19, 354
Venault de Charmilly, Peter Francis 14
vengeance narrative 4–5, 9–10, 15–17, 29, 32–33, 34, 36, 67–68, 97–98, 281–82, 475–76, 611
Vergès, Françoise 10n10, 95, 373–74
Vernet, André 516
Vilevolex, E. Sègny 422–23
Voltaire 159–60

Wakeman, George 438
Walcott, Derek, *Haitian Triology* 30n20
Waldstreicher, David 171–72
Walker, David 291n5, 294–95, 323–24
Wallez, M. 131n13
Walsh, John Patrick 30–31n20
Warner, Samuel 498n20
Washington, George 381–82, 511–12n32
Washington, Mary Helen 291
Weaver, Karol K. 207n5, 218n14
Webster, Daniel 508n28
Weiss, M. Lynn 350–51
Weissenthurn, Johanna Franul von 208n7

Weld, Theodore, *Slavery As It Is* 493–94
Weston, Helen 446–47
Wheatley, Phillis 140–41, 144–45, 293, 312, 345, 382, 488n8
"white" 12–14, 16, 19, 34, 113
theories of "white" supremacy 528
White, Ed 292–93
White, Hayden 5n4, 35–36
Whiteman, Maxwell 293
Whitlock, Gillian 227
Wigmoore, Francis 317, 327
Wilberforce, William 151, 290n4
Williams, Eric 65, 117
Williams-Wynn, Frances 137–38
Willoughby, Lord Francis 80n3
Wimpffen, Baron de 49, 89, 153
Wimsatt, W.K. 571–72, 574
Winant, Howard 18–19, 145
Woertendyke, Gretchen 255
Wolosky, Shira 583
Wood, Marcus 427–28
Woolf, Virginia 251
Wordsworth, William 375, 419, 511n31, 512–13
Wright, John 141–42
Wright, W.W. 434–35

Yellin, Jean Fagan 154n4, 278n19
Young, Robert 7, 67, 86–87, 90–91, 199, 222–23n5, 224–25
Youngquist, Paul 50n2, 57
Yudell, Michael 86n9

Zamora, Margarita 8n7
Zantop, Susan 334
Ziarek, Ewa 453
Zorada see Jouannet, Emilie